Official

BASEBALL GUIDE

1983 EDITION

Editor/Baseball Guide
LARRY WIGGE

Contributing Editors/Baseball Guide
CARL CLARK
DAVE SLOAN
CRAIG CARTER

President-Chief Executive Officer
RICHARD WATERS

Editor
DICK KAEGEL

Director of Books and Periodicals
RON SMITH

Published by

The Sporting News

1212 North Lindbergh Boulevard
P.O. Box 56 — St. Louis, Mo. 63166

Copyright © 1983
The Sporting News Publishing Company
a Times Mirror company

ISBN 0-89204-111-0   ISSN 0078-3838

TABLE OF CONTENTS

For Index to Contents See Page 476

(Index to Minor League Cities on Page 477)

ON THE COVER: Milwaukee Shortstop Robin Yount was named American League Most Valuable Player and The Sporting News' Major League Player of the Year last season as he led the Brewers to their first-ever World Series appearance.

—**Photo by Richard Pilling**

Baseball Shocks Doomsayers, Attains New Popularity Heights

By CLIFFORD KACHLINE

One year after the first midseason strike in its history, major league baseball attained new heights in popularity. Four down-to-the-wire divisional races, milestone performances by several players, a dramatic World Series and increased promotional efforts combined to produce all-time attendance records in 1982. The results served to confound the doomsayers who felt the previous summer's 50-day player walkout would seriously damage the fans' enthusiasm.

While reaching new plateaus at the gate and in television audiences, the sport in many ways mirrored the world's troubled economic and political picture. Even with the banner attendance figures, a number of teams encountered serious financial difficulties as a consequence of escalating player salaries. In addition, the game's political superstructure was left in turmoil when a small minority of club owners succeeded in blocking the retention of Bowie Kuhn as commissioner.

Year's end found the magnates busily engaged in trying to restructure baseball from the top and in seeking solutions to the problems that were being magnified by the rapidly-growing disparity in revenue among the 26 clubs. Despite the sport's overall prosperity, observers were in general agreement that management faced some of the most serious decisions in the long history of the game. Baseball never was healthier on the field or at the box office, but at the leadership level there was chaos.

For the ninth time in 14 years, the major leagues enjoyed record attendance. After playing to an all-time high of 1,428,748 customers for spring training games, the two leagues attracted 44,587,874 paid customers during the championship season. This was a million more than the previous record set in 1979. Both circuits exceeded their old marks. The American League's 14 teams drew 23,080,449 fans as compared to 21,507,425 for the 12-team National League. Over a 10-week stretch (excluding the All-Star break) starting June 2, the turnstiles averaged 2 million per week. The biggest one-week total was 2,303,766 for the August 9-15 period. Counting in-season exhibitions, the All-Star Game, League Championship Series

Montreal catcher Gary Carter (above) and the Mets' George Foster landed $2 million-plus yearly contracts in 1982.

and the World Series, the majors' total attendance came to 47,166,267.

Seven teams established seasonal gate records. The Los Angeles Dodgers set the pace with an astounding 3,608,881 for 80 home dates—an average of 45,111. Their Freeway rivals, the California Angels, ranked second with 2,807,360. Five other clubs topped the 2-million figure—the Philadelphia Phillies, Montreal Expos, Kansas City Royals, St. Louis Cardinals and New York Yankees, in that order. In the process, the Expos and world champion Cardinals achieved new peaks. The Milwaukee Brewers, American League champions, Oakland A's and Atlanta Braves also set records. The only team to fail to reach the one-million plateau was the Minnesota Twins with 921,186.

Despite the impressive attendance totals and soaring television revenue, numerous clubs finished deep in the red. Peter Bavasi, former major league executive who formed his own sports management consulting firm, wrote in a September 12 guest column in the New York Times that "consolidating operating losses (in the majors) are expected to be nearly $40 million this season." Skyrocketing salaries, an over-aggressive approach to winning and a heavy load of payments to players who were released contributed to the deficits. Nearly 20 players were understood to have contracts calling for a million dollars or more per season. Late in the year, a few clubs announced the launching of austerity programs to reduce costs, while many teams decided to raise ticket prices 50 cents to $1 across the board.

Because most clubs are privately-owned corporations or partnerships, they are not required to make financial data public. Nevertheless, in a number of instances, disclosures or comments by a member of management provided an insight into the financial situation of various organizations.

The Texas Rangers, Pittsburgh Pirates and Cleveland Indians were among the teams deepest in the red. President Eddie Chiles and Executive Vice-President Sam Meason estimated the Rangers lost between $5 and $6 million on an attendance of 1,154,432. The heavy deficit came on top of reported losses of $4.5 million in 1981 and $2 million in 1980, Chiles' first year as majority owner. The flow of red ink prompted speculation that Chiles might be ready to sell, but late in the year he was said to be prepared to shell out another $750,000 to buy out Mack Rankin, the Rangers' third largest investor.

The Pirates, with a gate of 1,024,106, also were believed to have lost more than $5 million in '82, while Cleveland officials indicated the Indians expected to wind up the year with a deficit of about $5 million. This led to rumors that Edward J. DeBartolo, an Ohioan and the nation's largest owner of shopping malls, might attempt to purchase the Indians from Steve O'Neill. DeBartolo, who owns the Pittsburgh Penguins of the National Hockey League and whose son Edward owns the San Francisco 49ers of the National Foot-

ball League, was rebuffed in his bid to buy the Chicago White Sox in 1980 because of his holdings in several race tracks.

After dropping an estimated $3 million in 1981, the White Sox' new ownership of Jerry Reinsdorf and Eddie Einhorn reportedly lost an additional $4 million in '82. Their new cable TV venture, Sports-Vision, still had not reaped the benefits they anticipated.

Across town, the Chicago Cubs' new owners, The Tribune Company, experienced a loss said to be close to $3 million in the first year of "The New Tradition." Approximately $1.3 million of this was the result of paying off contracts of players Ken Reitz, Mike Tyson and Rawly Eastwick, each of whom was released in spring training. "Our player payroll was one of the smallest in baseball at $5 million," Board Chairman Andrew McKenna said, "but it will go up. A fair amount of money went into the park (Wrigley Field), and we have more work to do on it." The bleak financial picture prompted the release of 12 front-office employees shortly after the season as part of an austerity move.

The Montreal Expos grossed an estimated $24 million with a record 2,318,292 home attendance and $8.1 million in television and radio revenue, yet lost close to $3 million, according to Hugh Hallward, a club director and minority stockholder. The club had an $11 million U.S. payroll that, according to President John McHale, ranked near the top in the major leagues. The obligation to pay players in U.S. funds and the difference in the exchange rates brought the Expos' cost of changing money to nearly $3 million, or almost $1 million more than anticipated. The super salaries of Gary Carter ($2 million-plus per year), Andre Dawson ($1.2 million), Al Oliver ($800,000) and Steve Rogers ($700,000) and the approximately $1.3 million paid to eight players who were released—Bill Lee, Stan Bahnsen, Fred Norman, Rodney Scott, John Milner, Tommy Hutton, Frank Taveras and Rowland Office—were factors in the Expos' huge deficit. Another was the $2.6 million rental fee on Olympic Stadium.

The A.L. West division-winning California Angels, with a player payroll of more than $9 million, lost around $1 million even with their record gate, according to General Manager Buzzie Bavasi. The presence of Reggie Jackson, signed the previous winter as a free agent, was a big boost to the Anaheim Stadium turnstiles, but it also exacted a financial toll. Besides a wage base of some $900,000, Reggie had a bonus clause in his contract calling for him to receive 50 cents on each ticket above the 2,400,000 level. This earned him an attendance bonus of $203,000. Reggie reportedly donated one game's worth of bonus money—around $12,000—to the Angels' six coaches.

Several other teams also were believed to have suffered heavy financial losses. The Minnesota Twins, however, were not one of them, even though they were the lone club to draw fewer than a million fans at home. After trading Roy Smalley, Butch Wynegar and Doug Corbett early in the season, the Twins carried 12 to 15 rookies and reduced their payroll to an estimated $1.9 million—less than Montreal's Gary Carter alone earned. President Calvin Griffith revealed the team would show a profit for the season. The $400,000 received by the Twins in the deal that sent Smalley to the New York Yankees helped balance the books.

The Los Angeles Dodgers, of course, figured to be the biggest winners in the profit sweepstakes. An advance sale of 26,000 season tickets provided a good start and contributed to a gross of around $20 million at the gate. In addition, the club took in an estimated $16 million or more from parking and concessions for an unprecedented income of $36 million, without including the lush broadcast and cable-TV package.

The wide disparity in income among clubs, particularly from new cable-TV sources, and proposals to restructure the game's hierarchy fueled the political upheaval that appeared destined to topple Kuhn from his $250,000-a-year position. Elected commissioner in 1969, he survived one crisis in 1975, the first time his contract came up for renewal. However, another mutiny erupted and, barring a minor miracle, the 56-year-old, 6-foot-5 Princeton lawyer's tenure as baseball boss was due to end at the expiration of his second term on August 12, 1983.

Peter O'Malley of the Dodgers, a strong Kuhn supporter like his late father, led a nearly year-long delaying action designed to calm or mollify the militants. Two of the nine signers of the "Dump Bowie" letter that appeared at the December 1981 winter meetings—Edward Bennett Williams of Baltimore and Ballard Smith of San Diego—were persuaded to swing over to the commissioner's side, but the other anti-Kuhn forces remained unswayed.

The most outspoken of the opposition were Nelson Doubleday of the New York Mets, August A. Busch, Jr., of St. Louis, John McMullen of Houston, Eddie Chiles of Texas and Ted Turner of Atlanta.

Money was the prime issue. All charged Kuhn lacked the business expertise required to lead baseball. Lou Susman, an attorney for Busch, was said to be the architect of much of the anti-Kuhn strategy.

"There are millions of dollars slipping away from us because Kuhn doesn't know how to run the business side of baseball," Doubleday told the New York Times' Joe Durso. Doubleday, who spent a record $21.1 million to buy the Mets in 1980, also was critical of revenue-sharing, which Kuhn supported, and of two members of the commissioner's staff.

"He (Kuhn) is surrounded by people who shouldn't be running the business," the Mets' owner said.

Of revenue-sharing, Doubleday commented: "I'm sympathetic to guys who need help. But it's more complicated than just giving them part of our local TV. If you're just supporting a bad operation, wherever it is, we're not interested."

For a brief time at midseason, Kuhn's job seemed safe and observers felt he would be voted a third term. The hopes of his followers were revived during a special two-day meeting the owners held in Chicago on June 14-15 to hear reports on restructuring of the sport's upper echelons and revenue-sharing. The optimism of the pro-commissioner group stemmed in part from indications that the opposition of two other signers of the "Dump Bowie" letter —George Argyros of Seattle and William Williams of Cincinnati seemed to have vanished.

After the first day's session, which was devoted to restructuring, Kuhn said he felt the meeting was "the most constructive day baseball has had in my 13 or 14 years as commissioner." He added that the changes proposed "would significantly strengthen the commissioner's office, and I have encouraged them right along."

Reflecting the sentiment of numerous owners, Dave Nightingale wrote in The Sporting News that Kuhn left the discussions "with (1) his powers virtually intact, (2) his job security much improved and (3) his enemies in disarray."

The optimism was shortlived as the behind-the-scenes struggle continued. Several weeks later, three of the commissioner's foes—Doubleday, Busch and McMullen—called for a special National League meeting on August 17, the day preceding the regular two-day joint conclave scheduled in San Diego. Their intent was obvious: To bring about the firing or resignation of Kuhn. American League owners also decided to meet that day.

Although no official word was released on the National League discussions, the media learned that Turner told his fellow owners that he would vote against Kuhn. This disclosure prompted a high-ranking Kuhn aide to comment: "It looks like the party is over for us." At the same time the American League was voting its support for the commissioner with the proviso that a Chief Operating Officer, Business Affairs (acronym COOBA) be hired to oversee such financial aspects as television contracts, marketing and revenue sharing. Under the A.L. plan, the COOBA would have been subordinate to the commissioner in the pecking order.

The joint meeting the next day lasted only 75 minutes and resulted in postponement of a decision on Kuhn. At the outset of the session, Bill Giles of Philadelphia quickly moved—amid cries of "Railroad" —that a vote be postponed.

The magnates then decided to set up a 10-man committee to discuss a compromise. Named to the committee were O'Malley, Doubleday, Busch, McKenna and Charles Bronfman (Montreal) from the National League and Williams, Argyros, Reinsdorf, Roy Eisenhardt (Oakland) and Haywood Sullivan (Boston) from the American League. After 45 minutes, the joint session was halted while the committee conferred. When the meeting resumed three hours later, the American League voted 11-3 and the National voted 7-5 in favor of the motion to delay a vote until November 1. The A.L. "no" votes were cast by Chiles, Argyros and George Steinbrenner (New York Yankees), while the "nays" in the N.L. came from Doubleday, Busch, McMullen, Turner and William Williams.

"I'm disappointed that things have not yet been resolved," Kuhn told the media after the meeting, "but baseball is a complicated game full of complicated people. I have no intention of resigning. . . . I think there is room in baseball for both a chief executive officer (meaning the commissioner) and for a chief operating officer (COOBA). And I think the COOBA can have a lot of power in certain areas without ever colliding with the CEO. But the CEO still must be in charge."

Several Kuhn supporters also spoke out. "If we were candid," said Bud Selig of Milwaukee, "Bowie Kuhn is not the problem. It starts with a lack of real understanding about our problems."

Saying the commissioner "has been tarred and feathered on many issues that he wasn't responsible for," Montreal's McHale added: "But there are two things

you have to give him high marks on: His defense of the integrity of the game and the growth of baseball. When he took over in 1969, major league baseball drew 25 million. Two years ago, it drew 43 million. That's not bad."

Many in the media also sided with Kuhn. "What really tickles me," wrote Dick Young of the New York Post, "is some club owners trying to blame Kuhn for the flow of red ink on so many ledgers. They (owners) are the guys who throw away millions of dollars to .220 hitters and sore-armed pitchers."

On being questioned about Doubleday's opposition to him because of the revenue-sharing issue, Kuhn responded: "Nelson (Doubleday) correctly perceives that I am a proponent of revenue sharing. You've got to have some system in which all teams can be competitive. I'm also thinking more about stabilizing costs."

With a three-fourths majority in each league required for re-election, it was obvious that an 11th-hour miracle was unlikely. Some Kuhn supporters felt a change in the Cincinnati vote was possible and still hoped to persuade Busch to switch sides. Bob Howsam, vice-chairman and former president of the Reds, was listed as a Kuhn backer. However, the Williams brothers—William and James—tended to go along with Howsam's successor as club head, Dick Wagner, who opposed the commissioner. In the case of Busch, Kuhn himself met with the Cardinals owner and his attorney, Susman, in an attempt to win the club's vote.

The final showdown came at the O'Hare Hyatt Regency Hotel in Chicago on November 1. Beating the public to the polls by one day, the owners met to cast their ballots. During the 27-minute session, McKenna presented a compromise proposed by the Cardinals. The plan, which the commissioner had agreed to, called for giving Kuhn a new three-year term beyond his current contract and provided for the inclusion in the baseball hierarchy of a business-oriented executive as chief operating officer. The COO would be located between Kuhn and all other departments in the baseball structure. American League owners voted 11-3 in favor of the proposal, but the National League ballot ended 7-5, two short of the required three-fourths. This represented a switch of only one vote—presumably McKenna's—since a straw poll at the August 18 meeting. Although the Cardinals proposed the compromise, they cast a negative vote after ascertaining that the plan had no chance of acceptance.

Kuhn immediately announced that he intended to serve out his term or until a successor was elected.

"It is true we are in some kind of stalemate, a sort of whirlpool from which I hope the sport can emerge quickly," he told the media. "Baseball can't restructure until it has a commissioner and it might not be able to get a commissioner until it is restructured. I support and will continue to support the idea that an incoming commissioner should need 75 percent of the vote. But I think it is unfair to demand that a commissioner in office should need more than a simple majority to retain his job. I guess the fact I got 70 percent of the vote—an overwhelming majority in most elections—after 14 years on the job is some kind of compliment."

The bottom line to Kuhn's demise, in the view of Nightingale of The Sporting News, was that he "never budged from one concept for his office: That the commissioner should not be subordinate to any individual." Kuhn conceded "that may have been the final straw that broke my back. But the concept of a 'dual' commissioner (involving a COO) always has been clearly unacceptable to me. To accept such would be a disservice to the office, a disservice to the game. And I don't want any part in hurting the great office of commissioner by accepting the 'dual' situation."

Texas Owner Eddie Chiles (above) and Atlanta Owner Ted Turner were among the more outspoken in the anti-Kuhn movement.

The reasons for the opposition to Kuhn were as varied as the eight men who voted against him. Besides doubts about his ability to deal with the increasingly complex business affairs and his support for revenue sharing, some owners were believed still to harbor lingering resentment against him because of his failure to settle the 1981 players' strike. Even though his hands in effect were tied because of the Player Relations Committee's mandate, Kuhn was nearly everyone's favorite whipping boy during the walkout.

As Hal Bock of the Associated Press pointed out, the most-frequently voiced comments at the time were: "How could the commissioner sit back and let the players walk out? . . . Pete Rozelle would never let it come to that (in the National Football League)." However, during football's 57-day players' strike that began on September 21, 1982, the NFL commissioner was equally silent.

The process of finding a successor to Kuhn was turned over to the Executive Council. That body in turn appointed a six-man search committee headed by one of its own members, Selig. Others named were Edward Bennett Williams, Bob Lurie, Dan Galbreath, Bronfman and

Peter Hardy of Toronto. In December, two more members were added—McMullen and Argyros. As the year came to a close, Selig said he already had the names of 15 possible candidates on file, all suggested by fellow club owners, and added that he expected interviews might begin early in '83. Meantime, several Kuhn supporters were continuing subtle efforts to change some of the opposition in hopes of yet gaining a third term for the incumbent.

In keeping with recent custom, Kuhn made the keynote speech at the opening session of the annual major-minor league convention in Hawaii on December 6. His apparent farewell address was a moving assessment of baseball's future and a stirring plea for recognition of various "imperatives." More than 1,500 executives, managers and other personnel were present to hear what he called his "annual poormouth speech," but he touched only briefly on the negative aspects of the industry.

"If we are going to solve our problems and achieve the growth of which this game is surely capable," Kuhn said, "then we must recognize that there are certain commandments, certain articles of faith which should be viewed as imperatives. Certainly the first imperative is protecting the integrity of the game. Unless we have integrity, we have nothing. . . . For example, we must be adamant that gambling influences will be barricaded outside the game, that legalized gambling on team sports will be fought with all our might and that the pernicious influence of illegal drugs will be battled at all times and at all levels.

"If maintaining baseball's integrity should be the first article of faith, then maintaining baseball as a family game is an imperative of nearly as great importance," he continued. "The ballpark must be preserved as a decent place for parents to take their children and ticket prices should be at a clearly competitive level so that families can afford to come.

"Another article of faith is the playing rules. Since 1903, there has been only one major change in the playing rules. No other game has been so preserved. Carnival types with no appreciation of the true merits of the game will always be heard crying for change and should be ignored.

"It should be an article of faith that the relationship between the clubs and players be improved," Kuhn added. "Whatever the unhappy passions of the past may have been, we must resolve that the future will be characterized by a far-ranging effort—a really far-ranging effort by both sides—to achieve a decent level of harmony.

"We must have a high quality of ownership which is dedicated to the welfare of the sport and interests of the fan and which is able to expertly carry out the complex demands of modern franchise operation. Indeed, quality of ownership may be the touchstone through which all of the articles of faith are achieved. Because that is so, we should be uncompromising in this area.

"Another imperative is the restructuring of baseball's administrative procedures and offices. . . . It gladdens my heart that the restructuring proposal calls for the continuation of a strong commissioner who will be empowered to move vigorously to protect our integrity and to foster cures for our persistent ills. Baseball should passionately resist the efforts of well-intended but wrong-minded people to diminish the stature and functions of the commissioner. We should bear in mind that all of us are only temporary caretakers for the baseball fans of the world. They indeed are our only permanency."

At the close of his 30-minute speech, Kuhn was given a standing ovation by the assembled baseball officials.

Because of the chaos caused by Kuhn's cashiering, a few owners expressed serious misgivings about the chances of reorganizing baseball's high command until a new commissioner was hired. It was hoped the full restructuring plan would be ready in time for the December meetings, but much of it was in a kind of limbo during the Kuhn furor.

"Clearly we are putting the cart before the horse," said Eisenhardt, co-chairman with O'Malley of the restructuring group, after the August sessions. "Restructuring should have been in place before the issue of the commissioner came up."

The Committee on Restructuring consisted of 12 owners, six appointed by each league at the December 1981 meetings. Its announced goal was to "bring baseball's superstructure into the Twentieth Century." Besides Eisenhardt and O'Malley, the committee was made up of Selig, Argyros, Reinsdorf, Sullivan and Steinbrenner from the American League and Bronfman, Ballard Smith, William Williams, Susman (representing Busch) and Bill Bartholomay from the National.

Early in the year, the committee contracted with representatives of the University of Pennsylvania's Wharton School to draw up a restructuring proposal. Ironically, Baseball commissioned a study by

After the fateful Chicago meeting that resulted in his ouster as baseball commissioner, Bowie Kuhn announced that he would serve out his term.

Wharton on the same subject in 1970 and then virtually ignored the consultants' findings.

After one of the early meetings, a committee member who requested anonymity told The Sporting News' Nightingale some of the reasons behind the deliberations.

"Baseball has the worst labor relations of any sport and it has the worst public relations image," he told Nightingale. "We lost $25 million last year (1981). There is dissension in the ranks. We have three law firms and two guys in charge of umpires and three guys in charge of public relations. We spend $250,000 a year on the commissioner's salary and we pay each of the league presidents $150,000. By the nature of our structure those three men often are at odds.

"So boil it down and we are paying out $550,000 a year in salaries to people who sometimes are in adversarial roles. We are subsidizing a situation that breeds divisiveness. No man can function as commissioner under our current structure. We should be doing things together. We can't get started on straightening things out

until we are reorganized as a business."

After holding at least half a dozen meetings over a six-month period, the Committee on Restructuring presented its report at the June 14 confab in Chicago. The owners unanimously endorsed the plan in concept and urged the committee to draft the documents and various amendments required to put it into effect. The report included the following recommendations:

• Creation of a 26-man board of directors (one from each club), which would meet quarterly rather than semi-annually.

• Creation of an eight-man Executive Committee with decision-making authority, with each member chairing a subcommittee dealing with one of the phases of the game. The commissioner would be accountable to the committee on a day-to-day basis.

• Elimination of separate league voting and decisions in favor of joint action by the 26 clubs.

• Inclusion of the two league offices, the Player Relations Committee and the Baseball Promotion Corp. in the commissioner's office complex, with each being directly accountable to the commissioner.

• Appointment of another executive to provide expertise in areas of tele-communications and merchandising.

• Reduction of the commissioner's term from seven years to five. (This later was reduced to three years in the unsuccessful compromise struck in an attempt to save Kuhn's job.)

• Combining the umpire staffs and public relations staffs of the two leagues.

The new chain of command and the new degree of "accountability" by the commissioner to the owners met with Kuhn's approval. Both he and Eisenhardt agreed that the strengthening of the commissioner's authority was a result of the previous year's players' strike, which demonstrated how little authority the sport's top office had in the situation.

"Not only would this (new setup) give the commissioner more authority, it would also give him more responsibility," Eisenhardt said. "There is no dissatisfaction with Ray Grebey (head of the Player Relations Committee). The owners just felt it important to have a chain of command."

On the matter of having the 26 clubs vote as a unit rather than by leagues, Eisenhardt explained: "We feel the present setup is damaging in three ways. A small number of clubs can vote no in one league and paralyze the other league. Most problems are a 26-club problem, a baseball problem. And the lack of meeting between the leagues prevents cross-pollination, which we feel is healthy." He pointed out the arrangement also would eliminate the expression "It's a league matter" and end the practice of the two leagues operating in a different fashion.

The role of the proposed Chief Operating Officer, Business Affairs (COOBA) was the subject of heated debate. At the August 17 owners' meeting it was decided that rather than merely assisting the commissioner, the COOBA would be directly in charge of marketing, promotions and media details. Later at the same session it was proposed that the COOBA would have separate and equal status with the commissioner and would report only to the board of directors and the Executive Committee.

The "dual" situation, of course, met with Kuhn's displeasure. During a World Series meeting between the commissioner and Susman, a further compromise was proposed whereby the COOBA would become simply COO and directly responsible to the commissioner, and the commissioner's term would be shortened to three years. But Susman was unable to sell the compromise to the four other National League opponents.

The restructuring committee made little appreciable progress at the December meetings in Hawaii, although it did get the owners to agree that future voting would be conducted jointly rather than by league in three areas. They are:

• Major League Rules involving the college draft, World Series and the protected lists, but not those sections dealing with territorial rights and playing rules.

• Professional Baseball Rules, which govern the relationship between the majors and minors.

• The amending of the Professional Baseball Agreement.

In all applicable situations, decisions would be made on a 28-vote basis by the 26 clubs, with each National League vote being worth 1 1/6 of an American League team's vote to give the two circuits equal strength in balloting.

Revenue sharing developed into an even more volatile issue than restructuring. The committee studying the subject presented its report—or actually two reports—at the second day of the June 14-15 Chicago conclave. One report was given by Giles on behalf of himself, McHale and Steinbrenner, whose teams operate in areas where broadcast revenues are largest, while the other was made by committee members Ballard Smith, Argyros and Ewing Kauffman of Kansas City, who represent smaller broadcast areas.

The Giles group proposed that the increased revenue from the national network TV package be placed in the Central Fund and distributed on the basis of 60 percent to clubs in the 13 smaller markets and 40 percent to the 13 larger markets or that 15 percent be skimmed off the top and divided among teams in the eight poorest media markets. The other group recommended that a pool be created by having all 26 teams contribute 25 percent of their gross revenues from gate receipts, so-called free television and pay-TV, with the kitty to be distributed equally among all teams.

The clubs already were sharing to some extent in ticket and cable-TV revenue and were dividing equally the income from the network TV packages. In the American League, the visiting team was receiving a 20 percent slice and the league office 4 percent on all tickets, while in the National the visitor's cut was 55.5 cents and the league office share was 16.5 cents per customer. In addition, visiting teams in both leagues received 25 percent of local subscription and cable-TV revenues.

Early in the season, at a gathering of sports editors in San Diego, Ballard Smith warned that some clubs were in danger of going out of business unless the disparity in income was corrected.

"I know of 15 clubs that have serious economic problems or would have if they didn't have ownership pumping in dollars," the Padres' president said. He added that the "terrible economic disorientation" was threatening baseball's competitive balance and said he felt the solution was a money-sharing system similar to that employed in the National Football League, where lucrative television revenue is divided equally among all teams.

The flap over revenue sharing and Kuhn actually claimed its first victim early in September when Tom Villante announced his resignation from the commissioner's staff effective December 1. As executive director of marketing and broadcasting for the last five years, he had been instrumental in negotiating the current national TV contracts with NBC, ABC and USA Cable Network as well as the agreement with CBS Radio. He had also created and produced the highly-successful campaign "Baseball Fever....Catch It."

Following the lead of former baseball executives Tal Smith and Peter Bavasi, Villante subsequently formed his own sports marketing firm in New York to specialize in sports telecommunications and marketing. Ironically, several major league teams were among his first clients.

In contrast to the magnates' wrangling over the role of commissioner, the Major League Baseball Players Association experienced smooth transition in leadership. Marvin Miller, who had served as executive director since 1966, announced that, at age 64, he wanted to retire. On December 8 at a meeting in Hawaii, the executive board of the Players Associaton unanimously elected Kenneth E. Moffett as Miller's successor.

Moffett, a 50-year-old Pennsylvania native, had been employed in the labor field since 1958 and was deputy director of the Federal Mediation and Conciliation Service. In 1981 he served as mediator in the baseball strike. Moffett was due to take over the Players Association office on January 1, 1983, although Miller planned to remain with the union on a full-time basis through the end of April "to make the transition as smooth as possible."

The staff of the Players Association experienced another change in personnel in December when Peter Rose, associate counsel, decided to leave to enter private law practice. He had worked for the union for five and a half years.

The complexity of the issues facing baseball was emphasized by two suits involving television. The first centered on the question of whether the players had any rights regarding the pictures of them that splash across the screen during game telecasts. The other was precipitated by the Atlanta Braves' success in winning the National League West title. The advent of cable and pay-TV added fuel in both instances.

In letters to the club owners and their TV licensees, Marvin Miller threatened to introduce a lawsuit to determine the players' rights to a share of television revenues unless serious discussions on the subject were begun by June 15. The Players Association director had contended for 10 years that his clients were being short-changed in this area. Ray Grebey, director of the Player Relations Committee, countered by going to court for the owners on June 14 with a request for a permanent injunction that would firmly establish that the clubs were sole owners of TV rights.

"This all was settled in the last Basic Agreement (signed in 1981)," Grebey said, "and now he (Miller) wants a second bite of the apple." The owners' suit was filed in the U.S. District Court for the Northern District of Illinois.

A few weeks later, Miller filed suit in Federal Court in New York. He charged the clubs had sold TV rights without obtaining the players' permission. At year's end, the issue remained unresolved. With the majors' annual income from local and national TV estimated in the range of $118 million, a rise of 32 percent over the previous year, the issue obviously was an important one.

Ted Turner's ownership of both the Braves and WTBS-TV, the Atlanta superstation, also led to legal entanglements for baseball. Under major league regulations, each team is permitted to televise locally any League Championship Series games in which it participates. The local team or station is allowed to use its own announcers and sell its own advertising. The arrangement is spelled out in the contracts under which NBC and ABC alternate each year in televising the LCS and World Series.

When it appeared that the Braves might gain a post-season berth, Turner launched plans to televise the games. However, because his superstation could be seen on cable hookup by 21 million homes throughout the U.S., it would mean that one-fourth of the nation would have an alternative to watching the ABC telecasts if WTBS-TV carried the Braves' Championship Series games. Such a situation obviously would greatly damage ABC ratings.

To protect ABC's exclusive rights, both the network and the Major League Baseball Television Committee (10 teams) filed suit to prohibit Turner's station from televising the games. The Atlanta owner lost the legal fight when U.S. District Judge Mary Johnson Lowe ruled against him in New York on October 3.

Telecasts of the games of two other clubs, the Mets and Cubs, likewise were carried by superstations and could be seen in wide areas of the country. Not including the Mets and Cubs, numerous teams had some form of subscription or pay-TV at season's start and others were entering into such contracts, thus potentially reducing the number of games on free television in the future. The importance of the medium's impact was emphasized by the $180,000 that NBC charged for each 30-second commercial during the '82 World Series.

On the playing field, there was as much action and excitement as off.

For the first time since the start of divisional play in 1969, all four races were decided by fewer than five games. As the season entered its final three weeks, the top three teams in the A.L. East were separated by four games and the first three in the A.L. West by 4½. In the N.L. East, the difference between the first and fourth-place teams was just 3½ games, while the top three clubs in the N.L. West were 5½ games apart. By the morning of September 15, with only 19 days remaining, a combined total of only 4½ games separated the four leaders from their nearest pursuers. The stirring finishes demonstrated the great parity in the four divisions, a factor that stimulated attendance.

An unseasonal snowstorm and the Atlanta Braves dominated the early-season schedule.

Baseball has frequently had to cope with cold and snow flurries in April, but this time the storm gods wreaked havoc on the sport. A blizzard that dumped approximately a foot of snow on Milwaukee, Chicago and New York on April 5-6 and lesser amounts on Detroit, Pittsburgh and Philadelphia wiped out the openers in those six cities.

For a five-day period, April 6-10, 17 games had to be called off because of the big snow—14 in the American League and five in the National. The Brewers, White Sox, Tigers and Pirates each lost their first three home dates, while Philadelphia had its first two wiped out. The Yankees' first five dates were postponed and the club didn't open the season until Easter Sunday (April 11).

Minneapolis' new Hubert H. Humphrey Metrodome did double duty during the snowstorm. While the Minnesota Twins entertained the Seattle Mariners in their opening series, two snowed-out teams obtained permission to play a pair of exhibitions there to keep in shape. They were the Toronto Blue Jays, who were booked to open in Detroit, and the White Sox.

Several of the other weather victims also made quick adjustments. The Red Sox, slated to open in Chicago, fled back to their spring training base at Winter Haven, Fla., for two days of workouts, the Brewers flew to Houston to drill in the Astrodome, the Yankees bused to West Point for indoor drills, the Texas Rangers worked out under the stands of New York's Shea Stadium and the Indians utilized Cleveland State's indoor facilities.

The Braves, under new Manager Joe Torre, broke from the gate with a rush, winning their first 13 games. The spurt established a National League record for consecutive victories at season's start. Only the year before the Oakland A's launched the campaign with 11 successive wins to set an American League record. The Braves' first loss came on April 22 when they bowed to Cincinnati, 2-1.

With superstation WTBS-TV beaming the games, Atlanta's spectacular start captured the attention of the nation's fans and the Braves soon became known as "America's Team." In midseason it was estimated the Braves' telecasts were drawing a nationwide audience of 1.5 million viewers for prime-time weeknight games and 1.2 million on weekends.

Two other victory-starved cities had their hopes lifted when the White Sox began the season with eight wins in a row and the San Diego Padres reeled off 11 straight victories April 14-27. The early going also saw the Cardinals put together 12 consecutive wins, while the Baltimore Orioles lost nine games in succession and the Texas Rangers 12. The unusual frequency of lengthy strings of victories and defeats prompted the media to call it "The Year of the Streak."

While the three other divisions were experiencing tight races, the Braves built their lead in the N.L. West to nine games over runnerup San Diego and 10½ over Los Angeles after a four-game sweep of

St. Louis reliever Bruce Sutter is mobbed by teammates after the Cardinals' 4-2, N.L. East-clinching victory against Montreal on September 27.

the Padres, July 27-29. But their success may also have contributed to their downfall.

Because of the large crowds being attracted to Atlanta Stadium, club officials decided to remove Chief Noc-A-Homa's teepee from the left-field bleachers on July 30 in order to accommodate more customers. The Braves promptly lost 15 of their next 16 games, including 11 in a row and eight straight to the Dodgers, before calls from superstitious fans prompted the club to reassemble the teepee at a cost of $3,000.

The Atlanta skid eventually extended to 19 defeats in 21 games and what had been a 10½-game cushion over the Dodgers was suddenly a four-game deficit. At the same time, the San Francisco Giants enjoyed a 10-game winning streak to climb into contention, and when the Dodgers lost eight in a row September 21-29, the N.L. West found itself with a three-way battle to the finish.

The lead changed hands—sometimes more than once—during the September stretch drive in all divisions except in the A.L. East, which, ironically, became a

first-place deadlock with one day to go. Three of the four races were settled on the final weekend of the season, including two on the last day.

The Cardinals became the first team to clinch when they sewed up the N.L. East on September 27 with a 4-2 victory at Montreal. They went on to finish three games in front of the runnerup Phillies. The California Angels sewed up the A.L. West on October 2 with a 6-4 conquest of Texas and wound up three games ahead of second-place Kansas City.

With two days remaining in the regular season, Atlanta, Los Angeles and San Francisco all had a chance in the N.L. West. The Dodgers eliminated the Giants during a 15-2 rout in San Francisco on October 2 as Atlanta was winning at San Diego, 4-2. In the season finale the next day, the Braves bowed to the Padres, 5-1. Torre's crew, now faced with a possible first-place playoff against Los Angeles, had to wait for 30 minutes before the Giants, sparked by Joe Morgan's three-run homer in the seventh inning, completed a 5-3 victory to eliminate the Dodgers.

The A.L. East ended in equally hectic

fashion. After leading the division for all but three days after the All-Star break, and being four games in front with only five to play, the Milwaukee Brewers suddenly found themselves in trouble. Beaten in the series windup at Boston on September 30, Harvey Kuenn's team arrived in Baltimore needing just one victory in the season-closing four-game set to wrap up the title.

But the Orioles almost pulled off a miracle. They swept the Friday night doubleheader, 8-3 and 7-1, and battered Milwaukee again on Saturday, 11-3. This left the clubs even going into closing day.

Led by Robin Yount's two homers and triple, the Brewers shook their slump just in time and won the October 3 finale, 10-2, behind Don Sutton. The victory by Harvey's Wallbangers, as the slugging Brewers were affectionately known, ruined the bid by Earl Weaver to capture another pennant in his farewell season as Orioles manager.

Milwaukee had another narrow escape in the A.L. Championship Series. The Angels won the first two games of the matchup in Anaheim, but the Brewers bounced back to become the first team to win a divisional playoff after an 0-2 start. However, after building a 3-2 lead in the World Series, their magic ended and the St. Louis Cardinals took Games 6 and 7 to become world champions.

Yount's heroics in the regular-season finale almost earned him the American League batting championship and at the same time contributed to a controversy. Going into the last game, Willie Wilson of Kansas City led Yount, .332 to .328, and Manager Dick Howser decided to have Wilson sit out the last contest. In the bottom of the ninth inning, with two away and Oakland leading, 6-3, A's Manager Billy Martin went to the mound "to buy time for Wilson," as he explained later. It developed that Howser was on the phone with the press box to determine Yount's status before deciding whether to send Wilson in as a pinch-hitter. Convinced that Yount would not get to bat again, Howser passed up using Wilson, and the Royals' outfielder won the batting crown by one point, .332 to .331.

As it turned out, Yount did get to bat again as Milwaukee staged a five-run uprising in the ninth inning, but he was hit by a pitch. A hit would have given the Brewer shortstop the batting championship by one-tenth of a point. The nefarious episode involving Wilson prompted an investigation by league President Lee MacPhail, but he decided no punitive action

was warranted and instead sent written warnings that such collusion would not be tolerated.

Yount wound up leading both leagues in hits (210), total bases (367) and slugging percentage (.578) and tied Hal McRae, Kansas City's designated hitter, for most doubles with 46. McRae captured American League RBI honors with 133, while the Brewers' Gorman Thomas and Reggie Jackson of California shared home run leadership at 39.

Al Oliver, obtained in a preseason deal with Texas, celebrated his return to the National League by winning the batting championship with a .331 average for Montreal. Oliver also topped the senior circuit in hits (204), doubles (43) and total bases (317) and tied Atlanta's Dale Murphy for RBI laurels with 109. Despite batting a meager .204, the Mets' Dave Kingman won the home run title with 37. Mike Schmidt of the Phillies led in slugging percentage with .547.

For the first time in major league history (excluding the strike-abbreviated 1981 season), only one pitcher attained the 20-victory level. He was Steve Carlton of the Phillies. Oddly, the 37-year-old lefthander got away to the worst start of his career. He lost his first four decisions, including two to the Mets, but still managed to compile a 23-11 record. Carlton also led National League pitchers in games started (38), complete games (19), innings pitched (295.2), shutouts (6) and strikeouts (286).

Steve Rogers, a 19-game winner for Montreal, captured the ERA crown at 2.40, while Atlanta's 43-year-old knuckleballer, Phil Niekro, had the best winning percentage (.810) on the strength of a 17-4 ledger.

The American League's biggest winner was LaMarr Hoyt, who chalked up a 19-15 record for the White Sox. Rick Sutcliffe of Cleveland was the circuit's earned-run leader with 2.96, Floyd Bannister of Seattle captured strikeout honors with 209 and Pete Vuckovich of Milwaukee and Jim Palmer of Baltimore tied for the top winning percentage (.750) with records of 18-6 and 15-5, respectively.

Bruce Sutter of St. Louis again led National League relief pitchers in saves with 36, while Dan Quisenberry of Kansas City paced American League firemen with 35.

Significant milestones were attained by several players, including Gaylord Perry, Pete Rose, Steve Garvey, Jim Kaat and Rickey Henderson.

Perry became only the 15th pitcher in the sport's annals—and the first since

Atlanta center fielder Dale Murphy hit 36 home runs and drove home 109 runs during his MVP season.

Seattle's Gaylord Perry (right) celebrates after becoming the 15th pitcher in major league history to win 300 games with a 7-3 win over the Yankees on May 6.

Early Wynn in 1963—to reach the 300-victory plateau. He notched No. 300 while pitching Seattle to a 7-3 decision over the Yankees at the Kingdome on May 6. At age 43, The Ancient Mariner, as the media dubbed him, was the majors' oldest active player until Manny Mota was reactivated by the Dodgers late in the season.

Shortly after the historic victory, Perry began wearing a sweatshirt that proclaimed "300 Wins is Nothing to Spit At." Unfortunately, the humor of the expression was blighted when, for the first time in his 21-year big-league career, the controversial veteran righthander was ejected from a game against Boston on August 23 by umpire Dave Phillips for allegedly throwing a spitball. Lee MacPhail subsequently suspended Perry for 10 days and fined him $250. After an appeal, MacPhail conducted a hearing and upheld the penalties. Perry finished the season with a 10-12 record and 307 career victories.

Rose achieved several milestones. The Phillies' 41-year-old dynamo equaled a National League record with his ninth 5-for-5 batting performance on April 28, be-

came only the fifth player to reach the 3,000 games level on June 20 and collected hit No. 3,772 on June 22 to pass Hank Aaron for second place behind Ty Cobb on the all-time list. Later in the season, Rose also moved ahead of Aaron as the career leader in at-bats.

Garvey became the fifth player in major league history to own a string of 1,000 consecutive games played on June 7. The Dodgers' first baseman closed the season with a streak of 1,107 appearances and needed only 10 more games to equal Billy Williams' N.L. record.

Kaat, 43-year-old southpaw with the Cardinals, established a longevity record for pitchers by working his 24th major league season.

Veterans weren't the only record-setters.

Henderson, only 23 during the season, earned season-long attention while becoming baseball's new base-stealing champion. In only his fourth season in the majors, the speedy Oakland outfielder broke Lou Brock's 1974 mark of 118 thefts by stealing 130. Henderson equaled his own 1980 A.L. standard on August 2 when he swiped No. 100 in the A's 106th game.

However, his assault on Brock's record was not without controversy. On August 24, in the final game of a home stand against Detroit, he stole two bases to reach 117. Later during that game, a suspicious thing happened. In the eighth inning, with the A's leading, 3-0, Fred Stanley was on second base and Henderson on first. Stanley took a big lead off second and wound up being trapped in a rundown. On a subsequent pitchout, Henderson took off for second, but was thrown out.

As a result, he had to wait until two nights later in Milwaukee to tie Brock, and then on August 27 he swiped four more bases against the Brewers for a record 122. Bruises from the many head-first slides slowed Henderson the last five weeks of the campaign, and he registered only eight more steals in his last 22 games to finish with 130.

Five teams changed managers during the season, one of them twice, and six named new skippers after the campaign. One of the latter switches resulted from Earl Weaver's decision to hang up his uniform after nearly 15 years at the Orioles helm.

In contrast to Baltimore's record of managerial stability, George Steinbrenner continued his revolving-door policy with Yankee dugout leaders. He fired two pilots during the season.

Bob Lemon was the first victim. Steinbrenner axed him for the second time (the first was in 1979) on April 25 with the Yankees showing a 6-8 record. The ouster came less than six months after the Hall of Famer had been assured that, barring health problems, he would lead the team for the entire season. Lemon returned to scouting duties in California and was replaced by Gene Michael, who had been scheduled to resume the reins in 1983 under a three-year contract.

Michael's second hitch at the New York helm, like his first a year earlier, was shortlived. On August 3 the Yankees dropped a twinight doubleheader to the White Sox, leaving them with a 44-42 ledger under Michael. Shortly after midnight, Steinbrenner announced he was bringing in Clyde King, his No. 1 troubleshooter, to manage the team the remainder of the season. It was the Yankees' ninth managerial change in Steinbrenner's turbulent 10-year regime as principal owner. Michael, who was offered a front-office job, joined Lemon and Martin as managers fired twice by the Yankee boss.

Baltimore's Earl Weaver decided to step down after 15 seasons as manager at the end of the '82 campaign.

The turmoil in the Yankees' ranks extended to the coaches and players. The erstwhile Bronx Bombers employed five different pitching coaches and three batting coaches during the course of the campaign. When Michael became manager, he brought in Stan Williams to replace Jerry Walker and join Jeff Torborg as co-pitching coaches. Williams in turn was fired on June 11 and succeeded by King. When the latter moved to the front office on July 19 as Steinbrenner's assistant, Sammy Ellis was brought up from Columbus (International) as pitching coach.

Mickey Vernon began the season as the club's batting coach, but was replaced the first week in June by Joe Pepitone. On August 24, Pepitone was shifted to the front office and Lou Piniella, veteran outfielder, took over the duties of hitting instructor.

The second club to change managers was Milwaukee. A slump that produced 14 defeats in 21 games left the Brewers with a 23-24 record on June 2, the date Bob (Buck) Rodgers was dismissed. Harvey Kuenn, the team's hitting coach since 1971, was appointed interim skipper. He quickly transformed the Brewers from an unhappy outfit into a loose, tension-free group, and they went on to capture the pennant. Despite four coronary bypasses in 1976, surgery for kidney failure in 1977 and the amputation of his right leg below the knee in 1980, Kuenn showed no ill effects from the stress of managing and was rehired for '83.

John McNamara, who led Cincinnati to the best record in the majors a year earlier, became the third manager to walk the plank. The Reds dumped him on July 21 in favor of coach Russ Nixon. Another coach, Joe Amalfitano, departed along with McNamara. At the time, the Reds were 34-58, the second-worst record in either league.

In a carnival-like scenario, Owner Eddie Chiles fired Don Zimmer as Texas skipper on July 26, but requested him to stay on for two more games. Coach Darrell Johnson took over on July 29 with the Rangers owning a 38-58 ledger. Chiles later barred Johnson from appearing on a radio station interview program hosted by broadcaster Brad Sham, who had criticized the dismissal of Zimmer.

Bill Virdon's seven-year stay as Houston manager ended August 10 when he was ousted. Bob Lillis, a coach with the Astros since 1973, replaced him with the team sporting a 49-62 record and in fifth place.

Weaver announced early in the year that he intended to retire at season's end from the Baltimore job that paid him nearly $200,000 a year. Although only 52, he was the dean of active managers, having succeeded Hank Bauer as the Orioles' boss in July of 1968. In his 14½ seasons, he compiled a .596 winning percentage—third best by any manager—while leading the Birds to six division titles, four pennants and one world championship as well as seven second-place finishes. In September, Weaver agreed to a two-year contract to remain with the Orioles as a consultant and scout.

Two incidents marred Weaver's farewell campaign. On July 17, the fiery dugout genius allegedly struck umpire Terry Cooney in the face during a dispute, prompting Lee MacPhail to suspend him a week and fine him $2,000. It was Weaver's sixth suspension in seven years. And then on the closing day, after the Orioles had won 33 of their last 43 games to deadlock for first place, Weaver saw his club beaten by Milwaukee in the decisive finale. Although the defeat dimmed the occasion, he twice was called back onto the field after the game as loyal Orioles fans cheered in tribute to his remarkable record.

Late in the season, Dave Garcia disclosed he planned to quit as Cleveland manager at the close of the campaign, and on closing day Jim Fanning resigned as Montreal skipper to return to the Expos' front office as vice-president for player development. Another job became vacant when Gene Mauch, stung by criticism from all sides for "over-managing," announced his resignation on October 22. In guiding the Angels to the A.L. West flag, he had won his first title in 23 years as a manager. The club's loss in the League Championship Series left management disappointed, and there was some question whether Mauch quit or actually was fired.

With one week left in the season, speculation developed about Billy Martin's status with Oakland. On September 27 it was revealed that both Cleveland and the Yankees had requested and been given permission to negotiate with him. Martin still had three years remaining on a five-year contract as manager and director of player development with Oakland, but it appeared he had worn out his welcome in his hometown.

Roy Eisenhardt, president of the A's, officially announced Martin's dismissal on October 20. It marked the sixth time in as many tries that Martin failed to hold a major league managerial job more than three years.

After winning the A.L. West title the previous season, the A's slipped badly in '82, finishing fifth. The frustrations took their toll on Martin. After a loss to Milwaukee on August 19, he allegedly tore his office apart, breaking up the furniture. His relationship with Eisenhardt apparently was never the same thereafter. That same day, Martin's attorney, Eddie Sapir, sought to have his five-year contract extended to 10 years, but was turned down. Besides earning $250,000 annually, Martin had the use of a $600,000 Bay Area home through 1990.

Shortly after the season ended, Gabe Paul, Cleveland president, reportedly offered Martin a three-year contract worth a minimum of $1 million to manage the Indians. Martin reportedly insisted on a five-year pact, and finally the Indians decided to quit chasing him.

Two Yankee coaches and a one-time Yankee skipper were chosen to fill three of the managerial vacancies. The first to be named was Virdon, who was appointed to the Montreal post on October 12. Mike Ferraro and Joe Altobelli, who served as Yankee coaches in '82, were hired as managers of Cleveland and Baltimore on November 4 and November 12, respectively.

Like Ferraro, Doug Rader earned his first chance to manage in the majors when he was signed by Texas on November 1 to succeed Darrell Johnson. Rader, who had piloted San Diego's Hawaii affiliate the last three seasons, thus became the Rangers' 11th manager in 11 years. California named John McNamara as Mauch's replacement on November 2, making him the Angels' sixth manager in seven years. Steve Boros, who had served as a coach with Montreal, became the third newcomer to major league managing ranks when he accepted the Oakland job on November 17.

And last but not least, Martin and Steinbrenner joined forces for the third time when Martin was named to the Yankees' managerial post January 11, 1983.

The problems facing managers and management in general were magnified by growing drug abuse. Although baseball has had a relatively clean record compared to some other sports, four players were arrested on drug charges in 1982 and three others voluntarily entered drug abuse programs.

The first incident to be reported involved Alan Wiggins, rookie San Diego outfielder. He was arrested at 2:30 a.m. July 21 by San Diego police on a charge of possessing one gram of cocaine. By midafternoon, after a conference with Padres President Ballard Smith, Wiggins had checked into an Orange County rehabilitation center for a 30-day treatment program. Upon his release, Commissioner Kuhn dealt him a 30-day suspension extending through September 19.

Another San Diego player encountered problems. He was second baseman Juan Bonilla. A few days after Wiggins' arrest, Smith spoke to Bonilla, who had been sidelined since May 19 with a fractured left wrist. Bonilla subsequently released a statement on August 7 saying that he had voluntarily joined Wiggins in the drug and alcohol clinic.

A pair of Cleveland pitchers, Len Barker and Ed Glynn, were picked up by two undercover police officers in Chicago the night of August 29 on marijuana charges. The Indians duo and teammate Dan Spillner were walking back to their hotel when the plainclothes policemen stopped them and charged Barker and Glynn with

Mike Ferraro took over as Cleveland manager on November 4.

exchanging a cigarette that "emitted an odor like marijuana." Spillner was allowed to continue on his way, but the others were taken to the police station, searched and booked. No drugs were found, and the pair denied having had marijuana.

In mid-September, outfielder Tim Raines of Montreal, whose performance was short of his brilliant 1981 rookie season, admitted that he had "used drugs" earlier in the year. After the season, the fleet 23-year-old entered the same Orange County clinic that Wiggins had attended for drug abuse. In a December 11 story in the Montreal Gazette, Raines made his first public admission of cocaine use and said it was a major factor in his poor season. Raines, whose salary had jumped from $35,000 as a rookie to $200,000, revealed that he had used more than $40,000 worth of cocaine in the first nine months of the year.

Narcotics officers arrested Ron LeFlore, White Sox outfielder, on September 30 after a search of his home allegedly uncovered drugs and firearms. Detectives claimed to have found 5.5 grams of Quaaludes and amphetamines as well as two belts with a .25 derringer concealed in the buckle of each. A police department spokesman said LeFlore, 34, had been under surveillance for three months. Charged with possession of a controlled substance and two counts of failing to register weapons, he was released on $3,000 bond. The White Sox promptly suspended him for the remaining three games of the season.

Manager Dick Howser of Kansas City and his hitting instructor, Rocky Colavito, also encountered difficulty with the law. After a night game on August 19, Colavito was driving away from Royals Stadium when his car was struck by another automobile. Rocky's 16-year-old son, Steve, and Howser were passengers in the Colavito vehicle. The Royals' manager and coach were charged with interfering with police officers who were called to the scene of the accident. After a hearing on October 12, Judge Leonard S. Hughes sentenced both Colavito and Howser to 90 days in jail and fined them $250 and $100, respectively. They remained free on bail pending an appeal.

Despite the heavy financial losses suffered by numerous clubs, there were no changes in ownership, at least among the controlling interests. However, several teams underwent important shifts in front-office personnel.

Shortly after the season opened, Whitey Herzog, who held the dual title of general manager and manager for a year and a half, relinquished his front-office duties with the St. Louis Cardinals. His assistant, Joe McDonald, was promoted to G.M. At the same time, the club tore up Herzog's contract and gave him a new three-year pact as manager through 1984. Several weeks later, the Cardinals elevated the 36-year-old Gary Blase from executive assistant to vice-president for business operations.

The Texas Rangers' dismal performance led Owner Chiles to fire Executive Vice-President Eddie Robinson on June 10. Chiles himself assumed the duties of general manager on an interim basis, but later turned most of them over to Paul Richards, Robinson's 73-year-old former assistant. Robinson, whose contract extended through 1983, subsequently went to work for the Yankees handling special assignments. In midseason, Chiles confirmed he had contacted Bud Wilkinson, former college and pro football coach, about becoming the Rangers' G.M. The position finally was filled on October 4 with the promotion of Joe Klein. Tom

Grieve, Klein's assistant, succeeded him as the Texas club's farm director.

N.E. (Pete) Hardy was named chief executive officer of the Toronto Blue Jays in July. The appointment filled the vacancy created by the resignation eight months earlier of Peter Bavasi. The 65-year-old Hardy had been vice chairman of the club's board of directors since 1976 and also was chairman of the board of John Labatt Ltd., owner of the Blue Jays.

On the heels of Martin's dismissal, the Oakland A's hired Bill Rigney on October 26 to serve as an assistant to President Eisenhardt on baseball matters. Eisenhardt also disclosed the A's would be run by a brain trust that includes, besides himself and Rigney, Executive Vice-President Wally Haas, Vice-President-General Counsel Sandy Alderson and Dick Wiencek and Walt Jocketty, directors of minor league personnel and operations, respectively.

Other front-office changes that occurred during the first half of the year included: Bill Turner retired after 31 years as assistant farm director of the Pittsburgh Pirates and was succeeded by Tom Kayser; Tony Siegle resigned as assistant G.M. at Houston to become executive assistant with the Philadelphia Phillies; Jerry Clothier was appointed vice-president, finance, by the Phillies; Andy MacPhail, son of American League President Lee MacPhail, was named assistant to Houston General Manager Al Rosen; Jack Brickhouse, who retired the previous winter as a Cubs' broadcaster, joined the Chicago club as vice-president for special assignments; Ike Ikuhara, a member of the Los Angeles Dodgers' staff since 1965, was named assistant to President Peter O'Malley; Sandy Johnson joined the San Diego Padres as director of scouting; Pat Nugent was elevated from assistant to General Manager John Mullen to assistant vice-president by the Atlanta Braves; Sal Artiaga resigned as business coordinator for player development of the Cincinnati Reds to join the National Association as administrator, and Bing Devine resigned as vice-president, baseball for the Montreal Expos to become president of the St. Louis football Cardinals.

Late in the season, Ralph Nelson, assistant to General Manager Tom Haller, was named director of minor league operations by the San Francisco Giants. He succeeded Jack Schwarz, who was moved upstairs as a consultant. In postseason personnel shifts, the turnover on the Yankees continued when Irv Kaze quit after two years as director of media relations to join the staff of the Los Angeles Raiders football team and Lou Saban, who had held the title of president of the Yankees since March 1981, resigned on December 23 to return to football as head coach of Central Florida College in Orlando.

Other postseason front-office changes included: Dan Tecklenburg resigned as business manager of the Cincinnati Reds and was succeeded by Doug Bureman, former traveling secretary; the Chicago Cubs as part of an economy move, dismissed 12 employees, including promotions director Buck Peden, traveling secretary Jim Davidovich and ticket manager Jerry Foran. At the same time, they gave assistant G.M. John Cox the added duties of traveling secretary and promoted Terry Barthelmas from director of stadium operations to vice-president of business operations; Jeff Odenwald resigned as director of marketing for the Seattle Mariners; Fred Claire was elevated to executive vice-president by the Los Angeles Dodgers; Hugh Alexander, special assignments scout, was promoted to player personnel advisor by the Philadelphia Phillies; Gene Kirby resigned as coordinator of broadcasting for the Montreal Expos; Danny Menendez, who had been the Expos' director of scouting, was shifted to supervisory scout of the southeastern U.S., and Juan Marichal was hired by Oakland as director of Latin-American scouting.

Sixty players became eligible at season's close to test the free-agent market, but 19 of them either quickly negotiated new contracts with their clubs or, as happened with several aging stars, were released outright.

Among those landing new pacts, Jason Thompson fared the best, signing a five-year, $5.5 million agreement with the Pittsburgh Pirates. The Detroit Tigers retained Chet Lemon and Larry Herndon by rewarding them with five-year, $3.3 million and four-year, $2.5 million contracts, respectively. Phil Niekro, Atlanta's 43-year-old pitching ace, opted to remain with the Braves under a one-year, $800,000 agreement.

The Los Angeles Dodgers failed in bids to sign two of the potential free agents before the re-entry process. Garvey, who had just finished a six-year, $1.971 million contract, was offered a three-year pact to remain with the club, but turned it down. In addition, the Dodgers, one of five clubs ineligible to select Type A players, worked out a conditional swap with the Seattle Mariners for southpaw Floyd Bannister, only to have it fall through when they couldn't satisfy his financial demands by the midnight November 2 deadline. In the deal, the Dodgers were to send pitchers Alejandro Pena and Steve Shirley and outfielder Mark Bradley to Seattle.

The seventh annual re-entry draft was held at the New York Sheraton on November 10. Of the 41 players still eligible, only three qualified as Type A players requiring extra compensation in the form of a choice from a pool of unprotected professional players. They were Bannister, Steve Kemp and John Lowenstein. There also were four Type B players—Bill Almon, Alan Ashby, Pete Falcone and Joe Nolan.

Bannister and another lefthanded pitcher, Terry Forster, were the most sought-after players. Each was selected by 16 teams. The Pirates made the largest number of selections, 22, while four clubs—Cincinnati, Minnesota, Detroit and the Dodgers—did not choose any. Twenty-one players were picked by fewer than four teams, excluding their own club, and thus became free to negotiate with any team.

Following is the list of 41 players involved in the re-entry process, with the number of teams selecting them shown in parentheses and an asterisk indicating whether the player was picked by his own team:

AMERICAN LEAGUE

Baltimore—John Lowenstein (7*), Joe Nolan (7*); Boston—Tom Burgmeier (10*); California—Don Baylor (6), Luis Tiant (0); Chicago—Bill Almon (4*), Steve Kemp (9*), Aurelio Rodriguez (2); Cleveland—Alan Bannister (3), Miguel Dilone (0), Rick Manning (6*); Detroit—None; Kansas City—Don Hood (0), Hal McRae (4*), Jamie Quirk (8*), Paul Splittorff (7*); Milwaukee—Bob McClure (12*); Minnesota—None; New York—None; Oakland—Dave McKay (0), Fred Stanley (1); Seattle—Floyd Bannister (16), Bruce Bochte (3), Al Cowens (9*); Texas—None; Toronto—Glenn Adams (1), Wayne Nordhagen (2).

NATIONAL LEAGUE

Atlanta—None; Chicago—Bump Wills (1); Cincinnati—Bob Shirley (13*); Houston—Alan Ashby (4*), Kiko Garcia (0), Randy Moffitt (1); Los Angeles—Terry Forster (16), Steve Garvey (9); Montreal—Woodie Fryman (5*), Mike Phillips (0), Joel Youngblood (8); New York—Pete Falcone (5*), Ron Hodges (6*), Ellis Valentine (1); Philadelphia—Bill Robinson (0); Pittsburgh—Omar Moreno (6*); St. Louis—Gene Tenace (9*); San Diego—Steve Swisher (0); San Francisco—Reggie Smith (0).

The biggest winners in the free-agent draft were Garvey and Steinbrenner. While the long-time Dodgers star signed the richest contract, the Yankee owner inked the maximum three players to bring to 19 the number of free agents he has corraled in seven years.

Garvey and his agent, Jerry Kapstein, agreed to a five-year pact with San Diego on December 21. It reportedly will pay the veteran first baseman $6.6 million over five years, exclusive of performance and attendance bonuses that could add another $575,000 annually and enable him to earn as much as $9.475 million over the duration of the contract.

Steinbrenner's first catch was designated hitter Baylor. Terms of his agreement are said to be worth $3.675 million over four years with an option on a fifth season that would increase the total to $4.175 million. The Yankee owner then signed Kemp to a five-year, $5.45 million contract and pitcher Shirley for four years and $1.5 million.

Moreno signed with Houston for a guaranteed $3.25 million over five years plus $275,000 annually in incentive bonuses, while Burgmeier accepted a two-year, $800,000 contract with Oakland and Falcone took a two-year, $650,000 deal with Atlanta.

McRae re-signed with Kansas City for three years for $1.75 million, including five bonuses of $5,000 each if he weighs 185 or less on the first day of spring training as well as on May 15, June 15, at the All-Star break and on closing day. Alan Ashby also remained with his old club, Houston, under a new four-year, $2 million contract.

Early in the year, several of the 1981 free agents also landed fat contracts. Reggie Jackson hauled in the biggest, signing a four-year pact with California on January 22 that called for a reported $975,000 per season, exclusive of an attendance clause.

The Chicago White Sox became the first team to receive compensation from the professional player pool for the loss of a free agent. Of the three Type A players in the '81 re-entry draft, two re-signed with their original clubs. the exception was pitcher Ed Farmer, who left the White Sox to join the Phillies. As compensation, the White Sox chose Joel Skinner, 20-year-old catcher belonging to the Pittsburgh organization, from the pool on February 2. The loss of Skinner, son of Pirate coach Bob Skinner, entitled the Pirates to receive $150,000 from the compensation pot.

One player passed up a chance for free agency early in '82. He was Rob Wilfong, Minnesota infielder. Confusion stemming from the previous summer's strike and the fact that bonuses were to be pro-rated resulted in the Twins sending him a contract that called for less than the 20 percent maximum salary cut. The mistake entitled Wilfong to free agency, but he chose instead to compromise by accepting a three-year contract.

A total of 104 players filed for salary arbitration in January. To be eligible for the arbitration process, a player must have had two years in the majors and not be under contract.

By the time the hearings began, all but 22 cases were resolved through negotiations. Six clubs—Boston, Detroit, Kansas City, the Yankees, Montreal and San Diego—hired Tal Smith, former Houston general manager, to represent them in the proceedings. His fee reportedly was $30,000 per arbitration. Of the eight cases he argued, the clubs won all but the one involving Willie Aikens. As a result, for the first time in four years the clubs won more cases (14) than the players (8). Still, the 14 players who lost came away with a whopping one-year average increase in salary from $137,857 to $253,071.

Data obtained by Murray Chass of the New York Times revealed the eight players who won their pay disputes submitted the following figures, with the club's offer in parentheses: Tom Hume, Cincinnati, $595,000 ($375,000); Rickey Henderson, Oakland, $535,000 ($350,000); Aikens, Kansas City, $375,000 ($275,000); Julio Cruz, Seattle, $375,000 ($200,000); Mario Soto, Cincinnati, $295,000 ($200,000); Steve Trout, Chicago White Sox, $250,000 ($175,000); Roger Erickson, Minnesota, $160,000 ($105,000), and Larry Bradford, Atlanta, $130,000 ($90,000).

Chass' figures for the 14 who had to accept the club's offer, with the player's requested amount in parentheses, were: Jack Morris, Detroit, $450,000 ($650,000); Carney Lansford, Boston, $440,000 ($650,000); Bump Wills, Texas, $355,000 ($450,000); Greg Minton, San Francisco, $343,000 ($495,000); Dan Quisenberry, Kansas City, $300,000 ($480,000); Ron Davis, New York Yankees, $300,000 ($575,000); Dave Stieb, Toronto, $250,000 ($325,000); Dave Revering, New York Yankees, $250,000 ($325,000); Bill Almon, Chicago White Sox, $220,000 ($340,000); Don Aase, California, $215,000 ($300,000); Bob Molinaro, Chicago White Sox, $120,000 ($165,000); Jamie Quirk, Kansas City, $115,000 ($180,000); Frank Pastore,

California designated hitter Don Baylor was Yankee Owner George Stein-brenner's first catch when the free-agent sweepstakes got underway.

Cincinnati, $95,000 ($175,000), and Bobby Brown, New York Yankees, $90,000 ($175,000).

One salary dispute that was submitted actually never went to arbitration. It involved Mike Flanagan, Baltimore pitcher. His agent put down a salary figure of $485,000 while the Orioles submitted

$500,000. It was only the second time in the seven-year history of salary arbitration that a player came in with a lower figure than the club.

In a special hearing late in March, arbitrator Tom Roberts ruled in favor of the St. Louis Cardinals' offer of $450,000 to newly-acquired shortstop Ozzie Smith, who had sought a $750,000 salary. A two-month delay in completing the bizarre three-stage trade that brought Smith to the Cardinals from San Diego, together with a no-trade clause in Smith's contract and a five-week honeymoon by his agent, led to the belated and unusual case.

After reaching the magic $1 million mark two years earlier, baseball's salary plateau jumped to $2 million in '82 when a pair of players landed contracts of that magnitude.

The first was George Foster. Entering his option year with Cincinnati at a $750,000 salary, Foster was traded to the New York Mets on February 10 after agreeing to a five-year contract worth at least $10.2 million. Five days later, Montreal's Gary Carter put his name to a seven-year extension of his pact that will be worth slightly more than $14 million through the 1989 season.

According to Chass, Foster's agreement called for a $1 million bonus and salaries for the five years of $1.45, $1.55, $1.65, $1.75 and $1.8 million plus various bonus clauses and two option years at $1.9 and $2 million, while Carter's contract included a $2 million signing bonus and salaries totaling about $12 million for seven years plus a potential $3 million in bonuses.

Data released late in the year by the Major League Players Association revealed the average player salary in '82 was $241,497. This represented an increase of 30 percent over the 1981 average of $185,651. The median pay amounted to $170,900.

Ray Grebey, who heads management's Player Relations Committee, contested the player-union figures. Grebey provided figures for rosters on opening day, 1982, which showed an average salary of $245,000. This does not include performance bonuses.

According to the Players Association, the California Angels' salary average moved from fourth place in 1981 to first in 1982.

A breakdown of the mean salaries of the 26 clubs for the four-year period 1979-1982 follows:

1981 Rank	Club	1982 Average	1981 Average	1980 Average	1979 Average	No. of Players
4	California	423,403	259,404	191,014	155,564	30
1	N.Y. Yankees	411,988	309,855	242,937	199,236	30
2	Philadelphia	390,370	289,971	221,274	197,926	26
5	Milwaukee	330,965	243,882	159,086	137,309	27
3	Houston	306,565	260,789	176,720	73,660	28
11	Montreal	299,192	195,958	158,196	142,829	27
20	Oakland	266,335	148,065	54,994	41,220	26
10	N.Y. Mets	263,539	201,303	126,488	93,607	28
22	Kansas City	258,091	112,910	100,453	91,583	28
8	Pittsburgh	251,234	206,359	199,185	174,439	29
13	Chi. White Sox	247,673	192,658	72,415	74,673	27
6	Boston	247,513	223,252	184,686	145,692	26
18	Baltimore	242,558	169,919	116,156	101,266	26
7	St. Louis	237,533	207,654	173,480	116,628	25
21	Chi. Cubs	220,662	125,117	160,209	104,116	25
14	Los Angeles	216,332	192,104	183,124	134,305	27
15	Cleveland	216,000	186,396	127,505	98,023	27
12	Atlanta	209,492	195,449	147,989	90,366	26
9	Cincinnati	203,532	201,557	162,655	165,144	26
16	San Francisco	198,438	185,939	148,265	120,737	27
17	Texas	186,424	178,131	148,792	128,806	27
19	Detroit	174,134	160,561	86,988	63,377	28
23	San Diego	137,946	103,106	138,978	103,819	28
24	Toronto	127,860	97,271	67,218	67,044	25
25	Seattle	114,405	95,263	82,244	61,830	30
26	Minnesota	67,335	85,736	80,358	70,703	27
	Average Salary	241,497	185,651	143,756	113,558	706
	Average number of players					26.7

Salary figures have been discounted for salary deferrals without interest at a rate of 9 percent per year for the period of delayed payments.

The hefty player salaries, besides taxing club budgets, also fattened the agents' fees. Bill Conlin of the Philadelphia Daily News estimated the agents' fees from existing contracts were in the neighborhood of $7 million for the year.

Major league umpires likewise achieved substantial gains in salary and benefits. In what was described as a "blockbuster deal," the attorney-negotiator for the Major League Umpires Association, Richie Phillips, and league presidents Lee MacPhail and Chub Feeney reached agreement on a four-year contract on April 5, just eight hours before the season opened. The 11th-hour settlement culminated five months of negotiations and averted the possibility of another strike.

Under terms of the contract, the umpires were assured of average increases in base pay of 40 percent in '82 and 60 percent over the four years. The minimum salary, previously $18,000, was immediately boosted to $26,000 and then to $28,000, $30,000 and $37,000 the next three seasons. Senior arbiters such as Doug Harvey and John Kibler were raised from $50,000 to $70,000 and will earn $75,000 in the final year of the contract.

The umpire's pension plan also was improved so it "outstrips the one the players have," according to Phillips. He said it calls for a 100 percent increase in benefits, while life insurance benefits and disability payments were hiked 50 percent and the per diem allowance was raised from $77 to $90. In addition, remuneration was set at $15,000 for working the World Series, $10,000 the League Championship Series, $7,500 for any division playoff and $2,500 for the All-Star Game.

Besides the hefty gains, the new contract also provided for the promotion of six minor league umpires who refused to work during the arbiters' 1979 strike. They were Rocky Roe, Randy Marsh, Mark Johnson, Charles Williams, Bob Davidson and Drew Cobel. Roe and Marsh had moved up in '81. Addition of the six hiked the number of umpires on the major league staffs to 60.

The entire package, it was estimated, will cost the two leagues $8 million over the life of the contract, but they did obtain two major concessions. The umpires agreed to a four-year pact instead of the proposed three years and gave the league presidents the right to assign umpires to the All-Star Game and postseason series on the basis of merit rather than according to a rotation plan.

The American League lost the services of its two senior umpires during the year.

Milwaukee pitcher Pete Vuckovich captured Cy Young honors with an 18-6 record.

Lou DiMuro, who was serving his 20th season, was fatally injured when struck by an automobile in Arlington, Tex., on June 6. Bill Haller, also a 20-year veteran, announced his retirement at the close of the World Series. A brother of the Giants' general manager, the 47-year-old Haller later was named assistant to Dick Butler, the league's umpire supervisor.

Although individual player honors for the year were widely distributed, Milwaukee's Robin Yount stood out as the dominant performer. He was a near-unanimous choice for Most Valuable Player in the American League and teammate Pete Vuckovich easily won the Cy Young prize in the annual polls of members of the Baseball Writers' Association. In the National League, Steve Carlton of Philadelphia captured an unprecedented fourth Cy Young Award and Atlanta's Dale Murphy won MVP laurels.

Listed first on all but one of the 28 ballots, Yount was a landslide winner over runnerup Eddie Murray of Baltimore, 385 points to 228, in the A.L. Most Valuable Player poll. Murphy, the top choice on 14 of 24 ballots, edged St. Louis' Lonnie Smith in the N.L. voting by a 283-218 margin. Results of the MVP voting in the two leagues, based on 14 points for first place, nine for second and on down to one point for 10th place, follow:

American League

Player—Club	1	2	3	4	5	6	7	8	9	10	Pts.
Robin Yount, Milwaukee	27	—	—	1	—	—	—	—	—	—	385
Eddie Murray, Baltimore	—	13	10	3	1	—	1	—	—	—	228
Doug DeCinces, California	—	7	8	3	3	1	1	1	—	—	178
Hal McRae, Kansas City	—	3	1	12	6	4	—	—	—	—	175
Cecil Cooper, Milwaukee	—	2	3	7	6	1	4	1	—	1	152
Reggie Jackson, California	1	2	2	—	4	3	3	1	2	1	107
Dwight Evans, Boston	—	—	—	—	4	1	3	3	3	1	57
Gorman Thomas, Milwaukee	—	—	1	—	2	2	2	1	1	1½	44½
Dan Quisenberry, Kansas City	—	—	—	—	1	1	3	3	3	1	39
Rickey Henderson, Oakland	—	—	1	1	—	2	—	—	4	5	38
Dave Winfield, New York	—	—	—	—	—	4	—	3	1	2	33
Paul Molitor, Milwaukee	—	—	—	—	1	1	2	—	4	2½	29½
Lance Parrish, Detroit	—	—	—	—	—	1	1	4	2	1	26
Brian Downing, California	—	—	—	—	—	2	2	1	—	1	22
Willie Wilson, Kansas City	—	—	—	—	—	1	1	2	—	1	16
Rollie Fingers, Milwaukee	—	—	1	—	—	—	—	1	—	1	12
Bob Boone, California	—	—	—	—	—	1	1	—	1	1	12
Pete Vuckovich, Milwaukee	—	—	—	1	—	—	1	—	—	—	11
Jim Rice, Boston	—	—	—	—	—	—	2	—	1	—	10
Toby Harrah, Cleveland	—	—	—	—	—	—	1	1	1	—	9
Harold Baines, Chicago	—	—	—	—	—	1	—	1	—	1	9
George Brett, Kansas City	—	1	—	—	—	—	—	—	—	—	9
Don Baylor, California	—	—	1	—	—	—	—	—	—	—	8
Andre Thornton, Cleveland	—	—	—	—	—	—	—	1	2	1	8
Bob Stanley, Boston	—	—	—	—	—	—	—	1	1	1	6
Jim Palmer, Baltimore	—	—	—	—	—	1	—	—	—	—	5
Damaso Garcia, Toronto	—	—	—	—	—	—	—	—	2	1	5
Rod Carew, California	—	—	—	—	—	1	—	—	—	—	5
Bill Caudill, Seattle	—	—	—	—	—	—	—	1	—	1	4
Buddy Bell, Texas	—	—	—	—	—	—	—	1	—	—	3
Cal Ripken, Baltimore	—	—	—	—	—	—	—	1	—	—	3
Carney Lansford, Boston	—	—	—	—	—	—	—	—	—	1	1
Rick Sutcliffe, Cleveland	—	—	—	—	—	—	—	—	—	1	1
Gary Ward, Minnesota	—	—	—	—	—	—	—	—	—	1	1

National League

Player—Club	1	2	3	4	5	6	7	8	9	10	Pts.
Dale Murphy, Atlanta	14	8	1	1	—	—	—	—	—	—	283
Lonnie Smith, St. Louis	8	1	8	3	2	—	—	—	—	—	218
Pedro Guerrero, Los Angeles	—	4	7	8	3	1	1	—	—	—	175
Al Oliver, Montreal	—	8	4	6	3	2	—	—	—	1	175
Bruce Sutter, St. Louis	2	3	2	2	2	5	1	1	2	1	134
Mike Schmidt, Philadelphia	—	—	—	1	1	1	7	1	2	1	54
Jack Clark, San Francisco	—	—	—	1	1	3	4	1	2	2	53
Greg Minton, San Francisco	—	—	—	1	2	3	1	—	3	—	44
Steve Carlton, Philadelphia	—	—	—	—	3	2	—	2	3	1	41
Bill Buckner, Chicago	—	—	—	—	1	2	3	1	2	3	38
Bill Madlock, Pittsburgh	—	—	1	1	—	2	—	2	2	2	37
Gary Carter, Montreal	—	—	—	—	—	1	2	7	—	1	35
Ozzie Smith, St. Louis	—	—	1	—	2	—	1	—	—	1	25
George Hendrick, St. Louis	—	—	—	—	2	—	1	—	2	—	20
Terry Kennedy, San Diego	—	—	—	—	—	1	2	2	—	1	20
Joe Morgan, San Francisco	—	—	—	—	1	1	1	—	—	2	17
Keith Hernandez, St. Louis	—	—	—	—	—	—	—	3	1	1	12
Jason Thompson, Pittsburgh	—	—	—	—	—	—	—	3	1	1	12
Gene Garber, Atlanta	—	—	—	—	—	—	—	—	2	2	6
Joaquin Andujar, St. Louis	—	—	—	—	1	—	—	—	—	—	6
Fernando Valenzuela, Los Ang.	—	—	—	—	—	—	—	—	1	1	3
Andre Dawson, Montreal	—	—	—	—	—	—	—	1	—	—	3
Chris Chambliss, Atlanta	—	—	—	—	—	—	—	—	—	2	2
Gary Matthews, Philadelphia	—	—	—	—	—	—	—	—	1	—	2
Ray Knight, Houston	—	—	—	—	—	—	—	—	—	1	1

Carlton received 20 first-place votes and four seconds to win the National League Cy Young balloting handily over Steve Rogers of Montreal, 112 points to 29. In capturing American League honors, Vuckovich was named on only 23 of 26 ballots but easily edged Jim Palmer of Baltimore, 87 to 59. A breakdown of the Cy Young poll in each league, based on a 5-3-1 vote system, follows:

American League

Pitcher-Club	1	2	3	Pts.
Vuckovich, Milwaukee	14	4	5	87
Palmer, Baltimore	4	12	3	59
Quisenberry, Kan. City	4	5	5	40
Stieb, Toronto	5	3	2	36
Sutcliffe, Cleveland	1	2	3	14
Zahn, California	-	1	4	7
Stanley, Boston	-	1	1	4
Caudill, Seattle	-	-	4	4
Petry, Detroit	-	-	1	1

National League

Pitcher-Club	1	2	3	Pts.
Carlton, Phila.	20	4	-	112
Rogers, Montreal	1	6	6	29
Valenzuela, Los Ang...	1	6	2½	25½
Sutter, St. Louis	2	3	6	25
P. Niekro, Atlanta	-	4	6	18
Minton, San Fran.	-	1	1	4
Andujar, St. Louis	-	-	1	1
Garber, Atlanta	-	-	1	1
Soto, Cincinnati	-	-	½	½

Cal Ripken, Baltimore infielder, was top choice in the Baseball Writers' balloting for American League Rookie of the Year. He received 24 first-place votes and four seconds to beat runnerup Kent Hrbek of Minnesota, 132 points to 90. Steve Sax of Los Angeles edged Pittsburgh's Johnny Ray, 63 to 57, in the National League rookie poll.

Whitey Herzog captured two of The Sporting News' most prestigious awards. The manager of the world champion Cardinals was voted Manager of the Year by his peers and also was chosen for The Sporting News Man of the Year honors. Other TSN honors went to Robin Yount as Major League Player of the Year and Harry Dalton, Milwaukee general manager, who was hailed as Executive of the Year. At the minor league level, TSN choices for No. 1 Man honors were: Player of the Year—Ron Kittle of Edmonton (Pacific Coast League), Manager of the Year—George Scherger of Indianapolis (American Association) and Executives of the Year—A. Ray Smith of Louisville (American Association) in Class AAA, Art

Whitey Herzog led his Cardinals to a World Series title and was named TSN's Man of the Year.

Clarkson of Birmingham (Southern) in Class AA and Bob Carruesco of Stockton (California) in Class A.

Other award winners chosen by The Sporting News included: A.L. Player and Pitcher of the Year—Yount and Stieb of Toronto, respectively; N.L. Player and Pitcher of the Year—Murphy of Atlanta and Carlton of Philadelphia, respectively; A.L. Rookie Player and Pitcher—Ripken of Baltimore and Ed Vande Berg of Seattle, respectively; N.L. Rookie Player and Pitcher—Ray of Pittsburgh and Steve Bedrosian of Atlanta, respectively; Comeback Player of the Year—Andre Thornton of Cleveland in the A.L. and Joe Morgan of San Francisco in the N.L.; Firemen of the Year—Quisenberry of Kansas City in the A.L. and Sutter of St. Louis in the N.L.

The All-Star Teams selected by The Sporting News for the two leagues consisted of the following:

American League: 1B—Cecil Cooper, Milwaukee; 2B—Damaso Garcia, Toron-

Steve Rogers won 19 games for Montreal and the N.L. earned-run average title (2.40).

to; SS—Robin Yount, Milwaukee; 3B—Doug DeCinces, California; LF—Dave Winfield, New York; CF—Gorman Thomas, Milwaukee; RF—Dwight Evans, Boston; C—Lance Parrish, Detroit; RHP—Dave Stieb, Toronto; LHP—Geoff Zahn, California; DH—Hal McRae, Kansas City.

National League: 1B—Al Oliver, Montreal; 2B—Manny Trillo, Philadelphia; SS—Ozzie Smith, St. Louis; 3B—Mike Schmidt, Philadelphia; LF—Lonnie Smith, St. Louis; CF—Dale Murphy, Atlanta; RF—Pedro Guerrero, Los Angeles; C—Gary Carter, Montreal; RHP—Steve Rogers, Montreal; LHP—Steve Carlton, Philadelphia.

The Hillerich & Bradsby Silver Slugger Awards for hitting prowess went to: 1B—Cooper, Milwaukee, in the American League and Oliver, Montreal, in the National; 2B—Garcia, Toronto and Morgan, San Francisco; SS—Yount, Milwaukee, and Dave Concepcion, Cincinnati; 3B—DeCinces, California, and Schmidt, Philadelphia; OF—Winfield, New York; Wilson, Kansas City, and Jackson, California, in the American and Murphy, Atlanta; Guerrero, Los Angeles, and Leon Durham, Chicago, in the National; C—Parrish, Detroit, and Carter, Montreal; P—Don Rob-

inson, Pittsburgh, and DH—McRae, Kansas City.

The Rawlings Gold Glove winners for fielding excellence, as chosen by the managers and coaches, were: 1B—Murray, Baltimore, in the American League and Keith Hernandez, St. Louis, in the National League; 2B—Frank White, Kansas City, and Trillo, Philadelphia; SS—Yount, Milwaukee, and Ozzie Smith, St. Louis; 3B—Buddy Bell, Texas, and Schmidt, Philadelphia; OF—Evans, Boston; Dwayne Murphy, Oakland, and Winfield, New York, in the American League and Andre Dawson, Montreal; Murphy, Atlanta, and Garry Maddox, Philadelphia, in the National League; C—Bob Boone, California, and Carter, Montreal, and P—Ron Guidry, New York, and Phil Niekro, Atlanta.

Silver Glove winners for fielding supremacy in the minors were: 1B—Chris Nyman, Edmonton (Pacific Coast); 2B—Steve Aragon, Wisconsin Rapids (Midwest); 3B—Robert Mariano, Fort Lauderdale (Florida State); SS—Roland Biancalana, Omaha (American Association); OF—Andres Mora, Saltillo-Laredo (Mexican), John Moses, Lynn (Eastern), and Ed Saavedra, Chattanooga (Southern); C—Tom Nieto, Arkansas (Texas); P—Fernando Gonzales, Alexandria (Carolina).

Louisville's record-breaking attendance highlighted the year's developments in minor leagues. After a nine-year stretch without professional baseball, the Kentucky city returned to the American Association in 1982 when A. Ray Smith shifted his franchise from Springfield, Ill. Louisville responded by turning out 868,418 customers, breaking the former National Association mark of 670,563 set by San Francisco of the Pacific Coast League in 1946. The remarkable showing also enabled the American Association to register a record gate of 2,407,526, topping the previous high set in 1948. Altogether, National Association clubs attracted 18,234,670 fans for the year, including 17,636,981 for the regular season.

An alleged pitch-tipping scheme led to a one-year suspension for one minor league player. Capping a five-month investigation, President Johnny Johnson of the National Association announced on February 3 that he was banning Angel Rodriguez, third-year catcher from Puerto Rico, for a year. The penalty was retroactive to August 21, 1981, when the Alexandria (Carolina) club sat Rodriguez down for supposedly tipping off opposing Latin-Americans in Spanish to upcoming pitches.

NATIONAL LEAGUE

Including

Team Reviews of 1982 Season

Team Day-by-Day Scores

1982 Standings, Home-Away Records

1982 Official N.L. Batting Averages

1982 Official N.L. Fielding Averages

1982 Official N.L. Pitching Averages

1982 Pitching Against Each Club

St. Louis' Joaquin Andujar, who describes himself as "one tough Dominican," was plenty tough on National League batters in 1982.

Consistency Makes Cards No. 1

By RICK HUMMEL

The Cardinals won their first pennant in 14 years—and their first World Series in 15—because of remarkable consistency. Until the last week of the 1982 season, when they already had clinched the National League East title, the Cardinals never lost more than three games in succession.

St. Louis' 12-game winning streak, which began in the second week of the season, jumped the Cardinals to the head of the class and the club's eight-game streak starting in mid-September broke the race open.

"The reason for it," said reliever Jim Kaat, "was because of the big guy (Bruce Sutter) in the bullpen. When you've got great defense, which we had, and a strong man in the bullpen, you know you're going to win consistently.

"It's just like playing golf. You don't have to make a lot of good shots. You just have to avoid making bad ones."

There were three new regulars in the Cardinals lineup—outfielders Lonnie Smith and Willie McGee and shortstop Ozzie Smith. When Keith Hernandez, George Hendrick and Darrell Porter struggled early in the season, McGee and the Smiths carried the Cardinals' offense.

Lonnie Smith, playing regularly for the first time in his career after being a spot player in Philadelphia, led the league in runs scored with 120, was second in steals with 68 and finished fourth in batting at .307.

Ozzie Smith made St. Louis fans forget Garry Templeton with his brilliant play at shortstop. Smith handled more chances per game than any other shortstop in the league and made just 13 errors, which was high in the Cardinal infield. The four regular infielders—Ozzie Smith, Keith Hernandez, Tom Herr and Ken Oberkfell—combined for only 44 errors.

McGee, acquired from the New York Yankees in October, 1981, for journeyman pitcher Bob Sykes, was called up from Louisville in May. He hit .296 in his first major league season and played a solid center field.

In the National League playoffs against Atlanta, McGee knocked in five runs and had a triple and home run in the pennant-clinching game. Then he played one of the most spectacular World Series games ever in Game 3. McGee hit two home runs, good for four runs, and saved a home run and a double with sparkling plays in the field.

The Wizard of Oz was terrific at shortstop for the Cardinals last season.

The starting pitching, featuring Joaquin Andujar, Bob Forsch, John Stuper, Dave LaPoint and Steve Mura, was far better than anyone had expected. Andujar, who finished 15-10, had a seven-game winning streak in the last two months of the season and then racked up three more victories in postseason play, including the pennant-clinching game and the seventh game of the World Series.

From August 12 on, Andujar's earned-run average was 1.68 and the Cardinals won 13 of the 14 games he started. Andujar finished tied for second in the league in ERA at 2.47.

Forsch likewise won 15 games, rookies Stuper and LaPoint combined for 18 (nine apiece) and Mura had 12 victories. Stuper earned the Cardinals' most important victory of the season in Game 6 of the Series when the Cardinals trailed, three games to two.

The bullpen, headed by Sutter and Doug

SCORES OF ST. LOUIS CARDINALS' 1982 GAMES

APRIL

6—At Hous.	W	14-3	Forsch	Ryan
7—At Hous.	L	2-3	Niekro	Martin
8—At Hous.	L	0-1	Knepper	Andujar
10—Pittsburgh	L	7-11	Scurry	Littell
11—Pittsburgh	W	7-6	Kaat	Romo
12—Pittsburgh	W	5-4	Martin	Griffin
13—At Chicago	W	4-3	Andujar	Martz
14—At Chicago	W	3-1	Rincon	Jenkins
15—At Chicago	W	6-1	Mura	Bird
16—Phila.	W	3-2	Forsch	Krukow
17—Phila.	W	6-0	Andujar	Carlton
18—Phila.	W	6-5‡	LaPoint	Brusstar
20—At Pitts.	W	7-4	Martin	Rhoden
21—At Pitts.	W	6-2	Mura	Candelaria
23—At Phila.	W	9-2	Forsch	Krukow
24—At Phila.	W	7-4	Bair	Farmer
25—At Phila.	L	4-8	Carlton	Rincon
26—Houston	L	2-6	Ryan	Martin
27—Houston	L	0-3	Ruhle	Mura
28—Houston	W	5-4	Forsch	Smith
30—At Cinn.	L	2-8	Pastore	Andujar

Won 14, Lost 7

MAY

1—At Cinn.	L	1-10	Soto	Rincon
2—At Cinn.	L	1-5	Leibrandt	Mura
2—At Cinn.	W	6-4	Martin	Price
3—Chicago	W	9-4	Bair	Noles
4—Chicago	W	7-4	Andujar	Jenkins
5—Chicago	W	7-6	Bair	Hernandez
7—Atlanta	L	3-6†	Garber	Martin
8—Atlanta	W	8-7	Sutter	Camp
9—Atlanta	L	0-3	Hanna	Andujar
10—Cincinnati	L	1-3	Pastore	Martin
11—Cincinnati	W	5-1	Mura	Soto
13—At Atlanta	W	10-9	Rincon	Dayley
14—At Atlanta	L	1-2	Garber	Bair
15—At Atlanta	W	7-6†	Sutter	Garber
16—At Atlanta	L	2-5	Mahler	Mura
18—At S. Diego	W	2-0	Forsch	Curtis
19—At S. Diego	L	4-5†	Boone	Sutter
20—At S. Diego	W	6-3	LaPoint	Welsh
21—At L.A.	W	6-3	Mura	Reuss
22—At L.A.	L	2-3	Power	Rincon
23—At L.A.	L	0-5	Welch	Forsch
24—At S. Fran.	W	6-0	Andujar	Gale
25—At S. Fran.	W	8-3	LaPoint	Martin
26—At S. Fran.	W	8-4	Mura	Hammaker
28—San Diego	W	5-2	Forsch	Eichelberger
29—San Diego	L	2-4	Curtis	Andujar
30—San Diego	W	6-5†	Sutter	Lucas
31—San Fran.	W	11-6	Martin	Martin

Won 17, Lost 11

JUNE

1—San Fran.	L	3-4‡	Minton	Kaat
2—San Fran.	W	1-0	Andujar	Laskey
4—Los Ang.	W	5-2	Forsch	Stewart
5—Los Ang.	L	2-6	Valenzuela	Mura
6—Los Ang.	L	3-5	Howe	Sutter
7—At Mon.	L	2-3	Burris	Sutter
8—At Mon.	W	5-4§	Sutter	Fryman
9—At Mon.	L	1-5	Gullickson	Forsch
11—At N.Y.	W	7-3	Andujar	Jones
12—At N.Y.	L	2-6	Swan	Mura
14—Montreal	W	2-1	Forsch	Gullickson
15—Montreal	W	3-2‡	Sutter	Burris
16—Montreal	L	3-8	Lea	LaPoint
18—New York	L	3-5	Orosco	Sutter
18—New York	W	5-4	Stuper	Lynch
19—New York	L	5-8	Hausman	Keener
20—New York	L	4-5†	Scott	Sutter
21—Phila.	W	7-5	Sutter	Reed
22—Phila.	W	3-2	Stuper	Lyle
23—Phila.	L	1-7	Krukow	Mura
24—Phila.	L	2-10	Carlton	Forsch
25—At Chicago	L	3-5	Jenkins	Andujar
26—At Chicago	W	4-1	LaPoint	Bird
26—At Chicago	W	2-1	Kaat	Smith
27—At Chicago	L	2-4	Ripley	Stuper
28—At Phila.	L	0-1	Carlton	Mura
29—At Phila.	W	15-3	Andujar	Ruthven
30—At Phila.	L	3-6	Christenson	Forsch

Won 12, Lost 16

JULY

2—Chicago	L	3-4	Kravec	LaPoint
3—Chicago	L	1-2	Filer	Andujar
4—Chicago	W	7-2	Stuper	Noles
5—At Cinn.	W	6-5†	Kaat	Hume
6—At Cinn.	W	3-1	Mura	Leibrandt

7—At Atlanta	L	2-3	Camp	Andujar
8—At Atlanta	W	5-2	Stuper	Mahler
9—At Hous.	W	3-2	LaPoint	Ryan
10—At Hous.	L	2-4	Niekro	Forsch
11—At Hous.	L	2-4	Knepper	Andujar
15—Cincinnati	L	3-7	Berenyi	Stuper
16—Cincinnati	W	6-4	Lahti	Hume
17—Cincinnati	W	4-2	Forsch	Soto
18—Cincinnati	W	6-5	Kaat	Leibrandt
19—Atlanta	L	1-4	Niekro	Andujar
20—Atlanta	L	6-8	Cowley	Lahti
21—Atlanta	W	8-0	Mura	Walk
23—Houston	W	6-2	Andujar	Niekro
24—Houston	W	5-1	Forsch	Knepper
25—Houston	W	4-3	Sutter	Sutton
27—New York	W	9-4	Lahti	Scott
28—New York	W	7-5	Keener	Lynch
29—At Mon.	L	3-4†	Fryman	Bair
30—At Mon.	L	4-5‡	Fryman	Bair
31—At Mon.	W	10-1	Mura	Burris

Won 15, Lost 10

AUGUST

1—At Mon.	L	4-5	Reardon	Lahti
2—Pittsburgh	L	2-4z	Romo	Kaat
3—Pittsburgh	W	4-2	Forsch	Robinson
4—Pittsburgh	L	2-5	Candelaria	LaPoint
5—Pittsburgh	W	7-3*	Mura	McWilliams
6—Montreal	L	3-5	Rogers	Andujar
7—Montreal	W	9-5	Kaat	Schatzeder
8—Montreal	L	1-2	Palmer	Forsch
9—At N.Y.	W	7-2	Lahti	Puleo
10—At N.Y.	W	7-2	Mura	Jones
12—At Pitts.	W	3-2	Andujar	Baumgarten
13—At Pitts.	L	4-7	Robinson	Forsch
14—At Pitts.	W	4-1	Stuper	Candelaria
15—At Pitts.	W	12-5	Mura	McWilliams
15—At Pitts.	W	5-2	LaPoint	Sarmiento
17—San Diego	W	3-2	Sutter	Lucas
18—San Diego	W	2-1	Forsch	Hawkins
19—San Diego	L	3-4	Dravecky	Stuper
20—San Fran.	L	7-8	Lavelle	Sutter
21—San Fran.	W	7-6	LaPoint	Laskey
22—San Fran.	W	5-4§	Lahti	Lavelle
23—Los Ang.	W	11-3	Forsch	Reuss
24—Los Ang.	L	2-5	Welch	Stuper
25—Los Ang.	L	3-11	Valenzuela	Mura
27—At S. Diego	W	2-1	Andujar	Lollar
29—At S. Diego	L	4-9	Curtis	Forsch
29—At S. Diego	W	5-3	Bair	Hawkins
30—At L.A.	W	3-2	Stuper	Valenzuela
31—At L.A.	L	1-4	Hooton	Mura

Won 17, Lost 12

SEPTEMBER

1—At L.A.	W	6-5x	Bair	Wright
3—At S. Fran.	L	2-3†	Minton	Sutter
4—At S. Fran.	L	4-5	Lavelle	Sutter
5—At S. Fran.	L	1-5	Breining	Stuper
6—Montreal	W	1-0	Andujar	Gullickson
7—Montreal	L	4-7	Smith	Lahti
8—Montreal	W	1-0	Forsch	Lea
10—New York	L	1-2	Swan	Stuper
11—New York	W	6-3	Andujar	Lynch
12—New York	L	1-4	Falcone	Mura
13—At Phila.	L	0-2	Carlton	Forsch
14—At Phila.	W	2-0	Stuper	Krukow
15—At Phila.	W	8-0	Andujar	Denny
17—At N.Y.	W	3-2†	Sutter	Allen
17—At N.Y.	W	7-1	Mura	Holman
18—At N.Y.	W	2-0	Forsch	Falcone
18—At N.Y.	W	6-2	Lahti	Terrell
19—At N.Y.	W	3-1	Stuper	Zachry
20—Phila.	W	4-1	Andujar	Denny
21—Phila.	L	2-5	Carlton	Rasmussen
22—Pittsburgh	W	2-1	LaPoint	Rhoden
23—Pittsburgh	L	3-5‡	Romo	Martin
24—Chicago	W	3-1	Stuper	Campbell
25—Chicago	W	5-1	Andujar	Noles
26—Chicago	L	1-6	Jenkins	Rasmussen
27—At Mon.	W	4-2	LaPoint	Gullickson
28—At Mon.	L	4-5†	Rogers	Lahti
29—At Pitts.	L	3-7	Romo	Stuper
30—At Pitts.	L	2-7	Sarmiento	Mura

Won 16, Lost 13

OCTOBER

2—At Chicago	L	4-8	Jenkins	Kaat
3—At Chicago	W	5-4y	Rasmussen	Kravec

Won 1, Lost 1

*5 innings. †10 innings. ‡11 innings. §12 innings. x13 innings. y14 innings. z17 innings.

Rookie Willie McGee was better than anyone expected as the Cardinals' regular center fielder.

The countdown toward the Cardinals' first East Division title ended September 27 in a 4-2 victory over Montreal, the division champion in strike-torn 1981. But Manager Whitey Herzog said there was no significance to beating the Expos.

"They weren't the Eastern Division champions last year," said Herzog, The Sporting News' Manager of the Year. "We beat them; we had a better record (59-43 overall mark compared with the Expos' 60-48). But we got the short end of the stick in the Bowie Kuhn sweepstakes (split-season format) and we couldn't do anything about it."

The Cardinals finished last in the major leagues in home runs, 67, the first division winner ever to do that. They became the second team in National League history to win a pennant and World Series despite finishing last in home runs, the 1965 Los Angeles Dodgers being the only other one.

Hendrick led the Cardinals with 19 home runs, slightly below his norm, but he knocked in 104 runs. Catcher Porter, who struggled through another off-year at bat, hit 12 home runs, but he saved his best for last when he was named the Most Valuable Player in both the Championship Series and the World Series.

Hernandez had just seven home runs but batted in 94 runs and matched his career batting average of .299.

Second baseman Herr, beset with leg injuries in the first half of the season, batted nearly .300 in the second half and finished at .266. Oberkfell closed with an eight-game hitting streak, winding up at .289. He extended that hitting streak to 13 games in postseason play.

The Cardinals' bench, featuring Dane Iorg, Mike Ramsey, Steve Braun, Gene Tenace and David Green, also contributed heavily. Iorg hit .294 during the season and .529 in the World Series as a designated hitter.

Ramsey was a valuable fill-in for Herr and Ozzie Smith, Braun hit nearly .300 as a pinch-hitter and Tenace had 16 extra-base hits among his 32 hits for the season. Green batted .283 as a fourth outfielder.

Then there was third-string catcher Glenn Brummer, who pulled off the most memorable play of the season August 22 when he stole home with two outs and two strikes in the 12th inning to beat the San Francisco Giants.

All this contributed to record attendance. The Cardinals drew 2,111,906 fans, marking the third time they had surpassed the 2,000,000 mark. The other two times, 1967 and 1968, they also were in the World Series.

Bair, had 31 victories and 47 saves in the regular season, with Sutter posting nine victories and 36 saves (high in the major leagues).

Sutter retired 13 men in succession in the league Championship Series as he got a victory and a save, and he piled up two more saves and a victory in the World Series, giving him 39 saves and 11 victories for the season.

"I don't think anybody will say next season that we didn't have a good pitching staff," said Sutter.

The Cardinals' team ERA was 3.37 and the staff was at its best in the eight-game winning streak, allowing only seven runs.

St. Louis was out of first place only twice after August 12, the last time being September 13 when the Cardinals were shut out by Philadelphia's Steve Carlton. But Stuper (with help from Sutter) and Andujar shut out the Phillies the next two nights and the Cardinals were on their way to nailing it down.

Phillies Start, Finish Slowly

By HAL BODLEY

For the Philadelphia Phillies, 1982 was the story of six agonizing weeks—the first three and the last three.

The recast Phillies, under new Manager Pat Corrales, lost 11 of their first 14 games and on April 24 were in last place in the National League East, nine games behind St. Louis (13-3).

After that, they picked up the pieces and fashioned a 76-50 record through September 10.

The Phils, who first gained sole possession of first place July 3, either led the East or shared the divisional lead for all but two days from July 11 through August 12. They last headed the division when Steve Carlton shut out the Cardinals on September 13. That victory over the Cards was one of only five Phils triumphs in a 16-game stretch, a span that doomed Philadelphia's hopes. The Phils finished 89-73, three games behind the Cardinals.

"When I look back on this season, I'll always remember our horrible start and the last three weeks," said Corrales, who was appointed to the job when Dallas Green became vice president and general manager of the Chicago Cubs. "It was hard to believe our bats went so cold."

"We got off to a lousy start and we didn't finish very well," said Bill Giles, who put together a syndicate that purchased the franchise in October of 1981 from the Carpenter family for $30 million. "For the five months in between, we were one of the best teams in the league; maybe the best. I find that encouraging.

"I don't think many people picked us to finish where we did. Second place, three games out, 16 games over .500. That's not too bad. If you had offered me that back in March, I might have taken it.

"It's just that when you get into first place in September, you feel you should stay there. If you don't, you feel let down."

The Phils, who had the best home record (51-30) of any National League team, had the best pitcher in baseball in Carlton.

At age 37, the lefthanded Carlton won a record fourth National League Cy Young Award. He had a 23-11 record, and was the majors' only 20-game winner.

Carlton led the league in victories (23), strikeouts (286), complete games (19), shutouts (six) and innings pitched (295⅔).

After losing his first four decisions for his worst start in 17-plus seasons, Carlton won 23 of his last 30 decisions.

Mike Krukow won 13 games for the Phils, and Dick Ruthven had 11 victories. Ron Reed was the big man in the bullpen, compiling 14 saves. Sid Monge, who had two saves, posted a 7-1 record.

Despite being hampered by numerous injuries, including a fractured toe and a cracked rib, two-time Most Valuable Player Mike Schmidt led the league in slugging percentage (.547), on-base percentage (.403) and walks (107). He finished third in the N.L. in home runs (35) and runs scored (108) and had a team-leading 87 runs batted in.

Catcher Bo Diaz, obtained from Cleveland in an off-season trade, finished his first year in the National League with 18 homers and 85 RBIs, most by a Phillies' catcher since Stan Lopata set club records of 32 and 95 in 1956.

Outfielder Gary Matthews had 19 homers and 83 RBIs.

Manny Trillo had a record-breaking season at second base, setting major league marks for most consecutive errorless games for a season (89) and most consecutive errorless chances (479).

Although first baseman Pete Rose slumped to a .271 average, he continued to establish milestones.

• On June 22 he collected his 3,772nd hit in the third inning off the Cardinals' John Stuper, moving into second place on the all-time hits list ahead of Hank Aaron.

• On July 19 he collected his 3,800th hit in the eighth inning against San Diego's Eric Show.

• On August 14 his first at-bat was his 12,365th, moving him into first place ahead of Aaron on the all-time list.

• On August 18 he had his 13,941st plate appearance, moving him into first place on the all-time list ahead of Aaron.

• On September 1 he made his 8,595th out, moving him into first place ahead of Aaron.

• On September 8 he played in his 3,077th game, also moving ahead of Aaron for first place on the National League all-time list.

In addition, Rose played in his 626th consecutive game last season, becoming only the second player in baseball history to have two streaks of 500 consecutive games played. Charlie Gehringer was the other.

Rose's 21-game hitting streak tied Houston's Dickie Thon for tops in the league. It was the seventh time in Rose's career he had compiled a hitting streak of

In his first season with the Phillies, Bo Diaz added more power to an already powerful lineup.

SCORES OF PHILADELPHIA PHILLIES' 1982 GAMES

APRIL			Winner	Loser	JULY			Winner	Loser
8—New York	L	2-7	Jones	Carlton	9—Los Ang.	L	4-6‡	Stewart	McGraw
9—Montreal	L	0-2	Rogers	Christenson	10—Los Ang.	W	4-2	Ruthven	Welch
10—Montreal	L	3-11	Gullickson	Ruthven	11—Los Ang.	W	4-3	Christenson	Valenzuela
11—Montreal	W	1-0	Krukow	Burris	15—At S. Fran.	W	2-1	Krukow	Gale
13—At N. Y.	L	2-5	Jones	Carlton	16—At S. Fran.	W	1-0	Carlton	Laskey
14—At N. Y.	L	1-8	Scott	Ruthven	17—At S. Fran.	W	5-3‡	R. Reed	Breining
15—At N. Y.	W	8-4x	Brusstar	Puleo	18—At S. Fran.	L	3-4	Hammaker	Christenson
16—At St. L.	L	2-3	Forsch	Krukow	19—At S. Diego	W	7-6	Monge	Curtis
17—At St. L.	L	0-6	Andujar	Carlton	20—At S. Diego	L	0-2	Montefusco	Carlton
18—At St. L.	L	5-6‡	LaPoint	Brusstar	21—At S. Diego	W	7-1	Ruthven	Lollar
19—At Mon.	W	2-0	Christenson	Sanderson	23—At L. A.	W	6-3	Altamirano	Stewart
21—At Mon.	L	2-5	Rogers	Carlton	24—At L. A.	L	2-3	Welch	Bystrom
23—St. Louis	L	2-9	Forsch	Krukow	25—At L. A.	W	1-0	Carlton	Reuss
24—St. Louis	L	4-7	Bair	Farmer	27—At Pitts.	L	0-4	McWilliams	Ruthven
25—St. Louis	W	8-4	Carlton	Rincon	28—At Pitts.	W	4-3	Christenson	Rhoden
27—At L.A.	L	0-3	Reuss	Christenson	29—Chicago	W	3-2	Krukow	Tidrow
28—At L.A.	W	9-3	Farmer	Howe	30—Chicago	W	3-1	Carlton	Jenkins
29—At L.A.	L	0-4	Hooton	Ruthven	31—Chicago	W	2-0	Bystrom	Ripley
30—At S. Diego	W	3-1†	Carlton	Eichelberger				**Won 16, Lost 9**	
			Won 6, Lost 13						
					AUGUST				
MAY					1—Chicago	L	2-7	Noles	Ruthven
1—At S. Diego	L	6-9	DeLeon	Christenson	2—Montreal	W	2-1	Christenson	Gullickson
2—At S. Diego	W	3-0	Krukow	Curtis	3—Montreal	W	3-2	Krukow	Palmer
3—At S. Fran.	W	5-3	Monge	Schatzeder	4—Montreal	W	5-4	Carlton	Sanderson
4—At S. Fran.	W	9-4	Carlton	Gale	5—Montreal	L	2-9	Lea	Bystrom
6—San Diego	W	12-7	Christenson	Eichelberger	6—At Chicago	L	2-4	Ripley	Ruthven
7—San Diego	W	5-2	Lyle	Lucas	7—At Chicago	L	2-3	Noles	Christenson
8—San Diego	W	5-1	Ruthven	Montefusco	8—At Chicago	L	5-8	Tidrow	McGraw
9—San Diego	L	0-6	Lollar	Carlton	9—Pittsburgh	W	4-3	Carlton	Tekulve
10—Los Ang.	W	9-8†	Brusstar	Niedenfuer	9—Pittsburgh	L	6-9z	Romo	R. Reed
11—Los Ang.	W	9-8	Altamirano	Reuss	10—Pittsburgh	W	9-5	Bystrom	Sarmiento
12—Los Ang.	W	11-3	R. Reed	Welch	11—Pittsburgh	W	4-1	Monge	Rhoden
13—San Fran.	W	8-1	Ruthven	Fowlkes	12—At Mon.	L	3-6	Gullickson	Christenson
14—San Fran.	W	2-0	Carlton	Gale	12—At Mon.	L	7-8	Fryman	Lyle
15—San Fran.	W	5-3	Christenson	Minton	13—At Mon.	L	2-3	Smith	Krukow
16—San Fran.	W	6-1	Krukow	Hammaker	14—At Mon.	W	15-11	J. Reed	Reardon
17—Houston	L	1-8	Ruhle	R. Reed	15—At Mon.	W	3-1	Bystrom	Rogers
18—Houston	L	1-2§	Smith	Farmer	17—At Hous.	L	0-2	Ruhle	Christenson
19—Houston	L	3-5	Knepper	Carlton	18—At Hous.	W	5-3y	McGraw	LaCoss
21—At Atlanta	L	6-7	Bedrosian	Lyle	19—At Hous.	L	6-7‡	Smith	Monge
22—At Atlanta	W	5-2	Krukow	McWilliams	20—At Cinn.	W	9-2	Ruthven	Harris
23—At Atlanta	W	2-1	Ruthven	Niekro	21—At Cinn.	L	3-10	Shirley	Bystrom
24—At Cinn.	W	9-1	Carlton	Seaver	22—At Cinn.	W	8-2	Christenson	Soto
25—At Cinn.	L	3-4	Harris	Farmer	23—At Atlanta	L	3-4	Camp	R. Reed
26—At Cinn.	L	0-2	Soto	Krukow	24—At Atlanta	L	7-9	Niekro	Carlton
29—Atlanta	W	1-0	Ruthven	Niekro	25—At Atlanta	W	11-9†	R. Reed	Garber
30—Atlanta	W	6-2	Carlton	Mahler	27—Cincinnati	L	1-8	Soto	Christenson
31—Cincinnati	W	5-4y	Monge	Shirley	28—Cincinnati	W	7-1	Krukow	Pastore
			Won 19, Lost 8		29—Cincinnati	W	3-1	Carlton	Berenyi
					30—Atlanta	W	6-1	Ruthven	Perez
JUNE					30—Atlanta	L	9-11§	Bedrosian	McGraw
1—Cincinnati	L	1-4*	Harris	Krukow	31—Atlanta	L	0-3	Boggs	Farmer
2—Cincinnati	W	4-2	Ruthven	Berenyi				**Won 15, Lost 17**	
4—At Hous.	L	3-8	Ruhle	Farmer					
5—At Hous.	W	5-3	Lyle	Smith	SEPTEMBER				
6—At Hous.	L	6-7	Ruhle	Brusstar	1—Atlanta	L	0-4	Camp	Krukow
7—Chicago	W	7-5	Monge	Smith	3—Houston	W	2-1	Carlton	Niekro
8—Chicago	W	5-2	Bystrom	Filer	4—Houston	W	4-2	Monge	Knepper
9—Chicago	W	4-2	Carlton	Jenkins	5—Houston	W	4-3	Altamirano	Ryan
11—Pittsburgh	L	0-1	Tekulve	Christenson	6—At Chicago	L	3-4	Bird	Krukow
12—Pittsburgh	L	2-9	Sarmiento	Krukow	7—At Chicago	W	7-5	McGraw	Campbell
14—At Chicago	L	11-12	Jenkins	Carlton	8—At Chicago	W	4-3	Carlton	Tidrow
15—At Chicago	L	5-8	Bird	Ruthven	10—At Pitts.	W	7-5	Ruthven	Candelaria
16—At Chicago	L	6-7‡	Tidrow	Brusstar	11—At Pitts.	L	9-10	Tekulve	R. Reed
17—At Pitts.	W	4-3‡	R. Reed	Scurry	12—At Pitts.	L	2-4	Rhoden	Christenson
18—At Pitts.	W	8-3	Krukow	Sarmiento	13—St. Louis	W	2-0	Carlton	Forsch
19—At Pitts.	W	8-3	Carlton	Robinson	14—St. Louis	L	0-2	Stuper	Krukow
20—At Pitts.	L	1-3	Tekulve	Ruthven	15—St. Louis	L	0-8	Andujar	Denny
21—At St. L.	L	5-7	Sutter	R. Reed	17—Pittsburgh	L	2-4	Rhoden	Carlton
22—At St. L.	L	2-3	Stuper	Lyle	18—Pittsburgh	W	5-4	Monge	Robinson
23—At St. L.	W	7-1	Krukow	Mura	19—Pittsburgh	L	1-8	Sarmiento	Krukow
24—At St. L.	W	10-2	Carlton	Forsch	20—At St. L.	L	1-4	Andujar	Denny
25—New York	W	1-0	Ruthven	Falcone	21—At St. L.	W	5-2	Carlton	Rasmussen
25—New York	W	5-3	Farmer	Zachry	22—At Mon.	L	4-11	Gullickson	Ruthven
26—New York	W	4-3	Bystrom	Jones	23—At Mon.	W	2-0‡	R. Reed	Rogers
26—New York	W	7-4	McGraw	Allen	24—At N.Y.	W	2-1	Krukow	Terrell
27—New York	W	8-3	Krukow	Swan	25—At N.Y.	L	1-2	Swan	Carlton
28—St. Louis	W	1-0	Carlton	Mura	26—At N.Y.	L	4-6	Puleo	Farmer
29—St. Louis	L	3-15	Andujar	Ruthven	27—Chicago	L	1-8	Martz	Bystrom
30—St. Louis	W	6-3	Christenson	Forsch	28—Chicago	W	3-2	Christenson	Bird
			Won 17, Lost 12		29—Montreal	W	4-0	Carlton	Smith
					30—Montreal	W	5-4	Altamirano	Reardon
JULY								**Won 14, Lost 13**	
2—At N. Y.	L	4-8	Swan	Bystrom					
4—At N. Y.	W	9-7	Carlton	Puleo	OCTOBER				
4—At N. Y.	W	7-2	Krukow	Jones	1—New York	L	0-1†	Leach	Altamirano
5—San Fran.	L	1-3	Laskey	Ruthven	2—New York	W	4-3	Altamirano	Zachry
6—San Fran.	W	3-2	Lyle	Breining	3—New York	W	4-1	Carlton	Lynch
7—San Diego	L	3-5	Lollar	Bystrom				**Won 2, Lost 1**	
8—San Diego	L	3-5	Montefusco	Krukow					

*7 innings.   †10 innings.   ‡11 innings.   §12 innings.   x13 innings.   y15 innings.   zSuspended game, completed August 10.

Second baseman Manny Trillo set a major league record of 89 consecutive games without an error as he won his third Gold Glove.

20 or more games, tying Ty Cobb for the most.

And in 1982, the 41-year-old Rose became only the fifth player to appear in 3,000 or more games.

As the Phils were rebounding from their difficult beginning, rookie outfielder Bob Dernier lit their fire. He was their leadoff batter and during one span batted well over .300. But more importantly, he stole 42 bases to break the Phils' rookie record of 33 set by Lonnie Smith, now with the Cards, in 1980.

Dernier, however, went into a slump in the second half of the season (he finished at .249) and some say this was what really cost the Phils.

"But not as much as the slump our big hitters had the final three weeks of the year," said Corrales. "Our pitching held up and so did our defense, but we just didn't get the big hit when we needed it."

During one late-season period, Schmidt, Diaz and Matthews were a collective 3-for-52.

But while they struggled, Greg Gross set a Phillies' club record with 19 pinch hits and also led the league with that number. Gross, who batted .358 as a pinch-hitter, erased the Phils' standard of 18 set by Rene Monteagudo in 1945 and equaled by Dave Philley in 1958.

Over the last seven seasons the Phils have won more games than any other National League team, 615. And for the seventh straight season they were runners-up in league home attendance, this time drawing 2,376,394 to Veterans Stadium.

But in the end, they would have been happy to trade some of those numbers for a few more victories in the beginning or at the end of a disappointing year.

Frustrated Expos Suffer a Fall

By IAN MacDONALD

Frustrating is the best word to use in summarizing the Montreal Expos' 1982 season.

The Expos produced some of the most glittering individual performances in the franchise's 14-year history, but collectively they came up short. After winning the National League East in 1981, Montreal slumped to third place in '82—six games behind first-place St. Louis and three behind runner-up Philadelphia.

Montreal, with a relatively young squad, had fallen just short of qualifying for the World Series in 1981, losing out on a ninth-inning home run in the fifth game of the N.L. Championship Series. Bolstered by the acquisition of Al Oliver on March 31, the Expos appeared primed to repeat as East Division titlists in '82.

While a six-game winning streak in June netted the Expos a share of first place with a 38-27 record, the club never established control. In fact, Montreal played sub-.500 ball (48-49) the rest of the season and was never higher than third place after June 28.

An unstable defense, injuries and a lack of timely hitting contributed greatly to the Expos' downfall. And the Oliver trade was a factor in the unraveling of the defense.

Oliver gave the Expos their first batting champion with a .331 average, led the league in hits (204), doubles (43) and total bases (317) and shared the N.L. lead in runs batted in (109) with Atlanta's Dale Murphy. He hit 22 homers.

To get Oliver, though, the Expos had to send established third baseman Larry Parrish and slugging prospect Dave Hostetler to the Texas Rangers. The trade, while giving Montreal the lefthanded punch it needed so badly, forced three defensive changes.

With Parrish gone, Tim Wallach (who had fought Terry Francona for the right-field job in spring training) took over at third. Incumbent first baseman Warren Cromartie was sent to right field, and one-time outfielder Oliver, whose shoulder problems made him less than a Gold Glove defender, was stationed at first base. ·

The defensive upheaval wasn't limited to those positions. The most troublesome spot was second base, a position at which the Expos tried seven players before obtaining Doug Flynn from Texas in August.

Rookie Wallace Johnson was given first shot at the job, but didn't measure up with the bat or glove. Before long, Tim Raines, Montreal's rookie outfield sensation of 1981, was tried at second, meaning the Expos, in effect, were playing with a pitcher, catcher, shortstop and six outfielders.

It wasn't the kind of defensive alignment that thrills pitchers.

Flynn put an end to what had become a merry-go-round at second base. He was steady afield and pesky at the plate (driving in 20 runs in 58 games).

The pitching staff endured—even prospered.

Steve Rogers posted a 19-8 record, led the N.L. with a 2.40 earned-run average and was second to Philadelphia's Steve Carlton in the Cy Young Award balloting. Righthanders Charlie Lea, Scott Sanderson and Bill Gullickson each won 12 games, and reliever Jeff Reardon notched 26 saves. The Montreal staff's 3.31 ERA was second in the majors to the Los Angeles Dodgers' 3.26.

Catcher Gary Carter didn't let the weight of a $2 million-a-year salary bog him down. Carter, the leading vote-getter for the All-Star Game, had career highs in average (.293), at-bats (557), runs (91), hits (163), total bases (284), doubles (32) and walks (78). He hit 29 homers and knocked in 97 runs.

Wallach came through with 28 homers and 97 RBIs; Raines led the league with 78 stolen bases, and shortstop Chris Speier batted .257 and drove in 60 runs.

Center fielder Andre Dawson, hobbled at times with hand and leg injuries, recorded his third straight .300-plus season. He batted .301 with 23 homers and 83 RBIs.

Big things were expected of rookie Francona, and he delivered—until tearing up a knee June 16 in St. Louis. Sidelined for the remainder of the year, Francona finished with a .321 average.

The frustrations took their toll on Manager Jim Fanning, who resigned on the final day of the season. But the fans weathered the disappointing 86-76 season setting a Montreal attendance record of 2,318,292.

In 1983, it will be up to new Manager Bill Virdon to find defensive cohesiveness avoid injuries and coax some timely hits out of the Expos.

This time, though, St. Louis—not Montreal—will be out to defend the N.L. East championship.

First baseman Al Oliver won the batting title and had a great season, but Montreal was a disappointment in the N.L. East.

SCORES OF MONTREAL EXPOS' 1982 GAMES

APRIL

Date		Score	Winner	Loser
9—At Phila.	W	2-0	Rogers	Christenson
10—At Phila.	W	11-3	Gullickson	Ruthven
11—At Phila.	L	0-1	Krukow	Burris
14—Pittsburgh	W	5-4	Sanderson	Solomon
15—Pittsburgh	L	3-4	Tekulve	Rogers
16—At N. Y.	W	4-3	Reardon	Orosco
17—At N. Y.	L	1-2	Puleo	Burris
18—At N. Y.	W	7-6	Lea	Jones
19—Phila.	L	0-2	Christenson	Sanderson
21—Phila.	W	5-2	Rogers	Carlton
23—New York	W	5-4	Reardon	Orosco
24—New York	L	0-1	Puleo	Burris
25—New York	W	5-2	Sanderson	Scott
27—At S. Fran.	W	3-2	Rogers	Holland
28—At S. Fran.	L	0-7	Laskey	Gullickson
29—At S. Fran.	L	3-7	Fowlkes	Burris
30—At L.A.	W	4-2	Sanderson	Valenzuela

Won 10, Lost 7

MAY

Date		Score	Winner	Loser
1—At L.A.	L	1-2	Reuss	Lea
2—At L.A.	W	13-1	Rogers	Welch
3—At S. Diego	W	8-2	Gullickson	Montefusco
4—At S. Diego	L	3-7	Lollar	Burris
6—Los Ang.	L	2-3	Reuss	Sanderson
7—Los Ang.	L	2-6	Welch	Rogers
8—Los Ang.	L	8-10	Howe	Gullickson
9—Los Ang.	L	4-5	Valenzuela	Burris
10—San Fran.	W	5-4	Fryman	Lavelle
11—San Fran.	L	4-5	Hammaker	Sanderson
12—San Fran.	L	2-3	Laskey	Rogers
13—San Diego	W	6-5†	Fryman	DeLeon
14—San Diego	W	8-7	Gorman	Show
15—San Diego	L	2-6	Welsh	Lea
16—San Diego	L	2-8	Eichelberger	Fryman
17—Atlanta	W	4-0	Rogers	Walk
18—Atlanta	L	4-6	Niekro	Gullickson
19—Atlanta	L	1-9	Dayley	Burris
21—At Cinn.	W	2-0	Lea	Soto
22—At Cinn.	W	4-2	Sanderson	Pastore
23—At Cinn.	W	4-2	Rogers	Berenyi
24—At Hous.	W	2-0	Gullickson	Knepper
25—At Hous.	W	6-1	Palmer	Ruhle
26—At Hous.	W	4-0*	Lea	LaCorte
28—Cincinnati	W	4-2	Sanderson	Berenyi
29—Cincinnati	W	4-1	Rogers	Price
30—Cincinnati	L	3-7	Shirley	Gullickson
31—Houston	W	10-0	Lea	Sutton

Won 15, Lost 13

JUNE

Date		Score	Winner	Loser
2—Houston	L	4-6	Ryan	Sanderson
3—At Pitts.	L	4-5*	Scurry	Smith
5—At Atlanta	L	1-2	Mahler	Gullickson
6—At Atlanta	W	6-3	Reardon	McWilliams
7—St. Louis	W	3-2	Burris	Sutter
8—St. Louis	L	4-5‡	Sutter	Fryman
9—St. Louis	W	5-1	Gullickson	Forsch
11—Chicago	W	9-8	Fryman	Campbell
12—Chicago	W	7-5	Burris	Hernandez
13—Chicago	W	5-3*	Fryman	Hernandez
14—At St. L.	L	1-2	Forsch	Gullickson
15—At St. L.	L	2-3†	Sutter	Burris
16—At St. L.	W	8-3	Lea	LaPoint
17—At Chicago	L	8-12	Proly	Palmer
18—At Chicago	W	4-0	Rogers	Filer
19—At Chicago	W	5-2	Burris	Hernandez
20—At Chicago	W	11-5	Sanderson	Bird
21—At N. Y.	W	5-1	Lea	Falcone
22—At N. Y.	W	4-3	Palmer	Jones
23—At N. Y.	W	5-0	Rogers	Swan
24—At N. Y.	L	1-3	Puleo	Gullickson
25—Pittsburgh	L	3-4	Robinson	Sanderson
25—Pittsburgh	L	7-9	Rhoden	Burris
26—Pittsburgh	L	5-14	Romo	Lea
27—Pittsburgh	W	5-2	Palmer	Candelaria
29—New York	L	4-5	Leach	Burris
30—New York	W	4-1	Gullickson	Falcone

Won 15, Lost 12

JULY

Date		Score	Winner	Loser
1—New York	L	1-2	Scott	Sanderson
2—At Pitts.	L	3-6	Candelaria	Lea
2—At Pitts.	L	2-7	McWilliams	Schatzeder
3—At Pitts.	L	2-4	Sarmiento	Palmer
4—At Pitts.	W	16-6	Rogers	Rhoden
4—At Pitts.	L	4-10	Robinson	Gullickson
5—San Diego	L	6-8	Chiffer	Sanderson
6—San Diego	L	1-5	Curtis	Burris
7—Los Ang.	L	1-3	Valenzuela	Lea
8—Los Ang.	W	7-3	Palmer	Pena

JULY

Date		Score	Winner	Loser
9—San Fran.	L	2-3	Hammaker	Rogers
10—San Fran.	W	8-4	Gullickson	Laskey
11—San Fran.	L	7-8*	Minton	Reardon
12—At S. Diego	W	6-2	Lea	Montefusco
16—At S. Diego	W	4-3	Rogers	Lollar
17—At S. Diego	W	4-1	Gullickson	Hawkins
18—At S. Diego	W	9-2	Palmer	Welsh
19—At L. A.	L	1-2	Romo	Sanderson
20—At L. A.	L	1-10	Reuss	Lea
21—At L. A.	W	4-1†	Rogers	Howe
23—At S. Fran.	W	8-7§	Burris	Lavelle
24—At S. Fran.	L	2-5	Hammaker	Palmer
25—At S. Fran.	L	2-3	Gale	Sanderson
27—At Chicago	W	4-3	Rogers	Martz
28—At Chicago	W	5-3	Gullickson	Noles
29—St. Louis	W	4-3*	Fryman	Bair
30—St. Louis	W	5-4†	Fryman	Bair
31—St. Louis	L	1-10	Mura	Burris

Won 13, Lost 15

AUGUST

Date		Score	Winner	Loser
1—St. Louis	W	5-4	Reardon	Lahti
2—At Phila.	L	1-2	Christenson	Gullickson
3—At Phila.	L	2-3	Krukow	Palmer
4—At Phila.	L	4-5	Carlton	Sanderson
5—At Phila.	W	9-2	Lea	Bystrom
6—At St. L.	W	5-3	Rogers	Andujar
7—At St. L.	L	5-9	Kaat	Schatzeder
8—At St. L.	W	2-1	Palmer	Forsch
9—Chicago	L	2-9	Jenkins	Sanderson
10—Chicago	L	3-5	Martz	Rogers
11—Chicago	W	3-0	Lea	Ripley
12—Phila.	W	6-3	Gullickson	Christenson
12—Phila.	W	8-7	Fryman	Lyle
13—Phila.	W	3-2	Smith	Krukow
14—Phila.	L	11-15	J. Reed	Reardon
15—Phila.	L	1-3	Bystrom	Rogers
17—At Atlanta	W	13-7	Lea	Walk
17—At Atlanta	W	3-2*	Reardon	Mahler
18—At Atlanta	W	12-2	Gullickson	Camp
19—At Atlanta	L	4-5	Niekro	Fryman
20—At Hous.	L	3-4*	Roberge	Reardon
21—At Hous.	L	3-5	Ryan	Burris
22—At Hous.	W	5-0	Lea	Ruhle
23—At Cinn.	L	2-6	Pastore	Gullickson
24—At Cinn.	W	5-1	Sanderson	Berenyi
25—At Cinn.	L	0-1	Shirley	Rogers
26—Houston	W	3-2	Reardon	Roberge
26—Houston	W	5-3	Reardon	Ruhle
28—Houston	L	0-2	Niekro	Lea
29—Houston	W	5-3	Sanderson	Knepper
30—Cincinnati	W	3-1	Rogers	Shirley
31—Cincinnati	L	1-2x	Leibrandt	Burris

Won 17, Lost 15

SEPTEMBER

Date		Score	Winner	Loser
1—Cincinnati	W	2-1	Lerch	Soto
3—Atlanta	L	3-4	Niekro	Lea
4—Atlanta	W	4-1	Sanderson	Perez
5—Atlanta	W	2-1	Rogers	Garber
6—At St. L.	L	0-1	Andujar	Gullickson
7—At St. L.	W	7-4	Smith	Lahti
8—At St. L.	L	0-1	Forsch	Lea
10—At Chicago	W	7-2	Rogers	Jenkins
11—At Chicago	W	10-6	Sanderson	Martz
12—At Chicago	W	11-3	Gullickson	Bird
14—New York	W	3-1	Lea	Zachry
15—New York	W	6-5†	Fryman	Sisk
16—New York	L	4-9	Swan	Sanderson
17—Chicago	L	1-3	Martz	Gullickson
18—Chicago	L	7-10	Tidrow	Fryman
19—Chicago	L	5-7	Tidrow	Smith
21—At N. Y.	L	1-2*	Orosco	Smith
21—At N. Y.	W	5-1	Sanderson	Swan
22—Phila.	W	11-4	Gullickson	Ruthven
23—Phila.	L	0-2†	R. Reed	Rogers
24—Pitts.	W	6-4	Lerch	Robinson
25—Pitts.	W	9-4	Sanderson	Sarmiento
26—Pitts.	L	0-3	McWilliams	Lea
27—St. Louis	L	2-4	LaPoint	Gullickson
28—St. Louis	W	5-4*	Rogers	Lahti
29—At Phila.	L	0-4	Carlton	Smith
30—At Phila.	L	4-5	Altamirano	Reardon

Won 14, Lost 13

OCTOBER

Date		Score	Winner	Loser
1—At Pitts.	W	8-5†	Fryman	Tunnell
2—At Pitts.	L	1-2	Tekulve	Gullickson
3—At Pitts.	W	6-1	Rogers	Robinson

Won 2, Lost 1

*10 innings. †11 innings. ‡12 innings. §13 innings. x14 innings.

Pitching Staff Ignites Pirates

By CHARLEY FEENEY

The 1982 Pittsburgh Pirates, who began the season with a mishmash starting pitching staff, were not considered contenders in the National League East.

True to form, the Pirates bungled their way through April and May and on the morning of June 1 were in last place with an 18-27 record, 11 games off the pace. But the pitching staff ignited a turnaround and by July 2 Pittsburgh had reached the plus side (37-36) and was only 3½ games out of first place.

Shortstop Dale Berra, hitting under .200 in early June, moved his average near .250. Don Robinson and John Candelaria, who weren't in the starting rotation when the season opened, became consistent winners. Pitchers Manny Sarmiento (called up from Portland) and Larry McWilliams (acquired from Atlanta) became big pluses to a staff that had two solid relievers in Kent Tekulve and Rod Scurry.

During the early weeks of the season, some players—but not enough—were getting the job done. Among them were rookie second baseman Johnny Ray, veteran third baseman Bill Madlock and first baseman Jason Thompson. However, right fielder Dave Parker continued to be injury-prone. A wrist injury kept him out of the lineup for nearly six weeks. When he recovered from torn cartilage in his right wrist, Parker hurt his right thumb and surgery was required. Parker finished the season with a .270 average and only 29 runs batted in.

The Pirates responded to adversity with a positive attitude, instilled by Manager Chuck Tanner.

"Attitude is the key," Tanner said as the Pirates remained in contention in July and August. "We didn't quit when things were going bad and now our attitude is paying off."

Attitude and the comeback made the Pirates a respectable club. They finished fourth with an 84-78 record, eight games back, and posted 42-39 records at home and on the road.

Ray was the most durable Pirate, playing in all 162 games. It marked only the second time a National League rookie had played in all of his team's games in a 162-game schedule (Dick Allen did it with Philadelphia in 1964).

Ray batted .281 and his defense, which in preseason reports wasn't supposed to be strong, was well above average. Madlock, with a .319 average, finished second to

John Candelaria rebounded from 1981 injuries to post a 12-7 record.

batting champion Al Oliver. Thompson batted .284 and had 31 homers, 101 RBIs and 101 walks. He became only the third Pirate in history to drive in 100 runs and get 100 walks in the same season. Ralph Kiner did it four straight years, beginning

Second baseman Johnny Ray became only the second National League rookie ever to play in all his team's games.

in 1948. Elbie Fletcher, in 1940, was the first Buc to accomplish the feat.

Tony Pena, the second-year catcher, appeared in 138 games and had a seesaw year at bat. He finished at .296, 10th best in the league. Pena batted over .400 in April and June. In May, he batted under .200; in July, he batted slightly over .200. There was nothing inconsistent about Pena's defense, though, and his backup, Steve Nicosia, did an excellent job and batted .280.

Center fielder Omar Moreno again had problems, hitting .245. He also had a bad back and his consecutive-game streak of 503 ended September 5 in Los Angeles. Lee Lacy and Mike Easler were supposed to be the platoon left fielders, but Parker's injuries gave Lacy a chance to play every day and he did a fine job. In 121 games, Lacy batted .312. Easler, supposedly a power man, hit 15 homers, but his 58 RBIs were surpassed by five teammates (Thompson, Madlock, Pena, Ray and Berra). Madlock had his best RBI season with 95, and Pena, Ray and Berra all drove in more than 60 runs.

The club's senior citizen, Willie Stargell, played his last season, mostly as a pinch-hitter. The 41-year-old team captain had 16 RBIs as a pinch-hitter and his three home runs raised his career homer total to 475 and tied him with Stan Musial for 14th place on the all-time list. Stargell finished with 1,540 career RBIs, putting him in 21st place on the all-time list.

When the season opened, Tanner appeared to have only one reliable starter— Rick Rhoden. After a slow start, Rhoden finished 11-14, but he could have reversed the record with a few breaks.

The Pirates acquired pitchers Ross Baumgarten and Paul Moskau during spring training. Baumgarten went 0-5 and Moskau was 1-3. Sarmiento, working as a starter and reliever, was 9-4 with one save and McWilliams was 6-5 as a Pirate.

Robinson, who was winless in 1981 and underwent surgery in October, 1981, won 15 games and had a chance for at least an 18-victory season. He lost his last five starts, however, and his record was 15-13. Candelaria, who had a 12-7 record and a 2.94 earned-run average, failed to win in September.

Tekulve, working in 85 games (most in the majors in 1982), posted a personal high in victories, 12, and had 20 saves. Scurry, a young lefthander who worked a full season in relief for the first time, was 4-5 with 14 saves and a 1.74 ERA. Enrique Romo, the long reliever, was 9-3 with a 4.36 ERA.

Two veteran pitchers, Eddie Solomon

Jason Thompson slugged 31 homers and had 101 RBIs for the Pirates.

and Tom Griffin, didn't make it through June. Solomon was traded to the Chicago White Sox for infielder Jim Morrison, who became a valuable extra man. Griffin was released.

Tanner juggled his batting order constantly and he often juggled his starting pitchers. What began as a mishmash operation developed into a good ball club. In fact, on the morning of September 15 the Pirates were 77-67 and only 3½ games behind first-place St. Louis. But seven losses in their next 10 games proved the Pirates —while respectable—were not championship-caliber in 1982.

SCORES OF PITTSBURGH PIRATES' 1982 GAMES

APRIL

Date	W/L	Score	Winner	Loser
10—At St. L.	W	11-7	Scurry	Littell
11—At St. L.	L	6-7	Kaat	Romo
12—At St. L.	L	4-5	Martin	Griffin
14—At Mon.	L	4-5	Sanderson	Solomon
15—At Mon.	W	4-3	Tekulve	Rogers
16—Chicago	W	7-6§	Romo	Hernandez
17—Chicago	L	2-10	Noles	Baumgarten
18—Chicago	L	1-5	Jenkins	Solomon
20—St. Louis	L	4-7	Martin	Rhoden
21—St. Louis	L	2-6	Mura	Candelaria
23—At Chicago	W	12-10	Solomon	Noles
24—At Chicago	W	8-5	Robinson	Martz
25—At Chicago	L	3-5	Martz	Rhoden
26—At Atlanta	W	6-4	Tekulve	McWilliams
27—At Atlanta	W	10-4	Griffin	Walk
28—At Atlanta	L	6-7†	Camp	Scurry
29—Houston	W	9-6	Romo	LaCoss
30—Houston	L	3-4	Sutton	Rhoden

Won 8, Lost 10

MAY

Date	W/L	Score	Winner	Loser
1—Houston	L	3-6	Ryan	Moskau
2—Houston	L	2-6	Niekro	Griffin
3—Atlanta	L	4-10	Niekro	Solomon
4—Atlanta	W	8-4	Robinson	Cowley
5—Atlanta	W	4-2	Rhoden	Mahler
7—At Cinn.	L	0-5	Soto	Moskau
8—At Cinn.	W	4-2z	Sarmiento	Shirley
9—At Cinn.	W	6-3	Robinson	Seaver
10—At Hous.	L	3-7	Sutton	Rhoden
11—At Hous.	L	2-4	Ryan	Griffin
13—Cincinnati	L	1-2	Price	Scurry
14—Cincinnati	W	8-7	Romo	Kern
15—Cincinnati	W	12-9	Rhoden	Pastore
16—Cincinnati	L	1-3	Soto	Solomon
18—At S. Fran.	L	1-2	Laskey	Candelaria
19—At S. Fran.	W	2-1	Robinson	Chris
20—At S. Fran.	L	1-3	Lavelle	Scurry
21—At S. Diego	L	5-7	Montefusco	Solomon
22—At S. Diego	L	3-12	Eichelberger	Moskau
23—At S. Diego	W	4-2	Candelaria	Curtis
24—At L.A.	W	9-3	Robinson	Niedenfuer
25—At L.A.	L	2-5	Valenzuela	Rhoden
26—At L.A.	L	2-3	Reuss	Solomon
28—San Fran.	L	5-10	Laskey	Candelaria
29—San Fran.	L	5-9	Barr	Robinson
30—San Fran.	W	7-6x	Solomon	Barr
31—Los Ang.	L	4-5	Howe	Tekulve

Won 10, Lost 17

JUNE

Date	W/L	Score	Winner	Loser
1—Los Ang.	W	3-1	Candelaria	Reuss
2—Los Ang.	W	8-7	Scurry	Romo
3—Montreal	W	5-4†	Scurry	Smith
4—San Diego	L	4-5	Curtis	Rhoden
6—San Diego	W	2-1	Tekulve	Lollar
7—At N.Y.	W	4-3§	Scurry	Allen
8—At N.Y.	W	6-2	Robinson	Orosco
9—At N.Y.	L	2-3	Allen	Tekulve
11—At Phila.	W	1-0	Tekulve	Christenson
12—At Phila.	W	9-2	Sarmiento	Krukow
14—New York	L	1-2	Falcone	Robinson
15—New York	W	13-3	Rhoden	Puleo
17—Phila.	L	3-4‡	R. Reed	Scurry
18—Phila.	L	3-8	Krukow	Sarmiento
19—Phila.	L	3-8	Carlton	Robinson
20—Phila.	W	3-1	Tekulve	Ruthven
21—Chicago	W	4-3	Moskau	Smith
22—Chicago	W	9-2	Candelaria	Martz
23—Chicago	L	5-6†	Campbell	Niemann
25—At Mon.	W	4-3	Robinson	Sanderson
25—At Mon.	W	9-7	Rhoden	Burris
26—At Mon.	W	14-5	Romo	Lea
27—At Mon.	L	2-5	Palmer	Candelaria
28—At Chicago	L	4-6	Tidrow	Romo
29—At Chicago	W	3-1	Rhoden	Jenkins
30—At Chicago	W	7-3	Robinson	Smith

Won 17, Lost 9

JULY

Date	W/L	Score	Winner	Loser
1—At Chicago	W	5-2	Romo	Campbell
2—Montreal	W	6-3	Candelaria	Lea
2—Montreal	W	7-2	McWilliams	Schatzeder
3—Montreal	W	4-2	Sarmiento	Palmer
4—Montreal	L	6-16	Rogers	Rhoden
4—Montreal	W	10-4	Robinson	Gullickson
5—Houston	L	4-6	Niekro	Baumgarten
6—Houston	W	1-0	McWilliams	Knepper
7—Cincinnati	L	3-6	Hume	Tekulve
8—Cincinnati	W	9-8	Tekulve	Price
9—At Atlanta	L	4-6	Diaz	Rhoden
10—At Atlanta	W	6-1	Robinson	Niekro
11—At Atlanta	W	3-1	McWilliams	Dayley
15—At Hous.	W	5-1	Candelaria	Sutton
16—At Hous.	L	2-4	Ryan	McWilliams
17—At Hous.	L	3-4†	Niekro	Tekulve
18—At Hous.	L	2-4	Knepper	Robinson
19—At Cinn.	W	5-4	Sarmiento	Pastore
20—At Cinn.	W	3-1	Candelaria	Berenyi
21—At Cinn.	W	3-2	McWilliams	Hume
23—Atlanta	W	6-0	Rhoden	Camp
24—Atlanta	L	3-4	Niekro	Robinson
25—Atlanta	W	8-0	Candelaria	Mahler
27—Phila.	W	4-0	McWilliams	Ruthven
28—Phila.	L	3-4	Christenson	Rhoden
29—At N.Y.	W	4-1	Robinson	Falcone
30—At N.Y.	W	5-1	Candelaria	Swan
31—At N.Y.	L	4-9	Puleo	Tekulve

Won 18, Lost 10

AUGUST

Date	W/L	Score	Winner	Loser
1—At N.Y.	W	4-3†	Tekulve	Leach
2—At St. L.	W	4-2a	Romo	Kaat
3—At St. L.	L	2-4	Forsch	Robinson
4—At St. L.	W	5-2	Candelaria	LaPoint
5—At St. L.	L	3-7*	Mura	McWilliams
6—New York	W	7-3	Sarmiento	Scott
6—New York	L	3-7	Jones	Baumgarten
7—New York	L	2-5	Zachry	Rhoden
8—New York	W	4-1	Robinson	Swan
9—At Phila.	L	3-4	Carlton	Tekulve
9—At Phila.	W	9-6b	Romo	R. Reed
10—At Phila.	L	5-9	Bystrom	Sarmiento
11—At Phila.	L	1-4	Monge	Rhoden
12—St. Louis	L	2-3	Andujar	Baumgarten
13—St. Louis	W	7-4	Robinson	Forsch
14—St. Louis	L	1-4	Stuper	Candelaria
15—St. Louis	L	5-12	Mura	McWilliams
15—St. Louis	L	2-5	LaPoint	Sarmiento
17—San Fran.	W	4-1	Robinson	Hammaker
18—San Fran.	L	9-16	Fowlkes	Robinson
19—San Fran.	W	6-1	Candelaria	Gale
20—Los Ang.	L	0-1	Valenzuela	McWilliams
21—Los Ang.	W	2-1	Tekulve	Howe
22—Los Ang.	W	4-3y	Robinson	Beckwith
23—San Diego	W	8-6	Candelaria	Hawkins
23—San Diego	L	3-5	Welsh	Baumgarten
24—San Diego	W	6-5‡	Tekulve	Eichelberger
25—San Diego	W	7-6	Tekulve	Chiffer
27—At S. Fran.	W	3-2	Rhoden	Laskey
28—At S. Fran.	L	2-4	Hammaker	Robinson
29—At S. Fran.	W	4-3	Candelaria	Martin
30—At S. Diego	L	1-2x	DeLeon	Tekulve
31—At S. Diego	W	7-1	Sarmiento	Montefusco

Won 17, Lost 16

SEPTEMBER

Date	W/L	Score	Winner	Loser
1—At S. Diego	L	1-4	Eichelberger	Rhoden
3—At L.A.	W	3-2	Robinson	Welch
4—At L.A.	W	1-0	Tunnell	Valenzuela
5—At L.A.	L	1-2†	Niedenfuer	Tekulve
6—New York	W	6-1	Rhoden	Falcone
7—New York	W	9-5	Sarmiento	Scott
8—New York	L	1-9	Ownbey	Robinson
10—Phila.	L	5-7	Ruthven	Candelaria
11—Phila.	W	10-9	Tekulve	R. Reed
12—Phila.	W	4-2	Rhoden	Christenson
13—Chicago	L	3-7	Ripley	Robinson
14—Chicago	W	15-5	Niemann	Noles
15—Chicago	L	2-7	Jenkins	Candelaria
17—At Phila.	W	4-2	Rhoden	Carlton
18—At Phila.	L	4-5	Monge	Robinson
19—At Phila.	W	8-1	Sarmiento	Krukow
20—At Chicago	L	1-3	Noles	McWilliams
21—At Chicago	L	0-1	Jenkins	Scurry
22—At St. L.	L	1-2	LaPoint	Rhoden
23—At St. L.	W	5-3‡	Romo	Martin
24—At Mon.	L	4-6	Lerch	Robinson
25—At Mon.	L	4-9	Sanderson	Sarmiento
26—At Mon.	W	3-0	McWilliams	Lea
27—At N.Y.	L	1-4	Holman	Rhoden
28—At N.Y.	L	2-3†	Orosco	Romo
29—St. Louis	W	7-3	Romo	Stuper
30—St. Louis	W	7-2	Sarmiento	Mura

Won 13, Lost 14

OCTOBER

Date	W/L	Score	Winner	Loser
1—Montreal	L	5-8‡	Fryman	Tunnell
2—Montreal	W	2-1	Tekulve	Gullickson
3—Montreal	L	1-6	Rogers	Robinson

Won 1, Lost 2

*5 innings. †10 innings. ‡11 innings. §12 innings. x13 innings. y14 innings. z15 innings. a17 innings. bSuspended game, completed August 10.

August Spree Buoys Cubs

By JOE GODDARD

The Chicago Cubs entered their New Tradition of ownership with a roar, tapered to a whimper and finished with a rush.

After Bump Wills homered on the second pitch of the season, the team suffered losing streaks of 13 and eight games, but an 18-10 record in August helped the Cubs finish in fifth place.

It was called progress.

The most satisfaction came in the final weeks when the Cubs helped to eliminate three teams from division contention. They beat both the Montreal Expos and Pittsburgh Pirates three straight, then put the finishing touches to the Philadelphia Phillies.

Cubs Executive Vice President and General Manager Dallas Green and Manager Lee Elia felt the late-season improvement—from August 1, the club had the fifth-best record in the major leagues —was nice, but just the beginning.

"Regardless of the standings, I believe this team is better than it was at this time last year," Green said.

Elia added, "Next year will bear the fruits of this year. It wasn't until the end of June that we squared away our pitching. We had trouble defensively in left field and at second base, and we weren't blessed with power hitters. We plan to change all that."

The season, the first under the Tribune Co. after 66 years with the Wrigley family, was made better by a couple of carryover Cubs, Bill Buckner and Leon Durham, newcomer Ryne Sandberg and recycled Ferguson Jenkins.

Buckner had an exemplary season, easily his finest in 12 years. He not only finished fifth in the league with a .306 average, but he reached 100-RBI and 200-hit milestones. Buckner had 105 RBIs. He also had 201 hits, 15 game-winning RBIs, stole 15 bases and struck out just once every 25 at-bats.

Durham was third in the league at .312 and the first to hit 20 homers and steal 20 bases. He finished with 22 and 28, respectively.

Jenkins, a free agent after six straight 20-victory years with the Cubs and eight seasons in the American League, returned to post a 14-15 record with a 3.15 earned-run average. Most of his losses were in tight games.

Sandberg was an immediate dividend from one of Green's many trades. He

Ryne Sandberg had an impressive rookie season in Chicago.

started 1-for-31 and at third base and finished with a .271 average and at second base, having moved over in September. By scoring 103 runs to rank fifth in the league, he set a club record for a rookie. He also stole 32 bases.

Lee Smith headed a bullpen that was in disarray in the first half, but one of the best in the league in the second. He had a 0.86 earned-run average and 15 of his 17 saves from July 8 on. Free agent Bill Campbell, Willie Hernandez, Mike Proly and Dick Tidrow had strong final months, too.

Starting pitching was a problem, with Randy Martz (11-10), Dickie Noles (10-13), Doug Bird (9-14) and Allen Ripley (5-7) showing occasional signs of effectiveness.

There were disappointments. Larry Bowa, one of many former Phillies, started slowly. Keith Moreland was on the cover of The Sporting News in May with an average over .350, but slumped markedly in the second half and ended at .261. Steve Henderson lost his left-field job by hitting .233.

It was a stormy season for Elia, who had been a coach under former Phillies Manager Green. He criticized Wills publicly, had a shoving disagreement with Buckner and said after late-season losses to the Mets, "After a while, you get tired of looking at garbage in your own backyard."

But at the end of the year, Elia was settled and encouraged. "I'll make no predictions about next year until the day we break training camp," he said, "and then I'll only say how much better we are than this year. And we will be better."

SCORES OF CHICAGO CUBS' 1982 GAMES

APRIL

Date		Score	Winner	Loser
5—At Cinn.	W	3-2*	Bird	Soto
7—At Cinn.	L	2-6	Berenyi	Noles
9—New York	W	5-0	Jenkins	Scott
10—New York	L	5-9	Zachry	Bird
11—New York	L	4-5	Falcone	Larson
12—New York	W	5-4	Noles	Swan
13—St. Louis	L	3-4	Andujar	Martz
14—St. Louis	L	1-3	Rincon	Jenkins
15—St. Louis	L	1-6	Mura	Bird
16—At Pitts.	L	6-7§	Romo	Hernandez
17—At Pitts.	W	10-2	Noles	Baumgarten
18—At Pitts.	W	5-1	Jenkins	Solomon
20—At N. York	L	2-3	Scott	Bird
21—At N. York	L	4-7	Swan	Campbell
23—Pittsburgh	L	10-12	Solomon	Noles
24—Pittsburgh	L	5-8	Robinson	Martz
25—Pittsburgh	W	5-3	Martz	Rhoden
27—Cincinnati	L	3-6	Berenyi	Larson
28—Cincinnati	W	6-0	Noles	Seaver
29—At Atlanta	L	0-3	Garber	Jenkins
30—At Atlanta	L	0-1	Bedrosian	Bird

Won 7, Lost 14

MAY

Date		Score	Winner	Loser
1—At Atlanta	W	5-1	Martz	Mahler
2—At Atlanta	L	3-10	Walk	Larson
3—At St. L.	L	4-9	Bair	Noles
4—At St. L.	L	4-7	Andujar	Jenkins
5—At St. L.	L	6-7	Bair	Hernandez
7—Houston	W	12-6	Martz	Ryan
8—Houston	W	3-2	Noles	Niekro
9—Houston	W	6-3	Hernandez	Moffitt
11—Atlanta	W	6-4	Bird	Mahler
12—Atlanta	L	3-6	Walk	Martz
13—At Hous.	W	5-0	Ripley	Niekro
14—At Hous.	W	6-3	Noles	Knepper
15—At Hous.	L	1-4	Sutton	Jenkins
16—At Hous.	W	2-1	Bird	Ryan
18—At L.A.	L	1-2	Niedenfuer	Campbell
19—At L.A.	L	1-4	Stewart	Noles
20—At L.A.	W	8-3	Jenkins	Valenzuela
21—At S. Fran.	W	6-4	Tidrow	Martin
22—At S. Fran.	W	2-1	Ripley	Hammaker
23—At S. Fran.	L	3-4†	Lavelle	Tidrow
23—At S. Fran.	L	3-6	Schatzeder	Larson
24—At S. Diego	L	2-8	Lollar	Noles
25—At S. Diego	L	1-2	Welsh	Bird
26—At S. Diego	W	5-3	Hernandez	DeLeon
28—Los Ang.	W	4-3	Martz	Welch
29—Los Ang.	W	3-2x	Smith	Pena
30—Los Ang.	L	0-7	Valenzuela	Jenkins
31—San Diego	L	7-9	Welsh	Bird

Won 14, Lost 14

JUNE

Date		Score	Winner	Loser
1—San Diego	L	1-9	Montefusco	Martz
2—San Diego	L	1-3	Eichelberger	Noles
4—San Fran.	L	3-4	Breining	Jenkins
5—San Fran.	L	1-2	Gale	Bird
6—San Fran.	L	3-5	Martin	Martz
7—At Phila.	L	5-7	Monge	Smith
8—At Phila.	L	2-5	Bystrom	Filer
9—At Phila.	L	2-4	Carlton	Jenkins
11—At Mon.	L	8-9	Fryman	Campbell
12—At Mon.	L	5-7	Burris	Hernandez
13—At Mon.	L	3-5†	Fryman	Hernandez
14—Phila.	W	12-11	Jenkins	Carlton
15—Phila.	W	8-5	Bird	Ruthven
16—Phila.	W	7-6‡	Tidrow	Brusstar
17—Montreal	W	12-8	Proly	Palmer
18—Montreal	L	0-4	Rogers	Filer
19—Montreal	L	2-5	Burris	Hernandez
20—Montreal	L	5-11	Sanderson	Bird
21—At Pitts.	L	3-4	Moskau	Smith
22—At Pitts.	L	2-9	Candelaria	Martz
23—At Pitts.	W	6-5†	Campbell	Niemann
25—St. Louis	W	5-3	Jenkins	Andujar
26—St. Louis	L	1-4	LaPoint	Bird
26—St. Louis	L	1-2	Kaat	Smith
27—St. Louis	W	4-2	Ripley	Stuper
28—Pittsburgh	W	6-4	Tidrow	Romo
29—Pittsburgh	L	1-3	Rhoden	Jenkins
30—Pittsburgh	L	3-7	Robinson	Smith

Won 8, Lost 20

JULY

Date		Score	Winner	Loser
1—Pittsburgh	L	2-5	Romo	Campbell
2—At St. L.	W	4-3	Kravec	LaPoint
3—At St. L.	W	2-1	Filer	Andujar
4—At St. L.	L	2-7	Stuper	Noles
5—At Atlanta	L	5-7	Hrabosky	Smith
6—At Atlanta	W	7-2	Bird	Dayley
7—At Hous.	L	1-5	Sutton	Ripley
8—At Hous.	W	5-3	Tidrow	Ruhle
9—Cincinnati	W	12-0	Jenkins	Shirley
10—Cincinnati	W	1-0	Noles	Berenyi
10—Cincinnati	L	5-6xa	Soto	Proly
11—Cincinnati	W	9-2	Bird	Seaver
15—Atlanta	L	4-11	Niekro	Jenkins
16—Atlanta	W	4-3†	Campbell	Garber
17—Atlanta	L	4-9	Walk	Noles
18—Atlanta	L	2-4	Camp	Bird
19—Houston	W	6-5†	Smith	LaCorte
20—Houston	W	5-3	Hernandez	Sutton
21—Houston	L	1-2	Ryan	Ripley
23—At Cinn.	W	7-5	Hernandez	Kern
24—At Cinn.	L	2-5	Pastore	Bird
25—At Cinn.	L	1-2	Berenyi	Jenkins
26—At Cinn.	L	2-4	Shirley	Ripley
27—Montreal	L	3-4	Rogers	Martz
28—Montreal	L	3-5	Gullickson	Noles
29—At Phila.	L	2-3	Krukow	Tidrow
30—At Phila.	L	1-3	Carlton	Jenkins
31—At Phila.	L	0-2	Bystrom	Ripley

Won 11, Lost 17

AUGUST

Date		Score	Winner	Loser
1—At Phila.	W	7-2	Noles	Ruthven
3—New York	W	5-0	Bird	Gaff
4—New York	L	4-7	Swan	Jenkins
5—New York	W	5-1	Martz	Puleo
6—Phila.	W	4-2	Ripley	Ruthven
7—Phila.	W	3-2	Noles	Christenson
8—Phila.	W	8-5	Tidrow	McGraw
9—At Mon.	W	9-2	Jenkins	Sanderson
10—At Mon.	W	5-3	Martz	Rogers
11—At Mon.	L	0-3	Lea	Ripley
12—At N.Y.	W	13-6	Proly	Orosco
13—At N.Y.	L	4-6	Orosco	Proly
14—At N.Y.	W	7-4	Proly	Falcone
15—At N.Y.	L	4-5	Lynch	Martz
15—At N.Y.	W	6-5	Proly	Orosco
17—Los Ang.	L	1-2zb	Reuss	Ripley
18—Los Ang.	L	4-7	Reuss	Bird
19—Los Ang.	W	8-2	Jenkins	Welch
20—San Diego	W	3-2	Martz	Montefusco
21—San Diego	L	0-2	Lollar	Ripley
22—San Diego	W	8-7	Tidrow	Lucas
23—San Fran.	W	8-5	Bird	Martin
24—San Fran.	W	8-4	Jenkins	Gale
25—San Fran.	W	4-2	Martz	Barr
27—At L.A.	L	4-9	Wright	Proly
28—At L.A.	L	1-7	Reuss	Noles
29—At L.A.	W	7-2	Jenkins	Welch
31—At S. Fran.	L	3-4	Holland	Hernandez

Won 18, Lost 10

SEPTEMBER

Date		Score	Winner	Loser
1—At S. Fran.	W	7-6	Campbell	Gale
3—At S. Diego	L	0-3	Show	Noles
4—At S. Diego	L	1-4	Lollar	Jenkins
5—At S. Diego	W	5-1	Martz	Dravecky
6—Phila.	W	4-3	Bird	Krukow
7—Phila.	L	5-7	McGraw	Campbell
8—Phila.	L	3-4	Carlton	Tidrow
10—Montreal	L	2-7	Rogers	Jenkins
11—Montreal	L	6-10	Sanderson	Martz
12—Montreal	L	3-11	Gullickson	Bird
13—At Pitts.	W	7-3	Ripley	Robinson
14—At Pitts.	L	5-15	Niemann	Noles
15—At Pitts.	W	7-2	Jenkins	Candelaria
17—At Mon.	W	3-1	Martz	Gullickson
18—At Mon.	W	10-7	Tidrow	Fryman
19—At Mon.	W	7-5	Tidrow	Smith
20—Pittsburgh	W	3-1	Noles	McWilliams
21—Pittsburgh	W	1-0	Jenkins	Scurry
22—New York	L	2-5	Holman	Martz
23—New York	L	4-5	Lynch	Bird
24—At St. L.	L	1-3	Stuper	Campbell
25—At St. L.	L	1-5	Andujar	Noles
26—At St. L.	W	6-1	Jenkins	Rasmussen
27—At Phila.	W	8-1	Martz	Bystrom
28—At Phila.	L	2-3	Christenson	Bird
29—At N.Y.	W	4-1	Proly	Terrell
30—At N.Y.	W	3-1	Noles	Gorman

Won 14, Lost 13

OCTOBER

Date		Score	Winner	Loser
2—St. Louis	W	8-4	Jenkins	Kaat
3—St. Louis	L	4-5y	Rasmussen	Kravec

Won 1, Lost 1

*8 innings. †10 innings. ‡11 innings. §12 innings. x13 innings. y14 innings. z21 innings. a Suspended game, completed July 11. b Suspended game, completed August 18.

Outfielder Leon Durham figures to have many more great seasons for the Cubs.

Mets' Season Truly Forgettable

By JACK LANG

No year in recent history was more disappointing for the Mets or their fans than 1982. It was a year in which the club went out and spent money in an attempt to beef up the offense. It was a year in which the Mets were supposed to present a formidable middle lineup. It was a year in which the Mets were supposed to climb from the depths and become contenders.

Much of the promise was founded on the acquisition of George Foster. The Mets gave up Jim Kern and Greg Harris to obtain the signing rights to Foster in February and they rewarded him with a five-year contract that guaranteed $10 million.

For the previous seven years with the Cincinnati Reds, Foster had hit 20 or more homers each year, including seasons in which he hit 52 and 40. Six straight years he had knocked in 90 or more runs, and three times he had 120 or more R.B.Is.

With Foster and Dave Kingman hitting third and fourth in the lineup, it was projected that the two of them would provide 70 or more homers. New Manager George Bamberger said in spring training that his only concern was who would bat fifth to protect his sluggers. But with Ellis Valentine and Joel Youngblood available, that problem seemingly would resolve itself.

What everyone seemed to overlook until it was too late was that while General Manager Frank Cashen provided a new manager and a new slugger, he forgot to provide new pitchers. The staff Bamberger took into the season was basically the same one that won only 41 games in the strike-shortened 1981 season and only 67 the year before.

If there was one mistake in judgment that Cashen made, it was in expecting Bamberger to work miracles with Pat Zachry, Pete Falcone, Randy Jones, Mike Scott and Craig Swan. Only with Swan was the former Baltimore pitching coach and Milwaukee manager able to apply his magic. Swan, with careful handling, came back from a torn rotator cuff to lead the Mets with an 11-7 record. The others failed dismally.

For the first 12 weeks of the season, Bamberger did work miracles. On June 20 the Mets were contenders with a 34-30 record after having taken three out of four from the Cardinals in St. Louis. But it was during that week that the Mets were dealt a blow which Bamberger later would single out as the catastrophe of the season. They lost Neil Allen.

The relief ace, who had 15 saves at the time and was battling the Cardinals' Bruce Sutter for the Fireman of the Year Award, was felled by a colon infection. Out for two weeks, he came back in a weakened condition and never was the same again. By the first week in August, Allen had 19 saves and a sore elbow. His problem was diagnosed as tendinitis and he was finished for the season.

It was while Allen was unavailable that the Mets lost 15 straight games and dropped into the East Division cellar. And that's where they finished.

"There is no doubt in my mind that Allen would have saved at least 35 games if we had him all year," Bamberger said upon signing a contract to return in 1983. "I know we would not have lost 15 in a row if we had him. The two worst things that happened to us all year was Allen getting sick and Foster having an off-year."

There were other contributing factors. The Mets never did resolve the right-field situation, letting Valentine and Youngblood battle it out for the job that neither could win. Youngblood was traded to Montreal in August and Valentine became a free agent at the end of the year.

The Mets' defense was as bad as there was in the league. The infield made 109 errors, with third baseman Hubie Brooks and shortstop Ron Gardenhire in particular providing little support for their pitchers. On the right side, Kingman was no help to the other infielders. He couldn't dig out low throws and had 18 errors.

Kingman did lead the league in home runs with 37 and he finished with 99 RBIs. But he batted only .204 and his long periods of non-production helped drag the team down. He had his worst dry spell in August when the Mets won only five of 29 games.

Following their 34-30 record, the Mets came home and lost three out of four to Montreal and then went to Philadelphia, where they spent a lost weekend. On June 25 and 26, employing only one catcher, they played consecutive twi-night doubleheaders followed by a single game the next day. John Stearns had to catch every inning of the five straight losses. It wore him out. Brooks, who had been playing with a slight hamstring problem, had to play all five games at third. He aggravated the injury so severely he was placed on the disabled list for a month.

By the All-Star Game, the Mets had slipped to 40-47. After the break, they lost

Mookie Wilson had a fine year at the plate and in center field for the '82 Mets.

SCORES OF NEW YORK METS' 1982 GAMES

APRIL			Winner	Loser
8—At Phila.	W	7-2	Jones	Carlton
9—At Chicago	L	0-5	Jenkins	Scott
10—At Chicago	W	9-5	Zachry	Bird
11—At Chicago	W	5-4	Falcone	Larson
12—At Chicago	L	4-5	Noles	Swan
13—Phila.	W	5-2	Jones	Carlton
14—Phila.	W	8-1	Scott	Ruthven
15—Phila.	L	4-8§	Brusstar	Puleo
16—Montreal	L	3-4	Reardon	Orosco
17—Montreal	W	2-1	Puleo	Burris
18—Montreal	L	6-7	Lea	Jones
20—Chicago	W	3-2	Scott	Bird
21—Chicago	W	7-4	Swan	Campbell
23—At Mon.	L	4-5	Reardon	Orosco
24—At Mon.	W	1-0	Puleo	Burris
25—At Mon.	L	2-5	Sanderson	Scott
27—At S. Diego	L	5-8	Show	Orosco
28—At S. Diego	W	5-4y	Falcone	Lucas
29—At S. Diego	L	0-6	Lollar	Puleo
30—At S. Fran.	L	4-5	Breining	Allen
		Won 10, Lost 10		

MAY				
1—At S. Fran.	L	3-6	Hammaker	Zachry
2—At S. Fran.	L	3-4	Holland	Lynch
2—At S. Fran.	W	2-0	Jones	Laskey
3—At L.A.	W	6-3‡	Lynch	Forster
4—At L.A.	L	1-2	Valenzuela	Allen
6—San Fran.	L	3-5	Minton	Orosco
7—San Fran.	W	3-2	Puleo	Laskey
8—San Fran.	L	3-8	Lavelle	Lynch
9—San Fran.	W	6-5	Swan	Minton
10—San Diego	W	3-2	Jones	Lucas
11—San Diego	W	6-0	Puleo	Eichelberger
13—Los Ang.	W	4-2	Falcone	Hooton
14—Los Ang.	L	1-4	Valenzuela	Jones
15—Los Ang.	W	6-4	Zachry	Power
16—Los Ang.	W	13-4	Scott	Reuss
17—Cincinnati	L	2-7	Leibrandt	Falcone
18—Cincinnati	W	7-4	Jones	Berenyi
19—Cincinnati	W	4-2	Zachry	Seaver
21—At Hous.	L	1-5	Sutton	Scott
22—At Hous.	W	6-5‡	Allen	Moffitt
23—At Hous.	W	2-0	Jones	Niekro
24—At Atlanta	W	5-3	Zachry	Dayley
25—At Atlanta	L	2-10	Mahler	Scott
26—At Atlanta	W	6-4	Swan	Camp
28—Houston	L	3-8	Ryan	Jones
29—Houston	L	2-5	Niekro	Zachry
30—Houston	W	9-5	Scott	Knepper
31—Atlanta	W	10-4	Puleo	Walk
		Won 17, Lost 11		

JUNE				
1—Atlanta	L	3-7	Dayley	Jones
2—Atlanta	L	1-3	Niekro	Falcone
4—At Cinn.	L	3-8	Seaver	Scott
5—At Cinn.	L	2-6	Soto	Puleo
6—At Cinn.	W	6-3	Swan	Pastore
7—Pittsburgh	L	3-4‡	Scurry	Allen
8—Pittsburgh	L	2-6	Robinson	Orosco
9—Pittsburgh	W	3-2	Allen	Tekulve
11—St. Louis	L	3-7	Andujar	Jones
12—St. Louis	W	6-2	Swan	Mura
14—At Pitts.	W	2-1	Falcone	Robinson
15—At Pitts.	L	3-13	Rhoden	Puleo
18—At St. L.	W	5-3	Orosco	Sutter
18—At St. L.	L	4-5	Stuper	Lynch
19—At St. L.	W	8-5	Hausman	Keener
20—At St. L.	W	5-4*	Scott	Sutter
21—Montreal	L	1-5	Lea	Falcone
22—Montreal	L	3-4	Palmer	Jones
23—Montreal	L	0-5	Rogers	Swan
24—Montreal	W	3-1	Puleo	Gullickson
25—At Phila.	L	0-1	Ruthven	Falcone
25—At Phila.	L	3-5	Farmer	Zachry
26—At Phila.	L	3-4	Bystrom	Jones
26—At Phila.	L	4-7	McGraw	Allen
27—At Phila.	L	3-8	Krukow	Swan
29—At Mon.	W	5-4	Leach	Burris
30—At Mon.	L	1-4	Gullickson	Falcone
		Won 9, Lost 18		

JULY				
1—At Mon.	W	2-1	Scott	Sanderson
2—Phila.	W	8-4	Swan	Bystrom
4—Phila.	L	7-9	Carlton	Puleo
4—Phila.	L	2-7	Krukow	Jones
5—Los Ang.	L	1-4	Welch	Falcone
6—Los Ang.	L	3-9	Stewart	Scott
7—San Fran.	L	2-3	Gale	Gaff

JULY			Winner	Loser
8—San Fran.	L	7-9	Martin	Orosco
9—San Diego	L	3-5	Chiffer	Puleo
9—San Diego	W	6-3	Zachry	Lucas
10—San Diego	W	9-7	Falcone	Curtis
11—San Diego	L	2-6	Lollar	Scott
15—At L.A.	W	5-2	Puleo	Reuss
16—At L.A.	L	6-7	Valenzuela	Zachry
17—At L.A.	L	5-6	Shirley	Allen
18—At L.A.	W	8-3	Scott	Welch
20—At S. Fran.	L	1-5	Gale	Puleo
21—At S. Fran.	W	6-2	Falcone	Laskey
23—At S. Diego	L	4-11	Hawkins	Gaff
24—At S. Diego	W	4-3	Allen	DeLeon
25—At S. Diego	L	2-3*	DeLeon	Allen
27—At St. L.	L	4-9	Lahti	Scott
28—At St. L.	L	5-7	Keener	Lynch
29—Pittsburgh	L	1-4	Robinson	Falcone
30—Pittsburgh	L	1-5	Candelaria	Swan
31—Pittsburgh	W	9-4	Puleo	Tekulve
		Won 9, Lost 17		

AUGUST				
1—Pittsburgh	L	3-4*	Tekulve	Leach
3—At Chicago	L	0-5	Bird	Gaff
4—At Chicago	W	7-4	Swan	Jenkins
5—At Chicago	L	1-5	Martz	Puleo
6—At Pitts.	L	3-7	Sarmiento	Scott
6—At Pitts.	W	7-3	Jones	Baumgarten
7—At Pitts.	W	5-2	Zachry	Rhoden
8—At Pitts.	L	1-4	Robinson	Swan
9—St. Louis	L	2-7	Lahti	Puleo
10—St. Louis	L	2-7	Mura	Jones
12—Chicago	L	6-13	Proly	Orosco
13—Chicago	W	6-4	Orosco	Proly
14—Chicago	L	4-7	Proly	Falcone
15—Chicago	W	5-4	Lynch	Martz
15—Chicago	L	5-6	Proly	Orosco
17—At Cinn.	L	2-9	Soto	Ownbey
18—At Cinn.	L	6-7x	Hayes	Scott
19—At Cinn.	L	1-3*	Kern	Hausman
20—At Atlanta	L	1-2*	Bedrosian	Zachry
21—At Atlanta	L	5-6	Walk	Jones
22—At Atlanta	L	9-10	Diaz	Orosco
23—At Hous.	L	0-2	Niekro	Zachry
24—At Hous.	L	4-5	Smith	Scott
25—At Hous.	L	4-5	Sutton	Lynch
27—Atlanta	L	8-9	Moore	Orosco
28—Atlanta	L	3-4	Camp	Scott
29—Atlanta	L	4-9	Niekro	Hausman
30—Houston	L	2-4	LaCorte	Swan
31—Houston	L	0-4	Ryan	Lynch
		Won 5, Lost 24		

SEPTEMBER				
1—Houston	W	5-1	Falcone	Ruhle
3—Cincinnati	L	0-1	Pastore	Ownbey
4—Cincinnati	W	3-2	Swan	Berenyi
5—Cincinnati	W	10-2	Lynch	Shirley
6—At Pitts.	L	1-6	Rhoden	Falcone
7—At Pitts.	L	5-9	Sarmiento	Scott
8—At Pitts.	W	9-1	Ownbey	Robinson
10—At St. L.	W	2-1	Swan	Stuper
11—At St. L.	L	3-6	Andujar	Lynch
12—At St. L.	W	4-1	Falcone	Mura
14—At Mon.	L	1-3	Lea	Zachry
15—At Mon.	L	5-6†	Fryman	Sisk
16—At Mon.	W	9-4	Swan	Sanderson
17—St. Louis	L	2-3*	Sutter	Allen
17—St. Louis	L	1-7	Mura	Holman
18—St. Louis	L	0-2	Forsch	Falcone
18—St. Louis	L	2-6	Lahti	Terrell
19—St. Louis	L	1-3	Stuper	Zachry
21—Montreal	W	2-1*	Orosco	Smith
21—Montreal	L	1-5	Sanderson	Swan
22—At Chicago	W	5-2	Holman	Martz
23—At Chicago	W	5-4	Lynch	Bird
24—Phila.	L	1-2	Krukow	Terrell
25—Phila.	W	2-1	Swan	Carlton
26—Phila.	W	6-4	Puleo	Farmer
27—Pittsburgh	W	4-1	Holman	Rhoden
28—Pittsburgh	W	3-2*	Orosco	Romo
29—Chicago	L	1-4	Proly	Terrell
30—Chicago	L	1-3	Noles	Gorman
		Won 14, Lost 15		

OCTOBER				
1—At Phila.	W	1-0*	Leach	Altamirano
2—At Phila.	L	3-4	Altamirano	Zachry
3—At Phila.	L	1-4	Carlton	Lynch
		Won 1, Lost 2		

*10 innings.   †11 innings.   ‡12 innings.   §13 innings.   x14 innings.   y15 innings.

If the Mets are to avoid a repeat of their disastrous 1982 season next year, George Foster (above) and Neil Allen, who was injured, will have to bounce back.

twice as many as they won (50 losses compared to 25 victories) and finished 32 games under .500 at 65-97.

The only pluses in an otherwise miserable season were the continued fine play of Mookie Wilson in center field, the promise of improved defense around second base that Brian Giles gave in the last six weeks and the young pitchers who came up in September and helped the Mets to a 14-15 record that month.

But Foster, who hit only 13 homers and drove in only 70 runs, was the major disappointment. Foster left 47 runners on third base with less than two out. The Mets continued to predict that Foster, who turned 34 in the off-season, would bounce back in 1983.

Remaining, of course, are questions about the pitching.

Atlanta Manager Joe Torre called Jerry Royster the team's most valuable player down the stretch last year.

Torre Right About His Braves

By TIM TUCKER

It was February 15, 1982, and Joe Torre had just stepped off a plane in West Palm Beach, Fla.

What, the new manager of the Atlanta Braves was asked, would he tell his players when they arrived?

"I'll tell them," Torre said without flinching, "that they're here to win the pennant . . . that there's no reason they can't win the division championship."

Division championship? The Braves?

The team that had finished six games under .500 overall in the split season of 1981 . . . the team that had made no off-season trades . . . the team that had failed to sign its only free-agent target, Reggie Jackson . . . the team with no semblance of a starting pitching rotation . . . the team with a shortstop who, the year before, hit .218 and committed 30 errors in 95 games?

But Torre was right. The 1982 Braves won the National League West, their first divisional championship since 1969.

For 13 years, the Braves had been little more than a laughingstock, a city's joke. They had been ripped and ridiculed, belittled and beaten.

But suddenly, they were champions.

They did it by winning 89 of 162 games, finishing one game ahead of the Dodgers. They did it by taking command with an unprecedented season-opening winning streak of 13 games, by surviving a startling midseason collapse that produced 19 losses in 21 games (including eight straight defeats to Los Angeles in a 10-day span) and by compiling a 5-2 record on the West Coast in the last week of the regular season.

How did it happen? Even to those who watched the season unfold, the answer is not easy. It is particularly difficult when one considers the inconsistency and instability of the starting pitchers.

Of the four pitchers who opened the season in the Braves' rotation, only one—Tommy Boggs—was in that role at the end. And Boggs missed four months because of a rotator-cuff injury.

Phil Niekro, who opened the season on the disabled list, joined the rotation April 23 and, again, was the ace of the staff. His knuckleball fluttering as well as ever, Niekro, 43, won 17 games and lost only four, led the staff in victories, starts, innings and strikeouts and, more significantly, pitched two straight shutouts in the crucial final week. As in 1969, when

Phil Niekro, the old pro, won 13 more games than he lost in 1982.

the Braves last were champions and he won 23 games, Niekro was indispensable.

Otherwise, the starting rotation was manipulated daily by Torre and his pitching coaches, Bob Gibson and Rube Walker. In April, the Braves got strong pitching from Rick Mahler and Bob Walk. Starting in late August, the Braves got some good games from Boggs and Pascual Perez. Between April and late August, there were productive spurts from Rick Camp and Ken Dayley. In all, the Braves used 12 starting pitchers.

"For a team without a starting pitching rotation, I think we did a heck of a job,"

SCORES OF ATLANTA BRAVES' 1982 GAMES

APRIL

Date		Score	Winner	Loser
6—At S. Diego	W	1-0	Mahler	Eichelberger
7—At S. Diego	W	6-4	Walk	Montefusco
9—Houston	W	6-2	Boggs	Sutton
10—Houston	W	8-6	McWilliams	Ruhle
11—Houston	W	5-0	Mahler	Ryan
12—At Cinn.	W	6-1	Walk	Berenyi
13—At Cinn.	W	8-5	Garber	Kern
14—At Cinn.	W	5-2*	Camp	Kern
16—At Hous.	W	5-3	McWilliams	Ryan
17—At Hous.	W	2-1	Hanna	Niekro
18—At Hous.	W	6-5	Hrabosky	Smith
20—Cincinnati	W	4-2	Bedrosian	Pastore
21—Cincinnati	W	4-3	Camp	Shirley
22—Cincinnati	L	1-2	Berenyi	Walk
23—San Diego	L	3-6‡	Chiffer	Camp
24—San Diego	L	4-6	Show	Garber
26—Pittsburgh	L	4-6	Tekulve	McWilliams
27—Pittsburgh	L	4-10	Griffin	Walk
28—Pittsburgh	W	7-6*	Camp	Scurry
29—Chicago	W	3-0	Garber	Jenkins
30—Chicago	W	1-0	Bedrosian	Bird

Won 16, Lost 5

MAY

Date		Score	Winner	Loser
1—Chicago	L	1-5	Martz	Mahler
2—Chicago	W	10-3	Walk	Larson
3—At Pitts.	W	10-4	Niekro	Solomon
4—At Pitts.	L	4-8	Robinson	Cowley
5—At Pitts.	L	2-4	Rhoden	Mahler
7—At St. L.	W	6-3*	Garber	Martin
8—At St. L.	L	7-8	Sutter	Camp
9—At St. L.	W	3-0	Hanna	Andujar
11—At Chicago	L	4-6	Bird	Mahler
12—At Chicago	W	6-3	Walk	Martz
13—St. Louis	L	9-10	Rincon	Dayley
14—St. Louis	W	2-1	Garber	Bair
15—St. Louis	L	6-7*	Sutter	Garber
16—St. Louis	W	5-2	Mahler	Mura
17—At Mon.	L	0-4	Rogers	Walk
18—At Mon.	W	6-4	Niekro	Gullickson
19—At Mon.	W	9-1	Dayley	Burris
21—Phila.	W	7-6	Bedrosian	Lyle
22—Phila.	L	2-5	Krukow	McWilliams
23—Phila.	L	1-2	Ruthven	Niekro
24—New York	L	3-5	Zachry	Dayley
25—New York	W	10-2	Mahler	Scott
26—New York	L	4-6	Swan	Camp
29—At Phila.	L	0-1	Ruthven	Niekro
30—At Phila.	L	2-6	Carlton	Mahler
31—At N.Y.	L	4-10	Puleo	Walk

Won 11, Lost 15

JUNE

Date		Score	Winner	Loser
1—At N.Y.	W	7-3	Dayley	Jones
2—At N.Y.	W	3-1	Niekro	Falcone
5—Montreal	W	2-1	Mahler	Gullickson
6—Montreal	L	3-6	Reardon	McWilliams
7—At L.A.	W	4-3	Niekro	Welch
8—At L.A.	W	4-3	Hanna	Hooton
9—At L.A.	W	11-5	Mahler	Stewart
11—At S. Fran.	W	5-3	Walk	Chris
12—At S. Fran.	W	10-5	Niekro	Gale
13—At S. Fran.	L	1-2	Martin	Dayley
13—At S. Fran.	W	5-1	Camp	Hammaker
14—At Hous.	L	0-9	Niekro	Mahler
15—At Hous.	W	7-0	Walk	Knepper
16—At Hous.	W	5-4*	Garber	Cappuzzello
18—San Fran.	W	8-3	Dayley	Martin
19—San Fran.	L	4-9	Lavelle	Garber
20—San Fran.	L	3-5	Laskey	Walk
21—San Fran.	W	7-6	Camp	Minton
22—Los Ang.	L	1-4	Stewart	Bedrosian
23—Los Ang.	W	7-2	Mahler	Valenzuela
24—Los Ang.	L	3-5	Reuss	Walk
25—At Cinn.	W	5-2	Niekro	Berenyi
26—At Cinn.	L	1-2	Seaver	Dayley
27—At Cinn.	W	2-0§	Garber	Hume
28—Houston	L	2-6	Ryan	Mahler
29—Houston	W	6-5†	Bedrosian	LaCoss
30—Houston	W	5-4	Diaz	Knepper

Won 18, Lost 9

JULY

Date		Score	Winner	Loser
2—Cincinnati	W	6-4	Dayley	Seaver
3—Cincinnati	W	4-2	Mahler	Soto
4—Cincinnati	W	4-1	Walk	Shirley
5—Chicago	W	7-5	Hrabosky	Smith
6—Chicago	L	2-7	Bird	Dayley
7—St. Louis	W	3-2	Camp	Andujar
8—St. Louis	L	2-5	Stuper	Mahler
9—Pittsburgh	W	6-4	Diaz	Rhoden
10—Pittsburgh	L	1-6	Robinson	Niekro
11—Pittsburgh	L	1-3	McWilliams	Dayley
15—At Chicago	W	11-4	Niekro	Jenkins
16—At Chicago	L	3-4*	Campbell	Garber
17—At Chicago	W	9-4	Walk	Noles
18—At Chicago	W	4-2	Camp	Bird
19—At St. L.	W	4-1	Niekro	Andujar
20—At St. L.	W	8-6	Cowley	Lahti
21—At St. L.	L	0-8	Mura	Walk
23—At Pitts.	L	0-6	Rhoden	Camp
24—At Pitts.	W	4-3	Niekro	Robinson
25—At Pitts.	L	0-8	Candelaria	Mahler
27—San Diego	W	9-2	Walk	Lollar
27—San Diego	W	8-6*	Bedrosian	Lucas
28—San Diego	W	8-6	Niekro	Hawkins
29—San Diego	W	6-2	Camp	Welsh
30—Los Ang.	L	9-10	Forster	Bedrosian
30—Los Ang.	L	2-8	Welch	Cowley
31—Los Ang.	L	0-3	Valenzuela	Perez

Won 16, Lost 11

AUGUST

Date		Score	Winner	Loser
1—Los Ang.	L	4-9	Stewart	Diaz
2—San Fran.	W	7-3	Walk	Breining
3—San Fran.	L	3-6	Minton	Garber
4—San Fran.	L	2-3	Lavelle	Bedrosian
5—At L.A.	L	2-3*	Forster	Garber
6—At L.A.	L	4-5*	Howe	Bedrosian
7—At L.A.	L	6-7†	Beckwith	Bedrosian
8—At L.A.	L	0-2	Welch	Camp
9—At S. Fran.	L	0-5	Barr	Perez
10—At S. Fran.	L	2-3	Laskey	Hrabosky
11—At S. Fran.	L	6-8‡	Breining	Diaz
12—At S. Diego	L	2-8	Welsh	Walk
13—At S. Diego	L	4-7	Dravecky	Camp
14—At S. Diego	W	6-5	Moore	Eichelberger
15—At S. Diego	L	5-6*	DeLeon	Bedrosian
17—Montreal	L	7-13	Lea	Walk
17—Montreal	L	2-3*	Reardon	Mahler
18—Montreal	L	2-12	Gullickson	Camp
19—Montreal	W	5-4	Niekro	Fryman
20—New York	W	2-1*	Bedrosian	Zachry
21—New York	W	6-5	Walk	Jones
22—New York	W	10-9	Diaz	Orosco
23—Phila.	W	4-3	Camp	R. Reed
24—Phila.	W	9-7	Niekro	Carlton
25—Phila.	L	9-11*	R. Reed	Garber
27—At N.Y.	W	9-8	Moore	Orosco
28—At N.Y.	W	4-3	Camp	Scott
29—At N.Y.	W	9-4	Niekro	Hausman
30—At Phila.	L	1-6	Ruthven	Perez
30—At Phila.	W	11-9‡	Bedrosian	McGraw
31—At Phila.	W	3-0	Boggs	Farmer

Won 13, Lost 18

SEPTEMBER

Date		Score	Winner	Loser
1—At Phila.	W	4-0	Camp	Krukow
3—At Mon.	W	4-3	Niekro	Lea
4—At Mon.	L	1-4	Sanderson	Perez
5—At Mon.	L	1-2	Rogers	Garber
6—San Fran.	L	2-8	Holland	Moore
7—San Fran.	L	2-3	Barr	Camp
8—Los Ang.	W	12-11*	Garber	Howe
9—Los Ang.	W	10-3	Mahler	Valenzuela
10—Cincinnati	W	8-2	Perez	Shirley
11—Cincinnati	L	3-4	Soto	Boggs
12—Cincinnati	W	4-3	Bedrosian	Harris
13—Houston	L	3-5	Niekro	Niekro
14—Houston	L	0-4	LaCoss	Mahler
15—Houston	L	4-5	Ryan	Boggs
17—At Cinn.	L	2-5	Soto	Camp
18—At Cinn.	W	5-4	Niekro	Pastore
19—At Cinn.	W	6-1	Perez	Berenyi
20—At Hous.	L	3-4	Smith	Garber
21—At Hous.	L	3-5	Ruhle	Camp
22—At Hous.	L	2-3	Smith	Garber
24—San Diego	W	11-6	Dayley	Griffin
25—San Diego	W	12-6	Moore	Eichelberger
26—San Diego	L	2-3	Lucas	Camp
27—At S. Fran.	W	7-0	Niekro	Martin
28—At S. Fran.	W	8-3	Perez	Laskey
29—At L.A.	W	4-3‡	Garber	Forster
30—At L.A.	L	3-10	Hooton	Camp

Won 13, Lost 14

OCTOBER

Date		Score	Winner	Loser
1—At S. Diego	W	4-0	Niekro	Show
2—At S. Diego	W	4-2	Perez	Montefusco
3—At S. Diego	L	1-5	Lollar	Camp

Won 2, Lost 1

*10 innings. †11 innings. ‡12 innings. §14 innings

Steve Bedrosian (above) was superb at killing opposing rallies while Bob Horner (below) helped prolong Atlanta's.

said Torre, whose strategy was to use the hottest available arm at each moment. Pitchers were spotted against certain teams, in certain parks, and the results were grand. Torre, for instance, went out of his way to pitch Niekro on the road; Niekro was 14-1 away, 3-3 at home.

Camp and Walk each won 11 games, and Mahler had nine victories.

The bullpen enabled the Braves to win despite the shaky rotation. Gene Garber, who had been on the trading block over the winter, had perhaps his finest big-league season, setting a team record with 30 saves and posting a 2.34 earned-run average. Steve Bedrosian, who had opened the season as a starter, developed into a hard-throwing, middle-inning complement to Garber and had 11 saves and a 2.42 ERA.

Atlanta struggled without an effective lefthander in the bullpen all summer, and by September the Braves had dispatched all their lefties, trading Larry McWilliams to Pittsburgh and Carlos Diaz to the Mets and releasing Al Hrabosky.

"The bullpen," Torre said as his team moved into the National League Championship Series, "got us where we are."

The offense helped, too.

To win the division, the Braves needed—and got—maximum offensive seasons from most of their everyday players. Atlanta led the league in home runs and set a team record for stolen bases.

Center fielder Dale Murphy clearly was the team's most valuable player, hitting 36 home runs (second in the N.L.), driving in 109 runs (good for a share of the league lead) and fielding superbly. Third baseman Bob Horner hit 32 home runs; first baseman Chris Chambliss hit a career-high 20 homers, and right fielder Claudell Washington had his second straight solid season (16 homers, 80 RBIs).

Shortstop Rafael Ramirez developed into a productive offensive player (.278 average, 52 RBIs), and he and second baseman Glenn Hubbard combined to help the Braves lead the major leagues in double plays. Ramirez did make 38 errors, however.

The bench was a big help. In August, Jerry Royster stepped off the bench, became the starting left fielder and hit .334 over the last two months of the season. In late September, when Horner was injured and Royster was forced to third base, Terry Harper moved into left field and hit .320 over a vital two-week period. Torre declared Royster "the team MVP the last eight weeks of the season."

It was a season unlike anything Atlanta baseball fans had reason to expect, although it was exactly what Torre told his players it could be. And being swept by St. Louis in the Championship Series did not detract from the accomplishments.

On a team loaded with stars, Pedro Guerrero may be the Dodgers' best.

Surge Not Enough for Dodgers

By GORDON VERRELL

On opening day, 1982, Terry Forster, the Los Angeles Dodgers' reliever who was attempting a comeback from two elbow operations, got a victory, his first in nearly three years.

The triumph was against the San Francisco Giants, 4-3, and the final out was a harmless, lazy fly ball by Joe Morgan.

Six months later, in the final game of the season, there was Forster vs. Morgan once again. And Morgan hit another ball, only this one wasn't lazy—or harmless.

It went for a three-run homer, jolting Forster and the Dodgers, 5-3, and preventing them from tying Atlanta for first place in the National League West.

Forster said the home run pitch to Morgan was "the worst pitch I've thrown in 12 years in the big leagues," and, unjustifiably, he placed the blame for the Dodgers' failure to defend their World Series championship entirely on his shoulders.

He shouldn't have, of course, for it was only because the Dodgers staged an incredible surge in August that they were able to overcome a rather uninspired first half and even be in the position to tie.

The Dodgers never contended through July, severely lacking the late-inning punch that was their earmark for so many summers.

And when the Dodgers arrived in Atlanta on July 30 for a doubleheader, they were in third place, 10½ games behind the Braves.

Yet, in the next 12 days, by winning 12 of 13 games—including eight straight over Atlanta—the Dodgers surged into first place, by one-half game over the Braves.

"Never have I seen a team gain so much ground in so short a time," said Dodgers Manager Tom Lasorda, as astounded as anyone.

By August 18, the lead was four games and it appeared the club had hit its stride.

In the next 6½ weeks, though, the Dodgers would lose the lead, regain it, lose it again and, finally, on the last day of the season, miss the opportunity for a one-game playoff with the Braves.

When the Dodgers lapsed into a complete, and certainly untimely, offensive slump in late September, it cost them the title.

The Dodgers pulled back into a three-game lead on September 20, having won eight of nine games, including seven straight. They were 20 games over .500 at 85-65.

Jerry Reuss matched his career high with 18 victories.

Then, in San Diego on September 21-22, the Dodgers lost twice, 3-0 and 2-1 (10 innings). Returning home, they lost three more to San Francisco, all by one run, then two to last-place Cincinnati, the losing streak climbing to seven.

And when Atlanta won a 12-inning, 4-3 game from the Dodgers on September 29, the Braves led by two games over Los Angeles and San Francisco—with only four games remaining.

As abruptly as the Dodgers fell into a batting slump, they erupted from it, crushing the Braves, 10-3, on September 30. The Dodgers then went to San Francisco, winning 4-0 and 15-2 and bringing the race to the final day, trailing the Braves by one game.

The Braves lost on the final day (at San Diego), but so did the Dodgers (at San Francisco). Los Angeles' defeat can be blamed on the same bugaboo that plagued

SCORES OF LOS ANGELES DODGERS' 1982 GAMES

APRIL

Date	W/L	Score	Winner	Loser
6—San Fran.	W	4-3	Forster	Lavelle
7—San Fran.	W	9-2	Welch	Breining
9—San Diego	L	4-7	Chiffer	Forster
10—San Diego	W	6-0	Valenzuela	Eichelberger
12—At Hous.	L	1-2†	LaCoss	Stewart
13—At Hous.	W	9-5	Welch	Knepper
14—At Hous.	L	1-2	Sutton	Hooton
15—At S. Diego	L	0-2	Eichelberger	Valenzuela
16—At S. Diego	L	3-8	Curtis	Reuss
17—At S. Diego	L	3-4	Show	Goltz
18—At S. Diego	L	3-9	DeLeon	Stewart
19—Houston	L	4-6	Sutton	Forster
20—Houston	W	10-2	Valenzuela	Ruhle
21—Houston	W	6-0	Reuss	Ryan
23—At S. Fran.	W	9-0	Welch	Fowlkes
24—At S. Fran.	W	7-6	Howe	Minton
25—At S. Fran.	L	3-6	Breining	Valenzuela
27—Phila.	W	3-0	Reuss	Christenson
28—Phila.	L	3-9	Farmer	Howe
29—Phila.	W	4-0	Hooton	Ruthven
30—Montreal	L	2-4	Sanderson	Valenzuela

Won 10, Lost 11

MAY

Date	W/L	Score	Winner	Loser
1—Montreal	W	2-1	Reuss	Lea
2—Montreal	L	1-13	Rogers	Welch
3—New York	L	3-6‡	Lynch	Forster
4—New York	W	2-1	Valenzuela	Allen
6—At Mon.	W	3-2	Reuss	Sanderson
7—At Mon.	W	6-2	Welch	Rogers
8—At Mon.	W	10-8	Howe	Gullickson
9—At Mon.	W	5-4	Valenzuela	Burris
10—At Phila.	L	8-9*	Brusstar	Niedenfuer
11—At Phila.	L	8-9	Altamirano	Reuss
12—At Phila.	L	3-11	R. Reed	Welch
13—At N. Y.	L	2-4	Falcone	Hooton
14—At N. Y.	W	4-1	Valenzuela	Jones
15—At N. Y.	L	4-6	Zachry	Power
16—At N. Y.	L	4-13	Scott	Reuss
18—Chicago	W	2-1	Niedenfuer	Campbell
19—Chicago	W	4-1	Stewart	Noles
20—Chicago	L	3-8	Jenkins	Valenzuela
21—St. Louis	L	3-6	Mura	Reuss
22—St. Louis	W	3-2	Power	Rincon
23—St. Louis	W	5-0	Welch	Forsch
24—Pittsburgh	L	3-9	Robinson	Niedenfuer
25—Pittsburgh	W	5-2	Valenzuela	Rhoden
26—Pittsburgh	W	3-2	Reuss	Solomon
28—At Chicago	L	3-4	Martz	Welch
29—At Chicago	L	2-3§	Smith	Pena
30—At Chicago	W	7-0	Valenzuela	Jenkins
31—At Pitts.	W	5-4	Howe	Tekulve

Won 15, Lost 13

JUNE

Date	W/L	Score	Winner	Loser
1—At Pitts.	L	1-3	Candelaria	Reuss
2—At Pitts.	L	7-8	Scurry	Romo
4—At St. L.	L	2-5	Forsch	Stewart
5—At St. L.	W	6-2	Valenzuela	Mura
6—At St. L.	W	5-3	Howe	Sutter
7—Atlanta	L	3-4	Niekro	Welch
8—Atlanta	L	3-4	Hanna	Hooton
9—Atlanta	L	5-11	Mahler	Stewart
10—Cincinnati	L	2-3	Kern	Valenzuela
11—Cincinnati	W	11-1	Reuss	Pastore
12—Cincinnati	W	4-3	Welch	Harris
13—Cincinnati	L	2-4	Berenyi	Hooton
14—At S. Diego	W	4-3†	Howe	Show
15—At S. Diego	W	3-0	Reuss	Curtis
16—At S. Diego	W	6-0	Welch	Lollar
18—At Cinn.	W	3-2†	Forster	Hume
19—At Cinn.	W	2-1	Valenzuela	Berenyi
20—At Cinn.	W	4-2	Reuss	Seaver
21—At Cinn.	L	2-10	Soto	Welch
22—At Atlanta	W	4-1	Stewart	Bedrosian
23—At Atlanta	L	2-7	Mahler	Valenzuela
24—At Atlanta	W	5-3	Reuss	Walk
25—At Hous.	L	5-7	LaCoss	Forster
26—At Hous.	W	4-1	Stewart	Sutton
27—At Hous.	W	7-3	Forster	Ruhle
28—San Diego	W	6-4	Valenzuela	Welsh
29—San Diego	L	5-7*	DeLeon	Shirley
30—San Diego	W	5-1	Welch	Eichelberger
30—San Diego	L	4-6	Show	Forster

Won 16, Lost 13

JULY

Date	W/L	Score	Winner	Loser
2—Houston	L	1-4	Sutton	Romo
3—Houston	W	5-4	Valenzuela	Roberge
4—Houston	L	0-3	Ryan	Reuss
5—At N. Y.	W	4-1	Welch	Falcone
6—At N. Y.	W	9-3	Stewart	Scott
7—At Mon.	W	3-1	Valenzuela	Lea
8—At Mon.	L	3-7	Palmer	Pena
9—At Phila.	W	6-4†	Stewart	McGraw
10—At Phila.	L	2-4	Ruthven	Welch
11—At Phila.	L	3-4	Christenson	Valenzuela
15—New York	L	2-5	Puleo	Reuss
16—New York	W	7-6	Valenzuela	Zachry
17—New York	W	6-5	Shirley	Allen
18—New York	L	3-8	Scott	Welch
19—Montreal	W	2-1	Romo	Sanderson
20—Montreal	W	10-1	Reuss	Lea
21—Montreal	L	1-4†	Rogers	Howe
23—Phila.	L	3-6	Altamirano	Stewart
24—Phila.	W	3-2	Welch	Bystrom
25—Phila.	L	0-1	Carlton	Reuss
26—At S. Fran.	L	1-6	Laskey	Valenzuela
27—At S. Fran.	W	7-3	Beckwith	Martin
28—At S. Fran.	L	2-6	Breining	Stewart
30—At Atlanta	W	10-9	Forster	Bedrosian
30—At Atlanta	W	8-2	Welch	Cowley
31—At Atlanta	W	3-0	Valenzuela	Perez

Won 14, Lost 12

AUGUST

Date	W/L	Score	Winner	Loser
1—At Atlanta	W	9-4	Stewart	Diaz
2—At Cinn.	L	1-5	Soto	Reuss
3—At Cinn.	W	4-0	Welch	Pastore
4—At Cinn.	W	8-2	Wright	Berenyi
5—Atlanta	W	3-2*	Forster	Garber
6—Atlanta	W	5-4*	Howe	Bedrosian
7—Atlanta	W	7-6†	Beckwith	Bedrosian
8—Atlanta	W	2-0	Welch	Camp
9—Cincinnati	W	3-2§	Stewart	Kern
10—Cincinnati	W	11-3	Valenzuela	Seaver
11—Cincinnati	L	1-2	Shirley	Hooton
12—San Fran.	W	6-2	Niedenfuer	Martin
13—San Fran.	W	6-1	Welch	Gale
14—San Fran.	L	2-4	Barr	Stewart
15—San Fran.	L	6-8	Laskey	Valenzuela
17—At Chicago	W	2-1za	Reuss	Ripley
18—At Chicago	W	7-4	Reuss	Bird
19—At Chicago	L	2-8	Jenkins	Welch
20—At Pitts.	W	1-0	Valenzuela	McWilliams
21—At Pitts.	L	1-2	Tekulve	Howe
22—At Pitts.	W	3-4x	Robinson	Beckwith
23—At St. L.	L	3-11	Forsch	Reuss
24—At St. L.	W	5-2	Welch	Stuper
25—At St. L.	W	11-3	Valenzuela	Mura
27—Chicago	W	9-4	Wright	Proly
28—Chicago	W	7-1	Reuss	Noles
29—Chicago	L	2-7	Jenkins	Welch
30—St. Louis	L	2-3	Stuper	Valenzuela
31—St. Louis	W	4-1	Hooton	Mura

Won 19, Lost 10

SEPTEMBER

Date	W/L	Score	Winner	Loser
1—St. Louis	L	5-6§	Bair	Wright
3—Pittsburgh	L	2-3	Robinson	Welch
4—Pittsburgh	L	0-1	Tunnell	Valenzuela
5—Pittsburgh	W	2-1*	Niedenfuer	Tekulve
6—At Cinn.	W	7-2	Reuss	Soto
7—At Cinn.	W	8-4	Stewart	Harris
8—At Atlanta	L	11-12*	Garber	Howe
9—At Atlanta	L	3-10	Mahler	Valenzuela
10—At Hous.	W	3-2	Howe	Ryan
11—At Hous.	W	5-3	Reuss	Ruhle
12—At Hous.	W	7-3	Stewart	DiPino
13—San Diego	W	4-3y	Reuss	Welsh
14—San Diego	W	1-0	Valenzuela	Show
15—San Diego	W	5-0	Hooton	Montefusco
17—Houston	W	9-2	Reuss	DiPino
18—Houston	L	0-2	Niekro	Welch
19—Houston	W	3-2	Valenzuela	LaCorte
21—At S. Diego	L	0-3	Montefusco	Hooton
22—At S. Diego	L	1-2*	DeLeon	Niedenfuer
24—San Fran.	L	2-3	Holland	Howe
25—San Fran.	L	4-5	McGaffigan	Valenzuela
26—San Fran.	L	2-3	Breining	Hooton
27—Cincinnati	L	1-6	Soto	Reuss
28—Cincinnati	L	3-4*	Hayes	Stewart
29—Atlanta	L	3-4‡	Garber	Forster
30—Atlanta	W	10-3	Hooton	Camp

Won 12, Lost 14

OCTOBER

Date	W/L	Score	Winner	Loser
1—At S. Fran.	W	4-0	Reuss	Breining
2—At S. Fran.	W	15-2	Welch	Martin
3—At S. Fran.	L	3-5	Minton	Niedenfuer

Won 2, Lost 1

*10 innings. †11 innings. ‡12 innings. §13 innings. x14 innings. y16 innings. z21 innings. aSuspended game, completed August 18.

Steve Sax was handed the second-base job in spring training and proved the Dodger brass right by capturing Rookie of the Year honors.

the Dodgers throughout the first half of the season and during the eight-game losing streak in September: blown opportunities.

The Dodgers had the bases loaded in the seventh inning of the final game, with one out and the scored tied, 2-2. But they failed to score.

That was nothing new. Against Atlanta on September 29, the Dodgers had the bases loaded, one out and failed to score. They lost, 4-3. One night earlier, against Cincinnati, the Dodgers had the bases loaded in the 10th inning, no one out and didn't score, losing, 4-3.

"I'll see those innings in my dreams—no, my nightmares—all winter," moaned Lasorda.

An ineffective bullpen hampered the

Dodgers from the start of the season. Then the starting pitchers, primarily Burt Hooton, had difficulty. Hooton wound up having arthroscopic knee surgery. He won only one game, a one-hitter over Philadelphia on April 29, before undergoing surgery June 21. He didn't win his second game until August 31.

Along with the pitching problems, the Dodgers set a Los Angeles club record for men left on base, 1,223, an average of better than 7½ per game.

One reason was the early-season failures of veterans Steve Garvey and Ron Cey, each playing under the cloud that 1982 might mark his last year with the Dodgers; Garvey because his contract expired, Cey because of whispers the club was ready to move Pedro Guerrero from right field to third base.

Both finished with respectable figures: Garvey had 86 runs batted in and 16 home runs; Cey 79 RBIs and 24 homers. But in the first half of the season, Cey drove in only 34 runs, Garvey 35.

Guerrero had a Most Valuable Player-type of season: 32 homers, one off Garvey's L.A. club record, 100 RBIs and a .304 average, highest on the club. Veteran outfielder Dusty Baker was consistent, finishing at .300 with 88 RBIs and 23 homers.

And shortstop Bill Russell, returning strongly from a winter of surgery on his hand and foot, responded with an excellent season (.274 and 46 RBIs) and played well in the field.

Steve Sax, who supplanted longtime second baseman Dave Lopes, set a club record for stolen bases by a rookie, 49, batted .282, and became the fourth consecutive Dodger voted N.L. Rookie of the Year.

Fernando Valenzuela, the cause celebre in 1981 when he was N.L. Cy Young Award winner, N.L. Rookie of the Year and The Sporting News' Player of the Year, overcame whatever negatives that lingered from a three-week salary holdout in the spring and won 19 games, though he failed three times in his bid for No. 20.

The so-called big three of Valenzuela (19-13), Jerry Reuss (whose 18-11 record matched his career high in victories) and Bob Welch (who at 16-11 had his winningest season) accounted for 53 of the Dodgers' 88 victories.

The disappointment of not winning the division was tempered, certainly, by the 3,608,881 fans who paid their way into Dodger Stadium in 1982, an all-time major league record and the third time in five years the Dodgers have topped the three-million mark.

Bullpen Lets Giants Stand Tall

By NICK PETERS

The skeptics laughed during spring training when Tom Haller, Giants' general manager, cautiously predicted the club could finish above .500 in 1982.

They howled when Manager Frank Robinson, not liberal with superlatives, boldly proclaimed, "We can win it all if things go right."

The cynics, forgetting that baseball is not a logical game, pointed to a completely revamped starting rotation and a retread first baseman, Reggie Smith, and collectively declared, "No way!"

But guess who laughed last? Haller and Robinson pulled a coup by making the Giants the most successful team in the majors over the final three months.

Moreover, they were in the pennant chase until the final weekend, reviving pennant fever in Northern California by going 20-7 in September. The Giants finished third, two games behind Atlanta, and were 12 games above .500 at 87-75.

There were heroes galore, of course, but the main reasons for the club's rise were a stout bullpen, a revitalized bench and a winning atmosphere partially attributed to veterans Joe Morgan and Smith.

The Giants exhibited character, rallying for 45 of their victories, including 27 on their final at-bats. They topped the majors in one-run games (66) and one-run victories (38).

By going 21-8 down the stretch, the Giants posted consecutive winning seasons for the first time since 1970-71. The spree included their first three-game sweep at Dodger Stadium in 15 years, and there was a measure of satisfaction in knocking the Dodgers out of a pennant playoff against Atlanta with a 5-3 victory on the final day of the season.

Morgan, whose dramatic home run ousted the Dodgers, was named the Giants' MVP by his teammates. At 39, he showed few signs of slowing down, batting a team-leading .289, swiping 24 bases in 28 tries, making only eight errors and setting a league career record for walks.

Smith, 37, made a big comeback. Despite injuries that limited him to 106 games, he batted .284 with 18 home runs. In 1981, with the Dodgers, he batted .200 in 41 games.

Jack Clark overcame a sluggish start to reach career highs with 27 home runs and 103 runs batted in, the first Giants player to top 100 in 11 years. Clark also had 21 game-winning RBIs, tying the Cardinals'

Keith Hernandez for the league lead.

Rookie Chili Davis belted 19 home runs and knocked in 76 runs despite batting leadoff much of the season. Fellow rookie Tom O'Malley moved into the third-base job and batted .275.

Thanks to newcomers Duane Kuiper and Champ Summers, pinch-hitting improved from .186, one homer and 18 RBIs in 1981 to .264, six homers and 43 RBIs. The bench accounted for some of the late-inning heroics.

Kuiper, kept on the bench by Morgan, didn't pout. He responded with a club-record 14 pinch hits, batting .318 in a pinch and .280 overall. Summers batted .323 with two homers and 11 RBIs as a pinch-hitter.

The club developed three promising starters in Fred Breining, Bill Laskey and Atlee Hammaker. Breining, a reliever until the final month, finished 11-6 with a 3.08 earned-run average.

Rookies Laskey and Hammaker were predictably inconsistent, but showed flashes of brilliance. Laskey, 12-8 at one point, finished 13-12 with a 3.14 ERA. Hammaker was 12-8 and 4.11. Neither was with the club on opening day.

But the bullpen was the pride of the team and the main reason for the strong finish, being directly involved (victory or save) in 68 victories. "We simply couldn't have done it without them," Robinson said.

There's no question Robinson taxed his relievers, but he had little choice given the inexperience of his starters. The manager had a penchant for pulling his starters early, but the moves usually paid off.

Greg Minton, an eccentric righthander, was at his finest, establishing club records with 30 saves and 78 appearances. He was 10-4 with a 1.83 ERA.

Al Holland, who opened the season as a starter, was back in his more effective relief role by early summer and finished fast, pitching 17⅔ hitless innings in September and finishing 7-3. Gary Lavelle (10-7, 2.67, eight saves) and Jim Barr (4-3, 3.29, two saves) also sparkled.

But the Giants hardly were an overnight success. Clark was languishing around .200 in the first two months before awakening with four home runs and 11 RBIs in two games at Pittsburgh, May 28-29.

That outburst seemed to buoy the club, but a three-game sweep by the Padres at Candlestick Park left the Giants reeling with a 32-42 record, 12½ games behind

Although he turned 39 during the season, Joe Morgan almost led the Giants to a Western Division title.

SCORES OF SAN FRANCISCO GIANTS' 1982 GAMES

APRIL			Winner	Loser
6—At L.A.	L	3-4	Forster	Lavelle
7—At L.A.	L	2-9	Welch	Breining
9—At Cinn.	L	0-7	Pastore	Schatzeder
10—At Cinn.	W	7-5*	Minton	Hume
11—At Cinn.	W	6-1	Holland	Leibrandt
13—San Diego	W	3-2	Fowlkes	Montefusco
14—San Diego	L	2-3	Lollar	Schatzeder
16—Cincinnati	W	6-1	Gale	Soto
17—Cincinnati	L	2-8	Berenyi	Holland
18—Cincinnati	W	4-2	Fowlkes	Seaver
19—At S. Diego	L	6-13	Eichelberger	Schatzeder
20—At S. Diego	L	4-8	Curtis	Gale
21—At S. Diego	L	6-7	Montefusco	Holland
23—Los Ang.	L	0-9	Welch	Fowlkes
24—Los Ang.	L	6-7	Howe	Minton
25—Los Ang.	W	6-3	Breining	Valenzuela
27—Montreal	L	2-3	Rogers	Holland
28—Montreal	W	7-0	Laskey	Gullickson
29—Montreal	W	7-3	Fowlkes	Burris
30—New York	W	5-4	Breining	Allen
		Won 9, Lost 11		

MAY				
1—New York	W	6-3	Hammaker	Zachry
2—New York	W	4-3	Holland	Lynch
2—New York	L	0-2	Jones	Laskey
3—Phila.	L	3-5	Monge	Schatzeder
4—Phila.	L	4-9	Carlton	Gale
6—At N.Y.	W	5-3	Minton	Orosco
7—At N.Y.	L	2-3	Puleo	Laskey
8—At N.Y.	W	8-3	Lavelle	Lynch
9—At N.Y.	L	5-6	Swan	Minton
10—At Mon.	L	4-5	Fryman	Lavelle
11—At Mon.	W	5-4	Hammaker	Sanderson
12—At Mon.	W	3-2	Laskey	Rogers
13—At Phila.	L	1-8	Ruthven	Fowlkes
14—At Phila.	L	0-2	Carlton	Gale
15—At Phila.	L	3-5	Christenson	Minton
16—At Phila.	L	1-6	Krukow	Hammaker
18—Pittsburgh	W	2-1	Laskey	Candelaria
19—Pittsburgh	L	1-2	Robinson	Chris
20—Pittsburgh	W	3-1	Lavelle	Scurry
21—Chicago	L	4-6	Tidrow	Martin
22—Chicago	L	1-2	Ripley	Hammaker
23—Chicago	W	4-3*	Lavelle	Tidrow
23—Chicago	W	6-3	Schatzeder	Larson
24—St. Louis	L	0-6	Andujar	Gale
25—St. Louis	L	3-8	LaPoint	Martin
26—St. Louis	L	4-8	Mura	Hammaker
28—At Pitts.	W	10-5	Laskey	Candelaria
29—At Pitts.	W	9-5	Barr	Robinson
30—At Pitts.	L	6-7§	Solomon	Barr
31—At St. L.	L	6-11	Martin	Martin
		Won 12, Lost 18		

JUNE				
1—At St. L.	W	4-3†	Minton	Kaat
2—At St. L.	L	0-1	Andujar	Laskey
4—At Chicago	W	4-3	Breining	Jenkins
5—At Chicago	W	2-1	Gale	Bird
6—At Chicago	W	5-3	Martin	Martz
8—Houston	W	7-3	Hammaker	Ryan
9—Houston	L	1-6	Niekro	Laskey
11—Atlanta	L	3-5	Walk	Chris
12—Atlanta	L	5-10	Niekro	Gale
13—Atlanta	W	2-1	Martin	Dayley
13—Atlanta	L	1-5	Camp	Hammaker
15—At Cinn.	W	4-3	Laskey	Seaver
16—At Cinn.	L	3-7	Soto	Barr
17—At Cinn.	L	2-4	Leibrandt	Gale
18—At Atlanta	L	3-8	Dayley	Martin
19—At Atlanta	W	9-4	Lavelle	Garber
20—At Atlanta	W	5-3	Laskey	Walk
21—At Atlanta	L	6-7	Camp	Minton
22—At Hous.	L	0-2	Ruhle	Gale
23—At Hous.	W	9-8	Breining	LaCorte
24—At Hous.	W	4-3*	Hammaker	Niekro
25—San Diego	L	2-3	Eichelberger	Laskey
26—San Diego	L	6-7x	Show	Lavelle
27—San Diego	L	2-4	Lollar	Gale
28—Cincinnati	W	7-1	Martin	Leibrandt
29—Cincinnati	W	3-0	Hammaker	Shirley
30—Cincinnati	W	7-6‡	Minton	Leibrandt
		Won 14, Lost 13		

JULY				
2—At S. Diego	W	8-4	Holland	Dravecky
2—At S. Diego	L	2-3	Lollar	Lavelle
3—At S. Diego	W	4-3x	Minton	Chiffer
4—At S. Diego	L	3-4	Dravecky	Hammaker

JULY			Winner	Loser
5—At Phila.	W	3-1	Laskey	Ruthven
6—At Phila.	L	2-3	Lyle	Breining
7—At N.Y.	W	3-2	Gale	Gaff
8—At N.Y.	W	9-7	Martin	Orosco
9—At Mon.	W	3-2	Hammaker	Rogers
10—At Mon.	L	4-8	Gullickson	Laskey
11—At Mon.	W	8-7*	Minton	Reardon
15—Phila.	L	1-2	Krukow	Gale
16—Phila.	L	0-1	Carlton	Laskey
17—Phila.	L	3-5†	R. Reed	Breining
18—Phila.	W	4-3	Hammaker	Christenson
20—New York	W	5-1	Gale	Puleo
21—New York	L	2-6	Falcone	Laskey
23—Montreal	L	7-8§	Burris	Lavelle
24—Montreal	W	5-2	Hammaker	Palmer
25—Montreal	W	3-2	Gale	Sanderson
26—Los Ang.	W	6-1	Laskey	Valenzuela
27—Los Ang.	L	3-7	Beckwith	Martin
28—Los Ang.	W	6-2	Breining	Stewart
30—At Hous.	L	1-3	Sutton	Gale
31—At Hous.	W	5-4	Laskey	Ruhle
31—At Hous.	L	0-5	LaCoss	Hammaker
		Won 14, Lost 12		

AUGUST				
1—At Hous.	W	4-2*	Minton	LaCorte
2—At Atlanta	L	3-7	Walk	Breining
3—At Atlanta	W	6-3	Minton	Garber
4—At Atlanta	W	3-2	Lavelle	Bedrosian
5—Houston	W	5-2	Laskey	Ruhle
6—Houston	W	7-6	Lavelle	Moffitt
7—Houston	W	9-2	Martin	Niekro
8—Houston	W	3-2	Breining	Knepper
8—Houston	W	8-3	Lavelle	LaCoss
9—Atlanta	W	5-0	Barr	Perez
10—Atlanta	W	3-2	Laskey	Hrabosky
11—Atlanta	W	8-6‡	Breining	Diaz
12—At L.A.	L	2-6	Niedenfuer	Martin
13—At L.A.	L	1-6	Welch	Gale
14—At L.A.	W	4-2	Barr	Stewart
15—At L.A.	W	8-6	Laskey	Valenzuela
17—At Pitts.	L	1-4	Rhoden	Hammaker
18—At Pitts.	W	16-9	Fowlkes	Robinson
19—At Pitts.	L	1-6	Candelaria	Gale
20—At St. L.	W	8-7	Lavelle	Sutter
21—At St. L.	L	6-7	LaPoint	Laskey
22—At St. L.	L	4-5‡	Lahti	Lavelle
23—At Chicago	L	5-8	Bird	Martin
24—At Chicago	L	4-8	Jenkins	Gale
25—At Chicago	L	2-4	Martz	Barr
27—Pittsburgh	L	2-3	Rhoden	Laskey
28—Pittsburgh	W	4-2	Hammaker	Robinson
29—Pittsburgh	L	3-4	Candelaria	Martin
31—Chicago	W	4-3	Holland	Hernandez
		Won 17, Lost 12		

SEPTEMBER				
1—Chicago	L	6-7	Campbell	Gale
3—St. Louis	W	3-2*	Minton	Sutter
4—St. Louis	W	5-4	Lavelle	Sutter
5—St. Louis	W	5-1	Breining	Stuper
6—At Atlanta	W	8-2	Holland	Moore
7—At Atlanta	W	3-2	Barr	Camp
8—At Hous.	L	1-8	Niekro	Hammaker
9—At Hous.	W	5-1	Martin	LaCoss
10—At S. Diego	W	5-1	Breining	Dravecky
11—At S. Diego	W	8-3	Laskey	Welsh
13—Cincinnati	L	4-5†	Price	Lavelle
14—Cincinnati	W	2-1	Hammaker	Berenyi
15—Cincinnati	W	5-4	Gale	Price
16—San Diego	W	9-3	Breining	Lollar
17—San Diego	L	2-4	Dravecky	Laskey
18—San Diego	W	4-1	Gale	Eichelberger
19—San Diego	W	4-3†	Holland	DeLeon
21—At Cinn.	L	5-6	Shirley	Breining
22—At Cinn.	W	2-0	Martin	Soto
23—At Cinn.	W	11-7	Hammaker	Pastore
24—At L.A.	W	3-2	Holland	Howe
25—At L.A.	W	5-4	McGaffigan	Valenzuela
26—At L.A.	W	3-2	Breining	Hooton
27—At Atlanta	L	0-7	Niekro	Martin
28—Atlanta	L	3-8	Perez	Laskey
29—Houston	W	6-1	Hammaker	Niekro
30—Houston	W	7-6	Lavelle	Boone
		Won 20, Lost 7		

OCTOBER				
1—Los Ang.	L	0-4	Reuss	Breining
2—Los Ang.	L	2-15	Welch	Martin
3—Los Ang.	W	5-3	Minton	Neidenfuer
		Won 1, Lost 2		

*10 innings.   †11 innings.   ‡12 innings.   §13 innings.   x15 innings.

San Francisco's Chili Davis was one of the best of the National League's star-studded rookie crop.

Atlanta, on June 27.

From that point, the Giants' 55-33 record was the finest in the major leagues.

"I see us making a move in the second half," Robinson vowed. "It would show progress if we finished above .500, and I feel we can do better than that."

How prophetic. However, on August 2, the day after Robinson was inducted into the Hall of Fame, a loss at Atlanta made the Giants 50-55, and they trailed the Braves by 13.

The next night, San Francisco launched a 10-game winning streak, the club's longest since 1966, and the Giants were only four games out on August 11. A 4-9 trip and a six-game losing streak dampened some enthusiasm, but the Giants rebounded to win 18 of 22 (beginning on August 31) and pulled within one game with one week to go.

Definitely a year to remember.

Padres Focus on Blessings

By PHIL COLLIER

The 1982 San Diego Padres equaled or exceeded almost everyone's preseason expectations, but they spent the last 11 weeks of play destroying earlier indications that they had become legitimate National League West contenders for the first time.

Fourteen games over .500 (50-36) and only two games behind first-place Atlanta at the All-Star break in mid-July, the Padres limped home at a 31-45 clip and might have been overtaken by fifth-place Houston if the season had lasted much longer.

Nevertheless, the Padres enjoyed only their second .500 season (81-81 record) in 14 years, vacated last place for the first time since 1979 and tied a club high with their fourth-place finish. Their home attendance (1,607,516) had been surpassed only by the 1978 team that drew 1,670,107 and finished fourth with a club-high 84 victories.

"I said in April that I thought we were capable of winning more than half of our games. I would have been disappointed if we had finished under .500," Dick Williams said after his first season as Padres' manager.

Jack McKeon, who took over as general manager in August of 1980, masterminded the trades that brought the Padres respectability. Four of the club's leading producers—Terry Kennedy, Garry Templeton, Sixto Lezcano and Luis DeLeon— were players he acquired from St. Louis.

Kennedy led the team in hitting (.295), home runs (21), doubles (42) and runs batted in (97). Templeton, while batting only .247, scored 76 runs, batted in 64 and had 27 steals. Lezcano supplied the right-handed batting punch the club needed, contributing 16 homers and 84 RBIs along with a .289 average. DeLeon, a rookie reliever, won nine of 14 decisions, compiled 15 saves and had a 2.03 ERA.

Lefthanded pitchers Tim Lollar and Chris Welsh, center fielder Ruppert Jones and outfielder-third baseman Joe Lefebvre, all acquired in a 1981 trade with the New York Yankees, made significant contributions. Lollar (16-9 record, 3.13 ERA) became the Padres' leading starter. Jones, in his option year, batted .283 with 12 homers and 61 RBIs. Welsh broke even in 16 decisions, and Lefebvre proved a handyman, though his statistics were not impressive.

Williams and new pitching coach Norm Sherry developed one of the N.L.'s youngest pitching staffs. DeLeon was part of a promising rookie contingent that included righthanders Eric Show (10-6 record, three saves, 2.64 ERA) and Floyd Chiffer (4-3 record, four saves, 2.95 ERA) as well as lefthander Dave Dravecky (5-3 record, two saves, 2.57 ERA).

Veteran righthander John (The Count) Montefusco was 10-11 and helped provide leadership.

However, the Padres were not without disappointments. Lefthander Gary Lucas, the club's most experienced reliever, logged 16 saves, but lost 10 of his 11 decisions. Righthander Juan Eichelberger, the Padres' opening-day pitcher, finished 7-14 with a 4.20 ERA. Third baseman Luis Salazar, who had batted over .300 in his first two years with the Padres, had eight home runs, 62 RBIs and 32 stolen bases, but hit only .242 and led the team in errors (29).

Jones, bothered by an ankle injury, tailed off badly after reaching the All-Star break with a .312 average, 11 homers and 50 RBIs. Rookie center fielder Alan Wiggins (.256 average, 33 steals) missed three months of play after being arrested on charges of cocaine possession and voluntarily entering a drug rehabilitation center. He was suspended for one month by the commissioner's office before returning in late September.

Second baseman Juan Bonilla, sensational as a rookie in 1981, suffered a compound fracture of his left wrist in a collision May 19, but returned in mid-September to prove that the Padres can count on him in 1983. Bonilla joined Wiggins in drug rehabilitation in mid-season.

Tim Flannery (.264) filled in well for Bonilla. Rookie Tony Gwynn batted .289 in his first 54 big-league games, most of them in left field, and the incumbent at the position, Gene Richards, hit .286 with 30 stolen bases.

The Padres lacked punch at first base (alternating Broderick Perkins, Randy Bass and Jody Lansford), and a lack of depth was evident late in the season when they lost Lezcano, Jones and Templeton because of injuries.

But, everything considered, it was a good year. The Padres shared the division lead for one day (April 27) after setting a club record with 11 consecutive victories and they held second place from April 28 until August 3. It was a foundation for better things in the future.

Catcher Terry Kennedy swung a big bat for the Padres as he led the team in batting average, home runs and RBIs.

SCORES OF SAN DIEGO PADRES' 1982 GAMES

APRIL			Winner	Loser
6—Atlanta	L	0-1	Mahler	Eichelberger
7—Atlanta	L	4-6	Walk	Montefusco
9—At L.A.	W	7-4	Chiffer	Forster
10—At L.A.	L	0-6	Valenzuela	Eichelberger
13—At S. Fran.	L	2-3	Fowlkes	Montefusco
14—At S. Fran.	W	3-2	Lollar	Schatzeder
15—Los Ang.	W	2-0	Eichelberger	Valenzuela
16—Los Ang.	W	8-3	Curtis	Reuss
17—Los Ang.	W	4-3	Show	Goltz
18—Los Ang.	W	9-3	DeLeon	Stewart
19—San Fran.	W	13-6	Eichelberger	Schatzeder
20—San Fran.	W	8-4	Curtis	Gale
21—San Fran.	W	7-6	Montefusco	Holland
23—At Atlanta	W	6-3‡	Chiffer	Camp
24—At Atlanta	W	6-4	Show	Garber
27—New York	W	8-5	Show	Orosco
28—New York	L	4-5x	Falcone	Lucas
29—New York	W	6-0	Lollar	Puleo
30—Phila.	L	1-3*	Carlton	Eichelberger
Won 13, Lost 6				

MAY				
1—Phila.	W	9-6	DeLeon	Christenson
2—Phila.	L	0-3	Krukow	Curtis
3—Montreal	L	2-8	Gullickson	Montefusco
4—Montreal	W	7-3	Lollar	Burris
6—At Phila.	L	7-12	Christenson	Eichelberger
7—At Phila.	L	2-5	Lyle	Lucas
8—At Phila.	L	1-5	Ruthven	Montefusco
9—At Phila.	W	6-0	Lollar	Carlton
10—At N.Y.	L	2-3	Jones	Lucas
11—At N.Y.	L	0-6	Puleo	Eichelberger
13—At Mon.	L	5-6†	Fryman	DeLeon
14—At Mon.	L	7-8	Gorman	Show
15—At Mon.	W	6-2	Welsh	Lea
16—At Mon.	W	8-2	Eichelberger	Fryman
18—St. Louis	L	0-2	Forsch	Curtis
19—St. Louis	W	5-4*	Boone	Sutter
20—St. Louis	L	3-6	LaPoint	Welsh
21—Pittsburgh	W	7-5	Montefusco	Solomon
22—Pittsburgh	W	12-3	Eichelberger	Moskau
23—Pittsburgh	L	2-4	Candelaria	Curtis
24—Chicago	W	8-2	Lollar	Noles
25—Chicago	W	2-1	Welsh	Jenkins
26—Chicago	L	3-5	Hernandez	DeLeon
28—At St. L.	L	2-5	Forsch	Eichelberger
29—At St. L.	W	4-2	Curtis	Andujar
30—At St. L.	L	5-6*	Sutter	Lucas
31—At Chicago	W	9-7	Welsh	Bird
Won 12, Lost 15				

JUNE				
1—At Chicago	W	9-1	Montefusco	Martz
2—At Chicago	W	3-1	Eichelberger	Noles
4—At Pitts.	W	5-4	Curtis	Rhoden
6—At Pitts.	L	1-2	Tekulve	Lollar
7—Cincinnati	W	6-5	Welsh	Harris
8—Cincinnati	W	4-1	Montefusco	Berenyi
9—Cincinnati	L	3-4	Seaver	Eichelberger
10—Houston	W	5-0	Curtis	Knepper
11—Houston	W	6-2	Lollar	Sutton
12—Houston	W	4-0	Welsh	Ruhle
13—Houston	W	5-4	Montefusco	Ryan
14—Los Ang.	L	3-4†	Howe	Show
15—Los Ang.	L	0-3	Reuss	Curtis
16—Los Ang.	L	0-6	Welch	Lollar
18—At Hous.	L	2-7	Ryan	Welsh
19—At Hous.	W	7-1	Montefusco	Niekro
20—At Hous.	L	4-8	LaCoss	Eichelberger
21—At Hous.	W	7-4	Show	LaCoss
22—At Cinn.	L	5-7	Price	Lucas
23—At Cinn.	L	4-5	Hume	Show
24—At Cinn.	W	7-6§	Show	Shirley
25—At S. Fran.	W	3-2	Eichelberger	Laskey
26—At S. Fran.	W	7-6x	Show	Lavelle
27—At S. Fran.	W	4-2	Lollar	Gale
28—At L.A.	L	4-6	Valenzuela	Welsh
29—At L.A.	W	7-5*	DeLeon	Shirley
30—At L.A.	L	1-5	Welsh	Eichelberger
30—At L.A.	W	6-4	Show	Forster
Won 17, Lost 11				

JULY				
2—San Fran.	L	4-8	Holland	Dravecky
2—San Fran.	W	3-2	Lollar	Lavelle
3—San Fran.	L	3-4x	Minton	Chiffer
4—San Fran.	W	4-3	Dravecky	Hammaker
5—At Mon.	W	8-6	Chiffer	Sanderson
6—At Mon.	W	5-1	Curtis	Burris
7—At Phila.	W	5-3	Lollar	Bystrom

JULY			Winner	Loser
8—At Phila.	W	5-3	Montefusco	Krukow
9—At N.Y.	W	5-3	Chiffer	Puleo
9—At N.Y.	L	3-6	Zachry	Lucas
10—At N.Y.	L	7-9	Falcone	Curtis
11—At N.Y.	W	6-2	Lollar	Scott
15—Montreal	L	2-6	Lea	Montefusco
16—Montreal	L	3-4	Rogers	Lollar
17—Montreal	L	1-4	Gullickson	Hawkins
18—Montreal	L	2-9	Palmer	Welsh
19—Phila.	L	6-7	Monge	Curtis
20—Phila.	W	2-0	Montefusco	Carlton
21—Phila.	L	1-7	Ruthven	Lollar
23—New York	W	11-4	Hawkins	Gaff
24—New York	L	3-4	Allen	DeLeon
25—New York	W	3-2*	DeLeon	Allen
27—At Atlanta	L	2-9	Walk	Lollar
27—At Atlanta	L	6-8*	Bedrosian	Lucas
28—At Atlanta	L	6-8	Niekro	Hawkins
29—At Atlanta	L	2-6	Camp	Welsh
30—At Cinn.	L	2-4	Berenyi	Montefusco
31—At Cinn.	W	5-4	Lollar	Seaver
31—At Cinn.	W	6-2	Show	Shirley
Won 13, Lost 16				

AUGUST				
1—At Cinn.	W	8-6	Curtis	Leibrandt
2—At Hous.	L	4-6	Niekro	Lucas
3—At Hous.	L	6-7†	Moffitt	DeLeon
4—At Hous.	W	5-2	Montefusco	Sutton
5—Cincinnati	L	2-4	Seaver	Lollar
6—Cincinnati	W	2-0	Show	Shirley
7—Cincinnati	W	4-1	Hawkins	Soto
8—Cincinnati	W	3-1	Dravecky	Pastore
9—Houston	L	3-4	Sutton	Montefusco
10—Houston	L	1-4	Ruhle	Lollar
11—Houston	L	0-3	Ryan	Show
12—Atlanta	W	8-2	Welsh	Walk
13—Atlanta	W	7-4	Dravecky	Camp
14—Atlanta	L	5-6	Moore	Eichelberger
15—Atlanta	W	6-5*	DeLeon	Bedrosian
17—At St. L.	L	2-3	Sutter	Lucas
18—At St. L.	L	1-2	Forsch	Hawkins
19—At St. L.	W	4-3	Dravecky	Stuper
20—At Chicago	L	2-3	Martz	Montefusco
21—At Chicago	W	2-0	Lollar	Ripley
22—At Chicago	L	7-8	Tidrow	Lucas
23—At Pitts.	L	6-8	Candelaria	Hawkins
23—At Pitts.	W	5-3	Welsh	Baumgarten
24—At Pitts.	L	5-6†	Tekulve	Eichelberger
25—At Pitts.	L	6-7	Tekulve	Chiffer
27—St. Louis	L	1-2	Andujar	Lollar
29—St. Louis	W	9-4	Curtis	Forsch
29—St. Louis	L	3-5	Bair	Hawkins
30—Pittsburgh	W	2-1§	DeLeon	Tekulve
31—Pittsburgh	L	1-7	Sarmiento	Montefusco
Won 13, Lost 17				

SEPTEMBER				
1—Pittsburgh	W	4-1	Eichelberger	Rhoden
3—Chicago	W	3-0	Show	Noles
4—Chicago	W	4-1	Lollar	Jenkins
5—Chicago	L	1-5	Martz	Dravecky
6—At Hous.	W	4-2	Welsh	Ruhle
7—At Hous.	L	3-4	DiPino	Eichelberger
8—At Cinn.	W	9-4	DeLeon	Lesley
9—At Cinn.	W	4-1	Lollar	Berenyi
10—San Fran.	L	1-5	Breining	Dravecky
11—San Fran.	L	3-8	Laskey	Welsh
13—At L.A.	L	3-4y	Reuss	Welsh
14—At L.A.	L	0-1	Valenzuela	Show
15—At L.A.	L	0-5	Hooton	Montefusco
16—At S. Fran.	L	3-9	Breining	Lollar
17—At S. Fran.	W	4-2	Dravecky	Laskey
18—At S. Fran.	L	1-4	Gale	Eichelberger
19—At S. Fran.	L	3-4†	Holland	DeLeon
21—Los Ang.	W	3-0	Montefusco	Hooton
22—Los Ang.	W	2-1*	DeLeon	Niedenfuer
24—At Atlanta	L	6-11	Dayley	Griffin
25—At Atlanta	L	6-12	Moore	Eichelberger
26—At Atlanta	W	3-2	Lucas	Camp
27—Houston	L	3-7	Ruhle	Welsh
28—Houston	W	3-0	Lollar	Knepper
29—Cincinnati	W	3-2*	DeLeon	Lesley
30—Cincinnati	L	4-6	Leibrandt	Chiffer
Won 12, Lost 14				

OCTOBER				
1—Atlanta	L	0-4	Niekro	Show
2—Atlanta	L	2-4	Perez	Montefusco
3—Atlanta	W	5-1	Lollar	Camp
Won 1, Lost 2				

*10 innings. †11 innings. ‡12 innings. §13 innings. x15 innings. y16 innings.

Astros' Big Hopes Shot Down

By HARRY SHATTUCK

Ah, the optimism of spring.

• "This is the year we go to the World Series," Chief Executive Officer John McMullen was saying in March, 1982.

• "We're much improved," General Manager Al Rosen was saying.

• "This is the best team I've ever managed in Houston," Bill Virdon was saying.

After winning the National League West Division championship in 1980 and the second-half West title in 1981, the Astros figured on celebrating long into October this time. Nothing else would do.

"We know we have the ability," catcher Alan Ashby said at spring training in Cocoa, Fla. "And we know we have a good attitude. We'll be very disappointed in ourselves if we don't win it this year."

The euphoria was short-lived.

Virdon and his athletes got the first sign of impending disaster when the Cardinals routed Nolan Ryan and beat the Astros, 14-3, on opening night in Houston.

By the end of April, ace reliever Joe Sambito, a prime reason for the Astros' steady development from a doormat to a contender, was sidelined by an elbow injury, not to pitch again all season.

By the end of May, Art Howe, Houston's leading hitter the previous season, was disabled because of a severe hamstring injury, never to regain his peak form.

By June 30, the Astros were 13 games below .500. By July, their fate as an also-ran was all but sealed. By mid-August, Virdon was gone, fired and replaced by coach Bob Lillis. By the end of August, stellar pitcher Don Sutton was gone, traded to Milwaukee for three minor leaguers. And by September, the talk in Houston was about next year.

The Astros finished fifth with a 77-85 record, 12 games behind Atlanta, and the season was such a complete washout that it's difficult to determine what went wrong most. The Astros didn't hit, field, run or pitch up to expectations.

Perhaps the best indicator of Houston's offensive frustrations was that Phil Garner led in home runs (13) and runs batted in (83). Nothing against Garner—he was a sparkplug all year—but at Pittsburgh he was known as "the best eighth-place hitter in baseball," while at Houston he eventually hit cleanup because nobody else drove in runs.

The Astros batted only .247 as a team, scored only 3.51 runs per game and hit

Ray Knight was leading the league in hitting before ailments sidelined him in September.

only 74 homers. They had no .300 hitters, though Ray Knight, their only All-Star, was well above that figure before a shoulder ailment and inner-ear infection took their toll in September. Knight finished at .294.

Pitching? The starting staff took its lumps frequently in April and early May. And though Joe Niekro (17 victories overall), Ryan (16) and Sutton (13 before being traded August 30) had good seasons, Bob Knepper was 5-15 and Vern Ruhle was 9-13. More costly was the collapse of what had been one of baseball's strongest, deepest bullpens. After nine appearances, Sambito had major surgery and was unavailable. Dave Smith was bothered continually by lower back soreness and didn't approach his previous level. And Frank LaCorte, until the final two months, simply had an off-season.

Speed? The team that approached 200 stolen bases in its previous two full seasons dropped to 140 during a year when opponents stressed aggressiveness. Often, four Houston singles were needed to produce a

Second basemen Phil Garner, with 13 home runs and 83 runs batted in, was the power man in a weak-hitting Astro lineup.

run.

And Houston's defense was not as consistent as anticipated. Center fielder Tony Scott struggled early in the season. Third baseman Knight's shoulder problem forced his move to first base. Left fielder Jose Cruz didn't have his best year defensively. And whether pitchers or catchers were to blame, and coaches suggested both, the Astros ranked 26th in the majors at retiring would-be base stealers, allowing opponents a 76 percent success rate.

There were highlights:

Dickie Thon replaced two-time All-Star shortstop Craig Reynolds in mid-June and, besides providing excellent defense, hit .276, becoming an effective leadoff man. Thon's 21-game hitting streak was the club's best and matched Pete Rose for the league's longest.

Garner and Knight, who like Thon were trade acquisitions made by Rosen in 1981, offered everything anybody had a right to expect.

Niekro, 37, and Ryan, 35, showed no reason why they can't remain among the game's elite pitchers for several more years.

Niekro finished in a second-place tie behind Montreal's Steve Rogers for the league's earned-run title with a 2.47 mark. He pitched five shutouts. Ryan increased his career strikeout total to 3,494, moving within 14 of Walter Johnson's major-league record.

Mike LaCoss, a tall, veteran righthander released by the Reds in spring training and signed as a 10th pitcher by the Astros, excelled so much in the bullpen that he was starting regularly in September. And LaCoss fared so well (6-6 record, 2.90 ERA) that he likely will get a shot in the rotation next year.

In September, infielder Bill Doran joined the Astros from Class AAA Tucson and impressed with his range afield and with his bat. And lefthanded starting pitcher Frank DiPino, obtained in the Sutton trade, showed that the deal may not be one-sided. DiPino struck out 10 Padres in five innings in his first Houston appearance.

The Astros did improve as the season progressed. After the All-Star break, their record was 40-37. After Lillis replaced Virdon August 10, they were 28-23.

Injuries certainly played a key role in the early problems, with six players spending time on the disabled list during the season.

Whatever the reasons, the Astros never approached those glowing spring forecasts.

Joe Niekro had 17 victories, five of them shutouts, and a 2.47 ERA in 1982.

SCORES OF HOUSTON ASTROS' 1982 GAMES

APRIL

Date		Score	Winner	Loser
6—St. Louis	L	3-14	Forsch	Ryan
7—St. Louis	W	3-2	Niekro	Martin
8—St. Louis	W	1-0	Knepper	Andujar
9—At Atlanta	L	2-6	Boggs	Sutton
10—At Atlanta	L	6-8	McWilliams	Ruhle
11—At Atlanta	L	0-5	Mahler	Ryan
12—Los Ang.	W	2-1†	LaCoss	Stewart
13—Los Ang.	L	5-9	Welch	Knepper
14—Los Ang.	W	2-1	Sutton	Hooton
16—Atlanta	L	3-5	McWilliams	Ryan
17—Atlanta	L	1-2	Hanna	Niekro
18—Atlanta	L	5-6	Hrabosky	Smith
19—At L.A.	W	6-4	Sutton	Forster
20—At L.A.	L	2-10	Valenzuela	Ruhle
21—At L.A.	L	0-6	Reuss	Ryan
23—Cincinnati	W	7-3	Niekro	Seaver
24—Cincinnati	L	2-3	Pastore	Knepper
25—Cincinnati	L	3-4*	Shirley	Moffitt
26—At St. L.	W	6-2	Ryan	Martin
27—At St. L.	W	3-0	Ruhle	Mura
28—At St. L.	L	4-5	Forsch	Smith
29—At Pitts.	L	6-9	Romo	LaCoss
30—At Pitts.	W	4-3	Sutton	Rhoden

Won 9, Lost 14

MAY

Date		Score	Winner	Loser
1—At Pitts.	W	6-3	Ryan	Moskau
2—At Pitts.	W	6-2	Niekro	Griffin
4—At Cinn.	L	2-5	Seaver	Knepper
5—At Cinn.	W	8-7	Sutton	Pastore
7—At Chicago	L	6-12	Martz	Ryan
8—At Chicago	L	2-3	Noles	Niekro
9—At Chicago	L	3-6	Hernandez	Moffitt
10—Pittsburgh	W	7-3	Sutton	Rhoden
11—Pittsburgh	W	4-2	Ryan	Griffin
13—Chicago	L	0-5	Ripley	Niekro
14—Chicago	L	3-6	Noles	Knepper
15—Chicago	W	4-1	Sutton	Jenkins
16—Chicago	L	1-2	Bird	Ryan
17—At Phila.	W	8-1	Ruhle	R. Reed
18—At Phila.	W	2-1‡	Smith	Farmer
19—At Phila.	W	5-3	Knepper	Carlton
21—New York	W	5-1	Sutton	Scott
22—New York	L	5-6‡	Allen	Moffitt
23—New York	L	0-2	Jones	Niekro
24—Montreal	L	0-2	Gullickson	Knepper
25—Montreal	L	1-6	Palmer	Ruhle
26—Montreal	L	0-4*	Lea	LaCorte
28—At N.Y.	W	8-3	Ryan	Jones
29—At N.Y.	W	5-2	Niekro	Zachry
30—At N.Y.	L	5-9	Scott	Knepper
31—At Mon.	L	0-10	Lea	Sutton

Won 12, Lost 14

JUNE

Date		Score	Winner	Loser
2—At Mon.	W	6-4	Ryan	Sanderson
4—Phila.	W	8-3	Ruhle	Farmer
5—Phila.	L	3-5	Lyle	Smith
6—Phila.	W	7-6	Ruhle	Brusstar
8—At S. Fran.	L	3-7	Hammaker	Ryan
9—At S. Fran.	W	6-1	Niekro	Laskey
10—At S. Diego	L	0-5	Curtis	Knepper
11—At S. Diego	L	2-6	Lollar	Sutton
12—At S. Diego	L	0-4	Welsh	Ruhle
13—At S. Diego	L	4-5	Montefusco	Ryan
14—Atlanta	W	9-0	Niekro	Mahler
15—Atlanta	L	0-7	Walk	Knepper
16—Atlanta	L	4-5*	Garber	Cappuzzello
18—San Diego	W	7-2	Ryan	Welsh
19—San Diego	L	1-7	Montefusco	Niekro
20—San Diego	W	8-4	LaCoss	Eichelberger
21—San Diego	L	4-7	Show	LaCoss
22—San Fran.	W	2-0	Ruhle	Gale
23—San Fran.	L	8-9	Breining	LaCorte
24—San Fran.	L	3-4*	Hammaker	Niekro
25—Los Ang.	W	7-5	LaCoss	Forster
26—Los Ang.	L	1-4	Stewart	Sutton
27—Los Ang.	L	3-7	Forster	Ruhle
28—At Atlanta	W	6-2	Ryan	Mahler
29—At Atlanta	L	5-6†	Bedrosian	LaCoss
30—At Atlanta	L	4-5	Diaz	Knepper

Won 10, Lost 16

JULY

Date		Score	Winner	Loser
2—At L.A.	W	4-1	Sutton	Romo
3—At L.A.	L	4-5	Valenzuela	Roberge
4—At L.A.	W	3-0	Ryan	Reuss
5—At Pitts.	W	6-4	Niekro	Baumgarten
6—At Pitts.	L	0-1	McWilliams	Knepper
7—Chicago	W	5-1	Sutton	Ripley

JULY

Date		Score	Winner	Loser
8—Chicago	L	3-5	Tidrow	Ruhle
9—St. Louis	L	2-3	LaPoint	Ryan
10—St. Louis	W	4-2	Niekro	Forsch
11—St. Louis	W	4-2	Knepper	Andujar
15—Pittsburgh	L	1-5	Candelaria	Sutton
16—Pittsburgh	W	4-2	Ryan	McWilliams
17—Pittsburgh	W	4-3*	Niekro	Tekulve
18—Pittsburgh	W	1-0	Knepper	Robinson
19—At Chicago	L	5-6*	Smith	LaCorte
20—At Chicago	L	3-5	Hernandez	Sutton
21—At Chicago	W	2-1	Ryan	Ripley
23—At St. L.	L	2-6	Andujar	Niekro
24—At St. L.	L	1-5	Forsch	Knepper
25—At St. L.	L	3-4	Sutter	Sutton
27—Cincinnati	W	3-2	Ryan	Leibrandt
28—Cincinnati	W	4-2	Niekro	Soto
29—Cincinnati	W	4-3	Moffitt	Harris
30—San Fran.	W	3-1	Sutton	Gale
31—San Fran.	L	4-5	Laskey	Ruhle
31—San Fran.	W	5-0	LaCoss	Hammaker

Won 15, Lost 11

AUGUST

Date		Score	Winner	Loser
1—San Fran.	L	2-4*	Minton	LaCorte
2—San Diego	W	6-4	Niekro	Lucas
3—San Diego	W	7-6†	Moffitt	DeLeon
4—San Diego	L	2-5	Montefusco	Sutton
5—At S. Fran.	L	2-5	Laskey	Ruhle
6—At S. Fran.	L	6-7	Lavelle	Moffitt
7—At S. Fran.	L	2-9	Martin	Niekro
8—At S. Fran.	L	2-3	Breining	Knepper
8—At S. Fran.	L	3-8	Lavelle	LaCoss
9—At S. Diego	W	4-3	Sutton	Montefusco
10—At S. Diego	W	4-1	Ruhle	Lollar
11—At S. Diego	W	3-0	Ryan	Show
13—At Cinn.	L	0-3	Pastore	Niekro
14—At Cinn.	W	2-0	Knepper	Berenyi
15—At Cinn.	W	7-3	Sutton	Seaver
16—At Cinn.	L	2-3†	Kern	Smith
17—Phila.	W	2-0	Ruhle	Christenson
18—Phila.	L	3-5§	McGraw	LaCoss
19—Phila.	W	7-6†	Smith	Monge
20—Montreal	W	4-3*	Roberge	Reardon
21—Montreal	W	5-3	Ryan	Burris
22—Montreal	L	0-5	Lea	Ruhle
23—New York	W	2-0	Niekro	Zachry
24—New York	W	5-4	Smith	Scott
25—New York	W	5-4	Sutton	Lynch
26—At Mon.	L	2-3	Reardon	Roberge
26—At Mon.	L	3-5	Reardon	Ruhle
28—At Mon.	W	2-0	Niekro	Lea
29—At Mon.	L	3-5	Sanderson	Knepper
30—At N.Y.	W	4-2	LaCorte	Swan
31—At N.Y.	W	4-0	Ryan	Lynch

Won 17, Lost 14

SEPTEMBER

Date		Score	Winner	Loser
1—At N.Y.	L	1-5	Falcone	Ruhle
3—At Phila.	L	1-2	Carlton	Niekro
4—At Phila.	L	2-4	Monge	Knepper
5—At Phila.	L	3-4	Altamirano	Ryan
6—San Diego	L	2-4	Welsh	Ruhle
7—San Diego	W	4-3	DiPino	Eichelberger
8—San Fran.	W	8-1	Niekro	Hammaker
9—San Fran.	L	1-5	Martin	LaCoss
10—Los Ang.	L	2-3	Howe	Ryan
11—Los Ang.	L	3-5	Reuss	Ruhle
12—Los Ang.	L	3-7	Stewart	DiPino
13—At Atlanta	W	5-3	Niekro	Niekro
14—At Atlanta	W	4-0	LaCoss	Mahler
15—At Atlanta	W	5-4	Ryan	Boggs
17—At L.A.	L	2-9	Reuss	DiPino
18—At L.A.	W	2-0	Niekro	Welch
19—At L.A.	L	4-5*	Valenzuela	LaCorte
20—Atlanta	W	4-3	Smith	Garber
21—Atlanta	W	5-3	Ruhle	Camp
22—Atlanta	W	3-2	Smith	Garber
24—At Cinn.	L	0-2	Berenyi	Niekro
25—At Cinn.	W	3-1	LaCoss	Scherrer
26—At Cinn.	W	4-0	Ryan	Shirley
27—At S. Diego	W	7-3	Ruhle	Welsh
28—At S. Diego	L	0-3	Lollar	Knepper
29—At S. Fran.	L	1-6	Hammaker	Niekro
30—At S. Fran.	L	6-7	Lavelle	Boone

Won 12, Lost 15

OCTOBER

Date		Score	Winner	Loser
1—Cincinnati	L	2-4	Shirley	Ryan
2—Cincinnati	W	4-2	DiPino	Soto
3—Cincinnati	W	3-0	Niekro	Pastore

Won 2, Lost 1

*10 innings.   †11 innings.   ‡12 innings.   §15 innings.

Cincinnati Is Left Red-Faced

By EARL LAWSON

The Cincinnati Reds, who compiled the best overall won-lost record during the strike-abbreviated 1981 season, had the dubious distinction of finishing 1982 with the most losses in the club's history—101—while winding up last in the National League West.

Only the Minnesota Twins of the American League West compiled a poorer record in the major leagues—60-102.

The Reds' dismal 61-victory season was accompanied by a drastic dip in attendance. The 79 home dates drew 1,326,528 cash customers, the lowest total since the Reds moved into Riverfront Stadium in mid-season of 1970 (excluding the shortened 1981 season when home attendance totaled 1,093,730).

Manager John McNamara was replaced by third-base coach Russ Nixon July 21 with the Reds mired in last place with a 34-58 record. The club went 27-43 under Nixon.

For the Reds, the season was downhill from the start. Their longest winning streak was four games; the longest losing streak was nine. The Reds were 8-12 in April, 11-16 in May, 12-16 in June, 7-21 in July, 13-16 in August and 10-20 for September-October.

Tom Seaver, a three-time Cy Young Award winner who compiled a 14-2 record in 1981, was 5-13 in 1982. Stricken with a lingering respiratory infection during spring training, Seaver didn't make his first start until mid-April. His season ended August 15 when an aching right shoulder forced him from a game with Houston after he had faced only three batters.

Johnny Bench, also plagued by nagging injuries, endured an equally disappointing season. After Reds' President Dick Wagner created an opening at third base for him by swapping Ray Knight to the Astros for Cesar Cedeno, Bench responded with a .258 batting mark, hit only 13 homers (second, though, on the club to Dan Driessen's 17) and drove home only 38 runs. His defensive play at third also was shaky.

Adding to the Reds' woes was a knee injury suffered by relief ace Tom Hume in late May. Hume was lost to the club following surgery shortly after the All-Star break.

However, it was Wagner's wholesale shakeup of the Reds' roster after the 1981 season that contributed most to the Reds demise.

"We knew at the time that we were taking calculated risks," said Wagner. "They just didn't pan out as we'd hoped."

Wagner didn't have to elaborate.

His unwillingness to give multi-year, multi-million dollar guaranteed contracts led to the departure of the three starting outfielders on the 1981 team. George Foster, one of the game's most prolific run producers the last six years, went to the New York Mets for pitchers Jim Kern and Greg Harris and catcher Alex Trevino.

Ken Griffey, like Foster a member of the Reds' 1975 and 1976 world champions, went to the New York Yankees for minor league pitching prospects Brian Ryder and Fred Toliver. Griffey was joined by right fielder Dave Collins, who opted for free agency and signed with the Yankees.

So, the Reds opened the 1982 season with a new outfield—rookie Paul Householder in right, Cedeno in center and Clint Hurdle, acquired from Kansas City in exchange for rookie righthander Scott Brown, in left field.

The season was hardly a month old before Hurdle was dispatched to the Reds' Indianapolis farm club of the American Association. Householder, a 23-year-old switch hitter and touted by Wagner as "one of the finest athletes I've seen to come into the majors in the past 10 years," finished with a .211 batting mark in 417 at-bats.

"The first legitimate center fielder we've had since Cesar Geronimo," was Wagner's comment after the Reds' acquisition of Cedeno.

Cedeno had predicted a banner season— a .300-plus average, 20 or more homers and 50 stolen bases. He batted .289, hit eight homers, drove in 57 runs and stole 16 bases.

The Reds had hoped Trevino would solve the catching problem that developed when Bench decided to call it quits behind the plate. He didn't.

Time and again good pitching was squandered because of a lack of an offense by a Reds' team that scored only 545 runs, the fewest in the league. Righthander Mario Soto compiled a 14-13 record and had a sparkling 2.79 earned-run average. His 274 strikeouts, topped only by Philadelphia's Steve Carlton, set a club record. Bruce Berenyi was 9-18 even though he wound up with a respectable 3.36 ERA.

There were times during the second half when the Reds fielded a lineup with four

Mario Soto won 14 games and was one of the few bright spots during the worst season in Cincinnati baseball history.

rookies—outfielders Householder, Duane Walker and Eddie Milner and second baseman Tom Lawless. The best of the lot was Milner, who batted .268 and stole 18 bases, tops on the club. And he sat out the last six weeks of the season after suffering a muscle pull in his thigh.

Mounting losses breeded discontent and grumbling.

"If I'd known the Reds were going to let both Foster and Griffey go, I'd never have signed my new contract," said All-Star shortstop Dave Concepcion, who had passed up free agency and signed a five-year, $4.7 million guaranteed contract at the end of the 1981 season.

Kern was traded to the White Sox in August after growing a beard, defying the Reds' long-standing, unwritten rule that called for players to be clean shaved.

"If there were any pluses," remarked Nixon as the season wound to an end, "it was that we had an opportunity to evaluate our youngsters on the club."

Unfortunately, though, only righthanded relief pitchers Brad Lesley and Ben Hayes, called up from Indianapolis after the All-Star break, drew high marks. Lesley's 0-2 record was accompanied by a 2.58 ERA compiled in 29 relief appearances. Hayes was 2-0 with a 1.97 ERA in 26 appearances.

SCORES OF CINCINNATI REDS' 1982 GAMES

APRIL

Date		Score	Winner	Loser
5—Chicago	L	2-3†	Bird	Soto
7—Chicago	W	6-2	Berenyi	Noles
9—San Fran.	W	7-0	Pastore	Schatzeder
10—San Fran.	L	5-7‡	Minton	Hume
11—San Fran.	L	1-6	Holland	Leibrandt
12—Atlanta	L	1-6	Walk	Berenyi
13—Atlanta	L	5-8	Garber	Kern
14—Atlanta	L	2-5‡	Camp	Kern
16—At S. Fran.	L	1-6	Gale	Soto
17—At S. Fran.	W	8-2	Berenyi	Holland
18—At S. Fran.	L	2-4	Fowlkes	Seaver
20—At Atlanta	L	2-4	Bedrosian	Pastore
21—At Atlanta	L	3-4	Camp	Shirley
22—At Atlanta	W	2-1	Berenyi	Walk
23—At Hous.	L	3-7	Niekro	Seaver
24—At Hous.	W	3-2	Pastore	Knepper
25—At Hous.	W	4-3‡	Shirley	Moffitt
27—At Chicago	W	6-3	Berenyi	Larson
28—At Chicago	L	0-6	Noles	Seaver
30—St. Louis	W	8-2	Pastore	Andujar

Won 8, Lost 12

MAY

Date		Score	Winner	Loser
1—St. Louis	W	10-1	Soto	Rincon
2—St. Louis	W	5-1	Leibrandt	Mura
3—St. Louis	L	4-6	Martin	Price
4—Houston	W	5-2	Seaver	Knepper
5—Houston	L	7-8	Sutton	Pastore
7—Pittsburgh	W	5-0	Soto	Moskau
8—Pittsburgh	L	2-4a	Sarmiento	Shirley
9—Pittsburgh	L	3-6	Robinson	Seaver
10—At St. L.	W	3-1	Pastore	Martin
11—At St. L.	L	1-5	Mura	Soto
13—At Pitts.	W	2-1	Price	Scurry
14—At Pitts.	L	7-8	Romo	Kern
15—At Pitts.	L	9-12	Rhoden	Pastore
16—At Pitts.	W	3-1	Soto	Solomon
17—At N.Y.	W	7-2	Leibrandt	Falcone
18—At N.Y.	L	4-7	Jones	Berenyi
19—At N.Y.	L	2-4	Zachry	Seaver
21—Montreal	L	0-2	Lea	Soto
22—Montreal	L	2-4	Sanderson	Pastore
23—Montreal	L	2-4	Rogers	Berenyi
24—Phila.	L	1-9	Carlton	Seaver
25—Phila.	W	4-3	Harris	Farmer
26—Phila.	W	2-0	Soto	Krukow
28—At Mon.	L	2-4	Sanderson	Berenyi
29—At Mon.	L	1-4	Rogers	Price
30—At Mon.	W	7-3	Shirley	Gullickson
31—At Phila.	L	4-5a	Monge	Shirley

Won 11, Lost 16

JUNE

Date		Score	Winner	Loser
1—At Phila.	W	4-1*	Harris	Krukow
2—At Phila.	L	2-4	Ruthven	Berenyi
4—New York	W	8-3	Seaver	Scott
5—New York	W	6-2	Soto	Puleo
6—New York	L	3-6	Swan	Pastore
7—At S. Diego	L	5-6	Welsh	Harris
8—At S. Diego	L	1-4	Montefusco	Berenyi
9—At S. Diego	W	4-3	Seaver	Eichelberger
10—At L.A.	W	3-2	Kern	Valenzuela
11—At L.A.	L	1-11	Reuss	Pastore
12—At L.A.	L	3-4	Welch	Harris
13—At L.A.	W	4-2	Berenyi	Hooton
15—San Fran.	L	3-4	Laskey	Seaver
16—San Fran.	W	7-3	Soto	Barr
17—San Fran.	W	4-2	Leibrandt	Gale
18—Los Ang.	L	2-3§	Forster	Hume
19—Los Ang.	L	1-2	Valenzuela	Berenyi
20—Los Ang.	L	2-4	Reuss	Seaver
21—Los Ang.	W	10-2	Soto	Welch
22—San Diego	W	7-5	Price	Lucas
23—San Diego	W	5-4	Hume	Show
24—San Diego	L	6-7y	Show	Shirley
25—Atlanta	L	2-5	Niekro	Berenyi
26—Atlanta	W	2-1	Seaver	Dayley
27—Atlanta	L	0-2z	Garber	Hume
28—At S. Fran.	L	1-7	Martin	Leibrandt
29—At S. Fran.	L	0-3	Hammaker	Shirley
30—At S. Fran.	L	6-7x	Minton	Leibrandt

Won 12, Lost 16

JULY

Date		Score	Winner	Loser
2—At Atlanta	L	4-6	Dayley	Seaver
3—At Atlanta	L	2-4	Mahler	Soto
4—At Atlanta	L	1-4	Walk	Shirley
5—St. Louis	L	5-6‡	Kaat	Hume
6—St. Louis	L	1-3	Mura	Leibrandt
7—At Pitts.	W	6-3	Hume	Tekulve
8—At Pitts.	L	8-9	Tekulve	Price
9—At Chicago	L	0-12	Jenkins	Shirley
10—At Chicago	L	0-1	Noles	Berenyi
10—At Chicago	W	6-5yb	Soto	Proly
11—At Chicago	L	2-9	Bird	Seaver
15—At St. L.	W	7-3	Berenyi	Stuper
16—At St. L.	L	4-6	Lahti	Hume
17—At St. L.	L	2-4	Forsch	Soto
18—At St. L.	L	5-6	Kaat	Leibrandt
19—Pittsburgh	L	4-5	Sarmiento	Pastore
20—Pittsburgh	L	1-3	Candelaria	Berenyi
21—Pittsburgh	L	2-3	McWilliams	Hume
23—Chicago	L	5-7	Hernandez	Kern
24—Chicago	W	5-2	Pastore	Bird
25—Chicago	W	2-1	Berenyi	Jenkins
26—Chicago	W	4-2	Shirley	Ripley
27—At Hous.	L	2-3	Ryan	Leibrandt
28—At Hous.	L	2-4	Niekro	Soto
29—At Hous.	L	3-4	Moffitt	Harris
30—San Diego	W	4-2	Berenyi	Montefusco
31—San Diego	L	4-5	Lollar	Seaver
31—San Diego	L	2-6	Show	Shirley

Won 7, Lost 21

AUGUST

Date		Score	Winner	Loser
1—San Diego	L	6-8	Curtis	Leibrandt
2—Los Ang.	W	5-1	Soto	Reuss
3—Los Ang.	L	0-4	Welch	Pastore
4—Los Ang.	L	2-8	Wright	Berenyi
5—At S. Diego	W	4-2	Seaver	Lollar
6—At S. Diego	L	0-2	Show	Shirley
7—At S. Diego	L	1-4	Hawkins	Soto
8—At S. Diego	L	1-3	Dravecky	Pastore
9—At L.A.	L	2-3y	Stewart	Kern
10—At L.A.	L	3-11	Valenzuela	Seaver
11—At L.A.	W	2-1	Shirley	Hooton
13—Houston	W	3-0	Pastore	Niekro
14—Houston	L	0-2	Knepper	Berenyi
15—Houston	L	3-7	Sutton	Seaver
16—Houston	W	3-2§	Kern	Smith
17—New York	W	9-2	Soto	Ownbey
18—New York	W	7-6z	Hayes	Scott
19—New York	W	3-1‡	Kern	Hausman
20—Phila.	L	2-9	Ruthven	Harris
21—Phila.	W	10-3	Shirley	Bystrom
22—Phila.	L	2-8	Christenson	Soto
23—Montreal	W	6-2	Pastore	Gullickson
24—Montreal	L	1-5	Sanderson	Berenyi
25—Montreal	W	1-0	Shirley	Rogers
27—At Phila.	W	8-1	Soto	Christenson
28—At Phila.	L	1-7	Krukow	Pastore
29—At Phila.	L	1-3	Carlton	Berenyi
30—At Mon.	L	1-3	Rogers	Shirley
31—At Mon.	W	2-1z	Leibrandt	Burris

Won 13, Lost 16

SEPTEMBER

Date		Score	Winner	Loser
1—At Mon.	L	1-2	Lerch	Soto
3—At N.Y.	W	1-0	Pastore	Ownbey
4—At N.Y.	L	2-3	Swan	Berenyi
5—At N.Y.	L	2-10	Lynch	Shirley
6—Los Ang.	L	2-7	Reuss	Soto
7—Los Ang.	L	4-8	Stewart	Harris
8—San Diego	L	4-9	DeLeon	Lesley
9—San Diego	L	1-4	Lollar	Berenyi
10—At Atlanta	L	2-8	Perez	Shirley
11—At Atlanta	W	4-3	Soto	Boggs
12—At Atlanta	L	3-4	Bedrosian	Harris
13—At S. Fran.	W	5-4§	Price	Lavelle
14—At S. Fran.	L	1-2	Hammaker	Berenyi
15—At S. Fran.	L	4-5	Gale	Price
17—Atlanta	W	5-2	Soto	Camp
18—Atlanta	L	4-5	Niekro	Pastore
19—Atlanta	L	1-6	Perez	Berenyi
21—San Fran.	W	6-5	Shirley	Breining
22—San Fran.	L	0-2	Martin	Soto
23—San Fran.	L	7-11	Hammaker	Pastore
24—Houston	W	2-0	Berenyi	Niekro
25—Houston	L	1-3	LaCoss	Scherrer
26—Houston	L	0-4	Ryan	Shirley
27—At L.A.	W	6-1	Soto	Reuss
28—At L.A.	W	4-3‡	Hayes	Stewart
29—At S. Diego	L	2-3‡	DeLeon	Lesley
30—At S. Diego	W	6-4	Leibrandt	Chiffer

Won 9, Lost 18

OCTOBER

Date		Score	Winner	Loser
1—At Hous.	W	4-2	Shirley	Ryan
2—At Hous.	L	2-4	DiPino	Soto
3—At Hous.	L	0-3	Niekro	Pastore

Won 1, Lost 2

*7 innings. †8 innings. ‡10 innings. §11 innings. x12 innings. y13 innings. z14 innings. a15 innings. bSuspended game, completed July 11.

National League Averages for 1982

CHAMPIONSHIP WINNERS IN PREVIOUS YEARS

1876—Chicago .788	1912—New York .682	1948—Boston .595
1877—Boston .646	1913—New York .664	1949—Brooklyn .630
1878—Boston .683	1914—Boston .614	1950—Philadelphia .591
1879—Providence .705	1915—Philadelphia .592	1951—New York† .624
1880—Chicago .798	1916—Brooklyn .610	1952—Brooklyn .627
1881—Chicago .667	1917—New York .636	1953—Brooklyn .682
1882—Chicago .655	1918—Chicago .651	1954—New York .630
1883—Boston .643	1919—Cincinnati .686	1955—Brooklyn .641
1884—Providence .750	1920—Brooklyn .604	1956—Brooklyn .604
1885—Chicago .777	1921—New York .614	1957—Milwaukee .617
1886—Chicago .726	1922—New York .604	1958—Milwaukee .597
1887—Detroit .637	1923—New York .621	1959—Los Angeles‡ .564
1888—New York .641	1924—New York .608	1960—Pittsburgh .617
1889—New York .659	1925—Pittsburgh .621	1961—Cincinnati .604
1890—Brooklyn .667	1926—St. Louis .578	1962—San Francisco§ .624
1891—Boston .630	1927—Pittsburgh .610	1963—Los Angeles .611
1892—Boston .680	1928—St. Louis .617	1964—St. Louis .574
1893—Boston .662	1929—Chicago .645	1965—Los Angeles .599
1894—Baltimore .695	1930—St. Louis .597	1966—Los Angeles .586
1895—Baltimore .669	1931—St. Louis .656	1967—St. Louis .627
1896—Baltimore .698	1932—Chicago .584	1968—St. Louis .599
1897—Boston .705	1933—New York .599	1969—New York (East)a .617
1898—Boston .685	1934—St. Louis .621	1970—Cincinnati (West)b .630
1899—Brooklyn .677	1935—Chicago .649	1971—Pittsburgh (East)c .599
1900—Brooklyn .603	1936—New York .597	1972—Cincinnati (West)b .617
1901—Pittsburgh .647	1937—New York .625	1973—New York (East)d .509
1902—Pittsburgh .741	1938—Chicago .586	1974—Los Angeles (West)b.. .630
1903—Pittsburgh .650	1939—Cincinnati .630	1975—Cincinnati (West)b .667
1904—New York .693	1940—Cincinnati .654	1976—Cincinnati (West)e .630
1905—New York .686	1941—Brooklyn .649	1977—Los Angeles (West)e.. .605
1906—Chicago .763	1942—St. Louis .688	1978—Los Angeles (West)e.. .586
1907—Chicago .704	1943—St. Louis .682	1979—Pittsburgh (East)d .605
1908—Chicago .643	1944—St. Louis .682	1980—Philadelphia (East)f .562
1909—Pittsburgh .724	1945—Chicago .636	1981—Los Angeles (West)g... .573
1910—Chicago .675	1946—St. Louis* .628	
1911—New York .647	1947—Brooklyn .610	

*Defeated Brooklyn, two games to none, in playoff for pennant. †Defeated Brooklyn, two games to one, in playoff for pennant. ‡Defeated Milwaukee, two games to none, in playoff for pennant. §Defeated Los Angeles, two games to one, in playoff for pennant. aDefeated Atlanta (West) in Championship Series. bDefeated Pittsburgh (East) in Championship Series. cDefeated San Francisco (West) in Championship Series. dDefeated Cincinnati (West) in Championship series. eDefeated Philadelphia (East) in Championship Series. fDefeated Houston (West) in Championship Series. gDefeated Montreal (East) in Championship Series.

STANDING OF CLUBS AT CLOSE OF SEASON

EAST DIVISION

Club	St.L.	Phil.	Mon.	Pitt.	Chi.	N.Y.	Atl.	Cin.	Hou.	L.A.	S.D.	S.F.	W.	L.	Pct.	G.B.
St. Louis	..	11	8	11	12	12	5	7	6	5	8	7	92	70	.568	......
Philadelphia	7	..	10	9	9	11	6	7	5	8	7	10	89	73	.549	3
Montreal	10	8	..	7	12	11	7	8	8	4	7	4	86	76	.531	6
Pittsburgh	7	9	11	..	9	10	8	8	3	7	6	6	84	78	.519	8
Chicago	6	9	6	9	..	9	4	6	9	5	4	6	73	89	.451	19
New York	6	7	7	8	9	..	3	5	4	6	6	4	65	97	.401	27

WEST DIVISION

Club	Atl.	L.A.	S.F.	S.D.	Hou.	Cin.	Chi.	Mon.	N.Y.	Phil.	Pitt.	St.L.	W.	L.	Pct.	G.B.
Atlanta	..	7	8	11	10	14	8	5	9	6	4	7	89	73	.549	......
Los Angeles	11	..	9	9	11	11	7	8	6	4	5	7	88	74	.543	1
San Francisco	10	9	..	8	13	12	6	8	8	2	6	5	87	75	.537	2
San Diego	7	9	10	..	9	12	8	5	6	5	6	4	81	81	.500	8
Houston	8	7	5	9	..	11	3	4	8	7	9	6	77	85	.475	12
Cincinnati	4	7	6	6	7	..	6	4	7	5	4	5	61	101	.377	28

Championship Series—St. Louis defeated Atlanta, three games to none.

RECORD AT HOME

EAST DIVISION

Club	Phil.	St.L.	Pitt.	Mon.	Chi.	N.Y.	S.F.	Hou.	L.A.	S.D.	Atl.	Cin.	W.	L.	Pct.
Philadelphia	.....	4-5	4-5	6-3	7-2	7-2	5-1	3-3	5-1	3-3	3-3	4-2	51	30	.630
St. Louis	6-3	.....	5-4	5-4	6-3	4-5	4-2	4-2	2-4	4-2	2-4	4-2	46	35	.568
Pittsburgh	4-5	3-6	.....	6-3	4-5	5-4	3-3	2-4	4-2	4-2	3-3	4-2	42	39	.519
Montreal	5-4	6-3	4-5	.....	4-5	5-4	2-4	4-2	1-5	2-4	3-3	4-2	40	41	.494
Chicago	7-2	3-6	4-5	1-8	.....	4-5	3-3	5-1	3-3	2-4	2-4	4-2	38	43	.469
New York	5-4	1-8	4-5	3-6	4-5	.....	2-4	2-4	3-3	4-2	1-5	4-2	33	48	.407

WEST DIVISION

Club	S.F.	Hou.	L.A.	S.D.	Atl.	Cin.	Phil.	St.L.	Pitt.	Mon.	Chi.	N.Y.	W.	L.	Pct.
San Francisco...		8-1	4-5	4-5	4-5	7-2	1-5	3-3	3-3	4-2	3-3	4-2	45	36	.556
Houston	4-5		3-6	5-4	4-5	6-3	4-2	4-2	5-1	2-4	2-4	4-2	43	38	.531
Los Angeles	4-5	5-4		6-3	5-4	4-5	3-3	3-3	3-3	3-3	4-2	3-3	43	38	.531
San Diego	5-4	5-4	6-3		4-5	6-3	2-4	2-4	4-2	1-5	4-2	4-2	43	38	.531
Atlanta	3-6	5-4	3-6	6-3		7-2	3-3	3-3	2-4	2-4	4-2	4-2	42	39	.519
Cincinnati	4-5	4-5	2-7	3-6	2-7		3-3	3-3	1-5	2-4	4-2	5-1	33	48	.407

RECORD ABROAD

EAST DIVISION

Club	Mon.	St.L.	Pitt.	Phil.	Chi.	N.Y.	Atl.	L.A.	S.F.	S.D.	Hou.	Cin.	W.	L.	Pct.
Montreal		4-5	3-6	3-6	8-1	6-3	4-2	3-3	2-4	5-1	4-2	4-2	46	35	.568
St. Louis	3-6		6-3	5-4	6-3	8-1	3-3	3-3	3-3	4-2	2-4	3-3	46	35	.568
Pittsburgh	5-4	4-5		5-4	5-4	5-4	4-2	3-3	3-3	2-4	1-5	5-1	42	39	.519
Philadelphia	4-5	3-6	5-4		2-7	4-5	3-3	3-3	5-1	4-2	2-4	3-3	38	43	.469
Chicago	5-4	3-6	5-4	2-7		5-4	2-4	2-4	3-3	2-4	4-2	2-4	35	46	.432
New York	4-5	5-4	4-5	2-7	5-4		2-4	3-3	2-4	2-4	2-4	1-5	32	49	.395

WEST DIVISION

Club	Atl.	L.A.	S.F.	S.D.	Hou.	Cin.	Mon.	St.L.	Pitt.	Phil.	Chi.	N.Y.	W.	L.	Pct.
Atlanta		4-5	5-4	5-4	5-4	7-2	3-3	4-2	2-4	3-3	4-2	5-1	47	34	.580
Los Angeles	6-3		5-4	3-6	6-3	7-2	5-1	4-2	2-4	1-5	3-3	3-3	45	36	.556
San Francisco...	6-3	5-4		4-5	5-4	5-4	4-2	2-4	3-3	1-5	3-3	4-2	42	39	.519
San Diego	3-6	3-6	5-4		4-5	6-3	4-2	2-4	2-4	3-3	4-2	2-4	38	43	.469
Houston	4-5	4-5	1-8	4-5		5-4	2-4	2-4	4-2	3-3	1-5	4-2	34	47	.420
Cincinnati	2-7	5-4	2-7	3-6	6-3		2-4	2-4	3-3	2-4	2-4	2-4	28	53	.346

SHUTOUT GAMES

Club	L.A.	Pitt.	St.L.	Atl.	Hou.	S.D.	Mon.	Chi.	Phil.	Cin.	N.Y.	S.F.	W.	L.	Pct.
Los Angeles	..	1	1	2	1	5	0	1	2	1	0	2	16	6	.727
Pittsburgh	1	..	0	2	1	0	1	0	2	0	0	0	7	3	.700
St. Louis	0	0	..	1	0	1	2	0	3	0	1	2	10	6	.625
Atlanta	0	0	1	..	2	2	0	2	2	1	0	1	11	10	.524
Houston	2	0	2	2	..	1	1	0	1	3	2	2	16	15	.516
San Diego	2	0	0	0	3	..	0	2	2	1	1	0	11	11	.500
Montreal	0	0	0	1	4	0	..	2	1	1	1	0	10	11	.476
Chicago	0	1	0	0	1	0	0	..	0	3	2	0	7	8	.467
Philadelphia	1	0	2	1	0	1	4	1	..	0	1	2	13	15	.464
Cincinnati	0	1	0	0	2	0	1	0	1	..	1	1	7	12	.368
New York	0	0	0	0	1	1	1	0	1	0	..	1	5	9	.357
San Francisco...	0	0	0	1	0	0	1	0	0	2	0	..	4	11	.267

OFFICIAL NATIONAL LEAGUE BATTING AVERAGES

Compiled by Elias Sports Bureau

CLUB BATTING

Club	Pct.	G.	AB.	R.	OR.	H.	TB.	2B.	3B.	HR.	RBI.	SH.	SF.	SB.	CS.	LOB.
Pittsburgh	.273	162	5614	724	696	1535	2289	272	40	134	688	78	67	161	75	1118
St. Louis	.264	162	5455	685	609	1439	1983	239	52	67	632	87	55	200	91	1147
Los Ang.	.264	162	5642	691	612	1487	2187	222	32	138	661	106	55	151	56	1223
Montreal	.262	162	5557	697	616	1454	2199	270	38	133	656	85	41	156	56	1153
Phila.	.260	162	5454	664	654	1417	2048	245	25	112	624	85	38	128	76	1098
Chicago	.260	162	5531	676	709	1436	2073	239	46	102	647	76	49	132	70	1094
S. Diego	.257	162	5575	675	658	1435	1999	217	52	81	611	86	47	165	77	1068
Atlanta	.256	162	5507	739	702	1411	2108	215	22	146	687	96	43	151	77	1124
S. Fran.	.253	162	5499	673	687	1393	2065	213	30	133	631	59	45	130	56	1173
Cincinnati	.251	162	5479	545	661	1375	1917	228	34	82	496	88	41	131	69	1122
N. York	.247	162	5510	609	723	1361	1931	227	26	97	568	64	53	137	58	1113
Houston	.247	162	5440	569	620	1342	1896	236	48	74	533	68	46	140	61	1092
Totals	.258	972	66263	7947	7947	17085	24695	2823	445	1299	7434	978	580	1782	822	13525

INDIVIDUAL BATTING

(Top Fifteen Qualifiers for Batting Championship—502 or More Plate Appearances)

*Bats lefthanded.   †Switch-hitter.

Player and Club	Pct.	G.	AB.	R.	H.	TB.	2B.	3B.	HR.	RBI.	GW.	SH.	SF.	SB.	CS.
Oliver, Albert, Mtl.*	.331	160	617	90	204	317	43	2	22	109	10	1	4	5	2
Madlock, Bill, Pitt.	.319	154	568	92	181	277	33	3	19	95	14	1	13	18	6
Durham, Leon, Chi.*	.312	148	539	84	168	281	33	7	22	90	9	0	2	28	14
Smith, Lonnie, St.L.	.307	156	592	120	182	257	35	8	8	69	9	3	4	68	26
Buckner, William, Chi.*	.306	161	657	93	201	290	34	5	15	105	15	1	10	15	5
Guerrero, Pedro, L.A.	.304	150	575	87	175	308	27	5	32	100	18	4	3	22	5
Dawson, Andre, Mtl	.301	148	608	107	183	303	37	7	23	83	14	4	6	39	10
Baker, Johnnie, L.A.	.300	147	570	80	171	261	19	1	23	88	16	2	9	17	10
Hernandez, Keith, St.L.*	.299	160	579	79	173	239	33	6	7	94	21	1	12	19	11

Player and Club	Pct.	G.	AB.	R.	H.	TB.	2B.	3B.	HR.	RBI.	GW.	SH.	SF.	SB.	CS.
Pena, Antonio, Pitt.	.296	138	497	53	147	216	28	4	11	63	11	3	2	2	5
Kennedy, Terrence, S.D.*	.295	153	562	75	166	273	42	1	21	97	15	3	8	1	0
Knight, C. Ray, Hou.	.294	158	609	72	179	245	36	6	6	70	11	1	13	2	5
Carter, Gary, Mtl.	.293	154	557	91	163	284	32	1	29	97	10	4	8	2	5
Morgan, Joseph, S.F.*	.289	134	463	68	134	203	19	4	14	61	10	1	3	24	4
Lezcano, Sixto, S.D.	.289	138	470	73	136	222	26	6	16	84	10	2	7	2	1
Oberkfell, Kenneth, St.L.*	.289	137	470	55	136	174	22	5	2	34	2	3	2	11	9

DEPARTMENTAL LEADERS: G—Garvey, Matthews, Murphy, J. Ray, Rose, 162; AB—Buckner, 657; R—Lo. Smith, 120; H—Oliver, 204; TB—Oliver, 317; 2B—Oliver, 43; 3B—Thon, 10; HR—Kingman, 37; RBI—Murphy, Oliver, 109; GW—Clark, K. Hernandez, 21; SH—Hubbard, 20; SF—Hendrick, 14; SB—Raines, 78; CS—Moreno, Lo. Smith, 26.

(All Players—Listed Alphabetically)

Player and Club	Pct.	G.	AB.	R.	H.	TB.	2B.	3B.	HR.	RBI.	GW.	SH.	SF.	SB.	CS.
Aguayo, Luis, Phila.	.268	50	56	11	15	29	1	2	3	7	0	1	0	1	1
Allen, Neil, N.Y.	.167	50	6	1	1	1	0	0	0	0	0	1	0	0	0
Altamirano, Porfirio, Phila.	.250	29	4	1	1	1	0	0	0	0	0	0	0	0	0
Alvarez, Jose, Atl.	.000	7	0	0	0	0	0	0	0	0	0	0	0	0	0
Andujar, Joaquin, St.L.†	.158	38	95	3	15	18	1	1	0	4	0	9	0	1	0
Ashby, Alan, Hous.†	.257	100	339	40	87	141	14	2	12	49	4	2	3	2	0
Backman, Walter, N.Y.†	.272	96	261	37	71	97	13	2	3	22	4	2	0	8	7
Bahnsen, Stanley, Phila.	.000	8	0	0	0	0	0	0	0	0	0	0	0	0	0
Bailor, Robert, N.Y.	.277	110	376	44	104	120	14	1	0	31	5	2	4	20	3
Bair, C. Douglas, St.L.	.077	63	13	0	1	1	0	0	0	0	0	2	0	0	0
Baker, Johnnie, L.A.	.300	147	570	80	171	261	19	1	23	88	16	2	9	17	10
Baller, Jay, Phila.	.000	4	0	0	0	0	0	0	0	0	0	0	0	0	0
Barr, James, S.F.	.250	53	32	1	8	9	1	0	0	3	0	2	0	0	0
Barranca, German, Cin.*	.255	46	51	11	13	20	1	3	0	2	0	1	0	2	0
Barrios, Jose, S.F.	.158	10	19	2	3	3	0	0	0	0	0	0	0	0	0
Bass, Kevin, Hou.†	.042	12	24	2	1	1	0	0	0	1	0	0	0	0	0
Bass, Randy, S.D.*	.200	13	30	1	6	9	0	0	1	8	0	0	1	0	0
Baumgarten, Ross, Pitt.*	.083	12	12	0	1	1	0	0	0	0	0	0	0	0	0
Beckwith, T. Joseph, L.A.*	.000	19	7	1	0	0	0	0	0	0	0	1	0	0	0
Bedrosian, Stephen, Atl.	.038	64	26	0	1	1	0	0	0	0	0	4	0	0	0
Belanger, Mark, L.A.	.240	54	50	6	12	13	1	0	0	4	0	2	0	1	0
Belliard, Rafael, Pitt.†	.500	9	2	3	1	1	0	0	0	0	0	0	0	1	0
Bench, Johnny, Cin.	.258	119	399	44	103	158	16	0	13	38	5	1	2	1	2
Benedict, Bruce, Atl.	.246	118	386	34	95	117	11	1	3	44	3	7	3	4	4
Benton, Alfred, Chi.	.143	4	7	0	1	1	0	0	0	1	0	0	0	0	0
Berenyi, Bruce, Cin.	.242	34	62	0	15	19	2	1	0	3	1	12	1	0	0
Bergman, David, S.F.*	.273	100	121	22	33	50	3	1	4	14	2	0	1	3	0
Berra, Dale, Pitt.	.263	156	529	64	139	204	25	5	10	61	6	8	9	6	6
Bevacqua, Kurt, S.D.	.252	64	123	15	31	40	9	0	0	24	2	1	4	2	0
Biittner, Lawrence, Cin.*	.310	97	184	18	57	76	9	2	2	24	1	2	3	1	0
Bird, J. Douglas, Chi.	.143	35	56	0	8	9	1	0	0	3	0	4	0	0	0
Blackwell, Timothy, Mtl.†	.190	23	42	2	8	12	2	1	0	3	0	0	0	0	0
Bochy, Bruce, N.Y.	.306	17	49	4	15	25	4	0	2	8	1	0	0	0	0
Boggs, Thomas, Atl.	.235	10	17	1	4	4	0	0	0	2	0	1	0	0	0
Bonilla, Juan, S.D.	.280	45	182	21	51	61	6	2	0	8	1	3	0	0	1
Boone, Daniel, S.D.-Hou.*	.167	20	6	0	1	2	1	0	0	0	0	0	0	0	0
Bowa, Lawrence, Chi.†	.246	142	499	50	123	152	15	7	0	29	1	9	1	8	3
Bradley, Mark, L.A.	.333	8	3	1	1	1	0	0	0	0	0	0	0	0	0
Braun, Stephen, St.L.*	.274	58	62	6	17	21	4	0	0	4	0	0	0	0	0
Breining, Fred, S.F.	.207	54	29	4	6	6	0	0	0	0	0	5	0	0	0
Brenly, Robert, S.F.	.283	65	180	26	51	69	4	1	4	15	1	1	2	6	2
Briggs, Daniel, Chi.*	.125	48	48	1	6	6	0	0	0	1	0	1	0	0	0
Brock, Gregory, L.A.*	.118	18	17	1	2	3	1	0	0	1	1	0	0	0	0
Brooks, Hubert, N.Y.	.249	126	457	40	114	145	21	2	2	40	7	3	5	6	3
Brummer, Glenn, St.L.	.234	35	64	4	15	19	4	0	0	8	0	0	2	0	0
Brusstar, Warren, Phila.	.000	22	2	0	0	0	0	0	0	0	0	0	0	0	0
Buckner, William, Chi.*	.306	161	657	93	201	290	34	5	15	105	15	1	10	15	5
Burris, B. Ray, Mtl.	.179	37	28	0	5	6	1	0	0	1	0	4	0	0	0
Butler, Brett, Atl.*	.217	89	240	35	52	54	2	0	0	7	1	3	0	21	8
Bystrom, Martin, Phila.	.125	19	24	2	3	4	1	0	0	0	0	3	0	0	0
Camp, Rick, Atl.	.024	51	41	0	1	2	1	0	0	0	0	5	0	0	0
Campbell, William, Chi.	.143	62	7	0	1	1	0	0	0	0	0	0	0	0	0
Candelaria, John, Pitt.†	.222	33	54	6	12	14	2	0	0	9	1	3	1	0	0
Cappuzzello, George, Hou.	.000	17	1	0	0	0	0	0	0	0	0	0	0	0	0
Carlton, Steven, Phila.*	.218	38	101	8	22	32	4	0	2	8	0	8	0	0	0
Carter, Gary, Mtl.	.293	154	557	91	163	284	32	1	29	97	10	4	8	2	5
Cedeno, Cesar, Cin.	.289	138	492	52	142	203	35	1	8	57	10	2	4	16	11
Cey, Ronald, L.A.	.254	150	556	62	141	238	23	1	24	79	11	2	8	3	2
Chambliss, C. Christopher, Atl.*	.270	157	534	57	144	233	25	2	20	86	11	0	6	7	3
Chiffer, Floyd, S.D.	.000	51	8	0	0	0	0	0	0	0	0	0	0	0	0
Chris, Michael, S.F.*	.143	9	7	0	1	1	0	0	0	1	0	1	0	1	0
Christenson, Larry, Phila.	.075	33	67	4	5	10	2	0	1	7	1	12	0	1	0
Clark, Jack, S.F.	.274	157	563	90	154	271	30	3	27	103	21	0	5	6	9
Concepcion, David, Cin.	.287	147	572	48	164	212	25	4	5	53	6	2	4	13	6
Cowley, Joseph, Atl.	.200	17	15	0	3	3	0	0	0	0	0	1	0	0	0
Cox, Larry, Chi.	.000	2	4	1	0	0	0	0	0	0	0	0	0	0	0

Player and Club	Pct.	G.	AB.	R.	H.	TB.	2B.	3B.	HR.	RBI.	GW.	SH.	SF.	SB.	CS.
Cromartie, Warren, Mtl.*	.254	144	497	59	126	198	24	3	14	62	13	1	4	3	0
Crow, Donald, L.A.	.000	4	4	0	0	0	0	0	0	0	0	0	0	0	0
Cruz, Hector, Chi.	.211	17	19	1	4	5	1	0	0	0	0	0	0	0	0
Cruz, Jose, Hou.*	.275	155	570	62	157	215	27	2	9	68	6	3	6	21	11
Curtis, John, S.D.*	.297	26	37	1	11	13	0	1	0	5	2	4	0	0	0
Davis, Charles, S.F.†	.261	154	641	86	167	263	27	6	19	76	8	7	6	24	13
Davis, Jody, Chi.	.261	130	418	41	109	169	20	2	12	52	4	4	7	0	1
Davis, Richard, Phila.-Pitt.	.228	67	145	12	33	54	5	2	4	17	1	1	4	2	0
Dawson, Andre, Mtl.	.301	148	608	107	183	303	37	7	23	83	14	4	6	39	10
Dayley, Kenneth, Atl.*	.250	20	20	1	5	5	0	0	0	1	0	1	0	0	1
DeJesus, Ivan, Phila.	.239	161	536	53	128	168	21	5	3	59	8	11	3	14	4
DeLeon, Luis, S.D.*	.091	61	11	0	1	2	1	0	0	0	0	1	0	0	0
Dempsey, Mark, S.F.	.000	3	1	0	0	0	0	0	0	0	0	0	0	0	0
Denny, John, Phila.	.167	4	6	0	1	1	0	0	0	0	0	0	0	0	0
Dernier, Robert, Phila.	.249	122	370	56	92	118	10	2	4	21	3	3	2	42	12
Diaz, Baudilio, Phila.	.288	144	525	69	151	236	29	1	18	85	12	1	7	3	6
Diaz, Carlos, Atl.-N.Y.	.000	23	3	0	0	0	0	0	0	0	0	0	0	0	0
DiPino, Frank, Hou.*	.000	6	8	0	0	0	0	0	0	0	0	1	0	0	0
Doran, William, Hou.†	.278	26	97	11	27	30	3	0	0	6	1	0	1	5	0
Dravecky, David, S.D.	.130	32	23	0	3	3	0	0	0	2	0	4	0	0	0
Driessen, Daniel, Cin.*	.269	149	516	64	139	217	25	1	17	57	6	0	6	11	6
Durham, Leon, Chi.*	.312	148	539	84	168	281	33	7	22	90	9	0	2	28	14
Easler, Michael, Pitt.*	.276	142	475	52	131	207	27	2	15	58	4	1	4	1	1
Edelen, B. Joe, Cin.	.500	9	2	0	1	1	0	0	0	0	0	0	0	0	0
Edwards, David, S.D.	.182	71	55	7	10	15	2	0	1	2	0	0	0	0	0
Eichelberger, Juan, S.D.	.091	31	55	0	5	8	1	1	0	3	1	5	0	1	0
Evans, Darrell, S.F.*	.256	141	465	64	119	195	20	4	16	61	5	3	6	5	4
Falcone, Peter, N.Y.*	.113	40	53	0	6	7	1	0	0	3	0	2	0	0	0
Farmer, Edward, Phila.	.000	47	11	0	0	0	0	0	0	0	0	2	0	0	0
Filer, Thomas, Chi.	.083	8	12	1	1	2	1	0	0	0	0	1	0	0	0
Flannery, Timothy, S.D.*	.264	122	379	40	100	125	11	7	0	30	4	6	6	1	0
Fletcher, Scott, Chi.	.167	11	24	4	4	4	0	0	0	1	0	0	0	1	0
Flynn, R. Douglas, Mtl.	.244	58	193	13	47	57	6	2	0	20	1	3	2	0	2
Forsch, Robert, St. L.	.205	36	73	7	15	20	3	1	0	3	0	14	0	0	0
Forster, Terry, L.A.*	.000	56	2	0	0	0	0	0	0	0	0	0	0	0	0
Foster, George, N.Y.	.247	151	550	64	136	202	23	2	13	70	6	0	6	1	1
Fowlkes, Alan, S.F.	.115	21	26	2	3	3	0	0	0	3	0	2	0	0	0
Franco, Julio, Phila.	.276	16	29	3	8	9	1	0	0	3	0	1	0	0	2
Francona, Terry, Mtl.*	.321	46	131	14	42	45	3	0	0	9	1	5	0	2	3
Frobel, Douglas, Pitt.*	.206	16	34	5	7	15	2	0	2	3	0	0	0	1	1
Fryman, Woodrow, Mtl.	.222	60	9	1	2	2	0	0	0	0	0	1	0	0	0
Gaff, Brent, N.Y.	.000	7	8	0	0	0	0	0	0	0	0	1	0	0	0
Gale, Richard, S.F.	.125	33	48	4	6	10	1	0	1	2	1	1	0	0	0
Garber, H. Eugene, Atl.	.133	69	15	1	2	2	0	0	0	0	0	2	0	0	0
Garcia, Alfonso, Hou.	.211	34	76	5	16	24	5	0	1	5	0	1	0	1	0
Gardenhire, Ronald, N.Y.	.240	141	384	29	92	120	17	1	3	33	3	12	5	5	6
Garner, Philip, Hou.	.274	155	588	65	161	249	33	8	13	83	15	0	7	24	13
Garrelts, Scott, S.F.	.000	1	0	0	0	0	0	0	0	0	0	0	0	0	0
Garvey, Steven, L.A.	.282	162	625	66	176	261	35	1	6	86	10	5	9	5	3
Gates, Michael, Mtl.*	.231	36	121	16	28	36	2	3	0	8	0	0	2	0	0
Giles, Brian, N.Y.	.210	45	138	14	29	43	5	0	3	10	1	0	2	6	1
Goltz, David, L.A.	.000	2	1	0	0	0	0	0	0	0	0	0	0	0	0
Gonzalez, Julio, St. L.	.241	42	87	9	21	31	3	2	1	7	1	1	0	1	1
Gorman, Thomas, Mtl.-N.Y.*	.000	8	1	0	0	0	0	0	0	0	0	1	0	0	0
Green, David, St. L.	.283	76	166	21	47	62	7	1	2	23	3	0	3	11	3
Griffin, Michael, S.D.	.000	7	1	0	0	0	0	0	0	0	0	0	0	0	0
Griffin, Thomas, Pitt.	.222	6	9	0	2	2	0	0	0	2	0	0	0	0	0
Gross, Gregory, Phila.*	.299	119	134	14	40	44	4	0	0	10	0	2	0	4	3
Guante, Cecilio, Pitt.	.000	10	5	1	0	0	0	0	0	0	0	0	0	0	0
Guerrero, Pedro, L.A.	.304	150	575	87	175	308	27	5	32	100	18	4	3	22	5
Gulden, Bradley, Mtl.*	.000	5	6	1	0	0	0	0	0	0	0	0	0	0	0
Gullickson, William, Mtl.	.122	34	82	5	10	13	3	0	0	6	0	9	0	0	0
Gwosdz, Douglas, S.D.	.176	7	17	1	3	3	0	0	0	0	0	0	0	0	0
Gwynn, Anthony, S.D.*	.289	54	190	33	55	74	12	2	1	17	3	4	1	8	3
Hall, Albert, Atl.†	.000	5	0	1	0	0	0	0	0	0	0	0	0	0	0
Hall, Melvin, Chi.*	.263	24	80	6	21	28	3	2	0	4	0	0	1	0	1
Hammaker, C. Atlee, S.F.†	.068	29	59	2	4	4	0	0	0	1	0	1	0	1	0
Hanna, Preston, Atl.	.400	20	5	1	2	3	1	0	0	1	0	0	0	0	0
Harper, Brian, Pitt.	.276	20	29	4	8	15	1	0	2	4	0	1	0	0	0
Harper, Terry, Atl.	.287	48	150	16	43	52	3	0	2	16	1	0	2	7	4
Harris, Greg, Cin.†	.167	35	18	0	3	3	0	0	0	3	0	0	0	0	0
Hausman, Thomas, N.Y.-Atl.	.000	24	2	0	0	0	0	0	0	0	0	0	0	0	0
Hawkins, M. Andrew, S.D.	.000	15	15	0	0	0	0	0	0	1	0	3	0	0	0
Hayes, Ben, Cin.	.000	26	4	0	0	0	0	0	0	0	0	2	0	0	0
Hebner, Richard, Pitt.*	.300	25	70	6	21	29	2	0	2	12	1	1	0	4	0
Heep, Daniel, Hou.*	.237	85	198	16	47	75	14	1	4	22	1	0	2	0	2
Henderson, Stephen, Chi.	.233	92	257	23	60	86	12	4	2	29	5	3	1	6	5
Hendrick, George, St. L.	.282	136	515	65	145	232	20	5	19	104	13	1	14	3	2
Hernandez, Guillermo, Chi.*	.000	75	3	1	0	0	0	0	0	0	0	1	0	1	0
Hernandez, Keith, St. L.*	.299	160	579	79	173	239	33	6	7	94	21	1	12	19	11

Player and Club	Pct.	G	AB	R	H	TB	2B	3B	HR	RBI	GW	SH	SF	SB	CS
Herr, Thomas, St. L.†	.266	135	493	83	131	158	19	4	0	36	7	3	5	25	12
Hinshaw, George, S.D.	.267	6	15	1	4	4	0	0	0	1	0	0	0	0	0
Hodges, Ronald, N.Y.*	.246	80	228	26	56	85	12	1	5	27	2	5	2	4	3
Holland, Alfred, S.F.	.059	58	34	0	2	2	0	0	0	0	0	3	0	0	0
Holman, R. Scott, N.Y.	.222	4	9	1	2	2	0	0	0	1	1	1	0	0	0
Hooton, Burt, L.A.	.086	21	35	3	3	7	1	0	1	1	1	6	0	0	0
Horner, J. Robert, Atl.	.261	140	499	85	130	250	24	0	32	97	13	0	3	3	5
Householder, Paul, Cin.†	.211	138	417	40	88	136	11	5	9	34	4	3	3	17	11
Howard, Michael, N.Y.†	.179	33	39	5	7	10	0	0	1	3	0	1	1	2	0
Howe, Arthur, Hou.	.238	110	365	29	87	119	15	1	5	38	5	4	3	2	0
Howe, Steven, L.A.*	.000	66	7	0	0	0	0	0	0	0	0	1	0	0	0
Hrabosky, Alan, Atl.	.333	31	3	0	1	1	0	0	0	0	0	0	0	0	0
Hubbard, Glenn, Atl.	.248	145	532	75	132	186	25	1	9	59	6	20	4	4	3
Hume, Thomas, Cin.	.000	46	5	0	0	0	0	0	0	0	0	0	0	0	0
Hurdle, Clinton, Cin.*	.206	19	34	2	7	8	1	0	0	1	0	0	0	0	1
Iorg, Dane, St. L.*	.294	102	238	17	70	86	14	1	0	34	5	0	3	0	1
Ivie, Michael, Hou.	.333	7	6	0	2	2	0	0	0	0	0	0	0	0	0
Jackson, Grant, Pitt.†	.000	1	0	0	0	0	0	0	0	0	0	0	0	0	0
James, Robert, Mtl.	.000	7	0	0	0	0	0	0	0	0	0	0	0	0	0
Jenkins, Ferguson, Chi.	.149	34	67	2	10	12	2	0	0	6	0	12	1	0	0
Johnson, Randall G., Atl.	.239	27	46	5	11	16	5	0	0	6	0	1	1	0	1
Johnson, Roy, Mtl.*	.219	17	32	2	7	9	2	0	0	2	0	1	0	0	0
Johnson, Wallace, Mtl.†	.193	36	57	5	11	15	0	2	0	2	1	0	0	4	1
Johnstone, John, L.A.-Chi.*	.241	119	282	40	68	114	14	1	10	45	7	1	4	0	2
Jones, Randall, N.Y.	.148	28	27	1	4	4	0	0	0	0	0	2	0	0	0
Jones, Ruppert, S.D.*	.283	116	424	69	120	180	20	2	12	61	9	3	3	18	15
Jorgensen, Michael, N.Y.*	.254	120	114	16	29	41	6	0	2	14	1	1	0	2	0
Kaat, James, St. L.*	.000	62	12	0	0	0	0	0	0	0	0	0	0	0	0
Keener, Jeffrey, St. L.*	.000	19	0	0	0	0	0	0	0	0	0	0	0	0	0
Kennedy, Junior, Chi.	.219	105	242	22	53	64	3	1	2	25	1	5	3	1	4
Kennedy, Terrence, S.D.*	.295	153	562	75	166	273	42	1	21	97	15	3	8	1	0
Kern, James, Cin.	.000	50	7	0	0	0	0	0	0	0	0	0	0	0	0
Kingman, David, N.Y.	.204	149	535	80	109	231	9	1	37	99	10	3	6	4	0
Knepper, Robert, Hou.*	.058	33	52	2	3	4	1	0	0	0	0	6	0	0	0
Knicely, Alan, Hou.	.188	59	133	10	25	33	2	0	2	12	2	1	0	0	1
Knight, C. Ray, Hou.	.294	158	609	72	179	245	36	6	6	70	11	1	13	2	5
Kravec, Kenneth, Chi.*	.000	13	3	0	0	0	0	0	0	0	0	0	0	0	0
Krenchicki, Wayne, Cin.*	.283	94	187	19	53	67	6	1	2	21	3	1	4	5	3
Krukow, Michael, Phila.	.181	33	72	3	13	14	1	0	0	2	1	5	0	0	0
Kuiper, Duane, S.F.*	.280	107	218	26	61	72	9	1	0	17	1	4	1	2	2
LaCorte, Frank, Hou.	.000	55	7	0	0	0	0	0	0	0	0	1	0	0	0
LaCoss, Michael, Hou.	.250	41	24	2	6	7	1	0	0	0	0	3	0	0	0
Lacy, Leondaus, Pitt.	.312	121	359	66	112	149	16	3	5	31	6	2	1	40	15
Lahti, Jeffrey, St. L.	.077	33	13	0	1	1	0	0	0	0	0	0	0	0	1
Lancellotti, Richard, S.D.*	.179	17	39	2	7	9	2	0	0	4	0	0	0	0	0
Landestoy, Rafael, Cin.†	.189	73	111	11	21	27	3	0	1	9	2	7	0	2	0
Landreaux, Kenneth, L.A.*	.284	129	461	71	131	189	23	7	7	50	5	8	6	31	10
Landrum, Terry, St. L.	.278	79	72	12	20	29	3	0	2	14	0	3	0	0	1
Lansford, Joseph, S.D.	.182	13	22	6	4	4	0	0	0	3	0	0	1	0	1
LaPoint, David, St. L.*	.053	42	38	2	2	2	0	0	0	1	0	8	0	0	0
Larson, Daniel, Chi.	.273	12	11	2	3	3	0	0	0	0	0	0	0	0	0
Laskey, William, S.F.	.129	32	62	1	8	8	0	0	0	4	0	4	0	0	1
Lavelle, Gary, S.F.	.154	68	13	1	2	3	1	0	0	2	0	2	0	0	0
Lawless, Thomas, Cin.	.212	49	165	19	35	41	6	0	0	4	0	2	0	16	5
Lea, Charles, Mtl.	.123	27	65	0	8	9	1	0	0	2	0	1	0	0	0
Leach, Terry, N.Y.	.125	21	8	0	1	1	0	0	0	0	0	1	0	0	0
Lee, William, Mtl.*	.000	7	0	0	0	0	0	0	0	0	0	0	0	0	0
Lefebvre, Joseph, S.D.*	.238	102	239	25	57	78	9	0	4	21	2	4	2	0	0
Leibrandt, Charles, Cin.	.080	36	25	1	2	2	0	0	0	1	0	4	0	0	0
LeMaster, Johnnie, S.F.	.216	130	436	34	94	116	14	1	2	30	3	5	2	13	4
Leonard, Jeffrey, S.F.	.259	80	278	32	72	117	16	1	9	49	4	0	5	18	5
Lerch, Randy, Mtl.*	.250	6	8	0	2	2	0	0	0	0	0	0	0	0	0
Lesley, Bradley, Cin.	.000	28	1	0	0	0	0	0	0	0	0	0	0	0	0
Lezcano, Sixto, S.D.	.289	138	470	73	136	222	26	6	16	84	10	2	7	2	1
Linares, Rufino, Atl.	.298	77	191	28	57	72	7	1	2	17	2	0	1	5	2
Littell, Mark, St. L.*	.000	16	2	0	0	0	0	0	0	0	0	0	0	0	0
Little, R. Bryan, Mtl.†	.214	29	42	6	9	9	0	0	0	3	0	0	1	2	1
Lollar, W. Timothy, S.D.*	.247	36	85	12	21	33	1	1	3	11	1	2	0	0	0
Loucks, Scott, Hou.	.224	44	49	6	11	13	2	0	0	3	1	0	0	4	1
Lucas, Gary, S.D.*	.000	65	14	0	0	0	0	0	0	1	0	3	0	0	0
Lyle, Albert, Phil.*	.500	34	2	0	1	1	0	0	0	0	0	0	0	0	0
Lynch, Edward, N.Y.	.000	43	33	2	0	0	0	0	0	0	0	3	0	0	0
Maddox, Garry, Phila.	.284	119	412	39	117	172	27	2	8	61	6	2	2	7	5
Madlock, Bill, Pitt.	.319	154	568	92	181	277	33	3	19	95	14	1	13	18	6
Mahler, Richard, Atl.	.190	39	58	5	11	14	0	0	1	4	0	11	0	0	0
Maldonado, Candido, L.A.	.000	6	4	0	0	0	0	0	0	0	0	0	0	0	0
Mankowski, Philip, N.Y.*	.229	13	35	2	8	9	1	0	0	4	1	0	2	0	1
Manuel, Jerry, S.D.	.200	2	5	0	1	3	0	1	0	1	0	0	0	0	0
Marshall, Michael, L.A.	.242	49	95	10	23	41	3	0	5	9	3	0	1	2	0
Martin, D. Renie, S.F.	.265	30	49	4	13	16	1	1	0	3	1	6	0	1	0

Player and Club	Pct.	G.	AB.	R.	H.	TB.	2B.	3B.	HR.	RBI.	GW.	SH.	SF.	SB.	CS.
Martin, John R., St. L.†	.091	24	11	1	1	1	0	0	0	0	0	2	0	0	0
Martz, Randy, Chi.*	.143	28	42	6	6	8	2	0	0	6	0	7	0	0	0
Matthews, Gary, Phila.	.281	162	616	89	173	263	31	1	19	83	17	0	6	21	4
Matuszek, Leonard, Phila.*	.077	25	39	1	3	4	1	0	0	3	0	0	1	0	1
May, Milton, S.F.*	.263	114	395	29	104	150	19	0	9	39	4	5	1	0	1
McGaffigan, Andrew, S.F.	.000	4	1	0	0	0	0	0	0	0	0	0	0	0	0
McGee, Willie, St. L.†	.296	123	422	43	125	165	12	8	4	56	7	2	1	24	12
McGraw, Frank, Phila.	.000	34	2	0	0	0	0	0	0	1	0	0	0	0	0
McWilliams, Larry, Atl.-Pitt.*	.184	47	38	1	7	7	0	0	0	0	0	10	0	0	0
Mills, J. Bradley, Mtl.*	.224	54	67	6	15	21	3	0	1	2	0	1	0	0	0
Milner, Eddie, Cin.*	.268	113	407	61	109	154	23	5	4	31	2	2	0	18	12
Milner, John, Mtl.-Pitt.*	.170	59	53	6	9	17	2	0	2	10	0	0	1	1	0
Minton, Gregory, S.F.†	.176	78	17	2	3	4	1	0	0	1	0	1	1	0	0
Moffitt, Randall, Hou.	.000	30	2	0	0	0	0	0	0	0	0	1	0	0	0
Molinaro, Robert, Chi.-Phila.*	.213	84	80	6	17	21	1	0	1	14	1	0	0	2	1
Monday, Robert, L.A.*	.257	104	210	37	54	101	6	4	11	42	7	1	3	2	1
Monge, Isidro, Phil.†	.111	47	9	1	1	1	0	0	0	0	0	2	0	0	0
Montanez, Guillermo, Pitt.-Phila.*	.208	54	48	4	10	11	1	0	0	2	0	0	0	0	0
Montefusco, John, S.D.	.086	32	58	2	5	6	1	0	0	2	0	6	0	0	0
Moore, Donnie, Atl.*	.000	16	1	0	0	0	0	0	0	0	0	0	0	0	0
Morales, Jose, L.A.	.300	35	30	1	9	13	1	0	1	8	0	0	0	0	0
Morales, Julio, Chi.	.284	65	116	14	33	51	2	2	4	30	5	0	1	1	2
Moreland, B. Keith, Chi.	.261	138	476	50	124	190	17	2	15	68	8	1	6	0	6
Moreno, Omar, Pitt.*	.245	158	645	82	158	203	18	9	3	44	3	10	6	60	26
Morgan, Joe, S.F.*	.289	134	463	68	134	203	19	4	14	61	10	1	3	24	4
Morrison, James, Pitt.	.279	44	86	10	24	42	4	1	4	15	3	2	3	2	0
Moskau, Paul, Pitt.	.091	13	11	1	1	1	0	0	0	0	0	1	0	0	0
Mota, Manuel, L.A.	.000	1	1	0	0	0	0	0	0	0	0	0	0	0	0
Mura, Stephen, St. L.	.057	35	53	3	3	3	0	0	0	3	0	10	0	0	0
Murphy, Dale, Atl.	.281	162	598	113	168	303	23	2	36	109	14	0	4	23	11
Nicosia, Steven, Pitt.	.280	39	100	6	28	34	3	0	1	7	0	2	1	0	1
Niedenfuer, Thomas, L.A.	.000	55	3	0	0	0	0	0	0	0	0	0	0	0	0
Niekro, Joseph, Hou.	.090	35	89	2	8	10	2	0	0	5	0	7	1	0	0
Niekro, Philip, Atl.	.195	35	87	6	17	24	4	0	1	7	0	3	1	0	0
Niemann, Randy, Pitt.*	1.000	20	2	1	2	2	0	0	0	0	0	0	0	0	0
Noles, Dickie, Chi.	.107	31	56	5	6	9	3	0	0	2	0	4	1	0	0
Nordhagen, Wayne, Pitt.	.500	1	4	0	2	2	0	0	0	0	0	0	0	0	0
Norman, Daniel, Mtl.	.212	53	66	6	14	23	3	0	2	7	0	0	0	0	1
Norman, Nelson, Pitt.†	.000	3	3	0	0	0	0	0	0	0	0	0	0	0	0
Oberkfell, Kenneth, St. L.*	.289	137	470	55	136	174	22	5	2	34	2	3	2	11	9
O'Berry, P. Michael, Cin.	.222	21	45	5	10	12	2	0	0	3	0	0	0	0	0
Oester, Ronald, Cin.†	.260	151	549	63	143	197	19	4	9	47	7	8	3	5	6
Office, Rowland, Mtl.*	.333	3	3	0	1	2	1	0	0	0	0	0	0	0	0
Oliver, Albert, Mtl.*	.331	160	617	90	204	317	43	2	22	109	10	1	4	5	2
O'Malley, Thomas, S.F.*	.275	92	291	26	80	106	12	4	2	27	3	1	1	0	3
Orosco, Jesse, N.Y.	.143	54	14	0	2	2	0	0	0	0	0	0	0	0	0
Orta, Jorge, L.A.*	.217	86	115	13	25	36	5	0	2	8	2	0	1	0	1
Ortiz, Adalberto, Pitt.	.200	7	15	1	3	4	1	0	0	0	0	0	0	0	0
Owen, Lawrence, Atl.	.333	2	3	1	1	2	1	0	0	0	0	0	0	0	0
Ownbey, Richard, N.Y.	.200	9	15	3	3	3	0	0	0	1	0	1	0	0	0
Palmer, David, Mtl.	.042	13	24	2	1	1	0	0	0	0	0	3	0	0	0
Paris, Kelly, St. L.	.103	12	29	1	3	3	0	0	0	0	0	1	0	1	0
Parker, David, Pitt.*	.270	73	244	41	66	109	19	3	6	29	6	0	3	7	5
Pastore, Frank, Cin.	.172	31	58	3	10	15	2	0	1	3	0	5	0	0	0
Pena, Alejandro, L.A.	.000	29	0	0	0	0	0	0	0	0	0	0	0	0	0
Pena, Antonio, Pitt.	.296	138	497	53	147	216	28	4	11	63	11	3	2	2	5
Perez, Pascual, Atl.	.167	16	18	2	3	5	2	0	0	0	0	5	0	0	0
Perkins, Broderick, S.D.*	.271	125	347	32	94	118	10	4	2	34	4	3	2	2	1
Pettini, Joseph, S.F.	.205	29	39	5	8	9	1	0	0	2	0	1	0	0	1
Phelps, Kenneth, Mtl.*	.250	10	8	0	2	2	0	0	0	0	0	0	0	0	0
Phillips, Michael, Mtl.*	.125	14	8	0	1	1	0	0	0	0	0	1	0	1	0
Pittman, Joseph, Hou.-S.D.	.250	70	128	16	32	35	3	0	0	7	1	3	0	8	3
Pladson, Gordon, Hou.	.000	2	0	0	0	0	0	0	0	0	0	0	0	0	0
Pocoroba, Biff, Atl.*	.275	56	120	5	33	46	7	0	2	22	5	0	0	0	0
Porter, Darrell, St. L.*	.231	120	373	46	86	150	18	5	12	48	6	1	3	1	1
Porter, Robert, Atl.*	.111	24	27	1	3	3	0	0	0	0	0	1	0	0	0
Power, Ted, L.A.	.000	12	6	0	0	0	0	0	0	0	0	1	0	0	0
Price, Joseph, Cin.	.333	59	3	0	1	1	0	0	0	0	0	2	0	0	0
Proly, Michael, Chi.	.286	44	14	0	4	5	1	0	0	1	0	5	0	0	0
Pruitt, Ronald, S.F.	.500	5	4	1	2	3	1	0	0	2	1	0	0	0	0
Puhl, Terry, Hou.*	.262	145	507	64	133	192	17	9	8	50	7	5	2	17	9
Pujols, Luis, Hou.	.199	65	176	8	35	57	6	2	4	15	1	5	0	0	3
Puleo, Charles, N.Y.	.125	36	48	3	6	6	0	0	0	0	0	6	0	0	0
Rabb, John, S.F.	.500	2	2	0	1	3	0	1	0	0	0	0	0	0	0
Raines, Timothy, Mtl.†	.277	156	647	90	179	239	32	8	4	43	9	6	1	78	16
Rajsich, Gary, N.Y.*	.259	80	162	17	42	62	8	3	2	12	0	2	0	1	3
Ramirez, Mario, S.D.	.174	13	23	1	4	5	1	0	0	1	0	0	0	0	0
Ramirez, Rafael, Atl.	.278	157	609	74	169	231	24	4	10	52	7	16	5	27	14
Ramsey, Michael, St. L.†	.230	112	256	18	59	74	8	2	1	21	2	11	0	6	5
Ransom, Jeffrey, S.F.	.159	15	44	5	7	7	0	0	0	3	0	0	1	0	0

Player and Club	Pct.	G.	AB.	R.	H.	TB.	2B.	3B.	HR.	RBI.	GW.	SH.	SF.	SB.	CS.
Rasmussen, Eric, St. L	.000	8	3	0	0	0	0	0	0	0	0	1	0	0	0
Ray, Johnny, Pitt.†	.281	162	647	79	182	247	30	7	7	63	8	13	5	16	7
Ray, Larry, Hou.*	.167	5	6	0	1	1	0	0	0	1	0	0	1	0	0
Reardon, Jeffrey, Mtl.	.100	75	10	0	1	2	1	0	0	1	0	1	0	0	0
Redus, Gary, Cin	.217	20	83	12	18	28	3	2	1	7	0	0	1	11	2
Reed, Jerry, Phila.	.000	7	0	0	0	0	0	0	0	0	0	0	0	0	0
Reed, Ronald, Phila.	.333	57	12	0	4	5	1	0	0	3	0	1	1	0	0
Reitz, Kenneth, Pitt	.000	7	10	0	0	0	0	0	0	0	0	0	0	0	0
Reuss, Jerry, L.A.*	.221	39	77	8	17	20	3	0	0	3	0	16	0	0	0
Reynolds, G. Craig, Hou.*	.254	54	118	16	30	41	2	3	1	7	0	3	1	3	1
Reynolds, Ronn, N.Y.	.000	2	4	0	0	0	0	0	0	0	0	0	0	0	0
Rhoden, Richard, Pitt	.265	36	83	10	22	37	6	0	3	12	2	2	1	0	0
Richards, Eugene, S.D.*	.286	132	521	63	149	187	13	8	3	28	1	1	2	30	20
Rincon, Andrew, St.L.	.100	11	10	3	1	1	0	0	0	1	0	1	0	0	0
Ripley, Allen, Chi.	.132	28	38	3	5	5	0	0	0	1	0	2	0	0	0
Roberge, Bertrand, Hou.	.000	22	1	0	0	0	0	0	0	0	0	0	0	0	0
Roberts, David A., Phila	.182	28	33	2	6	7	1	0	0	2	0	1	0	0	1
Robinson, Don, Pitt	.282	43	85	10	24	35	5	0	2	16	1	2	1	0	0
Robinson, William, Pitt.-Phila	.250	66	140	14	35	65	9	0	7	31	3	0	3	1	2
Roenicke, Ronald, L.A.†	.259	109	143	18	37	48	8	0	1	12	2	3	1	5	0
Rogers, Stephen, Mtl	.129	35	85	3	11	12	1	0	0	4	1	12	0	0	1
Romo, Enrique, Pitt	.300	46	10	2	3	5	2	0	0	0	0	1	0	0	0
Romo, Vicente, L.A.	.200	15	5	0	1	1	0	0	0	0	0	4	0	0	0
Roof, Eugene, St.L.†	.267	11	15	3	4	4	0	0	0	2	0	0	0	2	0
Rose, Peter, Phila.†	.271	162	634	80	172	214	25	4	3	54	8	8	3	8	8
Ross, Mark, Hou	.000	4	0	0	0	0	0	0	0	0	0	0	0	0	0
Royster, Jeron, Atl.	.295	108	261	43	77	100	13	2	2	25	1	5	3	14	6
Ruhle, Vernon, Hou.	.098	31	41	0	4	4	0	0	0	1	0	5	0	0	1
Runge, Paul, Atl	.000	4	2	0	0	0	0	0	0	0	0	0	0	0	0
Russell, William, L.A.	.274	153	497	64	136	169	20	2	3	46	3	8	4	10	2
Ruthven, Richard, Phila	.109	33	64	2	7	10	1	1	0	5	0	12	1	0	1
Ryan, L. Nolan, Hou	.120	35	83	5	10	10	0	0	0	3	0	6	0	0	0
Salazar, Luis, S.D.	.242	145	524	55	127	176	15	5	8	62	5	5	5	32	9
Sambito, Joseph, Hou.*	.000	10	1	0	0	0	0	0	0	0	0	0	0	0	0
Sanchez, Alejandro, Phila	.286	7	14	3	4	11	1	0	2	4	0	0	0	0	0
Sanchez, Orlando, St.L.*	.189	26	37	6	7	9	0	1	0	3	1	1	0	0	0
Sandberg, Ryne, Chi	.271	156	635	103	172	236	33	5	7	54	7	7	5	32	12
Sanderson, Scott, Mtl.	.140	32	57	5	8	14	3	0	1	6	0	16	0	0	0
Sarmiento, Manuel, Pitt	.191	35	47	2	9	9	0	0	0	4	1	7	0	0	0
Sax, David, L.A.	.000	2	2	0	0	0	0	0	0	0	0	0	0	0	0
Sax, Stephen, L.A.	.282	150	638	88	180	229	23	7	4	47	1	10	0	49	19
Schatzeder, Daniel, S.F.-Mtl.*	.231	39	13	0	3	3	0	0	0	1	0	0	0	0	0
Scherrer, William, Cin.*	.500	6	2	0	1	1	0	0	0	0	0	1	0	0	0
Schmidt, Michael, Phila	.280	148	514	108	144	281	26	3	35	87	13	0	7	14	7
Scioscia, Michael, L.A.*	.219	129	365	31	80	108	11	1	5	38	4	5	4	2	0
Scott, Anthony, Hou.†	.239	132	460	43	110	135	16	3	1	29	7	3	4	18	4
Scott, Michael, N.Y.	.146	37	48	2	7	11	4	0	0	3	0	0	0	0	0
Scott, Rodney, Mtl.†	.200	14	25	2	5	5	0	0	0	1	0	0	0	5	0
Scurry, Rodney, Pitt.*	.238	76	21	2	5	7	0	1	0	1	0	1	0	0	0
Seaver, G. Thomas, Cin	.176	22	34	3	6	8	2	0	0	0	0	5	0	0	0
Segelke, Herman, Chi	.000	3	0	0	0	0	0	0	0	0	0	0	0	0	0
Shirley, Robert, Cin	.143	41	42	1	6	6	0	0	0	2	0	5	0	0	0
Shirley, Steven, L.A.*	1.000	11	1	0	1	1	0	0	0	0	0	0	0	0	0
Show, Eric, S.D.	.146	47	41	2	6	6	0	0	0	0	0	2	0	0	0
Sinatro, Matthew, Atl	.136	37	81	10	11	16	2	0	1	4	0	2	0	0	1
Sisk, Douglas, N.Y.	.000	8	0	0	0	0	0	0	0	0	0	0	0	0	0
Smith, Bryn, Mtl	.000	47	8	2	0	0	0	0	0	0	0	1	0	0	0
Smith, C. Reginald, S.F.†	.284	106	349	51	99	164	11	0	18	56	10	0	3	7	0
Smith, Christopher, Mtl.†	.000	2	2	0	0	0	0	0	0	0	0	0	0	0	0
Smith, David, Hou	.000	49	2	0	0	0	0	0	0	0	0	0	0	0	0
Smith, James L., Pitt	.238	42	42	5	10	14	2	1	0	4	0	4	1	0	1
Smith, Kenneth, Atl.*	.293	48	41	6	12	13	1	0	0	3	1	0	0	0	0
Smith, Lee, Chi	.063	72	16	2	1	4	0	0	1	1	0	1	0	0	0
Smith, Lonnie, St.L.	.307	156	592	120	182	257	35	8	8	69	9	3	4	68	26
Smith, Osborne, St.L.†	.248	140	488	58	121	153	24	1	2	43	7	4	5	25	5
Solomon, Eddie, Pitt	.133	12	15	0	2	2	0	0	0	1	0	1	0	0	0
Soto, Mario, Cin	.167	37	84	5	14	18	4	0	0	5	0	11	0	0	0
Speier, Chris, Mtl	.257	156	530	41	136	191	26	4	7	60	4	3	4	1	6
Spilman, W. Harry, Hou.*	.279	38	61	7	17	28	2	0	3	11	2	0	0	0	0
Stargell, Wilver, Pitt.*	.233	74	73	6	17	30	4	0	3	17	1	0	2	0	0
Staub, Daniel, N.Y.*	.242	112	219	11	53	71	9	0	3	27	4	1	6	0	0
Stearns, John, N.Y.	.293	98	352	46	103	146	25	3	4	28	2	5	3	17	7
Stein, W. Randolph, Chi.	.000	6	0	0	0	0	0	0	0	0	0	0	0	0	0
Stenhouse, Michael, Mtl.*	.000	1	1	0	0	0	0	0	0	0	0	0	0	0	0
Stewart, David, L.A.	.179	45	39	3	7	8	1	0	0	2	0	5	0	0	0
Stuper, John, St.L.	.119	23	42	1	5	7	0	1	0	0	0	4	0	0	0
Sularz, Guy, S.F.	.228	63	101	15	23	29	3	0	1	7	1	1	0	3	0
Summers, John, S.F.*	.248	70	125	15	31	48	5	0	4	19	2	1	2	0	1
Sutter, H. Bruce, St.L.	.125	70	8	1	1	1	0	0	0	1	0	2	1	0	0
Sutton, Donald, Hou	.162	27	68	3	11	11	0	0	0	1	0	4	0	0	0

Player and Club	Pct.	G.	AB.	R.	H.	TB.	2B.	3B.	HR.	RBI.	GW.	SH.	SF.	SB.	CS.
Swan, Craig, N.Y.	.182	37	44	4	8	12	1	0	1	4	1	3	0	0	0
Sweet, Richard, N.Y.†	.333	3	3	0	1	1	0	0	0	0	0	0	0	0	0
Swisher, Steven, S.D.	.172	26	58	2	10	17	1	0	2	3	1	1	0	0	0
Tabler, Patrick, Chi.	.235	25	85	9	20	31	4	2	1	7	0	0	2	0	0
Taveras, Alejandro, L.A.	.333	11	3	1	1	2	1	0	0	2	0	0	0	0	0
Taveras, Franklin, Mtl.	.161	48	87	9	14	21	5	1	0	4	0	3	1	4	0
Tekulve, Kenton, Pitt.	.071	85	14	0	1	1	0	0	0	0	0	1	0	0	0
Templeton, Garry, S.D.†	.247	141	563	76	139	198	25	8	6	64	8	6	5	27	16
Tenace, F. Gene, St.L.	.258	66	124	18	32	62	9	0	7	18	3	0	1	1	1
Terrell, C. Walter, N.Y.*	.400	3	5	0	2	2	0	0	0	0	0	1	0	0	0
Thomas, Derrel, L.A.†	.265	66	98	13	26	30	2	1	0	2	0	1	0	2	3
Thompson, Jason, Pitt.*	.284	156	550	87	156	281	32	0	31	101	11	0	9	1	0
Thompson, V. Scot, Chi.*	.365	49	74	11	27	34	5	1	0	7	0	0	0	0	1
Thon, Richard, Hou.	.276	136	496	73	137	197	31	10	3	36	2	5	1	37	8
Tidrow, Richard, Chi.	.000	65	6	0	0	0	0	0	0	0	0	0	0	0	0
Tillman, Kerry, N.Y.	.154	12	13	4	2	3	1	0	0	0	0	0	0	1	0
Tingley, Ronald, S.D.	.100	8	20	0	2	2	0	0	0	0	0	1	0	0	0
Tolman, Timothy, Hou.	.192	15	26	4	5	10	2	0	1	3	1	0	0	0	0
Tomlin, David, Mtl.*	.000	1	0	0	0	0	0	0	0	0	0	0	0	0	0
Trevino, Alejandro, Cin	.251	120	355	24	89	108	10	3	1	33	2	5	4	3	1
Trillo, J. Manuel, Phila.	.271	149	549	52	149	175	24	1	0	39	6	9	1	8	10
Tunnell, B. Lee, Pitt.	.000	5	4	0	0	0	0	0	0	0	0	1	0	0	0
Unser, Delbert, Phila.*	.000	19	14	0	0	0	0	0	0	0	0	0	0	0	0
Vail, Michael, Cin	.254	78	189	9	48	72	10	1	4	29	3	0	2	0	0
Valentine, Ellis, N.Y.	.288	111	337	33	97	137	14	1	8	48	5	0	7	1	3
Valenzuela, Fernando, L.A.*	.168	38	95	6	16	19	0	0	1	9	1	10	2	0	0
Van Gorder, David, Cin	.182	51	137	4	25	30	3	1	0	7	0	2	0	1	0
Vargas, Hediberto, Pitt	.375	8	8	1	3	4	1	0	0	3	0	0	1	0	0
Venable, W. McKinley, S.F.*	.224	71	125	17	28	35	2	1	1	7	1	0	0	9	3
Veryzer, Thomas, N.Y.	.333	40	54	6	18	20	2	0	0	4	0	0	1	1	0
Virgil, Osvaldo, Phila	.238	49	101	11	24	39	6	0	3	8	1	0	0	0	1
Vukovich, George, Phila.*	.272	123	335	41	91	131	18	2	6	42	6	1	1	2	9
Walk, Robert, Atl.	.196	32	51	2	10	10	0	0	0	6	0	6	0	0	1
Walker, Duane, Cin.*	.218	86	239	26	52	77	10	0	5	22	1	3	4	9	3
Wallach, Timothy, Mtl	.268	158	596	89	160	281	31	3	28	97	9	5	4	6	4
Waller, E. Tyrone, Chi	.238	17	21	4	5	5	0	0	0	1	0	1	0	0	0
Walling, Dennis, Hou.*	.205	85	146	22	30	39	4	1	1	14	4	0	1	4	2
Walton, Reginald, Pitt	.200	13	15	1	3	4	1	0	0	0	0	0	0	0	0
Washington, Claudell, Atl.*	.266	150	563	94	150	234	24	6	16	80	14	1	6	33	10
Watson, Robert, Atl	.246	57	114	16	28	48	3	1	5	22	1	0	2	1	1
Welch, Robert, L.A.	.141	38	85	5	12	13	1	0	0	3	0	7	0	0	0
Wellman, Brad, S.F.	.250	6	4	1	1	1	0	0	0	0	0	0	0	0	0
Welsh, Christopher, S.D.*	.262	28	42	4	11	14	3	0	0	11	0	5	0	0	1
Whisenton, Larry, Atl.*	.238	84	143	21	34	57	7	2	4	17	2	0	2	2	2
White, Jerome, Mtl.†	.243	69	115	13	28	42	6	1	2	13	3	0	3	3	3
Wiggins, Alan, S.D.†	.256	72	254	40	65	77	3	3	1	15	4	6	0	33	6
Wills, Elliott, Chi.†	.272	128	419	64	114	158	18	4	6	38	4	2	5	35	10
Wilson, William, N.Y.†	.279	159	639	90	178	236	25	9	5	55	5	1	3	58	16
Wise, Richard, S.D.	.000	1	0	0	0	0	0	0	0	0	0	0	0	0	0
Wohlford, James, S.F.	.256	97	250	37	64	84	12	1	2	25	3	2	4	8	3
Woods, Gary, Chi	.269	117	245	28	66	95	15	1	4	30	3	4	0	3	3
Wright, J. Richard, L.A.*	.125	14	8	1	1	2	1	0	0	1	0	0	0	0	0
Yeager, Stephen, L.A.	.245	82	196	13	48	63	5	2	2	18	1	4	1	0	0
Youngblood, Joel, N.Y.-Mtl	.240	120	292	37	70	93	14	0	3	29	5	2	1	2	5
Zachry, Patrick, N.Y.	.079	36	38	3	3	3	0	0	0	0	0	2	0	0	0
Zuvella, Paul, Atl.	.000	2	1	0	0	0	0	0	0	0	0	0	0	0	0

AWARDED FIRST BASE ON INTERFERENCE: Benedict, Atl. 2 (Ashby, Brenly); Rose, Phila. 2 (An. Pena, Bochy); Chambliss, Atl. (Van Gorder); Garber, Atl. (May); Hendrick, St.L. (Benedict); Herr, St.L. (J. Davis); Householder, Cin. (Knicely); Howe, Hou. (Hodges); Perkins, S.D. (Brenly); Ray, Pitts. (T. Kennedy).

PLAYERS WITH TWO OR MORE CLUBS

(Alphabetically Arranged With Player's First Club on Top)

Player and Club	Pct.	G.	AB.	R.	H.	TB.	2B.	3B.	HR.	RBI.	GW.	SH.	SF.	Tot. BB.	Int. BB.	HP.	SO.	SB.	CS.	GI. DP.
Boone, S.D.	.200	10	5	0	1	2	1	0	0	0	0	0	0	0	0	0	0	0	0	0
Boone, Hou.	.000	10	1	0	0	0	0	0	0	0	0	0	0	0	0	0	1	0	0	0
Davis, Phila.	.279	28	68	5	19	30	3	1	2	7	0	0	1	2	0	0	9	1	0	4
Davis, Pitt	.182	39	77	7	14	24	2	1	2	10	1	1	3	5	0	0	9	1	0	1
Diaz, Atl	.000	19	3	0	0	0	0	0	0	0	0	0	0	0	0	0	1	0	0	0
Diaz, N.Y.	.000	4	0	0	0	0	0	0	0	0	0	0	0	0	0	0	0	0	0	0
Gorman, Mtl.	.000	5	0	0	0	0	0	0	0	0	0	0	0	0	0	0	0	0	0	0
Gorman, N.Y.	.000	3	1	0	0	0	0	0	0	0	1	0	0	0	0	0	0	0	0	0
Hausman, N.Y.	.000	21	2	0	0	0	0	0	0	0	0	0	0	0	0	0	1	0	0	0
Hausman, Atl.	.000	3	0	0	0	0	0	0	0	0	0	0	0	0	0	0	0	0	0	0
Johnstone, L.A.	.077	21	13	1	1	2	1	0	0	2	0	0	1	5	1	0	2	0	0	0
Johnstone, Chi	.249	98	269	39	67	112	13	1	10	43	7	1	3	40	8	0	41	0	2	3

Slg. Pct

.416

PLAYERS WITH TWO OR MORE CLUBS—Continued
(Alphabetically Arranged With Player's First Club on Top)

Player and Club	Pct.	G.	AB.	R.	H.	TB.	2B.	3B.	HR.	RBI.	GW.	SH.	SF.	Tot. BB.	Int. BB.	HP.	SO.	SB.	CS.	GI. DP.
McWilliams, Atl	.167	27	6	0	1	1	0	0	0	0	0	1	0	1	0	0	5	0	0	0
McWilliams, Pitt	.188	20	32	1	6	6	0	0	0	0	0	9	0	0	0	0	12	0	0	0
Milner, Mtl	.107	26	28	1	3	3	0	0	0	2	0	1	0	4	0	0	2	0	0	1
Milner, Pitt	.240	33	25	5	6	14	2	0	2	8	0	0	0	6	1	1	3	1	0	0
Molinaro, Chi	.197	65	66	6	13	17	1	0	1	12	1	0	0	6	1	0	5	1	1	0
Molinaro, Phila	.286	19	14	0	4	4	0	0	0	2	0	0	0	3	1	0	1	1	0	0
Montanez, Pitt	.281	36	32	4	9	10	1	0	0	1	0	0	0	3	3	0	3	0	0	2
Montanez, Phila	.063	18	16	0	1	1	0	0	0	1	0	0	0	1	0	0	3	0	0	0
Pittman, Hou.	.200	15	10	0	2	3	1	0	0	0	0	1	0	0	0	0	2	0	0	0
Pittman, S.D.	.254	55	118	16	30	32	2	0	0	7	1	2	0	9	2	0	13	8	3	3
Robinson, Pitt	.239	31	71	8	17	32	3	0	4	12	0	0	1	5	3	0	19	0	1	3
Robinson, Phila	.261	35	69	6	18	33	6	0	3	19	3	0	2	7	1	0	15	1	1	2
Schatzeder, S.F.	.125	13	8	0	1	1	0	0	0	1	0	0	0	0	0	0	4	0	0	0
Schatzeder, Mtl	.400	26	5	0	2	2	0	0	0	0	0	0	0	1	0	0	2	0	0	0
Youngblood, N.Y.	.257	80	202	21	52	73	12	0	3	21	2	1	0	8	1	5	37	0	4	4
Youngblood, Mtl.	.200	40	90	16	18	20	2	0	0	8	3	1	1	9	1	3	21	2	1	2

OFFICIAL MISCELLANEOUS NATIONAL LEAGUE BATTING RECORDS

CLUB MISCELLANEOUS BATTING RECORDS

Club	Slg. Pct.	G.	Tot. BB.	Int. BB.	HP.	SO.	GIDP.	ShO.
Pittsburgh	.408	162	447	72	28	862	116	3
Montreal	.396	162	503	72	35	816	107	11
Los Angeles	.388	162	528	83	30	804	98	6
Atlanta	.383	162	554	64	29	869	102	10
San Francisco	.376	162	607	70	17	915	131	11
Philadelphia	.376	162	506	66	24	831	134	15
Chicago	.375	162	460	62	25	869	97	8
St. Louis	.364	162	569	66	30	805	110	6
San Diego	.359	162	429	78	22	877	96	11
New York	.350	162	456	49	25	1005	112	9
Cincinnati	.350	162	470	50	21	817	143	12
Houston	.349	162	435	67	19	830	104	15
Totals	.373	972	5964	799	305	10300	1350	117

INDIVIDUAL MISCELLANEOUS BATTING RECORDS
(Top Fifteen Qualifiers for Slugging Championship)

Player—Club	Slg. Pct.	Tot. BB.	Int. BB.	HP.	SO.	GI DP.
Schmidt, Phila.	.547	107	17	7	131	11
Guerrero, L.A.	.536	65	16	5	89	7
Durham, Chi.	.521	66	14	2	77	11
Oliver, Mtl.	.514	61	15	4	59	11
Thompson, Pitt.	.511	101	7	2	107	11
Carter, Mtl.	.510	78	11	6	64	16
Murphy, Atl.	.507	93	9	3	134	10
Horner, Atl.	.501	66	3	4	75	13
Dawson, Mtl.	.498	34	4	8	96	8
Madlock, Pitt.	.488	48	16	4	39	12
Kennedy, S.D.	.486	26	9	5	91	7
Clark, S.F.	.481	90	7	1	91	20
Lezcano, S.D.	.472	78	10	2	69	11
Wallach, Mtl.	.471	36	4	4	80	15
Baker, L.A.	.458	56	5	3	62	7

DEPARTMENTAL LEADERS: Tot. BB—Schmidt, 107; Int. BB—K. Hernandez, 19; HP—L.Smith, 9; SO—Kingman, 156; GIDP—Matthews, 23.

(All Players—Listed Alphabetically)

Player—Club	Slg. Pct.	Tot. BB.	Int. BB.	HP.	SO.	GI DP.
Aguayo, Phila.	.518	5	1	1	7	1
Allen, N.Y.	.167	2	0	0	2	0
Altamirano, Phila.	.250	0	0	0	0	0
Alvarez, Atl.	.000	0	0	0	0	0
Andujar, St. L.	.189	0	0	0	44	2
Ashby, Hou.	.416	27	4	1	53	7
Backman, N.Y.	.372	49	1	0	47	6
Bahnsen, Phila.	.000	0	0	0	0	0
Bailor, N.Y.	.319	20	0	2	17	5
Bair, St. L.	.077	0	0	0	3	0
Baker, L.A.	.458	56	5	3	62	7
Baller, Phila.	.000	0	0	1	0	0
Barr, S.F.	.281	0	0	0	6	0
Barranca, Cin.	.392	2	0	0	9	1
Barrios, S.F.	.158	1	0	0	4	1
Bass, Hou.	.042	0	0	0	8	1
Bass, S.D.	.300	2	0	1	4	0
Baumgarten, Pitt.	.083	0	0	0	4	0
Beckwith, L.A.	.000	0	0	0	0	0
Bedrosian, Atl.	.038	1	0	0	6	0
Belanger, L.A.	.260	5	1	0	10	2
Belliard, Pitt.	.500	0	0	0	0	0
Bench, Cin.	.396	37	2	0	58	14
Benedict, Atl.	.303	37	9	3	40	10
Benton, Chi.	.143	0	0	0	1	0
Berenyi, Cin.	.306	0	0	0	16	0
Bergman, S.F.	.413	18	3	0	11	1
Berra, Pitt.	.386	33	12	4	83	15
Bevacqua, S.D.	.325	17	4	0	22	5
Biittner, Cin.	.413	17	2	2	16	9
Bird, Chi.	.161	0	0	0	20	1
Blackwell, Mtl.	.286	3	0	0	11	1
Bochy, N.Y.	.510	4	0	0	6	1
Boggs, Atl.	.235	0	0	0	4	0
Bonilla, S.D.	.335	11	0	1	15	2
Boone, S.D.-Hou.	.333	0	0	0	0	0
Bowa, Chi.	.305	39	5	1	38	10
Bradley, L.A.	.333	0	0	0	0	0
Braun, St. L.	.339	11	0	0	10	2

Player—Club	Slg. Pct.	Tot. BB.	Int. BB.	HP.	SO.	GI DP.
Breining, S.F.	.207	4	0	0	14	0
Brenly, S.F.	.383	18	4	1	26	2
Briggs, Chi.	.125	0	0	1	9	1
Brock, L.A.	.176	1	1	0	5	0
Brooks, N.Y.	.317	28	5	5	76	11
Brummer, St. L.	.297	0	0	0	12	0
Brusstar, Phila.	.000	0	0	0	2	0
Buckner, Chi.	.441	36	7	5	26	14
Burris, Mtl.	.214	3	0	0	10	0
Butler, Atl.	.225	25	0	0	35	1
Bystrom, Phila.	.167	1	0	0	12	0
Camp, Atl.	.049	2	0	0	23	0
Campbell, Chi.	.143	0	0	0	3	0
Candelaria, Pitt.	.259	6	0	0	20	1
Cappuzzello, Hou.	.000	0	0	0	0	0
Carlton, Phila.	.317	0	0	0	13	1
Carter, Mtl.	.510	78	11	6	64	16
Cedeno, Cin.	.413	41	2	4	41	15
Cey, L.A.	.428	57	6	4	99	16
Chambliss, Atl.	.436	57	13	0	57	11
Chiffer, S.D.	.000	0	0	0	2	0
Chris, S.F.	.143	0	0	0	3	0
Christenson, Phila.	.149	2	0	0	36	1
Clark, S.F.	.481	90	7	1	91	20
Concepcion, Cin.	.371	45	4	0	61	20
Cowley, Atl.	.200	0	0	0	4	0
Cox, Chi.	.000	2	1	0	1	0
Cromartie, Mtl.	.398	69	15	3	60	10
Crow, L.A.	.000	0	0	0	3	0
Cruz, Chi.	.263	2	0	0	4	1
Cruz, Hou.	.377	60	12	1	67	11
Curtis, S.D.	.351	0	0	0	15	0
Davis, S.F.	.410	45	2	2	115	13
Davis, Chi.	.404	36	4	1	92	6
Davis, Phila.-Pitt.	.372	7	0	0	18	5
Dawson, Mtl.	.498	34	4	8	96	8
Dayley, Atl.	.250	2	0	0	9	0
DeJesus, Phila.	.313	54	9	2	70	8
DeLeon, S.D.	.182	1	0	0	7	0
Dempsey, S.F.	.000	0	0	0	0	0
Denny, Phila.	.167	2	0	0	2	0
Dernier, Phila.	.319	36	0	1	69	6
Diaz, Phila.	.450	36	5	3	87	20
Diaz, Atl.-N.Y.	.000	0	0	0	1	0
DiPino, Hou.	.000	0	0	0	4	0
Doran, Hou.	.309	4	0	0	11	0
Dravecky, S.D.	.130	1	0	0	3	0
Driessen, Cin.	.421	82	8	2	62	8
Durham, Chi.	.521	66	14	2	77	11
Easler, Pitt.	.436	40	12	6	85	11
Edelen, Cin.	.500	0	0	0	0	0
Edwards, S.D.	.273	1	0	0	14	2
Eichelberger, S.D.	.145	1	0	0	22	2
Evans, S.F.	.419	77	7	2	64	8
Falcone, N.Y.	.132	0	0	0	24	1
Farmer, Phila.	.000	0	0	0	6	0
Filer, Chi.	.167	0	0	0	7	0
Flannery, S.D.	.330	30	10	2	32	4
Fletcher, Chi.	.167	4	0	0	5	0
Flynn, Mtl.	.295	4	0	0	23	6
Forsch, St. L.	.274	3	0	0	20	1
Forster, L.A.	.000	0	0	0	0	0
Foster, N.Y.	.367	50	9	2	123	13
Fowlkes, S.F.	.115	1	0	0	10	0
Franco, Phila.	.310	2	1	0	4	1
Francona, Mtl.	.344	8	0	0	11	2
Frobel, Pitt.	.441	1	0	0	11	0
Fryman, Mtl.	.222	0	0	0	1	0
Gaff, N.Y.	.000	2	0	0	3	0
Gale, S.F.	.208	5	0	0	34	0
Garber, Atl.	.133	2	0	0	6	0
Garcia, Hou.	.316	3	1	0	15	2
Gardenhire, N.Y.	.313	23	2	0	55	11
Garner, Hou.	.423	40	4	3	92	11
Garrelts, S.F.	.000	0	0	0	0	0
Garvey, L.A.	.418	20	10	1	86	10
Gates, Mtl.	.298	9	0	0	19	1
Giles, N.Y.	.312	12	1	0	29	0
Goltz, L.A.	.000	0	0	0	0	0

Player—Club	Slg. Pct.	Tot. BB.	Int. BB.	HP.	SO.	GI DP.
Gonzalez, St. L.	.356	1	0	1	24	2
Gorman, Mtl.-N.Y.	.000	0	0	0	0	0
Green, St. L.	.373	8	2	1	29	2
Griffin, S.D.	.000	0	0	0	1	0
Griffin, Pitt.	.222	0	0	0	3	0
Gross, Phila.	.328	19	3	0	8	6
Guante, Pitt.	.000	0	0	0	3	0
Guerrero, L.A.	.536	65	16	5	89	7
Gulden, Mtl.	.000	1	0	0	1	0
Gullickson, Mtl.	.159	1	0	0	22	2
Gwosdz, S.D.	.176	2	1	0	7	0
Gwynn, S.D.	.389	14	0	0	16	5
Hall, Atl.	.000	0	0	0	0	0
Hall, Chi.	.350	5	1	2	17	0
Hammaker, S.F.	.068	0	0	1	15	3
Hanna, Atl.	.600	0	0	0	0	0
Harper, Pitt.	.517	1	1	0	4	1
Harper, Atl.	.347	14	0	1	28	3
Harris, Cin.	.167	1	0	0	9	0
Hausman, N.Y.-Atl.	.000	0	0	0	1	0
Hawkins, S.D.	.000	0	0	0	8	0
Hayes, Cin.	.000	0	0	0	3	0
Hebner, Pitt.	.414	5	0	0	3	1
Heep, Hou.	.379	21	3	1	31	5
Henderson, Chi.	.335	22	3	0	64	4
Hendrick, St. L.	.450	37	8	1	80	13
Hernandez, Chi.	.000	1	0	0	3	0
Hernandez, St. L.	.413	100	19	2	67	10
Herr, St. L.	.320	57	2	2	56	5
Hinshaw, S.D.	.267	3	1	0	5	0
Hodges, N.Y.	.373	41	6	0	40	5
Holland, S.F.	.059	0	0	0	15	1
Holman, N.Y.	.222	0	0	0	3	1
Hooton, L.A.	.200	0	0	0	5	0
Horner, Atl.	.501	66	3	4	75	13
Householder, Cin.	.326	30	5	2	77	6
Howard, N.Y.	.256	6	0	1	7	0
Howe, Hou.	.326	41	15	1	45	10
Howe, L.A.	.000	0	0	0	3	0
Hrabosky, Atl.	.333	0	0	0	1	0
Hubbard, Atl.	.350	59	5	3	62	5
Hume, Cin.	.000	0	0	0	2	0
Hurdle, Cin.	.235	2	2	1	6	1
Iorg, St. L.	.361	23	3	0	23	11
Ivie, Hou.	.333	1	0	0	0	0
Jackson, Pitt.	.000	0	0	0	0	0
James, Mtl.	.000	0	0	0	0	0
Jenkins, Chi.	.179	0	0	0	23	0
Johnson, Atl.	.348	6	1	2	4	1
R. Johnson, Mtl.	.281	1	0	0	6	0
W. Johnson, Mtl.	.263	5	0	0	5	0
Johnstone, L.A.-Chi.	.404	45	9	0	43	3
Jones, N.Y.	.148	3	0	0	10	0
Jones, S.D.	.425	62	11	1	90	4
Jorgensen, N.Y.	.360	21	3	0	24	2
Kaat, St. L.	.000	1	0	0	4	0
Keener, St. L.	.000	0	0	0	0	0
Kennedy, Chi.	.264	21	1	0	34	9
Kennedy, S.D.	.486	26	9	5	91	7
Kern, Chi.	.000	1	0	0	5	0
Kingman, N.Y.	.432	59	9	4	156	11
Knepper, Hou.	.077	4	0	0	25	0
Knicely, Hou.	.248	14	3	1	30	4
Knight, Hou.	.402	48	9	5	58	16
Kravec, Chi.	.000	1	0	0	1	0
Krenchicki, Cin.	.358	13	1	0	23	3
Krukow, Phil.	.194	0	0	0	19	0
Kuiper, S.F.	.330	32	0	2	24	8
LaCorte, Hou.	.000	0	0	0	3	0
LaCoss, Hou.	.292	1	0	0	8	0
Lacy, Pitt.	.415	32	4	1	57	7
Lahti, St. L.	.077	0	0	0	8	0
Lancellotti, S.D.	.231	2	0	0	8	0
Landestoy, Cin.	.243	8	1	1	14	6
Landreaux, L.A.	.410	39	2	4	54	7
Landrum, St. L.	.403	8	0	1	18	1
Lansford, S.D.	.182	6	0	0	4	0
LaPoint, St. L.	.053	1	0	0	18	1
Larson, Chi.	.273	0	0	0	2	0

Player—Club	Slg. Pct.	Tot. BB.	Int. BB.	HP.	SO.	GI DP.
Laskey, S.F.	.129	2	0	0	34	1
Lavelle, S.F.	.231	0	0	0	4	0
Lawless, Cin.	.248	9	0	0	30	5
Lea, Mtl.	.138	5	0	0	22	4
Leach, N.Y.	.125	0	0	0	5	0
Lee, Mtl.	.000	0	0	0	0	0
Lefebvre, S.D.	.326	18	2	1	50	3
Leibrandt, Cin.	.080	1	0	0	13	1
LeMaster, S.F.	.266	31	10	0	78	14
Leonard, S.F.	.421	19	2	2	65	11
Lerch, Mtl.	.250	0	0	0	2	0
Lesley, Cin.	.000	0	0	0	0	0
Lezcano, S.D.	.472	78	10	2	69	11
Linares, Atl.	.377	7	0	1	29	10
Littell, St. L.	.000	0	0	0	2	0
Little, Mtl.	.214	4	0	0	6	1
Lollar, S.D.	.388	5	0	0	26	2
Loucks, Hou.	.265	3	0	0	17	1
Lucas, S.D.	.000	1	0	0	8	0
Lyle, Phila.	.500	1	0	0	1	0
Lynch, N.Y.	.000	1	0	0	18	0
Maddox, Phila.	.417	12	0	0	32	12
Madlock, Pitt.	.488	48	16	4	39	12
Mahler, Atl.	.241	4	0	0	17	0
Maldonado, L.A.	.000	1	1	0	2	0
Mankowski, N.Y.	.257	1	0	0	6	2
Manuel, S.D.	.600	1	0	0	0	0
Marshall, L.A.	.432	13	1	1	23	1
Martin, S.F.	.327	0	0	0	13	0
Martin, St. L.	.091	1	0	0	3	0
Martz, Chi.	.190	6	0	0	17	1
Matthews, Phila.	.427	66	1	2	87	23
Matuszek, Phila.	.103	1	0	1	10	3
May, S.F.	.380	28	8	0	38	4
McGaffigan, S.F.	.000	0	0	0	1	0
McGee, St.L.	.391	12	2	2	58	9
McGraw, Phila.	.000	0	0	0	0	0
McWilliams, Atl.-Pitt.	.184	1	0	0	17	0
Mills, Mtl.	.313	5	0	0	11	3
Milner, Cin.	.378	41	1	2	40	7
Milner, Mtl.-Pitt.	.321	10	1	1	5	1
Minton, S.F.	.235	0	0	0	7	0
Moffitt, Hou.	.000	0	0	0	0	0
Molinaro, Chi.-Phila.	.263	9	2	0	6	0
Monday, L.A.	.481	39	6	1	51	3
Monge, Phila.	.111	1	0	0	5	0
Montanez, Pitt.-Phila.	.229	4	3	0	6	2
Montefusco, S.D.	.103	4	0	0	30	1
Moore, Atl.	.000	0	0	0	1	0
Morales, L.A.	.433	4	0	0	8	1
Morales, Chi.	.440	9	1	0	7	5
Moreland, Chi.	.399	46	8	3	71	9
Moreno, Pitt.	.315	44	2	1	121	6
Morgan, S.F.	.438	85	4	2	60	3
Morrison, Pitt.	.488	5	0	0	14	4
Moskau, Pitt.	.091	0	0	0	2	1
Mota, L.A.	.000	0	0	0	0	0
Mura, St.L.	.057	1	0	1	10	1
Murphy, Atl.	.507	93	9	3	134	10
Nicosia, Pitt.	.340	11	4	0	13	1
Niedenfuer, L.A.	.000	1	0	0	0	0
Niekro, Hou.	.112	1	0	0	30	1
Niekro, Atl.	.276	0	0	0	16	4
Niemann, Pitt.	1.000	0	0	0	0	0
Noles, Chi.	.161	1	0	0	35	1
Nordhagen, Pitt.	.500	0	0	0	1	0
Norman, Mtl.	.348	7	0	0	20	0
Norman, Pitt.	.000	0	0	0	0	0
Oberkfell, St.L.	.370	40	6	1	31	11
O'Berry, Cin.	.267	10	0	0	13	1
Oester, Cin.	.359	35	8	0	82	16
Office, Mtl.	.667	0	0	0	1	0
Oliver, Mtl.	.514	61	15	4	59	11
O'Malley, S.F.	.364	33	9	1	39	11
Orosco, N.Y.	.143	0	0	0	4	1
Orta, L.A.	.313	12	3	1	13	1
Ortiz, Pitt.	.267	1	0	0	3	1
Owen, Atl.	.667	0	0	0	1	0
Ownbey, N.Y.	.200	2	0	0	4	0
Palmer, Mtl.	.042	0	0	0	7	0
Paris, St.L.	.103	0	0	0	7	1
Parker, Pitt.	.447	22	2	1	45	7
Pastore, Cin.	.259	1	0	0	17	0
Pena, L.A.	.000	0	0	0	0	0
Pena, Pitt.	.435	17	3	4	57	17
Perez, Atl.	.278	3	0	0	6	0
Perkins, S.D.	.340	26	10	3	20	6
Pettini, S.F.	.231	3	0	0	4	1
Phelps, Mtl.	.250	0	0	1	3	0
Phillips, Mtl.	.125	0	0	0	3	0
Pittman, Hou.-S.D.	.273	9	2	0	15	3
Pladson, Hou.	.000	0	0	0	0	0
Pocoroba, Atl.	.383	13	2	1	12	2
Porter, St.L.	.402	66	6	2	66	8
Porter, Atl.	.111	1	0	0	9	0
Power, L.A.	.000	0	0	0	5	0
Price, Cin.	.333	0	0	0	1	0
Proly, Chi.	.357	0	0	0	1	0
Pruitt, S.F.	.750	1	1	0	1	0
Puhl, Hou.	.379	51	2	2	49	6
Pujols, Hou.	.324	10	2	0	40	4
Puleo, N.Y.	.125	2	0	0	18	0
Rabb, S.F.	1.500	0	0	0	1	0
Raines, Mtl.	.369	75	9	2	83	6
Rajsich, N.Y.	.383	17	3	1	40	2
Ramirez, S.D.	.217	2	0	0	4	0
Ramirez, Atl.	.379	36	7	3	49	10
Ramsey, St.L.	.289	22	3	1	34	7
Ransom, S.F.	.159	6	0	0	7	3
Rasmussen, St.L.	.000	1	0	0	1	0
Ray, Pitt.	.382	36	1	1	34	8
Ray, Hou.	.167	0	0	0	4	0
Reardon, Mtl.	.200	0	0	0	8	0
Redus, Cin.	.337	5	0	0	21	0
J. Reed, Phila.	.000	0	0	0	0	0
R. Reed, Phila.	.417	2	0	0	4	0
Reitz, Pitt.	.000	0	0	1	4	0
Reuss, L.A.	.260	2	0	0	28	4
Reynolds, Hou.	.347	11	3	1	9	1
Reynolds, N.Y.	.000	1	0	0	1	0
Rhoden, Pitt.	.446	3	0	0	8	3
Richards, S.D.	.359	36	1	2	52	5
Rincon, St.L.	.100	1	0	0	6	0
Ripley, Chi.	.132	0	0	0	10	1
Roberge, Hou.	.000	0	0	0	1	0
Roberts, Phila.	.212	2	0	0	8	0
D. Robinson, Pitt.	.412	3	0	1	22	2
W. Robinson, Pitt.-Phila.	.464	12	4	0	34	5
Roenicke, L.A.	.336	21	3	2	32	2
Rogers, Mtl.	.141	11	0	0	32	0
Romo, Pitt.	.500	0	0	0	2	0
Romo, L.A.	.200	0	0	0	1	0
Roof, St.L.	.267	1	0	0	4	1
Rose, Phila.	.338	66	9	7	32	12
Ross, Hou.	.000	0	0	0	0	0
Royster, Atl.	.383	22	1	2	36	3
Ruhle, Hou.	.098	4	0	1	27	0
Runge, Atl.	.000	0	0	0	0	0
Russell, L.A.	.340	63	11	4	30	14
Ruthven, Phila.	.156	0	0	0	26	1
Ryan, Hou.	.120	5	0	0	37	1
Salazar, S.D.	.336	23	10	2	80	10
Sambito, Hou.	.000	0	0	0	1	0
Sanchez, Phila.	.786	0	0	0	4	0
Sanchez, St.L.	.243	5	0	0	5	0
Sandberg, Chi.	.372	36	3	4	90	7
Sanderson, Mtl.	.246	2	0	1	20	1
Sarmiento, Pitt.	.191	3	0	0	13	0
D. Sax, L.A.	.000	0	0	0	0	0
S. Sax, L.A.	.359	49	1	2	53	10
Schatzeder, S.F.-Mtl.	.231	1	0	0	6	0
Scherrer, Cin.	.500	1	0	0	0	0
Schmidt, Phila.	.547	107	17	3	131	11
Scioscia, L.A.	.296	44	11	1	31	8
Scott, Hou.	.293	15	4	1	56	11
Scott, N.Y.	.229	2	0	0	21	0
Scott, Mtl.	.200	3	0	0	2	0
Scurry, Pitt.	.333	0	0	0	8	0

Player—Club	Slg. Pct.	Tot. BB.	Int. BB.	HP.	SO.	GI DP.	Player—Club	Slg. Pct.	Tot. BB.	Int. BB.	HP.	SO.	GI DP.
Seaver, Cin.	.235	2	0	0	16	2	Thon, Hou.	.397	37	2	1	48	4
Segelke, Chi.	.000	0	0	0	0	0	Tidrow, Chi.	.000	0	0	0	3	0
Shirley, Cin.	.143	1	0	0	13	0	Tillman, N.Y.	.231	0	0	0	4	0
Shirley, L.A.	1.000	0	0	0	0	0	Tingley, S.D.	.100	0	0	0	7	0
Show, S.D.	.146	0	0	0	14	0	Tolman, Hou.	.385	4	0	0	3	1
Sinatro, Atl.	.198	4	0	0	9	3	Tomlin, Mtl.	.000	0	0	0	0	0
Sisk, N.Y.	.000	0	0	0	0	0	Trevino, Cin.	.304	34	11	3	34	16
B. Smith, Mtl	.000	2	0	0	1	0	Trillo, Phila.	.319	33	3	3	53	14
Smith, S.F.	.470	46	9	0	46	9	Tunnell, Pitt.	.000	0	0	0	3	0
C. Smith, Mtl.	.000	0	0	0	1	0	Unser, Phila.	.000	3	1	0	2	1
Smith, Hou.	.000	0	0	0	2	0	Vail, Cin.	.381	6	1	0	33	7
Smith, Pitt.	.333	5	0	0	7	0	Valentine, N.Y.	.407	5	0	1	38	11
Smith, Atl.	.317	6	0	0	13	0	Valenzuela, L.A.	.200	3	0	0	16	0
Smith, Chi.	.250	1	0	0	9	0	Van Gorder, Cin.	.219	14	2	1	19	4
L. Smith, St.L.	.434	64	2	9	74	11	Vargas, Pitt.	.500	0	0	0	2	0
O. Smith, St.L.	.314	68	12	2	32	10	Venable, S.F.	.280	7	0	0	16	2
Solomon, Pitt.	.133	0	0	0	7	0	Veryzer, N.Y.	.370	3	2	0	4	1
Soto, Cin.	.214	4	0	1	25	0	Virgil, Phila.	.386	10	0	0	26	3
Speier, Mtl.	.360	47	12	1	67	13	Vukovich, Phila.	.391	32	14	0	47	4
Spilman, Hou.	.459	5	0	0	10	1	Walk, Atl.	.196	6	0	0	17	0
Stargell, Pitt.	.411	10	1	0	24	1	Walker, Cin.	.322	27	0	2	58	1
Staub, N.Y.	.324	24	1	0	10	10	Wallach, Mtl.	.471	36	4	4	81	15
Stearns, N.Y.	.415	30	2	2	35	8	Waller, Chi.	.238	2	0	0	5	0
Stein, Chi.	.000	0	0	0	0	0	Walling, Hou.	.267	23	3	0	19	6
Stenhouse, Mtl.	.000	0	0	0	1	0	Walton, Pitt.	.267	1	0	1	1	0
Stewart, L.A.	.205	2	0	0	14	0	Washington, Atl.	.416	50	9	6	107	9
Stuper, St. L.	.167	1	0	0	24	0	Watson, Atl.	.421	14	2	0	20	4
Sularz, S.F.	.287	9	0	0	11	2	Welch, L.A.	.153	3	0	0	32	0
Summers, S.F.	.384	16	0	3	17	4	Wellman, S.F.	.250	0	0	0	1	0
Sutter, St.L.	.125	0	0	0	1	0	Welsh, S.D.	.333	3	0	0	13	1
Sutton, Hou.	.162	2	0	0	25	0	Whisenton, Atl.	.399	23	3	0	33	3
Swan, N.Y.	.273	7	0	0	15	1	White, Mtl.	.365	8	1	2	26	2
Sweet, N.Y.	.333	0	0	0	1	0	Wiggins, S.D.	.303	13	0	1	19	4
Swisher, S.D.	.293	5	0	0	24	0	Wills, Chi.	.377	46	3	5	76	4
Tabler, Chi.	.365	6	0	1	20	3	Wilson, N.Y.	.369	32	4	2	102	5
Taveras, L.A.	.667	0	0	0	1	0	Wise, S.D.	.000	0	0	0	0	0
Taveras, Mtl.	.241	7	0	0	6	2	Wohlford, S.F.	.336	30	4	0	36	9
Tekulve, Pitt.	.071	0	0	0	6	0	Woods, Chi.	.388	21	2	0	48	4
Templeton, S.D.	.352	26	7	1	82	19	Wright, L.A.	.250	0	0	0	2	0
Tenace, St.L.	.500	36	1	4	31	1	Yeager, L.A.	.321	13	3	1	28	3
Terrell, N.Y.	.400	0	0	0	2	0	Youngblood, N.Y.-Mtl.	.318	17	2	8	58	6
Thomas, L.A.	.306	10	1	0	12	2	Zachry, N.Y.	.079	1	0	0	17	0
Thompson, Pitt.	.511	101	7	2	107	11	Zuvella, Atl.	.000	0	0	0	0	0
Thompson, Chi.	.459	5	0	0	4	2							

OFFICIAL NATIONAL LEAGUE FIELDING AVERAGES

CLUB FIELDING

Club	Pct.	G.	PO.	A.	E.	TC.	DP.	TP.	PB.
St. Louis	.981	162	4396	2038	124	6558	169	0	14
Philadelphia	.981	162	4369	1821	121	6311	138	0	11
Montreal	.980	162	4382	1630	122	6134	117	0	8
Cincinnati	.980	162	4381	1763	128	6272	158	0	12
Chicago	.979	162	4342	1909	132	6383	110	0	13
Los Angeles	.979	162	4465	1946	139	6550	131	0	16
Atlanta	.979	162	4389	1922	137	6448	186	0	13
Houston	.978	162	4340	1827	136	6303	154	0	32
Pittsburgh	.977	162	4400	1858	145	6403	133	1	12
San Diego	.976	162	4428	1826	152	6406	142	0	11
San Francisco	.973	162	4396	1909	173	6478	125	0	7
New York	.972	162	4342	1836	175	6353	134	2	6
Totals	.978	972	52630	22285	1684	76599	1697	3	155

INDIVIDUAL FIELDING

*Throws lefthanded.

FIRST BASEMEN

Leader—Club	Pct.	G.	PO.	A.	E.	DP.
DRIESSEN, Cin.	.998	144	1239	78	3	123

(Listed Alphabetically)

Player—Club	Pct.	G.	PO.	A.	E.	DP.
Barrios, S.F.	1.000	7	47	0	0	4
Bass, S.D.	1.000	9	70	4	0	8
Bench, Cin.	1.000	8	53	4	0	7
Bergman, S.F.*	.991	69	308	20	3	18
Bevacqua, S.D.	.989	30	253	16	3	13
Biittner, Cin.*	.993	15	128	12	1	13
Bochy, N.Y.	1.000	1	2	0	0	0
Briggs, Chi.*	1.000	4	9	0	0	1
Brock, L.A.	1.000	3	9	0	0	0
Buckner, Chi.*	.993	161	1547	159	12	89
Cedeno, Cin.	1.000	1	0	1	0	0
Chambliss, Atl.	.993	151	1352	138	10	144
Concepcion, Cin.	1.000	1	9	0	0	1
Cromartie, Mtl.*	1.000	9	33	3	0	2
Driessen, Cin.	.998	144	1239	78	3	123
Durham, Chi.*	1.000	1	10	1	0	0
Edwards, S.D.	.000	1	0	0	0	0
Evans, S.F.	.993	49	396	49	3	31
Francona, Mtl.*	1.000	16	21	0	0	2
Garvey, L.A.	.995	158	1539	111	8	102
Hebner, Pitt.	1.000	4	27	1	0	1
Heep, Hou.*	.993	16	130	4	1	9
Hernandez, St. L.*	.994	158	1586	135	11	140
Howe, Hou.	.997	35	291	21	1	34
Iorg, St. L.	1.000	10	77	5	0	6
Jorgensen, N.Y.*	.991	56	106	5	1	14
Kennedy, S.D.	.984	12	111	10	2	7
Kingman, N.Y.	.986	143	1232	69	18	88
Knight, Hou.	.990	96	945	55	10	76
Lancellotti, S.D.*	1.000	7	59	2	0	7
Lansford, S.D.	.986	9	69	3	1	9
Leonard, S.F.	.400	1	2	0	3	0

Player—Club	Pct.	G.	PO.	A.	E.	DP.
Madlock, Pitt.	1.000	3	22	1	0	2
Marshall, L.A.	.981	13	100	5	2	6
Matuszek, Phila.	1.000	3	11	0	0	1
Milner, Mtl.-Pitt.*	1.000	6	24	2	0	5
Monday, L.A.*	1.000	4	24	3	0	2
Montanez, Pitt.-Phila.*	1.000	8	9	3	0	1
Oliver, Mtl.*	.986	159	1286	92	19	96
Perkins, S.D.*	.994	98	817	64	5	61
Porter, Atl.*	1.000	1	3	0	0	1
Rajsich, N.Y.*	1.000	2	10	1	0	1
Richards, S.D.*	.975	25	223	12	6	17
W. Robinson, Phila.	1.000	5	9	1	0	5
Rose, Phila.	.995	162	1428	123	8	114
Smith, S.F.	.982	99	792	78	16	61
Smith, Atl.	1.000	6	15	1	0	0
Spilman, Hou.	.989	11	86	5	1	5
Stargell, Pitt.*	1.000	8	43	3	0	2
Staub, N.Y.	1.000	18	129	15	0	12
Summers, S.F.	1.000	3	6	1	0	0
Tenace, St. L.	1.000	7	39	3	0	4
Thompson, Pitt.*	.993	155	1395	105	10	114
Thompson, Chi.*	1.000	4	3	1	0	0
Tolman, Hou.	1.000	1	10	1	0	2
Unser, Phila.*	1.000	5	9	1	0	1
Vargas, Pitt.	1.000	5	16	1	0	1
Wallach, Mtl.	.000	1	0	0	0	0
Walling, Hou.	.993	20	129	8	1	8
Watson, Atl.	1.000	27	206	8	0	18

TRIPLE PLAYS: Kingman, Staub, N.Y.; Thompson, Pitt.

FIRST BASEMEN WITH TWO OR MORE CLUBS

Player—Club	Pct.	G.	PO.	A.	E.	DP.
Milner, Mtl.*	1.000	5	23	2	0	4
Milner, Pitt.*	1.000	1	1	0	0	1
Montanez, Pitt.*	1.000	2	5	1	0	1
Montanez, Phila.*	1.000	6	4	2	0	0

SECOND BASEMEN

Leader—Club	Pct.	G.	PO.	A.	E.	DP.
TRILLO, Phila.	.994	149	343	441	5	101

(Listed Alphabetically)

Player—Club	Pct.	G.	PO.	A.	E.	DP.
Aguayo, Phila.	.966	21	21	36	2	3
Backman, N.Y.	.964	88	169	202	14	30
Bailor, N.Y.	.982	56	86	129	4	23
Barranca, Cin.	.824	6	5	9	3	1
Belanger, L.A.	1.000	1	0	1	0	0
Bonilla, S.D.	.975	45	99	134	6	26
Doran, Hou.	.975	26	41	78	3	17
Flannery, S.D.	.974	104	221	260	13	46
Flynn, Mtl.	.983	58	135	157	5	40
Garcia, Hou.	1.000	1	0	2	0	0
Gardenhire, N.Y.	1.000	1	1	1	0	0
Garner, Hou.	.980	136	273	429	14	90

Player—Club	Pct.	G.	PO.	A.	E.	DP.
Gates, Mtl.	1.000	36	53	91	0	18
Giles, N.Y.	.992	45	121	129	2	27
Gonzalez, St. L.	1.000	9	10	13	0	4
Herr, St. L.	.987	128	263	427	9	97
Howard, N.Y.	1.000	3	5	4	0	1
Hubbard, Atl.	.983	144	312	505	14	111
Johnson, Atl.	.955	13	20	44	3	7
W. Johnson, Mtl.	.952	13	22	18	2	4
Kennedy, Chi.	.978	71	109	160	6	25
Krenchicki, Cin.	1.000	9	5	10	0	3
Kuiper, S.F.	.978	51	101	124	5	24
Landestoy, Cin.	1.000	16	27	23	0	4
Lawless, Cin.	.978	47	87	136	5	35
Little, Mtl.	1.000	16	11	18	0	1
Manuel, S.D.	1.000	1	1	0	0	1
Morgan, S.F.	.989	120	254	364	7	69

SECOND BASEMEN—Continued

RF (handwritten)

Player—Club	Pct.	G.	PO.	A.	E.	DP.
Morrison, Pitt.	1.000	1	2	4	0	0
Norman, Pitt.	.000	2	0	0	0	0
Oberkfell, St. L.	1.000	1	2	1	0	0
Oester, Cin.	.972	118	258	325	17	72
O'Malley, S.F.	.000	1	0	0	0	0
Phillips, Mtl.	1.000	10	6	9	0	1
Pittman, S.D.	.964	30	39	68	4	14
Raines, Mtl.	.968	36	61	119	6	11
Ramirez, S.D.	1.000	1	0	1	0	0
Ramsey, St. L.	.963	43	93	115	8	25
Ray, Pitt.	.977	162	381	512	21	89
Roberts, Phila.	1.000	7	6	13	0	4
Royster, Atl.	.948	16	21	34	3	8
Sandberg, Chi. *6.33*	.993	24	57	95	1	9

Player—Club	Pct.	G.	PO.	A.	E.	DP.
S. Sax, L.A.	.977	149	347	452	19	83
Scott, Mtl.	.971	12	17	17	1	3
Smith, Pitt.	.833	3	3	2	1	1
Sularz, S.F.	.900	9	6	12	2	2
Taveras, L.A.	1.000	4	1	2	0	0
Taveras, Mtl.	.958	19	38	54	4	13
Thomas, L.A.	.986	18	28	44	1	8
Thon, Hou.	.000	1	0	0	0	0
Trillo, Phil.	.994	149	343	441	5	101
Veryzer, N.Y.	.962	26	21	30	2	4
Wellman, S.F.	1.000	2	0	1	0	0
Wiggins, S.D.	.000	1	0	0	0	0
Wills, Chi.	.963	103	199	297	19	45
Youngblood, N.Y.	.900	8	11	16	3	2

RF (handwritten)

TRIPLE PLAYS: Backman, Giles, N.Y.; Ray, Pitt.

.978 2221 4392 6168 234 = 4.75 (handwritten)

THIRD BASEMEN

Leader—Club	Pct.	G.	PO.	A.	E.	DP.
OBERKFELL, St. L.	.972	135	78	304	11	23

(Listed Alphabetically)

Player—Club	Pct.	G.	PO.	A.	E.	DP.
Aguayo, Phila.	1.000	5	2	4	0	0
Backman, N.Y.	.846	6	4	7	2	0
Bailor, N.Y.	.907	21	13	26	4	1
Bench, Cin.	.917	107	54	155	19	10
Berra, Pitt.	1.000	6	3	7	0	0
Bevacqua, S.D.	1.000	1	1	0	0	0
Braun, St. L.	.875	5	2	5	1	0
Brenly, S.F.	.000	1	0	0	0	0
Brooks, N.Y.	.931	126	89	237	24	17
Cey, L.A.	.963	149	93	320	16	23
Concepcion, Cin.	.000	1	0	0	0	0
DeJesus, Phila.	.926	7	6	19	2	1
Evans, S.F.	.933	84	59	150	15	12
Flannery, S.D.	.947	5	4	14	1	0
Franco, Phila.	1.000	2	0	2	0	0
Garcia, Hou.	1.000	2	1	0	0	0
Gardenhire, N.Y.	.000	1	0	0	0	0
Garner, Hou.	.940	18	12	35	3	4
Gonzalez, St. L.	.907	21	10	29	4	1
Guerrero, L.A.	.917	24	13	42	5	3
Hebner, Pitt.	.000	1	0	0	0	0
Horner, Atl.	.970	137	102	217	10	20
Howe, Hou.	.972	72	53	153	6	13
Iorg, St. L.	1.000	2	1	3	0	0
Johnson, Atl.	1.000	4	1	3	0	0
Kennedy, Chi.	1.000	7	1	8	0	0
Knicely, Hou.	.000	1	0	0	0	0
Knight, Hou.	.964	67	57	131	7	18
Krenchicki, Cin.	.955	70	35	93	6	7
Lacy, Pitt.	1.000	2	0	2	0	0
Landestoy, Cin.	1.000	21	12	31	0	7

Player—Club	Pct.	G.	PO.	A.	E.	DP.
Lefebvre, S.D.	.972	39	32	73	3	6
Madlock, Pitt.	.952	146	92	266	18	23
Mankowski, N.Y.	.957	13	2	20	1	2
Manuel, S.D.	1.000	1	0	1	0	0
Matuszek, Phila.	.750	8	1	8	3	0
Mills, Mtl.	.867	13	4	9	2	1
Moreland, Chi.	1.000	2	4	2	0	0
Morgan, S.F.	.750	3	1	2	1	0
Morrison, Pitt.	.964	26	15	39	2	2
Oberkfell, St. L.	.972	135	78	304	11	23
Oester, Cin.	.900	13	9	18	3	4
O'Malley, S.F.	.965	83	59	160	8	9
Paris, St. L.	.867	5	5	8	2	2
Pettini, S.F.	.000	1	0	0	0	0
Pittman, Hou.	1.000	3	1	1	0	0
Pocoroba, Atl.	1.000	2	1	0	0	0
Ramirez, S.D.	1.000	1	1	3	0	0
Ramsey, St. L.	.973	28	5	31	1	2
Reitz, Pitt.	1.000	4	0	6	0	0
Reynolds, Hou.	1.000	7	2	4	0	0
Roberts, Phila.	.818	11	2	7	2	0
Royster, Atl.	.943	62	31	51	5	3
Salazar, S.D.	.938	129	104	291	26	28
Sandberg, Chi.	.970	133	79	278	11	19
Schmidt, Phila.	.950	148	110	324	23	28
Smith, Pitt.	1.000	1	0	1	0	0
Stearns, N.Y.	.818	12	5	13	4	0
Sularz, S.F.	1.000	14	5	11	0	0
Tabler, Chi.	.949	25	23	33	3	3
Taveras, L.A.	1.000	4	0	5	0	0
Thomas, L.A.	1.000	14	4	3	0	0
Thon, Hou.	.905	8	6	13	2	2
Trevino, Cin.	.000	2	0	0	0	0
Wallach, Mtl.	.948	156	132	287	23	23
Waller, Chi.	.667	1	1	1	1	0
Youngblood, N.Y.	.000	1	0	0	0	0

RF (handwritten)

.951 2230 1442 3966 280 = 2.43 (handwritten)

SHORTSTOPS

Leader—Club	Pct.	G.	PO.	A.	E.	DP.
O. SMITH, St. L.	.984	139	279	535	13	101

(Listed Alphabetically)

Player—Club	Pct.	G.	PO.	A.	E.	DP.
Aguayo, Phila.	.867	15	4	9	2	2
Backman, N.Y.	.000	1	0	0	0	0
Bailor, N.Y.	.984	60	64	116	3	18
Belanger, L.A.	.953	44	20	62	4	4
Belliard, Pitt.	1.000	4	2	2	0	0
Berra, Pitt.	.961	153	238	498	30	77
Bowa, Chi.	.973	140	210	396	17	64
Concepcion, Cin.	.977	145	262	459	17	94
DeJesus, Phila.	.973	154	216	469	19	80
Evans, S.F.	.943	13	16	34	3	2
Flannery, S.D.	1.000	2	1	4	0	1
Fletcher, Chi.	1.000	11	11	23	0	3
Franco, Phila.	1.000	11	8	23	0	2
Garcia, Hou.	.946	21	28	60	5	13
Gardenhire, N.Y.	.956	135	234	398	29	68

Player—Club	Pct.	G.	PO.	A.	E.	DP.
Giles, N.Y.	1.000	2	1	4	0	1
Gonzalez, St. L.	1.000	1	1	2	0	0
Kennedy, Chi.	.936	28	28	60	6	10
Landestoy, Cin.	.000	2	0	0	0	0
LeMaster, S.F.	.963	130	223	382	23	63
Little, Mtl.	.960	10	10	14	1	1
Manuel, S.D.	.000	1	0	0	0	0
Morrison, Pitt.	.000	1	0	0	0	0
Norman, Pitt.	1.000	1	1	2	0	0
Oester, Cin.	.980	29	37	60	2	11
O'Malley, S.F.	1.000	1	1	1	0	1
Paris, St. L.	.913	4	4	17	2	2
Pettini, S.F.	.934	26	24	33	4	5
Phillips, Mtl.	1.000	2	2	1	0	0
Pittman, S.D.	.951	13	11	28	2	4
Ramirez, S.D.	.963	8	9	17	1	3
Ramirez, Atl.	.956	157	300	528	38	130
Ramsey, St. L.	.991	22	37	73	1	15
Reynolds, Hou.	.958	35	43	94	6	15

SHORTSTOPS—Continued

Player—Club	Pct.	G.	PO.	A.	E.	DP.	Player—Club	Pct.	G.	PO.	A.	E.	DP.
Royster, Atl.	.975	10	14	25	1	8	Taveras, Mtl.	.947	26	20	16	2	5
Russell, L.A.	.961	150	216	502	29	64	Templeton, S.D.	.961	136	220	422	26	70
Salazar, S.D.	.955	18	28	35	3	4	Thomas, L.A.	.842	6	5	11	3	6
Smith, Pitt.	.929	29	31	47	6	9	Thon, Hou.	.975	119	177	399	15	80
O. Smith, St. L.	.984	139	279	535	13	101	Veryzer, N.Y.	.868	16	19	14	5	0
Speier, Mtl.	.982	155	291	405	13	76	Youngblood, N.Y.	.667	1	1	1	1	0
Sularz, S.F.	.961	37	46	77	5	21	Zuvella, Atl.	.800	1	0	4	1	0
Taveras, L.A.	1.000	2	2	3	0	0							

.967 2227 3395 6365 338

= R.F. 4.38

TRIPLE PLAYS: Bailor, N.Y.; Berra, Pitt.

OUTFIELDERS

Leader—Club	Pct.	G.	PO.	A.	E.	DP.
MADDOX, Phila.	.992	111	253	8	2	4

(Listed Alphabetically)

Player—Club	Pct.	G.	PO.	A.	E.	DP.
Bailor, N.Y.	1.000	4	3	1	0	0
Baker, L.A.	.975	144	226	7	6	1
Bass, Hou.	.917	7	11	0	1	0
Bergman, S.F.*	.929	6	13	0	1	0
Bevacqua, S.D.	1.000	3	2	0	0	0
Biittner, Cin.*	.978	31	42	2	1	0
Bradley, L.A.	1.000	3	1	0	0	0
Braun, St. L.	1.000	8	4	0	0	0
Briggs, Chi.*	.875	10	5	2	1	0
Butler, Atl.*	1.000	77	129	2	0	0
Cedeno, Cin.	.990	131	301	4	3	2
Clark, S.F.	.980	155	281	10	6	2
Cromartie, Mtl.*	.979	136	275	10	6	1
Cruz, Chi.	1.000	4	1	0	0	0
Cruz, Hou.*	.964	155	340	9	13	3
Davis, S.F.	.972	153	404	16	12	4
Davis, Phila.-Pitt.	.984	44	62	0	1	0
Dawson, Mtl.	.982	147	419	8	8	2
Dernier, Phila.	.981	119	255	5	5	0
Durham, Chi.*	.963	143	301	11	12	1
Easler, Pitt.	.973	138	243	8	7	2
Edwards, S.D.	.944	45	34	0	2	0
Foster, N.Y.	.974	138	289	12	8	4
Francona, Mtl.*	.936	33	44	0	3	0
Frobel, Pitt.	1.000	12	18	0	0	0
Green, St. L.	.991	68	111	4	1	1
Gross, Phila.*	.983	71	55	3	1	0
Guerrero, L.A.	.976	137	269	11	7	6
Gwynn, S.D.*	.991	52	110	1	1	0
Hall, Chi.*	.939	22	42	4	3	1
Harper, Pitt.	1.000	8	10	0	0	0
Harper, Atl.	.987	41	74	4	1	1
Hebner, Pitt.	.964	21	25	2	1	0
Heep, Hou.*	1.000	39	62	2	0	1
Henderson, Chi.	.956	70	126	5	6	0
Hendrick, St. L.	.980	134	238	6	5	1
Hernandez, St. L.*	1.000	4	5	0	0	0
Hinshaw, S.D.	1.000	6	9	1	0	0
Householder, Cin.	.992	131	220	14	2	4
Howard, N.Y.	1.000	22	27	2	0	0
Hurdle, Cin.	.950	17	17	2	1	0
Iorg, St. L.	.971	63	99	2	3	0
R. Johnson, Mtl.*	1.000	11	18	0	0	0
Johnstone, Chi.	.982	86	154	8	3	0
Jones, S.D.*	.984	114	314	3	5	1
Jorgensen, N.Y.*	.962	16	25	0	1	0
Knicely, Hou.	.941	16	16	0	1	0
Lacy, Pitt.	.965	113	186	7	7	1
Lancellotti, S.D.*	.800	3	4	0	1	0
Landestoy, Cin.	1.000	3	2	0	0	0
Landreaux, L.A.	.986	117	281	3	4	1
Landrum, St. L.	1.000	56	50	2	0	1
Lefebvre, S.D.	1.000	36	38	1	0	0
Leonard, S.F.	.958	74	135	2	6	0
Lezcano, S.D.	.990	134	275	16	3	8
Linares, Atl.	1.000	53	92	4	0	1
Loucks, Hou.	.978	37	41	3	1	1
Maddox, Phila.	.992	111	253	8	2	4
Maldonado, L.A.	1.000	3	5	0	0	0
Marshall, L.A.	1.000	19	22	0	0	0
Matthews, Phila.	.966	162	268	14	10	2

Player—Club	RF	Pct.	G.	PO.	A.	E.	DP.
McGee, St. L.		.958	117	245	3	11	0
Milner, Cin.*		.987	107	215	8	3	1
Molinaro, Chi.		1.000	4	2	0	0	0
Monday, L.A.*		.943	57	62	4	4	0
Montanez, Pitt.*		.000	2	0	0	0	0
Morales, Chi.		1.000	41	72	5	0	1
Moreland, Chi.		.989	86	169	9	2	0
Moreno, Pitt.*		.983	157	396	10	7	3
Morrison, Pitt.		.000	2	0	0	0	0
Murphy, Atl.		.979	162	407	6	9	2
Nicosia, Pitt.		1.000	3	1	0	0	0
Nordhagen, Pitt.		1.000	1	2	0	0	0
Norman, Mtl.		.969	31	30	1	1	0
Office, Mtl.*		1.000	1	2	0	0	0
Orta, L.A.		.947	17	35	1	2	1
Parker, Pitt.		.957	63	108	2	5	1
Perkins, S.D.*		.933	11	14	0	1	0
Pittman, Hou.		1.000	1	1	0	0	0
Porter, Atl.*		1.000	4	4	0	0	0
Pruitt, S.F.		.000	1	0	0	0	0
Puhl, Hou.		.989	138	257	4	3	3
Rabb, S.F.		1.000	1	1	0	0	0
Raines, Mtl.		.992	120	232	7	2	1
Rajsich, N.Y.*		1.000	35	60	0	0	0
Ramsey, St.L.		.000	2	0	0	0	0
Ray, Hou.		1.000	1	1	0	0	0
Redus, Cin.		.970	20	29	3	1	0
Richards, S.D.*		.977	103	200	8	5	1
W. Robinson, Pitt.-Phila.		.984	41	60	3	1	0
Roenicke, L.A.*		.984	72	59	3	1	0
Roof, St. L.		1.000	5	5	0	0	0
Royster, Atl.		.953	25	39	2	2	1
Salazar, S.D.		1.000	1	1	0	0	0
Sanchez, Phila.		1.000	4	7	0	0	0
D. Sax, L.A.		1.000	1	1	0	0	0
Scott, Hou.		.982	129	262	7	5	0
Smith, Atl.		.000	3	0	0	0	0
L. Smith, St. L.		.970	149	303	16	10	3
Staub, N.Y.		.959	27	43	4	2	0
Summers, S.F.		.913	31	40	2	4	0
Thomas, L.A.		1.000	28	21	0	0	0
Thompson, Chi.*	1.65	1.000	23	36	2	0	1
Tillman, N.Y.		1.000	3	2	0	0	0
Tolman, Hou.		1.000	5	7	0	0	0
Unser, Phila.*		.000	2	0	0	0	0
Vail, Cin.		.988	52	72	7	1	0
Valentine, N.Y.		.983	98	159	10	3	4
Valenzuela, L.A.*		.000	1	0	0	0	0
Venable, S.F.		.986	53	66	6	1	2
Vukovich, Phila.		.977	102	168	4	4	3
Walker, Cin.*		.992	69	110	7	1	1
Wallach, Mtl.		.000	2	0	0	0	0
Waller, Chi.		1.000	7	9	0	0	0
Walling, Hou.		1.000	32	38	3	0	0
Walton, Pitt.		.000	2	0	0	0	0
Washington, Atl.*		.950	139	221	9	12	3
Watson, Atl.		1.000	2	2	0	0	0
Welch, L.A.		.000	1	0	0	0	0
Whisenton, Atl.*		.964	34	53	1	2	0
White, Mtl.		1.000	30	40	1	0	0
Wiggins, S.D.		.967	68	140	8	5	2
Wilson, N.Y.		.988	156	415	12	5	4
Wohlford, S.F.		.992	72	122	4	1	0
Woods, Chi.		1.000	103	161	6	0	1
Youngblood, N.Y.-Mtl.		.979	98	137	6	3	1

OUTFIELDERS WITH TWO OR MORE CLUBS

Player—Club	Pct.	G.	PO.	A.	E.	DP.
Davis, Phila.	1.000	16	29	0	0	0
Davis, Pitt.	.971	28	33	0	1	0
W. Robinson, Pitt.	1.000	22	39	0	0	0
W. Robinson, Phila.	.960	19	21	3	1	0
Youngblood, N.Y.	.969	63	88	5	3	1
Youngblood, Mtl.	1.000	35	49	1	0	0

(handwritten: RF .978 (1 12722 142 296 = 1.87 / 7057)

CATCHERS

Leader—Club	Pct.	G.	PO.	A.	E.	DP.	PB.
BENEDICT, Atl.	.993	118	602	73	5	9	9

(Listed Alphabetically)

(handwritten header: OSB ... SB GS ... PB)

Player—Club	Pct.	G.	PO.	A.	E.	DP.	PB.	SB	GS
Ashby, Hou. *(1.16)*	.977	95	530	55	14	10	9		90
Bench, Cin.	1.000	1	1	0	0	0	0		
Benedict, Atl. *(.86)*	.993	118	602	73	5	9	9	11	
Benton, Chi. *(2.00)*	1.000	4	20	1	0	2	0	0	1
Blackwell, Mtl. *(1.75)*	.985	18	58	9	1	1	4	2	8
Bochy, N.Y. *(1.00)*	.961	16	90	8	4	1	6	1	16
Brenly, S.F. *(1.10)*	.961	61	265	32	12	5	3	2	34/8
Brummer, St. L. *(.73)*	.970	32	88	8	3	1	1	1	15
Carter, Mtl. *(.65)*	.991	153	954	104	10	6	6	15	4
Cox, Chi. *(2.00)*	1.000	2	9	2	0	4	1	0	2
Crow, L.A. *(4.00)*	1.000	4	9	1	0	4	0	1	1
Davis, Phila. *(.78)*	.984	129	598	89	11	3	11	10	120
Diaz, Phila. *(.85)*	.989	144	850	80	11	5	7	10	135
Gulden, Mtl. *(.25)*	1.000	2	6	2	0	1	0		
Gwosdz, S.D. *(.25)*	1.000	7	34	2	0	1	0	0	4
Hodges, N.Y. *(.27)*	.980	74	362	35	8	6	3	4	3 65
Kennedy, S.D. *(.77)*	.990	139	666	56	7		0	2	11 9 133
Knicely, Hou. *(.75)*	.977	23	112	15	3	1	2	2 16	
Lefebvre, S.D.	1.000	3	2	0	0	0	0		
May, S.F. *(1.17)*	.987	110	552	61	8	1	5	41	01
Moreland, Chi. *(1.38)*	.975	44	211	27	6	2	3	54	79
Nicosia, Pitt. *(.71)*	.990	35	182	22	2	1	2	22	31
O'Berry, Cin. *(.57)*	.990	21	84	12	1	2	0	8	14
Ortiz, Pitt. *(.50)*	1.000	7	27	3	0	0	0	2	4
Owen, Atl.	1.000	2	2	1	0	0	0		
Pena, Pitt. *(.61)*	.982	137	763	89	16	6	10	78	127
Pocoroba, Atl. *(1.45)*	.988	36	143	16	2	2	1	42	29
Porter, St. L. *(.87)*	.983	111	469	64	9	8	7	94	108
Pruitt, S.F.	1.000	1	5	0	0	0	0		
Pujols, Hou. *(1.05)*	.991	64	295	39	3	3	20	59	56
Ransom, S.F. *(1.08)*	.988	14	71	8	1	1	0	14	13
Reynolds, N.Y. *(.50)*	1.000	2	3	0	0	0	0	1	2
Roberts, Phila. *(3.00)*	.938	10	15	0	1	0	0	3	1
Sanchez, St. L. *(1.83)*	1.000	15	34	4	0	1	0	11	6
Scioscia, L.A. *(.79)*	.986	123	631	57	10	10	14	84	107
Sinatro, Atl. *(1.18)*	1.000	35	112	25	0	1	3	26	22
Stearns, N.Y. *(.84)*	.987	81	379	61	6	9	2	66	79
Swisher, S.D.	.981	26	93	9	2	0	1		
Tenace, St. L. *(.94)*	.994	37	149	21	1	0	6	31	33
Tingley, S.D. *(1.86)*	.957	8	40	4	2	1	1	13	7
Trevino, Cin. *(.86)*	.979	116	725	61	17	7	9	89	104
Van Gorder, Cin. *(.14)*	.986	51	273	18	4	3	3	50	44
Virgil, Phila. *(1.23)*	.964	35	173	14	7	3	1	32	26
Yeager, L.A. *(.62)*	.990	76	338	42	4	8	1	37	54

(handwritten totals: 1730 1926 / .90 = OSB)

PITCHERS

Leader—Club	Pct.	G.	PO.	A.	E.	DP.
RHODEN, Pitt.	1.000	35	21	44	0	1

(Listed Alphabetically)

Player—Club	Pct.	G.	PO.	A.	E.	DP.
Allen, N.Y.	.900	50	1	8	1	1
Altamirano, Phila.	.909	29	2	8	1	0
Alvarez, Atl.	1.000	7	0	2	0	0
Andujar, St. L.	.932	38	17	51	5	3
Bahnsen, Phila.	1.000	8	1	1	0	0
Bair, St. L.	.957	63	9	13	1	1
Baller, Phila.	1.000	4	0	1	0	0
Barr, S.F.	.971	53	15	19	1	2
Baumgarten, Pitt.*	1.000	12	2	8	0	1
Beckwith, L.A.	1.000	19	2	2	0	0
Bedrosian, Atl.	.963	64	12	14	1	2
Berenyi, Cin.	.967	34	18	40	2	1
Bird, Chi.	1.000	35	19	19	0	0
Boggs, Atl.	.833	10	3	7	2	0
Boone, S.D.-Hou.*	.875	20	0	7	1	0
Breining, S.F.	.902	54	12	25	4	2
Brusstar, Phila.	1.000	22	1	4	0	1
Burris, Mtl.	.931	37	11	16	2	1
Bystrom, Phila.	.875	19	6	8	2	1
Camp, Atl.	.941	51	18	30	3	2
Campbell, Chi.	1.000	62	10	23	0	1
Candelaria, Pitt.*	.960	31	1	23	1	1
Cappuzzello, Hou.*	1.000	17	1	4	0	1
Carlton, Phila.*	.915	38	6	37	4	2
Chiffer, S.D.	1.000	51	5	10	0	0
Chris, S.F.*	1.000	9	2	10	0	0
Christenson, Phila.	.955	33	16	26	2	2
Cowley, Atl.	1.000	17	6	6	0	1
Curtis, S.D.*	.905	26	2	17	2	1
Dayley, Atl.*	1.000	20	3	5	0	0
DeLeon, S.D.	.912	61	13	18	3	1
Dempsey, S.F.	1.000	3	0	1	0	0
Denny, Phila.	1.000	4	1	7	0	1
Diaz, Atl.-N.Y.*	1.000	23	5	4	0	0
DiPino, Hou.*	1.000	6	0	2	0	0
Dravecky, S.D.*	1.000	31	7	24	0	3
Edelen, Cin.	1.000	9	2	1	0	0
Eichelberger, S.D.	.971	31	9	25	1	0
Falcone, N.Y.*	1.000	40	2	16	0	1
Farmer, Phila.	1.000	47	1	12	0	1
Filer, Chi.	1.000	8	13	10	0	2
Forsch, St. L.	.962	36	21	30	2	1
Forster, L.A.*	.957	56	4	18	1	0
Fowlkes, S.F.	.895	21	4	13	2	0
Fryman, Mtl.*	.957	60	6	16	1	2
Gaff, N.Y.	.778	7	2	5	2	1
Gale, S.F.	.976	33	10	31	1	1
Garber, Atl.	.909	69	13	27	4	5
Garrelts, S.F.	.000	1	0	0	0	0
Goltz, L.A.	1.000	2	0	2	0	0
Gorman, Mtl.-N.Y.*	1.000	8	2	2	0	0
Griffin, S.D.	1.000	7	0	1	0	0
Griffin, Pitt.	.857	6	0	6	1	0
Guante, Pitt.	1.000	10	1	2	0	0
Gullickson, Mtl.	.919	34	16	18	3	1
Hammaker, S.F.*	.976	29	5	35	1	0
Hanna, Atl.	1.000	20	1	3	0	0
Harris, Cin.	.913	34	8	13	2	2
Hausman, N.Y.-Atl.	.900	24	4	5	1	1
Hawkins, S.D.	.923	15	6	6	1	0
Hayes, Cin.	1.000	26	1	4	0	0
Hernandez, Chi.*	.964	75	5	22	1	1
Holland, S.F.*	.923	58	2	22	2	1
Holman, N.Y.	1.000	4	1	8	0	0
Hooton, L.A.	1.000	21	9	21	0	1
Howe, L.A.*	.950	66	2	17	1	0
Hrabosky, Atl.*	1.000	31	1	3	0	0
Hume, Cin.	.923	46	3	9	1	0
Jackson, Pitt.*	.000	1	0	0	0	0
James, Mtl.	1.000	7	1	0	0	0
Jenkins, Chi.	.923	34	18	30	4	0
Jones, Chi.	.974	28	7	31	1	3
Kaat, St. L.*	.917	62	8	14	2	0
Keener, St. L.	1.000	19	4	2	0	0
Kern, Cin.	1.000	50	3	15	0	0
Knepper, Hou.*	.976	33	8	32	1	3
Kravec, Chi.*	1.000	13	1	3	0	0
Krukow, Phila.	.982	33	19	35	1	1

PITCHERS—Continued

Player—Club	Pct.	G.	PO.	A.	E.	DP.
LaCorte, Hou.	.750	55	2	4	2	0
LaCoss, Hou.	.885	41	7	16	3	3
Lahti, St. L.	.960	33	9	15	1	1
LaPoint, St. L.*	.938	42	2	13	1	0
Larson, Chi.	1.000	12	10	7	0	2
Laskey, S.F.	.959	32	17	30	1	2
Lavelle, S.F.*	.944	68	8	26	2	0
Lea, Mtl.	.966	27	6	22	1	1
Leach, N.Y.	.889	21	0	8	1	0
Lee, Mtl.*	1.000	7	0	3	0	0
Leibrandt, Cin.*	.958	36	5	18	1	0
Lerch, Mtl.*	1.000	6	1	4	0	0
Lesley, Cin.	1.000	28	2	5	0	0
Littell, St. L.	.667	16	0	2	1	0
Lollar, S.D.*	1.000	34	7	38	0	4
Lucas, S.D.*	1.000	65	6	19	0	0
Lyle, Phila.*	.929	34	3	10	1	1
Lynch, N.Y.	1.000	43	6	18	0	0
Mahler, Atl.	.982	39	19	36	1	5
Martin, S.F.	.878	29	8	28	5	2
Martin, St. L.*	.909	24	2	8	1	0
Martz, Chi.	.977	28	15	27	1	1
McGaffigan, S.F.	.000	4	0	0	0	0
McGraw, Phila.*	1.000	34	4	7	0	1
McWilliams, Atl.-Pitt.*	1.000	46	9	40	0	2
Minton, S.F.	.917	78	11	22	3	2
Moffitt, Hou.	1.000	30	3	2	0	0
Monge, Phila.*	.950	47	5	14	1	0
Montefusco, S.D.	.930	32	11	29	3	0
Moore, Atl.	1.000	16	7	3	0	1
Moskau, Pitt.	1.000	13	3	4	0	0
Mura, St. L.	.947	35	14	22	2	3
Niedenfuer, L.A.	1.000	55	1	7	0	0
Niekro, Hou.	.955	35	22	42	3	2
Niekro, Atl.	.982	35	18	38	1	4
Niemann, Pitt.*	1.000	20	4	7	0	0
Noles, Chi.	.952	31	14	26	2	0
Orosco, N.Y.*	1.000	54	4	16	0	1
Ownbey, N.Y.	.800	8	1	7	2	0
Palmer, Mtl.	.944	13	7	10	1	1
Pastore, Cin.	.968	31	6	24	1	2
Pena, L.A.	.875	29	3	11	2	1
Perez, Atl.	.952	16	9	11	1	2
Pladson, Hou.	.000	2	0	0	0	0
Power, L.A.	1.000	12	3	5	0	0
Price, Cin.*	.818	59	1	8	2	0
Proly, Chi.	1.000	44	1	18	0	1
Puleo, N.Y.	.912	36	9	43	5	5
Rasmussen, St. L	1.000	8	0	4	0	0
Reardon, Mtl.	.938	75	6	9	1	0
J. Reed, Phila.	.500	7	0	1	1	0
R. Reed, Phila.	1.000	57	8	21	0	2
Reuss, L.A.*	.957	39	21	46	3	4
Rhoden, Pitt.	1.000	35	21	44	0	1
Rincon, St. L	1.000	11	5	3	0	1
Ripley, Chi.	.919	28	12	22	3	0
Roberge, Hou.	1.000	22	2	4	0	0
D. Robinson, Pitt.	.907	38	14	25	4	0
Rogers, Mtl.	.983	35	18	41	1	3
Romo, Pitt.	1.000	45	7	10	0	0
Romo, L.A.	1.000	15	2	8	0	0
Ross, Hou.	1.000	4	0	1	0	0
Ruhle, Hou.	.941	31	9	23	2	1
Ruthven, Phila.	.974	33	22	16	1	1
Ryan, Hou.	.955	35	9	33	2	1
Sambito, Hou.*	.800	9	0	4	1	1
Sanderson, Mtl.	.967	32	13	16	1	1
Sarmiento, Pitt.	.926	35	8	17	2	3
Schatzeder, S.F.-Mtl.*	.933	39	3	11	1	2
Scherrer, Cin.*	.750	5	0	3	1	0
Scott, N.Y.	.926	37	7	43	4	3
Scurry, Pitt.*	1.000	76	11	9	0	0
Seaver, Cin.	.900	21	7	11	2	1
Segelke, Chi.	1.000	3	1	0	0	0
Shirley, Cin.*	.946	41	4	31	2	1
Shirley, L.A.*	1.000	11	0	4	0	0
Show, S.D.	.929	47	4	35	3	1
Sisk, N.Y.	1.000	8	0	2	0	0
Smith, Mtl.	.944	47	2	15	1	0
Smith, Hou.	.833	49	3	7	2	2
Smith, Chi.	.950	72	9	10	1	2
Solomon, Pitt.	.600	11	0	3	2	0
Soto, Cin.	.929	35	10	29	3	1
Stein, Chi.	1.000	6	1	0	0	0
Stewart, L.A.	.912	45	15	16	3	2
Stuper, St. L.	.944	23	7	10	1	1
Sutter, St. L.	.955	70	6	15	1	5
Sutton, Hou.	.973	27	16	20	1	2
Swan, N.Y.	1.000	37	16	18	0	0
Tekulve, Pitt.	.974	85	11	27	1	2
Terrell, N.Y.	1.000	3	2	2	0	0
Tidrow, Chi.	1.000	65	6	7	0	0
Tomlin, Mtl.*	.000	1	0	0	0	0
Tunnell, Pitt.	1.000	5	1	4	0	0
Valenzuela, L.A.*	.977	37	20	64	2	4
Walk, Atl.	.829	32	12	17	6	2
Welch, L.A.	.957	36	19	26	2	0
Welsh, S.D.*	.947	28	7	29	2	4
Wise, S.D.	1.000	1	2	0	0	0
Wright, L.A.*	1.000	14	3	6	0	0
Zachry, N.Y.	.967	36	10	19	1	1

PITCHERS WITH TWO OR MORE CLUBS

Player—Club	Pct.	G.	PO.	A.	E.	DP.
Boone, S.D.*	.800	10	0	4	1	0
Boone, Hou.*	1.000	10	0	3	0	0
Diaz, Atl.*	1.000	19	5	3	0	0
Diaz, N.Y.*	1.000	4	0	1	0	0
Gorman, Mtl.*	1.000	5	1	1	0	0
Gorman, N.Y.*	1.000	3	1	1	0	0
Hausman, N.Y.	.857	21	3	3	1	1
Hausman, Atl.	1.000	3	1	2	0	0
McWilliams, Atl.*	1.000	27	3	14	0	1
McWilliams, Pitt.*	1.000	19	6	26	0	1
Schatzeder, S.F.*	1.000	13	1	7	0	0
Schatzeder, Mtl.*	.857	26	2	4	1	2

OFFICIAL NATIONAL LEAGUE PITCHING AVERAGES

CLUB PITCHING

Club	ERA.	G.	CG.	Sv.	ShO.	IP.	H.	BFP.	R.	ER.	HR.	SH.	SF.	HB.	Tot. BB.	Int. BB.	SO.	WP.	Bk.
Los Angeles	3.26	162	37	28	16	1488.1	1356	6185	612	539	81	96	35	22	468	89	932	35	10
Montreal	3.31	162	34	43	10	1460.2	1371	6083	616	538	110	72	48	22	448	49	936	47	8
St. Louis	3.37	162	25	47	10	1465.1	1420	6142	609	549	94	63	45	22	502	90	689	46	12
Houston	3.42	162	37	31	16	1465.2	1338	6038	620	549	87	68	40	33	479	40	899	61	11
San Diego	3.52	162	20	41	11	1476	1348	6197	658	578	139	88	48	27	502	39	765	28	12
Philadelphia	3.61	162	38	33	13	1456.1	1395	6103	654	584	86	70	54	28	472	70	1002	49	17
San Francisco	3.64	162	18	45	4	1456.1	1507	6232	687	592	109	94	61	25	466	89	810	33	19
Cincinnati	3.66	162	22	31	7	1460.1	1414	6220	661	594	105	88	44	27	570	85	998	50	11
Pittsburgh	3.81	162	19	39	7	1466.2	1434	6243	696	621	118	68	48	29	521	70	933	59	10
Atlanta	3.82	162	15	51	11	1463	1484	6206	702	621	126	86	48	24	582	62	813	37	7
New York	3.88	162	15	37	5	1447.1	1508	6271	723	624	119	91	45	17	502	49	759	32	13
Chicago	3.92	162	9	43	7	1447.1	1510	6182	709	630	125	94	59	29	452	67	764	32	15
TOTALS	3.60	972	289	469	117	17543.1	17085	74102	7947	7019	1299	978	580	305	5964	799	10300	509	145

NOTE: Total earned runs for six clubs do not agree with composite total of respective club's pitchers due to provisions of Scoring Rule Section 10:18 (i). The following differences are to be noted: Chicago pitchers add to 632, Cincinnati pitchers add to 595, Los Angeles pitchers add to 542, Montreal pitchers add to 540, Pittsburgh pitchers add to 623, San Francisco pitchers add to 597.

PITCHERS' RECORDS

(Top Fifteen Qualifiers for Earned-Run Leadership—162 or More Innings)

*Throws lefthanded.

Pitcher and Club	W.	L.	Pct.	ERA.	G.	GS.	CG.	ShO.	GF.	Sv.	IP.	H.	BFP.	R.	ER.	HR.	SH.	SF.	HB.	Tot. BB.	Int. BB.	SO.	WP.	Bk.
Rogers, Stephen, Montreal	19	8	.704	2.40	35	35	14	4	0	0	277	245	1122	84	74	12	13	6	6	65	7	179	3	0
Niekro, Joseph, Houston	17	12	.586	2.47	35	35	16	5	0	0	270	224	1067	79	74	12	13	5	5	64	7	130	19	3
Andujar, Joaquin, St. Louis	15	10	.600	2.47	38	37	9	5	1	0	265.2	237	1056	85	73	11	8	4	7	50	7	137	3	3
Soto, Mario, Cincinnati	14	13	.519	2.79	35	34	13	2	1	0	257.2	202	1033	88	80	19	12	8	4	71	12	274	6	1
Valenzuela, Fernando, Los Angeles*	19	13	.594	2.87	37	37	18	4	1	1	285	247	1156	105	91	13	9	6	2	83	12	199	4	0
Candelaria, John, Pittsburgh*	12	7	.632	2.94	31	30	4	0	0	1	174.2	166	704	62	57	13	5	6	4	37	3	133	1	1
Sutton, Donald, Houston	13	8	.619	3.00	27	27	4	1	0	0	195	169	784	75	65	10	4	5	5	46	5	139	9	0
Carlton, Steven, Philadelphia*	23	11	.676	3.10	38	38	19	6	0	0	295.2	253	1193	114	102	17	11	1	1	86	5	286	9	9
Reuss, Jerry, Los Angeles*	18	11	.621	3.11	39	37	8	4	0	0	254.2	232	1036	98	88	11	12	4	2	50	10	138	7	3
Krukow, Michael, Philadelphia	13	11	.542	3.12	33	33	4	2	0	0	208	211	893	87	81	20	9	10	3	82	10	138	13	1
Lollar, W. Timothy, San Diego*	16	9	.640	3.13	34	34	4	1	0	0	232.2	192	962	82	81	20	17	4	0	87	10	150	8	2
Laskey, William, San Francisco	13	12	.520	3.14	32	31	7	1	0	0	189.1	186	781	74	66	14	11	5	5	43	2	88	3	3
Jenkins, Ferguson, Chicago	14	15	.483	3.15	34	34	4	0	1	0	217.1	221	932	92	76	19	19	10	13	68	2	134	3	3
Ryan, L. Nolan, Houston	16	12	.571	3.16	35	35	10	3	0	0	250.1	196	1050	100	88	20	9	8	3	109	3	245	18	1
Lea, Charles, Montreal	12	10	.545	3.24	27	27	4	2	0	0	177.2	145	722	70	64	16	11	1	1	56	6	115	8	1

DEPARTMENTAL LEADERS: W—Carlton, 23; L—Berenyi, 23; Pct.—P. Niekro, .810; G—Tekulve, 85; GS—Carlton, 19; ShO—Carlton, 6; GF—Minton, 66; Sv—Sutter, 36; IP—Carlton, 295.2; H—Carlton, 253; BFP—Carlton, 1,193; R—D. Robinson, 123; ER—Bird, 109; HR—Bird, D. Robinson, 26; SH—Scott, 21; SF—Jenkins, 13; HB—Ryan, 8; Tot. BB—Ryan, 109; Int. BB—Tekulve, 23; SO—Carlton, 286; WP—J. Niekro, 19; Bk—Carlton, 9.

(All Pitchers—Listed Alphabetically)

Pitcher and Club	W.	L.	Pct.	ERA.	G.	GS.	CG.	ShO.	GF.	Sv.	IP.	H.	BFP.	R.	ER.	HR.	SH.	SF.	HB.	Tot. BB.	Int. BB.	SO.	WP.	Bk.
Allen, Neil, New York	3	7	.300	3.06	50	0	0	0	42	19	64.2	65	279	22	22	5	3	1	1	30	5	59	4	0
Altamirano, Porfirio, Philadelphia	5	0	.833	4.15	29	0	0	0	14	2	39	41	169	19	18	2	4	4	0	14	3	26	1	0
Alvarez, Jose, Atlanta	0	0	.000	4.70	7	0	0	0	2	0	7.2	8	29	4	4	1	1	0	0	2	1	6	0	0
Andujar, Joaquin, St. Louis	15	10	.600	2.47	38	37	9	5	1	0	265.2	237	1056	85	73	11	8	4	7	50	7	137	3	2

Pitcher and Club	W.	L.	Pct.	ERA.	G.	GS.	CG.	ShO.	GF.	Sv.	IP.	H.	BFP.	R.	ER.	HR.	SH.	SF.	HB.	Tot. BB.	Int. BB.	SO.	WP.	Bk.
Bahnsen, Stanley, Philadelphia	0	0	.000	1.35	8	0	0	0		0	13.1	8	48	8	2	0	0	1	0	3	0	9	2	0
Bair, C. Douglas, St. Louis	5	3	.625	2.55	63	0	0	0	33	8	91.2	69	372	27	26	7	4	4	1	36	13	68	0	0
Baller, Jay, Philadelphia	0	0	.000	3.38	4	1	0	0	1	0	8	7	35	4	3	1	1	0	1	2	0	7	1	1
Barr, James, San Francisco	4	3	.571	3.29	53	9	1	0	9	2	128.2	125	520	54	47	9	8	10	2	20	5	36	4	1
Baumgarten, Ross, Pittsburgh*	0	5	.000	6.55	12	10	0	0	1	0	44	60	208	33	32	3	1	3	2	27	1	17	0	1
Beckwith, T. Joseph, Los Angeles	2	6	.667	2.70	19	1	0	0	5	1	40	38	170	14	12	7	4	2	3	14	5	33	0	0
Bedrosian, Stephen, Atlanta	8	6	.571	2.42	64	3	0	0	30	11	137.2	102	567	90	37	8	2	7	3	57	5	123	16	0
Berenyi, Bruce, Cincinnati	9	18	.333	3.36	34	34	4	1	0	0	222.1	208	938	119	83	26	9	3	8	96	3	157	2	3
Bird, J. Douglas, Chicago	9	14	.391	5.14	35	33	2	0	1	0	191	230	819	122	109	21	17	3	2	30	1	71	1	0
Boggs, Thomas, Atlanta	2	2	.500	3.30	10	10	0	0	0	0	46.1	43	197	16	17	3	8	2	0	22	3	29	1	0
Boone, Daniel, San Diego-Houston*	1	2	.333	4.71	20	0	0	0	8	2	28.2	28	116	16	15	6	3	1	0	7	1	12	1	1
Breining, Fred, San Francisco	11	6	.647	3.08	54	9	2	0	16	0	143.1	146	613	61	49	14	2	3	1	52	10	98	3	0
Brusstar, Warren, Philadelphia	1	1	.500	4.76	22	0	0	0	16	2	22.2	31	102	12	12	2	15	1	0	5	3	12	6	1
Burris, B. Ray, Montreal	4	14	.222	4.73	37	15	2	0	9	0	123.2	143	550	77	65	18	8	2	2	53	7	55	7	0
Bystrom, Martin, Philadelphia	5	6	.455	4.85	19	16	1	0	0	0	89	93	387	53	48	6	2	6	1	35	4	50	3	0
Camp, Rick, Atlanta	11	13	.458	3.65	51	21	3	1	20	5	177.1	199	761	84	72	13	7	8	4	52	8	68	1	1
Campbell, William, Chicago	3	6	.333	3.69	51	0	0	0	39	8	100	89	421	44	41	6	8	4	0	40	13	71	9	3
Candelaria, John, Pittsburgh*	12	7	.632	2.94	62	30	1	0	6	0	174.2	166	704	62	57	17	2	7	0	37	3	133	0	0
Cappuzzello, George, Houston*	0	1	.000	2.79	17	0	0	0	6	0	19.1	16	81	14	6	2	7	2	3	7	1	13	0	0
Carlton, Steven, Philadelphia*	23	11	.676	3.10	38	38	19	6	0	0	295.2	253	1193	114	102	9	11	5	2	86	5	286	3	0
Chiffer, Floyd, San Diego	4	3	.571	2.95	51	0	0	0	18	6	79.1	73	340	33	26	2	4	3	1	34	2	48	4	3
Chris, Michael, San Francisco*	0	2	.000	4.85	6	6	0	0	0	0	26	23	124	16	14	6	4	1	0	26	1	10	2	0
Christenson, Larry, Philadelphia	9	10	.474	3.47	33	33	3	1	0	0	223	212	905	95	86	15	5	4	3	53	5	145	0	3
Cowley, Joseph, Atlanta	1	1	.500	4.47	17	8	0	0	4	0	52.1	53	221	27	26	6	6	7	1	16	2	27	0	0
Curtis, John, San Diego*	8	6	.571	4.10	26	18	0	1	5	1	116.1	121	502	62	53	15	3	1	0	46	5	54	4	4
Dayley, Kenneth, Atlanta*	5	6	.455	4.54	20	11	0	0	0	0	71.1	79	313	39	36	9	9	5	0	25	2	34	2	2
DeLeon, Luis, San Diego	9	5	.643	2.03	61	0	0	0	41	15	102	77	390	25	23	10	7	5	0	16	9	60	0	0
Dempsey, Mark, San Francisco	0	0	.000	7.94	3	1	0	0	0	0	5.2	11	28	5	5	1	0	1	0	2	0	4	0	0
Denny, John, Philadelphia	0	2	.000	4.03	4	4	0	0	0	0	22.1	18	94	12	10	3	1	0	1	10	1	19	0	0
Diaz, Carlos, Atlanta-New York*	3	2	.600	4.03	23	0	0	0	10	0	29	37	134	17	13	9	3	1	0	13	3	16	0	0
DiPino, Frank, Houston*	2	2	.500	6.04	6	0	0	0	0	0	28.1	32	122	20	19	4	2	1	1	11	1	25	1	0
Dravecky, David, San Diego*	5	3	.625	2.57	31	10	0	0	11	2	105	86	426	37	30	8	9	2	0	33	3	59	0	3
Edelen, B. Joe, Cincinnati	0	0	.000	8.80	9	0	0	0	2	0	15.1	22	74	15	15	2	1	1	0	8	3	11	1	0
Eichelberger, Juan, San Diego	7	14	.333	4.20	31	24	8	0	2	0	177.2	171	771	98	83	23	8	9	2	72	3	74	7	0
Falcone, Peter, New York*	8	10	.444	3.84	40	23	3	0	6	0	171	159	718	82	73	24	10	5	0	71	4	101	10	3
Farmer, Edward, Philadelphia	2	6	.250	4.86	47	4	0	0	14	6	76	66	336	44	41	5	2	2	4	50	11	58	3	0
Filer, Thomas, Chicago	1	0	.333	5.53	8	8	0	0	0	0	40.2	50	187	25	25	5	8	0	1	18	0	15	1	0
Forsch, Robert, St. Louis	15	9	.625	3.48	36	34	6	0	0	0	233	238	962	95	90	16	10	7	1	54	7	69	6	0
Forster, Terry, Los Angeles*	5	2	.455	3.04	56	0	0	0	13	3	83	66	349	38	28	3	6	5	0	31	9	52	2	2
Fowlkes, Alan, San Francisco	4	4	.667	5.19	21	15	1	0	2	0	85	111	387	55	49	12	3	3	5	24	6	50	3	0
Fryman, Woodrow, Montreal*	9	4	.692	3.75	60	0	0	0	34	12	69.2	66	292	36	29	3	7	3	2	26	4	46	2	0
Gaff, Brent, New York	0	0	.000	4.55	7	5	0	0	1	0	31.2	41	142	22	16	9	3	1	0	10	1	14	5	1
Gale, Richard, San Francisco	7	14	.333	4.23	33	29	3	0	0	0	170.1	193	765	91	80	4	11	12	1	81	11	102	2	0
Garber, H. Eugene, Atlanta	8	10	.444	2.34	69	0	0	0	56	30	119.1	100	480	40	31	0	9	5	2	32	16	68	0	0
Garrelts, Scott, San Francisco	0	1	.000	13.50	1	1	0	0	0	0	2	3	11	3	3	0	1	0	0	2	0	4	0	0
Goltz, David, Los Angeles	0	1	.000	4.91	2	0	0	0	0	0	16.1	6	17	5	5	0	0	1	0	4	0	3	0	0
Gorman, Thomas, Montreal-N.Y.*	1	1	.500	2.76	8	1	0	0	3	0	16.1	16	69	4	4	5	0	0	0	4	0	13	3	0
Griffin, Michael, San Diego	0	1	.000	3.48	7	7	0	0	0	0	10.1	9	41	4	4	1	0	0	0	15	0	4	1	0
Griffin, Thomas, Pittsburgh	1	3	.250	8.87	6	4	0	0	0	0	22.1	32	113	23	22	5	0	0	0	15	2	8	0	0
Guante, Cecilio, Pittsburgh	0	0	.000	3.33	10	0	0	0	1	0	27	28	117	16	10	1	0	4	0	5	0	26	0	0

Pitcher and Club	W.	L.	Pct.	ERA.	G.	GS.	CG.	ShO.	GF.	Sv.	IP.	H.	BFP.	R.	ER.	HR.	SH.	SF.	HB.	Tot. BB.	Int. BB.	SO.	WP.	Bk.
Gullickson, William, Montreal	12	14	.462	3.57	34	34	6	1	0	0	236.2	231	990	101	94	25	12	6	4	61	8	155	11	3
Hammaker, C. Atlee, San Francisco*	12	8	.600	4.11	29	27	4	1	0	0	175	189	725	86	80	16	9	4	2	28	2	102	2	4
Hanna, Preston, Atlanta	3	0	1.000	3.75	20	1	0	0	3	0	41.1	36	158	15	15	3	0	0	0	28	1	17	2	2
Harris, Greg, Cincinnati	2	6	.250	4.83	24	10	1	0	9	0	90.1	96	398	56	49	12	5	5	2	37	3	67	2	2
Hausman, Thomas, New York-Atlanta.	1	2	.333	4.46	24	10	0	0	14	2	40.1	37	181	20	20	4	6	5	2	10	3	18	1	0
Hawkins, M. Andrew, San Diego	2	5	.286	4.10	15	7	1	0	0	0	63.2	66	281	28	29	3	6	3	1	27	5	25	2	3
Hayes, Ben, Cincinnati	2	0	1.000	1.97	26	0	0	0	11	2	45.2	37	197	12	10	3	5	3	1	22	11	38	1	0
Hernandez, Guillermo, Chicago*	4	6	.400	3.00	75	0	0	0	30	10	75.1	74	312	26	25	12	8	3	1	24	6	54	6	0
Holland, Alfred, San Francisco*	7	3	.700	3.33	58	0	0	0	10	5	129.2	115	546	56	48	5	4	4	0	40	11	97	0	1
Holman, R. Scott, New York	2	1	.667	2.36	21	4	0	0	0	0	26.2	23	107	10	7	5	6	3	2	7	6	11	0	0
Hooton, Burt, Los Angeles	4	7	.364	4.03	21	21	2	2	0	0	120.2	130	514	57	54	5	10	6	0	33	2	51	4	0
Howe, Steven, Los Angeles*	7	5	.583	2.08	66	0	0	0	41	13	99.1	87	393	27	23	5	6	3	0	17	11	49	1	0
Hrabosky, Alan, Atlanta*	2	1	.667	5.54	31	0	0	0	7	3	37.1	41	166	25	23	2	5	0	3	21	2	20	0	0
Hume, Thomas, Cincinnati	2	6	.250	3.11	46	0	0	0	37	17	63.2	57	263	24	22	2	2	3	1	21	8	22	2	0
Jackson, Grant, Pittsburgh*	0	0	.000	13.50	7	0	0	0	1	0	0.2	1	3	1	1	0	0	0	0	0	0	1	0	0
James, Robert, Montreal	0	0	.000	6.00	7	0	0	0	0	0	9	10	44	6	6	0	1	2	0	8	2	11	0	0
Jenkins, Ferguson, Chicago	14	15	.483	3.15	34	34	4	1	0	0	217.1	221	932	92	76	19	10	13	5	68	2	134	3	3
Jones, Randall, New York*	7	7	.500	4.60	28	20	2	0	4	2	107.2	130	493	68	55	11	6	5	2	51	3	44	5	0
Kaat, James, St. Louis*	5	3	.625	4.08	62	2	0	0	12	2	75	79	321	40	34	4	2	6	0	23	9	35	2	2
Keener, Jeffrey, St. Louis	1	1	.500	1.61	19	0	0	0	3	0	22.1	19	104	8	4	1	7	2	2	19	4	25	0	0
Kern, James, Cincinnati	3	5	.375	2.84	50	0	0	0	26	1	76	61	335	27	24	3	3	3	3	48	14	43	9	2
Knepper, Robert, Houston*	5	15	.250	4.45	33	29	4	0	2	1	180	193	770	100	89	14	11	10	3	60	2	108	8	0
Kravec, Kenneth, Chicago*	5	11	.500	6.12	13	13	0	0	0	0	25	27	123	20	17	3	6	3	0	18	0	20	1	1
Krukow, Michael, Philadelphia	13	11	.542	3.12	33	33	7	2	0	0	208	211	893	87	72	8	3	6	3	82	10	138	1	1
LaCorte, Frank, Houston	5	6	.167	4.48	55	0	0	0	29	7	76.1	71	345	44	38	5	11	3	2	46	5	51	1	3
LaCoss, Michael, Houston	6	6	.500	2.90	41	8	0	0	11	0	115	107	488	41	37	3	5	2	3	54	6	51	5	3
Lahti, Jeffrey, St. Louis	5	4	.556	3.81	33	0	0	0	9	0	56.2	53	245	27	24	3	3	3	2	21	8	22	4	1
LaPoint, David, St. Louis*	9	3	.750	3.42	42	21	2	0	6	0	152.2	170	656	63	58	8	4	5	8	52	2	81	3	2
Larson, Daniel, Chicago	0	0	.000	5.67	12	6	0	0	2	0	39.2	51	183	30	25	4	17	1	3	18	1	22	1	2
Laskey, William, San Francisco	13	12	.520	3.14	32	31	7	1	0	0	189.1	186	781	74	66	14	5	7	4	43	2	88	2	2
Lavelle, Gary, San Francisco*	10	7	.588	2.67	68	0	0	0	35	8	104.2	97	432	35	31	6	11	5	2	29	12	76	2	1
Lea, Charles, Montreal	12	10	.545	3.24	27	27	4	2	0	0	177.2	145	722	70	64	16	11	1	0	56	6	115	8	8
Leach, Terry, New York	2	1	.667	4.17	21	0	0	0	12	3	45.1	46	194	21	21	1	5	0	0	18	5	30	0	0
Lee, William, Montreal*	0	0	.000	4.38	7	11	0	0	0	0	12.1	11	56	7	6	0	0	2	2	15	6	8	0	0
Leibrandt, Charles, Cincinnati*	5	7	.417	5.10	36	4	0	0	10	2	107.2	130	484	68	61	7	10	0	0	48	5	34	6	0
Lerch, Randy, Montreal*	2	2	.500	3.42	6	4	0	0	2	0	23.2	26	102	11	9	1	3	1	0	13	0	4	1	1
Lesley, Bradley, Cincinnati.	0	0	.000	2.58	28	0	0	0	19	4	38.1	27	151	13	11	0	1	2	0	15	1	29	0	1
Littell, Mark, St. Louis.	2	2	.500	5.23	16	0	0	0	6	0	20.2	22	98	14	12	0	2	0	0	12	4	7	1	1
Lollar, W. Timothy, San Diego*	16	9	.640	3.13	34	34	4	2	0	0	232.2	192	962	82	81	20	5	4	4	87	5	150	5	3
Lucas, Gary, San Diego*	1	10	.091	3.24	65	0	0	0	39	16	97.1	89	407	42	35	3	8	7	7	29	8	64	8	0
Lyle, Albert, Philadelphia*	3	3	.500	5.15	34	0	0	0	11	11	36.2	50	167	23	21	3	1	3	3	12	7	12	1	0
Lynch, Edward, New York	3	3	.500	3.55	43	12	0	0	9	2	139.1	145	585	57	55	18	6	1	3	40	3	51	8	3
Mahler, Richard, Atlanta	9	10	.474	4.21	39	33	5	0	3	0	205.1	213	857	91	96	14	6	4	5	62	5	105	1	2
Martin, D. Renie, San Francisco	7	10	.412	4.65	29	25	1	0	2	0	141.1	148	619	73	73	8	8	5	2	64	5	63	2	0
Martin, John R., St. Louis*	4	5	.444	4.23	24	7	0	0	3	0	66	56	276	31	31	6	6	1	0	30	3	21	1	0
Martz, Randy, Chicago	11	10	.524	4.21	28	24	2	0	2	0	147.2	157	629	80	69	17	10	3	3	36	4	40	0	0
McGaffigan, Andrew, San Francisco	3	0	1.000	0.00	4	0	0	0	1	0	8	5	30	1	0	0	0	0	1	1	0	4	0	0
McGraw, Frank, Philadelphia*	3	3	.500	4.31	34	0	0	0	25	5	39.2	50	181	19	19	3	4	3	1	12	2	25	3	1
McWilliams, Larry, Atlanta-Pitts.*	8	8	.500	3.84	46	20	2	2	6	1	159.1	158	678	79	68	12	9	6	6	44	6	118	3	1
Minton, Gregory, San Francisco	10	4	.714	1.83	78	0	0	0	66	30	123	108	496	29	25	5	6	4	2	58	17	58	7	0

Pitcher and Club	W.	L.	Pct.	ERA.	G.	GS.	CG.	ShO.	GF.	Sv.	IP.	H.	BFP.	R.	ER.	HR.	SH.	SF.	HB.	Tot. BB.	Int. BB.	SO.	WP.	Bk.
Moffitt, Randall, Houston	2	4	.333	3.02	30	0	0	0	19	3	41.2	36	179	15	14	3	2	1	1	13	3	20	0	0
Monge, Isidro, Philadelphia*	7	1	.875	3.75	47	0	0	0	12	2	72	70	305	35	30	8	8	4	3	22	3	43	3	0
Montefusco, John, San Diego	10	11	.476	4.00	32	32	1	0	0	0	184.1	177	770	93	82	17	9	11	3	41	2	83	2	1
Moore, Donnie, Atlanta	3	1	.750	4.23	16	0	0	0	5	1	27.2	32	121	13	13	7	2	1	2	7	3	17	0	1
Moskau, Paul, Pittsburgh	1	3	.250	4.37	13	5	0	0	2	0	35	43	152	21	17	7	1	1	0	8	0	15	2	1
Mura, Stephen, St. Louis	12	11	.522	4.05	35	30	7	1	2	0	184.1	196	795	89	83	16	2	9	0	80	4	84	9	1
Niedenfuer, Thomas, Los Angeles	3	4	.429	2.71	55	0	0	0	24	9	69.2	71	299	22	21	4	5	3	5	25	8	60	1	1
Niekro, Joseph, Houston	17	12	.586	2.47	35	35	16	0	0	0	270	224	1067	79	74	12	13	5	5	64	1	130	19	0
Niekro, Philip, Atlanta	17	4	.810	3.61	35	35	4	0	0	0	234.1	225	969	106	94	23	7	3	2	73	4	144	4	0
Niemann, Randy, Pittsburgh*	1	1	.500	5.09	20	0	0	0	8	0	35.1	34	157	22	20	1	3	1	2	17	1	26	4	1
Noles, Dickie, Chicago	10	13	.435	4.42	31	30	2	0	0	0	171	180	744	99	84	11	11	10	3	61	2	85	6	0
Orosco, Jesse, New York*	4	10	.286	2.72	54	0	0	0	22	4	109.1	92	451	37	33	2	4	2	2	40	8	89	4	6
Ownbey, Richard, New York	1	2	.333	3.75	8	8	2	0	0	0	50.1	44	232	23	21	5	3	3	0	43	1	28	4	0
Palmer, David, Montreal	6	4	.600	3.18	13	13	1	0	0	0	73.2	60	312	34	26	3	3	5	0	36	8	46	0	3
Pastore, Frank, Cincinnati	8	13	.381	3.97	31	29	3	1	0	0	188.1	210	812	86	83	13	10	3	0	57	7	94	6	0
Pena, Alejandro, Los Angeles	4	4	.500	4.79	29	0	0	0	11	0	35.2	37	160	24	19	2	2	1	1	21	3	20	4	1
Perez, Pascual, Atlanta	4	4	.500	3.06	16	11	0	0	2	0	79.1	85	333	35	27	4	5	5	0	17	0	29	1	0
Pladson, Gordon, Houston	0	2	.000	54.00	2	0	0	0	0	0	1.1	10	16	8	8	0	0	0	0	1	1	0	0	0
Power, Ted, Los Angeles	1	1	.500	6.68	12	4	0	0	4	0	33.2	38	160	27	25	4	4	1	0	23	8	15	3	1
Price, Joseph, Cincinnati*	3	4	.429	2.85	59	1	0	0	17	3	72.2	73	318	26	23	7	5	2	0	32	5	71	1	0
Proly, Michael, Chicago	5	3	.625	2.30	44	0	0	0	7	1	82	77	331	22	21	1	5	3	2	22	7	24	0	2
Puleo, Charles, New York	9	9	.500	4.47	36	24	1	0	6	0	171	179	759	99	85	13	10	3	0	90	4	98	3	0
Rasmussen, Eric, St. Louis	7	7	.500	4.42	8	0	0	0	8	1	18.1	21	83	13	9	0	0	1	2	8	4	15	2	0
Reardon, Jeffrey, Montreal	1	5	.636	2.06	75	0	0	0	53	26	109	87	444	28	25	6	8	3	0	36	8	86	0	0
Reed, Jerry, Philadelphia	5	5	.500	5.19	7	2	0	0	1	0	8.2	11	38	6	5	0	0	0	0	4	2	1	4	0
Reed, Ronald, Philadelphia	5	11	1.000	2.66	57	0	0	0	30	14	98	85	401	30	29	4	10	3	0	24	5	57	7	3
Reuss, Jerry, Los Angeles*	18	11	.621	3.11	39	37	8	3	0	0	254.2	232	1036	98	88	11	12	3	3	50	10	138	3	3
Rhoden, Richard, Pittsburgh	11	14	.440	4.14	35	35	6	1	0	0	230.1	239	983	115	106	14	12	2	2	70	8	128	9	2
Rincon, Andrew, St. Louis	2	3	.400	4.73	11	6	1	0	2	0	40	35	172	22	21	2	9	3	2	25	8	11	2	2
Ripley, Allen, Chicago	5	7	.417	4.26	28	19	0	0	5	0	122.2	130	512	61	58	12	7	0	0	38	6	57	7	3
Roberge, Bertrand, Houston	1	2	.333	4.21	22	0	0	0	13	3	25.2	29	110	12	12	0	2	1	0	6	3	18	6	1
Robinson, Don, Pittsburgh	15	13	.536	4.28	38	30	0	0	3	0	227	213	997	123	108	26	8	2	3	103	11	165	0	0
Rogers, Stephen, Montreal	19	8	.704	2.40	35	35	14	4	0	0	277	245	1122	84	74	4	12	8	6	65	7	179	17	1
Romo, Enrique, Pittsburgh	9	3	.750	4.36	45	0	0	0	14	1	86.2	81	373	43	42	11	13	2	6	36	8	58	3	0
Romo, Vicente, Los Angeles	1	0	.333	3.03	15	0	0	0	6	1	35.2	25	147	12	12	1	5	3	2	14	4	24	1	1
Ross, Mark, Houston	0	0	.000	1.50	4	0	0	0	2	0	6	3	21	1	1	0	0	0	0	4	0	4	0	0
Ruhle, Vernon, Houston	11	13	.409	3.93	31	21	3	2	3	1	149	169	625	81	65	12	8	4	4	24	10	56	0	0
Ruthven, Richard, Philadelphia	11	11	.500	3.79	33	33	8	3	0	0	204.1	189	849	99	86	18	5	11	6	59	3	115	0	0
Ryan, L. Nolan, Houston	16	12	.571	3.16	35	35	10	3	0	0	250.1	196	1050	100	88	20	8	3	3	109	8	245	6	5
Sambito, Joseph, Houston*	0	2	.000	0.71	9	0	0	0	7	0	12.2	7	47	2	1	0	3	0	0	2	3	7	0	0
Sanderson, Scott, Montreal*	12	12	.500	3.46	32	32	7	0	0	0	224	212	922	98	86	24	9	6	4	58	5	158	8	5
Sarmiento, Manuel, Pittsburgh	9	4	.692	3.39	35	17	0	0	6	0	164.2	153	678	69	62	7	3	7	2	46	9	81	5	0
Schatzeder, Daniel, S.F.-Mtl.*	1	6	.143	5.32	39	4	0	0	11	0	69.1	84	307	46	41	4	3	3	3	24	2	33	4	2
Scherrer, William, Cincinnati*	0	1	1.000	2.60	5	0	0	0	2	0	17.1	17	69	7	5	0	1	2	2	5	0	7	0	0
Scott, Michael, New York	7	13	.350	5.14	37	22	0	0	10	0	147	185	670	100	84	13	21	11	4	60	7	63	3	1
Scurry, Rodney, Pittsburgh*	4	5	.444	1.74	76	0	0	0	38	14	103.2	79	448	26	20	4	4	2	4	64	7	94	7	0
Seaver, G. Thomas, Cincinnati	5	13	.278	5.50	21	21	0	0	0	0	111.1	136	501	75	68	14	2	2	3	44	3	62	2	0
Segelke, Herman, Chicago	0	0	.000	8.31	3	1	0	0	1	0	4.1	6	25	4	4	1	0	0	0	4	0	4	1	0
Shirley, Robert, Cincinnati*	8	13	.381	3.60	41	20	1	0	6	0	152.2	138	647	74	61	17	9	5	3	73	13	89	2	1
Shirley, Steven, Los Angeles*	1	0	1.000	4.26	11	0	0	0	6	0	12.2	15	58	6	6	0	0	1	0	3	0	8	2	0
Show, Eric, San Diego	10	6	.625	2.64	47	14	2	1	12	3	150	117	611	49	44	10	13	6	5	48	3	88	2	0

Pitcher and Club	W.	L.	Pct.	ERA	G.	GS.	CG.	ShO.	GF.	Sv.	IP.	H.	BFP.	R.	ER.	HR.	SH.	SF.	HB.	Tot. BB.	Int. BB.	SO.	WP.	Bk.
Sisk, Douglas, New York	2	0	1.000	1.04	8	0	0	0	4	1	8.2	5	34	1	1	0	1	0	0	23	2	8	0	0
Smith, Bryn, Montreal	5	4	.556	4.20	47	1	0	0	16	3	79.1	81	335	43	37	5	1	4	0	25	5	50	5	1
Smith, David, Houston	5	4	.556	3.84	49	1	0	0	29	11	63.1	69	286	30	27	5	9	4	3	31	4	28	0	4
Smith, Lee, Chicago	2	5	.286	2.69	72	1	0	0	38	17	117	105	480	38	35	5	6	1	1	37	5	99	6	1
Solomon, Eddie, Pittsburgh	2	6	.250	6.75	11	10	0	0	1	0	46.2	69	221	38	35	9	1	2	1	18	1	18	1	0
Soto, Mario, Cincinnati	14	13	.519	2.79	35	34	13	2	1	0	257.2	202	1033	88	80	19	8	8	4	71	3	274	4	1
Stein, W. Randolph, Chicago	0	0	.000	3.48	6	0	0	0	2	0	10.1	7	43	4	4	2	0	1	0	7	2	8	1	0
Stewart, David, Los Angeles	9	8	.529	3.81	45	14	0	0	9	1	146.1	137	616	72	62	14	10	5	2	49	11	80	6	1
Stuper, John, St. Louis	9	7	.563	3.36	23	21	2	0	0	0	136.2	137	578	55	51	8	7	1	1	55	5	53	0	1
Sutter, H. Bruce, St. Louis	9	8	.529	2.90	70	0	0	0	58	36	102.1	88	424	38	33	8	10	1	2	34	13	61	4	0
Sutton, Donald, Houston	13	8	.619	3.00	27	27	4	2	0	0	195	169	784	75	65	10	4	5	3	46	4	139	5	1
Swan, Craig, New York	11	7	.611	3.35	37	21	2	0	6	1	166.1	165	691	70	62	7	7	3	0	37	4	67	3	0
Tekulve, Kenton, Pittsburgh	12	8	.600	2.87	85	0	0	0	64	20	128.2	113	541	47	41	3	10	5	3	46	23	66	0	1
Terrell, C. Walter, New York	8	8	.500	3.43	3	3	0	0	0	0	21	22	97	12	8	2	0	0	0	14	2	8	1	0
Tidrow, Richard, Chicago	8	3	.727	3.39	65	0	0	0	25	6	103.2	106	441	45	39	6	6	2	0	29	10	62	1	0
Tomlin, David, Montreal[*]	0	0	.000	4.50	3	0	0	0	0	0	2	1	7	1	1	0	0	2	0	2	0	4	0	0
Tunnell, B. Lee, Pittsburgh	1	1	.500	3.93	5	1	0	0	2	0	18.1	17	75	8	8	0	1	0	0	5	0	4	0	0
Valenzuela, Fernando, Los Angeles[*]	19	13	.594	2.87	37	37	18	4	0	0	285	247	1156	105	91	13	19	9	2	83	12	199	4	0
Walk, Robert, Atlanta	11	9	.550	4.87	32	27	3	1	1	0	164.1	179	717	101	89	19	8	6	5	59	2	84	7	1
Welch, Robert, Los Angeles	16	11	.593	3.36	36	36	9	3	0	0	235.2	199	965	94	88	19	7	4	5	81	5	176	5	1
Welch, Christopher, San Diego[*]	8	8	.500	4.91	28	20	3	0	7	1	139.1	146	618	88	76	16	5	2	0	63	2	48	2	0
Wise, Richard, San Diego	0	0	.000	9.00	1	0	0	0	0	0	2	5	9	2	2	0	0	0	0	1	0	2	0	0
Wright, J. Richard, Los Angeles[*]	2	1	.667	3.03	14	5	0	0	3	0	32.2	28	145	12	11	2	1	4	0	20	6	24	1	0
Zachry, Patrick, New York	6	9	.400	4.05	36	16	2	0	6	1	137.2	149	600	69	62	10	4	5	0	57	2	69	4	0

NOTE—Following pitchers combined to pitch shutout games: Atlanta (6)—Bedrosian and Garber, Boggs and Garber, Camp, Bedrosian, Garber, Camp and Garber, Hrabosky, Camp and Garber; Chicago (3)—Bystrom and Altamirano, Cowley, Garber, McWilliams and Camp, Cowley, Hanna, Bedrosian and Garber; Chicago (3)—Christenson and Farmer, Christenson, R. Reed, Farmer, McGraw and Altamirano; Pittsburgh Jenkins, Hernandez and Campbell, Jenkins and Smith, Ripley and Smith; Cincinnati (2)—Pastore and Lesley, Shirley and Lesley; Houston (6)—LaCoss and LaCorte 2, Knepper and Moffit, Knepper and Smith, Ruhle and Sambito, Ryan and Roberge; Los Angeles (3)—Valenzuela, Stewart and Goltz, Welch and Howe, Welch and Niedenfuer; Montreal (4)—Gullickson

and Fryman, Lea and Fryman, Lea, Fryman and Reardon, Lea and Reardon; New York (2)—Jones and Allen, Puleo, Falcone and Allen; Philadelphia (3)—Bystrom and Altamirano, Christenson and Farmer, Christenson, R. Reed, Farmer, McGraw and Altamirano; Pittsburgh (3)—Candelaria and Tekulve, McWilliams and Scurry, Tunnell, Scurry and Tekulve; St. Louis (2)—Forsch and Sutter, Stuper and Sutter; San Diego (5)—Lollar and DeLeon 2, Montefusco and DeLeon 2, Eichelberger and Lucas; San Francisco (1)—Martin and Holland.

PITCHERS WITH TWO OR MORE CLUBS
(Alphabetically Arranged With Pitcher's First Club on Top)

Pitcher and Club	W.	L.	Pct.	ERA	G.	GS.	CG.	ShO.	GF.	Sv.	IP.	H.	BFP.	R.	ER.	HR.	SH.	SF.	HB.	Tot. BB.	Int. BB.	SO.	WP.	Bk.
Boone, San Diego	1	0	1.000	5.63	10	0	0	0	4	1	16	21	69	10	10	2	1	0	0	3	0	8	0	0
Boone, Houston	0	1	.000	3.55	10	0	0	0	4	1	12.2	7	47	6	5	1	1	1	0	4	1	4	1	0
Diaz, Atlanta	3	2	.600	4.62	19	0	0	0	7	0	25.1	31	113	15	13	3	2	0	1	9	2	16	0	0
Diaz, New York	0	0	.000	0.00	4	0	0	0	3	0	3.2	6	21	2	0	0	0	1	0	4	1	0	0	0
Gorman, Montreal	1	0	1.000	5.14	5	1	0	0	0	0	7	8	33	4	4	4	0	0	0	4	0	6	1	0
Gorman, New York	0	1	.000	0.96	3	1	0	0	2	0	9.1	8	36	1	1	0	2	1	0	4	0	7	0	0
Hausman, New York	1	2	.333	4.42	21	0	0	0	12	0	36.2	44	162	26	18	4	3	1	2	6	1	16	1	0
Hausman, Atlanta	0	0	.000	4.91	3	0	0	0	2	0	3.2	6	19	2	2	0	0	0	1	4	2	2	0	0
McWilliams, Atlanta	2	3	.400	6.21	27	2	0	0	5	0	37.2	52	185	30	26	3	9	1	2	20	5	24	2	0
McWilliams, Pittsburgh	6	5	.545	3.11	19	18	2	2	0	1	121.2	106	493	49	42	3	6	2	4	24	1	94	2	0
Schatzeder, San Francisco	1	4	.200	7.29	13	3	0	0	1	0	33.1	47	155	30	27	1	1	2	2	12	1	18	2	0
Schatzeder, Montreal	0	2	.000	3.50	26	1	0	0	10	0	36	37	152	16	14	2	2	1	2	12	5	15	2	0

1982 N.L. Pitching Against Each Club

ATLANTA—89-73

Pitcher	Chi. W—L	Cin. W—L	Hou. W—L	L.A. W—L	Mtl. W—L	N.Y. W—L	Phil. W—L	Pitt. W—L	St.L. W—L	S.D. W—L	S.F. W—L	Totals W—L
Bedrosian	1—0	2—0	1—0	0—4	0—0	1—0	2—0	0—0	0—0	1—1	0—1	8—6
Boggs	0—0	0—1	1—1	0—0	0—0	0—0	1—0	0—0	0—0	0—0	0—0	2—2
Camp	1—0	2—1	0—1	0—2	0—1	1—1	2—0	1—1	1—1	1—4	2—1	11—13
Cowley	0—0	0—0	0—0	0—1	0—0	0—0	0—0	0—1	1—0	0—0	0—0	1—2
Dayley	0—1	1—1	0—0	0—0	1—0	0—0	0—0	0—1	0—1	1—0	1—1	5—6
Diaz	0—0	0—0	0—0	0—1	0—0	1—0	0—0	1—0	0—0	0—0	0—0	3—2
Garber	1—1	2—0	1—2	2—1	0—1	0—0	0—1	0—0	2—1	0—1	0—2	8—10
Hanna	0—0	0—0	1—0	1—0	0—0	0—0	0—0	0—0	0—0	1—0	0—0	3—0
Hrabosky	1—0	0—0	1—0	0—0	0—0	0—0	0—0	0—0	0—0	0—0	0—0	2—1
Mahler	0—2	1—0	1—3	3—0	1—1	0—0	0—1	0—2	1—1	1—0	0—0	9—10
McWilliams	0—0	0—0	2—0	0—0	0—1	0—0	0—0	0—1	0—1	0—0	0—0	2—3
Moore	0—0	0—0	0—0	0—0	0—0	1—0	0—0	0—0	0—0	2—0	0—1	3—1
Niekro	1—0	2—0	0—1	1—0	3—0	2—0	1—2	2—1	1—0	2—0	2—0	17—4
Perez	0—0	2—0	0—0	0—1	0—1	0—0	0—1	0—0	0—0	1—0	1—1	4—4
Walk	3—0	2—1	1—0	0—1	0—2	1—1	1—0	0—1	0—1	2—1	2—1	11—9
Totals	8—4	14—4	10—8	7—11	5—7	9—3	6—6	4—8	7—5	11—7	8—10	89—73

No Decisions—Alvarez, Hausman.

CHICAGO—73-89

Pitcher	Atl. W—L	Cin. W—L	Hou. W—L	L.A. W—L	Mtl. W—L	N.Y. W—L	Phil. W—L	Pitt. W—L	St.L. W—L	S.D. W—L	S.F. W—L	Totals W—L
Bird	2—2	2—1	1—0	0—1	0—2	1—3	2—1	0—0	0—2	0—1	1—1	9—14
Campbell	1—0	0—0	0—0	0—1	0—1	0—1	0—1	1—1	0—1	0—0	1—0	3—6
Filer	0—0	0—0	0—0	0—0	0—1	0—0	0—1	0—0	1—0	0—0	0—0	1—2
Hernandez	0—0	1—0	2—0	0—0	0—3	0—0	0—0	0—1	0—1	1—0	0—1	4—6
Jenkins	0—2	1—1	0—1	3—1	1—1	1—1	1—2	3—1	3—2	0—2	1—1	14—15
Kravec	0—0	0—0	0—0	0—0	0—0	0—0	0—0	0—0	1—1	0—0	0—0	1—1
Larson	0—1	0—1	0—0	0—0	0—0	0—1	0—0	0—0	0—0	0—0	0—1	0—4
Martz	1—1	0—0	1—0	1—0	2—2	1—2	1—0	1—2	0—1	2—1	1—1	11—10
Noles	0—1	2—1	2—0	0—2	0—1	2—0	2—0	2—2	0—3	0—3	0—0	10—13
Proly	0—0	0—1	0—0	0—1	1—0	4—1	0—0	0—0	0—0	0—0	0—0	5—3
Ripley	0—0	0—1	1—2	0—1	0—1	0—0	1—1	1—0	1—0	0—1	0—0	5—7
Smith	0—1	0—0	0—0	0—0	0—0	0—0	0—1	0—2	0—1	0—0	0—0	2—5
Tidrow	0—0	0—0	1—0	0—0	2—0	0—0	2—2	1—0	0—0	1—0	1—1	8—3
Totals	4—8	6—6	9—3	5—7	6—12	9—9	9—9	9—9	6—12	4—8	6—6	73—89

No Decisions—Segelke, Stein.

CINCINNATI—61-101

Pitcher	Atl. W—L	Chi. W—L	Hou. W—L	L.A. W—L	Mtl. W—L	N.Y. W—L	Phil. W—L	Pitt. W—L	St.L. W—L	S.D. W—L	S.F. W—L	Totals W—L
Berenyi	1—3	3—1	1—1	1—2	0—3	0—2	0—2	0—1	1—0	1—2	1—1	9—18
Harris	0—1	0—0	0—1	0—2	0—0	0—0	2—1	0—0	0—0	0—1	0—0	2—6
Hayes	0—0	0—0	0—0	1—0	0—0	1—0	0—0	0—0	0—0	0—0	0—0	2—0
Hume	0—1	0—0	0—0	0—1	0—0	0—0	0—0	1—1	0—2	1—0	0—1	2—6
Kern	0—2	0—1	1—0	1—1	0—0	0—1	0—0	0—0	0—0	0—0	0—0	3—5
Leibrandt	0—0	0—0	0—1	0—0	1—0	1—0	0—0	0—0	1—2	1—1	1—3	5—7
Lesley	0—0	0—0	0—0	0—0	0—0	0—0	0—0	0—0	0—2	0—0	0—0	0—2
Pastore	0—2	1—0	2—2	0—2	1—1	1—1	0—1	0—2	2—0	0—1	1—1	8—13
Price	0—0	0—0	0—0	0—0	0—0	0—0	0—0	1—1	0—1	1—0	1—1	3—4
Scherrer	0—0	0—0	0—1	0—0	0—0	0—0	0—0	0—0	0—0	0—0	0—0	0—1
Seaver	1—1	0—2	1—2	0—2	0—0	1—1	0—1	0—1	0—0	2—1	0—2	5—13
Shirley	0—3	1—1	2—1	1—0	2—1	0—1	1—1	0—1	0—0	0—3	1—1	8—13
Soto	2—1	1—1	0—2	3—1	0—2	2—0	2—1	2—0	1—2	0—1	1—2	14—13
Totals	4—14	6—6	7—11	7—11	4—8	7—5	5—7	4—8	5—7	6—12	6—12	61—101

No Decisions—Edelen.

HOUSTON—77-85

Pitcher	Atl. W—L	Chi. W—L	Cin. W—L	L.A. W—L	Mtl. W—L	N.Y. W—L	Phil. W—L	Pitt. W—L	St.L. W—L	S.D. W—L	S.F. W—L	Totals W—L
Boone	0—0	0—0	0—0	0—0	0—0	0—0	0—0	0—0	0—0	0—0	0—1	0—1
Cappuzzello	0—1	0—0	0—0	0—0	0—0	0—0	0—0	0—0	0—0	1—0	0—0	2—2
DiPino	0—0	0—0	1—0	0—2	0—0	0—0	0—0	0—0	0—0	1—0	0—0	2—2
Knepper	0—2	0—1	1—2	0—1	0—2	0—1	1—1	1—1	2—1	0—2	0—1	5—15
LaCorte	0—0	0—1	0—0	0—0	0—1	1—0	0—0	0—0	0—0	0—0	0—2	1—5
LaCoss	1—1	1—0	1—0	2—0	0—0	0—0	0—1	0—1	0—0	1—1	1—2	6—6
Moffitt	0—0	0—1	1—1	0—0	0—0	0—0	0—0	0—0	1—0	0—0	0—1	2—4
Niekro	2—1	0—2	3—2	0—2	1—0	2—1	0—1	3—0	2—1	1—1	2—3	17—12
Roberge	0—0	0—0	0—0	0—1	1—1	0—0	0—0	0—0	0—0	0—0	0—0	1—2
Ruhle	1—1	0—1	0—0	0—3	0—0	0—1	4—0	0—0	1—0	2—2	1—2	9—13
Ryan	2—2	1—2	1—2	2—0	2—0	2—0	0—1	3—0	1—2	2—1	0—1	16—12
Smith	2—1	0—0	0—1	0—0	0—0	1—0	2—1	0—0	0—1	0—0	0—0	5—4
Sutton	0—1	2—1	2—0	3—1	0—1	2—0	0—0	2—1	0—1	1—2	1—0	13—8
Totals	8—10	3—9	11—7	7—11	4—8	8—4	7—5	9—3	6—6	9—9	5—13	77—85

No Decisions—Pladson, Ross, Sambito.

LOS ANGELES—88-74

Pitcher	Atl. W—L	Chi. W—L	Cin. W—L	Hou. W—L	Mtl. W—L	N.Y. W—L	Phil. W—L	Pitt. W—L	St.L. W—L	S.D. W—L	S.F. W—L	Totals W—L
Beckwith	1—0	0—0	0—0	0—0	0—0	0—0	0—0	0—1	0—0	0—0	1—0	2—1
Forster	2—1	0—0	1—0	1—2	0—0	0—1	0—0	0—0	0—0	0—2	1—0	5—6
Goltz	0—0	0—0	0—0	0—0	0—0	0—0	0—0	0—0	0—0	0—1	0—0	0—1
Hooton	1—1	0—0	0—2	0—1	0—0	0—1	1—0	0—0	1—0	1—1	0—1	4—7
Howe	1—1	0—0	0—0	1—0	1—1	0—0	0—1	1—1	1—0	1—0	1—1	7—5
Niedenfuer	0—0	1—0	0—0	0—0	0—0	0—0	0—1	1—1	0—0	0—1	1—1	3—4
Pena	0—0	0—1	0—0	0—0	0—1	0—0	0—0	0—0	0—0	0—0	0—0	0—2
Power	0—0	0—0	0—0	0—0	0—0	0—1	0—0	0—0	1—0	0—0	0—0	1—1
Reuss	1—0	3—0	3—2	3—1	3—0	0—2	1—2	1—1	1—2	2—1	1—0	18—11
Romo	0—0	0—0	0—0	0—1	1—0	0—0	0—0	0—1	0—0	0—0	0—0	1—2
Shirley	0—0	0—0	0—0	0—0	0—0	1—0	0—0	0—0	0—0	0—1	0—0	1—1
Stewart	2—1	1—0	2—1	2—1	0—0	0—0	1—0	1—1	0—0	0—1	0—1	9—8
Valenzuela	1—2	1—1	2—1	3—0	2—1	3—0	0—1	2—1	2—1	3—1	0—4	19—13
Welch	2—1	0—3	2—1	1—1	1—1	1—1	1—2	0—1	2—0	2—0	4—0	16—11
Wright	0—0	1—0	1—0	0—0	0—0	0—0	0—0	0—0	0—1	0—0	0—0	2—1
Totals	11—7	7—5	11—7	11—7	8—4	6—6	4—8	5—7	7—5	9—9	9—9	88—74

No Decisions—None.

MONTREAL—86-76

Pitcher	Atl. W—L	Chi. W—L	Cin. W—L	Hou. W—L	L.A. W—L	N.Y. W—L	Phil. W—L	Pitt. W—L	St.L. W—L	S.D. W—L	S.F. W—L	Totals W—L
Burris	0—1	2—0	0—1	0—1	0—1	0—3	0—1	0—1	1—2	0—2	1—1	4—14
Fryman	0—1	2—1	0—0	0—0	0—0	1—0	1—0	1—0	2—1	1—1	1—0	9—4
Gorman	0—0	0—0	0—0	0—0	0—0	0—0	0—0	0—0	0—0	1—0	0—0	1—0
Gullickson	1—2	2—1	0—2	1—0	0—1	1—1	3—1	0—2	1—3	2—0	1—1	12—14
Lea	1—1	1—0	1—0	3—1	0—3	3—0	1—0	0—3	1—1	1—1	0—0	12—10
Lerch	0—0	0—0	1—0	0—0	0—0	0—0	0—0	1—0	0—0	0—0	0—0	2—0
Palmer	0—0	0—1	0—0	1—0	1—0	0—0	0—1	1—1	1—0	1—0	0—1	6—4
Reardon	2—0	0—0	0—0	2—1	0—0	2—0	0—2	0—0	1—0	0—0	0—1	7—4
Rogers	2—0	3—1	3—1	0—0	2—1	1—0	2—2	2—1	2—0	1—0	1—2	19—8
Sanderson	1—0	2—1	3—0	1—1	1—2	2—2	0—2	2—1	0—0	0—1	0—2	12—12
Schatzeder	0—0	0—0	0—0	0—0	0—0	0—0	0—0	0—1	0—1	0—0	0—0	0—2
Smith	0—0	0—1	0—0	0—0	0—0	0—1	1—1	0—1	1—0	0—0	0—0	2—4
Totals	7—5	12—6	8—4	8—4	4—8	11—7	8—10	7—11	10—8	7—5	4—8	86—76

No Decisions—James, Lee, Tomlin.

NEW YORK—65-97

Pitcher	Atl. W—L	Chi. W—L	Cin. W—L	Hou. W—L	L.A. W—L	Mtl. W—L	Phil. W—L	Pitt. W—L	St.L. W—L	S.D. W—L	S.F. W—L	Totals W—L
Allen	0—0	0—0	0—0	1—0	0—2	0—0	0—1	1—1	0—1	1—1	0—1	3—7
Falcone	0—1	1—1	0—1	1—0	1—1	0—2	0—1	1—2	1—1	2—0	1—0	8—10
Gaff	0—0	0—1	0—0	0—0	0—0	0—0	0—0	0—0	0—0	0—1	0—1	0—3
Gorman	0—0	0—1	0—0	0—0	0—0	0—0	0—0	0—0	0—0	0—0	0—0	0—1
Hausman	0—1	0—0	0—1	0—0	0—0	0—0	0—0	1—0	0—0	0—0	0—0	1—2
Holman	0—0	1—0	0—0	0—0	0—0	0—0	0—0	1—0	0—1	0—0	0—0	2—1
Jones	0—2	0—0	1—0	1—1	0—1	0—2	2—2	1—0	0—2	1—0	1—0	7—10
Leach	0—0	0—0	0—0	0—0	0—0	1—0	1—0	0—1	0—0	0—0	0—0	2—1
Lynch	0—0	2—0	1—0	0—2	1—0	0—0	0—1	0—0	0—3	0—0	0—2	4—8
Orosco	0—2	1—2	0—0	0—0	0—0	1—2	0—0	1—1	1—0	0—1	0—2	4—10
Ownbey	0—0	0—0	0—2	0—0	0—0	0—0	0—0	1—0	0—0	0—0	0—0	1—2
Puleo	1—0	0—1	0—1	0—0	1—0	3—0	1—2	1—1	0—1	1—2	1—1	9—9
Scott	0—2	1—1	0—2	1—2	2—1	1—1	1—0	0—2	1—1	0—1	1—0	7—13
Sisk	0—0	0—0	0—0	0—0	0—0	0—1	0—0	0—0	0—0	0—0	0—0	0—1
Swan	1—0	2—1	2—0	0—1	0—0	1—2	2—1	0—2	2—0	0—0	1—0	11—7
Terrell	0—0	0—1	0—0	0—0	0—0	0—0	0—1	0—0	0—1	0—0	0—0	0—3
Zachry	1—1	1—0	1—0	0—2	1—1	0—1	0—2	1—0	0—1	1—0	0—1	6—9
Totals	3—9	9—9	5—7	4—8	6—6	7—11	7—11	8—10	6—12	6—6	4—8	65—97

No Decisions—Diaz.

PHILADELPHIA—89-73

Pitcher	Atl. W—L	Chi. W—L	Cin. W—L	Hou. W—L	L.A. W—L	Mtl. W—L	N.Y. W—L	Pitt. W—L	St.L. W—L	S.D. W—L	S.F. W—L	Totals W—L
Altamirano	0—0	0—0	0—0	1—0	2—0	1—0	1—1	0—0	0—0	0—0	0—0	5—1
Brusstar	0—0	0—1	0—0	0—1	1—0	0—0	1—0	0—0	0—1	0—0	0—0	2—3
Bystrom	0—0	2—1	0—1	0—0	0—1	1—1	1—1	1—0	0—0	0—1	0—0	5—6
Carlton	1—1	3—1	2—0	1—1	1—0	2—1	2—3	2—1	5—1	1—2	3—0	23—11
Christenson	0—0	1—1	1—1	0—1	1—1	2—2	0—0	1—2	1—0	1—1	1—1	9—10
Denny	0—0	0—0	0—0	0—0	0—0	0—0	0—0	0—0	0—2	0—0	0—0	0—2
Farmer	0—1	0—0	0—1	0—2	1—0	0—0	0—1	1—0	0—0	1—0	0—0	2—6
Krukow	1—1	1—1	1—2	0—0	0—0	2—1	3—0	1—2	1—3	1—1	2—0	13—11
Lyle	0—1	0—0	0—0	1—0	0—0	0—1	0—0	0—0	0—1	1—0	1—0	3—3
McGraw	0—1	1—1	0—0	1—0	0—1	0—0	1—0	0—0	0—0	0—0	0—0	3—3
Monge	0—0	1—0	1—0	1—1	0—0	0—0	0—0	2—0	0—0	1—0	1—0	7—1
Reed, J.	0—0	0—0	0—0	0—0	0—0	0—0	1—0	0—0	0—0	0—0	0—0	1—0
Reed, R.	1—1	0—0	0—0	0—1	1—0	0—0	0—0	0—0	1—2	0—1	1—0	5—5
Ruthven	3—0	0—3	2—0	0—0	1—1	0—2	1—1	1—2	0—1	2—0	1—1	11—11
Totals	6—6	9—9	7—5	5—7	8—4	10—8	11—7	9—9	7—11	7—5	10—2	89—73

No Decisions—Bahnsen, Baller.

PITTSBURGH—84-78

Pitcher	Atl. W—L	Chi. W—L	Cin. W—L	Hou. W—L	L.A. W—L	Mtl. W—L	N.Y. W—L	Phil. W—L	St.L. W—L	S.D. W—L	S.F. W—L	Totals W—L
Baumgarten	0—0	0—1	0—0	0—1	0—0	0—0	0—1	0—0	0—1	0—1	0—0	0—5
Candelaria	1—0	1—1	1—0	1—0	1—0	1—1	1—0	0—1	1—2	2—0	2—2	12—7
Griffin	1—0	0—0	0—0	0—2	0—0	0—0	0—0	0—0	0—1	0—0	0—0	1—3
McWilliams	1—0	0—1	1—0	1—1	0—1	2—0	0—0	1—0	0—2	0—0	0—0	6—5
Moskau	0—0	1—0	0—1	0—1	0—0	0—0	0—0	0—0	0—1	0—0	0—0	1—3
Niemann	0—0	1—1	0—0	0—0	0—0	0—0	0—0	0—0	0—0	0—0	0—0	1—1
Rhoden	2—1	1—1	1—0	0—2	0—1	1—1	2—2	2—2	0—2	0—2	2—0	11—14
Robinson, D.	2—1	2—1	1—0	0—1	3—0	2—2	3—2	0—2	1—1	0—0	1—3	15—13
Romo	0—0	2—1	1—0	1—0	0—0	1—0	0—1	1—0	3—1	0—0	0—0	9—3
Sarmiento	0—0	0—0	2—0	0—0	0—0	1—1	2—0	2—2	1—1	1—0	0—0	9—4
Scurry	0—1	0—1	0—1	0—0	1—0	1—0	1—0	0—1	1—0	0—0	0—1	4—5
Solomon	0—1	1—1	0—1	0—0	0—1	0—1	0—0	0—0	0—0	0—1	1—0	2—6
Tekulve	1—0	0—0	1—1	0—1	1—2	2—0	1—2	3—1	0—0	3—1	0—0	12—8
Tunnell	0—0	0—0	0—0	0—0	1—0	0—1	0—0	0—0	0—0	0—0	0—0	1—1
Totals	8—4	9—9	8—4	3—9	7—5	11—7	10—8	9—9	7—11	6—6	6—6	84—78

No Decisions—Guante, Jackson.

ST. LOUIS—92-70

Pitcher	Atl. W—L	Chi. W—L	Cin. W—L	Hou. W—L	L.A. W—L	Mtl. W—L	N.Y. W—L	Phil. W—L	Pitt. W—L	S.D. W—L	S.F. W—L	Totals W—L
Andujar	0—3	3—2	0—1	1—2	0—0	1—1	2—0	4—0	1—0	1—1	2—0	15—10
Bair	0—1	2—0	0—0	0—0	1—0	0—2	0—0	1—0	0—0	1—0	0—0	5—3
Forsch	0—0	0—0	1—0	3—1	2—1	2—2	1—0	2—3	1—1	3—1	0—0	15—9
Kaat	0—0	1—1	2—0	0—0	0—0	1—0	0—0	0—0	1—1	0—0	0—1	5—3
Keener	0—0	0—0	0—0	0—0	0—0	0—0	0—1	1—1	0—0	0—0	0—0	1—1
Lahti	0—1	0—0	1—0	0—0	0—0	0—3	3—0	0—0	0—0	0—0	1—0	5—4
LaPoint	0—0	1—1	0—0	1—0	0—0	0—1	1—0	1—0	2—1	1—0	2—0	9—3
Littell	0—0	0—0	0—0	0—0	0—0	0—0	0—0	0—0	0—0	0—0	0—0	0—1
Martin	0—1	0—0	1—1	0—2	0—0	0—0	0—0	0—0	2—1	0—0	1—0	4—5
Mura	1—1	1—0	2—1	0—1	1—3	1—0	2—2	0—2	3—1	0—0	1—0	12—11
Rasmussen	0—0	1—1	0—0	0—0	0—0	0—0	0—0	0—1	1—0	0—0	0—0	1—2
Rincon	1—0	0—0	0—1	0—0	0—1	0—0	0—0	0—1	0—0	0—0	0—0	2—3
Stuper	1—0	2—1	0—1	0—0	1—1	0—0	2—1	2—0	1—1	0—1	0—1	9—7
Sutter	2—0	0—0	0—0	1—0	0—1	2—1	1—2	1—0	0—0	2—1	0—3	9—8
Totals	5—7	12—6	7—5	6—6	5—7	8—10	12—6	11—7	11—7	8—4	7—5	92—70

No Decisions—None.

SAN DIEGO—81-81

Pitcher	Atl. W—L	Chi. W—L	Cin. W—L	Hou. W—L	L.A. W—L	Mtl. W—L	N.Y. W—L	Phil. W—L	Pitt. W—L	St.L. W—L	S.F. W—L	Totals W—L
Boone	0—0	0—0	0—0	0—0	0—0	0—0	0—0	0—0	0—0	1—0	0—0	1—0
Chiffer	1—0	0—0	0—1	0—0	1—0	1—0	1—0	0—0	0—1	0—0	0—1	4—3
Curtis	0—0	0—0	1—0	1—0	1—1	1—0	0—1	0—2	1—1	2—1	1—0	8—6
DeLeon	1—0	0—1	2—0	0—1	3—0	0—1	1—1	1—0	1—0	0—0	0—1	9—5
Dravecky	1—0	0—1	1—0	0—0	0—0	0—0	0—0	0—0	1—0	2—2	0—0	5—3
Eichelberger	0—3	1—0	0—1	0—2	1—2	1—0	0—1	0—2	2—1	0—1	2—1	7—14
Griffin	0—1	0—0	0—0	0—0	0—0	0—0	0—0	0—0	0—0	0—0	0—0	0—1
Hawkins	0—1	0—0	1—0	0—0	0—0	0—1	1—0	0—0	0—1	0—2	0—0	2—5
Lollar	1—1	3—0	2—1	2—1	0—1	1—1	2—0	2—1	0—1	0—1	3—1	16—9
Lucas	1—1	0—1	0—1	0—1	0—0	0—0	0—3	0—1	0—0	0—2	0—0	1—10
Montefusco	0—2	1—1	1—1	3—1	1—1	0—2	0—0	2—1	1—1	0—0	1—1	10—11
Show	1—1	1—0	3—1	1—1	2—2	0—1	1—0	0—0	0—0	0—0	1—0	10—6
Welsh	1—1	2—0	1—0	2—2	0—2	1—1	0—0	0—0	1—0	0—1	0—1	8—8
Totals	7—11	8—4	12—6	9—9	9—9	5—7	6—6	5—7	6—6	4—8	10—8	81—81

No Decisions—Wise.

SAN FRANCISCO—87-75

Pitcher	Atl. W—L	Chi. W—L	Cin. W—L	Hou. W—L	L.A. W—L	Mtl. W—L	N.Y. W—L	Phil. W—L	Pitt. W—L	St.L. W—L	S.D. W—L	Totals W—L
Barr	2—0	0—1	0—1	0—0	1—0	0—0	0—0	0—0	1—1	0—0	0—0	4—3
Breining	1—1	1—0	0—1	2—0	3—2	0—0	1—0	0—2	0—0	1—0	2—0	11—6
Chris	0—1	0—0	0—0	0—0	0—0	0—0	0—0	0—0	0—1	0—0	0—0	0—2
Fowlkes	0—0	0—0	1—0	0—0	0—1	1—0	0—0	0—1	1—0	0—0	1—0	4—2
Gale	0—1	1—2	2—1	0—2	0—1	1—0	2—0	0—3	0—1	0—1	1—2	7—14
Hammaker	0—1	0—1	3—0	3—2	0—0	3—0	1—0	1—1	1—1	0—1	0—1	12—8
Holland	1—0	1—0	1—1	0—0	1—0	0—1	0—1	0—0	0—0	0—0	2—1	7—3
Laskey	2—1	0—0	1—0	2—1	2—0	2—1	0—3	1—1	2—1	0—2	1—2	13—12
Lavelle	2—0	1—0	0—1	3—0	0—1	0—2	1—0	0—0	1—0	2—1	0—2	10—7
Martin	1—2	1—2	2—0	2—0	0—3	0—0	1—0	0—0	0—2	0—0	0—0	7—10
McGaffigan	0—0	0—0	0—0	0—0	1—0	0—0	0—0	0—0	0—0	0—0	0—0	1—0
Minton	1—1	0—0	2—0	1—0	1—1	1—0	1—1	0—1	0—0	2—0	1—0	10—4
Schatzeder	0—0	1—0	0—1	0—0	0—0	0—0	0—0	0—1	0—0	0—0	0—2	1—4
Totals	10—8	6—6	12—6	13—5	9—9	8—4	8—4	2—10	6—6	5—7	8—10	87—75

No Decisions—Dempsey, Garrelts.

AMERICAN LEAGUE

Including

Team Reviews of 1982 Season

Team Day-by-Day Scores

1982 Standings, Home-Away Records

1982 Official A.L. Batting Averages

1982 Official A.L. Fielding Averages

1982 Official A.L. Pitching Averages

1982 Pitching Against Each Club

Cecil Cooper was his usual devastating self in '82, compiling a .313 average and collecting 32 home runs while driving in 121 runs.

Fun? Brewers Drink to That

By TOM FLAHERTY

On June 2, the new manager of the Milwaukee Brewers had a simple message for his players.

"Have fun," said Harvey Kuenn after taking over the struggling Brewers, who were 23-24 and tied for fifth place in the American League East when Buck Rodgers was fired.

The Brewers followed Kuenn's advice and had the most fun of any team in the franchise's 13-year history in Milwaukee. They finished with a 72-43 record under Kuenn, won their first division title (in 1981, the Brewers won the second half of the split season), their first A.L. Championship Series (three games to two over the California Angels) and came within one victory of a World Series title (losing to the St. Louis Cardinals in seven games).

The Brewers hit 216 home runs and scored 891 runs in earning a new nickname, "Harvey's Wallbangers."

More than anything, it was the Year of the Robin in County Stadium.

Robin Yount performed brilliantly at shortstop while having an offensive year that had Brewer fans chanting, "MVP! MVP!" every time he came to the plate.

Yount quietly shrugged off all of the attention.

Gorman Thomas and Ben Oglivie (below) combined for 73 home runs during the 1982 season.

"It's not just one player," he said over and over. "It's the whole team. Everybody on this team is the most valuable player."

What may sound like false modesty was typical Yount, a down-to-earth young man who just enjoys doing what he does very well—playing baseball.

And he was right. It wasn't a one-man production, even though one man did just a little more producing than anyone else.

Yount's name appeared under the league leaders in almost every category. But he was joined by a lot of teammates.

Gorman Thomas hit 39 homers to share the league lead with California's Reggie Jackson, and Ben Oglivie added 34 and Cecil Cooper 32. Cooper, Thomas, Oglivie and Yount each drove in more than 100 runs. Ted Simmons just missed with 97.

Cooper, who hit .313, was over .300 for the sixth straight year.

But Yount had more fun than anybody, just missing the batting title by a point with a .331 average and finishing among the league leaders in almost everything. The Brewer shortstop led the league in total bases with 367, slugging percentage at .578 and hits with 210, and shared the lead in doubles with 46. Yount, Cooper and

SCORES OF MILWAUKEE BREWERS' 1982 GAMES

APRIL			Winner	Loser
9—At Toronto	W	15-4	Vuckovich	Bomback
10—At Toronto	L	2-3*	Jackson	Fingers
11—At Toronto	W	14-5	McClure	Clancy
13—At Cleve.	W	9-8*	Fingers	Lewallyn
14—At Cleve.	L	2-6	Denny	Vuckovich
15—At Cleve.	L	1-8	Blyleven	Caldwell
16—Texas	L	1-4*	Darwin	Fingers
17—Texas	L	3-5	Tanana	McClure
18—Texas	L	6-9	Darwin	Vuckovich
21—Toronto	W	3-1	Lerch	Leal
22—Toronto	W	7-0	Caldwell	Bomback
23—At Texas	W	2-1	Haas	Honeycutt
24—At Texas	W	4-1	Vuckovich	Schmidt
25—At Texas	W	11-6	Bernard	Matlack
27—Chicago	L	2-11	Hoyt	Lerch
28—Chicago	W	2-1	Fingers	Burns
30—At Minn.	L	4-7	Erickson	Haas
			Won 9, Lost 8	

MAY				
1—At Minn.	W	6-5	Vuckovich	Corbett
2—At Minn.	W	11-4	Lerch	Williams
3—Kan. City	L	2-3	Splittorff	Caldwell
4—Kan. City	W	9-5	Slaton	Jackson
5—Kan. City	L	2-3*	Quisenberry	Fingers
6—Minnesota	W	6-3	Vuckovich	Havens
7—Minnesota	W	4-1	Lerch	Williams
8—Minnesota	W	12-1	Caldwell	Felton
9—Minnesota	W	6-2	Slaton	Redfern
10—At Kan. C.	L	2-3	Blue	Fingers
11—At Kan. C.	L	3-17	Gura	Augustine
12—At Kan. C.	L	7-9	Leonard	Lerch
13—At Chicago	L	2-13	Hoyt	Caldwell
14—At Chicago	W	2-1	Slaton	Dotson
15—At Chicago	W	8-3	Bernard	Burns
16—At Chicago	L	1-6	Trout	Lerch
18—California	L	1-4	Renko	Caldwell
19—California	L	2-7	Kison	Slaton
20—California	W	4-1	Haas	Zahn
21—Seattle	W	4-1	McClure	Perry
22—Seattle	L	1-7	Nelson	Lerch
23—Seattle	L	5-6†	Caudill	Fingers
25—Oakland	L	5-10	Keough	Haas
26—Oakland	L	2-7	Underwood	McClure
27—At Calif.	W	4-3	Vuckovich	Forsch
28—At Calif.	L	5-6	Corbett	Bernard
29—At Calif.	L	4-5*	Sanchez	Easterly
30—At Calif.	W	7-3	Slaton	Kison
31—At Seattle	L	4-5†	Stanton	Augustine
			Won 13, Lost 16	

JUNE				
1—At Seattle	W	2-1	Vuckovich	Nelson
2—At Seattle	W	5-2	Caldwell	Bannister
4—At Oak.	W	10-1	Haas	Keough
5—At Oak.	W	11-3	McClure	Beard
6—At Oak.	W	7-2	Vuckovich	Underwood
7—Baltimore	L	2-7	Palmer	Caldwell
8—Baltimore	L	2-4	McGregor	Lerch
9—Baltimore	L	3-8	Flanagan	Haas
10—Baltimore	W	9-7	Fingers	T. Martinez
11—Detroit	W	8-6	Vuckovich	Lopez
12—Detroit	L	3-7	Wilcox	Caldwell
13—Detroit	W	13-5	Lerch	Underwood
14—At Balt.	L	4-9	McGregor	Haas
15—At Balt.	W	6-3	McClure	Flanagan
16—At Balt.	T	2-2	....	....
17—At Detroit	W	3-2†	Caldwell	Tobik
18—At Detroit	W	5-2	Lerch	Wilcox
19—At Detroit	W	10-3	Haas	Morris
20—At Detroit	W	7-5	Augustine	Ujdur
21—New York	W	6-2	McClure	Righetti
22—New York	W	3-2	Vuckovich	Erickson
23—New York	L	2-3	Morgan	Caldwell
25—At Boston	W	9-3	Slaton	Hurst
26—At Boston	W	11-10	Fingers	Clear
27—At Boston	W	7-5	McClure	Torrez
28—At Boston	L	7-9	Stanley	Vuckovich
29—At N.Y.	W	11-4	Caldwell	Guidry
30—At N.Y.	W	9-7‡	Fingers	Rawley
			Won 20, Lost 7	

JULY				
1—At N.Y.	L	3-5	Morgan	Haas
2—Boston	W	14-5	McClure	Torrez
3—Boston	W	7-0	Vuckovich	Rainey
4—Boston	L	1-4	Eckersley	Caldwell
5—At Chicago	W	10-4	Slaton	Hoyt
7—Minnesota	L	8-11	Havens	McClure
8—Minnesota	L	0-3	O'Connor	Vuckovich

JULY			Winner	Loser
9—Kan. City	W	9-6	Caldwell	Splittortt
10—Kan. City	W	7-0	Lerch	Blue
11—Kan. City	W	8-5	Haas	Gura
15—Chicago	W	8-4	Slaton	Lamp
15—Chicago	W	5-4	Caldwell	Hoyt
16—Chicago	W	5-3	Haas	Koosman
17—Chicago	W	5-2	Ladd	Barojas
18—Chicago	W	9-3	Lerch	Barnes
19—At Minn.	L	4-6	Williams	Augustine
20—At Minn.	L	3-5	O'Connor	Caldwell
21—At Minn.	W	10-4	Haas	Viola
23—At Kan. C.	L	3-4	Quisenberry	Fingers
24—At Kan. C.	W	7-4	Vuckovich	Botelho
25—At Kan. C.	L	4-6	Gura	Lerch
26—At Texas	L	1-3	Hough	Caldwell
27—At Texas	W	8-2	Haas	Honeycutt
28—At Texas	W	3-2	McClure	Tanana
29—Cleveland	L	1-5‡	Spillner	Slaton
30—Cleveland	L	2-7	Sorensen	Lerch
31—Cleveland	W	4-2	Caldwell	Waits
			Won 16, Lost 11	

AUGUST				
1—Cleveland	L	1-4	Whitson	Haas
1—Cleveland	W	7-2	Slaton	Anderson
2—At Toronto	L	4-9	Stieb	McClure
3—At Toronto	W	7-4	Vuckovich	Clancy
4—At Toronto	W	8-0	Caldwell	Gott
6—At Cleve.	W	5-2*	Haas	Glynn
7—At Cleve.	L	3-4†	Glynn	Slaton
8—At Cleve.	W	7-6	Bernard	Barker
9—Texas	W	9-1	Caldwell	Medich
10—Texas	W	11-3	Slaton	Hough
11—Texas	L	3-6	Schmidt	Haas
12—Toronto	W	7-1	McClure	Gott
12—Toronto	W	4-3	Lerch	Murray
13—Toronto	W	3-1	Vuckovich	Leal
14—Toronto	L	2-4	Stieb	Caldwell
15—Toronto	L	2-3	Clancy	Slaton
17—At Oak.	L	6-10	Langford	Haas
18—At Oak.	L	2-3†	Beard	McClure
19—At Oak.	W	10-6	Vuckovich	Keough
20—At Seattle	W	6-5	Caldwell	Moore
21—At Seattle	W	3-2	Medich	Clark
22—At Seattle	W	8-5	Slaton	Bannister
23—At Calif.	L	3-5	Witt	McClure
24—At Calif.	W	7-3	Vuckovich	Renko
26—Oakland	W	10-3	Caldwell	Kingman
27—Oakland	W	5-4	Medich	Hanna
28—Oakland	L	6-7	Langford	Ladd
29—Oakland	W	8-1	McClure	Norris
30—Seattle	L	2-3*	Vande Berg	Slaton
31—Seattle	W	8-2	Caldwell	Clark
			Won 19, Lost 11	

SEPTEMBER				
1—Seattle	W	7-3	Medich	Stanton
2—Cleveland	W	2-1	Haas	Sutcliffe
2—Cleveland	L	2-4	Spillner	Sutton
3—California	L	2-5	John	McClure
4—California	W	8-2	Vuckovich	Tiant
5—California	W	8-5	Caldwell	Zahn
6—Detroit	L	5-6*	Wilcox	Medich
7—Detroit	W	4-0	Sutton	Petry
8—Detroit	W	9-7	Haas	Ujdur
9—At N.Y.	L	4-5*	May	Ladd
10—At N.Y.	W	5-3	Caldwell	Guidry
11—At N.Y.	L	2-14	Righetti	Medich
12—At N.Y.	L	8-9	Kaufman	Easterly
13—At Detroit	L	3-4†	Lopez	Ladd
14—At Detroit	W	6-3	Medich	Rucker
15—At Detroit	W	5-3	Vuckovich	Morris
17—New York	W	14-0	Caldwell	Wever
18—New York	W	6-4	McClure	Howell
19—New York	W	14-1	Sutton	Rawley
20—Boston	W	4-3†	Vuckovich	Stanley
21—Boston	L	3-4*	Clear	Medich
22—Boston	W	3-1	Caldwell	Denman
24—Baltimore	W	15-6	Sutton	Flanagan
25—Baltimore	L	2-7	Palmer	Vuckovich
26—Baltimore	L	2-5	D. Martinez	Caldwell
28—At Boston	W	9-3	Medich	Rainey
29—At Boston	W	6-3	McClure	Clear
30—At Boston	L	4-9	Eckersley	Slaton
			Won 17, Lost 11	

OCTOBER				
1—At Balt.	L	3-8	D. Martinez	Vuckovich
1—At Balt.	L	1-7	Davis	Caldwell
2—At Balt.	L	3-11	Stewart	Medich
3—At Balt.	W	10-2	Sutton	Palmer
			Won 1, Lost 3	

*10 innings. †11 innings. ‡12 innings.

Paul Molitor learned a new position and scored a major league-leading 136 runs.

Molitor, in fact, finished one, two, three in the league in hits.

Molitor led the league in runs scored with 136, and Yount was second with 129. Cooper, who scored 104 runs, finished sixth.

Despite all the offense, the Brewers made their fans—the True Blue Brew Crew—a very nervous lot before the regular season ended with a big victory October 3.

The Brewers, tied for the division lead at the All-Star break, seized sole possession of first place two days after the break and led by 6½ games late in August. But they lost Rollie Fingers, their bullpen ace, when he injured his arm September 2, and the Baltimore Orioles steadily chopped at their lead.

The Brewers went into Baltimore for the final four games of the season holding a three-game lead. All they needed was one victory to clinch the division title. They got it, but not until the season finale.

It probably was appropriate that Don Sutton was the winning pitcher in the game that clinched the title.

General Manager Harry Dalton, making another of his big deals, obtained Sutton from the Houston Astros on August 30 as pennant insurance. Sutton posted a 4-1

record down the stretch, but the pennant insurance paid a double indemnity on that big day in Baltimore.

With the addition of Sutton, the Brewers, whose pitching had often been maligned in the past, boasted one of the best starting staffs in the league.

Pete Vuckovich tied for second in the league with 18 victories and had just six losses while posting a 3.34 earned-run average. Mike Caldwell, after a slow start, blossomed under the patient Kuenn and had a 17-13 record and 3.91 ERA.

Bob McClure, getting a chance to start for the first time in his career, was 12-7.

Moose Haas, one of the best pitchers in the league two years ago, was inconsistent and finished the season in the bullpen after Sutton and Doc Medich were added to the staff. Haas still finished with an 11-8 record.

Despite the injury, Fingers managed 29 saves and became the first relief pitcher in history to save 300 or more games. He had run his career total to 301 before his forced absence.

With Fingers out, Dwight Bernard and rookie Pete Ladd got the ball in clutch situations and did the job more often than not. Bernard finished with six saves, and Ladd had three.

But maybe the most important contribution came from Jim Slaton, the veteran righthander who had been a starter all of his career.

Slaton pitched long relief, short relief and made an occasional start and turned in a 10-6 record, six saves and a 3.29 ERA.

There were a couple of important defensive changes, too.

Molitor, changing positions for the second straight season, moved to third base. One season is too early to judge the success of the move defensively, but the Brewers' leadoff hitter had an injury-free season for the first time in three years and had one of his best offensive years, batting .302 and hitting 19 home runs.

Second baseman Jim Gantner's average slipped to .295 in the final week of the season or all four Brewer infielders would have hit .300 or better.

The big payoff from moving Molitor, however, was opening up right field for Charlie Moore. Moore, a part-time player throughout his career, impressed more than one scout with his defensive ability, and his strong arm cut down a dozen runners who dared to challenge him.

The Brewers' rocking, rollicking game drew 1,978,896 fans to County Stadium. Kuenn's advice was good advice. Everybody had fun in 1982.

Weaver, Orioles Come Up Short

By JIM HENNEMAN

Earl Weaver didn't lack for personal goals at the start of the 1982 season. In his last year as manager of the Baltimore Orioles, he needed one more 100-victory season to match the record of six set by Joe McCarthy. He had a chance to move ahead of Frank Selee and into second place, behind McCarthy, in winning percentage, and there also was the possibility of a seventh divisional championship and fifth pennant in his 14th full season as manager.

He missed on each count, but only after the Orioles came within one victory of writing a fantasy finish to Weaver's illustrious career. "It would have been nice to tie McCarthy, because anybody would like to be mentioned in the same breath with him," said Weaver, "but winning the division and having a chance to go to another World Series was the only thing that really mattered."

Though the Orioles didn't make it to postseason play, under ordinary circumstances what they accomplished would have been remarkable. But it was far from an ordinary year, and not only because it was Weaver's last.

After chasing the Milwaukee Brewers throughout the second half of the season, the Orioles pulled into a tie on the next-to-last day. Baltimore had beaten Milwaukee five straight times, finally erasing a 7½-game deficit that had confronted the Orioles six weeks earlier. It meant the entire campaign was riding on the final game of the year. When it all fell apart as the Brewers registered a 10-2 victory, the letdown was awesome.

In retrospect, however, the Orioles lost the division race long before that last day and the fact they emerged with 94 victories was astounding. To do it they had to record the hottest streak in the club's 29-year history, winning 27 of 32 games from August 19 to September 20, and post the best record in the major leagues after the All-Star break, 50-30.

The furious finish was the result of several outstanding performances, most notably by first baseman Eddie Murray, veteran pitcher Jim Palmer, rookie infielder Cal Ripken and veteran outfielder John Lowenstein.

Easily the club's most valuable player for the second year in a row, Murray continued to torment American League pitchers and enjoyed his best overall season in a remarkably consistent six-year

career. He hit .316 (fourth in the league), had 32 home runs (tied for fifth), 110 runs batted in (sixth), 302 total bases (seventh), a .395 on-base percentage (fifth), a .549 slugging percentage (third) and 20 game-winning RBIs (tied for second). Murray's homer total matched his previous high and made him only the third switch-hitter in history to have more than one 30-homer season.

Rebounding from only the second losing year of his career, Palmer tied for the league lead in winning percentage (.750) with a 15-5 record, and his 3.13 earned-run average was third. At age 36, the three-time Cy Young Award winner was 13-2 with a 2.33 ERA after June 7 and was easily the club's most dependable starter. He tied a career high with 11 consecutive victories between May 30 and September 8, and also notched the sixth one-hitter of his career.

After a miserable start that saw him hitting only .117 through May 1, Ripken more than lived up to his advance notices. He slugged 28 home runs, drove in 93 runs and scored 90. He finished with a .264 average and made only 19 errors, despite the fact he started the season at third base and moved to shortstop on July 1.

Lowenstein, who has been a regular only one season of his 12-year career, probably was baseball's most effective platoon player. He has filled that role the last four years with the Orioles, but never more productively than he did in 1982. His career highs included average (.320), home runs (24), RBIs (66), runs scored (69) and walks (54). In addition, he handled 204 chances in the outfield without making an error.

"Murray and Ripken give this organization a great cornerstone, maybe the best in the game," said Weaver, reflecting on the year and also looking to the future. "They have the capabilities of doing the same thing that Brooks and Frank (Robinson) did for the Orioles. Both are excellent defensive players, though that tends to get overshadowed by their offense, and very intelligent players. They should give this club a good nucleus for the future.

"And Palmer," Weaver added, "is still Palmer. He's a master. I know he has at least 37 wins left in him (the number he needs to reach 300) and I wouldn't be surprised to see him still winning three or four years from now.

"Lowenstein is one of those players every team needs in order to win," Weav-

Hard-hitting Eddie Murray (below) helped Earl Weaver (above) come close in his final season as Orioles manager.

er said. "He knows what his role is, and keeps himself prepared. I can't imagine anyone in baseball, playing under the same conditions, who could have done a better job than he did. He adds an awful lot to the club."

The Orioles tied a major league mark with three pinch-hit home runs with the bases loaded. They hit 11 pinch homers overall, setting an American League record, with Benny Ayala, Terry Crowley, Jim Dwyer and Gary Roenicke hitting two apiece.

Of the club records that fell, the most significant was set by reliever Tippy Martinez, who made 76 appearances, 23 more than his previous high. The little lefthander, who assumed virtually the entire late-inning burden the last month of the season after Tim Stoddard was felled by a knee injury, had an 8-8 record and recorded a personal-high 16 saves. He hit his peak during July, when he made 16 appearances without allowing a run.

Ken Singleton's .251 average and Al Bumbry's .262 mark topped the Orioles' disappointments. And while their won-lost records were fair to good, pitchers Scott McGregor (14-12), Mike Flanagan (15-11) and Dennis Martinez (16-12) also never reached the heights expected of them. All five players experienced physical problems during the season, and the injuries were largely responsible for the club's poor start.

The Orioles lost nine straight games during the season's first month and that stretch, coupled with a combined road

record of 1-17 against Kansas City (0-6), Chicago (0-6) and Boston (1-5), proved disastrous.

SCORES OF BALTIMORE ORIOLES' 1982 GAMES

APRIL			Winner	Loser
5—Kan. City	W	13-5	Stewart	Leonard
10—Boston	L	0-2	Eckersley	McGregor
10—Boston	W	5-3	D. Martinez	Ojeda
11—Boston	L	0-6	Tudor	Flanagan
13—At Kan. C.	L	5-6	Frost	Stewart
14—At Kan. C.	L	3-4	Frost	Stanhouse
17—At Chicago	L	1-3	Burns	D. Martinez
17—At Chicago	L	6-10	Hoyt	T. Martinez
18—At Chicago	L	4-6	Hoyt	McGregor
20—At Boston	L	3-8	Ojeda	Flanagan
21—At Boston	L	5-6	Eckersley	D. Martinez
23—Chicago	L	2-4	Hoyt	Palmer
24—Chicago	W	7-4	Stewart	Hickey
25—Chicago	W	2-1	D. Martinez	Trout
28—Oakland	L	2-6	Norris	Flanagan
28—Oakland	W	5-1	McGregor	Keough
29—Oakland	L	6-9	Beard	T. Martinez
30—California	W	9-4	Palmer	Bahnsen
Won 6, Lost 12				

MAY				
1—California	L	4-6§	Aase	T. Martinez
2—California	W	6-4	McGregor	Moreno
3—Seattle	W	6-0	Flanagan	Moore
4—Seattle	L	3-4	Nelson	Stewart
6—At Calif.	W	9-2	Grimsley	Aase
7—At Calif.	W	5-3	McGregor	A. Moreno
8—At Calif.	L	2-7	Renko	Flanagan
9—At Calif.	L	4-8	Kison	D. Martinez
10—At Oak.	L	6-7*	Beard	Grimsley
11—At Oak.	W	7-1	McGregor	Langford
12—At Oak.	L	4-5	Beard	Stoddard
13—At Seattle	W	3-1	D. Martinez	Beattie
14—At Seattle	W	11-4	Stewart	Nelson
15—At Seattle	L	2-3	Caudill	McGregor
16—At Seattle	W	5-4*	T. Martinez	Perry
18—Minnesota	L	7-8	Castillo	Palmer
19—Minnesota	W	4-2	Stewart	Filson
20—Minnesota	W	6-0	McGregor	Redfern
21—At Toronto	W	3-0	Flanagan	Gott
22—At Toronto	W	6-0	D. Martinez	Stieb
23—At Toronto	L	1-7	Leal	Stewart
24—At Toronto	W	7-5	McGregor	Clancy
25—At Texas	W	10-3	Palmer	Medich
26—At Texas	L	3-5	Matlack	D. Martinez
27—At Texas	W	6-0	Stewart	Tanana
29—Toronto	W	3-1	Flanagan	Leal
29—Toronto	L	10-11	McLaughlin	Stoddard
30—Toronto	L	0-6	Gott	Palmer
31—Texas	W	8-7	D. Martinez	Matlack
Won 17, Lost 12				

JUNE				
2—Texas	L	1-4	Tanana	Stewart
4—At Minn.	L	0-6	Havens	McGregor
5—At Minn.	W	3-1	Flanagan	Williams
6—At Minn.	W	7-5†	Stoddard	Davis
7—At Milw.	W	7-2	Palmer	Caldwell
8—At Milw.	W	4-2	McGregor	Lerch
9—At Milw.	W	8-3	Flanagan	Haas
10—At Milw.	L	7-9	Fingers	T. Martinez
11—New York	W	9-4	D. Martinez	Morgan
12—New York	W	5-3	T. Martinez	Rawley
14—Milwaukee	W	9-4	McGregor	Haas
15—Milwaukee	L	3-6	McClure	Flanagan
16—Milwaukee	T	2-2	.....	.....
18—At N.Y.	W	4-1	Palmer	Morgan
19—At N.Y.	L	3-4x	LaRoche	Davis
20—At N.Y.	W	5-3†	T. Martinez	Gossage
21—At Cleve.	W	7-0	D. Martinez	Waits
22—At Cleve.	L	6-8	Sorensen	Stewart
23—At Cleve.	W	3-1	Palmer	Denny
24—Detroit	L	1-7	Ujdur	McGregor
25—Detroit	W	5-2	Flanagan	Petry
26—Detroit	W	4-1	D. Martinez	Wilcox
27—Detroit	W	13-1	Palmer	Morris
29—Cleveland	L	2-9	Denny	McGregor
30—Cleveland	L	0-9	Sutcliffe	Flanagan
Won 15, Lost 9				

JULY				
1—Cleveland	L	2-6	Barker	D. Martinez
2—At Detroit	W	5-4	Palmer	Underwood
3—At Detroit	W	8-3	Davis	Ujdur
4—At Detroit	L	1-6	Petry	Flanagan
5—At Calif.	W	8-5	McGregor	Forsch
6—At Calif.	W	3-2	D. Martinez	Corbett
7—At Seattle	L	7-8	Caudill	Stoddard
8—At Seattle	L	3-4	Moore	Flanagan
9—At Oak.	W	7-5	McGregor	Keough

JULY			Winner	Loser
10—At Oak.	L	1-3	Underwood	D. Martinez
11—At Oak.	W	8-7	Davis	Kingman
15—Seattle	W	3-2	McGregor	Beattie
16—Seattle	L	0-6	Bannister	D. Martinez
17—Seattle	W	8-4	Davis	Perry
18—Seattle	W	4-3	Stewart	Moore
19—California	L	5-6	Renko	McGregor
20—California	L	4-7	Goltz	D. Martinez
21—California	W	8-7	Stewart	Hassler
23—Oakland	W	2-1	Palmer	Keough
24—Oakland	W	5-4§	T. Martinez	Owchinko
25—Oakland	W	6-2	D. Martinez	Kingman
26—Chicago	W	6-2	Flanagan	Koosman
27—Chicago	W	5-3	T. Martinez	Hickey
28—Chicago	W	2-1	McGregor	Dotson
29—At Kan. C.	L	2-7	Botelho	D. Martinez
30—At Kan. C.	L	3-4	Gura	Stewart
31—At Kan. C.	L	0-2	Blue	Flanagan
Won 16, Lost 11				

AUGUST				
1—At Kan. C.	L	2-4	Castro	T. Martinez
2—Boston	L	2-5	Tudor	McGregor
3—Boston	W	7-2	D. Martinez	Rainey
3—Boston	L	6-7	Clear	Grimsley
4—Boston	W	4-2	Flanagan	Stanley
5—Kan. City	W	5-1	Palmer	Blue
6—Kan. City	L	1-3	Frost	Davis
6—Kan. City	W	0-4	Hood	McGregor
7—Kan. City	W	6-5	T. Martinez	Quisenberry
8—Kan. City	W	10-6	Stoddard	Armstrong
9—At Chicago	L	5-9	Hickey	T. Martinez
10—At Chicago	L	4-9	Burns	McGregor
11—At Chicago	L	1-4	Dotson	D. Martinez
13—At Boston	L	2-5	Tudor	Flanagan
14—At Boston	W	5-2*	T. Martinez	Clear
15—At Boston	L	0-8	Stanley	McGregor
16—At Boston	L	4-9	Burgmeier	Davis
17—At Minn.	W	8-4	Flanagan	O'Connor
18—At Minn.	L	5-6*	Davis	Stoddard
19—At Minn.	L	3-9	Castillo	McGregor
20—At Texas	W	4-2‡	T. Martinez	Comer
21—At Texas	W	8-6	Stoddard	Matlack
22—At Texas	W	10-3	Palmer	Honeycutt
24—Toronto	W	7-3*	D. Martinez	McLaughlin
25—Toronto	W	8-3	Flanagan	Clancy
26—Toronto	W	12-5	Davis	Gott
27—Texas	W	3-1	Palmer	Smithson
27—Texas	L	3-4	Comer	Stewart
28—Texas	W	8-3	D. Martinez	Schmidt
29—Texas	W	3-2	Flanagan	Tanana
30—At Toronto	W	6-3	Davis	Eichhorn
31—At Toronto	W	1-0	Palmer	Leal
Won 18, Lost 14				

SEPTEMBER				
1—At Toronto	W	5-2	D. Martinez	Stieb
3—Minnesota	W	4-2	Flanagan	O'Connor
4—Minnesota	W	3-0	Palmer	Castillo
5—Minnesota	W	5-4	Davis	Redfern
6—At N.Y.	W	8-2	McGregor	Righetti
7—At N.Y.	W	7-2	Flanagan	Morgan
8—At N.Y.	L	5-10	Howell	Palmer
9—At Cleve.	L	0-3	Anderson	D. Martinez
10—At Cleve.	W	3-2§	Stewart	Spillner
11—At Cleve.	W	8-1	Flanagan	Sorensen
12—At Cleve.	L	0-3	Sutcliffe	T. Martinez
13—New York	W	8-7	Boddicker	May
14—New York	W	5-4	Flinn	Rawley
14—New York	W	5-3	Davis	Morgan
15—New York	W	8-5	Welchel	Guidry
16—New York	W	3-1	Palmer	Righetti
17—Cleveland	L	3-5	Sutcliffe	D. Martinez
18—Cleveland	W	5-2	McGregor	Anderson
19—Cleveland	W	4-2*	Flanagan	Glynn
20—Detroit	W	3-1	Stewart	Morris
21—Detroit	L	1-11	Wilcox	Davis
23—Detroit	L	5-10	Rucker	Stewart
24—At Milw.	L	6-15	Sutton	Flanagan
25—At Milw.	W	7-2	Palmer	Vuckovich
26—At Milw.	W	5-2	D. Martinez	Caldwell
28—At Detroit	L	6-9	Rucker	Stewart
29—At Detroit	L	2-3	Tobik	T. Martinez
30—At Detroit	W	6-5	Flinn	Tobik
Won 19, Lost 9				

OCTOBER				
1—Milwaukee	W	8-3	D. Martinez	Vuckovich
1—Milwaukee	W	7-1	Davis	Caldwell
2—Milwaukee	W	11-3	Stewart	Medich
3—Milwaukee	L	2-10	Sutton	Palmer
Won 3, Lost 1				

*10 innings.　†11 innings.　‡12 innings.　§13 innings.　x16 innings.

Rookie Cal Ripken started slowly, but was an offensive catalyst during the Orioles' frantic stretch run.

The big inning, a trademark of past Boston teams, was missing in 1982. Only Jim Rice (right) and Dwight Evans (above) were legitimate power threats.

Bullpen Rescues Boston's Year

By JOE GIULIOTTI

They didn't have power, speed or starting pitching, yet the Boston Red Sox—with Manager Ralph Houk pulling the strings on the team's one strength, its bullpen—had a chance to do the impossible.

Teams have won without power or speed, but it's not often a club contends without effective starting pitching. The Red Sox, however, were an exception to the rule and remained in the fight for the East Division title until the middle of September, eventually finishing third, six games behind.

The Red Sox, in fact, opened a five-game lead June 23, defeating the Detroit Tigers, but suffered their biggest loss of the year in that game when third baseman Carney Lansford severely sprained his left ankle trying for an inside-the-park home run. He was never the same after that—and neither were the Red Sox.

Boston played .500 ball (48-48) from that day until the Red Sox ended the season with four straight victories, three against the Yankees in New York.

Lansford returned after missing 25 games, but had trouble running and never regained top form.

"People can talk about our lack of starting pitching and that was correct, but had Lansford not gotten hurt we still would have been able to overcome it," Houk said.

John Tudor was, by far, the most effective starter, posting a 13-10 record. But he didn't become a consistent winner until August (going 7-2 in his last 11 starts). The only other Red Sox starter to win in double figures—Dennis Eckersley—finished at .500 with a 13-13 record.

The other starters—Mike Torrez, Bruce Hurst, Chuck Rainey and Bobby Ojeda—were 23-27 with only four complete games, three by Rainey.

The Red Sox didn't have the big innings that were the team's trademark in past years. With the exception of Dwight Evans (32 homers) and Jim Rice (24), there was little power as the team's 136 home runs—just 67 in Fenway Park—indicate.

Boston, though, was an exciting and interesting team. The Red Sox pecked away most of the season and won over the fans with a comeback style that saw them win 19 games on the last at-bat and erase deficits to go on to victory 14 times after the seventh inning.

Houk's four-man bullpen saved the season. Bob Stanley, who set an American League record for a reliever by pitching 168⅓ innings, had 12 victories, 14 saves and an earned-run average of 3.10. Without him, the Red Sox may have been a last-place team.

Mark Clear was unhittable through June when he had six victories and 11 saves. Despite recording only three saves after June 17, he ended with a team-high 14 victories. Yet, plagued with wildness, Clear was not nearly as effective in the second half.

Veteran Tom Burgmeier, used mainly in long relief, was 7-0 with two saves and a 2.29 ERA. Luis Aponte, the fourth member of the bullpen brigade, was 2-2 with three saves. But Aponte's record is deceiving because he kept games close until Houk turned to Stanley and Clear.

Offensively, the Sox were paced by Evans, who had the best year of his 10-year career. In addition to his homer output, Evans knocked in 98 runs, drew 112 walks, had 37 doubles and was outstanding as usual in right field.

Rice played hurt (two severe hamstring pulls) most of the second half. While he didn't exhibit his usual power, Rice still drove in 97 runs.

The offensive surprise was Wade Boggs, the rookie who didn't get a chance to play until Lansford was hurt. Boggs hit .349 in 338 at-bats and finished the season as the regular first baseman.

Second baseman Jerry Remy batted .280 and was excellent in the field, and shortstop Glenn Hoffman was superb defensively (but batted only .209). Center fielder Reid Nichols showed promise, hitting .302 in 92 games. And 43-year-old Carl Yastrzemski, who will return for one last season, ended at .275 with 16 homers and 72 RBIs despite an August slump in which he batted .144 with no home runs and five RBIs.

Lansford finished at .301 with 11 homers. Dave Stapleton (.264) got off to a terrible start and never put it together until the final month.

The Red Sox had problems in the catching department with Rich Gedman batting .249 and Gary Allenson, who did the job defensively, finishing at .205.

But the Achilles' heel was pitching.

Houk, who got late-season looks at pitchers Brian Denman, Dennis (Oil Can) Boyd, Mike Brown and Steve Crawford (who didn't pitch until August because of elbow surgery), promises the pitching will be better in 1983. It will have to be.

SCORES OF BOSTON RED SOX' 1982 GAMES

APRIL

Date		Score	Winner	Loser
10—At Balt.	W	2-0	Eckersley	McGregor
10—At Balt.	L	3-5	D. Martinez	Ojeda
11—At Balt.	W	6-0	Tudor	Flanagan
12—Chicago	L	2-3	Dotson	Torrez
14—Chicago	L	4-5	Trout	Stanley
15—Chicago	L	4-8	Lamp	Ojeda
16—Toronto	L	0-2	Leal	Eckersley
17—Toronto	W	5-4	Tudor	Bomback
18—Toronto	W	4-3	Aponte	Jackson
19—Toronto	L	4-5	Murray	Clear
20—Baltimore	W	8-3	Ojeda	Flanagan
21—Baltimore	W	6-5	Eckersley	D. Martinez
23—At Toronto	W	5-4	Tudor	Clancy
24—At Toronto	W	8-7	Torrez	Stieb
25—At Toronto	W	5-4x	Clear	McLaughlin
26—At Chicago	W	3-2	Aponte	Dotson
26—At Chicago	W	5-0	Rainey	Escarrega
27—Kan. City	W	7-5	Stanley	Frost
28—Kan. City	L	5-8	Leonard	Tudor
30—Texas	W	7-1	Torrez	Hough

Won 13, Lost 7

MAY

Date		Score	Winner	Loser
1—Texas	W	6-5x	Clear	Comer
2—Texas	W	6-0	Eckersley	Medich
3—Minnesota	W	6-2	Rainey	Felton
4—Minnesota	W	5-3	Hurst	Redfern
5—Minnesota	L	2-3	Erickson	Torrez
6—At Texas	W	5-2	Stanley	Honeycutt
7—At Texas	L	0-1	Medich	Eckersley
8—At Texas	W	2-1	Rainey	Matlack
9—At Texas	W	1-0	Stanley	Tanana
10—At Minn.	W	9-5	Burgmeier	Erickson
11—At Minn.	L	6-10	Castillo	Ojeda
12—At Minn.	W	4-1	Eckersley	Davis
13—At Kan. C.	L	2-11	Frost	Rainey
15—At Kan. C.	W	10-5	Torrez	Blue
16—At Kan. C.	L	0-5	Leonard	Ojeda
18—Seattle	L	0-3	Bannister	Eckersley
19—Seattle	W	6-5x	Clear	Caudill
20—Seattle	W	11-2	Tudor	Moore
21—Oakland	W	8-7	Burgmeier	Langford
22—Oakland	W	7-4	Stanley	McLaughlin
23—Oakland	W	6-0*	Eckersley	Norris
25—California	L	2-10	Kison	Tudor
27—At Seattle	L	6-10	Nelson	Torrez
28—At Seattle	W	3-2	Eckersley	Bannister
29—At Seattle	L	2-4	Moore	Hurst
30—At Seattle	L	1-2	Beattie	Tudor
31—At Oak.	W	5-2	Ojeda	McLaughlin

Won 17, Lost 10

JUNE

Date		Score	Winner	Loser
1—At Oak.	L	2-3	Langford	Rainey
2—At Oak.	L	0-5	Norris	Eckersley
4—At Calif.	W	11-4§	Clear	Corbett
5—At Calif.	W	7-2	Tudor	Kison
6—At Calif.	W	5-1	Ojeda	Forsch
8—New York	W	4-3‡	Clear	Frazier
9—New York	W	3-2	Hurst	John
10—New York	L	3-5	Righetti	Tudor
11—Cleveland	W	6-2	Burgmeier	Sorensen
12—Cleveland	W	6-4	Stanley	Denny
14—At N.Y.	L	1-5	Guidry	Eckersley
15—At N.Y.	L	4-5	Gossage	Clear
16—At N.Y.	L	1-4†	Righetti	Tudor
17—At Cleve.	W	6-3	Torrez	Sorensen
18—At Cleve.	L	3-10	Denny	Eckersley
19—At Cleve.	W	7-3	Rainey	Sutcliffe
20—At Cleve.	L	4-5y	Spillner	Aponte
21—Detroit	W	5-1	Tudor	Petry
22—Detroit	W	5-4§	Clear	Tobik
23—Detroit	W	10-4	Eckersley	Morris
25—Milwaukee	L	3-9	Slaton	Hurst
26—Milwaukee	L	10-11	Fingers	Clear
27—Milwaukee	L	5-7	McClure	Torrez
28—Milwaukee	W	9-7	Stanley	Vuckovich
29—At Detroit	W	4-2	Eckersley	Ujdur
30—At Detroit	L	3-12	Petry	Hurst

Won 14, Lost 12

JULY

Date		Score	Winner	Loser
1—At Detroit	L	4-5	Wilcox	Stanley
2—At Milw.	L	5-14	McClure	Torrez
3—At Milw.	L	0-7	Vuckovich	Rainey
4—At Milw.	W	4-1	Eckersley	Caldwell
5—At Kan. C.	W	4-3§	Stanley	Armstrong
5—At Kan. C.	L	3-4	Hood	Ojeda
6—At Kan. C.	L	2-6	Blue	Tudor
7—At Texas	W	8-5	Torrez	Hough
8—At Texas	W	3-0	Rainey	Honeycutt
9—Minnesota	L	1-4	Viola	Eckersley
10—Minnesota	W	5-4	Hurst	Castillo
11—Minnesota	L	3-7	Havens	Clear
15—Kan. City	W	5-3	Burgmeier	Gura
16—Kan. City	W	7-3	Eckersley	Blue
17—Kan. City	W	8-4	Clear	Quisenberry
18—Kan. City	L	0-9	Botelho	Tudor
19—Texas	W	9-5	Clear	Darwin
21—Texas	L	3-6	Hough	Eckersley
21—Texas	W	6-1	Torrez	Honeycutt
23—At Minn.	L	4-8	Castillo	Hurst
24—At Minn.	L	3-5	Havens	Stanley
25—At Minn.	W	5-0	Torrez	Williams
26—Toronto	W	3-2	Eckersley	Gott
27—Toronto	L	1-3	Leal	Tudor
28—Toronto	W	9-7	Ojeda	Jackson
29—At Chicago	W	7-3	Rainey	Lamp
30—At Chicago	L	6-9	Hoyt	Torrez
31—At Chicago	L	5-7	Burns	Eckersley

Won 14, Lost 14

AUGUST

Date		Score	Winner	Loser
1—At Chicago	L	2-4	Koosman	Hurst
2—At Balt.	W	5-2	Tudor	McGregor
3—At Balt.	L	2-7	D. Martinez	Rainey
3—At Balt.	W	7-6	Clear	Grimsley
4—At Balt.	L	2-4	Flanagan	Stanley
6—Chicago	L	3-6	Koosman	Hurst
7—Chicago	L	3-7	Dotson	Tudor
8—Chicago	W	12-6	Burgmeier	Trout
9—At Toronto	L	2-4	Schrom	Eckersley
10—At Toronto	L	0-4	Stieb	Torrez
11—At Toronto	L	3-4	Jackson	Stanley
13—Baltimore	W	5-2	Tudor	Flanagan
14—Baltimore	L	2-5‡	T. Martinez	Clear
15—Baltimore	W	8-0	Stanley	McGregor
16—Baltimore	W	9-4	Burgmeier	Davis
17—At Calif.	L	2-10	Tiant	Ojeda
18—At Calif.	W	4-1	Tudor	Witt
19—At Calif.	L	5-8	Kison	Clear
20—At Oak.	L	3-4	Beard	Clear
21—At Oak.	L	5-12	Owchinko	Stanley
22—At Oak.	W	4-2	Denman	Langford
23—At Seattle	W	4-3	Clear	Caudill
24—At Seattle	W	5-4x	Burgmeier	Caudill
26—California	L	1-10	Forsch	Torrez
26—California	W	4-3	Stanley	Zahn
27—California	L	6-7	Steirer	Denman
28—California	W	7-6‡	Clear	Kison
29—California	W	9-3	Eckersley	Renko
30—Oakland	W	9-7	Clear	Underwood
31—Oakland	W	4-0	Rainey	Hanna

Won 15, Lost 15

SEPTEMBER

Date		Score	Winner	Loser
1—Oakland	W	7-4	Denman	Owchinko
3—Seattle	W	10-8	Tudor	Bannister
4—Seattle	L	3-4	Perry	Hurst
5—Seattle	W	6-5‡	Clear	Caudill
6—At Cleve.	W	10-3	Torrez	Sorensen
7—At Cleve.	L	4-5‡	Spillner	Clear
8—At Cleve.	L	0-2	Whitson	Tudor
10—Detroit	L	4-6	Morris	Eckersley
11—Detroit	W	13-3	Torrez	Wilcox
12—Detroit	W	10-7	Stanley	Tobik
13—Cleveland	L	1-3	Whitson	Boyd
13—Cleveland	L	3-4§	Brennan	Aponte
14—Cleveland	W	12-1	Tudor	Heaton
15—Cleveland	L	4-7	Barker	Eckersley
16—At Detroit	L	2-4	Wilcox	Torrez
17—At Detroit	L	1-5	Petry	Denman
18—At Detroit	W	6-2	Stanley	Ujdur
19—At Detroit	W	6-4	Tudor	Rucker
20—At Milw.	L	3-4§	Vuckovich	Stanley
21—At Milw.	W	4-3‡	Clear	Medich
22—At Milw.	L	1-3	Caldwell	Denman
24—New York	W	4-2	Tudor	Howell
25—New York	L	2-6	Rawley	Eckersley
26—New York	W	5-2	Stanley	Guidry
27—New York	L	3-10	Righetti	Denman
28—Milwaukee	L	3-9	Medich	Rainey
29—Milwaukee	L	3-6	McClure	Clear
30—Milwaukee	W	9-4	Eckersley	Slaton

Won 13, Lost 15

OCTOBER

Date		Score	Winner	Loser
1—At N.Y.	W	3-2x	Crawford	Morgan
2—At N.Y.	W	5-0	Denman	Righetti
3—At N.Y.	W	5-3§	Brown	May

Won 3, Lost 0

*5½ innings.   †6 innings.   ‡10 innings.   §11 innings.   x12 innings.   y14 innings.

Sparky, Tigers Find No Relief

By TOM GAGE

Through it all, particularly the ninth-inning home runs that sent the Tigers sulking off the field time after time, Detroit had the best pitching staff in the American League in 1982.

Statistically, that is.

The Tigers ended the season with a 3.80 earned-run average, first in the league, but found a way to finish fourth in the East Division. They haven't finished higher than fourth since 1973, except for their runner-up showing in the second half of 1981's split season.

What went wrong this time?

Plenty.

There were early injuries that had Manager Sparky Anderson scrambling for a patchwork bullpen. There were inexplicable slumps, such as Kevin Saucier losing his control and ending up in the Florida Instructional League trying to get it back.

There was a June swoon, during which the Tigers lost 15 of 17 games and went from first place (34-18) to fourth (36-33). And there were the usual final weeks that meant nothing except trying to spoil the hopes of contending clubs.

The Tigers finished 12 games behind the Milwaukee Brewers, and for all the reasons at his fingertips, Anderson stressed only one. No bullpen.

"We lost 28 games from the seventh inning on," Anderson said. "If we ever found a way to shut the door, it would have been us everybody was chasing, not Milwaukee or Baltimore."

The bullpen suffered one setback after another, starting with Aurelio Lopez' sore shoulder in spring training. Dave Rozema, 3-0 at the time with a 1.63 ERA, went out for the season May 14 when he tore knee ligaments during a brawl with the Minnesota Twins. The Tigers can't even count on his return for 1983.

Elias Sosa gave up too many home runs, and Pat Underwood was too inconsistent. And while Dave Tobik posted nine saves in his best year as a Tiger, he needed help.

"I couldn't ask him to do everything," said Anderson. "It would have been easy to burn him out."

Just when the Tigers felt they had experienced the worst of luck, one more setback came. Lopez returned from Evansville healthy again, his arm problems over. He saved three games and won two in the first two weeks of September, and Anderson thought one of his problems might be solved.

"One relief pitcher would have made the difference," he said. "Just one guy who could come in and lock it up for us. Lopez is throwing great again, he's going to make my winter a lot shorter."

Anderson's winter wasn't short. While the Tigers were flying to Baltimore for their second-to-last road swing, Lopez was in General Manager Jim Campbell's office with his resignation. Citing personal problems, Lopez retired and returned to Mexico.

While the bullpen kept the Tigers from finishing as high as they expected—in the spring, Anderson called the 1982 Tigers his best team since the World Series years in Cincinnati—there were positive developments.

Lance Parrish hit 32 home runs, setting an American League record for catchers. Larry Herndon proved a great bargain after being obtained from San Francisco for pitcher Dan Schatzeder. Herndon finished with 23 home runs, 88 runs batted in and a .292 batting average.

The starting rotation combined for 54 victories, with Jack Morris winning 17 games, Dan Petry 15, Milt Wilcox 12 and rookie Jerry Ujdur 10. Petry won only one game in the last six weeks because of back problems, Wilcox suffered several injuries and Ujdur got a late start after returning from Evansville, but by the time the season ended, the Tigers felt they did not have to look for another starting pitcher during the winter.

Lou Whitaker (.286 average) became the leadoff hitter the Tigers have needed since Ron LeFlore left, Alan Trammell salvaged his season by hitting more than .300 after the All-Star break, and several young imports from Evansville developed into certain starters for 1983.

Howard Johnson returned from the minors in August, relaxed at the plate and hit .316 overall while establishing himself as the starting third baseman. Glenn Wilson, who hit .292 in 84 games for Detroit and contributed 12 homers, figures to play either center or right field in '83, depending on Kirk Gibson's wrist problems. And first base candidate Mike Laga showed promise after his late-season recall.

Gibson is a question mark because of the injuries that have plagued him, but the Tigers still foresee stardom for the former Michigan State football star.

"It's incredible to say, but we still haven't seen what he can do a full year," Anderson said of Gibson.

SCORES OF DETROIT TIGERS' 1982 GAMES

APRIL

Date		Score	Winner	Loser
9—At Kan. C.	L	2-4	Gura	Morris
10—At Kan. C.	L	2-5	Leonard	Petry
11—At Kan. C.	W	2-1	Rozema	Blue
12—At Toronto	L	5-9	Leal	Wilcox
13—At Toronto	W	4-2	Morris	Murray
14—At Toronto	L	4-5	Jackson	Saucier
15—Toronto	W	4-2	Saucier	Stieb
16—New York	L	2-10	Guidry	Underwood
17—New York	W	5-3	Morris	John
18—New York	W	5-2	Petry	Righetti
19—Kan. City	W	3-2	Saucier	Quisenberry
20—Kan. City	W	8-0	Wilcox	Blue
21—Kan. City	W	4-1	Underwood	Gura
22—At N.Y.	W	3-1	Morris	John
23—At N.Y.	W	9-1	Petry	Righetti
24—At N.Y.	W	7-2	Pashnick	Alexander
25—At N.Y.	L	1-3	Rawley	Wilcox
27—At Minn.	W	5-2	Morris	Jackson
28—At Minn.	L	2-4	Redfern	Petry
29—At Chicago	L	2-3	Lamp	Pashnick
30—At Chicago	W	6-4†	Saucier	Koosman

Won 13, Lost 8

MAY

Date		Score	Winner	Loser
1—At Chicago	W	5-2	Petry	Dotson
2—At Chicago	L	3-10	Hoyt	Morris
4—Texas	W	4-3	Rozema	Darwin
5—Texas	W	6-4	Sosa	Comer
7—Chicago	L	5-8	Hoyt	Morris
8—Chicago	L	4-7	Koosman	Sosa
9—Chicago	L	3-4	Dotson	Pashnick
10—At Texas	W	3-1	Wilcox	Hough
13—Minnesota	W	6-2	Morris	Pacella
14—Minnesota	W	4-2†	Rozema	Davis
15—Minnesota	W	5-4*	Sosa	Jackson
16—Minnesota	W	7-6	Tobik	Felton
18—Oakland	W	11-9	Underwood	Beard
19—Oakland	W	6-3	Petry	Keough
20—Oakland	W	11-3	Wilcox	Underwood
21—California	L	7-9	Forsch	Underwood
22—California	W	5-1	Morris	Moreno
23—California	L	2-7	Renko	Petry
25—At Seattle	L	6-7	Caudill	Sosa
26—At Seattle	L	2-4	Perry	Morris
28—At Oak.	W	6-4	Tobik	Langford
29—At Oak.	W	7-4	Wilcox	Norris
30—At Oak.	W	5-2	Morris	Keough
30—At Oak.	L	3-10	McCatty	Underwood
31—At Calif.	W	4-3	Sosa	Corbett

Won 16, Lost 9

JUNE

Date		Score	Winner	Loser
1—At Calif.	W	2-1	Petry	Forsch
2—At Calif.	W	5-4	Lopez	Corbett
4—Seattle	L	0-4	Beattie	Morris
6—Seattle	W	10-2	Petry	Perry
8—Cleveland	W	8-3	Underwood	Sutcliffe
9—Cleveland	W	2-1	Morris	Barker
9—Cleveland	W	4-3§x	Pashnick	Anderson
11—At Milw.	L	6-8	Vuckovich	Lopez
12—At Milw.	W	7-3	Wilcox	Caldwell
13—At Milw.	L	5-13	Lerch	Underwood
14—At Cleve.	L	0-5	Barker	Morris
14—At Cleve.	L	1-2	Sutcliffe	Ujdur
17—Milwaukee	L	2-3†	Caldwell	Tobik
18—Milwaukee	L	2-5	Lerch	Wilcox
19—Milwaukee	L	3-10	Haas	Morris
20—Milwaukee	L	5-7	Augustine	Ujdur
21—At Boston	L	1-5	Tudor	Petry
22—At Boston	L	4-5†	Clear	Tobik
23—At Boston	L	4-10	Eckersley	Morris
24—At Balt.	W	7-1	Ujdur	McGregor
25—At Balt.	L	2-5	Flanagan	Petry
26—At Balt.	L	1-4	D. Martinez	Wilcox
27—At Balt.	L	1-13	Palmer	Morris
29—Boston	L	2-4	Eckersley	Ujdur
30—Boston	W	12-3	Petry	Hurst

Won 9, Lost 16

JULY

Date		Score	Winner	Loser
1—Boston	W	5-4	Wilcox	Stanley
2—Baltimore	L	4-5	Palmer	Underwood
3—Baltimore	L	3-8	Davis	Ujdur
4—Baltimore	W	6-1	Petry	Flanagan
5—Minnesota	L	3-5	Castillo	Wilcox
6—Minnesota	W	11-6	Morris	Redfern
7—At Chicago	L	0-7	Lamp	Ujdur
8—At Chicago	L	2-3	Hoyt	Petry
9—At Texas	L	2-3	Darwin	Tobik
9—At Texas	L	1-3	Medich	Pashnick

JULY

Date		Score	Winner	Loser
10—At Texas	L	5-6	Darwin	Tobik
10—At Texas	W	6-0	Morris	Hough
11—At Texas	W	3-2	Ujdur	Darwin
15—At Minn.	W	18-2	Petry	O'Connor
16—At Minn.	W	6-3	Morris	Viola
17—At Minn.	W	8-4	Ujdur	Castillo
18—At Minn.	L	1-6	Havens	Underwood
19—Chicago	L	0-6	Lamp	Wilcox
20—Chicago	W	1-0	Petry	Hoyt
21—Chicago	L	3-9‡	Barojas	Tobik
23—Texas	L	1-3	Tanana	Morris
24—Texas	W	3-1	Pashnick	Medich
25—Texas	W	7-2	Petry	Darwin
25—Texas	W	7-6	Rucker	Schmidt
26—At N.Y.	W	5-3	Ujdur	Morgan
27—At N.Y.	L	5-6	May	Morris
28—At N.Y.	L	7-8	Frazier	James
30—At Toronto	L	5-6‡	Murray	James
31—At Toronto	L	0-1*	Gott	Rucker

Won 13, Lost 16

AUGUST

Date		Score	Winner	Loser
1—At Toronto	W	8-5	Morris	Leal
2—At Kan. C.	L	5-6*	Quisenberry	Tobik
3—At Kan. C.	L	5-6	Armstrong	Underwood
4—At Kan. C.	W	7-1	Petry	Gura
5—Toronto	W	5-2	Ujdur	Leal
5—Toronto	W	7-4	Rucker	Jackson
6—Toronto	W	6-0	Morris	Stieb
7—Toronto	L	4-7	Clancy	Pashnick
8—Toronto	L	4-7	Gott	Underwood
8—Toronto	L	4-7	Geisel	Rucker
9—New York	L	7-9	LaRoche	Rucker
10—New York	W	10-1	Ujdur	Alexander
11—New York	W	3-2‡	Tobik	Frazier
13—Kan. City	W	10-1	Wilcox	Frost
14—Kan. City	L	0-1	Gura	Petry
15—Kan. City	L	1-6	Leonard	Ujdur
16—Seattle	W	3-1	Morris	Bannister
17—Seattle	L	4-5	Clark	Wilcox
17—Seattle	W	3-2	Pashnick	Stoddard
18—Seattle	W	7-2	Petry	Perry
20—At Calif.	W	8-6	Ujdur	Forsch
21—At Calif.	L	1-13	Zahn	Morris
22—At Calif.	L	5-6	Sanchez	Rucker
23—At Oak.	W	5-1	Petry	Norris
24—At Oak.	L	0-3	Keough	Ujdur
26—At Seattle	L	4-5	Caudill	Morris
27—At Seattle	W	6-1	Wilcox	Beattie
28—At Seattle	L	3-4	Musselman	Tobik
29—At Seattle	W	6-2	Ujdur	Perry
31—California	L	0-11	Zahn	Morris

Won 15, Lost 15

SEPTEMBER

Date		Score	Winner	Loser
1—California	W	5-3	Wilcox	Forsch
2—California	L	2-3	Lopez	Witt
3—Oakland	W	6-3	Ujdur	Langford
4—Oakland	L	3-4	Norris	Sosa
5—Oakland	W	8-1	Morris	Keough
6—At Milw.	W	6-5*	Wilcox	Medich
7—At Milw.	L	0-4	Sutton	Petry
8—At Milw.	L	7-9	Haas	Ujdur
10—At Boston	W	6-4	Morris	Eckersley
11—At Boston	L	3-13	Torrez	Wilcox
12—At Boston	L	7-10	Stanley ·	Tobik
13—Milwaukee	W	4-3†	Lopez	Ladd
14—Milwaukee	L	3-6	Medich	Rucker
15—Milwaukee	L	3-5	Vuckovich	Morris
16—Boston	W	4-2	Wilcox	Torrez
17—Boston	W	5-1	Petry	Denman
18—Boston	L	2-6	Stanley	Ujdur
19—Boston	L	4-6	Tudor	Rucker
20—At Balt.	L	1-3	Stewart	Morris
21—At Balt.	W	11-1	Wilcox	Davis
23—At Balt.	W	10-5	Rucker	Stewart
24—Cleveland	L	2-6	Brennan	Ujdur
25—Cleveland	W	4-0	Morris	Heaton
26—Cleveland	L	3-4	Barker	Wilcox
28—Baltimore	W	9-6	Rucker	Stewart
29—Baltimore	W	3-2	Tobik	T. Martinez
30—Baltimore	L	5-6	Flinn	Tobik

Won 14, Lost 13

OCTOBER

Date		Score	Winner	Loser
1—At Cleve.	L	2-3	Barker	Wilcox
1—At Cleve.	W	4-2	Underwood	Anderson
2—At Cleve.	L	0-2	Brennan	Petry
2—At Cleve.	W	4-1	Rucker	Reed
3—At Cleve.	W	9-1	Ujdur	Sutcliffe

Won 3, Lost 2

*10 innings. †11 innings. ‡12 innings. §18 innings. xSuspended game, completed September 24.

Lance Parrish earned a spot in the record books by hitting 32 home runs, the most ever by an American League catcher.

Dave Winfield was the only Yankee regular to put together an outstanding season.

Confusion Takes Toll on Yanks

By MOSS KLEIN

The most appropriate summation of the New York Yankees' disappointing season may have been provided by an incident in Oakland in May.

Dave Collins, a first-year Yankee who was continually confused by the season's chaotic events, motioned a reporter to his locker. "Which one's Espino?" Collins said, referring to catcher Juan Espino, who had been called up from the minors the previous day in Anaheim. "I haven't met him yet."

The reporter smiled. "You missed your chance," he told Collins. "He's gone already. He's back at Columbus."

"This team is amazing," Collins said. "I've never seen a team operate this way. I still don't know half the players."

The confusion never ended for Collins or his teammates. The defending American League champions finished in fifth place in the East Division with a 79-83 record—their lowest standing since 1969 and their worst record since 1967. They were never closer than six games from first place after June 2. The only time the Yankees' record climbed as high as five games above .500 was September 12—and that was followed by a nine-game losing streak, the longest skid by the Yankees since 1953.

"Overall, it was embarrassing for those of us who have played on good teams here to go through what we went through this year," said Lou Piniella, a nine-year Yankee.

The dominant themes of the Yankees' season, once again, were change and unrest. And the dominant character, once again, was Owner George Steinbrenner.

During spring training, Steinbrenner predicted that "this will be the best-balanced team in my 10 years here. This team has a chance to be awesome." But as the season progressed, the only thing that was awesome was the number of moves that Steinbrenner made in his desperate—and futile—effort to find a winning formula. And when the season neared its end, Steinbrenner said, "There'll be a lot of changes made before next season."

The Yankees went through three managers, tying the club record set in 1946, five pitching coaches, three hitting instructors and 42 players. And none of the combinations clicked.

Bob Lemon, who had been promised by Steinbrenner that he would get a full season "win or lose," was fired on April 25

Ace reliever Rich Gossage compiled 30 saves despite sitting out more than a month.

after the Yankees got off to a 6-8 start. Gene Michael, who had been replaced by Lemon in September of 1981, returned and lasted 86 games. Michael was fired following an August 3 doubleheader loss to the Chicago White Sox—during which Steinbrenner, embarrassed over his team's play, ordered a public address announcement offering free tickets for future games to the 34,172 fans.

Clyde King, Steinbrenner's longtime

SCORES OF NEW YORK YANKEES' 1982 GAMES

APRIL

Date		Winner	Loser
11—Chicago	L 6-7x	Hickey	Gossage
11—Chicago	L 0-2	Burns	John
12—At Texas	W 10-7	Righetti	Tanana
13—At Texas	W 6-3	Morgan	Honeycutt
14—At Texas	L 1-4	Hough	Pacella
16—At Detroit	W 10-2	Guidry	Underwood
17—At Detroit	L 3-5	Morris	John
18—At Detroit	L 2-5	Petry	Righetti
20—At Chicago	W 11-2	Morgan	Trout
21—At Chicago	W 1-0	Guidry	Dotson
22—Detroit	L 1-3	Morris	John
23—Detroit	L 1-9	Petry	Righetti
24—Detroit	L 2-7	Pashnick	Alexander
25—Detroit	W 3-1	Rawley	Wilcox
27—California	L 1-3†	Moreno	Guidry
28—California	W 6-0	John	Forsch
29—California	L 0-2	Zahn	Rawley
30—Seattle	L 3-6	Perry	Gossage
	Won 7, Lost 11		

MAY

Date		Winner	Loser
1—Seattle	W 5-1	Frazier	Beattie
2—Seattle	W 4-2	Guidry	Bannister
3—Oakland	L 2-5	Keough	John
4—Oakland	L 7-9y	Owchinko	LaRoche
6—At Seattle	L 3-7	Perry	Alexander
7—At Seattle	L 2-5	Bannister	Morgan
8—At Seattle	W 9-4	Guidry	Beattie
9—At Seattle	W 3-0	John	Nelson
10—At Calif.	L 1-2	Zahn	May
11—At Calif.	W 3-2	Righetti	Forsch
12—At Calif.	W 6-5	Rawley	Moreno
13—At Oak.	W 6-4	Guidry	Underwood
14—At Oak.	W 7-4	Morgan	Keough
15—At Oak.	L 3-7	Langford	May
16—At Oak.	L 6-7	McCatty	Righetti
17—At Kan. C.	L 0-7	Gura	Erickson
18—At Kan. C.	W 6-2	Guidry	Frost
19—At Kan. C.	W 3-2	John	Splittorff
21—Minnesota	W 12-1	May	Havens
22—Minnesota	W 1-0	Righetti	Jackson
23—Minnesota	W 4-2	Guidry	Castillo
25—Toronto	W 8-0	John	Gott
26—Toronto	L 0-7	Stieb	May
28—At Minn.	W 10-5	Gossage	Davis
29—At Minn.	W 6-4	Rawley	Havens
30—At Minn.	W 8-6‡	Gossage	Boris
31—At Toronto	L 4-5	Stieb	Erickson
	Won 17, Lost 10		

JUNE

Date		Winner	Loser
1—At Toronto	L 2-5	Murray	Rawley
2—At Toronto	W 12-6y	Rawley	McLaughlin
3—At Toronto	L 1-3	Leal	John
4—Kan. City	L 3-4	Splittorff	Righetti
6—Kan. City	L 1-14	Blue	Morgan
8—At Boston	L 3-4‡	Clear	Frazier
9—At Boston	L 2-3	Hurst	John
10—At Boston	W 5-3	Righetti	Tudor
11—At Balt.	L 4-9	D. Martinez	Morgan
12—At Balt.	L 3-5	T. Martinez	Rawley
14—Boston	W 5-1	Guidry	Eckersley
15—Boston	W 5-4	Gossage	Clear
16—Boston	W 4-1*	Righetti	Tudor
18—Baltimore	L 1-4	Palmer	Morgan
19—Baltimore	W 4-3z	LaRoche	Davis
20—Baltimore	L 3-5§	T. Martinez	Gossage
21—At Milw.	L 2-6	McClure	Righetti
22—At Milw.	L 2-3	Vuckovich	Erickson
23—At Milw.	W 3-2	Morgan	Caldwell
24—Cleveland	L 2-5	Spillner	Guidry
25—Cleveland	W 11-3	John	Barker
26—Cleveland	W 4-3a	LaRoche	Whitson
27—Cleveland	L 3-4	Sorensen	Erickson
29—Milwaukee	L 4-11	Caldwell	Guidry
30—Milwaukee	L 7-9x	Fingers	Rawley
	Won 9, Lost 16		

JULY

Date		Winner	Loser
1—Milwaukee	W 5-3	Morgan	Haas
2—At Cleve.	W 3-1	Erickson	Waits
3—At Cleve.	W 10-6	Frazier	Spillner
4—At Cleve.	W 3-2	Frazier	Denny
5—At Seattle	L 4-5	Vande Berg	Frazier
6—At Seattle	W 8-7x	May	Vande Berg
7—At Oak.	W 5-3	Erickson	Langford
8—At Oak.	L 3-6	Norris	Alexander
9—At Calif.	L 1-4	John	Guidry
10—At Calif.	L 6-12	Forsch	Guidry
11—At Calif.	L 1-2	Hassler	Gossage

JULY

Date		Winner	Loser
15—Oakland	W 2-1	Gossage	Beard
16—Oakland	W 6-2	Erickson	Langford
17—Oakland	W 4-1	Rawley	Keough
18—Oakland	W 7-3	Guidry	Kingman
19—Seattle	W 5-3	John	Nelson
20—Seattle	L 5-6	Caudill	Rawley
21—Seattle	L 5-6x	Caudill	Frazier
22—Texas	W 4-3	Erickson	Butcher
23—California	W 6-3	Rawley	Zahn
24—California	W 6-5	May	Kison
25—California	L 4-6	Mahler	John
26—Detroit	L 3-5	Ujdur	Morgan
27—Detroit	W 6-5	May	Morris
28—Detroit	W 8-7	Frazier	James
30—At Texas	W 4-0	Guidry	Medich
31—At Texas	L 2-3	Hough	Alexander
	Won 17, Lost 10		

AUGUST

Date		Winner	Loser
1—At Texas	L 2-4	Honeycutt	Morgan
3—Chicago	L 0-1	Trout	Rawley
3—Chicago	L 2-14	Dotson	Erickson
4—Chicago	W 6-2	Guidry	Hoyt
4—Chicago	L 0-7	Burns	John
5—Texas	L 2-7	Hough	Alexander
6—Texas	W 6-0	Righetti	Honeycutt
7—Texas	W 9-1	Morgan	Tanana
8—Texas	L 4-6	Darwin	Rawley
8—Texas	W 8-5	John	Schmidt
9—At Detroit	W 9-7	LaRoche	Rucker
10—At Detroit	L 1-10	Ujdur	Alexander
11—At Detroit	L 2-3x	Tobik	Frazier
12—At Chicago	L 1-2	Koosman	Morgan
13—At Chicago	W 4-3	John	Trout
14—At Chicago	L 0-6	Hoyt	Rawley
15—At Chicago	L 4-6	Lamp	Gossage
16—Kan. City	W 2-0	Righetti	Blue
16—Kan. City	W 4-3	May	Black
17—Kan. City	L 4-8	Splittorff	Morgan
18—Kan. City	W 9-2	John	Frost
20—Toronto	W 4-2	Rawley	Stieb
21—Toronto	L 1-3	Clancy	Guidry
22—Toronto	W 3-1	Righetti	Gott
23—Toronto	W 4-3	LaRoche	Leal
24—Minnesota	L 0-5	Viola	John
25—Minnesota	W 8-1	Rawley	Castillo
26—Minnesota	W 7-2	Guidry	Havens
27—At Toronto	L 3-10	Leal	Righetti
28—At Toronto	L 2-3§	Murray	LaRoche
29—At Toronto	W 8-2	John	Clancy
30—At Minn.	W 8-2	Rawley	Viola
31—At Minn.	W 3-1	Guidry	Havens
	Won 17, Lost 16		

SEPTEMBER

Date		Winner	Loser
1—At Minn.	L 2-7	Williams	Righetti
3—At Kan. C.	L 3-5	Blue	Howell
4—At Kan. C.	W 3-2	Rawley	Gura
5—At Kan. C.	W 18-7	Guidry	Leonard
6—Baltimore	L 2-8	McGregor	Righetti
7—Baltimore	L 2-7	Flanagan	Morgan
8—Baltimore	W 10-5	Howell	Palmer
9—Milwaukee	W 5-4‡	May	Ladd
10—Milwaukee	L 3-5	Caldwell	Guidry
11—Milwaukee	W 14-2	Righetti	Medich
12—Milwaukee	W 9-8	Kaufman	Easterly
13—At Balt.	L 7-8	Boddicker	May
14—At Balt.	L 4-5	Flinn	Rawley
14—At Balt.	L 3-5	Davis	Morgan
15—At Balt.	L 5-8	Welchel	Guidry
16—At Balt.	L 1-3	Palmer	Righetti
17—At Milw.	L 0-14	Caldwell	Wever
18—At Milw.	L 4-6	McClure	Howell
19—At Milw.	L 1-14	Sutton	Rawley
21—Cleveland	L 8-9	Reed	May
21—Cleveland	W 6-2	Righetti	Sorensen
22—Cleveland	L 0-5†	Sutcliffe	Alexander
24—At Boston	L 2-4	Tudor	Howell
25—At Boston	W 6-2	Rawley	Eckersley
26—At Boston	L 2-5	Stanley	Guidry
27—At Boston	W 10-3	Righetti	Denman
28—At Cleve.	W 6-4	Alexander	Sutcliffe
29—At Cleve.	W 13-6	Howell	Sorensen
30—At Cleve.	W 7-5	Morgan	Spillner
	Won 12, Lost 17		

OCTOBER

Date		Winner	Loser
1—Boston	L 2-3x	Crawford	Morgan
2—Boston	L 0-5	Denman	Righetti
3—Boston	L 3-5§	Brown	May
	Won 0, Lost 3		

*6 innings. †7 innings. ‡10 innings. §11 innings. x12 innings. y13 innings. z16 innings. a17 innings.

troubleshooter and three-time pitching coach, replaced Michael and impressed the players with his friendly yet firm approach and his strategic moves. But during the final week of the season, it was disclosed that Steinbrenner had sought and received permission from the Oakland A's to talk with Manager Billy Martin, a two-time Yankees manager.

Martin, who last managed the Yankees in 1979, would have hardly recognized the team that finished the 1982 season. The roster included eight players from '79.

Steinbrenner's grand plan entering the season was to implement a speed game. He made no effort to keep free agent Reggie Jackson, who took his productive bat to California and helped the Angels win the A.L. West. Ken Griffey and Collins, former Cincinnati teammates, were brought in to aid the speed approach but the new game plan never got out of the starting block. Before spring training ended, Steinbrenner began to worry that the team wouldn't have enough power and he attempted to change course in midstream.

Steinbrenner's ensuing moves, which produced seven trades in seven weeks beginning March 24, resulted in mass confusion. By the time the season ended, nine trades involving 30 players had been made.

"The changes we kept making did more harm than good," said veteran pitcher Rudy May. "You can't keep filtering players in and out. You have to develop a closeness, a chemistry. There are too many guys on this team who don't know anything about each other."

Gone were such Yankees heroes as first baseman Bob Watson (to Atlanta), reliever Ron Davis (to Minnesota), shortstop Bucky Dent (to Texas) and, finally, pitcher Tommy John (to California). The new Yankees included catcher Butch Wynegar, infielder Roy Smalley, outfielder-first baseman Lee Mazzilli, pitcher Roger Erickson and first baseman John Mayberry.

In addition to the trades, the Yankees employed a steady shuttle from Columbus, their Class AAA team in the International League. By season's end, 19 players had played for the Yankees and Columbus, including veteran pitcher Dave LaRoche, who made four round trips. "I'm honorary captain of the Columbus-Yankees team," LaRoche said.

Dave Winfield (.280 batting average, 37 homers and 106 runs batted in) was the only Yankee to have an outstanding season. Part-timers Piniella (.307, six homers, 37 RBIs) and Oscar Gamble (.272, 18 homers, 57 RBIs) were productive as designated hitters. Center fielder Jerry Mumphrey batted .300 and contributed nine homers and 68 RBIs (both career highs); second baseman Willie Randolph hit .280, and Smalley was second to Winfield with 20 homers.

But catchers Rick Cerone and Wynegar had injury-plagued seasons, third baseman Graig Nettles hit only .232 with 18 homers and 55 RBIs, and Griffey—who received a $6.25 million, six-year contract after being acquired from the Reds—batted .277, 30 points below his career average.

Except for reliever Rich Gossage (30 saves despite missing more than a month with tendinitis), the pitchers were disappointments. Ron Guidry (14-8 record and 3.81 earned-run average) and Dave Righetti (11-10, 3.79) were inconsistent. Shane Rawley (11-10, 4.06) was shifted from the bullpen to the starting rotation and showed potential.

Naturally, the frustrating season produced outbursts from distraught players. Gossage was the most vociferous, referring to Steinbrenner as "the Fat Man" and charging that the owner "treats us like animals" and "has made being here unbearable."

Doyle Alexander perhaps epitomized the frustration—and a bit of the humor—of the season. The veteran pitcher, acquired from the San Francisco Giants in March as a replacement for injured Rick Reuschel, had a disastrous season. He was 1-7 with a 6.08 ERA and his victory didn't come until September 28.

Alexander, who missed two months after suffering a broken knuckle when he punched the dugout wall in Seattle on May 6, was the target of abuse by Steinbrenner because of his failures and his refusal to pitch for Columbus.

After Alexander was knocked out of a game in Detroit on August 10, Steinbrenner telephoned the press box and issued a statement in which he said Alexander was being ordered to New York to undergo a physical.

"I'm afraid that some of my players will get hurt playing defense behind him," said Steinbrenner, a remark that stunned even Yankee veterans who were hardened to the owner's criticism.

Alexander responded by saying, "I want to make it clear that I'm going to see a medical doctor, not a psychiatrist. People have been known to go crazy on this team, but I'm not there yet."

It was that kind of season.

Second baseman Damaso Garcia enjoyed an outstanding season and finished with a .310 batting mark.

Blue Jays Take Major Step

By NEIL MacCARL

The Toronto Blue Jays made their biggest stride toward respectability in 1982 under new Manager Bobby Cox.

Cox quickly put his stamp on the team. He platooned players at several positions, made liberal use of his bench, let the players run and established a pride in performance that saw the Blue Jays win more games—they finished 78-84—than ever before and gain a share of sixth place in the American League East with Cleveland.

In fact, Toronto finished just one game behind fifth-place New York, the 1981 A.L. champion.

The Blue Jays had a winning record (44-37) at home for the first time, and they drew 1,275,978 fans to Exhibition Stadium (an increase of 1,775 per game over the 1981 average).

It was more enjoyable in the stands, too, with the sale of beer beginning late in July.

The offensive spark was provided by second baseman Damaso Garcia, the leadoff hitter who led the team with a .310 average and set club records in hits (185), runs scored (89) and stolen bases (54) despite missing three weeks after being struck on the left hand by a pitch.

Garcia, who played in 147 games, was amazingly consistent. Only once did he go hitless in two straight games. He had a team-record 20-game batting streak, and other streaks of 12, 14 and 17 games.

He had something up his sleeve for most of the season. After Garcia injured his left elbow while sliding in early May, trainer Ken Carson fitted him with a rubber sleeve to protect the elbow and the infielder could not have played without it.

Willie Upshaw hit so well in spring training that he won the first-base job from veteran John Mayberry. Upshaw led the team in home runs (21), runs batted in (75) and game-winning RBIs (a team-record 14).

Rookie outfielder Jesse Barfield impressed with his strong and accurate throwing arm, and he was the Blue Jays' chief threat against lefthanded pitching. Fifteen of Barfield's 18 home runs came off lefthanders.

After failing to hit major league pitching, basketball star Danny Ainge returned to the backcourt and the Blue Jays were left without a third baseman.

Holdover Garth Iorg and newcomer Rance Mulliniks shared the position, combining for 55 extra-base hits and 71 RBIs. They had 11 game-winning RBIs:

Cox also platooned his catchers, and the Ernie Whitt-Buck Martinez duo produced 21 home runs and 79 RBIs. Whitt, who hit only one homer in 1981, counted 11. Martinez' 10 homers doubled his previous high.

Outfielders also were platooned, with Barfield and Hosken Powell sharing right. At times, Barry Bonnell (among the A.L.'s leading hitters early in the season before finishing at .293) shared left with Al Woods. Lloyd Moseby was the regular center fielder until late in the season, but he struggled all year (batting .236).

Cox was like a magician pulling rabbits out of a hat in using pinch-hitters. Toronto's pinch batters totaled 71 hits (tying a league record) and knocked in 53 runs.

Shortstop Alfredo Griffin played in all 162 games and made only seven errors from mid-June until the end of the season.

Under pitching coach Al Widmar, the Blue Jays used a four-man starting rotation. The three regulars—Dave Stieb, Jim Clancy and Luis Leal—had the best record of any three starters on any team in the league, graded on earned-run average, hits, walks and strikeouts per nine innings.

Stieb led the league in innings pitched (288⅓), complete games (19) and shutouts (five) and set a Blue Jays record with 17 victories.

Clancy had his best season with 16 victories. In the final week of the season, he retired 24 straight Minnesota Twins before Randy Bush got a broken-bat single leading off the ninth inning. Leal won 12, also a career high.

Rookie Jim Gott, drafted from the St. Louis Cardinals' organization, demonstrated great potential, winning five games. Three were shutouts, although only one—a 1-0 triumph over Detroit in 10 innings—was a complete game. Gott experienced some difficulty with a recurring blister problem.

The bullpen of Joey McLaughlin, Roy Lee Jackson and Dale Murray combined for 24 victories and 25 saves, and Murray set a Toronto record with 11 saves.

Jerry Garvin, the only lefthanded pitcher on the staff for most of the year, was ineffective.

Toronto won season series from New York, Detroit, Kansas City, Texas, Oakland and Minnesota, with an 8-4 record against the Royals among the year's bright spots.

SCORES OF TORONTO BLUE JAYS' 1982 GAMES

APRIL

Date			Winner	Loser
9—Milwaukee	L	4-15	Vuckovich	Bomback
10—Milwaukee	W	3-2*	Jackson	Fingers
11—Milwaukee	L	5-14	McClure	Clancy
12—Detroit	W	9-5	Leal	Wilcox
13—Detroit	L	2-4	Morris	Murray
14—Detroit	W	5-4	Jackson	Saucier
15—At Detroit	L	2-4	Saucier	Stieb
16—At Boston	W	2-0	Leal	Eckersley
17—At Boston	L	4-5	Tudor	Bomback
18—At Boston	L	3-4	Aponte	Jackson
19—At Boston	W	5-4	Murray	Clear
21—At Milw.	L	1-3	Lerch	Leal
22—At Milw.	L	0-7	Caldwell	Bomback
23—Boston	L	4-5	Tudor	Clancy
24—Boston	L	7-8	Torrez	Stieb
25—Boston	L	4-5‡	Clear	McLaughlin
27—Texas	W	8-4	Murray	Medich
28—Texas	W	6-4	Clancy	Tanana
29—At Kan. C.	W	7-0	Stieb	Splittorff
30—At Kan. C.	L	7-8	Jackson	Jackson

Won 8, Lost 12

MAY

Date			Winner	Loser
1—At Kan. C.	L	7-8	Jackson	Bomback
2—At Kan. C.	W	7-5	Clancy	Leonard
4—At Chicago	L	3-4	Burns	Stieb
5—At Chicago	L	1-4	Trout	Leal
7—Kan. City	W	6-4	McLaughlin	Leonard
8—Kan. City	W	2-1	Bomback	Frost
9—Kan. City	W	2-0	Stieb	Splittorff
10—Chicago	L	3-6	Burns	McLaughlin
11—Chicago	W	9-4	Clancy	Trout
12—Chicago	L	2-9	Lamp	Bomback
13—At Texas	L	3-4	Darwin	Stieb
14—At Texas	L	3-4†	Mirabella	Jackson
15—At Texas	W	5-2	Clancy	Tanana
16—At Texas	L	1-2*	Darwin	Jackson
18—At Cleve.	L	5-6	Spillner	Murray
19—At Cleve.	W	8-5	Garvin	Barker
20—At Cleve.	W	2-0	Clancy	Sorensen
21—Baltimore	L	0-3	Flanagan	Gott
22—Baltimore	L	0-6	D. Martinez	Stieb
23—Baltimore	W	7-1	Leal	Stewart
24—Baltimore	L	5-7	McGregor	Clancy
25—At N.Y.	L	0-8	John	Gott
26—At N.Y.	W	7-0	Stieb	May
29—At Balt.	L	1-3	Flanagan	Leal
29—At Balt.	W	11-10	McLaughlin	Stoddard
30—At Balt.	W	6-0	Gott	Palmer
31—New York	W	5-4	Stieb	Erickson

Won 13, Lost 14

JUNE

Date			Winner	Loser
1—New York	W	5-2	Murray	Rawley
2—New York	L	6-12§	Rawley	McLaughlin
3—New York	W	3-1	Leal	John
4—Cleveland	L	3-6	Barker	Murray
6—Cleveland	W	5-1	Stieb	Sorensen
6—Cleveland	L	5-7	Glynn	Garvin
7—Cleveland	W	7-3	Leal	Denny
8—California	L	4-11	Zahn	Gott
9—California	W	5-4	McLaughlin	Corbett
11—Oakland	W	2-1	Clancy	Kingman
12—Oakland	L	1-8	Langford	Stieb
13—Oakland	L	5-7	Underwood	Jackson
14—Oakland	L	2-4	Keough	Gott
15—At Calif.	W	2-0	Clancy	Witt
16—At Calif.	L	1-7	Renko	Stieb
17—At Calif.	L	8-10	Kison	Leal
18—At Oak.	W	6-4	McLaughlin	Keough
19—At Oak.	W	3-1‡	McLaughlin	Owchinko
20—At Oak.	W	3-2	Stieb	Langford
21—At Seattle	L	4-5	Moore	Leal
22—At Seattle	L	5-6	Clark	Jackson
23—At Seattle	W	5-3†	McLaughlin	Stanton
26—Minnesota	L	3-4	Davis	Stieb
27—Minnesota	W	3-2	McLaughlin	Felton
29—Seattle	L	1-4	Bannister	Clancy
30—Seattle	L	4-10	Beattie	Stieb

Won 12, Lost 14

JULY

Date			Winner	Loser
1—Seattle	L	3-4	Perry	Leal
2—At Minn.	W	9-4	Murray	Havens
3—At Minn.	L	1-2	O'Connor	Clancy
4—At Minn.	L	3-4	Little	Stieb
5—At Texas	L	2-3	Matlack	Leal
6—At Texas	W	4-3	Murray	Tanana
7—At Kan. C.	L	1-3	Gura	Clancy

JULY

Date			Winner	Loser
8—At Kan. C.	W	5-4	Stieb	Armstrong
9—Chicago	W	7-6	Murray	Dotson
10—Chicago	L	5-6	Escarrega	Gott
11—Chicago	L	7-16	Burns	Clancy
15—Texas	W	5-1	Stieb	Honeycutt
16—Texas	W	6-0	Clancy	Hough
17—Texas	W	11-3	Jackson	Butcher
18—Texas	W	5-4*	McLaughlin	Darwin
19—Kan. City	W	4-2	Leal	Black
20—Kan. City	W	9-2	Stieb	Gura
21—Kan. City	L	7-9	Blue	Clancy
22—At Chicago	L	2-3	Burns	McLaughlin
23—At Chicago	W	7-1	Leal	Barnes
24—At Chicago	W	8-1	Stieb	Lamp
25—At Chicago	L	3-5	Hoyt	Clancy
26—At Boston	L	2-3	Eckersley	Gott
27—At Boston	W	3-1	Leal	Tudor
28—At Boston	L	7-9	Ojeda	Jackson
30—Detroit	W	6-5‡	Murray	James
31—Detroit	W	1-0*	Gott	Rucker

Won 15, Lost 12

AUGUST

Date			Winner	Loser
1—Detroit	L	5-8	Morris	Leal
2—Milwaukee	W	9-4	Stieb	McClure
3—Milwaukee	L	4-7	Vuckovich	Clancy
4—Milwaukee	L	0-8	Caldwell	Gott
5—At Detroit	L	2-5	Ujdur	Leal
5—At Detroit	L	4-7	Rucker	Jackson
6—At Detroit	L	0-6	Morris	Stieb
7—At Detroit	W	7-4	Clancy	Pashnick
8—At Detroit	W	7-4	Gott	Underwood
8—At Detroit	W	7-4	Geisel	Rucker
9—Boston	W	4-2	Schrom	Eckersley
10—Boston	W	4-0	Stieb	Torrez
11—Boston	W	4-3	Jackson	Stanley
12—At Milw.	L	1-7	McClure	Gott
12—At Milw.	L	3-4	Lerch	Murray
13—At Milw.	L	1-3	Vuckovich	Leal
14—At Milw.	W	4-2	Stieb	Caldwell
15—At Milw.	W	3-2	Clancy	Slaton
16—Cleveland	W	2-1	Gott	Waits
17—Cleveland	L	5-6	Spillner	McLaughlin
17—Cleveland	L	5-9	Sutcliffe	Geisel
20—At N.Y.	L	2-4	Rawley	Stieb
21—At N.Y.	W	3-1	Clancy	Guidry
22—At N.Y.	L	1-3	Righetti	Gott
23—At N.Y.	L	3-4	LaRoche	Leal
24—At Balt.	L	3-7*	D. Martinez	McLaughlin
25—At Balt.	L	3-8	Flanagan	Clancy
26—At Balt.	L	5-12	Davis	Gott
27—New York	W	10-3	Leal	Righetti
28—New York	W	3-2†	Murray	LaRoche
29—New York	L	2-8	John	Clancy
30—Baltimore	L	3-6	Davis	Eichhorn
31—Baltimore	L	0-1	Palmer	Leal

Won 13, Lost 20

SEPTEMBER

Date			Winner	Loser
1—Baltimore	L	2-5	D. Martinez	Stieb
3—At Cleve.	L	2-3	Anderson	Clancy
4—At Cleve.	L	3-4	Brennan	Murray
5—At Cleve.	W	6-5	Leal	Barker
6—At Oak.	W	3-1	Stieb	Kingman
7—At Oak.	W	2-1	Clancy	D'Acquisto
8—At Oak.	W	6-5	Jackson	Conroy
10—At Calif.	L	2-6	Zahn	Leal
11—At Calif.	L	1-4	Forsch	Stieb
12—At Calif.	L	2-3	John	Clancy
15—Oakland	W	3-2	Leal	Conroy
15—Oakland	W	12-11	Jackson	Hanna
16—California	W	2-1‡	Jackson	Sanchez
17—California	W	6-2	Clancy	John
18—California	L	6-8	Sanchez	Murray
19—California	L	1-5	Kison	Eichhorn
20—At Minn.	L	1-4	Castillo	Leal
21—At Minn.	W	5-1	Stieb	Viola
22—At Minn.	W	3-2*	Clancy	Havens
24—At Seattle	L	2-3	Vande Berg	Murray
25—At Seattle	L	0-7	Clark	Leal
26—At Seattle	W	6-2	Stieb	Bannister
28—Minnesota	W	3-0	Clancy	Viola
28—Minnesota	W	4-3*	Jackson	Davis
29—Minnesota	L	0-8	Havens	Eichhorn
30—Minnesota	W	6-4	Leal	O'Connor

Won 14, Lost 12

OCTOBER

Date			Winner	Loser
1—Seattle	W	2-0	Stieb	Bannister
2—Seattle	W	3-0	Gott	Stoddard
3—Seattle	W	5-2	Clancy	Caudill

Won 3, Lost 0

*10 innings.   †11 innings.   ‡12 innings.   §13 innings.

Contender Status Eludes Tribe

By TERRY PLUTO

In the spring, Cleveland Indians President Gabe Paul said the 1982 Indians were not another .500 team.

Paul was right. The Indians finished the year with a 78-84 record, tied for sixth and last place in the American League East with the Toronto Blue Jays. It was a bitter disappointment for Paul and the Indians' fans, who thought Cleveland might have its first contender since 1959.

Cleveland had its annual dose of major injuries.

Pitcher Bert Blyleven went 2-2 and then suffered a major elbow injury. After surgery to repair a muscle that literally had dropped off the bone, Blyleven missed the rest of the season.

Bake McBride was counted on as the team's regular right fielder. The Indians, though, were concerned about McBride's often troublesome knees. McBride's knees were fine—but his eyes went bad. He did not play after May 21 because of a severe infection.

Rick Waits was bothered by a ligament problem in his right knee. He went 2-13 before undergoing surgery in late September.

There were other flops.

John Denny, re-signed from the free-agent pool for $2 million over three years, went 6-11 with a 5.01 earned-run average. Bothered by an ailing shoulder, Denny was traded to Philadelphia in September for three minor leaguers. Miguel Dilone hit only .235, after batting .290 and .341 in the previous two seasons. A .300 hitter in his first three years with Cleveland, Mike Hargrove slipped to .271.

The new keystone combination of shortstop Jerry Dybzinski and second baseman Jack Perconte bombed, with neither getting into 100 games. The Indians, who tried eight keystone combinations overall, made eight fewer double plays than any team in the major leagues.

In their biggest off-season trade, the Indians swapped catcher Bo Diaz to Philadelphia for outfielder Lonnie Smith. Twenty minutes later, Smith was dealt to St. Louis for pitchers Lary Sorensen and Silvio Martinez. While Smith and Diaz went on to star with their respective clubs, Sorensen was 10-15 with a 5.61 ERA and Martinez ended up on the disabled list in the minor leagues. Sorensen was 1-8 with an 8.54 ERA in his last 10 appearances.

Dave Garcia, whose Indians compiled a

Rick Sutcliffe rebounded from a bad start to win the A.L. earned-run average title.

247-244 record in his 3½ years as manager, announced in early September that he would not return in 1983. During most of the summer, there were rumors Garcia would be replaced. It never happened, but the whispers seemed to have an unsettling effect on the club.

Toby Harrah and Andre Thornton nevertheless had the best seasons of their careers, and rookie Von Hayes had his moments.

Harrah batted .304 with 25 homers, 78 runs batted in, 100 runs scored and 17 stolen bases in 20 attempts. His .400 on-base percentage was second in the American League.

After injuries kept him out of the 1980 season and limited him to 69 games in 1981, Thornton rebounded to hit 32 homers with 116 RBIs, 109 walks (he led the league with 18 intentional passes) and a .273 batting average. He knocked in the most runs of any Cleveland player in the last 28 years and missed only one game.

Hayes drove in 82 runs while batting .250 and hitting 14 homers. He stole 32 bases. Dan Spillner, Rick Sutcliffe and Len Barker were pitching mainstays.

Spillner, who tied a club record with 21 saves, was 12-10 with a team-leading 2.49 ERA.

After his first three outings of the season, Sutcliffe had a 14.53 ERA and seemed headed to the minors. Instead, he developed a slider and finished with a 14-8 record and league-leading 2.96 ERA. Barker won a team-high 15 games and was second in the league in strikeouts with 187.

SCORES OF CLEVELAND INDIANS' 1982 GAMES

APRIL

Date		W/L	Score	Winner	Loser
10—Texas		L	3-8	Hough	Waits
11—Texas		W	13-1	Barker	Medich
13—Milwaukee		L	8-9	Fingers	Lewallyn
14—Milwaukee		W	6-2	Denny	Vuckovich
15—Milwaukee		W	8-1	Blyleven	Caldwell
16—Kan. City		L	1-3	Blue	Barker
17—Kan. City		L	10-12	Frost	Waits
18—Kan. City		W	8-2	Denny	Black
20—At Texas		W	9-4	Blyleven	Hough
21—At Texas		L	2-4	Medich	Waits
22—At Texas		W	4-3	Barker	Tanana
23—At Kan. C.		L	6-11	Jackson	Sorensen
24—At Kan. C.		L	1-5	Splittorff	Denny
25—At Kan. C.		L	3-6	Gura	Blyleven
27—Seattle		L	4-7‡	Caudill	Spillner
28—Seattle		W	6-1	Barker	Moore
29—Seattle		W	5-1	Sorensen	Nelson
30—Oakland		L	0-8	Langford	Denny

Won 8, Lost 10

MAY

Date		W/L	Score	Winner	Loser
1—Oakland		L	2-8	Jones	Blyleven
2—Oakland		L	2-5	Norris	Waits
3—California		L	4-5	Aase	Spillner
4—California		W	6-5	Sorensen	Zahn
6—At Oak.		L	2-4	McCattty	Denny
7—At Oak.		W	15-6	Sutcliffe	Langford
8—At Oak.		W	8-5	Barker	Norris
9—At Oak.		W	14-2	Sorensen	Keough
10—At Seattle		L	4-6	Vande Berg	Sutcliffe
11—At Seattle		W	5-4y	Whitson	Caudill
12—At Seattle		W	8-5	Sutcliffe	Bannister
13—At Calif.		L	2-3§	Hassler	Spillner
14—At Calif.		L	2-5	Kison	Sorensen
15—At Calif.		L	6-9	Witt	Brennan
16—At Calif.		L	0-3	Forsch	Denny
18—Toronto		W	6-5	Spillner	Murray
19—Toronto		L	5-8	Garvin	Barker
20—Toronto		L	0-2	Clancy	Sorensen
21—At Chicago		L	2-3*	Burns	Spillner
22—At Chicago		L	3-7	Trout	Denny
23—At Chicago		W	6-4y	Spillner	Koosman
24—At Minn.		W	9-2	Barker	Redfern
25—At Minn.		W	7-0	Sorensen	Havens
26—At Minn.		W	2-1	Spillner	Davis
28—Chicago		W	5-2	Denny	Trout
29—Chicago		W	5-2	Sutcliffe	Hoyt
30—Chicago		W	4-2	Barker	Lamp
31—Minnesota		W	9-4	Sorensen	Filson

Won 15, Lost 13

JUNE

Date		W/L	Score	Winner	Loser
1—Minnesota		W	6-4	Glynn	Davis
2—Minnesota		W	4-2	Sutcliffe	Castillo
4—At Toronto		W	6-3	Barker	Murray
6—At Toronto		L	1-5	Stieb	Sorensen
6—At Toronto		W	7-5	Glynn	Garvin
7—At Toronto		L	3-7	Leal	Denny
8—At Detroit		L	3-8	Underwood	Sutcliffe
9—At Detroit		L	1-2	Morris	Barker
9—At Detroit		L	3-4ab	Pashnick	Anderson
11—At Boston		L	2-6	Burgmeier	Sorensen
12—At Boston		L	4-6	Stanley	Denny
14—Detroit		W	5-0	Barker	Morris
14—Detroit		W	2-1	Sutcliffe	Ujdur
17—Boston		L	3-6	Torrez	Sorensen
18—Boston		W	10-3	Denny	Eckersley
19—Boston		L	3-7	Rainey	Sutcliffe
20—Boston		W	5-4y	Spillner	Aponte
21—Baltimore		L	0-7	D. Martinez	Waits
22—Baltimore		W	8-6	Sorensen	Stewart
23—Baltimore		L	1-3	Palmer	Denny
24—At N.Y.		W	5-2	Spillner	Guidry
25—At N.Y.		L	3-11	John	Barker
26—At N.Y.		L	3-4z	LaRoche	Whitson
27—At N.Y.		W	4-3	Sorensen	Erickson
29—At Balt.		W	9-2	Denny	McGregor
30—At Balt.		W	9-0	Sutcliffe	Flanagan

Won 13, Lost 13

JULY

Date		W/L	Score	Winner	Loser
1—At Balt.		W	6-2	Barker	D. Martinez
2—New York		L	1-3	Erickson	Waits
3—New York		L	6-10	Frazier	Spillner
4—New York		L	2-3	Frazier	Denny
5—At Oak.		L	0-2	Underwood	Sutcliffe
6—At Oak.		L	3-7	Kingman	Barker
7—At Calif.		W	8-6	Waits	Witt
8—At Calif.		L	1-5	Goltz	Sorensen
9—At Seattle		W	7-4	Denny	Bannister
10—At Seattle		W	7-1	Sutcliffe	Beattie

JULY

Date		W/L	Score	Winner	Loser
11—At Seattle		W	4-3	Barker	Caudill
15—California		L	2-8	Goltz	Waits
16—California		L	0-15	Forsch	Denny
17—California		W	10-4	Glynn	Corbett
18—California		W	5-4	Glynn	Corbett
19—Oakland		W	5-4	Spillner	Beard
20—Oakland		L	4-6	Norris	Waits
21—Oakland		L	4-6	Underwood	Denny
23—Seattle		W	4-3‡	Spillner	Vande Berg
24—Seattle		L	0-9	Moore	Barker
25—Seattle		W	5-3	Sorensen	Beattie
26—Kan. City		L	1-8	Blue	Brennan
27—Kan. City		L	1-8	Frost	Waits
28—Kan. City		W	4-2	Sutcliffe	Castro
29—At Milw.		W	5-1§	Spillner	Slaton
30—At Milw.		W	7-2	Sorensen	Lerch
31—At Milw.		L	2-4	Caldwell	Waits

Won 13, Lost 14

AUGUST

Date		W/L	Score	Winner	Loser
1—At Milw.		W	4-1	Whitson	Haas
1—At Milw.		L	2-7	Slaton	Anderson
2—Texas		W	6-2	Sutcliffe	Tanana
3—Texas		W	2-0	Barker	Schmidt
3—Texas		L	4-5†	Matlack	Spillner
4—Texas		W	8-4	Anderson	Medich
6—Milwaukee		L	2-5†	Haas	Glynn
7—Milwaukee		W	4-3‡	Glynn	Slaton
8—Milwaukee		L	6-7	Bernard	Barker
9—At Kan. C.		L	2-12	Gura	Sorensen
10—At Kan. C.		L	1-5	Armstrong	Waits
11—At Kan. C.		L	0-8	Hood	Whitson
13—At Texas		L	7-8	Darwin	Spillner
14—At Texas		L	2-3	Butcher	Barker
15—At Texas		W	6-4	Sorensen	Hough
16—At Toronto		L	1-2	Gott	Waits
17—At Toronto		W	6-5	Spillner	McLaughlin
17—At Toronto		W	9-5	Sutcliffe	Geisel
20—Minnesota		W	7-5	Barker	Redfern
21—Minnesota		L	3-4	Williams	Sorensen
22—Minnesota		W	4-3	Sutcliffe	O'Connor
23—Chicago		W	5-4	Spillner	Escarrega
24—Chicago		W	14-7	Waits	Hoyt
25—Chicago		L	1-5	Dotson	Barker
27—At Minn.		L	3-5	Williams	Sorensen
28—At Minn.		L	0-10	O'Connor	Sutcliffe
29—At Minn.		L	3-6	Castillo	Spillner
30—At Chicago		L	1-4	Dotson	Waits
31—At Chicago		L	6-14	Hickey	Barker

Won 12, Lost 17

SEPTEMBER

Date		W/L	Score	Winner	Loser
1—At Chicago		L	0-6	Koosman	Sorensen
2—At Milw.		L	1-2	Haas	Sutcliffe
2—At Milw.		W	4-2	Spillner	Sutton
3—Toronto		W	3-2	Anderson	Clancy
4—Toronto		W	4-3	Brennan	Murray
5—Toronto		L	5-6	Leal	Barker
6—Boston		L	3-10	Torrez	Sorensen
7—Boston		W	5-4†	Spillner	Clear
8—Boston		W	2-0	Whitson	Tudor
9—Baltimore		W	3-0	Anderson	D. Martinez
10—Baltimore		L	2-3x	Stewart	Spillner
11—Baltimore		L	1-8	Flanagan	Sorensen
12—Baltimore		W	3-0	Sutcliffe	T. Martinez
13—At Boston		W	3-1	Whitson	Boyd
13—At Boston		W	4-3‡	Brennan	Aponte
14—At Boston		L	1-12	Tudor	Heaton
15—At Boston		W	7-4	Barker	Eckersley
17—At Balt.		W	5-3	Sutcliffe	D. Martinez
18—At Balt.		L	2-5	McGregor	Anderson
19—At Balt.		L	2-4†	Flanagan	Glynn
21—At N.Y.		W	9-8	Reed	May
21—At N.Y.		L	2-6	Righetti	Sorensen
22—At N.Y.		W	5-0*	Sutcliffe	Alexander
24—At Detroit		W	6-2	Brennan	Ujdur
25—At Detroit		L	0-4	Morris	Heaton
26—At Detroit		W	4-3	Barker	Wilcox
28—New York		L	4-6	Alexander	Sutcliffe
29—New York		L	6-13	Howell	Sorensen
30—New York		L	5-7	Morgan	Spillner

Won 15, Lost 14

OCTOBER

Date		W/L	Score	Winner	Loser
1—Detroit		W	3-2	Barker	Wilcox
1—Detroit		L	2-4	Underwood	Anderson
2—Detroit		W	2-0	Brennan	Petry
2—Detroit		L	1-4	Rucker	Reed
3—Detroit		L	1-9	Ujdur	Sutcliffe

Won 2, Lost 3

*7 innings. †10 innings. ‡11 innings. §12 innings. x13 innings. y14 innings. z17 innings. a18 innings. bSuspended game, completed September 24.

Andre Thornton enjoyed the best season of his career, hitting 32 homers and driving in 116 runs.

Reggie Jackson changed uniforms and produced another Reggie Jackson-like season.

Angels on Cloud Nine in West

By JOHN STREGE

The American League West title was won in the winter, when the California Angels made a series of transactions that paid off in the summer.

The Angels acquired stars to complement their superstars, and brought in Reggie Jackson to join them.

The additions of Jackson, Doug DeCinces, Bob Boone and Tim Foli helped the Angels to their greatest season.

They won 93 games, most in club history. They attracted more than 2.8 million fans, an American League record. And they won the West Division championship for the second time in club history, only to fall one victory short of their first World Series appearance when they lost to Milwaukee in the A.L. Championship Series.

"It was," Vice President Buzzie Bavasi said simply, "a good year."

In agreement was Manager Gene Mauch, who previously had managed 22 major league teams without a champion.

The first transaction the Angels made, at the winter meetings in Hollywood, Fla., was the purchase of catcher Boone from the Philadelphia Phillies. Boone caught 143 games and was the only catcher in the major leagues to throw out more than 50 percent of potential base stealers.

Then, the Angels dealt rookie outfielder Brian Harper to the Pittsburgh Pirates for Foli, who was projected as California's utility infielder. When All-Star shortstop Rick Burleson tore his rotator cuff 11 games into the season, Foli became the regular shortstop and played superbly. In 139 games at shortstop, he committed just 10 errors.

The acquisition of DeCinces was more out of Mauch's desire to rid himself of right fielder Dan Ford, never a favorite of the manager. "I didn't really know how good DeCinces was until this season," Mauch said.

DeCinces became a star. The third baseman batted .301 with 30 home runs and 97 runs batted in, all career highs.

Last, but not least, the Angels signed Jackson, a free agent, to a four-year, $3.6 million contract. At age 36, Jackson proved he was not through. He hit 39 homers, tying Milwaukee's Gorman Thomas for the A.L. lead, and drove in 101 runs, tops on the Angels.

Mauch was the man behind the transactions that produced the second West crown in four years for Owner Gene Autry. He

The Angels received an unexpected boost from 18-game winner Geoff Zahn.

also was the man behind the deal that might have lost it for the Angels.

When he learned that Minnesota relief pitcher Doug Corbett was available in early May, Mauch recommended the Angels get him at any price. The price was steep—promising rookie outfielder Tom Brunansky went to the Twins in a four-player deal.

In his first six outings for the Angels, Corbett had four saves and a victory. Then, he began to hang his sinker. He lost seven straight games, and at one point was sent to the Angels' Spokane farm club. He never again was a factor in the Angels' season.

Corbett did, however, typify California's year. The Angels won the A.L. West by three games over Kansas City, and maybe

SCORES OF CALIFORNIA ANGELS' 1982 GAMES

APRIL

Date		Score	Winner	Loser
6—At Oak.	L	2-3‡	Jones	Aase
7—At Oak.	W	7-0	Zahn	Norris
8—At Oak.	W	8-6y	Sanchez	Jones
9—At Minn.	L	1-2	Williams	Moreno
10—At Minn.	W	8-1	Renko	Jackson
11—At Minn.	L	1-3	Redfern	Forsch
13—Seattle	W	4-3za	Sanchez	Nelson
14—Seattle	W	2-1†	Renko	Vande Berg
15—Seattle	W	3-2	Moreno	Perry
16—Minnesota	W	4-2†	Aase	Corbett
17—Minnesota	W	6-2	Forsch	Felton
18—Minnesota	W	5-2	Zahn	Erickson
19—At Seattle	W	3-1	Witt	Nelson
20—At Seattle	L	4-6	Perry	Moreno
21—At Seattle	L	3-5	Bannister	Renko
23—Oakland	W	7-2	Forsch	Keough
24—Oakland	W	4-2	Zahn	McCatty
25—Oakland	W	5-1	Witt	Langford
27—At N.Y.	W	3-1*	Moreno	Guidry
28—At N.Y.	L	0-6	John	Forsch
29—At N.Y.	W	2-0	Zahn	Rawley
30—At Balt.	L	4-9	Palmer	Bahnsen

Won 15, Lost 7

MAY

Date		Score	Winner	Loser
1—At Balt.	W	6-4x	Aase	T. Martinez
2—At Balt.	L	4-6	McGregor	Moreno
3—At Cleve.	W	5-4	Aase	Spillner
4—At Cleve.	L	5-6	Sorensen	Zahn
6—Baltimore	L	2-9	Grimsley	Aase
7—Baltimore	L	3-5	McGregor	Moreno
8—Baltimore	W	7-2	Renko	Flanagan
9—Baltimore	W	8-4	Kison	D. Martinez
10—New York	W	2-1	Zahn	May
11—New York	L	2-3	Righetti	Forsch
12—New York	L	5-6	Rawley	Moreno
13—Cleveland	W	3-2§	Hassler	Spillner
14—Cleveland	W	5-2	Kison	Sorensen
15—Cleveland	W	9-6	Witt	Brennan
16—Cleveland	W	3-0	Forsch	Denny
18—At Milw.	W	4-1	Renko	Caldwell
19—At Milw.	W	7-2	Kison	Slaton
20—At Milw.	L	1-4	Haas	Zahn
21—At Detroit	W	9-7	Forsch	Underwood
22—At Detroit	L	1-5	Morris	Moreno
23—At Detroit	W	7-2	Renko	Petry
25—At Boston	W	10-2	Kison	Tudor
27—Milwaukee	L	3-4	Vuckovich	Forsch
28—Milwaukee	W	6-5	Corbett	Bernard
29—Milwaukee	W	5-4†	Sanchez	Easterly
30—Milwaukee	L	3-7	Slaton	Kison
31—Detroit	L	3-4	Sosa	Corbett

Won 16, Lost 11

JUNE

Date		Score	Winner	Loser
1—Detroit	L	1-2	Petry	Forsch
2—Detroit	L	4-5	Lopez	Corbett
4—Boston	L	4-11‡	Clear	Corbett
5—Boston	L	2-7	Tudor	Kison
6—Boston	L	1-5	Ojeda	Forsch
8—At Toronto	W	11-4	Zahn	Gott
9—At Toronto	L	4-5	McLaughlin	Corbett
10—At Chicago	L	6-7	Barojas	Goltz
11—At Chicago	W	6-5	Kison	Dotson
12—At Chicago	W	3-0	Forsch	Trout
13—At Chicago	W	7-4	Zahn	Lamp
15—Toronto	L	0-2	Clancy	Witt
16—Toronto	W	7-1	Renko	Stieb
17—Toronto	W	10-8	Kison	Leal
18—Chicago	W	7-2	Moreno	Lamp
19—Chicago	L	6-7	Dotson	Zahn
20—Chicago	W	3-1	Witt	Hoyt
21—Texas	W	10-2	Renko	Hough
22—Texas	L	0-4	Honeycutt	Kison
23—Texas	W	5-3	Forsch	Medich
24—Kan. City	W	7-2	Zahn	Creel
25—Kan. City	L	6-8†	Quisenberry	Moreno
26—Kan. City	W	6-5§	Forsch	Quisenberry
27—Kan. City	W	9-1	Goltz	Black
29—At Texas	W	2-1	Zahn	Medich
30—At Texas	L	3-5	Schmidt	Aase

Won 14, Lost 12

JULY

Date		Score	Winner	Loser
1—At Texas	L	2-7	Tanana	Witt
2—At Kan. C.	L	2-5	Blue	Renko
3—At Kan. C.	L	2-6	Gura	Goltz
4—At Kan. C.	L	1-6	Black	Zahn
5—Baltimore	L	5-8	McGregor	Forsch
6—Baltimore	L	2-3	D. Martinez	Corbett
7—Cleveland	L	6-8	Waits	Witt

JULY

Date		Score	Winner	Loser
8—Cleveland	W	5-1	Goltz	Sorensen
9—New York	W	4-1	Zahn	John
10—New York	W	12-6	Forsch	Guidry
11—New York	W	2-1	Hassler	Gossage
15—At Cleve.	W	8-2	Goltz	Waits
16—At Cleve.	W	15-0	Forsch	Denny
17—At Cleve.	L	4-10	Glynn	Corbett
18—At Cleve.	L	4-5	Glynn	Corbett
19—At Balt.	W	6-5	Renko	McGregor
20—At Balt.	W	7-4	Goltz	D. Martinez
21—At Balt.	L	7-8	Stewart	Hassler
23—At N.Y.	L	3-6	Rawley	Zahn
24—At N.Y.	L	5-6	May	Kison
25—At N.Y.	W	6-4	Mahler	John
26—Oakland	L	8-11	Beard	Sanchez
27—Oakland	W	8-7x	Goltz	Owchinko
28—Oakland	W	13-1	Witt	Keough
29—Seattle	W	3-1	Renko	Moore
30—Seattle	W	2-0	Forsch	Beattie
31—Seattle	L	3-9	Bannister	Goltz

Won 13, Lost 14

AUGUST

Date		Score	Winner	Loser
1—Seattle	W	9-4	Zahn	Bordi
2—Minnesota	L	7-9	Little	Sanchez
3—Minnesota	L	4-5	Havens	Renko
4—Minnesota	W	8-6	Goltz	Felton
5—Minnesota	L	6-8	O'Connor	Tiant
6—At Seattle	W	11-9	Sanchez	Bannister
7—At Seattle	W	3-1	Witt	Perry
8—At Seattle	W	9-5	Renko	Moore
10—At Minn.	L	2-5	Redfern	Forsch
11—At Minn.	W	6-3	Zahn	Felton
12—At Minn.	W	3-1	Tiant	Viola
13—At Oak.	W	9-0	Witt	Norris
14—At Oak.	L	1-10	Keough	Renko
15—At Oak.	L	2-3	Underwood	Goltz
16—At Oak.	W	8-4	Zahn	McCatty
17—Boston	W	10-2	Tiant	Ojeda
18—Boston	L	1-4	Tudor	Witt
19—Boston	W	8-5	Kison	Clear
20—Detroit	L	6-8	Ujdur	Forsch
21—Detroit	W	13-1	Zahn	Morris
22—Detroit	W	6-5	Sanchez	Rucker
23—Milwaukee	W	5-3	Witt	McClure
24—Milwaukee	L	3-7	Vuckovich	Renko
26—At Boston	W	10-1	Forsch	Torrez
26—At Boston	L	3-4	Stanley	Zahn
27—At Boston	W	7-6	Steirer	Denman
28—At Boston	L	6-7†	Clear	Kison
29—At Boston	L	3-9	Eckersley	Renko
31—At Detroit	W	11-0	Zahn	Morris

Won 17, Lost 12

SEPTEMBER

Date		Score	Winner	Loser
1—At Detroit	L	3-5	Wilcox	Forsch
2—At Detroit	L	3-6	Lopez	Witt
3—At Milw.	W	5-2	John	McClure
4—At Milw.	L	2-8	Vuckovich	Tiant
5—At Milw.	L	5-8	Caldwell	Zahn
6—Chicago	W	8-6	Renko	Kern
7—Chicago	L	4-7	Hoyt	John
8—Chicago	L	3-5	Dotson	Curtis
10—Toronto	W	6-2	Zahn	Leal
11—Toronto	W	4-1	Forsch	Stieb
12—Toronto	W	3-2	John	Clancy
13—At Chicago	W	6-4	Sanchez	Hickey
14—At Chicago	W	7-0	Kison	Lamp
15—At Chicago	L	3-8	Koosman	Zahn
16—At Toronto	L	1-2§	Jackson	Sanchez
17—At Toronto	L	2-6	Clancy	John
18—At Toronto	W	8-6	Sanchez	Murray
19—At Toronto	W	5-1	Kison	Eichhorn
20—Kan. City	W	3-2	Zahn	Gura
21—Kan. City	W	2-1	Forsch	Quisenberry
22—Kan. City	W	8-5	John	Blue
23—At Texas	L	4-5	Darwin	Witt
24—At Texas	W	10-1	Kison	Honeycutt
25—At Texas	W	6-5	Goltz	Darwin
26—At Texas	L	5-7	Hough	Forsch
27—At Kan. C.	W	3-2	John	Blue
28—At Kan. C.	L	4-5	Armstrong	Goltz
29—At Kan. C.	L	5-6	Tufts	Sanchez

Won 15, Lost 13

OCTOBER

Date		Score	Winner	Loser
1—Texas	W	4-0	Zahn	Butcher
2—Texas	W	6-4	Goltz	Hough
3—Texas	W	7-6	Mahler	Darwin

Won 3, Lost 0

*7 innings.   †10 innings.   ‡11 innings.   §12 innings.   x13 innings.   y16 innings.   z20 innings.   aSuspended game, completed April 14.

Third baseman Doug DeCinces surprised Manager Gene Mauch with the best season of his career.

could have won it by considerably more. They lost 27 games from the seventh inning on, and made a season-long search for a bullpen stopper.

Don Aase was the man early in the season, until he hurt his elbow. Luis Sanchez was the man late in the season. He won seven games and saved five.

In between, the Angels were desperate, but were saved by their own penchant for coming back.

A lesser team might have folded, but this was a team of veterans—and a team of winners. All nine regulars had played on at least one divisional champion.

Brian Downing enjoyed his finest season. He hit .281 with 28 homers and 84 RBIs while batting leadoff. A converted catcher, Downing played 158 games in left field without committing an error.

Fred Lynn rebounded from a dismal 1981 season and, in his second year with California, hit .299 with 21 homers and 86 RBIs. He contributed mightily to the Angels' stretch drive, despite playing with a cracked rib.

Rod Carew hit .319, the 14th consecutive season he exceeded .300.

Don Baylor batted only .263, but had a league-high 21 game-winning RBIs (and 93 RBIs overall).

The pitching staff, expected to be the Angels' downfall, was a surprise, the bullpen notwithstanding. The team earned-run average, 3.82, was second best in the league.

Geoff Zahn won a career-high 18 games. Ken Forsch added 13 victories, Steve Renko finished 11-6, Bruce Kison was 10-5 and Tommy John, acquired from the New York Yankees on August 31, won four key games in September and added another in the A.L. Championship Series against Milwaukee.

Two of John's victories came against Kansas City, which lost four of six games to the Angels in the last two weeks of the season.

Designated hitter Hal McRae remained healthy and recorded a major league-leading 133 RBIs.

Royals Come Painfully Close

By MIKE McKENZIE

Year of the Crutch? Year of the Choke? How best to summarize the Kansas City Royals of 1982?

Were they the frumps who, come playoff time, found September lodged in their windpipes and, therefore, were out a championship?

Or, were they overachievers who should count their blessings for even staying close to a perch in autumn that hardly anybody could foresee for them in springtime?

The Oakland A's were supposed to be the scourge of the American League West. The Royals were rated from second to fourth in the division, depending on variables called the Chicago White Sox and California Angels.

Scarcely a soul dared pick the Royals No. 1. Yet, halfway through September they had a two-game lead. And, after blowing the lead and allowing the margin for defeat to dwindle to zero, they finished in a flourish that had ace relief pitcher Dan Quisenberry alluding to the Miracle Mets of '69: "Maybe there's room for two miracles in this century."

The Angels, who built a 4½-game lead over Kansas City on September 27, did not lock out the Royals until the day before the season ended.

By then the Royals should have named Alan Alda as honorary manager. Alda portrays television's Dr. Hawkeye Pierce, and the Royals' roster was befitting any M*A*S*H episode.

In shortsighted viewing, the last 2½ weeks of the season can be lifted as a microcosm of the Royals' plight. They lost 10 of 11 games and it cost them 6½ games in the standings. They embarked on a trip September 17 and lost the first six and went 1-8 before returning home. "We played bad," said designated hitter Hal McRae, "and blew it."

But in a broader view, that crash landing—which resulted in a 90-72 record and three-game deficit—merely was a period, not an exclamation point. The ugly finish bode the Royals no more evil than other ill-fated stretches: i.e., a seven-game losing streak and nine losses in 10 games in July; seven losses in nine games from August 31 to September 10; or the 4-8 standing in the season series with the Toronto Blue Jays.

Also telling were the 0-4 records that Kansas City compiled against Dave Stieb (Toronto) and Tommy John (New York

and California).

The eternal optimist who manages the Royals, Dick Howser, summed up the year:

"I'm not much on sour grapes. I think of the season only in terms of game one through 162—not one incident, one loss, one call, or one player move. I can think of a lot more positive things that happened than negative."

The brighter moments in the eyes of Howser and a record Royals audience of more than 2.3 million included:

• Willie Wilson leading the league in batting average, .332, and triples, 15. He overcame a pulled hamstring that sidelined him for all but two games from April 5 to May 9, and a beaning in the cheek by Dan Petry of Detroit on August 4. He sat out the last day of the season while Robin Yount got three hits, leaving the Milwaukee shortstop a point short in the batting race.

• McRae leading the league in runs batted in, 133, a record for the club and for designated hitters.

• Quisenberry leading the league in saves, 35, a club record that, along with a 9-7 won-lost record, earned him The Sporting News' Fireman of the Year award for the second time in the last three seasons.

• John Wathan setting a major league record for stolen bases by a catcher, 36.

• The club leading the league in batting average, .285, hits, doubles and triples.

Further, the year was the most productive ever offensively for second baseman Frank White (.298 and 45 doubles) and shortstop U.L. Washington (.286, 10 home runs, 60 RBIs), already recognized for their defensive cohesiveness.

Amos Otis, whose temper and injury problems left him sitting most of September, hit .286 with 88 RBIs and tied for second in game-winning RBIs in the league with 20.

McRae's .308 batting average, 46 doubles and personal-high 27 home runs—along with the RBIs that topped George Brett's previous club high of 118 and Rusty Staub's previous league high of 121 by a designated hitter—made him one of the A.L.'s offensive standouts.

Brett had 21 homers, 82 RBIs and a .301 average.

Also prominent in the "uppers" of the Royals' season were Jerry Martin in solidifying right field (15 home runs, good de-

SCORES OF KANSAS CITY ROYALS' 1982 GAMES

APRIL			Winner	Loser
5—At Balt.	L	5-13	Stewart	Leonard
9—Detroit	W	4-2	Gura	Morris
10—Detroit	W	5-2	Leonard	Petry
11—Detroit	L	1-2	Rozema	Blue
13—Baltimore	W	6-5	Frost	Stewart
14—Baltimore	W	4-3	Frost	Stanhouse
16—At Cleve.	W	3-1	Blue	Barker
17—At Cleve.	W	12-10	Frost	Waits
18—At Cleve.	L	2-8	Denny	Black
19—At Detroit	L	2-3	Saucier	Quisenberry
20—At Detroit	L	0-8	Wilcox	Blue
21—At Detroit	L	1-4	Underwood	Gura
23—Cleveland	W	11-6	Jackson	Sorensen
24—Cleveland	W	5-1	Splittorff	Denny
25—Cleveland	W	6-3	Gura	Blyleven
27—At Boston	L	5-7	Stanley	Frost
28—At Boston	W	8-5	Leonard	Tudor
29—Toronto	L	0-7	Stieb	Splittorff
30—Toronto	W	8-7	Jackson	Jackson

Won 11, Lost 8

MAY				
1—Toronto	W	8-7	Jackson	Bomback
2—Toronto	L	5-7	Clancy	Leonard
3—At Milw.	W	3-2	Splittorff	Caldwell
4—At Milw.	L	5-9	Slaton	Jackson
5—At Milw.	W	3-2*	Quisenberry	Fingers
7—At Toronto	L	4-6	McLaughlin	Leonard
8—At Toronto	L	1-2	Bomback	Frost
9—At Toronto	L	0-2	Stieb	Splittorff
10—Milwaukee	W	3-2	Blue	Fingers
11—Milwaukee	W	17-3	Gura	Augustine
12—Milwaukee	W	9-7	Leonard	Lerch
13—Boston	W	11-2	Frost	Rainey
15—Boston	L	5-10	Torrez	Blue
16—Boston	W	5-0	Leonard	Ojeda
17—New York	W	7-0	Gura	Erickson
18—New York	L	2-6	Guidry	Frost
19—New York	L	2-3	John	Splittorff
21—Texas	W	3-0	Leonard	Tanana
22—Texas	L	1-3‡	Hough	Quisenberry
23—Texas	W	5-3	Armstrong	Honeycutt
24—At Chicago	L	1-3	Hoyt	Splittorff
25—At Chicago	W	7-4	Creel	Dotson
26—At Chicago	L	5-7	Burns	Gura
28—At Texas	L	2-8	Hough	Frost
29—At Texas	W	14-1	Splittorff	Honeycutt
30—At Texas	L	1-8	Medich	Creel
31—Chicago	W	11-4	Gura	Burns

Won 14, Lost 13

JUNE				
1—Chicago	W	4-3	Blue	Dotson
2—Chicago	W	7-6†	Armstrong	Barojas
4—At N.Y.	W	4-3	Splittorff	Righetti
6—At N.Y.	W	14-1	Blue	Morgan
7—At Minn.	W	5-4*	Quisenberry	Redfern
8—At Minn.	W	9-4	Gura	O'Connor
9—At Minn.	W	8-5	Splittorff	Williams
10—At Minn.	L	7-8	Redfern	Armstrong
11—Seattle	W	3-2‡	Quisenberry	Vande Berg
12—Seattle	L	2-3	Nelson	Creel
13—Seattle	L	1-7	Bannister	Gura
14—Minnesota	W	3-0	Splittorff	Havens
15—Minnesota	W	7-4	Black	Williams
16—Minnesota	L	2-5	Viola	Blue
18—At Seattle	W	4-1	Gura	Caudill
19—At Seattle	L	3-10	Beattie	Creel
20—At Seattle	W	7-5	Splittorff	Perry
21—At Oak.	L	3-4	Beard	Blue
22—At Oak.	W	2-1	Black	Keough
23—At Oak.	W	1-0	Gura	Kingman
24—At Calif.	L	2-7	Zahn	Creel
25—At Calif.	W	8-6*	Quisenberry	Moreno
26—At Calif.	L	5-6‡	Forsch	Quisenberry
27—At Calif.	L	1-9	Goltz	Black
28—Oakland	L	4-8	Langford	Gura
29—Oakland	W	7-2	Hood	Beard
30—Oakland	L	0-4	Keough	Splittorff

Won 16, Lost 11

JULY				
2—California	W	7-2	Blue	Renko
3—California	W	6-2	Gura	Goltz
4—California	W	6-1	Black	Zahn
5—Boston	L	3-4†	Stanley	Armstrong
5—Boston	W	4-3	Hood	Ojeda
6—Boston	W	6-2	Blue	Tudor
7—Toronto	W	3-1	Gura	Clancy
8—Toronto	L	4-5	Stieb	Armstrong

JULY				Winner	Loser
9—At Milw.	L	6-9	Caldwell	Splittorff
10—At Milw.	L	0-7	Lerch	Blue
11—At Milw.	L	5-8	Haas	Gura
15—At Boston	L	3-5	Burgmeier	Gura
16—At Boston	L	3-7	Eckersley	Blue
17—At Boston	L	4-8	Clear	Quisenberry
18—At Boston	W	9-0	Botelho	Tudor
19—At Toronto	L	2-4	Leal	Black
20—At Toronto	L	2-9	Stieb	Gura
21—At Toronto	W	9-7	Blue	Clancy
23—Milwaukee	W	4-3	Quisenberry	Fingers
24—Milwaukee	L	4-7	Vuckovich	Botelho
25—Milwaukee	W	6-4	Gura	Lerch
26—At Cleve.	W	8-1	Blue	Brennan
27—At Cleve.	W	8-1	Frost	Waits
28—At Cleve.	L	2-4	Sutcliffe	Castro
29—Baltimore	W	7-2	Botelho	D. Martinez
30—Baltimore	W	4-3	Gura	Stewart
31—Baltimore	W	2-0	Blue	Flanagan

Won 15, Lost 12

AUGUST				
1—Baltimore	W	4-2	Castro	T. Martinez
2—Detroit	W	6-5*	Quisenberry	Tobik
3—Detroit	W	6-5	Armstrong	Underwood
4—Detroit	L	1-7	Petry	Gura
5—At Balt.	L	1-5	Palmer	Blue
6—At Balt.	W	3-1	Frost	Davis
6—At Balt.	W	4-0	Hood	McGregor
7—At Balt.	L	5-6	T. Martinez	Quisenberry
8—At Balt.	L	6-10	Stoddard	Armstrong
9—Cleveland	W	12-2	Gura	Sorensen
10—Cleveland	W	5-1	Armstrong	Waits
11—Cleveland	W	8-0	Hood	Whitson
13—At Detroit	L	1-10	Wilcox	Frost
14—At Detroit	W	1-0	Gura	Petry
15—At Detroit	W	6-1	Leonard	Ujdur
16—At N.Y.	L	0-2	Righetti	Blue
16—At N.Y.	L	3-4	May	Black
17—At N.Y.	W	8-4	Splittorff	Morgan
18—At N.Y.	L	2-9	John	Frost
19—Chicago	W	3-0	Gura	Hoyt
20—Chicago	W	13-5	Leonard	Escarrega
21—Chicago	W	4-3	Quisenberry	Barojas
22—Chicago	L	3-12	Koosman	Splittorff
23—At Texas	L	2-5	Schmidt	Armstrong
24—At Texas	W	5-3	Gura	Tanana
25—At Texas	W	4-3	Leonard	Butcher
26—At Texas	W	5-3	Black	Hough
27—At Chicago	W	7-1	Splittorff	Koosman
28—At Chicago	W	10-1	Blue	Burns
29—At Chicago	W	7-4	Gura	Hoyt
30—Texas	W	8-3	Leonard	Butcher
31—Texas	L	0-6	Hough	Black

Won 21, Lost 11

SEPTEMBER				
1—Texas	L	3-7	Smithson	Splittorff
3—New York	W	5-3	Blue	Howell
4—New York	L	2-3	Rawley	Gura
5—New York	L	7-18	Guidry	Leonard
6—At Seattle	L	2-6	Bannister	Black
7—At Seattle	L	2-5	Moore	Splittorff
8—At Seattle	W	6-2	Blue	Beattie
10—Minnesota	L	0-5	Castillo	Gura
11—Minnesota	W	9-3	Leonard	Viola
12—Minnesota	W	18-7	Tufts	Felton
13—Seattle	W	8-0	Blue	Moore
14—Seattle	W	5-2	Castro	Beattie
15—Seattle	W	5-4†	Quisenberry	Caudill
16—Seattle	L	2-4	Vande Berg	Leonard
17—At Minn.	L	4-5	Havens	Splittorff
18—At Minn.	L	5-11	Williams	Blue
19—At Minn.	L	4-9	O'Connor	Castro
20—At Calif.	L	2-3	Zahn	Gura
21—At Calif.	L	1-2	Forsch	Quisenberry
22—At Calif.	L	5-8	John	Blue
24—At Oak.	W	7-4	Gura	Codiroli
25—At Oak.	L	3-10	Underwood	Leonard
26—At Oak.	L	4-5	Beard	Quisenberry
27—California	L	2-3	John	Blue
28—California	W	5-4	Armstrong	Goltz
29—California	W	6-5	Tufts	Sanchez
30—Oakland	W	11-4	Splittorff	Norris

Won 11, Lost 16

OCTOBER				
1—Oakland	W	12-7	Castro	Kingman
2—Oakland	W	5-4	Quisenberry	Underwood
3—Oakland	L	3-6	Kingman	Gura

Won 2, Lost 1

*10 innings.　†11 innings.　‡12 innings.

fense), the steady play of veterans Greg Pryor, Cesar Geronimo (23 RBIs on 32 hits) and Lee May when pressed into emergency duty, and the emergence of several unknown quantities from the minor league system. Infielder Onix Concepcion, catcher Don Slaught, outfielder Steve Hammond and pitchers Mike Armstrong, Don Hood and Derek Botelho all had significant moments.

Willie Aikens, who had only four home runs and 30 RBIs at the All-Star break, came on strong in the stretch and finished with 17 homers and 74 RBIs.

In pitching, Larry Gura matched his personal high of 18 victories, and Paul Splittorff came through strong until developing back problems in July. Dennis Leonard was injured almost half the season, and Vida Blue was inconsistent (13-12 record). Dave Frost won three in relief, three starting, and Don Hood won his only three starts of the last several years, filling voids at critical times.

Frost, before the season, and Bill Castro, in midseason, were free-agent signees who helped the Royals survive seemingly insurmountable problems that included, among many things, perhaps the most devastating injury of the year—Leonard's broken fingers.

A victory May 21 might well be the hinge upon which the Royals' entire season hung. A line drive by Buddy Bell of Texas smashed into Leonard's right hand, which he had flung in front of his face in self-defense. The ball shattered his index and middle fingers. He missed 79 days, 16 starts, and won just 10 games, about half what is expected of him. Leonard had been the most effective righthanded pitcher in the league over the previous five seasons.

Although Howser steadfastly refused to lean on the injury excuse, the factor cannot be ignored in replaying the hand of '82.

Twenty-two players missed games with an assortment of 36 injuries. A dozen went on the disabled list.

Howser was able to field his favorite lineup—Wathan catching, Aikens at first base, White at second, Washington at short, Brett at third, Wilson in left field, Otis in center, Martin in right and McRae at designated hitter—just 43 times, barely one-fourth of the schedule.

Pitchers missed 34 scheduled starts, position players missed 278 games. Armstrong, the rookie in middle relief, said, "What is most vivid in my mind is seeing people falling down all the time."

Pitcher Mike Jones, counted on as a starter, missed the whole season with a

Willie Wilson overcame injuries to win his first batting title.

broken neck from a December auto accident. Newly acquired rookie reliever Scott Brown also rode out the season on the disabled list with a bad elbow.

Both utility infielders who made the squad in spring training, Concepcion and Tim Ireland, started the year on the disabled list. Aikens (sprained hand) and Washington (back spasms) joined them in April. And Wilson missed all but five at-bats in the first 26 games because of a pulled hamstring.

Otis suffered an abdominal muscle pull in May that plagued him the rest of the season, and he also was suspended five days for throwing his bat after he was hit in the helmet September 1 by a pitch from Mike Smithson of Texas. Otis missed the last nine games when a groin muscle pull felled him.

Wathan broke a foot, Frost required knee surgery and Slaught needed surgery to repair torn ligaments in his left thumb.

During the devastating September—which began with three losses at Minnesota, followed by three defeats in Anaheim (the Royals and Angels were tied for first place entering the series)—six Royals were hurt. As a result, Ron Johnson and Bombo Rivera, fresh up from Omaha, were thrust into duty when the title was still on the line.

Add to that handicap the Royals' slumping pitching—Gura, Blue and Leonard in their last 13 combined starts got one victory—and the picture was bleak.

Harold Baines handled his share of the offensive load by driving in 105 runs.

Good News, Bad News for Sox

By DAVE VAN DYCK

What kind of season was 1982 for the Chicago White Sox?

It was one that began with Manager Tony LaRussa predicting an American League West championship, only to come within one game of being fired. It was a season that saw the White Sox' record—the best in the majors in late May at 28-14—dip to 49-49 by late July. A season in which center fielder Ron LeFlore hit almost .300 halfway through the year, then sat the rest of the way. A season in which the White Sox finished with their second highest attendance ever (more than 1.5 million), but lost $3 million. A season in which LaMarr Hoyt won his first nine decisions, then lost 15 of his last 25.

"Good team, but not great," said LaRussa of Chicago's 87-75 record and third-place finish in the West Division. It was the best season for the White Sox since 1977 and the second best since 1972. It could have been better if the White Sox, who finished six games behind California, had beaten Kansas City (Chicago was 3-10 against the Royals) and the rest of the West Division (38-40 compared with 49-35 against the East).

Scheduled to start the season April 6 but snowed out until April 11, the White Sox made up for lost time by winning their first eight games. Hoyt carried the team, and by May 24 his 14 consecutive triumphs over two seasons had set a club record. But while the hitters remained consistent, the pitchers were like yo-yos.

By the All-Star break, the White Sox were two games behind California and one behind Kansas City. Hoyt was 11-7 and Richard Dotson 3-10. Pitching coach Ron Schueler was fired and replaced by veteran minor league instructor Ken Silvestri. The slide continued until the Sox had fallen to the season-low .500 mark.

The front office refused to give LaRussa a vote of confidence and rumors had player personnel director Bobby Winkles ready to take over. The team quashed the rumors. It won 15 of the next 18 games and, again, the pitching staff was the key. In the 20 games from July 18 to August 7, the staff posted a 2.51 earned-run average. LaRussa's job was saved and it appeared the season was, too, although the White Sox would never see first place again.

The effective pitching ended as suddenly as it started when, on August 8, Steve Trout gave up four runs without getting an out in Boston. The next night against Baltimore, Hoyt gave up five runs in 1⅔ innings.

Silvestri, hired on an interim basis, would be replaced after the season. And the Chicago staff would end up like the team: Part good, part bad.

Trout didn't pitch during the last month, banished to the bullpen with a 6-9 record and 4.26 ERA. The team's best pitcher, Britt Burns, ended his season at home in Alabama nursing a sore shoulder that hindered him in the last month. Still, Burns finished 13-5. Reliever Kevin Hickey didn't go home, but couldn't pitch the last 10 days because of a sore shoulder. Hoyt wound up his strange season with a 19-15 record and the most victories in the A.L.

Dotson and veterans Jerry Koosman and Dennis Lamp left for the winter feeling good. Dotson won eight of his last 13 games. Koosman was 11-7 and the most consistent pitcher at the end. Lamp finished with a career-high tying 11 victories after splitting his season between the bullpen and the starting rotation.

The hitting was consistently good compared with the pitching, except for a streak when both fell apart. That dry spell started in mid-August with the Sox three games out of first place and facing a trip to Texas, Kansas City and Cleveland. The White Sox finished it 3-7, then were outscored 24-6 in three losses to the Royals at Comiskey Park. The skid left Chicago nine games behind first-place Kansas City.

The White Sox still nurtured pennant hopes September 12 when, 3½ games back, they played the A's in Oakland. Already smarting over the loss of Burns (who started only one more game), the White Sox then lost their leader, second baseman Tony Bernazard, for the rest of the season when he broke his leg against the A's.

Bernazard's worth was evident in the final statistics. Although he missed the last 21 games, Bernazard finished second on the club in runs scored, third in walks, fourth in stolen bases and fifth in runs batted in.

Chicago's batting load was shouldered by Harold Baines, Steve Kemp, Greg Luzinski and Carlton Fisk.

Baines had his first 100-RBI season (105) and Luzinski finished with 102 RBIs, the first time the White Sox had two

SCORES OF CHICAGO WHITE SOX' 1982 GAMES

APRIL

Date		Score	Winner	Loser
11—At N.Y.	W	7-6§	Hickey	Gossage
11—At N.Y.	W	2-0	Burns	John
12—At Boston	W	3-2	Dotson	Torrez
14—At Boston	W	5-4	Trout	Stanley
15—At Boston	W	8-4	Lamp	Ojeda
17—Baltimore	W	3-1	Burns	D. Martinez
17—Baltimore	W	10-6	Hoyt	T. Martinez
18—Baltimore	W	6-4	Hoyt	McGregor
20—New York	L	2-11	Morgan	Trout
21—New York	L	0-1	Guidry	Dotson
23—At Balt.	W	4-2	Hoyt	Palmer
24—At Balt.	L	4-7	Stewart	Hickey
25—At Balt.	L	1-2	D. Martinez	Trout
26—Boston	L	2-3	Aponte	Dotson
26—Boston	L	0-5	Rainey	Escarrega
27—At Milw.	W	11-2	Hoyt	Lerch
28—At Milw.	L	1-2	Fingers	Burns
29—Detroit	W	3-2	Lamp	Pashnick
30—Detroit	L	4-6‡	Saucier	Koosman

Won 11, Lost 8

MAY

Date		Score	Winner	Loser
1—Detroit	L	2-5	Petry	Dotson
2—Detroit	W	10-3	Hoyt	Morris
4—Toronto	W	4-3	Burns	Stieb
5—Toronto	W	4-1	Trout	Leal
7—At Detroit	W	8-5	Hoyt	Morris
8—At Detroit	W	7-4	Koosman	Sosa
9—At Detroit	W	4-3	Dotson	Pashnick
10—At Toronto	W	6-3	Burns	McLaughlin
11—At Toronto	L	4-9	Clancy	Trout
12—At Toronto	W	9-2	Lamp	Bomback
13—Milwaukee	W	13-2	Hoyt	Caldwell
14—Milwaukee	L	1-2	Slaton	Dotson
15—Miwaukee	L	3-8	Bernard	Burns
16—Milwaukee	W	6-1	Trout	Lerch
17—Texas	W	8-6	Lamp	Honeycutt
18—Texas	W	10-2	Hoyt	Medich
19—Texas	W	6-5	Barojas	Darwin
21—Cleveland	W	3-2*	Burns	Spillner
22—Cleveland	W	7-3	Trout	Denny
23—Cleveland	L	4-6y	Spillner	Koosman
24—Kan. City	W	3-1	Hoyt	Splittorff
25—Kan. City	L	4-7	Creel	Dotson
26—Kan. City	W	7-5	Burns	Gura
28—At Cleve.	L	2-5	Denny	Trout
29—At Cleve.	L	2-5	Sutcliffe	Hoyt
30—At Cleve.	L	2-4	Barker	Lamp
31—At Kan. C.	L	4-11	Gura	Burns

Won 17, Lost 10

JUNE

Date		Score	Winner	Loser
1—At Kan. C.	L	3-4	Blue	Dotson
2—At Kan. C.	L	6-7‡	Armstrong	Barojas
4—At Texas	L	3-4	Hough	Hoyt
5—At Texas	W	2-1	Burns	Honeycutt
6—At Texas	L	4-5	Schmidt	Koosman
7—Oakland	W	6-5‡	Hickey	Beard
8—Oakland	W	5-4	Barojas	McLaughlin
9—Oakland	L	4-5	Keough	Hoyt
10—California	W	7-6	Barojas	Goltz
11—California	L	5-6	Kison	Dotson
12—California	L	0-3	Forsch	Trout
13—California	L	4-7	Zahn	Lamp
15—At Oak.	W	7-0	Hoyt	Kingman
16—At Oak.	W	7-6†	Barojas	Beard
17—At Oak.	W	11-7	Trout	Norris
18—At Calif.	L	2-7	Moreno	Lamp
19—At Calif.	W	7-6	Dotson	Zahn
20—At Calif.	L	1-3	Witt	Hoyt
21—Minnesota	W	5-4	Barojas	Felton
22—Minnesota	W	6-5	Solomon	Felton
23—Minnesota	L	3-6	Boris	Barojas
25—At Seattle	L	0-1	Beattie	Hoyt
26—At Seattle	W	13-3	Burns	Perry
27—At Seattle	L	5-6	Nelson	Trout
28—At Minn.	W	8-7	Lamp	Williams
29—At Minn.	L	5-12	Viola	Dotson
30—At Minn.	L	3-4	Castillo	Hoyt

Won 12, Lost 15

JULY

Date		Score	Winner	Loser
1—At Minn.	L	2-9	Redfern	Burns
3—Seattle	W	7-6	Koosman	Stanton
4—Seattle	L	1-3	Bannister	Dotson
5—Milwaukee	L	4-10	Slaton	Hoyt
7—Detroit	W	7-0	Lamp	Ujdur
8—Detroit	W	3-2	Hoyt	Petry
9—At Toronto	L	6-7	Murray	Dotson
10—At Toronto	W	6-5	Escarrega	Gott
11—At Toronto	W	16-7	Burns	Clancy
15—At Milw.	L	4-8	Slaton	Lamp
15—At Milw.	L	4-5	Caldwell	Hoyt
16—At Milw.	L	3-5	Haas	Koosman
17—At Milw.	L	2-5	Ladd	Barojas
18—At Milw.	L	3-9	Lerch	Barnes
19—At Detroit	W	6-0	Lamp	Wilcox
20—At Detroit	L	0-1	Petry	Hoyt
21—At Detroit	W	9-3§	Barojas	Tobik
22—Toronto	W	3-2	Burns	McLaughlin
23—Toronto	L	1-7	Leal	Barnes
24—Toronto	L	1-8	Stieb	Lamp
25—Toronto	W	5-3	Hoyt	Clancy
26—At Balt.	L	2-6	Flanagan	Koosman
27—At Balt.	L	3-5	T. Martinez	Hickey
28—At Balt.	L	1-2	McGregor	Dotson
29—Boston	L	3-7	Rainey	Lamp
30—Boston	W	9-6	Hoyt	Torrez
31—Boston	W	7-5	Burns	Eckersley

Won 11, Lost 16

AUGUST

Date		Score	Winner	Loser
1—Boston	W	4-2	Koosman	Hurst
3—At N.Y.	W	1-0	Trout	Rawley
3—At N.Y.	W	14-2	Dotson	Erickson
4—At N.Y.	L	2-6	Guidry	Hoyt
4—At N.Y.	W	7-0	Burns	John
6—At Boston	W	6-3	Koosman	Hurst
7—At Boston	W	7-3	Dotson	Tudor
8—At Boston	L	6-12	Burgmeier	Trout
9—Baltimore	W	9-5	Hickey	T. Martinez
10—Baltimore	W	9-4	Burns	McGregor
11—Baltimore	W	4-1	Dotson	D. Martinez
12—New York	W	2-1	Koosman	Morgan
13—New York	L	3-4	John	Trout
14—New York	W	6-0	Hoyt	Rawley
15—New York	W	6-4	Lamp	Gossage
16—At Texas	W	6-1	Dotson	Honeycutt
17—At Texas	L	3-4‡	Darwin	Lamp
18—At Texas	L	1-11	Tanana	Trout
19—At Kan. C.	L	0-3	Gura	Hoyt
20—At Kan. C.	L	5-13	Leonard	Escarrega
21—At Kan. C.	L	3-4	Quisenberry	Barojas
22—At Kan. C.	W	12-3	Koosman	Splittorff
23—At Cleve.	L	4-5	Spillner	Escarrega
24—At Cleve.	L	7-14	Waits	Hoyt
25—At Cleve.	W	5-1	Dotson	Barker
27—Kan. City	L	1-7	Splittorff	Koosman
28—Kan. City	L	1-10	Blue	Burns
29—Kan. City	L	4-7	Gura	Hoyt
30—Cleveland	W	4-1	Dotson	Waits
31—Cleveland	W	14-6	Hickey	Barker

Won 17, Lost 13

SEPTEMBER

Date		Score	Winner	Loser
1—Cleveland	W	6-0	Koosman	Sorensen
2—Texas	W	6-5†	Kern	Comer
3—Texas	W	7-5	Brusstar	Schmidt
4—Texas	W	4-0	Dotson	Tanana
5—Texas	L	7-10	Matlack	Barojas
6—At Calif.	L	6-8	Renko	Kern
7—At Calif.	W	7-4	Hoyt	John
8—At Calif.	W	5-3	Dotson	Curtis
10—At Oak.	W	9-3	Lamp	Norris
11—At Oak.	W	2-0	Koosman	Codiroli
12—At Oak.	L	2-4	Langford	Hoyt
13—California	L	4-6	Sanchez	Hickey
14—California	L	0-7	Kison	Lamp
15—California	W	8-3	Koosman	Zahn
16—Oakland	W	6-3	Hoyt	Baker
18—Oakland	L	1-2	Codiroli	Dotson
18—Oakland	L	4-5	Beard	Barojas
19—Oakland	W	8-3	Koosman	Hanna
20—At Seattle	L	2-5	Clark	Hoyt
21—At Seattle	L	4-5	Caudill	Hickey
22—At Seattle	L	4-8	Stoddard	Dotson
23—At Seattle	W	12-4	Koosman	Moore
24—Minnesota	W	3-2x	Brusstar	Boris
25—Minnesota	W	13-1	Hoyt	O'Connor
26—Minnesota	L	1-2	Castillo	Dotson
27—Seattle	L	4-8	Perry	Koosman
27—Seattle	W	4-1	Kern	Stoddard
28—Seattle	W	3-1	Lamp	Moore
29—Seattle	W	6-5	Hoyt	Nunez

Won 17, Lost 12

OCTOBER

Date		Score	Winner	Loser
1—At Minn.	L	2-3	Castillo	Dotson
2—At Minn.	W	5-3	Lamp	Viola
3—At Minn.	W	6-1	Hoyt	Havens

Won 2, Lost 1

*7 innings.   †10 innings.   ‡11 innings.   §12 innings.   x13 innings.   y14 innings.

Second baseman Tony Bernazard (above) was the heart of the White Sox while LaMarr Hoyt's 19 victories topped the American League.

players with 100 or more in 46 years. Kemp missed by two of giving the White Sox three 100-RBI men for the first time. Fisk hit 14 homers and drove in 65 runs.

The offense got an unexpected lift from Rudy Law, who replaced LeFlore in center field. LeFlore, one of the game's best offensive players, was suspended twice, once for three days, once for three hours. In the last month of the season, he appeared only as a pinch-runner. But part of the reason was Law, who compiled a .318 average and a team-high 36 stolen bases in 121 games as the leadoff man.

The White Sox' future also was brightened by the late-season showings of Ron Kittle and Greg Walker, who joined the club after their Class AAA season at Edmonton.

Outfielder Kittle, who had 50 home runs in the Pacific Coast League, hit one homer and knocked in seven runs in 29 at-bats. First baseman Walker, who missed most of the summer with a broken wrist, produced two home runs and seven RBIs while going 7 for 17.

Bill Caudill (right) rose from obscurity and established several Mariners' relief records.

Mariners Not Adrift This Time

By TRACY RINGOLSBY

When he looked at his club coming out of spring training, Seattle Manager Rene Lachemann admitted that—on paper—there wasn't much to look at.

The Mariners, never better than a sixth-place team in the American League West (except for a fifth-place finish in the second half of 1981's split season), were expected to battle the Minnesota Twins for the sixth and seventh positions in 1982.

Entering their sixth A.L. season, the Mariners had four players whom other major-league teams coveted—Floyd Bannister, Richie Zisk, Julio Cruz and Bruce Bochte—and one of them was being forced to play out of position. Bochte moved from first base to left field to make room for rookie Jim Maler. The rest of the roster was a conglomeration of fringe major leaguers, journeyman minor leaguers and untested rookies.

Lachemann had a feeling it wouldn't be long before he was history.

"To be honest with you," Lachemann said, "coming out of spring training I wanted to stay away from 100 losses. And if the club had that type of record, I didn't figure the manager would stay around very long."

Not only did the Mariners stay away from 100 losses, but Lachemann was re-hired for 1983 after the club enjoyed its most successful season. Despite a season-ending, six-game losing streak, the Mariners were 76-86, winning nine more games than any of their predecessors and finishing fourth in the American League West.

The '82 Mariners were at the .500 level later than any team in club history (59-59 on August 17) and were an unprecedented seven games over .500 (45-38) on July 8, having won 15 of 25 games in June, their best month in history.

The pitching staff, which set a club ERA record at 4.23 in 1981 despite finishing last in the major leagues in that department, developed into one of the better staffs in the A.L. Not only was this staff the first Mariner contingent to give up fewer hits (1,431) than innings pitched (1,476⅓), but it finished fourth in the league in ERA (3.88) and became the first A.L. team to surpass 1,000 strikeouts (1,002) since the 1973 California Angels. Bannister led the A.L. with 209 strikeouts and won 12 games.

The offense, supposedly a weak point because of the loss of Tom Paciorek, Jeff Burroughs and Dan Meyer during the previous winter, outscored the 1981 Mariners (4.0 runs per game to 3.9), and Seattle's .254 batting average was the second highest in club history.

The Mariners enjoyed box-office success, too. Their attendance exceeded one million for the first time since 1977, the club's first year, as 1,070,404 fans paid their way into the Kingdome.

Much of the Mariners' success can be attributed to Lachemann's skillful use of players that other clubs had written off.

While Jim Beattie set a Mariner ERA record for a starting pitcher (3.34), Bill Caudill rewrote the club's relief record books. Caudill, excess baggage with the Chicago Cubs, won more games (12) and saved more games (26) than any previous Mariner reliever. His 2.35 ERA was the lowest in club history. And his 111 strikeouts in 95⅔ innings proved the best ratio in the big leagues.

Todd Cruz, who had bounced from Philadelphia to Kansas City to California to the Chicago White Sox in the previous three years, saved the Mariners "at least 80 runs" with his defense, according to Lachemann. And he hit 16 home runs and had 57 runs batted in, tying with Bochte for the club lead in game-winning RBIs with nine.

Gaylord Perry, who at age 43 received a spring-training invitation from only the Mariners, brought the club more national recognition when he became the 15th 300-game winner in big-league history in May. Perry, suspended 10 days in September for throwing spitballs, was 10-12 overall. He had a 10-2 record in games in which Seattle scored four runs or more, and also set a Mariner record in April with 13 strikeouts against California (which stood as the A.L. season high).

And Al Cowens, who at age 30 was written off as a platoon player and sold by the Detroit Tigers to Seattle for $60,000 in the final days of spring training, set Mariner records in doubles (39), extra-base hits (67) and assists by an outfielder (14). He also led the club in RBIs (78) and finished second to Zisk in home runs with 20.

For the first time, the Mariners got a major lift from their farm system.

Lefthanded reliever Ed Vande Berg set a major-league record for rookies with 18 appearances, finished second to Caudill in ERA at 2.37 and set a Mariner record for victories by a rookie, compiling a 9-4 rec-

SCORES OF SEATTLE MARINERS' 1982 GAMES

APRIL			Winner	Loser	JULY			Winner	Loser
6—At Minn.	W	11-7	Bannister	Redfern	7—Baltimore	W	8-7	Caudill	Stoddard
7—At Minn.	L	5-7	Erickson	Beattie	8—Baltimore	W	4-3	Moore	Flanagan
8—At Minn.	L	1-4	Havens	Nelson	9—Cleveland	L	4-7	Denny	Bannister
9—At Oak.	L	3-5	McCatty	Perry	10—Cleveland	L	1-7	Sutcliffe	Beattie
11—At Oak.	W	6-3x	Caudill	McLaughlin	11—Cleveland	L	3-4	Barker	Caudill
11—At Oak.	L	1-3	Langford	Moore	15—At Balt.	L	2-3	McGregor	Beattie
13—At Calif.	L	3-4yz	Sanchez	Nelson	16—At Balt.	W	6-0	Bannister	D. Martinez
14—At Calif.	L	1-2*	Renko	Vande Berg	17—At Balt.	L	4-8	Davis	Perry
15—At Calif.	L	2-3	Moreno	Perry	18—At Balt.	L	3-4	Stewart	Moore
16—Oakland	W	5-0	Bannister	Norris	19—At N.Y.	L	3-5	John	Nelson
17—Oakland	L	3-10	Keough	Moore	20—At N.Y.	W	6-5	Caudill	Rawley
18—Oakland	W	4-3	Vande Berg	Underwood	21—At N.Y.	W	6-5‡	Caudill	Frazier
19—California	L	1-3	Witt	Nelson	23—At Cleve.	L	3-4†	Spillner	Vande Berg
20—California	W	6-4	Perry	Moreno	24—At Cleve.	W	9-0	Moore	Barker
21—California	W	5-3	Bannister	Renko	25—At Cleve.	L	3-5	Sorensen	Beattie
22—Minnesota	W	8-4	Moore	Redfern	26—Minnesota	L	4-10	O'Connor	Bannister
23—Minnesota	L	4-12	Erickson	Nunez	27—Minnesota	W	9-7	Clark	Pacella
24—Minnesota	W	3-2	Vande Berg	Davis	28—Minnesota	W	6-2	Perry	Castillo
25—Minnesota	W	5-4†	Caudill	Felton	29—At Calif.	L	1-3	Renko	Moore
27—At Cleve.	W	7-4†	Caudill	Spillner	30—At Calif.	L	0-2	Forsch	Beattie
28—At Cleve.	L	1-6	Barker	Moore	31—At Calif.	W	9-3	Bannister	Goltz
29—At Cleve.	L	1-5	Sorensen	Nelson			**Won 12, Lost 14**		
30—At N.Y.	W	6-3	Perry	Gossage					
		Won 11, Lost 12			AUGUST				
					1—At Calif.	L	4-9	Zahn	Bordi
MAY					2—At Oak.	L	5-6	Keough	Stanton
1—At N.Y.	L	1-5	Frazier	Beattie	3—At Oak.	W	3-2	Moore	Langford
2—At N.Y.	L	2-4	Guidry	Bannister	4—At Oak.	W	5-2	Beattie	Kingman
3—At Balt.	L	0-6	Flanagan	Moore	4—At Oak.	L	3-8	McCatty	Bordi
4—At Balt.	W	4-3	Nelson	Stewart	6—California	L	9-11	Sanchez	Bannister
6—New York	W	7-3	Perry	Alexander	7—California	L	1-3	Witt	Perry
7—New York	W	5-2	Bannister	Morgan	8—California	L	5-9	Renko	Moore
8—New York	L	4-9	Guidry	Beattie	9—Oakland	L	4-9	Kingman	Beattie
9—New York	L	0-3	John	Nelson	10—Oakland	W	4-2	Vande Berg	McCatty
10—Cleveland	W	6-4	Vande Berg	Sutcliffe	11—Oakland	W	7-4	Bannister	Langford
11—Cleveland	L	4-5§	Whitson	Caudill	13—At Minn.	L	1-3	Castillo	Perry
12—Cleveland	L	5-8	Sutcliffe	Bannister	14—At Minn.	W	3-1	Stanton	Havens
13—Baltimore	L	1-3	D. Martinez	Beattie	15—At Minn.	W	10-2	Beattie	Felton
14—Baltimore	L	4-11	Stewart	Nelson	16—At Detroit	L	1-3	Morris	Bannister
15—Baltimore	W	3-2	Caudill	McGregor	17—At Detroit	W	5-4	Clark	Wilcox
16—Baltimore	L	4-5*	T. Martinez	Perry	17—At Detroit	L	2-3	Pashnick	Stoddard
18—At Boston	W	3-0	Bannister	Eckersley	18—At Detroit	L	2-7	Petry	Perry
19—At Boston	L	5-6‡	Clear	Caudill	20—Milwaukee	L	5-6	Caldwell	Moore
20—At Boston	L	2-11	Tudor	Moore	21—Milwaukee	L	2-3	Medich	Clark
21—At Milw.	L	1-4	McClure	Perry	22—Milwaukee	L	5-8	Slaton	Bannister
22—At Milw.	W	7-1	Nelson	Lerch	23—Boston	L	3-4	Clear	Caudill
23—At Milw.	W	6-5†	Caudill	Fingers	24—Boston	L	4-5‡	Burgmeier	Caudill
25—Detroit	W	7-6	Caudill	Sosa	26—Detroit	W	5-4	Caudill	Morris
26—Detroit	W	4-2	Perry	Morris	27—Detroit	L	1-6	Wilcox	Beattie
27—Boston	W	10-6	Nelson	Torrez	28—Detroit	W	4-3	Musselman	Tobik
28—Boston	L	2-3	Eckersley	Bannister	29—Detroit	L	2-6	Ujdur	Perry
29—Boston	W	4-2	Moore	Hurst	30—At Milw.	W	3-2*	Vande Berg	Slaton
30—Boston	W	2-1	Beattie	Tudor	31—At Milw.	L	2-8	Caldwell	Clark
31—Milwaukee	W	5-4†	Stanton	Augustine			**Won 10, Lost 19**		
		Won 14, Lost 14							
					SEPTEMBER				
JUNE					1—At Milw.	L	3-7	Medich	Stanton
1—Milwaukee	L	1-2	Vuckovich	Nelson	3—At Boston	L	8-10	Tudor	Bannister
2—Milwaukee	L	2-5	Caldwell	Bannister	4—At Boston	W	4-3	Perry	Hurst
4—At Detroit	W	4-0	Beattie	Morris	5—At Boston	L	5-6*	Clear	Caudill
6—At Detroit	L	2-10	Petry	Perry	6—Kan. City	W	6-2	Bannister	Black
7—At Texas	W	6-0	Nelson	Matlack	7—Kan. City	W	5-2	Moore	Splittorff
8—At Texas	W	2-1§	Caudill	Mirabella	8—Kan. City	L	2-6	Blue	Beattie
9—At Texas	W	4-3†	Vande Berg	Comer	10—At Texas	W	5-2	Perry	Tanana
11—At Kan. C.	L	2-3‡	Quisenberry	Vande Berg	11—At Texas	L	2-5	Hough	Bannister
12—At Kan. C.	W	3-2	Nelson	Creel	12—At Texas	W	1-0	Stoddard	Smithson
13—At Kan. C.	W	7-1	Bannister	Gura	13—At Kan. C.	L	0-8	Blue	Moore
14—Texas	W	4-0	Beattie	Matlack	14—At Kan. C.	L	2-5	Castro	Beattie
15—Texas	L	2-5	Tanana	Moore	15—At Kan. C.	L	4-5†	Quisenberry	Caudill
16—Texas	W	7-2	Perry	Hough	16—At Kan. C.	W	4-2	Vande Berg	Leonard
17—Texas	L	1-5	Honeycutt	Nelson	17—Texas	W	6-0	Stoddard	Smithson
18—Kan. City	L	1-4	Gura	Caudill	18—Texas	L	4-10	Mason	Moore
19—Kan. City	W	10-3	Beattie	Creel	19—Texas	W	9-7	Nunez	Honeycutt
20—Kan. City	L	5-7	Splittorff	Perry	20—Chicago	W	5-2	Clark	Hoyt
21—Toronto	W	5-4	Moore	Leal	21—Chicago	W	5-4	Caudill	Hickey
22—Toronto	W	6-5	Clark	Jackson	22—Chicago	W	8-4	Stoddard	Dotson
23—Toronto	L	3-5†	McLaughlin	Stanton	23—Chicago	L	4-12	Koosman	Moore
25—Chicago	W	1-0	Beattie	Hoyt	24—Toronto	W	3-2	Vande Berg	Murray
26—Chicago	L	3-13	Burns	Perry	25—Toronto	W	7-0	Clark	Leal
27—Chicago	W	6-5	Nelson	Trout	26—Toronto	L	2-6	Stieb	Bannister
29—At Toronto	W	4-1	Bannister	Clancy	27—At Chicago	W	8-4	Perry	Koosman
30—At Toronto	W	10-4	Beattie	Stieb	27—At Chicago	L	1-4	Kern	Stoddard
		Won 15, Lost 10			28—At Chicago	L	1-3	Lamp	Moore
					29—At Chicago	L	5-6	Hoyt	Nunez
JULY							**Won 14, Lost 14**		
1—At Toronto	W	4-3	Perry	Leal					
3—At Chicago	L	6-7	Koosman	Stanton	OCTOBER				
4—At Chicago	W	3-1	Bannister	Dotson	1—At Toronto	L	0-2	Stieb	Bannister
5—New York	W	5-4	Vande Berg	Frazier	2—At Toronto	L	0-3	Gott	Stoddard
6—New York	L	7-8‡	May	Vande Berg	3—At Toronto	L	2-5	Clancy	Caudill
							Won 0, Lost 3		

*10 innings.   †11 innings.   ‡12 innings.   §14 innings.   x16 innings.   y20 innings.   zSuspended game, completed April 14.

The Mariners paid Detroit $60,000 for Al Cowens, who proceeded to set three team records and lead the club in RBIs.

ord with five saves.

Mike Moore, the No. 1 selection in the June 1981 draft, made the club in spring training and was a regular in the rotation for the entire season. His 7-14 record gave Seattle reason for hope, particularly because he pitched into the seventh inning in 12 of his last 16 starts.

Bob Stoddard, the final cut in spring training, returned in mid-August and became Seattle's most consistent starter in the final weeks. He was 3-3, but only once gave up more than four runs, pitching two complete games (including a shutout of Texas) and registering a 2.41 ERA in his nine starts.

And there was Dave Henderson, who struggled when the center-field job was

given to him a year earlier and wound up back in the minor leagues. This time, Henderson was around for the whole year, playing 104 games and finishing fourth on the Mariners with 14 home runs.

Mariner veterans had their moments, too.

Bochte, who batted a team-leading .297, set a club record with seven straight hits against Chicago in September. Zisk had 21 home runs and a 21-game hitting streak (tying the club record). And second baseman Cruz not only surpassed 40 stolen bases for the fifth straight year with 46, but he had career highs with eight home runs and 49 RBIs.

In the final analysis Seattle's odd mixture of talent was worth looking at.

Center fielder Dwayne Murphy hit only .238, but still slugged 27 home runs and drove in 94 runs.

A's Thankful for Henderson

By KIT STIER

From the beginning it was clear that 1982 was going to be a long and dreadful season for the Oakland A's.

Anemic bats and sore-armed pitchers plagued the A's the entire season. The team that bolted to a 17-1 record and won the American League West in 1981 never got its engine turned over in '82 and tumbled into fifth place.

The A's set a franchise attendance record when 1,735,489 fans turned out at the Oakland Coliseum for 78 home dates. But all those fans really had to cheer about were the exploits of Rickey Henderson, who tied Lou Brock's season stolen base record of 118 on August 26 in Milwaukee. The next night the fleet left fielder stole four bases to break the mark Brock had set in 1974 with the St. Louis Cardinals.

After breaking Brock's record, Henderson was slowed—and at times sidelined—by a jammed shoulder. He finished with 130 thefts.

Henderson might have gotten a good jump out of the starting blocks, but the rest of the A's were still complaining about their horrible spring training camp at the All-Star break.

The A's were rained out of five exhibition games and lost several days of practice because of the weather. It also didn't help that Manager Billy Martin invited 100 players to the major league camp in Phoenix.

Many of the players, especially pitchers, complained they never got in shape. During the season, eight A's spent time on the disabled list and others missed playing time because of assorted injuries.

Another trend was set for the season when the A's and California Angels played for 3 hours, 31 minutes in the season opener at the Coliseum. The A's played 43 other games that topped the three-hour mark, including three that exceeded five hours. The average time of an A's game was 2:52. Billy Ball had turned to Boring Ball.

On their way to a 68-94 record, the third worst mark since the team moved to California from Kansas City in 1968, the A's lost six straight on three occasions and five straight twice. From August 22 through September 16 they dropped 18 of 22 games.

The main reason for Oakland's troubles was the pitching staff.

Steve McCatty, runner-up in the Cy Young Award voting in 1981, left spring training with a sore right shoulder and never recovered. He was on the disabled list, appeared in just 21 games and finished with a 6-3 record.

Mike Norris, 7-11, also was on the disabled list (because of tendinitis). Rick Langford, 11-16, had a sore right elbow late in the season. Nothing was physically wrong with Matt Keough, but he went 11-18 with a 5.72 earned-run average.

The one bright spot on the pitching staff was Tom Underwood, who spent the season shuffling between the bullpen and the starting rotation. On a staff that finished with a 4.54 ERA, Underwood had a 3.29 ERA with a 10-6 record and seven saves.

The starting staff was in such disarray that Martin was forced to press relievers Dave Beard, Preston Hanna and Jeff Jones into starting assignments.

Beard, who started twice, pitched well at times and finished with a 10-9 record, 11 saves and a 3.44 ERA. The 11 saves were the most by an A's pitcher since Elias Sosa recorded 14 in 1978.

Jones had a 3-1 record, but appeared in just 18 games because of a sore right shoulder. He was never placed on the disabled list, but did not pitch after September 1.

Injuries weren't limited to the pitching staff. Catcher Mike Heath started the season on the disabled list. During the season, Jim Spencer (who was released in June), Mickey Klutts, Tony Armas and Cliff Johnson also spent time on the sideline.

It had been said that if anything ever happened to the A's starting outfielders, the club would be in trouble. How true.

Center fielder Dwayne Murphy missed 10 games with injuries and one because he was in Martin's doghouse. Right fielder Armas spent time on the disabled list with a pulled thigh muscle and missed 24 games. Henderson missed 13 games.

Those injuries forced Martin to use Jeff Burroughs, Joe Rudi and Dan Meyer in the outfield on several occasions. Martin often muttered about how terrible it was to use designated hitters on defense.

If the A's team ERA was sky high, their team batting average was subterranean. The A's hit a collective .236, easily the lowest in the major leagues.

The three outfielders were responsible for 65 of the club's 149 home runs and 234 of its 659 runs batted in. One shiny spot on offense was Burroughs, who was signed as a free agent on the first day of the season and batted a team-leading .277. He also

SCORES OF OAKLAND ATHLETICS' 1982 GAMES

APRIL

Date		Score	Winner	Loser
6—California	W	3-2‡	Jones	Aase
7—California	L	0-7	Zahn	Norris
8—California	L	6-8y	Sanchez	Jones
9—Seattle	W	5-3	McCatty	Perry
11—Seattle	L	3-6y	Caudill	McLaughlin
11—Seattle	W	3-1	Langford	Moore
13—At Minn.	W	8-3	Keough	Erickson
14—At Minn.	W	7-5§	Jones	Arroyo
15—At Minn.	L	5-11	Williams	Langford
16—At Seattle	L	0-5	Bannister	Norris
17—At Seattle	W	10-3	Keough	Moore
18—At Seattle	L	3-4	Vande Berg	Underwood
19—Minnesota	L	2-5	Davis	Langford
20—Minnesota	W	4-3y	Beard	Castillo
21—Minnesota	W	5-2	Underwood	Jackson
23—At Calif.	L	2-7	Forsch	Keough
24—At Calif.	L	2-4	Zahn	McCatty
25—At Calif.	L	1-5	Witt	Langford
28—At Balt.	W	6-2	Norris	Flanagan
28—At Balt.	L	1-5	McGregor	Keough
29—At Balt.	W	9-6	Beard	T. Martinez
30—At Cleve.	W	8-0	Langford	Denny

Won 11, Lost 11

MAY

Date		Score	Winner	Loser
1—At Cleve.	W	8-2	Jones	Blyleven
2—At Cleve.	W	5-2	Norris	Waits
3—At N.Y.	W	5-2	Keough	John
4—At N.Y.	W	9-7x	Owchinko	LaRoche
6—Cleveland	W	4-2	McCatty	Denny
7—Cleveland	L	6-15	Sutcliffe	Langford
8—Cleveland	L	5-8	Barker	Norris
9—Cleveland	L	2-14	Sorensen	Keough
10—Baltimore	W	7-6†	Beard	Grimsley
11—Baltimore	L	1-7	McGregor	Langford
12—Baltimore	W	5-4	Beard	Stoddard
13—New York	L	4-6	Guidry	Underwood
14—New York	L	4-7	Morgan	Keough
15—New York	W	7-3	Langford	May
16—New York	W	7-6	McCatty	Righetti
18—At Detroit	L	9-11	Underwood	Beard
19—At Detroit	L	3-6	Petry	Keough
20—At Detroit	L	3-11	Wilcox	Underwood
21—At Boston	L	7-8	Burgmeier	Langford
22—At Boston	L	4-7	Stanley	McLaughlin
23—At Boston	L	0-6*	Eckersley	Norris
25—At Milw.	W	10-5	Keough	Haas
26—At Milw.	W	7-2	Underwood	McClure
28—Detroit	L	4-6	Tobik	Langford
29—Detroit	L	4-7	Wilcox	Norris
30—Detroit	L	2-5	Morris	Keough
30—Detroit	W	10-3	McCatty	Underwood
31—Boston	L	2-5	Ojeda	McLaughlin

Won 12, Lost 16

JUNE

Date		Score	Winner	Loser
1—Boston	W	3-2	Langford	Rainey
2—Boston	W	5-0	Norris	Eckersley
4—Milwaukee	L	1-10	Haas	Keough
5—Milwaukee	L	3-11	McClure	Beard
6—Milwaukee	L	2-7	Vuckovich	Underwood
7—At Chicago	L	5-6‡	Hickey	Beard
8—At Chicago	L	4-5	Barojas	McLaughlin
9—At Chicago	W	5-4	Keough	Hoyt
11—At Toronto	L	1-2	Clancy	Kingman
12—At Toronto	W	8-1	Langford	Stieb
13—At Toronto	W	7-5	Underwood	Jackson
14—At Toronto	W	4-2	Keough	Gott
15—Chicago	L	0-7	Hoyt	Kingman
16—Chicago	L	6-7†	Barojas	Beard
17—Chicago	L	7-11	Trout	Norris
18—Toronto	L	4-6	McLaughlin	Keough
19—Toronto	L	1-3§	McLaughlin	Owchinko
20—Toronto	L	2-3	Stieb	Langford
21—Kan. City	W	4-3	Beard	Blue
22—Kan. City	L	1-2	Black	Keough
23—Kan. City	L	0-1	Gura	Kingman
24—At Texas	L	1-2	Matlack	Langford
25—At Texas	W	6-2	McCatty	Tanana
26—At Texas	L	2-5	Hough	Keough
27—At Texas	L	4-10	Honeycutt	Kingman
28—At Kan. C.	W	8-4	Langford	Gura
29—At Kan. C.	L	2-7	Hood	Beard
30—At Kan. C.	W	4-0	Keough	Splittorff

Won 10, Lost 18

JULY

Date		Score	Winner	Loser
2—Texas	L	0-7	Hough	Kingman
3—Texas	W	5-3	Langford	Honeycutt
4—Texas	L	4-11	Medich	Keough
5—Cleveland	W	2-0	Underwood	Sutcliffe
6—Cleveland	W	7-3	Kingman	Barker
7—New York	L	3-5	Erickson	Langford
8—New York	W	6-3	Norris	Alexander
9—Baltimore	L	5-7	McGregor	Keough
10—Baltimore	W	3-1	Underwood	D. Martinez
11—Baltimore	L	7-8	Davis	Kingman
15—At N.Y.	L	1-2	Gossage	Beard
16—At N.Y.	L	2-6	Erickson	Langford
17—At N.Y.	L	1-4	Rawley	Keough
18—At N.Y.	L	3-7	Guidry	Kingman
19—At Cleve.	L	4-5	Spillner	Beard
20—At Cleve.	W	6-4	Norris	Waits
21—At Cleve.	W	6-4	Underwood	Denny
23—At Balt.	L	1-2	Palmer	Keough
24—At Balt.	L	4-5x	T. Martinez	Owchinko
25—At Balt.	L	2-6	D. Martinez	Kingman
26—At Calif.	W	11-8	Beard	Sanchez
27—At Calif.	L	7-8x	Goltz	Owchinko
28—At Calif.	L	1-13	Witt	Keough
29—Minnesota	W	5-0	Langford	Havens
30—Minnesota	W	4-3†	Kingman	Davis
31—Minnesota	W	3-2	Underwood	Felton

Won 11, Lost 15

AUGUST

Date		Score	Winner	Loser
1—Minnesota	L	7-8	Pacella	Beard
2—Seattle	W	6-5	Keough	Stanton
3—Seattle	L	2-3	Moore	Langford
4—Seattle	L	2-5	Beattie	Kingman
4—Seattle	W	8-3	McCatty	Bordi
6—At Minn.	W	4-1	Norris	Viola
7—At Minn.	W	7-1	Keough	Castillo
8—At Minn.	W	5-2	Underwood	Havens
9—At Seattle	W	9-4	Kingman	Beattie
10—At Seattle	L	2-4	Vande Berg	McCatty
11—At Seattle	L	4-7	Bannister	Langford
13—California	L	0-9	Witt	Norris
14—California	W	10-1	Keough	Renko
15—California	W	3-2	Underwood	Goltz
16—California	L	4-8	Zahn	McCatty
17—Milwaukee	W	10-6	Langford	Haas
18—Milwaukee	W	3-2‡	Beard	McClure
19—Milwaukee	L	6-10	Vuckovich	Keough
20—Boston	W	4-3	Beard	Clear
21—Boston	W	12-5	Owchinko	Stanley
22—Boston	L	2-4	Denman	Langford
23—Detroit	L	1-5	Petry	Norris
24—Detroit	W	3-0	Keough	Ujdur
26—At Milw.	L	3-10	Caldwell	Kingman
27—At Milw.	L	4-5	Medich	Hanna
28—At Milw.	W	7-6	Langford	Ladd
29—At Milw.	L	1-8	McClure	Norris
30—At Boston	L	7-9	Clear	Underwood
31—At Boston	L	0-4	Rainey	Hanna

Won 14, Lost 15

SEPTEMBER

Date		Score	Winner	Loser
1—At Boston	L	4-7	Denman	Owchinko
3—At Detroit	L	3-6	Ujdur	Langford
4—At Detroit	W	4-3	Norris	Sosa
5—At Detroit	L	1-8	Morris	Keough
6—Toronto	L	1-3	Stieb	Kingman
7—Toronto	L	1-2	Clancy	D'Acquisto
8—Toronto	L	5-6	Jackson	Conroy
10—Chicago	L	3-9	Lamp	Norris
11—Chicago	L	0-2	Koosman	Codiroli
12—Chicago	W	4-2	Langford	Hoyt
15—At Toronto	L	2-3	Leal	Conroy
15—At Toronto	L	11-12	Jackson	Hanna
16—At Chicago	L	3-6	Hoyt	Baker
18—At Chicago	W	2-1	Codiroli	Dotson
18—At Chicago	W	5-4	Beard	Barojas
19—At Chicago	L	3-8	Koosman	Hanna
20—Texas	L	3-10	Tanana	Keough
21—Texas	W	6-1	Conroy	Hough
22—Texas	W	5-3	Baker	Smithson
24—Kan. City	L	4-7	Gura	Codiroli
25—Kan. City	W	10-3	Underwood	Leonard
26—Kan. City	W	5-4	Beard	Quisenberry
27—At Texas	L	1-4	Smithson	Langford
28—At Texas	W	5-4	Conroy	Mason
29—At Texas	L	3-5	Henke	Beard
30—At Kan. C.	L	4-11	Splittorff	Norris

Won 9, Lost 17

OCTOBER

Date		Score	Winner	Loser
1—At Kan. C.	L	7-12	Castro	Kingman
2—At Kan. C.	L	4-5	Quisenberry	Underwood
3—At Kan. C.	W	6-3	Kingman	Gura

Won 1, Lost 2

*5½ innings. †10 innings. ‡11 innings. §12 innings. x13 innings. y16 innings.

Tom Underwood shuffled between the bullpen and the starting rotation, compiling a 10-6 record with seven saves.

hit 16 homers and drove in 48 runs.

The infield, which Martin described as a "bunch of Pac-Men who gobbled up grounders and spit them out again," was not much better at the plate than it was afield.

There was little run production from third basemen Wayne Gross and Klutts. Shortstop Fred Stanley, who became a regular when the A's traded Rob Picciolo

to Milwaukee, has never been known as a hitter and wound up at .193. Davey Lopes, acquired during the off-season, hit .242 and had 11 homers, while Meyer drove in 59 runs and had eight home runs.

The catchers also failed to contribute much to Oakland's offense. Jeff Newman hit only .199 and had just six homers. Heath batted .242 with three homers.

It was that kind of year.

Rookie Dave Hostetler provided the highlight of the Rangers' season by hitting 22 home runs in his first 72 games.

Bottom Drops Out on Rangers

By JIM REEVES

Never has a Texas Rangers season started with such optimism and ended with such despair.

Losing isn't new to the Rangers, but such total incompetence—as reflected by a 64-98 record in 1982—hadn't been seen at Arlington Stadium since 1973, when the Rangers lost 105 games. Billy Martin developed the "Turnaround Gang"—a club that went 84-76—in 1974, and Texas had been a contending, or at least competitive, club in the American League West since. The Rangers even finished second to Oakland in the overall standings during strike-split 1981.

But the bottom dropped out in 1982, and Executive Vice-President Eddie Robinson and Manager Don Zimmer plunged through Owner Eddie Chiles' trapdoor.

It was Robinson, under mandate from the club's board of directors last spring, who traded Al Oliver to Montreal for Larry Parrish (who was converted from third baseman to outfielder) and rookie first baseman Dave Hostetler.

It was Robinson who dealt the club's top two minor league pitching prospects—Ron Darling and Walt Terrell—to the New York Mets for outfielder Lee Mazzilli.

And it was Robinson who paid with his job when both deals backfired.

Zimmer quickly found Mazzilli to be less than adequate in left field, and shoulder and wrist injuries curtailed his use at designated hitter. Parrish got off to the worst start of his career and Hostetler began the season at Class AAA Denver. By the time Hostetler arrived in Arlington May 29 and Parrish finally began to hit in July, it was too late to save Robinson.

Chiles fired the veteran baseball executive June 10. Zimmer escaped Chiles' wrath, but it was only a temporary reprieve. Zimmer was dismissed July 28 in a colossal public relations foulup; he managed three games after getting the word from Chiles.

It was typical of the Rangers' haphazard and miserable season.

The Rangers' season opener was delayed by a blizzard in New York, but by mid-April Texas had put together a modest four-game winning streak, including a three-game sweep of the Brewers in Milwaukee. It was not a portent of things to come.

Milwaukee repaid the Rangers with a three-game sweep of its own in Arlington, launching Texas' 12-game losing streak that lasted from April 22 through May 6. The Rangers finally stepped off the down escalator when Doc Medich and Danny Darwin posted a 12-hit shutout and Bobby Johnson's home run off Dennis Eckersley beat Boston, 1-0.

The Rangers never seemed to recover from the losing streak and Parrish, trying to adjust to new contact lenses, was hitting .160 in late June with one homer and six RBIs.

But Parrish wasn't Zimmer's only problem. Mazzilli missed most of the first half of the season with injuries, didn't play well when he was healthy and eventually was traded to the New York Yankees for shortstop Bucky Dent. Pat Putnam, counted on to supply offensive punch, didn't. Rookie second baseman Mike Richardt suffered tonsillitis and went on the disabled list in June. And shortstop Mark Wagner didn't hit and sat out the second half of the season with a pulled muscle.

Catcher Jim Sundberg hit well early, then slumped badly in the middle of the season. Buddy Bell was forced to play with a right knee that needed arthroscopic surgery as soon as the season ended.

Rookie center fielder George Wright showed flashes of brilliance defensively, but the switch-hitter struggled from the left side of the plate. With Mazzilli in and out of the lineup and Parrish in a slump, the outfield was in disarray.

The pitching staff realized quickly there would be little run support and began pressing. Veteran Frank Tanana experienced the worst season (7-18) of his career and Rick Honeycutt, losing his sinker, slipped to 5-17. The bullpen was unreliable.

Hostetler gave the Rangers a lift, hitting 22 homers in his first 72 games. There was talk of him making a late rush for Rookie of the Year honors, but he didn't hit a homer after August 17.

There were a few bright spots. Despite his sore knee, Bell hit a team-high .296 with 13 homers and tied Hostetler for the club's runs-batted-in lead with 67. Parrish came on strong in the second half, finishing at .264 with 17 homers and 62 RBIs. Wright began hitting better from the left side and successfully made the jump from Class AA to the big leagues, hitting .264 with 11 homers and 50 RBIs, mostly as a leadoff hitter. Sundberg rallied in September to hit .251 and matched his career high

SCORES OF TEXAS RANGERS' 1982 GAMES

APRIL

Date		Score	Winner	Loser
10—At Cleve.	W	8-3	Hough	Waits
11—At Cleve.	L	1-13	Barker	Medich
12—New York	L	7-10	Righetti	Tanana
13—New York	L	3-6	Morgan	Honeycutt
14—New York	W	4-1	Hough	Pacella
16—At Milw.	W	4-1*	Darwin	Fingers
17—At Milw.	W	5-3	Tanana	McClure
18—At Milw.	W	9-6	Darwin	Vuckovich
20—Cleveland	L	4-9	Blyleven	Hough
21—Cleveland	W	4-2	Medich	Waits
22—Cleveland	L	3-4	Barker	Tanana
23—Milwaukee	L	1-2	Haas	Honeycutt
24—Milwaukee	L	1-4	Vuckovich	Schmidt
25—Milwaukee	L	6-11	Bernard	Matlack
27—At Toronto	L	4-8	Murray	Medich
28—At Toronto	L	4-6	Clancy	Tanana
30—At Boston	L	1-7	Torrez	Hough

Won 6, Lost 11

MAY

Date		Score	Winner	Loser
1—At Boston	L	5-6‡	Clear	Comer
2—At Boston	L	0-6	Eckersley	Medich
4—At Detroit	L	3-4	Rozema	Darwin
5—At Detroit	L	4-6	Sosa	Comer
6—Boston	L	2-5	Stanley	Honeycutt
7—Boston	W	1-0	Medich	Eckersley
8—Boston	L	1-2	Rainey	Matlack
9—Boston	L	0-1	Stanley	Tanana
10—Detroit	L	1-3	Wilcox	Hough
13—Toronto	W	4-3	Darwin	Stieb
14—Toronto	W	4-3†	Mirabella	Jackson
15—Toronto	L	2-5	Clancy	Tanana
16—Toronto	W	2-1*	Darwin	Jackson
17—At Chicago	L	6-8	Lamp	Honeycutt
18—At Chicago	L	2-10	Hoyt	Medich
19—At Chicago	L	5-6	Barojas	Darwin
21—At Kan. C.	L	0-3	Leonard	Tanana
22—At Kan. C.	W	3-1‡	Hough	Quisenberry
23—At Kan. C.	L	3-5	Armstrong	Honeycutt
25—Baltimore	L	3-10	Palmer	Medich
26—Baltimore	W	5-3	Matlack	D. Martinez
27—Baltimore	L	0-6	Stewart	Tanana
28—Kan. City	W	8-2	Hough	Frost
29—Kan. City	L	1-14	Splittorff	Honeycutt
30—Kan. City	W	8-1	Medich	Creel
31—At Balt.	L	7-8	D. Martinez	Matlack

Won 8, Lost 18

JUNE

Date		Score	Winner	Loser
2—At Balt.	W	4-1	Tanana	Stewart
4—Chicago	W	4-3	Hough	Hoyt
5—Chicago	L	1-2	Burns	Honeycutt
6—Chicago	W	5-4	Schmidt	Koosman
7—Seattle	L	0-6	Nelson	Matlack
8—Seattle	L	1-2§	Caudill	Mirabella
9—Seattle	L	3-4†	Vande Berg	Comer
12—Minnesota	W	4-3	Honeycutt	Castillo
13—Minnesota	W	10-4	Medich	O'Connor
14—At Seattle	L	0-4	Beattie	Matlack
15—At Seattle	W	5-2	Tanana	Moore
16—At Seattle	L	2-7	Perry	Hough
17—At Seattle	W	5-1	Honeycutt	Nelson
18—At Minn.	W	3-2	Medich	Castillo
19—At Minn.	W	6-3	Matlack	Redfern
20—At Minn.	L	1-4	Havens	Tanana
21—At Calif.	L	2-10	Renko	Hough
22—At Calif.	W	4-0	Honeycutt	Kison
23—At Calif.	L	3-5	Forsch	Medich
24—Oakland	W	2-1	Matlack	Langford
25—Oakland	L	2-6	McCatty	Tanana
26—Oakland	W	5-2	Hough	Keough
27—Oakland	W	10-4	Honeycutt	Kingman
29—California	L	1-2	Zahn	Medich
30—California	W	5-3	Schmidt	Aase

Won 14, Lost 11

JULY

Date		Score	Winner	Loser
1—California	W	7-2	Tanana	Witt
2—At Oak.	W	7-0	Hough	Kingman
3—At Oak.	L	3-5	Langford	Honeycutt
4—At Oak.	W	11-4	Medich	Keough
5—Toronto	W	3-2	Matlack	Leal
6—Toronto	L	3-4	Murray	Tanana
7—Boston	L	5-8	Torrez	Hough
8—Boston	L	0-3	Rainey	Honeycutt
9—Detroit	W	3-2	Darwin	Tobik
9—Detroit	W	3-1	Medich	Pashnick
10—Detroit	W	6-5	Darwin	Tobik
10—Detroit	L	0-6	Morris	Hough
11—Detroit	L	2-3	Ujdur	Darwin
15—At Toronto	L	1-5	Stieb	Honeycutt
16—At Toronto	L	0-6	Clancy	Hough
17—At Toronto	L	3-11	Jackson	Butcher
18—At Toronto	L	4-5*	McLaughlin	Darwin
19—At Boston	L	5-9	Clear	Darwin
21—At Boston	W	6-3	Hough	Eckersley
21—At Boston	L	1-6	Torrez	Honeycutt
22—At N.Y.	L	3-4	Erickson	Butcher
23—At Detroit	W	3-1	Tanana	Morris
24—At Detroit	L	1-3	Pashnick	Medich
25—At Detroit	L	2-7	Petry	Darwin
25—At Detroit	L	6-7	Rucker	Schmidt
26—Milwaukee	W	3-1	Hough	Caldwell
27—Milwaukee	L	2-8	Haas	Honeycutt
28—Milwaukee	L	2-3	McClure	Tanana
30—New York	L	0-4	Guidry	Medich
31—New York	W	3-2	Hough	Alexander

Won 11, Lost 19

AUGUST

Date		Score	Winner	Loser
1—New York	W	4-2	Honeycutt	Morgan
2—At Cleve.	L	2-6	Sutcliffe	Tanana
3—At Cleve.	L	0-2	Barker	Schmidt
3—At Cleve.	W	5-4*	Matlack	Spillner
4—At Cleve.	L	4-8	Anderson	Medich
5—At N.Y.	W	7-2	Hough	Alexander
6—At N.Y.	L	0-6	Righetti	Honeycutt
7—At N.Y.	L	1-9	Morgan	Tanana
8—At N.Y.	W	6-4	Darwin	Rawley
8—At N.Y.	L	5-8	John	Schmidt
9—At Milw.	L	1-9	Caldwell	Medich
10—At Milw.	L	3-11	Slaton	Hough
11—At Milw.	W	6-3	Schmidt	Haas
13—Cleveland	W	8-7	Darwin	Spillner
14—Cleveland	W	3-2	Butcher	Barker
15—Cleveland	L	4-6	Sorensen	Hough
16—Chicago	L	1-6	Dotson	Honeycutt
17—Chicago	W	4-3†	Darwin	Lamp
18—Chicago	W	11-1	Tanana	Trout
20—Baltimore	L	2-4‡	T. Martinez	Comer
21—Baltimore	L	6-8	Stoddard	Matlack
22—Baltimore	L	3-10	Palmer	Honeycutt
23—Kan. City	W	5-2	Schmidt	Armstrong
24—Kan. City	L	3-5	Gura	Tanana
25—Kan. City	L	3-4	Leonard	Butcher
26—Kan. City	L	3-5	Black	Hough
27—At Balt.	L	1-3	Palmer	Smithson
27—At Balt.	W	4-3	Comer	Stewart
28—At Balt.	L	3-8	D. Martinez	Schmidt
29—At Balt.	L	2-3	Flanagan	Tanana
30—At Kan. City	L	3-8	Leonard	Butcher
31—At Kan. City	W	6-0	Hough	Black

Won 12, Lost 20

SEPTEMBER

Date		Score	Winner	Loser
1—At Kan. City	W	7-3	Smithson	Splittorff
2—At Chicago	L	5-6*	Kern	Comer
3—At Chicago	L	5-7	Brusstar	Schmidt
4—At Chicago	L	0-4	Dotson	Tanana
5—At Chicago	W	10-7	Matlack	Barojas
6—Minnesota	W	4-3	Smithson	Havens
6—Minnesota	W	11-7	Hough	Cooper
7—Minnesota	L	1-8	Williams	Comer
8—Minnesota	W	2-0	Matlack	O'Connor
10—Seattle	L	2-5	Perry	Tanana
11—Seattle	W	5-2	Hough	Bannister
12—Seattle	L	0-1	Stoddard	Smithson
13—At Minn.	L	0-2	Williams	Mason
14—At Minn.	L	2-3	O'Connor	Matlack
15—At Minn.	L	2-10	Castillo	Tanana
16—At Minn.	W	8-2	Hough	Viola
17—At Seattle	L	0-6	Stoddard	Smithson
18—At Seattle	W	10-4	Mason	Moore
19—At Seattle	L	7-9	Nunez	Honeycutt
20—At Oak.	W	10-3	Tanana	Keough
21—At Oak.	L	1-6	Conroy	Hough
22—At Oak.	L	3-5	Baker	Smithson
23—California	W	5-4	Darwin	Witt
24—California	L	1-10	Kison	Honeycutt
25—California	L	5-6	Goltz	Darwin
26—California	W	7-5	Hough	Forsch
27—Oakland	W	4-1	Smithson	Langford
28—Oakland	L	4-5	Conroy	Mason
29—Oakland	W	5-3	Henke	Beard

Won 13, Lost 16

OCTOBER

Date		Score	Winner	Loser
1—At Calif.	L	0-4	Zahn	Butcher
2—At Calif.	L	4-6	Goltz	Hough
3—At Calif.	L	6-7	Mahler	Darwin

Won 0, Lost 3

*10 innings. †11 innings. ‡12 innings. §14 innings.

Knuckleballer Charlie Hough won a starting job and produced 16 victories.

in homers with 10.

Knuckleballer Charlie Hough established himself as a starter, posting a 16-13 record. Dave Schmidt pitched well in relief before elbow tenderness sidelined him for the final month, and rookie Mike Smithson showed he may be ready to pitch in the big leagues regularly in 1983, despite a 3-4 record and 5.01 ERA. He beat Kansas City and Baltimore when those teams were in pennant races.

Seeking to rebound, Chiles promoted Rangers' farm director Joe Klein to general manager, restoring some credibility to a front office that had spent the season shredding whatever public relations image it had.

"We've got a lot of work to do," Klein said, "but nobody on my staff is afraid of work."

Rookie Kent Hrbek, the early-season talk of the American League, finished with a .301 average, 23 home runs and 92 RBIs.

Twins Point to 44-48 Finish

By PATRICK REUSSE

The Minnesota Twins started the 1982 season on one highly optimistic note, drawing a club-record 52,279 fans to the new Hubert H. Humphrey Metrodome.

For the Twins, the opening-night result —Seattle 11, Minnesota 7—proved much more symbolic than the attendance. When the season was over, the Twins had compiled the worst record, 60-102, among the 26 major league teams. And, despite the new domed stadium, Minnesota finished last in attendance in the majors for the third consecutive season, drawing 921,186.

In 21 previous seasons in Minnesota, the Twins had never lost more than 90 games, but in 1982 they capitulated in the season's opening weeks by purging the roster of high-salaried veterans with multi-year contracts.

In April, the Twins sent shortstop Roy Smalley to the New York Yankees for relief pitcher Ron Davis, two minor leaguers and $400,000 in cash. Then, in a period of two days in May, the Twins traded four veterans—pitchers Doug Corbett and Roger Erickson, catcher Butch Wynegar and infielder Rob Wilfong. The most significant player obtained in return was Tom Brunansky, a young outfielder acquired from the California Angels.

It took a long stretch of defeats before the Twins responded to the roster shuffling. From April 30 until June 26, Minnesota failed to win two games in succession. During that eight-week period, the Twins went 7-41. Included was a club-record losing streak of 14 games, which stretched from May 19 through June 2. During May, the Twins were 3-26, the second worst month in the majors since the turn of the century. (The Philadelphia A's went 2-28 in July, 1916.)

When the Twins bottomed out at 16-54, there was speculation the club might break the 1962 New York Mets' mark for the worst record (40-120) since the advent of the 162-game schedule. But Minnesota, with improved starting pitching and a second-half surge by outfielder Gary Ward, played more respectably during the season's final three months, winning 44 and losing 48 and finishing four games behind sixth-place Texas in the American League West.

Kent Hrbek, a rookie first baseman promoted late in the 1981 season from Class A, was the Twins' focal point during the distressing early weeks. While his team-mates struggled, Hrbek stayed among the league leaders in the major categories—average, home runs and runs batted in. Hrbek was the Twins' representative on the American League All-Star Team.

Hrbek had 15 home runs by June 10, but then cooled off. He hit only four home runs from then until September 6, but Hrbek still finished with 23 home runs, 92 runs batted in and a .301 average.

Ward, 28, a second-year left fielder, came on when Hrbek slowed down and he carried the Twins during the period of improved play. Ward finished with 68 extra-base hits—33 doubles, seven triples and a club-leading 28 home runs. He batted .289 and drove in 91 runs.

Hrbek and Ward were two of four Minnesota players to hit over 20 home runs. Third baseman Gary Gaetti hit 25 and Brunansky had 20. Like Hrbek, Gaetti and Brunansky were rookies.

This marked the first time since 1965, Minnesota's World Series season, that the Twins had four players with 20 or more home runs. The team total of 148 home runs was the highest since 1970, when the Twins hit 153.

Part of the reason was the Metrodome, where 191 homers were struck (110 of them by the opposition). The Metrodome, though, did not lead the majors in homers; it was second to Detroit's Tiger Stadium, which had 208.

The Twins' pitching staff allowed 208 home runs overall, including a staff-leading 32 by starter Brad Havens.

As a team, the Twins had the worst ERA—4.72—in the major leagues and in the history of the franchise. Manager Billy Gardner finally settled on a reasonably effective starting rotation of Havens, Bobby Castillo, Jack O'Connor, Al Williams and rookie Frank Viola during the season's final weeks.

Castillo, obtained in January, 1982, from the Los Angeles Dodgers, was the Twins' most effective pitcher almost from the start. He finished 13-11, with a 3.66 earned-run average and a staff-leading 218⅔ innings. Williams, demoted for a time to the minor leagues, came back to win his last six decisions and was 9-7.

Davis, who replaced Corbett as the late-inning reliever, was an unimpressive 3-9 with an ERA of 4.42. Davis did have 22 saves; the rest of the bullpen totaled only eight.

One of those pitchers was Terry Felton. Felton had been with the Twins in 1980,

SCORES OF MINNESOTA TWINS' 1982 GAMES

APRIL

			Winner	Loser
6—Seattle	L	7-11	Bannister	Redfern
7—Seattle	W	7-5	Erickson	Beattie
8—Seattle	W	4-1	Havens	Nelson
9—California	W	2-1	Williams	Moreno
10—California	L	1-8	Renko	Jackson
11—California	W	3-1	Redfern	Forsch
13—Oakland	L	3-8	Keough	Erickson
14—Oakland	L	5-7‡	Jones	Arroyo
15—Oakland	W	11-5	Williams	Langford
16—At Calif.	L	2-4*	Aase	Corbett
17—At Calif.	L	2-6	Forsch	Felton
18—At Calif.	L	2-5	Zahn	Erickson
19—At Oak.	W	5-2	Davis	Langford
20—At Oak.	L	3-4x	Beard	Castillo
21—At Oak.	L	2-5	Underwood	Jackson
22—At Seattle	L	4-8	Moore	Redfern
23—At Seattle	W	12-4	Erickson	Nunez
24—At Seattle	L	2-3	Vande Berg	Davis
25—At Seattle	L	4-5†	Caudill	Felton
27—Detroit	L	2-5	Morris	Jackson
28—Detroit	W	4-2	Redfern	Petry
30—Milwaukee	W	7-4	Erickson	Haas
Won 9, Lost 13				

MAY

			Winner	Loser
1—Milwaukee	L	5-6	Vuckovich	Corbett
2—Milwaukee	L	4-11	Lerch	Williams
3—At Boston	L	2-6	Rainey	Felton
4—At Boston	L	3-5	Hurst	Redfern
5—At Boston	W	3-2	Erickson	Torrez
6—At Milw.	L	3-6	Vuckovich	Havens
7—At Milw.	L	1-4	Lerch	Williams
8—At Milw.	L	1-12	Caldwell	Felton
9—At Milw.	L	2-6	Slaton	Redfern
10—Boston	L	5-9	Burgmeier	Erickson
11—Boston	W	10-6	Castillo	Ojeda
12—Boston	L	1-4	Eckersley	Davis
13—At Detroit	L	2-6	Morris	Pacella
14—At Detroit	L	2-4†	Rozema	Davis
15—At Detroit	L	4-5*	Sosa	Jackson
16—At Detroit	L	6-7	Tobik	Felton
18—At Balt.	W	8-7	Castillo	Palmer
19—At Balt.	L	2-4	Stewart	Filson
20—At Balt.	L	0-6	McGregor	Redfern
21—At N.Y.	L	1-12	May	Havens
22—At N.Y.	L	0-1	Righetti	Jackson
23—At N.Y.	L	2-4	Guidry	Castillo
24—Cleveland	L	2-9	Barker	Redfern
25—Cleveland	L	0-7	Sorensen	Havens
26—Cleveland	L	1-2	Spillner	Davis
28—New York	L	5-10	Gossage	Davis
29—New York	L	4-6	Rawley	Havens
30—New York	L	6-8*	Gossage	Boris
31—At Cleve.	L	4-9	Sorensen	Filson
Won 3, Lost 26				

JUNE

			Winner	Loser
1—At Cleve.	L	4-6	Glynn	Davis
2—At Cleve.	L	2-4	Sutcliffe	Castillo
4—Baltimore	W	6-0	Havens	McGregor
5—Baltimore	L	1-3	Flanagan	Williams
6—Baltimore	L	5-7†	Stoddard	Davis
7—Kan. City	L	4-5*	Quisenberry	Redfern
8—Kan. City	L	4-9	Gura	O'Connor
9—Kan. City	L	5-8	Splittorff	Williams
10—Kan. City	W	8-7	Redfern	Armstrong
12—At Texas	L	3-4	Honeycutt	Castillo
13—At Texas	L	4-10	Medich	O'Connor
14—At Kan. C.	L	0-3	Splittorff	Havens
15—At Kan. C.	L	4-7	Black	Williams
16—At Kan. C.	W	5-2	Viola	Blue
18—Texas	L	2-3	Medich	Castillo
19—Texas	L	3-6	Matlack	Redfern
20—Texas	W	4-1	Havens	Tanana
21—At Chicago	L	4-5	Barojas	Felton
22—At Chicago	L	5-6	Solomon	Felton
23—At Chicago	W	6-3	Boris	Barojas
26—At Toronto	W	4-3	Davis	Stieb
27—At Toronto	L	2-3	McLaughlin	Felton
28—Chicago	L	7-8	Lamp	Williams
29—Chicago	W	12-5	Viola	Dotson
30—Chicago	W	4-3	Castillo	Hoyt
Won 8, Lost 17				

JULY

			Winner	Loser
1—Chicago	W	9-2	Redfern	Burns
2—Toronto	L	4-9	Murray	Havens
3—Toronto	W	2-1	O'Connor	Clancy
4—Toronto	W	4-3	Little	Stieb
5—At Detroit	W	5-3	Castillo	Wilcox
6—At Detroit	L	6-11	Morris	Redfern
7—At Milw.	W	11-8	Havens	McClure
8—At Milw.	W	3-0	O'Connor	Vuckovich
9—At Boston	W	4-1	Viola	Eckersley
10—At Boston	L	4-5	Hurst	Castillo
11—At Boston	W	7-3	Havens	Clear
15—Detroit	L	2-18	Petry	O'Connor
16—Detroit	L	3-6	Morris	Viola
17—Detroit	L	4-8	Ujdur	Castillo
18—Detroit	W	6-1	Havens	Underwood
19—Milwaukee	W	6-4	Williams	Augustine
20—Milwaukee	W	5-3	O'Connor	Caldwell
21—Milwaukee	L	4-10	Haas	Viola
23—Boston	W	8-4	Castillo	Hurst
24—Boston	W	5-3	Havens	Stanley
25—Boston	L	0-5	Torrez	Williams
26—At Seattle	W	10-4	O'Connor	Bannister
27—At Seattle	L	7-9	Clark	·Pacella
28—At Seattle	L	2-6	Perry	Castillo
29—At Oak.	L	0-5	Langford	Havens
30—At Oak.	L	3-4*	Kingman	Davis
31—At Oak.	L	2-3	Underwood	Felton
Won 14, Lost 13				

AUGUST

			Winner	Loser
1—At Oak.	W	8-7	Pacella	Beard
2—At Calif.	W	9-7	Little	Sanchez
3—At Calif.	W	5-4	Havens	Renko
4—At Calif.	L	6-8	Goltz	Felton
5—At Calif.	W	8-6	O'Connor	Tiant
6—Oakland	L	1-4	Norris	Viola
7—Oakland	L	1-7	Keough	Castillo
8—Oakland	L	2-5	Underwood	Havens
10—California	W	5-2	Redfern	Forsch
11—California	L	3-6	Zahn	Felton
12—California	L	1-3	Tiant	Viola
13—Seattle	W	3-1	Castillo	Perry
14—Seattle	L	1-3	Stanton	Havens
15—Seattle	L	2-10	Beattie	Felton
17—Baltimore	L	4-8	Flanagan	O'Connor
18—Baltimore	W	6-5*	Davis	Stoddard
19—Baltimore	W	9-3	Castillo	McGregor
20—At Cleve.	L	5-7	Barker	Redfern
21—At Cleve.	W	4-3	Williams	Sorensen
22—At Cleve.	L	3-4	Sutcliffe	O'Connor
24—At N.Y.	W	5-0	Viola	John
25—At N.Y.	L	1-8	Rawley	Castillo
26—At N.Y.	L	2-7	Guidry	Havens
27—Cleveland	W	5-3	Williams	Sorensen
28—Cleveland	W	10-0	O'Connor	Sutcliffe
29—Cleveland	W	6-3	Castillo	Spillner
30—New York	L	2-8	Rawley	Viola
31—New York	L	1-3	Guidry	Havens
Won 13, Lost 15				

SEPTEMBER

			Winner	Loser
1—New York	W	7-2	Williams	Righetti
3—At Balt.	L	2-4	Flanagan	O'Connor
4—At Balt.	L	0-3	Palmer	Castillo
5—At Balt.	L	4-5	Davis	Redfern
6—At Texas	L	3-4	Smithson	Havens
6—At Texas	L	7-11	Hough	Cooper
7—At Texas	W	8-1	Williams	Comer
8—At Texas	L	0-2	Matlack	O'Connor
10—At Kan. C.	W	5-0	Castillo	Gura
11—At Kan. C.	L	3-9	Leonard	Viola
12—At Kan. C.	L	7-18	Tufts	Felton
13—Texas	W	2-0	Williams	Mason
14—Texas	W	3-2	O'Connor	Matlack
15—Texas	W	10-2	Castillo	Tanana
16—Texas	L	2-8	Hough	Viola
17—Kan. City	W	5-4	Havens	Splittorff
18—Kan. City	W	11-5	Williams	Blue
19—Kan. City	W	9-4	O'Connor	Castro
20—Toronto	W	4-1	Castillo	Leal
21—Toronto	L	1-5	Stieb	Viola
22—Toronto	L	2-3*	Clancy	Havens
24—At Chicago	L	2-3§	Brusstar	Boris
25—At Chicago	L	1-13	Hoyt	O'Connor
26—At Chicago	W	2-1	Castillo	Dotson
28—At Toronto	L ·	0-3	Clancy	Viola
28—At Toronto	L	3-4*	Jackson	Davis
29—At Toronto	W	8-0	Havens	Eichhorn
30—At Toronto	L	4-6	Leal	O'Connor
Won 12, Lost 16				

OCTOBER

			Winner	Loser
1—Chicago	W	3-2	Castillo	Dotson
2—Chicago	L	3-5	Lamp	Viola
3—Chicago	L	1-6	Hoyt	Havens
Won 1, Lost 2				

*10 innings. †11 innings. ‡12 innings. §13 innings. x16 innings.

Outfielder Gary Ward surged in the second half and finished with 28 home runs and 91 RBIs.

compiling a 0-3 record before being sent to the minors. He made the team again in spring training, and served as a spot starter and long reliever. In the process, Felton compiled a 1982 record of 0-13, and his 16 straight defeats set a record for consecutive losses at the start of a career. Guy Morton, who lost his first 13 decisions for Cleveland in 1914, had held the record.

In addition to the pitching problems, the Twins managed only 38 stolen bases and allowed 128.

One of Minnesota's hopes for improved speed was rookie Jim Eisenreich. He opened the season in center field and was batting over .300 when he went out of the lineup with a nervous disorder on April 30. Eisenreich returned to action only briefly, and spent the final weeks of the season on the disabled list.

American League Averages for 1982

CHAMPIONSHIP WINNERS IN PREVIOUS YEARS

1900—Chicago* .607	1928—New York .656	1955—New York .623
1901—Chicago .610	1929—Philadelphia .693	1956—New York .630
1902—Philadelphia .610	1930—Philadelphia .662	1957—New York .636
1903—Boston .659	1931—Philadelphia .704	1958—New York .597
1904—Boston .617	1932—New York .695	1959—Chicago .610
1905—Philadelphia .622	1933—Washington .651	1960—New York .630
1906—Chicago .616	1934—Detroit .656	1961—New York .673
1907—Detroit .613	1935—Detroit .616	1962—New York .593
1908—Detroit .588	1936—New York .667	1963—New York .646
1909—Detroit .645	1937—New York .662	1964—New York .611
1910—Philadelphia .680	1938—New York .651	1965—Minnesota .630
1911—Philadelphia .669	1939—New York .702	1966—Baltimore .606
1912—Boston .691	1940—Detroit .584	1967—Boston .568
1913—Philadelphia .627	1941—New York .656	1968—Detroit .636
1914—Philadelphia .651	1942—New York .669	1969—Baltimore (East)‡ .673
1915—Boston .669	1943—New York .636	1970—Baltimore (East)‡ .667
1916—Boston .591	1944—St. Louis .578	1971—Baltimore (East)§ .639
1917—Chicago .649	1945—Detroit .575	1972—Oakland (West)a .600
1918—Boston .595	1946—Boston .675	1973—Oakland (West)b .580
1919—Chicago .629	1947—New York .630	1974—Oakland (West)b .556
1920—Cleveland .636	1948—Cleveland† .626	1975—Boston (East)c .594
1921—New York .641	1949—New York .630	1976—New York (East)d .610
1922—New York .610	1950—New York .636	1977—New York (East)d .617
1923—New York .645	1951—New York .636	1978—New York (East)d .613
1924—Washington .597	1952—New York .617	1979—Baltimore (East)e .642
1925—Washington .636	1953—New York .656	1980—Kansas City (West)f .599
1926—New York .591	1954—Cleveland .721	1981—New York (East)c .551
1927—New York .714		

*Not recognized as major league in 1900. †Defeated Boston in one-game playoff for pennant. ‡Defeated Minnesota (West) in Championship Series. §Defeated Oakland (West) in Championship Series. aDefeated Detroit (East) in Championship Series. bDefeated Baltimore (East) in Championship Series. cDefeated Oakland (West) in Championship Series. dDefeated Kansas City (West) in Championship Series. eDefeated California (West) in Championship Series. fDefeated New York (East) in Championship Series.

STANDING OF CLUBS AT CLOSE OF SEASON

EAST DIVISION

Club	Mil.	Balt.	Bos.	Det.	N.Y.	Tor.	Clv.	Cal.	Chi.	K.C.	Min.	Oak.	Sea.	Tex.	W.	L.	Pct.	G.B.
Milwaukee	..	4	9	10	8	9	6	6	9	5	7	7	8	7	95	67	.586	......
Baltimore	9	..	4	7	11	10	6	7	5	4	8	7	7	9	94	68	.580	1
Boston	4	9	..	8	7	7	6	7	4	6	6	8	7	10	89	73	.549	6
Detroit	3	6	5	..	8	6	7	7	3	6	9	9	6	8	83	79	.512	12
New York	5	2	6	5	..	6	9	5	4	7	10	7	6	7	79	83	.488	16
Toronto	4	3	6	7	7	..	6	4	4	8	7	9	5	8	78	84	.481	17
Cleveland	7	7	7	6	4	7	..	4	6	2	8	4	9	7	78	84	.481	17

WEST DIVISION

Club	Cal.	K.C.	Chi.	Sea.	Oak.	Tex.	Min.	Balt.	Bos.	Clv.	Det.	Mil.	N.Y.	Tor.	W.	L.	Pct.	G.B.
California	..	7	8	10	9	8	7	5	5	8	5	6	7	8	93	69	.574	......
Kansas City	6	..	10	7	7	7	7	8	6	10	6	7	5	4	90	72	.556	3
Chicago	5	3	..	6	9	8	7	7	8	6	9	3	8	8	87	75	.537	6
Seattle	3	6	7	..	7	9	8	5	5	3	6	4	6	7	76	86	.469	17
Oakland	4	6	4	6	..	5	10	5	4	8	3	5	5	3	68	94	.420	25
Texas	5	6	5	4	8	..	8	3	2	5	4	5	5	4	64	98	.395	29
Minnesota	6	6	6	5	3	5	..	4	6	4	3	5	2	5	60	102	.370	33

Tie Game—Milwaukee vs. Baltimore.
Championship Series—Milwaukee defeated California, three games to two.

RECORD AT HOME

EAST DIVISION

Club	Balt.	Bos.	Mil.	Det.	Tor.	N.Y.	Clev.	K.C.	Cal.	Chi.	Sea.	Tex.	Min.	Oak.	W.	L.	Pct.
Baltimore	.....	3-4	4-2	4-3	4-2	7-0	2-4	4-2	3-3	5-1	4-2	4-2	5-1	4-2	53	28	.654
Boston	5-1	....	2-5	5-1	4-3	4-3	3-3	4-2	3-3	1-5	4-2	5-1	3-3	6-0	49	32	.605
Milwaukee	2-5	4-2	.....	4-2	5-2	5-1	3-4	4-2	3-3	6-1	3-3	2-4	4-2	3-3	48	34	.585
Detroit	3-3	4-3	1-6	.....	4-3	4-2	4-2	4-2	3-3	1-5	4-2	5-1	5-1	5-1	47	34	.580
Toronto	1-6	3-3	2-4	4-2	.....	5-2	3-4	5-1	3-3	2-4	3-3	6-0	4-2	3-3	44	37	.543
New York	2-4	3-3	4-3	3-4	4-2	.....	3-4	3-3	3-3	1-5	3-3	4-2	5-1	4-2	42	39	.519
Cleveland	3-4	4-3	3-3	4-3	3-3	0-6	.....	2-4	3-3	5-1	4-2	4-2	1-5	1-5	41	40	.506

WEST DIVISION

Club	K.C.	Cal.	Chi.	Sea.	Tex.	Min.	Oak.	Balt.	Bos.	Mil.	Det.	Tor.	N.Y.	Clev.	W.	L.	Pct.
Kansas City	.....	5-1	6-1	4-3	3-3	4-2	4-3	6-0	4-2	5-1	4-2	3-3	2-4	6-0	56	25	.691
California	6-1	.....	3-3	6-1	5-1	4-3	5-1	2-4	2-4	3-3	2-4	5-1	4-2	5-1	52	29	.642
Chicago	2-4	2-5	.....	4-2	6-1	4-2	4-3	6-0	3-3	2-3	4-2	4-2	3-3	5-1	49	31	.613
Seattle	3-3	2-4	5-2	.....	4-3	5-2	4-2	3-3	3-3	1-5	4-2	4-2	3-3	1-5	42	39	.519
Texas	3-4	4-3	4-2	1-5	.....	5-1	5-2	1-5	1-5	1-5	3-3	4-2	3-3	3-3	38	43	.469
Minnesota	4-3	3-3	4-3	3-3	4-3	.....	1-5	3-3	3-3	3-3	2-4	3-3	1-5	3-3	37	44	.457
Oakland	3-3	3-4	1-5	4-3	3-3	5-2	.....	3-3	4-2	2-4	2-4	0-6	3-3	3-3	36	45	.444

RECORD ABROAD

EAST DIVISION

Club	Mil.	Balt.	Bos.	Clev.	N.Y.	Det.	Tor.	Cal.	Chi.	K.C.	Sea.	Oak.	Tex.	Min.	W.	L.	Pct.
Milwaukee	.....	2-4	5-2	3-3	3-4	6-1	4-2	3-3	3-2	1-5	5-1	4-2	5-1	3-3	47	33	.588
Baltimore	5-2	.....	1-5	4-3	4-2	3-3	6-1	4-2	0-6	0-6	3-3	3-3	5-1	3-3	41	40	.506
Boston	2-4	4-3	.....	3-4	3-3	3-4	3-3	4-2	3-3	2-4	3-3	2-4	5-1	3-3	40	41	.494
Cleveland	4-3	4-2	3-3	.....	4-3	2-4	4-3	1-5	1-5	0-6	5-1	3-3	3-3	3-3	37	44	.457
New York	1-5	0-7	3-4	6-0	.....	2-4	2-5	2-4	3-3	4-2	3-3	3-3	3-3	5-1	37	44	.457
Detroit	2-4	3-4	1-5	3-4	4-3	.....	2-4	2-4	2-4	2-4	4-2	3-3	4-2		36	45	.444
Toronto	2-5	2-4	3-4	3-3	2-4	3-4	.....	1-5	2-4	3-3	2-4	6-0	2-4	3-3	34	47	.420

WEST DIVISION

Club	Cal.	Chi.	K.C.	Sea.	Oak.	Tex.	Min.	Mil.	Balt.	Bos.	Clev.	N.Y.	Det.	Tor.	W.	L.	Pct.
California	.....	5-2	1-5	4-2	4-3	3-4	3-3	3-3	3-3	3-3	3-3	3-3	3-3	3-3	41	40	.506
Chicago	3-3	.....	1-6	2-5	5-1	2-4	3-4	1-6	1-5	5-1	1-5	5-1	4-2		38	44	.463
Kansas City	1-6	4-2	.....	3-3	3-3	4-3	3-4	2-4	2-4	2-4	4-2	3-3	2-4	1-5	34	47	.420
Seattle	1-6	2-4	3-4	.....	3-4	5-1	3-3	3-3	2-4	2-4	2-4	3-3	2-4	3-3	34	47	.420
Oakland	1-5	3-4	3-4	2-4	.....	2-5	5-1	3-3	2-4	0-6	5-1	2-4	1-5	3-3	32	49	.395
Texas	1-5	1-6	3-3	3-4	3-3	.....	3-4	4-2	2-4	1-5	2-4	2-4	1-5	0-6	26	55	.321
Minnesota	3-4	2-4	2-4	2-5	2-5	1-5	.....	2-4	1-5	3-3	1-5	1-5	1-5	2-4	23	58	.284

SHUTOUT GAMES

Club	Mil.	Cal.	Sea.	K.C.	Tor.	Chi.	Bos.	Clev.	Min.	Balt.	N.Y.	Oak.	Det.	Tex.	W.	L.	Pct.
Milwaukee	..	0	0	1	2	0	1	0	0	0	1	0	1	0	6	1	.857
California	0	..	1	0	0	2	0	2	0	0	1	2	1	1	10	3	.769
Seattle	0	0	..	0	1	1	1	1	0	1	0	1	1	4	11	6	.647
Kansas City	0	0	1	..	0	1	2	1	1	2	1	1	1	1	12	8	.600
Toronto	0	1	2	2	..	0	2	1	1	1	1	0	1	1	13	9	.591
Chicago	0	0	0	0	0	..	0	1	0	0	4	2	2	1	10	7	.588
Boston	0	0	0	0	0	1	..	0	1	3	1	2	0	3	11	9	.550
Cleveland	0	0	0	0	0	0	1	..	1	3	1	0	2	1	9	11	.450
Minnesota	1	0	0	1	1	0	0	1	..	1	1	0	0	1	7	9	.438
Baltimore	0	0	1	0	3	0	0	1	2	..	0	0	0	1	8	11	.421
New York	0	1	1	1	1	1	0	0	1	0	..	0	0	2	8	11	.421
Oakland	0	0	0	1	0	0	1	2	1	0	0	..	1	0	6	9	.400
Detroit	0	0	0	1	1	1	0	1	0	0	0	0	..	1	5	10	.333
Texas	0	1	0	1	0	0	1	0	1	0	0	1	0	..	5	17	.227

OFFICIAL AMERICAN LEAGUE BATTING AVERAGES

Compiled by Sports Information Center, North Quincy, Mass.

CLUB BATTING

Club	Pct.	G.	AB.	R.	OR.	H.	TB.	2B.	3B.	HR.	RBI.	SH.	SF.	SB.	CS.	LOB.
Kan. C	.285	162	5629	784	717	1603	2410	295	58	132	746	32	49	133	48	1120
Milw	.279	163	5733	891	717	1599	2606	277	41	216	843	56	46	84	52	1097
Boston	.274	162	5596	753	713	1536	2277	271	31	136	705	53	38	42	39	1179
Calif	.274	162	5532	814	670	1518	2396	268	26	186	760	114	56	55	53	1180
Chicago	.273	162	5575	786	710	1523	2301	266	52	136	747	54	50	136	58	1148
Detroit	.266	162	5590	729	685	1489	2337	237	40	177	684	41	39	93	66	1101
Balt	.266	163	5557	774	687	1478	2328	259	27	179	735	57	52	49	38	1207
Clev	.262	162	5559	683	748	1458	2074	225	32	109	639	74	40	151	68	1258
Toronto	.262	162	5526	651	701	1447	2117	262	45	106	605	48	50	118	81	1071
Minn	.257	162	5544	657	819	1427	2193	234	44	148	624	22	51	38	33	1109
N. York	.256	162	5526	709	716	1417	2199	225	37	161	666	55	49	69	45	1151
Seattle	.254	162	5626	651	712	1431	2146	259	33	130	614	42	35	131	82	1079
Texas	.249	162	5445	590	749	1354	1955	204	26	115	558	64	32	63	45	1082
Oakland	.236	162	5448	691	819	1286	1998	211	27	149	659	50	54	232	87	1052
Totals	.264	1135	77886	10163	10163	20566	31337	3493	519	2080	9585	762	641	1394	795	15834

INDIVIDUAL BATTING

(Top Fifteen Qualifiers for Batting Championship—502 or More Plate Appearances)

*Bats lefthanded.   †Switch-hitter.

Player and Club	Pct.	G.	AB.	R.	H.	TB.	2B.	3B.	HR.	RBI.	GW.	SH.	SF.	SB.	CS.
Wilson, Willie, K.C.†	.332	136	585	87	194	252	19	15	3	46	2	2	2	37	11
Yount, Robin, Milw	.331	156	635	129	210	367	46	12	29	114	12	4	10	14	3
Carew, Rodney, Calif*	.319	138	523	88	167	211	25	5	3	44	4	16	4	10	17
Murray, Eddie, Balt†	.316	151	550	87	174	302	30	1	32	110	20	0	6	7	2
Cooper, Cecil, Milw*	.313	155	654	104	205	345	38	3	32	121	15	4	6	2	3
Garcia, Damaso, Tor	.310	147	597	89	185	238	32	3	5	42	7	5	1	54	20
Rice, James, Bos	.309	145	573	86	177	283	24	5	24	97	15	0	3	0	1
McRae, Harold, K.C.	.308	159	613	91	189	332	46	8	27	133	13	1	2	4	4
Harrah, Colbert, Clev	.304	162	602	100	183	295	29	4	25	78	7	7	3	17	3
Molitor, Paul, Milw	.302	160	666	136	201	300	26	8	19	71	7	10	5	41	9
DeCinces, Douglas, Cal	.301	153	575	94	173	315	42	5	30	97	11	4	9	7	5
Lansford, Carney, Bos	.301	128	482	65	145	214	28	4	11	63	6	1	8	9	4
Hrbek, Kent, Minn*	.301	140	532	82	160	258	21	4	23	92	10	1	4	3	1
Brett, George, K.C.*	.301	144	552	101	166	279	32	9	21	82	13	0	5	6	1
Mumphrey, Jerry, N.Y.†	.300	123	477	76	143	214	24	10	9	68	11	3	3	11	3

DEPARTMENTAL LEADERS: G—D. Evans, Griffin, Harrah, 162; AB—Molitor, 666; R—Molitor, 136; H—Yount, 210; TB—Yount, 367; 2B—McRae, Yount, 46; 3B—W. Wilson, 15; HR—Thomas, Re. Jackson, 39; RBI—McRae, 133; GW—Baylor, 21; SH—Foli, 26; SF—Gaetti, 13; SB—R. Henderson, 130; CS—R. Henderson, 42.

(All Players—Listed Alphabetically)

Player and Club	Pct.	G.	AB.	R.	H.	TB.	2B.	3B.	HR.	RBI.	GW.	SH.	SF.	SB.	CS.
Adams, Glenn, Tor*	.258	30	66	2	17	24	4	0	1	11	1	0	3	0	0
Adams, Ricky, Calif	.143	8	14	1	2	2	0	0	0	0	0	1	0	1	0
Aikens, Willie, K.C.*	.281	134	466	50	131	213	29	1	17	74	7	0	5	0	1
Allenson, Gary, Bos	.205	92	264	25	54	83	11	0	6	33	4	3	1	0	3
Almon, William, Chi	.256	111	308	40	79	109	10	4	4	26	4	1	1	10	8
Armas, Antonio, Oak	.233	138	536	58	125	232	19	2	28	89	10	0	8	2	2
Ayala, Benigno, Balt	.305	64	128	17	39	63	6	0	6	24	3	0	0	1	1
Baines, Harold, Chi*	.271	161	608	89	165	285	29	8	25	105	9	2	9	10	3
Baker, David, Tor*	.250	9	20	3	5	6	1	0	0	2	1	1	0	0	0
Balboni, Stephen, N.Y.	.187	33	107	8	20	30	2	1	2	4	1	0	1	0	0
Bando, Christopher, Clev†	.212	66	184	13	39	56	6	1	3	16	1	1	3	0	0
Bannister, Alan, Clev	.267	101	348	40	93	123	16	1	4	41	3	6	1	18	5
Barfield, Jesse, Tor	.246	139	394	54	97	168	13	2	18	58	7	6	1	1	4
Barrett, Martin, Bos	.056	8	18	0	1	1	0	0	0	0	0	0	0	0	0
Bass, Kevin, Milw†	.000	18	9	4	0	0	0	0	0	0	0	1	0	0	0
Bass, Randy, Tex*	.208	16	48	5	10	15	2	0	1	6	2	0	2	0	0
Baylor, Donald, Calif	.263	157	608	80	160	258	24	1	24	93	21	0	8	10	4
Bell, David, Tex	.296	148	537	62	159	229	27	2	13	67	5	0	5	5	4
Bell, Kevin, Oak	.333	4	9	1	3	4	1	0	0	0	0	0	0	0	0
Beniquez, Juan, Calif	.265	112	196	25	52	76	11	2	3	24	3	16	0	3	0
Bernazard, Antonio, Chi†	.256	137	540	90	138	214	25	9	11	56	5	16	5	11	0
Biancalana, Roland, K.C.†	.500	3	2	0	1	3	0	1	0	0	0	0	0	0	0
Bochte, Bruce, Sea*	.297	144	509	58	151	208	21	0	12	70	9	4	3	8	5
Bogener, Terry, Tex*	.217	24	60	6	13	20	2	1	1	4	2	1	0	2	0
Boggs, Wade, Bos*	.349	104	338	51	118	149	14	1	5	44	3	4	4	1	0
Bonnell, R. Barry, Tor	.293	140	437	59	128	178	26	3	6	49	8	2	4	14	2
Bonner, Robert, Balt	.169	41	77	8	13	18	3	1	0	5	0	3	1	0	0
Boone, Robert, Calif	.256	143	472	42	121	159	17	0	7	58	9	23	5	0	2
Bosetti, Richard, Oak	.200	6	15	1	3	3	0	0	0	0	0	1	0	0	0
Bosley, Thaddis, Sea*	.174	22	46	3	8	9	1	0	0	2	0	0	0	3	1
Brett, George, K.C.*	.301	144	552	101	166	279	32	9	21	82	13	0	5	6	1

Player and Club	Pct.	G.	AB.	R.	H.	TB.	2B.	3B.	HR.	RBI.	GW.	SH.	SF.	SB.	CS.
Brookens, Thomas, Det	.231	140	398	40	92	140	15	3	9	58	10	2	5	5	9
Brouhard, Mark, Milw	.269	40	108	16	29	47	4	1	4	10	0	3	0	0	3
Brown, Darrell, Oak†	.333	8	18	2	6	8	0	1	0	3	0	1	0	1	0
Brown, Rogers, Sea†	.241	79	245	29	59	80	7	1	4	17	3	3	2	28	6
Brunansky, Thomas, Minn	.272	127	463	77	126	218	30	1	20	46	8	1	2	1	2
Bulling, Terry, Sea	.221	56	154	17	34	44	7	0	1	8	2	0	0	2	1
Bumbry, Alonza, Balt.	.262	150	562	77	147	190	20	4	5	40	3	10	2	10	5
Burleson, Richard, Calif	.156	11	45	4	7	8	1	0	0	2	0	2	0	0	0
Burroughs, Jeffrey, Oak	.277	113	285	42	79	144	13	2	16	48	5	1	3	1	3
Bush, R. Randall, Minn*	.244	55	119	13	29	49	6	1	4	13	3	0	1	0	0
Butera, Salvatore, Minn	.254	54	126	9	32	34	2	0	0	8	1	2	0	0	0
Cabell, Enos, Det	.261	125	464	45	121	150	17	3	2	37	6	2	2	15	6
Capra, Nick, Tex	.267	13	15	2	4	7	0	0	1	1	0	0	0	2	1
Carew, Rodney, Calif*	.319	138	523	88	167	211	25	5	3	44	4	16	4	10	17
Castillo, E. Manuel, Sea†	.257	138	506	49	130	170	29	1	3	49	5	2	9	2	8
Castillo, M. Carmelo, Clev	.208	47	120	11	25	35	4	0	2	11	2	1	0	0	0
Castillo, Martin, Det	.000	1	0	0	0	0	0	0	0	0	0	0	0	0	0
Castino, John, Minn	.241	117	410	48	99	141	12	6	6	37	1	3	2	2	5
Cerone, Richard, N.Y.	.227	89	300	29	68	93	10	0	5	28	5	4	5	0	2
Charboneau, Joseph, Clev	.214	22	56	7	12	22	2	1	2	9	1	0	1	0	0
Clark, Robert, Calif	.211	102	90	11	19	26	1	0	2	8	1	2	1	1	0
Collins, David, N.Y.†	.253	111	348	41	88	115	12	3	3	25	4	9	3	13	8
Concepcion, Onix, K.C.	.234	74	205	17	48	59	9	1	0	15	1	4	0	2	1
Cooper, Cecil, Milw*	.313	155	654	104	205	345	38	3	32	121	15	4	6	2	3
Cowens, Alfred, Sea	.270	146	560	72	151	266	39	8	20	78	3	1	3	11	7
Craig, Rodney, Clev†	.231	49	65	7	15	17	2	0	0	1	0	2	0	3	1
Crowley, Terrence, Balt*	.237	65	93	8	22	33	2	0	3	17	3	0	0	0	0
Cruz, Julio, Sea†	.242	154	549	83	133	189	22	5	8	49	2	6	2	46	13
Cruz, Todd, Sea	.230	136	492	44	113	185	20	2	16	57	9	11	4	2	10
Dauer, Richard, Balt	.280	158	558	75	156	208	24	2	8	57	7	11	6	0	1
Davis, Michael, Oak.*	.400	23	75	12	30	37	4	0	1	10	0	0	0	3	2
Davis, Richard, Tor	.286	3	7	0	2	2	0	0	0	2	0	0	1	0	0
DeCinces, Douglas, Cal	.301	153	575	94	173	315	42	5	30	97	11	4	9	7	5
DeJohn, Mark, Det.†	.190	24	21	1	4	6	2	0	0	1	0	3	0	1	0
Dempsey, J. Rikard, Balt	.256	125	344	35	88	120	15	1	5	36	7	7	5	0	3
Dent, Russell, N.Y.-Tex	.193	105	306	27	59	74	10	1	1	23	0	7	3	0	0
Dillard, Stephen, Chi	.171	16	41	1	7	12	3	1	0	5	0	0	0	0	1
Dilone, Miguel, Clev.†	.235	104	379	50	89	116	12	3	3	25	2	6	0	33	5
Downing, Brian, Cal	.281	158	623	109	175	300	37	2	28	84	6	3	8	2	1
Dwyer, James, Balt.*	.304	71	148	28	45	73	4	3	6	15	2	1	2	2	0
Dybzinski, Jerome, Clev	.231	80	212	19	49	59	6	2	0	22	1	7	3	3	5
Edler, David, Sea	.279	40	104	14	29	41	2	2	2	18	3	1	1	4	2
Edwards, Marshall, Milw.*	.247	69	178	24	44	56	4	1	2	14	1	5	2	10	4
Eisenreich, James, Minn.*	.303	34	99	10	30	42	6	0	2	9	0	0	0	0	0
Engle, R. David, Minn	.226	58	186	20	42	65	7	2	4	16	2	0	0	0	0
Espino, Juan, N.Y.	.000	3	2	0	0	0	0	0	0	0	0	0	0	0	0
Essian, James, Sea	.275	48	153	14	42	59	8	0	3	20	1	0	0	2	0
Evans, Barry, N.Y.	.258	17	31	2	8	11	3	0	0	2	0	0	0	0	0
Evans, Dwight, Bos	.292	162	609	122	178	325	37	7	32	98	7	3	2	3	2
Faedo, Leonardo, Minn	.243	90	255	16	62	79	8	0	3	22	3	2	2	1	0
Fahey, William, Det.*	.149	28	67	7	10	12	2	0	0	4	1	0	1	1	0
Ferguson, Joseph, Cal	.226	36	84	10	19	30	2	0	3	8	0	1	0	0	0
Firova, Dan, Sea	.000	3	5	0	0	0	0	0	0	0	0	0	0	0	0
Fischlin, Michael, Clev	.268	112	276	34	74	88	12	1	0	21	4	9	1	9	5
Fisk, Carlton, Chi	.267	135	476	66	127	192	17	3	14	65	4	4	4	17	2
Flynn, R. Douglas, Tex	.211	88	270	13	57	67	6	2	0	19	3	7	2	6	2
Foley, Marvis, Chi.*	.111	27	36	1	4	4	0	0	0	1	0	0	0	0	0
Foli, Timothy, Cal	.252	150	480	46	121	148	14	2	3	56	4	26	6	2	4
Foote, Barry, N.Y.	.146	17	48	4	7	12	5	0	0	2	1	0	1	0	0
Ford, Darnell, Balt	.235	123	421	46	99	156	21	3	10	43	4	2	3	5	2
Gaetti, Gary, Minn	.230	145	508	59	117	225	25	4	25	84	10	4	13	0	4
Gamble, Oscar, N.Y.*	.272	108	316	49	86	165	21	2	18	57	7	0	4	6	3
Gantner, James, Milw.*	.295	132	447	48	132	165	17	2	4	43	4	7	3	6	3
Garcia, Damaso, Tor	.310	147	597	89	185	238	32	3	5	42	7	5	1	54	20
Gedman, Richard, Bos.*	.249	92	289	30	72	105	17	2	4	26	2	4	0	0	1
Geronimo, Cesar, K.C.*	.269	53	119	14	32	56	6	3	4	23	3	0	4	2	0
Gibson, Kirk, Det.*	.278	69	266	34	74	118	16	2	8	35	6	1	1	9	7
Goodwin, Danny, Oak.*	.212	17	52	6	11	21	2	1	2	8	0	2	1	0	0
Gray, Gary, Sea	.257	80	269	26	69	108	14	2	7	29	4	0	0	1	1
Gray, Lorenzo, Chi	.286	17	28	4	8	9	1	0	0	0	0	0	0	1	0
Grich, Robert, Cal	.261	145	506	74	132	227	28	5	19	65	2	6	3	3	3
Griffey, G. Kenneth, N.Y.*	.277	127	484	70	134	197	23	2	12	54	9	1	3	10	4
Griffin, Alfredo, Tor.†	.241	162	539	57	130	169	20	8	1	48	3	11	4	10	8
Gross, Wayne, Oak.*	.251	129	386	43	97	138	14	0	9	41	3	7	3	3	1
Grubb, John, Tex.*	.279	103	308	35	86	114	13	3	3	26	2	2	3	0	3
Gulliver, Glenn, Balt.*	.200	50	145	24	29	39	7	0	1	5	2	3	0	0	0
Hairston, Jerry, Chi.†	.233	85	90	11	21	41	5	0	5	18	3	1	3	0	0
Hammond, Steven, K.C.*	.230	46	126	14	29	39	5	1	1	11	1	0	1	0	1
Hancock, R. Garry, Bos.*	.000	11	14	3	0	0	0	0	0	0	0	0	0	0	0
Hargrove, D. Michael, Clev.*	.271	160	591	67	160	200	26	1	4	65	8	4	6	2	2

Player and Club	Pct.	G.	AB.	R.	H.	TB.	2B.	3B.	HR.	RBI.	GW.	SH.	SF.	SB.	CS.
Harrah, Colbert, Clev	.304	162	602	100	183	295	29	4	25	78	7	7	3	17	3
Hassey, Ronald, Clev.*	.251	113	323	33	81	114	18	0	5	34	6	3	2	3	2
Hatcher, Michael, Minn.	.249	84	277	23	69	95	13	2	3	26	1	0	1	0	2
Hayes, Von, Clev.*	.250	150	527	65	132	205	25	3	14	82	11	8	2	32	13
Heath, Kelly, K.C.	.000	1	1	0	0	0	0	0	0	0	0	0	0	0	0
Heath, Michael, Oak	.242	101	318	43	77	112	18	4	3	39	4	2	4	8	3
Hebner, Richard, Det.*	.274	68	179	25	49	79	6	0	8	18	0	0	1	1	1
Henderson, David, Sea	.253	104	324	47	82	143	17	1	14	48	4	1	1	2	5
Henderson, Rickey, Oak	.267	149	536	119	143	205	24	4	10	51	5	0	2	130	42
Hernandez, Leonardo, Balt	.000	2	2	0	0	0	0	0	0	0	0	0	0	0	0
Hernandez, Pedro, Tor	.000	8	9	1	0	0	0	0	0	0	0	0	0	0	0
Herndon, Larry, Det	.292	157	614	92	179	295	21	13	23	88	7	2	4	12	9
Hill, Marc, Chi	.261	53	88	9	23	34	2	0	3	13	0	2	1	0	0
Hisle, Larry, Milw	.129	9	31	7	4	10	0	0	2	5	0	0	0	0	0
Hobson, Clell, N.Y.	.172	30	58	2	10	12	2	0	0	3	0	0	1	0	0
Hoffman, Glenn, Bos	.209	150	469	53	98	146	23	2	7	49	5	5	4	0	4
Hostetler, David, Tex	.232	113	418	53	97	181	12	3	22	67	10	0	5	2	2
Howell, Roy, Milw.*	.260	98	300	31	78	105	11	2	4	38	3	1	4	0	2
Hrbek, Kent, Minn.*	.301	140	532	82	160	258	21	4	23	92	10	1	4	3	1
Iorg, Garth, Tor	.285	129	417	45	119	152	20	5	1	36	4	2	7	3	2
Ireland, Timothy, K.C.	.143	7	7	2	1	1	0	0	0	0	0	0	0	0	0
Ivie, Michael, Det	.232	80	259	35	60	116	12	1	14	38	4	0	3	0	0
Jackson, Reginald, Cal.*	.275	153	530	92	146	282	17	1	39	101	8	0	4	4	5
Jackson, Ronnie, Cal	.331	53	142	15	47	59	6	0	2	19	1	4	1	0	1
Johnson, Anthony, Tor	.235	70	98	17	23	36	2	1	3	14	2	1	1	3	13
Johnson, Bobby, Tex	.125	20	56	4	7	15	2	0	2	7	2	2	0	0	1
Johnson, Clifford, Oak	.238	73	214	19	51	82	10	0	7	31	1	0	2	1	2
Johnson, Howard, Det.†	.316	54	155	23	49	66	5	0	4	14	0	1	0	7	4
Johnson, Lamar, Tex	.259	105	324	37	84	116	11	0	7	38	7	2	0	3	5
Johnson, Randall, Minn.*	.248	89	234	26	58	98	10	0	10	33	2	0	7	0	0
Johnson, Ronald, K.C.	.286	8	14	2	4	6	2	0	0	0	0	0	0	0	0
Jones, Lynn, Det	.223	58	139	15	31	36	3	1	0	14	0	3	1	0	2
Jurak, Edward, Bos	.333	12	21	3	7	7	0	0	0	7	1	0	1	0	0
Kearney, Robert, Oak	.169	22	71	7	12	15	3	0	0	5	0	0	2	0	0
Kelleher, Michael, Det-Cal	.160	36	50	9	8	9	1	0	0	1	0	3	0	1	1
Kemp, Steven, Chi.*	.286	160	580	91	166	248	23	1	19	98	14	1	6	7	7
Kittle, Ronald, Chi	.241	20	29	3	7	12	2	0	1	7	1	0	0	0	0
Klutts, Gene, Oak	.178	55	157	10	28	36	8	0	0	14	1	3	1	0	0
Kuntz, Russell, Chi	.192	21	26	4	5	6	1	0	0	3	0	0	0	0	0
LaFrancois, Roger, Bos.*	.400	8	10	1	4	5	1	0	0	1	0	0	0	0	0
Laga, Michael, Det.*	.261	27	88	6	23	41	9	0	3	11	1	0	0	1	0
Langford, J. Rick, Oak	.000	33	1	0	0	0	0	0	0	0	0	0	0	0	0
Lansford, Carney, Bos	.301	128	482	65	145	214	28	4	11	63	6	1	8	9	4
Laudner, Timothy, Minn	.255	93	306	37	78	120	19	1	7	33	2	2	1	0	2
Law, Rudy, Chi.*	.318	121	336	55	107	147	15	8	3	32	1	3	1	36	10
Law, Vance, Chi	.281	114	359	40	101	138	20	1	5	54	4	7	5	4	2
Leach, Richard, Det.*	.239	82	218	23	52	72	7	2	3	12	0	4	2	4	0
LeFlore, Ronald, Chi	.287	91	334	58	96	131	15	4	4	25	3	0	1	28	14
Lemon, Chester, Det	.266	125	436	75	116	195	20	1	19	52	3	4	1	1	4
Lopes, David, Oak	.242	128	450	58	109	167	19	3	11	42	1	2	3	28	12
Loviglio, John, Chi	.194	15	31	5	6	6	0	0	0	2	0	1	0	2	1
Lowenstein, John, Balt.*	.320	122	322	69	103	194	15	2	24	66	9	3	4	7	6
Luzinski, Gregory, Chi	.292	159	583	87	170	263	37	1	18	102	17	0	8	1	1
Lynn, Fredric, Cal.*	.299	138	472	89	141	244	38	1	21	86	12	5	7	7	8
Maler, James, Sea	.226	64	221	18	50	76	8	3	4	26	2	2	1	0	0
Manning, Richard, Clev.*	.270	152	562	71	152	198	18	2	8	44	3	2	1	12	8
Martin, Jerry, K.C.	.266	147	519	52	138	207	22	1	15	65	5	2	4	1	1
Martinez, John, Tor	.242	96	260	26	63	110	17	0	10	37	4	2	5	1	1
Mattingly, Donald, N.Y.*	.167	7	12	0	2	2	0	0	0	1	0	0	1	0	0
May, Lee, K.C.	.308	42	91	12	28	46	5	2	3	12	0	0	2	0	0
Mayberry, John, Tor.-N.Y.*	.218	86	248	27	54	91	7	0	10	30	2	0	2	0	0
Mazzilli, Lee, Tex.-N.Y.†	.251	95	323	43	81	121	10	0	10	34	2	0	0	13	9
McBride, Arnold, Clev.*	.365	27	85	8	31	40	3	3	0	13	1	0	1	2	2
McHenry, Vance, Sea	.000	3	1	0	0	0	0	0	0	0	0	0	0	0	0
McKay, David, Oak.†	.198	78	212	25	42	60	4	1	4	17	0	0	3	6	1
McRae, Harold, K.C.	.308	159	613	91	189	332	46	8	27	133	13	1	2	4	0
Mendoza, Mario, Tex	.118	12	17	1	2	2	0	0	0	0	0	1	0	0	0
Mercado, Orlando, Sea	.118	9	17	1	2	5	0	0	1	6	1	0	0	0	0
Meyer, Daniel, Oak.*	.240	120	383	28	92	139	17	3	8	59	10	3	5	1	1
Milbourne, Lawrence, NY-Min-Cle†	.257	125	416	40	107	136	13	5	2	26	2	7	8	3	7
Miller, Edward, Det.†	.040	14	25	3	1	1	0	0	0	0	0	1	0	0	3
Miller, Richard, Bos.*	.254	135	409	50	104	133	13	2	4	38	7	4	1	5	6
Mitchell, Robert, Minn.*	.249	124	454	48	113	142	11	6	2	28	1	2	1	8	9
Molitor, Paul, Milw	.302	160	666	136	201	300	26	8	19	71	7	10	5	41	9
Money, Donald, Milw	.284	96	275	40	78	146	14	3	16	55	4	5	0	0	2
Moore, Charles, Milw	.254	133	456	53	116	164	22	4	6	45	5	4	2	2	10
Moore, Kelvin, Oak	.224	21	67	6	15	24	1	1	2	6	0	0	2	0	1
Morales, Jose, Balt	.000	3	3	0	0	0	0	0	0	0	0	0	0	0	0
Moreno, Jose, Cal.†	.000	11	3	3	0	0	0	0	0	0	0	0	0	0	2
Morrison, James, Chi	.223	51	166	17	37	71	7	3	7	19	3	1	0	0	1

Player and Club	Pct.	G.	AB.	R.	H.	TB.	2B.	3B.	HR.	RBI.	GW.	SH.	SF.	SB.	CS.
Moseby, Lloyd, Tor.*	.236	147	487	51	115	180	20	9	9	52	2	3	2	11	7
Moses, John, Sea.†	.318	22	44	7	14	24	5	1	1	3	1	0	0	5	1
Mulliniks, S. Rance, Tor.*	.244	112	311	32	76	113	25	0	4	35	7	3	1	3	2
Mumphrey, Jerry, N.Y.†	.300	123	477	76	143	214	24	10	9	68	11	3	3	11	3
Murcer, Bobby, N.Y.*	.227	65	141	12	32	59	6	0	7	30	2	0	2	2	1
Murphy, Dwayne, Oak.*	.238	151	543	84	129	227	15	1	27	94	6	12	8	26	8
Murray, Eddie, Balt.†	.316	151	550	87	174	302	30	1	32	110	20	0	6	7	2
Nahorodny, William, Clev.	.223	39	94	6	21	40	5	1	4	18	2	1	1	0	0
Nettles, Graig, N.Y.*	.232	122	405	47	94	163	11	2	18	55	5	0	4	1	5
Newman, Jeffrey, Oak	.199	72	251	19	50	79	11	0	6	30	2	1	2	0	1
Nichols, T. Reid, Bos	.302	92	245	35	74	113	16	1	7	33	6	4	1	5	3
Nolan, Joseph, Balt.*	.233	77	219	24	51	78	7	1	6	35	4	1	6	1	1
Nordhagen, Wayne, Tor	.270	72	185	12	50	59	6	0	1	20	0	0	2	0	2
Norris, Michael, Oak	.000	29	0	1	0	0	0	0	0	0	0	0	0	0	0
Nyman, Christopher, Chi	.246	28	65	6	16	17	1	0	0	2	1	2	0	3	2
O'Brien, Peter, Tex.*	.239	20	67	13	16	34	4	1	4	13	1	0	1	1	0
Oglivie, Benjamin, Milw.*	.244	159	602	92	147	273	22	1	34	102	11	0	1	3	5
Otis, Amos, K.C.	.286	125	475	73	136	200	25	3	11	88	20	1	9	9	5
Paciorek, Thomas, Chi	.312	104	382	49	119	187	27	4	11	55	8	1	6	3	3
Page, Mitchell, Oak.*	.256	31	78	14	20	37	5	0	4	7	4	0	0	3	4
Pagel, Karl, Clev.*	.167	23	18	3	3	3	0	0	0	2	1	0	0	0	0
Parrish, Lance, Det	.284	133	486	75	138	257	19	2	32	87	10	0	2	3	4
Parrish, Larry, Tex	.264	128	440	59	116	182	15	0	17	62	7	0	4	5	2
Patterson, Michael, N.Y.*	.188	11	16	3	3	7	1	0	1	1	0	0	0	1	0
Perconte, John, Clev.*	.237	93	219	27	52	64	4	4	0	15	1	7	3	9	3
Perez, Atanasio, Bos	.260	69	196	18	51	87	14	2	6	31	4	0	0	0	1
Petralli, Eugene, Tor.†	.364	16	44	3	16	18	2	0	0	1	1	1	0	0	0
Pettis, Gary, Cal.†	.200	10	5	5	1	4	0	0	1	1	1	0	0	0	0
Phillips, K. Anthony, Oak.†	.210	40	81	11	17	23	2	2	0	8	0	5	0	2	3
Picciolo, Robert, Oak.-Milw	.243	40	70	10	17	19	2	0	0	4	0	4	0	1	0
Piniella, Louis, N.Y.	.307	102	261	33	80	117	17	1	6	37	3	2	1	0	1
Poquette, Thomas, K.C.*	.145	24	62	4	9	10	1	0	0	3	0	1	1	1	0
Powell, Hosken, Tor.*	.275	112	265	43	73	103	13	4	3	26	2	0	3	4	4
Pryor, Gregory, K.C.	.270	73	152	23	41	59	10	1	2	12	4	4	0	2	0
Putnam, Patrick, Tex.*	.230	43	122	14	28	42	8	0	2	9	0	0	0	0	2
Quirk, James, K.C.*	.231	36	78	8	18	24	3	0	1	5	1	0	1	0	0
Ramos, Domingo, Sea.	.154	8	26	3	4	6	2	0	0	1	0	1	0	0	0
Ramos, Roberto, N.Y.	.091	4	11	1	1	4	0	0	1	2	0	0	0	0	0
Randle, Leonard, Sea.†	.174	30	46	10	8	10	2	0	0	1	0	1	0	2	2
Randolph, William, N.Y.	.280	144	553	85	155	193	21	4	3	36	6	10	2	16	9
Rayford, Floyd, Balt.	.132	34	53	7	7	16	0	0	3	5	1	0	0	0	1
Remy, Gerald, Bos.*	.280	155	636	89	178	206	22	3	0	47	7	18	5	16	9
Revering, David, N.Y.-Tor-Sea*	.202	98	257	25	52	89	11	1	8	32	7	0	4	0	3
Rhomberg, Kevin, Clev.	.333	16	18	3	6	9	0	0	1	1	0	0	0	0	2
Rice, James, Bos.	.309	145	573	86	177	283	24	5	24	97	15	0	3	0	1
Richardt, Michael, Tex.	.241	119	402	34	97	116	10	0	3	43	1	5	4	9	1
Ripken, Calvin Jr., Balt.	.264	160	598	90	158	284	32	5	28	93	11	2	6	3	3
Rivera, Jesus, K.C.	.100	5	10	1	1	1	0	0	0	0	0	0	0	0	0
Rivers, John, Tex.*	.235	19	68	6	16	22	1	1	1	4	0	0	1	0	0
Roberts, Leon, Tex.-Tor.	.230	71	178	13	41	54	7	0	2	11	0	1	2	1	1
Robertson, Andre, N.Y.	.220	44	118	16	26	37	5	0	2	9	1	2	0	0	0
Rodriguez, Aurelio, Chi.	.241	118	257	24	62	88	15	1	3	31	3	8	0	0	0
Rodriguez, Edwin, N.Y.	.333	3	9	2	3	3	0	0	0	1	0	0	0	0	0
Roenicke, Gary, Balt.	.270	137	393	58	106	196	25	1	21	74	3	5	0	6	7
Romero, Edgardo, Milw.	.250	52	144	18	36	47	8	0	1	7	0	3	0	0	0
Rudi, Joseph, Oak.	.212	71	193	21	41	64	6	1	5	18	4	4	1	0	0
Ryal, Mark, K.C.*	.077	6	13	0	1	1	0	0	0	0	0	0	0	0	0
Sakata, Lenn, Balt.	.259	136	343	40	89	127	18	1	6	31	1	8	4	7	4
Sample, William, Tex.	.261	97	360	56	94	142	14	2	10	29	6	8	0	10	2
Sconiers, Daryl, Cal.*	.154	12	13	0	2	2	0	0	0	2	1	0	0	0	0
Scott, Rodney, N.Y.†	.192	10	26	5	5	5	0	0	0	0	0	1	0	2	0
Serna, Paul, Sea.	.225	65	169	15	38	50	3	0	3	8	2	3	1	0	5
Sexton, Jimmy, Oak.	.245	69	139	19	34	44	4	0	2	14	2	2	3	16	0
Shelby, John, Balt.†	.314	26	35	8	11	17	3	0	1	2	0	0	0	0	1
Simmons, Ted, Milw.†	.269	137	539	73	145	243	29	0	23	97	12	1	7	0	0
Simpson, Joe, Sea.*	.257	105	296	39	76	104	14	4	2	23	4	3	1	8	14
Singleton, Kenneth, Balt.†	.251	156	561	71	141	214	27	2	14	77	10	1	7	0	1
Skube, Robert, Milw.*	.667	4	3	0	2	2	0	0	0	0	0	0	0	0	0
Slaught, Donald, K.C.	.278	43	115	14	32	47	6	0	3	8	1	2	0	0	0
Smalley, Roy, Minn.-N.Y.†	.255	146	499	57	127	206	15	2	20	67	3	7	4	0	1
Smith, Raymond, Minn.	.217	9	23	1	5	7	0	1	0	1	0	0	0	0	0
Spencer, James, Oak.*	.168	33	101	6	17	28	3	1	2	5	2	0	1	0	0
Squires, Michael, Chi.*	.267	116	195	33	52	70	9	3	1	21	1	4	0	3	3
Stanley, Frederick, Oak.	.193	101	228	33	44	57	7	0	2	17	2	1	0	0	1
Stapleton, David, Bos.	.264	150	538	66	142	214	28	1	14	65	8	4	5	2	4
Stegman, David, N.Y.	.000	2	0	0	0	0	0	0	0	0	0	0	0	0	0
Stein, William, Tex.	.239	85	184	14	44	55	8	0	1	16	2	2	0	0	0
Strougther, Stephen, Sea.*	.170	26	47	4	8	12	1	0	1	3	0	0	0	0	0
Sullivan, Marc, Bos.	.333	2	6	0	2	2	0	0	0	0	0	0	0	0	0
Sundberg, James, Tex.	.251	139	470	37	118	180	22	5	10	47	5	9	1	2	6

Player and Club	Pct.	G.	AB.	R.	H.	TB.	2B.	3B.	HR.	RBI.	GW.	SH.	SF.	SB.	CS.
Sweet, Richard, Sea.†	.256	88	258	29	66	86	6	1	4	24	3	3	3	3	0
Thomas, J. Gorman, Milw.	.245	158	567	96	139	287	29	1	39	112	12	5	6	3	7
Thornton, Andre, Clev.	.273	161	589	90	161	285	26	1	32	116	15	3	5	6	7
Tolleson, J. Wayne, Tex.†	.114	38	70	6	8	9	1	0	0	2	0	3	0	1	1
Trammell, Alan, Det.	.258	157	489	66	126	193	34	3	9	57	6	9	6	19	8
Turner, John, Det.*	.248	85	210	21	52	79	3	0	8	27	6	0	2	1	3
Upshaw, Willie, Tor.*	.267	160	580	77	155	257	25	7	21	75	14	10	3	8	8
Valdez, Julio, Bos.†	.250	28	20	3	5	6	1	0	0	1	0	3	0	1	0
Vega, Jesus, Minn.	.266	71	199	23	53	74	6	0	5	29	0	1	4	6	1
Velez, Otoniel, Tor.	.192	28	52	4	10	14	1	0	1	5	0	0	0	1	0
Wagner, Mark, Tex.	.240	60	179	14	43	49	4	1	0	8	0	7	0	1	0
Walker, Gregory, Chi.*	.412	11	17	3	7	17	2	1	2	7	1	0	0	0	0
Ward, Gary, Minn.	.289	152	570	85	165	296	33	7	28	91	9	1	7	13	1
Washington, Ronald, Minn.	.271	119	451	48	122	166	17	6	5	39	4	2	3	3	3
Washington, U.L., K.C.†	.286	119	437	64	125	180	19	3	10	60	6	5	7	23	7
Wathan, John, K.C.	.270	121	448	79	121	147	11	3	3	51	5	3	1	36	9
Watson, Robert, N.Y.	.235	7	17	3	4	7	3	0	0	3	0	0	0	0	0
Wells, Gregory, Minn.	.204	15	54	5	11	16	1	2	0	3	0	0	2	0	0
Werner, Donald, Tex.	.203	22	59	4	12	4	2	0	0	3	0	3	0	0	0
Werth, Dennis, K.C.	.133	41	15	5	2	2	0	0	0	2	0	0	0	0	0
Whitaker, Louis, Det.*	.286	152	560	76	160	243	22	8	15	65	11	6	4	11	3
White, Frank, K.C.	.298	145	524	71	156	246	45	6	11	56	4	7	5	10	7
Whitt, L. Ernest, Tor.*	.261	105	284	28	74	125	14	2	11	42	5	1	5	3	1
Wilfong, Robert, Minn.-Cal.*	.208	80	183	24	38	50	5	2	1	16	1	3	0	4	2
Wilson, Glenn, Det.	.292	84	322	39	94	147	15	1	12	34	3	3	2	2	3
Wilson, Willie, K.C.†	.332	136	585	87	194	252	19	15	3	46	2	2	2	37	11
Winfield, David, N.Y.	.280	140	539	84	151	302	24	8	37	106	15	5	8	5	3
Wockenfuss, Johnny, Det.	.301	70	193	28	58	91	9	0	8	32	1	0	2	0	0
Woods, Alvis, Tor.*	.234	85	201	20	47	69	11	1	3	24	2	0	3	1	3
Wright, George, Tex.†	.264	150	557	69	147	210	20	5	11	50	3	8	1	3	7
Wynegar, Harold, Minn-NY†	.267	87	277	36	74	100	12	1	4	28	2	7	3	0	1
Yastrzemski, Carl, Bos.*	.275	131	459	53	126	198	22	1	16	72	9	0	3	0	1
Yost, Edgar, Milw.	.276	40	98	13	27	42	6	3	1	8	1	2	0	3	1
Young, Michael, Balt.†	.000	6	2	2	0	0	0	0	0	0	0	0	0	0	0
Yount, Robin, Milw.	.331	156	635	129	210	367	46	12	29	114	12	4	10	14	3
Zisk, Richard, Sea.	.292	131	503	61	147	240	28	1	21	62	8	0	3	2	1

The following pitchers neither had a plate appearance nor scored a run, but made appearances in addition to their games pitched as indicated: Fernando Arroyo, Minnesota—one game announced as a relief pitcher but did not pitch; Harry Black, Kansas City—one game as a pinch-runner; Samuel Stewart, Baltimore—one game announced as a relief pitcher but did not pitch; Milton Wilcox, Detroit—one game announced as a starting pitcher but did not pitch.

AWARDED FIRST BASE ON INTERFERENCE—Griffey, N.Y. (Heath); Otis, K.C. (Nolan); Sundberg, Tex. (Hill).

PLAYERS WITH TWO OR MORE CLUBS
(Alphabetically Arranged With Player's First Club on Top)

Player and Club	Pct.	G.	AB.	R.	H.	TB.	2B.	3B.	HR.	RBI.	GW.	SH.	SF.	Tot. BB.	Int. BB.	HP.	SO.	SB.	CS.	GI. DP.
Dent, N.Y.	.169	59	160	11	27	30	1	1	0	9	0	4	1	8	0	0	11	0	0	7
Dent, Tex.	.219	46	146	16	32	44	9	0	1	14	0	3	2	13	0	0	10	0	0	2
Kelleher, Det.	.000	2	1	0	0	0	0	0	0	0	0	0	0	0	0	0	0	0	0	0
Kelleher, Cal.	.163	34	49	9	8	9	1	0	0	1	0	3	0	5	0	1	5	1	1	5
Mayberry, Tor.	.273	17	33	7	9	15	0	0	2	3	0	0	1	7	1	1	5	0	0	0
Mayberry, N.Y.	.209	69	215	20	45	76	7	0	8	27	2	0	1	28	2	5	38	0	0	7
Mazzilli, Tex.	.241	58	195	23	47	67	8	0	4	17	1	0	0	28	0	1	26	11	6	4
Mazzilli, N.Y.	.266	37	128	20	34	54	2	0	6	17	1	0	0	15	0	1	15	2	3	2
Milbourne, N.Y.	.148	14	27	2	4	5	1	0	0	0	0	0	0	1	0	0	4	0	1	0
Milbourne, Minn.	.235	29	98	9	23	26	1	1	0	1	0	1	0	7	0	0	8	1	1	5
Milbourne, Clev.	.275	82	291	29	80	105	11	4	2	25	2	7	7	12	0	2	20	2	5	10
Picciolo, Oak.	.224	18	49	3	11	12	1	0	0	3	0	3	0	1	0	0	10	1	0	0
Picciolo, Milw.	.286	22	21	7	6	7	1	0	0	1	0	1	0	1	0	0	4	0	0	0
Revering, N.Y.	.150	14	40	2	6	8	2	0	0	2	1	0	1	3	2	0	4	0	0	3
Revering, Tor.	.215	55	135	15	29	50	6	0	5	18	4	0	2	22	1	0	30	0	3	2
Revering, Sea.	.207	29	82	8	17	31	3	1	3	12	2	0	1	9	0	0	17	0	0	3
Roberts, Tex.	.233	31	73	7	17	23	3	0	1	6	0	1	1	4	0	1	14	0	0	4
Roberts, Tor.	.229	40	105	6	24	31	4	0	1	5	0	0	1	7	0	0	16	1	1	3
Smalley, Minn.	.154	4	13	2	2	3	1	0	0	0	0	0	0	3	0	0	4	0	0	0
Smalley, N.Y.	.257	142	486	55	125	203	14	2	20	67	3	7	4	68	7	0	100	0	1	4
Wilfong, Minn.	.160	25	81	7	13	14	1	0	0	5	0	1	0	7	0	1	13	0	2	4
Wilfong, Cal.	.245	55	102	17	25	36	4	2	1	11	1	2	0	7	1	0	17	4	0	1
Wynegar, Minn.	.209	24	86	9	18	25	4	0	1	8	0	0	0	10	1	0	12	0	0	2
Wynegar, N.Y.	.293	63	191	27	56	75	8	1	3	20	2	7	3	40	1	1	21	0	1	7

OFFICIAL MISCELLANEOUS AMERICAN LEAGUE BATTING RECORDS

CLUB MISCELLANEOUS BATTING RECORDS

Club	Slg. Pct.	G.	Tot. BB.	Int. BB.	HP.	SO.	GIDP.	ShO.
Milwaukee	.455	163	484	42	18	714	106	1
California	.433	162	613	46	35	760	130	3
Kansas City	.428	162	442	37	25	758	140	8
Baltimore	.419	163	634	52	25	796	141	11
Detroit	.418	162	470	29	26	807	99	10
Chicago	.413	162	533	45	30	866	117	7
Boston	.407	162	547	34	28	736	171	9
New York	.398	162	590	45	24	719	152	11
Minnesota	.396	162	474	31	24	887	149	9
Toronto	.383	162	415	38	28	749	107	9
Seattle	.381	162	456	31	22	806	113	6
Cleveland	.373	162	651	48	35	625	143	11
Oakland	.367	162	582	20	20	948	95	9
Texas	.359	162	447	22	32	750	134	17
Totals	.402	1135	7338	520	372	10921	1797	121

INDIVIDUAL MISCELLANEOUS BATTING RECORDS
(Top Fifteen Qualifiers for Slugging Championship)

Player—Club	Slg. Pct.	Tot. BB.	Int. BB.	HP.	SO.	GI DP.
Yount, Milw.	.578	54	2	1	63	19
Winfield, N.Y.	.560	45	7	0	64	20
Murray, Balt.	.549	70	18	1	82	17
DeCinces, Cal.	.548	66	7	1	80	18
McRae, K.C.	.542	55	7	5	61	8
Evans, Bos.	.534	112	1	1	125	17
Re. Jackson, Cal.	.532	85	12	2	156	10
Parrish, Det.	.529	40	5	1	99	5
Cooper, Milw.	.528	32	7	0	53	4
Ward, Minn.	.519	37	4	1	105	16
Lynn, Cal.	.517	58	4	3	72	9
Thomas, Milw.	.506	84	5	4	143	10
Brett, K.C.	.505	71	14	1	51	12
Rice, Bos.	.494	55	6	7	98	29
Harrah, Clev.	.490	84	7	12	52	13

DEPARTMENTAL LEADERS: Tot. BB—R. Henderson, 116; Int. BB—Murray, Thornton, 18; HP—Lemon, 15; SO—Re. Jackson, 156; GIDP—Rice, 29.

(All Players—Listed Alphabetically)

Player—Club	Slg. Pct.	Tot. BB.	Int. BB.	HP.	SO.	GI DP.
Adams, Tor.	.364	4	0	0	5	3
Adams, Cal.	.143	0	0	1	2	1
Aikens, K.C.	.457	45	7	3	70	19
Allenson, Bos.	.314	38	1	1	39	6
Almon, Chi.	.354	25	0	1	49	4
Armas, Oak.	.433	33	5	1	128	14
Ayala, Balt.	.492	5	2	0	14	3
Baines, Chi.	.469	49	10	0	95	12
Baker, Tor.	.300	3	0	2	3	0
Balboni, N.Y.	.280	6	0	0	34	1
Bando, Clev.	.304	24	1	0	30	6
Bannister, Clev.	.353	42	1	1	41	4
Barfield, Tor.	.426	42	3	3	79	7
Barrett, Bos.	.056	0	0	0	1	1
Bass, Milw.	.000	1	0	0	1	0
Bass, Tex.	.313	1	0	1	7	1
Baylor, Cal.	.424	57	7	7	69	18
Bell, Tex.	.426	70	8	2	50	13
Bell, Oak.	.444	0	0	0	2	0
Beniquez, Cal.	.388	15	1	1	21	4
Bernazard, Chi.	.396	67	0	2	88	9
Biancalana, K.C.	1.500	1	0	0	0	1
Bochte, Sea.	.409	67	5	3	71	17
Bogener, Tex.	.333	4	0	2	8	3
Boggs, Bos.	.441	35	4	0	21	9
Bonnell, Tor.	.407	32	4	3	51	8
Bonner, Balt.	.234	3	0	0	12	3
Boone, Cal.	.337	39	2	0	34	9
Bosetti, Oak.	.200	0	0	0	1	1
Bosley, Sea.	.196	4	0	0	8	1
Brett, K.C.	.505	71	14	1	51	12
Brookens, Det.	.352	27	0	0	63	9
Brouhard, Milw.	.435	9	0	2	17	3
Brown, Oak.	.444	1	0	0	2	0
Brown, Sea.	.327	17	2	0	32	3
Brunansky, Minn.	.471	71	0	8	101	12
Bulling, Sea.	.286	19	2	0	16	6
Bumbry, Balt.	.338	44	4	0	77	12
Burleson, Cal.	.178	6	2	0	3	2
Burroughs, Oak.	.505	45	0	0	61	8
Bush, Minn.	.412	8	0	3	28	1
Butera, Minn.	.270	17	0	1	12	6
Cabell, Det.	.323	15	2	1	48	10
Capra, Tex.	.467	3	0	1	4	1
Carew, Cal.	.403	67	5	2	49	9
Castillo, Sea.	.336	22	2	2	35	11
Castillo, Clev.	.292	6	2	2	17	2
Castillo, Det.	.000	0	0	0	0	0
Castino, Minn.	.344	36	1	2	51	11
Cerone, N.Y.	.310	19	1	1	27	12
Charboneau, Clev.	.393	5	0	1	7	2
Clark, Cal.	.289	0	0	0	29	1
Collins, N.Y.	.330	28	3	5	49	6
Concepcion, K.C.	.288	5	0	1	18	6
Cooper, Milw.	.528	32	7	0	53	4
Cowens, Sea.	.475	46	3	1	81	12
Craig, Clev.	.262	4	0	0	6	5
Crowley, Balt.	.355	21	1	0	9	5
J. Cruz, Sea.	.344	57	1	3	71	6
T. Cruz, Sea.	.376	12	1	0	95	18
Dauer, Balt.	.373	50	1	1	34	15
Davis, Oak.	.493	2	0	0	8	0
Davis, Tor.	.286	0	0	0	1	1
DeCinces, Cal.	.548	66	7	1	80	18
DeJohn, Det.	.286	4	0	0	4	0
Dempsey, Balt.	.349	46	1	0	37	10
Dent, N.Y.-Tex.	.242	21	0	0	21	9
Dillard, Chi.	.293	1	0	0	5	1
Dilone, Clev.	.306	25	0	2	36	11
Downing, Cal.	.482	86	1	5	58	14
Dwyer, Balt.	.493	27	4	0	24	0
Dybzinski, Clev.	.278	21	0	3	25	7
Edler, Sea.	.394	11	1	0	13	3
Edwards, Milw.	.315	4	0	0	8	5
Eisenreich, Minn.	.424	11	0	1	13	1
Engle, Minn.	.349	10	0	1	22	6
Espino, N.Y.	.000	0	0	0	1	0
Essian, Sea.	.386	11	0	1	7	3
Evans, N.Y.	.355	6	0	1	6	0
Evans, Bos.	.534	112	1	1	125	17
Faedo, Minn.	.310	16	0	1	22	9
Fahey, Det.	.179	0	0	0	5	0
Ferguson, Cal.	.357	12	0	0	19	4

Player—Club	Slg. Pct.	Tot. BB.	Int. BB.	HP.	SO.	GI DP.	Player—Club	Slg. Pct.	Tot. BB.	Int. BB.	HP.	SO.	GI DP.
Firova, Sea.	.000	0	0	0	0	0	Lowenstein, Balt	.602	54	10	1	59	6
Fischlin, Clev.	.319	34	0	2	36	3	Luzinski, Chi	.451	89	11	6	120	19
Fisk, Chi.	.403	46	7	6	60	12	Lynn, Cal	.517	58	4	3	72	9
Flynn, Tex.	.248	4	0	0	14	3	Maler, Sea	.344	12	3	3	35	4
Foley, Chi.	.111	6	1	0	4	0	Manning, Clev	.352	54	5	0	60	11
Foli, Cal.	.308	14	1	2	22	7	Martin, K.C.	.399	38	0	2	138	8
Foote, N.Y.	.250	1	0	0	11	2	Martinez, Tor	.423	24	1	0	34	10
Ford, Balt.	.371	23	1	4	71	9	Mattingly, N.Y.	.167	0	0	0	1	2
Gaetti, Minn.	.443	37	2	3	107	16	May, K.C.	.505	14	1	0	18	0
Gamble, N.Y.	.522	58	2	4	47	4	Mayberry, Tor-N.Y.	.367	35	3	6	43	7
Gantner, Milw.	.369	26	3	2	36	6	Mazzilli, Tex-N.Y.	.375	43	0	2	41	6
Garcia, Tor.	.399	21	1	5	44	7	McBride, Clev	.471	2	1	0	12	2
Gedman, Bos.	.363	10	2	2	37	13	McHenry, Sea	.000	0	0	0	0	0
Geronimo, K.C.	.471	8	2	0	16	5	McKay, Oak	.283	11	0	0	35	0
Gibson, Det.	.444	25	2	1	41	2	McRae, K.C.	.542	55	7	5	61	8
Goodwin, Oak.	.404	2	0	0	13	3	Mendoza, Tex	.118	0	0	0	4	1
Gray, Sea.	.401	24	0	2	59	4	Mercado, Sea	.294	0	0	0	5	0
Gray, Chi.	.321	2	0	0	4	0	Meyer, Oak	.363	18	3	0	33	6
Grich, Cal.	.449	82	3	8	109	13	Milbourne, NY-Mn-Clv	.327	20	0	2	32	15
Griffey, N.Y.	.407	39	1	0	58	10	Miller, Det	.040	4	0	3	4	0
Griffin, Tor.	.314	22	0	0	48	7	Miller, Bos	.325	40	2	2	41	7
Gross, Oak.	.358	53	0	2	50	4	Mitchell, Minn	.313	54	4	2	53	6
Grubb, Tex.	.370	39	2	6	37	5	Molitor, Milw	.450	69	1	1	93	9
Gulliver, Balt.	.269	37	0	0	18	2	Money, Milw	.531	32	2	1	38	4
Hairston, Chi.	.456	9	0	0	15	3	Moore, Milw	.360	29	2	1	49	11
Hammond, K.C.	.310	4	0	0	18	7	Moore, Oak	.358	3	0	0	23	2
Hancock, Bos.	.000	1	0	0	1	0	Morales, Balt	.000	0	0	0	2	0
Hargrove, Clev.	.338	101	3	3	58	22	Moreno, Cal	.000	2	0	0	0	0
Harrah, Clev.	.490	84	7	12	52	13	Morrison, Chi	.428	13	0	0	15	5
Hassey, Clev.	.353	53	5	1	32	10	Moseby, Tor	.370	33	3	8	106	10
Hatcher, Minn.	.343	8	1	0	27	12	Moses, Sea	.545	4	0	0	5	0
Hayes, Clev.	.389	42	3	4	63	10	Mulliniks, Tor	.363	37	1	1	49	10
Heath, K.C.	.000	0	0	0	0	0	Mumphrey, N.Y.	.449	50	4	0	66	17
Heath, Oak.	.352	27	3	0	36	3	Murcer, N.Y.	.418	12	2	1	15	4
Hebner, Det.	.441	25	2	0	21	1	Murphy, Oak	.418	94	2	3	122	8
Henderson, Sea.	.441	36	2	0	67	5	Murray, Balt	.549	70	18	1	82	17
Henderson, Oak.	.382	116	1	2	94	5	Nahorodny, Clev	.426	2	0	0	9	3
Hernandez, Balt.	.000	0	0	0	2	0	Nettles, N.Y.	.402	51	4	1	49	11
Hernandez, Tor.	.000	0	0	0	3	1	Newman, Oak	.315	14	1	0	49	7
Herndon, Det.	.480	38	3	1	92	20	Nichols, Bos	.461	14	1	1	28	3
Hill, Chi.	.386	6	0	1	13	4	Nolan, Balt	.356	16	1	0	35	5
Hisle, Milw.	.323	5	0	0	13	2	Nordhagen, Tor	.319	10	1	0	22	6
Hobson, N.Y.	.207	1	0	0	14	2	Nyman, Chi	.262	3	0	0	9	3
Hoffman, Bos.	.311	30	5	5	69	15	O'Brien, Tex	.507	6	0	0	8	0
Hostetler, Tex.	.433	42	3	1	113	14	Oglivie, Milw	.453	70	13	4	81	6
Howell, Milw.	.350	21	2	0	39	2	Otis, K.C.	.421	37	3	2	65	17
Hrbek, Minn.	.485	54	12	0	80	17	Paciorek, Chi.	.490	24	3	9	53	6
Iorg, Tor.	.365	12	2	4	38	6	Page, Oak	.474	7	1	2	24	3
Ireland, K.C.	.143	1	0	0	1	0	Pagel, Clev	.167	7	1	0	11	0
Ivie, Det.	.448	24	3	2	51	5	Parrish, Det	.529	40	5	1	99	5
Re. Jackson, Cal.	.532	85	12	2	156	10	Parrish, Tex	.414	30	0	4	84	12
Ro. Jackson, Cal.	.415	10	0	2	12	3	Patterson, N.Y.	.438	2	0	0	6	0
Johnson, Tor.	.367	11	1	0	26	1	Perconte, Clev	.292	22	1	0	25	1
Johnson, Tex.	.268	3	0	1	22	3	Perez, Bos	.444	19	3	0	48	6
Johnson, Oak.	.383	26	2	2	41	3	Petralli, Tor	.409	4	0	0	6	1
Johnson, Det.	.426	16	1	1	30	3	Pettis, Cal	.800	0	0	0	2	0
Johnson, Tex.	.358	31	1	0	40	13	Phillips, Oak	.284	12	0	0	2	26	0
Johnson, Minn.	.419	30	2	0	46	3	Picciolo, Oak-Milw	.271	2	0	0	14	0
Johnson, K.C.	.429	4	0	0	3	0	Piniella, N.Y.	.448	18	6	1	18	12
Jones, Det.	.259	7	0	0	14	2	Poquette, K.C.	.161	4	0	1	5	0
Jurak, Bos.	.333	2	0	0	4	0	Powell, Tor	.389	12	2	0	23	4
Kearney, Oak.	.211	3	0	2	10	1	Pryor, K.C.	.388	10	0	0	20	5
Kelleher, Det-Cal	.180	5	0	1	5	5	Putnam, Tex	.344	10	1	1	18	3
Kemp, Chi.	.428	89	8	3	83	8	Quirk, K.C.	.308	3	0	0	15	2
Kittle, Chi.	.414	3	0	0	12	0	Ramos, Sea	.231	3	0	0	2	0
Klutts, Oak.	.229	9	0	0	18	4	Ramos, N.Y.	.364	0	0	0	3	0
Kuntz, Chi.	.231	2	0	0	8	1	Randle, Sea.	.217	4	0	0	4	1
LaFrancois, Bos.	.500	0	0	0	0	0	Randolph, N.Y.	.349	75	3	3	35	13
Laga, Det.	.466	4	0	0	23	1	Rayford, Balt	.302	6	0	0	14	0
Langford, Oak.	.000	0	0	0	0	0	Remy, Bos	.324	55	1	2	77	14
Lansford, Bos	.444	46	2	2	48	15	Revering, NY-Tor-Sea	.346	34	3	0	51	8
Laudner, Minn	.392	34	2	0	74	6	Rhomberg, Clev	.500	2	0	0	4	0
R. Law, Chi.	.438	23	0	0	41	5	Rice, Bos	.494	55	6	7	98	29
V. Law, Chi.	.384	26	1	1	46	10	Richardt, Tex	.289	23	1	1	42	13
Leach, Det.	.330	21	2	0	29	2	Ripken, Balt	.475	46	3	3	95	16
LeFlore, Chi.	.392	22	1	0	91	4	Rivera, K.C.	.100	0	0	0	2	0
Lemon, Det	.447	56	2	15	69	13	Rivers, Tex.	.324	0	0	0	7	1
Lopes, Oak	.371	40	1	1	51	14	Roberts, Tex-Tor	.303	11	1	1	30	7
Loviglio, Chi.	.194	1	0	0	4	0	Robertson, N.Y.	.314	8	0	0	19	4

Player—Club	Slg. Pct.	Tot. BB.	Int. BB.	HP.	SO.	GI DP.
Rodriguez, Chi	.342	11	0	1	35	7
Rodriguez, N.Y.	.333	1	0	0	1	0
Roenicke, Balt	.499	70	2	9	73	7
Romero, Milw	.326	8	0	0	16	4
Rudi, Oak	.332	24	0	1	35	2
Ryal, K.C.	.077	1	0	0	3	0
Sakata, Balt	.370	30	2	4	39	7
Sample, Tex	.394	27	0	3	35	4
Sconiers, Cal	.154	2	0	0	1	2
Scott, N.Y.	.192	4	0	0	2	1
Serna, Sea	.296	4	0	1	13	4
Sexton, Oak	.317	9	0	1	24	0
Shelby, Balt	.486	0	0	0	5	0
Simmons, Milw	.451	32	5	2	40	20
Simpson, Sea	.351	22	4	2	48	1
Singleton, Balt	.381	86	2	2	93	24
Skube, Milw	.667	0	0	0	0	0
Slaught, K.C.	.409	9	0	0	12	3
Smalley, Minn-NY	.413	71	8	0	104	4
Smith, Minn	.304	1	0	0	3	0
Spencer, Oak	.277	3	1	0	20	3
Squires, Chi	.359	14	3	0	13	4
Stanley, Oak	.250	29	0	1	32	4
Stapleton, Bos	.398	31	5	3	40	24
Stegman, N.Y.	.000	0	0	0	0	0
Stein, Tex	.299	12	0	2	23	4
Stroughter, Sea	.255	3	1	1	9	0
Sullivan, Bos	.333	0	0	0	2	0
Sundberg, Tex	.383	49	2	1	57	11
Sweet, Sea	.333	20	0	2	24	2
Thomas, Milw	.506	84	5	4	143	10
Thornton, Clev	.484	109	18	2	81	21
Tolleson, Tex	.129	5	0	0	14	1
Trammell, Det	.395	52	0	0	47	5
Turner, Det	.376	20	1	0	37	2
Upshaw, Tor	.443	52	8	1	91	11
Valdez, Bos	.300	0	0	0	7	0
Vega, Minn	.372	8	1	0	19	5
Velez, Tor	.269	13	0	0	15	1
Wagner, Tex	.274	10	0	0	28	6
Walker, Chi	1.000	2	0	0	3	0
Ward, Minn	.519	37	4	1	105	16
Washington, Minn	.368	14	0	0	79	11
Washington, K.C.	.412	38	0	0	48	4
Wathan, K.C.	.328	48	0	2	46	26
Watson, N.Y.	.412	3	0	0	0	1
Wells, Minn	.296	1	0	0	8	0
Werner, Tex	.237	3	0	0	7	1
Werth, K.C.	.133	0	0	0	2	1
Whitaker, Det	.434	48	4	1	58	8
White, K.C.	.469	16	1	2	65	12
Whitt, Tor	.440	26	5	0	34	5
Wilfong, Minn-Cal	.273	14	1	1	30	5
Wilson, Det	.457	15	0	0	51	8
Wilson, K.C.	.431	26	2	6	81	4
Winfield, N.Y.	.560	45	7	0	64	20
Wockenfuss, Det	.472	29	2	0	21	3
Woods, Tor	.343	21	4	0	20	3
Wright, Tex	.377	30	4	3	78	11
Wynegar, Minn-NY	.361	50	2	1	33	9
Yastrzemski, Bos	.431	59	1	2	50	12
Yost, Milw	.429	7	0	0	20	1
Young, Balt	.000	0	0	0	1	0
Yount, Milw	.578	54	2	1	63	19
Zisk, Sea	.477	49	4	1	89	9

OFFICIAL AMERICAN LEAGUE DESIGNATED HITTING

CLUB DESIGNATED HITTING

Club	Pct.	AB.	R.	H.	TB.	2B.	3B.	HR.	RBI.	SH.	SF.	BB.	HP.	SO.	SB.	CS.	GI DP.
Kansas City	.313	626	94	196	345	46	8	29	136	1	2	57	5	67	4	4	8
Boston	.293	625	76	183	282	36	3	19	102	0	6	74	3	86	0	2	18
Chicago	.291	605	96	176	279	39	2	20	105	0	8	91	6	126	4	3	19
Seattle	.279	634	83	177	285	34	1	24	77	1	3	60	3	118	5	4	9
New York	.275	625	67	172	289	31	1	28	109	2	8	63	2	81	7	5	12
Cleveland	.274	605	95	166	290	26	1	32	114	6	4	107	3	84	7	8	21
California	.261	637	85	166	274	25	1	27	103	0	8	61	7	75	10	4	20
Baltimore	.254	621	80	158	233	30	0	15	78	1	7	92	0	103	0	2	25
Detroit	.247	615	72	152	256	19	2	27	77	3	6	58	2	110	2	2	10
Oakland	.246	615	69	151	243	26	3	20	91	2	8	70	4	130	10	7	15
Minnesota	.244	618	74	151	240	27	4	18	84	1	14	45	3	89	1	2	12
Texas	.244	603	68	147	201	20	2	10	63	3	5	58	5	72	8	9	15
Milwaukee	.243	606	72	147	222	21	3	16	80	9	4	55	2	89	0	5	12
Toronto	.238	596	52	142	190	18	3	8	56	1	8	60	0	91	7	16	10
Totals	.265	8631	1083	2284	3629	398	34	293	1275	30	91	951	45	1321	65	73	206

INDIVIDUAL DESIGNATED HITTING
(Listed Alphabetically)

Player and Club	Pct.	G.	AB.	R.	H.	TB.	2B.	3B.	HR.	RBI.	SH.	SF.	BB.	HP.	SO.	SB.	CS.	GI DP.
Adams, Tor.	.266	27	64	2	17	24	4	0	1	11	0	3	4	0	5	0	0	1
Almon, Chi.	.000	1	0	0	0	0	0	0	0	0	0	0	0	0	0	0	1	0
Armas, Oak.	.250	1	4	0	1	1	0	0	0	0	0	0	0	0	1	0	0	0
Ayala, Balt.	.359	17	39	4	14	20	3	0	1	4	0	0	2	0	5	0	1	1
Balboni, N.Y.	.333	5	15	1	5	7	0	1	0	0	0	0	1	0	6	0	0	0
Bannister, Clev.	.750	1	4	0	3	3	0	0	0	3	1	0	0	0	0	0	0	0
Barfield, Tor.	.000	1	1	0	0	0	0	0	0	0	0	0	0	0	0	0	0	0
Bass, Milw.	.000	2	0	1	0	0	0	0	0	1	0	0	0	0	0	0	0	0
Bass, Tex.	.250	7	24	3	6	9	0	0	1	3	0	0	1	0	3	0	0	0
Baylor, Cal.	.263	155	608	79	160	258	24	1	24	93	0	8	55	7	69	10	4	18
Bell, Oak.	.000	1	0	0	0	0	0	0	0	0	0	0	0	0	0	0	0	0
Bochte, Sea.	.323	12	31	3	10	15	2	0	1	5	1	0	5	1	4	0	1	0
Bogener, Tex.	.357	4	14	2	5	7	0	1	0	2	1	0	1	0	0	0	0	0
Boggs, Bos.	.667	3	3	2	2	2	0	0	0	1	0	1	1	0	0	0	0	0
Bonnell, Tor.	.300	6	20	6	6	14	0	1	2	6	0	0	0	0	2	1	0	0
Brouhard, Milw.	.263	7	19	0	5	5	0	0	0	0	0	0	1	0	5	0	1	1
Brown, Oak.	.000	1	0	0	0	0	0	0	0	0	0	0	0	0	0	0	0	0

Player and Club	Pct.	G.	AB.	R.	H.	TB.	2B.	3B.	HR.	RBI.	SH.	SF.	BB.	HP.	SO.	SB.	CS.	GI DP.
Brown, Sea.	.500	3	2	1	1	1	0	0	0	0	0	0	0	0	0	1	0	0
Bumbry, Balt.	.000	1	1	0	0	0	0	0	0	0	0	0	0	0	0	0	0	0
Burroughs, Oak.	.268	48	157	21	42	69	7	1	6	23	0	2	26	0	37	1	2	3
Bush, Minn.	.265	26	83	9	22	37	4	1	3	9	0	1	5	3	15	0	0	1
Castillo, Clev.	.000	2	0	1	0	0	0	0	0	0	0	0	0	1	0	0	0	0
Castino, Minn.	.000	1	5	0	0	0	0	0	0	0	0	0	0	0	1	0	0	0
Charboneau, Clev.	1.000	1	1	0	1	1	0	0	0	0	0	0	0	0	0	0	0	0
Collins, N.Y.	1.000	1	1	0	1	1	0	0	0	0	0	0	0	0	0	0	0	0
Concepcion, K.C.	.000	1	0	1	0	0	0	0	0	0	0	0	0	0	0	0	0	0
Cooper, Milw.	.250	1	4	0	1	1	0	0	0	0	0	0	1	0	1	0	0	0
Cowens, Sea.	.000	1	0	1	0	0	0	0	0	0	0	0	0	0	0	0	0	0
Craig, Clev.	.000	4	3	1	0	0	0	0	0	0	1	0	0	0	1	1	0	0
Crowley, Balt.	.226	14	31	3	7	7	0	0	0	1	0	0	6	0	4	0	0	1
J. Cruz, Sea.	.000	2	0	0	0	0	0	0	0	0	0	0	0	0	0	0	0	0
Davis, Tor.	.000	1	3	0	0	0	0	0	0	0	0	0	0	0	1	0	0	0
Dempsey, Balt.	.000	1	0	0	0	0	0	0	0	0	0	0	1	0	0	0	0	0
Dilone, Clev.	.500	1	2	0	1	2	1	0	0	0	0	0	0	0	0	0	0	0
Dwyer, Balt.	.000	1	0	0	0	0	0	0	0	0	0	0	0	0	0	0	0	0
Edler, Sea.	.000	2	1	1	0	0	0	0	0	0	0	0	0	0	1	0	0	0
Edwards, Milw.	.222	6	9	4	2	2	0	0	0	1	1	0	1	0	1	0	1	1
Engle, Minn.	.208	20	72	10	15	23	3	1	1	6	0	0	3	0	8	0	0	3
Evans, Bos.	.000	1	4	0	0	0	0	0	0	0	0	0	1	0	1	0	0	0
Faedo, Minn.	.000	1	0	0	0	0	0	0	0	0	0	0	0	0	0	0	0	0
Foley, Chi.	.000	1	1	0	0	0	0	0	0	0	0	0	0	0	0	0	0	0
Ford, Balt.	.000	1	0	1	0	0	0	0	0	0	0	0	0	0	0	0	0	0
Gaetti, Minn.	.333	1	3	0	1	1	0	0	0	0	0	0	0	0	0	0	0	0
Gamble, N.Y.	.264	74	227	32	60	110	14	0	12	38	0	3	36	2	34	4	3	3
Garcia, Tor.	.000	4	0	0	0	0	0	0	0	0	0	0	0	0	0	0	3	0
Geronimo, K.C.	.500	1	2	0	1	1	0	0	0	0	0	0	0	0	0	0	0	0
Gibson, Det.	.182	4	11	1	2	2	0	0	0	0	1	0	0	0	4	0	0	0
Goodwin, Oak.	.200	15	50	5	10	19	1	1	2	8	2	1	2	0	12	0	0	3
Gray, Sea.	.245	14	53	6	13	22	3	0	2	8	0	0	4	1	15	0	0	0
Grich, Cal.	.000	1	4	0	0	0	0	0	0	0	0	0	0	0	1	0	0	1
Gross, Oak.	.000	1	0	0	0	0	0	0	0	0	0	0	1	0	0	0	0	0
Grubb, Tex.	.216	18	51	6	11	13	2	0	0	3	0	1	10	2	7	0	0	0
Hairston, Chi.	.000	2	0	0	0	0	0	0	0	0	0	0	0	0	0	0	0	0
Hammond, K.C.	.500	1	2	0	1	1	0	0	0	1	0	0	0	0	1	0	0	0
Hargrove, Clev.	.125	5	24	2	3	4	1	0	0	1	0	0	5	0	2	0	0	1
Hassey, Clev.	.167	2	6	0	1	1	0	0	0	0	0	0	0	0	0	0	0	0
Hatcher, Minn.	.240	29	96	11	23	35	5	2	1	12	0	0	3	0	11	0	1	3
Hebner, Det.	.262	20	61	8	16	34	0	0	6	8	0	0	8	0	7	0	0	0
Henderson, Oak.	.167	4	12	2	2	2	0	0	0	0	0	0	2	0	5	4	0	1
Hernandez, Tor.	.000	3	4	1	0	0	0	0	0	0	0	0	0	0	2	0	0	0
Herndon, Det.	.143	3	7	1	1	3	0	1	0	1	0	0	0	0	1	0	0	0
Hisle, Milw.	.100	8	30	6	3	6	0	0	1	3	0	0	5	0	13	0	0	2
Hobson, N.Y.	.194	15	36	2	7	8	1	0	0	2	0	1	0	0	9	0	0	1
Hostetler, Tex.	.364	3	11	3	4	5	1	0	0	0	0	0	1	0	3	0	0	0
Howell, Milw.	.258	84	279	29	72	97	11	1	4	37	1	4	20	0	37	0	1	2
Hrbek, Minn.	.333	2	6	3	2	6	1	0	1	1	0	0	0	0	2	0	0	0
Iorg, Tor.	.000	1	1	0	0	0	0	0	0	0	0	0	0	0	0	0	0	0
Ivie, Det.	.233	79	258	35	60	116	12	1	14	38	0	3	24	2	50	0	0	5
Re. Jackson, Cal.	.238	5	21	5	5	15	1	0	3	10	0	0	3	0	5	0	0	0
Johnson, Oak.	.239	48	163	15	39	60	6	0	5	23	0	2	23	2	31	0	2	1
Johnson, Tor.	.212	28	33	5	7	8	1	0	0	1	1	0	1	0	8	3	7	0
Johnson, Minn.	.265	67	211	25	56	93	10	0	9	32	0	7	28	0	37	0	0	3
Johnson, Det.	.231	10	26	4	6	7	1	0	0	1	1	0	3	0	7	1	1	1
L. Johnson, Tex.	.253	77	265	29	67	91	9	0	5	31	1	0	27	1	32	3	5	12
Jones, Det.	.000	1	1	0	0	0	0	0	0	0	0	0	0	0	0	0	0	1
Kemp, Chi.	.286	2	7	2	2	3	1	0	0	0	0	0	2	0	2	0	0	0
Kittle, Chi.	.000	3	2	1	0	0	0	0	0	0	0	0	1	0	1	0	0	0
Laga, Det.	.167	8	24	1	4	7	0	0	1	1	0	0	1	0	6	0	0	0
Lansford, Bos.	.367	13	49	8	18	25	4	0	1	10	0	2	4	0	5	0	0	2
R. Law, Chi.	.000	3	0	0	0	0	0	0	0	0	0	0	0	0	0	2	1	0
Leach, Det.	.000	4	4	0	0	0	0	0	0	0	0	1	0	0	2	0	0	0
LeFlore, Chi.	.000	2	0	2	0	0	0	0	0	0	0	0	0	0	0	1	0	0
Lemon, Det.	.200	1	5	1	1	2	1	0	0	2	0	0	0	0	0	0	0	1
Loviglio, Chi.	.000	2	0	2	0	0	0	0	0	0	0	0	0	0	0	0	0	0
Luzinski, Chi.	.291	156	581	87	169	262	37	1	18	101	0	8	88	6	119	1	1	19
Maler, Sea.	.200	5	10	0	2	2	0	0	0	0	0	0	0	0	3	0	0	0
Martin, K.C.	.400	3	10	2	4	10	0	0	2	2	0	0	0	0	3	0	0	0
May, K.C.	.333	2	3	0	1	1	0	0	0	0	0	0	2	0	2	0	0	0
Mayberry, Tor.-N.Y	.258	17	31	3	8	12	1	0	1	4	0	0	6	0	5	0	0	0
Mazzilli, Tex.-N.Y.	.288	33	125	18	36	56	5	0	5	18	0	0	18	0	10	5	3	1
McHenry, Sea.	.000	1	0	0	0	0	0	0	0	0	0	0	0	0	0	0	0	0
McRae, K.C.	.310	158	609	91	189	332	46	8	27	133	1	2	55	5	61	4	4	8
Mercado, Sea.	.000	1	0	0	0	0	0	0	0	0	0	0	0	0	0	0	0	0
Meyer, Sea.	.246	38	142	10	35	52	6	1	3	28	0	3	8	0	15	1	0	5
Milbourne, Clev.	.000	1	3	0	0	0	0	0	0	0	0	1	0	0	1	0	0	0
Miller, Det.	.000	1	1	0	0	0	0	0	0	0	0	0	0	0	0	0	0	0

Player and Club	Pct.	G.	AB.	R.	H.	TB.	2B.	3B.	HR.	RBI.	SH.	SF.	BB.	HP.	SO.	SB.	CS.	GI DP.
Molitor, Milw.	.208	6	24	5	5	5	0	0	0	0	1	0	1	0	2	0	0	1
Money, Milw.	.253	66	182	21	46	79	8	2	7	29	5	0	24	1	24	0	2	3
Moreno, Cal.	.000	1	0	0	0	0	0	0	0	0	0	0	1	0	0	0	0	0
Morrison, Chi.	.000	1	1	0	0	0	0	0	0	0	0	0	0	0	1	0	0	0
Murcer, N.Y.	.230	47	126	10	29	55	5	0	7	30	0	2	10	0	14	2	1	2
Murphy, Oak.	.333	1	3	0	1	1	0	0	0	0	0	0	0	0	1	0	0	0
Murray, Balt.	.000	2	0	1	0	0	0	0	0	0	0	0	0	0	0	0	0	0
Nettles, N.Y.	.100	3	10	0	1	1	0	0	0	0	0	0	0	0	3	0	0	1
Newman, Oak.	.333	1	3	0	1	2	1	0	0	2	0	0	0	0	0	0	0	0
Nichols, Bos.	.000	4	0	1	0	0	0	0	0	0	0	0	0	0	0	0	0	0
Nordhagen, Tor.	.282	60	149	10	42	46	4	0	0	11	0	1	8	0	20	0	2	5
Norris, Oak.	.000	1	0	1	0	0	0	0	0	0	0	0	0	0	0	0	0	0
O'Brien, Tex.	.143	4	14	2	2	5	0	0	1	2	0	1	1	0	5	0	0	0
Page, Oak.	.267	24	75	12	20	37	5	0	4	7	0	0	7	2	24	3	3	2
Pagel, Clev.	.000	1	1	0	0	0	0	0	0	0	0	0	0	0	1	0	0	0
Parrish, Tex.	.500	2	4	1	2	3	1	0	0	0	0	0	1	0	0	0	0	0
Patterson, N.Y.	.000	1	0	0	0	0	0	0	0	0	0	0	0	0	0	0	0	0
Perconte, Clev.	.000	2	0	1	0	0	0	0	0	0	0	0	0	0	0	0	0	0
Perez, Bos.	.267	46	172	16	46	75	13	2	4	25	0	0	18	0	38	0	1	5
Picciolo, Milw.	.000	1	1	0	0	0	0	0	0	0	0	0	0	0	1	0	0	0
Piniella, N.Y.	.344	55	131	15	45	69	9	0	5	22	1	1	7	0	7	0	0	4
Powell, Tor.	.298	19	47	6	14	18	2	1	0	4	0	0	1	0	4	0	0	0
Randle, Sea.	.000	13	3	8	0	0	0	0	0	0	0	0	2	0	0	2	2	0
Randolph, N.Y.	.571	1	7	1	4	4	0	0	0	1	0	0	1	0	0	0	0	0
Rayford, Balt.	.000	2	1	1	0	0	0	0	0	0	0	0	0	0	1	0	0	0
Revering, N.Y.-Tor.	.205	50	117	12	24	40	4	0	4	11	0	2	21	0	24	0	3	2
Rhomberg, Clev.	.400	4	5	2	2	5	0	0	1	1	0	0	0	0	2	0	1	0
Richardt, Tex.	.189	15	53	3	10	12	2	0	0	8	1	2	3	0	6	1	1	1
Rivers, Tex.	.231	16	65	5	15	21	1	1	1	4	0	1	0	0	7	0	0	1
Roberts, Tex.-Tor.	.167	22	54	1	9	10	1	0	0	2	0	1	2	0	6	1	0	1
Rudi, Oak.	.000	3	5	0	0	0	0	0	0	0	0	0	0	0	3	0	0	0
Sample, Tex.	.000	1	0	0	0	0	0	0	0	0	0	0	0	0	0	0	1	0
Sconiers, Cal.	.000	1	1	0	0	0	0	0	0	0	0	0	0	0	0	0	0	1
Serna, Sea.	.000	2	0	0	0	0	0	0	0	0	0	0	0	0	0	0	0	0
Sexton, Oak.	.000	5	1	3	0	0	0	0	0	0	0	0	0	0	1	1	0	0
Simmons, Milw.	.200	15	55	6	11	24	1	0	4	9	0	0	2	1	6	0	0	2
Singleton, Balt.	.250	148	548	69	137	206	27	0	14	73	1	7	83	0	93	0	1	23
Skube, Milw.	1.000	1	1	0	1	1	0	0	0	0	0	0	0	0	0	0	0	0
Smalley, N.Y.	.077	4	13	0	1	1	0	0	0	3	1	1	1	0	3	0	0	0
Stapleton, Bos.	.200	4	5	1	1	2	1	0	0	3	0	2	1	1	0	0	0	0
Stegman, N.Y.	.000	1	0	0	0	0	0	0	0	0	0	0	0	0	0	0	0	0
Stein, Tex.	.167	3	6	0	1	1	0	0	0	0	0	0	1	0	1	0	0	0
Stroughter, Sea.	.129	9	31	2	4	5	1	0	0	2	0	0	1	0	6	0	0	0
Thornton, Clev.	.279	152	556	88	155	274	24	1	31	109	3	4	102	2	77	6	7	20
Turner, Det.	.271	50	155	14	42	57	3	0	4	18	0	2	14	0	26	1	1	2
Upshaw, Tor.	.333	5	12	1	4	6	0	1	0	5	0	1	0	0	4	1	0	0
Valdez, Bos.	.000	3	0	1	0	0	0	0	0	0	0	0	0	0	0	0	0	0
Vega, Minn.	.265	39	117	13	31	44	4	0	3	22	1	4	5	0	11	1	1	2
Velez, Tor.	.204	24	49	4	10	14	1	0	1	5	0	0	12	0	12	1	0	1
Walker, Chi.	.385	4	13	2	5	14	1	1	2	4	0	0	0	0	3	0	0	0
Ward, Minn.	.000	2	8	0	0	0	0	0	0	0	0	0	1	0	2	0	0	0
Washington, K.C.	.000	1	0	0	0	0	0	0	0	0	0	0	0	0	0	0	0	0
Watson, N.Y.	.000	1	3	0	0	0	0	0	0	0	0	0	0	0	0	0	0	0
Wells, Minn.	.059	5	17	3	1	1	0	0	0	2	0	2	0	0	2	0	0	0
Whitaker, Det.	.000	1	1	0	0	0	0	0	0	0	0	0	0	0	0	0	0	0
Whitt, Tor.	.500	1	2	0	1	1	0	0	0	0	0	0	0	0	0	0	0	0
Wilfong, Cal.	.333	1	3	1	1	1	0	0	0	0	0	0	2	0	0	0	0	0
Wilson, Det.	.300	4	10	2	3	4	1	0	0	0	0	0	1	0	2	0	0	0
Winfield, N.Y.	.200	4	15	1	3	3	0	0	0	1	0	0	1	0	1	0	0	1
Wockenfuss, Det.	.333	17	51	5	17	24	1	0	2	8	0	1	7	0	5	0	0	0
Woods, Tor.	.190	10	21	2	4	5	1	0	0	0	0	0	6	0	0	0	1	0
Yastrzemski, Bos.	.296	102	392	47	116	178	18	1	14	63	0	2	49	2	42	0	1	11
Yost, Milw.	.000	1	1	0	0	0	0	0	0	0	0	0	0	0	0	0	0	0
Young, Balt.	.000	2	1	1	0	0	0	0	0	0	0	0	0	0	0	0	0	0
Yount, Milw.	1.000	1	1	0	1	2	1	0	0	1	0	0	0	0	0	0	0	0
Zisk, Sea.	.292	130	503	61	147	240	28	1	21	62	0	3	48	1	89	2	1	9

Note—The following players made no plate appearances as designated hitters and are listed in the designated hitting statistics only because they pinch-ran for the DH: Almon, Bell (Oak.), Brown (Oak.), Concepcion, Cowens, J. Cruz, Dwyer, Ford, Garcia, Hairston, R. Law, LeFlore, Loviglio, McHenry, Mercado, Murray, Nichols, Norris, Patterson, Perconte, Sample, Serna, Stegman, Valdez, Washington (K.C.).

Game-winning RBIs by designated hitters, listed alphabetically by club, follow: Baltimore (12)—Ayala 1, Crowley 1, Singleton 10. Boston (11)—Perez 3, Stapleton 1, Yastrzemski 7. California (22)—Baylor 21, Re. Jackson 1. Chicago (18)—Luzinski 17, Walker 1. Cleveland (14)—Thornton 14. Detroit (9)—Ivie 4, Turner 4, Wockenfuss 1. Kansas City (14)—Hammond 1, McRae 13. Milwaukee (5)—Howell 3, Money 1, Simmons 1. Minnesota (6)—Bush 2, Engle 1, Hatcher 1, Johnson 2. New York (11)—Gamble 5, Mayberry 1, Mazzilli 1, Murcer 2, Piniella 1, Randolph 1. Oakland (11)—Burroughs 4, Johnson 1, Meyer 2, Page 4. Seattle (9)—Gray 1, Zisk 8. Texas (8)—Bass 1, L. Johnson 6, Mazzilli 1. Toronto (6)—Adams 1, Revering 3, Upshaw 2.

OFFICIAL AMERICAN LEAGUE FIELDING AVERAGES

CLUB FIELDING

Club	Pct.	G.	PO.	A.	E.	TC.	DP.	TP.	PB.
Baltimore	.984	163	4387	1707	101	6195	140	0	7
California	.983	162	4392	1984	108	6484	171	0	4
Minnesota	.982	162	4299	1560	108	5967	162	1	6
Detroit	.981	162	4353	1844	117	6314	165	0	15
Texas	.981	162	4293	1916	121	6330	169	0	19
Boston	.981	162	4359	1830	121	6310	172	0	16
Cleveland	.980	162	4405	1740	123	6268	129	0	6
Milwaukee	.980	163	4402	1834	125	6361	185	0	12
Kansas City	.979	162	4293	1743	127	6163	140	0	6
New York	.979	162	4377	1701	128	6206	158	0	15
Toronto	.978	162	4331	1768	136	6235	146	0	7
Seattle	.978	162	4429	1773	139	6341	158	0	10
Chicago	.976	162	4317	1901	154	6372	173	0	13
Oakland	.974	162	4368	1647	160	6175	140	0	8
Totals	.980	1135	61005	24948	1768	87721	2208	1	144

INDIVIDUAL FIELDING

FIRST BASEMEN

*Throws lefthanded.

Leader—Club	Pct.	G.	PO.	A.	E.	DP.
MURRAY, Balt	.997	149	1269	97	4	106

(Listed Alphabetically)

Player—Club	Pct.	G.	PO.	A.	E.	DP.
Aikens, K.C.	.994	128	1048	75	7	95
Balboni, N.Y.	.990	26	194	13	2	23
Bochte, Sea.*	.997	34	267	21	1	38
Boggs, Bos	.994	49	460	49	3	40
Cabell, Det	.992	83	548	52	5	62
Carew, Cal.	.992	134	1339	94	12	115
Collins, N.Y.*	.985	52	384	23	6	30
Cooper, Milw.*	.997	154	1428	98	5	156
Crowley, Balt.*	.988	10	74	6	1	12
Gray, Sea	.984	60	476	31	8	36
Gross, Oak	.980	16	90	7	2	6
Hargrove, Clev.*	.996	153	1293	123	5	110
Hebner, Det	.990	40	286	25	3	15
Hobson, N.Y.	.951	11	37	2	2	3
Hostetler, Tex	.990	109	1099	48	12	102
Hrbek, Minn	.993	138	1174	88	9	125
Ro. Jackson, Cal	.994	37	315	19	2	37
Johnson, Oak	.987	11	66	8	1	7
L. Johnson, Tex	.982	12	105	4	2	6
Laga, Det.*	.994	19	163	4	1	18
Leach, Det.*	.995	56	410	28	2	36
Maler, Sea	.991	57	529	41	5	45
May, K.C.	.989	32	175	10	2	18
Mayberry, Tor.-N.Y.*	.996	67	494	26	2	52
Mazzilli, N.Y.	.995	23	179	7	1	26
Meyer, Oak	.990	58	373	31	4	38
Money, Milw.	1.000	11	62	11	0	9
Moore, Oak.*	.971	20	123	9	4	9
Murray, Balt	.997	149	1269	97	4	106
Nyman, Chi	.994	24	160	12	1	16
Paciorek, Chi	.993	102	833	66	6	85
Pagel, Clev.*	.970	10	30	2	1	2
Pryor, K.C.	1.000	14	22	4	0	1
Putnam, Tex	.990	39	285	24	3	26
Revering, N.Y.-Tor.-Sea .	.992	44	351	15	3	33
Roenicke, Balt	1.000	10	75	6	0	7
Rudi, Oak	.991	49	398	20	4	37
Spencer, Oak.*	.992	32	230	22	2	20

Player—Club	Pct.	G.	PO.	A.	E.	DP.
Squires, Chi.*	.995	109	512	48	3	59
Stapleton, Bos	.991	106	964	77	9	98
Upshaw, Tor.*	.989	155	1438	101	17	123
Vega, Minn	.974	18	106	8	3	9
Wells, Minn	.962	10	74	2	3	6
Werth, K.C.	.990	35	93	9	1	10
Wockenfuss, Det	1.000	17	122	3	0	9
Yastrzemski, Bos	1.000	14	116	10	0	12

TRIPLE PLAY: Hrbek.

(Fewer Than Ten Games)

Player—Club	Pct.	G.	PO.	A.	E.	DP.
Ayala, Balt	1.000	3	24	0	0	2
Bass, Tex.*	1.000	6	51	3	0	8
Davis, Oak.*	.919	7	30	4	3	5
Dwyer, Balt.*	1.000	1	6	0	0	0
Fisk, Chi	.909	2	9	1	1	1
Foley, Chi	1.000	1	2	0	0	0
Hassey, Clev	1.000	2	4	0	0	0
Hayes, Clev	1.000	4	15	0	0	2
Hill, Chi	1.000	1	1	0	0	0
Howell, Milw	.933	4	26	2	2	1
Johnson, K.C.	.976	7	39	2	1	3
B. Johnson, Tex	1.000	3	22	0	0	0
Mattingly, N.Y.*	1.000	1	4	0	0	0
Newman, Oak	.960	3	23	1	1	1
O'Brien, Tex.*	1.000	3	22	2	0	4
Perez, Bos	.857	2	5	1	1	0
Quirk, K.C.	1.000	6	33	6	0	5
Sconiers, Cal.*	1.000	3	23	1	0	5
Stein, Tex	1.000	2	7	0	0	1
Thornton, Clev	1.000	8	76	5	0	5
Wathan, K.C.	1.000	3	19	2	0	2
Watson, N.Y.	1.000	6	40	0	0	5

FIRST BASEMEN WITH TWO OR MORE CLUBS

Player—Club	Pct.	G.	PO.	A.	E.	DP.
Mayberry, Tor.	1.000	4	39	1	0	3
Mayberry, N.Y.	.996	63	455	25	2	49
Revering, N.Y.	1.000	13	113	2	0	7
Revering, Tor.	1.000	4	36	2	0	4
Revering, Sea	.986	27	202	11	3	22

SECOND BASEMEN

Leader—Club	Pct.	G.	PO.	A.	E.	DP.
WHITAKER, Det	.988	149	331	470	10	120

(Listed Alphabetically)

Player—Club	Pct.	G.	PO.	A.	E.	DP.
Bannister, Clev	.960	48	91	123	9	22
Bernazard, Chi	.985	137	353	443	12	116
Brookens, Det	.979	26	37	57	2	7
Castino, Minn	.995	96	193	228	2	63

Player—Club	Pct.	G.	PO.	A.	E.	DP.
Concepcion, K.C.	1.000	24	29	30	0	3
J. Cruz, Sea	.987	151	320	434	10	98
Dauer, Balt	.987	123	261	268	7	67
Dillard, Chi	.959	16	29	42	3	5
Flynn, Tex	.989	55	117	146	3	31
Gantner, Milw	.982	131	307	398	13	104
Garcia, Tor	.980	141	273	461	15	94
Grich, Cal.	.986	142	338	450	11	112

SECOND BASEMEN—Continued

Player—Club	Pct.	G.	PO.	A.	E.	DP.
Iorg, Tor	.986	30	57	81	2	17
V. Law, Chi.	.909	10	11	19	3	5
Lopes, Oak	.977	125	289	338	15	82
Loviglio, Chi	.964	13	24	30	2	5
McKay, Oak	.968	59	99	116	7	22
Milbourne, NY-Minn-Clev.	.979	92	186	238	9	52
Perconte, Clev	.976	82	131	199	8	23
Picciolo, Milw	1.000	11	6	3	0	1
Pryor, K.C.	1.000	15	25	23	0	7
Randolph, N.Y.	.981	142	352	380	14	100
Remy, Bos	.982	154	290	432	13	104
Richardt, Tex	.988	98	234	278	6	68
Robertson, N.Y.	.972	15	44	25	2	6
Romero, Milw	.975	39	97	96	5	30
Sakata, Balt	.977	83	106	145	6	34
Serna, Sea	.981	18	21	30	1	7
Stein, Tex	.957	34	46	65	5	21
Washington, Minn	.975	37	74	82	4	20
Whitaker, Det	.988	149	331	470	10	120
White, K.C.	.978	144	361	389	17	99
Wilfong, Minn.-Cal	.981	50	66	139	4	32

Player—Club	Pct.	G.	PO.	A.	E.	DP.
DeJohn, Det.	1.000	1	1	1	0	1
Evans, N.Y.	1.000	8	11	14	0	3
Fischlin, Clev.	1.000	6	3	3	0	1
Foli, Cal.	.947	8	12	24	2	6
Harrah, Clev.	.000	3	0	0	0	0
Heath, K.C.	1.000	1	1	2	0	1
Ireland, K.C.	1.000	4	1	5	0	1
Kelleher, Det.	1.000	1	0	1	0	0
Money, Milw.	.000	1	0	1	0	0
Moore, Milw.	1.000	1	0	1	0	0
Moreno, Cal.	1.000	2	2	2	0	0
Randle, Sea.	.833	6	3	7	2	2
Rodriguez, Chi.	1.000	3	1	4	0	1
Rodriguez, N.Y.	.875	3	2	12	2	1
Scott, N.Y.	1.000	4	5	8	0	0
Smalley, N.Y.	.000	1	0	0	0	0
Stanley, Oak.	1.000	2	4	3	0	1
Stapleton, Bos.	.980	9	28	22	1	3
Tolleson, Tex.	.000	1	0	0	0	0

(Fewer Than Ten Games)

Player—Club	Pct.	G.	PO.	A.	E.	DP.
Barrett, Bos.	1.000	7	11	21	0	4
Bonner, Balt.	.000	3	0	0	0	0
Castillo, Sea.	.960	9	13	11	1	6

SECOND BASEMEN WITH TWO OR MORE CLUBS

Players—Club	Pct.	G.	PO.	A.	E.	DP.
Milbourne, N.Y.	.944	3	9	8	1	4
Milbourne, Minn.	.981	26	49	52	2	14
Milbourne, Clev.	.981	63	128	178	6	34
Wilfong, Minn.	.980	22	31	67	2	19
Wilfong, Cal.	.982	28	35	72	2	13

THIRD BASEMEN

Leader—Club	Pct.	G.	PO.	A.	E.	DP.
BELL, Tex.	.976	145	131	396	13	35

(Listed Alphabetically)

Player—Club	Pct.	G.	PO.	A.	E.	DP.
Bell, Tex.	.976	145	131	396	13	35
Boggs, Bos.	.967	44	28	119	5	11
Brett, K.C.	.959	134	107	294	17	22
Brookens, Det	.939	113	72	206	18	20
Cabell, Det.	.925	59	44	91	11	7
Castillo, Sea.	.938	130	96	209	20	18
Castino, Minn.	.974	21	25	50	2	6
Dauer, Balt.	.991	61	28	86	1	8
DeCinces, Cal.	.961	153	112	399	21	41
Edler, Sea.	.922	31	20	51	6	4
Gaetti, Minn.	.963	142	106	286	15	35
Gray, Chi.	.864	16	9	10	3	2
Gross, Chi.	.970	108	113	182	9	25
Gulliver, Balt.	.970	50	34	97	4	6
Harrah, Clev.	.971	159	126	279	12	25
Iorg, Tor.	.946	100	57	155	12	13
Johnson, Det.	.901	33	25	39	7	6
Jurak, Bos.	.923	11	7	17	2	1
Klutts, Oak.	.946	49	41	82	7	6
Lansford, Bos.	.968	114	83	216	10	19
V. Law, Chi.	.937	39	19	55	5	3
McKay, Oak.	.931	16	19	35	4	1
Milbourne, N.Y.-Clev.	.955	12	4	17	1	1
Molitor, Milw.	.942	150	128	340	29	48
Money, Milw.	.923	16	10	38	4	2
Morrison, Chi.	.914	50	19	87	10	10
Mulliniks, Tor.	.938	102	60	137	13	13
Nettles, N.Y.	.934	113	73	255	23	23
Pryor, K.C.	.951	40	26	72	5	7
Rayford, Balt.	.898	27	11	42	6	2
Ripken, Balt.	.973	71	66	151	6	17
Rodriguez, Chi.	.969	112	78	204	9	19
Serna, Sea.	.972	15	9	26	1	3
Smalley, N.Y.	.953	53	28	113	7	11
Stein, Tex.	.986	28	13	55	1	5

TRIPLE PLAY: Gaetti.

(Fewer Than Ten Games)

Player—Club	Pct.	G.	PO.	A.	E.	DP.
Baker, Tor.	.808	8	5	16	5	2

Player—Club	Pct.	G.	PO.	A.	E.	DP.
Bando, Clev.	.000	2	0	0	0	0
Bannister, Clev.	.000	1	0	0	0	0
Bell, Oak.	.857	3	3	3	1	1
Bonnell, Tor.	1.000	9	2	4	0	1
J. Cruz, Sea.	1.000	1	1	3	0	0
DeJohn, Det.	.800	4	0	4	1	2
Dybzinski, Clev.	.875	3	2	5	1	1
Evans, N.Y.	1.000	6	2	10	0	0
Fischlin, Clev.	.750	8	2	1	1	0
Foley, Chi.	.000	2	0	0	0	0
Foli, Cal.	1.000	2	0	6	0	0
Hatcher, Minn.	1.000	5	3	10	0	1
Hayes, Clev.	1.000	5	2	8	0	0
Heath, Oak.	1.000	5	4	3	0	0
Hernandez, Tor.	.000	2	0	0	0	0
Hill, Chi.	.000	1	0	0	0	0
Ireland, K.C.	.000	1	0	0	0	0
Ro. Jackson, Cal.	1.000	9	2	12	0	0
Kelleher, Det.-Cal.	1.000	7	3	8	0	0
Newman, Oak.	1.000	1	4	0	0	0
Parrish, Tex.	.000	3	0	0	0	0
Petralli, Tor.	1.000	3	2	1	0	0
Putnam, Tex.	.000	1	0	0	0	0
Quirk, K.C.	.000	1	0	0	0	0
Randle, Sea.	.964	9	7	20	1	1
Rhomberg, Clev.	1.000	1	1	1	0	0
Robertson, N.Y.	.000	2	0	0	0	0
Romero, Milw.	.000	2	0	0	0	0
Sexton, Oak.	.923	8	7	17	2	1
Stapleton, Bos.	1.000	5	5	7	0	0
Tolleson, Tex.	1.000	4	0	2	0	0
Washington, Minn.	1.000	1	0	1	0	0
Wilfong, Cal.	.933	5	1	13	1	0
Wockenfuss, Det.	.000	1	0	0	0	0

THIRD BASEMEN WITH TWO OR MORE CLUBS

Player—Club	Pct.	G.	PO.	A.	E.	DP.
Kelleher, Det.	.000	1	0	0	0	0
Kelleher, Cal.	1.000	6	3	8	0	0
Milbourne, N.Y.	1.000	3	0	5	0	0
Milbourne, Clev.	.941	9	4	12	1	1

SHORTSTOPS

Leader—Club	Pct.	G.	PO.	A.	E.	DP.
FOLI, Cal.	.985	139	235	432	10	87

(Listed Alphabetically)

Player—Club	Pct.	G.	PO.	A.	E.	DP.
Almon, Chi.	.949	108	164	317	26	72
Bonner, Balt.	.959	38	33	61	4	9
Burleson, Cal.	.986	11	19	51	1	12
Concepcion, K.C.	.948	46	63	138	11	25
T. Cruz, Sea.	.963	136	215	439	25	98
DeJohn, Det.	.978	20	19	26	1	7
Dent, N.Y.-Tex.	.970	103	129	323	14	57
Dybzinski, Clev.	.957	77	118	239	16	39
Faedo, Minn.	.967	88	129	218	12	52
Fischlin, Clev.	.970	101	136	253	12	42
Flynn, Tex.	.962	35	44	108	6	17
Foli, Cal.	.985	139	235	432	10	87
Griffin, Tor.	.968	162	319	479	26	92
Hoffman, Bos.	.972	150	246	439	20	93
Kelleher, Cal.	.965	28	31	52	3	8
V. Law, Chi.	.953	85	126	239	18	44
Mendoza, Tex.	.882	12	14	16	4	6
Milbourne, N.Y.-Clev.	.886	30	20	42	8	6
Mulliniks, Tor.	.963	16	9	17	1	3
Phillips, Oak.	.953	39	46	95	7	17
Picciolo, Oak.-Milw.	.973	24	41	69	3	13
Ripken, Balt.	.972	94	155	289	13	47
Robertson, N.Y.	.966	27	40	73	4	21
Romero, Milw.	.920	10	6	17	2	4
Sakata, Balt.	.958	56	76	154	10	27
Serna, Sea.	.936	31	33	70	7	13
Sexton, Oak.	.957	47	56	101	7	18
Smalley, Minn.-N.Y.	.979	93	114	254	8	44
Stanley, Oak.	.963	98	112	223	13	42
Stapleton, Bos.	.973	27	35	73	3	14
Tolleson, Tex.	.958	26	47	68	5	20
Trammell, Det.	.978	157	259	459	16	97
Valdez, Bos.	.976	22	16	24	1	5
Wagner, Tex.	.955	60	77	197	13	32

Player—Club	Pct.	G.	PO.	A.	E.	DP.
Washington, K.C.	.961	117	173	371	22	63
Washington, Minn.	.972	91	127	186	9	38
Yount, Milw.	.969	154	253	489	24	95

(Fewer Than Ten Games)

Player—Club	Pct.	G.	PO.	A.	E.	DP.
Adams, Cal.	.947	8	6	12	1	4
Bannister, Clev.	1.000	2	1	0	0	0
Bell, Tex.	1.000	4	0	1	0	0
Biancalana, K.C.	1.000	3	2	8	0	1
Brookens, Det.	1.000	9	7	13	0	0
J. Cruz, Sea.	1.000	2	1	1	0	0
DeCinces, Cal.	.667	2	1	1	1	0
Evans, N.Y.	1.000	4	1	2	0	0
Gaetti, Minn.	.714	2	0	5	2	1
Harrah, Clev.	.000	2	0	0	0	0
McHenry, Sea.	.500	1	1	0	1	0
McKay, Oak.	1.000	3	2	2	0	1
Molitor, Milw.	.842	4	6	10	3	0
Murphy, Oak.	1.000	1	0	4	0	0
Pryor, K.C.	1.000	7	5	13	0	3
Ramos, Sea.	.920	8	9	14	2	0
Rodriguez, Chi.	1.000	2	0	1	0	0
Scott, N.Y.	.963	6	9	17	1	5
Stein, Tex.	1.000	6	1	2	0	1
Wilfong, Cal.	1.000	2	1	2	0	0

SHORTSTOPS WITH TWO OR MORE CLUBS

Player—Club	Pct.	G.	PO.	A.	E.	DP.
Dent, N.Y.	.962	58	74	177	10	27
Dent, Tex.	.980	45	55	146	4	30
Milbourne, N.Y.	.917	9	3	8	1	0
Milbourne, Clev	.879	21	17	34	7	6
Picciolo, Oak	.979	18	34	58	2	11
Picciolo, Milw	.947	6	7	11	1	2
Smalley, Minn.	1.000	4	5	16	0	2
Smalley, N.Y.	.977	89	109	238	8	42

OUTFIELDERS

Leaders—Club	Pct.	G.	PO.	A.	E.	DP.
DOWNING, Calif	1.000	158	321	9	0	0
LOWENSTEIN, Balt	1.000	112	202	2	0	0

(Listed Alphabetically)

Player—Club	Pct.	G.	PO.	A.	E.	DP.
Armas, Oak	.983	135	333	9	6	1
Ayala, Balt	.972	25	35	0	1	0
Baines, Chi*	.980	161	326	10	7	4
Bannister, Clev.	.991	55	115	1	1	0
Barfield, Tor	.963	137	217	15	9	4
Bass, Milw	1.000	14	7	0	0	0
Beniquez, Calif	.983	107	113	4	2	1
Bochte, Sea*	.988	99	161	5	2	1
Bogener, Tex*	1.000	16	22	0	0	0
Bonnell, Tor	.979	125	232	3	5	0
Bosley, Sea*	1.000	19	12	1	0	0
Brett, K.C.	1.000	12	23	1	0	1
Brouhard, Milw	.986	30	69	2	1	0
Brown, Sea	.968	68	148	5	5	1
Brunansky, Minn	.986	127	343	8	5	0
Bumbry, Balt.	.986	147	404	9	6	1
Burroughs, Oak	.981	34	52	0	1	0
Castillo, Clev	.978	43	91	0	2	0
Charboneau, Clev.	.955	18	21	0	1	0
Clark, Calif	1.000	102	88	2	0	0
Collins, N.Y.*	.992	60	114	5	1	0
Cowens, Sea	.987	145	280	14	4	1
Craig, Clev.	.966	22	28	0	1	0
Davis, Oak*	.946	13	35	0	2	0
Dilone, Clev	.964	97	187	3	7	1
Downing, Calif	1.000	158	321	9	0	0
Dwyer, Balt*	.976	49	81	0	2	0
Edwards, Milw*	.984	54	119	2	2	1
Eisenreich, Minn*	.973	30	72	0	2	0
Engle, Minn	.985	34	63	3	1	1
Evans, Bos	.973	161	346	9	10	3

Player—Club	Pct.	G.	PO.	A.	E.	DP.
Ford, Balt	.975	119	263	6	7	2
Gamble, N.Y.	1.000	29	59	6	0	1
Geronimo, K.C.*	1.000	44	93	3	0	0
Gibson, Det*	.994	64	167	4	1	3
Griffey, N.Y.*	.983	125	282	8	5	2
Grubb, Tex	.965	77	135	4	5	1
Hairston, Chi	1.000	36	34	2	0	1
Hammond, K.C.	1.000	37	81	3	0	1
Hatcher, Minn	.988	47	78	7	1	0
Hayes, Clev	.981	139	306	9	6	4
Heath, Oak	.938	10	14	1	1	0
Henderson, Oak*	.977	144	379	2	9	0
Henderson, Sea	.985	101	249	11	4	4
Herndon, Det	.983	155	328	11	6	3
Re. Jackson, Calif*	.972	139	200	6	6	1
Johnson, Tor	.979	29	45	2	1	0
Jones, Det	1.000	56	86	3	0	2
Kemp, Chi*	.976	154	280	6	7	1
Kuntz, Chi	1.000	21	21	0	0	0
R. Law, Chi*	.973	94	215	2	6	0
Leach, Det*	1.000	14	20	1	0	0
LeFlore, Chi	.939	83	179	7	12	1
Lemon, Det	.984	121	242	11	4	2
Lowenstein, Balt	1.000	111	202	2	0	0
Lynn, Calif*	.991	133	317	6	3	3
Manning, Clev	.978	152	387	10	9	1
Martin, K.C.	.980	142	333	4	7	2
Mazzilli, Tex-N.Y.	.949	28	55	1	3	1
McBride, Clev	1.000	22	37	0	0	0
Meyer, Oak	.938	11	14	1	1	0
Miller, Bos*	.983	127	277	6	5	2
Mitchell, Minn*	.997	121	350	8	1	3
Moore, Milw	.988	115	231	13	3	6
Moseby, Tor.	.992	145	361	4	3	0
Moses, Sea*	.947	19	16	2	1	0
Mumphrey, N.Y.	.986	123	336	5	5	2

OUTFIELDERS—Continued

Player—Club	Pct.	G.	PO.	A.	E.	DP.	Player—Club	Pct.	G.	PO.	A.	E.	DP.
Murphy, Oak	.983	147	452	14	8	3	Howell, Milw	1.000	2	2	0	0	0
Nichols, Bos	.989	82	169	9	2	4	Ireland, K.C.	.750	2	3	0	1	0
Nordhagen, Tor	1.000	10	15	1	0	1	Johnson, Minn*	1.000	2	2	0	0	0
O'Brien, Tex*	1.000	11	17	1	0	1	Johnson, Det	1.000	9	11	1	0	0
Oglivie, Milw*	.982	159	359	15	7	3	Jurak, Bos	.000	1	0	0	0	0
Otis, K.C.	.997	125	308	5	1	1	Kittle, Chi	1.000	5	3	0	0	0
Parrish, Tex	.962	124	190	12	8	4	Langford, Oak	1.000	1	1	0	0	0
Piniella, N.Y.	1.000	40	68	2	0	1	V. Law, Chi.	.000	1	0	0	0	0
Poquette, K.C.	.957	23	44	1	2	0	Lopes, Oak	1.000	6	6	0	0	0
Powell, Tor*	.974	75	111	2	3	0	Mattingly, N.Y.*	1.000	6	11	1	0	0
Rice, Bos	.969	145	273	10	9	3	McRae, K.C.	.500	1	1	0	1	0
Roberts, Tex-Tor	1.000	44	66	0	0	0	Miller, Det	1.000	8	13	1	0	0
Roenicke, Balt	.990	125	288	7	3	0	Nyman, Chi	1.000	2	1	0	0	0
Rudi, Oak	.947	14	18	0	1	0	Paciorek, Chi.	1.000	6	2	0	0	0
Sample, Tex	.981	91	196	6	4	1	Parrish, Det	.000	1	0	0	0	0
Shelby, Balt	1.000	24	20	1	0	1	Patterson, N.Y.	1.000	9	5	0	0	0
Simpson, Sea*	.984	97	177	7	3	0	Pettis, Calif	1.000	8	5	1	0	0
Thomas, Milw	.991	157	427	11	4	4	Putnam, Tex	1.000	1	2	0	0	0
Turner, Det*	.909	13	10	0	1	0	Quirk, K.C.	.000	1	0	0	0	0
Ward, Minn	.989	150	343	13	4	3	Rhomberg, Clev.	.900	7	8	1	1	1
Wilson, K.C.	.987	135	376	4	5	0	Richardt, Tex	1.000	6	19	1	0	0
Wilson, Det	.987	80	215	8	3	1	Rivera, K.C.	1.000	3	4	0	0	0
Winfield, N.Y.	.974	135	279	17	8	2	Romero, Milw	1.000	1	0	0	0	0
Wockenfuss, Det	1.000	10	15	1	0	0	Ryal, K.C.*	.900	5	9	0	1	0
Woods, Tor*	.970	64	96	2	3	1	Singleton, Balt	1.000	5	10	0	0	0
Wright, Tex	.981	149	398	14	8	3	Skube, Milw*	.000	1	0	0	0	0

.982 (Fewer Than Ten Games) 160 295=2.17

Player—Club	Pct.	G.	PO.	A.	E.	DP.
Boggs, Bos	1.000	1	1	0	0	0
Bosetti, Oak	1.000	6	14	2	0	0
Brookens, Det	1.000	1	3	0	0	0
Brown, Oak	1.000	7	9	0	0	0
Bush, Minn*	1.000	6	7	0	0	0
Cabell, Det	.000	3	0	0	0	0
Capra, Tex	1.000	9	14	2	0	1
Castino, Minn	1.000	6	12	0	0	0
Davis, Tor	1.000	1	2	0	0	0
Edler, Sea	1.000	2	4	2	0	0
Ferguson, Calif	1.000	2	1	0	0	0
Hancock, Bos*	1.000	7	4	0	0	0
Hernandez, Tor	.000	1	0	0	0	0

Player—Club	Pct.	G.	PO.	A.	E.	DP.
Stapleton, Bos	.000	1	0	0	0	0
Stein, Tex	1.000	1	5	0	0	0
Stroughter, Sea	1.000	3	7	1	0	0
Sundberg, Tex	1.000	1	5	0	0	0
Vega, Minn	.000	1	0	0	0	0
Wilfong, Calif	1.000	3	1	1	0	0
Yastrzemski, Bos	1.000	2	3	0	0	0
Young, Balt	1.000	1	1	0	0	0

.983 165 211 14 4 = 1.36

OUTFIELDERS WITH TWO OR MORE CLUBS

Player—Club	Pct.	G.	PO.	A.	E.	DP.
Mazzilli, Tex	.945	26	51	1	3	1
Mazzilli, N.Y.	1.000	2	4	0	0	0
Roberts, Tex	1.000	28	42	0	0	0
Roberts, Tor	1.000	16	24	0	0	0

Grand total .982 299 = 2.15

CATCHERS

Player—Club	Pct.	G.	PO.	A.	E.	DP.	PB.
SIMMONS, Milw	.995	121	570	62	3	8	8

(Listed Alphabetically)

Player—Club	Pct.	G.	PO.	A.	E.	DP.	PB.
Allenson, Bos	.992	91	454	39	4	8	6
Bando, Clev	.990	63	268	23	3	1	2
Boone, Calif	.989	143	650	87	8	8	2
Bulling, Sea	.991	56	304	24	3	5	2
Butera, Minn	.988	53	230	26	3	5	3
Cerone, N.Y.	.989	89	509	25	6	5	11
Dempsey, Balt	.991	124	491	46	5	8	5
Essian, Sea	.994	48	282	26	2	1	1
Fahey, Det	1.000	28	85	16	0	2	3
Ferguson, Calif	.993	32	138	13	1	2	2
Fisk, Chi	.994	133	639	62	4	7	10
Foley, Chi	.980	15	45	4	1	0	0
Foote, N.Y.	.973	17	71	2	2	0	2
Gedman, Bos	.977	86	397	29	10	5	10
Hassey, Clev	.993	105	562	38	4	6	4
Heath, Oak	.973	90	350	50	11	8	5
Hill, Chi	.993	49	135	15	1	2	3
B. Johnson, Tex	1.000	14	70	5	0	1	3
Kearney, Oak	.970	22	114	14	4	1	0
Laudner, Minn	.976	93	454	41	12	5	2
Martinez, Tor	.988	93	382	35	5	8	2
Moore, Milw	.960	20	86	9	4	2	1
Nahorodny, Clev	1.000	35	111	11	0	2	0
Newman, Oak	.989	67	320	27	4	5	3
Nolan, Balt	.978	72	292	22	7	2	2
Parrish, Det	.989	132	627	76	8	8	11
Petralli, Tor	.981	12	49	3	1	0	0

Player—Club	Pct.	G.	PO.	A.	E.	DP.	PB.
Quirk, K.C.	1.000	29	77	6	0	0	1
Simmons, Milw	.995	121	570	62	3	8	8
Slaught, K.C.	.994	43	156	7	1	1	1
Sundberg, Tex	.991	132	607	69	6	15	16
Sweet, Sea	.993	83	431	26	3	6	7
Wathan, K.C.	.980	120	463	38	10	3	4
Werner, Tex	.980	22	91	5	2	2	0
Whitt, Tor	.982	98	406	30	8	0	5
Wockenfuss, Det	.981	24	91	10	2	0	1
Wynegar, Minn-N.Y.	.991	86	523	26	5	10	3
Yost, Milw	.977	39	121	6	3	2	3

TRIPLE PLAY: Butera.

(Fewer Than Ten Games)

Player—Club	Pct.	G.	PO.	A.	E.	DP.	PB.
Castillo, Det	1.000	1	1	0	0	0	0
Espino, Sea	1.000	3	4	0	0	0	0
Firova, Sea	.900	3	8	1	1	0	0
Fischlin, Clev	1.000	1	1	0	0	0	0
LaFrancois, Bos	1.000	8	15	0	0	0	0
Mercado, Sea	1.000	8	31	1	0	0	0
Ramos, N.Y.	1.000	4	21	1	0	0	0
Rayford, Balt	1.000	2	0	1	0	0	0
Smith, Minn	1.000	9	44	2	0	0	0
Sullivan, Bos	1.000	2	9	2	0	1	0
Werth, K.C.	1.000	2	1	0	0	0	0

CATCHER WITH TWO OR MORE CLUBS

Player—Club	Pct.	G.	PO.	A.	E.	DP.	PB.
Wynegar, Minn	.986	24	128	9	2	4	1
Wynegar, N.Y.	.993	62	395	17	3	6	2

PITCHERS

Leader—Club	Pct.	G.	PO.	A.	E.	DP.
PETRY, Det.	1.000	35	28	48	0	4

(Listed Alphabetically)

Player—Club	Pct.	G.	PO.	A.	E.	DP.
Aase, Cal.	1.000	24	3	5	0	0
Alexander, N.Y.	.923	16	3	9	1	1
Andersen, Sea.	1.000	40	8	14	0	2
Anderson, Clev.	.947	25	10	8	1	0
Aponte, Bos.	1.000	40	11	16	0	3
Armstrong, K.C.	1.000	52	9	8	0	1
Arroyo, Minn.-Oak.	.929	16	3	10	1	1
Augustine, Milw.*	1.000	20	0	4	0	1
Bannister, Sea.	.950	35	8	30	2	1
Barker, Clev.	.962	33	23	27	2	1
Barojas, Chi.	1.000	61	10	28	0	2
Beard, Oak.	.875	54	3	11	2	1
Beattie, Sea.	.974	28	16	21	1	2
Bernard, Milw.	1.000	47	3	8	0	0
Black, K.C.*	.947	22	6	12	1	1
Blue, K.C.*	.947	31	14	22	2	0
Boitano, Tex.	1.000	19	1	3	0	0
Bomback, Tor.	1.000	16	6	9	0	0
Boris, Minn.	1.000	23	2	4	0	0
Brennan, Clev.	1.000	30	9	13	0	2
Brusstar, Chi.	1.000	10	1	5	0	0
Burgmeier, Bos.*	.974	40	17	20	1	4
Burns, Chi.*	.889	28	2	14	2	0
Butcher, Tex.	1.000	18	7	19	0	3
Caldwell, Milw.*	.984	35	13	48	1	5
Castillo, Minn.	.929	40	20	19	3	1
Castro, K.C.	1.000	21	6	4	0	0
Caudill, Sea.	1.000	70	3	5	0	1
Clancy, Tor.	.953	40	14	27	2	2
Clark, Sea.*	1.000	37	7	20	0	3
Clear, Bos.	.857	55	7	11	3	0
Comer, Tex.	.947	37	3	15	1	1
Corbett, Minn.-Cal.	.962	43	13	12	1	0
D'Acquisto, Oak.	1.000	11	0	2	0	2
Darwin, Tex.	1.000	56	5	19	0	0
Davis, Balt.	.947	29	6	12	1	0
Davis, Minn.	1.000	63	6	10	0	1
Denny, Clev.	1.000	21	12	19	0	2
Dotson, Chi.	.974	34	13	24	1	1
Easterly, Milw.*	1.000	28	3	7	0	0
Eckersley, Bos.	.977	33	21	21	1	2
Erickson, Minn.-N.Y.	.952	23	6	14	1	0
Escarrega, Chi.	1.000	38	6	7	0	1
Felton, Minn.	.909	48	5	5	1	0
Fingers, Milw.	1.000	50	4	10	0	1
Flanagan, Balt.*	1.000	36	7	38	0	1
Forsch, Cal.	.894	37	13	29	5	2
Frazier, N.Y.	.885	63	6	17	3	2
Frost, K.C.	.917	21	5	6	1	1
Garvin, Tor.*	1.000	32	5	17	0	0
Geisel, Tor.*	1.000	16	0	3	0	0
Glynn, Clev.*	1.000	47	1	4	0	0
Goltz, Cal.	1.000	28	4	5	0	0
Gossage, N.Y.	1.000	56	2	6	0	1
Gott, Tor.	.960	30	6	18	1	2
Grimsley, Balt.*	.929	21	2	11	1	1
Guidry, N.Y.*	1.000	34	7	19	0	1
Gura, K.C.*	.966	37	7	50	2	6
Haas, Milw.	1.000	32	14	18	0	1
Hanna, Oak.	.857	23	1	5	1	1
Hassler, Cal.*	.955	54	2	19	1	2
Havens, Minn.*	1.000	33	4	18	0	0
Hickey, Chi.*	.962	60	5	20	1	4
Honeycutt, Tex.*	.950	30	3	35	2	0
Hood, K.C.*	.944	30	6	11	1	0
Hough, Tex.	.980	34	14	35	1	4
Hoyt, Chi.	1.000	39	16	26	0	3
Hurst, Bos.*	.966	28	6	22	1	1
Jackson, K.C.*	.857	20	1	5	1	0
Jackson, Minn.*	.727	13	1	7	3	1
Jackson, Tor.	1.000	48	6	12	0	0
James, Det.	.571	12	0	4	3	0
John, N.Y.-Cal.*	.967	37	10	48	2	1
Jones, Oak.	1.000	18	3	3	0	0

Player—Club	Pct.	G.	PO.	A.	E.	DP.
Keough, Oak.	.906	34	9	20	3	2
Kern, Chi.	1.000	13	3	3	0	0
Kingman, Oak.	.923	23	3	9	1	0
Kison, Cal.	.977	33	19	24	1	2
Koosman, Chi.*	.973	42	12	24	1	3
Ladd, Milw.	1.000	16	1	0	0	0
Lamp, Chi.	.906	44	9	39	5	6
Langford, Oak.	.964	32	15	39	2	3
LaRoche, N.Y.*	1.000	25	1	3	0	0
Leal, Tor.	1.000	38	17	31	0	2
Leonard, K.C.	.919	21	16	18	3	2
Lerch, Milw.*	.895	21	4	13	2	0
Little, Minn.*	1.000	33	0	3	0	0
Lopez, Det.	1.000	19	3	5	0	0
Lyle, Chi.*	1.000	11	1	1	0	0
F. Martinez, Balt.*	1.000	76	6	10	0	1
J.D. Martinez, Balt.	.981	40	13	38	1	2
Matlack, Tex.*	1.000	33	4	24	0	1
May, N.Y.*	.955	41	2	19	1	1
McCatty, Oak.	1.000	21	12	13	0	0
McClure, Milw.*	.900	34	4	23	3	3
McGregor, Balt.*	1.000	37	11	30	0	1
McLaughlin, Tor.	1.000	44	6	10	0	3
McLaughlin, Oak.	1.000	21	2	8	0	2
Medich, Tex.-Milw.	1.000	31	8	27	0	0
Mirabella, Tex.*	.889	40	2	6	1	2
Moore, Sea.	.889	28	13	27	5	2
Moreno, Cal.*	.833	13	2	8	2	0
Morgan, N.Y.	1.000	30	4	26	0	3
Morris, Det.	.983	37	26	31	1	2
Murray, Tor.	.949	56	5	32	2	2
Musselman, Sea.	.833	12	1	4	1	0
Nelson, Sea.	.968	22	10	20	1	4
Norris, Oak.	.956	28	22	21	2	1
O'Connor, Minn.*	1.000	23	3	6	0	0
Ojeda, Bos.*	.900	22	2	7	1	0
Owchinko, Oak.*	1.000	54	7	7	0	1
Pacella, N.Y.-Minn.	1.000	24	3	2	0	0
Palmer, Balt.	.964	36	16	37	2	3
Pashnik, Det.	1.000	28	6	12	0	1
Perry, Sea.	.939	32	11	35	3	1
Petry, Det.	1.000	35	28	48	0	4
Quisenberry, K.C.	.970	72	18	46	2	3
Rainey, Bos.	.973	27	17	19	1	0
Rawley, N.Y.*	.971	47	5	29	1	1
Redfern, Minn.	1.000	27	8	13	0	2
Renko, Cal.	.885	31	9	14	3	4
Righetti, N.Y.*	.885	33	5	18	3	1
Rucker, Det.*	.824	27	4	10	3	2
Sanchez, Cal.	.952	46	1	19	1	1
Saucier, Det.*	.833	31	6	4	2	4
Schmidt, Tex.	.900	33	2	16	2	2
Senteney, Tor.	1.000	11	1	1	0	0
Slaton, Milw.	1.000	39	6	16	0	0
Sorensen, Clev.	.905	32	10	28	4	2
Sosa, Det.	1.000	38	3	13	0	0
Spillner, Clev.	.929	65	6	7	1	0
Splittorff, K.C.*	.969	29	7	24	1	4
Stanhouse, Balt.	1.000	17	2	5	0	1
Stanley, Bos.	.966	48	13	43	2	4
Stanton, Sea.	.920	56	10	13	2	1
Steirer, Cal.	1.000	10	2	5	0	0
Stewart, Balt.	.969	38	10	21	1	3
Stieb, Tor.	.976	38	27	53	2	6
Stoddard, Balt.	.889	50	2	6	1	0
Sutcliffe, Clev.	.979	34	14	32	1	1
Tanana, Tex.*	.974	30	8	30	1	0
Tobik, Det.	.941	51	8	8	1	1
Torrez, Bos.	.963	31	12	14	1	0
Trout, Chi.*	.871	25	9	18	4	2
Tudor, Bos.*	.957	32	5	39	2	4
Tufts, K.C.*	1.000	10	1	0	0	0
Ujdur, Det.	.941	25	11	21	2	2
Underwood, Det.*	.957	33	1	21	1	1
Underwood, Oak.*	.909	56	9	11	2	0
Vande Berg, Sea.*	.960	78	5	19	1	3
Viola, Minn.*	.889	22	1	15	2	0
Vuckovich, Milw.	.929	30	13	39	4	1

PITCHERS—Continued

Player—Club	Pct.	G.	PO.	A.	E.	DP.
Waits, Clev.*	1.000	25	6	23	0	1
Whitson, Clev.	1.000	40	4	8	0	0
Wilcox, Det.	.961	29	11	38	2	5
Williams, Minn.	.925	26	14	23	3	0
Witt, Cal.	.905	33	14	24	4	3
Zahn, Cal.*	.950	34	3	35	2	1

TRIPLE PLAY: Felton.

(Fewer Than Ten Games)

Player—Club	Pct.	G.	PO.	A.	E.	DP.
Agosto, Chi.*	1.000	1	0	1	0	0
Bahnsen, Cal.	.000	7	0	0	1	0
Bailey, Det.*	1.000	8	1	2	0	0
Baker, Oak.	.750	5	0	3	1	0
Barnes, Chi.*	1.000	6	0	4	0	0
Berenguer, Det.	.000	2	0	0	0	0
Blyleven, Clev.	1.000	4	2	2	0	0
Boddicker, Balt.	.889	7	5	3	1	0
Bohnet, Clev.*	1.000	3	1	2	0	0
Bordi, Sea.	1.000	7	1	1	0	0
Botelho, K.C.	1.000	8	1	2	0	0
Boyd, Bos.	1.000	3	0	1	0	0
Brown, Bos.	.000	3	0	0	0	0
Codiroli, Oak.	1.000	3	3	3	0	0
Conroy, Oak.*	.667	5	1	3	2	0
Cooper, Minn.	1.000	6	1	1	0	0
Crawford, Bos.	1.000	5	0	1	0	0
Creel, K.C.	1.000	9	1	8	0	1
Curtis, Cal.*	1.000	8	0	1	0	0
Denman, Bos.	1.000	9	6	5	0	0
Eichhorn, Tor.	1.000	7	1	3	0	0
Farr, Tex.	1.000	5	0	2	0	0
Filson, Minn.*	.000	5	0	0	0	0
Flinn, Balt.	1.000	5	2	0	0	0
Gleaton, Sea.*	1.000	3	1	0	0	0
Gumpert, Det.	.000	5	0	0	0	0
Heaton, Clev.*	1.000	8	2	3	0	0
Henke, Tex.	1.000	8	2	2	0	0
Howell, N.Y.	1.000	6	2	2	0	0
Jones, Milw.	1.000	4	1	0	0	0
Kaufman, N.Y.	1.000	7	1	0	0	0
Kinney, Oak.*	1.000	3	0	1	0	0
Lewallyn, Clev.	1.000	4	2	0	0	0
Lewis, N.Y.	.000	1	0	0	0	0
Mahler, Cal.*	1.000	6	0	1	0	0
Mason, Tex.*	1.000	4	1	5	0	0
McGlothen, N.Y.	1.000	4	1	1	0	0
Nunez, Sea.	.875	8	2	5	1	0
Porter, Milw.	.000	3	0	0	0	0
Reed, Clev.	1.000	6	1	2	0	0
Rothschild, Det.	.000	2	0	0	0	0
Rozema, Det.	1.000	8	7	5	0	0
Schrom, Tor.	.000	6	0	0	0	0
Siwy, Chi.	.000	2	0	0	0	0
Smithson, Tex.	1.000	8	2	3	0	0
Solomon, Chi.	.000	6	0	0	0	0
Stoddard, Sea.	1.000	9	0	14	0	1
Sutton, Milw.	1.000	7	6	8	0	1
Tiant, Cal.	1.000	6	1	0	0	0
Welchel, Balt.	.000	2	0	0	0	0
Wever, N.Y.	.000	1	0	0	0	0
Wihtol, Clev.	1.000	6	0	1	0	0
Wright, K.C.	.750	7	1	2	1	0

PITCHERS WITH TWO OR MORE CLUBS

Player—Club	Pct.	G.	PO.	A.	E.	DP.
Arroyo, Minn.	1.000	6	2	6	0	1
Arroyo, Oak.	.833	10	1	4	1	0
Corbett, Minn.	1.000	10	5	4	0	0
Corbett, Cal.	.941	33	8	8	1	0
Erickson, Minn.	1.000	7	2	9	0	0
Erickson, N.Y.	.900	16	4	5	1	0
John, N.Y.	.960	30	8	40	2	1
John, Cal.	1.000	7	2	8	0	0
Medich, Tex.	1.000	21	5	21	0	0
Medich, Milw.	1.000	10	3	6	0	0
Pacella, N.Y.	1.000	3	0	1	0	0
Pacella, Minn.	1.000	21	3	1	0	0

OFFICIAL AMERICAN LEAGUE PITCHING AVERAGES

CLUB PITCHING

Club	ERA.	G.	CG.	ShO.	Sv.	IP.	H.	BFP.	R.	ER.	HR.	SH.	SF.	HB.	Tot. BB.	Int. BB.	SO.	WP.	Bk.
Detroit	3.80	162	45	5	27	1451	1371	6115	685	613	172	50	35	23	554	50	740	53	4
California	3.82	162	40	10	27	1464	1436	6158	670	621	124	47	32	42	482	33	728	36	4
Chicago	3.87	162	30	10	41	1439	1502	6146	710	618	99	56	41	26	460	30	753	28	13
Seattle	3.88	162	23	11	39	1476.1	1431	6251	712	636	173	62	33	25	547	23	1002	47	9
Toronto	3.95	162	41	13	25	1443.2	1428	6141	701	633	147	46	31	25	493	29	776	38	3
Milwaukee	3.98	163	34	6	47	1467.2	1514	6247	717	649	152	52	51	21	511	27	717	44	8
Baltimore	3.99	163	38	8	34	1462.1	1436	6185	687	648	147	52	46	22	488	41	719	35	6
New York	3.99	162	24	8	39	1459	1471	6220	716	647	113	69	59	22	491	40	939	41	15
Boston	4.03	162	23	11	33	1453	1557	6246	713	651	155	46	43	35	478	36	816	24	6
Kansas City	4.08	162	16	12	45	1431	1443	6109	717	649	163	46	54	26	471	30	650	43	11
Cleveland	4.11	162	31	9	30	1468.1	1433	6307	748	670	122	56	66	22	589	32	882	56	8
Texas	4.28	162	32	5	24	1431	1554	6191	749	681	128	69	51	41	483	68	690	34	4
Oakland	4.54	162	42	6	22	1456	1506	6430	819	735	177	71	54	30	648	21	697	58	8
Minnesota	4.72	162	26	7	30	1433	1484	6256	819	752	208	40	45	12	643	60	812	45	12
Totals	4.07	1135	445	121	463	20335	20566	87002	10163	9203	2080	762	641	372	7338	520	10921	582	111

(BFP total includes three batsmen awarded first base because of interference.)

NOTE—Totals for earned runs for several clubs do not agree with the composite totals for all pitchers of each respective club due to instances in which provisions of Section 10.18 (i) of the Scoring Rules were applied. The following differences are to be noted: Boston pitchers add to 652; Cleveland, 672; Detroit, 615; Milwaukee, 650; Minnesota, 759; New York, 648; Seattle, 640; Texas, 684.

PITCHERS' RECORDS

(Top Fifteen Qualifiers for Earned-Run Leadership—162 or More Innings)

Pitcher and Club	W.	L.	Pct.	ERA.	G.	GS.	CG.	ShO.	GF.	Sv.	IP.	H.	BFP.	R.	ER.	HR.	SH.	SF.	HB.	Tot. BB.	Int. BB.	SO.	WP.	Bk.
Sutcliffe, Richard, Cleveland	14	8	.636	2.96	34	27	6	0	3	1	216	174	887	81	71	16	7	8	4	98	2	142	6	1
Stanley, Robert, Boston	12	7	.632	3.10	48	0	0	0	33	14	168.1	161	700	60	58	11	4	4	5	50	6	83	2	0
Palmer, James, Baltimore	15	5	.750	3.13	36	32	8	2	1	1	227	195	920	85	79	22	5	8	3	63	1	103	1	0
Petry, Daniel, Detroit	15	9	.625	3.22	35	35	8	1	0	0	246	220	1031	116	88	15	8	3	4	100	5	132	9	1
Stieb, David, Toronto	17	14	.548	3.25	38	38	19	5	0	0	288.1	271	1187	96	104	27	10	3	5	75	4	141	3	1
Vuckovich, Peter, Milwaukee	18	6	.750	3.34	30	30	9	1	0	0	223.2	234	971	96	83	14	9	3	1	102	0	105	6	2
Beattie, James, Seattle	8	12	.400	3.34	28	26	6	0	1	0	172.1	149	715	73	64	13	6	5	3	65	0	140	6	0
Bannister, Floyd, Seattle*	12	13	.480	3.43	35	35	5	3	0	0	247	225	1022	112	94	32	10	5	7	77	0	209	6	2
Witt, Michael, California	8	6	.571	3.51	33	26	5	1	4	0	179.2	177	748	77	70	8	6	7	2	47	3	85	8	0
Hoyt, D. LaMarr, Chicago	19	15	.559	3.53	39	32	14	1	2	2	239.2	248	995	104	94	17	6	7	2	48	3	124	4	1
Wilcox, Milton, Detroit	12	10	.545	3.62	32	30	9	0	1	0	193.2	187	833	91	78	18	7	5	8	85	5	112	5	1
Tudor, John, Boston*	13	11	.565	3.63	30	29	6	1	1	0	195.2	215	847	90	79	20	8	9	4	59	7	146	0	2
Castillo, Robert, Minnesota	13	11	.542	3.66	40	25	7	0	6	0	218.2	194	903	96	89	26	4	0	3	85	7	123	1	1
Uidur, Gerald, Detroit	10	10	.500	3.69	25	25	7	0	0	0	178	150	732	76	73	29	8	5	3	69	1	86	5	1
John, Thomas, New York-California*	14	12	.538	3.69	37	33	10	2	2	2	221.2	239	918	102	91	15	7	3	3	39	4	68	7	2

*Throws lefthanded.

DEPARTMENTAL LEADERS: W—Hoyt, 19; L—Keough, Tanana, 18; Pct.—Palmer, Vuckovich, .750; G—Vande Berg, 78; GS—Clancy, 40; CG—Stieb, 19; ShO—Stieb, 5; GF—Quisenberry, 68; Sv—Quisenberry, 35; IP—Stieb, 288.1; H—Stieb, 271; BFP—Stieb, 1,187; R—Keough, 144; ER—Keough, 133; HR—Keough, 38; SH—Rawley, 16; SF—Haas, Medich, 11; Tot. BB—Righetti, 108; Int. BB—R. Davis, 12; SO—Bannister, 209; WP—Perry, 13; Bk—Black, 7.

(All Pitchers—Listed Alphabetically)

Pitcher and Club	W.	L.	Pct.	ERA.	G.	GS.	CG.	ShO.	GF.	Sv.	IP.	H.	BFP.	R.	ER.	HR.	SH.	SF.	HB.	Tot. BB.	Int. BB.	SO.	WP.	Bk.
Aase, Donald, California	3	3	.500	3.46	24	0	0	0	18	4	52	45	212	20	20	5	4	0	0	23	2	40	2	0
Agosto, Juan, Chicago*	0	3	.000	18.00	1	0	0	0	0	0	2	7	13	4	4	1	0	0	0	2	0	1	0	0
Alexander, Doyle, New York	1	7	.125	6.08	16	11	1	0	3	0	66.2	81	293	52	45	14	4	3	2	14	2	26	2	0
Andersen, Larry, Seattle	0	0	.000	5.99	40	1	0	0	14	0	79.2	100	354	56	53	16	2	4	4	23	2	32	1	4
Anderson, Karl, Cleveland	3	4	.429	3.35	25	5	1	0	12	0	80.2	84	353	37	30	4	5	4	1	30	2	44	4	0
Aponte, Luis, Boston	2	2	.500	3.18	40	0	0	0	28	6	85	78	349	31	30	5	5	2	1	25	3	44	4	0
Armstrong, Michael, K.C.	5	5	.500	3.20	52	0	0	0	25	0	112.2	88	466	45	40	9	4	2	3	43	1	75	7	2
Arroyo, Fernando, Minnesota-Oakland	0	1	.000	5.25	16	2	0	0	9	0	36	40	155	22	21	6	1	2	0	13	2	13	4	1
Augustine, Gerald, Milwaukee*	1	3	.250	5.08	20	0	0	0	5	1	62	63	270	43	35	13	2	4	0	26	2	22	3	0
Bahnsen, Stanley, California	0	1	.000	4.66	8	3	0	0	0	0	9.2	13	50	6	5	0	5	1	1	8	1	5	0	0
Bailey, Howard, Detroit*	0	0	.000	0.00	8	1	0	0	5	0	10	3	37	0	0	0	5	1	0	2	0	3	0	0
Baker, Steve, Oakland	0	0	.000	4.56	8	2	0	0	0	0	25.2	30	110	14	13	3	2	1	1	4	0	14	0	0
Bannister, Floyd, Seattle*	12	13	.480	3.43	35	35	5	0	0	0	247	225	1022	112	94	32	10	5	3	77	0	209	6	7
Barker, Leonard, Cleveland	15	11	.577	3.90	33	33	5	3	0	0	244.2	211	1021	117	106	17	10	9	3	88	2	187	10	0
Barnes, Richard, Chicago*	0	2	.000	4.76	6	2	0	0	0	0	17	21	79	15	9	1	2	1	2	4	0	6	0	0
Barojas, Salome, Chicago	6	6	.500	3.54	61	0	0	0	42	21	106.2	96	446	43	42	9	4	4	3	46	6	56	4	5
Beard, David, Oakland	10	9	.526	3.44	54	0	0	0	39	11	91.2	85	397	41	35	9	6	3	1	35	6	73	4	2
Beattie, James, Seattle	8	12	.400	3.34	28	26	6	1	0	0	172.1	149	715	73	64	13	6	9	3	65	0	140	5	0
Berenguer, Juan, Detroit	0	0	.000	6.75	47	2	0	0	19	0	6.2	5	34	5	5	0	0	1	1	5	1	8	0	0
Bernard, Dwight, Milwaukee	3	1	.750	3.76	22	1	0	0	19	6	79	78	335	39	33	4	5	5	1	27	0	45	1	0
Black, Harry, Kansas City*	4	6	.400	4.58	31	14	0	0	0	0	88.1	92	386	48	45	8	4	3	5	34	6	40	4	0
Blue, Vida, Kansas City*	13	12	.520	3.78	31	31	5	2	0	0	181	163	773	80	76	20	5	4	1	80	3	103	4	0
Blyleven, Rikalbert, Cleveland	2	2	.500	4.87	4	4	0	0	0	0	20.1	16	89	14	11	2	3	2	1	11	0	19	0	0
Boddicker, Michael, Baltimore	0	0	.000	3.51	7	3	0	0	0	0	25.2	25	110	10	10	2	1	0	2	7	2	20	0	0
Bohnet, John, Cleveland*	0	0	.000	6.94	7	0	0	0	3	0	11.2	11	53	9	9	1	0	1	0	2	0	4	0	0
Boitano, Danny, Texas*	0	0	.000	5.34	19	0	0	0	10	0	30.1	33	136	19	18	5	1	2	3	13	0	28	4	0
Bomback, Mark, Toronto	1	5	.167	6.03	16	8	0	0	3	0	59.2	87	287	44	40	10	3	2	3	25	3	22	3	4
Bordi, Richard, Seattle	0	2	.000	8.31	7	0	0	0	2	0	13	18	60	12	12	4	4	3	0	10	0	10	2	0
Boris, Paul, Minnesota	1	2	.333	3.99	23	0	0	0	12	0	49.2	46	215	24	22	8	4	3	3	19	3	30	0	0
Botelho, Derek, Kansas City*	2	1	.667	4.13	8	4	0	0	3	0	24	25	100	11	11	2	3	6	2	8	0	12	2	0
Boyd, Dennis, Boston	0	1	.000	5.40	3	3	0	0	0	0	8.1	11	37	5	5	2	4	2	0	2	0	8	1	0
Brennan, Thomas, Cleveland	2	1	.667	4.27	30	4	0	0	14	2	92.2	112	393	51	44	0	2	6	0	10	1	46	4	1
Brown, Michael, Boston	2	0	1.000	0.00	3	0	0	0	3	0	6	7	24	0	0	0	0	0	0	1	0	8	0	0
Brusstar, Warren, Chicago	4	0	1.000	3.44	40	0	0	0	14	2	18.1	19	78	7	7	2	0	3	2	3	0	44	1	0
Burgmeier, Thomas, Boston*	7	0	1.000	2.29	40	0	0	0	17	2	94.1	98	413	30	26	6	2	3	6	22	7	8	1	0
Burns, R. Britt, Chicago*	13	5	.722	4.04	28	28	5	1	0	0	169.1	168	736	89	76	12	10	2	2	67	3	116	0	1
Butcher, John, Texas	1	5	.167	4.87	18	13	2	0	3	1	102.1	102	406	53	51	10	2	4	2	34	4	39	9	0
Caldwell, R. Michael, Milwaukee*	17	13	.567	3.91	35	34	12	3	0	0	258	269	1064	119	112	30	10	9	4	58	3	75	0	1
Castillo, Robert, Minnesota	13	11	.542	3.66	40	25	6	1	6	0	218.2	194	903	96	89	26	8	2	2	85	7	123	2	0
Castro, William, Kansas City	3	2	.600	3.45	21	0	0	0	7	0	75.2	72	322	34	29	8	5	2	0	20	4	37	2	0
Caudill, William, Seattle	12	9	.571	2.35	70	0	0	0	64	26	95.2	65	380	25	25	9	5	3	2	35	1	111	2	1
Clancy, James, Toronto	16	14	.533	3.71	40	40	11	3	0	0	266.2	251	1100	122	110	26	5	4	1	77	2	139	6	0
Clark, Bryan, Seattle*	5	2	.714	2.75	37	5	1	1	2	0	114.2	104	491	44	35	6	7	5	2	58	6	70	4	0
Clear, Mark, Boston	14	9	.609	3.00	55	0	0	0	44	14	105	92	467	39	35	11	8	7	1	61	6	109	3	1
Codiroli, Christopher, Oakland	1	2	.333	4.32	37	3	1	0	0	0	16.2	16	70	8	8	2	1	6	0	4	0	23	3	0
Comer, Steven, Texas	1	6	.143	5.10	28	3	0	0	22	6	97	133	441	64	55	11	8	1	2	36	9	17	3	0
Conroy, Timothy, Oakland*	1	1	.500	3.55	6	5	1	0	0	0	25.1	20	110	13	10	1	1	1	0	18	2	5	1	0
Cooper, Donald, Minnesota	0	1	.000	9.53	6	0	0	0	2	0	11.1	14	57	12	12	0	1	0	0	11	0	5	1	0
Corbett, Douglas, Minn-Calif	1	9	.100	5.13	43	1	0	0	23	11	79	73	334	45	45	11	3	0	0	35	6	52	4	2

Pitcher and Club	W.	L.	Pct.	ERA.	G.	GS.	CG.	ShO.	GF.	Sv.	IP.	H.	BFP.	R.	ER.	HR.	SH.	SF.	HB.	Tot. BB.	Int. BB.	SO.	WP.	Bk.
Crawford, Steve, Boston	1	0	1.000	2.00	5		0	0	4	0	9	14	41	3	2	0	0	0	0	3	0	6	0	0
Creel, S. Keith, Kansas City*	1	4	.200	5.40	9	6	0	0	1	0	41.2	43	190	28	25	8	2	0	2	25	0	13	4	0
Curtis, John, California*	0	1	.000	6.00	8		0	0	0	0	12	16	54	8	8	0	1	2	0	3	2	10	2	0
D'Acquisto, John, Oakland	0	1	.000	5.29	11		0	0	6	1	17	20	78	11	10	1	0	0	0	9	0	7	2	1
Darwin, Danny, Texas	10	8	.556	3.44	56	1	0	0	41	7	89	95	394	38	34	6	6	5	2	37	8	61	2	1
Davis, George, Baltimore	8	4	.667	3.49	29	1	0	0	7	0	100.2	96	412	40	39	8	2	6	0	28	8	67	2	1
Davis, Ronald, Minnesota*	3	9	.250	4.42	63		0	0	53	22	106	106	458	53	52	16	1	2	1	47	12	89	5	0
Denman, Brian, Boston	3	4	.429	4.78	9	9	1	0	0	0	49	55	206	32	26	6	2	1	2	9	3	9	1	2
Denny, John, Cleveland	6	11	.353	5.01	21	21	2	1	0	0	138.1	126	609	80	77	11	1	3	1	73	2	94	5	2
Dotson, Richard, Chicago	11	15	.423	3.84	34	31	5	1	0	0	196.2	219	867	97	84	19	7	6	5	73	4	109	5	0
Easterly, James, Milwaukee*	2	2	.500	4.70	28		0	0	11	2	30.2	39	142	19	16	6	0	0	0	15	0	16	2	0
Eckersley, Dennis, Boston	13	13	.500	3.73	33	33	11	3	0	0	224.1	228	926	101	93	31	4	4	1	43	3	127	1	0
Eichhorn, Mark, Toronto	0	3	.000	5.45	7		0	0	0	0	38	40	171	28	23	4	1	2	0	14	1	16	3	3
Erickson, Roger, Minnesota-New York	8	8	.500	4.61	23	18	2	0	1	0	111.1	142	496	65	57	11	10	7	1	29	2	49	3	1
Escarrega, Ernesto, Chicago*	1	3	.250	3.67	38	2	0	0	15	1	73.2	73	300	33	30	3	3	4	0	16	2	33	0	0
Farr, James, Texas*	0	3	.000	2.50	5		0	0	0	0	18	20	80	8	5	0	1	1	0	7	1	6	1	0
Felton, Terry, Minnesota	0	13	.000	4.99	48	6	0	0	20	3	117.1	99	517	71	65	18	3	4	0	76	8	92	2	0
Filson, W. Peter, Minnesota*	5	6	.455	8.76	5		0	0	0	0	12.1	17	63	12	12	2	0	2	1	8	1	10	0	0
Fingers, Roland, Milwaukee	5	6	.455	2.60	50		0	0	45	29	79.2	63	318	23	23	5	4	6	0	20	5	71	0	0
Flanagan, Michael, Baltimore*	15	11	.577	3.97	36	35	11	0	0	0	236	233	991	110	104	24	5	6	2	76	1	103	4	2
Flinn, John, Baltimore	2	1	.667	1.32	5		0	0	3	0	13.2	13	53	3	2	1	0	0	0	3	1	13	9	0
Forsch, Kenneth, California	13	11	.542	3.87	37	35	12	4	0	0	228	225	955	108	98	25	8	6	1	57	5	73	1	2
Frazier, George, New York	4	4	.500	3.47	63		0	0	26	3	111.2	103	466	51	43	7	8	2	5	39	0	69	1	0
Frost, David, Kansas City	6	6	.500	5.51	21	14	0	0	0	0	81.2	103	368	53	50	10	1	4	1	30	2	26	4	0
Garvin, T. Jared, Toronto*	1	1	.500	7.25	32	2	0	0	13	0	58.1	81	274	48	47	6	2	2	2	26	2	35	1	0
Geisel, J. David, Toronto*	1	1	.500	3.98	16		0	0	6	0	31.2	32	142	15	14	3	0	1	0	17	0	22	4	0
Gleaton, Jerry, Seattle*	0	2	.000	13.50	3		0	0	0	0	4.2	7	24	3	7	2	0	0	0	2	0	1	2	0
Glynn, Edward, Cleveland*	5	2	.714	4.17	47		0	0	24	4	49.2	43	219	27	23	6	4	2	0	30	5	54	0	1
Goltz, David, California	8	5	.615	4.08	28	7	1	0	16	3	86	82	365	43	39	4	2	4	2	32	2	49	0	0
Gossage, Richard, New York	4	5	.444	2.23	56		0	0	43	30	93	63	356	23	23	5	2	2	2	28	8	102	7	0
Gott, James, Toronto	5	10	.333	4.43	30	23	0	0	0	0	136	134	600	76	67	15	8	2	2	66	5	82	5	0
Grimsley, Ross, Baltimore*	1	2	.333	5.25	21		0	0	3	0	60	65	257	35	35	7	3	2	2	22	0	18	2	0
Guidry, Ronald, N.Y.*	14	8	.636	3.81	34	33	6	0	0	0	222	216	935	104	94	21	3	6	2	69	5	162	4	1
Gumpert, David, Detroit	0	0	.000	27.00	3		0	0	2	0	2	7	13	6	6	2	1	0	0	2	1	0	2	0
Gura, Lawrence, Kansas City*	18	12	.600	4.03	37	37	8	0	0	0	248	251	1042	124	111	31	4	7	2	64	2	98	8	0
Haas, Bryan, Milwaukee	11	8	.579	4.47	32	27	3	0	0	0	193.1	232	825	101	96	15	5	11	1	39	1	104	2	0
Hanna, Preston, Oakland	2	1	.667	5.59	23		0	0	8	1	48.1	54	228	34	30	5	2	5	3	33	4	32	0	0
Hassler, Andrew, California*	1	2	.333	2.78	54	2	0	0	19	4	71.1	58	302	24	22	3	5	3	0	40	5	38	6	0
Havens, Bradley, Minnesota*	10	14	.417	4.31	33	32	4	2	0	0	208.2	201	893	112	100	32	6	4	1	80	4	129	6	1
Heaton, Neal, Cleveland*	0	2	.000	5.23	8	4	0	0	0	0	31	32	142	21	18	1	0	0	2	16	2	14	0	0
Henke, Thomas, Texas	1	0	1.000	1.15	8		0	0	6	0	15.2	14	67	2	2	0	1	2	0	8	0	9	5	0
Hickey, Kevin, Chicago*	4	4	.500	3.00	60		0	0	20	6	78	73	327	32	26	4	0	4	3	30	6	38	4	1
Honeycutt, Fredrick, Texas*	5	17	.227	3.51	30	26	4	1	0	1	164	201	728	103	96	20	4	8	0	54	4	64	6	0
Hood, Donald, Kansas City*	4	0	1.000	5.27	34	3	0	0	17	0	66.2	71	288	31	26	7	3	3	0	22	3	31	3	1
Hough, Charles, Texas	16	13	.552	3.95	34	34	12	2	0	0	228	217	954	111	100	21	7	2	0	72	5	128	9	0
Howell, Jay, New York	1	3	.250	7.71	6	6	0	0	0	0	28	25	138	24	22	1	1	2	0	18	3	21	1	0
Hoyt, D. LaMarr, Chicago	19	15	.559	3.53	39	32	14	0	0	0	239.2	248	995	104	94	17	6	7	2	48	0	124	4	0
Hurst, Bruce, Boston*	3	7	.300	5.77	28	19	0	0	4	0	117	161	535	87	75	16	4	1	2	40	3	53	0	0
Jackson, Darrell, Minnesota*	0	5	.000	6.25	13	7	0	0	0	0	44.2	51	202	33	31	6	2	1	0	24	3	16	3	1
Jackson, Grant, Kansas City*	3	1	.750	5.17	20		0	0	10	0	38.1	42	180	27	22	7	1	1	2	21	4	15	2	1

Pitcher and Club	W.	L.	Pct.	ERA.	G.	GS.	CG.	ShO.	GF.	Sv.	IP.	H.	BFP.	R.	ER.	HR.	SH.	SF.	HB.	Tot. BB.	Int. BB.	SO.	WP.	Bk.
Jackson, Roy, Toronto	8	8	.500	3.06	48	2	0	0	24	6	97	77	394	37	33	7	3	4	0	31	4	71	1	0
James, Robert, Detroit	0	2	.000	5.03	12	1	0	0	2	0	19.2	22		13	11	4	0	0	3	8	1	20	4	0
John, Thomas, New York-California*	14	12	.538	3.69	37	33	10	2	2	0	221.2	239	918	102	91	15	8	7	0	39	0	68	7	2
Jones, Douglas, Milwaukee*	0	1	.000	10.13	4	0	0	0	2	0	2.2	5	14	5	3	1	1	0	3	1	1	1	0	
Jones, Jeffrey, Oakland	3	1	.750	5.11	18	2	0	0	7	0	37	44	177	29	21	6	0	0	0	26	1	18	3	0
Kaufman, Curt, New York	1	0	1.000	5.19	7	0	0	0	5	0	8.2	4	40	5	5	1	0	0	5	6	1	1	0	0
Keough, Matthew, Oakland	11	18	.379	5.72	34	34	10	2	0	3	209.1	233	946	144	133	38	10	9	3	101	1	75	10	3
Kern, James, Chicago	2	1	.667	5.14	13	1	0	0	7	0	28	20	112	16	16	3	1	1	7	12	0	23	2	0
Kingman, Brian, Oakland	4	12	.250	4.48	23	20	3	0	1	1	122.2	131	548	64	61	11	1	7	0	57	0	46	2	2
Kinney, Dennis, Oakland*	0	5	.000	8.31	16	0	0	0	11	1	4.1	9	24	9	4	1	1	0	5	4	0	0	0	0
Kison, Bruce, California	10	5	.667	3.17	33	16	3	0	12	3	142	120	582	54	50	15	5	5	0	44	3	86	5	0
Koosman, Jerry, Chicago*	11	7	.611	3.84	42	19	3	1	11	0	173.1	194	726	81	74	5	5	6	2	38	3	88	4	2
Ladd, Peter, Milwaukee	1	3	.250	4.00	16	0	0	0	11	5	18	16	75	16	8	5	1	0	0	6	3	12	1	0
Lamp, Dennis, Chicago	11	8	.579	3.99	44	27	3	2	0	0	189.2	206	817	96	84	9	12	2	6	59	1	78	5	0
Langford, J. Rick, Oakland	11	16	.407	4.21	32	31	15	1	0	0	237.1	265	1006	121	111	33	6	5	2	49	2	79	4	1
LaRoche, David, New York*	4	2	.667	3.42	25	0	0	0	15	0	50	54	212	19	19	4	1	1	1	11	1	31	0	0
Leal, Luis, Toronto	12	15	.444	3.93	38	38	10	0	0	0	249.2	250	1055	113	109	24	9	3	3	79	3	111	5	1
Leonard, Dennis, Kansas City	10	6	.625	5.10	21	21	2	0	0	0	130.2	145	579	82	74	20	6	0	2	46	3	58	4	0
Lerch, Randy, Milwaukee*	8	7	.533	4.97	21	20	1	0	0	0	108.2	123	493	68	60	8	3	5	6	51	1	33	2	0
Lewallyn, Dennis, Cleveland	0	0	.000	6.97	4	0	0	0	15	0	10.1	13	45	8	8	3	0	0	0	3	0	3	0	0
Lewis, James, New York	0	0	.000	54.00	1	0	0	0	0	0	0.2	3	9	7	4	0	0	0	0	0	0	0	1	0
Little, D. Jeffery, Minnesota*	2	0	1.000	4.01	33	0	0	0	15	0	36.1	33	165	20	17	6	2	0	0	27	3	26	6	1
Lopez, Aurelio, Detroit	3	1	.750	5.27	19	0	0	0	9	0	41	41	176	27	24	8	0	2	3	19	0	26	4	0
Lyle, Albert, Chicago*	0	0	.000	3.00	6	0	0	0	6	0	12	11	50	4	4	0	1	0	0	7	0	6	1	1
Mahler, Michael, California*	2	8	.200	1.13	1	0	0	0	0	0	8	9	37	4	1	0	0	0	0	6	0	5	0	0
Martinez, Felix, Baltimore*	8	2	.800	3.41	76	0	0	0	44	16	95	81	389	39	36	6	7	1	6	37	5	78	4	3
Martinez, J. Dennis, Baltimore	16	12	.571	4.21	40	39	10	2	0	0	252	262	1093	123	118	30	11	7	7	87	2	111	7	1
Mason, Michael, Texas*	1	4	.200	5.09	13	4	1	0	0	1	23	21	96	13	13	3	1	1	0	9	1	8	2	1
Matlack, Jonathon, Texas*	7	7	.500	3.53	33	23	4	0	0	1	147.2	158	622	64	58	14	5	5	3	37	4	78	2	0
May, Rudolph, New York*	6	3	.667	2.89	41	8	1	0	11	0	106	109	438	43	34	4	9	4	0	14	5	85	2	1
McCatty, Steven, Oakland	6	3	.632	3.99	21	6	4	0	22	1	128.2	124	570	62	57	16	4	4	4	70	4	66	5	0
McClure, Robert, Milwaukee*	12	7	.632	4.22	34	20	5	0	0	0	172.2	160	734	90	81	21	6	4	4	74	4	99	5	0
McGlothen, Lynn, New York	0	2	.000	10.80	4	0	0	0	1	0	5	3	26	6	6	1	0	0	0	2	0	2	0	0
McGregor, Scott, Baltimore*	14	12	.538	4.61	37	37	17	7	0	0	226.1	238	957	126	116	31	5	5	2	52	6	84	3	5
McLaughlin, Joey, Toronto	8	6	.571	3.21	44	0	0	0	34	8	70	54	290	27	25	7	3	6	1	30	3	49	2	0
McLaughlin, Michael, Oakland	0	2	.000	4.84	21	2	0	0	6	0	48.1	51	223	31	26	3	3	0	0	27	3	27	2	0
Medich, George, Texas-Milwaukee	12	15	.444	5.04	31	31	7	0	0	0	185.2	203	828	110	104	12	7	11	3	93	6	73	8	1
Mirabella, Paul, Texas*	7	14	.333	4.80	40	27	6	1	19	3	50.2	46	217	28	27	4	8	2	2	22	0	29	6	0
Moore, Michael, Seattle	7	14	.300	5.36	28	27	0	0	0	0	144.1	159	651	91	86	21	4	4	1	79	5	73	6	0
Moreno, Angel, California*	3	11	.389	4.74	13	8	2	1	2	0	49.1	55	218	31	26	7	1	2	2	23	1	22	1	1
Morgan, Michael, New York	7	11	.515	4.37	30	23	2	0	2	0	150.1	167	661	77	73	15	2	4	1	67	7	71	6	0
Morris, John, Detroit	17	16	.515	4.06	37	37	17	3	0	0	266.1	247	1107	131	120	37	4	5	2	96	5	135	10	1
Murray, Dale, Toronto	8	7	.533	3.16	56	0	0	0	33	11	111	115	470	48	39	3	5	1	1	32	7	60	4	2
Musselman, R. Ronald, Seattle	1	0	1.000	3.45	12	0	0	0	8	0	15.2	18	69	6	6	3	0	1	1	6	2	9	0	1
Nelson, W. Eugene, Seattle	6	11	.400	4.62	22	19	2	0	0	0	122.2	133	545	70	63	16	6	2	2	60	6	71	4	1
Norris, Michael, Oakland	7	11	.389	4.76	28	28	7	1	0	0	166.1	154	735	103	88	25	3	3	6	84	1	83	7	3
Nunez, Edwin, Seattle	1	2	.333	4.58	8	5	0	0	0	0	35.1	36	153	18	18	13	0	0	0	16	0	27	0	2
O'Connor, Jack, Minnesota*	8	3	.471	4.29	23	19	6	1	3	0	126	122	543	63	60	13	4	2	2	57	4	56	4	1
Ojeda, Robert, Boston*	4	6	.400	5.63	22	14	0	0	6	0	78.1	95	352	53	49	13	2	1	1	29	5	52	7	1
Owchinko, Robert, Oakland*	2	4	.333	5.21	54	0	0	0	23	3	102	111	463	60	59	11	5	0	0	52	5	67	4	1

Pitcher and Club	W.	L.	Pct.	ERA.	G.	GS.	CG.	ShO.	GF.	Sv.	IP.	H.	BFP.	R.	ER.	HR.	SH.	SF.	HB.	Tot. BB.	Int. BB.	SO.	WP.	Bk.
Pacella, John, N. York-Minn.	1	3	.250	7.30	24	2	0	0	7	2	61.2	74	295	56	50	14	0	6	3	46	1	22	4	0
Palmer, James, Baltimore	15	5	.750	3.13	36	32	8	2	1	2	227	195	920	85	79	22	5	2	4	63	4	103	2	1
Pashnick, Larry, Detroit	4	4	.500	4.01	28	13	1	0	6	0	94.1	110	403	46	42	17	5	4	1	25	1	19	4	1
Perry, Gaylord, Seattle	10	12	.455	4.40	32	32	8	1	0	0	216.2	245	923	117	106	27	7	8	2	54	4	116	3	0
Petry, Daniel, Detroit	15	9	.625	3.22	35	35	8	0	0	0	246	220	1031	98	88	15	8	8	4	100	5	132	13	0
Porter, Charles, Milwaukee	0	0	.000	4.91	3	0	0	0	1	0	3.2	3	13	2	2	0	0	0	0	1	0	3	0	0
Quisenberry, Daniel, Kansas City	9	7	.563	2.57	72	0	0	0	68	35	136.2	126	529	43	39	9	10	7	2	12	2	46	2	0
Rainey, Charles, Boston	7	5	.583	5.02	27	25	3	0	0	0	129	146	573	75	72	12	7	5	5	63	5	57	7	0
Rawley, Shane, New York*	11	10	.524	4.06	47	17	3	0	15	3	164	165	699	79	74	14	16	9	2	54	5	111	2	0
Redfern, Peter, Minnesota	5	11	.313	6.58	27	13	2	0	5	0	94.1	122	438	74	69	10	4	3	1	51	3	40	4	1
Reed, Jerry, Cleveland	1	1	.500	3.45	6	1	0	0	1	0	15.2	15	63	6	6	1	0	0	0	1	0	10	0	0
Renko, Steven, California	11	6	.647	4.44	31	23	4	0	4	1	156	163	665	78	77	17	3	5	2	51	4	81	3	0
Righetti, David, New York*	11	10	.524	3.79	33	27	4	0	0	0	183	155	804	88	77	11	8	8	1	108	4	163	9	0
Rothschild, Lawrence, Detroit	0	0	.000	13.50	2	0	0	0	0	0	2.2	4	14	4	4	1	0	0	0	2	0	0	0	0
Rozema, David, Detroit	3	0	1.000	1.63	8	2	0	0	3	1	27.2	17	107	5	5	2	2	0	1	7	1	15	0	0
Rucker, David, Detroit*	5	4	.555	3.38	27	0	0	0	8	0	64	62	274	26	24	4	2	2	2	23	3	31	1	0
Sanchez, Luis, California	7	4	.636	3.21	46	0	0	0	25	5	92.2	89	388	36	33	3	7	7	2	34	4	58	1	0
Saucier, Kevin, Detroit*	3	1	.750	3.12	31	1	0	0	14	5	40.1	35	173	15	14	1	0	0	0	29	4	23	3	0
Schmidt, David, Texas	4	6	.400	3.20	33	8	0	0	14	5	109.2	118	462	45	39	5	4	9	3	25	5	69	2	0
Schrom, Kenneth, Toronto	1	0	1.000	5.87	6	0	0	0	1	0	15.1	23	71	11	10	3	6	3	1	15	3	8	1	0
Senteney, Steve, Toronto	0	0	.000	4.91	11	1	0	0	3	1	22	29	100	16	12	1	0	0	0	6	1	20	1	0
Siwy, James, Chicago	0	0	.000	10.29	2	0	0	0	0	0	7	10	32	8	8	1	0	1	0	5	0	3	0	0
Slaton, James, Milwaukee	10	6	.625	3.29	39	7	3	0	21	0	117.2	117	494	48	43	14	6	2	3	41	3	59	2	0
Smithson, B. Mike, Texas	3	4	.429	5.01	8	8	3	1	0	0	46.2	51	199	26	26	5	1	2	2	13	0	24	1	0
Solomon, Eddie, Chicago	1	0	1.000	3.68	8	0	0	0	4	0	7.1	7	31	7	3	1	0	0	0	2	0	2	0	3
Sorensen, Lary, Cleveland	10	15	.400	5.61	32	30	6	0	0	0	189.1	251	849	130	118	19	3	9	3	55	6	62	2	0
Sosa, Elias, Detroit	3	3	.500	4.43	38	0	0	0	27	4	61	64	260	31	30	5	8	7	0	18	8	24	1	0
Spillner, Daniel, Cleveland	12	10	.545	2.49	65	0	0	1	54	21	133.2	117	557	44	37	9	3	0	1	45	7	90	0	3
Splittorff, Paul, Kansas City*	10	10	.500	4.28	29	28	0	0	0	0	162	166	692	83	77	14	3	5	0	57	1	74	5	0
Stanhouse, Donald, Baltimore	0	0	.000	5.40	17	0	0	0	33	0	26.2	29	125	16	16	3	4	0	1	15	0	8	5	0
Stanley, Robert, Boston	12	7	.632	3.10	48	1	0	0	18	14	168.1	161	694	60	58	11	10	4	3	50	6	83	5	0
Stanton, Michael, Seattle	2	4	.333	4.16	56	1	0	0	18	7	71.1	70	302	37	33	5	2	4	1	21	0	49	5	0
Steirer, Ricky, California	1	1	.500	3.76	10	2	0	0	2	0	26.1	25	117	14	11	2	5	2	0	11	3	14	1	0
Stewart, Samuel, Baltimore	10	9	.526	4.14	38	0	1	1	16	5	139	140	607	68	64	9	10	6	2	62	4	69	0	1
Stieb, David, Toronto	17	14	.548	3.25	38	38	19	5	0	0	288.1	271	1187	116	104	27	7	3	6	75	8	141	2	1
Stoddard, Robert, Seattle	3	3	.500	2.41	9	9	2	1	0	0	67.1	48	259	22	18	7	0	3	1	18	0	24	0	0
Stoddard, Timothy, Baltimore	3	4	.429	4.02	50	0	0	0	38	12	56	53	249	26	25	4	7	1	1	29	6	42	3	0
Sutcliffe, Richard, Cleveland	14	8	.636	2.96	34	27	6	1	3	0	216	174	887	81	71	16	1	3	3	98	2	142	3	1
Sutton, Donald, Milwaukee	4	1	.800	3.29	7	7	2	0	0	0	56	55	228	21	20	8	3	7	1	18	0	36	2	0
Tanana, Frank, Texas*	7	18	.280	4.21	30	30	7	0	0	0	194.1	199	832	102	91	16	13	8	0	55	10	87	6	0
Tiant, Luis, California	2	2	.500	5.76	6	5	0	0	0	0	29.2	39	135	20	19	3	1	4	0	8	0	30	0	1
Tobik, David, Detroit	4	9	.308	3.56	51	1	0	0	31	9	98.2	86	406	45	39	8	8	7	6	38	8	63	2	0
Torrez, Michael, Boston	9	9	.500	5.23	31	31	6	0	0	0	175.2	196	782	107	102	20	5	3	2	74	1	84	4	1
Trout, Steven, Chicago*	6	9	.400	4.26	25	19	5	0	3	0	120.1	130	537	76	57	9	5	5	6	50	3	62	3	1
Tudor, John, Boston*	13	10	.565	3.63	32	30	7	1	0	0	195.2	215	847	90	79	20	8	3	0	59	0	146	3	0
Tufts, Robert, Kansas City*	2	0	1.000	4.50	10	0	0	0	6	1	20	24	86	10	10	0	0	8	0	3	0	13	0	0
Ujdur, Gerald, Detroit	10	10	.500	3.69	25	25	2	0	0	0	178	150	732	76	73	29	2	5	3	69	4	86	5	1
Underwood, Patrick, Detroit*	4	8	.333	4.73	33	12	2	0	6	0	99	108	428	66	52	17	6	2	6	22	2	43	6	0
Underwood, Thomas, Oakland*	10	6	.625	3.29	56	0	0	0	20	7	153	136	651	66	56	11	12	2	1	68	4	79	5	2
Vande Berg, Edward, Seattle*	9	4	.692	2.37	78	0	0	0	27	5	76	54	303	21	20	5	6	2	2	32	7	60	3	2

Pitcher and Club	W.	L.	Pct.	ERA.	G.	GS.	CG.	ShO.	GF.	Sv.	IP.	H.	BFP.	R.	ER.	HR.	SH.	SF.	HB.	Tot. BB.	Int. BB.	SO.	WP.	Bk.
Viola, Frank, Minnesota*	4	10	.286	5.21	22	22	3	1	0	0	126	152	543	77	73	22	2	0	4	38	2	84	4	1
Vuckovich, Peter, Milwaukee	18	6	.750	3.34	30	30	9	1	0	0	223.2	234	971	96	83	14	9	4	5	102	1	105	6	0
Waits, M. Richard, Cleveland*	2	13	.133	5.40	25	21	2	0	0	0	115	128	510	74	69	13	7	3	1	57	3	44	4	0
Welchel, Donald, Baltimore	1	0	1.000	8.31	4	1	0	0	0	0	4.1	22	18	6	4	1	0	1	0	7	0	3	0	0
Wever, Stefan, New York	0	1	.000	27.00	1	1	0	0	0	0	2.2	6	18	9	8	1	0	0	0	3	0	2	3	0
Whitson, Eddie, Cleveland	4	2	.667	3.26	40	6	1	1	18	2	107.2	91	467	43	39	6	7	8	1	58	3	61	4	0
Wihtol, Alexander, Cleveland	0	0	.000	4.63	6	0	0	0	4	0	11.2	9	50	6	6	1	0	1	1	7	0	8	0	1
Wilcox, Milton, Detroit	12	10	.545	3.62	29	29	9	3	0	0	193.2	187	833	91	78	18	0	5	7	85	5	112	5	1
Williams, Alberto, Minnesota	9	7	.563	4.22	26	26	5	1	0	0	153.2	166	666	74	72	18	7	7	7	55	5	61	6	2
Witt, Michael, California	8	6	.571	3.51	33	26	3	0	2	0	179.2	177	748	77	70	8	8	5	0	47	2	85	8	1
Wright, James, Kansas City	0	0	.000	5.32	7	0	0	0	3	0	23.2	32	108	18	14	3	2	0	0	6	0	9	0	1
Zahn, Geoffrey, California*	18	8	.692	3.73	34	34	12	4	0	0	229.1	225	944	100	95	18	4	3	0	65	5	81	2	0

NOTE—Following pitchers combined to pitch shutout games: Baltimore (1)—Flanagan, Stoddard and F. Martinez; Boston (3)—Torrez and Clear, Torrez and Stanley, Tudor, Stanley and Clear; Chicago (3)—Burns and Barojas, Koosman and Barojas, Trout, Barojas, Hickey and Lamp; Cleveland (5)—Barker and Spillner, Brennan and Spillner, Denny and Anderson, Sutcliffe and Glynn, Sutcliffe and Whitson; Kansas City (7)—Leonard and Quisenberry 2, Botelho and Armstrong, Gura and Quisenberry, Hood and Quisenberry, Splittorff, Hood and Quisenberry, Splittorff and Quisenberry; Minnesota (3)—Havens, and Felton, O'Connor and Davis, Williams and Davis; New York (5)—Righetti and Gossage 2, Guidry and May, John and Gossage, Righetti and LaRoche; Oakland (1)—Underwood and Beard; Seattle (3)—Beattie and Stanton, Beattie, Vande Berg and Caudill, Stoddard and Caudill; Texas (2)—Matlack, Darwin and Mirabella, Medich and Darwin; Toronto (4)—Gott and Jackson 2, Clancy and McLaughlin, Leal and Jackson.

PITCHERS WITH TWO OR MORE CLUBS

(Alphabetically Arranged With Pitcher's First Club on Top)

Pitcher and Club	W.	L.	Pct.	ERA.	G.	GS.	CG.	ShO.	GF.	Sv.	IP.	H.	BFP.	R.	ER.	HR.	SH.	SF.	HB.	Tot. BB.	Int. BB.	SO.	WP.	Bk.
Arroyo, Minnesota	0	1	.000	5.27	6	0	0	0	2	0	13.2	17	61	8	8	2	1	1	0	6	1	4	1	0
Arroyo, Oakland	0	0	.000	5.24	10	0	0	0	6	0	22.1	23	94	14	13	4	0	1	1	7	0	9	3	0
Corbett, Minnesota	0	2	.000	5.32	10	0	0	0	5	3	22	27	100	13	13	3	1	0	0	10	5	15	2	1
Corbett, California	1	7	.125	5.05	33	0	0	0	18	8	57	46	234	32	32	8	3	0	0	25	5	37	2	1
Erickson, Minnesota	4	3	.571	4.87	7	7	2	0	0	0	40.2	56	188	29	22	6	1	2	0	12	1	12	2	0
Erickson, New York	4	5	.444	4.46	16	11	0	1	1	1	70.2	86	308	36	35	5	7	5	1	17	1	37	5	1
John, New York	10	10	.500	3.66	30	26	9	2	0	0	186.2	190	766	84	76	11	7	7	3	34	3	54	5	2
John, California	4	2	.667	3.86	7	7	1	0	1	0	35	49	152	18	15	4	4	1	0	5	0	14	2	0
Medich, Texas	7	11	.389	5.06	21	21	2	0	0	0	122.2	146	557	73	69	8	9	9	3	61	5	37	4	1
Medich, Milwaukee	5	4	.556	5.00	10	10	1	0	0	0	63	57	271	37	35	4	0	2	1	32	1	36	4	0
Pacella, New York	0	1	.000	7.20	3	1	0	0	0	0	10	13	51	8	8	0	3	0	0	9	1	2	2	0
Pacella, Minnesota	1	2	.333	7.32	21	1	0	0	7	2	51.2	61	244	48	42	14	0	3	0	37	0	20	2	0

1982 A.L. Pitching Against Each Club

BALTIMORE—94-68

Pitcher	Bos. W-L	Cal. W-L	Chi. W-L	Clev. W-L	Det. W-L	K.C. W-L	Mil. W-L	Min. W-L	N.Y. W-L	Oak. W-L	Sea. W-L	Tex. W-L	Tor. W-L	Totals W-L
Boddicker...	0-0	0-0	0-0	0-0	0-0	0-0	0-0	0-0	1-0	0-0	0-0	0-0	0-0	1-0
Davis.........	0-1	0-0	0-0	0-0	1-1	0-1	1-0	1-0	1-1	1-0	1-0	0-0	2-0	8-4
Flanagan....	1-3	0-1	1-0	2-1	1-1	0-1	1-2	3-0	1-0	0-1	1-1	1-0	3-0	15-11
Flinn..........	0-0	0-0	0-0	0-0	1-0	0-0	0-0	0-0	1-0	0-0	0-0	0-0	0-0	2-0
Grimsley.....	0-1	1-0	0-0	0-0	0-0	0-0	0-0	0-0	0-0	0-1	0-0	0-0	0-0	1-2
D. Martinez	2-1	1-2	1-2	1-3	1-0	0-1	2-0	0-0	1-0	1-1	1-1	2-1	3-0	16-12
T. Martinez	0-0	0-1	1-2	0-1	0-1	1-1	0-1	0-0	2-0	1-1	1-0	1-0	0-0	8-8
McGregor...	0-3	3-1	1-2	1-1	0-1	0-1	2-0	1-2	1-0	3-0	1-1	0-0	1-0	14-12
Palmer........	0-0	1-0	0-1	1-0	2-0	1-0	2-1	1-1	2-1	1-0	0-0	3-0	1-1	15-5
Stanhouse...	0-0	0-0	0-0	0-0	0-0	0-1	0-0	0-0	0-0	0-0	0-0	0-0	0-0	0-1
Stewart	0-0	1-0	1-0	1-1	1-2	1-2	1-0	1-0	0-0	0-0	2-1	1-2	0-0	10-9
Stoddard....	0-0	0-0	0-0	0-0	0-0	1-0	0-0	1-1	0-0	0-1	0-1	1-0	0-1	3-4
Welchel	0-0	0-0	0-0	0-0	0-0	0-0	0-0	0-0	1-0	0-0	0-0	0-0	0-0	1-0
Totals	4-9	7-5	5-7	6-7	7-6	4-8	9-4	8-4	11-2	7-5	7-5	9-3	10-3	94-68

BOSTON—89-73

Pitcher	Balt. W-L	Cal. W-L	Chi. W-L	Clev. W-L	Det. W-L	K.C. W-L	Mil. W-L	Min. W-L	N.Y. W-L	Oak. W-L	Sea. W-L	Tex. W-L	Tor. W-L	Totals W-L
Aponte	0-0	0-0	1-0	0-2	0-0	0-0	0-0	0-0	0-0	0-0	0-0	0-0	1-0	2-2
Boyd..........	0-0	0-0	0-0	0-1	0-0	0-0	0-0	0-0	0-0	0-0	0-0	0-0	0-0	0-1
Brown.........	0-0	0-0	0-0	0-0	0-0	0-0	0-0	0-0	1-0	0-0	0-0	0-0	0-0	1-0
Burgmeier...	1-0	0-0	1-0	1-0	0-0	1-0	0-0	1-0	0-0	1-0	1-0	0-0	0-0	7-0
Clear..........	1-1	2-1	0-0	0-1	1-0	1-0	1-2	0-1	1-1	1-1	3-0	2-0	1-1	14-9
Crawford....	0-0	0-0	0-0	0-0	0-0	0-0	0-0	0-0	1-0	0-0	0-0	0-0	0-0	1-0
Denman......	0-0	0-1	0-0	0-0	0-1	0-0	0-1	0-0	1-1	2-0	0-0	0-0	0-0	3-4
Eckersley...	2-0	1-0	0-1	0-2	2-1	1-0	2-0	1-1	0-2	1-1	1-1	1-2	1-2	13-13
Hurst	0-0	0-0	0-2	0-0	0-1	0-0	0-1	2-1	1-0	0-2	0-0	0-0	0-0	3-7
Ojeda.........	1-1	1-1	0-1	0-0	0-0	0-2	0-0	0-1	0-0	1-0	0-0	0-0	1-0	4-6
Rainey	0-1	0-0	2-0	1-0	0-0	0-1	0-2	1-0	0-0	1-1	0-0	2-0	0-0	7-5
Stanley.......	1-1	1-0	0-1	1-0	2-1	2-0	1-1	0-0	1-1	0-1	0-0	2-0	0-1	12-7
Torrez........	0-0	0-1	0-2	2-0	1-1	1-0	0-2	1-1	0-0	0-0	0-1	3-0	1-1	9-9
Tudor	3-0	2-1	0-1	1-1	2-0	0-3	0-0	0-0	1-2	0-0	2-1	0-0	2-1	13-10
Totals	9-4	7-5	4-8	6-7	8-5	6-6	4-9	6-6	7-6	8-4	7-5	10-2	7-6	89-73

CALIFORNIA—93-69

Pitcher	Balt. W-L	Bos. W-L	Chi. W-L	Clev. W-L	Det. W-L	K.C. W-L	Mil. W-L	Min. W-L	N.Y. W-L	Oak. W-L	Sea. W-L	Tex. W-L	Tor. W-L	Totals W-L
Aase..........	1-1	0-0	0-0	1-0	0-0	0-0	0-0	1-0	0-0	0-1	0-0	0-1	0-0	3-3
Bahnsen.....	0-1	0-0	0-0	0-0	0-0	0-0	0-0	0-0	0-0	0-0	0-0	0-0	0-0	0-1
Corbett	0-1	0-1	0-0	0-2	0-2	0-0	0-1	0-0	0-0	0-0	0-0	0-0	0-1	1-7
Curtis.........	0-0	0-0	0-1	0-0	0-0	0-0	0-0	0-0	0-0	0-0	0-0	0-0	0-0	0-1
Forsch........	0-1	1-1	0-1	2-0	1-3	2-0	0-1	1-2	1-2	1-0	1-0	1-1	1-0	13-11
Goltz..........	1-0	0-0	0-1	2-0	0-0	1-2	0-0	1-0	0-0	1-1	0-1	2-0	0-0	8-5
Hassler	0-1	0-0	0-0	1-0	0-0	0-0	0-0	0-0	1-0	0-0	0-0	0-0	0-0	2-1
John..........	0-0	0-0	0-1	0-0	0-0	2-0	1-0	0-0	0-0	0-0	0-0	1-1	0-0	4-2
Kison	1-0	2-2	2-0	1-0	0-0	0-0	1-1	0-0	0-1	0-0	0-0	1-1	2-0	10-5
Mahler........	0-0	0-0	0-0	0-0	0-0	0-0	0-0	0-0	1-0	0-0	0-0	1-0	0-0	2-0
Moreno.......	0-2	0-0	1-0	0-0	0-1	0-1	0-0	0-1	1-1	0-0	1-1	0-0	0-0	3-7
Renko.........	2-0	0-1	1-0	0-0	1-0	0-1	1-1	1-1	0-0	0-1	3-1	1-0	1-0	11-6
Sanchez......	0-0	0-0	1-0	0-0	1-0	0-1	1-0	0-1	0-0	1-1	2-0	0-0	1-1	7-4
Steirer	0-0	1-0	0-0	0-0	0-0	0-0	0-0	0-0	0-0	0-0	0-0	0-0	0-0	1-0
Tiant	0-0	1-0	0-0	0-0	0-0	0-0	0-1	1-1	0-0	0-0	0-0	0-0	0-0	2-2
Witt...........	0-0	0-1	1-0	1-1	0-1	0-0	1-0	0-0	0-0	3-0	2-0	0-2	0-1	8-6
Zahn..........	0-0	0-1	1-2	0-1	2-0	2-1	0-2	2-0	3-1	3-0	1-0	2-0	2-0	18-8
Totals	5-7	5-7	8-5	8-4	5-7	7-6	6-6	7-6	7-5	9-4	10-3	8-5	8-4	93-69

CHICAGO—87-75

Pitcher	Balt. W-L	Bos. W-L	Cal. W-L	Clev. W-L	Det. W-L	K.C. W-L	Mil. W-L	Min. W-L	N.Y. W-L	Oak. W-L	Sea. W-L	Tex. W-L	Tor. W-L	Totals W-L
Barnes........	0-0	0-0	0-0	0-0	0-0	0-0	0-1	0-0	0-0	0-0	0-0	0-0	0-1	0-2
Barojas.......	0-0	0-0	1-0	0-0	1-0	0-2	0-1	1-1	0-0	2-1	0-0	1-1	0-0	6-6
Brusstar.....	0-0	0-0	0-0	0-0	0-0	0-0	0-0	1-0	0-0	0-0	0-0	1-0	0-0	2-0
Burns.........	2-0	1-0	0-0	1-0	0-0	1-2	0-2	0-1	2-0	0-0	1-0	1-0	4-0	13-5
Dotson........	1-1	2-1	2-1	2-0	1-1	0-2	0-0	0-3	1-1	0-1	0-2	2-0	0-1	11-15
Escarrega ..	0-0	0-1	0-0	0-1	0-0	0-1	0-0	0-0	0-0	0-0	0-0	0-0	1-0	1-3
Hickey........	1-2	0-1	0-1	1-0	0-0	0-0	0-0	0-0	1-0	1-0	0-1	0-0	0-0	4-4
Hoyt..........	3-0	1-0	1-1	0-2	3-1	1-2	2-2	2-1	1-1	2-2	1-2	1-1	1-0	19-15
Kern..........	0-0	0-0	0-1	0-0	0-0	0-0	0-0	0-0	0-0	1-0	1-0	0-0	0-0	2-1
Koosman.....	0-1	2-0	1-0	1-1	1-1	1-1	0-1	0-0	1-0	2-0	2-1	0-1	0-0	11-7
Lamp.........	0-0	1-1	0-3	0-1	3-0	0-0	0-1	2-0	1-0	1-0	1-1	1-1	1-1	11-8
Solomon	0-0	0-0	0-0	0-0	0-0	0-0	0-0	1-0	0-0	0-0	0-0	0-0	0-0	1-0
Trout.........	0-1	1-1	0-1	1-1	0-0	0-0	1-0	0-0	1-2	1-0	0-1	0-1	1-1	6-9
Totals	7-5	8-4	5-8	6-6	9-3	3-10	3-9	7-6	8-4	9-4	6-7	8-5	8-4	87-75

No Decisions: Agosto, Lyle, Siwy.

CLEVELAND—78-84

Pitcher	Balt. W-L	Bos. W-L	Cal. W-L	Chi. W-L	Det. W-L	K.C. W-L	Mil. W-L	Min. W-L	N.Y. W-L	Oak. W-L	Sea. W-L	Tex. W-L	Tor. W-L	Totals W-L
Anderson....	1-1	0-0	0-0	0-0	0-2	0-0	0-1	0-0	0-0	0-0	0-0	1-0	1-0	3-4
Barker.......	1-0	1-0	0-0	1-2	3-1	0-1	0-1	2-0	0-1	1-1	2-1	3-1	1-2	15-11
Blyleven.....	0-0	0-0	0-0	0-0	0-0	0-1	1-0	0-0	0-0	0-1	0-0	1-0	0-0	2-2
Brennan......	0-0	1-0	0-1	0-0	2-0	0-1	0-0	0-0	0-0	0-0	0-0	0-0	1-0	4-2
Denny	1-1	1-1	0-2	1-1	0-0	1-1	1-0	0-0	0-1	0-3	1-0	0-0	0-1	6-11
Glynn..........	0-1	0-0	2-0	0-0	0-0	0-0	1-1	1-0	0-0	0-0	0-0	0-0	1-0	5-2
Heaton	0-0	0-1	0-0	0-0	0-1	0-0	0-0	0-0	0-0	0-0	0-0	0-0	0-0	0-2
Lewallyn.....	0-0	0-0	0-0	0-0	0-0	0-0	0-1	0-0	0-0	0-0	0-0	0-0	0-0	0-1
Reed..........	0-0	0-0	0-0	0-0	0-1	0-0	0-0	0-0	1-0	0-0	0-0	0-0	0-0	1-1
Sorensen....	1-1	0-3	1-2	0-1	0-0	0-2	1-0	2-2	1-2	1-0	2-0	1-0	0-2	10-15
Spillner	0-1	2-0	0-2	2-1	0-0	0-0	2-0	1-1	1-2	1-0	1-1	0-2	2-0	12-10
Sutcliffe.....	3-0	0-1	0-0	1-0	1-2	1-0	0-1	2-1	1-1	1-1	2-1	1-0	1-0	14-8
Waits..........	0-1	0-0	1-1	1-1	0-0	0-3	0-1	0-0	0-1	0-2	1-0	0-2	0-1	2-13
Whitson......	0-0	2-0	0-0	0-0	0-0	0-1	1-0	0-0	0-1	0-0	1-0	0-0	0-0	4-2
Totals	7-6	7-6	4-8	6-6	6-7	2-10	7-6	8-4	4-9	4-8	9-3	7-5	7-6	78-84

No Decisions: Bohnet, Gumpert, Wihtol.

DETROIT—83-79

Pitcher	Balt. W-L	Bos. W-L	Cal. W-L	Chi. W-L	Clev. W-L	K.C. W-L	Mil. W-L	Min. W-L	N.Y. W-L	Oak. W-L	Sea. W-L	Tex. W-L	Tor. W-L	Totals W-L
James.........	0-0	0-0	0-0	0-0	0-0	0-0	0-0	0-0	0-1	0-0	0-0	0-0	0-1	0-2
Lopez.........	0-0	0-0	2-0	0-0	0-0	0-0	1-1	0-0	0-0	0-0	0-0	0-0	0-0	3-1
Morris........	0-2	1-1	1-2	0-2	2-1	0-1	0-2	4-0	2-1	2-0	1-3	1-1	3-0	17-16
Pashnick.....	0-0	0-0	0-0	0-2	1-0	0-0	0-0	0-0	1-0	0-0	1-0	1-1	0-1	4-4
Petry.........	1-1	2-1	1-1	2-1	0-1	1-2	0-1	1-1	2-0	2-0	2-0	1-0	0-0	15-9
Rozema	0-0	0-0	0-0	0-0	0-0	1-0	0-0	1-0	0-0	0-0	0-0	1-0	0-0	3-0
Rucker.......	2-0	0-1	0-1	0-0	1-0	0-0	0-1	0-0	0-1	0-0	0-0	1-0	1-2	5-6
Saucier.......	0-0	0-0	0-0	1-0	0-0	1-0	0-0	0-0	0-0	0-0	0-0	1-1	0-1	3-1
Sosa	0-0	0-0	1-0	0-1	0-0	0-0	0-0	1-0	0-0	0-1	0-1	1-0	0-0	3-3
Tobik.........	1-1	0-2	0-0	0-1	0-0	0-1	0-1	1-0	1-0	1-0	0-1	0-2	0-0	4-9
Ujdur	1-1	0-2	1-0	0-1	1-2	0-1	0-2	1-0	2-0	1-1	1-0	1-0	0-0	10-10
Underwood.	0-1	0-0	0-1	0-0	2-0	1-1	0-1	0-1	0-1	1-1	0-0	0-0	0-1	4-8
Wilcox.......	1-1	2-1	1-0	0-1	0-2	2-0	2-1	0-1	0-1	2-0	1-1	1-0	0-1	12-10
Totals	6-7	5-8	7-5	3-9	7-6	6-6	3-10	9-3	8-5	9-3	6-6	8-4	6-7	83-79

No Decisions: Bailey, Berenguer, Rothschild.

KANSAS CITY—90-72

Pitcher	Balt. W-L	Bos. W-L	Cal. W-L	Chi. W-L	Clev. W-L	Det. W-L	Mil. W-L	Min. W-L	N.Y. W-L	Oak. W-L	Sea. W-L	Tex. W-L	Tor. W-L	Totals W-L
Armstrong..	0-1	0-1	1-0	1-0	1-0	1-0	0-0	0-1	0-0	0-0	0-0	1-1	0-1	5-5
Black	0-0	0-0	1-1	0-0	0-1	0-0	0-0	1-0	0-1	1-0	0-1	1-1	0-1	4-6
Blue	1-1	1-2	1-2	2-0	2-0	0-2	1-1	0-2	2-1	0-1	2-0	0-0	0-1	13-12
Botelho.......	1-0	1-0	0-0	0-0	0-0	0-0	0-1	0-0	0-0	0-0	0-0	0-0	0-0	2-1
Castro	1-0	0-0	0-0	0-0	0-1	0-0	0-0	0-1	1-0	1-0	0-0	0-0	0-0	3-2
Creel..........	0-0	0-0	0-1	1-0	0-0	0-0	0-0	0-0	0-0	0-0	0-2	0-1	1-0	1-4
Frost	3-0	1-1	0-0	0-0	2-0	0-1	0-0	0-2	0-0	0-0	0-0	0-1	0-1	6-6
Gura...........	1-0	0-1	1-1	3-1	2-0	2-2	2-1	1-1	2-2	1-1	1-0	1-1	1-1	18-12
Hood..........	1-0	1-0	0-0	0-0	1-0	0-0	0-0	0-0	1-0	0-0	0-0	0-0	0-0	4-0
Jackson......	0-0	0-0	0-0	0-0	0-0	1-0	0-0	0-1	0-0	0-0	0-0	2-0	0-0	3-1
Leonard......	0-1	2-0	0-0	1-0	0-0	2-0	1-0	1-0	0-1	0-1	0-1	3-0	0-2	10-6
Quisenberry	0-1	0-1	1-2	1-0	0-0	1-1	2-0	1-0	0-0	1-1	2-0	0-1	0-0	9-7
Splittorff ...	0-0	0-0	0-0	1-2	1-0	0-0	1-1	2-1	2-1	1-1	1-1	1-1	0-2	10-10
Tufts	0-0	0-0	1-0	0-0	0-0	0-0	0-0	1-0	0-0	0-0	0-0	0-0	0-0	2-0
Totals	8-4	6-6	6-7	10-3	10-2	6-6	7-5	7-6	5-7	7-6	7-6	7-6	4-8	90-72

No Decisions: Wright.

MILWAUKEE—95-67

Pitcher	Balt. W-L	Bos. W-L	Cal. W-L	Chi. W-L	Clev. W-L	Det. W-L	K.C. W-L	Min. W-L	N.Y. W-L	Oak. W-L	Sea. W-L	Tex. W-L	Tor. W-L	Totals W-L
Augustine ...	0-0	0-0	0-0	0-0	0-0	1-0	0-1	0-1	0-0	0-0	0-1	0-0	0-0	1-3
Bernard......	0-0	0-0	0-1	1-0	1-0	0-0	0-0	0-0	0-0	0-0	0-0	1-0	0-0	3-1
Caldwell.....	0-3	1-1	1-1	1-1	1-1	1-1	1-1	1-1	3-1	1-0	3-0	1-1	2-1	17-13
Easterly......	0-0	0-0	0-1	0-0	0-0	0-0	0-0	0-0	0-1	0-0	0-0	0-0	0-0	0-2
Fingers	1-0	1-0	0-0	1-0	1-0	0-0	0-3	0-0	1-0	0-0	0-1	0-1	0-1	5-6
Haas	0-2	0-0	1-0	1-0	2-1	2-0	1-0	1-1	0-1	1-2	0-0	2-1	0-0	11-8
Ladd...........	0-0	0-0	0-0	1-0	0-0	0-1	0-0	0-0	0-1	0-1	0-0	0-0	0-0	1-3
Lerch..........	0-0	0-0	0-0	1-2	0-1	2-0	1-2	2-0	0-0	0-0	0-0	0-0	2-0	8-7
Medich.......	0-1	1-1	0-0	0-0	0-0	1-1	0-0	0-0	0-1	1-0	2-0	0-0	0-0	5-4
McClure......	1-0	3-0	0-2	0-0	0-0	0-0	0-0	0-1	2-0	2-2	1-0	1-1	2-1	12-7
Slaton........	0-0	1-1	1-1	3-0	1-2	0-0	1-0	1-0	0-0	0-0	1-1	1-0	0-1	10-6
Sutton........	2-0	0-0	0-0	0-0	0-1	1-0	0-0	0-0	1-0	0-0	0-0	0-0	0-0	4-1
Vuckovich...	0-2	2-1	3-0	0-0	0-1	2-0	1-0	2-1	1-0	2-0	1-0	1-1	3-0	18-6
Totals	4-9	9-4	6-6	9-3	6-7	10-3	5-7	7-5	8-5	7-5	8-4	7-5	9-4	95-67

No Decisions: Jones, Porter.

MINNESOTA—60-102

Pitcher	Balt. W-L	Bos. W-L	Calif. W-L	Chi. W-L	Clev. W-L	Det. W-L	K.C. W-L	Mil. W-L	N.Y. W-L	Oak. W-L	Sea. W-L	Tex. W-L	Tor. W-L	Totals W-L
Arroyo	0-0	0-0	0-0	0-0	0-0	0-0	0-0	0-0	0-0	0-1	0-0	0-0	0-0	0-1
Boris	0-0	0-0	0-0	1-1	0-0	0-0	0-0	0-0	0-1	0-0	0-0	0-0	0-0	1-2
Castillo	2-1	2-1	0-0	3-0	1-1	1-1	1-0	0-0	0-2	0-2	1-1	1-2	1-0	13-11
Cooper	0-0	0-0	0-0	0-0	0-0	0-0	0-0	0-0	0-0	0-0	0-0	0-1	0-0	0-1
Corbett	0-0	0-0	0-1	0-0	0-0	0-0	0-0	0-1	0-0	0-0	0-0	0-0	0-0	0-2
Davis	1-1	0-1	0-0	0-0	0-2	0-1	0-0	0-0	0-1	1-1	0-1	0-0	1-1	3-9
Erickson	0-0	1-1	0-1	0-0	0-0	0-0	0-0	1-0	0-0	0-1	2-0	0-0	0-0	4-3
Felton	0-0	0-1	0-3	0-2	0-0	0-1	0-1	0-1	0-1	0-0	0-2	0-0	0-1	0-13
Filson	0-1	0-0	0-0	0-0	0-1	0-0	0-0	0-0	0-0	0-0	0-0	0-0	0-0	0-2
Havens	1-0	2-0	1-0	0-1	0-1	1-0	1-1	1-1	0-0	0-2	1-1	1-1	1-2	10-14
Jackson	0-0	0-0	0-1	0-0	0-0	0-2	0-0	0-0	0-1	0-1	0-0	0-0	0-0	0-5
Little	0-0	0-0	1-0	0-0	0-0	0-0	0-0	0-0	0-0	0-0	0-0	0-0	1-0	2-0
O'Connor	0-2	0-0	1-0	0-0	1-1	0-1	1-1	2-0	0-0	0-0	1-0	1-2	1-1	8-9
Pacella	0-0	0-0	0-0	0-0	0-0	0-1	0-0	0-0	0-0	1-0	0-1	0-0	0-0	1-2
Redfern	0-2	0-1	2-0	1-0	0-2	1-1	1-1	0-1	0-0	0-0	0-2	0-1	0-0	5-11
Viola	0-0	1-0	0-1	1-1	0-0	0-1	1-1	0-1	1-1	0-1	0-0	0-1	0-2	4-10
Williams	0-1	0-1	1-0	0-1	2-0	0-0	1-2	1-2	1-0	1-0	0-1	2-0	0-0	9-7
Totals	4-8	6-6	6-7	6-7	4-8	3-9	6-7	5-7	2-10	3-10	5-8	5-8	5-7	60-102

NEW YORK—79-83

Pitcher	Balt. W-L	Bos. W-L	Cal. W-L	Chi. W-L	Clev. W-L	Det. W-L	K.C. W-L	Mil. W-L	Min. W-L	Oak. W-L	Sea. W-L	Tex. W-L	Tor. W-L	Totals W-L
Alexander	0-0	0-0	0-0	0-0	1-1	0-2	0-0	0-0	0-0	0-1	0-1	0-2	0-0	1-7
Erickson	0-0	0-0	0-0	0-1	1-1	0-0	0-1	0-1	0-0	2-0	0-0	1-0	0-1	4-5
Frazier	0-0	0-1	0-0	0-0	2-0	1-1	0-0	0-0	0-0	0-0	1-2	0-0	0-0	4-4
Gossage	0-1	1-0	0-1	0-2	0-0	0-0	0-0	0-0	2-0	1-0	0-1	0-0	0-0	4-5
Guidry	0-1	1-1	0-2	2-0	0-1	1-0	2-0	0-2	3-0	2-0	2-0	1-0	0-1	14-8
Howell	1-0	0-1	0-0	0-0	1-0	0-0	0-1	0-1	0-0	0-0	0-0	0-0	0-0	2-3
John	0-0	0-1	1-2	1-2	0-0	0-2	2-0	0-0	0-1	0-1	2-0	1-0	2-1	10-10
Kaufman	0-0	0-0	0-0	0-0	0-0	0-0	0-0	1-0	0-0	0-0	0-0	0-0	0-0	1-0
LaRoche	1-0	0-0	0-0	0-0	1-0	1-0	0-0	0-0	0-0	0-1	0-0	0-0	1-1	4-2
May	0-1	0-1	1-1	0-0	0-1	1-0	1-0	1-0	1-0	0-1	1-0	0-0	0-1	6-6
Morgan	0-4	0-1	0-0	1-1	1-0	0-1	0-2	2-0	0-0	1-0	0-0	2-1	0-0	7-11
Pacella	0-0	0-0	0-0	0-0	0-0	0-0	0-0	0-0	0-0	0-0	0-1	0-0	0-0	0-1
Rawley	0-2	1-0	2-1	0-2	0-0	1-0	1-0	0-2	3-0	1-0	0-1	0-1	2-1	11-10
Righetti	0-2	3-1	1-0	0-0	1-0	0-2	1-1	1-1	1-1	0-1	0-0	2-0	1-1	11-10
Wever	0-0	0-0	0-0	0-0	0-0	0-0	0-0	0-1	0-0	0-0	0-0	0-0	0-0	0-1
Totals	2-11	6-7	5-7	4-8	9-4	5-8	7-5	5-8	10-2	7-5	6-6	7-5	6-7	79-83

No Decisions: Lewis, McGlothen.

OAKLAND—68-94

Pitcher	Balt. W-L	Bos. W-L	Cal. W-L	Chi. W-L	Clev. W-L	Det. W-L	K.C. W-L	Mil. W-L	Min. W-L	N.Y. W-L	Sea. W-L	Tex. W-L	Tor. W-L	Totals W-L
Baker	0-0	0-0	0-0	0-1	0-0	0-0	0-0	0-0	0-0	0-0	0-0	1-0	0-0	1-1
Beard	3-0	1-0	1-0	1-2	0-1	0-1	2-1	1-1	1-1	0-1	0-0	0-1	0-0	10-9
Codiroli	0-0	0-0	0-0	1-1	0-0	0-0	0-1	0-0	0-0	0-0	0-0	0-0	0-0	1-2
Conroy	0-0	0-0	0-0	0-0	0-0	0-0	0-0	0-0	0-0	0-0	0-0	2-0	0-2	2-2
D'Acquisto	0-0	0-0	0-0	0-0	0-0	0-0	0-0	0-0	0-0	0-0	0-0	0-0	0-1	0-1
Hanna	0-0	0-1	0-0	0-1	0-0	0-0	0-0	0-1	0-0	0-0	0-0	0-0	0-1	0-4
Jones	0-0	0-0	1-1	0-0	1-0	0-0	0-0	0-0	1-0	0-0	0-0	0-0	0-0	3-1
Keough	0-3	0-0	1-2	1-0	0-1	1-3	1-1	1-2	2-0	1-2	2-0	0-3	1-1	11-18
Kingman	0-2	0-0	0-0	0-1	1-0	0-0	1-2	0-1	1-0	0-1	1-1	0-2	0-2	4-12
Langford	0-1	1-2	0-1	1-0	1-1	0-2	1-0	2-0	1-2	1-2	1-2	1-2	1-1	11-16
McCatty	0-0	0-0	0-2	0-0	1-0	1-0	0-0	0-0	0-0	1-0	2-1	1-0	0-0	6-3
McLaughlin	0-0	0-2	0-0	0-1	0-0	0-0	0-0	0-0	0-0	0-0	0-1	0-0	0-0	0-4
Norris	1-0	1-1	0-2	0-2	2-1	1-2	0-1	0-1	1-0	1-0	0-1	0-0	0-0	7-11
Owchinko	0-1	1-1	0-1	0-0	0-0	0-0	0-0	0-0	0-0	1-0	0-0	0-0	0-1	2-4
Underwood	1-0	0-1	1-0	0-0	2-0	0-1	1-1	1-1	3-0	0-1	0-1	0-0	1-0	10-6
Totals	5-7	4-8	4-9	4-9	8-4	3-9	6-7	5-7	10-3	5-7	6-7	5-8	3-9	68-94

No Decisions: Arroyo, Kinney.

SEATTLE—76-86

Pitcher	Balt. W-L	Bos. W-L	Cal. W-L	Chi. W-L	Clev. W-L	Det. W-L	K.C. W-L	Mil. W-L	Min. W-L	N.Y. W-L	Oak. W-L	Tex. W-L	Tor. W-L	Totals W-L
Bannister	1-0	1-2	2-1	1-0	0-2	0-1	2-0	0-2	1-1	1-1	2-0	0-1	1-2	12-13
Beattie	0-2	1-0	0-1	1-0	0-2	1-1	1-2	0-0	1-1	0-2	1-1	1-0	1-0	8-12
Bordi	0-0	0-0	0-1	0-0	0-0	0-0	0-0	0-0	0-0	0-0	0-1	0-0	0-0	0-2
Caudill	2-0	0-4	0-0	1-0	1-2	2-0	0-2	1-0	1-0	2-0	1-0	1-0	0-1	12-9
Clark	0-0	0-0	0-0	1-0	0-0	1-0	0-0	0-2	1-0	0-0	0-0	2-0	0-0	5-2
Moore	1-2	1-1	0-2	0-2	1-1	0-0	1-1	0-1	1-0	0-0	1-2	0-2	1-0	7-14
Musselman	0-0	0-0	0-0	0-0	0-0	1-0	0-0	0-0	0-0	0-0	0-0	0-0	0-0	1-0
Nelson	1-1	1-0	0-2	1-0	0-1	0-0	1-0	1-1	0-1	0-2	0-0	1-1	0-0	6-9
Nunez	0-0	0-0	0-0	0-1	0-0	0-0	0-0	0-0	0-1	0-0	0-0	1-0	0-0	1-2
Perry	0-2	1-0	1-2	1-1	0-0	1-3	0-1	0-1	1-1	2-0	0-1	2-0	1-0	10-12
Stanton	0-0	0-0	0-0	0-1	0-0	0-0	0-0	1-1	1-0	0-0	0-1	0-0	0-1	2-4
Stoddard	0-0	0-0	0-0	1-1	0-0	0-1	0-0	0-0	0-0	0-0	0-0	2-0	0-1	3-3
Vande Berg	0-0	0-0	0-1	0-0	1-1	0-0	1-1	1-0	1-0	1-1	2-0	1-0	1-0	9-4
Totals	5-7	5-7	3-10	7-6	3-9	6-6	6-7	4-8	8-5	6-6	7-6	9-4	7-5	76-86

No Decisions: Andersen, Gleaton.

TEXAS—64-98

Pitcher	Balt. W-L	Bos. W-L	Cal. W-L	Chi. W-L	Clev. W-L	Det. W-L	K.C. W-L	Mil. W-L	Min. W-L	N.Y. W-L	Oak. W-L	Sea. W-L	Tor. W-L	Totals W-L
Butcher	0-0	0-0	0-1	0-0	1-0	0-0	0-2	0-0	0-0	0-1	0-0	0-0	0-1	1-5
Comer	1-1	0-1	0-0	0-1	0-0	0-1	0-0	0-0	0-1	0-0	0-0	0-1	0-0	1-6
Darwin	0-0	0-1	1-2	1-1	1-0	2-3	0-0	2-0	0-0	1-0	0-0	0-0	2-1	10-8
Henke	0-0	0-0	0-0	0-0	0-0	0-0	0-0	0-0	0-0	0-0	1-0	0-0	0-0	1-0
Honeycutt	0-1	0-3	1-1	0-3	0-0	0-0	0-2	0-2	1-0	1-2	1-1	1-1	0-1	5-17
Hough	0-0	1-2	1-2	1-0	1-2	0-2	3-1	1-1	2-0	3-0	2-1	1-1	0-1	16-13
Mason	0-0	0-0	0-0	0-0	0-0	0-0	0-0	0-0	0-1	0-0	0-1	1-0	0-0	1-2
Matlack	1-2	0-1	0-0	1-0	1-0	0-0	0-0	0-1	2-1	0-0	1-0	0-2	1-0	7-7
Medich	0-1	1-1	0-2	0-1	1-2	1-1	1-0	0-1	2-0	0-1	1-0	0-0	0-1	7-11
Mirabella	0-0	0-0	0-0	0-0	0-0	0-0	0-0	0-0	0-0	0-0	0-0	0-1	1-0	1-1
Schmidt	0-1	0-0	1-0	1-1	0-1	0-1	1-0	1-1	0-0	0-1	0-0	0-0	0-0	4-6
Smithson	0-1	0-0	0-0	0-0	0-0	0-0	1-0	0-0	1-0	0-0	1-1	0-2	0-0	3-4
Tanana	1-2	0-1	1-0	1-1	0-2	1-0	0-2	1-1	0-2	0-2	1-1	1-1	0-3	7-18
Totals	3-9	2-10	5-8	5-8	5-7	4-8	6-7	5-7	8-5	5-7	8-5	4-9	4-8	64-98

No Decisions: Boitano, Farr.

TORONTO—78-84

Pitcher	Balt. W-L	Bos. W-L	Cal. W-L	Chi. W-L	Clev. W-L	Det. W-L	K.C. W-L	Mil. W-L	Min. W-L	N.Y. W-L	Oak. W-L	Sea. W-L	Tex. W-L	Totals W-L
Bomback	0-0	0-1	0-0	0-1	0-0	0-0	1-1	0-2	0-0	0-0	0-0	0-0	0-0	1-5
Clancy	0-2	0-1	2-1	1-2	1-1	1-0	1-2	1-2	2-1	1-1	2-0	1-1	3-0	16-14
Eichhorn	0-1	0-0	0-1	0-0	0-0	0-0	0-0	0-0	0-1	0-0	0-0	0-0	0-0	0-3
Garvin	0-0	0-0	0-0	0-0	1-1	0-0	0-0	0-0	0-0	0-0	0-0	0-0	0-0	1-1
Geisel	0-0	0-0	0-0	0-0	0-1	1-0	0-0	0-0	0-0	0-0	0-0	0-0	0-0	1-1
Gott	1-2	0-1	0-1	0-1	1-0	2-0	0-0	0-2	0-0	0-2	0-1	1-0	0-0	5-10
Jackson	0-0	1-2	1-0	0-0	0-0	1-1	0-1	1-0	1-0	0-0	2-1	0-1	1-2	8-8
Leal	1-2	2-0	0-2	1-1	2-0	1-2	1-0	0-2	1-1	2-1	1-0	0-3	0-1	12-15
McLaughlin	1-1	0-1	1-0	0-2	0-1	0-0	1-0	0-0	1-0	0-1	2-0	1-0	1-0	8-6
Murray	0-0	1-0	0-1	1-0	0-3	1-1	0-0	0-1	1-0	2-0	0-0	0-1	2-0	8-7
Schrom	0-0	1-0	0-0	0-0	0-0	0-0	0-0	0-0	0-0	0-0	0-0	0-0	0-0	1-0
Stieb	0-2	1-1	0-2	1-1	1-0	0-2	4-0	2-0	1-2	2-1	2-1	2-1	1-1	17-14
Totals	3-10	6-7	4-8	4-8	6-7	7-6	8-4	4-9	7-5	7-6	9-3	5-7	8-4	78-84

No Decisions: Senteney.

Outfielder Lonnie Smith of the Cardinals (right) and Shortstop Robin Yount of the Brewers had great seasons in 1982 as they propelled their teams to divisional and Championship Series triumphs.

1982 CHAMPIONSHIP SERIES

Including

National League Review

National League Box Scores

National League Composite Box Score

American League Review

American League Box Scores

American League Composite Box Score

The Atlanta Braves' dugout reflects the futility of their situation late in their 7-0 loss to the Cardinals in Game 1 of the N.L. Championship Series.

Cardinals Sweep Past Braves

By LARRY WIGGE

Darrell Porter squirmed when a flock of reporters approached his spot in the locker room at Atlanta Stadium on October 10. The veteran catcher had just helped the St. Louis Cardinals sweep the Atlanta Braves in the 1982 National League Championship Series.

Porter had been an inspirational leader. The pitchers gave him credit for pulling together an otherwise questionable staff and making the unit a meaningful contributor to the Cardinals' success.

And, more importantly, Porter turned in his best offensive showing since leaving Kansas City following the 1980 season to sign a huge free-agent contract with the Cardinals. He reached base safely 10 times (five hits and five walks) in 14 plate appearances. He drove in a run, scored once in each of the three games and tied a Championship Series record (for a three-game series) with three doubles.

But Porter, who had set his life straight after years of alcohol and drug abuse, was reluctant to accept the fact that he had been chosen the series' Most Valuable Player.

"I'm a .230 hitter and no one should have to count on a .230 hitter," he said. "I used to be an awfully consistent player. But not anymore. But my life is on the upswing and has been since 1980 (when he entered a drug rehabilitation center)."

Actually, Porter batted .231 during the 1982 season after hitting .224 in 1981 for the Cardinals. But he was the driving force in the Cardinals' first Championship Series appearance. His teammates nodded with approval at the MVP choice. Finally, Porter opened up and accepted the accolades.

"I'm getting to know who I am again," he said. "For the last five or six months I've been feeling good."

But wasn't a .231 average an empty figure for a man who was feeling good?

"I went into this Championship Series totally relaxed," Porter continued. "I feel comfortable at the plate. But I don't even want to ask anyone what I'm doing differently up there, I'm just going to keep doing what I'm doing. I just want to have some fun. I want to relax."

Cardinals' Manager Whitey Herzog steadfastly remained in Porter's corner during the catcher's two seasons in St. Louis, even if the fans chose to boo him lustily for the most part.

With the N.L. pennant on the line, the Cardinals' much-maligned Darrell Porter played his best.

"People can say what they want, but five (1977-78, 1980-81-82) of the last six years his teams have won the division," said Herzog, obviously considering the Cardinals "champions" in 1981 because their overall record in the split season was the best in the East Division (still, the Cards didn't qualify for the '81 playoffs).

"He must be doing something right," saluted Herzog.

There were other Cardinal players who did things right, too.

Rain aborted Game 1 in which the Braves, behind pitching ace Phil Niekro, were leading the Cardinals 1-0 after 4½ innings. The postponement erased Niekro and Joaquin Andujar of the Cardinals as the opening-game pitchers. Bob Forsch then treated the St. Louis fans to a dazzling three-hit shutout one night later as the Cardinals jumped in front in the series with a 7-0 victory.

Forsch, who struck out six batters and walked none, became the third man to pitch a shutout in the first game of a league Championship Series. The others were Baltimore's Jim Palmer in 1973 and Don Sutton of Los Angeles in 1974. (Cincinnati's Gary Nolan and Clay Carroll combined for a first-game shutout in 1970, beating Pittsburgh 3-0 in 10 innings.)

Forsch helped offensively, too. He had two singles, hit a sacrifice fly in a five-run sixth inning that spelled the exit of starter-loser Pascual Perez and scored the game's final run in the eighth.

"Right now, the shutout is more important, but tomorrow, I'll come back here talking about the hits," Forsch said with a laugh. Forsch limited the Braves to singles by Claudell Washington in the third and sixth and a fifth-inning single by Bruce Benedict. He retired the last 11 Braves in order.

Game 1 also brought attention to a spindly youngster named Willie McGee. McGee was a speedster who got away from New York Yankees Owner George Steinbrenner. He was frozen on the Yankees' Double A roster at Nashville (Southern League) before Steinbrenner dealt him to the Cardinals for pitcher Bob Sykes during the previous October.

McGee, the fastest of the Cardinals, made headlines for not coming home on what should have been an inside-the-park home run when his third-inning drive into the right-field corner skipped away from Washington.

McGee admitted later that he got caught up in the excitement and forgot to look for third-base coach Chuck Hiller, who was waving the rookie home.

"The words I said can't be repeated," said a smiling McGee, who scored on Ozzie Smith's sacrifice fly. That was the only run Forsch needed.

However, the Cardinals broke it open in the sixth, setting a Championship Series record for most hits in an inning (six) and tying the mark for most runs (five). George Hendrick, McGee and Ozzie Smith produced run-scoring singles to highlight the outburst.

Prior to the series there hadn't been a rainout at Busch Memorial Stadium since August of 1976, but Game 2 also was delayed a day by more heavy thunderstorms.

Though the Cardinals scored a run off Niekro in the first inning of the second contest, the Braves took command in the third. Rafael Ramirez singled home Benedict, who had walked and advanced to second on a sacrifice, and then came all the way around himself when the ball got past McGee in center field and went to the wall for a three-base error.

With knuckleballer Niekro (14-1 on the road and 17-4 overall during the regular season) pitching well after his washed-out effort of three days earlier, the Braves increased their lead to 3-1 in the fifth on a single by Glenn Hubbard, Benedict's double and a sacrifice fly by Niekro.

After the Cardinals scored once in the sixth, the Braves tried to put the game away in the eighth when Dale Murphy singled to left and stole second. After Chris Chambliss was given an intentional walk, Herzog called on his relief ace, Bruce Sutter. Murphy tried to surprise the Cardinals with an attempted steal of third base, but Porter cut him down. Then Sutter struck out Bob Horner and induced Jerry Royster to tap back to the mound.

The Cardinals pecked away at the lead, getting their sixth-inning run on Porter's second double of the game, which chased Keith Hernandez home from first base. And with Gene Garber pitching in the eighth for the Braves, Porter drew a one-out walk, went to third on a single by Hendrick and scored the tying run on McGee's high bounder up the middle. Atlanta shortstop Ramirez got to the ball, but the only man he could retire was Hendrick at second base.

Momentum seemingly had swung to the Cardinals.

David Green, who went into to play left field in the eighth and was inserted in the pitcher's spot in the batting order when Herzog brought in Sutter, opened the ninth with a single to left. Tom Herr sacrificed Green to second, bringing Ken Oberkfell to the plate.

Oberkfell, who had a .289 average during the regular season but a .600 mark over his career against Garber (6 for 10, including a July 7 homer at Atlanta), was given a chance to bat even though Sutter was scheduled to be the next hitter.

When Oberkfell lashed a liner just over the glove of a leaping Brett Butler in center field, the Cardinals had themselves a 4-3 victory and a 2-0 lead in the series.

Asked if he expected to be walked, Oberkfell replied: "That was the last thing in my mind. I was just up there to hit the first thing that looked good enough to hit. When I looked up, I thought he (Butler) might catch it. I would have been surprised that anybody would not bother to pitch to me when you consider how few RBIs I've had (34 in the regular season)."

Oberkfell's .600 average against Garber was news to Oberkfell, Garber and Torre.

"I didn't want to face Hernandez in that situation," said Torre, obviously thinking one hitter beyond Sutter's spot in the order. Herzog, who said he would have

Ace reliever Bruce Sutter had a win and a save in the three-game St. Louis sweep.

used Dane Iorg to bat for Sutter, agreed with Torre's strategy.

If the come-from-behind effort by the Cardinals in Game 2 hadn't finished off the Braves, then a four-run outburst in the second inning of Game 3 at Atlanta did.

Hernandez began the uprising with a single to left. Porter walked. Hendrick lined a single to right-center field to score Hernandez. McGee then split the gap in right-center for a triple, making the score 3-0. Ozzie Smith boosted the lead to four runs with a single to left-center. Exit Atlanta starter Rick Camp.

The Redbirds added a run in the fifth on a leadoff double by Herr and a two-out single by Hernandez. And McGee hit a bases-empty homer in the ninth.

The only runs the Braves could manage against Andujar came in the seventh when Atlanta had four singles, scoring on a double-play grounder by Chambliss and a single by Hubbard. Sutter quelled that rally, and retired the last seven batters for a 6-2 triumph.

Sutter, who was the winning pitcher in Game 2, retired 13 men in succession in his 4⅓ innings of Championship Series work.

When Porter was named the MVP of the series, he pointed to a corner of the locker

room where several Cardinal pitchers were standing. "They're the ones," he said.

The St. Louis moundsmen limited the Braves to just five runs in three games. Atlanta, which had 146 homers in the regular season, had none in the series. In fact, the Braves had only one extra-base hit. More importantly, Cardinal pitchers held the Braves' three leading run-producers, Murphy, Horner and Chambliss, to four hits—all singles—and no RBIs in 32 at-bats.

It was the second visit to the N.L. Championship Series for the Braves, who were swept by the New York Mets in 1969.

The Cardinals, on the other hand, became the sixth team to sweep an N.L. series. Better yet, they had earned their first visit to the World Series since 1968 when they lost to the Detroit Tigers.

GAME OF THURSDAY, OCTOBER 7, AT ST. LOUIS (N)

Atlanta	AB.	R.	H.	RBI.	PO.	A.
Washington, rf	4	0	2	0	3	0
Ramirez, ss	4	0	0	0	1	2
Murphy, cf	4	0	0	0	4	0
Chambliss, 1b	3	0	0	0	8	1
Horner, 3b	3	0	0	0	0	2
Royster, lf	3	0	0	0	2	0
Hubbard, 2b	3	0	0	0	0	3
Benedict, c	3	0	1	0	5	0
Perez, p	2	0	0	0	0	1
Bedrosian, p	0	0	0	0	0	0
Moore, p	0	0	0	0	1	0
Whisenton, ph	1	0	0	0	0	0
Walk, p	0	0	0	0	0	0
Totals	30	0	3	0	24	9

St. Louis	AB.	R.	H.	RBI.	PO.	A.
Herr, 2b	5	0	2	0	2	2
Oberkfell, 3b	5	0	1	1	0	3
L. Smith, lf	3	1	1	1	0	0
Green, lf	0	0	0	0	0	0
Hernandez, 1b	4	1	1	0	10	0
Hendrick, rf	4	1	1	1	3	0
Porter, c	4	1	2	0	6	1
McGee, cf	4	2	2	1	3	0
O. Smith, ss	3	0	1	2	3	4
Forsch, p	3	1	2	1	0	2
Totals	35	7	13	7	27	12

Atlanta	0 0 0	0 0 0	0 0 0—0
St. Louis	0 0 1	0 0 5	0 1 x—7

Atlanta	IP.	H.	R.	ER.	BB.	SO.
Perez (Loser)	5*	7	4	4	1	2
Bedrosian	⅔	3	2	2	1	1
Moore	1⅓	1	0	0	0	1
Walk	1	2	1	1	1	1

St. Louis	IP.	H.	R.	ER.	BB.	SO.
Forsch (Winner)	9	3	0	0	0	6

*Pitched to three batters in sixth.

Game-winning RBI—O. Smith.

Error—Oberkfell. Left on bases—Atlanta 3, St. Louis 11. Two-base hit—Porter. Three-base hit—McGee. Caught stealing—Washington. Sacrifice flies—O. Smith, Forsch, L. Smith. Hit by pitcher—By Moore (L. Smith). Wild pitch—Bedrosian. Umpires—Williams, Engel, Wendelstedt, Froemming, Rennert and Runge. Time—2:25. Attendance—53,008.

GAME OF SATURDAY, OCTOBER 9, AT ST. LOUIS (N)

Atlanta	AB.	R.	H.	RBI.	PO.	A.
Washington, rf	3	0	0	0	2	1
Ramirez, ss	4	1	1	1	2	5
Murphy, cf-lf	4	0	1	0	1	0
Chambliss, 1b	3	0	0	0	12	1
Horner, 3b	4	0	0	0	1	0
Butler, cf	0	0	0	0	0	0
Royster, lf-3b	4	0	2	0	0	0
Hubbard, 2b	3	1	1	0	1	4
Benedict, c	2	1	1	0	5	2
Niekro, p	0	0	0	1	1	1
Pocoroba, ph	1	0	0	0	0	0
Garber, p	1	0	0	0	0	1
Totals	29	3	6	2	25	15

St. Louis	AB.	R.	H.	RBI.	PO.	A.
Herr, 2b	3	0	0	0	2	2
Oberkfell, 3b	5	1	1	1	1	0
L. Smith, lf	4	0	1	0	1	0
Sutter, p	0	0	0	0	0	2
Hernandez, 1b	4	1	1	0	11	1
Porter, c	2	1	2	1	5	1
Hendrick, rf	4	0	2	1	0	0
McGee, cf	4	0	0	1	6	0
O. Smith, ss	2	0	1	0	0	3
Stuper, p	1	0	0	0	0	0
Braun, ph	1	0	0	0	0	0
Bair, p	0	0	0	0	0	1
Green, lf	1	1	1	0	0	0
Totals	31	4	9	3	27	10

```
Atlanta ..................... 0 0 2   0 1 0   0 0 0—3
St. Louis .................. 1 0 0   0 0 1   0 1 1—4
```
One out when winning run scored.

Atlanta	IP.	H.	R.	ER.	BB.	SO.
Niekro	6	6	2	2	4	5
Garber (Loser)	2⅓	3	2	2	1	2

St. Louis	IP.	H.	R.	ER.	BB.	SO.
Stuper	6	4	3	2	1	4
Bair	1*	2	0	0	3	0
Sutter (Winner)	2	0	0	0	0	1

*Pitched to two batters in eighth.

Game-winning RBI—Oberkfell.

Error—McGee. Left on bases—Atlanta 6, St. Louis 9. Two-base hits—Porter 2, Benedict. Stolen bases—O. Smith, Murphy. Caught stealing—Murphy. Sacrifice hits—Stuper, Niekro, Hubbard, Herr. Sacrifice fly—Niekro. Wild pitch—Niekro. Passed ball—Benedict. Umpires—Engel, Wendelstedt, Froemming, Rennert, Runge and Williams. Time—2:46. Attendance—53,408.

GAME OF SUNDAY, OCTOBER 10, AT ATLANTA (N)

St. Louis	AB.	R.	H.	RBI.	PO.	A.
Herr, 2b	5	1	1	0	2	6
Oberkfell, 3b	5	0	1	0	1	1
L. Smith, lf	4	0	1	0	1	0
Hernandez, 1b	4	1	2	1	14	0
Porter, c	3	1	1	0	4	1
Hendrick, rf	5	1	1	1	1	0
McGee, cf	5	2	2	3	3	0
O. Smith, ss	4	0	3	1	1	4
Andujar, p	1	0	0	0	0	1
Sutter, p	1	0	0	0	0	0
Totals	37	6	12	6	27	13

Atlanta	AB.	R.	H.	RBI.	PO.	A.
Ramirez, ss	3	0	1	0	2	4
Royster, lf	4	0	0	0	2	0
Washington, rf	2	0	1	0	0	0
Harper, pr-rf	1	1	0	0	0	0
Horner, 3b	4	0	1	0	1	3
Chambliss, 1b	4	0	0	0	10	3
Murphy, cf	3	1	2	0	3	0
Hubbard, 2b	3	0	1	1	3	4
Benedict, c	3	0	0	0	6	0
Camp, p	0	0	0	0	0	0
Perez, p	1	0	0	0	0	0
Moore, p	0	0	0	0	0	0
Whisenton, ph	1	0	0	0	0	0
Mahler, p	0	0	0	0	0	1
Bedrosian, p	0	0	0	0	0	0
Butler, ph	1	0	0	0	0	0
Garber, p	0	0	0	0	0	0
Totals	30	2	6	1	27	15

```
St. Louis .................. 0 4 0   0 1 0   0 0 1—6
Atlanta ..................... 0 0 0   0 0 0   2 0 0—2
```

St. Louis	IP.	H.	R.	ER.	BB.	SO.
Andujar (Winner)	6⅔	6	2	2	2	4
Sutter (Save)	2⅓	0	0	0	0	0

Atlanta	IP.	H.	R.	ER.	BB.	SO.
Camp (Loser)	1*	4	4	4	1	0
Perez	3⅔	3	1	1	1	2
Moore	1⅓	1	0	0	0	0
Mahler	1⅔	3	0	0	2	0
Bedrosian	⅓	0	0	0	0	1
Garber	1	1	1	1	0	1

*Pitched to five batters in second.

Game-winning RBI—Hendrick.

Error—Ramirez. Double plays—St. Louis 3. Left on bases—St. Louis 11, Atlanta 3. Two-base hit—Herr. Three-base hit—McGee. Home run—McGee. Sacrifice hits—Andujar 2, L. Smith. Wild pitches—Andujar 2. Balk—Andujar. Umpires—Wendelstedt, Froemming, Rennert, Runge, Williams and Engel. Time—2:51. Attendance—52,173.

ST. LOUIS CARDINALS' BATTING AND FIELDING AVERAGES

Player—Position	G.	AB.	R.	H.	TB.	2B.	3B.	HR.	RBI.	B.A.	PO.	A.	E.	F.A.
Green, lf	2	1	1	1	1	0	0	0	0	1.000	0	0	0	.000
Forsch, p	1	3	1	2	2	0	0	0	1	.667	0	2	0	1.000
Porter, c	3	9	3	5	8	3	0	0	1	.556	15	3	0	1.000
O. Smith, ss	3	9	0	5	5	0	0	0	3	.556	4	11	0	1.000
Hernandez, 1b	3	12	3	4	4	0	0	0	1	.333	35	1	0	1.000
McGee, cf	3	13	4	4	11	0	2	1	5	.308	12	0	1	.923
Hendrick, rf	3	13	2	4	4	0	0	0	2	.308	5	0	0	1.000
L. Smith, lf	3	11	1	3	3	0	0	0	1	.273	2	0	0	1.000
Herr, 2b	3	13	1	3	4	1	0	0	0	.231	6	10	0	1.000
Oberkfell, 3b	3	15	3	3	3	0	0	0	2	.200	2	4	1	.857
Bair, p	1	0	0	0	0	0	0	0	0	.000	0	1	0	1.000
Sutter, p	2	1	0	0	0	0	0	0	0	.000	0	2	0	1.000
Andujar, p	1	1	0	0	0	0	0	0	0	.000	0	1	0	1.000
Braun, ph	1	1	0	0	0	0	0	0	0	.000	0	0	0	.000
Stuper, p	1	1	0	0	0	0	0	0	0	.000	0	0	0	.000
Totals	3	103	17	34	45	4	2	1	16	.330	81	35	2	.983

ATLANTA BRAVES' BATTING AND FIELDING AVERAGES

Player—Position	G.	AB.	R.	H.	TB.	2B.	3B.	HR.	RBI.	B.A.	PO.	A.	E.	F.A.
Washington, rf	3	9	0	3	3	0	0	0	0	.333	5	1	0	1.000
Murphy, cf-lf	3	11	1	3	3	0	0	0	0	.273	8	0	0	1.000
Benedict, c	3	8	1	2	3	1	0	0	0	.250	16	2	0	1.000
Hubbard, 2b	3	9	1	2	2	0	0	0	1	.222	4	11	0	1.000
Ramirez, ss	3	11	1	2	2	0	0	0	1	.182	5	11	1	.941
Royster, lf-3b	3	11	0	2	2	0	0	0	0	.182	4	0	0	1.000
Horner, 3b	3	11	0	1	1	0	0	0	0	.091	2	5	0	1.000
Bedrosian, p	2	0	0	0	0	0	0	0	0	.000	0	0	0	.000
Moore, p	2	0	0	0	0	0	0	0	0	.000	1	0	0	1.000
Camp, p	1	0	0	0	0	0	0	0	0	.000	0	0	0	.000
Mahler, p	1	0	0	0	0	0	0	0	0	.000	0	1	0	1.000
Niekro, p	1	0	0	0	0	0	0	0	1	.000	1	1	0	1.000
Walk, p	1	0	0	0	0	0	0	0	0	.000	0	0	0	.000
Butler, cf-ph	2	1	0	0	0	0	0	0	0	.000	0	0	0	.000
Garber, p	2	1	0	0	0	0	0	0	0	.000	0	1	0	1.000
Pocoroba, ph	1	1	0	0	0	0	0	0	0	.000	0	0	0	.000
Harper, pr-rf	1	1	1	0	0	0	0	0	0	.000	0	0	0	.000
Whisenton, ph	2	2	0	0	0	0	0	0	0	.000	0	0	0	.000
Perez, p	2	3	0	0	0	0	0	0	0	.000	0	1	0	1.000
Chambliss, 1b	3	10	0	0	0	0	0	0	0	.000	30	5	0	1.000
Totals	3	89	5	15	16	1	0	0	3	.169	76	39	1	.991

ST. LOUIS CARDINALS' PITCHING RECORDS

Pitcher	G.	GS.	CG.	IP.	H.	R.	ER.	BB.	SO.	HB.	WP.	W.	L.	Pct.	ERA.
Forsch	1	1	1	9	3	0	0	0	6	0	0	1	0	1.000	0.00
Sutter	2	0	0	4⅓	0	0	0	1	0	0	0	1	0	1.000	0.00
Bair	1	0	0	1	2	0	0	3	0	0	0	0	0	.000	0.00
Andujar	1	1	0	6⅔	6	2	2	2	4	0	2	1	0	1.000	2.70
Stuper	1	1	0	6	4	3	2	1	4	0	0	0	0	.000	3.00
Totals	3	3	1	27	15	5	4	6	15	0	2	3	0	1.000	1.33

Shutout—Forsch. Save—Sutter.

ATLANTA BRAVES' PITCHING RECORDS

Pitcher	G.	GS.	CG.	IP.	H.	R.	ER.	BB.	SO.	HB.	WP.	W.	L.	Pct.	ERA.
Moore	2	0	0	2⅔	2	0	0	0	1	1	0	0	0	.000	0.00
Mahler	1	0	0	1⅔	3	0	0	2	0	0	0	0	0	.000	0.00
Niekro	1	1	0	6	6	2	2	4	5	0	1	0	0	.000	3.00
Perez	2	1	0	8⅔	10	5	5	2	4	0	0	0	1	.000	5.19
Garber	2	0	0	3⅓	4	3	3	1	3	0	0	0	1	.000	8.10
Walk	1	0	0	1	3	1	1	1	1	0	0	0	0	.000	9.00
Bedrosian	2	0	0	1	3	2	2	1	2	0	1	0	0	.000	18.00
Camp	1	1	0	1	4	4	4	1	0	0	0	0	1	.000	36.00
Totals	3	3	0	25⅓	35	17	17	12	16	1	2	0	3	.000	6.04

No shutouts or saves.

COMPOSITE SCORE BY INNINGS

St. Louis	1	4	1	0	1	6	0	2	2 — 17
Atlanta	0	0	2	0	1	0	2	0	0 — 5

Game-winning RBIs—O. Smith, Oberkfell, Hendrick.
Sacrifice hits—Andujar 2, Stuper, Niekro, Hubbard, Herr, L. Smith.
Sacrifice flies—O. Smith, Forsch, L. Smith, Niekro.
Stolen bases—O. Smith, Murphy.
Caught stealing—Washington, Murphy.
Double plays—Oberkfell, Herr and Hernandez; Herr and Hernandez; Herr, O. Smith and Hernandez.
Left on bases—St. Louis 11, 9, 11—31; Atlanta 3, 6, 3—12.
Hit by pitcher—By Moore (L. Smith).
Passed ball—Benedict.
Balk—Andujar.
Time of games—First game, 2:25; second game, 2:46; third game, 2:51.
Attendance—First game, 53,008; second game, 53,408; third game, 52,173.
Umpires—Williams, Engel, Wendelstedt, Froemming, Rennert and Runge.
Official scorers—Jack Herman, St. Louis Globe-Democrat; Randy Donaldson.

Reserve Mark Brouhard helped keep Milwaukee hopes alive with a Game 4 performance that included a home run and a Championship Series-record four runs scored.

Brewers Beat Angels, Odds

By LARRY WIGGE

In many postseason games in the American League over the past decade, the man you expected to see celebrating was Reggie Jackson. But it didn't happen in 1982.

Jackson didn't have a chance to wave his magic wand in the ninth inning October 10 with California trailing Milwaukee, 4-3, in the fifth and decisive game of the A.L. Championship Series. Instead, he was left in the on-deck circle watching Peter Ladd retire Rod Carew for the final out as the Brewers captured the first A.L. pennant in the franchise's 14 years.

History confronted Manager Harvey Kuenn's Brewers with at least 15 good reasons why they should fail in their bid for a comeback triumph in the series. Entering the 1982 major league playoffs, 15 teams had fallen behind two games to none in Championship Series play and then dropped into oblivion. And the Atlanta Braves became No. 16 a few hours after Milwaukee nailed down its pennant.

The Brewers, Harvey's Wallbangers, had beaten the odds after losing the first two games of the series at Anaheim and then trailing late in Game 5. Their tenacity proved the Brewers were more than what the cold, hard total of 216 home runs might have suggested.

In Game 1, the Angels looked like the champions, devastating Mike Caldwell and the Brewers, 8-3, behind five runs batted in by Don Baylor and a complete-game effort by 39-year-old lefthander Tommy John.

Baylor drove home the game's first run with a sacrifice fly in the opening inning. But Milwaukee bolted to a 3-1 advantage on a towering two-run homer by Gorman Thomas in the second and a run-scoring groundout by Cecil Cooper in the third.

Baylor, who set a league record with 21 game-winning RBIs during the season, followed an RBI single by Bobby Grich with a two-run triple in the third to put the Angels ahead, 4-3. In the fourth, he singled home two more runs. The five RBIs matched a Championship Series record established by Paul Blair of Baltimore in 1969 and equaled by Bob Robertson of Pittsburgh in 1971.

Fred Lynn, who had three hits in the game, provided a fifth-inning homer for the Angels.

Pitching for a team that wasn't supposed to have exceptional starters, John

Game 1 heroes for California were winning pitcher Tommy John (left) and Don Baylor (center), who drove in five runs.

and second-game starter Bruce Kison made the experts take another look.

Kison limited the Brewers to five hits in Game 2, struck out eight, issued no walks and induced 14 Milwaukee batters to ground out as the Angels gained a 2-0 cushion in the series with a 4-2 triumph.

Tim Foli drove home the game's first run with a single in the second inning. Bob Boone followed with a suicide squeeze bunt, giving California a 2-0 lead. In the third, Jackson performed some of his autumn magic with a long homer over the center-field wall. Boone produced the final California run with a sacrifice fly in the fourth.

The only runs the Brewers could muster came on a two-run, inside-the-park home run by Paul Molitor in the fifth inning.

Shortstop Foli wasn't ready to celebrate, remembering a comeback that didn't fall short.

"When I was at Pittsburgh in 1979, we were down 3-1 to Baltimore in the World Series," Foli said. "We had to face Flanagan, McGregor and Palmer—and we wound up winning it."

Milwaukee catcher Ted Simmons didn't think his team was finished.

"Remember the mini-series (divisional playoff after the split season) last year with the New York Yankees?" Simmons asked. "We lost the first two games at home, then went to New York where we won two and nearly took the series. Remember? We were leading in the fifth game. I'm convinced it can be done."

"By no stretch of the imagination do I feel like we have it made," Foli continued. "With that lineup, they (the Brewers) are capable of doing anything."

The change of scenery seemed to agree with the Brewers when the series shifted to Milwaukee after a day off for travel. The Brewers roared to a 5-0 cushion after seven innings in Game 3 and had veteran Don Sutton on the mound.

After Robin Yount walked to lead off the fourth inning, Cooper doubled him home. Simmons singled Cooper to third before Thomas produced the second run with a sacrifice fly to center. A single by Ben Oglivie preceded another sacrifice fly, this one by Don Money. The Brewers added to that 3-0 lead when Molitor collected his second two-run homer in as many games in the seventh.

But then the Brewers got a scare.

Boone led off the California eighth with a long drive to left field. Oglivie leaped for the ball, but he had it snatched from his grasp by a fan who was leaning over the grandstand wall. Umpire Larry Barnett ruled that the fan caught the ball behind the fence (although an instant replay on television showed that the spectator leaned over the wall).

The controversial call gave the Angels new life. With one out, Carew singled. Then, with two outs, Lynn and Baylor stroked run-scoring doubles to cut the Milwaukee lead to 5-3.

With the .300-hitting Doug DeCinces at the plate, Milwaukee's Kuenn normally would call on relief ace Rollie Fingers. But Fingers had not pitched since September 2 and his availability was still a giant question mark because of an elbow injury. So Kuenn chose Ladd to replace Sutton.

Ladd, who had been summoned by the Brewers from their Triple-A club at Vancouver in July, possessed a 90-miles-per-hour fastball. But Milwaukee supporters also remembered two home runs Ladd served up in key games down the stretch in the A.L. East race.

Ladd got DeCinces to ground to third and then disposed of the Angels in order in the ninth.

The next afternoon, following a rain delay at the start, pitcher Moose Haas got the call for the Brewers and John was back for the Angels after only three days rest despite the fact 13-game winner Ken Forsch was available (Forsch never pitched in the series).

But the name to remember in Game 4 was Mark Brouhard, a substitute left fielder for Oglivie (who was bothered by a rib injury). Brouhard hadn't played since September 11 and hadn't started since September 5. But in this pressure assignment, Brouhard scored four times, had a single, double and homer and drove in three runs to key the Brewers' 9-5 victory that evened the series at two games apiece.

Brouhard had been sent to the minors as late as August 12. He returned on August 30, just prior to the deadline for being eligible for the playoffs.

"I don't even know where I am," said Brouhard, who batted only 108 times during the regular season with a .269 average and 10 RBIs. "It really helped me to get down there (Vancouver of the Pacific Coast League) and get the rust off my seat."

Walks to Simmons and Money preceded Brouhard's RBI single in the second inning. When Lynn made a poor throw from center field and DeCinces made another error on the same play, the Brewers had scored three runs. They scored three more in the fourth on a wild pitch, a run-scoring single by Jim Gantner and a groundout by Molitor.

When the rains came again in the fifth inning, Haas wondered whether he would make the record book; he had a no-hitter going. But when play resumed in the sixth, Lynn cracked a run-scoring double to cut the Milwaukee margin to 6-1.

Gantner provided another RBI single in the Milwaukee half of the sixth, but the Angels rallied for four runs in the eighth and knocked Haas from the mound when Baylor smashed a bases-loaded homer.

Slaton took the mound and retired five straight batters, while Brouhard put the game out of reach with his two-run homer in the eighth.

The moment of truth was at hand.

The Angels opened Game 5 with a double by Brian Downing, who later scored on a single by Lynn. But the Brewers gave no quarter, scoring in their half of the first on a double by Molitor, a grounder and a sacrifice fly by Simmons.

Lynn, who had 11 hits in the playoffs and was the series' Most Valuable Player, drove home the second California run with a single in the third. Boone extended the Angels' lead to 3-1 in the fourth with an RBI single.

But Oglivie, back in the lineup, belted a long home run over the right-field wall in the Brewers' fourth.

With one out in the Angels' fifth, Jackson drew a walk from Milwaukee starter Pete Vuckovich. Lynn and Baylor followed with singles. But any threat of the Angels adding to their 3-2 lead was squelched when Brewers' catcher-turned-right fielder Charlie Moore nailed Jackson at third base with a perfect throw following Lynn's hit.

"When I ran by the ball, it took a real big hop," Jackson said. "I thought the play might be close but I never thought I'd be out."

"I knew it was a good throw when I let it go," said Moore, who had 13 assists in the regular season, "but I wasn't sure how good it was until I saw the umpire's hand go up."

Kison, who had a lifetime September-October record of 32-8, pitched five innings before giving way to hard-throwing Luis Sanchez. Sanchez mowed down the Brewers in the sixth and then retired Money to lead off the seventh before running into trouble.

Moore's bloop hit dropped in the middle of the infield, just out of the reach of a diving Grich at second base. First-base umpire Al Clark ruled that Grich had caught the ball, but was overruled by home-plate umpire Don Denkinger.

Gantner followed with a single up the middle and, after Molitor fouled out for the second out, Yount fouled off several two-strike pitches before working Sanchez for a walk to load the bases.

Cooper, who had gone 2-for-19 and was hitless in his previous nine at-bats, strolled to the plate. He had been a .313 hitter during the regular season. Nearly everyone in the ballpark expected California Manager Gene Mauch to bring in lefthander Andy Hassler, but the veteran skipper stayed with Sanchez.

The 1-and-1 pitch to Cooper was a fastball, tailing away but slightly up in the strike zone, and Cooper stroked it to left field. In a Carlton Fisk imitation (from the 1975 World Series), Cooper implored the looping hit to get down safely. It did, with Moore and Gantner scoring to give the Brewers a 4-3 lead.

"I thought it might carry too far and be the third out," said Cooper. "When it didn't, I had the most satisfying hit of my life."

Two more bits of drama were left, however.

Marshall Edwards, a 5-foot-9 backup outfielder, was inserted in center field for Thomas (bothered by a knee injury) in the eighth. Baylor, the second batter in the inning, crashed a long drive off reliever Bob McClure. Edwards went into full flight at the wall in left-center to snare the potentially troublesome smash.

Then in the ninth, after a leadoff pinch single by Ron Jackson, Ladd was called on to make his third appearance of the series. Boone sacrificed pinch-runner Rob Wilfong to second base. Downing then grounded to third, before Carew bounced to Yount at shortstop.

"I saw every bounce going into Robin's glove," Ladd said. "And I saw every inch of his throw to first base."

GAME OF TUESDAY, OCTOBER 5, AT CALIFORNIA (N)

Milwaukee	AB.	R.	H.	RBI.	PO.	A.
Molitor, 3b	4	1	1	0	0	0
Yount, ss	4	0	1	0	4	1
Cooper, 1b	4	0	1	1	6	0
Simmons, c	4	1	2	0	7	0
Thomas, cf	4	1	1	2	3	0
Oglivie, lf	4	0	0	0	2	0
Money, dh	3	0	0	0	0	0
Moore, rf	3	0	1	0	1	0
Gantner, 2b	4	0	0	0	0	3
Caldwell, p	0	0	0	0	0	2
Slaton, p	0	0	0	0	1	0
Ladd, p	0	0	0	0	0	0
Bernard, p	0	0	0	0	0	0
Totals	34	3	7	3	24	6

California	AB.	R.	H.	RBI.	PO.	A.
Downing, lf	4	2	1	0	1	0
Beniquez, lf	0	0	0	0	1	0
DeCinces, 3b	4	2	1	0	2	5
Grich, 2b	3	1	2	1	1	3
Baylor, dh	3	1	2	5	0	0
Re. Jackson, rf	4	0	1	0	0	0
Clark, rf	0	0	0	0	1	0
Lynn, cf	4	1	3	1	4	0
Carew, 1b	4	0	0	0	8	2
Foli, ss	4	0	0	0	1	1
Boone, c	4	1	1	0	5	0
John, p	0	0	0	0	3	1
Totals	34	8	10	8	27	12

Milwaukee .... 021 000 000—3
California............................. 104 210 00x—8

Milwaukee	IP.	H.	R.	ER.	BB.	SO.
Caldwell (Loser)	3*	7	6	5	1	2
Slaton	3	3	2	1	1	2
Ladd	1	0	0	0	0	3
Bernard	1	0	0	0	0	0

California	IP.	H.	R.	ER.	BB.	SO.
John (Winner)	9	7	3	3	1	5

*Pitched to one batter in fourth.

Game-winning RBI—Baylor.
Errors—Caldwell, Molitor. Double play—Milwaukee 1. Left on bases—Milwaukee 6, California 5. Two-base hits—Cooper, Grich. Three-base hit—Baylor. Home runs— Thomas, Lynn. Sacrifice fly —Baylor. Hit by pitcher—By John (Moore). Wild pitch—Caldwell. Umpires—Barnett, Kunkel, Garcia, Palermo, Denkinger and Clark. Time—2:31. Attendance—64,406.

GAME OF WEDNESDAY, OCTOBER 6, AT CALIFORNIA (N)

Milwaukee	AB.	R.	H.	RBI.	PO.	A.
Molitor, 3b	4	1	2	2	1	1
Yount, ss	4	0	1	0	2	3
Cooper, 1b	4	0	0	0	5	1
Simmons, c	4	0	0	0	5	0
Oglivie, lf	4	0	0	0	1	0
Thomas, cf	3	0	0	0	3	0
Howell, dh	3	0	0	0	0	0
Moore, rf	3	1	2	0	3	0
Gantner, 2b	3	0	0	0	4	2
Vuckovich, p	0	0	0	0	0	1
Totals	32	2	5	2	24	8

California	AB.	R.	H.	RBI.	PO.	A.
Downing, lf	3	0	0	0	1	0
Beniquez, lf	0	0	0	0	0	0
Carew, 1b	4	0	0	0	14	0
Re. Jackson, rf	3	1	1	1	1	0
Clark, rf	0	0	0	0	0	0
Lynn, cf	4	1	2	0	1	0
Baylor, dh	3	0	0	0	0	0
DeCinces, 3b	3	2	1	0	1	1
Grich, 2b	2	0	1	0	1	5
Foli, ss	2	0	1	1	0	2
Boone, c	1	0	0	2	8	1
Kison, p	0	0	0	0	0	0
Totals	25	4	6	4	27	9

Milwaukee .... 000 020 000—2
California .... 021 100 00x—4

Milwaukee	IP.	H.	R.	ER.	BB.	SO.
Vuckovich (Loser)	8	6	4	4	4	4

California	IP.	H.	R.	ER.	BB.	SO.
Kison (Winner)	9	5	2	2	0	8

Game-winning RBI—Foli.
Errors—None. Double plays—Milwaukee 2. Left on bases—Milwaukee 3, California 5. Two-base hit—DeCinces. Home runs—Re. Jackson, Molitor. Sacrifice hits—Boone, Foli. Sacrifice fly—Boone. Hit by pitcher—By Vuckovich (Grich). Umpires—Kunkel, Garcia, Palermo, Denkinger, Clark and Barnett. Time—2:06. Attendance—64,179.

GAME OF FRIDAY, OCTOBER 8, AT MILWAUKEE

California	AB.	R.	H.	RBI.	PO.	A.
Downing, lf	4	0	0	0	2	0
Carew, 1b	4	1	2	0	4	0
Re. Jackson, rf	4	0	1	0	0	0
Lynn, cf	3	1	2	1	4	0
Baylor, dh	3	0	1	1	0	0
DeCinces, 3b	4	0	1	0	3	1
Grich, 2b	4	0	0	0	2	2
Foli, ss	3	0	0	0	3	1
Wilfong, ph	1	0	0	0	0	0
Boone, c	4	1	1	1	6	0
Zahn, p	0	0	0	0	0	0
Witt, p	0	0	0	0	0	1
Hassler, p	0	0	0	0	0	0
Totals	34	3	8	3	24	5

Milwaukee	AB.	R.	H.	RBI.	PO.	A.
Molitor, 3b	4	1	1	2	1	4
Yount, ss	2	1	1	0	0	4
Cooper, 1b	4	1	1	1	12	0
Simmons, c	4	1	1	0	11	0
Thomas, cf	3	0	0	0	2	0
Oglivie, lf	3	0	1	0	0	0
Money, dh	1	0	0	1	0	0
Edwards, pr-dh	0	1	0	0	0	0
Moore, rf	2	0	1	0	0	0
Gantner, 2b	3	0	0	0	1	1
Sutton, p	0	0	0	0	0	0
Ladd, p	0	0	0	0	0	0
Totals	26	5	6	5	27	10

California .... 000 000 030—3
Milwaukee .... 000 300 20x—5

California	IP.	H.	R.	ER.	BB.	SO.
Zahn (Loser)	3⅔	4	3	3	1	2
Witt	3	2	2	2	2	3
Hassler	1⅓	0	0	0	0	1

Milwaukee	IP.	H.	R.	ER.	BB.	SO.
Sutton (Winner)	7⅔	8	3	3	2	9
Ladd (Save)	1⅓	0	0	0	0	2

Game-winning RBI—Cooper.
Errors—None. Double plays—California 1, Milwaukee 1. Left on bases—California 6, Milwaukee 4. Two-base hits—Lynn, Baylor, Cooper. Home runs—Molitor, Boone. Stolen base—Carew. Sacrifice hit—Moore. Sacrifice flies—Thomas, Money. Hit by pitcher—By Zahn (Oglivie). Umpires—Garcia, Palermo, Denkinger, Clark, Barnett and Kunkel. Time—2:41. Attendance—50,135.

GAME OF SATURDAY, OCTOBER 9, AT MILWAUKEE

California	AB.	R.	H.	RBI.	PO.	A.
Downing, lf	4	1	1	0	0	0
Carew, 1b	2	1	1	0	10	2
Re. Jackson, rf	4	1	0	0	0	0
Lynn, cf	3	1	1	1	4	0
Baylor, dh	4	1	1	4	0	0
DeCinces, 3b	4	0	0	1	1	3
Grich, 2b	3	0	0	0	3	5
Foli, ss	4	0	1	0	2	3
Boone, c	4	0	0	0	4	2
John, p	0	0	0	0	0	0
Goltz, p	0	0	0	0	0	0
Sanchez, p	0	0	0	0	0	0
Totals	32	5	5	5	24	15

Milwaukee	AB.	R.	H.	RBI.	PO.	A.
Molitor, 3b	4	0	0	1	0	3
Yount, ss	4	0	1	0	2	2
Cooper, 1b	4	0	0	0	5	1
Simmons, c	3	1	0	0	9	1
Thomas, cf	2	0	0	0	5	0
Money, dh	3	2	2	0	0	0
Edwards, pr-dh	0	1	0	0	0	0
Brouhard, lf	4	4	3	3	1	0
Moore, rf	2	1	1	0	2	0
Gantner, 2b	4	0	2	2	3	0
Haas, p	0	0	0	0	0	0
Slaton, p	0	0	0	0	0	0
Totals	30	9	9	6	27	7

California .... 000 001 040—5
Milwaukee .... 030 301 02x—9

California	IP.	H.	R.	ER.	BB.	SO.
John (Loser)	3⅓	4	6	4	5	1
Goltz	3⅔	4	3	3	2	2
Sanchez	1	1	0	0	0	0

Milwaukee	IP.	H.	R.	ER.	BB.	SO.
Haas (Winner)	7⅓	5	5	4	5	7
Slaton (Save)	1⅔	0	0	0	0	1

*Pitched to two batters in eighth.
Game-winning RBI—Brouhard.
Errors—Lynn, DeCinces 2, Yount, Cooper. Double play—California 1. Left on bases—California 5, Milwaukee 5. Two-base hits—Lynn, Carew, Brouhard. Home runs—Baylor, Brouhard. Stolen base—Edwards. Caught stealing—Carew, Molitor, Thomas. Sacrifice hit—Moore. Wild pitches—John 3. Passed ball—Boone. Umpires—Palermo, Denkinger, Clark, Barnett, Kunkel and Garcia. Time—3:10. Attendance—51,003.

GAME OF SUNDAY, OCTOBER 10, AT MILWAUKEE

California	AB.	R.	H.	RBI.	PO.	A.
Downing, lf	4	1	1	0	1	0
Carew, 1b	3	0	0	0	7	0
Re. Jackson, rf	3	0	0	0	1	0
Lynn, cf	4	0	3	2	3	0
Baylor, dh	4	0	1	0	0	0
DeCinces, 3b	4	1	3	0	2	2
Grich, 2b	3	0	0	0	3	2
Foli, ss	3	0	0	0	0	0
Ro. Jackson, ph	1	0	1	0	0	0
Wilfong, pr	0	0	0	0	0	0
Boone, c	3	1	2	1	7	0
Kison, p	0	0	0	0	0	0
Sanchez, p	0	0	0	0	0	0
Hassler, p	0	0	0	0	0	1
Totals	32	3	11	3	24	5

Milwaukee	AB.	R.	H.	RBI.	PO.	A.
Molitor, 3b	3	1	2	0	2	3
Yount, ss	2	0	0	0	3	2
Cooper, 1b	4	0	1	2	9	1
Simmons, c	3	0	0	1	4	2
Oglivie, lf	4	1	1	1	2	0
Thomas, cf	3	0	0	0	0	0
Edwards, cf	1	0	0	0	2	0
Money, dh	4	0	0	0	0	0
Moore, rf	3	1	1	0	1	1
Gantner, 2b	2	1	1	0	4	2
Vuckovich, p	0	0	0	0	0	2
McClure, p	0	0	0	0	0	0
Ladd, p	0	0	0	0	0	1
Totals	29	4	6	4	27	14

```
California ............................. 1 0 1  1 0 0  0 0 0—3
Milwaukee ........................... 1 0 0  1 0 0  2 0 x—4
```

California	IP.	H.	R.	ER.	BB.	SO.
Kison	5	3	2	1	3	4
Sanchez (Loser)	1⅔	3	2	2	1	1
Hassler	1⅓	0	0	0	0	1

Milwaukee	IP.	H.	R.	ER.	BB.	SO.
Vuckovich	6⅓	9	3	3	3	4
McClure (Winner)	1⅔*	2	0	0	0	0
Ladd (Save)	1	0	0	0	0	0

*Pitched to one batter in ninth.
Game-winning RBI—Cooper.
Errors—Oglivie 2, Molitor, Cooper, DeCinces.
Double plays—California 1, Milwaukee 2. Left on bases—California 8, Milwaukee 6. Two-base hits

Paul Molitor's two-run homer in Game 3 helped the Brewers break the ice against the Angels.

—Downing, DeCinces, Molitor. Home run—Oglivie. Stolen base—Molitor. Caught stealing—DeCinces. Sacrifice hits—Downing, Grich, Boone. Sacrifice fly—Simmons. Umpires—Denkinger, Clark, Barnett, Kunkel, Garcia and Palermo. Time—3:01. Attendance—54,968.

MILWAUKEE BREWERS' BATTING AND FIELDING AVERAGES

Player—Position	G.	AB.	R.	H.	TB.	2B.	3B.	HR.	RBI.	B.A.	PO.	A.	E.	F.A.
Brouhard, lf	1	4	4	3	7	1	0	1	3	.750	1	0	0	1.000
Moore, rf	5	13	3	6	6	0	0	0	0	.462	7	1	0	1.000
Molitor, 3b	5	19	4	6	13	1	0	2	5	.316	4	11	2	.882
Yount, ss	5	16	1	4	4	0	0	0	0	.250	11	12	1	.958
Gantner, 2b	5	16	1	3	3	0	0	0	2	.188	12	8	0	1.000
Money, dh	4	11	2	2	2	0	0	0	1	.182	0	0	0	.000
Simmons, c	5	18	3	3	3	0	0	0	1	.167	36	3	0	1.000
Cooper, 1b	5	20	1	3	5	2	0	0	4	.150	37	3	2	.952
Oglivie, lf	4	15	1	2	5	0	0	1	1	.133	5	0	2	.714
Thomas, cf	5	16	1	1	4	0	0	1	3	.063	13	0	0	1.000
Edwards, pr-dh-cf	3	0	2	0	0	0	0	0	0	.000	2	0	0	1.000
Ladd, p	3	0	0	0	0	0	0	0	0	.000	0	1	0	1.000
Slaton, p	2	0	0	0	0	0	0	0	0	.000	1	0	0	1.000
Vuckovich, p	2	0	0	0	0	0	0	0	0	.000	0	3	0	1.000
Bernard, p	1	0	0	0	0	0	0	0	0	.000	0	0	0	.000
Caldwell, p	1	0	0	0	0	0	0	0	0	.000	0	2	1	.667
Haas, p	1	0	0	0	0	0	0	0	0	.000	0	0	0	.000
McClure, p	1	0	0	0	0	0	0	0	0	.000	0	0	0	.000
Sutton, p	1	0	0	0	0	0	0	0	0	.000	0	1	0	1.000
Howell, dh	1	3	0	0	0	0	0	0	0	.000	0	0	0	.000
Totals	5	151	23	33	52	4	0	5	20	.219	129	45	8	.956

CALIFORNIA ANGELS' BATTING AND FIELDING AVERAGES

Player—Position	G.	AB.	R.	H.	TB.	2B.	3B.	HR.	RBI.	B.A.	PO.	A.	E.	F.A.
Ro. Jackson, ph	1	1	0	1	1	0	0	0	0	1.000	0	0	0	.000
Lynn, cf	5	18	5	11	16	2	0	1	5	.611	16	0	1	.941
DeCinces, 3b	5	19	5	6	8	2	0	0	0	.316	9	12	3	.875
Baylor, dh	5	17	2	5	11	1	1	1	10	.294	0	0	0	.000
Boone, c	5	16	3	4	7	0	0	1	4	.250	30	3	0	1.000
Grich, 2b	5	15	1	3	4	1	0	0	1	.200	10	17	0	1.000
Carew, 1b	5	17	2	3	4	1	0	0	0	.176	43	4	0	1.000
Downing, lf	5	19	3	3	4	1	0	0	0	.158	5	0	0	1.000
Foli, ss	5	16	0	2	2	0	0	0	1	.125	6	7	0	1.000
Re. Jackson, rf	5	18	2	2	5	0	0	1	2	.111	2	0	0	1.000
Beniquez, lf	2	0	0	0	0	0	0	0	0	.000	1	0	0	1.000
Clark, rf	2	0	0	0	0	0	0	0	0	.000	1	0	0	1.000
Hassler, p	2	0	0	0	0	0	0	0	0	.000	0	1	0	1.000
John, p	2	0	0	0	0	0	0	0	0	.000	3	1	0	1.000
Kison, p	2	0	0	0	0	0	0	0	0	.000	0	0	0	.000
Sanchez, p	2	0	0	0	0	0	0	0	0	.000	0	0	0	.000
Goltz, p	1	0	0	0	0	0	0	0	0	.000	0	0	0	.000
Witt, p	1	0	0	0	0	0	0	0	0	.000	0	1	0	1.000
Zahn, p	1	0	0	0	0	0	0	0	0	.000	0	0	0	.000
Wilfong, ph-pr	2	1	0	0	0	0	0	0	0	.000	0	0	0	.000
Totals	5	157	23	40	62	8	1	4	23	.255	126	46	4	.977

MILWAUKEE BREWERS' PITCHING RECORDS

Pitcher	G.	GS.	CG.	IP.	H.	R.	ER.	BB.	SO.	HB.	WP.	W.	L.	Pct.	ERA
Ladd	3	0	0	3⅓	0	0	0	0	5	0	0	0	0	.000	0.00
McClure	1	0	0	1⅔	2	0	0	0	0	0	0	1	0	1.000	0.00
Bernard	1	0	0	1	0	0	0	0	0	0	0	0	0	.000	0.00
Slaton	2	0	0	4⅔	3	2	1	1	3	0	0	0	0	.000	1.93
Sutton	1	1	0	7⅔	8	3	3	2	9	0	0	1	0	1.000	3.52
Vuckovich	2	2	1	14⅓	15	7	7	7	8	0	0	0	1	.000	4.40
Haas	1	1	0	7⅓	5	5	4	5	7	0	0	1	0	1.000	4.91
Caldwell	1	1	0	3	7	6	5	1	2	0	1	0	1	.000	15.00
Totals	5	5	1	43	40	23	20	16	34	0	1	3	2	.600	4.19

No shutouts. Saves—Ladd 2, Slaton.

CALIFORNIA ANGELS' PITCHING RECORDS

Pitcher	G.	GS.	CG.	IP.	H.	R.	ER.	BB.	SO.	HB.	WP.	W.	L.	Pct.	ERA
Hassler	2	0	0	2⅔	0	0	0	0	2	0	0	0	0	.000	0.00
Kison	2	2	1	14	8	4	3	3	12	0	0	1	0	1.000	1.93
John	2	2	1	12⅓	11	9	7	6	6	1	3	1	1	.500	5.11
Witt	1	0	0	3	2	2	2	3	2	0	0	0	0	.000	6.00
Sanchez	2	0	0	2⅔	4	2	2	1	1	0	0	0	1	.000	6.75
Goltz	1	0	0	3⅔	4	3	3	2	2	0	0	0	0	.000	7.30
Zahn	1	1	0	3⅔	4	3	3	1	2	1	0	0	1	.000	7.30
Totals	5	5	2	42	33	23	20	15	28	2	3	2	3	.400	4.29

No shutouts or saves.

COMPOSITE SCORE BY INNINGS

Milwaukee	1	5	1	7	2	1	4	2	0	—	23
California	2	2	6	4	1	1	0	7	0	—	23

Game-winning RBIs—Cooper 2, Baylor, Foli, Brouhard.

Sacrifice hits—Boone 2, Moore 2, Foli, Downing, Grich.

Sacrifice flies—Baylor, Boone, Thomas, Money, Simmons.

Stolen bases—Carew, Edwards, Molitor.

Caught stealing—Carew, Molitor, Thomas, DeCinces.

Double plays—Gantner, Yount and Cooper 2; Yount (unassisted); Yount, Gantner and Cooper; De-Cinces, Grich and Carew; Molitor and Cooper; Grich, Carew, Foli, Carew and DeCinces; DeCinces and Grich; Molitor, Gantner and Cooper.

Left on bases—Milwaukee 6, 3, 4, 5, 6—24; California 5, 5, 6, 5, 8—29.

Hit by pitcher—By John (Moore), by Vuckovich (Grich), by Zahn (Oglivie).

Passed ball—Boone.

Balks—None.

Time of games—First game, 2:31; second game, 2:06; third game, 2:41; fourth game, 3:10; fifth game, 3:01.

Attendance—First game, 64,406; second game, 64,179; third game, 50,135; fourth game, 51,003; fifth game, 54,968.

Umpires—Barnett, Kunkel, Garcia, Palermo, Denkinger and Clark.

Official scorers—Ed Munson, Pancho Palesse.

1982 WORLD SERIES

Including

Review of 1982 Series

Official Play-by-Play, Each Game

Official Composite Box Score

World Series MVP Darrell Porter delivers a victory hug to Bruce Sutter after the Cardinals relief ace had shut the door on Milwaukee in Game 7.

Cards Deck 'Mighty Brewers'

By LARRY WIGGE

Away from the madding crowd that was celebrating on the field and on the streets outside Busch Memorial Stadium after the St. Louis Cardinals had captured their ninth World Series in 13 appearances, Keith Hernandez took a moment to reminisce.

Foremost on his mind, of course, was his single to center field with the bases loaded and one out in the sixth inning that drove in two runs to erase a 3-1 Milwaukee lead and sparked the Cardinals to a 6-3 victory in the seventh game of the 1982 World Series. Also important to Hernandez, however, was a confrontation with a boyhood chum and lifelong friend.

When Hernandez came to the plate in perhaps the most crucial spot in the Cardinals' season, he wasn't thinking about his first 15 hitless at-bats or the two key errors he committed in the early part of the Series. Nor was he thinking about how he had battled back to go 6-for-11 thereafter, or how nice it would be to celebrate his 29th birthday with a key hit. Instead, he was thinking about Brewers' lefthanded reliever Bob McClure, his longtime friend, who was to serve up the key two-run single.

"Yeah, I thought about it a lot," Hernandez said of McClure. "I grew up about 100 feet from him in San Francisco. I played with him in grammar school, junior high. He was always the best pitcher. And then he moved to Terra Nova, and we moved to Millbrae where I went to Capuchino High.

"I remember I hit against him in a Little League championship game at Linda Mar. I went 2-for-3, one bleeder, one line drive. I was 10 and he was 11."

But this meeting in 1982 wasn't Little League stuff.

"I had to try to block all of that out of my mind when I came to the plate," Hernandez said. "I worked the count to 3-and-1." Then. . . .

Hernandez said he didn't hear the deafening roar of the crowd when he slapped a single to center, scoring Ozzie and Lonnie Smith. Nor did he hear the cheers when George Hendrick followed with a single to right to score pinch-runner Mike Ramsey with what proved to be the winning run.

"I was looking for a double play," a solemn McClure said later. "It didn't work out that way."

Cardinals first baseman Keith Hernandez won his Game 7 confrontation with boyhood chum Bob McClure.

McClure said he thought he had faced Hernandez twice when the two were in the American Association in 1974, but Hernandez didn't recall any meeting between the two since high school. A hard-throwing lefthander, McClure said he tried hard "the first time I faced Keith (a walk on four pitches leading off the eighth inning of Game 2). This time I tried to get our friendship out of my mind."

The record book will show clearly that Hernandez got the best of McClure on October 20, 1982. But to Hernandez, the feeling of bat connecting with ball was more personal.

After most of the crowd of reporters had departed the winners' locker room, Hernandez pulled a cover off his locker room stall and pointed to a photo on the floor. It was a picture of Hernandez and McClure, arm in arm, taken before Game 6. McClure had written a note on the photo.

"Can't get you out," he penned. "Best wishes, Bob McClure."

When the 79th World Series began October 12, the story lines were expected to focus on Milwaukee's power vs. the Cardinals' speed. Another interesting confrontation was built in.

It had been 22 months since Cardinals Manager Whitey Herzog, also general manager at the time, had traded established veterans Ted Simmons, Rollie Fingers and Pete Vuckovich to the Brewers for Sixto Lezcano, Lary Sorensen (both since departed) and minor leaguers Dave LaPoint and David Green.

Those in the trade proved only sidebar material, though, for writers from throughout the country.

You wouldn't have believed it was going to be a St. Louis series based on the Game 1 final score of 10-0 in favor of the Brewers.

"All I can say," Herzog said, "is I'm glad we didn't have to play a doubleheader today the way we played."

Mike Caldwell, a lefthander who had a brief trial with the Cardinals in the spring of 1977, shackled the Redbirds on three hits. Meanwhile, the top two men in the Milwaukee batting order were wearing out Bob Forsch and three relievers.

Leadoff man Paul Molitor set a Series record with five hits and Robin Yount, who follows Molitor in the potent Brewers' lineup, smacked four. It was the first time since 1946—and only the third time in history—that one team had two four-hit performances in the same game. The '46 Cards, in fact, had three players—Joe Garagiola, Enos Slaughter and Whitey Kurowski—collect four hits in the same game.

Oh, yes, Simmons belted a fifth-inning home run against his former teammates.

Simmons hit another homer in Game 2, but that contest might best be remembered as the call of the wild. Milwaukee Manager Harvey Kuenn called on Peter Ladd to pitch in relief in the last of the eighth with two men on, one out and the score tied, 4-4. It was the same Ladd who performed so admirably in filling in for the injured Rollie Fingers in the A.L. Championship Series. But this time the hard-throwing righthander walked Lonnie Smith and pinch-hitter Steve Braun to force in the winning run. Ladd fumed at plate umpire Bill Haller's call on a 3-2 pitch to Smith.

Game 3 featured the exploits of Willie McGee, St. Louis' rookie center fielder. The will-of-the-wisp not only clubbed two home runs to key the Cardinals' 6-2 victory, but he also flagged down a couple of long drives, by Molitor leading off Milwaukee's first inning and by Gorman Thomas with a man on base and one out in the ninth.

"I don't know if anyone has ever played a better World Series game than Willie," said a smiling Herzog. "He hit two homers and was all over the field. If he doesn't make that catch in the ninth, Mr. Sutter's in trouble." But St. Louis relief ace Bruce Sutter escaped, notching the first of his two Series saves.

McGee became only the third rookie to hit two home runs in a Series game, following Charlie Keller of the 1939 New York Yankees and Tony Kubek of the '57 Yanks.

The other key moment in Game 3 came with one out in the bottom of the seventh when Simmons crashed a single off the right kneecap of St. Louis pitcher Joaquin Andujar. The Cardinals' righthander had to be carried off the field, and his availability for the remainder of the Series was in question. Using Sutter for 2⅓ innings for the second straight game, Herzog opened himself for some criticism when Game 4 took shape.

The Cardinals threatened to take a 3-1 lead in the Series with one run in the first inning and three in the second of Game 4. The Redbirds, in fact, entered the last of the seventh with a 5-1 lead.

But after LaPoint retired Thomas on a foul pop, Ben Oglivie hit a grounder to Hernandez, who flipped to LaPoint for what should have been the second out. Instead, LaPoint dropped the throw as he crossed the bag.

Don Money followed with a single. After Charlie Moore popped to short (for what-should have been the end of the inning), Jim Gantner doubled home Oglivie. Doug Bair replaced LaPoint and walked Molitor. Then Yount sent a check-swing single to right, scoring Money and Gantner. Before the inning was history, Cecil Cooper would drive in the tying run with an infield single off Jim Kaat and Gorman Thomas (battling a 5-for-56 slump) would single home two more runs of Jeff Lahti, giving the Brewers six runs in the inning and a 7-5 victory to even the Series at two games apiece. A tired Sutter wasn't available to quell the rally.

"When Keith's throw hit my glove it felt like a brick and it dropped to the ground like one, too," recalled LaPoint.

There were no check-swing hits for Yount in Game 5 as the Brewers defeated the Cardinals, 6-4, to take a 3-2 lead in games. Yount, the American League's Most Valuable Player, rapped a shot off St. Louis starter Bob Forsch's leg for a single in the first inning and eventually scored. In the third, he doubled to set the stage for Milwaukee's second run. He singled in the fifth to keep alive another rally that had netted the Brewers their third run. And in the seventh he rifled a homer over the right-center field wall.

Yount, who hit .331 with 29 homers and 114 runs batted in during the regular season, went 4-for-4. With his four-hit performance in Game 1, it was the first time any player had managed two such games in one Series.

Caldwell gained his second victory of the Series, even though he surrendered 14 hits in 8⅓ innings.

With their backs to the wall and veteran Don Sutton pitching for the Brewers against rookie John Stuper, the Redbirds played like a team possessed in Game 6.

The Cardinals had homers by Darrell Porter, who was named the Series MVP, and Hernandez, who drove in four runs in Game 6, in their 13-1 victory. The game also was spiced with controversy when Lonnie Smith tried to steal home in the third inning. He was called out, but television replays seemed to indicate otherwise. There also was a 26-minute rain delay in the bottom of the fifth and another delay of 2 hours, 13 minutes one inning later when the Cardinals scored six times and increased their cushion to 13-0.

Through it all, however, the focal point was Stuper. The 25-year-old righthander not only outdueled Sutton, but he endured both rain delays and pitched the entire game while yielding only four hits. He lost his shutout bid in the ninth inning.

"There's a fine line between being a hero and being just plain stupid," acknowledged Stuper when asked whether he might be jeopardizing his career by pitching so long. "I wouldn't have gone back

out there if I didn't think I could do the job."

The Series had advanced to the point of no return.

Though the Cardinals opened a 1-0 lead in the fourth inning of Game 7, Oglivie blasted a long home run in the fifth to tie the score. Andujar, pitching despite a swollen right knee, hurt himself in the sixth when he fielded Molitor's bunt and threw wildly to first base, the throw hitting the runner and Jim Gantner scoring from second base on the error. Later in the inning, Cecil Cooper got Molitor home with a sacrifice fly to put the Brewers on top, 3-1.

Then, with one out in the Cardinals' sixth, Ozzie Smith singled. Lonnie Smith doubled, sending Ozzie to third. McClure replaced Vuckovich on the mound for the Brewers and walked pinch-hitter Gene Tenace, setting the stage for Hernandez' game-tying single and Hendrick's decisive hit.

"I can't think of a better way to end it," said Dane Iorg, who set a Series record for designated hitters with nine hits. "The best hitting lineup in baseball against the best reliever (Sutter) in the game with a one-run lead. Nobody could have written the script any better."

The Cards, though, rewrote the script by adding to their lead.

Sutter, who entered the game in the eighth after Andujar was removed by Herzog following a shouting match with Milwaukee's Gantner, had a 6-3 edge by the time the ninth rolled around, the Cardinals getting two eighth-inning runs on singles by Porter and Braun. Sutter, who retired all six batters he faced, struck out Thomas to end the game.

"I knew Whitey had a plan when he traded for me (in December, 1980) and I also knew he wasn't going to let anything get in his way of winning it all," said Sutter. "It was fun watching all of that develop.

"I don't think it will really hit me . . . what we have done . . . until this winter. I'll be sitting up there on a deer stand, and I'll start yelling. I won't get any deer, but I'll have a good time."

"I told Whitey and the rest of the guys before the game that they could ice up the champagne, that there was no way the Brewers were going to beat me," said Andujar, holding an ice pack on his injured knee.

"I've got all winter to rest my knee. There's no way Whitey could have kept One Tough Dominican (his pet nickname for himself) out of this game."

Game 1

At St. Louis
October 12

Milwaukee (A.L.)	AB.	R.	H.	PO.	A.	E.
Molitor, 3b	6	1	5	0	2	0
Yount, ss	6	1	4	1	1	0
Cooper, 1b	4	1	0	14	3	0
Simmons, c	5	1	2	3	0	0
Oglivie, lf	4	1	0	0	0	0
Thomas, cf	4	0	1	2	0	0
Howell, dh	2	0	0	0	0	0
aMoney, dh	2	1	1	0	0	0
Moore, rf	5	2	2	4	0	0
Gantner, 2b	4	2	2	0	7	0
Caldwell, p	0	0	0	3	1	0
Totals	42	10	17	27	14	0

St. Louis (N.L.)	AB.	R.	H.	PO.	A.	E.
Herr, 2b	3	0	0	2	5	0
L. Smith, lf	4	0	0	2	0	0
Hernandez, 1b	4	0	0	14	1	1
Hendrick, rf	4	0	0	1	0	0
Tenace, dh	3	0	0	0	0	0
Porter, c	3	0	2	3	0	0
Green, cf	3	0	0	2	0	0
Oberkfell, 3b	3	0	1	0	4	0
O. Smith, ss	3	0	0	3	3	0
Forsch, p	0	0	0	0	0	0
Kaat, p	0	0	0	0	0	0
LaPoint, p	0	0	0	0	0	0
Lahti, p	0	0	0	0	0	0
Totals	30	0	3	27	13	1

Milwaukee	2 0 0	1 1 2	0 0 4—10
St. Louis	0 0 0	0 0 0	0 0 0— 0

Milwaukee	IP.	H.	R.	ER.	BB.	SO.
Caldwell (W)	9	3	0	0	1	3

St. Louis	IP.	H.	R.	ER.	BB.	SO.
Forsch (L)	5⅔	10	6	4	1	1
Kaat	1⅓	1	0	0	1	1
LaPoint	1⅔	3	2	2	1	0
Lahti	⅓	3	2	2	0	1

Bases on balls—Off Caldwell 1 (Herr), off Forsch 1 (Cooper), off Kaat 1 (Thomas), off La-Point 1 (Oglivie).

Strikeouts—By Caldwell 3 (L. Smith 2, Tenace), by Forsch 1 (Simmons), by Kaat 1 (Cooper), by Lahti 1 (Yount).

Game-winning RBI—None.

aFlied out for Howell in seventh. Runs batted in—Molitor 2, Yount 2, Simmons, Thomas, Money, Gantner 2. Two-base hits—Moore, Yount, Porter. Three-base hit—Gantner. Home run—Simmons. Sacrifice hit—Gantner. Hit by pitcher—By Forsch (Howell). Double play—Hernandez, O. Smith and Hernandez. Left on bases—Milwaukee 10, St. Louis 4. Umpires—Weyer (N.L.) plate, Haller (A.L.) first, Kibler (N.L.) second, Phillips (A.L.) third, Davidson (N.L.) left, Evans (A.L.) right. Time—2:30. Attendance—53,723.

FIRST INNING

Milwaukee—Molitor grounded to Herr. Yount lined a single to left. Cooper walked, Yount advancing to second. Simmons was called out on strikes. Oglivie's smash toward Hernandez took one bounce before going under the first baseman's glove into right field; Yount scored and Cooper advanced to third on the error. Thomas hit a ground ball single that Ozzie Smith backhanded in short left as Cooper scored and Oglivie advanced to second. Howell was hit by a pitch, loading the bases. Moore fouled out to Hernandez. Two runs, two hits, one error, three left.

St. Louis—Herr grounded to Yount. Lonnie Smith grounded to Molitor. Hernandez grounded to Gantner. No runs, no hits, no errors, none left.

SECOND INNING

Milwaukee—Gantner flied to Green. Molitor beat out a ground ball to Ozzie Smith's right for a single. Yount blooped a single to center, Molitor stopping at second. Cooper popped to Ozzie Smith. Simmons popped to Herr. No runs, two hits, no errors, two left.

St. Louis—Hendrick flied to Thomas. Tenace popped to Cooper. Porter lined a double to right center. Green lined to Cooper. No runs, one hit, no errors, one left.

THIRD INNING

Milwaukee—Oglivie grounded to Herr. Thomas grounded to Oberkfell. Howell grounded to Herr. No runs, no hits, no errors, none left.

St. Louis—Oberkfell grounded to Gantner. Ozzie Smith bounced to Gantner, who made a leaping throw to first from the sliding pit in front of second base. Herr popped to Yount. No runs, no hits, no errors, none left.

FOURTH INNING

Milwaukee—Moore lined a double into the left-field corner. Gantner sacrificed Moore to third, Hernandez making the play unassisted. Molitor drove in Moore with a broken-bat single to second but was thrown out, Ozzie Smith to Herr, trying to stretch the hit into a double. Yount grounded to Oberkfell. One run, two hits, no errors, none left.

St. Louis—Lonnie Smith struck out. Hernandez grounded to Gantner. Hendrick hit a sharp grounder to the right of Cooper, who fielded the ball and threw to Caldwell covering first for the out. No runs, no hits, no errors, none left.

FIFTH INNING

Milwaukee—Cooper flied to Lonnie Smith. Simmons, after hitting a long foul ball into the right-field stands, blasted Forsch's next pitch over the right-field wall for a home run. Oglivie grounded to Herr. Thomas, on a checked swing, rolled out to Hernandez. One run, one hit, no errors, none left.

St. Louis—Tenace bounced out, Caldwell to Cooper. Porter grounded out, Cooper to Caldwell. Green grounded to Molitor. No runs, no hits, no errors, none left.

SIXTH INNING

Milwaukee—Howell grounded to Hernandez. Moore grounded to Ozzie Smith. Gantner lined a single to right. Molitor singled to left, Gantner stopping at second. Yount's soft fly dropped near the right-field line for a double, Gantner and Molitor scoring. Kaat replaced Forsch on the mound for St. Louis. Cooper struck out. Two runs, three hits, no errors, one left.

St. Louis—Oberkfell grounded to Gantner. Ozzie Smith flied to Thomas. Herr walked. Lonnie Smith struck out. No runs, no hits, no errors, one left.

SEVENTH INNING

Milwaukee—Simmons grounded a single to center. Oglivie grounded into a double play, Hernandez to Ozzie Smith to Hernandez. Thomas walked. Money batted for Howell and flied to Hendrick, who made a running catch in right center. No runs, one hit, no errors, one left.

St. Louis—Hernandez grounded out, Cooper to Caldwell. Hendrick grounded to Gantner. Tenace was called out on strikes. No runs, no hits, no errors, none left.

EIGHTH INNING

Milwaukee—LaPoint replaced Kaat on the mound for the Cardinals. Moore flied to Lonnie Smith. Gantner grounded to Oberkfell, who had to go far to his left to make the play. Molitor's grounder through the box was stopped behind second by a diving Ozzie Smith, who made no throw as Molitor tied a World Series record with his fourth hit. Yount collected his fourth hit with a single to right, Molitor stopping at second. Cooper forced Yount, Herr to Ozzie Smith. No runs, two hits, no errors, two left.

St. Louis—Porter grounded a single to center. Green hit a long fly over Moore's head, but Moore made a fine running catch on the warning track. Oberkfell grounded a single to center, Porter stopping at second. Ozzie Smith lined to Moore. Herr flied to Moore. No runs, two hits, no errors, two left.

NINTH INNING

Milwaukee—Simmons flied to Green. Oglivie walked. Thomas was nipped at first after bouncing to Oberkfell, Oglivie advancing to second. Money grounded a single to left—Ozzie Smith just missed making a diving stop—to score Oglivie. Lahti replaced LaPoint on the mound for St. Louis. Moore hit a high chopper over the mound for a single, Money stopping at second. Gantner's grounder scooted past Herr and rolled into deep right center for a triple, Money and Moore scoring. Molitor drove in Gantner and set a Series record with his fifth hit, a grounder in the hole between third and short. Yount was called out on strikes. Four runs, four hits, no errors, one left.

St. Louis—Lonnie Smith flied to Moore. Hernandez grounded to Gantner. Hendrick fouled out to Cooper. No runs, no hits, no errors, none left.

Game 2

At St. Louis
October 13

Milwaukee (A.L.)	AB.	R.	H.	PO.	A.	E.
Molitor, 3b	5	1	2	0	1	0
Yount, ss	4	1	1	4	3	0
Cooper, 1b	5	0	3	9	2	0
Simmons, c	3	1	1	5	0	0
Oglivie, lf	4	0	1	2	0	1
Thomas, cf	3	0	0	1	0	0
Howell, dh	4	1	0	0	0	0
Moore, rf	4	0	2	3	0	0
Gantner, 2b	3	0	0	0	3	0
Sutton, p	0	0	0	0	0	0
McClure, p	0	0	0	0	0	0
Ladd, p	0	0	0	0	0	0
Totals	35	4	10	24	9	1

St. Louis (N.L.)	AB.	R.	H.	PO.	A.	E.
Herr, 2b	3	1	1	2	1	0
Oberkfell, 3b	3	1	2	0	3	0
bTenace	1	0	0	0	0	0
Ramsey, 3b	0	0	0	0	0	0
Hernandez, 1b	3	0	0	7	2	0
Hendrick, rf	3	2	0	0	0	0
Porter, c	4	0	2	8	1	0
L. Smith, lf	3	0	0	1	0	0
Iorg, dh	2	0	1	0	0	0
aGreen, dh	1	0	0	0	0	0
cBraun, dh	0	0	0	0	0	0
McGee, cf	4	1	0	4	0	0
O. Smith, ss	4	0	2	5	3	0
Stuper, p	0	0	0	0	0	0
Kaat, p	0	0	0	0	0	0
Bair, p	0	0	0	0	0	0
Sutter, p	0	0	0	0	0	0
Totals	31	5	8	27	10	0

Milwaukee .... 012　010　000—4
St. Louis............................... 002　002　01*—5

Milwaukee	IP.	H.	R.	ER.	BB.	SO.
Sutton	6	5	4	4	1	3
McClure (L)	1⅓	2	1	1	2	2
Ladd	⅔	1	0	0	2	0

St. Louis	IP.	H.	R.	ER.	BB.	SO.
Stuper	4*	6	4	4	3	3
Kaat	⅔	1	0	0	0	0
Bair	2	1	0	0	0	3
Sutter (W)	2⅓	2	0	0	1	1

*Pitched to one batter in fifth.

Bases on balls—Off Sutton 1 (Hendrick), off McClure 2 (Herr, Hernandez), off Ladd 2 (L. Smith, Braun), off Stuper 3 (Yount, Thomas, Gantner), off Sutter 1 (Simmons).

Strikeouts—By Sutton 3 (Hendrick, Herr, L. Smith), by McClure 2 (Green, McGee), by Stuper 3 (Oglivie, Howell, Molitor), by Bair 3 (Thomas, Howell, Molitor), by Sutter 1 (Howell).

Game-winning RBI—Braun.

aStruck out for Iorg in seventh. bFlied out for Oberkfell in seventh. cWalked with bases loaded for Green in eighth. Runs batted in—Yount, Cooper, Simmons, Moore, Herr, Oberkfell, Porter 2, Braun. Two-base hits—Moore, Herr, Yount, Porter, Cooper. Home run—Simmons. Stolen bases—Molitor, McGee, Oberkfell, O. Smith. Caught stealing—Molitor. Wild pitches—Stuper 2. Double play—Hernandez, O. Smith and Hernandez. Left on bases—Milwaukee 8, St. Louis 7. Umpires—Haller (A.L.) plate, Kibler (N.L.) first, Phillips (A.L.) second, Davidson (N.L.) third, Evans (A.L.) left, Weyer (N.L.) right. Time—2:54. Attendance—53,723.

FIRST INNING

Milwaukee—Molitor grounded to Oberkfell. Yount walked. With Yount running, Cooper singled to left, Yount advancing to third. Simmons grounded into a double play, Hernandez to Ozzie Smith to Hernandez. No runs, one hit, no errors, one left.

St. Louis—Herr flied to Oglivie. Oberkfell flied to Moore. Hernandez flied to Moore. No runs, no hits, no errors, none left.

SECOND INNING

Milwaukee—Oglivie struck out. Thomas walked. Howell forced Thomas, Hernandez to Ozzie Smith. With Moore batting, Howell advanced to second on Stuper's wild pitch. Moore lined a double to the wall in left center, Howell scoring. Gantner flied to McGee. One run, one hit, no errors, one left.

St. Louis—Hendrick struck out. Porter grounded to Gantner. Lonnie Smith grounded to Yount. No runs, no hits, no errors, none left.

THIRD INNING

Milwaukee—Molitor grounded a single to center. On Stuper's first pitch to Yount, Molitor stole second without drawing a throw as Porter was unable to glove a low fastball. With the count to Yount 1-1, Stuper threw a wild pitch, Molitor advancing to third. Yount grounded to Herr, Molitor scoring. Cooper popped to Ozzie Smith. Simmons drilled a home run into the right-field bleachers. Oglivie singled to right. Thomas forced Oglivie, Oberkfell to Herr. Two runs, three hits, no errors, one left.

St. Louis—Iorg bounced a single to right. Cooper made a diving stop of McGee's grounder and threw to Yount to force Iorg. With Ozzie Smith batting, McGee stole second. Smith grounded to Yount, McGee advancing to third. Herr cracked a ground-rule double to right center, McGee scoring. Oberkfell lined a single to right, Herr scoring.

Hernandez fouled out to Oglivie. Two runs, three hits, no errors, one left.

FOURTH INNING

Milwaukee—Howell struck out. Moore grounded to Oberkfell. Gantner walked. Molitor struck out. No runs, no hits, no errors, one left.

St. Louis—Hendrick popped to Cooper. Porter grounded to Gantner. Lonnie Smith grounded to Molitor. No runs, no hits, no errors, none left.

FIFTH INNING

Milwaukee—Yount doubled high off the left-field wall. Kaat replaced Stuper on the mound for St. Louis. Cooper singled to left center, Yount scoring. Simmons flied to McGee. Oglivie popped to Ozzie Smith. Bair replaced Kaat on the mound for St. Louis. Thomas struck out. One run, two hits, no errors, one left.

St. Louis—Iorg grounded to Gantner. McGee popped to Yount. Ozzie Smith grounded to Yount. No runs, no hits, no errors, none left.

SIXTH INNING

Milwaukee—Howell struck out. Moore flied to McGee. Gantner popped to Ozzie Smith. No runs, no hits, no errors, none left.

St. Louis—Herr was called out on strikes. Oberkfell singled to center. On Sutton's first pitch to Hernandez, Oberkfell stole second. Hernandez flied to Moore, Oberkfell advancing to third after the catch. Hendrick walked. With Hendrick running, Porter lined a 1-2 pitch into the left-field corner for a double; Oberkfell and Hendrick scored, Porter advanced to third when Oglivie made an errant throw. Lonnie Smith struck out. Two runs, two hits, one error, one left.

SEVENTH INNING

Milwaukee—Molitor struck out. Yount flied to Lonnie Smith. Cooper doubled down the right-field line. Sutter replaced Bair on the mound for St. Louis. Simmons was walked intentionally. Dashing in front of second base, Ozzie Smith fielded Oglivie's bouncer and threw to Hernandez for the out. No runs, one hit, no errors, two left.

St. Louis—McClure replaced Sutton on the mound for Milwaukee. Green batted for Iorg and struck out. McGee struck out. Ozzie Smith singled to center. With Herr batting and the count 1-2, Smith stole second as Simmons made a high throw after calling for a pitchout. Herr walked. Tenace batted for Oberkfell and flied to Thomas. No runs, one hit, no errors, two left.

EIGHTH INNING

Milwaukee—Ramsey came in to play third base for St. Louis. Thomas fouled out to Porter. Howell struck out. Moore chopped the ball over Ramsey's head for a single. Gantner grounded to Hernandez at the bag. No runs, one hit, no errors, one left.

St. Louis—Hernandez walked. Hendrick forced Hernandez, Cooper to Yount. Porter singled to center, Hendrick stopping at second. Ladd replaced McClure on the mound for Milwaukee. Lonnie Smith walked on a 3-2 pitch that just missed the outside corner, loading the bases. Braun batted for Green and walked on four pitches, Hendrick scoring and the bases remaining loaded. McGee lined to Yount. Ozzie Smith's grounder struck Braun on the heel; though Braun was out, ending the inning, Smith was credited with a single. One run, two hits, no errors, three left.

NINTH INNING

Milwaukee—Molitor pushed a bunt down the

first-base line for a single. With Yount batting, Molitor was caught stealing, Porter to Herr, who dug out a low throw. Yount grounded to Ozzie Smith. Cooper flied to McGee. No runs, one hit, no errors, none left.

Game 3

At Milwaukee
October 15

St. Louis (N.L.)	AB.	R.	H.	PO.	A.	E.
Herr, 2b	5	0	0	1	3	0
Oberkfell, 3b	4	0	0	1	1	0
Hernandez, 1b	4	0	0	8	0	1
xHendrick, rf	2	1	1	3	0	0
Porter, c	4	0	0	6	0	0
L. Smith, lf	4	2	2	1	0	0
Green, lf	0	0	0	0	0	0
Iorg, dh	4	1	1	0	0	0
McGee, cf	3	2	2	6	0	0
O. Smith, ss	3	0	0	1	3	0
Andujar, p	0	0	0	0	1	0
Kaat, p	0	0	0	0	0	0
Bair, p	0	0	0	0	0	0
Sutter, p	0	0	0	0	0	0
Totals	33	6	6	27	8	1

Milwaukee (A.L.)	AB.	R.	H.	PO.	A.	E.
Molitor, 3b	4	0	0	1	0	0
Yount, ss	3	1	0	5	5	0
Cooper, 1b	4	1	1	14	0	1
Simmons, c	4	0	1	1	1	1
Oglivie, lf	4	0	0	4	0	0
Thomas, cf	4	0	1	2	0	0
Howell, dh	2	0	0	0	0	0
aMoney, dh	1	0	0	0	0	0
Moore, rf	3	0	0	0	0	0
Gantner, 2b	3	0	2	0	6	1
Vuckovich, p	0	0	0	0	2	0
McClure, p	0	0	0	0	0	0
Totals	32	2	5	27	14	3

St. Louis .... 0 0 0   0 3 0   2 0 1—6
Milwaukee .... 0 0 0   0 0 0   0 2 0—2

St. Louis	IP.	H.	R.	ER.	BB.	SO.
Andujar (W)	6⅓	3	0	0	1	3
Kaat	⅓	1	0	0	0	1
Bair	0*	0	0	0	1	0
Sutter (S)	2⅓	1	2	2	1	1

Milwaukee	IP.	H.	R.	ER.	BB.	SO.
Vuckovich (L)	8⅔	6	6	4	3	1
McClure	⅓	0	0	0	0	0

*Pitched to one batter in seventh.

Bases on balls—Off Andujar 1 (Moore), off Bair 1 (Money), off Sutter 1 (Yount), off Vuckovich 3 (Hendrick, McGee, O. Smith).

Strikeouts—By Andujar 3 (Thomas, Molitor, Oglivie), by Kaat 1 (Oglivie), by Sutter 1 (Money), by Vuckovich 1 (Porter).

Game-winning RBI—McGee.

xAwarded first base on catcher's interference. aWalked for Howell in seventh. Runs batted in—McGee 4, O. Smith, Cooper 2. Two-base hits—Gantner, L. Smith, Iorg. Three-base hit—L. Smith. Home runs—McGee 2, Cooper. Caught stealing—Hendrick. Double play—Herr, O. Smith and Hernandez. Left on bases—St. Louis 4, Milwaukee 6. Umpires—Kibler (N.L.) plate, Phillips (A.L.) first, Davidson (N.L.) second, Evans (A.L.) third, Weyer (N.L.) left, Haller (A.L.) right. Time—2:53. Attendance—56,556.

FIRST INNING

St. Louis—Herr popped to Yount. Oberkfell lined to Oglivie. Hernandez grounded to Gantner. No runs, no hits, no errors, none left.

Milwaukee—Molitor flied to McGee, who made a leaping catch at the 402-foot mark. Yount flied to Hendrick. Cooper grounded to Herr. No runs, no hits, no errors, none left.

SECOND INNING

St. Louis—Hendrick hit a two-hop single down the third-base line. Porter was retired on a dribbler, Vuckovich to Cooper, Hendrick advancing to second. Lonnie Smith bounced to Yount, Hendrick advancing to third. Iorg bounced out, Vuckovich to Cooper. No runs, one hit, no errors, one left.

Milwaukee—Simmons bounced out, Andujar to Hernandez. Oglivie lined to Hendrick. Thomas struck out. No runs, no hits, no errors, none left.

THIRD INNING

St. Louis—McGee grounded to Yount. Ozzie Smith grounded to Yount. Herr grounded to Gantner. No runs, no hits, no errors, none left.

Milwaukee—Howell grounded to Ozzie Smith. Moore walked. Gantner doubled to right, Moore stopping at third. Molitor struck out. Yount grounded to Herr. No runs, one hit, no errors, two left.

FOURTH INNING

St. Louis—Oberkfell fouled out to Molitor. Hernandez fouled out to Oglivie. Hendrick walked. With Porter batting, Hendrick was caught stealing, Simmons to Yount. No runs, no hits, no errors, none left.

Milwaukee—Cooper flied to McGee. Simmons flied to Hendrick. Oglivie struck out. No runs, no hits, no errors, none left.

FIFTH INNING

St. Louis—Porter was called out on strikes. Lonnie Smith doubled to left center. Iorg's grounder was booted by Cooper, Smith advancing to third. McGee belted a home run to right, Smith and Iorg scoring ahead of him. Ozzie Smith flied to Thomas. Herr grounded to Gantner. Three runs, two hits, one error, none left.

Milwaukee—Thomas popped to Herr. Howell grounded to Oberkfell. Moore grounded to Ozzie Smith. No runs, no hits, no errors, none left.

SIXTH INNING

St. Louis—Oberkfell popped to Yount. Hernandez grounded to Gantner. Hendrick grounded to Yount. No runs, no hits, no errors, none left.

Milwaukee—Gantner lined a single to right. Molitor flied to McGee. Yount grounded into a double play, Herr to Ozzie Smith to Hernandez. No runs, one hit, no errors, none left.

SEVENTH INNING

St. Louis—Porter popped to Yount. Lonnie Smith tripled to right center and scored when Gantner's relay throw struck him and bounced into the third-base dugout. Iorg flied to Thomas. McGee unloaded another home run to right field, the 31st time a player had hit two or more homers in a World Series game. Ozzie Smith popped to Yount. Two runs, two hits, one error, none left.

Milwaukee—Cooper flied to McGee. Simmons singled, smashing the ball off Andujar's right kneecap on one bounce. Andujar was carried off the field, and Kaat came in to pitch. Oglivie was called out on strikes. Thomas lined a single to left, Simmons stopping at second. After Money was announced as a pinch-hitter for Howell, Bair replaced Kaat on the mound for St. Louis. Money walked, loading the bases. Sutter replaced Bair on the mound for St. Louis. Oberkell, on the top step of the third-base dugout, made a backhanded catch of Moore's foul popup. No runs, two hits, no errors, three left.

EIGHTH INNING

St. Louis—Herr grounded to Gantner. Oberkfell flied to Oglivie. Hernandez grounded to Yount. No runs, no hits, no errors, none left.

Milwaukee—Gantner flied to Lonnie Smith. Molitor fouled out to Porter. Yount walked. Cooper hit a home run to right, Yount scoring ahead of him. Simmons grounded to Hernandez. Two runs, one hit, no errors, none left.

NINTH INNING

St. Louis—Simmons tipped Herndrick's bat as he lifted a fly to Oglivie, and Hendrick was awarded first base on catcher's interference. Porter, trying to sacrifice, popped up and Cooper made a diving catch in foul territory. Lonnie Smith flied to Oglivie. Iorg's drive to right bounced off the warning track and was touched by a fan for a ground-rule double, Hendrick stopping at third. (St. Louis Manager Herzog argued that Hendrick should have been allowed to score.) McGee was walked intentionally, loading the bases. Ozzie Smith walked, Hendrick scoring and the bases remaining loaded. McClure replaced Vuckovich on the mound for Milwaukee. Herr grounded to Gantner. One run, one hit, one error, three left.

Milwaukee—Green replaced Lonnie Smith in left field for St. Louis. Oglivie's grounder was fumbled by Hernandez for an error. Thomas drove the ball to deep left center, but McGee made a leaping catch to rob him of a home run. Money was called out on strikes. Moore flied to McGee. No runs, no hits, one error, one left.

Game 4

**At Milwaukee
October 16**

St. Louis (N.L.)	AB.	R.	H.	PO.	A.	E.
Herr, 2b	4	0	0	1	1	0
Oberkfell, 3b	2	2	1	0	2	0
bTenace	1	0	0	0	0	0
Hernandez, 1b	4	0	0	8	1	0
Hendrick, rf	4	0	1	1	0	0
Porter, c	3	0	1	5	0	0
L. Smith, lf	4	1	1	2	0	0
Iorg, dh	4	0	2	0	0	0
aGreen, dh	0	0	0	0	0	0
McGee, cf	4	1	1	4	0	0
O. Smith, ss	3	1	1	3	1	0
LaPoint, p	0	0	0	0	2	1
Bair, p	0	0	0	0	0	0
Kaat, p	0	0	0	0	0	0
Lahti, p	0	0	0	0	1	0
Totals	33	5	8	24	8	1

Milwaukee (A.L.)	AB.	R.	H.	PO.	A.	E.
Molitor, 3b	4	1	0	1	0	0
Yount, ss	4	1	2	3	3	1
Cooper, 1b	4	1	2	10	0	0
Simmons, c	2	0	0	6	0	0
Thomas, cf	4	0	1	4	0	0
Oglivie, lf	3	1	1	1	0	0
Money, dh	4	2	2	0	0	0
Moore, rf	4	0	1	0	0	0
Gantner, 2b	4	1	1	1	5	1
Haas, p	0	0	0	1	2	0
Slaton, p	0	0	0	0	0	0
McClure, p	0	0	0	0	0	0
Totals	33	7	10	27	10	2

St. Louis		1 3 0	0 0 1	0 0 0—5		
Milwaukee		0 0 0	0 1 0	6 0*—7		

St. Louis	IP.	H.	R.	ER.	BB.	SO.
LaPoint	6⅔	7	4	1	1	3
Bair (L)	0*	1	2	2	1	0
Kaat	0*	1	1	1	1	0
Lahti	1⅓	1	0	0	1	0

Milwaukee	IP.	H.	R.	ER.	BB.	SO.
Haas	5⅓	7	5	4	2	3
Slaton (W)	2	1	0	0	2	1
McClure (S)	1⅔	0	0	0	0	2

*Pitched to two batters in seventh.

Bases on balls—Off LaPoint 1 (Simmons), off Bair 1 (Molitor), off Kaat 1 (Simmons), off Lahti 1 (Oglivie), off Haas 2 (O. Smith, Oberkfell), off Slaton 2 (Oberkfell, Porter).

Strikeouts—By LaPoint 3 (Simmons, Money, Molitor), by Haas 3 (Herr, Hernandez, Porter), by Slaton 1 (L. Smith), by McClure 2 (Herr, Tenace).

Game-winning RBI—Thomas.

aRan for Iorg in eighth. bStruck out for Oberkfell in ninth. Runs batted in—Herr 2, Hendrick, Iorg, Yount 2, Cooper, Thomas 2, Gantner. Two-base hits—Oberkfell, Money, L. Smith, Iorg, Gantner. Three-base hit—Oglivie. Stolen bases—McGee, Oberkfell. Sacrifice fly—Herr. Wild pitches—Haas, Kaat. Double plays—Herr and Hernandez; O. Smith and Hernandez; Gantner, Yount and Cooper; Gantner and Cooper. Left on bases—St. Louis 6, Milwaukee 6. Umpires—Phillips (A.L.) plate, Davidson (N.L.) first, Evans (A.L.) second, Weyer (N.L.) third, Haller (A.L.) left, Kibler (N.L.) right. Time—3:04. Attendance—56,560.

FIRST INNING

St. Louis—Herr was called out on strikes. Oberkfell lashed a double down the right-field line. Hernandez struck out. Hendrick hit a bouncer to the left of Yount that glanced off his glove into short center for a single, Oberkfell scoring. Porter singled to center, Hendrick stopping at second. Lonnie Smith forced Hendrick, Molitor unassisted. One run, three hits, no errors, two left.

Milwaukee—Molitor grounded to Oberkfell. Yount chopped a single past third. With Yount running on a 3-2 pitch, Cooper lined into a double play, Herr to Hernandez. No runs, one hit, no errors, none left.

SECOND INNING

St. Louis—Iorg flied to Thomas. McGee singled to left. On a 2-2 pitchout with Ozzie Smith batting, McGee stole second. Smith walked. With Herr batting, McGee advanced to third and Smith to second on a wild pitch by Haas. Herr hit a long fly to center; Thomas made the catch but then slipped on the warning track and both McGee and Smith were able to score. Herr was credited with two runs batted in. Oberkfell walked. With Hernandez batting, Oberkfell stole second. Hernandez' sharp grounder skidded between Gantner's legs for an error; Oberkfell scored and Hernandez raced to second. Hendrick fouled out to Cooper. Three runs, one hit, one error, one left.

Milwaukee—Simmons struck out. Thomas flied to McGee. Oglivie tripled off the wall in left center. Money struck out. No runs, one hit, no errors, one left.

THIRD INNING

St. Louis—Porter rolled out, Haas to Cooper. Lonnie Smith lined to Haas. Iorg popped to Yount. No runs, no hits, no errors, none left.

Milwaukee—Moore flied to McGee. Gantner grounded to Oberkfell. Molitor struck out. No runs, no hits, no errors, none left.

FOURTH INNING

St. Louis—McGee grounded to Yount. Ozzie Smith bunted toward third for a single. Herr flied to Thomas. With Oberkfell batting, Smith was picked off, Haas to Cooper. No runs, one hit, no errors, none left.

Milwaukee—Yount bounced out, LaPoint to Hernandez. Cooper grounded a single to the right of Ozzie Smith. Simmons walked, Cooper advancing to second. Thomas fouled out to Porter. Oglivie grounded to Hernandez. No runs, one hit, no errors, two left.

FIFTH INNING

St. Louis—Oberkfell grounded to Gantner. Hernandez grounded to Yount. Hendrick flied to Thomas. No runs, no hits, no errors, none left.

Milwaukee—Money doubled to left center. Moore's lazy fly ball fell in front of McGee for a single, Money stopping at third. Gantner's grounder up the middle was turned into a double play by Ozzie Smith, who stepped on second as he caught the ball, then threw to Hernandez for the second out while Money scored. Molitor flied to McGee. One run, two hits, no errors, none left.

SIXTH INNING

St. Louis—Porter struck out. Lonnie Smith lined a double into the left-field corner. Iorg doubled to right center, Smith scoring. Slaton replaced Haas on the mound for Milwaukee. McGee flied to Oglivie. Ozzie Smith grounded to Yount, but Yount's throw pulled Cooper off the bag, Iorg advancing to third. Herr lined to Yount. One run, two hits, one error, two left.

Milwaukee—Yount's drive back to the box was snared on the short hop by LaPoint, who threw to Hernandez for the out. Cooper flied to Hendrick. Simmons flied to McGee. No runs, no hits, no errors, none left.

SEVENTH INNING

St. Louis—Oberkfell walked. Hernandez grounded into a double play, Gantner to Yount to Cooper. Hendrick grounded to Gantner. No runs, no hits, no errors, none left.

Milwaukee—Thomas fouled out to Porter. Oglivie reached after grounding to Hernandez when LaPoint, covering first, dropped Hernandez' throw. Money singled to right, Oglivie stopping at second. Moore popped to Ozzie Smith. Gantner doubled to right center, Oglivie scoring and Money stopping at third. Bair replaced LaPoint on the mound for St. Louis. Molitor walked, loading the bases. Yount, on a 2-1 pitch high and tight, lined a checked-swing single to right; Money and Gantner scored and Molitor advanced to third. Kaat replaced Bair on the mound for St. Louis. Cooper lined a one-hop single off the glove of a diving Oberkfell; Molitor scored and Yount stopped at second. With Simmons batting, Yount advanced to third and Cooper to second on a wild pitch by Kaat. Lahti replaced Kaat on the mound for St. Louis with a 2-1 count on Simmons and walked him intentionally, loading the bases. Thomas lined a single to left center; Yount and Cooper scored, Simmons advanced to third and Thomas raced to second on the throw to third. Oglivie was walked intentionally, loading the bases. Money lined to Lonnie Smith. Six runs, five hits, one error, three left.

EIGHTH INNING

St. Louis—Porter walked. Lonnie Smith struck out. Iorg lined a single to center, Porter advancing to third. Green ran for Iorg. McClure replaced Slaton on the mound for Milwaukee. McGee grounded into a double play, Gantner taking the ball at second and throwing to Cooper in time to nip McGee. No runs, one hit, no errors, one left.

Milwaukee—Moore bounced out, Lahti to Hernandez. Gantner lined to Ozzie Smith. Molitor flied to Lonnie Smith. No runs, no hits, no errors, none left.

NINTH INNING

St. Louis—Ozzie Smith grounded to Gantner. Herr was called out on strikes. Tenace batted for Oberkfell and struck out. No runs, no hits, no errors, none left.

Game 5

**At Milwaukee
October 17**

St. Louis (N.L.)	AB.	R.	H.	PO.	A.	E.
L. Smith, dh	5	0	2	0	0	0
Green, lf	5	2	2	2	0	0
Hernandez, 1b	4	1	3	5	1	0
Hendrick, rf	5	0	3	1	0	0
Porter, c	5	0	1	5	1	0
bRamsey	0	0	0	0	0	0
McGee, cf	5	0	1	4	0	0
Oberkfell, 3b	4	0	3	0	2	0
aTenace	1	0	0	0	0	0
Herr, 2b	4	0	0	3	2	1
O. Smith, ss	3	1	0	3	2	0
Forsch, p	0	0	0	1	0	1
Sutter, p	0	0	0	0	0	0
Totals	41	4	15	24	8	2

Milwaukee (A.L.)	AB.	R.	H.	PO.	A.	E.
Molitor, 3b	4	1	1	2	5	0
Yount, ss	4	2	4	3	3	0
Cooper, 1b	4	0	1	8	2	0
Simmons, c	3	0	0	4	1	0
Oglivie, lf	4	1	2	1	0	0
Thomas, cf	4	0	0	3	0	0
Money, dh	3	1	0	0	0	0
Moore, rf	4	1	2	1	0	0
Gantner, 2b	4	0	1	4	4	1
Caldwell, p	0	0	0	1	1	0
McClure, p	0	0	0	0	0	0
Totals	34	6	11	27	16	1

St. Louis	0 0 1	0 0 0	1 0 2—4
Milwaukee	1 0 1	0 1 0	1 2 *—6

St. Louis	IP.	H.	R.	ER.	BB.	SO.
Forsch (L)	7	8	4	3	2	3
Sutter	1	3	2	2	1	2

Milwaukee	IP.	H.	R.	ER.	BB.	SO.
Caldwell (W)	8⅓	14	4	4	2	3
McClure (S)	⅔	1	0	0	0	1

Bases on balls—Off Forsch 2 (Molitor, Simmons), off Sutter 1 (Money), off Caldwell 2 (Hernandez, O. Smith).

Strikeouts—By Forsch 3 (Thomas, Money, Oglivie), by Sutter 2 (Simmons, Thomas), by Caldwell 3 (Green, Porter, McGee), by McClure 1 (McGee).

Game-winning RBI—Cooper.

aFlied out for Oberkfell in ninth. bRan for Porter in ninth. Runs batted in—Hernandez 2, Hendrick 2, Molitor, Yount, Cooper, Simmons, Moore, Gantner. Two-base hits—Hernandez 2, Yount, Moore, Green. Three-base hit—Green. Home run —Yount. Stolen base—L. Smith. Caught stealing—L. Smith, Oglivie. Double plays—Porter and Herr; Oberkfell, Herr and Hernandez; Molitor and Cooper. Left on bases—St. Louis 12, Milwaukee 7. Umpires—Davidson (N.L.) plate, Evans (A.L.) first, Weyer (N.L.) second, Haller (A.L.) third, Kibler (N.L.) left, Phillips (A.L.) right. Time— 3:02. Attendance—56,562.

FIRST INNING

St. Louis—Lonnie Smith lined a single off Caldwell's glove. Smith stole second as Green struck out on a 1-2 pitch. With Hernandez batting, Smith was caught stealing, Simmons to Molitor. Her-

Mike Caldwell shut out the Cardinals in Game 1 and returned to the victory circle in Game 5.

nandez lined a single to right. Hendrick forced Hernandez, Molitor to Gantner. No runs, two hits, no errors, one left.

Milwaukee—Molitor flied to McGee. Yount lined a single off Forsch's left foot. Cooper lined a single to right, Yount stopping at second. With a 2-2 count on Simmons, Forsch tried to pick off Yount but threw the ball high and to the left of Ozzie Smith and into center field; Yount advanced to third and Cooper to second on the error. Simmons grounded to Hernandez, Yount scoring and Cooper going to third. Oglivie flied to McGee. One run, two hits, one error, one left.

SECOND INNING

St. Louis—Porter grounded to Gantner. McGee grounded to Molitor. Oberkfell singled to center. Herr forced Oberkfell, Yount to Gantner. No runs, one hit, no errors, one left.

Milwaukee—Thomas flied to McGee on the warning track. Money bounced to Ozzie Smith. Moore lined to Ozzie Smith. No runs, no hits, no errors, none left.

THIRD INNING

St. Louis—Ozzie Smith hit a line drive off Caldwell's glove, but Gantner fielded the rebound and threw to Cooper for the out. Lonnie Smith grounded to Yount, who made a nice play ranging to his left. Green tripled when his blooper to right rolled past a diving Moore. Hernandez doubled home Green as Thomas nearly made a diving catch in left center. Hendrick's bouncer up the middle was stopped by a diving Gantner, Hernandez stopping at third on the single. Porter grounded to Gantner. One run, three hits, no errors, two left.

Milwaukee—Gantner popped to Ozzie Smith. Molitor walked. Yount lined a double into the left-field corner, Molitor stopping at third. Cooper's grounder toward first took a nasty hop, but Hernandez was able to glove it and throw to Forsch for the out, Molitor scoring and Yount advancing to third. Simmons flied to Green. One run, one hit, no errors, one left.

FOURTH INNING

St. Louis—McGee grounded to Molitor. Oberkfell lined a single to right. Herr's grounder was booted by Gantner, Oberkfell advancing to second on the error. Ozzie Smith grounded into a double play, Molitor stepping on third and throwing to Cooper to end the inning. No runs, one hit, one error, one left.

Milwaukee—Oglivie grounded a single to center. Thomas struck out and Oglivie, who was running on the 3-2 pitch, was caught stealing, Porter to Herr. Money was called out on strikes. No runs, one hit, no errors, none left.

FIFTH INNING

St. Louis—Moore made an outstanding diving catch of Lonnie Smith's sinking liner to right center. Green flied to Thomas. Hernandez walked. Hendrick flied to Thomas. No runs, no hits, no errors, one left.

Milwaukee—Moore drilled a double down the left-field line. Gantner grounded to Herr, Moore advancing to third. Molitor lined a single between Oberkfell and Ozzie Smith, Moore scoring. Yount singled on a sharp grounder that Oberkfell knocked down on the third-base line, Molitor advancing to second. Cooper flied to Hendrick. Simmons walked, loading the bases. Oglivie struck out. One run, three hits, no errors, three left.

SIXTH INNING

St. Louis—Porter struck out. McGee lined a single to right. Oberkfell forced McGee, Gantner to Yount. Herr forced Oberkfell, Yount unassisted. No runs, one hit, no errors, one left.

Milwaukee—Thomas' grounder bounced off Herr's chest for an error. Money grounded into a double play, Oberkfell to Herr to Hernandez. Moore grounded to Oberkfell. No runs, no hits, one error, none left.

SEVENTH INNING

St. Louis—Ozzie Smith walked. Lonnie Smith singled to right, Ozzie Smith stopping at second. Green flied to Thomas in short center. Hernandez forced Lonnie Smith, Cooper to Yount, Ozzie Smith advancing to third. After Moore almost made a running catch of his pop foul near the stands, Hendrick grounded a single to center, Ozzie Smith scoring and Hernandez stopping at second. Cooper dived to his right to grab Porter's

Rookie John Stuper shrugged off the pressure and pitched the Cardinals to a Game 6 victory.

grounder, then threw while on his knees to Caldwell covering first for the out. One run, two hits, no errors, two left.

Milwaukee—Gantner popped to Ozzie Smith. Molitor fouled out to Green. Yount lined a home run into the right-field bleachers to become the first player with two four-hit games in a World Series. (Yount had four hits in Game 1). Cooper flied to McGee. One run, one hit, no errors, none left.

EIGHTH INNING

St. Louis—McGee struck out. Oberkfell grounded a single to left. Herr forced Oberkfell, Yount to Gantner. Ozzie Smith forced Herr, Gantner unassisted. No runs, one hit, no errors, one left.

Milwaukee—Sutter replaced Forsch on the mound for St. Louis. Simmons struck out. Oglivie grounded a single to the right of Herr. Thomas struck out. Money walked, Oglivie advancing to second. Moore lined a single to right center, Oglivie scoring and Money advancing to third. Gantner lined a single to right center, Money scoring and Moore advancing to third. Molitor forced Gantner, Ozzie Smith to Herr. Two runs, three hits, no errors, two left.

NINTH INNING

St. Louis—Lonnie Smith bounced to Molitor. Green bounced a double over Molitor. Hernandez lashed a double to right center, Green scoring. Hendrick grounded a single to center, Hernandez scoring. McClure replaced Caldwell on the mound for Milwaukee. Porter lined a single to right, Hendrick stopping at second. McGee struck out. Ramsey ran for Porter. Tenace batted for Oberkfell and flied to Oglivie. Two runs, four hits, no errors, two left.

Game 6

At St. Louis
October 19

Milwaukee (A.L.)	AB.	R.	H.	PO.	A.	E.
Molitor, 3b	4	0	1	0	0	0
Yount, ss	4	0	0	0	3	2
Cooper, 1b	4	0	0	8	2	0
Simmons, c	2	0	0	4	0	0
Yost, c	0	0	0	1	0	0
Oglivie, lf	4	0	1	5	0	0
Thomas, cf	3	0	0	0	0	0
aEdwards, cf	0	0	0	0	0	0
Money, dh	3	0	0	0	0	0
Moore, rf	3	0	1	2	0	0
Gantner, 2b	3	1	1	3	2	2
Sutton, p	0	0	0	1	2	0
Slaton, p	0	0	0	0	0	0
Medich, p	0	0	0	0	0	0
Bernard, p	0	0	0	0	0	0
Totals	30	1	4	24	9	4

St. Louis (N.L.)	AB.	R.	H.	PO.	A.	E.
L. Smith, lf	3	1	1	1	0	0
Green, lf	1	1	0	0	0	0
Oberkfell, 3b	5	1	0	1	4	1
Hernandez, 1b	5	2	2	8	0	0
Hendrick, rf	5	2	2	3	0	0
Porter, c	4	1	1	2	0	0
Brummer, c	0	0	0	0	0	0
Iorg, dh	4	3	3	0	0	0
McGee, cf	4	1	1	5	0	0
Herr, 2b	3	1	2	1	2	0
O. Smith, ss	4	0	0	5	3	0
Stuper, p	0	0	0	1	1	0
Totals	38	13	12	27	10	1

Milwaukee	000	000	001—	1		
St. Louis	020	326	00*—	13		

Milwaukee	IP.	H.	R.	ER.	BB.	SO.
Sutton (L)	4⅓	7	7	5	0	2
Slaton	⅔	0	0	0	0	0
Medich	2	5	6	4	1	0
Bernard	1	0	0	0	0	1

St. Louis	IP.	H.	R.	ER.	BB.	SO.
Stuper (W)	9	4	1	1	2	2

Bases on balls—Off Medich 1 (Green), off Stuper 2 (Simmons, Yost).

Strikeouts—By Sutton 2 (L. Smith, Hendrick), by Bernard 1 (Green), by Stuper 2 (Gantner, Thomas).

Game-winning RBI—None.

aRan for Thomas in eighth. Runs batted in—Hernandez 4, Hendrick, Porter 2, McGee, Herr 2. Two-base hits—Iorg 2, Herr, Gantner. Three-base hit—Iorg. Home runs—Porter, Hernandez. Stolen base—L. Smith. Caught stealing—L. Smith. Sacrifice hit—Herr. Wild pitches—Medich 2, Stuper. Balk—Sutton. Double plays—Oberkfell, Herr and Hernandez; Herr, O. Smith and Hernandez. Left on bases—Milwaukee 4, St. Louis 3. Umpires—Evans (A.L.) plate, Weyer (N.L.) first, Haller (A.L.) second, Kibler (N.L.) third, Phillips (A.L.) left, Davidson (N.L.) right. Time—2:21. Attendance—53,723.

FIRST INNING

Milwaukee—Molitor popped to Ozzie Smith. Yount lined to Stuper. Cooper flied to Lonnie Smith. No runs, no hits, no errors, none left.

St. Louis—Lonnie Smith was called out on strikes. Oberkfell flied to Moore. Hernandez grounded out, Cooper to Sutton. No runs, no hits, no errors, none left.

SECOND INNING

Milwaukee—Simmons walked. Oglivie singled to center, Simmons stopping at second. Thomas flied to McGee. Money grounded into a double play, Oberkfell to Herr to Hernandez. No runs, one hit, no errors, one left.

St. Louis—Hendrick struck out. Porter grounded to Gantner. Iorg doubled when Oglivie, racing into the left-field corner, was unable to hold on to his long fly. McGee's grounder scooted under Yount's glove for an error, Iorg scoring. Herr drilled a double off the right-field wall; McGee scored, sliding home just ahead of an excellent throw by Moore. Ozzie Smith grounded to Yount. Two runs, two hits, one error, one left.

THIRD INNING

Milwaukee—Moore singled to left center. Gantner struck out. Molitor grounded into a double play, Herr to Ozzie Smith to Hernandez. No runs, one hit, no errors, none left.

St. Louis—Gantner booted Lonnie Smith's grounder to his left for an error. With Oberkfell batting, Smith stole second. Oberkfell popped to Gantner. Hernandez grounded to Gantner, Smith advancing to third. On Sutton's first pitch to Hendrick, Smith made an unsuccessful attempt to steal home. No runs, no hits, one error, none left.

FOURTH INNING

Milwaukee—Yount flied to Hendrick. Cooper popped to Ozzie Smith. Simmons flied to Hendrick. No runs, no hits, no errors, none left.

St. Louis—Hendrick singled to center. With Porter batting, Hendrick advanced to second on a balk by Sutton. Porter belted a home run to right, Hendrick scoring ahead of him. Iorg lined a triple down the right-field line. The light shower had begun in the third inning turned into a driving rain. McGee grounded to Yount, Iorg holding third. With Iorg charging toward the plate on a suicide squeeze, Herr laid down a perfect sacrifice bunt; Iorg scored as Herr was retired, Sutton to Cooper. Ozzie Smith grounded to Cooper. Three runs, three hits, no errors, none left.

FIFTH INNING

Milwaukee—Oglivie flied to McGee. Thomas struck out. Money grounded to Oberkfell. No runs, no hits, no errors, none left.

St. Louis—Lonnie Smith's blooper to right fell for a single. Oberkfell grounded out, Sutton to Cooper, Smith advancing to second. Hernandez blasted a home run into the bleachers in right center, Smith scoring ahead of him. Slaton replaced Sutton on the mound for Milwaukee, but before he could take his warmup pitches time was called and the field covered because of rain. After a rain delay of 26 minutes, Hendrick popped to Gantner. Porter flied to Oglivie. Two runs, two hits, no errors, none left.

SIXTH INNING

Milwaukee—Green replaced Lonnie Smith in left field for St. Louis. Moore lined to Ozzie Smith. Gantner flied to Hendrick. Molitor grounded to Oberkfell. No runs, no hits, no errors, none left.

St. Louis—Medich replaced Slaton on the mound for Milwaukee. Iorg doubled to left center. With McGee batting, Iorg advanced to third on a wild pitch. McGee grounded a single to right, Iorg scoring. Herr hit a bloop single to left, McGee stopping at second. With Ozzie Smith batting, McGee advanced to third and Herr to second on another wild pitch. Smith grounded to Cooper, with both runners holding. With Green batting and the count 2-2, a heavy rain again forced play to be halted, for two hours and 13 minutes. When

High on the Cardinals' hero list were (left to right) designated hitter Dane Iorg, center fielder Willie McGee and left fielder Lonnie Smith.

play resumed, Green walked, loading the bases. Oberkfell forced McGee, Cooper to Simmons, the bases remaining loaded. Hernandez singled to right; Herr and Green scored and Oberkfell advanced to third. Hendrick singled to right; Oberkfell scored, Hernandez advanced to third and Hendrick took second on Moore's high throw to third. Gantner misplayed Porter's grounder for an error, Hernandez and Hendrick scoring. Iorg lined to Oglivie. Six runs, five hits, one error, one left.

SEVENTH INNING

Milwaukee—Yount grounded to Ozzie Smith. Cooper grounded to Ozzie Smith. Simmons grounded out, Stuper to Hernandez. No runs, no hits, no errors, none left.

St. Louis—Yost replaced Simmons behind the plate for Milwaukee. McGee flied to Oglivie. Herr flied to Oglivie. Ozzie Smith flied to Oglivie. No runs, no hits, no errors, none left.

EIGHTH INNING

Milwaukee—Oglivie flied to McGee. Thomas grounded to Oberkfell, whose throw pulled Hernandez off the bag for an error. Edwards ran for Thomas. Money popped to Ozzie Smith. Moore popped to Oberkfell. No runs, no hits, one error, one left.

St. Louis—Edwards remained in the game to play center field for Milwaukee and Bernard replaced Medich on the mound. Green struck out. Oberkfell grounded to Yount, whose throw pulled Cooper off the bag for an error. Hernandez flied to Moore. Hendrick forced Oberkfell, as Yount fielded the ball behind second and made a backhanded flip to Gantner. No runs, no hits, one error, one left.

NINTH INNING

Milwaukee—Brummer replaced Porter behind the plate for St. Louis. Gantner cracked a double into the left-field corner. Molitor singled to center, Gantner stopping at third. With Yount batting, Gantner scored and Molitor advanced to second on a wild pitch by Stuper. Yount grounded to Oberkfell, Molitor holding second. Cooper flied to McGee. Yost walked. Oglivie flied to McGee. One run, two hits, no errors, two left.

Game 7

At St. Louis
October 20

Milwaukee (A.L.)	AB.	R.	H.	PO.	A.	E.
Molitor, 3b	4	1	2	0	1	0
Yount, ss	4	0	1	4	1	0
Cooper, 1b	3	0	1	8	1	0
Simmons, c	4	0	0	5	0	0
Oglivie, lf	4	1	1	0	0	0
Thomas, cf	4	0	0	3	0	0
Howell, dh	3	0	0	0	0	0
Moore, rf	3	0	1	3	0	0
Gantner, 2b	3	1	1	1	6	0
Vuckovich, p	0	0	0	0	0	0
McClure, p	0	0	0	0	0	0
Haas, p	0	0	0	0	0	0
Caldwell, p	0	0	0	0	0	0
Totals	32	3	7	24	9	0

St. Louis (N.L.)	AB.	R.	H.	PO.	A.	E.
L. Smith, lf	5	2	3	4	0	0
Oberkfell, 3b	3	0	0	1	5	0
aTenace	0	0	0	0	0	0
bRamsey, 3b	1	1	0	0	0	0
Hernandez, 1b	3	1	2	12	2	0
Hendrick, rf	5	0	2	1	1	0
Porter, c	5	0	1	4	0	0
Iorg, dh	3	0	2	0	0	0
cGreen, dh	0	0	0	0	0	0
dBraun, dh	2	0	1	0	0	0
McGee, cf	5	1	1	1	0	0
Herr, 2b	3	0	1	1	5	0
O. Smith, ss	4	1	2	2	2	0
Andujar, p	0	0	0	1	1	1
Sutter, p	0	0	0	0	1	0
Totals	39	6	15	27	17	1

Milwaukee	000	012	000—3
St. Louis	000	103	02*—6

Milwaukee	IP.	H.	R.	ER.	BB.	SO.
Vuckovich	5⅓	10	3	3	2	3
McClure (L)	⅓	2	1	1	1	0
Haas	2	1	2	2	1	1
Caldwell	⅓	2	0	0	0	0

St. Louis	IP.	H.	R.	ER.	BB.	SO.
Andujar (W)	7	7	3	2	0	1
Sutter (S)	2	0	0	0	0	2

Bases on balls—Off Vuckovich 2 (Herr, Hernandez), off McClure 1 (Tenace), off Haas 1 (Hernandez). Strikeouts—By Vuckovich 3 (Oberkfell, Porter, Hernandez), by Haas 1 (Ramsey), by Andujar 1 (Thomas), by Sutter 2 (Yount, Thomas). Game-winning RBI—Hendrick. aWalked for Oberkfell in sixth. bRan for Tenace and scored in sixth. cAnnounced as pinch-hitter for Iorg in sixth. dGrounded out for Green in sixth. Runs batted in—Cooper, Oglivie, L. Smith, Hernandez 2, Hendrick, Porter, Braun. Two-base hits—Gantner, L. Smith 2. Home run—Oglivie. Sacrifice fly—Cooper. Double plays—None. Left on bases—Milwaukee 3, St. Louis 13. Umpires—Weyer (N.L.) plate, Haller (A.L.) first, Kibler (N.L.) second, Phillips (A.L.) third, Davidson (N.L.) left, Evans (A.L.) right. Time—2:50. Attendance—53,723.

FIRST INNING

Milwaukee—Molitor flied to Hendrick. Yount bounced to Oberkfell. Cooper grounded to Oberkfell, Hernandez making a good pickup of a low throw. No runs, no hits, no errors, none left.

St. Louis—Lonnie Smith flied to Moore. Oberkfell struck out. Hernandez beat out a high bouncer to Gantner for a single. Hendrick fouled out to Simmons. No runs, one hit, no errors, one left.

SECOND INNING

Milwaukee—Simmons flied to Lonnie Smith. Oglivie grounded to Oberkfell. Thomas flied to McGee. No runs, no hits, no errors, none left.

St. Louis—Porter was called out on strikes. Gantner made a diving stop of Iorg's grounder up the middle, but Iorg beat the throw to first for a single. McGee flied to Thomas. Herr walked, Iorg advancing to second. Ozzie Smith bounced an infield single over the mound, loading the bases. Lonnie Smith flied to Moore. No runs, two hits, no errors, three left.

THIRD INNING

Milwaukee—Howell grounded out, Hernandez to Andujar. Moore grounded to Herr. Gantner grounded to Ozzie Smith. No runs, no hits, no errors, none left.

St. Louis—Oberkfell grounded to Cooper. Hernandez walked. Hendrick grounded a single between Molitor and Yount, Hernandez stopping at second. Porter flied to Moore at the wall in right, Hernandez advancing to third and Hendrick to second after the catch. Iorg grounded to Gantner. No runs, one hit, no errors, two left.

FOURTH INNING

Milwaukee—Molitor grounded a single to the left of Herr. Yount forced Molitor, Oberkfell to Herr. Cooper grounded a single to right; Yount tried to advance to third but was thrown out, Hendrick to Oberkfell, Cooper holding first. Simmons fouled out to Porter. No runs, two hits, no errors, one left.

St. Louis—McGee lined a single to center. Herr lined a single to right center, McGee advancing to third. Ozzie Smith popped to Gantner. Lonnie Smith bounced a single into the hole between third and short; McGee scored and Herr stopped at second when Yount made a backhanded stop. Oberkfell forced Smith, Cooper to Yount, Herr advancing to third. Hernandez struck out. One run, three hits, no errors, two left.

FIFTH INNING

Milwaukee—Oglivie smashed a home run deep into the right-field bleachers. Thomas flied to Lonnie Smith on the warning track. Howell grounded to Oberkfell. Moore grounded to Herr. One run, one hit, no errors, none left.

St. Louis—Hendrick grounded to Yount. Porter popped to Yount. Iorg's bouncer up the middle struck second base and hopped to Yount, who couldn't make a play. McGee flied to Thomas. No runs, one hit, no errors, one left.

SIXTH INNING

Milwaukee—Gantner doubled to right center. Molitor, sacrificing, bunted toward third; Andujar fielded the ball, but his off-balance throw to Herr covering first hit Molitor and rolled down the right-field line, Gantner scoring and Molitor taking second. Molitor was credited with a single and Andujar was charged with an error. Yount hit a high bouncer between Herr and Hernandez for a single, Molitor advancing to third. Cooper flied to Lonnie Smith in deep left, Molitor scoring after the catch. Simmons forced Yount, Hernandez to Ozzie Smith. Herr, going to his right, made a diving stop of Oglivie's grounder and flipped to Ozzie Smith to force Simmons. Two runs, three hits, one error, one left.

St. Louis—Herr grounded to Molitor. Ozzie Smith sliced a single to left. Lonnie Smith ground-

A line drive knocked Joaquin Andujar out of the box in Game 3, but the 'One Tough Dominican' returned in style in the finale.

ed a double past Molitor and into the left-field corner, Ozzie Smith stopping at third. McClure replaced Vuckovich on the mound for Milwaukee. Tenace batted for Oberkfell and walked, loading the bases. Ramsey ran for Tenace. Hernandez singled to right center, Ozzie Smith and Lonnie Smith scoring and Ramsey advancing to third. Hendrick (after hitting a grounder to Molitor that was foul by about a foot—Molitor's throw home would have nailed Ramsey) lined a single to right, Ramsey scoring and Hernandez stopping at second. Porter forced Hendrick, Gantner to Yount, Hernandez advancing to third. After Green was announced as a pinch-hitter for Iorg, Haas replaced McClure on the mound for Milwaukee. Braun batted for Green and rolled to Gantner. Three runs, four hits, no errors, two left.

SEVENTH INNING

Milwaukee—Ramsey ramained in the game to play third for St. Louis. Thomas struck out. Howell hit a long fly to left which Lonnie Smith tracked circuitously, finally making a lunging backhanded catch on the warning track. Moore bounced a single to deep short. Gantner grounded out, Andujar to Hernandez. Gantner and Andujar then engaged in a heated argument. Andujar dropped his glove in preparation for fisticuffs but was headed off by home plate umpire Lee Weyer.

Neither player was ejected. No runs, one hit, no errors, one left.

St. Louis—McGee grounded to Gantner. Herr lined to Yount. Ozzie Smith grounded to Gantner. No runs, no hits, no errors, none left.

EIGHTH INNING

Milwaukee—Sutter replaced Andujar on the mound for St. Louis. Molitor grounded to Ozzie Smith. Yount struck out on a pitch in the dirt. Cooper grounded to Herr. No runs, no hits, no errors, none left.

St. Louis—Lonnie Smith's liner bounced over the right-field wall for a ground-rule double. Ramsey, trying to sacrifice with two strikes, bunted foul for a strikeout. Hernandez was walked intentionally. Hendrick flied to Thomas. Caldwell replaced Haas on the mound for Milwaukee. Porter lined a single to right, Smith scoring and Hernandez advancing to third. Braun singled to center, Hernandez scoring and Porter stopping at second. McGee grounded to Gantner. Two runs, three hits, no errors, two left.

NINTH INNING

Milwaukee—Simmons bounced out, Sutter to Hernandez. Oglivie grounded to Herr. Thomas struck out. No runs, no hits, no errors, none left.

ST. LOUIS CARDINALS' BATTING AND FIELDING AVERAGES

Player—Position	G.	AB.	R.	H.	TB.	2B.	3B.	HR.	RBI.	BB.	IBB.	SO.	B.A.	PO.	A.	E.	F.A.
Iorg, dh	5	17	4	9	15	4	1	0	1	0	0	0	.529	0	0	0	.000
Braun, ph-dh	2	2	0	1	1	0	0	0	2	1	0	0	.500	0	0	0	.000
Hendrick, rf	7	28	5	9	9	0	0	0	5	2	0	2	.321	10	1	0	1.000
L. Smith, lf-dh	7	28	6	9	15	4	1	0	1	1	0	5	.321	11	0	0	1.000
Oberkfell, 3b	7	24	4	7	8	1	0	0	1	2	0	1	.292	3	21	1	.960
Porter, c	7	28	1	8	13	2	0	1	5	1	0	4	.286	33	2	0	1.000
Hernandez, 1b	7	27	4	7	12	2	0	1	8	4	1	2	.259	62	7	2	.972
McGee, cf	6	25	6	6	12	0	0	2	5	1	1	3	.240	24	0	0	1.000
O. Smith, ss	7	24	3	5	5	0	0	0	1	3	0	0	.208	22	17	0	1.000
Green, cf-ph-dh-lf-pr	7	10	3	2	5	1	1	0	0	1	0	3	.200	4	0	0	1.000
Herr, 2b	7	25	2	4	6	2	0	0	5	3	0	3	.160	11	19	1	.968
Andujar, p	2	0	0	0	0	0	0	0	0	0	0	0	.000	1	2	1	.750
Bair, p	3	0	0	0	0	0	0	0	0	0	0	0	.000	0	0	0	.000
Brummer, c	1	0	0	0	0	0	0	0	0	0	0	0	.000	0	0	0	.000
Forsch, p	2	0	0	0	0	0	0	0	0	0	0	0	.000	1	0	1	.500
Kaat, p	4	0	0	0	0	0	0	0	0	0	0	0	.000	0	0	0	.000
Lahti, p	2	0	0	0	0	0	0	0	0	0	0	0	.000	0	1	0	1.000
LaPoint, p	2	0	0	0	0	0	0	0	0	0	0	0	.000	0	2	1	.667
Ramsey, 3b-pr	3	1	1	0	0	0	0	0	0	0	0	1	.000	0	0	0	.000
Stuper, p	2	0	0	0	0	0	0	0	0	0	0	0	.000	1	1	0	1.000
Sutter, p	4	0	0	0	0	0	0	0	0	0	0	0	.000	0	1	0	1.000
Tenace, dh-ph	5	6	0	0	0	0	0	0	0	1	0	2	.000	0	0	0	.000
Totals	7	245	39	67	101	16	3	4	34	20	2	26	.273	183	74	7	.973

Green—Struck out for Iorg in seventh inning of second game; ran for Iorg in eighth inning of fourth game; announced as pinch-hitter for Iorg in sixth inning of seventh game.

Tenace—Flied out for Oberkfell in seventh inning of second game; struck out for Oberkfell in ninth inning of fourth game; flied out for Oberkfell in ninth inning of fifth game; walked for Oberkfell in sixth inning of seventh game.

Braun—Walked with bases loaded for Green in eighth inning of second game; grounded out for Green in sixth inning of seventh game.

Ramsey—Ran for Porter in ninth inning of fifth game; ran for Tenace and scored in sixth inning of seventh game.

MILWAUKEE BREWERS' BATTING AND FIELDING AVERAGES

Player—Position	G.	AB.	R.	H.	TB.	2B.	3B.	HR.	RBI.	BB.	IBB.	SO.	B.A.	PO.	A.	E.	F.A.
Yount, ss	7	29	6	12	18	3	0	1	6	2	0	2	.414	20	19	3	.929
Molitor, 3b	7	31	5	11	11	0	0	0	3	2	0	4	.355	4	9	0	1.000
Moore, rf	7	26	3	9	12	3	0	0	2	1	0	0	.346	13	0	0	1.000
Gantner, 2b	7	24	5	8	14	4	1	0	4	1	0	1	.333	9	33	5	.894
Cooper, 1b	7	28	3	8	12	1	0	1	6	1	0	1	.286	71	10	1	.988
Money, ph-dh	5	13	4	3	4	1	0	0	1	2	0	3	.231	0	0	0	.000
Oglivie, lf	7	27	4	6	11	0	1	1	1	2	1	4	.222	13	0	1	.929
Simmons, c	7	23	2	4	10	0	0	2	3	5	2	3	.174	28	2	1	.968
Thomas, cf	7	26	0	3	3	0	0	0	3	2	0	7	.115	15	0	0	1.000
Bernard, p	1	0	0	0	0	0	0	0	0	0	0	0	.000	0	0	0	.000
Caldwell, p	3	0	0	0	0	0	0	0	0	0	0	0	.000	4	2	0	1.000
Edwards, pr-cf	1	0	0	0	0	0	0	0	0	0	0	0	.000	0	0	0	.000
Haas, p	2	0	0	0	0	0	0	0	0	0	0	0	.000	1	2	0	1.000
Howell, dh	4	11	1	0	0	0	0	0	0	0	0	3	.000	0	0	0	.000
Ladd, p	1	0	0	0	0	0	0	0	0	0	0	0	.000	0	0	0	.000
McClure, p	5	0	0	0	0	0	0	0	0	0	0	0	.000	0	0	0	.000
Medich, p	1	0	0	0	0	0	0	0	0	0	0	0	.000	0	0	0	.000
Slaton, p	2	0	0	0	0	0	0	0	0	0	0	0	.000	0	0	0	.000
Sutton, p	2	0	0	0	0	0	0	0	0	0	0	0	.000	1	2	0	1.000
Vuckovich, p	2	0	0	0	0	0	0	0	0	0	0	0	.000	0	2	0	1.000
Yost, c	1	0	0	0	0	0	0	0	0	1	0	0	.000	1	0	0	1.000
Totals	7	238	33	64	95	12	2	5	29	19	3	28	.269	180	81	11	.960

Money—Flied out for Howell in seventh inning of first game; walked for Howell in seventh inning of third game.

Edwards—Ran for Thomas in eighth inning of sixth game.

ST. LOUIS CARDINALS' PITCHING RECORDS

Pitcher	G.	GS.	CG.	IP.	H.	R.	ER.	HR.	BB.	IBB.	SO.	HB.	WP.	W.	L.	Pct.	ERA.
Andujar	2	2	0	13⅓	10	3	2	1	1	0	4	0	0	2	0	1.000	1.35
LaPoint	2	1	0	8⅓	10	6	3	0	2	0	3	0	0	0	0	.000	3.24
Stuper	2	2	1	13	10	5	5	1	5	0	5	0	3	1	0	1.000	3.46
Kaat	4	0	0	2⅓	4	1	1	0	2	1	2	0	1	0	0	.000	3.86
Sutter	4	0	0	7⅔	6	4	4	1	3	1	6	0	0	1	0	1.000	4.70
Forsch	2	2	0	12⅔	18	10	7	2	3	0	4	1	0	0	2	.000	4.97
Bair	3	0	0	2	2	2	2	0	2	0	3	0	0	1	0	1.000	9.00
Lahti	2	0	0	1⅔	4	2	2	0	1	1	1	0	0	0	0	.000	10.80
Totals	7	7	1	61	64	33	*23	5	19	3	28	1	4	4	3	.571	3.39

No Shutouts. Saves—Sutter 2.

*Individual earned runs do not add to team total because of rule 10.18 (i) being applied in Game 4.

MILWAUKEE BREWERS' PITCHING RECORDS

Pitcher	G.	GS.	CG.	IP.	H.	R.	ER.	HR.	BB.	IBB.	SO.	HB.	WP.	W.	L.	Pct.	ERA.
Slaton	2	0	0	2⅔	1	0	0	0	2	0	1	0	0	1	0	1.000	0.00
Bernard	1	0	0	1	0	0	0	0	0	0	1	0	0	0	0	.000	0.00
Ladd	1	0	0	⅔	1	0	0	0	2	0	0	0	0	0	0	.000	0.00
Caldwell	3	2	1	17⅔	19	4	4	0	3	0	6	0	0	2	0	1.000	2.04
McClure	5	0	0	4⅓	5	2	2	0	3	0	5	0	0	0	2	.000	4.15
Vuckovich	2	2	0	14	16	9	7	2	5	1	4	0	0	0	1	.000	4.50
Haas	2	1	0	7⅓	8	7	6	0	3	1	4	0	1	0	0	.000	7.36
Sutton	2	2	0	10⅓	12	11	9	2	1	0	5	0	0	0	1	.000	7.84
Medich	1	0	0	2	5	6	4	0	1	0	0	0	2	0	0	.000	18.00
Totals	7	7	1	60	67	39	32	4	20	2	26	0	3	3	4	.429	4.80

Shutout—Caldwell. Saves—McClure 2.

COMPOSITE SCORE BY INNINGS

St. Louis	1	5	3	4	5	12	3	3	3 — 39
Milwaukee	3	1	3	1	5	4	7	4	5 — 33

Game-winning RBI—Braun, McGee, Thomas, Cooper, Hendrick.

Sacrifice hits—Gantner, Herr.

Sacrifice flies—Herr, Cooper.

Stolen bases—McGee 2, Oberkfell 2, L. Smith 2, Molitor, O. Smith.

Caught stealing—L. Smith 2, Molitor, Hendrick, Oglivie.

Awarded first base on catcher's interference—Hendrick.

Double plays—Hernandez, O. Smith and Hernandez 2; Oberkfell, Herr and Hernandez 2; Herr, O. Smith and Hernandez 2; Herr and Hernandez; O. Smith and Hernandez; Gantner, Yount and Cooper; Gantner and Cooper; Porter and Herr; Molitor and Cooper.

Passed balls—None.

Hit by pitcher—By Forsch (Howell).

Balk—Sutton.

Bases on balls—Off Stuper 5 (Yount, Thomas, Gantner, Simmons, Yost), off Forsch 3 (Cooper, Molitor, Simmons), off Sutter 3 (Simmons, Yount, Money), off Bair 2 (Money, Molitor), off Kaat 2 (Thomas, Simmons), off LaPoint 2 (Oglivie, Simmons), off Andujar 1 (Moore), off Lahti 1 (Oglivie), off Vuckovich 5 (Hendrick, McGee, O. Smith, Herr, Hernandez), off Caldwell 3 (Herr, Hernandez, O. Smith), off Haas 3 (O. Smith, Oberkfell, Hernandez), off McClure 3 (Herr, Hernandez, Tenace), off Ladd 2 (L. Smith, Braun), off Slaton 2 (Oberkfell, Porter), off Medich 1 (Green), off Sutton 1 (Hendrick).

Strikeouts—By Sutter 6 (Thomas 2, Howell, Money, Simmons, Yount), by Stuper 5 (Oglivie, Howell, Molitor, Gantner, Thomas), by Andujar 4 (Thomas 2, Molitor, Oglivie), by Forsch 4 (Simmons, Thomas, Money, Oglivie), by Bair 3 (Thomas, Howell, Molitor), by LaPoint 3 (Simmons, Money, Molitor), by Kaat 2 (Cooper, Oglivie), by Lahti 1 (Yount), by Caldwell 6 (L. Smith 2, Tenace, Green, Porter, McGee), by McClure 5 (McGee 2, Green, Herr, Tenace), by Sutton 5 (Hendrick 2, L. Smith 2, Herr), by Haas 4 (Herr, Hernandez, Porter, Ramsey), by Vuckovich 4 (Porter 2, Oberkell, Hernandez), by Bernard 1 (Green), by Slaton 1 (L. Smith).

Left on bases—St. Louis 49—4, 7, 4, 6, 12, 3, 13; Milwaukee 44—10, 8, 6, 6, 7, 4, 3.

Time of games—First game, 2:30; second game, 2:54; third game, 2:53; fourth game, 3:04; fifth game, 3:02; sixth game, 2:21; seventh game, 2:50.

Attendance—First game, 53,723; second game, 53,723; third game, 56,556; fourth game, 56,560; fifth game, 56,562; sixth game, 53,723; seventh game, 53,723.

Umpires—Weyer (N.L.), Haller (A.L.), Kibler (N.L.), Phillips (A.L.), Davidson (N.L.), Evans (A.L.).

Official scorers—Jack Herman, St. Louis Globe-Democrat; Dave Nightingale, The Sporting News; Dick Young, New York Post.

1982 ALL-STAR GAME

Including

Review of 1982 Game

Official Box Score

Official Play-by-Play

Results of Previous Games

N.L. Wins in Canada, Too

By LARRY WIGGE

Dave Concepcion didn't point to the left-field stands to show the world where he was going to deposit his next home run. And there wasn't a sick kid in a hospital bed gasping for breath, waiting to hear Concepcion fulfill a promise to hit a home run.

No, any comparison between Concepcion and Babe Ruth (who once delivered on a vow to hit a home run for an ailing youngster) would be lacking. Except, however, that Concepcion, the Cincinnati Reds' shortstop, did predict he would hit a home run July 13 in the 53rd All-Star Game at Olympic Stadium in Montreal.

Typical of the soft-spoken shortstop, it was only a whispered conversation with Philadelphia second baseman Manny Trillo. But on a night when the Nationals drubbed the Americans for the 11th consecutive time and the 19th time in their last 20 meetings, it was a delicious tidbit for history to take note of.

Concepcion lashed a two-out, two-run homer over the left-field barrier in the second inning for his first All-Star home run, sending the Nationals to a 4-1 victory over the Americans.

"When Gary Carter was up," Concepcion said with a smile, "I turned to Manny and I said, 'I got the feeling I'm gonna hit one out of the park.'

"We tease around a lot. And Manny started laughing because he knew I only had one homer all year (in 328 at-bats). But I told him I was going to do it and I did it."

The Americans, tired of hearing about the N.L. superiority in the midsummer classic, had opened a 1-0 lead in the first inning on singles by Rickey Henderson (the first of three hits by the Oakland outfielder) and Kansas City's George Brett and a sacrifice fly by California's Reggie Jackson.

Boston's Dennis Eckersley then zipped through the first five batters he faced before walking Atlanta's Dale Murphy to set the stage for Concepcion's called shot.

"Even though I retired the first five batters, my control was off," Eckersley confided later. "I walked Murphy on four pitches and then served up a hanging slider to Concepcion and he yanked it out."

It seemed fitting that Concepcion, a Venezuelan, was chosen the game's Most Valuable Player since Montreal was playing host to the first All-Star Game on foreign soil.

"It makes me feel like a winner again," Concepcion said. The 34-year-old veteran, hitting .293 at the All-Star break, was referring to the troubled times (33-53 record) that had befallen his Reds.

"I've been in four World Series, but this had to be one of the biggest moments in my career," Concepcion said. "My wife asked me before we came here when I was going to win the MVP. She said I'd been in the majors for 13 years and it was about time I won the MVP. So I guess you should say I did it for Delia."

The Nationals added another run in the third when San Diego's Ruppert Jones slammed a pinch triple off the right-center field wall and scored on a short sacrifice fly to right by Philadelphia's Pete Rose.

Rose, who had been around long enough to remember the American League's last All-Star victory at Detroit in 1971, observed, "Each league has a certain amount of superstars. Mike Schmidt would hit homers in any league and Rickey Henderson could steal bases on Mars. . . . I don't know about the other guys, but I've never looked upon the All-Star Game as a showcase. To me it's a matter of pride, and I go out and play as hard as I would any other game."

Much to the delight of the 59,057 partisan fans, the N.L. counted its final run in the sixth with the aid of two of Montreal's favorite players. Al Oliver of the Expos bounced a leadoff double over the third-base bag and was able to advance to third when the ball skipped by Henderson in left field for an error. After Kansas City's Dan Quisenberry retired the next two batters, Montreal's Carter lined a single to center.

"We're going to keep it going for as long as we can," Carter said of the N.L.'s domination. "I can't pinpoint one thing, but there's a lot of intensity and confidence in the clubhouse before the game. And when we get between the white lines, that has an overwhelming effect."

Montreal's Steve Rogers pitched three innings and was credited with the victory, though he permitted the only American League run. Philadelphia's Steve Carlton and Cincinnati's Mario Soto followed with two-inning stints, with each pitcher striking out four batters.

The A.L. collected eight hits (as many as the N.L.) and had five walks, but hit into one double play and left 11 runners on

Montreal fans enjoyed their first fling with an All-Star cast that included Expo Steve Rogers, the 1982 Classic's winning pitcher.

base. The only inning the Americans did not have at least one baserunner was the second.

With two runners aboard and one out in the fourth, Chicago's Carlton Fisk and Cleveland's Andre Thornton were strikeout victims of Carlton. Detroit's Lance Parrish doubled off the center-field wall to open the seventh. One out later, Henderson beat out a soft roller to Los Angeles second baseman Steve Sax, Parrish advancing to third. But Soto struck out Kansas City's Willie Wilson and Buddy Bell of Texas to end the threat.

All was not negative for the Americans, however. Parrish, who took over behind the plate in the fifth inning, had the A.L.'s only extra-base hit and exhibited a shotgun arm. He gunned down three would-be base stealers (Trillo in the fifth, St. Louis' Ozzie Smith in the seventh and Oliver in the eighth). It was a record. But Parrish lamented not being able to get a hit off San Francisco reliever Greg Minton with two men on and two outs in the eighth.

Meanwhile, Kansas City's Brett wondered aloud: "I just wish we would win one of these game so that people would stop asking questions about why we never beat the National League."

AMERICANS	AB.	R.	H.	RBI.	PO.	A.
Henderson (A's), lf	4	1	3	0	3	0
Lynn (Angels), cf	2	0	0	0	0	0
Wilson (Royals), cf	2	0	0	0	1	0
mHrbek (Twins), ph	1	0	0	0	0	0
Brett (Royals), 3b	2	0	2	0	0	0
cBell (Rangers), ph-3b	3	0	0	0	0	1
Jackson (Angels), rf	1	0	0	1	3	0
Winfield (Yankees), rf	2	0	1	0	0	0
Cooper (Brewers), 1b	2	0	1	0	5	0
fMurray (O's), ph-1b	1	0	0	0	4	0
Yount (Brewers), ss	3	0	0	0	0	2
Grich (Angels), 2b	1	0	0	0	2	2
gYastr'ski (R. Sox), ph	1	0	0	0	0	0
Quisenb'ry (Royals), p	0	0	0	0	0	0
kMcRae (Royals), ph	0	0	0	0	0	0
Fingers (Brewers), p	0	0	0	0	0	0
Fisk (White Sox), c	2	0	0	0	2	0
Parrish (Tigers), c	2	0	1	0	2	3
Eckersley (Red Sox), p	1	0	0	0	0	0
bThornton (Ind.), ph	1	0	0	0	0	0
Clancy (Blue Jays), p	0	0	0	0	0	0
Bannister (M's), p	0	0	0	0	0	0
White (Royals), 2b	1	0	0	0	2	1
lOglivie (Brewers), ph	1	0	0	0	0	0
Totals	33	1	8	1	24	9

NATIONALS	AB.	R.	H.	RBI.	PO.	A.
Raines (Expos), lf	1	0	0	0	0	0
Carlton (Phillies), p	0	0	0	0	0	1
eHorner (Braves), ph	1	0	0	0	0	0
Soto (Reds), p	0	0	0	0	0	0
jThompson (Pir.), ph	1	0	0	0	0	0
Valenzuela (Dodg.), p	0	0	0	0	0	0
Minton (Giants), p	0	0	0	0	0	0
Howe (Dodgers), p	0	0	0	0	0	0
Hume (Reds), p	0	0	0	0	0	0
Rose (Phillies), 1b	1	0	0	1	4	0
Oliver (Expos), 1b	2	1	2	0	2	0
Dawson (Expos), cf	4	0	1	0	4	0

NATIONALS	AB.	R.	H.	RBI.	PO.	A.
Schmidt (Phillies), 3b	1	0	0	0	0	0
Knight (Astros), 3b	3	0	0	0	1	4
Carter (Expos), c	3	0	1	1	7	0
hPena (Pirates), pr-c	1	0	0	0	3	0
Stearns (Mets), c	0	0	0	0	0	0
Murphy (Braves), rf	2	1	0	0	2	0
Concepcion (Reds), ss	3	1	1	2	1	1
iO. Smith (Cards) 1, pr-ss	0	0	0	0	1	1
Trillo (Phillies), 2b	2	0	1	0	0	1
dSax (Dodgers), pr-2b	1	0	1	0	2	0
Rogers (Expos), p	0	0	0	0	0	0
aJones, (Padres), ph	1	1	1	0	0	0
Baker (Dodgers), lf	2	0	0	0	0	0
L. Smith (Cards), lf	0	0	0	0	1	0
Totals	29	4	8	4	27	8

Americans .... 1 0 0　0 0 0　0 0 0—1
Nationals .... 0 2 1　0 0 1　0 0 x—4

AMERICANS	IP.	H.	R.	ER.	BB.	SO.
Eckersley (Red Sox)	3	2	3	3	2	1
Clancy (Blue Jays)	1	0	0	0	0	0
Bannister (Mariners)	1	1	0	0	0	0
Quisenberry (Royals)	2	3	1	1	0	1
Fingers (Brewers)	1	2	0	0	0	0

NATIONALS	IP.	H.	R.	ER.	BB.	SO.
Rogers (Expos)	3	4	1	1	0	2
Carlton (Phillies)	2	1	0	0	2	4
Soto (Reds)	2	3	0	0	0	4
Valenzuela (Dodgers)	⅔	0	0	0	2	0
Minton (Giants)	⅔	0	0	0	1	0
Howe (Dodgers)	⅓	0	0	0	0	0
Hume (Reds)	⅓	0	0	0	0	0

Winning pitcher—Rogers. Losing pitcher—Eckersley. Save—Hume.

Game-winning RBI—Concepcion.

aTripled for Rogers in third. bStruck out for Eckersley in fourth. cStruck out for Brett in fifth. dRan for Trillo in fifth. eFlied out for Carlton in fifth. fFlied out for Cooper in sixth. gStruck out for Grich in sixth. hRan for Carter in sixth. iRan for Concepcion in seventh. jGrounded out for Soto in seventh. kWalked for Quisenberry in eighth. lFlied out for White in ninth. mFlied out for Wilson in ninth. Errors—Sax, Henderson, Bell. Double play—Carlton, Concepcion and Rose. Left on bases—Americans 11, Nationals 4. Two-base hits—Oliver, Parrish. Three-base hit—Jones. Home run—Concepcion. Stolen bases—Raines, Pena, Henderson. Caught stealing—Sax, O. Smith, Oliver. Sacrifice flies—Jackson, Rose. Wild pitch—Rogers. Bases on balls—Off Carlton 2 (Yount, Grich), off Valenzuela 2 (Murray, McRae), off Minton 1 (Henderson), off Eckersley 2 (Murphy, Raines). Strikeouts—By Rogers 2 (Yount, Grich), by Carlton 4 (Cooper, Fisk, Thornton, Bell), by Soto 4 (Yastrzemski, White, Wilson, Bell), by Eckersley 1 (Raines), by Quisenberry 1 (Knight). Umpires—Harvey (N.L.) plate, Springstead (A.L.) first base, McSherry (N.L.) second base, McKeon (A.L.) third base, Montague (N.L.) left field, Reilly (A.L.) right field. Time—2:53. Attendance—59,057. Official scorers—Ian MacDonald, Montreal Gazette; Dick O'Connor, Peninsula Times Tribune (Palo Alto, Calif.); Charlie Scoggins, Lowell (Mass.) Sun. Players listed on rosters but not used: A.L.—Clear, Gossage, Guidry, Harrah; N.L.—Durham, Niekro.

FIRST INNING

Americans—Henderson singled to left. Lynn flied to Dawson. Brett lined a single to left, Henderson stopping at second. With Jackson batting, Rogers threw a wild pitch, the runners advancing to second and third. Jackson flied to Dawson,

Henderson scoring after the catch and Brett remaining at second. Cooper bounced an infield single past the second-base side of the mound and Brett advanced to third. Yount struck out. One run, three hits, no errors, two left.

Nationals—Raines struck out. Rose lined to Henderson. Dawson flied to Jackson. No runs, no hits, no errors, none left.

SECOND INNING

Americans—Grich was called out on strikes. Fisk flied to Dawson. Eckersley grounded to Trillo. No runs, no hits, no errors, none left.

Nationals—Schmidt fouled out to Fisk. Carter grounded to Grich. Murphy walked. Concepcion lined a home run down the left-field line, Murphy scoring ahead of him. Trillo grounded to Yount. Two runs, one hit, no errors, none left.

THIRD INNING

Americans—Knight replaced Schmidt at third base for the Nationals. Henderson grounded to Knight. Lynn grounded to Rose, who made the play unassisted. Brett grounded a single up the middle. Jackson popped to Knight. No runs, one hit, no errors, one left.

Nationals—Jones batted for Rogers and tripled off the base of the wall in right-center. Raines walked. With Rose batting, Raines stole second without drawing a throw. Rose flied to Jackson; Jones tagged and scored on a close play at the plate, Raines remaining at second. Dawson grounded to Grich, Raines advancing to third. Knight popped to Grich. One run, one hit, no errors, one left.

FOURTH INNING

Americans—Baker came in to play left field and Carlton to pitch for the Nationals; Baker assumed the ninth spot in the order and Carlton the first. Cooper struck out. Yount walked. Grich walked, Yount advancing to second. Fisk struck out. Thornton batted for Eckersley and struck out. No runs, no hits, no errors, two left.

Nationals—Clancy came in to pitch for the Americans and Wilson replaced Lynn in center field. Carter grounded to Yount. Murphy flied to Jackson. Concepcion grounded to Cooper, who made the play unassisted. No runs, no hits, no errors, none left.

FIFTH INNING

Americans—Henderson singled to right. Wilson grounded into a double play, Carlton to Concepcion to Rose. Bell batted for Brett and struck out. No runs, one hit, no errors, none left.

Nationals—Bannister replaced Clancy on the mound for the Americans, Parrish replaced Fisk behind the plate, Winfield replaced Jackson in right field and Bell remained in the game to play third base. Trillo singled up the middle. Sax ran for Trillo. With Baker batting, Sax was caught stealing, Parrish to Grich. Baker flied to Henderson. Horner batted for Carlton and flied to Henderson. No runs, one hit, no errors, none left.

SIXTH INNING

Americans—Soto came in to pitch for the Nationals, Oliver replaced Rose at first base and Sax remained in the game to play second base. Winfield bounced a single over the mound and into center field. Murray batted for Cooper and flied to Murphy. Yount forced Winfield at second, Knight to Sax, who then threw the ball into the first-base dugout trying for a double play; Yount advanced to second on the error. Yastrzemski batted for Grich and struck out. No runs, one hit, one error, one left.

Nationals—Quisenberry replaced Bannister on the mound for the Americans, White came in to play second base and Murray remained in the game to play first base; Quisenberry assumed the seventh spot in the batting order and White the ninth. Oliver doubled down the left-field line and went to third when Henderson overran the ball for an error. Dawson grounded to Murray, who made the play unassisted as Oliver held third. Knight struck out. Carter singled to center and Oliver scored as Wilson narrowly missed making a diving catch. Pena ran for Carter. With Murphy batting, Pena stole second. Murphy grounded to Bell. One run, two hits, one error, one left.

SEVENTH INNING

Americans—Pena remained in the game to catch for the Nationals. Parrish doubled off the center-field wall. White struck out. Henderson dribbled a single to the right of the mound, Parrish advancing to third. With Wilson batting, Henderson stole second without drawing a throw. Wilson struck out. Bell struck out. No runs, two hits, no errors, two left.

Nationals—Concepcion grounded to Bell, who booted the ball for an error. Ozzie Smith ran for Concepcion. With Sax batting, Smith was caught stealing on a pitchout, Parrish to White. Sax beat out a high chopper to third for a single. Baker flied to Wilson. Thompson batted for Soto and grounded to White. No runs, one hit, one error, one left.

EIGHTH INNING

Americans—Valenzuela came in to pitch for the Nationals, and Smith remained in the game to play shortstop. Winfield grounded to Knight. Murray walked. Yount forced Murray, Knight to Sax. McRae batted for Quisenberry and walked, Yount advancing to second. Minton replaced Valenzuela on the mound. Parrish hit a slow bouncer over the mound that looked like a sure hit, but Smith made a sensational play, scooping up the ball on the run and throwing out Parrish. No runs, no hits, no errors, two left.

Nationals—Fingers came in to pitch for the Americans. Oliver singled to right. With Dawson batting, Oliver was caught stealing, Parrish to White. Dawson singled to center. Knight grounded to Murray, Dawson advancing to second as Murray went to the bag. Pena fouled out to Parrish, who made an excellent running catch near the first-base dugout. No runs, two hits, no errors, one left.

NINTH INNING

Americans—Lonnie Smith replaced Baker in left field and Stearns replaced Pena behind the plate for the Nationals. Oglivie batted for White and flied to Lonnie Smith. Henderson walked. After Hrbek was announced as a pinch-hitter for Wilson, Howe replaced Minton on the mound for the Nationals. Hrbek flied to Dawson in short center. Hume replaced Howe on the mound. Bell flied to Murphy. No runs, no hits, no errors, one left.

RESULTS OF PREVIOUS GAMES

1933—At Comiskey Park, Chicago, July 6. Americans 4, Nationals 2. Managers—Connie Mack, John McGraw. Winning pitcher—Lefty Gomez. Losing pitcher—Bill Hallahan. Attendance—47,595.

1934—At Polo Grounds, New York, July 10. Americans 9, Nationals 7. Managers—Joe Cronin, Bill Terry. Winning pitcher—Mel Harder. Losing pitcher—Van Mungo. Attendance—48,363.

1935—At Municipal Stadium, Cleveland, July 8. Americans 4, Nationals 1. Managers—Mickey Cochrane, Frankie Frisch. Winning pitcher—Lefty Gomez. Losing pitcher—Bill Walker. Attendance—69,831.

1936—At Braves Field, Boston, July 7. Nationals 4, Americans 3. Managers—Charlie Grimm, Joe McCarthy. Winning pitcher—Dizzy Dean. Losing pitcher—Lefty Grove. Attendance—25,556.

1937—At Griffith Stadium, Washington, July 7. Americans 8, Nationals 3. Managers—Joe McCarthy, Bill Terry. Winning pitcher—Lefty Gomez. Losing pitcher—Dizzy Dean. Attendance—31,391.

1938—At Crosley Field, Cincinnati, July 6. Nationals 4, Americans 1. Managers—Bill Terry, Joe McCarthy. Winning pitcher—Johnny Vander Meer. Losing pitcher—Lefty Gomez. Attendance—27,067.

1939—At Yankee Stadium, New York, July 11. Americans 3, Nationals 1. Managers—Joe McCarthy, Gabby Hartnett. Winning pitcher—Tommy Bridges. Losing pitcher—Bill Lee. Attendance—62,892.

1940—At Sportsman's Park, St. Louis, July 9. Nationals 4, Americans 0. Managers—Bill McKechnie, Joe Cronin. Winning pitcher—Paul Derringer. Losing pitcher—Red Ruffing. Attendance—32,373.

1941—At Briggs Stadium, Detroit, July 8. Americans 7, Nationals 5. Managers—Del Baker, Bill McKechnie. Winning pitcher—Ed Smith. Losing pitcher—Claude Passeau. Attendance—54,674.

1942—At Polo Grounds, New York, July 6. Americans 3, Nationals 1. Managers—Joe Cronin, Leo Durocher. Winning pitcher—Spud Chandler. Losing pitcher—Mort Cooper. Attendance—34,178.

1943—At Shibe Park, Philadelphia, July 13 (night game). Americans 5, Nationals 3. Managers—Joe McCarthy, Billy Southworth. Winning pitcher—Dutch Leonard. Losing pitcher—Mort Cooper. Attendance—31,938.

1944—At Forbes Field, Pittsburgh, July 11 (night game). Nationals 7, Americans 1. Managers—Billy Southworth, Joe McCarthy. Winning pitcher—Ken Raffensberger. Losing pitcher—Tex Hughson. Attendance—29,589.

1945—No game played.

1946—At Fenway Park, Boston, July 9. Americans 12, Nationals 0. Managers—Steve O'Neill, Charlie Grimm. Winning pitcher—Bob Feller. Losing pitcher—Claude Passeau. Attendance—34,906.

1947—At Wrigley Field, Chicago, July 8. Americans 2, Nationals 1. Managers—Joe Cronin, Eddie Dyer. Winning pitcher—Frank Shea. Losing pitcher—Johnny Sain. Attendance—41,123.

1948—At Sportsman's Park, St. Louis, July 13. Americans 5, Nationals 2. Managers—Bucky Harris, Leo Durocher. Winning pitcher—Vic Raschi. Losing pitcher—Johnny Schmitz. Attendance—34,009.

1949—At Ebbets Field, Brooklyn, July 12. Americans 11, Nationals 7. Managers—Lou Boudreau, Billy Southworth. Winning pitcher—Virgil Trucks. Losing pitcher—Don Newcombe. Attendance—32,577.

1950—At Comiskey Park, Chicago, July 11. Nationals 4, Americans 3 (14 innings). Managers—Burt Shotton, Casey Stengel. Winning pitcher—Ewell Blackwell. Losing pitcher—Ted Gray. Attendance—46,127.

1951—At Briggs Stadium, Detroit, July 10. Nationals 8, Americans 3. Managers—Eddie Sawyer, Casey Stengel. Winning pitcher—Sal Maglie. Losing pitcher—Ed Lopat. Attendance—52,075.

1952—At Shibe Park, Philadelphia, July 8. Nationals 3, Americans 2 (five innings—rain). Managers—Leo Durocher, Casey Stengel. Winning pitcher—Bob Rush. Losing pitcher—Bob Lemon. Attendance—32,785.

1953—At Crosley Field, Cincinnati, July 14. Nationals 5, Americans 1. Managers—Chuck Dressen, Casey Stengel. Winning pitcher—Warren Spahn. Losing pitcher—Allie Reynolds. Attendance—30,846.

1954—At Municipal Stadium, Cleveland, July 13. Americans 11, Nationals 9. Managers—Casey Stengel, Walter Alston. Winning pitcher—Dean Stone. Losing pitcher—Gene Conley. Attendance—68,751.

1955—At Milwaukee County Stadium, Milwaukee, July 12. Nationals 6, Americans 5 (12 innings). Managers—Leo Durocher, Al Lopez. Winning pitcher—Gene Conley. Losing pitcher—Frank Sullivan. Attendance—45,643.

1956—At Griffith Stadium, Washington, July 10. Nationals 7, Americans 3. Managers—Walter Alston, Casey Stengel. Winning pitcher—Bob Friend. Losing pitcher—Billy Pierce. Attendance—28,843.

1957—At Busch Stadium, St. Louis, July 9. Americans 6, Nationals 5. Managers—Casey Stengel, Walter Alston. Winning pitcher—Jim Bunning. Losing pitcher—Curt Simmons. Attendance—30,693.

1958—At Memorial Stadium, Baltimore, July 8. Americans 4, Nationals 3. Managers—Casey Stengel, Fred Haney. Winning pitcher—Early Wynn. Losing pitcher—Bob Friend. Attendance—48,829.

1959 (first game)—At Forbes Field, Pittsburgh, July 7. Nationals 5, Americans 4. Managers—Fred Haney, Casey Stengel. Winning pitcher—Johnny Antonelli. Losing pitcher—Whitey Ford. Attendance—35,277.

1959 (second game)—At Memorial Coliseum, Los Angeles, August 3. Americans 5, Nationals 3. Managers—Casey Stengel, Fred Haney. Winning pitcher—Jerry Walker. Losing pitcher—Don Drysdale. Attendance—55,105.

1960 (first game)—At Municipal Stadium, Kansas City, July 11. Nationals 5, Americans 3. Managers—Walter Alston, Al Lopez. Winning pitcher—Bob Friend. Losing pitcher—Bill Monbouquette. Attendance—30,619.

1960 (second game)—At Yankee Stadium, New York, July 13. Nationals 6, Americans 0. Managers—Walter Alston, Al Lopez. Winning pitcher—Vernon Law. Losing pitcher—Whitey Ford. Attendance—38,362.

1961 (first game)—At Candlestick Park, San Francisco, July 11. Nationals 5, Americans 4 (10 innings). Managers—Danny Murtaugh, Paul Richards. Winning pitcher—Stu Miller. Losing pitcher—Hoyt Wilhelm. Attendance—44,115.

1961 (second game)—At Fenway Park, Boston, July 31. Americans 1, Nationals 1 (nine-inning tie, stopped by rain). Managers—Paul Richards, Danny Murtaugh. Attendance—31,851.

1962 (first game)—At District of Columbia Stadium, Washington, July 10. Nationals 3, Americans 1. Managers—Fred Hutchinson, Ralph Houk. Winning pitcher—Juan Marichal. Losing pitcher—Camilo Pascual. Attendance—45,480.

1962 (second game)—At Wrigley Field, Chicago, July 30. Americans 9, Nationals 4. Managers—Ralph Houk, Fred Hutchinson. Winning pitcher—Ray Herbert. Losing pitcher—Art Mahaffey. Attendance—38,359.

MVP Dave Concepcion (13) gets a big greeting from National League team-mates after his two-run homer.

1963—At Municipal Stadium, Cleveland, July 9. Nationals 5, Americans 3. Managers—Alvin Dark, Ralph Houk. Winning pitcher—Larry Jackson. Losing pitcher—Jim Bunning. Attendance—44,160.

1964—At Shea Stadium, New York, July 7. Nationals 7, Americans 4. Managers—Walter Alston, Al Lopez. Winning pitcher—Juan Marichal. Losing pitcher—Dick Radatz. Attendance—50,850.

1965—At Metropolitan Stadium, Bloomington (Minnesota), July 13. Nationals 6, Americans 5. Managers—Gene Mauch, Al Lopez. Winning pitcher—Sandy Koufax. Losing pitcher—Sam McDowell. Attendance—46,706.

1966—At Busch Memorial Stadium, St. Louis, July 12. Nationals 2, Americans 1 (10 innings). Managers—Walter Alston, Sam Mele. Winning pitcher—Gaylord Perry. Losing pitcher—Pete Richert. Attendance—49,936.

1967—At Anaheim Stadium, Anaheim (California), July 11. Nationals 2, Americans 1 (15 innings). Managers—Walter Alston, Hank Bauer. Winning pitcher—Don Drysdale. Losing pitcher—Jim Hunter. Attendance—46,309.

1968—At Astrodome, Houston, July 9 (night). Nationals 1, Americans 0. Managers—Red Schoendienst, Dick Williams. Winning pitcher—Don Drysdale. Losing pitcher—Luis Tiant. Attendance—48,321.

1969—At Robert F. Kennedy Memorial Stadium, Washington, July 23. Nationals 9, Americans 3. Managers—Red Schoendienst, Mayo Smith. Winning pitcher—Steve Carlton. Losing pitcher—Mel Stottlemyre. Attendance—45,259.

1970—At Riverfront Stadium, Cincinnati, July 14 (night). Nationals 5, Americans 4 (12 innings). Managers—Gil Hodges, Earl Weaver. Winning pitcher—Claude Osteen. Losing pitcher—Clyde Wright. Attendance—51,838.

1971—At Tiger Stadium, Detroit, July 13 (night). Americans 6, Nationals 4. Managers—Earl Weaver, George (Sparky) Anderson. Winning pitcher—Vida Blue. Losing pitcher—Dock Ellis. Attendance—53,559.

1972—At Atlanta Stadium, Atlanta, July 25 (night). Nationals 4, Americans 3 (10 innings). Managers—Danny Murtaugh, Earl Weaver. Win-

ning pitcher—Tug McGraw. Losing pitcher—Dave McNally. Attendance—53,107.

1973—At Royals Stadium, Kansas City, July 24 (night). Nationals 7, Americans 1. Managers—George (Sparky) Anderson, Dick Williams. Winning pitcher—Rick Wise. Losing pitcher—Bert Blyleven. Attendance—40,849.

1974—At Three Rivers Stadium, Pittsburgh, July 23 (night). Nationals 7, Americans 2. Managers—Yogi Berra, Dick Williams. Winning pitcher—Ken Brett. Losing pitcher—Luis Tiant. Attendance—50,706.

1975—At Milwaukee County Stadium, Milwaukee, July 15 (night). Nationals 6, Americans 3. Managers—Walter Alston, Alvin Dark. Winning pitcher—Jon Matlack. Losing pitcher—Jim Hunter. Attendance—51,480.

1976—At Veterans Stadium, Philadelphia, July 13 (night). Nationals 7, Americans 1. Managers—George (Sparky) Anderson, Darrell Johnson. Winning pitcher— Randy Jones. Losing pitcher—Mark Fidrych. Attendance—63,974.

1977—At Yankee Stadium, New York, July 19 (night). Nationals 7, Americans 5. Managers—Alfred (Billy) Martin, George (Sparky) Anderson. Winning pitcher—Don Sutton. Losing pitcher—Jim Palmer. Attendance—56,683.

1978—At San Diego Stadium, San Diego, July 11. Nationals 7, Americans 3. Managers—Alfred (Billy) Martin, Thomas Lasorda. Winning pitcher—Bruce Sutter. Losing pitcher—Rich Gossage. Attendance—51,549.

1979—At Kingdome, Seattle, July 17, Nationals 7, Americans 6. Managers—Chuck Tanner, Bob Lemon. Winning pitcher—Bruce Sutter. Losing pitcher—Jim Kern. Attendance—58,905.

1980—At Dodger Stadium, Los Angeles, July 8, Nationals 4, Americans 2. Managers—Chuck Tanner, Earl Weaver. Winning pitcher—Jerry Reuss. Losing pitcher—Tommy John. Attendance—56,088.

1981—At Municipal Stadium, Cleveland, August 9, Nationals 5, Americans 4. Managers—Dallas Green, Jim Frey. Winning pitcher—Vida Blue. Losing pitcher—Rollie Fingers. Attendance—72,086.

TSN Player of the Year Robin Yount blasted American League pitching for 210 hits, 29 homers, 114 RBIs and a .331 average as he led the Brewers to the World Series.

BATTING, PITCHING

FEATURES

Including

Low-Hit Pitching Performances

Top Strikeout Performances

Baseball's Top Firemen

Pitchers Winning 1-0 Games

Multi-Home Run Performances

Batters Hitting Grand Slams

Top One-Game Hitting Performances

Baseball's Top Pinch-Hitters

Top Performances in Debuts

Homers by Parks

Award Winners

Hall of Fame Electees

Hall of Famers List, Years Selected

No pitcher was able to throw a no-hitter in 1982, but Philadelphia's Steve Carlton, who won his fourth Cy Young Award, had three two-hitters.

Pitchers Shut Out in No-Hit Bids

By CARL CLARK

There were only 49 low-hit games in the major leagues in 1982, the fewest in a full season (there were 33 in the truncated '81 season) since 1962, when 32 were pitched. American League pitchers tossed six one-hitters and 16 two-hitters; National League pitchers turned in eight one-hitters and 19 two-hitters.

For the first time since 1949, no one pitched a no-hitter. While Harvey Haddix gave up a game-deciding double in the 13th inning against Milwaukee on May 26, 1959, the Pittsburgh pitcher is still credited with a no-hitter for having pitched 12 perfect innings against the Braves. Haddix's performance was the low no-hitter in '59.

Jerry Reuss of Los Angeles pitched two one-hitters and Philadelphia's Steve Carlton, en route to an unprecedented fourth Cy Young Award, pitched three two-hitters.

In each of Reuss' one-hitters, the hit was a first-inning double. Art Howe had Houston's only hit in Reuss' 6-0 victory over the Astros on April 21. Reuss recorded an 11-1 victory over Cincinnati on June 11, retiring 27 consecutive batters after Eddie Milner's leadoff hit.

Carlton took a no-hitter into the eighth inning against the Giants on May 14, but, with two out, Bob Brenly and Johnnie LeMaster singled. Carlton, who never has pitched a no-hitter though he holds the N.L. record for one-hitters with six, settled for a two-hitter and a 2-0 victory.

Excellently conditioned at age 37, Carlton finished the season robustly, winning six games in the final month. Included in those victories were his other two-hitters. In a 2-1 victory over the Astros on September 3, Carlton struck out 12, walked none and allowed only a single by Danny Heep and a home run by Howe. Singles by Joel Youngblood and Tim Raines were the Expos' only hits in Carlton's 4-0 triumph over Montreal on September 29.

Three other N.L. pitchers—the Astros' Nolan Ryan, Atlanta's Rick Mahler and the Expos' Charlie Lea—took part in more than one low-hit game.

Mahler pitched a two-hitter against San Diego on opening night, the Braves winning 1-0, and worked the first seven innings of a one-hitter against Montreal on September 5. The Expos' only hit was a solo homer by Al Oliver in the second inning, but Montreal beat the Braves, 2-1, scoring the winning run in the ninth inning off Gene Garber with the help of a hit batsman and an error by shortstop Rafael Ramirez.

Ryan posted the eighth one-hitter of his major league career in a 3-0 victory over San Diego on August 11. Only Terry Kennedy's fifth-inning single kept Ryan from recording his sixth no-hitter. Twenty days later, Ryan came even closer to a no-hitter. He held the Mets hitless for seven innings before Ron Hodges singled. Bob Bailor singled in the ninth, and Ryan wound up with a two-hitter and 4-0 victory.

Lea limited Cincinnati to two hits on May 21. Woodie Fryman relieved him in the ninth and wrapped up the 2-0 triumph. In his next start, at Houston on May 26, Lea gave up just one hit in nine innings, retiring 26 consecutive batters after Craig Reynolds singled in the first inning, but was lifted for a pinch-hitter in the 10th inning with the score 0-0. The Expos rallied for four runs, Lea picking up the victory when Jeff Reardon retired the Astros on one hit, another single by Reynolds.

Dave Stieb pitched two-hitters for Toronto on August 10 and September 6. He beat Boston, 4-0, allowing early-inning singles to Carney Lansford and Gary Allenson, and defeated Oakland, 3-1, giving up a home run to Tony Armas in the seventh inning and a single to Jeff Burroughs in the eighth.

Detroit's Jack Morris pitched one two-hitter and had a hand in another. The only

---

No No-Hitters For First Time Since '49

The 1982 season was not without its pitching highlights; however, for the first time since 1949 no pitchers hurled a no-hit game. In fact, it was only the 13th time since the turn of the century that the majors went through an entire season without having a no-hitter pitched.

Oddly enough, the American League has gone through five seasons without a no-hitter since Bert Blyleven, then of the Texas Rangers, blanked the California Angels, 6-0, September 22, 1977. Ironically, that same season was the first time there were no no-hitters in the National League.

Were it not for lone first-inning doubles in two of his starts, Los Angeles' Jerry Reuss could have pitched two no-hitters last season.

safeties off Morris in his 8-1 victory over Oakland on September 5 were a home run by Dwayne Murphy in the third inning and a single by Burroughs in the seventh. Morris pitched the first seven innings of the Tigers' 5-1 victory over the Angels on May 22. Tim Foli had both Angels hits, a home run in the sixth inning and a single off Dave Tobik in the eighth.

No one came closer to a no-hitter in '82 than Toronto's Jim Clancy, who threw eight hitless innings in the first game of a September 28 doubleheader against Minnesota. The Twins' only hit in the 3-0 defeat was a broken-bat single leading off the ninth by designated hitter Randy Bush.

The only double low-hit game was the Mets' 1-0, 10-inning triumph over the Phillies on October 1. In his only start of the season, Terry Leach went all the way for the Mets, striking out seven. He walked six, but Luis Aguayo's fifth-inning triple was the Phillies' only hit. John Denny, who had worked the first five innings of a Cleveland two-hitter on September 9, pitched the first nine innings for the Phillies, allowing one hit, Dave Kingman's single in the second. The Mets broke through in the 10th against Porfirio Altamirano. Kingman walked and his pinch-runner, Rusty Tillman, advanced to third on Gary Rajsich's single and scored on Hubie Brooks' sacrifice fly.

A complete list of one- and two-hit games follows:

NATIONAL LEAGUE
One-Hit Games

April 21—Reuss, Los Angeles vs. Houston, 6-0—
Howe, double in first.

April 28—Noles, Chicago vs. Cincinnati, 6-0—
Milner, single in fourth.

April 29—Hooton, Los Angeles vs. Philadelphia,
4-0—DeJesus, single in fourth.

June   2—Eichelberger, San Diego vs. Chicago, 3-
1—Thompson, single in second.

June 11—Reuss, Los Angeles vs. Cincinnati, 11-1
—Milner, double in first.

Aug. 11—Ryan, Houston vs. San Diego, 3-0—
Kennedy, single in fifth.

Sept.   5—Mahler (seven innings) and Garber
(one and two-thirds innings), Atlanta vs. Montreal, 1-2—Oliver,
homer in second.

Oct.   1—Leach, New York vs. Philadelphia, 1-0
—Aguayo, triple in fifth.

Two-Hit Games

April   6—Mahler, Atlanta vs. San Diego, 1-0—Salazar, single in second; Jones, double
in ninth.

May 14—Carlton, Philadelphia vs. San Francisco, 2-0—Brenly, single in eighth; Le-
Master, single in eighth.

May 17—Rogers, Montreal vs. Atlanta, 4-0—
Horner, single in second; Smith, single in eighth.

May 21—Lea (eight innings) and Fryman (one
inning), Montreal vs. Cincinnati, 2-
0—Driessen, single in sixth; Driessen, single in ninth.

May 26—Lea (nine innings) and Reardon (one
inning), Montreal vs. Houston, 4-0—
Reynolds, single in first; Reynolds,
single in 10th.

June 10—Curtis, San Diego vs. Houston, 5-0—
Knight, single in fourth; Knicely,
single in fifth.

July 20—Montefusco (seven innings) and De-
Leon (two innings), San Diego vs.
Philadelphia, 2-0—Diaz, single in
fifth; Carlton, single in sixth.

Aug.   5—Martz, Chicago vs. New York, 5-1—
Hodges, single in second; Hodges,
single in eighth.

Aug. 17—Rhoden, Pittsburgh vs. San Francisco,
4-1—Davis, double in sixth; Morgan,
single in sixth.

Aug. 20—Valenzuela, Los Angeles vs. Pittsburgh,
1-0—Berra, single in first; Ray, single in fifth.

Aug. 21—Lollar (eight innings) and DeLeon (one
inning), San Diego vs. Chicago, 2-0
—Durham, double in second; Sandberg, single in sixth.

Aug. 31—Ryan, Houston vs. New York, 4-0—
Hodges, single in eighth; Bailor, single in ninth.

Sept.   3—Carlton, Philadelphia vs. Houston, 2-1—
Heep, single in second; Howe, homer
in fifth.

Sept. 14—LaCoss (seven innings) and LaCorte
(two innings), Houston vs. Atlanta,
4-0—Mahler, single in third; Washington, single in third.

Sept. 18—Niekro, Houston vs. Los Angeles, 2-0—
Thomas, single in fourth; Cey, single
in eighth.

Sept. 22—Martin (seven innings) and Holland
(two innings), San Francisco vs.
Cincinnati, 2-0—Driessen, single in
second; Trevino, single in fifth.

Sept. 27—Niekro, Atlanta vs. San Francisco, 7-0
—Evans, single in fourth; Clark, triple in sixth.

Sept. 29—Carlton, Philadelphia vs. Montreal, 4-0
—Youngblood, single in fifth;
Raines, single in ninth.

Oct.   1—Denny (nine innings) and Altamirano
(one inning), Philadelphia vs. New
York, 0-1—Kingman, single in second; Rajsich, single in 10th.

AMERICAN LEAGUE
One-Hit Games

April 10—Leonard (five and two-thirds innings),
Jackson (one and one-third in-
nings) and Quisenberry (two innings), Kansas City vs. Detroit, 5-2
—Gibson, single in sixth.

April 20—Wilcox, Detroit vs. Kansas City, 8-0—
Martin, single in second.

May 30—Gott (six innings) and Jackson (three
innings), Toronto vs. Baltimore, 6-0
—Dempsey, single in fifth.

Sept.   4—Palmer, Baltimore vs. Minnesota, 3-0—
Gaetti, single in fifth.

Sept. 13—Blue, Kansas City vs. Seattle, 8-0—
Brown, single in sixth.

Sept. 28—Clancy, Toronto vs. Minnesota, 3-0
(first game)—Bush, single in ninth.

Two-Hit Games

May 22—Morris (seven innings) and Tobik (two
innings), Detroit vs. California, 5-1
—Foli, homer in sixth; Foli, single in
eighth.

June   4—Beattie, Seattle vs. Detroit, 4-0—Brookens, single in sixth; Lemon, single in
eighth.

June   7—Nelson, Seattle vs. Texas, 6-0—Bell, single in seventh; Hostetler, single in
eighth.

July   2—Hough, Texas vs. Oakland, 7-0—
Murphy, single in first; Klutts, single in second.

July   4—Black (seven innings) and Armstrong
(two innings), Kansas City vs. California, 6-1—Baylor, single in fourth;
Clark, homer in fifth.

July   9—Zahn, California vs. New York, 4-1—
Mumphrey, triple in fifth; Ran-
dolph, single in ninth.

July 16—Bannister, Seattle vs. Baltimore, 6-0—
Roenicke, double in second; Sakata,
single in seventh.

July 21—Torrez (eight innings) and Stanley (one
inning), Boston vs. Texas, 6-1 (second game)—Richardt, double in
third; Werner, single in third.

July 23—Tanana (six and two-thirds innings)
and Schmidt (two and one-third innings), Texas vs. Detroit, 3-1—
Lemon, single in fifth; Brookens,
double in sixth.

Aug.   4—Burns, Chicago vs. New York, 7-0 (second game)—Nettles, single in sec-
ond; Cerone, single in sixth.

Aug. 10—Stieb, Toronto vs. Boston, 4-0—Lansford, single in second; Allenson, single in third.

Sept.   5—Morris, Detroit vs. Oakland, 8-1—
Murphy, homer in third; Burroughs,
single in seventh.

Sept.   6—Stieb, Toronto vs. Oakland, 3-1—
Armas, homer in seventh; Burroughs, single in eighth.

Sept.   9—Denny (five innings) and Anderson
(four innings), Cleveland vs. Baltimore, 3-0—Dwyer, double in first;
Singleton, single in third.

Sept. 17—Stoddard, Seattle vs. Texas, 6-0—
Wright, single in first; Bell, single in
first.

Sept. 22—Sutcliffe (six innings) and Glynn (one
inning), Cleveland vs. New York, 5-
0 (stopped by rain)—Randolph, single in first; Randolph, single in
fourth.

Carlton, Soto Go on Strikeout Binge

By LARRY WIGGE

Allowing 10 hits and walking two is not a typical Steve Carlton performance. And when you permit the leadoff batter to reach base in five of the nine innings, you are supposed to be on the losing end of the score.

But, attesting to Carlton's greatness, he survived all of those obstacles and still pitched the Phillies to a 4-2 victory over the Cubs June 9.

That was just one of 23 victories in 1982 for Carlton, the four-time Cy Young lefthander who was the only pitcher in the majors to top the 20-win plateau.

Carlton overcame the odds that day with a devastating strikeout pitch. He fanned 16 Cubs' batters, including Ryne Sandberg four times and Junior Kennedy and Steve Henderson three times each. Only Bill Buckner and Gary Woods, who had three hits apiece, escaped Carlton's knockout punch.

Cincinnati's Mario Soto, the only other hurler to strike out 15 or more batters in '82, was the model of consistency August 17 when he defeated the Mets, 9-2, striking out 15 batters while walking none. The 15 strikeouts were the most in Soto's career and pushed him over the 200 level, making him the first Reds' pitcher to pass 200 strikeouts in one season since Tom Seaver did it in 1978.

Carlton, who shares the major league record of 19 strikeouts in a game (1969 for the Cardinals against the Mets) with Seaver, fell just one strikeout short of the Phillies' club record set by Art Mahaffey in 1961.

Cincinnati's Mario Soto pitched all his team's 10-strikeout gems.

The stylish Philadelphia lefthander struck out 10 or more batters 11 times in 1982. Houston's Nolan Ryan accomplished the feat 10 times, extending his major league record to 145. Soto had nine games of at least 10 strikeouts, while Cleveland's Len Barker led American League hurlers with four multi-strikeout games.

The 10-strikeout plateau was reached 67 times in '82. Following is a listing of all the pitchers who achieved 10 strikeouts in a game with the number of times accomplished:

AMERICAN LEAGUE: Baltimore—None. Boston (2)—Eckersley, Tudor. California—None. Chicago—None. Cleveland (4)—Barker 4. Detroit (2)—Morris, Petry. Kansas City—None. Milwaukee—None. Minnesota (2)—Castillo, Viola. New York (1)—Guidry. Oakland—None. Seattle (6)—Bannister 2, Beattie 2, Perry 2. Texas—None. Toronto (1)—Clancy.

NATIONAL LEAGUE: Atlanta—None. Chicago—None. Cincinnati (9)—Soto 9. Houston (13)—Ryan 10, Sutton 2, DiPino. Los Angeles (2)—Valenzuela, Welch. Montreal (5)—Gullickson 2, Sanderson 2, Rogers. New York (1)—Puleo. Philadelphia (14)—Carlton 11, Christenson 3. Pittsburgh (2)—McWilliams, D. Robinson. St. Louis—None. San Diego (2)—Lollar 2. San Francisco (1)—Breining.

Following is a recap of the 15-strikeout games:

Date	Pitcher—Club—Opp.	Place	IP.	H.	R.	ER.	BB.	SO.	Result
June 9—	Carlton, Phillies vs. Cubs	Phil.	9	10	2	2	2	16	W 4-2
Aug. 17—	Soto, Reds vs. Mets	Cin.	9	4	2	2	0	15	W 9-2

Sutter, Quisenberry Top Firemen

By LARRY WIGGE

The bases are loaded, Mike Schmidt is at the plate with one out and the St. Louis Cardinals are clinging to a 2-0 lead in the last of the eighth inning. Schmidt can put the game out of reach with a homer and give the Philadelphia Phillies a 1½-game lead in the National League East Division. Even a single would tie the contest.

The Phillies had to feel pretty good with that situation September 14 at Veterans Stadium, even if Schmidt was facing Bruce Sutter. Facing the previous batter, Sutter had given up an infield single to load the bases.

The key to a good relief pitcher, though, is to give a little and then slam the door. Sutter did just that. Sutter got two quick strikes. Schmidt worked the count to 2-2. Sutter then got Schmidt to bounce back to the mound and he started a pitcher-to-home-to-first double play that ended the inning.

The Cardinals went on to win that night and the next night, and then swept a five-game series in New York en route to capturing their East Division title. In looking back on the season, St. Louis fans won't forget that confrontation between Sutter and Schmidt.

Sutter's impact on the Cardinals World Championship push was immense. After the All-Star break, he appeared in 33 games, pitched 50⅓ innings and permitted only eight earned runs (a 1.43 ERA) while saving 18 games and winning three.

With 36 saves and nine relief wins, Sutter won The Sporting News Fireman of the Year Award in the National League for 1982. It was the third time in the last

National League

Pitcher—Club	Saves	Relief Wins	Tot. Pts.	Pitcher—Club	Saves	Relief Wins	Tot. Pts.
Sutter, St. Louis	36	9	45	Hrabosky, Atlanta	3	2	5
Minton, San Francisco	30	10	40	Kern, Cincinnati	2	3	5
Garber, Atlanta	30	8	38	Lahti, St. Louis	0	5	5
Reardon, Montreal	26	7	33	Lyle, Philadelphia	2	3	5
Tekulve, Pittsburgh	20	12	32	Moffitt, Houston	3	2	5
DeLeon, San Diego	15	9	24	Proly, Chicago	1	4	5
Allen, New York	19	3	22	B. Smith, Montreal	3	2	5
Fryman, Montreal	12	9	21	Brusstar, Philadelphia	2	2	4
Howe, Los Angeles	13	7	20	Diaz, Atl.-New York	1	3	4
Hume, Cincinnati	17	2	19	Hayes, Cincinnati	2	2	4
Smith, Chicago	17	2	19	Leach, New York	3	1	4
Bedrosian, Atlanta	11	7	18	Leibrandt, Cincinnati	2	2	4
Lavelle, San Francisco	8	10	18	Lesley, Cincinnati	4	0	4
R. Reed, Philadelphia	14	4	18	Moore, Atlanta	1	3	4
Scurry, Pittsburgh	14	4	18	Roberge, Houston	3	1	4
Lucas, San Diego	16	1	17	Ruhle, Houston	1	3	4
Smith, Houston	11	5	16	Sambito, Houston	4	0	4
Hernandez, Chicago	10	4	14	Scott, New York	3	1	4
Tidrow, Chicago	6	8	14	Swan, New York	1	3	4
Bair, St. Louis	8	5	13	Barr, San Francisco	2	1	3
Niedenfuer, Los Angeles	9	3	12	Beckwith, Los Angeles	1	2	3
Campbell, Chicago	8	3	11	Boone, San Diego-Houston	2	1	3
Holland, San Francisco	5	5	10	Dravecky, San Diego	2	1	3
Romo, Pittsburgh	1	9	10	Falcone, New York	2	1	3
Camp, Atlanta	5	4	9	Hanna, Atlanta	0	3	3
Monge, Philadelphia	2	7	9	LaCoss, Houston	0	3	3
Show, San Diego	3	6	9	Lynch, New York	2	1	3
Chiffer, San Diego	4	4	8	McWilliams, Atlanta-Pittsburgh	2	1	3
Forster, Los Angeles	3	5	8	Puleo, New York	1	2	3
LaCorte, Houston	7	1	8	Sarmiento, Pittsburgh	1	2	3
McGraw, Philadelphia	5	3	8	Zachry, New York	1	2	3
Orosco, New York	4	4	8	Dayley, Atlanta	0	2	2
Altamirano, Philadelphia	2	5	7	Martz, Chicago	1	1	2
Farmer, Philadelphia	6	1	7	Niemann, Pittsburgh	1	1	2
Stewart, Los Angeles	1	6	7	Perez, Atlanta	0	2	2
Breining, San Francisco	0	6	6	Reuss, Los Angeles	0	2	2
Burris, Montreal	2	4	6	D. Robinson, Pittsburgh	0	2	2
Kaat, St. Louis	2	4	6	Shirley, Cincinnati	0	2	2
Price, Cincinnati	3	3	6				

One save—Candelaria, Pittsburgh; Forsch, St. Louis; Harris, Cincinnati; Knepper, Houston; Romo, Los Angeles; Sisk, New York.

One relief win—Cowley, Atlanta; Curtis, San Diego; Fowlkes, San Francisco; Gale, San Francisco; Gorman, Montreal-New York; Hammaker, San Francisco; Hausman, New York-Atlanta; Keener, St. Louis; Kravec, Chicago; LaPoint, St. Louis; Martin, St. Louis; McGaffigan, San Francisco; Rasmussen, St. Louis; J. Reed, Philadelphia; Rincon, St. Louis; Schatzeder, S.F.-Montreal; Shirley, Los Angeles; Solomon, Pittsburgh; Soto, Cincinnati; Welsh, San Diego; Wright, Los Angeles.

four seasons he had captured the award. After missing out in 1981, Kansas City's Dan Quisenberry won his second American League award. He had 35 saves and nine wins.

With one point being awarded for each save and each relief win, Sutter's 45 points were five better than San Francisco's Greg Minton, who finished with 30 saves and 10 wins. Atlanta's Gene Garber had 30 saves and eight wins for 38 points.

In the American League, Quisenberry's 44-point total was six points better than Seattle's Bill Caudill, who had 26 saves and 12 wins. The A.L. winner in 1981, Rollie Fingers of Milwaukee, missed the final month of the season but still finished in a third-place tie with New York's Rich Gossage, each compiling 34 points. Dan Spillner of Cleveland had 33.

That the Royals finished three games behind the California Angels in the A.L. West Division was a tribute to Quisenberry. His brilliance out of the bullpen carried a spotty starting staff that accounted for only 16 complete games all season, fewest in the A.L. The submarining righthander again displayed impeccable control, walking only 12 batters in 136⅔ innings. He didn't issue a walk in his first 19 appearances.

In winning his third Fireman of the Year Award, Sutter tied Fingers and Mike Marshall for the career record. Since The Sporting News initiated the award in 1960, only Ron Perranoski (with Minnesota in 1969-70), Bill Campbell (with Minnesota in 1976 and Boston in '77), Marshall (with Montreal in '73 and Los Angeles in '74) and Fingers (with San Diego in '77 and '78) had previously won two consecutive awards.

American League

Pitcher—Club	Saves	Relief Wins	Tot. Pts.	Pitcher—Club	Saves	Relief Wins	Tot. Pts.
Quisenberry, Kansas City	35	9	44	Koosman, Chicago	3	2	5
Caudill, Seattle	26	12	38	Owchinko, Oakland	3	2	5
Fingers, Milwaukee	29	5	34	Aponte, Boston	3	1	4
Gossage, New York	30	4	34	Brennan, Cleveland	2	2	4
Spillner, Cleveland	21	12	33	Kern, Chicago	3	1	4
Clear, Boston	14	14	28	Ladd, Milwaukee	3	1	4
Barojas, Chicago	21	6	27	LaRoche, New York	0	4	4
Stanley, Boston	14	12	26	Mirabella, Texas	3	1	4
Davis, Minnesota	22	3	25	Rozema, Detroit	1	3	4
T. Martinez, Baltimore	16	8	24	Rucker, Detroit	0	4	4
Beard, Oakland	11	10	21	Tufts, Kansas City	2	2	4
Murray, Toronto	11	8	19	Underwood, Detroit	3	1	4
Darwin, Texas	7	10	17	Davis, Baltimore	0	3	3
McLaughlin, Toronto	8	8	16	Felton, Minnesota	3	0	3
Stoddard, Baltimore	12	3	15	Frost, Kansas City	0	3	3
R.L. Jackson, Toronto	6	8	14	Hoyt, Chicago	0	3	3
Vande Berg, Seattle	5	9	14	Matlack, Texas	1	2	3
Tobik, Detroit	9	4	13	Pacella, Minnesota	2	1	3
Corbett, Minn.-California	11	1	12	Sutcliffe, Cleveland	1	2	3
Sanchez, California	5	7	12	Whitson, Cleveland	2	1	3
Slaton, Milwaukee	6	6	12	Anderson, Cleveland	0	2	2
Stewart, Baltimore	5	7	12	Brusstar, Chicago	0	2	2
Underwood, Oakland	7	5	12	Castillo, Minnesota	0	2	2
Armstrong, Kansas City	6	5	11	Castro, Kansas City	1	1	2
Hickey, Chicago	6	4	10	Clark, Seattle	0	2	2
Bernard, Milwaukee	6	3	9	Easterly, Milwaukee	2	0	2
Burgmeier, Boston	2	7	9	Escarrega, Chicago	1	1	2
Glynn, Cleveland	4	5	9	Flinn, Baltimore	0	2	2
Schmidt, Texas	6	3	9	Haas, Milwaukee	1	1	2
Stanton, Seattle	7	2	9	Hood, Kansas City	1	1	2
Aase, California	4	3	7	Jackson, Kansas City	0	2	2
Goltz, California	3	4	7	Jones, Oakland	0	2	2
May, New York	3	4	7	Kingman, Oakland	1	1	2
Rawley, New York	3	4	7	Kison, California	1	1	2
Saucier, Detroit	5	2	7	Little, Minnesota	0	2	2
Sosa, Detroit	4	3	7	Mahler, California	0	2	2
Comer, Texas	6	0	6	McClure, Milwaukee	0	2	2
Hassler, California	4	2	6	A. Moreno, California	0	2	2
Lamp, Chicago	5	1	6	Morgan, New York	0	2	2
Lopez, Detroit	3	3	6	Redfern, Minnesota	0	2	2
Frazier, New York	1	4	5	Renko, California	0	2	2

One save—Anderson, Seattle; Bailey, Detroit; Barnes, Chicago; Butcher, Texas; Curtis, California; Erickson, New York; Gumpert, Detroit; Lyle, Chicago; Palmer, Baltimore; Righetti, New York.

One relief win—Augustine, Milwaukee; Boddicker, Baltimore; Boris, Minnesota; Brown, Boston; Crawford, Boston; Forsch, California; Garvin, Toronto; Geisel, Toronto; Grimsley, Baltimore; Henke, Texas; Kaufman, New York; McLaughlin, Oakland; Musselman, Seattle; Ojeda, Boston; Pashnick, Detroit; Reed, Cleveland; Schrom, Toronto; Solomon, Chicago; Waits, Cleveland; Welchel, Baltimore; Witt, California.

Phillies Captured Six 1-0 Decisions

By CARL CLARK

A pitcher with 285 major league victories, more than 3,000 strikeouts and four Cy Young Awards doesn't need much support. Sometimes one run suffices, as it did three times for Philadelphia's Steve Carlton in 1982.

The Phillies won six 1-0 games, the most in the majors, and Carlton pitched three of them. He defeated St. Louis on June 28, San Francisco on July 16 and Los Angeles on July 25. In those 27 innings, Carlton gave up only 15 hits and struck out 17.

There were 23 1-0 games in the National League. The American League had 12, its fewest since 1958 when, as an eight-team league, it had 11.

Dick Ruthven won two 1-0 games for the Phillies, defeating Atlanta on May 29 and New York in the first game of a June 25 doubleheader.

The only other N.L. pitchers who won two 1-0 games were Fernando Valenzuela of Los Angeles and Joaquin Andujar of St. Louis. Each also lost a 1-0 decision.

Andujar blanked San Francisco on June 2 and Montreal on September 6, but lost to Houston on April 8 when the Astros scored an unearned run in the eighth inning.

Valenzuela, who now has a 4-2 record in 1-0 games, defeated San Diego on September 14 and split decisions against Pittsburgh. Both Pirates games were decided by home runs. On August 20, Valenzuela made Ron Cey's second-inning homer off Larry McWilliams stand up. Lee Lacy's first-inning homer was the Pirates' margin of victory on September 4.

(Seven 1-0 games were decided by home runs, two by Lacy, who also connected against Philadelphia's Larry Christenson in the ninth inning June 11.)

Larry Gura won two 1-0 games for Kansas City, at Oakland on June 23 and at Detroit on August 14. Both times the Royals scored the winning run in the ninth inning.

The Expos finished third in the N.L. in runs but lost five 1-0 games. Ray Burris took two of those losses. The Giants' Bill Laskey and the White Sox' LaMarr Hoyt also lost two 1-0 games.

Extra innings were needed to decide two 1-0 games. Toronto, behind Jim Gott, defeated Detroit in 10 innings on July 31; Jesse Barfield drove in the winning run with a two-out pinch single off reliever Dave Rucker. Jerry Ujdur pitched the first nine innings for Detroit. The Mets edged the Phillies on October 1, scoring in the 10th inning on Hubie Brooks' sacrifice fly. Terry Leach, making his only start after 20 relief appearances, went all the way for the Mets. Porfirio Altamirano, who relieved John Denny in the 10th, was the loser.

The complete list of 1-0 games, including the winning and losing pitchers and the inning in which the run was scored, follows:

AMERICAN LEAGUE (12)

Date	Winner	Loser	Inning
APRIL—			
21 —	Guidry, N.Y.	*Dotson, Chi.	5
MAY—			
7 —	*Medich, Tex.	Eckersley, Bos.	5
9 —	*Stanley, Bos.	*Tanana, Tex.	6
22 —	*Righetti, N.Y.	*Jackson, Minn.	5
JUNE—			
23 —	Gura, K.C.	*Kingman, Oak.	9
25 —	*Beattie, Sea.	Hoyt, Chi.	6
JULY—			
20 —	Petry, Det.	Hoyt, Chi.	7
31 —	Gott, Tor.	*Rucker, Det.	10
AUGUST—			
3† —	*Trout, Chi.	*Rawley, N.Y.	5
14 —	Gura, K.C.	*Petry, Det.	9
31 —	Palmer, Balt.	Leal, Tor.	1
SEPTEMBER—			
12 —	*Stoddard, Sea.	*Smithson, Tex.	1

NATIONAL LEAGUE (23)

Date	Winner	Loser	Inning
APRIL—			
6 —	Mahler, Atl.	*Eichelberger, S.D.	5
8 —	*Knepper, Hou.	*Andujar, St.L.	8
11 —	Krukow, Phila.	Burris, Mont.	8
24 —	*Puleo, N.Y.	*Burris, Mont.	7
30 —	*Bedrosian, Atl.	*Bird, Chi.	6
MAY—			
29 —	Ruthven, Phila.	Niekro, Atl.	6
JUNE—			
2 —	Andujar, St.L.	Laskey, S.F.	3
11 —	*Tekulve, Pitts.	Christenson, Phila.	9
25† —	Ruthven, Phila.	Falcone, N.Y.	9
28 —	Carlton, Phila.	*Mura, St.L.	5
JULY—			
6 —	McWilliams, Pitts.	Knepper, Hou.	2
10 —	Noles, Chi.	Berenyi, Cin.	4
16 —	Carlton, Phila.	*Laskey, S.F.	5
25 —	Carlton, Phila.	*Reuss, L.A.	2
AUGUST—			
20 —	Valenzuela, L.A.	*McWilliams, Pitts.	2
25 —	*Shirley, Cin.	Rogers, Mont.	8
SEPTEMBER—			
3 —	*Pastore, Cin.	Ownbey, N.Y.	4
4 —	*Tunnell, Pitts.	Valenzuela, L.A.	1
6 —	Andujar, St.L.	*Gullickson, Mont.	9
8 —	Forsch, St.L.	*Lea, Mont.	3
14 —	Valenzuela, L.A.	*Show, S.D.	1
21 —	*Jenkins, Chi.	*Scurry, Pitts.	7
OCTOBER—			
1 —	Leach, N.Y.	*Altamirano, Phila.	10

*Did not pitch complete game.
†First game of doubleheader.

DeCinces Hits Three Homers Twice

By LARRY WIGGE

Doug DeCinces was flattered when a representative of Baseball's Hall of Fame called to ask for the bat he used to hit three homers against the Seattle Mariners August 8. But the California Angels third baseman figured that could wait. He wasn't finished with his good-luck bat.

The call came after DeCinces had become only the seventh player in major league history and just the second American Leaguer to connect for a pair of three-homer games in the same season.

Ted Williams is the only other A.L. performer to hit three homers twice in the same season, doing it for the Red Sox in 1957. Johnny Mize had a pair of three-homer games for the Cardinals in 1938 and again in 1940. Ralph Kiner of the Pirates accomplished the feat in 1947, while Willie Mays did it for the Giants in 1961, Willie Stargell for the Pirates in 1971 and Dave Kingman for the Cubs in 1979.

Actually, DeCinces, who had hit three homers against the Twins on August 3, erupted for the fastest pair of three-homer games on record. The five-day difference beat a seven-day differential by Mize in July of 1938. The only other player to accomplish this unusual trick in the same month was Stargell, who connected 11 days apart in April of 1971.

Against the Twins, DeCinces had a solo homer in the first, a two-run blast in the third and another solo shot in the eighth. The Angels, however, lost, 5-4.

California didn't waste DeCinces' Seattle performance. The third baseman hit solo homers in the first and third innings and added a two-run clout in the eighth in a 9-5 victory.

Detroit's Larry Herndon was one of four other A.L. batters with three homers in a game. Herndon's performance was notable because he tied a record May 18 when he powered the Tigers to an 11-9 triumph over Oakland with homers in his first three at-bats. That gave him four consecutive homers over two games, the 15th such accomplishment in history.

Paul Molitor hit three solo homers May 12, but his Milwaukee club lost at Kansas City, 9-7. Another Brewer, Ben Oglivie, exploded for three homers in a 7-5 victory at Detroit June 20. The Tigers also fell victim to Harold Baines' three-homer explosion July 7. Baines included a grand slam in his production, leading the White Sox to a 7-0 victory.

The National League had produced at least one three-homer game every year from 1946 through 1980, but failed to accomplish the feat for the second straight season.

Milwaukee shortstop Robin Yount led the major leagues with seven multi-homer games.

Following is a list of players who had two-homer games in 1982 and the number of times they did it:

AMERICAN LEAGUE: Baltimore (4)—Murray 2, Lowenstein, Roenicke. Boston (4)—Evans 2, Nichols, Rice. California (11)—DeCinces 5, Baylor 2, Downing 2, Boone, Re. Jackson. Chicago (8)—Baines 3, Fisk, Kemp, Luzinski, Morrison, Paciorek. Cleveland (2)—Thornton 2. Detroit (13)—Parrish 4, Whitaker 3, Herndon 2, Lemon 2, Hebner, Ivie. Kansas City (5)—Aikens 2, McRae, Otis, Washington. Milwaukee (20)—Yount 7, Thomas 6, Cooper 3, Molitor, Money, Oglivie, Simmons. Minnesota (3)—Brunansky, Bush, Gaetti. New York (8)—Winfield 4, Smalley 3, Nettles. Oakland (3)—Armas, Lopes, Meyer. Seattle (3)—Edler, Serna, Zisk. Texas (7)—Hostetler 3, Bell 2, Parrish, Sample. Toronto (3)—Upshaw 2, Mayberry.

NATIONAL LEAGUE: Atlanta (9)—Horner 4, Murphy 2, Ramirez, Washington, Watson. Chicago (7)—Durham 2, Buckner, Davis, Johnstone, Moreland, Sandberg. Cincinnati (5)—Driessen 2, Cedeno, Oester, Walker. Houston (4)—Ashby 2, Puhl, Spilman. Los Angeles (5)—Baker 2, Guerrero, Landreaux, Monday. Montreal (10)—Carter 3, Wallach 3, Dawson 2, Cromartie, Oliver. New York (2)—Kingman 2. Philadelphia (3)—Diaz 2, Matthews. Pittsburgh (4)—Thompson 2, Parker, Pena. St. Louis (3)—Hendrick 2, Porter. San Diego (4)—Kennedy 2, Lezcano 2. San Francisco (6)—Clark 3, Brenly, May, Smith.

A recap of the three-homer games:

Date	Player—Club—Opp.	Place	AB.	R.	H.	2B.	3B.	HR.	RBI.	Result
May 12	Molitor, Brewers vs. Royals	A	5	3	4	0	0	3	4	L 7-9
May 18	Herndon, Tigers vs. A's	H	4	3	3	0	0	3	7	W 11-9
June 20	Oglivie, Brewers vs. Tigers	A	3	3	3	0	0	3	5	W 7-5
July 7	Baines, White Sox vs. Tigers	H	4	3	3	0	0	3	6	W 7-0
Aug. 3	DeCinces, Angels vs. Twins	H	5	3	3	0	0	3	4	L 4-5
Aug. 8	DeCinces, Angels vs. Mariners	A	5	3	3	0	0	3	4	W 9-5

Parrish Leads Grand-Slam Barrage

By CARL CLARK

Seldom did a week of the American League's 1982 season pass without a grand slam. One week, five were hit, three by Texas' Larry Parrish. Baltimore hit eight overall; California, Minnesota, New York and Seattle five each. Every club contributed at least one grand slam to the league total of 48, which fell only two short of the record, set in 1979.

Parrish struggled the first three months of the season, batting .197 with only two home runs and eight runs batted in. He broke loose, however, against Oakland on July 4. He hit a three-run homer off Matt Keough in the third inning and a grand slam off Fernando Arroyo in the fourth for seven RBIs in an 11-4 victory. Three days later, he again connected with the bases loaded, this time against Boston's Mark Clear. His first-inning grand slam off Milt Wilcox in the first game of a July 10 doubleheader helped the Rangers defeat Detroit, 6-5.

Parrish thus became the third player to hit three grand slams in one calendar week. Lou Gehrig (Yankees, 1931) and Jim Northrup (Detroit, 1968) are the others. Northrup and Rudy York of the 1938 Tigers are the only players besides Parrish who have hit three grand slams in a calendar month (Gehrig's week overlapped months).

Six A.L. batters hit two grand slams in 1982: Brian Downing, California; Harold Baines, Chicago; Alan Trammell, Detroit; Gary Gaetti, Minnesota; Roy Smalley, New York and Eddie Murray, Baltimore. It was the second consecutive season that Murray had hit two.

Baines' grand slams were part of his hottest week. In the White Sox' 7-0 victory over Detroit on July 7, Baines drove in six runs with solo homers in the fifth and seventh innings and a grand slam in the eighth. He hit two homers off lefthander Jerry Garvin, one with the bases empty and one with the bases full, in a 16-7 romp over Toronto on July 11.

Three of the Orioles' grand slams were struck by pinch-hitters. That tied the major league record shared by four National League teams. Terry Crowley's pinch homer in the ninth off Kansas City's Mike Armstrong on August 8 was one of two grand slams that the Orioles hit with the score tied in the bottom of the last inning. Joe Nolan gave the Orioles a 7-3 victory over Toronto on August 24 with a two-out blast in the 10th.

Armstrong gave up three grand slams in all. (The record is four.) Touched for two were Garvin, Boston's Tom Burgmeier, Elias Sosa of Detroit, Jim Slaton of Milwaukee and Minnesota's Ron Davis.

The National League was comparatively tranquil with only 23 grand slams. Montreal's Tim Wallach was the lone player to hit two, and the team leader was Pittsburgh with five. When Richie Hebner and Bill Madlock teed off in the Pirates' 15-5 victory over Chicago on September 14, it was the 31st time in major league history that a team had hit two grand slams in the same game.

Notes: Tom Brunansky hit an inside-the-park grand slam for Minnesota on July 19. It was his second inside-the-park home run of the season and came when his sinking liner skipped past center fielder Gorman Thomas. . . . Orlando Mercado's grand slam for Seattle on September 19 was his first major league hit. . . . Pitcher Scott Sanderson belted a grand slam in Montreal's 10-6 victory over the Cubs on September 11. It was Sanderson's first major league homer, and his grand slam was the first of four that Cubs' pitchers allowed in an eight-day span.

The complete list of grand slams, with the inning in which each was hit in parentheses, follows:

AMERICAN LEAGUE (48)

APRIL—
5 —Murray, Baltimore vs. Leonard, Kansas City.....	(3)
9 —Otis, Kansas City vs. Morris, Detroit	(1)
24 —Barfield, Toronto vs. Burgmeier, Boston.............	(8)
27 —LeFlore, Chicago vs. Slaton, Milwaukee.............	(2)

MAY—
1 —Smalley, New York vs. Caudill, Seattle	(8)
10 —Ward, Minnesota vs. Torrez, Boston	(4)
10 —Roenicke, Baltimore vs. McCatty, Oakland	(6)
16 —Trammell, Detroit vs. Havens, Minnesota...........	(2)
18 —Burroughs, Oakland vs. Sosa, Detroit.................	(7)
22 —Maler, Seattle vs. Lerch, Milwaukee	(3)
28 —Nettles, New York vs. Davis, Minnesota..............	(9)
29† —Ayala, Baltimore vs. Garvin, Toronto	(7)
31 —Miller, Boston vs. McLaughlin, Oakland.............	(4)

JUNE—
2 —Murcer, New York vs. Bomback, Toronto	(13)
10 —Hrbek, Minnesota vs. Armstrong, Kansas City...	(5)
14 —Ford, Baltimore vs. Easterly, Milwaukee...........	(7)
19 —Kemp, Chicago vs. Sanchez, California	(5)
25 —Smalley, New York vs. Barker, Cleveland	(3)

JULY—
2 —Cooper, Milwaukee vs. Burgmeier, Boston	(7)
4 —Parrish, Texas vs. Arroyo, Oakland......................	(4)
6 —McRae, Kansas City vs. Tudor, Boston	(1)
7 —Baines, Chicago vs. Sosa, Detroit..........................	(8)
7 —Parrish, Texas vs. Clear, Boston	(9)
10* —Parrish, Texas vs. Wilcox, Detroit	(1)
11 —Baines, Chicago vs. Garvin, Toronto.....................	(2)
15 —Lynn, California vs. Waits, Cleveland	(3)
19 —Brunansky, Minnesota vs. Augustine, Milw.......	(3)
21 Oglivie, Milwaukee vs. Boris, Minnesota............	(4)
26 —Gaetti, Minnesota vs. Bannister, Seattle	(1)
27 —Edler, Seattle vs. Little, Minnesota......................	(6)
29 —Thornton, Cleveland vs. Slaton, Milwaukee........	(12)
30 —Trammell, Detroit vs. Clancy, Toronto	(4)

Texas' Larry Parrish became only the third player in history to hit three grand slams in the same calendar week during July 4-10 last season.

AUGUST—
6 —Re. Jackson, California vs. Vande Berg, Seattle. (6)
8 —Crowley, Baltimore vs. Armstrong, Kansas City (9)
11 —Baylor, California vs. Davis, Minnesota.............. (7)
15 —T. Cruz, Seattle vs. Redfern, Minnesota .... (6)
21 —Armas, Oakland vs. Stanley, Boston .... (6)
22 —Henderson, Seattle vs. Haas, Milwaukee .... (1)
24 —Nolan, Baltimore vs. McLaughlin, Toronto......... (10)
26 —Murray, Baltimore vs. Schrom, Toronto.............. (3)
31 —Downing, California vs. Pashnick, Detroit.......... (5)

SEPTEMBER—
6 —Downing, California vs. Koosman, Chicago........ (2)
13 —Winfield, New York vs. D. Martinez, Baltimore. (5)
14† —Ripken, Baltimore vs. Morgan, New York .... (6)
19 —Lansford, Boston vs. Tobik, Detroit .... (8)
19 —Gaetti, Minnesota vs. Armstrong, Kansas City... (5)
19 —Mercado, Seattle vs. Comer, Texas .... (5)
30 —Aikens, Kansas City vs. Owchinko, Oakland....... (7)

NATIONAL LEAGUE (23)

APRIL—
10 —L. Smith, St. Louis vs. Rhoden, Pittsburgh.......... (4)
25 —Leonard, San Fran. vs. Stewart, Los Ang. .... (8)
27 —Pena, Pittsburgh vs. Alvarez, Atlanta.................. (5)

MAY—
1 —Driessen, Cincinnati vs. Kaat, St. Louis .... (7)
4 —Easler, Pittsburgh vs. Cowley, Atlanta................ (3)

22 —Puhl, Houston vs. Allen, New York .... (9)
29 —Clark, San Fran. vs. D. Robinson, Pitts............... (5)

JUNE—
19 —Davis, San Francisco vs. Bedrosian, Atlanta ...... (9)
29 —Hendrick, St. Louis vs. Farmer, Philadelphia..... (8)
30* —Baker, Los Angeles vs. Eichelberger, San Diego. (5)

JULY—
20 —McGee, St. Louis vs. Dayley, Atlanta................... (1)

AUGUST—
1 —Chambliss, Atlanta vs. Beckwith, Los Angeles ... (1)
5 —Wallach, Montreal vs. Lyle, Philadelphia............ (8)
14 —Robinson, Philadelphia vs. Burris, Montreal...... (8)
15* —Milner, Pittsburgh vs. Mura, St. Louis .... (7)
22 —Maddox, Philadelphia vs. Soto, Cincinnati .... (3)

SEPTEMBER—
8 —Hodges, New York vs. Jackson, Pittsburgh......... (9)
9 —Benedict, Atlanta vs. Valenzuela, Los Angeles... (6)
11 —Sanderson, Montreal vs. Martz, Chicago............ (3)
14 —Hebner, Pittsburgh vs. Noles, Chicago .... (3)
14 —Madlock, Pittsburgh vs. Proly, Chicago.............. (4)
18 —Wallach, Montreal vs. Bird, Chicago .... (3)

OCTOBER—
1 —Monday, Los Angeles vs. Breining, San Fran...... (8)
*First game of doubleheader.
†Second game of doubleheader.

Lefebvre Only Player To Get Six Hits

By CARL CLARK

The Padres' Joe Lefebvre, in a 4-3, 16-inning loss to the Dodgers on September 13, became the first National Leaguer in five years to collect six hits in a game and the 33rd N.L. player since 1900—only St. Louis' Jim Bottomley has done it twice, in 1924 and 1931—to record six or more hits in a game. Twenty-two major leaguers had five hits in a game in 1982, with San Diego's Gene Richards accomplishing the feat two times.

Lefebvre's first three hits—singles in the first and eighth innings and a two-run homer in the third—were off Bob Welch. Lefebvre picked up his other hits in extra innings. He singled off Joe Beckwith in the 12th, and touched Dave Stewart for a double in the 14th and a single in the 16th. Lefebvre was retired twice.

Ironically, five of the Padres' nine other hits that night were produced by Richards, the last man before Lefebvre to get six hits in an N.L. contest. In 1977, Richards went 6-for-7 in a 15-inning loss to the Expos.

Leading off ahead of Lefebvre against Los Angeles, Richards had four singles and a triple in eight at-bats. In a 9-7 loss to the Mets on July 10, Richards went 5-for-5 and drove in three runs.

Pete Rose's .271 batting average was his lowest since 1964, but the Phillies' first baseman continued his assault on the record books. His 5-for-5 performance against the Dodgers April 28 was the ninth five-hit game of his career, tying Max Carey's N.L. record. In June, Rose hit safely in 21 consecutive games (32-for-86, .372), the longest streak in the league last season. It was his seventh streak of 20 or more games, matching Ty Cobb's major league mark.

Dickie Thon of the Astros had a 21-game string, too, but didn't create nearly so much havoc during his as Jason Thompson, George Hendrick and Al Oliver did in shorter streaks. Thompson batted .453, hit eight homers and drove in 24 runs for the Pirates in a 17-game stretch beginning in late April. The Expos' Oliver knocked in 16 runs and batted .446 over 15 games in August. In a 15-game binge in midseason, Hendrick batted .362 and drove in 20 runs for the Cardinals.

The majors' longest hitting streak, 25 games, belonged to the Angels' Rod Carew. From May 23 through June 21, Carew had 41 hits in 99 at-bats for a .414 average. His streak was halted by Rang-

Joe Lefebvre . . . Padres' six-hit man.

ers lefthander Rick Honeycutt. Carew posted a .373 average and scored 19 runs in a 19-game tear that began in mid-August.

(Toby Harrah might have matched Carew's 25-game streak but for an impropriety. Harrah hit safely in the Indians' first 14 games, getting 23 hits in 54 at-bats for a .426 average. When Harrah singled in the first inning against Seattle's Floyd Bannister on April 27, it appeared he had extended his streak to 15 games. Umpire Bill Kunkel, however, nullified the hit and ejected Harrah for using an illegal bat. Harrah went on to collect hits in each of his next 10 games. Matt Keough and Jeff Jones of the A's stopped that streak May 9, but Harrah began another one the next night that reached 16 games, in which he batted .415.)

Two other players had two streaks of 15 or more games. Twins rookie Kent Hrbek ran off 23 games beginning April 17; stopped in five at-bats by the Tigers' Dan Petry and Dave Rozema May 14, he began another streak, one that reached 17 games before he went 0-for-1 with three walks against the Royals on June 14. Hrbek batted .308 with five homers and 17 RBIs in the first streak, .406 (28-for-69) with five homers and 19 RBIs in the second. Damaso Garcia of the Blue Jays had streaks of 20 and 17 games. In the shorter streak, Garcia scored in 11 consecutive games.

The only other 20-game streak was turned in by the Mariners' Richie Zisk. As in his 15-game streak in 1981, Zisk hit with power, clubbing eight homers in 21 games. He batted .420 (37-for-88) and drove in 21 runs.

The Angels' Fred Lynn topped even that in an 18-game spree in July. With 29 hits (seven of them homers) in 69 at-bats (.420), Lynn drove in 28 runs and scored 18.

Streaks of 15 or more games also were recorded by these players: 19 games—Pedro Guerrero, Dodgers; Glenn Wilson, Tigers; 18 games—Billy Sample, Rangers; 17 games—Cecil Cooper, Brewers; Larry Herndon, Tigers; Paul Molitor, Brewers; Jerry Royster, Braves; Lonnie Smith, Cardinals; Willie Wilson, Royals; 16 games—Ron Cey, Dodgers; Ray Knight, Astros; Gary Roenicke, Orioles; Steve Sax, Dodgers; 15 games—Buddy Bell, Rangers; Jack Clark, Giants; Chili Davis, Giants; Mike Easler, Pirates; Steve Garvey, Dodgers; Tony Gwynn, Padres; Keith Hernandez, Cardinals; Gary Matthews, Phillies; Tom O'Malley, Giants; John Stearns, Mets; George Wright, Rangers.

Bill Buckner of the Cubs paced the majors in games with four or more hits. He had seven.

The complete list of players with four or more hits in one game follows:

AMERICAN LEAGUE: Baltimore (9)—Murray 4, Ford 2, Bumbry, Ripken, Roenicke. Boston (8)—Rice 4, Boggs, Evans, Lansford, Yastrzemski. California (8)—Carew 2, Downing 2, Re. Jackson 2, Baylor, DeCinces. Chicago (5)—Luzinski 2, Paciorek 2, Rodriguez. Cleveland (9)—Harrah 4, Bando, Bannister, Dilone, Hassey, Manning. Detroit (12)—Gibson 2, Lemon 2, Whitaker 2, Wockenfuss 2, Ca-bell, Herndon, Ivie, Wilson. Kansas City (14)—Brett 3, Wilson 3, Aikens 2, McRae 2, Otis, Quirk, Wathan, White. Milwaukee (21)—Cooper 5, Molitor 5, Yount 5, Simmons 2, Howell, Moore, Oglivie, Thomas. Minnesota (11)—Washington 3, Gaetti 2, Ward 2, Hrbek, Johnson, Vega, Wilfong. New York (9)—Griffey 2, Randolph 2, Winfield 2, Collins, Piniella, Smalley. Oakland (3)—Armas, Burroughs, Meyer. Seattle (10)—Bochte 3, Cowens 2, Zisk 2, T. Cruz, Essian, Moses. Texas (10)—Wright 3, Bell 2, Hostetler 2, Bass, Grubb, Parrish. Toronto (8)—Bonnell 2, Garcia 2, Griffin 2, Moseby, Whitt.

NATIONAL LEAGUE: Atlanta (17)—Hubbard 3, Horner 2, Ramirez 2, Royster 2, Washington 2, Chambliss, Linares, Murphy, Pocoroba, Watson, Whisenton. Chicago (15)—Buckner 7, Henderson 2, Bowa, Durham, Moreland, Sandberg, Thompson, Wills. Cincinnati (7)—Milner 2, Driessen, Oester, Trevino, Van Gorder, Walker. Houston (5)—Garner 2, Cruz, Spilman, Thon. Los Angeles (9)—Garvey 3, Cey 2, Baker, Landreaux, Monday, Orta. Montreal (15)—Oliver 5, Carter 2, Dawson 2, Cromartie, Francona, Raines, Speier, Wallach, White. New York (9)—Wilson 3, Stearns 2, Brooks, Foster, Staub, Valentine. Philadelphia (18)—Diaz 6, Matthews 3, Rose 3, Vukovich 3, Dernier 2, Maddox. Pittsburgh (13)—Ray 5, Berra 2, Madlock 2, Pena 2, Moreno, Thompson. St. Louis (9)—L. Smith 3, Herr 2, McGee 2, Gonzalez, Iorg. San Diego (11)—Richards 4, Lezcano 2, Bonilla, Gwynn, Jones, Kennedy, Lefebvre. San Francisco (11)—Clark 2, Wohlford 2, Bergman, Davis, Evans, Kuiper, Morgan, O'Malley, Smith.

The records of all players with five or more hits in a game follow:

Date	Player—Club—Opp.	Place	AB.	R.	H.	2B.	3B.	HR.	RBI.	Result
April 10	Bonnell, Blue Jays vs. Brewers (10 inn.)	H	5	1	5	1	0	0	1	W 3-2
April 11*	Essian, Mariners vs. A's (16 innings)	A	6	1	5	2	0	0	4	W 6-3
April 13‡	Baylor, Angels vs. Mariners (20 innings)	H	9	2	5	1	0	0	1	W 4-3
April 17†	Murray, Orioles vs. White Sox	A	5	2	5	0	0	0	0	L 6-10
April 28	Rose, Phillies vs. Dodgers	A	5	1	5	1	0	0	1	W 9-3
May 8	Baker, Dodgers vs. Expos	A	6	2	5	0	0	2	5	W 10-8
May 14	Gibson, Tigers vs. Twins (11 innings)	H	6	1	5	0	0	1	2	W 4-2
May 20	Herndon, Tigers vs. A's	H	5	2	5	0	2	0	1	W 11-3
May 29	McRae, Royals vs. Rangers	A	5	2	5	0	0	0	3	W 14-1
June 6	Aikens, Royals vs. Yankees	A	6	1	5	3	0	0	4	W 14-1
June 9	Pocoroba, Braves vs. Dodgers	A	5	0	5	1	0	0	5	W 11-5
June 12	Horner, Braves vs. Giants	A	5	0	5	2	0	0	1	W 10-5
June 19	Foster, Mets vs. Cardinals	A	5	2	5	1	0	1	1	W 8-5
June 19	Garcia, Blue Jays vs. A's (12 innings)	A	5	1	5	0	0	0	1	W 3-1
July 2	Yount, Brewers vs. Red Sox	H	5	3	5	1	0	0	1	W 14-5
July 10	Richards, Padres vs. Mets	A	5	2	5	0	0	1	3	L 7-9
July 17	Morgan, Giants vs. Phillies (11 innings)	H	6	0	5	0	0	2	1	L 3-5
Aug. 2	Herr, Cardinals vs. Pirates (17 innings)	H	9	1	5	1	0	0	1	L 2-4
Aug. 5	Raines, Expos vs. Phillies	A	6	3	5	0	0	0	0	W 9-2
Aug. 22	Ripken, Orioles vs. Rangers	A	5	2	5	0	0	1	2	W 10-3
Aug. 25	Maddox, Phillies vs. Braves (10 innings)	A	6	1	5	0	0	0	1	W 11-9
Sept. 8	Washington, Braves vs. Dodgers (10 inn.)	H	6	3	5	1	0	1	4	W 12-11
Sept. 13	Richards, Padres vs. Dodgers (16 innings)	A	8	2	5	0	1	0	0	L 3-4
Sept. 13	Lefebvre, Padres vs. Dodgers (16 innings)	A	8	1	6	1	0	1	2	L 3-4

*First game of doubleheader. †Second game of doubleheader. ‡Suspended game, completed April 14.

Orioles Came Through in Pinch

By LARRY WIGGE

The Baltimore Orioles had fallen behind 3-0 after three innings of their season's finale with the Milwaukee Brewers October 3, but nobody on the Baltimore bench was throwing in the towel.

Manager Earl Weaver's judicious use of his potent bench had been one of the keys that permitted the Orioles to rally from 7½ games behind and pull into a tie with the Brewers for the A.L. East Division lead with one game remaining.

Even though the Orioles finally succumbed to the Brewers, Baltimore's reserves were in for some plaudits. The O's, in fact, set an A.L. record with 11 pinch-homers and they tied a major league mark by hitting three pinch-grand slams (Benny Ayala, Dan Ford and Terry Crowley).

The Angels' Ron Jackson was the A.L. pinch-hitting leader with 6-for-11, a .545 average. Jeff Burroughs of the A's had four pinch-homers (to lead the majors) and 12 RBIs, while Bill Stein of the Rangers led the A.L. with 12 pinch-hits.

Mike Easler of the Pirates was the National League pinch-hitting leader with a .500 average, going 5-for-10. Pittsburgh teammate Willie Stargell led the N.L. with three pinch-homers and knocked in 16 runs. Greg Gross topped the majors with 19 pinch-hits, setting a Phillies' club record held since 1945 by Rene Monteagudo, who had 18.

Jose Morales of the Dodgers and Crowley of the O's each surpassed the 100-hit level on the all-time pinch-hitting list. Morales has 108 and Crowley 103.

Following is a listing of all pinch-hitters with at least 10 at-bats in 1982:

NATIONAL LEAGUE PINCH-HITTING
(Compiled by Elias Sports Bureau)
Club Pinch-Hitting

Club	AB.	H.	HR.	RBI.	Pct.	Club	AB.	H.	HR.	RBI.	Pct.
St. Louis	202	54	1	29	.267	Philadelphia	189	41	0	23	.217
San Francisco	227	60	6	43	.264	Chicago	269	58	6	41	.216
Pittsburgh	236	61	7	40	.258	Houston	179	38	1	12	.212
San Diego	182	42	4	32	.231	Atlanta	220	45	4	33	.205
New York	243	56	3	38	.230	Montreal	198	39	4	22	.197
Cincinnati	251	57	2	34	.227	Los Angeles	270	49	4	32	.181
						TOTALS	2666	600	42	379	.225

Individual Pinch-Hitting
(10 or More At-Bats)

Player-Club	AB.	H.	HR.	RBI.	Pct.	Player-Club	AB.	H.	HR.	RBI.	Pct.
Easler, Pittsburgh	10	5	0	1	.500	Bergman, S.F.	21	5	0	1	.238
Baalor, New York	13	6	0	2	.462	Lefebvre, S.D.	34	8	1	3	.235
May, San Fran.	13	6	1	2	.462	Pocoroba, Atlanta	17	4	0	9	.235
Chambliss, Atlanta	11	5	2	8	.455	Barranca, Cin.	39	9	0	0	.231
Harper, Pittsburgh	12	5	1	1	.417	Lacy, Pittsburgh	13	3	0	3	.231
McGee, St. Louis	15	6	0	5	.400	Spilman, Houston	26	6	1	2	.231
Perkins, San Diego	29	11	0	7	.379	Smith, Atlanta	35	8	0	2	.229
Gross, Phila.	53	19	0	7	.358	Landrum, St. Louis	18	4	0	2	.222
Bevacqua, S.D.	26	9	0	10	.346	Vukovich, Phila.	23	5	0	6	.217
Green, St. Louis	12	4	0	1	.333	Virgil, Phila.	14	3	0	0	.214
Hodges, New York	12	4	0	1	.333	Staub, New York	57	12	1	13	.211
Morales, Chicago	30	10	2	11	.333	Molinaro, Chi-Phi	67	14	1	13	.209
Morgan, San Fran.	12	4	0	4	.333	Montanez, Pit-Phi	43	9	0	2	.209
Summers, S.F.	31	10	2	11	.323	Davis, Phila.-Pitt.	24	5	0	2	.208
Kuiper, San Fran.	44	14	0	5	.318	Biittner, Cincinnati	49	10	0	5	.204
Landestoy, N.Y.	35	11	1	5	.314	Cruz, Chicago	15	3	0	0	.200
Jorgensen, N.Y.	48	15	1	8	.313	Scott, Houston	10	2	0	1	.200
Morales, L.A.	30	9	1	8	.300	Walling, Houston	30	6	0	3	.200
Roenicke, L.A.	44	13	0	3	.295	Robinson, Pit-Phi	26	5	1	7	.192
Braun, St. Louis	41	12	0	3	.293	W. Johnson, Mon.	21	4	0	0	.190
Wills, Chicago	21	6	1	4	.286	Flannery, S.D.	16	3	0	0	.188
Vail, Cincinnati	29	8	0	9	.276	Morrison, Pitt.	16	3	0	1	.188
Heep, Houston	23	6	0	3	.261	Valentine, N.Y.	16	3	0	4	.188
Iorg, St. Louis	27	7	0	5	.259	Wohlford, S.F.	27	5	0	3	.185
Thompson, Chi.	27	7	0	2	.259	Foster, New York	11	2	0	2	.182
Linares, Atlanta	31	8	0	2	.258	Woods, Chicago	22	4	0	4	.182
White, Montreal	39	10	1	7	.256	Whisenton, Atlanta	45	8	1	4	.178
Krenchicki, Cin.	28	7	1	7	.250	Venable, San Fran.	17	3	0	1	.176
Mills, Montreal	40	10	1	1	.250	Evans, San Fran.	12	2	1	4	.167
Ramsey, St. Louis	16	4	0	3	.250	Milner, Mon.-Pitt.	43	7	2	10	.163
Stargell, Pitts.	56	14	3	16	.250	Brock, Los Angeles	13	2	0	1	.154
Tenace, St. Louis	12	3	0	1	.250	Edwards, S.D.	20	3	1	1	.150
Watson, Atlanta	24	6	1	8	.250	Marshall, L.A.	20	3	1	2	.150
Henderson, Chi.	25	6	0	2	.240	Orta, Los Angeles	60	9	1	5	.150

Individual Pinch-Hitting—Continued
(10 or More At-Bats)

Player—Club	AB.	H.	HR.	RBI.	Pct.	Player—Club	AB.	H.	HR.	RBI.	Pct.
Norman, Montreal.	21	3	0	3	.143	Landreaux, L. A.	11	1	0	1	.091
Walker, Cincinnati	14	2	0	3	.143	Gonzales, St. Louis.	12	1	0	0	.083
Pittman, Hou.-S.D.	15	2	0	0	.133	Porter, Atlanta	16	1	0	0	.063
Y'blood, N.Y.-Mon.	15	2	0	3	.133	Knicely, Houston ...	17	1	0	0	.059
J'stone, L.A.-Chi. ...	26	3	0	2	.115	Matuszek, Phila	17	1	0	1	.059
Monday, L.A.	35	4	1	8	.114	Rajsich, New York	35	2	1	1	.057
Briggs, Chicago	37	4	0	0	.108	Unser, Phila.	11	0	0	0	.000
Householder, Cin....	10	1	0	1	.100	Walton, Pittsburgh	10	0	0	0	.000

AMERICAN LEAGUE PINCH-HITTING
(Compiled by Sports Information Center)

Club Pinch-Hitting

Club	AB.	H.	HR.	RBI.	Pct.	Club	AB.	H.	HR.	RBI.	Pct.
California	65	22	1	17	.338	Detroit	126	26	5	24	.206
Toronto	262	71	4	53	.271	Cleveland	117	24	2	18	.205
Baltimore	188	47	11	45	.250	Seattle	95	19	1	11	.200
Oakland	144	34	4	20	.236	Minnesota................	116	22	2	13	.190
Texas.......................	115	27	2	17	.235	New York................	140	26	3	14	.186
Milwaukee	82	19	1	8	.232	Boston	88	16	2	10	.182
Chicago...................	131	28	2	22	.214	Kansas City	73	12	1	16	.164
						Totals	1742	393	41	288	.226

Individual Pinch-Hitting
(10 or More At-Bats)

Player-Club	AB.	H.	HR.	RBI.	Pct.	Player-Club	AB.	H.	HR.	RBI.	Pct.
Ro. Jackson, Calif..	11	6	0	0	.545	Crowley, Balt..........	35	7	2	10	.200
Lynn, California	10	5	0	6	.500	Murcer, New York	30	6	2	7	.200
Nordhagen, Tor......	26	11	0	8	.423	Cabell, Detroit........	10	2	0	3	.200
Iorg, Toronto..........	22	9	0	5	.409	Geronimo, K.C........	10	2	0	3	.200
Aikens, Kan. City...	10	4	1	5	.400	Bonnell, Toronto	22	4	0	3	.182
Martinez, Toronto..	10	4	0	4	.400	Hammond, K.C.	11	2	0	3	.182
Ayala, Baltimore ...	24	9	2	10	.375	Hayes, Cleveland ...	11	2	0	1	.182
Wockenfuss, Det. ...	11	4	2	5	.364	Ivie, Detroit	11	2	0	1	.182
Piniella, New York	25	9	0	4	.360	R. Law, Chicago.....	17	3	0	0	.176
Stein, Texas............	34	12	1	8	.353	Turner, Detroit........	24	4	1	4	.167
Burroughs, Oak......	33	11	4	12	.333	Howell, Milwaukee	12	2	0	1	.167
Powell, Toronto......	30	10	0	3	.333	Nolan, Baltimore ...	12	2	1	2	.167
Whitt, Toronto........	21	7	2	3	.333	Kittle, Chicago	13	2	0	3	.154
Bando, Cleveland ...	12	4	0	2	.333	Woods, Toronto	20	3	0	3	.150
Boggs, Boston	13	4	0	1	.308	Leach, Detroit	14	2	0	1	.143
Gross, Oakland.......	20	6	0	3	.300	Meyer, Oakland	29	4	0	1	.138
Hassey, Cleveland..	10	3	0	3	.300	Mulliniks, Toronto.	22	3	0	5	.136
Johnson, Toronto ...	10	3	0	1	.300	Bush, Minnesota.....	25	3	0	2	.120
Moore, Milwaukee.	10	3	0	1	.300	Gamble, New York	18	2	0	0	.111
Lowenstein, Balt....	17	5	1	6	.294	Craig, Cleveland	19	2	0	0	.105
Barfield, Toronto ...	21	6	2	8	.286	Wilfong, Min.-Cal..	19	2	0	2	.105
Grubb, Texas..........	14	4	0	0	.286	Revering,					
Roenicke, Balt.	18	5	2	6	.278	N.Y.-Tor.-Sea.....	20	2	0	2	.100
Roberts, Tex.-Tor..	15	4	1	5	.267	Nettles, New York.	10	1	0	1	.100
L. Johnson, Texas..	19	5	0	1	.263	Strougher, Seattle	10	1	0	0	.100
Dwyer, Baltimore..	23	6	2	2	.261	Money, Milwaukee	21	2	0	0	.095
Johnson, Oakland ..	20	5	0	3	.250	Johnson, Minn.	22	2	1	2	.091
Vega, Minnesota	20	5	0	2	.250	Castillo, Seattle	11	1	0	2	.091
Hobson, New York.	12	3	0	0	.250	Foley, Chicago........	11	1	0	1	.091
Perez, Boston	21	5	2	6	.238	Dilone, Cleveland...	12	1	0	2	.083
Hairston, Chicago..	47	11	0	9	.234	Mazzilli, Tex.-N.Y.	12	1	0	0	.083
Engle, Minnesota...	13	3	0	3	.231	Yastrzemski, Bos...	15	1	0	1	.067
Ford, Baltimore	18	4	1	4	.222	Sweet, Seattle	18	1	0	2	.056
Hebner, Detroit	14	3	0	1	.214	Rudi, Oakland	10	0	0	0	.000
Squires, Chicago.....	14	3	0	4	.214						

PINCH-HOMERS FOR 1982

. NATIONAL LEAGUE: Atlanta (4)—Chambliss 2, Watson, Whisenton. Chicago (6)—Morales 2, Durham, Molinaro, Moreland, Wills. Cincinnati (2)—Krenchicki, Landestoy. Houston (1)—Spilman. Los Angeles (4)—Marshall, Monday, Morales, Orta. Montreal (4)—Mills, Oliver, Wallach, White. New York (3)—Jorgensen, Rajsich, Staub. Philadelphia (0). Pittsburgh (7)—Stargell 3, Milner 2, Harper, Robinson. St. Louis (1)—Hernandez. San Diego (4)—Edwards, Kennedy, Lefebvre, Templeton. San Francisco (6)—Summers 2, Davis, Evans, May, Smith.

AMERICAN LEAGUE: Baltimore (11)—Ayala 2, Crowley 2, Dwyer 2, Roenicke 2, Ford, Lowenstein, Nolan. Boston (2)—Perez 2. California (1)—Carew. Chicago (2)—Hairston 2. Cleveland (2)—Charboneau, Nahorodny. Detroit (5)—Wockenfuss 2, Brookens, Johnson, Turner. Kansas City (1)—Aikens. Milwaukee (1)—Hisle. Minnesota (2)—Johnson, Ward. New York (3)—Murcer 2, Mayberry. Oakland (4)—Burroughs 4. Seattle (1)—Gray. Texas (2)—Roberts, Stein. Toronto (4)—Barfield 2, Whitt 2.

Pitchers Dominate Debut List

By CARL CLARK

Lee Tunnell, one of 142 players who made their major league debuts in 1982, never will forget his first outing for the Pirates. Working against Fernando Valenzuela before 49,541 fans at Dodger Stadium September 4 (almost as many as watched him all season at Portland, where he was 12-9), Tunnell, given a run by Lee Lacy's first-inning homer, shut out Los Angeles for seven innings, allowing just four singles. Rod Scurry and Kent Tekulve completed the 1-0 triumph.

The Royals' Derek Botelho also pitched seven scoreless innings in his first game, a 9-0 victory over the Red Sox July 18. He allowed Boston only three singles before Mike Armstrong finished up for Kansas City.

Salome Barojas, purchased by the White Sox after six years in the Mexican League, burst onto the scene with saves in his first five games. He did not yield an earned run in his first eight appearances, giving up only four hits in 14 innings.

Bill Laskey of the Giants, after making his first appearance in relief, blanked the Expos 7-0 in his first start April 28. Laskey limited Montreal to three singles and drove in a run.

Switch-hitting center fielder George Wright sparked the Rangers' 8-3 opening-day victory over Cleveland. Wright had three hits—a single, double and home run —in four at-bats, scored two runs and drove in three.

The White Sox had the oldest rookie, 32-year-old pitcher Ernesto Escarrega. Like Barojas, Escarrega came up from the Mexican League.

The Mariners unveiled the youngest newcomer, plus a real veteran of the minor leagues. Edwin Nunez was 18 when he pitched against the Twins April 7. Outfielder Steve Stroughter, 30, who began his professional career in 1971, finally reached the majors 11 years, seven leagues, nine teams and 1,236 games later.

An alphabetical list of the players who made their big-league debuts in 1982 follows. More than a quarter of them are native Californians.

Player	Pos.	Club	Date and Place of Birth	Debut
Adams, Ricky Lee	SS	California	1-21-59—Upland, Calif.	9-15
Altamirano, Porfirio	P	Philadelphia	5-17-52—Esteli, Nicaragua	5- 9
Anderson, Karl Adam	P	Cleveland	5-27-56—Westbury, N.Y.	6-11
Baker, David Glenn	3B	Toronto	11- 8-56—Des Moines, Ia.	9-12
Baller, Jay Scott	P	Philadelphia	10- 6-60—Stayton, Ore.	9-19
Barnes, Richard Monroe	P	Chicago A.L.	7-21-59—Palm Beach, Fla.	7-18
Barojas, Salome	P	Chicago A.L.	6-16-57—Cordoba Veracruz, Mex.	4-11
Barrett, Martin Glenn	2B	Boston	6-23-58—Arcadia, Calif.	9- 6
Barrios, Jose Manuel	1B	San Francisco	6-26-57—New York, N.Y.	4-23
Bass, Kevin Charles	OF	Milw.-Hous.	5-12-59—Menlo Park, Calif.	4- 9
Belliard, Rafael Leonidas	SS	Pittsburgh	10-24-61—P. Nuevo, Mao, D.R.	9- 6
Biancalana, Roland Amer.	SS	Kansas City	2- 2-60—Larkspur, Calif.	9-12
Bogener, Terry Wayne	OF	Texas	9-28-55—Hannibal, Mo.	6-14
Boggs, Wade Anthony	3B-1B	Boston	6-15-58—Omaha, Neb.	4-10
Bohnet, John Kelly	P	Cleveland	1- 8-61—Pasadena, Calif.	5-10
Boris, Paul Stanley	P	Minnesota	12-13-55—Irvington, N.J.	5-21
Botelho, Derek Wayne	P	Kansas City	8- 2-56—Long Beach, Calif.	7-18
Boyd, Dennis Ray	P	Boston	10- 6-59—Meridian, Miss.	9-13
Brock, Gregory Allen	1B	Los Angeles	6-14-57—McMinnville, Ore.	9- 1
Brown, Michael Gary	P	Boston	3- 4-59—Haddon Township, N.J.	9-16
Bush, Robert Randall	DH-OF	Minnesota	10- 5-58—Dover, Del.	5- 1
Capra, Nick Lee	OF	Texas	3- 8-58—Denver, Colo.	9- 6
Castillo, Monte Carmelo	OF	Cleveland	6- 8-58—S. F. de Macoris, D.R.	7-17
Chiffer, Floyd John	P	San Diego	4-20-56—Glen Cove, N.Y.	4- 7
Codiroli, Christopher Allen	P	Oakland	3-26-58—Oxnard, Calif.	9-11
Cowley, Joseph Alan	P	Atlanta	8-15-58—Lexington, Ky.	4-13
Creel, Steven Keith	P	Kansas City	2- 4-59—Dallas, Tex.	5-25
Crow, Donald Leroy	C	Los Angeles	8-18-58—Yakima, Wash.	7-25
Davis, George Earl	P	Baltimore	12-26-61—Dallas, Tex.	4-29
Dayley, Kenneth Grant	P	Atlanta	2-25-59—Jerome, Idaho	5-13
DeJohn, Mark Stephen	SS	Detroit	9-18-53—Middletown, Conn.	4-28
Dempsey, Mark Steven	P	San Francisco	12-17-57—Dayton, O.	9- 4
Denman, Brian John	P	Boston	2-12-56—Minneapolis, Minn.	8-22
Diaz, Carlos Antonio Jr.	P	Atlanta	1- 7-58—Kaneohe, Hawaii	6-30
Doran, William Donald	2B	Houston	5-28-58—Cincinnati, O.	9- 6
Dravecky, David Francis	P	San Diego	2-14-56—Youngstown, O.	6-15
Eichhorn, Mark Anthony	P	Toronto	11-21-60—San Jose, Calif.	8-30
Eisenreich, James Michael	OF	Minnesota	4-18-59—St. Cloud, Minn.	4- 6
Escarrega, Ernesto	P	Chicago A.L.	12-27-49—L. Mochis, Sinaloa, Mex.	4-26
Espino, Juan	C	New York A.L.	3-16-56—Bonao, D.R.	6-25

White Sox reliever Salome Barojas broke in with five straight saves and did not allow an earned run in his first eight appearances.

Player	Pos.	Club	Date and Place of Birth	Debut
Farr, James Alfred	P	Texas	5-18-56—Waverly, N.Y.	9- 7
Filer, Thomas Carson	P	Chicago N.L.	12- 1-56—Philadelphia, Pa.	6- 8
Filson, William Peter	P	Minnesota	9-28-58—Darby, Pa.	5-15
Fowlkes, Alan Kim	P	San Francisco	8- 8-58—Brawley, Calif.	4- 7
Franco, Julio Cesar	SS-3B	Philadelphia	8-23-58—S.P. de Macoris, D.R.	4-23
Frobel, Douglas Steven	OF	Pittsburgh	6- 6-59—Ottawa, Ont., Canada	9- 5
Gaff, Brent Allen	P	New York N.L.	10- 5-58—Fort Wayne, Ind.	7- 7
Garrelts, Scott William	P	San Francisco	10-30-61—Urbana, Ill.	10- 2
Gott, James William	P	Toronto	8- 3-59—Hollywood, Calif.	4- 9
Gray, Lorenzo	3B	Chicago A.L.	3- 4-58—Mound Bayou, Miss.	7- 8
Guante, Cecilio	P	Pittsburgh	2- 1-61—Villa Mella, D.R.	5- 1
Gulliver, Glenn James	3B	Baltimore	10-15-54—Detroit, Mich.	7-17
Gumpert, David Lawrence	P	Detroit	5- 5-58—South Haven, Mich.	7-25
Gwynn, Anthony Keith	OF	San Diego	5- 9-60—Los Angeles, Calif.	7-19
Hammond, Steven Ben	OF	Kansas City	5- 9-57—Atlanta, Ga.	6-28
Hawkins, Melton Andrew	P	San Diego	1-21-60—Waco, Tex.	7-17
Hayes, Ben Joseph	P	Cincinnati	8- 4-57—Niagara Falls, N.Y.	6-25
Heath, Kelly Mark	2B	Kansas City	9- 4-57—Plattsburgh, N.Y.	4-20
Heaton, Neal	P	Cleveland	3- 3-60—Jamaica, N.Y.	9- 3
Henke, Thomas Anthony	P	Texas	12-21-57—Kansas City, Mo.	9-10
Hernandez, Leonardo Jesus	3B	Baltimore	11- 6-59—El Milagro, Venezuela	9-19
Hinshaw, George Addison	OF	San Diego	10-23-59—Los Angeles, Calif.	9-19

Player	Pos.	Club	Date and Place of Birth	Debut
Johnson, Howard Michael	3B	Detroit	11-29-60—Clearwater, Fla.	4-14
Johnson, Randall Glenn	2B-3B	Atlanta	6-10-56—Escondido, Calif.	4-27
Johnson, Ronald David	1B	Kansas City	3-23-56—Long Beach, Calif.	9-12
Johnson, Roy Edward	OF	Montreal	6-27-59—Parkin, Ark.	7- 3
Jones, Douglas Reid	P	Milwaukee	6-24-57—Lebanon, Ind.	4- 9
Jurak, Edward James	3B	Boston	10-24-57—Los Angeles, Calif.	6-30
Kaufman, Curt Gerrard	P	New York A.L.	7-19-57—Omaha, Neb.	9-10
Keener, Jeffrey Bruce	P	St. Louis	1-14-59—Pana, Ill.	6- 8
Kittle, Ronald Dale	OF	Chicago A.L.	1- 5-58—Gary, Ind.	9- 2
LaFrancois, Roger Victor	C	Boston	8- 2-56—Norwich, Conn.	5-27
Laga, Michael Russell	1B	Detroit	6-14-60—Ridgewood, N.J.	9- 1
Lahti, Jeffrey Allen	P	St. Louis	10- 8-56—Oregon City, Ore.	6-27
Lancellotti, Richard A.	1B-OF	San Diego	7- 5-56—Providence, R.I.	8-27
Lansford, Joseph Dale	1B	San Diego	1-15-61—San Jose, Calif.	7-31
Laskey, William Alan	P	San Francisco	12-20-57—Toledo, O.	4-23
Lawless, Thomas James	2B	Cincinnati	12-19-56—Erie, Pa.	7-15
Lesley, Bradley Jay	P	Cincinnati	9-11-58—Turlock, Calif.	7-31
Little, Richard Bryan	2B-SS	Montreal	10- 8-59—Houston, Tex.	7-29
Mason, Michael Paul	P	Texas	11-21-58—Faribault, Minn.	9-13
Mattingly, Donald Arthur	OF	New York A.L.	4-20-61—Evansville, Ind.	9- 8
McGee, Willie Dean	OF	St. Louis	11- 2-58—San Francisco, Calif.	5-10
Mercado, Orlando	C	Seattle	11- 7-61—Arecibo, P.R.	9-13
Moore, Michael Wayne	P	Seattle	11-26-59—Eakly, Okla.	4-11
Moses, John William	OF	Seattle	8- 9-57—Los Angeles, Calif.	8-23
Musselman, Ralph Ronald	P	Seattle	11-11-54—Wilmington, N.C.	8-18
Nunez, Edwin	P	Seattle	5-27-63—Humacao, P.R.	4- 7
Nyman, Christopher C.	1B	Chicago A.L.	6- 6-55—Pomona, Calif.	7-28
O'Brien, Peter Michael	OF	Texas	2- 9-58—Santa Monica, Calif.	9- 3
O'Malley, Thomas Patrick	3B	San Francisco	12-25-60—Orange, N.J.	5- 8
Ortiz, Adalberto Jr.	C	Pittsburgh	10-24-59—Humacao, P.R.	9-20
Ownbey, Richard Wayne	P	New York N.L.	10-20-57—Corona, Calif.	8-17
Paris, Kelly Jay	SS-3B	St. Louis	10-17-57—Encino, Calif.	9- 1
Pashnick, Larry John	P	Detroit	4-25-58—Lincoln Park, Mich.	4-10
Petralli, Eugene James Jr.	C	Toronto	9-25-59—Sacramento, Calif.	9- 4
Pettis, Gary George	OF	California	4- 3-58—Oakland, Calif.	9-13
Phillips, Keith Anthony	SS	Oakland	4-25-59—Atlanta, Ga.	5-10
Rabb, John Andrew	C-OF	San Francisco	6-23-60—Los Angeles, Calif.	9- 4
Rajsich, Gary Louis	OF	New York N.L.	10-28-54—Youngstown, O.	4- 9
Ray, Larry Dale	OF	Houston	3-11-58—Madison, Ind.	9-10
Redus, Gary Eugene	OF	Cincinnati	11- 1-56—Athens, Ala.	9- 7
Reynolds, Ronn Dwayne	C	New York N.L.	9-28-58—Wichita, Kan.	9-29
Rhomberg, Kevin Jay	2B-OF	Cleveland	11-22-55—Dubuque, Ia.	9- 1
Rodriguez, Edwin	2B	New York A.L.	8-14-60—Ponce, P.R.	9-28
Ross, Mark Joseph	P	Houston	8- 8-57—Galveston, Tex.	9-12
Ryal, Mark Dwayne	OF	Kansas City	4-28-60—Henryetta, Okla.	9- 7
Sanchez, Alejandro	OF	Philadelphia	2-26-59—San Pedro, D.R.	9- 6
Sax, David John	C-OF	Los Angeles	9-22-58—Sacramento, Calif.	9- 1
Scherrer, William Joseph	P	Cincinnati	1-20-58—Tonawanda, N.Y.	9- 7
Segelke, Herman Neils	P	Chicago N.L.	4-24-58—San Mateo, Calif.	4- 7
Senteney, Steve Leonard	P	Toronto	8- 7-57—Indianapolis, Ind.	6- 6
Shirley, Steven Brian	P	Los Angeles	10-12-56—San Francisco, Calif.	6-21
Sisk, Douglas Randall	P	New York N.L.	9-26-57—Renton, Wash.	9- 6
Siwy, James	P	Chicago A.L.	9-20-58—Central Falls, R.I.	8-20
Skube, Robert Jacob	OF	Milwaukee	10- 8-57—Northridge, Calif.	9-17
Slaught, Donald Martin	C	Kansas City	9-11-59—Long Beach, Calif.	7- 6
Smith, James Lorne	SS-2B	Pittsburgh	9- 8-54—Santa Monica, Calif.	4-12
Smithson, Billy Mike	P	Texas	1-21-55—Centerville, Tenn.	8-27
Steirer, Ricky Francis	P	California	8-27-56—Baltimore, Md.	8- 5
Stenhouse, Michael Steven	OF	Montreal	5-29-60—Pueblo, Colo.	10- 3
Stroughter, Stephen Lewis	OF	Seattle	3-15-52—Visalia, Calif.	4- 7
Stuper, John Anton	P	St. Louis	5- 9-57—Butler, Pa.	6- 1
Sullivan, Marc Cooper	C	Boston	7-25-58—Quincy, Mass.	10- 1
Terrell, Charles Walter	P	New York N.L.	5-11-58—Jeffersonville, Ind.	9- 8
Tillman, Kerry Jerome	OF	New York N.L.	8-29-60—Jacksonville, Fla.	6- 6
Tingley, Ronald Irvin	C	San Diego	5-27-59—Presque Isle, Me.	9-25
Tunnell, Byron Lee	P	Pittsburgh	10-30-60—Tyler, Tex.	9- 4
Vande Berg, Edward John	P	Seattle	10-26-58—Redlands, Calif.	4- 7
Van Gorder, David Thomas	C	Cincinnati	3-27-57—Los Angeles, Calif.	6-15
Vargas, Hediberto	1B	Pittsburgh	2-23-59—Guanica, P.R.	9- 8
Viola, Frank John Jr.	P	Minnesota	4-19-60—Hempstead, N.Y.	6- 6
Walker, Duane Allen	OF	Cincinnati	3-13-57—Pasadena, Tex.	5-25
Walker, Gregory Lee	1B	Chicago A.L.	10- 6-59—Douglas, Ga.	9-18
Welchel, Donald Ray	P	Baltimore	2- 3-57—Atlanta, Tex.	9-15
Wellman, Brad Eugene	2B	San Francisco	8-17-59—Lodi, Calif.	9- 4
Wever, Stefan Matthew	P	New York A.L.	4-22-58—Morgurg, Germany	9-17
Wilson, Glenn Dwight	OF	Detroit	12-22-58—Baytown, Tex.	4-15
Wright, George Dewitt	OF	Texas	12-22-58—Oklahoma City, Okla.	4-10
Wright, James Richard	P	Los Angeles	11-22-58—Paris, Tex.	7-28
Young, Michael Darren	OF	Baltimore	3-20-60—Hayward, Calif.	9-14
Zuvella, Paul	SS	Atlanta	10-31-58—San Mateo, Calif.	9- 4

Homers by Parks for 1982
National League

	At Atl.	At Chi.	At Cin.	At Hou.	At L.A.	At Mont.	At N.Y.	At Phil.	At Pitt.	At St.L.	At S.D.	At S.F.	Totals 1982	1981
Atlanta...............	95	5	4	3	6	4	7	2	4	3	7	6	146	64
Chicago.............	4	53	5	0	1	11	8	6	8	2	2	2	102	57
Cincinnati..........	4	4	37	0	1	6	4	4	6	3	9	4	82	64
Houston	4	2	2	31	4	2	5	2	5	3	7	7	74	45
Los Angeles........	17	5	11	4	57	7	5	6	5	4	8	9	138	82
Montreal............	9	12	3	5	1	59	11	7	9	5	5	7	133	81
New York..........	7	6	4	0	6	3	48	1	6	9	4	3	97	57
Philadelphia	4	7	5	1	2	5	4	57	5	8	9	5	112	69
Pittsburgh.........	9	3	4	1	3	8	5	7	77	5	8	4	134	55
St. Louis.............	4	6	1	5	0	6	5	5	4	27	2	2	67	50
San Diego	13	5	4	1	4	4	2	4	5	1	33	5	81	32
San Francisco....	11	7	4	6	7	9	4	2	8	5	15	55	133	63
1982 Totals	181	115	84	57	92	124	108	103	142	75	109	109	1299	...
1981 Totals	78	79	67	25	71	62	68	80	58	48	36	47	...	719

AT ATLANTA (181): Atlanta (95)—Horner 25, Murphy 24, Chambliss 11, Washington 8, Hubbard 7, Ramirez 7, Watson 3, Benedict 2, Linares 2, Pocoroba 2, Whisenton 2, Mahler, Royster. **Chicago** (4)—Davis 2, Moreland, Smith. **Cincinnati** (4)—Bench, Biittner, Concepcion, Driessen. **Houston** (4)—Cruz, Puhl, Pujols, Thon. **Los Angeles** (17)—Baker 5, Garvey 3, Guerrero 3, Cey 2, Landreaux 2, Sax 2. **Montreal** (9)—Dawson 4, Wallach 3, Carter, Speier. **New York** (7)—Kingman 2, Backman, Brooks, Foster, Giles, Valentine. **Philadelphia** (4)—Matthews 2, DeJesus, Maddox. **Pittsburgh** (9)—Thompson 3, Easler 2, Madlock 2, Moreno, Pena. **St. Louis** (4)—Hendrick, Landrum, Oberkfell, L. Smith. **San Diego** (13)—Lezcano 4, Kennedy 2, Richards 2, Jones, Lollar, Salazar, Swisher, Templeton. **San Francisco** (11)—Davis 3, Evans 2, Smith 2, Clark, May, Morgan, O'Malley.

AT CHICAGO (115): Atlanta (5)—Murphy 2, Benedict, Chambliss, Whisenton. **Chicago** (53)—Buckner 9, Durham 9, Moreland 8, Johnstone 7, Davis 6, Sandberg 5, Morales 3, Wills 3, Woods 2, Kennedy. **Cincinnati** (4)—Bench, Milner, Oester, Vail. **Houston** (2)—Garner, Heep. **Los Angeles** (5)—Guerrero 3, Garvey, Orta. **Montreal** (12)—Cromartie 3, Oliver 3, Wallach 2, Carter, Sanderson, Speier, White. **New York** (6)—Foster 2, Giles, Kingman, Stearns, Swan. **Philadelphia** (7)—Schmidt 4, Matthews 2, Rose. **Pittsburgh** (3)—Berra, Stargell, Thompson. **St. Louis** (6)—Porter 2, Gonzalez, Hendrick, L. Smith, O. Smith. **San Diego** (5)—Jones 2, Gwynn, Kennedy, Lezcano. **San Francisco** (7)—Davis 3, Brenly, Gale, Smith, Sularz.

AT CINCINNATI (84): Atlanta (4)—Chambliss, Horner, Murphy, Royster. **Chicago** (5)—Moreland 2, Sandberg, Wills, Woods. **Cincinnati** (37)—Driessen 7, Cedeno 6, Householder 6, Bench 5, Oester 4, Concepcion 3, Walker 3, Milner, Pastore, Redus. **Houston** (2)—Garner, Scott. **Los Angeles** (11)—Cey 2, Garvey 2, Landreaux 2, Baker, Guerrero, Monday, Roenicke, Scioscia. **Montreal** (3)—Cromartie 2, Carter. **New York** (4)—Foster, Hodges, Staub, Youngblood. **Philadelphia** (5)—Maddox 2, Diaz, Robinson, Schmidt. **Pittsburgh** (4)—Berra 2, Stargell, Thompson. **St. Louis** (1)—Tenace. **San Diego** (4)—Lezcano 4. **San Francisco** (4)—Clark 2, Davis, Smith.

AT HOUSTON (57): Atlanta (3)—Chambliss, Ramirez, Washington. **Chicago**—None. **Cincinnati** —None. **Houston** (31)—Garner 6, Ashby 5, Puhl 5, Howe 4, Cruz 3, Knicely 2, Heep, Pujols, Spilman, Thon, Tolman, Walling. **Los Angeles** (4)—Baker 2, Cey, Hooton. **Montreal** (5)—Dawson 2, Carter, Oliver, Wallach. **New York**—None. **Philadelphia** (1)—Maddox. **Pittsburgh** (1)—Parker. **St. Louis** (5) —Hendrick 2, Porter 2, L. Smith. **San Diego** (1)—Lefebvre. **San Francisco** (6)—Clark 3, Bergman, Evans, Smith.

AT LOS ANGELES (92): Atlanta (6)—Washington 2, Chambliss, Harper, Murphy, Whisenton. **Chicago** (1)—Davis. **Cincinnati** (1)—Householder. **Houston** (4)—Knight 2, Pujols 2. **Los Angeles** (57) —Guerrero 15, Cey 10, Baker 7, Monday 7, Garvey 5, Marshall 2, Russell 2, Sax 2, Scioscia 2, Yeager 2, Landreaux, Morales, Orta. **Montreal** (1)—Wallach. **New York** (6)—Kingman 4, Backman, Wilson. **Philadelphia** (2)—Christenson, Schmidt. **Pittsburgh** (3)—Lacy, Madlock, Thompson. **St. Louis**— None. **San Diego** (4)—Edwards, Kennedy, Lefebvre, Perkins. **San Francisco** (7)—Evans 2, Clark, Davis, Leonard, Morgan, Smith.

AT MONTREAL (124): Atlanta (4)—Chambliss, Horner, Murphy, Washington. **Chicago** (11)—Buckner 2, Durham 2, Moreland 2, Johnstone, Morales, Sandberg, Tabler, Wills. **Cincinnati** (6)—Milner 2, Oester 2, Driessen, Vail. **Houston** (2)—Ashby, Heep. **Los Angeles** (7)—Baker 3, Garvey 2, Guerrero, Marshall. **Montreal** (59)—Carter 16, Oliver 12, Wallach 11, Dawson 9, Cromartie 4, Norman 2, Speier 2, Mills, Raines, White. **New York** (3)—Gardenhire, Kingman, Wilson. **Philadelphia** (5)—Schmidt 2, Diaz, Maddox, Robinson. **Pittsburgh** (8)—Morrison 2, Pena 2, Thompson 2, Parker, D. Robinson. **St. Louis** (6)—Hendrick 2, Hernandez 2, McGee, Porter. **San Diego** (4)—Bass, Jones, Kennedy, Templeton. **San Francisco** (9)—Clark 2, May 2, Morgan 2, Evans, Smith, Summers.

AT NEW YORK (108): Atlanta (7)—Washington 3, Murphy, Ramirez, Sinatro, Watson. **Chicago** (8)—Buckner 3, Durham 3, Henderson 2. **Cincinnati** (4)—Bench 2, Driessen 2. **Houston** (5)—Ashby, Heep, Knight, Puhl, Thon. **Los Angeles** (5)—Cey 2, Baker, Guerrero, Marshall. **Montreal** (11)—Carter 4, Cromartie 3, Oliver 2, Dawson, Speier. **New York** (48)—Kingman 19, Foster 7, Valentine 4, Hodges 3, Jorgensen 2, Rajsich 2, Staub 2, Wilson 2, Youngblood 2, Backman, Bochy, Brooks, Gardenhire, Howard. **Philadelphia** (4)—Aguayo, Schmidt, Virgil, Vukovich. **Pittsburgh** (5)—Madlock 2, Davis, Lacy, Pena. **St. Louis** (5)—Porter 3, Green, Hendrick. **San Diego** (2)—Lollar, Richards. **San Francisco** (4)—Davis, LeMaster, O'Malley, Smith.

AT PHILADELPHIA (103): Atlanta (2)—Murphy, Watson. **Chicago** (6)—Durham 2, Buckner, Johnstone, Molinaro, Woods. **Cincinnati** (4)—Driessen 2, Krenchicki, Landestoy. **Houston** (2)—Howe, Knight. **Los Angeles** (6)—Guerrero 4, Baker, Monday. **Montreal** (7)—Wallach 4, Carter, Dawson, Oliver. **New York** (1)—Gardenhire. **Philadelphia** (57)—Schmidt 17, Diaz 11, Matthews 10, Dernier 3, Maddox 3, Vukovich 3, Aguayo 2, Rose 2, Sanchez 2, Carlton, Davis, DeJesus, Virgil. **Pittsburgh** (7)—

Easler 3, Berra, Harper, Lacy, Madlock. **St. Louis (5)**—Hendrick 2, Hernandez, Porter, O. Smith. **San Diego (4)**—Jones, Kennedy, Salazar, Templeton. **San Francisco (2)**—Clark, Summers.

AT PITTSBURGH (142): Atlanta (4)—Horner, Hubbard, Murphy, Washington. **Chicago (8)**—Durham 3, Davis 2, Johnstone, Moreland, Wills. **Cincinnati (6)**—Biittner, Cedeno, Driessen, Krenchicki, Vail, Walker. **Houston (5)**—Cruz 2, Garner 2, Puhl. **Los Angeles (5)**—Cey 2, Garvey, Monday, Scioscia. **Montreal (9)**—Carter 2, Dawson 2, Raines 2, Wallach 2, Cromartie. **New York (6)**—Kingman 4, Hodges, Valentine. **Philadelphia (5)**—Schmidt 3, Matthews 2. **Pittsburgh (77)**—Thompson 17, Madlock 13, Easler 9, Ray 6, Pena 5, Berra 4, Parker 4, B. Robinson 3, Frobel 2, Hebner 2, Lacy 2, Morrison 2, Rhoden 2, Davis, Milner, Moreno, Nicoscia, D. Robinson, Stargell. **St. Louis (4)**—L. Smith 2, Green, Tenace. **San Diego (5)**—Kennedy 3, Lezcano 2. **San Francisco (8)**—Clark 5, Davis, Leonard, May.

AT ST. LOUIS (75): Atlanta (3)—Horner 2, Hubbard. **Chicago (2)**—Durham 2. **Cincinnati (3)**—Bench, Driessen, Householder. **Houston (3)**—Cruz 2, Knight. **Los Angeles (4)**—Garvey, Guerrero, Russell, Valenzuela. **Montreal (5)**—Dawson 2, Wallach 2, Cromartie. **New York (9)**—Kingman 4, Bochy, Foster, Giles, Stearns, Valentine. **Philadelphia (8)**—Diaz 2, DeJesus, Matthews, Robinson, Schmidt, Virgil, Vukovich. **Pittsburgh (5)**—Milner, Ray, Rhoden, B. Robinson, Thompson. **St. Louis (27)**—Hendrick 10, Hernandez 4, Porter 3, L. Smith 3, Tenace 3, McGee 2, Oberkfell, Ramsey. **San Diego (1)**—Jones. **San Francisco (5)**—Brenly 2, Leonard 2, Morgan.

AT SAN DIEGO (109): Atlanta (7)—Chambliss 3, Harper, Horner, Murphy, Niekro. **Chicago (2)**—Davis, Moreland. **Cincinnati (9)**—Bench 3, Cedeno, Concepcion, Driessen, Oester, Vail, Walker. **Houston (7)**—Ashby 5, Garner, Knight. **Los Angeles (8)**—Baker 3, Cey, Garvey, Guerrero, Landreaux, Marshall. **Montreal (5)**—Carter 2, Oliver, Speier, Wallach. **New York (4)**—Kingman, Stearns, Valentine, Wilson. **Philadelphia (9)**—Diaz 3, Schmidt 3, Davis, Dernier, Matthews. **Pittsburgh (8)**—Thompson 3, Berra 2, Easler, Harper, Pena. **St. Louis (2)**—Tenace 2. **San Diego (33)**—Kennedy 10, Jones 6, Salazar 6, Lezcano 5, Lefebvre 2, Templeton 2, Lollar, Wiggins. **San Francisco (15)**—Clark 3, Davis 3, Morgan 3, Evans 2, Bergman, Leonard, May, Wohlford.

AT SAN FRANCISCO (109): Atlanta (6)—Murphy 3, Chambliss, Horner, Ramirez. **Chicago (2)**—Durham, Kennedy. **Cincinnati (4)**—Driessen, Householder, Oester, Trevino. **Houston (7)**—Garner 2, Spilman 2, Cruz, Garcia, Reynolds. **Los Angeles (9)**—Cey 4, Guerrero 2, Landreaux, Monday, Scioscia. **Montreal (7)**—Dawson 2, Oliver 2, Raines, Speier, Wallach. **New York (3)**—Foster, Kingman, Stearns. **Philadelphia (5)**—Schmidt 2, Carlton, Matthews, Vukovich. **Pittsburgh (4)**—Thompson 2, Moreno, Pena. **St. Louis (2)**—Landrum, McGee. **San Diego (5)**—Kennedy 2, Perkins, Swisher, Templeton. **San Francisco (55)**—Smith 10, Clark 9, Evans 8, Davis 6, Morgan 6, Leonard 4, May 4, Bergman 2, Summers 2, Brenly, LeMaster, Venable, Wohlford.

American League

	At Balt.	At Bos.	At Cal.	At Chi.	At Clev.	At Det.	At K.C.	At Mil.	At Min.	At N.Y.	At Oak.	At Sea.	At Tex.	At Tor.	Totals 1982	1981
Baltimore	87	4	10	3	4	9	5	13	12	5	4	8	9	6	179	88
Boston	8	67	5	4	7	10	2	3	7	3	4	8	4	4	136	90
California	7	8	99	4	10	9	5	8	3	3	8	8	9	5	186	97
Chicago	2	6	5	51	2	11	7	7	7	7	8	9	4	10	136	76
Cleveland	6	4	3	0	49	1	3	9	7	1	8	9	4	5	109	39
Detroit	10	5	5	3	4	108	3	3	11	6	7	5	4	3	177	65
Kansas City	10	10	6	3	4	3	61	5	10	6	4	6	1	3	132	61
Milwaukee	10	16	11	5	6	13	11	89	12	10	12	6	5	10	216	96
Minnesota	3	3	6	5	3	9	5	2	81	3	4	12	9	3	148	47
New York	10	10	1	2	6	7	7	4	11	73	8	9	7	6	161	100
Oakland	7	4	4	5	6	11	8	4	10	2	71	9	3	5	149	104
Seattle	5	6	3	2	5	5	2	2	6	2	5	78	4	5	130	89
Texas	7	2	7	4	6	5	3	4	6	6	9	8	43	5	115	49
Toronto	2	4	3	3	1	7	3	0	8	1	2	7	3	62	106	61
1982 Totals	174	149	168	94	113	208	125	153	191	128	154	182	109	132	2080	...
1981 Totals	96	99	87	64	52	87	44	62	72	71	103	105	45	75	...	1062

AT BALTIMORE (174): Baltimore (87)—Murray 18, Ripken 11, Lowenstein 10, Singleton 9, Roenicke 6, Ford 5, Bumbry 4, Dauer 4, Dwyer 4, Ayala 3, Nolan 3, Sakata 3, Crowley 2, Dempsey 2, Gulliver, Rayford, Shelby. **Boston (8)**—Evans 2, Rice 2, Stapleton 2, Lansford, Yastrzemski. **California (7)**—Baylor 2, Re. Jackson 2, Boone, Ferguson, Lynn. **Chicago (2)**—Hairston, Kemp. **Cleveland (6)**—Hayes 3, Manning, Nahorodny, Thornton. **Detroit (10)**—Herndon 3, Ivie 2, Gibson, Johnson, Lemon, Parrish, Whitaker. **Kansas City (10)**—Brett 4, Washington 3, Martin, McRae, White. **Milwaukee (10)**—Yount 4, Oglivie 2, Simmons 2, Cooper, Thomas. **Minnesota (3)**—Brunansky, Gaetti, Ward. **New York (10)**—Smalley 4, Winfield 3, Mazzilli, Randolph, Robertson. **Oakland (7)**—Armas 2, Lopes 2, Johnson, Meyer, Murphy. **Seattle (5)**—Henderson 2, Zisk 2, Stroughter. **Texas (7)**—Parrish 2, Bass, Hostetler, L. Johnson, Roberts, Sample. **Toronto (2)**—Johnson, Revering.

AT BOSTON (149): Baltimore (4)—Lowenstein, Ripken, Roenicke, Sakata. **Boston (67)**—Evans 19, Rice 9, Stapleton 7, Yastrzemski 7, Hoffman 6, Perez 5, Boggs 4, Lansford 4, Allenson 3, Gedman, Miller, Nichols. **California (8)**—Downing 2, Grich 2, Baylor, Carew, DeCinces, Foli. **Chicago (6)**—Fisk 2, Bernazard, Kemp, Paciorek, Rodriguez. **Cleveland (4)**—Thornton 2, Harrah, Hassey. **Detroit (5)**—Lemon 2, Gibson, Whitaker, Wockenfuss. **Kansas City (10)**—McRae 4, Brett 2, Martin 2, Washington, White. **Milwaukee (16)**—Thomas 4, Cooper 3, Oglivie 2, Howell, Molitor, Money, Moore, Simmons, Yost, Yount. **Minnesota (3)**—Gaetti 3. **New York (10)**—Cerone 2, Winfield 2, Balboni, Griffey, Mayberry, Mumphrey, Murcer, Piniella. **Oakland (4)**—Armas, Johnson, McKay, Page. **Seattle (6)**—Cowens 2, Bochte, Brown, T. Cruz, Gray. **Texas (2)**—Sundberg 2. **Toronto (4)**—Bonnell, Griffin, Moseby, Whitt.

AT CALIFORNIA (168): Baltimore (10)—Roenicke 3, Ripken 2, Dempsey, Ford, Murray, Rayford, Singleton. **Boston (5)**—Gedman 2, Allenson, Lansford, Rice. **California (99)**—Re. Jackson 21, DeCinces 17, Downing 15, Baylor 13, Lynn 13, Grich 8, Boone 5, Beniquez, Carew, Clark, Ferguson, Foli,

Ro. Jackson, Pettis. **Chicago** (5)—Bernazard 2, Kemp, Luzinski, Paciorek. **Cleveland** (3)—Hayes 2, Nahorodny. **Detroit** (5)—Gibson, Herndon, Leach, Wilson, Wockenfuss. **Kansas City** (6)—McRae 2, Aikens, May, Otis, Washington. **Milwaukee** (11)—Cooper 3, Simmons 2, Howell, Molitor, Money, Oglivie, Thomas, Yount. **Minnesota** (6)—Ward 2, Eisenreich, Hrbek, Laudner, Washington. **New York** (1)—Winfield. **Oakland** (4)—Gross, Henderson, Lopes, Murphy. **Seattle** (3)—T. Cruz, Simpson, Zisk. **Texas** (7)—Hostetler 2, O'Brien 2, Bell, Parrish, Sundberg. **Toronto** (3)—Barfield, Garcia, Revering.

AT CHICAGO (94): Baltimore (3)—Roenicke 2, Dwyer. **Boston** (4)—Allenson, Evans, Hoffman, Yastrzemski. **California** (4)—Beniquez, Downing, Re. Jackson, Lynn. **Chicago** (51)—Luzinski 13, Baines 11, Fisk 7, Kemp 4, LeFlore 3, Morrison 3, Almon 2, Hairston 2, V. Law 2, Bernazard, Hill, Squires, Walker. **Cleveland**—None. **Detroit** (3)—Herndon, Ivie, Parrish. **Kansas City** (3)—Aikens, Brett, Geronimo. **Milwaukee** (5)—Thomas 2, Yount 2, Howell. **Minnesota** (5)—Laudner 2, Brunansky, Gaetti, Johnson. **New York** (2)—Cerone, Mazzilli. **Oakland** (5)—Armas 3, Burroughs, Sexton. **Seattle** (2)—Brown, T. Cruz. **Texas** (4)—L. Johnson, Parrish, Sundberg, Wright. **Toronto** (3)—Barfield 2, Upshaw.

AT CLEVELAND (113): Baltimore (4)—Murray 2, Ripken 2. **Boston** (7)—Evans 2, Rice 2, Yastrzemski 2, Stapleton. **California** (10)—DeCinces 2, Downing 2, Grich 2, Lynn 2, Baylor, Re. Jackson. **Chicago** (2)—Bernazard 2. **Cleveland** (49)—Harrah 17, Thornton 16, Hayes 3, Bannister 2, Castillo 2, Dilone 2, Hassey 2, Bando, Manning, Milbourne, Nahorodny, Rhomberg. **Detroit** (4)—Herndon, Parrish, Trammell, Wockenfuss. **Kansas City** (4)—McRae 2, Brett, May. **Milwaukee** (5)—Cooper, Molitor, Money, Simmons, Thomas, Yount. **Minnesota** (3)—Hrbek 2, Ward. **New York** (6)—Winfield 4, Mumphrey, Nettles. **Oakland** (6)—Newman 2, Burroughs, Gross, Murphy, Rudi. **Seattle** (5)—Brown, Cowens, T. Cruz, Henderson, Zisk. **Texas** (6)—Bell 2, Wright 2, Parrish, Sundberg. **Toronto** (1)—Mulliniks.

AT DETROIT (208): Baltimore (9)—Ripken 4, Ford, Murray, Nolan, Rayford, Singleton. **Boston** (10)—Evans 2, Nichols 2, Rice 2, Allenson, Lansford, Miller, Yastrzemski. **California** (9)—Downing 2, Grich 2, Re. Jackson 2, Boone, DeCinces, Foli. **Chicago** (11)—Paciorek 3, Luzinski 2, Morrison 2, Baines, Hill, R. Law, V. Law. **Cleveland** (1)—Harrah. **Detroit** (108)—Parrish 22, Lemon 12, Ivie 10, Herndon 9, Whitaker 9, Wilson 9, Turner 7, Hebner 6, Trammell 5, Brookens 4, Gibson 4, Laga 3, Wockenfuss 3, Cabell 2, Leach 2, Johnson. **Kansas City** (3)—Martin 2, Pryor. **Milwaukee** (13)—Oglivie 4, Molitor 2, Thomas 2, Yount 2, Cooper, Money, Simmons. **Minnesota** (9)—Brunansky 2, Engle 2, Hrbek 2, Johnson 2, Castino. **New York** (7)—Gamble 2, Smalley 2, Murcer, Nettles, Winfield. **Oakland** (11)—Goodwin 2, Gross 2, Henderson 2, Murphy 2, Armas, Burroughs, McKay. **Seattle** (5)—T. Cruz 2, Cowens, Gray, Revering. **Texas** (5)—Bell, Hostetler, Mazzilli, Putnam, Wright. **Toronto** (7)—Upshaw 2, Adams, Johnson, Mulliniks, Powell, Whitt.

AT KANSAS CITY (125): Baltimore (5)—Roenicke 2, Murray, Ripken, Sakata. **Boston** (2)—Stapleton, Yastrzemski. **California** (5)—Baylor 2, Re. Jackson 2, Clark. **Chicago** (7)—Baines 3, Kemp 3, Morrison. **Cleveland** (3)—Harrah, Nahorodny, Thornton. **Detroit** (3)—Lemon 2, Herndon. **Kansas City** (61)—McRae 12, Aikens 11, Brett 9, White 7, Martin 6, Otis 5, Geronimo 3, Washington 2, Wathan 2, Wilson 2, May, Quirk. **Milwaukee** (11)—Molitor 3, Yount 2, Brouhard, Cooper, Edwards, Money, Oglivie, Thomas. **Minnesota** (5)—Ward 2, Brunansky, Hatcher, Vega. **New York** (7)—Winfield 3, Smalley 2, Griffey, Piniella. **Oakland** (8)—Murphy 3, Armas, Burroughs, McKay, Rudi, Stanley. **Seattle** (2)—T. Cruz, Henderson. **Texas** (3)—Bell 2, Wright. **Toronto** (3)—Barfield, Martinez, Upshaw.

AT MILWAUKEE (153): Baltimore (13)—Dauer 2, Murray 2, Ripken 2, Ayala, Dempsey, Lowenstein, Nolan, Roenicke, Sakata, Singleton. **Boston** (3)—Stapleton 2, Evans. **California** (8)—Downing 2, Grich 2, Re. Jackson 2, Baylor, DeCinces. **Chicago** (7)—Baines, Fisk, Kemp, R. Law, LeFlore, Paciorek, Rodriguez. **Cleveland** (9)—Hargrove 2, Harrah 2, Hayes 2, Thornton 2, Manning. **Detroit** (3)—Brookens 2, Herndon. **Kansas City** (5)—Slaught 2, Martin, McRae, Pryor. **Milwaukee** (89)—Thomas 19, Oglivie 16, Cooper 12, Molitor 9, Yount 9, Simmons 7, Money 6, Moore 3, Brouhard 2, Gantner 2, Hisle 2, Edwards, Romero. **Minnesota** (2)—Gaetti, Laudner. **New York** (4)—Smalley 2, Piniella, Winfield. **Oakland** (4)—Murphy 2, Gross, Page. **Seattle** (2)—Cowens, Maler. **Texas** (4)—Wright 2, Hostetler, L. Johnson. **Toronto**—None.

AT MINNESOTA (191): Baltimore (12)—Lowenstein 3, Murray 3, Roenicke 2, Ayala, Crowley, Dauer, Ripken. **Boston** (7)—Rice 4, Boggs, Gedman, Lansford. **California** (3)—Baylor 2, DeCinces. **Chicago** (7)—Baines, Bernazard, Fisk, Kemp, Kittle, Paciorek, Walker. **Cleveland** (7)—Hayes 2, Thornton 2, Bannister, Hassey, Manning. **Detroit** (11)—Parrish 4, Brookens 2, Hebner, Herndon, Johnson, Trammell, Whitaker. **Kansas City** (10)—Otis 3, Aikens 2, White 2, Martin, McRae, Washington. **Milwaukee** (12)—Money 3, Oglivie 2, Simmons 2, Thomas 2, Yount 2, Moore. **Minnesota** (81)—Ward 16, Gaetti 15, Hrbek 11, Brunansky 10, Johnson 7, Washington 4, Vega 3, Bush 2, Castino 2, Engle 2, Faedo 2, Hatcher 2, Laudner 2, Eisenreich, Mitchell, Wynegar. **New York** (11)—Nettles 3, Gamble 2, Griffey, Mayberry, Mumphrey, Piniella, Smalley, Winfield. **Oakland** (10)—Armas 3, Meyer 2, Gross, Henderson, Lopes, Rudi, Spencer. **Seattle** (5)—Maler 2, Cowens, T. Cruz, Essian, Zisk. **Texas** (6)—Bell 2, Bogener, Hostetler, L. Johnson, Parrish. **Toronto** (8)—Moseby 3, Martinez 2, Upshaw 2, Barfield.

AT NEW YORK (128): Baltimore (5)—Ayala, Lowenstein, Murray, Nolan, Ripken. **Boston** (3)—Evans 2, Rice. **California** (3)—Re. Jackson 2, Grich. **Chicago** (7)—Baines, Bernazard, Hairston, Kemp, R. Law, Morrison, Rodriguez. **Cleveland** (1)—Bannister. **Detroit** (6)—Gibson, Herndon, Lemon, Parrish, Turner, Wockenfuss. **Kansas City** (6)—McRae 2, Aikens, Brett, Slaught, Washington. **Milwaukee** (10)—Cooper 3, Oglivie 2, Brouhard, Moore, Thomas. **Minnesota** (3)—Brunansky, Castino, Ward. **New York** (73)—Winfield 14, Gamble 11, Nettles 10, Griffey 8, Smalley 8, Mumphrey 6, Mazzilli 3, Murcer 3, Collins 2, Mayberry 2, Cerone, Patterson, Piniella, Ramos, Randolph, Wynegar. **Oakland** (2)—Burroughs 2. **Seattle** (2)—Bochte, Zisk. **Texas** (6)—Hostetler, Grubb, Parrish, Rivers. **Toronto** (1)—Moseby.

AT OAKLAND (154): Baltimore (4)—Lowenstein, Murray, Ripken, Roenicke. **Boston** (4)—Miller 2, Evans, Lansford. **California** (8)—Downing 3, DeCinces 2, Re. Jackson, Lynn, Wilfong. **Chicago** (8)—Kemp 3, Baines 2, Fisk 2, Luzinski. **Cleveland** (8)—Thornton 4, Hargrove, Harrah, Hassey, Manning. **Detroit** (7)—Herndon 2, Whitaker 2, Brookens, Parrish, Wilson. **Kansas City** (4)—Martin 2, McRae, Washington. **Milwaukee** (12)—Yount 3, Cooper 2, Oglivie 2, Simmons 2, Thomas 2, Gantner. **Minnesota** (4)—Brunansky, Gaetti, Hrbek, Ward. **New York** (8)—Gamble 2, Winfield 2, Balboni, Mayberry, Robertson, Wynegar. **Oakland** (71)—Murphy 15, Armas 14, Burroughs 6, Henderson 5, Lopes 5, Johnson 4, Gross 3, Heath 3, Meyer 3, Newman 3, Moore 2, Page 2, Rudi 2, Davis, McKay, Sexton, Stanley.

Seattle (5)—Bochte 2, Zisk 2, Cowens. **Texas** (9)—Parrish 3, Bell, Capra, L. Johnson, Richardt, Sample, Sundberg. **Toronto** (2)—Barfield, Revering.

AT SEATTLE (182): **Baltimore** (8)—Lowenstein 3, Ford 2, Bumbry, Dauer, Singleton. **Boston** (8)—Nichols 4, Evans, Lansford, Stapleton, Yastrzemski. **California** (8)—DeCinces 3, Downing, Grich, Re. Jackson, Ro. Jackson, Lynn. **Chicago** (9)—Kemp 2, V. Law 2, Bernazard, Fisk, Hairston, Hill, Paciorek. **Cleveland** (9)—Charboneau 2, Harrah 2, Bando, Hargrove, Hayes, Milbourne, Thornton. **Detroit** (5)—Herndon 2, Hebner, Johnson, Wilson. **Kansas City** (6)—Brett 3, Otis 2, Aikens. **Milwaukee** (6)—Cooper 3, Yount 2, Simmons. **Minnesota** (12)—Castino 2, Gaetti 2, Hrbek 2, Ward 2, Brunansky, Faedo, Mitchell, Vega. **New York** (9)—Mayberry 3, Winfield 2, Gamble, Griffey, Murcer, Wynegar. **Oakland** (9)—Burroughs 2, Lopes 2, Meyer 2, Armas, Murphy, Spencer. Cruz 8, T. Cruz 8, Henderson 8, Zisk 8, Bochte 7, Gray 5, Castillo 3, Serna 3, Sweet 3, Edler 2, Essian 2, Revering 2, Brown, Bulling, Maler, Mercado, Moses, Simpson. **Texas** (8)—Hostetler 2, Dent, B. Johnson, Parrish, Sample, Sundberg, Wright. **Toronto** (7)—Upshaw 3, Barfield, Garcia, Martinez, Whitt.

AT TEXAS (109): **Baltimore** (9)—Murray 2, Ripken 2, Roenicke 2, Ford, Lowenstein, Singleton. **Boston** (4)—Rice 2, Evans, Perez. **California** (9)—DeCinces 2, Lynn 2, Baylor, Beniquez, Carew, Ferguson, Re. Jackson. **Chicago** (4)—Baines 3, Paciorek. **Cleveland** (4)—Thornton 2, Hayes, Manning. **Detroit** (4)—Ivie, Lemon, Trammell, Wockenfuss. **Kansas City** (1)—Wathan. **Milwaukee** (5)—Thomas 2, Gantner, Howell, Money. **Minnesota** (9)—Hrbek 3, Brunansky 2, Bush 2, Gaetti, Ward. **New York** (7)—Nettles 2, Cerone, Collins, Piniella, Randolph, Winfield. **Oakland** (3)—Burroughs, Johnson, Murphy. **Seattle** (4)—Zisk 2, Bochte, Henderson. **Texas** (43)—Hostetler 10, Sample 7, Parrish 6, Bell 3, Sundberg 3, Wright 3, Grubb 2, L. Johnson 2, Mazzilli 2, O'Brien 2, B. Johnson, Putnam, Stein. **Toronto** (3)—Bonnell, Upshaw, Velez.

AT TORONTO (132): **Baltimore** (6)—Lowenstein 3, Dempsey, Dwyer, Roenicke. **Boston** (4)—Yastrzemski 2, Lansford, Rice. **California** (5)—Re. Jackson 3, Baylor, Grich. **Chicago** (10)—Almon 2, Baines 2, Bernazard 2, Paciorek 2, Kemp, Luzinski. **Cleveland** (5)—Manning 2, Bando, Dilone, Thornton. **Detroit** (5)—Parrish, Trammell, Whitaker. **Kansas City** (3)—Hammond, McRae, Wilson. **Milwaukee** (10)—Cooper 2, Molitor 2, Oglivie 2, Simmons 2, Money, Thomas. **Minnesota** (3)—Hrbek, Laudner, Ward. **New York** (6)—Winfield 2, Mazzilli, Murcer, Nettles, Smalley. **Oakland** (5)—Armas 2, Burroughs, Henderson, Newman. **Seattle** (5)—Zisk 3, Henderson, Sweet. **Texas** (5)—Richardt 2, Bell, Hostetler, Mazzilli. **Toronto** (62)—Barfield 11, Upshaw 11, Whitt 8, Martinez 6, Bonnell 4, Moseby 4, Garcia 3, Woods 3, Mayberry 2, Mulliniks 2, Powell 2, Revering 2, Iorg, Johnson, Nordhagen, Roberts.

The Sporting News AWARDS

THE SPORTING NEWS MVP AWARDS

AMERICAN LEAGUE   NATIONAL LEAGUE

Year	Player	Club	Points	Player	Club	Points
1929	Al Simmons, Philadelphia, of		40	No selection		
1930	Joseph Cronin, Washington, ss		52	William Terry, New York, 1b		47
1931	H. Louis Gehrig, New York, 1b		40	Charles Klein, Philadelphia, of		40
1932	James Foxx, Philadelphia, 1b		46	Charles Klein, Philadelphia, of		46
1933	James Foxx, Philadelphia, 1b		49	Carl Hubbell, New York, p		64
1934	H. Louis Gehrig, New York, 1b		51	Jerome Dean, St. Louis, p		57
1935	Henry Greenberg, Detroit, 1b		64	J. Floyd Vaughan, Pitts., ss		42
1936	H. Louis Gehrig, New York, 1b		55	Carl Hubbell, New York, p		61
1937	Charles Gehringer, Detroit, 2b		78	Joseph Medwick, St. Louis, of		70
1938	James Foxx, Boston, 1b		05	Ernest Lombardi, Cincinnati, c		229
1939	Joseph DiMaggio, N. York, of		280	William Walters, Cincinnati, p		303
1940	Henry Greenberg, Detroit, of		292	Frank McCormick, Cinn., 1b		274
1941	Joseph DiMaggio, N. York, of		291	Adolph Camilli, Brooklyn, 1b		300
1942	Joseph Gordon, New York, 2b		270	Morton Cooper, St. Louis, p		263
1943	Spurgeon Chandler, N. Y., p		246	Stanley Musial, St. Louis, of		267
1944	Robert Doerr, Boston, 2b			Martin Marion, St. Louis, ss		
1945	Edward J. Mayo, Detroit, 2b			Thomas Holmes, Boston, of		

THE SPORTING NEWS PLAYER, PITCHER OF YEAR

AMERICAN LEAGUE   NATIONAL LEAGUE

1948—Louis Boudreau, Cleveland, ss
    Robert Lemon, Cleveland, p
1949—Theodore Williams, Boston, of
    Ellis Kinder, Boston, p
1950—Philip Rizzuto, New York, ss
    Robert Lemon, Cleveland, p
1951—Ferris Fain, Philadelphia, 1b
    Robert Feller, Cleveland, p
1952—Luscious Easter, Cleveland, 1b
    Robert Shantz, Philadelphia, p
1953—Albert Rosen, Cleveland, 3b
    Erv (Bob) Porterfield, Wash., p
1954—Roberto Avila, Cleveland, 2b
    Robert Lemon, Cleveland, p
1955—Albert Kaline, Detroit, of
    Edward Ford, New York, p
1956—Mickey Mantle, New York, of
    W. William Pierce, Chicago, p
1957—Theodore Williams, Boston, of
    W. William Pierce, Chicago, p
1958—Jack Jensen, Boston, of
    Robert Turley, New York, p
1959—J. Nelson Fox, Chicago, 2b
    Early Wynn, Chicago, p
1960—Roger Maris, New York, of
    Charles Estrada, Baltimore, p
1961—Roger Maris, New York, of
    Edward Ford, New York, p
1962—Mickey Mantle, New York, of
    Richard Donovan, Cleveland, p
1963—Albert Kaline, Detroit, of
    Edward Ford, New York, p
1964—Brooks Robinson, Baltimore, 3b
    Dean Chance, Los Angeles, p
1965—Pedro (Tony) Oliva, Minn., of
    James Grant, Minnesota, p
1966—Frank Robinson, Baltimore, of
    James Kaat, Minnesota, p
1967—Carl Yastrzemski, Boston, of
    Jim Lonborg, Boston, p
1968—Ken Harrelson, Boston, of
    Denny McLain, Detroit, p
1969—Harmon Killebrew, Minn., 1b-3b
    Denny McLain, Detroit, p
1970—Harmon Killebrew, Minn., 3b
    Sam McDowell, Cleveland, p
1971—Pedro (Tony) Oliva, Minn., of
    Vida Blue, Oakland, p
1972—Richie Allen, Chicago, 1b
    Wilbur Wood, Chicago, p

1948—Stanley Musial, St. Louis, of-1b
    John Sain, Boston, p
1949—Enos Slaughter, St. Louis, of
    Howard Pollet, St. Louis, p
1950—Ralph Kiner, Pittsburgh, of
    C. James Konstanty, Phila., p
1951—Stanley Musial, St. Louis, of
    Elwin Roe, Brooklyn, p
1952—Henry Sauer, Chicago, of
    Robin Roberts, Philadelphia, p
1953—Roy Campanella, Brooklyn, c
    Warren Spahn, Milwaukee, p
1954—Willie Mays, New York, of
    John Antonelli, New York, p
1955—Edwin Snider, Brooklyn, of
    Robin Roberts, Philadelphia, p
1956—Henry Aaron, Milwaukee, of
    Donald Newcombe, Brooklyn, p
1957—Stanley Musial, St. Louis, 1b
    Warren Spahn, Milwaukee, p
1958—Ernest Banks, Chicago, ss
    Warren Spahn, Milwaukee, p
1959—Ernest Banks, Chicago, ss
    Samuel Jones, San Francisco, p
1960—Richard Groat, Pittsburgh, ss
    Vernon Law, Pittsburgh, p
1961—Frank Robinson, Cincinnati, of
    Warren Spahn, Milwaukee, p
1962—Maurice Wills, Los Angeles, ss
    Donald Drysdale, Los Angeles, p
1963—Henry Aaron, Milwaukee, of
    Sanford Koufax, Los Angeles, p
1964—Kenton Boyer, St. Louis, 3b
    Sanford Koufax, Los Angeles, p
1965—Willie Mays, San Francisco, of
    Sanford Koufax, Los Angeles, p
1966—Roberto Clemente, Pittsburgh, of
    Sanford Koufax, Los Angeles, p
1967—Orlando Cepeda, St. Louis, 1b
    Mike McCormick, San Fran., p
1968—Pete Rose, Cincinnati, of
    Bob Gibson, St. Louis, p
1969—Willie McCovey, San Fran., 1b
    Tom Seaver, New York, p
1970—Johnny Bench, Cin., c
    Bob Gibson, St. Louis, p
1971—Joe Torre, St. Louis, 3b
    Ferguson Jenkins, Chicago, p
1972—Billy Williams, Chicago, of
    Steve Carlton, Philadelphia, p

PLAYER, PITCHER OF YEAR—Continued

AMERICAN LEAGUE	NATIONAL LEAGUE
1973—Reggie Jackson, Oakland, of Jim Palmer, Baltimore, p	1973—Bobby Bonds, San Francisco, of Ron Bryant, San Francisco, p
1974—Jeff Burroughs, Texas, of Jim Hunter, Oakland, p	1974—Lou Brock, St. Louis, of Mike Marshall, Los Angeles, p
1975—Fred Lynn, Boston, of Jim Palmer, Baltimore, p	1975—Joe Morgan, Cincinnati, 2b Tom Seaver, New York, p
1976—Thurman Munson, New York, c Jim Palmer, Baltimore, p	1976—George Foster, Cincinnati, of Randy Jones, San Diego, p
1977—Rod Carew, Minnesota, 1b Nolan Ryan, California, p	1977—George Foster, Cincinnati, of Steve Carlton, Philadelphia, p
1978—Jim Rice, Boston, of Ron Guidry, New York, p	1978—Dave Parker, Pittsburgh, of Vida Blue, San Francisco, p
1979—Don Baylor, California, of Mike Flanagan, Baltimore, p	1979—Keith Hernandez, St. Louis, 1b Joe Niekro, Houston, p
1980—George Brett, Kansas City, 3b Steve Stone, Baltimore, p	1980—Mike Schmidt, Philadelphia, 3b Steve Carlton, Philadelphia, p
1981—Tony Armas, Oakland, of Jack Morris, Detroit, p	1981—Andre Dawson, Montreal, of Fernando Valenzuela, Los Angeles, p
1982—Robin Yount, Milwaukee, ss Dave Stieb, Toronto, p	1982—Dale Murphy, Atlanta, of Steve Carlton, Philadelphia, p

FIREMAN (Relief Pitcher) OF THE YEAR

Year	Player	Club	Player	Club
1960	Mike Fornieles, Boston		Lindy McDaniel, St. Louis	
1961	Luis Arroyo, New York		Stu Miller, San Francisco	
1962	Dick Radatz, Boston		Roy Face, Pittsburgh	
1963	Stu Miller, Baltimore		Lindy McDaniel, Chicago	
1964	Dick Radatz, Boston		Al McBean, Pittsburgh	
1965	Eddie Fisher, Chicago		Ted Abernathy, Chicago	
1966	Jack Aker, Kansas City		Phil Regan, Los Angeles	
1967	Minnie Rojas, California		Ted Abernathy, Cincinnati	
1968	Wilbur Wood, Chicago		Phil Regan, L.A.-Chicago	
1969	Ron Perranoski, Minnesota		Wayne Granger, Cincinnati	
1970	Ron Perranoski, Minnesota		Wayne Granger, Cincinnati	
1971	Ken Sanders, Milwaukee		Dave Giusti, Pittsburgh	
1972	Sparky Lyle, New York		Clay Carroll, Cincinnati	
1973	John Hiller, Detroit		Mike Marshall, Montreal	
1974	Terry Forster, Chicago		Mike Marshall, Los Angeles	
1975	Rich Gossage, Chicago		Al Hrabosky, St. Louis	
1976	Bill Campbell, Minnesota		Rawly Eastwick, Cincinnati	
1977	Bill Campbell, Boston		Rollie Fingers, San Diego	
1978	Rich Gossage, New York		Rollie Fingers, San Diego	
1979	Mike Marshall, Minnesota Jim Kern, Texas		Bruce Sutter, Chicago	
1980	Dan Quisenberry, Kansas City		Rollie Fingers, San Diego Tom Hume, Cincinnati	
1981	Rollie Fingers, Milwaukee		Bruce Sutter, St. Louis	
1982	Dan Quisenberry, Kansas City		Bruce Sutter, St. Louis	

THE SPORTING NEWS ROOKIE AWARDS

1946—Combined selection—Delmer Ennis, Philadelphia, N. L., of
1947—Combined selection—Jack Robinson, Brooklyn, 1b
1948—Combined selection—Richie Ashburn, Philadelphia, N. L., of

Year	Player	Club	Player	Club
1949	Roy Sievers, St. Louis, of		Donald Newcombe, Brooklyn, p	
1950	Combined selection—Edward Ford, New York, A. L., p			
1951	Orestes Minoso, Chicago, of		Willie Mays, New York, of	
1952	Clinton Courtney, St. Louis, c		Joseph Black, Brooklyn, p	
1953	Harvey Kuenn, Detroit, ss		James Gilliam, Brooklyn, 2b	
1954	Robert Grim, New York, p		Wallace Moon, St. Louis, of	
1955	Herbert Score, Cleveland, p		William Virdon, St. Louis, of	
1956	Luis Aparicio, Chicago, ss		Frank Robinson, Cincinnati, of	
1957	Anthony Kubek, New York, inf-of (No pitcher named)		Edward Bouchee, Philadelphia, 1b Jack Sanford, Philadelphia, p	
1958	Albert Pearson, Washington, of Ryne Duren, New York, p		Orlando Cepeda, San Francisco, 1b Carlton Willey, Milwaukee, p	
1959	W. Robert Allison, Washington, of		Willie McCovey, San Francisco, 1b	
1960	Ronald Hansen, Baltimore, ss		Frank Howard, Los Angeles, of	
1961	Richard Howser, Kansas City, ss Donald Schwall, Boston, p		Billy Williams, Chicago, of Kenneth Hunt, Cincinnati, p	
1962	Thomas Tresh, New York, of-ss		Kenneth Hubbs, Chicago, 2b	
1963	Peter Ward, Chicago, 3b Gary Peters, Chicago, p		Peter Rose, Cincinnati, 2b Raymond Culp, Philadelphia, p	
1964	Pedro (Tony) Oliva, Minn., of Wallace Bunker, Baltimore, p		Richard Allen, Philadelphia, 3b William McCool, Cincinnati, p	

THE SPORTING NEWS ROOKIE AWARDS—Continued

AMERICAN LEAGUE

Year   Player   Club
1965—Curtis Blefary, Baltimore, of
      Marcelino Lopez, California, p
1966—Tommie Agee, Chicago, of
      James Nash, Kansas City, p
1967—Rod Carew, Minnesota, 2b
      Tom Phoebus, Baltimore, p
1968—Del Unser, Washington, of
      Stan Bahnsen, New York, p
1969—Carlos May, Chicago, of
      Mike Nagy, Boston, p
1970—Roy Foster, Cleveland, of
      Bert Blyleven, Minnesota, p
1971—Chris Chambliss, Cleveland, 1b
      Bill Parsons, Milwaukee, p
1972—Carlton Fisk, Boston, c
      Dick Tidrow, Cleveland, p
1973—Al Bumbry, Baltimore, of
      Steve Busby, Kansas City, p
1974—Mike Hargrove, Texas, 1b
      Frank Tanana, California, p
1975—Fred Lynn, Boston, of
      Dennis Eckersley, Cleveland, p
1976—Butch Wynegar, Minnesota, c
      Mark Fidrych, Detroit, p
1977—Mitchell Page, Oakland, of
      Dave Rozema, Detroit, p
1978—Paul Molitor, Milwaukee, 2b
      Rich Gale, Kansas City, p
1979—Pat Putnam, Texas, 1b
      Mark Clear, California, p
1980—Joe Charboneau, Cleveland, of
      Britt Burns, Chicago, p
1981—Rich Gedman, Boston, c
      Dave Righetti, New York, p
1982—Cal Ripken, Baltimore, ss-3b
      Ed Vande Berg, Seattle, p

NATIONAL LEAGUE

Player   Club
Joseph Morgan, Houston, 2b
Frank Linzy, San Francisco, p
Tommy Helms, Cincinnati, 3b
Donald Sutton, Los Angeles, p
Lee May, Cincinnati, 1b
Dick Hughes, St. Louis, p
Johnny Bench, Cincinnati, c
Jerry Koosman, New York, p
Coco Laboy, Montreal, 3b
Tom Griffin, Houston, p
Bernie Carbo, Cincinnati, of
Carl Morton, Montreal, p
Earl Williams, Atlanta, c
Reggie Cleveland, St. Louis, p
Dave Rader, San Francisco, c
Jon Matlack, New York, p
Gary Matthews, San Fran., of
Steve Rogers, Montreal, p
Greg Gross, Houston, of
John D'Acquisto, San Francisco, p
Gary Carter, Montreal, of-c
John Montefusco, San Francisco, p
Larry Herndon, San Francisco, of
Butch Metzger, San Diego, p
Andre Dawson, Montreal, of
Bob Owchinko, San Diego, p
Bob Horner, Atlanta, 3b
Don Robinson, Pittsburgh, p
Jeff Leonard, Houston, of
Rick Sutcliffe, Los Angeles, p
Lonnie Smith, Philadelphia, of
Bill Gullickson, Montreal, p
Tim Raines, Montreal, of
Fernando Valenzuela, Los Angeles, p
Johnny Ray, Pittsburgh, 2b
Steve Bedrosian, Atlanta, p

MAJOR LEAGUE EXECUTIVE

Year Executive   Club
1936—Branch Rickey, St. Louis NL
1937—Edward Barrow, New York AL
1938—Warren Giles, Cincinnati NL
1939—Larry MacPhail, Brooklyn NL
1940—W. O. Briggs, Sr., Detroit AL
1941—Edward Barrow, New York AL
1942—Branch Rickey, St. Louis NL
1943—Clark Griffith, Washington AL
1944—Wm. O. DeWitt, St. Louis AL
1945—Philip K. Wrigley, Chicago NL
1946—Thomas A. Yawkey, Boston AL
1947—Branch Rickey, Brooklyn NL
1948—Bill Veeck, Cleveland AL
1949—Robt. Carpenter, Phila'phia NL
1950—George Weiss, New York AL
1951—George Weiss, New York AL
1952—George Weiss, New York AL
1953—Louis Perini, Milwaukee NL
1954—Horace Stoneham, N. York NL
1955—Walter O'Malley, Brooklyn NL
1956—Gabe Paul, Cincinnati NL
1957—Frank Lane, St. Louis NL
1958—Joe L. Brown, Pittsburgh NL
1959—E. J. (Buzzie) Bavasi, L.A. NL

Year Executive   Club
1960—George Weiss, New York AL
1961—Dan Topping, New York AL
1962—Fred Haney, Los Angeles AL
1963—Vaughan (Bing) Devine, St.L.NL
1964—Vaughan (Bing) Devine, St.L.NL
1965—Calvin Griffith, Minnesota AL
1966—Lee MacPhail, Commissioner's
      Office
1967—Dick O'Connell, Boston AL
1968—James Campbell, Detroit AL
1969—John Murphy, New York NL
1970—Harry Dalton, Baltimore AL
1971—Cedric Tallis, Kansas City AL
1972—Roland Hemond, Chicago AL
1973—Bob Howsam, Cincinnati NL
1974—Gabe Paul, New York AL
1975—Dick O'Connell, Boston AL
1976—Joe Burke, Kansas City AL
1977—Bill Veeck, Chicago AL
1978—Spec Richardson, San Fran. NL
1979—Hank Peters, Baltimore AL
1980—Tal Smith, Houston NL
1981—John McHale, Montreal NL
1982—Harry Dalton, Milwaukee AL

MAJOR LEAGUE MANAGER

Year Manager   Club
1936—Joe McCarthy, New York AL
1937—Bill McKechnie, Boston NL
1938—Joe McCarthy, New York AL
1939—Leo Durocher, Brooklyn NL
1940—Bill McKechnie, Cincinnati NL
1941—Billy Southworth, St. Louis NL
1942—Billy Southworth, St. Louis NL

Year Manager   Club
1943—Joe McCarthy, New York AL
1944—Luke Sewell, St. Louis AL
1945—Ossie Bluege, Washington AL
1946—Eddie Dyer, St. Louis NL
1947—Bucky Harris, New York AL
1948—Bill Meyer, Pittsburgh NL
1949—Casey Stengel, New York AL

Year	Manager	Club	Year	Manager	Club
1950	Red Rolfe, Detroit AL		1967	Dick Williams, Boston AL	
1951	Leo Durocher, New York NL		1968	Mayo Smith, Detroit AL	
1952	Eddie Stanky, St. Louis NL		1969	Gil Hodges, New York NL	
1953	Casey Stengel, New York AL		1970	Danny Murtaugh, Pittsb'gh NL	
1954	Leo Durocher, New York NL		1971	Charlie Fox, San Francisco NL	
1955	Walter Alston, Brooklyn NL		1972	Chuck Tanner, Chicago AL	
1956	Birdie Tebbetts, Cincinnati NL		1973	Gene Mauch, Montreal NL	
1957	Fred Hutchinson, St. Louis NL		1974	Bill Virdon, New York AL	
1958	Casey Stengel, New York AL		1975	Darrell Johnson, Boston AL	
1959	Walter Alston, Los Angeles NL		1976	Danny Ozark, Philadelphia NL	
1960	Danny Murtaugh, Pitts. NL		1977	Earl Weaver, Baltimore AL	
1961	Ralph Houk, New York AL		1978	George Bamberger, Milw'kee AL	
1962	Bill Rigney, Los Angeles AL		1979	Earl Weaver, Baltimore AL	
1963	Walter Alston, Los Angeles NL		1980	Bill Virdon, Houston NL	
1964	Johnny Keane, St. Louis NL		1981	Billy Martin, Oakland AL	
1965	Sam Mele, Minnesota AL		1982	Whitey Herzog, St. Louis NL	
1966	Hank Bauer, Baltimore AL				

MAJOR LEAGUE PLAYER

Year	Player	Club	Year	Player	Club
1936	Carl Hubbell, New York NL		1960	Bill Mazeroski, Pittsburgh NL	
1937	Johnny Allen, Cleveland AL		1961	Roger Maris, New York AL	
1938	Johnny Vander Meer, Cinn. NL		1962	Maury Wills, Los Angeles NL	
1939	Joe DiMaggio, New York AL			Don Drysdale, Los Angeles NL	
1940	Bob Feller, Cleveland AL		1963	Sandy Koufax, Los Angeles NL	
1941	Ted Williams, Boston AL		1964	Ken Boyer, St. Louis NL	
1942	Ted Williams, Boston AL		1965	Sandy Koufax, Los Angeles NL	
1943	Spud Chandler, New York AL		1966	Frank Robinson, Baltimore AL	
1944	Marty Marion, St. Louis NL		1967	Carl Yastrzemski, Boston AL	
1945	Hal Newhouser, Detroit AL		1968	Denny McLain, Detroit AL	
1946	Stan Musial, St. Louis NL		1969	Willie McCovey, San Fran. NL	
1947	Ted Williams, Boston AL		1970	Johnny Bench, Cin. NL	
1948	Lou Boudreau, Cleveland AL		1971	Joe Torre, St. Louis NL	
1949	Ted Williams, Boston AL		1972	Billy Williams, Chicago NL	
1950	Phil Rizzuto, New York AL		1973	Reggie Jackson, Oakland AL	
1951	Stan Musial, St. Louis NL		1974	Lou Brock, St. Louis NL	
1952	Robin Roberts, Philadelphia NL		1975	Joe Morgan, Cincinnati NL	
1953	Al Rosen, Cleveland AL		1976	Joe Morgan, Cincinnati NL	
1954	Willie Mays, New York NL		1977	Rod Carew, Minnesota AL	
1955	Duke Snider, Brooklyn NL		1978	Ron Guidry, New York AL	
1956	Mickey Mantle, New York AL		1979	Willie Stargell, Pittsburgh NL	
1957	Ted Williams, Boston AL		1980	George Brett, Kansas City AL	
1958	Bob Turley, New York AL		1981	Fernando Valenzuela, Los Angeles NL	
1959	Early Wynn, Chicago AL		1982	Robin Yount, Milwaukee AL	

MINOR LEAGUE EXECUTIVE (HIGHER CLASSIFICATIONS)
(Restricted to Class AAA Starting in 1963)

Year	Executive	Club	Year	Executive	Club
1936	Earl Mann, Atlanta, Southern		1960	Ray Winder, Little Rock, Sou.	
1937	Robt. LaMotte, Savannah, Sally		1961	Elten Schiller, Omaha, A.A.	
1938	Louis McKenna, St. Paul, A.A.		1962	Geo. Sisler, Jr., Rochester, Int.	
1939	Bruce Dudley, Louisville, A.A.		1963	Lewis Matlin, Hawaii, PCL	
1940	Roy Hamey, Kansas City, A.A.		1964	Ed. Leishman, San Diego, PCL	
1941	Emil Sick, Seattle, PCL		1965	Harold Cooper, Columbus, Int.	
1942	Bill Veeck, Milwaukee, A.A.		1966	John Quinn, Jr., Hawaii, PCL	
1943	Clar. Rowland, Los Angeles, PCL		1967	Hillman Lyons, Richmond, Int.	
1944	William Mulligan, Seattle, PCL		1968	Gabe Paul, Jr., Tulsa, PCL	
1945	Bruce Dudley, Louisville, A.A.		1969	Bill Gardner, Louisville, Int.	
1946	Earl Mann, Atlanta, Southern		1970	Dick King, Wichita, A.A.	
1947	Wm. Purnhage, Waterloo, I.I.I.		1971	Carl Steinfeldt, Jr., Roch'ter, Int.	
1948	Ed. Glennon, Bir'ham, Southern		1972	Don Labbruzzo, Evansville, A.A.	
1949	Ted Sullivan, Indianapolis, A.A.		1973	Merle Miller, Tucson, PCL	
1950	Cl. (Brick) Laws, Oakland, PCL		1974	John Carbray, Sacramento, PCL	
1951	Robert Howsam, Denver, West.		1975	Stan Naccarato, Tacoma, PCL	
1952	Jack Cooke, Toronto, Int.		1976	Art Teece, Salt Lake City, PCL	
1953	Richard Burnett, Dallas, Texas		1977	George Sisler, Jr., Col'bus, Int.	
1954	Edward Stumpf, Indpls., A.A.		1978	Willie Sanchez, Albu'que, PCL	
1955	Dewey Soriano, Seattle, PCL		1979	George Sisler, Jr., Col'bus, Int.	
1956	Robert Howsam, Denver, A.A.		1980	Jim Burris, Denver, A.A.	
1957	John Stiglmeier, Buffalo, Int.		1981	Pat McKernan, Albuquerque, PCL	
1958	Ed. Glennon, Bir'ham, Southern		1982	A. Ray Smith, Louisville, A.A.	
1959	Ed. Leishman, Salt Lake, PCL				

MINOR LEAGUE EXECUTIVE (LOWER CLASSIFICATIONS)
(Separate Awards for Class AA and Class A Started in 1963)

Year Executive   Club
1950—H. Cooper, Hutch'son, West. A.
1951—O. W. (Bill) Hayes, T'ple, B.S.
1952—Hillman Lyons, Danville, MOV
1953—Carl Roth, Peoria, III
1954—James Meaghan, Cedar R., III
1955—John Petrakis, Dubuque, MOV
1956—Marvin Milkes, Fresno, Calif.
1957—Richard Wagner, L'coln, West.
1958—Gerald Waring, Macon, Sally
1959—Clay Dennis, Des Moines, III
1960—Hubert Kittle, Yakima, Northw.
1961—David Steele, Fresno, California
1962—John Quinn, Jr., S. Jose, Calif.
1963—Hugh Finnerty, Tulsa, Texas
      Ben Jewell, M. Valley, Pioneer
1964—Glynn West, Birmingham, Sou.
      Jas. Bayens, Rock Hill, W. Car.
1965—Dick Butler, Dallas-Ft.W., Tex.
      Ken. Blackman, Quad C., Midw.
1966—Tom Fleming, Evansville, South.
      Cappy Harada, Lodi, California
1967—Robt. Quinn, Reading, East.
      Pat Williams, Spar'burg, W. C.
1968—Phil Howser, Charlotte, South.
      Merle Miller, Burlington, Midw.
1969—Charlie Blaney, Albuq., Texas
      Bill Gorman, Visalia, Calif.

Year Executive   Club
1970—Carl Sawatski, Arkansas, Texas
      Bob Williams, Bakersfield, Calif.
1971—Miles Wolff, Savannah, Dixie A.
      Ed Holtz, Appleton, Midwest
1972—John Begzos, S. Antonio, Texas
      Bob Piccinini, Modesto, Calif.
1973—Dick Kravitz, Jacksonville, Sou.
      Fritz Colschen, Clinton, Midw.
1974—Jim Paul, El Paso, Texas
      Bing Russell, Portland, N'west
1975—Jim Paul, El Paso, Texas
      Cordy Jensen, Eugene, N'west
1976—Woodrow Reid, Chat'ooga, Sou.
      Don Buchheister, Ced. Rap., Mid.
1977—Jim Paul, El Paso, Texas
      Harry Pells, Quad Cities, Midw.
1978—Larry Schmittou, Nashville, Sou.
      Dave Hersh, Appleton, Midwest
1979—Bill Rigney Jr., Midland, Tex.
      Tom Romenesko, G'sboro, W.C.
1980—Frances Crockett, C'lotte, Sou.
      Tom Romenesko, G'sboro, W.C.
1981—Allie Prescott, Memphis, Southern
      Dan Overstreet, Hagerstown, Caro.
1982—Art Clarkson, Birmingham, Sou.
      Bob Carruesco, Stockton, Calif.

MINOR LEAGUE MANAGER

Year Manager   Club
1936—Al Sothoron, Milwaukee, A.A.
1937—Jake Flowers, Salis'y, East. Sh.
1938—Paul Richards, Atlanta, South.
1939—Bill Meyer, Kansas City, A.A.
1940—Larry Gilbert, Nashville, South.
1941—Burt Shotton, Columbus, A.A.
1942—Eddie Dyer, Columbus, A.A.
1943—Nick Cullop, Columbus, A.A.
1944—Al Thomas, Baltimore, Int.
1945—Lefty O'Doul, San Fran., PCL
1946—Clay Hopper, Montreal, Int.
1947—Nick Cullop, Milwaukee, A.A.
1948—Casey Stengel, Oakland, PCL
1949—Fred Haney, Hollywood, PCL
1950—Rollie Hemsley, Columbus, A.A.
1951—Charlie Grimm, Milw., A.A.
1952—Luke Appling, Memphis, South.
1953—Bobby Bragan, Hollywood, PCL
1954—Kerby Farrell, Indpls., A.A.
1955—Bill Rigney, Minneapolis, A.A.
1956—Kerby Farrell, Indpls., A.A.
1957—Ben Geraghty, Wichita, A.A.
1958—Cal Ermer, Birmingham, South.
1959—Pete Reiser, Victoria, Texas

Year Manager   Club
1960—Mel McGaha, Toronto, Int.
1961—Kerby Farrell, Buffalo, Int.
1962—Ben Geraghty, Jackson'le, Int.
1963—Rollie Hemsley, Indpls., Int.
1964—Harry Walker, Jacks'vle., Int.
1965—Grady Hatton, Okla. City, PCL
1966—Bob Lemon, Seattle, PCL
1967—Bob Skinner, San Diego, PCL
1968—Jack Tighe, Toledo, Int.
1969—Clyde McCullough, Tide., Int.
1970—Tom Lasorda, Spokane, PCL
1971—Del Rice, Salt Lake City, PCL
1972—Hank Bauer, Tidewater, Int.
1973—Joe Morgan, Charleston, Int.
1974—Joe Altobelli, Rochester, Int.
1975—Joe Frazier, Tidewater, Int.
1976—Vern Rapp, Denver, A.A.
1977—Tommy Thompson, Arkan., Tex.
1978—Les Moss, Evansville, A.A.
1979—Vern Benson, Syracuse, Int.
1980—Hal Lanier, Springfield, A.A.
1981—Del Crandall, Albuquerque, PCL
1982—George Scherger, Indianapolis, A.A.

MINOR LEAGUE PLAYER

Year Player   Club
1936—Jn. Vander Meer, Durham, Pied.
1937—Charlie Keller, Newark, Int.
1938—Fred Hutchinson, Seattle, PCL
1939—Lou Novikoff, Tulsa-Los A'les.
1940—Phil Rizzuto, Kansas City, A.A.
1941—John Lindell, Newark, Int.
1942—Dick Barrett, Seattle, PCL
1943—Chet Covington, Scranton, East.
1944—Rip Collins, Albany, Eastern
1945—Gil Coan, Chattanooga, South.
1946—Sibby Sisti, Indianapolis, A.A.
1947—Hank Sauer, Syracuse, Int.
1948—Gene Woodling, S. F., PCL
1949—Orie Arntzen, Albany, Eastern
1950—Frank Saucier, San Ant'o, Tex.

Year Player   Club
1951—Gene Conley, Hartford, Eastern
1952—Bill Skowron, Kans. City, A.A.
1953—Gene Conley, Toledo, A.A.
1954—Herb Score, Indianapolis, A.A.
1955—John Murff, Dallas, Texas
1956—Steve Bilko, Los Angeles, PCL
1957—Norm Siebern, Denver, A.A.
1958—Jim O'Toole, Nashville, South.
1959—Frank Howard, Victoria-Spok.
1960—Willie Davis, Spokane, PCL
1961—Howie Koplitz, Bir'ham, South.
1962—Bob Bailey, Columbus, Int.
1963—Don Buford, Indianapolis, Int.
1964—Mel Stottlemyre, Richm'd., Int.
1965—Joe Foy, Toronto, International

MINOR LEAGUE PLAYER—Cont.

Year	Player	Club
1966	Mike Epstein, Rochester, Int.	
1967	Johnny Bench, Buffalo, Int.	
1968	Merv Rettenmund, Roch'ter, Int.	
1969	Danny Walton, Okla. City, A.A.	
1970	Don Baylor, Rochester, Int.	
1971	Bobby Grich, Rochester, Int.	
1972	Tom Paciorek, Albuq'que, PCL	
1973	Steve Ontiveros, Phoenix, PCL	
1974	Jim Rice, Pawtucket, Int.	

Year	Player	Club
1975	Hector Cruz, Tulsa, A.A.	
1976	Pat Putnam, Asheville, W. Car.	
1977	Ken Landreaux, S.L.C., PCL-El Paso, Tex.	
1978	Champ Summers, Indi'polis, A.A.	
1979	Mark Bomback, Vancouver, PCL	
1980	Tim Raines, Denver, A.A.	
1981	Mike Marshall, Albuquerque, PCL	
1982	Ron Kittle, Edmonton, PCL	

Baseball Writers' Association Awards
Most Valuable Player Citations

CHALMERS AWARD

AMERICAN LEAGUE

Year	Player	Club	Points
1911	Tyrus Cobb, Detroit, of	64
1912	Tristram Speaker, Boston, of	59
1913	Walter Johnson, Washington, p	54
1914	Edward Collins, Phila., 2b	63

NATIONAL LEAGUE

Player	Club	Points
Frank Schulte, Chicago, of	29
Lawrence Doyle, N. Y., 2b	48
Jacob Daubert, Brooklyn, 1b	50
John Evers, Boston, 2b	50

LEAGUE AWARDS

AMERICAN LEAGUE

Year	Player	Club	Points
1922	George Sisler, St. Louis, 1b	59
1923	George Ruth, New York, of	64
1924	Walter Johnson, Washington, p	55
1925	Roger Peckinpaugh, Wash., ss	45
1926	George Burns, Cleveland, 1b	63
1927	H. Louis Gehrig, New York, 1b	56
1928	Gordon Cochrane, Phila., c	53
1929	No selection	

NATIONAL LEAGUE

Player	Club	Points
No selection	
No selection	
Arthur Vance, Brooklyn, p	74
Rogers Hornsby, St. Louis, 2b	73
Robert O'Farrell, St. Louis, c	79
Paul Waner, Pittsburgh, of	72
James Bottomley, St. Louis, 1b	76
Rogers Hornsby, Chicago, 2b	60

BASEBALL WRITERS' ASSOCIATION MVP AWARDS

AMERICAN LEAGUE

Year	Player	Club	Points
1931	Robert Grove, Philadelphia, p	78
1932	James Foxx, Philadelphia, 1b	75
1933	James Foxx, Philadelphia, 1b	74
1934	Gordon Cochrane, Detroit, c	67
1935	Henry Greenberg, Detroit, 1b	*80
1936	H. Louis Gehrig, New York, 1b	73
1937	Charles Gehringer, Detroit, 2b	78
1938	James Foxx, Boston, 1b	305
1939	Joseph DiMaggio, N. York, of	280
1940	Henry Greenberg, Detroit, of	292
1941	Joseph DiMaggio, N. York, of	291
1942	Joseph Gordon, New York, 2b	270
1943	Spurgeon Chandler, N. Y., p	246
1944	Harold Newhouser, Detroit, p	236
1945	Harold Newhouser, Detroit, p	236
1946	Theodore Williams, Boston, of	224
1947	Joseph DiMaggio, N. York, of	202
1948	Louis Boudreau, Cleveland, ss	324
1949	Theodore Williams, Boston, of	272
1950	Philip Rizzuto, New York, ss	284
1951	Lawrence Berra, New York, c	184
1952	Robert Shantz, Phila., p	280
1953	Albert Rosen, Cleveland, 3b	*336
1954	Lawrence Berra, New York, c	230
1955	Lawrence Berra, New York, c	218
1956	Mickey Mantle, N. Y., of	*336
1957	Mickey Mantle, New York, of	233
1958	Jack Jensen, Boston, of	233
1959	J. Nelson Fox, Chicago, 2b	295
1960	Roger Maris, New York, of	225
1961	Roger Maris, New York, of	202
1962	Mickey Mantle, New York, of	234
1963	Elston Howard, New York, c	248
1964	Brooks Robinson, Balti., 3b	269
1965	Zoilo Versalles, Minn., ss	275

NATIONAL LEAGUE

Player	Club	Points
Frank Frisch, St. Louis, 2b	65
Charles Klein, Phila., of	78
Carl Hubbell, New York, p	77
Jerome Dean, St. Louis, p	78
Charles Hartnett, Chicago, c	75
Carl Hubbell, New York, p	60
Joseph Medwick, St. Louis, of	70
Ernest Lombardi, Cincinnati, c	229
William Walters, Cincinnati, p	303
Frank McCormick, Cinn., 1b	274
Adolph Camilli, Brooklyn, 1b	300
Morton Cooper, St. Louis, p	263
Stanley Musial, St. Louis, of	267
Martin Marion, St. Louis, ss	190
Philip Cavarretta, Chicago, 1b	279
Stanley Musial, St. Louis, 1b	319
Robert Elliott, Boston, 3b	205
Stanley Musial, St. Louis, of	303
Jack Robinson, Brooklyn, 2b	264
C. James Konstanty, Phila., p	286
Roy Campanella, Brooklyn, c	243
Henry Sauer, Chicago, of	226
Roy Campanella, Brooklyn, c	297
Willie Mays, New York, of	283
Roy Campanella, Brooklyn, c	226
Donald Newcombe, Brkn., p	223
Henry Aaron, Milwaukee, of	239
Ernest Banks, Chicago, ss	283
Ernest Banks, Chicago, ss	232½
Richard Groat, Pittsburgh, ss	276
Frank Robinson, Cincinnati, of	219
Maurice Wills, Los Angeles, ss	209
Sanford Koufax, Los Angeles, p	237
Kenton Boyer, St. Louis, 3b	243
Willie Mays, San Francisco, of	224

BASEBALL WRITERS' ASSOCIATION MVP AWARDS—Cont.

AMERICAN LEAGUE			NATIONAL LEAGUE		
Year	Player Club	Points	Player Club		Points
1966—Frank Robinson, Balti., of		*280	Roberto Clemente, Pitts., of		218
1967—Carl Yastrzemski, Boston, of		275	Orlando Cepeda, St. Louis, 1b		*280
1968—Dennis McLain, Detroit, p		*280	Robert Gibson, St. Louis, p		242
1969—Harmon Killebrew, Minn., 1-3b		294	Willie McCovey, San Fran., 1b		265
1970—John (Boog) Powell, Balt., 1b		234	Johnny Bench, Cincinnati, c		326
1971—Vida Blue, Oakland, p		268	Joseph Torre, St. Louis, 3b		318
1972—Richie Allen, Chicago, 1b		321	Johnny Bench, Cincinnati, c		263
1973—Reggie Jackson, Oak., of		*336	Pete Rose, Cincinnati, of		274
1974—Jeff Burroughs, Texas, of		248	Steve Garvey, Los Angeles, 1b		270
1975—Fred Lynn, Boston, of		326	Joe Morgan, Cincinnati, 2b		321½
1976—Thurman Munson, N. Y., c		304	Joe Morgan, Cincinnati, 2b		311
1977—Rod Carew, Minn., 1b		273	George Foster, Cincinnati, of		291
1978—Jim Rice, Boston, of		352	Dave Parker, Pittsburgh, of		320
1979—Don Baylor, California, of		347	Willie Stargell, Pittsburgh, 1b		216
			Keith Hernandez, St. Louis, 1b		216
1980—George Brett, Kansas City, 3b		335	Mike Schmidt, Philadelphia, 3b		*336
1981—Rollie Fingers, Milwaukee, p		319	Mike Schmidt, Philadelphia, 3b		321
1982—Robin Yount, Milwaukee, ss		385	Dale Murphy, Atlanta, of		283

*Unanimous selection.

BASEBALL WRITERS' ASSOCIATION ROOKIE AWARDS

1947—Combined selection—Jack Robinson, Brooklyn, 1b.
1948—Combined selection—Alvin Dark, Boston, N. L., ss.

Year	Player Club	Votes	Player Club		Votes
1949—Roy Sievers, St. Louis, of		10	Donald Newcombe, Brkn, p		21
1950—Walter Dropo, Boston, 1b		15	Samuel Jethroe, Boston, of		11
1951—Gilbert McDougald, N. Y., 3b		13	Willie Mays, New York, of		18
1952—Harry Byrd, Philadelphia, p		9	Joseph Black, Brooklyn, p		19
1953—Harvey Kuenn, Detroit, ss		23	James Gilliam, Brooklyn, 2b		11
1954—Robert Grim, New York, p		15	Wallace Moon, St. Louis, of		17
1955—Herbert Score, Cleveland, p		18	William Virdon, St. Louis, of		15
1956—Luis Aparicio, Chicago, ss		22	Frank Robinson, Cincinnati, of		*24
1957—Anthony Kubek, N. Y., inf-of		23	John Sanford, Philadelphia, p		16
1958—Albert Pearson, Washington, of		14	Orlando Cepeda, S. Fran., 1b		*†21
1959—W. Robert Allison, Wash., of		18	Willie McCovey, San Fran., 1b		*24
1960—Ronald Hansen, Baltimore, ss		22	Frank Howard, Los Angeles, of		12
1961—Donald Schwall, Boston, p		7	Billy Williams, Chicago, of		10
1962—Thomas Tresh, New York, of-ss		13	Kenneth Hubbs, Chicago, 2b		19
1963—Gary Peters, Chicago, p		10	Peter Rose, Cincinnati, 2b		17
1964—Pedro (Tony) Oliva, Minn., of		19	Richard Allen, Philadelphia, 3b		18
1965—Curtis Blefary, Baltimore, of		12	James Lefebvre, Los Ang., 2b		13
1966—Tommie Agee, Chicago, of		16	Tommy Helms, Cincinnati, 3b		12
1967—Rod Carew, Minnesota, 2b		19	Tom Seaver, New York, p		11
1968—Stan Bahnsen, New York, p		17	Johnny Bench, Cincinnati, c		10½
1969—Lou Piniella, Kansas City, of		9	Ted Sizemore, Los Angeles, 2b		14
1970—Thurman Munson, N. Y., c		23	Carl Morton, Montreal, p		11
1971—Chris Chambliss, Cleveland, 1b		11	Earl Williams, Atlanta, c		18
1972—Carlton Fisk, Boston, c		*24	Jon Matlack, New York, p		19
1973—Al Bumbry, Baltimore, of		13½	Gary Matthews, San Fran., of		11
1974—Mike Hargrove, Texas, 1b		16½	Bake McBride, St. Louis, of		16
1975—Fred Lynn, Boston, of		23	John Montefusco, San Fran., p		12
1976—Mark Fidrych, Detroit, p		22	Butch Metzger, San Diego, p		11
			Pat Zachry, Cincinnati, p		11
1977—Eddie Murray, Balt., dh-1b		12½	Andre Dawson, Montreal, of		10
1978—Lou Whitaker, Detroit, 2b		21	Bob Horner, Atlanta, 3b		12½
1979—John Castino, Minn., 3b		7	Rick Sutcliffe, L.A., p		20
Alfredo Griffin, Tor., ss		7			
1980—Joe Charboneau, Clev., of		103	Steve Howe, L.A., p		80
1981—Dave Righetti, N. Y., p		127	Fernando Valenzuela, L. A., p		107
1982—Cal Ripken, Balt., ss-3b		132	Steve Sax, L.A., 2b		63

*Unanimous selection. †Three writers did not vote.

The Phillies' Steve Carlton, who won his fourth Cy Young Award in 1982, may be the best pitcher in baseball today.

CY YOUNG MEMORIAL AWARD

Year	Pitcher Club	Votes
1956	Donald Newcombe, Brkn	10
1957	Warren Spahn, Milwaukee	15
1958	Robert Turley, N. Y., A. L.	5
1959	Early Wynn, Chicago, A.L.	13
1960	Vernon Law, Pittsburgh	8
1961	Edward Ford, N.Y., A.L.	9
1962	Don Drysdale, L.A., N.L.	14
1963	Sanford Koufax, L.A., N.L.	*20
1964	Dean Chance, L. A., A. L.	17
1965	Sanford Koufax, L.A., N.L.	*20
1966	Sanford Koufax, L.A., N.L.	*20

Year	Pitcher Club	Votes
1967	A. L.—Jim Lonborg, Boston	18
	N. L.—M. McCormick, S. F.	18
1968	A. L.—Dennis McLain, Det.	*20
	N. L.—Bob Gibson, St. L.	*20
1969	A. L.—Dennis McLain, Det.	10
	Mike Cuellar, Balt.	10
	N. L.—Tom Seaver, N. Y.	23
1970	A. L.—Jim Perry, Minn.	†55
	N. L.—Bob Gibson, St. L.	†118
1971	A. L.—Vida Blue, Oakland	†98
	N. L.—Fergy Jenkins, Chi.	†97

Year	Pitcher Club	Votes
1972	A. L.—Gaylord Perry, Cleve.	†64
	N. L.—Steve Carlton, Phil.	*†120
1973	A. L.—Jim Palmer, Balt.	†88
	N. L.—Tom Seaver, N. Y.	†71
1974	A. L.—Jim Hunter, Oakland	†90
	N. L.—Mike Marshall, L. A.	†96
1975	A. L.—Jim Palmer, Balt.	†98
	N. L.—Tom Seaver, N. Y.	†98
1976	A. L.—Jim Palmer, Balt.	†108
	N. L.—Randy Jones, S. D.	†96
1977	A. L.—Sparky Lyle, N.Y.	†56½
	N. L.—Steve Carlton, Phil.	*†104
1978	A. L.—Ron Guidry, N.Y.	*†140
	N. L.—Gaylord Perry, S.D.	‡116
1979	A. L.—Mike Flanagan, Balt.	†136
	N. L.—Bruce Sutter, Chi.	†72
1980	A. L.—Steve Stone, Balt.	100
	N. L.—Steve Carlton, Phil.	118
1981	A. L.—Rollie Fingers, Milwaukee	126
	N. L.—Fernando Valenzuela, L.A.	70
1982	A. L.—Pete Vuckovich, Milwaukee	87
	N. L.—Steve Carlton, Philadelphia	112

*Unanimous selection. †Point system used.

Brooks, Marichal Head for Hall

By LARRY WIGGE

Lee May was a slugging first baseman for the Cincinnati Reds in 1970. He watched in amazement as third baseman Brooks Robinson almost singlehandedly stole the World Series for the Baltimore Orioles that year with one spectacular play after another.

If you can't beat 'em, join 'em. May did and, in October of 1977, when the Orioles honored Robinson before his retirement, May was called out to make a "special presentation."

When May strolled onto the field with a used vacuum cleaner, the meaning was obvious. What Brooks didn't scoop up in his 23 years in the major leagues couldn't be scooped up by a vacuum cleaner.

For a .267 lifetime hitter to enter Baseball's Hall of Fame on his first ballot as Brooks Robinson did in 1983, there had to be something special about his fielding.

Robinson became only the 14th player to be elected his first time on the ballot, gaining the honor with a whopping 91.9 percent when 344 of 374 voting members of the Baseball Writers' Association of America placed his name on their ballots.

In addition to Robinson, high-kicking righthander Juan Marichal, who won 20 games six times and had a 243-142 lifetime record, also was elected.

Marichal, who failed in two previous ballots, received 313 votes. Harmon Killebrew finished third with 269 votes (12 short of the required 75 percent or 281 votes), while Luis Aparicio had 252 votes, Hoyt Wilhelm 243, Don Drysdale 242 and Gil Hodges 237.

"I played 23 years and I never had five games as good as those five I had against Cincinnati in the 1970 Series," Robinson said when notified of his election. "All five of those games were seen around the country on TV. I'm sure it enhanced my reputation. I know one thing, this sure was a blow for the defensive ballplayer."

Robinson batted .429 in the '70 Series and was named Most Valuable Player. He won MVP honors in the American League in 1964 when he put together his best offensive totals: 28 homers, a league-leading 118 RBIs and a .317 average.

Robinson hit 268 homers and had 2,848 career hits. But more importantly, he was named winner of 16 consecutive Gold Gloves for exceptional fielding from 1960 through 1975. He played in 18 All-Star games.

Marichal spent 14 of his 16 seasons with

Baltimore's Brooks Robinson.

the San Francisco Giants. He had a career earned-run average of 2.89, baffling National League hitters with a wide assortment of pitches and deliveries.

Marichal, the first Hall of Famer from the Dominican Republic, hurled a no-hitter against the Houston Colt .45s on June 15, 1963. He set a record with six opening-day victories. Twice he led the N.L. in innings pitched (321 in 1963 and 326 in 1968). He led the league with a 25-8 record in 1963 and duplicated the feat with a 26-9 record in 1968. His 2.10 ERA in 1969 also led the league.

Marichal had his biggest success in the years when Hall of Famers Sandy Koufax and Bob Gibson were walking away with all the pitching awards. But there was no question Marichal belonged in the same elite class.

Critics claim Marichal didn't gain immediate election to the Hall of Fame because of a 1965 incident when he slugged Dodgers' catcher John Roseboro over the head with a bat. He was suspended for eight games and fined $1,750. But Marichal denied the incident hurt his chances.

"I don't think that hurt me," Marichal

San Francisco's Juan Marichal.

said. "It is all forgotten, especially with John and me. We are very good friends. He came to the Dominican Republic last October and played in my golf tournament. He also was my house guest."

Roseboro sent Marichal a thank-you note, saying: "After 20 years I hope we can now be 'amigos' for the rest of our lives."

The election of Robinson and Marichal swelled the Hall of Fame membership to 180.

The complete Hall of Fame voting totals, with 281 votes needed for election, follows:

Robinson, 344; Marichal, 313; Killebrew, 269; Aparicio, 252; Wilhelm, 243; Drysdale, 242; Hodges, 237; Nelson Fox, 173; Billy Williams, 153; Red Schoendienst, 146; Jim Bunning, 138; Harvey Kuenn, 77, Maury Wills, 77; Tony Oliva, 75; Roger Maris, 69; Orlando Cepeda, 59; Bill Mazeroski, 48; Lew Burdette, 43; Elston Howard, 32; Elroy Face, 32; Don Larsen, 22; Joe Torre, 20; Thurman Munson, 18; Richie Allen, 14; Vada Pinson, 12; Jim Perry, 7; Boog Powell, 5; Ray Sadecki, 2; Dave Guisti, 1; Tommy Helms, 1; Felix Millan, 1.

The following failed to receive any votes: Mike Cuellar, Larry Dierker, Pat Dobson, Al Downing, Joe Hoerner, Randy Hundley, Carlos May, Ken McMullen, Bill Melton, Gary Nolan, Doug Rader, Cookie Rojas, Diego Segui, Bill Singer, Jimmy Wynn.

Following is a complete list of those enshrined in the Hall of Fame prior to 1983 with the vote by which each enrollee was elected:

1936—Tyrus Cobb (222), John (Honus) Wagner (215), George (Babe) Ruth (215), Christy Mathewson (205), Walter Johnson (189), named by Baseball Writers Association of America. Total ballots cast, 226.

1937—Napoleon Lajoie (168), Tristram Speaker (165), Denton (Cy) Young (153), named by the BBWAA. Total ballots cast, 201. George Wright, Morgan G. Bulkeley, Byron Bancroft Johnson, John J. McGraw, Cornelius McGillicuddy (Connie Mack), named by Centennial Commission.

1938—Grover C. Alexander (212), named by BBWAA. Total ballots, 262. Henry Chadwick, Alexander J. Cartwright, named by Centennial Commission.

1939—George Sisler (235), Edward Collins (213), William Keeler (207), Louis Gehrig, named by BBWAA. (Gehrig by special election after retirement from game was announced). Total ballots cast, 274. Albert G. Spalding, Adrian C. Anson, Charles A. Comiskey, William (Buck) Ewing, Charles Radbourn, William A. (Candy) Cummings, named by committee of old-time players and writers.

1942—Rogers Hornsby (182), named by BBWAA. Total ballots cast, 233.

1944—Judge Kenesaw M. Landis, named by committee on old timers.

1945—Hugh Duffy, Jimmy Collins, Hugh Jennings, Ed Delahanty, Fred Clarke, Mike Kelly, Wilbert Robinson, Jim O'Rourke, Dennis (Dan) Brouthers and Roger Bresnahan, named by committee on old timers.

1946—Jesse Burkett, Frank Chance, Jack Chesbro, Johnny Evers, Clark Griffith, Tom McCarthy, Joe McGinnity, Eddie Plank, Joe Tinker, Rube Waddell and Ed Walsh, named by committee on old timers.

1947—Carl Hubbell (140), Frank Frisch (136), Gordon (Mickey) Cochrane (128) and Robert (Lefty) Grove (123), named by BBWAA. Total ballots, 161.

1948—Herbert J. Pennock (94) and Harold (Pie) Traynor (93), named by BBWAA. Total ballots cast, 121.

1949—Charles Gehringer (159), named by BBWAA in runoff election. Total ballots cast, 187. Charles (Kid) Nichols and Mordecai (Three-Finger) Brown, named by committee on old timers.

1951—Mel Ott (197) and Jimmie Foxx (179), named by BBWAA. Total ballots cast, 226.

1952—Harry Heilmann (203) and Paul

Waner (195), named by BBWAA. Total ballots cast, 234.

1953—Jerome (Dizzy) Dean (209) and Al Simmons (199), named by BBWAA. Total ballots cast, 264. Charles Albert (Chief) Bender, Roderick (Bobby) Wallace, William Klem, Tom Connolly, Edward G. Barrow and William Henry (Harry) Wright, named by the new Committee on Veterans.

1954—Walter (Rabbit) Maranville (209), William Dickey (202) and William Terry (195), named by BBWAA. Total ballots cast, 252.

1955—Joe DiMaggio (223), Ted Lyons (217), Arthur (Dazzy) Vance (205) and Charles (Gabby) Hartnett (195), named by BBWAA. Total ballots cast, 251. J. Franklin (Home Run) Baker and Ray Schalk, named by Committee on Veterans.

1956—Hank Greenberg (164) and Joe Cronin (152), named by BBWAA. Total ballots cast, 193.

1957—Joseph V. McCarthy and Sam Crawford, named by Committee on Veterans.

1959—Zachariah (Zack) Wheat, named by Committee on Veterans.

1961—Max Carey and William Hamilton, named by Committee on Veterans.

1962—Bob Feller (150) and Jackie Robinson (124), named by BBWAA. Total ballots cast, 160. Bill McKechnie and Edd Roush, named by Committee on Veterans.

1963—Eppa Rixey, Edgar (Sam) Rice, Elmer Flick and John Clarkson, named by Committee on Veterans.

1964—Luke Appling (189), named by BBWAA in runoff election. Total ballots cast, 225. Urban (Red) Faber, Burleigh Grimes, Tim Keefe, Heinie Manush, Miller Huggins and John Montgomery Ward, named by Committee on Veterans.

1965—James (Pud) Galvin, named by Committee on Veterans.

1966—Ted Williams (282), named by BBWAA. Total ballots cast, 302. Casey Stengel, named by Committee on Veterans.

1967—Charles (Red) Ruffing (266), named by BBWAA in runoff election. Total ballots cast, 306. Branch Rickey and Lloyd Waner, named by Committee on Veterans.

1968—Joseph (Ducky) Medwick (240), named by BBWAA. Total ballots cast, 283. Leon (Goose) Goslin and Hazen (Kiki) Cuyler, named by Committee on Veterans.

1969—Stan (The Man) Musial (317) and Roy Campanella (270), named by BBWAA. Total ballots cast, 340. Stan Coveleski and Waite Hoyt, named by Committee on Veterans.

1970—Lou Boudreau (232), named by BBWAA. Total ballots cast, 300. Earle Combs, Jesse Haines and Ford Frick, named by Committee on Veterans.

1971—Chick Hafey, Rube Marquard, Joe Kelley, Dave Bancroft, Harry Hooper, Jake Beckley and George Weiss, named by Committee on Veterans. Satchel Paige, named by Special Committee on Negro Leagues.

1972—Sandy Koufax (344), Yogi Berra (339) and Early Wynn (301), named by BBWAA. Total ballots cast, 396. Lefty Gomez, Will Harridge and Ross Youngs, named by Committee on Veterans. Josh Gibson and Walter (Buck) Leonard, named by Special Committee on Negro Leagues.

1973—Warren Spahn (316), named by BBWAA. Total ballots cast, 380. Roberto Clemente (393), in special election by BBWAA in which 424 ballots were cast. Billy Evans, George Kelly and Mickey Welch, named by Committee on Veterans. Monte Irvin, named by Special Committee on Negro Leagues.

1974—Mickey Mantle (322) and Whitey Ford (284), named by BBWAA. Total ballots cast, 365. Jim Bottomley, Sam Thompson and Jocko Conlan, named by Committee on Veterans. James (Cool Papa) Bell, named by Special Committee on Negro Leagues.

1975—Ralph Kiner (273), named by BBWAA. Total ballots cast, 362. Earl Averill, Bucky Harris and Billy Herman, named by Committee on Veterans. William (Judy) Johnson, named by Special Committee on Negro Leagues.

1976—Robin Roberts (337) and Bob Lemon (305), named by BBWAA. Total ballots cast, 388. Roger Connor, Cal Hubbard and Fred Lindstrom, named by Committee on Veterans. Oscar Charleston, named by Special Committee on Negro Leagues.

1977—Ernie Banks (321), named by BBWAA. Total ballots cast, 383. Joe Sewell, Al Lopez and Amos Rusie, named by Committee on Veterans. Martin Dihigo and John Henry Lloyd, named by Special Committee on Negro Leagues.

1978—Eddie Mathews (301), named by BBWAA. Total ballots cast, 379. Larry MacPhail and Addie Joss, named by Committee on Veterans.

1979—Willie Mays (409), named by BBWAA. Total ballots cast, 432. Hack Wilson and Warren Giles, named by Committee on Veterans.

1980—Al Kaline (340) and Duke Snider (333), named by BBWAA. Total ballots cast, 385. Chuck Klein and Tom Yawkey, named by Committee on Veterans.

1981—Bob Gibson (337), named by BBWAA. Total ballots cast, 401. Johnny Mize and Rube Foster, named by Committee on Veterans.

1982—Henry Aaron (406) and Frank Robinson (370), named by BBWAA. Total ballots cast, 415. Albert B. (Happy) Chandler and Travis Jackson, named by Committee on Veterans.

BASEBALL RE-ENTRY DRAFT

MINOR LEAGUE DRAFT

MAJOR LEAGUE TRANSACTIONS

NECROLOGY

Seattle lefthander Floyd Bannister was the most sought-after commodity in the free-agent market. After being drafted by 16 teams, Bannister signed with the Chicago White Sox.

Garvey, Bannister Strike Gold

By LARRY WIGGE

Let's see now. Modern math would tell us that $6.5 million over the next five years is roughly equivalent to 1.083 million Big Macs sold each year for the next five years.

That's what they call the bottom line in the business world. More specifically, however, that might be the bottom line facing San Diego Padres Owner Ray Kroc when he looks at his investment in former Los Angeles Dodgers star first baseman Steve Garvey.

After 12 seasons with the Dodgers (where he averaged .301), Garvey turned down a four-year contract worth $5 million and went through baseball's seventh annual re-entry draft for free agents November 10. After that, he sat back and watched the Chicago Cubs, San Francisco Giants and Padres up the ante for his services for the next five years.

Naturally, the Padres expect Garvey to continue his star status in San Diego and come out of the deal in the black. Ticket sales showed an immediate boost after the Padres signed Garvey on December 21, just one day before he celebrated his 34th birthday.

While Garvey was the most established star available among the 41 free agents who went through the re-entry draft in 1982, Floyd Bannister, a southpaw hurler who led the American League in strikeouts with 209 for the Seattle Mariners in '82, was the most popular player.

Bannister, who had a 12-13 won-lost mark in '82 and a 51-68 ledger for five big-league seasons with Houston and Seattle, was chosen by 16 clubs.

With a hard-throwing lefthanded starting pitcher becoming such a rare commodity in today's marketplace, the St. Louis Cardinals, New York Yankees, Philadelphia Phillies, Kansas City Royals and Chicago White Sox battled down to the wire for Bannister.

On December 14, Bannister accepted a five-year package worth $4.5 million from the White Sox. And presumably, he turned down an extra $1 million offer because his family preferred to live in Chicago.

George Steinbrenner remained the most active member in baseball's annual re-entry proceedings by signing three more free agents. He lured outfielder-designated hitter Don Baylor away from the California Angels and also brought White Sox outfielder Steve Kemp and Cincinnati lefthander Bob Shirley into the Yankees fold.

Bannister and Kemp, along with Baltimore's John Lowenstein, were the only Type A players in the draft. Signing them required compensation of a player from the free-agent pool as well as a first-round draft choice.

The Atlanta Braves signed a pair of lefthanded pitchers from the re-entry list, starter Pete Falcone from the New York Mets and reliever Terry Forster from the Dodgers. Bill Almon of the White Sox, Alan Ashby of the Houston Astros, Falcone and Joe Nolan of the Baltimore Orioles were classified as Type B players in the draft and compensation of a draft choice would be due the club losing the free agent.

Other key players who switched clubs included: Reliever Tom Burgmeier, who left the Red Sox to join Oakland; Almon, who also signed with the A's; Pittsburgh outfielder Omar Moreno, who signed with Houston, and Cardinals catcher Gene Tenace, who agreed to terms with the Pirates.

Ashby, Kansas City designated hitter Hal McRae, Montreal reliever Woodie Fryman and Milwaukee lefthander Bob McClure headed a long list of players who had re-signed with their 1982 clubs.

Reggie Smith, who was the starting first baseman for the Giants in '82, accepted a multi-year pact with Tokyo Giants of the Japanese League.

Following is a list of the 41 players eligible for the 1982 re-entry draft. The number in parentheses following the player's name indicates the number of clubs that selected that player. Those clubs that chose to retain the rights to a free agent are listed in capital letters:

Type A Players

Floyd Bannister (16)—Braves, Orioles, Cubs, White Sox, Indians, Astros, Royals, Brewers, Mets, Yankees, Phillies, Pirates, Cardinals, Padres, Rangers, Blue Jays.

Steve Kemp (9)—Orioles, Cubs, WHITE SOX, Indians, Astros, Yankees, Phillies, Pirates, Rangers.

John Lowenstein (7)—ORIOLES, Royals, Brewers, Pirates, Giants, Rangers, Blue Jays.

Type B Players

Bill Almon (4)—WHITE SOX, Indians, Yankees, Pirates.

Alan Ashby (4)—ASTROS, Yankees, Pirates, Giants.

Pete Falcone (5)—Braves, Angels, METS, Pirates, Blue Jays.

Joe Nolan (7)—ORIOLES, Astros, Mets, Phillies, Cardinals, Giants, Rangers.

The San Diego Padres are hoping their new, eight-time All Star first baseman can do for them what he did for the L.A. Dodgers.

Others

Glenn Adams (1)—Mariners.

Alan Bannister (3)—Phillies, Pirates, Giants.

Don Baylor (6)—Orioles, Astros, Brewers, Yankees, Pirates, Rangers.

Bruce Bochte (3)—Royals, Giants, Blue Jays.

Tom Burgmeier (10)—RED SOX, White Sox, Astros, Brewers, Mets, A's, Pirates, Cardinals, Rangers, Blue Jays.

Al Cowens (9)—Orioles, Royals, Mets, Yankees, Pirates, Giants, MARINERS, Rangers, Blue Jays.

Miguel Dilone (0)—None.

Terry Forster (16)—Braves, Red Sox, Angels, Cubs, White Sox, Indians, Astros, Brewers, Expos, Mets, Yankees, Pirates, Cardinals, Padres, Giants, Rangers.

Woodie Fryman (5)—Brewers, EXPOS, Phillies, Pirates, Cardinals.

Kiko Garcia (0)—None.

Steve Garvey (9)—Cubs, White Sox, Astros, Yankees, Pirates, Padres, Giants, Mariners, Rangers.

Ron Hodges (6)—Orioles, Cubs, Astros, METS, Cardinals, Rangers.

Don Hood (0)—None.

Rick Manning (6)—White Sox, INDIANS, Astros, Brewers, Pirates, Rangers.

Bob McClure (12)—Braves, Orioles, Red Sox, Angels, White Sox, Astros, BREWERS, Mets, A's, Phillies, Pirates, Cardinals.

Dave McKay (0)—None.

Hal McRae (4)—Angels, ROYALS, Yankees, Pirates.

Randy Moffitt (1)—Blue Jays.

Omar Moreno (6)—Angels, Cubs, Astros, Yankees, PIRATES, Rangers.

Wayne Nordhagen (2)—Cubs, Mariners.

Mike Phillips (0)—None.

Jamie Quirk (8)—Cubs, ROYALS, Mets, Yankees, Pirates, Cardinals, Mariners, Rangers.

Bill Robinson (0)—None.

Aurelio Rodriguez (2)—Cubs, Yankees.

Bob Shirley (13)—Braves, Orioles, Cubs, White Sox, REDS, Brewers, Expos, Yankees, Phillies, Pirates, Mariners, Rangers, Blue Jays.

Reggie Smith (0)—None.

Paul Splittorff (7)—ROYALS, Yankees, Pirates, Cardinals, Giants, Rangers, Blue Jays.

Fred Stanley (1)—Blue Jays.

Steve Swisher (0)—None.

Gene Tenace (9)—Red Sox, Indians, Royals, Mets, Yankees, Phillies, Pirates, CARDINALS, Rangers.

Luis Tiant (0)—None.

Ellis Valentine (1)—Pirates.

Bump Wills (1)—Yankees.

Joel Youngblood (8)—Cubs, Astros, Yankees, Phillies, Pirates, Giants, Mariners, Rangers.

NOTE—The following players, selected by fewer than four clubs (excluding a player's former club), are free to negotiate with any club: Adams, Almon, Ashby, A. Bannister, Bochte, Dilone, Garcia, Hood, McKay, McRae, Moffitt, Nordhagen, Phillips, Robinson, Rodriguez, Smith, Stanley, Swisher, Tiant, Valentine, Wills.

A's, Jays Take Two in Draft

Nine players were selected in baseball's annual major league draft, conducted December 6 in Honolulu, Hawaii. Players with three years in the minors who were left off the parent club's 40-man roster were eligible to be purchased by another major league club for $25,000.

With clubs drafting in inverse order of their 1982 records by leagues, the Reds had the first choice and selected catcher Dann Bilardello from the Dodgers' organization. Bilardello hit .285 with 17 home runs at San Antonio (Texas) in '82. He threw out 42 basestealers in 96 games.

The Twins tapped lefthanded pitcher Paul Gibson, 3-3 at Birmingham, the Tigers' Southern League affiliate. Gibson had 12 saves and struck out 71 batters in 77 innings.

The A's and Blue Jays were the only teams to take more than one player. Oakland selected infielders Luis Quinones and German Rivera. Quinones, a shortstop in the Padres' system, batted .292 at Amarillo (Texas); Rivera, who played shortstop and third base for San Antonio, hit .289 with 15 homers. Toronto selected two pitchers: Jim Acker of the Braves' organization and Mercedes Esquer of the Padres' organization.

Of the nine players selected, only outfielder Joe Simpson and pitcher Odell Jones had major league experience. Simpson, selected by the Royals, batted .257 in 105 games with Seattle. Jones, chosen by the Rangers, had pitched for Pittsburgh and Seattle. In '82, he was 16-9 for Portland, Pittsburgh's Pacific Coast League farm.

Draft choices in order of selection:

FIRST ROUND

Reds—Catcher Dann Bilardello from Albuquerque (Pacific Coast) of the Dodgers' organization.

Twins—Pitcher Paul Gibson from Evansville (American Association) of the Tigers' organization.

Rangers—Pitcher Odell Jones from Portland (Pacific Coast) of the Padres' organization.

A's—Infielder Luis Quinones from Hawaii (Pacific Coast) of the Padres' organization.

Blue Jays—Pitcher Jim Acker from Richmond (International) of the Braves' organization.

Royals—Outfielder Joe Simpson from Salt Lake City (Pacific Coast) of the Mariners' organization.

Cardinals—Pitcher Kurt Kepshire from Indianapolis (American Association) of the Reds' organization.

SECOND ROUND

A's—Infielder German Rivera from Albuquerque (Pacific Coast) of the Dodgers' organization.

Blue Jays—Pitcher Mercedes Esquer from Portland (Pacific Coast) of the Pirates' organization.

Major League Attendance for 1982

NATIONAL LEAGUE			AMERICAN LEAGUE		
	Home	Away		Home	Away
Atlanta	1,801,985	1,985,595	Baltimore	1,613,031	1,622,107
Chicago	1,249,278	1,827,275	Boston	1,950,124	1,752,071
Cincinnati	1,326,528	1,745,770	California	2,807,360	1,897,660
Houston	1,558,555	1,585,541	Chicago	1,567,787	1,657,869
Los Angeles	3,608,881	2,250,191	Cleveland	1,044,021	1,476,546
Montreal	2,318,292	1,564,412	Detroit	1,636,058	1,610,612
New York	1,323,036	1,624,181	Kansas City	2,284,464	1,602,561
Philadelphia	2,376,394	1,848,941	Milwaukee	1,978,896	1,831,965
Pittsburgh	1,024,106	1,766,903	Minnesota	921,186	1,452,080
St. Louis	2,111,906	1,850,533	New York	2,041,219	2,206,859
San Diego	1,607,516	1,740,929	Oakland	1,735,489	1,709,054
San Francisco	1,200,948	1,717,154	Seattle	1,070,404	1,354,339
			Texas	1,154,432	1,514,425
Total	21,507,425	21,507,425	Toronto	1,275,978	1,392,301
			Total	23,080,449	23,080,449

Smith Swap Put Cards on Top

By CARL CLARK

One of the most important transactions of 1982 had its origins in incidents of the previous year.

Garry Templeton, the brilliant but erratic shortstop of the Cardinals, said in May that he would like to be traded, preferably to San Diego. Then on August 26, Templeton gave the Cardinals reason to reevaluate their reluctance to honor that request when he made a series of obscene gestures at fans who had booed him for failing to run out a ground ball. Templeton was fined and suspended, and agreed to undergo psychiatric examination.

"I promised him I would try to trade him," Whitey Herzog said in November. "I'd really like not to trade him. I think we'd have a better ball club if he would clean up his act and play like he can."

Herzog, then the Cardinals' general manager as well as field manager, had changed his tune by mid-December. "I can't win a pennant with that boy," he said. "I feel I might win a world championship if I get a shortstop who goes out there every day and hounds that ball."

That ball hound was Ozzie Smith, who was available because the Padres feared they would lose him to free agency after the 1983 season. Blocking a swap was the no-trade clause in Smith's one-year contract. That contract had expired, but Smith's agent, Ed Gottlieb, said, "The no-trade clause is for ad infinitum." Smith was willing to accept the trade, however, if the Cardinals would raise his salary to $750,000.

The clubs waited for Smith to act. If Smith filed for arbitration, his new contract would not have a no-trade clause. If he didn't file, the Padres would renew his contract with the maximum cut of 20 percent. Finally, on February 11, the impasse was broken; Smith would okay the trade, and his '82 salary would be decided by special arbitration. Smith sought $750,000, the Cardinals offered $450,000.

Not only did the decision go in the Cardinals' favor, but they got that world championship, too. Surprisingly, Smith hit for a higher average than Templeton (.248 to .247). Not so surprisingly, Smith accepted 159 more chances than Templeton, made 13 fewer errors and participated in 31 more double plays. He won his third consecutive Gold Glove and a place on The Sporting News National League All-Star team.

In other preseason deals of import, the

Third baseman Doug DeCinces paid big dividends for California in his first season as the Angels captured the A.L. West title.

Angels landed third baseman Doug DeCinces and the Expos pried loose Al Oliver from the Rangers.

DeCinces, whom California acquired from the Orioles for outfielder Dan Ford, had his finest season as the Angels won the American League West title. He hit .301 with 30 home runs and 97 runs batted in and finished third in the voting for the league's Most Valuable Player Award.

The Expos, after getting Oliver for outfielder-third baseman Larry Parrish and first baseman Dave Hostetler, were heavy favorites to take the N.L. East crown. They failed, but Oliver was blameless. The

Little did San Diego's Ozzie Smith and St. Louis' Garry Templeton, shown here in a 1981 game, realize that they would be traded for each other less than a year later.

35-year-old first baseman won his first batting title with a .331 average, hit 22 homers and drove in 109 runs. He placed fourth in the N.L. MVP balloting.

The Mariners probably weren't expecting Bill Caudill to make like Goose Gossage when they obtained him from the Yankees on April 1 along with pitcher Gene Nelson and outfielder Bobby Brown for Shane Rawley. Caudill, however, taking Rawley's role as the short man in the Mariners' bullpen, won 12 games and saved 26. His strikeout ratio, 10.4 per nine innings, was the best in the majors.

The next trades of consequence were made in late August. Locked in tight races, the Angels and Brewers needed pitching help. Both got it. The Brewers traded outfielder Kevin Bass and pitchers Mike Madden and Frank DiPino, all of whom were playing for Vancouver (Pacific Coast), to the Astros for Don Sutton. The Angels picked up Tommy John from the Yankees for minor league pitcher Dennis Rasmussen. Sutton and John won four games apiece for their new teams. Sutton's 10-2 victory over the Orioles on the last day of the season gave the Brewers the A.L. East title.

There wasn't much action at the winter meetings in Honolulu, Hawaii. Certainly not enough to satisfy a wheeler-dealer like Herzog.

"You go to the World Series," Herzog said, "and teams say, 'Let's wait for free agency before we make a deal.' You go to the winter meetings and they say, 'Let's wait until the interleague period in the spring.' They all think they've got pennant winners. I can't believe they won't get off their butts."

The Phillies didn't wear out any chairs. They traded second baseman Manny Trillo, infielder Julio Franco, outfielder George Vukovich, pitcher Jay Baller and minor league catcher Gerry Willard to the Indians for outfielder Von Hayes. A few days after the meetings had ended, they sent pitcher Mike Krukow and minor leaguers Mark Davis, a pitcher, and Charles Penigar, an outfielder, to the Giants for second baseman Joe Morgan and reliever Al Holland.

The 24-year-old Hayes, who the Phillies believe has enormous potential, hit .250 with 14 homers and 82 RBIs in '82, his first full season in the majors.

"I'm flattered to be traded for someone like Manny Trillo," said Hayes. "He's one of the best second basemen in the game. (Trillo made only five errors in '82. In one stretch, he went a record 89 games without an error.) It would have been a fair swap for Cleveland if they traded me for Trillo straight up."

Indians President Gabe Paul disagreed.

"Without Baller and Franco," he said, "there was no deal." Franco, 24, batted .300, hit 21 homers and had 33 stolen bases at Oklahoma City (American Association). One scout called Baller, 9-8 with a 2.68 ERA at Reading (Eastern), "the best pitching prospect I've seen in three years." Baller struck out 155 batters in 151⅓ innings.

Morgan hit .289 with 14 homers and 24 stolen bases but is 39 years old and could not come to terms with the Giants. Holland was 7-3 and had five saves.

"Before we went to the winter meetings, we wrote down the names of the players we wanted most," said Phillies President Bill Giles. "Those players were Von Hayes, Joe Morgan and Al Holland. Now, we have them all."

Only one other major trade was consummated at the winter meetings. The Red Sox traded third baseman Carney Lansford, the A.L. batting champ in 1981, outfielder Garry Hancock and pitcher Jerry King to the A's for outfielder Tony Armas and catcher Jeff Newman. Armas, named A.L. Player of the Year by The Sporting News in 1981, has hit 85 homers the past three seasons. A right fielder for Oakland, Armas will play center field for Boston.

Dick Wagner finished dismantling the Big Red Machine. Unwilling to meet George Foster's contract demands, the Reds president traded him to the Mets in February for catcher Alex Trevino and pitchers Greg Harris and Jim Kern. After signing a $10 million pact, Foster proceeded to hit .247 with just 13 homers and 70 RBIs. Even in the shortened '81 season, Foster had 22 homers and 90 RBIs. In December, the Reds returned Tom Seaver to the Mets for pitcher Charlie Puleo and minor leaguers Lloyd McClendon and Jason Felice. Seaver had been with the Reds since June, 1977, and had posted a 75-46 (.620) record. He slumped to 5-13 in '82, however, his first losing record in 16 seasons.

"When I left the Mets' organization," said Seaver, "I didn't really think I would be back. It's just starting to dawn on me that I'm a Met again and I couldn't be happier. This (1983) will be a year of mission for me."

A chronological listing of major league deals and free-agent signings in 1982 follows:

January 6—Rangers signed pitcher Frank Tanana, a re-entry free agent formerly with the Red Sox.

January 6—Dodgers traded pitcher Bobby Castillo and outfielder Bobby Mitchell to Twins for catcher Scotti Madison and pitcher Paul Voigt, who was assigned to Albuquerque.

January 8—Mets traded pitcher Ray Searage to Indians for shortstop Tom Veryzer.

January 12—Expos signed catcher Tim Blackwell, a re-entry free agent formerly with the Cubs.

January 12—Expos re-signed shortstop Chris Speier, a re-entry free agent.

January 12—Angels released outfielder Larry Harlow.

January 15—Rangers signed first baseman Lamar Johnson, a re-entry free agent formerly with the White Sox.

January 15—Indians re-signed pitcher Rick Waits, a re-entry free agent.

January 15—Mariners re-signed pitcher Glenn Abbott, a re-entry free agent.

January 19—Indians released catcher-outfielder Ron Pruitt.

January 19—Royals signed outfielder Tom Poquette, a re-entry free agent formerly with the Rangers.

January 19—Tigers released infielder Stan Papi.

January 19—Expos traded pitcher Grant Jackson to Royals for first baseman Ken Phelps, who was assigned to Wichita.

January 20—Phillies re-signed pitcher Ron Reed, a re-entry free agent.

January 20—Indians signed catcher Bill Nahorodny, a free agent, and assigned him to Charleston, W. Va.

January 20—Indians re-signed pitcher Sid Monge, a re-entry free agent.

January 22—Angels signed outfielder Reggie Jackson, a re-entry free agent formerly with the Yankees.

January 23—Astros re-signed outfielder Tony Scott, a re-entry free agent.

January 25—Phillies re-signed pitcher Larry Christenson, a re-entry free agent.

January 26—Red Sox' Pawtucket affiliate purchased pitcher John Verhoeven from Twins.

January 27—Phillies traded shortstop Larry Bowa and infielder Ryne Sandberg to Cubs for shortstop Ivan DeJesus.

January 27—Indians purchased catcher Craig Stimac from Padres and assigned him to Charleston, W. Va.

January 28—Angels traded outfielder Dan Ford to Orioles for third baseman Doug DeCinces and pitcher Jeff Schneider.

January 28—Phillies signed pitcher Ed Farmer, a re-entry free agent formerly with the White Sox.

January 29—Angels re-signed catcher Ed Ott, a re-entry free agent.

January 29—Indians released pitcher Wayne Garland.

February 1—Cardinals traded pitcher Donnie Moore to Braves for pitcher Dan Morogiello; Moore, on Louisville roster, was assigned to Richmond, and Morogiello, on Richmond roster, was assigned to Louisville.

February 2—Rangers signed pitcher Jim Gideon, a free agent, and assigned him to Denver.

February 3—Royals' Omaha affiliate signed pitcher Dave Frost, a free agent.

February 5—Brewers released pitcher Reggie Cleveland.

February 5—Astros signed pitcher Randy Moffitt, a free agent, and assigned him to Tucson.

February 8—Dodgers traded second baseman Davey Lopes to A's for second baseman Lance Hudson; Hudson, on Modesto roster, was assigned to Lodi.

February 8—Indians purchased pitcher Mike Stanton from Cardinals' Louisville affiliate and assigned him to Charleston, W. Va.; released him February 13.

February 9—Reds traded pitcher Paul Moskau to Orioles for a player to be named; Reds acquired infielder Wayne Krenchicki to complete deal, February 16.

February 9—Reds signed pitcher Andy Replogle, a free agent, and assigned him to Indianapolis; released him April 5.

February 10—Reds traded outfielder George Foster to Mets for catcher Alex Trevino and pitchers Jim Kern and Greg Harris.

February 11—Padres traded shortstop Ozzie Smith to Cardinals for shortstop Garry Templeton.

February 11—White Sox signed infielder Pete Mackanin, a re-entry free agent formerly with the Twins; released him March 29.

February 12—Tigers signed outfielder Jerry Turner, a re-entry free agent formerly with the White Sox.

February 13—Indians re-signed pitcher John Denny, a re-entry free agent.

February 13—White Sox signed infielder Steve Dillard and catcher Dave Richards, free agents, and assigned them to Edmonton.

February 16—Indians traded pitcher Sid Monge to Phillies for outfielder Bake McBride.

February 16—Giants signed catcher-outfielder Ron Pruitt, a free agent, and assigned him to Phoenix.

February 19—Cubs re-signed pitcher Dick Tidrow, a re-entry free agent.

February 19—Cardinals traded pitcher Luis DeLeon to Padres for pitcher Al Olmsted, completing deal of December 10, 1981, in which Cardinals traded outfielder Sixto Lezcano and a player to be named to Padres for pitcher Steve Mura and a player to be named; Olmsted, on Hawaii roster, was assigned to Louisville.

February 19—Orioles signed pitcher Jesse Jefferson, a re-entry free agent formerly with the Blue Jays, and assigned him to Rochester; released him April 1.

February 19—Orioles acquired outfielder Rick Lisi from Rangers for a player to be named; Rangers acquired pitcher Steve Luebber to complete deal, February 23. Lisi was assigned to Rochester, Luebber to Denver.

February 22—Yankees purchased third baseman Barry Evans from Padres and assigned him to Columbus, O.

February 24—A's traded pitcher Craig Minetto to Orioles for pitcher Allen Edwards. Minetto was assigned to Rochester; Edwards, on Rochester roster, was assigned to West Haven.

February 25—Padres released pitcher John Littlefield.

February 25—Red Sox signed pitcher Mark Fidrych, a free agent, and assigned him to Pawtucket.

February 27—Giants signed outfielder Reggie Smith, a re-entry free agent formerly with the Dodgers.

March 1—Tigers traded pitchers Jack Smith and Mark Fellows and outfielder Darrell Brown to A's for infielder Jeff Cox and catcher Scott Meyer. Cox and Meyer, on Tacoma roster, were assigned to Evansville; Brown, on Evansville roster, was assigned to Tacoma, and Fellows, on Lakeland roster, was assigned to Madison.

March 2—Royals acquired pitcher Bud Black from Mariners to complete deal of October 23, 1981, in which Royals traded infielder Manny Castillo to Mariners for a player to be named.

March 4—Giants traded third baseman-first baseman Enos Cabell and cash to Tigers for outfielder-first baseman Champ Summers.

March 5—Brewers traded outfielder Thad Bosley to Mariners for pitcher Mike Parrott.

March 5—Mariners signed pitcher Gaylord Perry, a free agent.

March 6—Padres signed pitcher John Montefusco, a re-entry free agent formerly with the Braves.

March 10—Tigers' Evansville affiliate purchased pitcher Mark Lee from Pirates.

March 10—Tigers signed catcher Kevin Pasley, a free agent, and assigned him to Evansville.

March 15—Cubs released second baseman Mike Tyson.

March 15—Expos traded outfielder-first baseman Dan Briggs to Cubs for a player to be named; Expos acquired pitcher Mike Griffin and assigned him to Wichita to complete deal, March 26.

March 20—White Sox purchased pitcher Geoff Combe from Reds and assigned him to Edmonton.

March 21—White Sox traded pitchers Butch Edge and Ross Baumgarten to Pirates for infielder Vance Law and pitcher Ernie Camacho. Edge was assigned to Portland, Camacho to Edmonton.

March 23—Braves released outfielder Brian Asselstine.

March 23—Braves traded outfielder Eddie Miller to Tigers for pitcher Roger Weaver, who was assigned to Richmond.

March 24—Angels traded third baseman Butch

Hobson to Yankees for pitcher Bill Castro.

March 24—Royals traded pitcher Jeff Schattinger to White Sox for infielder Greg Pryor.

March 24—Yankees traded first baseman Dennis Werth to Royals for pitcher Scot Behan; Behan, on Sarasota roster, was assigned to Fort Lauderdale.

March 25—Blue Jays traded pitcher Phil Huffman to Royals for shortstop Rance Mulliniks; Huffman was assigned to Omaha.

March 25—Blue Jays acquired pitcher Dave Geisel from Cubs to complete deal of December 12, 1981, in which Blue Jays traded pitcher Paul Mirabella for a player to be named.

March 26—Rangers released pitcher Bob Lacey.

March 26—Padres released pitcher John Urrea.

March 26—Reds traded catcher Joe Nolan to Orioles for pitcher Brooks Carey and outfielder Dallas Williams; Carey and Williams were assigned to Indianapolis.

March 26—Rangers traded second baseman Bump Wills to Cubs for pitcher Paul Mirabella, a player to be named and cash; Rangers acquired pitcher Paul Semall and assigned him to Denver to complete deal, April 21.

March 26—Indians released infielder Dave Rosello.

March 26—Twins released first baseman-outfielder Tim Corcoran.

March 26—Phillies released pitcher Dave Rajsich.

March 28—Astros traded catcher-infielder Dave Roberts to Phillies for pitcher Steve Dunnegan, who was assigned to Columbus, Ga.

March 28—Blue Jays released pitcher Juan Berenguer and Nino Espinosa and third baseman Ted Cox.

March 28—Mariners purchased outfielder Al Cowens from Tigers.

March 28—Tigers released pitcher George Cappuzzello.

March 29—Braves released pitchers Rick Matula and Larry Bradford and infielder Luis Gomez.

March 29—Brewers released pitcher Mike Parrott.

March 29—Cubs acquired outfielder Bob Molinaro from White Sox to complete deal of August 15, 1981, in which Cubs traded pitcher Lynn McGlothen to White Sox for a player to be named.

March 29—Phillies reclaimed catcher Miguel Ibarra from Cubs, who had selected Ibarra from Oklahoma City in the 1981 major league draft.

March 29—Cardinals reclaimed pitcher Rafael Pimentel from Cubs, who had selected Pimentel from Springfield in the 1981 major league draft.

March 29—Phillies released pitcher Mike Proly and catcher Don McCormack.

March 29—Reds released oufielder Sam Mejias.

March 29—Pirates sold outfielder Matt Alexander to Mexico City Tigers.

March 29—Giants released pitcher Doug Capilla.

March 29—Mariners released shortstop Jim Anderson and pitcher Ken Clay.

March 29—Astros reclaimed infielder Clifton Wherry from Padres, who had selected Wherry from Tucson in the 1981 major league draft.

March 30—Expos traded pitcher Elias Sosa to Tigers for a player to be named; deal was later completed by a cash settlement.

March 30—Giants traded pitchers Vida Blue and Bob Tufts to Royals for pitchers Atlee Hammaker, Craig Chamberlain and Renie Martin and a player to be named; Chamberlain was assigned to Phoenix, Tufts to Omaha. Giants acquired second baseman Brad Wellman and assigned him to Phoenix to complete deal, April 19.

March 30—Giants traded pitcher Doyle Alexander to Yankees for pitcher Andy McGaffigan and outfielder Ted Wilborn; McGaffigan and Wilborn were assigned to Phoenix.

March 30—Rangers released catcher-first baseman John Ellis.

March 30—Dodgers traded outfielder Rudy Law to White Sox for outfielder Cecil Espy and pitcher Bert Geiger; Espy was assigned to Vero Beach, Geiger to Albuquerque.

March 31—Blue Jays reclaimed catcher Ramon Lora from Dodgers, who had selected Lora from Syracuse in the 1981 major league draft.

March 31—Expos traded third baseman-outfielder Larry Parrish and first baseman Dave Hostetler to Rangers for first baseman-outfielder Al Oliver.

April 1—Cardinals traded pitcher Bob Shirley to Reds for pitchers Jose Brito and Jeff Lahti; Brito and Lahti were assigned to Louisville.

April 1—Yankees acquired pitcher Bill Caudill from Cubs as partial completion of August 19, 1981 deal in which Yankees traded infielder Pat Tabler to Cubs for two players to be named (Yankees acquired pitcher Jay Howell from Cubs' Iowa affiliate to complete deal, August 2).

April 1—Yankees traded pitchers Gene Nelson and Bill Caudill, cash and a player to be named to Mariners for pitcher Shane Rawley; Mariners acquired outfielder Bobby Brown and assigned him to Salt Lake City to complete deal, April 6.

April 1—Cubs released third baseman Ken Reitz, pitcher Rawly Eastwick and catcher Larry Cox.

April 1—White Sox purchased pitcher Salome Barojas from Mexico City Reds.

April 1—Mets traded outfielder Lee Mazzilli to Rangers for pitchers Ron Darling and Walt Terrell; Darling and Terrell were assigned to Tidewater.

April 1—Angels signed catcher Jerry Narron, a free agent, and assigned him to Spokane.

April 2—Yankees reclaimed pitcher Paul Boris from Twins, who had selected Boris from Columbus, O., in the 1981 major league draft.

April 2—Indians released outfielder Pat Kelly.

April 2—Expos released pitcher Stan Bahnsen.

April 2—White Sox traded outfielder Wayne Nordhagen to Blue Jays for third baseman Aurelio Rodriguez.

April 2—Pirates released catcher Gary Alexander.

April 2—Giants released second baseman Rennie Stennett.

April 2—Mariners released pitcher Dick Drago.

April 3—Pirates purchased pitcher Paul Moskau from Orioles.

April 4—Royals purchased pitcher Mike Armstrong from Padres.

April 4—Astros signed pitcher George Cappuzzello, a free agent, and assigned him to Tucson.

April 5—Giants signed pitcher Jim Barr, a free agent.

April 5—Mets released third baseman Mike Cubbage.

April 5—Orioles signed pitchers Ross Grimsley and Don Stanhouse, free agents.

April 5—Yankees re-signed outfielder Bobby Murcer, a re-entry free agent.

April 5—Yankees traded catcher Brad Gulden to Expos for catcher Bobby Ramos. Gulden was assigned to Wichita; Ramos, on Wichita roster, was assigned to Columbus, O.

April 6—Astros purchased pitcher Mike LaCoss from Reds.

April 6—Angels released shortstop Fred Patek and pitchers Bill Castro and John D'Acquisto.

April 7—A's signed outfielder Jeff Burroughs, a re-entry free agent formerly with the Mariners.

April 8—Angels signed pitcher Stan Bahnsen, a free agent.

April 9—Pirates purchased outfielder Reggie Walton from Mariners' Salt Lake City affiliate and assigned him to Portland.

April 9—Rangers traded pitcher John Henry Johnson to Red Sox for pitcher Mike Smithson; Johnson was assigned to Pawtucket, Smithson to Denver.

April 10—Twins traded shortstop Roy Smalley to Yankees for pitchers Ron Davis and Paul Boris and shortstop Greg Gagne; Boris was assigned to Toledo, Gagne to Orlando.

April 11—Angels signed first baseman Ron Jackson, a re-entry free agent formerly with the Tigers, and assigned him to Spokane.

April 13—White Sox released pitcher Lynn McGlothen.

April 16—Padres released pitcher Rick Wise.

April 21—Angels purchased infielder Mick Kelleher from Tigers.

April 23—Yankees traded first baseman Bob Watson to Braves for pitcher Scott Patterson, who was assigned to Columbus, O.

April 27—Dodgers released pitcher Dave Goltz.

April 27—Braves signed pitcher John D'Acquisto, a free agent and assigned him to Richmond; released him July 27.

April 28—Royals purchased outfielder Steve Hammond from Braves' Richmond affiliate and assigned him to Omaha.

April 28—Orioles traded catcher-designated hitter Jose Morales to Dodgers for third baseman Leo Hernandez; Hernandez, on Albuquerque roster, was assigned to Charlotte.

April 30—Astros released first baseman Mike Ivie.

May 2—A's signed pitcher Bill Castro, a free agent, and assigned him to Tacoma; released him June 25.

May 5—Blue Jays traded first baseman John Mayberry to Yankees for first baseman Dave Revering and third baseman Jeff Reynolds; Reynolds, on Nashville roster, was assigned to Knoxville.

May 5—Expos released outfielder Rowland Office.

May 6—Tigers signed first baseman Mike Ivie, a free agent.

May 8—Expos released second baseman Rodney Scott.

May 9—Expos released pitcher Bill Lee.

May 9—Royals signed pitcher Mike Parrott, a free agent, and assigned him to Jacksonville.

May 12—Twins traded pitcher Doug Corbett and second baseman Rob Wilfong to Angels for outfielder Tom Brunansky, pitcher Mike Walters and cash; Walters was assigned to Toledo.

May 12—Twins traded catcher Butch Wynegar and pitcher Roger Erickson to Yankees for infielder Larry Milbourne and pitchers John Pacella and Pete Filson. Pacella and Filson were on the Columbus, O., roster.

May 14—Angels released pitcher Stan Bahnsen.

May 14—A's traded second baseman Rob Picciolo to Brewers for pitcher Mike Warren and first baseman John Evans. Warren, on Stockton roster, was assigned to Modesto; Evans, on Vancouver roster, was assigned to Tacoma.

May 14—Phillies signed outfielder Rowland Office, a free agent, and assigned him to Oklahoma City.

May 15—Pirates released pitcher Tom Griffin.

May 16—Pirates signed third baseman Ken Reitz, a free agent.

May 16—Astros signed outfielder Bob Pate, a free agent, and assigned him to Tucson.

May 17—Rangers purchased first baseman-outfielder Randy Bass from Padres.

May 18—Twins released pitcher Fernando Arroyo.

May 18—Yankees' Columbus, O., affiliate signed outfielder Bobby Bonds and pitcher Lynn McGlothen, free agents; Bonds was released June 21.

May 21—Mariners purchased catcher Rick Sweet from Mets.

May 22—Expos traded infielder Jerry Manuel, on Wichita roster, to Padres for pitcher Kim Seaman; Seaman, on Hawaii roster, was assigned to Wichita.

May 24—Angels signed pitcher Dave Goltz, a free agent.

May 24—Dodgers purchased pitcher Vicente Romo from Coatzacoalcos.

May 25—Dodgers released outfielder Jay Johnstone.

May 25—A's signed pitcher Fernando Arroyo, a free agent.

May 30—Expos released infielder Mike Phillips.

May 31—Phillies' Oklahoma City affiliate signed pitcher Stan Bahnsen, a free agent.

June 1—Cubs signed outfielder Jay Johnstone, a free agent.

June 5—Pirates released third baseman Ken Reitz.

June 7—Rangers released shortstop Mario Mendoza.

June 8—Phillies released outfielder Del Unser.

June 8—Astros traded infielder Joe Pittman to Padres for pitcher Dan Boone.

June 8—Padres traded infielder Jerry Manuel to Expos for a player to be named; Padres acquired pitcher Mike Griffin to complete deal, August 30.

June 14—White Sox traded third baseman Jim Morrison to Pirates for pitcher Eddie Solomon.

June 15—Yankees signed second baseman Rodney Scott, a free agent, and assigned him to Columbus, O.

June 15—Expos purchased pitcher Dan Schatzeder from Giants.

June 15—Phillies traded outfielder Dick Davis to Blue Jays for outfielder Wayne Nordhagen, then traded Nordhagen to Pirates for first baseman-outfielder Bill Robinson.

June 22—Pirates acquired outfielder Dick Davis from Blue Jays for a player to be named; Blue Jays acquired outfielder Wayne Nordhagen to complete deal, June 25.

June 28—Mariners released infielder Lenny Randle.

June 28—A's released first baseman Jim Spencer.

June 30—Braves traded pitcher Larry McWilliams to Pirates for pitcher Pascual Perez and a player to be named; Perez, on Portland roster, was assigned to Richmond. Braves acquired shortstop Carlos Rios and assigned him to Richmond to complete deal, September 8.

July 1—Pirates released first baseman Willie Montanez.

July 3—Twins traded infielder Larry Milbourne to Indians for outfielder Larry Littleton; Littleton, on Charleston, W. Va. roster, was assigned to Toledo.

July 6—Royals signed pitcher Bill Castro, a free agent.

July 6—Expos released first baseman John Milner.

July 6—Braves released pitcher Preston Hanna.

July 6—White Sox released pitcher Eddie Solomon.

July 9—Royals released pitcher Grant Jackson.

July 15—Blue Jays purchased outfielder Leon Roberts from Rangers.

July 15—A's signed pitcher Preston Hanna, a free agent.

July 15—Orioles released pitcher Don Stanhouse; Stanhouse signed with Orioles' Rochester affiliate July 23.

July 21—Royals released outfielder Tom Poquette.

July 26—Twins released pitcher Darrell Jackson.

July 27—A's Tacoma affiliate released pitcher Fernando Arroyo.

July 29—Pirates signed first baseman John Milner, a free agent.

July 29—White Sox' Edmonton affiliate signed pitcher Fernando Arroyo, a free agent.

August 2—Angels purchased pitcher Luis Tiant from Tabasco.

August 2—Rangers traded infielder Doug Flynn to Expos for future considerations.

August 2—Blue Jays' first baseman Dave Revering was granted free agency when he refused an option to the minors.

August 2—Yankees acquired pitcher Jay Howell from Cubs' Iowa affiliate to complete deal of August 19, 1981, in which Yankees traded infielder Pat Tabler to Cubs for two players to be named (Yankees had acquired pitcher Bill Caudill as partial completion of deal, April 1).

August 4—Mets traded outfielder Joel Youngblood to Expos for a player to be named; Mets acquired pitcher Tom Gorman from Expos' Wichita affiliate and assigned him to Tidewater to complete deal, August 16.

August 6—Mariners signed first baseman Dave Revering, a free agent.

August 8—Rangers traded outfielder Lee Mazzilli to Yankees for shortstop Bucky Dent.

August 10—Phillies' Oklahoma City affiliate signed first baseman Willie Montanez, a free agent.

August 11—Brewers purchased pitcher Doc Medich from Rangers.

August 12—A's signed pitcher John D'Acquisto, a free agent, and assigned him to Tacoma.

August 13—Expos released shortstop Frank Taveras.

August 14—Expos purchased pitcher Randy Lerch from Brewers.

August 16—Tigers traded third baseman-first baseman Richie Hebner to Pirates for a player to be named.

August 21—White Sox purchased pitcher Sparky Lyle from Phillies.

August 23—Reds traded pitcher Jim Kern to White Sox for two players to be named; Reds acquired third baseman Wade Rowdon and outfielder Leo Garcia to complete deal, September 7. Rowdon and Garcia were on Appleton roster.

August 23—Yankees purchased outfielder-infielder Pedro Hernandez from Blue Jays and assigned him to Columbus, O.

August 25—Yankees released infielder Rodney Scott.

August 30—Astros traded pitcher Don Sutton to Brewers for three players to be named; Astros acquired outfielder Kevin Bass and pitchers Mike Madden and Frank DiPino to complete deal, September 3.

August 30—Braves released pitcher Al Hrabosky.

August 30—White Sox purchased pitcher Warren Brusstar from Phillies.

August 30—Blue Jays released pitcher Ken Schrom.

August 31—Angels purchased pitcher John Curtis from Padres.

August 31—Yankees traded pitcher Tommy John to Angels for future considerations; Yankees acquired pitcher Dennis Rasmussen, on Spokane roster, to complete deal, November 24.

September 1—Phillies purchased outfielder Bob Molinaro from Cubs.

September 1—Dodgers activated coach Manny Mota, a pinch-hitter.

September 6—A's released outfielder Rick Bosetti.

September 7—Blue Jays released outfielder Otto Velez.

September 7—Reds traded infielder German Barranca to Tigers for a player to be named; Barranca was assigned to Evansville.

September 8—Expos purchased pitcher Dave Tomlin from Reds' Indianapolis affiliate.

September 10—Pirates signed pitcher Grant Jackson, a free agent.

September 10—Mets traded pitcher Tom Hausman to Braves for pitcher Carlos Diaz.

September 12—Indians traded pitcher John Denny to Phils for outfielder Wil Culmer and pitchers Jerry Reed and Roy Smith; Smith and Culmer were on Oklahoma City roster.

September 20—Yankees released pitcher Lynn McGlothen.

October 4—Pirates released pitchers Paul Moskau and Grant Jackson.

October 7—Padres purchased pitcher Elias Sosa from Tigers.

October 7—Expos purchased first baseman-outfielder Rick Lancellotti from Padres and assigned him to Wichita.

October 8—Tigers released outfielders Rick Peters and Jerry Turner.

October 12—White Sox released pitcher Sparky Lyle.

October 15—Giants released pitcher Bill Bordley.

October 15—Reds purchased pitcher Ted Power from Dodgers' Albuquerque affiliate.

October 15—Giants traded pitcher Al Hargesheimer to Cubs for pitcher Herman Segelke, who was on Iowa roster; Hargesheimer, on Phoenix roster, was assigned to Iowa.

October 15—Padres traded pitcher Tom Tellmann to Brewers for pitchers Weldon Swift and Tim Cook.

October 19—Orioles released pitchers Don Stanhouse and Ross Grimsley.

October 20—Yankees released pitcher Dave LaRoche.

October 23—Dodgers released shortstop Mark Belanger.

October 26—Yankees purchased catcher Brad Gulden from Expos' Wichita affiliate.

October 27—Blue Jays purchased third baseman Tucker Ashford from Yankees' Columbus affiliate.

November 1—Red Sox released first baseman Tony Perez.

November 1—Twins traded pitcher John Pacella to Rangers for pitcher Len Whitehouse.

November 2—Indians released catcher Bill Nahorodny.

November 2—Royals released pitcher Dave Frost and first baseman Dennis Werth.

November 3—Padres released outfielder Dave Edwards.

November 3—Expos purchased catcher Bobby Ramos from Yankees.

November 4—Phillies released first baseman Willie Montanez and pitcher Stan Bahnsen.

November 4—A's released third baseman Mickey Klutts.

November 5—A's traded designated hitter Cliff Johnson to Blue Jays for outfielder Al Woods.

November 5—Mets released pitcher Randy Jones.

November 15—Reds released outfielder Clint Hurdle.

November 15—Royals re-signed designated hitter Hal McRae, a re-entry free agent.

November 16—A's signed pitcher Tom Burgmeier, a re-entry free agent formerly with the Red Sox.

November 18—Indians traded pitcher Ed Whitson to Padres for pitcher Juan Eichelberger and first baseman-outfielder Broderick Perkins.

November 29—Cubs purchased infielder Jay Loviglio from White Sox.

December 1—Braves signed pitcher Terry Forster, a re-entry free agent formerly with the Dodgers.

December 1—Yankees signed designated hitter Don Baylor, a re-entry free agent formerly with the Angels.

December 1—Pirates signed catcher-first baseman Gene Tenace, a re-entry free agent formerly with the Cardinals.

December 2—Cardinals released infielder Julio Gonzalez.

December 3—Astros re-signed catcher Alan Ashby, a re-entry free agent.

December 6—Reds released outfielder-first baseman Larry Biittner.

December 6—Brewers re-signed pitcher Bob McClure, a re-entry free agent.

December 6—A's traded outfielder Tony Armas and catcher Jeff Newman to Red Sox for third baseman Carney Lansford, outfielder Garry Hancock and pitcher Jerry King.

December 8—White Sox sold pitcher Ernesto Escarrega to Mexico City Reds.

December 9—Indians traded outfielder Von Hayes to Phillies for second baseman Manny Trillo, outfielder George Vukovich, infielder Julio Franco, pitcher Jay Baller and catcher Gerry Willard.

December 9—Indians traded shortstop Larry Milbourne to Phillies for a player to be named.

December 9—Yankees traded outfielder-first baseman Dave Collins, pitcher Mike Morgan, first baseman Fred McGriff and cash to Blue Jays for pitcher Dale Murray and outfielder Tom Dodd.

December 9—Yankees signed outfielder Steve Kemp, a re-entry free agent formerly with the White Sox.

December 9—Cubs traded outfielder Steve Henderson to Mariners for pitcher Rich Bordi.

December 10—Astros signed outfielder Omar Moreno, a re-entry free agent formerly with the Pirates.

December 10—Hankyo Braves of Japan signed second baseman Bump Wills, a re-entry free agent formerly with the Cubs.

December 10—Cubs traded pitcher Doug Bird to Red Sox for pitcher Chuck Rainey.

December 10—Mets traded pitcher Mike Scott to Astros for first baseman-outfielder Danny Heep.

December 10—Cubs traded infielder Tye Waller to White Sox for pitcher Reggie Patterson.

December 10—Cubs signed outfielder Wayne Nordhagen, a re-entry free agent formerly with the Blue Jays.

December 10—Blue Jays traded third baseman Dave Baker to Twins for pitcher Don Cooper; Baker was assigned to Toledo, Cooper to Syracuse.

December 13—A's released outfielder Darrell Brown and infielder Kevin Bell.

December 13—White Sox signed pitcher Floyd Bannister, a re-entry free agent formerly with the Mariners.

December 13—Rangers released pitcher Steve Comer.

December 14—Giants traded second baseman Joe Morgan and pitcher Al Holland to Phillies for pitchers Mike Krukow and Mark Davis and outfielder Charles Penigar.

December 15—Indians re-signed outfielder Rick Manning, a re-entry free agent.

December 15—Yankees signed pitcher Bob Shirley, a re-entry free agent formerly with the Reds.

December 15—Indians traded pitcher Ray Searage to Padres for a player to be named.

December 16—Reds traded pitcher Tom Seaver to Mets for pitcher Charlie Puleo, catcher Lloyd McClendon and outfielder Jason Felice.

December 20—Braves signed pitcher Pete Falcone, a re-entry free agent formerly with the Mets.

December 20—A's released pitcher Preston Hanna.

December 21—Padres signed first baseman Steve Garvey, a re-entry free agent formerly with the Dodgers.

December 21—Rangers traded first baseman Pat Putnam to Mariners for pitcher Ron Musselman.

December 22—Yankees traded first baseman-outfielder Lee Mazzilli to Pirates for catcher John Holland, pitcher Tim Burke, infielder Jose Rivera and outfielder Don Aubin. Burke was assigned to Columbus, O.; Holland, Rivera and Aubin were assigned to Nashville.

December 23—Expos re-signed pitcher Woodie Fryman, a re-entry free agent.

December 28—Mets traded pitcher Pat Zachry to Dodgers for outfielder Jorge Orta.

December 29—Rangers signed outfielder-first baseman Larry Biittner, a free agent.

December 30—Royals re-signed pitcher Paul Splittorff, a re-entry free agent.

Paige, L. Waner Died in '82

Foremost among the baseball men who died in 1982 were the legendary Satchel Paige and the always dependable Lloyd Waner, both members of the Hall of Fame.

Paige, who didn't make his major league debut until he was 42—at least 42, Bill Veeck would say—was named to the Hall of Fame in 1971 by a special committee set up to select the top players from black baseball. Paige won a modest 28 games in the American League, but pitching year-round in his prime, supplementing his work in the Negro leagues with barnstorming and forays into Latin America, he almost certainly had won more than 1,500 games before he ever stepped onto a major league diamond.

A righthander with a wicked fastball and pinpoint control, Paige began his professional career in 1926 with the Chattanooga Black Lookouts of the Negro Southern League. In 1931 he joined the Pittsburgh Crawfords. Players like Josh Gibson, Oscar Charleston and Judy Johnson made the Crawfords a powerhouse, and Paige won at least 90 games in three seasons with them. Though the records are sketchy, he is believed to have won 31 games and pitched 16 shutouts in 1933.

Satchel spent the 1934 and '35 seasons with a semipro club that operated out of Bismarck, N.D. One of its exhibitions was at Yankee Stadium against Dizzy Dean and a team of major league regulars. Before 30,000 fans, Paige bested Dean, 1-0, in 13 innings.

"If Satch and I were pitching on the same team," said Dean, "we'd cinch the pennant by July 4 and go fishing until World Series time."

After pitching Bismarck to the championship in the first National Baseball Congress tournament in 1935, Paige again hooked up with the Crawfords. A year later, however, he jumped the club again to pitch first in Venezuela and then the Dominican Republic. When he returned to the States in 1938, he found that his contract belonged to the Kansas City Monarchs. That was fine with Paige, since he had kept a home in Kansas City for many years.

Ten years and several championships later, Paige still was going strong for the Monarchs and Veeck, owner of the Cleveland Indians, was looking for another pitcher. Abe Saperstein, who ran the Harlem Globetrotters and did some scouting for Veeck, recommended Paige. An im-

Lloyd Waner was a Hall of Famer with both bat and glove.

pressive tryout convinced Veeck, and a few days later, July 9, 1948, Paige became the first black pitcher in the American League.

How old was he? Well, Veeck claimed to have a 1921 newspaper clipping which said that Paige struck out 17 men "with his customary ease," suggesting that Paige already had established a reputation at that early date. "Satch," Veeck said, "I'm just sorry you didn't come up in your prime. You'd have been one of the greatest righthanders baseball has ever known." Satch's usual reply to such lamentations: "Age is a question of mind over matter. If you don't mind, it doesn't matter."

Paige played an important role in the Indians' capture of the 1948 pennant. In 21 appearances, most of them in relief, he had a 6-1 record with a 2.47 ERA. Cleveland defeated the Boston Braves in the World Series, but Paige made only a token appearance.

Paige finished 4-7 in 1949 and was released. He went back to barnstorming with an assurance from Veeck, who had sold the Indians, that another job was his as soon as Veeck got back into baseball.

The wait wasn't long. Veeck bought the

A pair of Hall of Famers, Rogers Hornsby and Satchel Paige, were teamed up during the 1952 season. Hornsby was the St. Louis Browns manager while Paige was a relief specialist.

St. Louis Browns in 1951 and Paige joined the club in July. He posted a 3-4 record with a last-place team and managed a 12-10 mark for a seventh-place club the next season. He faltered in 1953, finishing 3-9 for another bad club. Veeck sold out and Satch was out of a job again.

Paige pitched only one more game in the majors, three scoreless innings for Charley Finley's Kansas City A's in 1965, but did turn in three solid seasons for Veeck at Miami (International League), winning 31 games from 1956-58.

Paige returned to the majors one more time, to coach for the Atlanta Braves in 1968-69 so he could qualify for the minimum pension. He died at Kansas City on June 8. He was 75.

Lloyd Waner, who with his older brother Paul battered National League pitching for more than a decade, died at Oklahoma City on July 22. He was 76.

Lloyd, like Paul a lefthanded-hitting outfielder, holds the record for most hits by a rookie. He rapped 223 for Pittsburgh in 1927 and led the league in runs scored (133) while batting .355. Not bad for a 140-pound reed who had been released by the San Francisco Seals two years earlier. Paul, who had persuaded the Pirates to give Lloyd a chance, batted a league-leading .380 that season, his second with Pittsburgh, as the Pirates won the pennant. Lloyd hit .400 and Paul .333 in the World Series, but the Yankees swept the Pirates. It would be the brothers' only Series appearance.

Lloyd hit .335 in 1928 and .353 in 1929, when he led the league in triples with 20. Appendicitis shelved him for most of the 1930 season, but he came back strong in 1931, leading the league in hits with 214. He went on to hit over .300 in five of the next seven seasons.

In 1941, his 15th season with the Pirates, Lloyd was traded to the Boston Braves for pitcher Nick Strincevich. He also played for Cincinnati, the Philadelphia Phillies and Brooklyn before returning to the Pirates in 1944. He retired after the 1945 season.

Lloyd's batting accomplishments—2,458 hits and a .316 average—overshadowed his defensive play, but with Lloyd in center field and Paul in right, few balls found the gaps and few runners took liberties. Lloyd led N.L. outfielders in putouts four times and had as many as 22 assists in a season. Third baseman Pie Traynor, the Waners' teammate for 11 years, said Lloyd was a better center fielder than Willie Mays. "Mays plays too deep," Traynor said. "Mays gives you all those balls in back of second base. Lloyd played a natural center field and could go in and grab those balls."

Lloyd was elected to the Hall of Fame in 1967, 15 years after the induction of Paul, who died in 1965. "It was the biggest thrill and the biggest surprise I ever had," Lloyd said. "I just wish Paul had been here to see it."

Frank McCormick, Jackie Jensen and Ken Boyer, all of whom received Most Valuable Player citations for their powerful and timely hitting, also died in 1982.

A slick-fielding first baseman who was with Cincinnati for 10 of his 13 major league seasons, McCormick was at his best from 1938-40. He led the league in hits each season and averaged 120 runs batted in. In 1940, his MVP season, he drove in 127 runs and helped the Reds win their first world championship in 21 years. McCormick also played for the Philadelphia Phillies and Boston Braves. He later scouted and coached for the Reds and for several years was a member of their TV announcing crew. McCormick died in November at the age of 71.

Jensen always was ticketed for stardom. An All-America fullback at the University of California, he passed up his senior year to sign a $75,000 contract with the Oakland Oaks of the Pacific Coast League. The New York Yankees, hoping he would be their next center fielder, purchased his contract in 1950. Jensen and Manager Casey Stengel proved incompatible, however, and in May of 1952 Jensen was traded to Washington.

He did well for the Senators but was traded to the Boston Red Sox after two seasons. Jensen blossomed in Boston. In his first year, he hit 25 home runs, drove in 117 runs and stole a league-leading 22 bases. In seven seasons with the Red Sox, Jensen led the league in RBIs three times. His 35 homers and 122 RBIs in 1958 made him the A.L.'s MVP.

But Jensen was a reluctant star. Fear of flying and marital problems (Jensen's wife was diving champion Zoe Ann Olsen) deprived him of the joy that should have been his. "It's the money—and nothing but the money—that keeps me in baseball today," he once said. Eventually, even that wasn't enough to hold him. He retired after the 1959 season, at age 32, though he did make a brief comeback in 1961.

His marriage could not be saved and Jensen later regretted his early exit. "I thought that being at home year-round might be the answer, that the old life would come back," he told Atlanta writer Furman Bisher in 1974. "It was a terrible mistake."

Jensen was 55 when he died of a heart attack in Charlottesville, Va.

Boyer, one of three brothers who played major league baseball, was signed as a pitcher, but the Cardinals quickly changed their plans for him after he batted .455 in his first minor league season. He worked his way up the ladder as a third baseman, reaching St. Louis in 1955. Except for one season in center field, Boyer manned the hot corner for the Cardinals for 11 years. He batted .300 or better five times, hit 20 or more homers eight times, won five Gold Glove awards and played in 10 All-Star games. In 1964 he won the MVP award on the strength of a league-leading 119 RBIs. In the World Series that year, against the Yankees and his brother Clete, Ken led the Cardinals to a seven-game victory with two home runs, one a grand slam off Al Downing that gave the Cardinals a 4-3 victory in Game 4. Including four seasons with the New York Mets, Chicago White Sox and Los Angeles Dodgers, Boyer belted 282 homers and drove in 1,141 runs.

When he could no longer play, Boyer, a natural leader, turned to managing. After a minor league apprenticeship, he took over the Cardinals in 1978. The Cardinals posted an 86-76 record in 1979, but in 1980 Boyer was fired when the Cardinals lost 33 of their first 51 games. He had been hired to manage St. Louis' American Association club at Louisville for 1982 before tests revealed malignant tumors in both lungs. Boyer succumbed to the cancer in September. He was 51.

Dixie Walker and Wally Post also lost battles with cancer. Walker, who was 71, spent his most productive years with the Brooklyn Dodgers, winning a batting title in 1944 and an RBI crown in 1945. The outfielder's clutch hitting—he drove in more than 1,000 runs—and affability made him a favorite of the Brooklyn fans, the most fervent in baseball. His younger brother, Harry, a former N.L. outfielder and manager, now coaches at the University of Alabama in Birmingham. Initial casting called for Post to be a pitcher, but his vast power forced the Reds to reconsider. Post became an outfielder and hit 210 homers in the majors, most of them for Cincinnati. He was 52.

Heart failure was responsible for Bob Johnson's demise. Johnson, who was 75, spent most of his career with the Philadelphia Athletics. A capable outfielder, he drove in more than 100 runs for the A's in every season from 1935-41 and finished his career with 288 homers and 1,283 RBIs.

Bill DeWitt, the only general manager to have pennant-winning clubs in both major leagues, died in Cincinnati on March 3. He was 79. DeWitt got his first job in 1916 as an office boy for Branch Rickey, then general manager of the Browns. He followed Rickey to the Cardinals the next year and in 1925 became the club's treasurer. DeWitt returned to the Browns in 1936 as general manager. He was named Executive of the Year by The Sporting News in 1944, when under his guidance, the Browns won the only pennant of their 40-year history.

DeWitt and his brother Charley bought a controlling interest in the Browns in 1949, but financial straits forced them to sell their interest to Bill Veeck in 1951. DeWitt became president of the Detroit Tigers in 1959. His term was brief, but he made some controversial deals (Harvey Kuenn for Rocky Colavito, Manager Jimmy Dykes for Indians Manager Joe Gordon) and acquired Norm Cash from the White Sox via the Indians for Steve Demeter, who never had another hit in the majors.

In 1961, DeWitt became the G.M. at Cincinnati and the Reds won their first N.L. pennant in 21 years. But that was far in the past to the Reds fans who were outraged when DeWitt traded Frank Robinson to the Orioles after the 1965 season. "An Old 30," DeWitt called him. Robinson won MVP honors in 1966 and led Baltimore to four A.L. pennants.

DeWitt sold his interest in the Reds after the 1966 season. Since 1972 he had been a member of the Hall of Fame Veterans Committee.

Walter (Red) Smith, nonpareil among American sportswriters, won a Pulitzer Prize in 1976 for "distinguished commentary." His work for the New York Herald-Tribune and the New York Times was notable for its clarity and erudition. Accuracy and integrity were his hallmarks. Smith died in January at Stamford, Conn. He was 76.

Other personalities who died in 1982 included Bob Short, former owner of the Washington Senators and Texas Rangers; Roy Hofheinz, who was instrumental in Houston's attainment of a National League franchise; Joe Dugan, third baseman for the Yankee juggernauts of the 1920s; Ray Fisher, a pitcher for the New York Highlanders/Yankees and Cincinnati who became a successful coach at the University of Michigan; Dave Malarcher and Webster McDonald, standouts in the Negro leagues;·28-year-old heart attack victim Francisco Barrios, a pitcher in the Chicago White Sox' organization from 1974-81; former A.L. umpire Nestor Chylak; and Lou DiMuro, who was in his 20th season as an A.L. umpire. DiMuro was struck by an automobile while he was crossing a street near Arlington Stadium, where a few hours earlier he had worked the Rangers' June 6 night game against the White Sox.

An alphabetical list of baseball deaths in 1982 follows:

James Audrey (Jimmy) Adair, 75, shortstop for the Chicago Cubs in 1931 and a longtime coach and scout, of a heart attack at Dallas, Tex., December 9; coached for the Chicago White Sox in 1951-52, Baltimore from 1956-60 and Houston from 1962-65; scouted for Baltimore, the Kansas City and Oakland A's and the Kansas City Royals.

Bob Addie, 71, Washington sportswriter for nearly 40 years, of cardiac arrest, at Washington, D.C., January 18; covered the Senators from the early 1950s until the club moved to Texas in 1971; his "Addie's Atoms" were a weekly feature of The Sporting News from the early '50s through the late '60s; retired in 1977.

Dale Leonard Alderson, 64, righthander who lost his only decision in 16 games for the Chicago Cubs in 1943-44, at Garden Grove, Calif., February 12.

William Morgan (Bill) Andrus, 74, third baseman who appeared in six games for Washington in 1931 and the Philadelphia Phillies in 1937, at Washington, D.C., March 12.

Robert Schley (Bob) Barrett, 82, infielder for the Chicago Cubs from 1923-25, Brooklyn in 1925 and 1927, and the Boston Red Sox in 1929, at Atlanta, Ga., January 18; a .260 hitter in 239 games, he saw extensive action only in 1927, when he played third base for the Dodgers and batted .259.

Francisco Javier Barrios, 28, righthanded pitcher in the Chicago White Sox' organization from 1974 until his release in September, 1981, of a heart attack at the home of his parents in Hermosillo, Mexico, April 9; worked in two games for the White Sox in 1974 and joined them as a starter in 1976; pitched 129 games for the Sox and had a 38-38 record with a 4.15 ERA; 14-7 in 1977, he began having shoulder problems and underwent surgery for a torn rotator cuff in 1979; in 1976 he pitched the final four innings of a no-hitter against Oakland (Blue Moon Odom pitched the first five); a few months prior to his release, he was charged with possession of cocaine and began voluntary treatment; several major league clubs had expressed interest in signing Barrios for the 1982 season, as he had pitched five shutouts in his last six starts for the Hermosillo Orangepickers of the Mexican Pacific League.

David Irenus (Red) Barron, 82, an outfielder who played 10 games for the Boston Braves in 1929, at Atlanta, Ga., October 4; he was an All-Southern Conference running back at Georgia Tech from 1919-22.

John Frederick (Sheriff) Blake, 83, righthander who was a regular on the Chicago Cubs' staff from 1924-31, at Beckley, W. Va., October 31; broke into the majors in 1920 with Pittsburgh but appeared in only six games and had no record; his record with the Cubs was 81-92, but included a 17-11 mark in 1928, when he led the National League in shutouts with four; the Cubs traded him to the Phillies in 1931 after he lost his first four decisions; finished 4-5 with Philadelphia, then spent the next five seasons in the minors before surfacing briefly with the St. Louis Cardinals and Browns in 1937; his major league record was 87-102; appeared in two World Series games with the Cubs in 1929 and had an 0-1 record.

Porter Blinn, 62, Cincinnati's scouting supervisor for New England, at Hartford, Conn., April 17; he had been with the Reds' organization since 1970.

Alonzo D. Boone, 72, pitcher for several Negro League clubs, including the Cleveland Buckeyes when they won pennants in 1945 and '47, at Cleveland, O., April 10; managed the Buckeyes from 1948 until they folded several years later.

Lute Joseph Boone, 92, infielder who batted .209 in 314 games for the New York Yankees (1913-16) and Pittsburgh (1918), at Pittsburgh, Pa., July 29.

Kenton Lloyd (Ken) Boyer, 51, the National League's Most Valuable Player in 1964 when he led the St. Louis Cardinals to a pennant and a seven-game World Series victory over the New York Yankees, of lung cancer, at St. Louis, Mo., September 7; a solid third baseman for the Cardinals from 1955-65, he also managed the club in all or parts of three seasons (1978-80) and had been

hired to pilot St. Louis' American Association club at Louisville for 1982 before it was learned late in 1981 that he had inoperable malignancies in both lungs; batted .300 or better five times en route to a career average of .287; slugged 282 home runs and drove in 1,141 runs; won five Gold Glove awards; played in 10 All-Star games, batting .348 (8-for-23) with two homers; in his MVP season he batted .295, hit 24 homers and drove in a league-leading 119 runs; hit two homers in the '64 World Series, one a grand slam off Al Downing in Game 4 that accounted for all the Cardinals' runs in a 4-3 victory that tied the Series at two games apiece; slumped to .260 in 1965, his lowest full-season average in the majors, and was traded after the season to the New York Mets for third baseman Charlie Smith and pitcher Al Jackson; the Mets dealt him to the Chicago White Sox midway through the 1967 season, and Chicago released him early in 1968; he then signed with Los Angeles and played two seasons before retiring; coached for the Cardinals in 1971-72 and managed in their minor league system in 1970 and from 1973-76; managed Rochester, Baltimore's International League affiliate, in 1977 and for 10 games in 1978 before taking over the Cardinals; he was fired in 1980 after St. Louis got off to an 18-33 start—his record with the Cardinals was 166-191 (.465); all six of his brothers played professional baseball, two of them in the majors—Clete was a third baseman for the Yankees, Kansas City Athletics and Atlanta, and Cloyd pitched for the Cardinals from 1949-52 and the Athletics in 1955.

Clarence Wilbur (Buster) Bray, 69, outfielder who played four games for the Boston Braves in 1941, September 4.

Leo David Callahan, 91, outfielder who batted .221 in 114 games for Brooklyn in 1913 and the Philadelphia Phillies in 1919, at Erie, Pa., May 2.

Elijah (Eli) Chism, 65, outfielder with the Cleveland Buckeyes and Birmingham Black Barons of the old Negro leagues, at St. Louis, Mo., April 4.

Nestor Chylak Jr., 59, American League umpire for 25 years, at Dunmore, Pa., February 17; began umpiring in Organized Baseball in 1947 and reached the majors in 1954; worked in five World Series (1957-60-66-71-77), five All-Star games (1957, both games in 1960, 1964 and 1973) and three Championship Series (1969-72-73); retired as an active umpire after the '78 season and became the A.L.'s assistant supervisor of umpires.

Alva Warren (Al) Cicotte, 52, righthander who had a 10-13 record with six major league clubs in the late 1950s and early '60s, at Westlake, Mich., November 29; pitched for the New York Yankees in 1957, Detroit and Washington in 1958, Cleveland in 1959, the St. Louis Cardinals in 1961 and Houston in 1962; Topps Minor League Player of the Year in 1960 when he was 16-7 for Toronto and had the International League's lowest ERA, 1.97; grandnephew of Eddie Cicotte, pitcher for the Chicago White Sox from 1912-20 and one of the men who allegedly conspired to throw the 1919 World Series.

Henry (Percy) Dawson, 92, general manager at Norfolk (Piedmont) from 1934-50 and a long-time scout for the New York Yankees and Philadelphia Phillies, at Richmond, Va., January 17; owner and operator of the Richmond Colts of the old Virginia League in the 1920s, he later was credited with scouting and signing Lew Burdette, Bob Porterfield, Bobby Richardson and Jim Coates.

William O. (Bill) DeWitt, 79, the only general manager to have pennant-winning clubs in both major leagues, at Cincinnati, O., March 3; in a career that spanned more than 50 years, he served as farm director of the St. Louis Cardinals, general manager and owner of the St. Louis Browns, assistant general manager of the New York Yankees, president of the Detroit Tigers, general manager and owner of the Cincinnati Reds and board chairman of the Chicago White Sox; he got his start in baseball in 1916 when Branch Rickey, general manager of the Browns, hired him as his office boy; when Rickey made a lateral move to the Cardinals the next year, DeWitt went along and in 1925 became the club's treasurer; in 1936 Rickey was asked to find a buyer for the Browns —he did and convinced him to hire DeWitt, now in charge of the Cardinals' farm system, as general manager; under DeWitt, the Browns won the only pennant of their 40-year history, in 1944, and DeWitt was named Executive of the Year; he and his brother Charley bought a controlling interest in the club in 1949, but attendance problems forced them to sell their interest to Bill Veeck; in 1953, DeWitt became an assistant to Yankees G.M. George Weiss, with the understanding that he would succeed Weiss upon his expected retirement—instead, Weiss signed a new five-year contract in 1956, and DeWitt was let go; he was named president of the Tigers in 1959 (he had administered a plan to help struggling minor league clubs in the interim), but the job lasted just one year; he landed on his feet, however, as Cincinnati, which hadn't won a flag since 1940, took the National League crown in 1961, his first year as general manager; the next spring, he purchased the club from the estate of Powel Crosley for $4.6 million; calling Frank Robinson "an old 30," he traded the popular outfielder to the Orioles after the 1965 season—Robinson won MVP honors in 1966; sold his interest in the Reds after the 1966 season for a $2 million profit; later had interests in the World Hockey Association's Cincinnati Stingers and the Kentucky Colonels of the American Basketball Association; he was one of the largest investors in the syndicate that purchased the White Sox in 1975; served as board chairman of Cincinnati's Riverfront Stadium and since 1972 had been a member of the Hall of Fame Veterans Committee.

Leo Louis Dickerman, 84, righthanded pitcher for Brooklyn in 1923-24 and the St. Louis Cardinals in 1924-25, at Atkins, Ark., April 30; had a 19-27 record in 89 games.

Louis John (Lou) DiMuro, 50, American League umpire since 1963, struck by an automobile while crossing a street near Arlington (Tex.) Stadium, June 7; he was walking alone after working the Rangers' June 6 night game against the White Sox when the accident occurred; umpired in two World Series (1969, '76) and four All-Star games (1965-67-72-81).

Joseph Anthony (Jumpin' Joe) Dugan, 85, third baseman for the New York Yankees during the 1920s, at Norwood, Mass., July 7; signed by Connie Mack in 1917 for $500, he played five seasons with the Philadelphia Athletics; he was traded to the Boston Red Sox early in 1922 and then to New York later that season; remained with the Yankees for seven seasons, then returned to the Red Sox on waivers in 1929; played briefly with Detroit in 1931 before retiring; regarded as an excellent defensive player, he also compiled a career average of .280; batted .267 in five World Series with the Yankees; scouted for the Red Sox from 1955-66; his nickname came from the fact that he left the A's, then a terrible club, at every opportunity, returning to New Haven, Conn., to visit his parents and friends.

Edward Joseph (Ed) Edelen, 69, righthander who pitched in two games for Washington in 1932, at La Plata, Md., February 1.

Russell Earl (Red) Evans, 75, righthander who compiled a 1-11 record in 41 games, most as a reliever, with the Chicago White Sox in 1936 and

Brooklyn in 1939, at Lakeview, Ark., June 18; named Most Valuable Player in the Southern Association in 1938, when he won 21 games for New Orleans.

Raymond Lyle (Ray) Fisher, 95, righthander who had a 97-93 record and 2.82 ERA in 10 seasons with the New York Highlanders/Yankees and Cincinnati, and who went on to become the most successful baseball coach in University of Michigan history, at Ann Arbor, Mich., November 3; pitched for New York from 1910-17 and Cincinnati in 1919-20; best seasons were 1915, when he was 18-11 with a 2.11 ERA, and 1919, when he finished 14-5 with a 2.17 ERA to help the Reds win the National League pennant; offered a contract in 1921 that contained a $1,000 pay cut, he grudgingly signed but soon accepted the coaching position at Michigan—because he was under contract the Reds placed him on the ineligible list and when he wanted to rejoin the team during the summer, Commissioner Landis informed him that he was banned from the game for life; Landis' reasons were nebulous, but included the fact that Fisher had considered a contract offer from an "outlaw league" team in Franklin, Pa.; he was cleared in 1980 by Commissioner Kuhn, who, after being petitioned by Fisher's supporters, told him he should consider himself "a retired player in good standing"; in his 38 years at Michigan (1921-58), his teams won nine Big 10 titles outright and shared four others; the highlight of his coaching career came in 1953 when Michigan won the NCAA championship.

Grover A. Froese, 66, American League umpire from June 1952 through the 1954 season and later a scout for the Philadelphia Phillies, of a heart attack, at Bay Shore, N.Y., July 20.

Albert Frank (Pudgy) Gould, 89, 5-foot, 6½-inch righthander who had a 10-11 record for Cleveland in 1916-17, at San Jose, Calif., August 8; pitched two no-hit games for Muscatine in the old Central Association in 1914.

William B. (Bill) Haeffner, 87, catcher for the Philadelphia Athletics in 1915, Pittsburgh in 1920 and the New York Giants in 1928, at Delaware County, Pa., January 27; in 59 games he batted .194.

James Harrison (Truck) Hannah, 90, catcher for the New York Yankees from 1918-20, at Fountain Valley, Calif., in April; batted .235 in 244 games.

Harvey R. Hansen Sr., 81, one of 11 partners who bought the Detroit Tigers from the Walter O. Briggs family in 1956 for $5.5 million, at Boca Raton, Fla., November 7; he was club president from 1957 until 1959, when he sold his interests in the Tigers to Knorr Broadcasting Co.

Anthony Spencer (Spence) Harris, 82, outfielder who batted .249 in four seasons in the majors, in August; played for the Chicago White Sox in 1925-26, Washington in 1929 and the Philadelphia Athletics in 1930.

Roy M. Hofheinz, 70, the promoter and politician chiefly responsible for getting a National League franchise for Houston and president of that club from 1963-71, after suffering what apparently was a heart attack, at Houston, Tex., November 21; elected Harris County's youngest judge ever at the age of 24, he twice was elected mayor of Houston, the first time when he was 40; teamed with business partner R.E. (Bob) Smith, an oilman and rancher, to back and promote the construction of the world's first domed athletic stadium, the $31.6 million Astrodome; with construction financed by a bond issue passed in 1960, he was able to convince the N.L.'s expansion committee the same year to award the city a franchise—the Colt .45s were born two years later and in 1965 moved into the Astrodome as the Astros;

gained control of the Houston Sports Authority, the parent company that built the dome and nearby Astroworld amusement park, when he bought out Smith for $7.5 million in 1965; in 1970 he suffered a massive stroke that left him partially paralyzed and confined to a wheelchair; mounting debts forced him in 1975 to relinquish control of his organization to Six Flags Corporation under a long-term lease arrangement.

James McDaniel Hopper, 62, righthander who had an 0-1 record in two games for Pittsburgh in 1946, at Charlotte, N.C., January 23.

James Hensel (Hank) Hulvey, 84, losing pitcher in his only major league appearance, for the Philadelphia Athletics in 1923, at Mount Sidney, Va., April 9.

Thomas Carr (Whitey) Hurd, 58, righthanded reliever who had a 13-10 record for the Boston Red Sox from 1954-56, of cancer, at Waterloo, Ia., September 5; in 1955, he was 8-6 with a 3.01 ERA and five saves.

Irvine Franklin (Irv) Jeffries, 76, infielder for the Chicago White Sox in 1930-31 and the Philadelphia Phillies in 1934, at Louisville, Ky., June 8; appeared in 175 games and batted .234; later managed in the minors and scouted for the White Sox in the late 1940s.

Jack Eugene (Jackie) Jensen, 55, the American League's Most Valuable Player in 1958 as an outfielder for the Boston Red Sox, of a heart attack, at Charlottesville, Va., July 14; one of the first big-money bonus babies, he passed up his senior year at the University of California, where he had been an All-America fullback, to sign with the Oakland Oaks of the Pacific Coast League in 1949; the New York Yankees purchased his contract the next year—looked upon as Joe DiMaggio's successor in center field, he didn't measure up to standards and was traded to Washington in May of 1952; although he turned in two respectable seasons for the Senators, he was traded again, to the Red Sox for pitcher Mickey McDermott and outfielder Tom Umphlett; in his first season with Boston, Jensen hit 25 home runs, drove in 117 runs and stole a league-leading 22 bases; he played six more seasons for the Red Sox and drove in more than 100 runs in four of those seasons and hit 20 or more home runs in five; in his MVP season he batted .286 and his 35 homers and 122 RBIs were career highs; fear of flying (during his last few seasons he rode trains on Red Sox trips) and his failing marriage to diving champion Zoe Ann Olsen caused him to retire after the 1959 season, at age 32, but he made a brief comeback in 1961; he averaged .279 over 11 seasons, hit 199 home runs, drove in 929 runs and stole 143 bases; suffered his first heart attack in 1969, when he was baseball coach at the University of Nevada-Reno; after his recovery, he coached at the University of California until he was fired in 1976; in recent years he had run a baseball camp for youngsters and a Christmas tree farm.

Arthur Gilbert (Art) Johnson, 85, lefthander whose major league career consisted of three scoreless innings for the 1927 New York Giants, at Sarasota, Fla., June 7.

Earl W. Johnson, 79, one of the four Chicago businessmen who were the major investors in the Philadelphia and Kansas City Athletics in the 1950s, at Bridgman, Mich., October 23; he and his brother, Arnold, were co-owners of the team from 1954-61; they moved the A's to Kansas City in 1955, Arnold serving as president and Earl as treasurer until the club was sold to Charley Finley after the 1960 season.

Henry Ward Johnson, 76, righthander who compiled a 63-56 record in 249 major league games encompassing 12 seasons, at Bradenton, Fla., August 20; pitched for the New York Yankees in 1925-26 and from 1928-32, the Boston Red Sox from 1933-35, the Philadelphia Athletics in 1936 and Cincinnati in 1939; though he had a winning record, his career ERA was 4.75; best season was 1928, when he was 14-9 and beat Lefty Grove four times.

Robert Lee (Indian Bob) Johnson, 75, outfielder who batted .296 with 288 homers and 1,283 runs batted in over 13 seasons with the Philadelphia Athletics, Washington and the Boston Red Sox, of heart failure, at Tacoma, Wash., July 6; played for Philadelphia from 1933-42, driving in 100 or more runs in seven of those years; traded to the Senators in 1943, he batted .265, the lowest average of his career, but bounced back the following season at Boston with a .324 mark and 106 RBIs; turned in a solid season in 1945 but was released because of the Red Sox's commitment to younger players; returned to the minors, playing in the Pacific Coast League until a knee injury forced his retirement in 1948; named to the American League All-Star team six times; shares the major league record for most RBIs in an inning, six, accomplishing the feat with the A's in 1937; younger brother of Roy Johnson, an outfielder who played for Detroit, the Boston Red Sox, New York Yankees and Boston Bees.

Anthony Charles (Tony) Kaufmann, 81, righthander who had a 64-62 record in 202 major league games in the 1920s and early '30s, and who later managed, coached and scouted in the St. Louis Cardinals' organization, at Elgin, Ill., June 4; pitched for the Chicago Cubs from 1921 through July of 1927, when he was traded to the Philadelphia Phillies; a month later, the Phillies sold him to the Cardinals; he pitched one game for the Cardinals that season and four games in 1928; after he batted .402 as a pitcher-outfielder for Rochester in 1928, the New York Giants drafted him and used him as an outfielder and pinch-runner in 1929, but he managed only one hit in 32 at-bats; he returned to the Cardinals' organization the next season, pitching for the parent club in 1930-31 and 1935; best seasons were 1923, when he won 14 and lost 10, and 1924, when he finished 16-11; managed for the Cardinals at Decatur and Rochester, was a Cardinals scout from 1942-46, a coach from 1947-49 and a scout again from 1950-61.

Hugo Emil Klaerner, 73, righthander who had an 0-2 record in three games for the Chicago White Sox in 1934, at Fredericksburg, Tex., January 3.

Robert Troxell (Ray) Knode, 81, first baseman for Cleveland from 1923-26, at Battle Creek, Mich., April 13; hit .266 in 109 games; younger brother of Mike Knode, who played for the St. Louis Browns in 1920.

Joseph H. LaCour, 62, attorney who had served as secretary for the Boston Red Sox since 1965, at Boston, Mass., April 15.

Peter John (Pete) Layden, 62, outfielder who batted .250 in 41 games for the St. Louis Browns in 1948, at Edna, Tex., July 18; he was an outstanding fullback for the University of Texas from 1939-41.

Pete Leyva, 88, onetime owner of the El Paso (Texas League) franchise and later a scout for the St. Louis Cardinals, Pittsburgh and Brooklyn, at El Paso, Tex., in May.

Alfredo Modesto Lefevre, 83, infielder in 17 games for the New York Giants in 1920, at Glen Cove, N.Y., January 21.

Hillman Lyons, 60, twice cited by The Sporting News as a minor league executive of the year, at Murray, Ky., March 7; the awards were bestowed in 1952, for his direction of Danville (Mississippi-Ohio Valley League), and in 1967, when he was the general manager of the International League champion at Richmond; he was director of customer services for Milwaukee in 1963-64 and scouted for Detroit and Montreal; served as G.M. at Macon in 1981.

Dave Malarcher, 87, star third baseman in the Negro leagues with the Chicago American Giants, at Chicago, Ill., May 11; a defensive standout, he also batted .344 in 1920 and .346 in 1925; managed the Giants to three pennants.

Charles Kennon (Buck) Marrow, 73, righthanded pitcher for Detroit in 1932 and Brooklyn in 1937-38, at Newport News, Va., November 21; had a 3-8 record in 39 games.

Frank Andrew McCormick, 71, the National League's Most Valuable Player in 1940, of cancer, at Manhasset, N.Y., November 21; a standout first baseman who spent 10 of his 13 seasons in the major leagues with Cincinnati, he hit .309 and drove in 127 runs in 1940 and helped the Reds to their first world championship in 21 years; led the league in hits in each of his first three full seasons with Cincinnati (1938-40); batted .331 with 128 RBIs in 1939; in 1940 he led the league in doubles with 44, his third consecutive season with 40 or more; the Reds sold him to the Philadelphia Phillies after the 1945 season for $40,000; he was released by the Phillies during the 1947 season and was immediately signed by the Boston Braves, with whom he completed his playing career in 1948; he had a career average of .299 with 128 home runs and 954 RBIs; managed in the minors from 1949-51, then rejoined the Reds as a scout (1952-55), as a coach (1956-57) and as a member of the TV announcing crew (1958 through the mid-60s).

Clyde Edward McCullough, 65, National League catcher for 15 seasons in the 1940s and '50s, and later a minor league manager and major league coach, of a heart attack, at San Francisco, Calif., September 18; at the time of his death, he was traveling with the Padres, whom he had joined in the spring as bullpen coach; played for the Cubs from 1940-48 (he missed the 1944-45 seasons while serving in the Navy, though he was discharged in time to make a pinch-hitting appearance in the '45 World Series) and from 1953-56; in the interim, he was with Pittsburgh; one of the top defensive catchers in the majors during his career, he batted .252 in 1,098 games; he was The Sporting News' minor league manager of the year in 1969 after guiding Tidewater to the International League championship; coached for Washington in 1960, Minnesota in 1961 and the New York Mets in 1963 and was a minor league instructor in the Mets' system from 1974-76.

Webster McDonald, 82, righthander who was one of the top pitchers in the old Negro leagues, at Philadelphia, Pa., June 12; with his underhanded delivery, he hurled the Chicago American Giants to two pennants; also pitched for the Baltimore Black Sox, Homestead Grays and Philadelphia Hilldales; he was a player on and manager of the Philadelphia Stars' 1934 pennant winner.

Frank B. McGowan, 79, former major league outfielder who was New England scouting supervisor for the Baltimore Orioles from 1954-73, at Hamden, Conn., May 6; played for the Philadelphia Athletics in 1922-23, the St. Louis Browns in 1928-29 and the Boston Bees in 1937, batting .262 in 375 games; he was named most valuable player in the International League in 1936, when he batted .356, hit 23 homers and drove in 111 runs for Buffalo; managed in the I.L. at Baltimore in 1932-33; he is a member of the I.L. Hall of Fame.

Casimir Eugene (Cass) Michaels (nee Kwietniewski), 56, infielder who had a .262 average over 12 major league seasons, most of them with the Chicago White Sox in the 1940s, at Grosse Pointe, Mich., November 12; played two games

with the White Sox in 1943, when he was only 17, and was the club's regular shortstop by 1945; batted .308 for the Sox in 1949 while playing in all 154 games; also played for Washington (1950-52), the St. Louis Browns (1952) and the Philadelphia Athletics (1952-53); returned to Chicago in 1954 but retired when he was suffering a fractured skull that season when he was hit by a pitch thrown by the Athletics' Marion Fricano; scouted for the White Sox in 1955-56.

Marvin Milkes, 58, former major league executive, at Los Angeles, Calif., January 31; his first job in organized ball was as assistant general manager for Fresno of the California League in 1946; 10 years later, as the general manager for Fresno, he won The Sporting News' award for executive of the year for the lower minors; after that he worked his way up the ladder until he reached the majors in 1961 as vice-president of the Los Angeles Angels; became the first G.M. of the Seattle Pilots, who folded after their expansion season in 1969; the franchise was purchased by a Milwaukee group, and Milkes moved, too, but soon resigned with four years remaining on his five-year contract; since that time, he had been involved in player representation and in professional soccer administration.

William Francis (Bill) Miller, 71, a righthander who was defeated in his only major league appearance, for the St. Louis Browns in 1937, at Hannibal, Mo., February 26.

Edwin Willis (Eddie) Morgan, 67, outfielder and first baseman for the St. Louis Cardinals in 1936 and Brooklyn in 1937, at Lakewood, O., June 27; hit .212 in 39 games.

Edward Joseph (Eddie) Mulligan, 87, infielder for the Chicago Cubs in 1915-16, the Chicago White Sox in 1921-22 and Pittsburgh in 1928, at San Rafael, Calif., March 15; batted .232 in 351 games in the majors and was the White Sox' shortstop the day Charley Robertson threw his perfect game at Detroit in 1922; he is best remembered, however, for his 17 years in the Pacific Coast League—he played for eight Coast clubs and set PCL records at third base for most games, most putouts, most assists and most chances accepted; managed at San Diego and Salt Lake City; owned Salt Lake franchise from 1940 until 1949, when he bought the Sacramento club; president of the California League from 1956-75.

Bill O'Donnell, 56, play-by-play announcer for Baltimore since 1966, of cancer, at Johns Hopkins Hospital, Baltimore, Md., October 29; a 32-year veteran of sports broadcasting, he began the 1982 season in the broadcast booth, but quit early in the year because of his illness.

Leroy Robert (Satchel) Paige, 75, already a legend when he became the first black to pitch in the American League as a 42-year-old in 1948, at Kansas City, Mo., June 8; well past his prime when he joined Cleveland (regarded by many as the premier pitcher of his time, he would have been pitching in the majors as early as the 1930s but for the color barrier), he nevertheless won six games and lost only one for the Indians in '48—in 21 appearances, most of them in relief, he had a 2.47 ERA; spent one more year with Cleveland, then pitched for the St. Louis Browns from 1951-53 and made one appearance (three scoreless innings) for the Kansas City Athletics in 1965; he had a 12-10 record for the Browns in 1952, and his final major league mark was 28-31 with a 3.29 ERA; those figures, however, are but the tip of an iceberg because, though records are not available, Paige almost certainly won more than 1,500 games pitching in the Negro leagues and winter leagues in South and Central America and the Caribbean; in recognition of this, a special committee set up to select top stars of the old Negro leagues for the Hall of Fame made him its first choice, in 1971; his first pro job was with the Chattanooga Black Lookouts of the Negro Southern League in 1926; pitched for the Birmingham Black Barons and Nashville Elite Giants before joining the Pittsburgh Crawfords in 1931; in three seasons with the Crawfords, considered one of the best teams ever—black or white—he probably won at lest 90 games; barnstormed with a semipro team from Bismarck, N.D., in 1934-35—the team lost only once during the '35 season and won the first National Baseball Congress tournament as Satch won four games and the most valuable player award; he was back with the Crawfords in 1936 but jumped the club again in 1937, going first to Venezuela and then to the Dominican Republic and Mexico; from 1939 until he signed with the Indians in '48, Paige did most of his pitching for the Kansas City Monarchs of the Negro American League, winning 21 games without a defeat in 1946; coached for Atlanta in 1968-69, when he was employed so he could qualify for the minimum pension.

Ervin Martin (Erv) Palica, 54, righthanded pitcher for Brooklyn from 1947-54 (except for military service in '52) and Baltimore in 1955-56, of a heart attack, May 29; as a spot starter and reliever he posted a 41-55 record with a 4.22 ERA; his best season was 1950, when he won 13 games and lost eight.

Henry Stephen Peploski, 74, infielder who played in six games for the Boston Braves in 1929, at Dover, N.J., January 28; younger brother of Pepper Peploski, who played briefly for Detroit in 1913.

Clarence Anthony (Bud) Podbielan, 58, righthanded relief pitcher who had a 25-42 record in 172 games with Brooklyn (1949-52), Cincinnati (1952-57) and Cleveland (1959), at Syracuse, N.Y., October 27; after he failed to replace Hugh Casey in the Brooklyn bullpen, the Reds made him a starter in 1953-54, but his record over the two seasons was 13-26; suffered a fractured right wrist the next season, did not return until 1957 and never won another game in the majors.

Walter Charles (Wally) Post, 52, whose 210 major league home runs included many tapemeasure shots, of cancer, at St. Henry, O., January 5; he started out as a pitcher in the Cincinnati system, compiling a 17-7 record at Muncie in the Ohio State League in 1947, but his ability as a hitter caused the Reds to switch him to the outfield; MVP seasons at Buffalo (International) in 1951 and Indianapolis (American Association) in 1953 won him a place in the Reds' outfield and as a rookie in 1954 he hit 18 homers and drove in 83 runs; the following year, he belted 40 homers, drove in 109 runs and batted .309, 43 points above his career average; he cracked 36 homers and 20 homers the next two seasons, then was traded to the Philadelphia Phillies for Harvey Haddix; traded back to the Reds in 1960, he helped them to the 1961 pennant with 17 homers and 62 RBIs, and in the five-game World Series loss to the Yankees he collected six hits, including one home run, in 18 at-bats; the Reds sold him to Minnesota early in 1963 and he ended his career the following year after five games with Cleveland.

Dr. Hubert Shelby (Shucks) Pruett, 81, lefthanded pitcher whose seven years in the majors were distinguished only by his mastery of Babe Ruth, of cancer, at Ladue, Mo., January 28; he struck out Ruth 10 of the first 13 times he faced him as a rookie with the St. Louis Browns in 1922; primarily a reliever throughout his career, his 7-7 record and 2.33 ERA in his rookie season was his best year; finished his career with a 29-48 mark and 4.63 ERA, pitching for St. Louis from 1922-24, the Philadelphia Phillies in 1927-28, the New

York Giants in 1930 and the Boston Braves in 1932.

Melvin Joseph Queen, 64, righthanded pitcher for the New York Yankees in 1942-44-46-47 and Pittsburgh in 1947-48 and from 1950-52, at Fort Smith, Ark., April 4; pitched in 146 games, 77 as a starter, and was 27-40 with a 5.09 ERA; his only winning season was 1944, when he was 6-3; scouted for Cincinnati in the early 1960s; father of Melvin Douglas Queen, who pitched for Cincinnati and California in the 1960s and early '70s.

Joseph F. (Joe) Reardon, 76, who joined the Philadelphia Phillies as minor league business administrator shortly after the club was acquired by Robert Carpenter Sr. in 1943, and who, as director of minor league operations over the next 10 years, assembled the team that won the 1950 National League pennant, at Scranton, Pa., June 25; helped develop such players as Robin Roberts, Curt Simmons and Richie Ashburn.

Chester Franklin (Buster) Ross, 79, lefthander who compiled a 7-12 record in three seasons with the Boston Red Sox, 1924-26, at Mayfield, Ky., April 24.

Edward Joseph (Ebba) St. Claire, 61, catcher for the Boston and Milwaukee Braves from 1951-53 and the New York Giants in 1954, at Whitehall, N.Y., August 22; batted .249 in 164 games.

Erik Oliver Sax, 77, third baseman who played in 16 games for the St. Louis Browns in 1928, at Newark, N.J., March 21.

Ray W. Scarborough, 64, righthander who had an 80-85 record in 10 American League seasons, at Mount Olive, N.C., July 1; pitched only 1½ seasons in the minors before joining Washington midway through the 1942 season; enlisted in the Navy in 1943, had two sub-.500 seasons in 1946-47 after his release from service, but then won 15 and lost 8 with a 2.82 ERA in 1948; he was 13-11 the following season, but was traded to Chicago early in 1950 and then to Boston in 1951; New York obtained him in a waiver deal in August of 1952 and he had a 5-1 record after joining the Yankees, who won the pennant by two games; released by New York in August of 1953, he signed with Detroit, but retired after that season; scouted for Baltimore for 10 years before joining California in a similar capacity in 1973; in 1978 he joined Milwaukee, for whom he was a special assignments scout at the time of his death.

Paul Frederick Schreiber, 79, righthander who pitched 10 games for Brooklyn in 1922-23 and two games for the New York Yankees in 1945, at Sarasota, Fla., January 28; coached or pitched batting practice for the Yankees from 1932-45; joined the Boston Red Sox in 1946, pitching batting practice for two years, then coaching until 1959, when he became a scout; retired in 1964.

Ray Solomon Shearer, 52, outfielder who played two games for Milwaukee in 1957, at Manchester, Pa., February 22.

Benjamin Cowan Shields, 79, lefthanded pitcher for the New York Yankees in 1924-25, the Boston Red Sox in 1930 and the Philadelphia Phillies in 1931, at Woodruff, S.C., January 23; appeared in only 13 games in those seasons, winning all four of his decisions.

Robert E. (Bob) Short, 65, owner of the Washington Senators/Texas Rangers from late 1968 through 1973, of cancer, at Minneapolis, Minn., November 20; a self-made millionaire through the successful operation of trucking, hotel and legal businesses, he purchased the Senators, a 1961 expansion club, for $10 million; brought in Ted Williams as manager, but sub-.500 records and poor attendance in 1970-71 caused him to move the club to Texas, charging the Washington community with non-support; two years later, he sold his

Wally Post was MVP in the International League with Buffalo in 1951.

majority interest in the Rangers to Brad Corbett for $10 million; owned the Minneapolis/Los Angeles Lakers of the National Basketball Association from 1957-65; in 1978, he ran for Hubert Humphrey's Senate seat from Minnesota—he defeated Donald Fraser in the Democratic primary, but lost to Republican David Durenberger in the general election.

Caesar J. Sinibaldi, 71, former minor league catcher and a scout for Baltimore since 1979, at Albany, Calif., August 27; scouted for Oakland from 1972-77 and San Francisco in 1978; signed Mike Norris to his first contract with the A's.

Walter Wellesley (Red) Smith, 76, Pulitzer Prize winner as a sports columnist for the New York Times, at Stamford, Conn., January 15; he won the Prize in 1976 for "distinguished commentary"—the only other sportswriter to receive the award was the Times' Arthur Daley in 1956; Smith began his newspaper career in 1928 as a general news reporter for the Milwaukee Sentinel; later that year he moved to the copy desk of the St. Louis Star and when several members of the sports staff were fired, he was asked to fill one of the vacancies; he went on to write for the Philadelphia Record, the New York Herald-Tribune and other New York publications before joining the Times in 1971; his erudition and command of the English language was such that he was a consultant for several dictionaries and encyclopedias; ever more liberal as he grew older, he regularly scolded professional sports management for its callous attitude in labor relations, lamented what he felt were the International Olympic Committee's anachronistic definitions of amateurism, and ridiculed Commissioner Bowie Kuhn.

Monty Franklin Pierce Stratton, 70, Chicago White Sox righthander whose promising pitching career was cut short by a hunting accident that cost him a leg in 1938, of cancer, at Greenville, Tex., September 29; he seemed to be on the brink of stardom after posting 15-5 and 15-9 marks in 1937-38, but while hunting rabbits on his mother's farm near Greenville, he accidentally discharged the .22-caliber pistol he was carrying; the slug logged in his right knee, severing the main artery, and the leg was amputated the following day; coached for the White Sox the next three seasons; in 1946 he signed with Sherman in the old Class C East Texas League and had an 18-8 record; with Waco (Big State League, Class B) in 1947, he was 7-7; his struggle to regain the heights as a pitcher interested Hollywood moviemakers and "The Monty Stratton Story," released in 1949 and starring Jimmy Stewart in the title role, received Photoplay's gold medal as best picture of the year.

John Patrick (Jackie) Tobin, 61, infielder in 84 games for the 1945 Boston Red Sox, at Oakland, Calif., January 18; younger brother of Jim Tobin, pitcher for Pittsburgh, the Boston Braves and Detroit from 1937-45.

Fred (Dixie) Walker, 71, outfielder whose clutch hitting for the Brooklyn Dodgers made him "The People's Cherce," died of cancer, at Birmingham, Ala., May 17; spent 18 seasons in the major leagues, but it was in his years with the Dodgers (1939-47) that he won a batting title (.357 in 1944), a runs-batted-in championship (124 in 1945) and swung the bat with enough authority to wind up with a .306 career average; came to the Dodgers after seven-plus seasons in the American League with the New York Yankees in 1931 and 1933-36, the Chicago White Sox from 1936-38 and Detroit in 1938-39; the Yankees, who bought him off the Class D Greenville roster in 1930 for the then-record price of $25,000, regarded him as a likely successor to Babe Ruth or Earl Combs—until he tore muscles in his right shoulder in 1933; traded to the White Sox in 1936, he injured his shoulder again and underwent surgery; drove in 95 runs for Chicago in 1937 and batted .308 for Detroit in 1938, but after he tore knee cartilage the next season, the Dodgers were able to purchase his contract for $7,500; in his years with the Dodgers, he hit .300 or better seven times and collected 725 of his 1,023 career RBIs; closed out his career with Pittsburgh in 1948-49; managed in the minors at Atlanta, Houston, Rochester and Toronto, and coached for the St. Louis Cardinals in 1953, Milwaukee/Atlanta from 1963-68 and the Dodgers from 1969-76; scouted for Milwaukee from 1960-62; older brother of Harry Walker, former National League outfielder and manager and now baseball coach at the University of Alabama in Birmingham; son of Ewart Walker, pitcher for Washington from 1909-1912, and nephew of Ernie Walker, outfielder for the St. Louis Browns from 1913-15.

Harvey Willos (Hub) Walker, 76, outfielder with Detroit in 1931, 1935 and 1945 and Cincinnati in 1936-37, at San Jose, Calif., November 26; batted .263 in 297 games; pinch hit twice in 1945 World Series, getting one hit in two at-bats.

Lloyd James (Little Poison) Waner, 76, half of the Hall of Fame brother combination that patrolled the outfield for Pittsburgh in the 1920s and '30s, at Oklahoma City, Okla., July 22; his brother Paul, who collected 3,152 hits in 20 major league seasons, was elected to the Hall of Fame in 1952 and died in 1965; Lloyd, who had 2,459 hits and batted .316, was chosen for the Hall of Fame by the Veterans' Committee in 1967; Lloyd, three years younger than Paul, joined the Pirates in 1927 and made such an impression on Manager Donie Bush that Bush switched Kiki Cuyler to left field and inserted Lloyd in center, next to Paul in right; Lloyd responded with a rookie record 223 hits, 198 of which were singles (another record), and led the league in runs scored (133) while batting .355; the Pirates won the 1927 National League pennant and Lloyd batted .400 (6-for-15) in the World Series, which the Yankees won in four games—it was the Waners' only Series appearance; Lloyd batted .335 in 1928, then boosted that to .353 the next season, when he led the league in triples with 20; a spring bout with appendicitis caused him to miss all but 68 games of the 1930 season, but he came back strong in 1931, leading the league in hits with 214; he batted over .300 in 11 of his 18 major league seasons; Lloyd was in his 15th season for the Pirates when he was traded to Boston in 1941 for pitcher Nick Strincevich; a month later, he was traded to Cincinnati, which released him after the season; he played 101 games for the Philadelphia Phillies in 1942, spent the 1943 season on the voluntarily retired list, then hit .321 in 34 games in 1944 for Brooklyn and Pittsburgh, who signed him after the Dodgers gave him his release in June; ended his career the next season with the Pirates, being used sparingly as a pinch-hitter; scouted for Pittsburgh until 1949, and was employed by Baltimore in the same capacity in 1955.

Lester Evans (Wimpy) Willis, 75, lefthander who had an 0-2 record and 3.48 ERA in 22 games for the 1947 Cleveland Indians, January 22.

George Rowland (Pinky) Woods, 62, righthanded pitcher for the Boston Red Sox from 1943-45, at Los Angeles, Calif., October 30; won 13 games and lost 21 in 85 appearances, 44 as a starter.

William Henry (Bill) Zuber, 69, righthander who pitched for four American League clubs in the 1930s and '40s, at Cedar Rapids, Ia.; pitched for Cleveland in 1936 and from 1938-40, Washington in 1941-42, New York from 1943-46 and Boston in 1946-47; in 224 games, 159 of those in relief, he had a 43-42 record with a 4.28 ERA; pitched two innings for the Red Sox in the 1946 World Series.

LEAGUE AND CLUB INFORMATION

Including

Major League Directory

National League Directory

National League Team Directories

American League Directory

American League Team Directories

Major League Players Association Directory

Major League Farm Systems

Minor League Presidents

Directory of Organized Baseball

MAJOR LEAGUES

COMMISSIONER—Bowie K. Kuhn
SECRETARY-TREASURER—Alexander H. Hadden
HEADQUARTERS—75 Rockefeller Plaza
New York, N. Y. 10019
Telephone—586-7400 (area code 212)
Teletype—710-581-4279

EXECUTIVE COUNCIL—Bowie K. Kuhn, Commissioner; Leland S. MacPhail, Jr., President of American League; Charles S. Feeney, President of National League; Jerry Reinsdorf, Allan H. Selig, Haywood C. Sullivan and Edward Bennett Williams, representatives of American League, and Daniel M. Galbreath, Robert A. Lurie, Peter F. O'Malley and Ballard F. Smith, Jr., representatives of National League.

ADMINISTRATOR—William A. Murray
SPECIAL ASSISTANTS TO THE COMMISSIONER—
Joseph L. Reichler, Monte Irvin
DIRECTOR OF INFORMATION—Robert A. Wirz
DIRECTOR OF SECURITY—Horace J. (Harry) Gibbs
CONTROLLER—Donald C. Marr, Jr.
ASSISTANTS TO ADMINISTRATOR—George E. Pfister, Miguel A. Rodriguez
ADMINISTRATIVE ASSISTANT—Miguel A. Rodriguez
ASSISTANT COUNSEL—Edwin M. Durso
ASSOCIATE DIRECTOR OF INFORMATION, MEDIA—Charles B. Adams
ASSISTANT DIRECTOR OF INFORMATION—Richard Cerrone
OFFICE MANAGER—Mary Ann Burns
BOOKKEEPER—Rita Datz

NATIONAL ASSOCIATION REPRESENTATIVES—John Johnson, President of the National Association, and members of National Association Executive Committee.

NATIONAL ASSOCIATION
OF PROFESSIONAL BASEBALL LEAGUES

PRESIDENT-TREASURER—John H. Johnson
ADMINISTRATOR—Sal Artiaga
VICE-PRESIDENT—Harold Cooper
DIRECTOR OF PROMOTIONS—Bob Sparks
HEADQUARTERS—201 Bayshore Dr. S.E., P. O. Box A
St. Petersburg, Fla. 33731
Telephone—822-6937 (area code 813)
Teletype—810-863-0361

EXECUTIVE COMMITTEE—Harold Cooper, Chairman, President of the International League; Jimmy Bragan, President of the Southern League, George G. MacDonald, Jr., President of the Florida State League.

National League
Organized 1876

CHARLES S. FEENEY
President and Treasurer

JOHN J. McHALE
Vice-President

PHYLLIS B. COLLINS
Secretary

BLAKE CULLEN
Administrator and Public Relations Director

KATY FEENEY
Assistant Public Relations Director

LOUIS H. KREMS
Business Manager

JOSEPHINE TROY
Administrative Assistant

Headquarters—1 Rockefeller Plaza, New York, N. Y. 10020

Telephone—582-4213 (area code 212)

UMPIRES—Fred Brocklander, Jerry Crawford, Jerry Dale, David Davidson, Robert Davidson, Robert Engel, Bruce Froemming, Eric Gregg, Lanny Harris, H. Douglas Harvey, John Kibler, Randy Marsh, John McSherry, Ed Montague, Dave Pallone, Frank Pulli, Jim Quick, Lawrence (Dutch) Rennert, Paul Runge, Dick Stello, Terry Tata, Ed Vargo, Harry Wendelstedt, Joe West, Lee Weyer, Charles Williams, William G. Williams.

OFFICIAL STATISTICIANS—Elias Sports Bureau, Inc., 500 5th Ave., Suite 2114, New York, N. Y. 10036. Telephone (212) 869-1530.

Players cannot be transferred from one major league club to another after June 15 to the close of the championship season except through regular waiver channels.

WAIVER PRICE, $20,000. Interleague waivers, $20,000, except for selected players and draft-excluded players.

National League President Charles S. Feeney.

ATLANTA BRAVES

Chairman of the Board—William C. Bartholomay

President—R.E. (Ted) Turner, III
Executive Vice-President—Allison Thornwell, Jr.
Vice-President and General Manager—John W. Mullen
Vice-President and Business Manager—Charles S. Sanders
Vice-President, Player Development—Henry L. Aaron
Assistant Vice-President, Scouting—Paul L. Snyder, Jr.
Assistant Vice-President, Baseball—Patrick R. Nugent
Director of Broadcasting—Ernie Johnson
Manager of Broadcast Sales and Administration—Wayne Long
Ticket Distribution Manager—Ed Newman
Director of Public Relations, Promotions—Wayne Minshew
Director of Publications and Publicity Manager—Bob Korch
Director of Stadium Operations and Security—Joe Shirley
Director of Matrix Operations—Bob Larson
Assistant Controller—Martin Mathews
Traveling Secretary and Equipment Manager—Bill Acree
Director of Ticket Sales—Andre DeLorenzo
Group Sales Manager—Larry Cancro
Manager—Joe Torre
Club Physician—Dr. David T. Watson
Executive Offices—P.O. Box 4064, Atlanta, Ga. 30302
Telephone—522-7630 (area code 404)

SCOUTS—Mike Arbuckle, Sam Berry, Forrest (Smoky) Burgess, Stu Cann, Joe Caputo, Harold Cronin, Lou Fitzgerald, Rod Gilbreath, Pedro Gonzalez, John Groth, Willie Harris, Gene Hassell, Ted Henkel, Herb Hippauf, Burney R. (Dickey) Martin, Bob Mavis, Rance Pless, Bob Scruggs, Bill Serena, Charles Smith, Tony Stiel, Bob Turzilli, Bob Wadsworth, Wesley Westrum, William R. Wight, Don Williams, H.F. (Red) Wooten.

PARK LOCATION—Atlanta-Fulton County Stadium, on Capitol Avenue at the junction of Interstate Highways 20, 75 and 85.

Seating capacity—52,785.

FIELD DIMENSIONS—Home plate to left field at foul line, 330 feet; to center field, 402 feet; to right field at foul line, 330 feet.

CHICAGO CUBS

Chairman of the Board, President and Treasurer—Andrew J. McKenna

Executive Vice-President and General Manager—Dallas Green
Vice-President, Business Operations—Terry Barthelmas
Director of Minor Leagues and Scouting—Gordon Goldsberry
Vice-President, Planning and Special Projects—Mark McGuire
Vice-President, Media Relations and Operations—Jeff Odenwald
Vice-President, Marketing and Advertising—Bing Hampton
Vice-President, Ticket Sales—Patty Cox Hampton
Special Assistant to Exec. V.P. and V.P., Business Operations—E. R. Saltwell
Assistant to Exec. V.P. and Traveling Secretary—John Cox
Director of Scouting—A. B. (Vedie) Himsl
Chief Accounting Officer—Joseph A. Kirchen
Secretary—Stanley J. Gradowski, Jr.
Director, Public Relations and Publications—Bob Ibach
Director, Group Sales—Frank Maloney
Director, Stadium Operations—Robert Hubberts
Manager of Promotions—Mary Beth Hughes
Manager of Advertising—Valentine Judge
Associate Director, Minor Leagues—William Harford
Assistant Director, Publications and Statistics—Ned Colletti
Assistant Director, Stadium Operations/Facilities—Lubie Veal
Vice-President, Special Assignments—Jack Brickhouse
Legal Counsel—Judge Robert C. Cannon
Manager—Lee Elia
Executive Offices—Wrigley Field, N. Clark and Addison Streets, Chicago, Ill. 60613
Telephone—281-5050 (area code 312)

SCOUTS—Billy Blitzer, William Capps, B. Bill Champion, Bill Darden, Brandon Davis, Tom Davis, Frank DeMoss, Edward DiRamio, Walt Dixon, Larry Grefer, Gene Handley, John Hennessy, Thomas Hinkle, Roy Johnson, John Jorgensen, Douglas Laumann, Douglas Mapson, Julio Navarro, Gary Nickels, John O'Neil, Andrew Pienovi, Evo Pusich, Eric Soderholm, Joaquin Velilla, H.D. Wilson, James Zerilla.

PARK LOCATION—Wrigley Field, Addison Street, N. Clark Street, Waveland Avenue and Sheffield Avenue.

Seating capacity—37,272.

FIELD DIMENSIONS—Home plate to left field at foul line, 355 feet; to center field, 400 feet; to right field at foul line, 353 feet.

CINCINNATI REDS

Chairmen—James R. Williams, William J. Williams

Vice-Chairman—Robert L. Howsam
President and Chief Executive Officer—Richard Wagner
Vice-President, Marketing—Roger Ruhl
Assistant General Manager—Woody Woodward
Vice-President, Player Personnel—Sheldon Bender
Business Manager—Doug Bureman
Director, Scouting—Larry Doughty
Special Assignment Scout—Ray Shore
Controller—D.L. Porco
Special Assistant, Publicity-Promotions—Gordy Coleman
Director, Stadium Operations—Doug Duennes
Director, Publicity—Jim Ferguson
Director, Advertising—Sue Kountz
Director, Promotions—Greg McCollam
Director, Ticket Department—Bill Stewart
Director, Season Tickets and Customer Relations—Janet Wendel
Director, Group Sales—Ted Williams
Director, Broadcasting—Jim Winters
Traveling Secretary—Steve Cobb
Assistant, Player Development and Scouting—Joe Nichols
Chairman Emeritus—Louis Nippert
Manager—Russ Nixon
Executive Offices—100 Riverfront Stadium, Cincinnati, O. 45202
Telephone—421-4510 (area code 513)

SCOUTS—Larry Barton, Jr., Gene Bennett, Cameron Bonifay, Dave Calaway, Bill Clark, Martin Daily, Larry D'Amato, Roger Ferguson, Elmer Gray, Edwin Howsam, Julian Mock, Chet Montgomery, Greg Riddoch, Ed Roebuck, Johnny Sierra, Neil Summers, Fred Uhlman, Mickey White, George Zuraw.

PARK LOCATION—Riverfront Stadium, downtown Cincinnati, bounded by Second Street to Ohio River and from Walnut Street to Broadway.

Seating capacity—52,392.

FIELD DIMENSIONS—Home plate to left field at foul line, 330 feet; to center field, 404 feet; to right field at foul line, 330 feet.

HOUSTON ASTROS

Board of Directors—John J. McMullen, Jack T. Trotter, T.H. Neyland

President and General Manager—Albert L. Rosen
Vice-President, Baseball Operations—Bob Kennedy
Administrative Asst. to the President and Traveling Secretary—Donald Davidson
Assistant to the General Manager—Andy MacPhail
Director of Minor League Operations—William J. Wood
Director of Scouting—Lynwood Stallings
Assistant, Minor League Operations and Scouting—Dan O'Brien, Jr.
Director of Public Relations—Mike Ryan
Asst. Director of Public Relations—Rick Rivers
Director of Broadcasting and Promotions—Art Elliott
Promotions, Scoreboard Operations—Paul Darst
Broadcast and Promotions Sales—Hugh Pickett, Lou Korpas
Director of Ticket Sales—Larry Serota
Manager, Season Ticket Sales—M.M. (Buddy) Hancken
Manager, Group Sales—Donna deGruyter
Administrative Asst., Major League Operations—Sandra Zimmerman
Administrative Asst. Minor League Operations—Ev Goldberg
Secretary, Public Relations—Beverly Rains
Club Physicians—Drs. Harold H. Brelsford, Hatch Cummings
Public Address Announcer—J. Fred Duckett
Manager—Bob Lillis
Executive Offices—Astrodome, P.O. Box 288
Houston, Tex. 77001
Telephone—799-9500 (area code 713)
HOUSTON SPORTS ASSOCIATION, INC.
President and Chief Operating Officer—Robert G. Harter
Vice-President, Administration—E. Michael Crowley
Vice-President, Engineering—W. Gary Keller
Vice-President, Public Relations and Advertising—Ben Gillespie
Vice-President, Corporate Affairs—Jim McConn
Executive Vice-President, Event Sales and Management—Jimmie Fore
Director, Special Projects—Jim Weidler
Director, Service and Administration—Bill Boyd
Treasurer—A. Eugene Stoffel
Controller—Adam C. Richards
Financial Analyst—Bill Boyd
Ticket Manager—Charles T. Wall

SCOUTS—Clary Anderson, Stan Benjamin, Jack Bloomfield, C.V. Davis, Paul Florence, Ben Galante, Carl Greene, Bill Hallauer, Bob Hartsfield, Deacon Jones, Bob Kennedy, Jr., David Lakey, Gordon Lakey, Julio Linares, Walter Matthews, William Melendez, Domingo Mercedes, Dan O'Brien, Jr., Tony Pacheco, Lynwood Stallings, Reggie Waller, Paul Weaver, Harrison Wickel.

PARK LOCATION—Astrodome, Kirby and Interstate Loop 610

Seating capacity—45,000.

FIELD DIMENSIONS—Home plate to left field at foul line, 340 feet; to center field, 406 feet; to right field at foul line, 340 feet.

LOS ANGELES DODGERS

Board of Directors—Peter O'Malley, President; Harry M. Bardt;
Roland Seidler, Jr., Vice-President and Treasurer;
Mrs. Roland (Terry) Seidler, Secretary

President—Peter O'Malley
Executive Vice-President—Fred Claire
Vice-President, Player Personnel—Al Campanis
Vice-President, Minor League Operations—William P. Schweppe
Vice-President, Marketing—Merritt Willey
Special Consultant—Walter Alston
Controller and Assistant Treasurer—Ken Hasemann
Assistant Secretary—Irene Tanji
Director, Advertising, Novelties and Souvenirs—Danny Goodman
Director, Dodgertown—Charles Blaney
Director, Stadium Operations—Bob Smith
Director, Ticket Department—Walter Nash
Director, Stadium Club and Transportation—Bob Schenz
Director, Dodger Network—David Van de Walker
Director, Scouting—Ben Wade
Director, Publicity—Steve Brener
Director, Publications—Toby Zwikel
Director, Community Relations—Don Newcombe
Community Relations—Roy Campanella, Lou Johnson
Director, Ticket Marketing and Promotions—Barry Stockhamer
Director, Community Services and Special Events—Bill Shumard
Assistant to the President—Ike Ikuhara
Traveling Secretary—Billy DeLury
Auditor—Michael Strange
Manager—Tom Lasorda
Club Physicians—Dr. Frank Jobe, Dr. Robert Woods
Executive Offices—Dodger Stadium, 1000 Elysian Park Avenue,
Los Angeles, Calif. 90012
Telephone—224-1500 (area code 213)

SCOUTS—Rafael Avila, Boyd Bartley, Bob Bishop, Gib Bodet, Mike Brito, Bob Darwin, Paul Duval, Eddie Fajardo, Jim Garland, Dick Hanlon, Dennis Haren, Gail Henley, Elvio Jimenez, Tony John, Tim Johnson, Hank Jones, John Keenan, Ron King, Steve Lembo, Ed Liberatore, Carl Lowenstine, Dale McReynolds, Tommy Mixon, John O'Neil, Regie Otero, Medardo Perez, Bill Pleis, Jerry Stephenson, Dick Teed, Corito Varona, Guy Wellman.

PARK LOCATION—Dodger Stadium, 1000 Elysian Park Avenue.

Seating capacity—56,000.

FIELD DIMENSIONS—Home plate to left field at foul line, 330 feet; to center field, 395 feet; to right field at foul line, 330 feet.

MONTREAL EXPOS

Board of Directors—Charles R. Bronfman, Lorne C. Webster,
John J. McHale, Sydney Maislin, Paul Beaudry, Hugh Hallward,
Charlemagne Beaudry, E. Leo Kolber, Melvin W. Griffin,
Louis R. Desmarais, Arnold Ludwick, Honorary Treasurer

Chairman of the Board—Charles R. Bronfman
President and Chief Executive Officer—John J. McHale
Vice-President, Player Development, Scouting—Jim Fanning
Director of Minor League Operations—Bob Gebhard
Director, Team Travel—Peter Durso
Director, Business Operations—Gerry Trudeau
Director of Marketing—Rene Guimond
Director of Finance—Dennis Bodin
Publicists—Monique Giroux, Richard Griffin
Field Coordinator, Player Development—Pat Daugherty
Coordinator, Spring Training—Kevin McHale
Manager—Bill Virdon
Club Physician—Dr. Robert Brodrick
Mailing Address—P. O. Box 500, Station M, Montreal, Quebec,
Canada H1V 3P2
Telephone—253-3434 (area code 514)

SCOUTS—(Special assignment)—Charlie Fox, Carroll (Whitey) Lockman, Ed
Lopat; (Supervisors)—Danny Menendez, Bob Fontaine, Jr.; (Regular)—Bill Adair,
Jesus Alou, Terry Boyle, Harry Bright, Cliff Ditto, Mercer Harris, Dick Lemay, Eddie
Lyons, Roy McMillan, Walter Millies, John (Red) Murff, Herb Newberry, Bob Oldis,
Frank Perez, Ron Piche, Harry Pritikin, Earl Rapp.

PARK LOCATION—Olympic Stadium, 4545 Pierre de Coubertin, Montreal, Quebec, Canada H1V 3N7.

Seating capacity—58,838.

FIELD DIMENSIONS—Home plate to left field at foul line, 325 feet; to center
field, 404 feet; to right field at foul line, 325 feet.

NEW YORK METS

Chairman of the Board—Nelson Doubleday

Directors—Nelson Doubleday, Fred Wilpon, Walter E. Freese
John W. O'Donnell, John C. Herndon, John T. Sargent
President & Chief Executive Officer—Fred Wilpon
Exec. Vice-President, G.M. & Chief Operating Officer—J. Frank Cashen
Vice-President, Administration—James Nagourney
Vice-President, Baseball Operations—James Lou Gorman
Vice-President—Alan E. Harazin
Vice-President and Controller—Harold W. O'Shaughnessy
Special Asst. to the G.M. & Team Travel Director—Arthur Richman
Director of Operations—Bob Mandt
Director of Scouting—Joseph McIlvaine
Ticket Manager—Bill Ianniciello
Director of Minor League Operations—Stephen Schryver
Director of Public Relations—Jay Horwitz
Director of Promotions—Tim Hamilton
Stadium Manager—John McCarthy
Manager—George Bamberger
Club Physician—Dr. James C. Parkes II
Team Trainer—Larry Mayol
Executive Offices—William A. Shea Stadium, Roosevelt
Avenue and 126th Street, Flushing, N.Y. 11368
Telephone—507-6387 (area code 212)

SCOUTS—Carmen Fusco, Roland Johnson, Dean Jongewaard, Buddy Kerr, Dave Madison, Joe Mason, Rich Miller, Harry Minor, Robert Minor, Bill Monbouquette, Danny Monzon, Julian Morgan, Roy Partee, Carlos Pascual, Junior Roman, Terry Ryan, Bob Scheffing, Marvin Scott, Jim Terrell, Eddy Toledo, Ollie Vanek, Bob Wellman, Len Zanke, Jack Zduriencik.

PARK LOCATION—William A. Shea Stadium, Roosevelt Avenue and 126th Street, Flushing, N. Y. 11368.

Seating capacity—55,300.

FIELD DIMENSIONS—Home plate to left field at foul line, 338 feet; to center field, 410 feet; to right field at foul line, 338 feet.

PHILADELPHIA PHILLIES

President—Bill Giles

Partners—The Taft Baseball Co., John Drew Betz, Tri-Play Associates,
Fitz Eugene Dixon Jr., Mrs. Rochelle Levy, Robert D. Hedberg
Vice-President and General Manager—Paul Owens
Executive Vice-President—David Montgomery
Vice-President, Finance—Jerry Clothier
Vice-President, Public Relations—Larry Shenk
Secretary and Counsel—William Y. Webb
Director of Minor Leagues and Scouting—Jim Baumer
Executive Assistant—Tony Siegle
Player Personnel Advisor—Hugh Alexander
Assistant to the President—Mrs. Cathy Halpin
Ticket Manager—Ray Krise
Director of Promotions—Frank Sullivan
Director of Advertising—Tom Hudson
Traveling Secretary—Eddie Ferenz
Director of Ticket Sales—Richard Deats
Asst. Director of Minor Leagues and Scouting—Jack Pastore
Director of Community Relations and Broadcaster—Chris Wheeler
Assistant Public Relations Director—Vince Nauss
Director of Marketing—Dennis Lehman
Director of Stadium Operations—Mike DiMuzio
Executive Secretary to Minor Leagues—Bill Gargano
Club Physician—Dr. Phillip Marone
Club Trainer—Jeff Cooper
Strength and Flexibility Instructor—Gus Hoefling
Manager—Pat Corrales
Executive Offices—Philadelphia Veterans Stadium
Mailing Address—P.O. Box 7575, Philadelphia, Pa. 19101
Telephone—463-6000 (area code 215)

SCOUTS—(Special assignment)—Hugh Alexander and Wilbur Johnson. (Regular)—Francisco Acevedo, Oliver Bidwell, Edward Bockman, Carlos Cervo, George Farson, Doug Gassaway, Charles Gault, Bill Harper, Dick Lawlor, Anthony Lucadello, Gene Martin, Luis Peraza, Bob Reasonover, Scott Reid, Joe Reilly, Tony Roig, Andy Seminick, Elmer Valo, Randy Waddill, Don Williams, Bob Zuk.

PARK LOCATION—Philadelphia Veterans Stadium, Broad Street and Pattison Avenue.

Seating capacity—65,454.

FIELD DIMENSIONS—Home plate to left field at foul line, 330 feet; to center field, 408 feet; to right field at foul line, 330 feet.

PITTSBURGH PIRATES

President—Daniel M. Galbreath

Chairman of the Board—John W. Galbreath
Directors—Daniel M. Galbreath, David M. Roderick, Thomas
P. Johnson, Thomas P. Johnson, Jr., James M. Johnson, James
W. Phillips, Willard F. Rockwell, Jr., James H. Higgins
Executive Vice-President—Harding Peterson
Vice-President, Administration—Joseph M. O'Toole
Vice-President, Public Relations and Marketing—Jack Schrom
Vice-President and Secretary—Thomas P. Johnson
Assistant to Vice-President for Sales and Promotions—Olin J. DePolo
Treasurer, Assistant Secretary—Douglas G. McCormick
Assistant to the Vice-Presidents—Milt Graff
Director of Publicity—Edward A. Wade
Assistant Directors of Publicity—Sally O'Leary, Thomas Bird
Radio and TV Coordinator—Greg Brown
Director of Minor League Clubs—Branch B. Rickey, III
Assistant Director of Scouting—Jon Neiderer
Assistant Director of Minor League Clubs—Tom Kayser
Director of Season and Group Sales—Steve Greenberg
Season and Group Sales Department—Mark Ferraco, Lisa D'Amico
Assistant Director of Promotions—Kathy Saba
Assistant to the Treasurer—Kenneth C. Curcio
Ticket Manager—Richard C. Holland
Manager—Chuck Tanner
Traveling Secretary—Charles Muse
Club Physicians—Drs. Joseph Coroso, Jack Failla
Team Trainer—Tony Bartirome
Pirates Equipment Mgr.—John Hallahan
Executive Offices—Three Rivers Stadium, P.O. Box 6415
Pittsburgh, Pa. 15212
Telephone—323-5000 (area code 412)

SCOUTS—(Special assignment scouts)—Gene Baker, Kelvin Bowles, Joe L. Brown, Bill Bryk, Joe Consoli, Pablo Cruz, George Detore, Angel Figueroa, Jerry Gardner, Pete Gebrian, Fred Goodman, Howie Haak, Bob Johnson, Carlton Keller, Jose Luna, Jim Maxwell, Jeff McKay, Steve Oleschuk, Earl Silverthorn, Bob Whalen, Lenny Yochim. (Scouting assistants)—Ronnie Ahlhorn, Ossie Alvarez, Calvin Biron, Willie Bojos, Paul Bordi, Bill Bryan, Curt Bryan, Dave Buccolo, Joe Buccolo, F. (Kid) Carr, Maxie Carroll, Bill Cayavec, Frank Coimbre, Cecil Cole, Jean Cote, Nick Creola, Frank Curorke, Jim Emerson, Chuck Faris, Ed Farnum, Bigjack Fogerty, Steve Gilliland, John Gordon, Fred Hannum, Chris Healy, Leroy Hill, Bill Hirsch, Leo Hirsch, Bud Hoff, Woody Hunt, Fred Jiminez, Jim Lehman, Kevin Lester, Rip Lowe, J.D. McCord, Tom Myers, Sam Narron, John Nix, Boyd Odom, George Omachi, Angel Ortiz, Bobby Prescott, Dick Probola, Ron Rahr, Harold Ray, Don Reed, Luis Rivera, Doug Robbins, Andre Rodgers, Mark Runyan, Ken Saybel, George Schmidt, John Sloan, Don Suriano, Cloy Sykes, John Tucker, Roy Velasco, Tom Venditelli, Jim Walker, Joe Walker, Bill White, Bill Wigle, Jim Williams, Tom Work, Fred Wright, Ed Zeidler, Jack Zilles.

PARK LOCATION—Three Rivers Stadium, 600 Stadium Circle.

Seating capacity—54,499.

FIELD DIMENSIONS—Home plate to left field at foul line, 335 feet; to center field, 400 feet; to right field at foul line, 335 feet.

ST. LOUIS CARDINALS

Chairman of the Board, President and Chief Executive Officer—
August A. Busch, Jr.

Vice-Presidents—August A. Busch, III, Fred L. Kuhlmann, Margaret S. Busch
Senior Vice-President—Stan Musial
Secretary and Treasurer—John L. Hayward
Assistant Secretary—Richard Schwartz
Assistant Treasurer—H. F. Suellentrop
Board of Directors—Adolphus A. Busch, IV, August A. Busch, Jr., August A. Busch, III, Frederic E. Giersch, Jr., Louis B. Hager, John Hayward, Ben Kerner, Fred L. Kuhlmann, J.W. McAfee, Stanley F. Musial, W.R. Persons, Jack Pickens, Walter C. Reisinger, Margaret S. Busch
General Manager—Joe McDonald
Manager—Whitey Herzog
Vice-President, Business Operations—Gary Blase
Controller—John McMinn
Director of Administration—Joe McShane
Director of Player Development—Lee Thomas
Director of Scouting—Fred McAlister
Director of Minor League Operations—Paul Fauks
Director of Promotions—Marty Hendin
Director of Public Relations—Jim Toomey
Assistant Director of Public Relations—Robin Monsky
Director of Sales—Joe Cunningham
Director of Season Ticket Sales—Sue Ann McClaren
Director of Tickets and Operations—Mike Bertani
Assistant Director of Tickets—Josephine Arnold
Administrative Assistant to G.M.—Judy Lovelace
Traveling Secretary—C.J. Cherre
Club Physician—Dr. Stan London
Executive Offices—Busch Stadium, 250 Stadium Plaza,
St. Louis, Mo. 63102
Telephone—421-3060 (area code 314)

SCOUTS—(Supervisors)—Jim Belz, Vern Benson, Willie Calvino, Steve Flores, Joe Frazier, Rich Hacker, Jim Johnston, Hank Kelly, Marty Keough, Marty Maier, Tom McCormack, Mo Mozzali, Mike Roberts, Hal Smith, Charles (Tim) Thompson. (Regular)—Ted Baker, James Brown, Walker Cress, Roberto Diaz, Cecil Espy, Ray Goodman, Jim Holden, Darren Holt, Henry Krause, Thornton Lee, Frank Matthews, Virgil Melvin, Albert Osorio, Ed Pebley, Victor Perez, Joe Popek, Larry Schultz, Bart Shelly, George Silvey, John Skurski, Bill Warren.

PARK LOCATION—Busch Stadium, Broadway, Walnut Street, Stadium Plaza and Spruce Street.

Seating capacity—50,100.

FIELD DIMENSIONS—Home plate to left field at foul line, 330 feet; to center field, 414 feet; to right field at foul line, 330 feet.

SAN DIEGO PADRES

Board of Directors—Ray A. Kroc, Chairman; Joan Kroc, Ballard F. Smith, Jr.

President and Treasurer—Ballard F. Smith, Jr.
Senior Vice-President, Business Operations—Elten F. Schiller
Vice-President, Baseball Operations—Jack McKeon
Administrative Assistant—Rhoda Polley
Vice-President, Chief Financial Officer—Dick Freeman
Accounting Dept. Supervisor—Sondra Welch
Director of Player Development—Bob Cluck
Director of Scouting—Sandy Johnson
Major League Scout, Special Assignments—Dick Hager
Administrator, Minor Leagues and Scouting—Tom Romenesko
Director of Public Relations—Bob Chandler
Assistants—Be Barnes, Jim Geschke
Director of Broadcasting—Jerry Coleman
Director of Group Sales—Tom Mulcahy
Director of Promotions—Andy Strasberg
Director of Ticket Sales—Dave Gilmore
Traveling Secretary—John Mattei
Manager—Dick Williams
Club Physician—Scripps Clinic
Executive Offices—P. O. Box 2000, San Diego, Calif. 92120
Telephone—283-4494 (area code 619)

SCOUTS—Aquiles Angulo, Dave Bartosch, Ken Bracey, Billy Castell, Ray Coley, Manny Crespo, Grisha Davida, Bill Earnhart, Denny Galehouse, Tony Garcia, Dick Hager, Bernie Healy, Al Heist, Donald Hennelly, Edgar Jewell, Jim Marshall, Bill McKeon, Kelly McKeon, Luis Rosa, Brad Sloan, Bob Stamsos, Vince Valecce, Bob Warner, Hank Zacharias.

PARK LOCATION—San Diego Stadium, 9949 Friars Road.

Seating capacity—51,309.

FIELD DIMENSIONS—Home plate to left field at foul line, 330 feet; to center field, 420 feet; to right field at foul line, 330 feet.

SAN FRANCISCO GIANTS

President—Robert A. Lurie

Vice-President, Baseball Operations—Thomas F. Haller
Vice-President, Business Operations—Patrick J. Gallagher
Vice-President, Administration—Corey Busch
Asst. Vice-President, Baseball Operations/Minor Leagues—Ralph E. Nelson, Jr.
Director of Player Personnel and Scouting—Bob Fontaine
Field Director of Player Development—Jim Lefebvre
Minor League Consultant—Jack Schwarz
Asst. Field Director of Player Personnel and Development—Robert L. Miller
Director of Publicity—Duffy Jennings
Director of Community and Public Relations—Stu Smith
Director of Marketing—Laurence M. Baer
Director of Stadium Operations—Don Foreman
Ticket Manager—Arthur Schulze
Accounting Manager—Ron Mosher
Director of Sales—Bob Gaillard
Traveling Secretary/Statistician—Dirk Smith
Speakers Bureau—Joe Orengo
Community Representative—Mike Sadek
Team Photographer—Dennis Desprois
Manager—Frank Robinson
Executive Offices—Candlestick Park, San Francisco, Calif. 94124
Telephone—468-3700 (area code 415)

SCOUTS—Everett (Rocky) Bridges, Edward A. Barberis, Ernie Beck, Dave Clark, Mark Conkin, Terry Christman, Harry Craft, Dutch Deutsch, Jack DiGrace, Ruben Decena, Nino Escalera, Jack French, Robert Folkins, Maurice D. Fisher, George M. Genovese, Grady Hatton, Carl Hubbell, Herman Hannah, Richard Klaus, Harvey Koepf, Andy Korenek, Jim Lyke, Horacio Martinez, Marty Miller, Bob Miller, Hugh Poland, Bill Parese, Ken (Squeaky) Parker, Veto Ramirez, Del Rice, Walt Ripley, Hank Sauer, Marvin Stendel, LeGrant Scott, John Shafer, Gene Thompson, Dick Wilson, Joe Winstead, Tom Zimmer.

PARK LOCATION—Candlestick Point, Bayshore Freeway.

Seating capacity—58,000.

FIELD DIMENSIONS—Home plate to left field at foul line, 335 feet; to center field, 400 feet; to right field at foul line, 335 feet.

American League
Organized 1900

LELAND S. MacPHAIL, Jr.
President

JOSEPH E. CRONIN
Chairman

CALVIN R. GRIFFITH, JOHN E. FETZER, GENE AUTRY
Vice-Presidents

ROBERT O. FISHEL
Secretary and
Assistant to the President

DONALD C. MARR, Jr.
Controller

RICHARD BUTLER
Supervisor of Umpires

ROBERT F. HOLBROOK
Special Assistant

STEPHANIE VARDAVAS
Manager, Waivers & Player Records Department

PHYLLIS MERHIGE
Assistant Public Relations Director

TESS BASTA, ROBERT GRIM
Administrators

Headquarters—280 Park Avenue, New York, N. Y. 10017

Telephone—682-7000 (area code 212)

ASSISTANT SUPERVISORS OF UMPIRES—Nestor Chylak, William Haller, Henry Soar.

UMPIRES—Lawrence Barnett, Nicholas Bremigan, Joseph Brinkman, Drew Cable, Alan Clark, Terrance Cooney, Derryl Cousins, Donald Denkinger, James Evans, Dale Ford, Richard Garcia, Russell Goetz, Ted Hendry, Kenneth Kaiser, Greg Kosc, William Kunkel, George Maloney, Larry McCoy, James McKean, Durwood Merrill, Jerome Neudecker, Stephen Palermo, Dallas Parks, David Phillips, Michael Reilly, John (Rocky) Roe, John Shulock, Martin Springstead, Vic Voltaggio.

OFFICIAL STATISTICIANS—Sports Information Center, 1776 Heritage Drive, No. Quincy, Mass. 02171. Telephone—(617) 328-4674.

Players cannot be transferred from one major league to another after June 15 to close of the championship season except through regular waiver channels.

WAIVER PRICE, $20,000. Interleague waivers, $20,000, except for selected players and draft-excluded players.

American League President Leland S. MacPhail Jr.

BALTIMORE ORIOLES

Chairman of the Board and President—Edward Bennett Williams

Executive Vice-President, General Manager—Henry J. Peters
Vice-President, Stadium Operations—Jack Dunn, III
Vice-President, Finance—Joseph P. Hamper, Jr.
Treasurer—Gerald T. Gabrys
Secretary, General Counsel—Lawrence Lucchino
Directors—Edward Bennett Williams, Joseph P. DiMaggio, Jack Dunn, III,
Gerald T. Gabrys, Charles H. Hoffberger, Jerold C. Hoffberger,
Zanvyl Kreiger, Lawrence Lucchino, Henry J. Peters, Peter P. Weidenbruch, Jr.
Special Assistant to the General Manager—James J. Russo
Director of Business Affairs—Robert R. Aylward
Public Relations Director—Robert W. Brown
Traveling Secretary—Philip E. Itzoe
Director, Player Development and Scouting—Thomas A. Giordano
Director of Sales—Jon Richardson
Promotions Director—Drew M. Sheinman
Ticket Office Manager—Timothy Geraghty
Assistant Public Relations Director—John C. Blake
Assistant Director, Player Development and Scouting—John J. McCall
Director, Florida Operations—Ralph A. Morcroft
Assistant Ticket Manager—Joseph B. Codd
Washington Area Representative—Joseph D. Felperin
Baltimore Sales Representative—Herbert C. Fett
Consultant; President, Orioles Foundation—Herbert E. Armstrong
Manager—Joseph S. Altobelli
Club Physician—Dr. Leonard Wallenstein
Executive Offices—Memorial Stadium, Baltimore, Md. 21218
Telephone—243-9800 (area code 301)

SCOUTS—(Major League)—Jim Russo, John Stokoe, Earl Weaver, Bill Werle.
(Regular)—Jack Baker, Joe Bowman, Dan Cressman, Ray Crone, Ed Crosby, Joe
DeLucca, Jim Driscoll, Jose Garcia, Jim Gilbert, John Hagemann, Myron Hayworth,
Len Johnston, Mark Just, Bill Lawlor, George Lauzerique, Earl McKenzie, Minne
Mendoza, Lamar North, Jim Pamlayne, Robert Roselli, Jack Sanford, William Teed,
Tommy Thompson, Pete Torrez, Herman Welsh, Jerry Zimmerman.

PARK LOCATION—Memorial Stadium, 33rd Street, Ellerslie Avenue, 36th
Street, and Ednor Road.

Seating capacity—53,209.

FIELD DIMENSIONS—Home plate to left field at foul line, 309 feet; to center
field, 405 feet; to right field at foul line, 309 feet.

BOSTON RED SOX

President—Jean R. Yawkey

Executive Vice-President, General Manager—Haywood C. Sullivan
Executive Vice-President, Administration—Edward G. LeRoux, Jr.
Treasurer—James M. Olivier, Jr.
V. P., Player Development Director—Edward F. Kenney
Scouting Director—Edward M. Kasko
Traveling Secretary—John J. Rogers
Public Relations Director—George Sullivan
Publicity Director—Richard L. Bresciani
Marketing Director—James P. Healey
Group Sales Director—Leslie Cargill
Assistant Publicity Director—John E. McCarthy
Executive Assistant—Joseph F. McDermott
Assistant Treasurer—John J. Reilly
Ticket Director—Arthur J. Moscato
Promotions Director—Wayne Thornton
Consultant, Player Relations—John L. Harrington
Consultant, Organizational Hitting Instructor—Theodore S. Williams
Superintendent, Grounds & Maintenance—Joseph Mooney
Manager—Ralph G. Houk
Club Physician—Dr. Arthur M. Pappas
Executive Offices—24 Yawkey Way, Boston, Mass. 02215
Telephone—267-9440 (area code 617)

SCOUTS—Milton Bolling, Ray Boone, Wayne Britton, George Digby, Howard (Danny) Doyle, Bill Enos, Larry Flynn, Earl Johnson, Charles Koney, Wilfrid (Lefty) Lefebvre, Don Lenhardt, Tommy McDonald, Felix Maldonado, Frank Malzone, Sam Mele, Ramon Naranjo, Willie Paffen, Philip Rossi, Edward Scott, Matt Sczesny, Joe Stephenson, Larry Thomas, Charlie Wagner.

PARK LOCATION—Fenway Park, Yawkey Way, Lansdowne Street and Ipswich Street.

Seating capacity—33,536.

FIELD DIMENSIONS—Home plate to left field at foul line, 315 feet; to center field, 420 feet; to right field at foul line, 302 feet; average right-field distance, 382 feet.

CALIFORNIA ANGELS

President and Chairman of the Board—Gene Autry

Executive Vice-President—E.J. Bavasi
Assistant to the Chairman of the Board—Arthur E. Patterson
Vice-President and Chief Administrative Officer—Mike Port
Director Public Relations and Promotions—Tom Seeberg
Director of Accounting—Jim Kaczmarek
Director Scouting & Player Development—Larry Himes
Director of Minor League Operations—Bill Bavasi
Director Ticket Development—Carl Gordon
Director Group Sales—Lynn Kirchmann Biggs
Director Stadium Operations—Jean (Corky) Lippert
Traveling Secretary—Frank Sims
Assistant Director Public Relations—Tim Mead
Assistant Ticket Director—Bob Terzes
Stadium Operations—Kevin Uhlich
Film Coordinator and Special Statistics—George Goodale
Medical Director—Dr. Robert K. Kerlan
Orthopedist—Dr. Lewis Yocum
Trainers—Rick Smith, Ned Bergert
Manager—John McNamara
Executive Offices—Anaheim Stadium, 2000 State College Blvd.,
Anaheim, Calif. 92806
Telephone—937-6700 (area code 714) or 625-1123 (area code 213)

SCOUTS—Edmundo Borrome, George Brunet, Vince Capece, Joe Carpenter, Lloyd Christopher, Lou Cohenour, Alex Cosmidis, Pompeyo Davillo, Bob Gardner, Al Goldis, Steve Gruwell, Harry Hayes, Rick Ingalls, Nick Kamzic, Joe Maddon, Vic Power, Philip Rizzo, Cookie Rojas, Lou Snipp.

PARK LOCATION—Anaheim Stadium, 2000 State College Blvd.

Seating capacity—65,158.

FIELD DIMENSIONS—Home plate to left field at foul line, 333 feet; to center field, 404 feet; to right field at foul line, 333 feet.

CHICAGO WHITE SOX

Chairman, Board of Directors—Jerry M. Reinsdorf
President—Eddie M. Einhorn
Executive Vice-President, General Manager—Roland A. Hemond
Executive Vice-President—Howard C. Pizer
Vice-President, Marketing—Michael D. McClure
Vice-President, Broadcasting and Special Projects—Laureen Ong Fadil
Vice-President, Baseball Administration—Jack Gould
Assistant General Manager—David Dombrowski
Director of Player Development—Bob Winkles
Assistant to Vice-President, Marketing—Stephen M. Schanwald
Director of Public Relations—Charles A. Shriver
Sales Manager—Millie Johnson
Director, Season Sales—Jeff Overton
Director of Broadcast Sales—Edwin M. Doody
Controller—Timothy L. Buzard
Traveling Secretary—Glen Rosenbaum
Ticket Manager—Robert K. Devoy
Director, Group Sales and Park Entertainment—George M. Koch
Assistant Director of Public Relations—Kenneth M. Valdiserri
Director of Latin American Baseball Operations—Angel Vasquez
Administrative Assistant, Baseball Operations—William E. Smith, Jr.
General Counsel—Allan B. Muchin
Trainer—Herman Schneider
Assistant Trainer—Brandt McFarlin
Team Physicians—Drs. Richard D. Corzatt, James B. Boscardin, Hugo Cuadros
Manager—Tony LaRussa
Equipment/Club House Mgr., White Sox—Willie Thompson
Equipment/Club House Mgr., Visitors—John MacNamara, Jr.
Director of Park Operations—David M. Schaffer
Groundskeepers—Gene and Roger Bossard
P.A. Announcer—Wayne Mesmer
Organist—Nancy Faust
Executive Offices—Comiskey Park, Dan Ryan at 35th Street, Chicago, Ill. 60616
Telephone—924-1000 (area code 312)

SCOUTS—(Advance)—Loren Babe. (Special Assignment)—Jerry Krause, Fred Shaffer. (Supervisor)—Walt Widmayer. (Regular)—James Busby, Bobby Gardner, Jr., Eric Gluck, Bennie Huffman, Joseph Ingalls, Bart Johnson, Leo Labossiere, Marvin Lane, Dario Lodigiani, Terry Logan, Larry Monroe, Rich Morales, Fern Paredes, Silvano Quezada, Thomas Roberts, Cucho Rodriguez, Mark Servais, Duane Shaffer, George Sobek, Lynn Squires, Kenneth Stauffer, Angel Vazquez (Castro), Stan Zielinski.

PARK LOCATION—Comiskey Park, Dan Ryan at 35th Street, Chicago, Ill. 60616.

Seating capacity—43,695.

FIELD DIMENSIONS—Home plate to left field at foul line, 341 feet; to center field, 401 feet; to right field at foul line, 341 feet.

CLEVELAND INDIANS

President and Chief Executive Officer—Gabe Paul

Chairman of the Board—F.J. (Steve) O'Neill
Directors—F.J. O'Neill, C.C. Tippit, Dudley S. Blossom, III, Alva T. Bonda,
Walter Laich, Gabe Paul, Arnold Pinkney, Phillip Seghi, Maurice Stonehill
Vice-President and General Manager—Phillip D. Seghi
Vice-President, Player Development and Scouting—Bob Quinn
Treasurer—Dudley S. Blossom, III
Secretary and Club Legal Counsel—Armond D. Arnson
Manager—Mike Ferraro
Traveling Secretary—Mike Seghi
Director of Public Relations—Bob DiBiasio
Director of Marketing—Joann Klonowski
Director of Sales—Tom Pulchinski
Director of Stadium Operations—Dan Zerbey
Ticket Director—Jerry Waring
Controller—Jason Rosenthal
Public Relations—Bob Feller
Special Assistant to the President—Ron Mottl
Special Assistant to General Manager—Dan Carnevale
Special Assignment Representative—Birdie Tebbetts
Asst. Public Relations Director—Pete Spudich
Minor League Administrator—Joe Pavia
Asst. Farm Director—Phil Thomas
Trainer—Jim Warfield
Club Physicians—Drs. William Wilder, Earl Brightman
Club Dentist—Dr. Marvin Schermer
Equipment Manager—Cy Buynak
Groundskeeper—Marshall Bossard
Executive Offices—Cleveland Stadium, Cleveland, Ohio 44114
Telephone—861-1200 (area code 216)

SCOUTS—Hector Acevedo, Jack Cassini, Red Gaskill, Leon Hamilton, Luis Issac,
Frank Lucchesi, Bobby Malkmus, Jim Miller, Woody Smith, Gary Sutherland, Jack
Vallely, Gene Woodling.

PARK LOCATION—Cleveland Stadium, Boudreau Blvd.

Seating capacity—74,208.

FIELD DIMENSIONS—Home plate to left field at foul line, 320 feet; to center
field, 400 feet; to right field at foul line, 320 feet.

DETROIT TIGERS

Owner & Chairman of the Board—John E. Fetzer

President & General Manager—James A. Campbell
Vice-President/Finance & Secretary-Treasurer—Alexander C. Callam
Vice-President/Operations—William E. Haase
Vice-President/Baseball—William R. Lajoie
Director of Public Relations—Dan Ewald
Director of Ticket Sales—Jerry Bucholtz
Box Office Treasurer—William H. Willis
Director of Stadium Operations—Ralph E. Snyder
Field Director/Player Development—Walter A. Evers
Administrator, Player Development—David Miller
Scouting Director—George Bradley
Traveling Secretary—Bill Brown
Assistant Director of Public Relations—Bob Miller
Asst. Dir. of Public Relations/Special Events—Lew Martin
Asst. Dir. of Public Relations/Community Affairs—Vince Desmond
Executive Secretary/Baseball—Alice Sloane
Executive Secretary/Operations—Hazel McLane
Consultants—Richard B. Ferrell, Edward G. Katalinas
Asst. Director of Stadium Operations—Frank Feneck
Manager—Sparky Anderson
Club Physician—Clarence S. Livingood M.D.
Orthopedic Consultant—Robert A. Teitge M.D.
Executive Offices—Tiger Stadium, Detroit, Mich. 48216
Telephone—962-4000 (area code 313)

SCOUTS—Rick Arnold, John (Red) Barkley, Ray Bellino, Wayne Blackburn, Bart Braun, Joe Henderson, Roger Jongewaard, Joe Lewis, Orlando Pena, Jax Robertson, William Schudlich, John Young. (Scouting consultants)—Richard Ferrell, Ed Katalinas, Frank Skaff, Jack Tighe.

PARK LOCATION—Tiger Stadium, Michigan Avenue, Cochrane Avenue, Kaline Drive and Trumbull Avenue.

Seating capacity—52,806.

FIELD DIMENSIONS—Home plate to left field at foul line, 340 feet; to center field, 440 feet; to right field at foul line, 325 feet.

KANSAS CITY ROYALS

Board of Directors
Joe Burke, William Deramus III, Charles Hughes, Ewing Kauffman,
Mrs. Ewing Kauffman, Earl Smith

Chairman of the Board—Ewing Kauffman
President—Joe Burke
Executive Vice-President and General Manager—John Schuerholz
Executive Vice-President, Administration—Spencer (Herk) Robinson
Vice-President, Controller—Dale Rohr
Vice-President and Legal Counsel—Phil Koury
Director of Public Relations—Dean Vogelaar
Director of Marketing and Broadcasting—Bryan Burns
Traveling Secretary/Lancer Coordinator—Bill Beck
Assistant Director of Publications—Will Rudd
Director of Scouting and Player Development—Dick Balderson
Assistant Director of Scouting and Player Development—Dean Taylor
Director of Ticket Operations—Stacy Sherrow
Director of Season Ticket Sales—Joe Grigoli
Season Ticket Coordinator—Debbie Gooding
Director of Group Sales/Special Events—Rush Limbaugh
Director of Event Personnel—Chris Muehlbach
Stadium Engineer—George Humphrey
Stadium Maintenance Coordinator—Bob Frank
Accountants—Tom Pfannenstiel, Ken Willeke
Manager—Dick Howser
Equipment Manager—Al Zych
Groundskeeper—George Toma
Team Physician—Dr. Paul Meyer
Trainer—Mickey Cobb
Executive Offices—Royals Stadium, Harry S Truman Sports Complex
Mailing Address—P. O. Box 1969, Kansas City, Mo. 64141
Telephone—921-8000 (area code 816)

SCOUTS—Carl Blando, Al Diez, Tom Ferrick, Rosey Gilhousen, Ken Gonzales, Guy Hansen, Ron Hopkins, Al Kubski, Brian Murphy, George Noga, Rich Schlenker, Jerry Stephens, Art Stewart, Jerry Terrell, Red Whitsett.

PARK LOCATION—Royals Stadium, Harry S Truman Sports Complex.

Seating capacity—40,628.

FIELD DIMENSIONS—Home plate to left field at foul line, 330 feet; to center field, 410 feet; to right field at foul line, 330 feet.

MILWAUKEE BREWERS

President, Chief Executive Officer—Allan H. (Bud) Selig

Executive Vice-President, General Manager—Harry Dalton
Vice-President, Marketing—Richard Hackett
Vice-President, Administration—Thomas J. Ferguson
Vice-President, Broadcast Operations—William Haig
Vice-President, Finance—Richard Hoffmann
Vice-President, Stadium Operations—Gabe Paul, Jr.
Assistant General Manager—Walter Shannon
Special Assistants to the General Manager—Dee Fondy, Sal Bando
Director of Player Procurement—Ray Poitevint
Coordinator of Minor League Operations—Bruce Manno
Administrative Assistant for Scouting and Player Development—Dan Duquette
Director of Publicity—Tom Skibosh
Assistant Director of Stadium Operations and Advertising—Jack Hutchinson
Ticket Sales Director—Tim Trovato
Director of the Speakers Bureau—John Counsell
Assistant Director of Publicity—Mario Ziino
Ticket Office Manager—John Barnes
Director of Ticket Office Computer Operations—Alice Boettcher
Director of Special Events—Mark Paget
Manager—Harvey Kuenn
Club Physician—Dr. Paul Jacobs
Trainers—Freddie Frederico, John Adam
Superintendent of Grounds and Maintenance—Harry Gill
Assistant Groundskeeper—Gary Vandenberg
Equipment Manager—Bob Sullivan
P.A. Announcer—Bob Betts
Organist—Frank Charles
Executive Offices—Milwaukee Brewers Baseball Club
Milwaukee County Stadium, Milwaukee, Wis. 53214
Telephone—933-1818 (area code 414)

SCOUTS—Scouting supervisors: Julio Blanco-Herrera, Nelson Burbrink, Felix Delgado, Tom Gamboa, Roland LeBlanc, Walter Youse. Regular scouts: Fred Beene, Tom Bourque, Ken Califano, Gerry Craft, Dick Ehrig, Charles Fitzgerald, Dick Foster, Hy Gomberg, Larry Hisle, Gene Kerns, Frank Kolarek, Billy Moffitt, Johnny Neun, Ken Richardson, Lee Sigman, Harry Smith, Milt Sobel, Sam Suplizio, Paul Tretiak.

PARK LOCATION—Milwaukee County Stadium, S. 46th St. off Bluemound Rd.

Seating capacity—53,192.

FIELD DIMENSIONS—Home plate to left field at foul line, 315 feet; to center field, 402 feet; to right field at foul line, 315 feet.

MINNESOTA TWINS

Chairman of Board, President—Calvin R. Griffith

Vice-President—Mrs. Thelma Griffith Haynes
Executive Vice-President—Clark Griffith
Executive Vice-President—Bruce G. Haynes
Director—H. Gabriel Murphy
Director—Eugene V. Young
Director—Wheelock Whitney
Executive Vice-President—Howard T. Fox, Jr.
Executive Vice-President—William S. Robertson
Vice-President—James K. Robertson
Vice-President, Farm Director—George Brophy
Assistant Farm Director—Jim Rantz
Controller—Jack Alexander
Director of Public Relations—Tom Mee
Director of Sales—Gil Lansdale
Traveling Secretary—Mike Robertson
Manager—Billy Gardner
Club Physicians—Dr. Leonard J. Michienzi and Dr. Harvey O'Phelan
Executive Offices—Hubert H. Humphrey Metrodome, 501 Chicago Ave. South,
Minneapolis, Minn. 55415
Telephone—375-1366 (area code 612)

SCOUTS—Floyd Baker, Ellsworth Brown, Spud Chandler, Ellis Clary, Edward Dunn, Jesse Flores, Jr., Jesse Flores, Sr., Angelo Giuliani, Lee Irwin, Hank Izquierdo, William Messmann, Marvin Olson, Spencer (Red) Robbins, Stanley Rogers, Herb Stein.

PARK LOCATION—Hubert H. Humphrey Metrodome, 501 Chicago Ave. South.

Seating capacity—55,122.

FIELD DIMENSIONS—Home plate to left field at foul line, 343 feet; to center field, 408 feet; to right field at foul line, 327 feet.

NEW YORK YANKEES

Principal Owner—George M. Steinbrenner III

Limited Partners—Harold Bowman, Lester Crown, Michael Friedman,
Marvin Goldklang, Barry Halper, Leonard L. Kleinman, Harvey Leighton,
Daniel McCarthy, Harry Nederlander, Robert Nederlander,
William J. O'Neill, William Rose, Edward Rosenthal,
Jack Satter, Charlotte Witkind
President—Eugene J. McHale
Executive Vice-President—Cedric Tallis
Manager—Billy Martin
Administrative Vice-President and Treasurer—David Weidler
Vice-President, Baseball Operations—Bill Bergesch
Vice-President—Ed Weaver
Director of Player Development and Scouting—Murray Cook
Director of Scouting—Bobby Hofman
Traveling Secretary—Bill Kane
Administrative Assistant—Gerry Murphy
Director of Media Relations—Ken Nigro
Director of Publications—David Szen
Director of Public Relations—John Fugazy
Public Relations Assistants—Betsy Leesman, Bob Pelegrino, Lou D'Ermilio
Stadium Manager—Patrick Kelly
Executive Director of Ticket Operations—Frank Swaine
Ticket Director—Michael Rendine
Assistant Ticket Director—Jim Hodge
Director, Customer Services and Asst. Stadium Manager—Jim Naples
Baseball Operations Assistants—Mike Barnett, John Dato,
Bob Kalaf, Roy Krasik, Doug Melvin
Director of Group Sales—Joe Novelino
Director of Accounting—Bill Nahabedian
Stadium Superintendent—Jimmy Esposito
Spring Training Coordinator—Marsh Samuel
Team Photographer—John Woodward
Director, Yankee Alumni Association—Jim Ogle
Club Physician—Dr. John J. Bonamo
P.A. Announcer—Bob Sheppard
Organist—Eddie Layton
Executive Offices—Yankee Stadium, Bronx, N.Y. 10451
Telephone—293-4300 (area code 212)
Ticket Information—293-6000 (area code 212)

SCOUTS—Luis Arroyo, Hank Bauer, Joe Begani, Ollie Brown, Howard Cassidy,
Al Cuccinello, Whitey DeHart, Joe DiCarlo, Henry Dotterer, Fred Ferreria, Whitey
Ford, Jack Gillis, Tom Greenwade, Dick Groch, Jim Gruzdis, Roy Hamey, Jim
Hegan, Gary Hughes, John Kennedy, Clyde King, Bob Lemon, Don Lindeberg, Jack
Llewellyn, Gene Michael, Jim Naples, Sr., Bob Nieman, Frank O'Rourke, Meade
Palmer, Gust Poulos, Eddie Robinson, Russ Sehon, Robert Shaw.

PARK LOCATION—Yankee Stadium, E: 161st St. and River Ave., Bronx, N.Y.
10451.

Seating capacity—57,545.

FIELD DIMENSIONS—Home plate to left field at foul line, 312 feet; to center
field, 417 feet; to right field at foul line, 310 feet.

OAKLAND A's

President—Roy Eisenhardt

Executive Vice-President—Walter J. Haas
Vice-President and General Counsel—Sandy Alderson
Vice-President, Baseball Administration—Carl A. Finley
Vice-President, Business Operations—Andy Dolich
Vice-President, Minor League Player Development—Dick Wiencek
Vice-President, Finance—James T. Lawrence
Assistant to the President, Baseball Matters—Bill Rigney
Director of Major League Scouting—Charlie Metro
Director of Minor League Operations—Walt Jocketty
Traveling Secretary, Director of Press Relations—Mickey Morabito
Director of Media Relations—Rick Moxley
Director of Sales and Telecommunications—David Rubinstein
Director of Marketing and Merchandising—Roger Moskowitz
Director of Ticket Operations—Raymond B. Krise Jr.
Director of Special Projects—Earl Robinson
Director of Youth Programs-Speakers Bureau—Craig Amerkhanian
Director of Stadium Operations—Jorge Costa
Director of Public Relations—Daniel Orum
Executive Assistant—Sharon Jones
Business Operations Coordinator—Sharon Kelly
Ticket Manager—Bettina Flores
Director of Broadcast Operations—Bill King
Director of Ticket Sales—Steve Page
Assistant Director of Press Relations-Statistician—Jay Alves
Managing Editor, Publications—Art Worthington
Manager—Steve Boros
Team Physician—Dr. Thomas E. Richmond
Trainer—Barry Weinberg, Jack Homel
Equipment Manager—Frank Ciensczyk
Visiting Clubhouse Manager—Steve Vucinich
Marketing Representatives—Tom Cordova, Clarence Jackson, Doris Messina,
Larry Sindall, Tony Stevens
Executive Offices—Oakland-Alameda County Coliseum, Oakland, Calif. 94621
Telephone—638-4900 (area code 415)

SCOUTS—Albert Elliott, Jr., Frank Franchi, Grady Fuson, Fred Hatfield, Juan Marichal, Edwin Mathews, Mickey McDermott, Jethro McIntyre, Charlie Metro, Mel Nelson, Camilo Pascual, James Perry, Charles Silvera, Ed Stevens, Mike Wallace, Gary Wiencek, Del Wilber.

PARK LOCATION—Oakland-Alameda County Coliseum, Nimitz Freeway and Hegenberger Road.

Seating capacity—50,219.

FIELD DIMENSIONS—Home plate to left field at foul line, 330 feet; to center field, 397 feet; to right field at foul line, 330 feet.

SEATTLE MARINERS

Principal Owner—George L. Argyros

Limited Partners—Stanley Golub, Danny Kaye, Walter Schoenfeld, Lester M. Smith
President—Daniel F. O'Brien
Director of Player Development—Hal Keller
Vice-President, Sales and Marketing—Bill Long
Director of Sales—Al (Moose) Clauson
Director of Team Travel—Lee Pelekoudas
Director of Stadium Operations—Craig Barrick
Director of Public Relations—Randy Adamack
Manager—Rene Lachemann
Manager of Publicity—Bob Porter
Manager of Promotions—Steve Krause
Manager of Broadcast Services—Melody Tucker
Manager of Community Relations—Jeff Klein
Manager of Stadium Entertainment—Randy Stearns
Assistant Director of Player Development—Jeff Scott
Assistant Director of Player Development for Instruction—Bill Haywood
Controller—Brian Beggs
Office Manager—Janet Croft
Club Physicians—Drs. Larry Pedegana, James Trombold
Club Dentist—Dr. Richard Leshgold
Head Groundkeeper—Wilbur Woo
P.A. Announcer—Gary Spinnell
Executive Offices—P.O. Box 4100
100 South King Street, Suite 300, Seattle, Washington 98104
Telephone—628-3555 (area code 206)

SCOUTS—John Cole, Amado Dinzy, Bob Harrison, Bill Kearns, Jose "Coco" Laboy, Jeff Malinoff, Orlando Martinez, Whitey Piurek, Rip Tutor, Steve Vrablik.

PARK LOCATION—Kingdome, 201 South King Street, Seattle, Washington.

Seating capacity—59,438.

FIELD DIMENSIONS—Home plate to left field at foul line, 316 feet; to center field, 410 feet; to right field at foul line, 316 feet.

TEXAS RANGERS

Chairman of the Board, President, Chief Executive Officer—Eddie Chiles

Vice Chairman, General Counsel, Secretary—Dee J. Kelly
Vice President and General Manager—Joe Klein
Special Assistant to the Vice-President, Baseball Operations—Paul Richards
Executive Vice-President, Business Operations—Samuel G. Meason
Vice-President, Marketing—James T. Medick
Directors—Dee J. Kelly, Mack Rankin,
William H. Seay, Charles S. Sharp
Treasurer—Charles F. Wangner
Executive Director, Texas Rangers Network—Roy Parks
Director of Player Development—Tom Grieve
Director of Media Relations—Burton Hawkins
Director of Public Relations—Allan Charnish
Director of Advertising and Promotions—Harry Campbell
Director of Ticket Management—Mary Ann Bosher
Director of Security—John Welaj
Director of Maintenance and Crowd Control—Matt Stolley
Traveling Secretary—Dan Schimek
Manager—Doug Rader
Administrative Assistant and Director of Speakers Bureau—Bobby Bragan
Administrative Assistant—Wayne Krivsky
Sabremetrician—Craig Wright
Physical Fitness Consultant—Dr. Eugene Coleman
Director of Physical Fitness Programs—Mike Fitzsimmons
Medical Director—Dr. B. J. Mycoskie
Field Superintendent—John Oliveria
Public Address Announcer—Mitch Carr
Executive Offices—Arlington Stadium, P.O. Box 1111,
1500 Copeland Road, Arlington, Tex. 76010
Telephone—273-5222 (area code 817)

SCOUTS—Harley Anderson, Lee Anthony, Joseph Branzell, Jackie Brathwaite, Paddy Cottrell, Dick Gernert, Cesar Guttierez, Andy Hancock, Sid Hudson, Stan Jakubowski, Gary Johnson, Joseph Lewis, Joseph Marchese, Cotton Nix, Connie Ryan, Rick Schroeder, Fred Velasquez.

PARK LOCATION—Arlington Stadium, 1500 Copeland Road, Arlington, Tex.

Seating capacity—41,284.

FIELD DIMENSIONS—Home plate to left field at foul line, 330 feet; to center field, 400 feet; to right field at foul line, 330 feet.

TORONTO BLUE JAYS

Chief Executive Officer—N. E. Hardy

Board of Directors—L. G. Greenwood, N. E. Hardy,
R. Howard Webster, P. N. T. Widdrington
Chairman of the Board—R. Howard Webster
Vice-President, Business Operations—Paul Beeston
Vice-President, Baseball Operations—Pat Gillick
Executive Coordinator, Baseball Operations—Bobby Mattick
Director, Public Relations—Howard Starkman
Director, Operations—Ken Erskine
Director, Ticket Operations—George Holm
Administrator, Player Personnel—Elliott Wahle
Trainer-Director, Team Travel—Ken Carson
Director, Group Sales—Maureen Haffey
Director, Player Development—Billy Smith
Director, Canadian Scouting—Bob Prentice
Assistant Director, Public Relations—Gary Oswald
Assistant Director, Operations—Gord Ash
Assistant Director, Ticket Operations—Len Frejlich
Director, Security—Fred Wootton
Equipment Manager—Jeff Ross
Coordinator, Promotions & Group Services—John MacLachlan
Supervisor, Grounds—Dave Hamilton
Manager—Bobby Cox
Team Physician—Dr. Ron Taylor
Executive Offices—Exhibition Stadium, Exhibition Place,
Toronto, Ontario
Mailing Address—Box 7777, Adelaide St. P. O., Toronto, Ont. M5C 2K7
Telephone—595-0077 (area code 416)

SCOUTS—Ellis Dungan, Robert Engle (Eastern Regional Scouting Director),
Joe Ford, Epy Guerrero, Jack Hayes, Jim Hughes, Al LaMacchia (Senior Scouting
Supervisor), Duane Larson (off-season), Larry Maxie, Ben McLure, Wayne Morgan
(Western Regional Scouting Director), Paul Ricciarini, Don Welke, Bob Wilbur, Tim
Wilkin, Dave Yoakum.

PARK LOCATION—Exhibition Stadium on the grounds of Exhibition Place. En-
trances to Exhibition Place via Lakeshore Boulevard, Queen Elizabeth Way High-
way and Dufferin and Bathurst Streets.

Seating capacity—43,737.

FIELD DIMENSIONS—Home plate to left field at foul line, 330 feet; to center
field, 400 feet; to right field at foul line, 330 feet.

ROBIN YOUNT
● MILWAUKEE BREWERS ●
MAJOR LEAGUE
PLAYER OF THE YEAR

HARRY DALTON
● MILWAUKEE BREWERS ●
MAJOR LEAGUE EXECUTIVE

WHITEY HERZOG
● ST. LOUIS CARDINALS ●
MAJOR LEAGUE MANAGER

GEORGE SCHERGER
● INDIANAPOLIS ●
MINOR LEAGUE MANAGER

The Sporting News

No. **1**

MEN

of

1982

RON KITTLE
● EDMONTON ●
MINOR LEAGUE PLAYER

A. RAY SMITH
● LOUISVILLE ●
MINOR LEAGUE EXECUTIVE
IN CLASS AAA

ART CLARKSON
● BIRMINGHAM ●
MINOR LEAGUE EXECUTIVE
IN CLASS AA

BOB CARRUESCO
● STOCKTON ●
MINOR LEAGUE EXECUTIVE
IN CLASS A

Major League Players Association

1370 Avenue of the Americas
Suite 2602
New York, N.Y. 10019
Telephone—(212) 581-8484

Kenneth E. Moffett—Executive Director
Donald Fehr—General Counsel
Peter Rose—Associate Counsel
Administrator—Arthur Schack
Staff—Millie Ciuro, John Hess and Joyce Reiss.

EXECUTIVE BOARD

Steve Renko—American League Representative
Phil Garner—National League Representative
Ted Simmons—Pension Committee
Steve Rogers—Pension Committee
Plus all remaining player representatives

NATIONAL LEAGUE PLAYER REPRESENTATIVES

Phil Niekro—Atlanta Braves
Bill Buckner—Chicago Cubs
Frank Pastore—Cincinnati Reds
Bob Knepper—Houston Astros
Burt Hooton—Los Angeles Dodgers
Steve Rogers—Montreal Expos
Mike Jorgensen—New York Mets
Greg Gross—Philadelphia Phillies
Kent Tekulve—Pittsburgh Pirates
Keith Hernandez—St. Louis Cardinals
Gary Lucas—San Diego Padres
Rich Gale—San Francisco Giants

AMERICAN LEAGUE PLAYER REPRESENTATIVES

Scott McGregor—Baltimore Orioles
Mark Clear—Boston Red Sox
Don Aase—California Angels
Greg Luzinski—Chicago White Sox
Mike Hargrove—Cleveland Indians
Jack Morris—Detroit Tigers
Dan Quisenberry—Kansas City Royals
Ted Simmons—Milwaukee Brewers
Ron Davis—Minnesota Twins
Dave Winfield—New York Yankees
To be Announced—Oakland A's
Jim Beattie—Seattle Mariners
Rick Honeycutt—Texas Rangers
Buck Martinez—Toronto Blue Jays

Major League Farm Systems for '83

AMERICAN LEAGUE

BALTIMORE (4): AAA—Rochester. AA—Charlotte. A—Hagerstown. Rookie—Bluefield.

BOSTON (5): AAA—Pawtucket. AA—New Britain, Conn. A—Elmira, Winston-Salem, Winter Haven.

CALIFORNIA (5): AAA—Edmonton. AA—Nashua. A—Peoria, Redwood, Salem.

CHICAGO (5): AAA—Denver. AA—Glens Falls. A—Appleton, Niagara Falls. Rookie—Sarasota.

CLEVELAND (4): AAA—Charleston, W. Va. AA—Buffalo. A—Batavia, Waterloo.

DETROIT (4): AAA—Evansville. AA—Birmingham. A—Lakeland. Rookie—Bristol, Va.

KANSAS CITY (6): AAA—Omaha. AA—Jacksonville. A—Fort Myers, Charleston, S. C. Rookie—Sarasota, Butte.

MILWAUKEE (5): AAA—Vancouver. AA—El Paso. A—Beloit, Stockton. Rookie—Paintsville.

MINNESOTA (5): AAA—Toledo. AA—Orlando. A—Visalia, Wisconsin Rapids. Rookie—Elizabethton.

NEW YORK (5): AAA—Columbus, O. AA—Nashville. A—Ft. Lauderdale, Greensboro, Oneonta.

OAKLAND (6): AAA—Tacoma. AA—Albany. A—Idaho Falls, Madison, Medford, Modesto.

SEATTLE (5): AAA—Salt Lake City. AA—Chattanooga. A—Bakersfield, Bellingham, Wausau.

TEXAS (4): AAA—Oklahoma City. AA—Tulsa. A—Burlington. Rookie—Sarasota.

TORONTO (6): AAA—Syracuse. AA—Knoxville. A—Florence, Kinston. Rookie—Bradenton, Medicine Hat.

NATIONAL LEAGUE

ATLANTA (5): AAA—Richmond. AA—Savannah. A—Anderson, Durham. Rookie—Bradenton.

CHICAGO (6): AAA—Iowa. AA—Midland. A—Geneva, Quad Cities, Salinas. Rookie—Pikeville.

CINCINNATI (6): AAA—Indianapolis. AA—Waterbury. A—Cedar Rapids, Eugene, Tampa. Rookie—Billings.

HOUSTON (6): AAA—Tucson. AA—Columbus, Ga. A—Asheville, Auburn, Daytona Beach. Rookie—Sarasota.

LOS ANGELES (6): AAA—Albuquerque. AA—San Antonio. A—Lodi, Vero Beach. Rookie—Lethbridge, Sarasota.

MONTREAL (6): AAA—Wichita. AA—Memphis. A—Gastonia, Jamestown, West Palm Beach. Rookie—Calgary.

NEW YORK (6): AAA—Tidewater. AA—Jackson. A—Columbia, S.C., Little Falls, Lynchburg. Rookie—Kingsport.

PHILADELPHIA (6): AAA—Portland. AA—Reading. A—Bend, Peninsula, Spartanburg. Rookie—Helena.

PITTSBURGH (5): AAA—Hawaii. AA—Lynn. A—Alexandria, Greenwood. Rookie—Bradenton.

ST. LOUIS (7): AAA—Louisville. AA—Arkansas. A—Erie, Macon, St. Petersburg, Springfield. Rookie—Johnson City.

SAN DIEGO (6): AAA—Las Vegas. AA—Beaumont, Tex. A—Miami, Reno, Salem. Rookie—Bradenton.

SAN FRANCISCO (5): AAA—Phoenix. AA—Shreveport. A—Clinton, Fresno. Rookie—Great Falls.

Minor League Presidents for '83

CLASS AAA

American Association—Joe Ryan, P. O. Box 382, Wichita, Kan. 67201

International League—Harold Cooper, Box 608, Grove City, Ohio 43123

Mexican League—Roberto Avila, Angel Pola No. 16, Col. del Periodista, Mexico 10, D. F., Mexico

Pacific Coast League—Bill Cutler, 2101 E. Broadway Rd., Tempe, Ariz. 85282

CLASS AA

Eastern League—Charles Eshbach, Box 318, Bristol, Conn. 06010

Southern League—Jimmy Bragan, 235 Main St., Suite 200, Trussville, Ala. 35173

Texas League—Carl Sawatski, 1501 N. University, Suite 412, Little Rock, Ark. 72207

CLASS A

California League—Joe Gagliardi, 1060 Willow, San Jose, Calif. 95125

Carolina League—Jim Mills, 219 W. Chatham St., Apex, N.C. 27502

Florida State League—George MacDonald, Jr., P. O. Box 414, Lakeland, Fla. 33802

Midwest League—William K. Walters, P. O. Box 444, Burlington, Ia. 52601

New York-Pennsylvania League—Vincent M. McNamara, 220 Brookside Drive, Buffalo, N. Y. 14220.

Northwest League—Bob Freitas, 1840 Tabor Street, Eugene, Ore. 97401

South Atlantic League—John H. Moss, P. O. Box 49, Kings Mountain, N. C. 28086

ROOKIE CLASSIFICATION

Appalachian League—Bill Halstead, 157 Carson Lane, Bristol, Va. 24201

Gulf Coast League—Thomas J. Saffell, 420 Golden Gate Point, Apt. 18, Sarasota, Fla. 33577

Pioneer League—Ralph C. Nelles, P. O. Box 1144, Billings, Mont. 59103

OFFICIAL MINOR LEAGUE AVERAGES

Including

Official Averages of All Class AAA, Class AA, Class A and Rookie Leagues

National Association President John Johnson.

American Association

CLASS AAA

**Leading Batter
ROY JOHNSON
Wichita**

**League President
JOE RYAN**

**Leading Pitcher
JAY HOWELL
Iowa**

CHAMPIONSHIP WINNERS IN PREVIOUS YEARS

1902—Indianapolis .683	1937—Columbus† .584	1958—Charleston .589
1903—St. Paul .657	1938—St. Paul .596	Minneapolis (3rd)‡ .536
1904—St. Paul .646	Kansas City (2nd)‡ .556	1959—Louisville§ .599
1905—Columbus .658	1939—Kansas City .695	Omaha§ .516
1906—Columbus .615	Louisville (4th)‡ .490	Minneapolis (2nd)‡ .586
1907—Columbus .584	1940—Kansas City .625	1960—Denver .571
1908—Indianapolis .601	Louisville (4th)‡ .500	Louisville (2nd)‡ .556
1909—Louisville .554	1941—Columbus† .621	1961—Indianapolis .573
1910—Minneapolis .637	1942—Kansas City .549	Louisville (2nd)‡ .533
1911—Minneapolis .600	Columbus (3rd)‡ .532	1962—Indianapolis .605
1912—Minneapolis .636	1943—Milwaukee .596	Louisville (4th)‡ .486
1913—Milwaukee .599	Columbus (3rd)‡ .532	1963-1968—Did not operate.
1914—Milwaukee .590	1944—Milwaukee .667	1969—Omaha .607
1915—Minneapolis .597	Louisville (3rd)‡ .574	1970—Omaha° .529
1916—Louisville .605	1945—Milwaukee .604	Denver .504
1917—Indianapolis .588	Louisville (3rd)‡ .545	1971—Indianapolis .604
1918—Kansas City .589	1946—Louisville† 601	Denver° .521
1919—St. Paul .610	1947—Kansas City .608	1972—Wichita .621
1920—St. Paul .701	Milwaukee (3rd)‡ .513	Evansville° .593
1921—Louisville .583	1948—Indianapolis .649	1973—Iowa .610
1922—St. Paul .641	St. Paul (3rd)‡ .558	Tulsa° .504
1923—Kansas City .675	1949—St. Paul .608	1974—Indianapolis .578
1924—St. Paul .578	Indianapolis (2nd)‡ .604	Tulsa° .567
1925—Louisville .635	1950—Minneapolis .584	1975—Evansville° .566
1926—Louisville .629	Columbus (3rd)‡ .549	Denver .596
1927—Toledo .601	1951—Milwaukee† .623	1976—Denver° .632
1928—Indianapolis .593	1952—Milwaukee .656	Omaha .574
1929—Kansas City .665	Kansas City (2nd)‡ .578	1977—Omaha .563
1930—Louisville .608	1953—Toledo .584	Denver° .522
1931—St. Paul .623	Kansas City (2nd)‡ .571	1978—Indianapolis .578
1932—Minneapolis .595	1954—Indianapolis .625	Omaha° .489
1933—Columbus° .604	Louisville (2nd)‡ .556	1979—Evansville° .574
Minneapolis .562	1955—Minneapolis† .597	Oklahoma City .533
1934—Minneapolis .570	1956—Indianapolis† .597	1980—Denver .676
Columbus° .556	1957—Wichita .604	Springfield° .551
1935—Minneapolis .591	Denver (2nd)‡ .584	1981—Omaha .581
1936—Milwaukee† .584		Denver° .559

*Won playoff (East vs. West). †Won championship and four-team playoff. ‡Won four-team playoff. §Respective Eastern and Western division winners.

STANDING OF CLUBS AT CLOSE OF SEASON, AUGUST 29

EASTERN DIVISION

Club	Ind.	Iowa	Lou.	Evan.	Den.	O.C.	Oma.	Wich.	W.	L.	T.	Pct.	G.B.
Indianapolis (Reds)	.....	15	10	14	9	10	9	8	75	61	0	.551	....
Iowa (Cubs)	9	.....	14	12	7	11	9	11	73	62	0	.541	1½
Louisville (Cardinals)	14	10	.....	10	8	11	11	9	73	62	0	.541	1½
Evansville (Tigers)	10	11	14	.....	8	10	9	6	68	65	0	.511	5½

WESTERN DIVISION

Club	Oma.	Wich.	Den.	O.C.	Evan.	Ind.	Iowa	Lou.	W.	L.	T.	Pct.	G.B.
*Omaha (Royals)	.....	13	16	16	7	7	7	5	71	66	0	.518	....
*Wichita (Expos)	12	.....	13	15	10	8	5	7	70	67	0	.511	1
Denver (Rangers)	8	11	.....	18	7	7	9	8	68	67	0	.504	2
Oklahoma City (Phillies)	6	9	8	.....	5	6	5	4	43	91	0	.321	26½

*Omaha and Wichita ended the regular season tied. Omaha defeated Wichita, 2-0, in a one-game playoff on August 30 to advance to the league championship series against Indianapolis.

Iowa club represented Des Moines, Iowa.

Major league affiliations in parentheses.

Playoff—Indianapolis defeated Omaha, four games to two, to win league championship.

Regular-Season Attendance—Denver, 537,914; Evansville, 118,139; Indianapolis, 213,965; Iowa, 203,169; Louisville, 868,418; Oklahoma City, 180,932; Omaha, 178,235; Wichita, 106,754. Total, 2,407,526.

Managers: Denver, Rich Donnelly; Evansville, Roy Majtyka; Indianapolis, George Scherger; Iowa, Jim Napier; Louisville, Joe Frazier; Oklahoma City, Ron Clark, Ellis Deal, Tony Taylor; Omaha, Joe Sparks; Wichita, Felipe Alou.

All-Star Team: 1B—Phelps, Wichita; 2B—Lawless, Indianapolis; 3B—Tabler, Iowa; SS—Paris, Louisville; OF—Hall, Iowa; Johnson, Wichita; Redus, Indianapolis; DH—Calise, Louisville; C—Benton, Iowa, and Wieghaus, Wichita; RHP—Howell, Iowa; LHP—Tufts, Omaha.

(Compiled by Ed Williams, League Statistician, Shawnee, Okla.)

CLUB BATTING

Club	Pct.	G.	AB.	R.	OR.	H.	TB.	2B.	3B.	HR.	RBI.	GW.	SH.	SF.	HP.	BB.	Int. BB.	SO.	SB.	CS.	LOB.
Wichita	.300	137	4709	829	806	1412	2227	230	45	165	772	66	38	42	30	570	42	622	101	44	1026
Iowa	.294	135	4444	749	714	1305	2069	262	41	140	699	66	58	33	34	456	32	742	128	76	879
Denver	.281	135	4439	771	753	1247	2051	222	54	158	716	60	42	41	38	582	33	713	71	41	994
Omaha	.276	137	4543	651	603	1252	1907	213	44	118	594	63	37	42	28	467	33	759	138	68	956
Indianapolis	.273	136	4516	709	648	1235	1891	227	48	111	655	66	91	45	24	502	36	768	149	55	964
Oklahoma City	.267	134	4321	567	783	1152	1687	213	41	80	517	38	44	29	29	412	30	584	139	76	875
Louisville	.264	135	4477	674	648	1184	1815	208	36	117	615	59	38	30	32	509	22	809	112	56	930
Evansville	.257	133	4307	648	643	1109	1836	218	34	147	612	63	58	40	45	452	31	812	132	57	843

INDIVIDUAL BATTING

(Leading Qualifiers for Batting Championship—367 or More Plate Appearances)

*Bats lefthanded.   †Switch-hitter.

Player and Club	Pct.	G.	AB.	R.	H.	TB.	2B.	3B.	HR.	RBI.	GW.	SH.	SF.	HP.	BB.	Int. BB.	SO.	SB.	CS.
Johnson, Roy, Wichita*	.367	102	376	73	138	211	19	6	14	76	7	3	3	3	46	5	39	21	4
Tabler, Patrick, Iowa	.342	129	441	89	151	256	32	11	17	105	5	3	9	3	85	4	74	15	7
Johnson, Ronald, Omaha	.336	137	494	65	166	232	27	3	11	73	10	0	1	3	55	3	46	1	2
Phelps, Kenneth, Wichita*	.3333	132	453	112	151	320	23	4	46	141	15	3	0	10	108	12	99	2	4
Redus, Gary, Indianapolis	.3326	122	439	112	146	265	29	9	24	93	8	2	9	4	51	3	93	54	5
Hall, Melvin, Iowa*	.329	133	502	116	165	307	34	6	32	125	17	4	6	1	42	9	70	19	9
Paris, Kelly, Louisville	.328	129	482	71	158	233	32	5	11	83	10	2	4	6	24	1	52	20	8
Smith, Christopher, Wichita†	.326	115	445	79	145	232	27	9	14	84	10	0	5	0	44	4	27	3	4
Rivera, Jesus, Omaha	.318	126	468	92	149	263	23	5	27	91	5	0	3	1	57	4	101	33	6
Johnson, Howard, Evansville	.317	98	366	70	116	209	16	4	23	67	11	3	6	4	46	5	62	35	9

Departmental Leaders: G—Ron Johnson, 137; AB—Williams, 514; R—Hall, 116; H—Ron Johnson, 166; TB—Phelps, 320; 2B—Hall, 34; 3B—Tabler, 11; HR—Phelps, 46; RBI—Phelps, 141; GWRBI—Hall, 17; SH—Fiala, 20; SF—Redus, Tabler, 9; HP—Laga, 13; BB—Phelps, 108; IBB—Phelps, Ryal, 12; SO—Calise, 156; SB—Redus, 54; CS—Williams, 15.

(All Players—Listed Alphabetically)

Player and Club	Pct.	G.	AB.	R.	H.	TB.	2B.	3B.	HR.	RBI.	GW.	SH.	SF.	HP.	BB.	Int. BB.	SO.	SB.	CS.
Anderson, James, Denver	.314	128	488	95	153	237	30	3	16	83	7	7	7	7	45	1	52	4	1
Ashmore, Mitchell, Omaha	.000	1	1	0	0	0	0	0	0	0	0	0	0	0	0	0	0	0	0
Aviles, Ramon, 8 Den.-88 Ok.C.	.262	96	305	40	80	95	10	1	1	26	3	6	3	0	33	3	23	3	5
Babitt, Mack, Wichita	.282	31	71	13	20	23	1	1	0	3	1	4	0	0	6	0	10	5	1
Barnes, William, Indianapolis	.305	18	59	8	18	28	5	1	1	3	0	2	0	1	0	1	6	1	2
Barranca, German, Indianapolis*	.299	36	107	18	32	45	4	0	3	7	0	1	0	0	17	1	16	7	6
Barrow, Melvin, Denver	.241	36	87	17	21	31	6	2	0	6	1	3	1	1	6	0	18	2	1
Bass, Randy, Denver*	.290	68	214	43	62	128	10	1	18	45	3	0	1	4	49	4	47	0	1
Benton, Alfred, Iowa	.330	85	291	36	96	154	17	4	11	57	8	2	2	11	1	45	6	3
Bertoni, Jeffrey, Evansville	.270	70	244	34	66	108	15	3	7	35	4	4	2	3	20	1	57	3	4
Biancalana, Roland, Omaha†	.251	130	415	56	104	144	16	9	2	36	3	6	3	1	44	2	77	18	7
Bjorkman, George, Louisville	.208	108	317	59	66	131	19	2	14	43	3	5	3	6	78	3	103	9	5
Bogener, Terry, Denver*	.321	76	243	44	78	117	17	5	4	31	2	1	1	34	1	24	2	4
Boitano, Danny, Denver	1.000	32	1	1	1	1	0	0	0	1	0	0	0	0	0	0	0	0	0
Bonham, William, Indianapolis	.000	1	1	0	0	0	0	0	0	0	0	0	0	0	0	0	1	0	0
Borucki, Raymond, Ok. City	.244	22	82	6	20	22	2	0	0	8	0	0	1	0	4	1	10	0	1
Bradford, Larry, 21 Lou.-14 Ok.C.	.000	35	0	0	0	0	0	0	0	0	1	0	0	0	0	0	0	0	0
Brewer, Michael, Omaha	.286	18	56	10	16	24	5	0	1	7	0	0	1	3	0	14	5	0
Briggs, Daniel, Iowa*	.303	8	33	6	10	13	3	0	0	6	1	0	0	0	6	0	3	0	0
Brummer, Glenn, Louisville	.107	8	28	2	3	6	0	0	1	2	0	0	0	0	0	0	7	0	0
Bruno, Joseph, Ok. City*:	.239	83	293	39	70	90	10	2	2	23	2	7	1	0	37	2	41	12	6
Burroughs, Darren, Ok. City	1.000	22	1	0	1	1	0	0	0	0	0	0	0	0	0	0	0	0	0
Calise, Michael, Louisville	.272	119	404	73	110	228	19	0	33	91	7	0	0	0	68	3	156	3	0
Capilla, Douglas, Wichita*	.000	11	2	0	0	0	0	0	0	0	0	0	0	0	0	0	0	0	0
Capra, Nick, Denver	.281	121	416	82	117	179	15	10	9	40	4	4	1	1	71	0	72	29	13
Carey, Brooks, Indianapolis*	.200	22	20	0	4	4	0	0	0	1	0	0	0	0	0	0	0	0	0
Carlucci, Richard, Indianapolis*	.174	51	23	3	4	7	0	0	1	4	0	1	0	0	2	0	10	0	0
Carrion, Leonel, Wichita	.205	29	88	11	18	25	2	1	1	12	2	2	1	1	11	0	13	4	0

Player and Club	Pct.	G.	AB.	R.	H.	TB.	2B.	3B.	HR.	RBI.	GW.	SH.	SF.	HP.	BB.	Int. BB.	SO.	SB.	CS.
Castillo, Martin, Evansville	.242	116	388	52	94	156	20	3	12	56	3	3	1	2	50	1	92	7	5
Cato, Keefe, Indianapolis	.152	21	33	4	5	5	0	0	0	2	0	6	0	0	·1	0	9	0	0
Christmas, Stephen, Indianapolis	.306	85	252	31	77	114	14	1	7	37	4	2	1	0	14	2	16	1	0
Colletti, Manuel, Omaha†	.211	7	19	3	4	4	0	0	0	1	0	0	0	0	5	0	3	0	0
Corcoran, Timothy, Ok. City°	.289	120	433	60	125	184	28	5	7	69	4	2	2	2	48	4	39	4	3
Corey, Mark, Evansville	.167	14	42	4	7	12	2	0	1	3	0	1	0	0	5	0	19	1	0
Cowger, Tracy, Denver	.133	12	30	3	4	5	1	0	0	1	0	1	0	1	3	0	6	0	0
Cox, Jeffrey, 50 Evan.-21 Omaha	.225	71	191	40	43	50	5	1	0	18	0	5	4	3	36	2	18	12	4
Cruz, Hector, Iowa	.263	10	38	5	10	21	5	0	2	9	0	0	1	1	0	0	13	0	0
Culmer, Wilfred, Okla. City	.288	119	403	58	116	184	16	5	14	58	4	1	4	2	40	5	82	14	11
Davis, Mark, Okla. City°	.000	21	1	0	0	0	0	0	0	0	0	0	0	0	0	0	1	0	0
Dawley, William, Indianapolis	.197	30	61	4	12	17	3	1	0	5	0	6	0	1	1	0	16	1	0
DeJohn, Mark, Evansville†	.182	57	159	18	29	42	3	2	2	16	2	3	2	1	19	0	29	1	3
DeSa, Joseph, Louisville°	.275	130	487	72	134	208	26	3	14	75	8	2	3	4	48	1	63	1	2
Dewey, Duane, Omaha	.220	20	50	9	11	24	4	0	3	8	0	2	0	0	4	0	15	0	0
Djakonow, Powel, Evansville	.255	47	141	18	36	54	6	0	4	20	1	5	1	3	24	0	41	1	1
Dowless, Michael, Indianapolis	.200	26	35	5	7	12	3	1	0	1	0	6	0	0	7	0	17	0	0
Downs, Kelly, Oklahoma City	.000	32	2	0	0	0	0	0	0	0	0	0	0	0	0	0	2	0	0
Doyle, Jeffrey, Louisville†	.246	119	415	53	102	151	17	4	8	49	7	10	2	2	46	2	31	9	2
Dues, Hal, Wichita	.200	16	5	0	1	1	0	0	0	0	0	0	0	0	0	0	2	0	0
Edelen, Joe, Indianapolis	.091	15	22	4	2	5	0	0	1	2	0	1	0	0	0	0	10	0	0
Edler, David, Omaha	.305	71	262	40	80	130	11	6	9	51	4	3	4	2	33	0	53	8	8
Engle, Ricky, Wichita°	.500	26	2	2	1	4	0	0	1	1	0	0	0	0	0	0	0	0	0
Esasky, Nicholas, Indianapolis	.264	105	341	59	90	192	15	3	27	62	4	0	2	1	45	4	118	1	2
Farkas, Ronald, Indianapolis	.249	108	301	32	75	102	13	1	4	49	5	4	5	0	45	0	46	2	0
Fiala, Neil, Indianapolis°	.269	128	420	66	113	142	16	2	3	50	1	20	3	5	70	0	37	11	9
Filkins, Leslie, Evansville°	.257	117	389	59	100	168	28	2	12	52	8	1	2	2	51	4	64	5	5
Fletcher, Scott, Iowa	.313	129	502	90	157	201	26	3	4	60	6	14	1	9	46	1	62	20	8
Foley, Thomas, Indianapolis°	.269	129	427	65	115	177	20	9	8	63	11	3	7	2	42	8	48	1	2
Followell, Vern, Evansville†	.235	103	327	46	77	98	10	1	3	35	3	9	1	0	29	1	25	6	2
Franco, Julio, Ok. City	.300	120	463	80	139	231	19	5	21	66	8	2	2	3	39	1	56	33	11
Frias, Jose, Wichita	.139	15	36	1	5	6	1	0	0	4	0	2	0	0	0	0	5	0	0
Fuentes, Michael, Wichita	.000	1	2	0	0	0	0	0	0	0	0	0	0	0	2	0	0	0	0
Gates, Eddie, Evansville	.176	22	51	7	9	20	2	0	3	11	1	0	1	2	10	0	15	1	0
Gates, Joseph, Denver°	.125	8	16	7	2	3	1	0	0	0	0	0	0	0	0	0	1	0	1
Gates, Michael, Wichita°	.331	64	248	52	82	118	8	5	6	35	1	2	0	3	30	1	14	9	6
Glynn, Eugene, Wichita	.263	10	19	4	5	7	0	1	0	3	0	0	0	1	0	0	4	0	0
Gonzales, Daniel, 41 Den.-41 Ok.C.°	.284	82	275	31	78	109	19	3	2	31	2	0	2	2	18	3	27	0	3
Gonzalez, Jose, Louisville†	.357	8	28	5	10	12	2	0	0	4	2	0	0	0	1	0	4	0	1
Gorman, Thomas, Wichita°	.000	23	7	0	0	0	0	0	0	0	0	1	0	0	0	0	0	0	0
Grant, Thomas, Iowa°	.265	122	389	53	103	171	25	5	11	59	3	5	3	5	57	1	79	7	8
Grapenthin, Richard, Wichita	.000	20	1	0	0	0	0	0	0	0	0	0	0	0	0	0	0	0	0
Green, David, Louisville	.345	46	174	45	60	100	5	4	9	40	7	7	0	1	18	2	23	7	6
Griffin, Michael, Wichita	.200	28	5	0	1	1	0	0	0	0	0	0	1	0	0	0	3	0	0
Gulden, Bradley, Wichita°	.288	64	212	37	61	102	16	2	7	35	5	1	3	1	21	3	25	1	1
Hall, Melvin, Iowa°	.329	133	502	116	165	307	34	6	32	125	17	4	6	1	42	9	70	19	9
Hammond, Steven, Omaha°	.379	36	132	24	50	75	13	0	4	13	2	2	0	1	11	2	17	1	0
Hampton, Rafael, Evansville	.190	17	58	10	11	18	0	2	1	3	0	0	0	1	12	0	7	5	1
Hamric, Russell, Ok. City	.257	120	447	51	115	153	25	2	3	35	2	10	2	4	22	1	37	8	13
Harris, Greg, Indianapolis†	.100	8	20	0	2	3	1	0	0	3	0	2	0	0	0	0	3	0	0
Hayes, Ben, Indianapolis	.000	41	9	0	0	0	0	0	0	0	0	0	2	0	0	0	5	0	0
Hayes, William, Iowa	.249	75	245	36	61	124	16	1	15	40	7	1	2	5	22	0	68	3	1
Heath, Kelly, Omaha	.238	106	361	48	86	137	14	2	11	41	4	5	5	3	31	1	58	5	5
Hicks, Joseph, Iowa	.311	66	244	29	76	129	19	2	10	52	2	1	3	0	18	1	68	4	2
Holt, Roger, Denver°	.239	128	414	54	99	126	16	4	1	37	7	11	1	2	42	3	46	4	3
Hostetler, David, Denver	.266	36	128	24	34	78	8	0	12	36	4	0	3	1	20	1	32	0	0
Hurdle, Clinton, Indianapolis°	.245	88	261	38	64	118	18	0	12	58	7	3	5	3	58	7	63	3	1
Ibarra, Miguel, Oklahoma City	.267	21	60	8	16	19	3	0	0	9	0	1	0	1	4	0	8	1	1
Ireland, Timothy, Omaha	.248	86	315	45	78	106	10	3	4	33	5	3	5	4	36	0	54	6	9
Isales, Orlando, Indianapolis	.277	113	242	35	67	96	17	3	2	42	5	1	3	3	25	3	28	10	2
Jirschele, Michael, Denver	.311	14	45	6	14	23	3	3	0	5	0	1	0	0	2	0	8	0	0
Johnson, Bobby, Denver	.249	99	305	57	76	162	10	5	22	76	4	0	5	3	62	2	88	3	4
Johnson, Howard, Evansville†	.317	98	366	70	116	209	16	4	23	67	11	3	6	2	46	5	62	35	9
Johnson, Ronald, Omaha	.336	137	494	65	166	232	27	3	11	73	10	0	1	3	55	3	46	1	2
Johnson, Roy, Wichita°	.367	102	376	73	138	211	19	6	14	76	7	3	3	3	46	5	39	21	4
Johnson, Wallace, Wichita†	.352	76	298	62	105	143	12	4	6	36	5	2	4	0	42	4	16	16	2
Jones, Robert, Denver°	.318	82	261	44	83	148	19	5	12	51	4	1	3	7	39	1	42	1	2
Kable, David, Louisville°	.207	116	368	47	76	134	17	1	13	53	6	0	2	4	47	5	99	5	1
Keatley, Gregory, Omaha	.198	83	268	23	53	77	10	1	4	28	4	4	3	0	29	1	55	1	1
Kenaga, Jeffrey, Evansville°	.261	116	410	60	107	200	29	5	18	68	1	4	2	3	25	6	61	4	0
Kennedy, Kevin, Louisville	.111	4	9	0	1	1	0	0	0	1	0	1	0	0	2	0	2	0	0
Kepshire, Kurt, Indianapolis°	.000	5	1	0	0	0	0	0	0	0	0	0	0	0	0	0	1	0	0
Kubski, Gilbert, Indianapolis°	.247	48	85	11	21	33	7	1	1	11	1	4	0	0	11	2	14	0	0
Laga, Michael, Evansville°	.250	126	444	77	111	234	15	3	34	90	15	0	6	13	47	9	117	5	2
Landrum, Terry, Louisville	.202	25	94	10	19	23	2	0	6	11	1	1	2	6	0	26	3	2	
Lavigne, Randall, Iowa	.257	76	230	29	59	84	9	2	4	29	3	3	2	1	17	0	63	7	5
Lawless, Thomas, Indianapolis	.308	86	351	76	108	144	18	6	2	28	0	2	1	1	39	2	48	35	7
Leach, Richard, Evansville°	.289	11	38	6	11	13	2	0	0	2	0	0	1	0	5	0	4	0	1
Lesley, Bradley, Indianapolis	.200	40	10	1	2	2	0	0	0	1	0	0	0	0	1	0	2	0	0
Little, Bryan, Wichita†	.286	99	388	67	111	133	13	3	1	35	1	4	2	2	60	1	19	20	9
Littlejohn, Dennis, Denver	.270	53	159	27	43	59	4	0	4	15	2	2	1	0	21	0	31	1	0
Lombarski, Thomas, Oklahoma City°	.265	87	260	30	69	95	16	2	2	22	2	2	4	0	37	2	33	12	3
Lopez, Juan, Evansville	.355	29	107	16	38	49	8	0	1	8	0	2	0	0	5	0	12	2	3
Lyons, William, Louisville	.268	29	82	8	22	34	4	1	2	9	0	2	1	0	9	0	9	0	2
Mackanin, Peter, Denver	.268	116	377	54	101	180	17	7	16	73	4	2	2	2	31	5	76	5	1
Manuel, Jerry, Wichita†	.255	71	263	31	67	98	22	0	3	37	5	3	2	1	15	0	34	2	1
Martin, Jared, Iowa°	.211	17	38	5	8	9	1	0	0	3	0	0	0	4	1	0	5	1	1
Matuszek, Leonard, Oklahoma City°	.290	67	231	41	67	112	16	4	7	46	2	0	5	3	36	6	36	9	3
McCann, Francis, Wichita	.237	62	114	12	27	40	7	0	2	15	1	0	3	0	11	1	28	1	1
McCormack, Donald, Evansville	.234	76	192	21	45	69	11	2	3	26	2	0	2	0	19	1	32	0	1
McDonald, Manuel, Oklahoma City	.225	83	262	16	59	74	10	1	1	26	4	3	1	2	12	0	24	3	4
McEnaney, William, Denver°	.000	54	0	1	0	0	0	0	0	0	0	0	0	0	0	1	0	0	0

Player and Club	Pct.	G.	AB.	R.	H.	TB.	2B.	3B.	HR.	RBI.	GW.	SH.	SF.	HP.	BB.	Int. BB.	SO.	SB.	CS.
McGee, Willie, Louisville†	.291	13	55	11	16	25	2	2	1	3	0	1	0	0	2	0	7	5	1
Miller, Edward, Evansville†	.278	76	281	51	78	128	23	3	7	40	6	7	4	10	27	0	64	27	8
Mills, Bradley, Wichita°	.471	4	17	3	8	8	0	0	0	6	0	1	0	1	0	3	0	0	
Mills, Rhadames, Louisville	.233	115	339	47	79	105	10	5	2	22	1	6	0	3	42	1	62	16	5
Montanez, Guillermo, Oklahoma City°	.323	8	31	3	10	15	2	0	1	5	0	0	0	1	1	0	4	0	1
Motley, Darryl, Omaha	.254	114	409	51	104	152	12	6	8	52	10	2	4	5	25	1	55	16	4
Mueller, Willard, Wichita	.000	56	1	0	0	0	0	0	0	0	0	0	0	0	0	0	0	0	0
Murray, Richard, Wichita	.288	80	285	48	82	141	18	1	13	54	2	0	2	3	13	0	43	3	2
Mustad, Eric, Wichita	.000	1	1	0	0	0	0	0	0	0	0	0	0	0	0	0	1	0	0
Neufang, Gerald, Denver	.250	4	12	2	3	4	1	0	0	1	0	1	0	0	2	0	0	0	0
Norman, Daniel, Wichita	.348	8	23	5	8	16	2	0	2	7	0	0	1	0	4	1	4	2	0
O'Berry, Michael, Indianapolis	.190	45	105	11	20	25	3	1	0	5	1	2	2	0	6	0	15	0	0
O'Brien, Peter, Denver°	.310	128	477	92	148	246	21	1	25	102	8	1	8	1	56	4	65	0	2
Office, Rowland, Oklahoma City°	.183	26	93	12	17	20	3	0	0	5	1	0	1	2	12	1	18	6	2
Ojeda, Luis, Louisville	.227	9	22	1	5	5	0	0	0	1	0	0	0	0	1	0	3	0	0
O'Keefe, Richard, Indianapolis°	.000	4	1	0	0	0	0	0	0	0	0	0	0	0	0	0	0	0	0
Olmsted, Alan, Louisville	.333	28	3	0	1	1	0	0	0	0	0	0	0	0	0	0	0	0	0
Orensky, Herbert, Oklahoma City°	.187	52	150	13	28	44	4	3	2	16	1	1	1	0	19	1	30	3	1
Paris, Kelly, Louisville	.328	129	482	71	158	233	32	5	11	83	10	2	4	6	24	1	52	20	8
Pasley, Kevin, Evansville	.273	5	11	0	3	4	1	0	0	0	0	0	0	0	1	0	0	0	0
Penniall, David, 12 Lou.-47 Evns.	.277	59	173	26	48	70	5	1	5	26	1	4	2	0	16	1	27	6	2
Perkins, Craig, Denver	.000	1	2	0	0	0	0	0	0	0	0	0	0	0	0	0	2	0	0
Phelps, Kenneth, Wichita°	.333	132	453	112	151	320	23	4	46	141	15	0	3	10	108	12	99	2	4
Phillips, Michael, Wichita°	.277	46	137	15	38	45	2	1	1	9	1	2	0	1	13	2	10	1	1
Poole, Stine, Evansville	.229	16	35	5	8	13	2	0	1	7	0	1	0	0	3	0	8	0	0
Putnam, Patrick, Denver°	.310	80	281	47	87	152	20	3	13	60	7	0	2	5	36	5	34	1	0
Quintana, Luis, Wichita°	.250	56	4	0	1	2	1	0	0	1	0	0	0	0	0	0	0	0	0
Ramos, Richard, Wichita	.200	24	10	1	2	2	0	0	0	0	0	0	0	0	0	0	2	0	0
Rasmussen, James, Oklahoma City	.000	25	3	0	0	0	0	0	0	0	0	0	0	0	0	0	2	0	0
Redus, Gary, Indianapolis	.333	122	439	112	146	265	29	9	24	93	8	2	9	4	51	3	93	54	5
Reed, Jerry, Oklahoma City	.000	25	2	0	0	0	0	0	0	0	0	0	0	0	0	0	0	0	0
Rivera, Jesus, Omaha	.318	126	468	92	149	263	23	5	27	91	5	0	3	1	57	4	101	33	6
Rodriguez, Luis, Oklahoma City	.167	20	60	3	10	11	1	0	0	4	0	0	0	0	6	0	11	2	1
Rohn, Daniel, Iowa°	.275	107	364	85	100	152	20	4	8	32	3	5	1	3	66	3	37	26	10
Roof, Eugene, Louisville†	.306	119	458	78	140	186	27	5	3	49	2	2	5	3	74	4	64	13	12
Rooney, Patrick, Wichita	.271	99	358	60	97	167	13	3	17	52	2	0	2	3	20	1	80	4	1
Ryal, Mark, Omaha°	.285	129	473	69	135	226	27	2	20	77	8	4	6	2	42	12	76	4	11
Ryder, Brian, Indianapolis	.154	34	26	2	4	5	1	0	0	1	0	2	0	0	6	0	11	0	0
Salas, Mark, Louisville	.182	7	22	1	4	4	0	0	0	1	0	0	0	0	0	0	4	0	0
Sanchez, Alejandro, Oklahoma City	.306	88	320	57	98	175	24	7	13	46	2	1	1	3	14	2	68	28	6
Sanchez, Orlando, Louisville°	.235	41	132	14	31	49	9	0	3	14	3	1	1	0	7	0	21	0	1
Santana, Rafael, Louisville	.286	121	430	65	123	153	15	3	3	53	0	3	6	1	27	0	46	16	6
Sattler, William, Wichita	.500	26	4	0	2	2	0	0	0	2	0	0	0	0	0	0	2	0	0
Scherrer, William, Indianapolis°	.231	22	26	4	6	6	0	0	0	2	1	3	0	0	0	0	7	0	0
Seaman, Kim, Wichita	.000	43	2	0	0	0	0	0	0	0	0	0	0	0	0	0	2	0	0
Sheridan, Patrick, Omaha°	.252	41	135	8	34	44	8	1	0	13	1	0	2	0	16	3	33	0	0
Silverio, Luis, Omaha	.260	93	312	49	81	121	17	1	7	35	5	1	3	1	38	1	55	29	9
Slaught, Donald, Omaha	.267	53	206	29	55	79	10	1	4	16	1	3	2	0	8	1	21	6	3
Smith, Christopher, Wichita†	.326	115	445	79	145	232	27	9	14	84	10	0	5	0	44	4	27	3	4
Sofield, Richard, Denver°	.278	15	36	6	10	15	3	1	0	3	1	1	0	2	1	6	0	0	
Soriano, Hilario, Wichita	.241	24	58	6	14	22	2	0	2	7	0	1	1	0	1	0	12	0	0
Stenhouse, Michael, Wichita°	.289	134	436	94	126	232	25	3	25	80	5	2	8	0	101	6	70	6	6
Stockstill, David, Denver°	.000	1	3	0	0	0	0	0	0	0	0	0	0	0	0	0	0	0	0
Strain, Joseph, Iowa	.293	80	266	48	78	96	13	1	1	24	2	3	2	1	25	1	18	8	8
Tabler, Patrick, Iowa	.342	129	441	89	151	256	32	11	17	105	5	3	9	3	85	4	74	15	7
Thompson, Scot, Iowa°	.344	29	93	17	32	44	6	0	2	11	0	1	1	0	10	0	7	2	1
Toliver, Freddie, Indianapolis°	.000	4	3	0	0	0	0	0	0	1	0	0	0	0	2	0	0	0	
Tolleson, Wayne, Denver†	.241	71	266	48	64	91	9	3	4	27	2	5	3	0	40	1	49	19	6
Tomlin, David, Indianapolis°	.313	66	16	2	5	6	1	0	0	2	2	1	0	1	0	7	0	0	
Ulrich, Jeffrey, 44 OkC-10 Wich	.215	54	149	13	32	41	7	1	0	16	2	4	3	1	10	0	20	0	0
Upton, Jack, Iowa	.251	113	387	58	97	154	18	0	13	47	5	3	1	3	25	2	47	2	5
Van Gorder, David, Indianapolis	.264	54	174	21	46	65	7	0	4	29	3	3	3	0	17	1	25	0	1
Venner, Gary, Denver°	.400	2	5	1	2	3	1	0	0	0	0	0	0	0	0	0	0	0	0
Walker, Duane, Indianapolis°	.287	36	115	21	33	53	6	1	4	19	4	3	2	0	22	2	29	4	2
Waller, Tyrone, Iowa	.268	106	381	47	102	154	18	2	10	40	3	5	0	0	26	1	83	9	8
Wellman, Brad, Omaha	.292	6	24	5	7	13	3	0	1	3	1	0	0	1	3	0	4	1	1
Werner, Donald, Denver	.438	8	16	2	7	12	2	0	1	2	0	0	0	0	1	0	1	0	0
Werth, Dennis, Omaha	.207	23	29	4	6	9	1	1	0	2	0	0	0	0	10	1	7	1	0
Wieghaus, Thomas, 88 Wich-23 OkC	.292	111	390	48	114	156	17	2	7	49	4	6	0	4	23	1	58	1	2
Wieser, Daniel, Omaha†	.284	28	81	12	23	37	2	3	2	14	0	1	1	1	15	1	14	1	1
Willard, Daniel, Oklahoma City°	.232	36	95	13	22	33	5	0	2	14	0	0	1	2	27	1	18	1	1
Williams, Dallas, Indianapolis°	.300	132	514	75	154	217	26	8	7	74	9	7	2	4	23	3	55	18	15
Willis, Michael, Oklahoma City°	.000	56	1	0	0	0	0	0	0	0	0	0	0	0	0	0	0	0	0
Wilson, Glenn, Evansville	.279	42	165	24	46	87	7	2	10	33	3	0	2	0	9	0	37	4	4
Wolters, Michael, Louisville	.176	34	91	7	16	18	2	0	0	8	1	1	1	0	4	0	19	4	1
Young, Kip, Indianapolis	.188	20	16	1	3	3	0	0	0	0	0	2	0	0	0	0	4	0	1
Younger, Stanley, Evansville°	.267	52	165	18	44	52	8	0	0	9	0	3	1	0	9	1	30	10	4

The following pitchers, listed alphabetically by club, with games in parentheses, had no plate appearances, primarily through use of designated hitters:

DENVER—Babcock, Robert (14); Butcher, John (8); Cruz, Victor (44); Farr, James (26); Hudson, Anthony (2); Kainer, Donald (1); Kerrigan, Joseph (48); Lazorko, Jack (15); Long, Dennis (2); Matula, Richard (36); Mercer, Mark (13); Rajsich, David (19); Semall, Paul (32); Smithson, Mike (29); Whitehouse, Leonard (31).

EVANSVILLE—Bailey, Howard (26); Berenguer, Juan (25); Cary, Charles (1); Dacko, Mark (26); Gumpert, David (2); James, Robert (9); Lee, Mark (18); Lopez, Aurelio (12); Luebber, Stephen (28); Moore, David (15); Pashnick, Larry (3); Robbins, Bruce (11); Rothschild, Lawrence (45); Rucker, David (30); Ruiz, August (44); Saucier, Kevin (10); Ujdur, Gerald (8); Wirth, Alan (3).

IOWA—Blyth, Robert (11); Earley, William (28); Filer, Thomas (17); Gerlach, James (27); Howell, Jay (20); Jones, Larry (42); Knapp, Christian (17); Kravec, Kenneth (14); Larson, Daniel (17); Lefferts, Craig (18); Parker, Mark (26); Proly, Michael (17); Pryce, Kenneth (5); Segelke, Herman (27); Stein, Randolph (43).

LOUISVILLE—Brito, Jose (36); Citarella, Ralph (28); Davis, Christopher (14); Fulgham, John (10); Horton, Ricky (8); Johnson, Jerry (12); Keener, Jeffrey (9); Kinnunen, Michael (16); Lahti, Jeffrey (21); Littell, Mark (1); Martin, John (12); Miller, Dyar (46); Morogiello, Daniel (57); Rasmussen, Eric (4); Rincon, Andrew (18); Stuper, John (8); Winfield, Steven (17).

OKLAHOMA CITY—Altamirano, Porfirio (6); Bahnsen, Stanley (23); Brusstar, Warren (22); Carman, Donald (10); Culver, George (1); Decker, Marty (10); Faulk, Kelly (14); Reelhorn, Jonathon (29); Sutton, Johnny (3).

OMAHA—Armstrong, Michael (15); Black, Harry (4); Botelho, Derek (5); Botting, Ralph (3); Creel, Keith (18); Fischer, Daniel (26); Frost, David (4); Hood, Donald (8); Huffman, Phillip (9); Kelly, William (29); Leonard, Dennis (3); Miscik, Dennis (4); Parrott, Michael (22); Schuler, David (32); Tufts, Robert (59); Wills, Frank (41); Wright, James (12); Yuhas, Vincent (13).

WICHITA—Abone, Joseph (23); Bargar, Greg (9); Dixon, Thomas (3); MacPherson, Bruce (8); Smith, Bryn (3); Tenenini, Robert (30).

GRAND SLAM HOME RUNS—Bass, Esasky, Hurdle, Murray, 2 each; Benton, Castillo, Djakonow, Fletcher, E. Gates, Green, Gulden, Hall, Hayes, H. Johnson, Kable, Laga, Mackanin, O'Brien, Phelps, Rooney, C. Smith, Stenhouse, Tabler, Wieghaus, 1 each.

AWARDED FIRST BASE ON CATCHER'S INTERFERENCE—Aviles 2 (Benton, Bjorkman); Bertoni 2 (Bjorkman, Christmas); W. Hayes (Slaught); Lopez (Bjorkman); Sheridan (Cowger); Tolleson (Benton); Younger (Christmas).

CLUB FIELDING

Club	Pct.	G.	PO.	A.	E.	DP.	PB.	Club	Pct.	G.	PO.	A.	E.	DP.	PB.
Louisville	.9763	135	3497	1442	120	134	15	Omaha	.9705	137	3517	1393	149	123	9
Denver	.9761	135	3389	1504	120	138	13	Iowa	.9701	135	3412	1393	148	109	13
Evansville	.9720	133	3423	1503	142	123	22	Wichita	.9695	137	3530	1402	155	131	8
Indianapolis	.9717	136	3525	1393	143	114	14	Oklahoma City	.963	134	3325	1479	187	109	12

INDIVIDUAL FIELDING

*Throws lefthanded.

FIRST BASEMEN

Player and Club	Pct.	G.	PO.	A.	E.	DP.	Player and Club	Pct.	G.	PO.	A.	E.	DP.
Barnes, Indianapolis	1.000	2	11	0	0	0	Kable, Louisville*	.991	81	712	53	7	57
Bass, Denver	1.000	6	60	5	0	6	Kubski, Indianapolis	.931	7	27	0	2	2
Bertoni, Evansville	1.000	2	11	0	0	2	Laga, Evansville*	.985	125	1135	68	18	93
Calise, Louisville	.988	18	149	14	2	13	Lombarski, Oklahoma City	.992	40	330	28	3	18
Castillo, Evansville	.957	2	20	2	1	3	J. Lopez, Evansville	1.000	1	4	0	0	0
Christmas, Indianapolis	1.000	1	1	0	0	0	Mackanin, Denver	.947	4	16	2	1	1
Corcoran, Oklahoma City*	.977	19	165	7	4	20	Matuszek, Oklahoma City	.987	64	560	59	8	55
Culmer, Oklahoma City	.946	11	97	9	6	5	McCormack, Evansville	.960	9	43	5	2	3
DeSa, Louisville*	.988	49	367	32	5	43	McDonald, Oklahoma City	1.000	1	0	1	0	0
Djakonow, Evansville	.964	4	26	1	1	5	Montanez, Oklahoma City*	1.000	1	15	1	0	1
Farkas, Indianapolis	.995	54	383	28	2	33	Murray, Wichita	1.000	21	118	10	0	6
Fiala, Indianapolis	.992	90	667	52	6	63	O'Brien, Denver*	.991	41	312	34	3	24
Followell, Evansville	1.000	1	1	0	0	0	Phelps, Wichita*	.988	123	1047	74	14	108
Hicks, Iowa	.989	21	165	11	2	13	Putnam, Denver	.988	73	625	48	8	74
Hostetler, Denver	.978	14	123	8	3	12	Roof, Louisville	1.000	1	3	0	0	1
Hurdle, Indianapolis	1.000	2	3	0	0	0	Ryal, Omaha*	1.000	1	2	0	0	0
Ireland, Omaha	.936	11	40	4	3	4	C. Smith, Omaha	1.000	2	3	0	0	0
Isales, Indianapolis	.988	13	72	7	1	5	Thompson, Iowa*	.952	6	37	3	2	2
B. Johnson, Denver	1.000	7	55	5	0	5	UPTON, Iowa	.993	111	932	84	7	85
Ron Johnson, Omaha	.980	128	1044	74	23	100	Werth, Omaha	1.000	20	59	5	0	4

SECOND BASEMEN

Player and Club	Pct.	G.	PO.	A.	E.	DP.	Player and Club	Pct.	G.	PO.	A.	E.	DP.
Aviles, 1 Denver-13 Okla. City	.972	14	36	33	2	5	HOLT, Denver	.983	122	259	384	11	92
Babitt, Wichita	.946	25	37	50	5	18	Ireland, Omaha	.945	11	25	27	3	7
Barranca, Indianapolis	.966	26	36	77	4	12	W. Johnson, Wichita	.957	40	81	76	7	14
Bertoni, Evansville	.962	34	82	94	7	20	Lawless, Indianapolis	.976	80	170	236	10	46
Borucki, Oklahoma City	.941	3	8	8	1	2	Little, Wichita	.990	24	43	57	1	12
Colletti, Omaha	.917	3	5	6	1	1	J. Lopez, Evansville	.953	25	38	64	5	14
Cox, 48 Evansville-9 Omaha	.968	57	124	179	10	45	Mackanin, Denver	.938	16	24	36	4	8
Djakonow, Evansville	.944	7	14	20	2	7	Manuel, Wichita	1.000	6	15	12	0	4
Doyle, Louisville	.977	101	198	273	11	62	Paris, Louisville	1.000	3	4	6	0	2
Farkas, Indianapolis	1.000	3	7	0	0	0	Phillips, Wichita	.935	10	16	27	3	4
Fiala, Indianapolis	.993	37	58	93	1	22	Rodriguez, Oklahoma City	.895	5	9	8	2	1
Followell, Evansville	.992	29	53	75	1	14	Rohn, Iowa	.982	84	168	222	7	41
Frias, Wichita	.944	4	8	9	1	3	Santana, Louisville	.989	41	82	103	2	27
J. Gates, Denver	1.000	3	7	12	0	2	Strain, Iowa	.979	59	116	169	6	34
M. Gates, Wichita	.978	57	121	149	6	38	Wellman, Omaha	1.000	6	14	23	0	2
Hamric, Oklahoma City	.966	118	221	343	20	64	Wieser, Omaha	.937	11	28	31	4	5
Heath, Omaha	.968	104	229	283	17	61	Wolters, Louisville	1.000	1	2	6	0	1

THIRD BASEMEN

Player and Club	Pct.	G.	PO.	A.	E.	DP.	Player and Club	Pct.	G.	PO.	A.	E.	DP.
Anderson, Denver	.923	74	41	128	14	15	Lyons, Louisville	1.000	24	15	33	0	3
Aviles, 3 Denver-57 Okla. City	.934	60	38	90	9	9	Mackanin, Denver	.908	62	34	95	13	5
Babitt, Wichita	1.000	2	1	0	0	0	Manuel, Wichita	.953	31	23	58	4	2
Barnes, Indianapolis	.951	11	14	25	2	2	McCann, Wichita	.949	61	34	59	5	6
Bertoni, Evansville	.960	11	5	19	1	0	McDonald, Oklahoma City	.912	61	43	112	15	9
Borucki, Oklahoma City	.949	19	17	39	3	3	J. Mills, Wichita	.800	4	4	8	3	2
Castillo, Evansville	.962	24	14	36	2	3	R. Mills, Louisville	.875	3	1	6	1	0
Cox, Omaha	1.000	5	4	4	0	1	Murray, Wichita	.862	43	33	61	15	8
Djakonow, Evansville	.842	22	17	47	12	5	Ojeda, Louisville	.917	9	5	6	1	1
Doyle, Louisville	.914	15	10	22	3	1	Paris, Louisville	.920	7	6	17	2	1
Edler, Omaha	.907	70	53	113	17	7	Phillips, Wichita	.667	3	0	4	2	1
ESASKY, Indianapolis	.915	101	77	150	21	13	Rodriguez, Oklahoma City	.895	4	2	15	2	0
Farkas, Indianapolis	.971	38	21	45	2	5	Rohn, Iowa	1.000	3	2	11	0	0
Followell, Evansville	1.000	12	3	9	0	1	Santana, Louisville	.966	73	58	139	7	16
Frias, Wichita	.917	9	3	8	1	1	C. Smith, Wichita	.946	21	12	23	2	2
M. Gates, Wichita	.882	9	8	7	2	1	Stockstill, Denver	1.000	1	0	1	0	0
Ireland, Omaha	.959	56	35	104	6	5	Tabler, Iowa	.906	127	112	215	34	11
Jirschele, Denver	1.000	1	0	1	0	0	Waller, Iowa	1.000	10	10	11	0	0
H. Johnson, Denver	.895	82	48	139	22	19	Wieser, Omaha	.750	10	4	11	5	1
Lombarski, Oklahoma City	.500	3	0	1	1	0	Wolters, Louisville	.911	20	13	28	4	1
J. Lopez, Evansville	1.000	2	0	4	0	0							

SHORTSTOPS

Player and Club	Pct.	G.	PO.	A.	E.	DP.
Anderson, Denver	.948	54	89	168	14	38
Aviles, 11 OKC-1 Den	.939	12	17	29	3	5
Bertoni, Evansville	.957	24	46	66	5	13
BIANCALANA, Omaha	.969	129	204	357	18	79
DeJohn, Evansville	.984	56	73	170	4	29
Fiala, Indianapolis	.923	5	4	8	1	1
Fletcher, Iowa	.957	129	224	357	26	78
Foley, Indianapolis	.955	128	227	343	27	70
Followell, Evansville	.964	59	87	182	10	33
Franco, Oklahoma City	.930	118	211	350	42	63
Frias, Wichita	1.000	4	1	6	0	1
Glynn, Wichita	1.000	2	2	6	0	1
Gonzalez, Louisville	.971	8	15	18	1	5
Heath, Omaha	1.000	1	3	2	0	0
Holt, Denver	1.000	2	5	7	0	2
Ireland, Omaha	.957	13	30	37	3	9
Jirschele, Denver	.981	12	18	35	1	9
Lawless, Indianapolis	.909	11	15	15	3	2
Little, Wichita	.959	79	122	248	16	58
Manuel, Wichita	.952	35	58	82	7	21
Paris, Louisville	.952	118	198	341	27	77
Phillips, Wichita	.954	32	58	86	7	17
Rodriguez, Oklahoma City	.971	6	11	22	1	0
Rohn, Iowa	.938	6	12	18	2	4
Santana, Louisville	.966	17	23	33	2	8
Strain, Iowa	.857	2	2	4	1	0
Tolleson, Denver	.980	71	97	195	6	14

OUTFIELDERS

Player and Club	Pct.	G.	PO.	A.	E.	DP.
Barrow, Denver	.982	33	50	4	1	0
Bogener, Denver°	.982	68	107	5	2	2
Brewer, Omaha	.976	16	37	3	1	1
Briggs, Iowa°	1.000	8	15	1	0	0
Bruno, Oklahoma City°	.970	81	156	5	5	2
Capra, Denver	.990	121	275	11	3	2
Carrion, Wichita	.944	28	50	1	3	1
Castillo, Evansville	1.000	15	16	1	0	0
Corcoran, Oklahoma City°	.971	94	165	4	5	0
Corey, Evansville	.955	13	20	1	1	0
Cowger, Denver	1.000	4	5	0	0	0
H. Cruz, Iowa	1.000	4	6	1	0	0
Culmer, Oklahoma City	.934	58	81	4	6	0
DeSa, Louisville°	.962	90	121	6	5	3
Djakonow, Evansville	1.000	2	2	0	0	0
Farkas, Indianapolis	1.000	2	1	0	0	0
Filkins, Evansville°	.988	110	155	9	2	3
Fuentes, Wichita	1.000	1	6	0	0	0
E. Gates, Evansville	1.000	8	6	0	0	0
Glynn, Wichita	.750	3	3	0	1	0
Gonzalez, 30 OkC-40 Den	.964	70	105	3	4	2
Grant, Iowa	.958	103	147	13	7	5
Green, Louisville	.992	46	111	17	1	2
Gulden, Wichita	.833	5	5	0	1	0
Hall, Iowa°	.973	131	317	13	9	1
Hammond, Omaha	.978	26	42	2	1	0
Hampton, Evansville	1.000	17	32	3	0	0
Hurdle, Indianapolis	.967	78	110	7	4	2
Ireland, Omaha	1.000	2	1	0	0	0
Isales, Indianapolis	.929	84	94	10	8	1
H. Johnson, Evansville	.955	23	21	0	1	0
Roy Johnson, Wichita°	.968	102	238	4	8	2
W. Johnson, Wichita	.909	37	47	3	5	0
R. Jones, Denver°	.984	77	120	5	2	2
Kable, Louisville°	1.000	7	9	1	0	0
Kenaga, Evansville	.981	83	149	5	3	0
Kubski, Indianapolis	.962	20	24	1	1	0
Landrum, Louisville	.958	25	46	0	2	0
Lavigne, Iowa	.972	68	99	7	3	1
Lombarski, Oklahoma city	.939	22	29	2	2	0
Mackanin, Denver	1.000	3	1	0	0	0
Manuel, Wichita	1.000	3	3	0	0	0
Martin, Iowa°	.933	11	14	0	1	0
McDonald, Oklahoma City	.941	19	31	1	2	0
McGee, Louisville	.976	13	40	0	1	0
E. Miller, Evansville	.982	76	158	4	3	1
R. Mills, Louisville	.985	107	253	15	4	1
Motley, Omaha	.987	102	216	4	3	1
Murray, Wichita	.966	19	28	0	1	0
Norman, Wichita	1.000	6	12	0	0	0
O'Brien, Denver°	.956	80	106	3	5	1
Office, Oklahoma City°	.968	26	60	0	2	0
Penniall, 41 Evan-11 Lou	.989	52	86	1	1	0
Putnam, Denver	1.000	2	2	0	0	0
Redus, Indianapolis	.971	118	223	10	7	0
Rivera, Omaha	.976	41	79	3	2	1
Rodriguez, Oklahoma City	1.000	5	4	1	0	0
ROOF, Louisville	.991	117	220	7	2	3
Rooney, Wichita	.980	99	185	7	4	1
Ryal, Omaha°	.977	125	240	18	6	1
A. Sanchez, Oklahoma City	.948	87	155	10	9	1
O. Sanchez, Louisville	1.000	14	20	0	0	0
Sheridan, Omaha	1.000	32	92	3	0	1
Silverio, Omaha	.995	89	180	2	1	0
C. Smith, Wichita	.931	20	24	3	2	0
Sofield, Denver	1.000	13	16	0	0	0
Stenhouse, Wichita	.976	130	243	6	6	0
Thompson, Iowa°	.750	5	3	0	1	0
Walker, Indianapolis°	.973	36	68	3	2	0
Waller, Iowa	.971	93	156	9	5	1
Wieser, Omaha	1.000	4	2	1	0	1
Williams, Indianapolis°	.987	128	300	12	4	5
Wilson, Evansville	.971	41	96	6	3	0
Wolters, Louisville	1.000	10	11	2	0	0
Younger, Evansville°	.963	15	25	1	1	0

CATCHERS

Player and Club	Pct.	G.	PO.	A.	E.	DP.	PB.
Benton, Iowa	.966	68	354	38	14	2	10
Bjorkman, Louisville	.980	103	530	60	12	10	10
Brummer, Louisville	1.000	8	34	6	0	0	0
Castillo, Evansville	.982	86	475	78	10	6	14
Christmas, Indianapolis	.974	75	408	39	12	4	7
Cowger, Denver	.902	7	36	1	4	0	0
Dewey, Omaha	.955	18	78	6	4	0	1
Gulden, Wichita	.979	44	214	20	5	3	3
W. Hayes, Iowa	.990	69	438	37	5	2	3
Ibarra, Oklahoma City	1.000	3	12	3	0	0	0
B. JOHNSON, Denver	.992	79	456	49	4	5	8
Keatley, Omaha	.975	82	457	47	13	4	4
Kennedy, Louisville	.950	4	18	1	1	0	0
Littlejohn, Denver	.992	43	226	32	2	3	4
McCormack, Evansville	.992	51	228	24	2	3	8
Neufang, Denver	.913	4	16	5	2	1	0
O'Berry, Indianapolis	.979	36	172	18	4	3	3
Orensky, Oklahoma City	.983	41	207	22	4	0	3
Pasley, Evansville	.929	3	11	2	1	0	0
Perkins, Denver	1.000	1	5	0	0	0	0
Poole, Evansville	.951	15	72	6	4	1	0
Salas, Louisville	.950	6	16	3	1	1	0
O. Sanchez, Louisville	.959	25	123	17	6	2	5
Slaught, Omaha	.980	40	216	25	5	5	3
Soriano, Omaha	1.000	16	61	10	0	2	0
Ulrich, 39 Ok.C.-10 Wich.	.982	49	240	35	5	4	3
Van Gorder, Indianapolis	.990	52	260	36	3	6	4
Venner, Denver	1.000	2	6	1	0	0	0
Werner, Denver	.978	8	41	4	1	0	1
Werth, Omaha	.000	1	0	0	0	0	0
Wieghaus, 85 Wich.-22 Ok.C.	.991	107	605	64	6	6	6
Willard, Oklahoma City	.962	35	169	35	8	6	5

PITCHERS

Player and Club	Pct.	G.	PO.	A.	E.	DP.
Abone, Wichita	1.000	23	3	9	0	0
Altamirano, Oklahoma City	.800	6	1	3	1	0
Armstrong, Omaha	.857	15	2	4	1	1
Babcock, Denver	.923	14	1	11	1	1
Bahnsen, Oklahoma City	1.000	23	4	7	0	0
Bailey, Evansville°	.978	26	10	35	1	1
Bargar, Wichita	1.000	9	5	4	0	0
Berenguer, Evansville	.957	25	3	19	1	0
Black, Omaha°	1.000	4	1	4	0	0
Blyth, Iowa	1.000	11	0	1	0	0
Boitano, Denver	.600	32	0	3	2	1
Botelho, Omaha	1.000	15	4	15	0	0
Botting, Omaha°	1.000	3	0	2	0	0
Bradford, 21 Lou.-14 Ok.C.°	.833	35	0	5	1	0
Brito, Louisville	.826	36	3	16	4	1
Brusstar, Oklahoma City	1.000	22	3	6	0	1
Burroughs, Oklahoma City°	1.000	22	2	11	0	0
Butcher, Denver	1.000	8	3	13	0	1
Capilla, Wichita°	1.000	11	2	6	0	0
Carey, Indianapolis°	.889	21	0	8	1	0
Carlucci, Indianapolis	1.000	51	3	20	0	2
Carman, Oklahoma City°	1.000	10	1	7	0	0
Cary, Evansville°	1.000	1	0	1	0	0
Cato, Indianapolis	1.000	16	7	15	0	0

PITCHERS—Continued

Player and Club	Pct.	G.	PO.	A.	E.	DP.	Player and Club	Pct.	G.	PO.	A.	E.	DP.
Citarella, Louisville	1.000	28	8	24	0	1	Martin, Louisville*	.955	11	6	15	1	0
Corcoran, Oklahoma City*	1.000	2	0	1	0	0	Matula, 17 Evan-19 Den	.971	36	15	19	1	1
Creel, Omaha	.857	18	5	13	3	2	McEnaney, Denver*	1.000	54	6	13	0	2
V. Cruz, Denver	1.000	44	2	5	0	1	Mercer, Denver*	1.000	13	0	2	0	0
Culver, Oklahoma City	1.000	1	1	0	0	0	D. Miller, Louisville	.875	46	1	6	1	0
Dacko, Evansville	1.000	26	13	28	0	2	Miscik, Omaha*	1.000	4	0	5	0	1
C. Davis, Louisville	1.000	14	0	3	0	0	Moore, Evansville	1.000	15	1	6	0	1
M. Davis, Oklahoma City*	1.000	21	2	19	0	0	Morogiello, Louisville*	1.000	57	1	9	0	1
Dawley, Indianapolis	.923	29	16	20	3	2	Mueller, Wichita	1.000	56	3	2	0	0
Decker, Oklahoma City	.667	10	1	1	1	0	O'Keefe, Indianapolis*	1.000	4	0	1	0	0
Dixon, Wichita	1.000	3	1	5	0	0	OLMSTED, Louisville*	1.000	28	16	31	0	3
Dowless, Indianapolis	.905	26	8	11	2	1	Parker, Iowa	.929	26	6	7	1	0
Downs, Oklahoma City	.900	32	11	25	4	1	Parrott, Omaha	.947	22	7	11	1	0
Dues, Wichita	1.000	16	12	13	0	1	Pashnick, Evansville	1.000	3	0	1	0	0
Earley, Iowa*	1.000	28	6	16	0	1	Proly, Iowa	1.000	17	2	9	0	0
Edelen, Indianapolis	.769	13	3	7	3	0	Pryce, Iowa	1.000	5	0	2	0	0
Engle, Wichita*	.636	24	0	7	4	0	Quintana, Wichita*	1.000	56	7	18	0	4
Farr, Denver	.981	26	16	37	1	2	Rajsich, Denver*	.958	19	7	16	1	2
Faulk, Oklahoma City	1.000	14	3	10	0	2	Ramos, Wichita	1.000	24	7	16	0	1
Filer, Iowa	.963	17	6	20	1	0	E. Rasmussen, Louisville	1.000	4	1	4	0	0
Fischer, Omaha	.970	26	9	23	1	1	J. Rasmussen, Okla City	.917	25	8	14	2	1
Frost, Omaha	1.000	4	3	0	0	0	Reed, Oklahoma City	.895	25	18	33	6	5
Fulgham, Louisville	.923	10	4	8	1	1	Reelhorn, Oklahoma City	.962	29	16	34	2	2
Gerlach, Iowa	.929	27	8	18	2	1	Rincon, Louisville	.968	18	13	17	1	1
Gorman, Wichita*	.960	23	4	20	1	0	Robbins, Evansville*	.929	11	3	10	1	0
Grapenthin, Wichita	1.000	20	2	3	0	0	Rothschild, Evansville	1.000	45	4	12	0	1
Griffin, Wichita	.905	28	2	17	2	0	Rucker, Evansville*	1.000	30	6	14	0	2
Gumpert, Evansville	1.000	2	0	1	0	0	Ruiz, Evansville*	.900	44	4	23	3	3
Harris, Indianapolis	.800	8	7	9	4	0	Ryder, Indianapolis	1.000	34	7	17	0	0
B. Hayes, Indianapolis	1.000	41	8	8	0	1	Sattler, Wichita	.889	26	7	25	4	3
Hood, Omaha*	1.000	8	3	12	0	2	Saucier, Evansville*	.909	10	1	9	1	0
Horton, Louisville*	1.000	8	2	5	0	0	Scherrer, Indianapolis*	.913	19	3	18	2	0
Howell, Iowa	.886	20	9	22	4	0	Schuler, Omaha*	1.000	32	8	15	0	1
Huffman, Omaha	1.000	9	0	8	0	0	Seaman, Wichita*	.909	43	1	9	1	0
James, Evansville	.500	9	0	1	1	0	Segelke, Iowa	.926	27	11	14	2	1
J. Johnson, Louisville	.909	12	2	8	1	1	Semall, 2 Iowa-30 Den	1.000	32	15	22	0	5
L. Jones, Iowa	.952	42	3	17	1	1	B. Smith, Wichita	1.000	3	1	10	0	3
Keener, Louisville	1.000	9	1	0	0	0	Smithson, Denver	.950	29	8	30	2	3
Kelly, Omaha	1.000	29	12	20	0	4	Stein, Iowa	.889	43	6	10	2	0
Kepshire, Indianapolis	1.000	5	1	1	0	0	Stuper, Louisville	1.000	8	5	15	0	0
Kerrigan, 31 OC-17 Den	1.000	48	9	20	0	1	Sutton, Oklahoma City	1.000	3	2	2	0	1
Kinnunen, Louisville*	1.000	16	1	13	0	1	Tenenini, Wichita	1.000	30	3	6	0	0
Knapp, Iowa	.941	17	7	9	1	0	Toliver, Indianapolis	.875	4	1	6	1	0
Kravec, Iowa*	.923	14	4	8	1	0	Tomlin, Indianapolis*	1.000	64	3	15	0	1
Lahti, Louisville	1.000	21	2	7	0	0	Tufts, Omaha*	.941	59	2	14	1	2
Larson, Iowa	1.000	17	11	16	0	3	Ujdur, Evansville	1.000	8	6	8	0	0
Lazorko, Denver	.857	23	4	8	2	1	Whitehouse, Denver*	.973	30	11	25	1	3
Lee, Evansville	1.000	18	1	3	0	0	Willis, Oklahoma City*	1.000	56	6	15	0	0
Lefferts, Iowa*	.923	18	4	8	1	1	Wills, Denver	.909	41	7	13	2	0
Leonard, Omaha	1.000	3	1	0	0	0	Winfield, Louisville	1.000	17	4	6	0	0
Lesley, Indianapolis	1.000	40	2	8	0	1	Wirth, Evansville	1.000	3	1	1	0	1
A. Lopez, Evansville	1.000	12	0	3	0	0	Wright, Omaha	.882	12	8	7	2	1
Luebber, 13 Den-15 Evans	.950	28	1	27	2	1	Young, Indianapolis	1.000	16	7	7	0	1
MacPherson, Wichita	1.000	8	1	1	0	0	Yuhas, Omaha	.929	13	3	10	1	1
Martin, Iowa*	1.000	1	0	1	0	0							

The following players had no accepted recorded chances at the positions indicated; therefore, are not listed in the fielding averages for those particular positions: Aviles, of; Babitt, ss; Benton, of; Bertoni, p; Bonham, p; Dawley, of; Earley, 1b; Farkas, ss; Fiala, 3b; Franco, 3b; Glynn, 2b; Hudson, p; Kainer, p; Kubski, p; Littell, p; Long, p; Lyons, 1b, 2b, of; McDonald, c; Mustad, p; O'Berry, 1b, of; Rohn, of; Tabler, 1b; Werth, c.

CLUB PITCHING

Club	ERA	G.	CG	ShO.	Sv.	IP.	H.	R.	ER.	HR.	HB.	BB.	Int. BB.	SO.	WP.	Bk.
Omaha	4.03	137	24	10	24	1172.1	1162	603	525	109	27	489	33	703	25	11
Evansville	4.29	137	25	4	27	1141	1189	643	544	92	43	519	24	734	80	15
Louisville	4.37	135	33	6	28	1165.2	1168	648	566	122	35	467	26	662	62	13
Indianapolis	4.43	136	20	9	35	1175	1228	648	578	132	27	486	46	788	49	6
Iowa	4.89	135	19	10	30	1137.1	1208	714	618	144	37	497	33	755	50	10
Denver	5.39	135	26	3	25	1129.2	1289	753	676	145	29	463	33	735	44	5
Oklahoma City	5.42	134	16	2	17	1141	1307	783	668	114	31	533	42	700	51	21
Wichita	5.45	137	18	3	28	1176.2	1345	806	712	178	31	496	22	732	40	10

PITCHERS' RECORDS
(Leading Qualifiers for Earned-Run Average Leadership—109 or More Innings)

*Throws lefthanded.

Pitcher—Club	W.	L.	Pct.	ERA.	G.	GS.	CG.	GF.	ShO.	Sv.	IP.	H.	R.	ER.	HR.	HB.	BB.	Int. BB.	SO.	WP
Howell, Iowa	13	4	.765	2.36	20	20	5	0	2	0	141.1	102	45	37	9	2	48	1	139	3
Olmsted, Louisville*	9	9	.500	3.63	28	24	9	2	1	0	161.1	158	79	65	18	6	44	0	43	3
Dawley, Indianapolis	11	7	.611	3.82	29	28	6	0	1	0	179	196	86	76	22	8	44	4	106	5
Fischer, Omaha	3	3	.500	3.85	26	10	2	7	1	0	110	119	57	47	12	2	43	6	44	7
Bailey, Evansville*	11	10	.524	4.158	26	26	4	0	2	0	153.2	169	89	71	14	10	64	2	83	13
Dacko, Evansville	12	10	.545	4.162	26	26	6	0	1	0	173	199	94	80	14	3	54	3	86	7
Farr, Denver	13	8	.619	4.27	26	26	7	0	1	0	173	200	95	82	14	1	49	5	90	10
Reed, Oklahoma City	6	7	.462	4.37	25	17	2	4	0	0	131.2	135	78	64	12	2	59	3	73	6
Creel, Omaha	6	8	.429	4.40	18	17	3	0	0	0	114.2	120	69	56	12	1	67	1	56	7
Luebber, 13 Den-15 Evns	7	10	.412	4.48	28	19	4	5	0	0	122.2	127	74	61	11	2	61	3	83	11
Brito, Louisville	5	8	.385	4.51	36	15	2	13	1	4	119.2	107	64	60	13	2	62	5	94	5

Departmental Leaders: G—Tomlin, 64; GS—Dawley, 28; CG—Berenguer, Olmsted, 9; GF—Tufts, 46; ShO—Bailey, Howell, Kelly, Scherrer, Stuper, 2; Sv—Cruz, Lesley, 14; W—Citarella, 15; L—Downs, 15; Pct.—Howell, .765; IP—Dawley, 179; H—Farr, 200; R—Downs, 116; ER—Semall, 97; HR—Sattler, 28; HB—Bailey, 10; BB—Wills, 81; IBB—Lesley, Matula, 8; SO—Smithson, 144; WP—Bailey, 13.

(All Pitchers—Listed Alphabetically)

Pitcher—Club	W.	L.	Pct.	ERA.	G.	GS.	CG.	GF.	ShO.	Sv.	IP.	H.	R.	ER.	HR.	HB.	BB.	Int. BB.	SO.	WP.
Abone, Wichita	2	2	.500	6.86	23	1	0	5	0	2	40.2	63	38	31	8	1	15	1	19	2
Altamirano, Oklahoma City	1	0	1.000	0.64	6	0	0	5	0	0	14	12	3	1	1	0	3	1	17	2
Armstrong, Omaha	4	2	.667	3.21	15	0	0	12	0	3	28	19	12	10	1	0	20	0	27	2
Babcock, Denver	3	1	.750	3.16	14	0	0	5	0	1	25.2	29	11	9	1	2	14	2	22	1
Bahnsen, Oklahoma City	4	3	.571	4.89	23	1	0	11	0	1	46	42	26	25	7	0	28	5	31	1
Bailey, Evansville°	11	10	.524	4.16	26	26	4	0	2	0	153.2	169	89	71	14	10	64	2	83	13
Bargar, Wichita	0	4	.000	11.20	9	8	1	0	0	0	31.1	53	45	39	8	2	22	0	18	3
Berenguer, Evansville	11	10	.524	4.61	25	24	9	0	1	0	156.1	152	85	80	12	6	80	0	127	6
Bertoni, Evansville	0	0	.000	0.00	1	0	0	1	0	0	1	0	0	0	0	0	0	0	1	0
Black, Omaha°	3	1	.750	2.48	4	4	3	0	1	0	29	23	9	8	2	0	10	0	20	0
Blyth, Iowa	2	0	1.000	6.75	11	0	0	6	0	0	13.1	17	11	10	3	1	12	0	13	0
Boitano, Denver	6	5	.545	4.31	32	1	0	20	0	6	48	51	29	23	6	1	23	6	42	4
Bonham, Indianapolis	0	0	.000	4.50	1	1	0	0	0	0	4	2	2	2	0	0	3	0	3	0
Botelho, Omaha	7	5	.583	4.19	15	15	3	0	0	0	105.1	86	51	49	15	3	37	0	74	0
Botting, Omaha°	1	0	1.000	9.00	3	2	0	1	0	0	10	14	10	10	2	0	4	0	7	0
Bradford, 21 Lou-14 OkC°	2	3	.400	4.48	35	5	0	14	0	2	70.1	81	39	35	3	1	35	4	48	2
Brito, Louisville	5	8	.385	4.51	36	15	2	13	1	4	119.2	107	64	60	13	2	62	5	94	9
Brusstar, Oklahoma City	4	2	.667	2.57	22	0	0	20	0	5	28	25	11	8	1	1	14	2	13	1
Burroughs, Oklahoma City°	2	7	.222	5.66	22	12	1	4	0	0	76.1	99	59	48	7	5	43	2	65	3
Butcher, Denver	5	1	.833	2.75	8	8	1	0	0	0	59	54	20	18	5	0	14	0	31	1
Capilla, Wichita°	2	2	.500	6.38	11	7	0	3	0	0	36.2	36	28	26	7	1	32	0	24	0
Carey, Indianapolis°	2	5	.286	8.89	21	7	0	3	0	0	55.2	80	57	55	14	4	37	1	44	2
Carlucci, Indianapolis	2	2	.500	3.11	51	0	0	17	0	9	92.2	93	38	32	7	0	41	4	73	5
Carman, Oklahoma City°	0	1	.000	6.82	10	5	0	2	0	0	33	37	29	25	2	3	23	1	29	1
Cary, Evansville°	1	0	1.000	5.40	1	1	0	0	0	0	5	6	3	3	1	0	3	0	5	1
Cato, Indianapolis	6	4	.600	3.58	16	15	2	0	0	0	88	83	46	35	10	5	25	4	49	3
Citarella, Louisville	15	6	.714	4.88	28	25	4	1	0	0	153	171	95	83	18	6	62	0	82	10
Corcoran, Oklahoma City°	0	0	.000	9.00	2	0	0	1	0	0	3	6	3	3	0	0	1	0	0	0
Creel, Omaha	6	8	.429	4.40	18	17	3	0	0	0	114.2	120	69	56	12	1	67	1	56	1
Cruz, Denver	3	3	.500	3.86	44	0	0	31	0	14	56	48	28	24	8	1	25	2	62	2
Culver, Oklahoma City	0	0	.000	27.00	1	0	0	1	0	0	1	3	3	3	0	0	2	0	0	0
Dacko, Evansville	12	10	.545	4.16	26	26	6	0	0	0	173	199	94	80	14	3	54	3	86	7
C. Davis, Louisville	0	1	.000	5.49	14	0	0	4	0	0	19.2	20	12	12	3	2	6	2	9	1
M. Davis, Oklahoma City°	5	12	.294	6.24	21	19	3	1	1	0	96.2	111	75	67	15	2	50	1	95	5
Dawley, Indianapolis	11	7	.611	3.82	29	28	6	0	1	0	179	196	86	76	22	8	48	4	106	5
Decker, Oklahoma City	0	3	.000	7.98	10	0	0	4	0	0	14.2	17	15	13	1	0	11	0	19	1
Dixon, Wichita	1	1	.500	4.00	3	3	0	0	0	0	18	15	8	8	1	0	6	0	13	0
Dowless, Indianapolis	10	7	.588	5.48	26	23	4	2	0	0	133	150	90	81	18	2	58	4	72	2
Downs, Oklahoma City	2	15	.118	5.34	32	25	5	2	0	1	156.2	182	116	93	14	4	72	7	70	4
Dues, Wichita	5	3	.625	4.63	16	15	2	0	0	0	91.1	93	54	47	8	2	48	3	34	3
Earley, Iowa°	4	2	.667	3.41	28	3	1	10	1	4	66	61	28	25	4	3	27	6	33	1
Edelen, Indianapolis	3	4	.429	5.37	13	13	0	0	0	0	55.1	79	39	33	7	0	18	5	28	2
Engle, Wichita°	3	3	.500	8.07	24	8	0	1	0	0	64.2	85	65	58	10	1	50	0	41	1
Farr, Denver	13	8	.619	4.27	26	26	7	0	1	0	173	200	95	82	14	1	49	5	90	10
Faulk, Oklahoma City	1	4	.250	4.43	14	3	0	4	0	1	40.2	50	22	20	2	2	17	1	14	4
Filer, Iowa	6	7	.462	6.73	17	16	3	0	0	0	92.1	109	74	69	14	1	31	1	51	5
Fischer, Omaha	3	3	.500	3.85	26	10	2	7	1	0	110	119	57	47	12	2	43	6	44	1
Frost, Omaha	1	0	1.000	4.76	4	4	0	0	0	0	22.2	21	12	12	1	2	4	0	12	1
Fulgham, Louisville	4	3	.571	7.01	10	10	0	0	0	0	51.1	73	42	40	9	0	21	0	26	2
Gerlach, Iowa	2	4	.333	4.82	27	6	1	15	0	2	74.2	78	47	40	9	0	29	5	30	0
Gorman, Wichita°	8	7	.533	5.20	23	16	6	5	1	1	119.1	131	77	69	19	4	35	1	69	5
Grapenthin, Wichita	2	2	.500	4.73	20	2	0	8	0	3	32.1	36	21	17	5	0	16	1	23	1
Griffin, Wichita	8	7	.533	5.93	28	24	2	3	1	1	136.2	166	99	90	24	4	24	1	88	3
Gumpert, Evansville	1	0	1.000	0.00	2	0	0	2	0	0	5.2	0	0	0	0	0	3	0	2	0
Harris, Indianapolis	4	1	.800	3.00	8	8	3	0	1	0	48	27	18	16	2	2	24	0	44	3
Hayes, Indianapolis	5	5	.500	2.73	41	2	0	17	0	6	69.1	57	24	21	5	1	40	5	61	5
Hood, Omaha°	2	2	.500	4.34	8	6	1	1	1	0	37.1	34	19	18	1	0	19	2	21	1
Horton, Louisville°	2	3	.400	6.69	8	6	0	1	0	0	36.1	47	31	27	6	4	11	0	37	3
HOWELL, Iowa	13	4	.765	2.36	20	20	5	0	2	0	141.1	102	45	37	9	2	48	1	139	3
Hudson, Denver	0	0	.000	2.45	2	0	0	1	0	0	3.2	5	1	1	0	0	0	0	3	0
Huffman, Omaha	3	4	.429	5.63	9	8	2	0	1	0	38.1	42	31	24	6	2	16	0	13	0
James, Evansville	1	1	.500	2.08	9	1	0	6	0	4	21.2	9	6	5	0	2	14	0	30	4
Johnson, Louisville	0	4	.000	4.96	12	7	2	4	0	1	45.1	48	29	25	5	3	17	3	21	2
Jones, Iowa	5	6	.455	3.97	42	1	0	23	0	5	88.1	91	45	39	12	0	51	4	70	9
Kainer, Denver	0	1	.000	22.50	1	1	0	0	0	0	2	7	5	5	2	0	0	0	1	0
Keener, Louisville	1	0	1.000	5.91	9	0	0	3	0	1	10.2	15	8	7	1	0	5	0	6	3
Kelly, Omaha	6	12	.333	4.98	29	19	2	4	2	2	132	145	79	73	16	3	40	5	60	0
Kepshire, Indianapolis	0	0	.000	5.00	5	0	0	2	0	0	9	7	5	5	2	0	5	1	8	0
Kerrigan, 31 OkC-17 Den	1	5	.167	5.38	48	1	0	22	0	2	97	117	61	58	8	0	39	4	52	3
Kinnunen, Louisville°	2	3	.400	4.72	16	5	1	3	0	1	47.2	50	29	25	7	3	21	2	21	4
Knapp, Iowa	6	6	.500	8.10	17	17	2	0	1	0	90	122	85	81	22	5	48	1	46	4
Kravec, Iowa°	2	6	.250	6.98	14	14	0	0	0	0	68.1	76	59	53	14	3	39	0	53	1
Kubski, Indianapolis	0	0	.000	9.00	1	0	0	1	0	0	2	4	2	2	1	0	2	0	1	0
Lahti, Louisville	3	2	.600	4.45	21	0	0	12	0	3	30.1	27	15	15	3	1	7	3	17	2
Larson, Iowa	7	5	.583	4.80	17	16	3	1	0	0	99.1	113	59	53	9	6	43	2	68	3
Lazorko, Denver	1	2	.333	6.85	23	1	0	7	0	1	43.1	63	38	33	8	5	23	4	32	3
Lee, Evansville	1	2	.333	7.25	18	0	0	13	0	2	22.1	26	19	18	0	4	13	2	8	2
Lefferts, Iowa°	8	5	.615	3.05	18	14	3	0	1	0	97.1	97	50	33	8	3	25	1	71	3
Leonard, Omaha	1	2	.333	7.40	3	3	1	0	0	0	20.2	19	17	17	4	1	9	1	13	3
Lesley, Indianapolis	6	4	.600	3.62	40	0	0	29	0	14	59.2	55	27	24	6	1	25	8	47	1
Littell, Louisville	0	1	.000	3.00	1	1	0	0	0	0	3	2	2	1	0	0	5	0	2	0
Long, Denver	0	0	.000	10.80	2	0	0	2	0	0	1.2	2	2	2	0	0	3	0	0	0
Lopez, Denver	4	0	1.000	1.76	12	2	0	4	0	0	30.2	23	6	6	3	1	10	0	30	6
Luebber, 13 Den-15 Evns	7	10	.412	4.48	28	19	4	5	0	1	122.2	127	74	61	11	2	61	3	83	11
MacPherson, Wichita	2	1	.667	4.50	8	0	0	2	0	0	12	18	10	6	1	0	9	2	4	0
Jared Martin, Iowa°	0	0	.000	0.00	1	0	0	1	0	0	2	0	0	0	0	0	1	0	0	0
John Martin, Iowa	5	3	.625	3.47	11	11	6	0	0	0	83	62	37	32	6	1	38	1	41	2
Matula, 17 Evns-19 Den	3	8	.273	5.62	36	10	0	11	0	0	113.2	141	91	71	16	4	49	8	52	4
McEnaney, Denver°	4	4	.500	4.93	54	4	1	18	0	2	76.2	89	44	42	13	2	24	1	42	2
Mercer, Denver°	1	0	1.000	8.80	13	0	0	2	0	0	15.1	21	15	15	2	0	8	0	8	1
Miller, Louisville	3	1	.750	2.91	46	0	0	32	0	10	55.2	34	21	18	7	1	21	3	44	1

Pitcher—Club	W.	L.	Pct.	ERA	G.	GS.	CG.	GF.	ShO.	Sv.	IP.	H.	R.	ER.	HR.	HB.	BB.	Int. BB.	SO.	WP.
Miscik, Omaha*	0	1	.000	4.22	4	0	0	1	0	0	10.2	10	5	5	1	0	4	0	5	1
Moore, Evansville	1	2	.333	6.36	15	12	1	1	0	0	63.2	84	49	45	10	2	27	0	35	4
Morogiello, Louisville*	5	4	.556	4.50	57	1	0	15	0	6	80	102	44	40	7	1	22	2	43	5
Mueller, Wichita	3	9	.250	4.66	56	0	0	41	0	12	75.1	80	43	39	10	1	34	4	46	3
Mustad, Wichita	0	0	.000	3.00	1	1	0	0	0	0	3	1	1	1	0	0	0	0	3	0
O'Keefe, Indianapolis*	0	0	.000	10.38	4	0	0	2	0	0	4.1	7	5	5	1	0	6	0	3	0
Olmsted, Louisville*	9	9	.500	3.63	28	24	9	2	1	0	161.1	158	79	65	18	6	44	0	43	3
Parker, Iowa	1	3	.250	6.54	26	6	0	7	0	2	63.1	94	51	46	11	1	28	4	34	5
Parrott, Omaha	3	3	.500	2.75	22	7	2	9	0	4	72	68	28	22	4	1	25	3	40	0
Pashnick, Evansville	1	1	.500	3.80	3	3	0	0	0	0	21.1	21	13	9	3	0	9	0	9	0
Proly, Iowa	2	1	.667	5.01	17	0	0	16	0	7	23.1	23	18	13	1	1	5	2	7	0
Pryce, Iowa	1	1	.500	3.90	5	5	1	0	1	0	27.2	35	19	12	1	1	3	0	16	1
Quintana, Wichita*	9	5	.643	4.18	56	0	0	21	0	7	94.2	95	49	44	9	3	46	3	85	4
Rajsich, Denver*	5	6	.455	6.15	19	14	3	1	0	0	86.1	96	64	59	13	1	47	0	52	6
Ramos, Wichita	10	7	.588	5.15	24	23	6	0	0	0	136.1	147	87	78	24	3	51	1	81	0
E. Rasmussen, Louisville	2	2	.500	4.13	4	4	0	0	0	0	28.1	27	13	13	1	1	9	0	20	1
J. Rasmussen, Oklahoma City	8	13	.381	6.94	25	21	2	1	0	0	118	145	97	91	16	4	61	2	74	8
Reed, Oklahoma City	6	7	.462	4.37	25	17	2	4	0	0	131.2	135	78	64	12	2	59	3	73	6
Reelhorn, Oklahoma City	2	13	.133	5.00	29	21	1	4	0	1	136.2	164	100	76	17	6	57	6	68	4
Rincon, Louisville	5	8	.385	5.09	18	18	4	0	1	0	116.2	115	80	66	13	2	61	2	75	7
Robbins, Evansville*	3	3	.500	5.85	11	11	0	0	0	0	52.1	54	40	34	2	3	40	0	42	9
Rothschild, Evansville	6	4	.600	3.65	45	0	0	29	0	10	69	73	34	28	7	2	30	3	45	4
Rucker, Evansville*	4	1	.800	3.39	30	0	0	22	0	6	58.1	53	27	22	2	4	29	5	42	3
Ruiz, Evansville*	2	4	.333	4.82	44	2	0	16	0	3	93.1	110	61	50	8	3	50	2	60	5
Ryder, Indianapolis	6	8	.429	5.74	34	16	0	2	0	0	109.2	122	77	70	13	0	60	1	50	8
Sattler, Wichita	10	6	.625	5.39	26	26	0	0	0	0	145.1	171	99	87	28	6	49	0	90	7
Saucier, Evansville*	0	4	.000	7.36	10	3	0	4	0	1	22	18	19	18	1	1	23	1	17	1
Scherrer, Indianapolis*	6	4	.600	4.06	19	12	4	2	2	0	88.2	68	43	40	7	1	32	1	81	4
Schuler, Omaha*	6	2	.750	3.10	32	5	1	9	1	0	107.1	123	39	37	7	4	23	5	87	2
Seaman, Wichita*	1	6	.143	6.32	43	0	0	18	0	2	57	62	41	40	9	2	34	2	56	5
Segelke, Iowa	7	9	.438	5.92	27	17	0	5	0	0	117	131	88	77	21	5	76	3	64	11
Semall, 2 Ia-30 Den	6	10	.375	6.97	32	18	5	7	0	1	125.1	157	103	97	15	3	64	4	66	2
B. Smith, Wichita	2	0	1.000	1.90	3	3	1	0	0	0	23.2	21	5	5	1	0	2	0	15	0
Smithson, Denver	11	7	.611	4.54	29	24	8	3	0	0	152.2	149	82	77	21	6	47	2	144	6
Stein, Iowa	7	3	.700	3.80	43	0	0	30	0	10	71	59	35	30	6	5	31	3	59	4
Stuper, Louisville*	7	1	.875	1.46	8	8	5	0	2	0	61.2	49	11	10	1	0	16	0	42	2
Sutton, Oklahoma City	1	1	.500	5.40	3	3	1	0	0	0	20	22	12	12	1	0	10	0	13	2
Tenenini, Wichita	2	2	.500	4.17	30	0	0	12	0	0	58.1	72	36	27	5	1	23	3	23	3
Toliver, Indianapolis	2	2	.500	3.92	4	4	0	0	0	0	20.2	20	10	9	0	0	13	2	19	4
Tomlin, Indianapolis*	9	2	.818	3.53	64	0	0	36	0	5	91.2	96	39	36	10	2	30	5	67	4
Tufts, Omaha*	10	6	.625	1.60	59	0	0	46	0	12	95.1	74	28	17	3	4	30	7	52	4
Ujdur, Evansville	2	4	.333	3.80	8	7	1	1	0	0	47.1	42	23	20	5	0	14	0	30	5
Whitehouse, Denver*	4	8	.333	6.30	30	20	1	1	1	0	121.1	146	97	85	14	3	45	1	65	0
Willis, Oklahoma City*	7	6	.538	7.00	56	2	1	33	0	6	91.1	131	81	71	14	2	46	7	61	4
Wills, Omaha	7	10	.412	5.20	41	12	2	23	0	3	107.1	110	71	62	8	4	81	2	77	7
Winfield, Louisville	3	0	1.000	2.70	17	0	0	3	0	0	30	27	14	9	2	1	16	0	13	4
Wirth, Evansville	2	1	.667	2.40	3	3	0	0	0	0	15	16	4	4	1	0	8	0	6	0
Wright, Omaha	5	2	.714	3.41	12	12	2	0	0	0	63.1	60	28	24	8	0	20	1	45	1
Young, Indianapolis	3	6	.333	4.76	16	7	1	3	0	1	64.1	82	40	34	7	1	19	1	32	1
Yuhas, Omaha	4	2	.667	4.48	13	13	0	0	0	0	68.1	75	38	34	6	0	37	0	50	1

BALKS—Reelhorn, 6; Downs, Ruiz, Sattler, 5 each; Bailey, Citarella, 4 each; Horton, Howell, Wright, 3 each; Burroughs, Dacko, M. Davis, Earley, Filer, Fischer, Hayes, Kinnunen, Kravec, Moore, Olmsted, Quintana, Sutton, 2 each; Berenguer, Boitano, Botelho, Brito, Butcher, Carey, Carlucci, Creel, Decker, Dowless, Dues, Farr, Hood, Huffman, James, Jones, Kelly, Mercer, Ramos, J. Rasmussen, Seaman, Smithson, Toliver, Willis, Winfield, Yuhas, 1 each.

COMBINATION SHUTOUTS—Robbins-Lee, Evansville; Dawley-Young, Young-Tomlin-Lesley, Dowless-Lesley, Hayes-Lesley, Scherrer-Lesley, Indianapolis; Segelke-Proly, Earley-Stein, Lefferts-Stein, Filer-Earley-Stein, Iowa; Rasmussen-Morogiello-Brito-Miller, Louisville; Wright-Miscik, Yuhas-Tufts, Botelho-Tufts-Schuler-Kelly, Omaha; Griffin-Quintana-Mueller, Wichita.

NO-HIT GAME—None.

International League

CLASS AAA

Leading Batter
GREGORY WELLS
Toledo

League President
HAROLD COOPER

Leading Pitcher
JAMES LEWIS
Columbus

CHAMPIONSHIP WINNERS IN PREVIOUS YEARS

1884—Trenton .520	1927—Buffalo .667	1956—Toronto .566
1885—Syracuse .584	1928—Rochester .549	Rochester (2nd)† .553
1886—Utica .646	1929—Rochester .613	1957—Toronto .575
1887—Toronto .644	1930—Rochester .629	Buffalo (2nd)† .571
1888—Syracuse .723	1931—Rochester .601	1958—Montreal‡ .588
1889—Detroit .649	1932—Newark .649	1959—Buffalo .582
1890—Detroit .617	1933—Newark .622	Havana (3rd)† .523
1891—Buffalo (reg. season) .727	Buffalo (4th)† .494	1960—Toronto‡ .649
Buffalo (supplem'l) .680	1934—Newark .608	1961—Columbus .597
1892—Providence .615	Toronto (3rd)† .559	Buffalo (3rd)† .559
Binghamton° .667	1935—Montreal .597	1962—Jacksonville .610
1893—Erie .606	Syracuse (2nd)† .565	Atlanta (3rd)† .539
1894—Providence .696	1936—Buffalo‡ .610	1963—Syracuse x .533
1895—Springfield .687	1937—Newark‡ .717	Indianapolis‡ .562
1896—Providence .602	1938—Newark‡ .684	1964—Jacksonville .589
1897—Syracuse .632	1939—Jersey City .582	Rochester (4th)† .532
1898—Montreal .586	Rochester (2nd)† .556	1965—Columbus .582
1899—Rochester .624	1940—Rochester .611	Toronto (3rd)† .556
1900—Providence .616	Newark (2nd)† .594	1966—Rochester .565
1901—Rochester .642	1941—Newark .649	Toronto (2nd-tied)† .558
1902—Toronto .669	Montreal (2nd)† .584	1967—Richmond .574
1903—Jersey City .642	1942—Newark .601	Toledo (3rd)† .525
1904—Buffalo .657	Syracuse (3rd)† .513	1968—Toledo .565
1905—Providence .638	1943—Toronto .625	Jacksonville (4th)† .514
1906—Buffalo .607	Syracuse (3rd)† .536	1969—Tidewater .563
1907—Toronto .619	1944—Baltimore‡ .553	Syracuse (3rd)† .536
1908—Baltimore .593	1945—Montreal .621	1970—Syracuse‡ .600
1909—Rochester .596	Newark (2nd)† .582	1971—Rochester‡ .614
1910—Rochester .601	1946—Montreal‡ .649	1972—Louisville .563
1911—Rochester .645	1947—Jersey City .610	Tidewater (3rd)† .545
1912—Toronto .595	Syracuse (3rd)† .575	1973—Charleston .586
1913—Newark .625	1948—Montreal‡ .614	Pawtucket y† .534
1914—Providence .617	1949—Buffalo .584	1974—Memphis .613
1915—Buffalo .632	Montreal (3rd)† .545	Rochester x‡ .611
1916—Buffalo .586	1950—Rochester .609	1975—Tidewater‡ .610
1917—Toronto .604	Baltimore (3rd)† .556	1976—Rochester .638
1918—Toronto .693	1951—Montreal‡ .617	Syracuse (2nd)† .590
1919—Baltimore .671	1952—Montreal .629	1977—Pawtucket .571
1920—Baltimore .719	Rochester (3rd)† .619	Charleston (2nd)‡ .557
1921—Baltimore .717	1953—Rochester .630	1978—Charleston .607
1922—Baltimore .689	Montreal (2nd)† .586	Richmond (4th)† .511
1923—Baltimore .677	1954—Toronto .630	1979—Columbus‡ .612
1924—Baltimore .709	Syracuse (4th)§ .510	1980—Columbus‡ .593
1925—Baltimore .633	1955—Montreal .617	1981—Columbus‡ .633
1926—Toronto .657	Rochester (4th)† .497	

°Won split-season playoff. †Won four-team playoff. ‡Won championship and four-team playoff. §Defeated Havana in game to decide fourth place, then won four-team playoff. xLeague was divided into Northern, Southern divisions. yLeague divided into American, National divisions. (NOTE—Known as Eastern League in 1884, New York State League in 1885, International League in 1886-87, International Association in 1888, International League in 1889-90, Eastern Association in 1891, and Eastern League from 1892 until 1912.)

STANDING OF CLUBS AT CLOSE OF SEASON, SEPTEMBER 3

Club	Rich.	Col.	Tide.	Roch.	Paw.	Syr.	Tol.	Char.	W.	L.	T.	Pct.	G.B.
Richmond (Braves)	....	11	10	11	13	13	16	8	82	57	0	.590	......
Columbus (Yankees)	9	....	11	11	12	7	16	13	79	61	0	.564	3½
Tidewater (Mets)	9	9	....	11	9	11	9	16	74	63	0	.540	7
Rochester (Orioles)	9	9	9	....	12	13	11	9	72	68	0	.514	10½
Pawtucket (Red Sox)	7	8	9	8	....	11	10	14	67	71	0	.486	14½
Syracuse (Blue Jays)	7	13	9	7	9	....	9	10	64	76	0	.457	18½
Toledo (Twins)	4	4	11	9	10	11	....	11	60	80	0	.429	22½
Charleston (Indians)	12	7	4	11	6	10	9	....	59	81	0	.421	23½

Major league affiliations in parentheses.

Tidewater club represented Norfolk and Portsmouth, Va.

Playoffs—Rochester defeated Richmond, three games to none; Tidewater defeated Columbus, three games to none; Tidewater defeated Rochester, three games to none, to win league championship and Governor's Cup.

Regular-Season Attendance—Charleston, 145,337; Columbus, 400,899; Pawtucket, 204,724; Richmond, 257,611; Rochester, 361,312; Syracuse, 184,483; Tidewater, 148,271; Toledo, 150,184. Total, 1,852,861. Playoffs, 26,929. No all-star game.

Managers—Charleston, Doc Edwards; Columbus, Frank Verdi; Pawtucket, Joe Morgan; Richmond, Eddie Haas; Rochester, Lance Nichols; Syracuse, Jim Beauchamp; Tidewater, Jack Aker; Toledo, Cal Ermer.

All-Star Team: 1B—Wells, Toledo; 2B—Barrett, Pawtucket; 3B—Ashford, Columbus; SS—Fernandez, Syracuse; OF—Mattingly, Columbus; Hancock, Pawtucket; Shelby, Rochester; C—Petralli, Syracuse; DH—Brant, Columbus; P—McMurtry, Richmond; Rel.P—Kaufman, Columbus; Manager—Haas, Richmond.

(Compiled by Howe News Bureau, Boston, Mass.)

CLUB BATTING

Club	Pct.	G.	AB.	R.	OR.	H.	TB.	2B.	3B.	HR.	RBI.	GW.	SH.	SF.	HP.	BB.	Int. BB.	SO.	SB.	CS.	LOB.
Richmond	.284	139	4667	771	652	1324	2047	190	40	151	716	78	29	35	50			802	189	59	1084
Columbus	.283	140	4690	769	732	1327	2061	218	36	148	717	69	52	49	34	663	34	733	102	59	1090
Syracuse	.274	140	4572	638	696	1253	1770	194	31	87	584	58	45	49	34	487	23	581	83	47	979
Charleston	.273	140	4713	647	673	1285	1874	180	47	105	603	54	73	36	27	559	41	816	126	88	1052
Toledo	.273	140	4585	633	720	1250	1873	205	41	112	587	56	56	30	25	553	30	610	67	55	1019
Pawtucket	.269	138	4509	626	704	1212	1762	176	16	114	569	55	65	45	24	530	31	689	146	59	1021
Tidewater	.265	137	4530	637	530	1201	1737	197	39	87	578	67	49	41	29	530	41	656	196	102	966
Rochester	.259	140	4562	646	660	1182	1881	182	41	145	591	61	58	49	32	568	37	902	96	56	1025

INDIVIDUAL BATTING

(Leading Qualifiers for Batting Championship—378 or More Plate Appearances)

*Bats lefthanded.   †Switch-hitter.

Player and Club	Pct.	G.	AB.	R.	H.	TB.	2B.	3B.	HR.	RBI.	GW.	SH.	SF.	HP.	BB.	Int. BB.	SO.	SB.	CS.
Wells, Gregory, Toledo	.336	136	541	78	182	306	30	5	28	107	7	0	4	1	35	3	47	9	8
Ashford, Thomas, Columbus	.331	137	540	98	179	252	35	4	10	101	11	1	6	1	64	6	57	5	6
Adams, Glenn, Syracuse*	.330	101	348	52	115	169	21	0	11	51	13	0	4	2	52	4	41	0	1
Tillman, Kerry, Tidewater	.322	108	404	60	130	167	10	6	5	54	9	0	2	3	37	2	57	26	18
Mattingly, Donald, Columbus*	.315	130	476	67	150	208	24	2	10	75	7	5	6	2	50	5	24	1	2
Bonaparte, Elijah, Toledo*	.306	111	399	59	122	159	15	8	2	30	3	2	2	0	45	3	50	20	13
Rhomberg, Kevin, Charleston	.304	100	382	64	116	142	16	5	0	26	1	11	3	0	73	1	55	45	23
Fernandez, Octavio, Syracuse†	.302	134	523	78	158	203	21	6	4	56	5	8	4	1	42	1	31	22	13
Barrett, Martin, Pawtucket	.300	131	477	72	143	187	27	1	5	57	3	11	6	1	73	1	27	28	13
Jacoby, Brook, Richmond	.299	134	501	74	150	231	21	3	18	58	9	2	2	3	45	2	106	1	2
Norrid, Timothy, Charleston*	.299	126	442	61	132	197	18	4	13	65	7	5	4	1	71	15	48	3	5

Departmental Leaders: G—R. Jones, 139; AB—Shelby, 548; R—Runge, 106; H—Wells, 182; TB—Wells, 306; 2B—Ashford, 35; 3B—Hall, 15; HR—Balboni, 32; RBI—Wells, 107; GWRBI—Keller, Wynne, 14; SH—Oquendo, 14; SF—Hancock, 8; HP—Brant, 14; BB—Runge, 95; IBB—Norrid, 15; SO—Young, 140; SB—Hall, 62; CS—Rhomberg, 23.

(All Players—Listed Alphabetically)

Player and Club	Pct.	G.	AB.	R.	H.	TB.	2B.	3B.	HR.	RBI.	GW.	SH.	SF.	HP.	BB.	Int. BB.	SO.	SB.	CS.
Adams, Glenn, Syracuse*	.330	101	348	52	115	169	21	0	11	51	13	0	4	2	52	4	41	0	1
Alfaro, Jesus, Rochester	.250	4	12	1	3	3	0	0	0	0	0	0	1	0	0	1	0	0	0
Alvarez, Roberto, Columbus	.125	2	8	1	1	1	0	0	0	0	0	0	0	0	0	1	0	0	0
Anicich, Michael, Tidewater	.175	16	57	4	10	12	2	0	0	4	0	1	0	0	18	0	0		
Ashford, Thomas, Columbus	.331	137	540	98	179	252	35	4	10	101	11	1	6	1	64	6	57	5	6
Ault, Douglas, Syracuse*	.241	50	137	11	33	50	5	0	4	29	5	1	3	0	10	0	11	0	1
Baker, David, Syracuse*	.279	116	369	52	103	174	19	2	16	63	7	4	6	7	46	1	61	0	2
Baker, Ricky, Charleston†	.255	49	188	24	48	66	4	4	2	25	3	8	3	1	21	2	23	13	4
Balboni, Stephen, Columbus	.284	83	313	57	89	204	17	1	32	86	11	0	6	2	38	2	68	0	1
Barrett, Martin, Pawtucket	.300	131	477	72	143	187	27	1	5	57	3	11	6	1	73	1	27	28	13
Beamon, Charles, Syracuse*	.286	127	416	69	119	168	23	1	8	53	7	0	4	2	47	3	55	12	4
Bell, Jorge, Syracuse	.200	37	125	11	25	47	5	4	3	19	1	2	1	2	1	0	42	2	2
Beltre, Sergio, Tidewater	.244	13	41	6	10	12	0	1	0	3	0	0	0	3	1	9	2	1	
Biercevicz, Gregory, Tidewater	.000	22	1	0	0	0	0	0	0	0	0	0	0	0	0	0	0	0	0
Bochy, Bruce, Tidewater	.227	81	251	32	57	113	11	0	15	52	4	0	6	0	19	1	47	2	3
Bockhorn, Glen, Richmond	.400	2	5	2	2	8	0	0	2	3	0	0	0	0	0	2	0	0	
Boddicker, Michael, Rochester	1.000	21	1	0	1	2	1	0	0	2	1	0	0	0	0	0	0	0	0
Bonaparte, Elijah, Toledo*	.306	111	399	59	122	159	15	8	2	30	3	2	2	0	45	3	50	20	13
Bonds, Bobby, Columbus	.179	28	84	10	15	27	6	0	2	7	0	1	1	0	15	0	29	2	1
Bonner, Robert, Rochester	.206	48	155	12	32	39	1	0	2	18	1	3	2	0	11	0	33	4	1
Booker, Roderick, Toledo*	.250	104	292	38	73	83	8	1	0	19	1	7	3	2	31	2	36	5	6
Bourjos, Christopher, Rochester	.261	78	241	33	63	96	10	4	5	33	4	4	1	2	26	1	35	5	5
Bowen, Samuel, 60-Paw.-27 Chstn	.218	87	289	40	63	112	11	1	12	29	0	1	4	3	42	2	72	1	1
Brant, Marshall, Columbus	.280	132	482	86	135	251	21	1	31	96	9	2	4	14	66	4	111	0	1
Brooks, Craig, Pawtucket*	.203	69	177	18	36	50	6	1	2	16	2	3	2	2	21	1	59	2	1
Burns, Michael, Pawtucket	.000	28	2	0	0	0	0	0	0	0	0	0	0	0	0	0	2	0	0
Bush, R. Randall, Toledo*	.325	49	160	21	52	90	14	0	8	27	4	2	2	1	26	4	20	2	0
Bustabad, Juan, Pawtucket*	.266	133	440	61	117	126	5	2	0	23	1	12	4	2	50	3	62	24	9
Butler, Brett, Richmond*	.363	41	157	22	57	74	8	3	1	22	0	0	1	1	22	3	19	12	9
Butterfield, Brian, Columbus†	.417	13	36	4	15	16	1	0	0	2	0	0	0	0	3	0	1	0	0
Callahan, Patrick, Columbus	.237	28	76	14	18	27	4	1	1	10	2	3	1	0	8	0	16	0	2
Cannon, Joseph, J., Syracuse*	.222	31	90	13	20	29	1	1	2	10	0	1	1	5	0	21	2	0	

Player and Club	Pct.	G.	AB.	R.	H.	TB.	2B.	3B.	HR.	RBI.	GW.	SH.	SF.	HP.	BB.	Int. BB.	SO.	SB.	CS.
Castillo, M. Carmelo, Charleston	.278	71	281	46	78	119	12	1	9	39	5	5	3	0	23	4	54	12	7
Chapman, Kelvin, Tidewater	.280	101	329	53	92	124	13	2	5	40	7	6	4	5	43	2	42	25	8
Charboneau, Joseph, Charleston	.234	20	77	8	18	24	1	1	1	5	0	0	1	2	11	1	13	0	0
Christensen, James, Toledo	.268	98	310	38	83	134	19	4	8	49	6	7	1	1	19	0	43	4	2
Colbern, Michael, Richmond	.150	6	20	2	3	4	1	0	0	2	1	0	0	0	2	0	3	0	0
Corey, Mark, Rochester	.000	1	2	0	0	0	0	0	0	0	0	0	0	0	0	0	2	0	0
Cubbage, Michael, Tidewater*	.268	113	369	54	99	157	28	0	10	54	7	0	5	2	76	11	71	2	4
Curry, Stephen, Richmond	.250	2	4	1	1	2	1	0	0	1	0	0	0	0	1	0	1	1	0
Darling, Ronald, Tidewater	.000	27	1	0	0	0	0	0	0	0	0	0	0	0	0	0	1	0	0
David, Andre, Toledo*	.140	15	43	4	6	9	1	1	0	0	0	0	0	0	1	0	8	0	1
Davis, Michael, Tidewater	.266	113	402	55	107	174	19	0	16	63	5	1	7	4	35	2	58	12	2
DeLeon, Luis, Charleston†	.298	106	356	49	106	140	11	7	3	30	2	9	1	5	24	2	60	10	6
Dempsey, Peter, Syracuse	.253	95	281	40	71	109	15	1	7	31	1	3	3	2	20	2	51	2	3
Derryberry, Timothy, Rochester*	.234	97	291	45	68	128	7	1	17	49	4	6	5	6	52	8	89	1	0
Doyle, Brian, 11 Syr.-50 Chstn*	.256	61	211	21	54	60	4	1	0	23	2	5	1	0	16	1	9	5	3
Duff, David, Tidewater	.235	7	17	4	4	5	1	0	0	0	0	0	0	0	3	0	3	0	0
Dugas, Shanie, Charleston*	.205	37	122	20	25	47	9	2	3	13	1	1	0	0	27	1	37	3	1
Dybzinski, Jerome, Charleston	.299	30	107	14	32	46	6	1	2	12	2	3	1	4	9	0	11	1	2
Engle, R. David, Toledo	.441	9	34	14	15	33	1	1	5	12	1	0	1	0	7	0	5	0	0
Espino, Juan, Columbus	.282	54	163	30	46	67	10	1	3	27	1	2	1	3	21	0	24	1	0
Evans, Barry, Columbus	.276	69	239	27	66	104	14	3	6	39	2	1	4	1	24	1	31	1	1
Fernandez, Octavio, Syracuse†	.302	134	523	78	158	203	21	6	4	56	5	8	4	1	42	1	31	22	13
Fitzgerald, Michael, Tidewater	.245	94	302	33	74	99	9	2	4	36	5	8	2	1	41	1	55	9	4
Flores, Gilberto, Tidewater	.332	83	256	47	85	98	11	1	0	24	4	1	0	3	43	1	27	23	8
Foote, Barry, Columbus	.385	7	26	1	10	15	2	0	1	5	0	0	1	0	1	0	7	0	0
Gaudet, James, Syracuse	.143	6	14	0	2	2	0	0	0	1	0	0	0	0	0	0	2	0	0
Gentile, Gene, Pawtucket*	.292	115	349	57	102	176	21	4	15	70	7	0	2	0	45	5	74	4	4
Giles, Brian, Tidewater	.278	108	352	48	98	171	32	4	11	54	3	5	0	4	37	0	81	16	7
Graham, Daniel, Rochester*	.272	112	356	43	97	148	14	2	11	50	7	3	5	0	50	5	72	2	0
Graham, Lee, Pawtucket*	.290	125	472	76	137	170	16	1	5	43	4	4	3	2	57	3	43	46	12
Gulliver, Glenn, Rochester*	.295	85	268	48	79	128	9	2	12	35	6	2	3	0	90	2	35	7	4
Hall, Albert, Richmond†	.263	129	528	97	139	196	18	15	3	42	3	2	1	4	74	3	62	62	11
Hammond, Steven, Richmond*	.200	4	10	0	2	2	0	0	0	0	0	0	0	0	0	0	2	0	0
Hancock, R. Garry, Pawtucket*	.294	123	449	53	132	219	18	3	21	71	8	2	8	1	24	5	28	2	5
Harer, Wayne, Columbus†	.252	75	222	39	56	73	9	1	2	19	2	7	3	0	27	0	25	4	3
Harper, Terry, Richmond	.384	37	146	25	56	99	12	2	9	42	2	0	2	1	24	4	20	6	1
Hart, J. Michael, 33-Roch-71-Col†	.286	104	311	50	89	148	16	2	13	36	1	0	3	0	75	7	71	1	5
Hernandez, Leonardo, Richmond	.317	53	202	29	64	113	10	3	11	43	3	0	3	1	13	1	28	7	5
Hernandez, Pedro, 61-Syr.-3-Colum.	.247	64	198	18	49	63	4	2	2	19	2	1	4	2	8	0	24	4	3
Hobson, Clell, Columbus	.325	27	83	17	27	46	5	1	4	20	1	2	0	0	18	0	13	0	1
Howard, Michael, Tidewater†	.286	99	332	62	95	142	12	10	5	33	2	3	1	2	58	8	37	17	12
Jacoby, Brook, Richmond	.299	134	501	74	150	231	21	3	18	58	9	2	2	3	45	2	106	1	2
Jimenez, Alfonso, Toledo	.226	37	115	7	26	29	3	0	0	12	2	2	3	1	13	1	14	1	4
Johnson, Randall, Richmond	.364	7	22	5	8	18	1	0	3	7	0	0	1	1	4	0	6	0	2
Jones, Ricky, Rochester	.230	139	457	66	105	163	15	2	13	51	3	8	6	3	36	1	91	4	3
Jurak, Edward, Pawtucket	.296	81	284	39	84	127	14	1	9	43	6	3	1	4	42	0	46	8	1
Keller, Charles, Richmond	.285	122	410	77	117	221	20	0	28	93	14	2	4	2	81	4	98	1	0
Komminsk, Brad, Richmond*	.353	5	17	4	6	13	1	0	2	5	1	0	0	0	2	0	5	0	1
Koza, David, Pawtucket	.259	123	390	60	101	169	14	0	18	72	10	5	6	4	34	2	81	0	2
Landis, Craig, Richmond	.211	24	57	11	12	25	1	0	4	12	2	0	0	2	7	0	13	1	0
Laudner, Timothy, Toledo	.169	20	71	4	12	20	2	0	2	12	0	0	0	0	11	0	15	0	1
Lickert, John, Pawtucket	.252	115	349	37	88	119	11	1	6	37	7	10	1	1	32	1	39	3	1
Lisi, Riccardo, Rochester	.231	93	294	34	68	97	9	1	6	40	5	2	4	6	22	1	54	4	6
Littleton, Larry, 72-Char.-62-Tol. ...'	.274	134	431	59	118	193	18	9	13	71	3	5	3	3	64	1	81	5	3
Logan, Daniel, Rochester*	.288	124	393	53	113	199	23	3	19	68	10	0	5	0	45	6	88	2	1
LoGrande, Angelo, Charleston	.293	125	484	65	142	219	26	0	17	67	4	2	4	2	35	2	101	0	0
Lora, Ramon, Syracuse	.340	16	50	6	17	28	3	1	2	14	0	0	1	1	6	0	7	0	0
MacDonald, Ronald, Tidewater	.282	38	131	24	37	51	6	1	2	25	1	4	2	3	14	0	18	1	2
Machemer, David, Toledo	.249	104	354	51	88	110	14	1	2	37	2	2	2	2	65	2	26	9	6
MacWhorter, Keith, Pawtucket	.000	40	1	0	0	0	0	0	0	0	0	0	0	0	0	0	1	0	0
Mankowski, Phillip, Tidewater*	.275	106	375	37	103	139	20	2	4	46	5	1	2	2	41	6	29	8	3
Manrique, Fred, Syracuse	.251	103	362	41	91	116	9	2	4	37	2	2	1	2	17	0	45	5	3
Mattingly, Donald, Columbus*	.315	130	476	67	150	208	24	2	10	75	7	5	6	2	50	5	24	1	2
McMullen, Ricky, Tidewater	.267	8	15	1	4	4	0	0	0	1	0	1	1	0	1	0	2	0	2
Mesa, Ivan, Toledo	.193	64	161	16	31	42	0	1	3	13	2	5	0	1	18	1	21	6	1
Mitchell, Robert, Toledo*	.349	12	43	10	15	25	7	0	1	5	0	1	1	0	9	0	1	1	0
Murray, Richard, Charleston	.242	40	153	21	37	51	2	0	4	22	4	0	0	2	20	0	40	3	0
Nahorodny, William, Charleston	.291	15	55	9	16	36	2	0	6	18	2	0	1	1	6	1	7	1	0
Nandin, Robert, Syracuse†	.282	49	170	21	48	55	7	0	0	16	2	3	1	0	15	0	12	15	1
Nixon, Otis, Columbus†	.280	59	207	43	58	62	4	0	0	14	2	7	1	0	49	0	41	46	13
Norrid, Timothy, Charleston*	.299	126	442	61	132	197	18	4	13	65	7	5	4	1	71	15	48	3	5
Oquendo, Jose, Tidewater†	.214	114	337	40	72	86	3	3	0	22	1	14	1	0	41	1	50	24	16
Owen, Lawrence, Richmond	.208	58	178	21	37	57	5	0	5	26	4	5	1	1	20	0	38	1	0
Pacho, Juan, Charleston	.000	3	7	0	0	0	0	0	0	0	0	0	1	0	0	0	2	0	0
Pagel, Karl, Charleston*	.331	50	157	39	52	93	12	1	9	33	0	0	2	0	46	4	47	1	1
Parks, Danny, Pawtucket	.000	28	2	0	0	0	0	0	0	0	0	0	0	0	0	0	1	0	0
Patterson, Michael, Columbus*	.252	96	326	61	82	159	14	12	13	37	4	4	2	1	58	6	75	19	6
Perry, Gerald, Richmond*	.297	133	492	94	146	221	22	4	15	92	9	2	5	1	91	11	79	39	12
Petralli, Eugene, Syracuse†	.289	126	395	57	114	166	19	3	9	58	5	3	7	2	73	6	54	2	2
Plante, Daniel, Columbus	1.000	1	1	0	1	1	0	0	0	0	0	0	0	0	0	0	0	0	0
Poe, Richard, Tidewater*	.105	11	38	0	4	4	0	0	0	2	0	0	0	0	1	0	5	0	0
Porter, Robert, Richmond*	.300	84	290	39	87	126	9	3	8	56	2	2	4	0	48	8	40	3	3
Ramos, Roberto, Columbus	.232	63	198	22	46	61	9	0	2	14	0	0	1	2	28	0	35	2	0
Rayford, Floyd, Rochester	.250	3	12	1	3	6	0	0	1	2	0	0	0	0	0	0	2	0	1
Rey, Everett, Charleston	.243	45	136	8	33	41	6	1	0	16	4	4	0	0	8	0	30	0	3
Reynolds, Michael, Richmond*	.143	5	7	1	1	1	0	0	0	0	0	0	0	0	0	0	2	0	0
Rhomberg, Kevin, Charleston	.304	100	382	64	116	142	16	5	0	26	1	11	3	0	73	1	55	45	23
Rivera, David, Charleston	.225	97	320	31	72	117	6	6	9	57	8	2	3	1	28	0	79	3	8
Robertson, Andre, Columbus	.203	57	202	28	41	63	7	3	3	26	4	3	4	1	40	1	40	1	4
Robinson, Bruce, Columbus*	.120	15	25	1	3	3	0	0	0	1	0	0	1	0	5	0	2	0	0
Rodriguez, Victor, Rochester	.247	87	300	26	74	88	10	2	0	18	2	7	1	0	11	0	31	3	3
Rosello, David, Charleston	.251	111	395	53	99	127	12	2	4	38	0	6	3	2	62	1	71	9	10

Player and Club	Pct.	G.	AB.	R.	H.	TB.	2B.	3B.	HR.	RBI.	GW.	SH.	SF.	HP.	BB.	Int. BB.	SO.	SB.	CS.
Royster, Willie, Rochester	.198	59	167	19	33	37	1	0	1	10	0	3	3	4	8	3	28	8	2
Ruiz, Manuel, Richmond	.343	27	67	8	23	30	4	0	1	6	1	0	0	0	8	0	11	2	0
Runge, Paul, Richmond	.280	134	507	106	142	224	25	6	15	71	7	2	2	4	95	1	106	18	5
Saferight, Harry, Toledo°	.228	75	219	22	50	71	6	0	5	30	3	0	0	1	21	4	26	1	0
Schmidt, David, Pawtucket	.229	70	153	25	35	50	6	0	3	23	2	2	3	3	34	1	46	2	1
Schmitz, Daniel, Columbus°	.295	63	207	28	61	71	5	1	1	29	1	2	3	0	33	4	15	2	0
Schoppee, David, Pawtucket	.000	54	1	0	0	0	0	0	0	0	0	0	0	0	0	0	0	0	0
Scott, Richard, Columbus	.500	5	10	2	5	8	0	0	1	1	0	2	0	0	1	0	2	0	0
Scott, Rodney, Columbus†	.366	30	112	19	41	54	2	1	3	15	3	1	1	0	20	0	10	7	7
Shelby, John, Rochester†	.279	133	548	92	153	239	26	6	16	52	4	12	3	1	51	1	115	34	16
Simunic, Douglas, Charleston	.000	3	12	0	0	0	0	0	0	0	0	0	0	1	0	3	0	0	
Sinatro, Matthew, Richmond	.252	72	246	39	62	95	7	1	8	29	5	2	1	1	30	0	45	13	4
Smith, Garry, Columbus	.235	30	68	9	16	31	4	1	3	11	3	0	1	1	11	0	19	0	1
Smith, Kenneth, Richmond°	.264	43	129	24	34	61	3	0	8	25	7	0	1	1	30	6	32	11	1
Smith, Raymond, Toledo	.272	94	305	25	83	118	13	2	6	43	5	10	2	4	18	1	10	3	4
Snider, Kelly, Toledo°	.273	111	381	54	104	150	14	1	10	36	3	1	3	3	60	7	54	0	0
Sodders, Michael, Toledo	.213	37	122	17	26	38	6	0	2	7	1	1	1	1	18	0	28	1	0
Sofield, Richard, Toledo°	.236	85	297	43	70	109	14	5	5	33	4	4	2	2	33	0	52	3	4
Stegman, David, Columbus	.272	115	383	71	104	156	18	2	10	53	5	4	1	2	66	2	41	11	5
Stimac, Craig, Charleston	.296	101	399	58	118	168	19	2	9	56	6	4	4	1	18	1	39	8	9
Sullivan, Marc, Pawtucket	.200	4	10	0	2	2	0	0	0	0	0	0	0	0	1	0	0	0	0
Tarver, Laschelle, Tidewater°	.250	3	8	1	2	2	0	0	0	0	0	0	0	0	1	0	1	1	0
Taylor, Michael, Charleston°	.250	36	124	17	31	42	3	1	2	9	2	3	0	0	13	3	27	5	4
Teufel, Timothy, Toledo	.282	45	149	25	42	78	10	4	6	20	3	5	2	2	15	0	23	1	1
Tevlin, Creighton, Syracuse°	.274	134	463	63	127	147	18	1	0	48	2	8	6	1	70	4	41	5	2
Thompson, Milton, Richmond°	.167	3	6	2	1	1	0	0	0	0	0	0	0	0	1	1	3	1	0
Tillman, Kerry, Tidewater	.322	108	404	60	130	167	10	6	5	54	9	0	2	3	37	2	57	26	18
Ullger, Scott, Toledo	.290	115	352	77	102	168	16	4	14	60	6	5	3	0	78	0	74	0	2
Valle, John, Rochester	.269	91	242	42	65	122	15	3	12	51	6	5	4	2	35	1	29	3	1
Vargas, Leonel, Richmond	.266	115	413	54	110	164	16	1	12	70	5	1	7	3	29	5	69	9	1
Velez, Otoniel, Syracuse	.258	7	19	1	3	4	1	0	0	0	0	0	0	0	3	0	11	0	0
Verhoeven, John, 18 Paw-25 Syr	.000	43	1	0	0	0	0	0	0	0	0	0	0	0	0	0	1	0	0
Walker, Cleotha, Pawtucket†	.251	133	494	71	124	195	22	2	15	66	4	3	3	0	60	7	99	25	9
Webster, Mitchell, Syracuse†	.281	137	513	95	144	218	21	7	13	68	4	6	2	8	67	2	55	12	11
Wells, Gregory, Toledo	.336	136	541	78	182	306	30	5	28	107	7	0	4	1	35	3	47	9	8
Westmoreland, Claude, Toledo	.333	19	39	2	13	20	2	1	1	9	2	0	0	5	2	14	0	1	
Whitmer, Daniel, Syracuse	.120	30	75	6	9	17	2	0	2	7	1	3	0	1	4	0	18	0	0
Wilson, James, Pawtucket	.244	96	275	29	67	93	8	0	6	26	1	9	3	2	23	1	32	1	0
Wirth, Alan, Rochester	.000	10	1	0	0	0	0	0	0	0	0	0	0	0	0	0	1	0	0
Wynne, Marvell, Tidewater°	.230	130	512	76	118	177	15	7	10	65	14	4	7	0	36	5	45	28	12
Young, Michael, Rochester†	.265	137	502	86	133	225	22	11	16	62	5	3	4	6	82	3	140	11	7
Zuvella, Paul, Richmond	.281	133	455	63	128	174	15	2	9	54	6	9	3	4	39	2	41	8	7

The following pitchers, listed alphabetically by club, with games in parentheses, had no plate appearances, primarily through use of designated hitters:

CHARLESTON—Anderson, Karl (11); Bohnet, John (9); Christenson, Gary (13); Combe, Geoff (23); Glaser, Gordon (32); Glynn, Edward (7); Heaton, Neal (29); Hrynko, Larry (41); Lewallyn, Dennis (41); Martinez, Silvio (4); Munninghoff, Scott (4); Nuismer, Jack (30); Pietroburgo, Robert (62); Searage, Raymond (38); Wihtol, Alexander (26).

COLUMBUS—Alexander, Doyle (1); Browning, Michael (4); Bruhert, Michael (29); Cochran, Gregory (25); Hernaiz, Jesus (4); Howell, Jay (5); Kaufman, Curt (55); LaRoche, David (17); Lewis, James (32); May, Rudolph (1); McGlothen, Lynn (22); Pacella, John (6); Patterson, Scott (29); Righetti, David (4); Serum, Gary (36); Sykes, Robert (15); Wehrmeister, David (36); Werly, James (26).

PAWTUCKET—Burtt, Dennis (25); Crawford, Steven (10); Denman, Brian (20); Dorsey, James (22); Fidrych, Mark (20); Johnson, John Henry (29); King, Jerome (17); Moloney, William (53).

RICHMOND—Alvarez, Jose (36); Boggs, Thomas (3); Brizzolara, Anthony (32); Cole, Timothy (23); Cowley, Joseph (9); D'Acquisto, John (17); Dayley, Kenneth (13); Diaz, Carlos (31); Field, Gregory (1); Fore, Charles (15); Gibson, James (15); Jones, Craig (2); McMurtry, Craig (32); Moore, Donnie (36); Perez, Pascual (5); Pettaway, Felix (10); Smith, Michael (10); Twitty, Jeffrey (9); Weaver, Roger (29).

ROCHESTER—Brown, Mark (3); Camacho, Ernie (8); Davis, George (4); Flinn, John (39); Ford, David (20); Grimsley, Ross (6); MacPherson, Bruce (6); Minetto, Craig (55); Ramirez, Allan (24); Rowe, Thomas (5); Smith, Mark (2); Snell, Nathaniel (37); Speck, Clifford (31); Stanhouse, Donald (15); Stoddard, Timothy (5); Swaggerty, William (29); Torrez, Peter (5); Welchel, Donald (30).

SYRACUSE—Baker, James (11); Barlow, Michael (3); Bomback, Mark (9); Cerutti, John (6); Eichhorn, Mark (27); Garvin, Jared (4); Geisel, David (21); Littlefield, John (14); O'Keeffe, Richard (14); Riccelli, Frank (3); Schneider, Jeffrey (34); Schrom, Kenneth (27); Senteney, Steve (44); Todd, Jackson (28); Wilson, Gary (5); Wright, James (5).

TIDEWATER—Dixon, Thomas (22); Dye, Scott (20); Gaff, Brent (23); Gorman, Thomas (4); Hausman, Mark (3); Holman, Scott (24); Leach, Terry (30); Ownbey, Richard (23); Ratzer, Steven (47); Terrell, Walter (21); Vonohlen, David (36).

TOLEDO—Boris, Paul (17); Cooper, Donald (28); Dooner, Glenn (54); Filson, Peter (23); Fregin, Douglas (5); Hodge, Eddie (5); Jackson, Darrell (5); Korczyk, Steven (39); Kromy, Ted (10); Little, Jeffrey (25); Mapel, Steven (3); Mulligan, Robert (11); O'Connor, Jack (12); Veselic, Robert (15); Viola, Frank (8); Walters, Michael (41); Williams, Albert (3); Williams, Richard (18); Young, Kip (9).

GRAND SLAM HOME-RUNS—Balboni, 3; Graham, Logan, Rivera, Valle, Vargas, 2 each; Ashford, Barrett, Bochy, Bourjos, Brant, Bush, Espino, Giles, Gulliver, Harper, Keller, Komminsk, Koza, Laudner, Lickert, Lisi, Littleton, Mattingly, Norrid, Perry, Porter, Runge, K. Smith, Sofield, Tillman, 1 each.

AWARDED FIRST BASE ON CATCHER'S INTERFERENCE—Webster, 6 (Graham 2, Callahan, Royster, R. Smith, Stimac); Dempsey, 2 (Graham, Lickert); Saferight, 2 (Callahan, Whitmer); Callahan (Petralli); Cubbage (Espino); Giles (Schmidt); Graham (Owen); R. Jones (Nahorodny); Lisi (Lickert); Oquendo (Petralli); Rey (Petralli); Runge (Graham); Taylor (Petralli); Walker (Owen).

CLUB FIELDING

Club	Pct.	G.	PO.	A.	E.	DP.	PB.	Club	Pct.	G.	PO.	A.	E.	DP.	PB.
Rochester	.975	140	3613	1601	135	154	24	Syracuse	.972	140	3560	1520	146	142	3
Tidewater	.974	137	3593	1554	135	147	11	Pawtucket	.970	138	3526	1563	160	147	14
Columbus	.973	140	3650	1422	142	128	9	Charleston	.967	140	3676	1671	183	163	17
Richmond	.973	139	3596	1438	138	134	14	Toledo	.967	140	3570	1596	176	148	10

INDIVIDUAL FIELDING
FIRST BASEMEN

°Throws lefthanded.

Player and Club	Pct.	G.	PO.	A.	E.	DP.	Player and Club	Pct.	G.	PO.	A.	E.	DP.
Anicich, Tidewater	1.000	10	78	5	0	6	Baker, Syracuse	1.000	4	34	2	0	5
Ault, Syracuse°	.974	29	178	12	5	20	Balboni, Columbus	.983	50	426	38	8	42

FIRST BASEMEN—Continued

Player and Club	Pct.	G.	PO.	A.	E.	DP.	Player and Club	Pct.	G.	PO.	A.	E.	DP.
Beamon, Syracuse*	.989	117	865	98	11	96	MacDonald, Tidewater	1.000	16	140	8	0	13
Brant, Columbus	.990	79	648	66	7	55	Mankowski, Tidewater	.958	9	87	5	4	7
CUBBAGE, Tidewater	.994	94	813	70	5	89	Mattingly, Columbus*	1.000	10	72	4	0	8
Davis, Tidewater	1.000	4	22	5	0	4	Murray, Charleston	.985	27	239	26	4	31
Dempsey, Syracuse	1.000	6	19	0	0	2	Nahorodny, Charleston	1.000	1	9	1	0	1
Fitzgerald, Tidewater	.978	11	82	6	2	10	Norrid, Charleston	.991	64	585	56	6	64
Gaudet, Syracuse	1.000	2	10	2	0	1	Pagel, Charleston	.990	18	174	15	2	23
Hancock, Pawtucket*	.994	41	294	20	2	28	Perry, Richmond	.986	131	1110	94	17	106
Harer, Columbus*	1.000	1	6	1	0	0	Petralli, Syracuse	.978	6	41	3	1	3
Hobson, Columbus	.940	6	43	4	3	4	Porter, Richmond*	1.000	2	14	2	0	1
Howard, Tidewater	1.000	1	7	1	0	2	Snider, Toledo*	.995	19	170	14	1	18
Keller, Richmond	.985	8	62	3	1	9	Stimac, Charleston	.990	13	85	14	1	12
Koza, Pawtucket*	.987	117	918	63	13	99	Ullger, Toledo	1.000	2	7	2	0	1
Lisi, Rochester	1.000	2	5	2	0	0	Valle, Rochester	.992	55	351	21	3	29
Logan, Rochester*	.993	112	942	64	7	108	Wells, Toledo	.986	122	1138	83	17	108
LoGrande, Charleston	.970	27	240	18	8	16	Wilson, Pawtucket	1.000	1	1	0	0	0

SECOND BASEMEN

Player and Club	Pct.	G.	PO.	A.	E.	DP.	Player and Club	Pct.	G.	PO.	A.	E.	DP.
Alfaro, Rochester	.933	4	6	8	1	4	Machemer, Toledo	.949	33	59	90	8	23
Alvarez, Columbus	1.000	2	2	2	0	2	Manrique, Syracuse	.962	78	169	208	15	48
Ashford, Columbus	1.000	9	27	24	0	8	McMullen, Tidewater	1.000	1	1	4	0	0
Baker, Syracuse	.971	8	14	19	1	3	Mesa, Toledo	.959	17	21	50	3	6
BARRETT, Pawtucket	.985	130	303	415	11	99	Nandin, Syracuse	.967	36	83	92	6	26
Bonner, Rochester	.997	48	110	175	1	29	Nixon, Columbus	.967	41	72	136	7	23
Booker, Toledo	.912	18	39	54	9	11	Rayford, Rochester	1.000	2	2	6	0	6
Butterfield, Columbus	.892	13	24	34	7	3	Reynolds, Richmond	1.000	3	4	5	0	2
Chapman, Tidewater	.970	56	109	149	8	31	Rhomberg, Charleston	.970	75	192	235	13	51
Christensen, Toledo	.994	37	69	108	1	19	Robertson, Columbus	.941	2	9	7	1	0
Doyle, 11 Syr.-29 Charleston	.976	40	77	128	5	37	Rodriguez, Rochester	.965	87	189	273	17	63
Dugas, Charleston	.984	36	68	113	3	20	Rosello, Charleston	.947	5	8	10	1	5
Evans, Columbus	.979	19	26	67	2	9	Ruiz, Richmond	1.000	4	5	7	0	0
Giles, Tidewater	.973	94	203	301	14	64	Runge, Richmond	.977	134	318	412	17	84
Gulliver, Rochester	.952	11	9	11	1	1	Schmitz, Columbus	.964	39	77	111	7	25
L. Hernandez, Rochester	1.000	1	0	1	0	1	Scott, Columbus	.951	17	33	45	4	6
P. Hernandez, 17 Syr.-3 Col	.936	20	37	36	5	8	Teufel, Toledo	.988	44	99	139	3	36
Johnson, Richmond	1.000	1	7	2	0	2	Walker, Pawtucket	.980	12	17	32	1	3

THIRD BASEMEN

Player and Club	Pct.	G.	PO.	A.	E.	DP.	Player and Club	Pct.	G.	PO.	A.	E.	DP.
ASHFORD, Columbus	.955	127	113	187	14	17	Lisi, Rochester	.882	25	11	34	6	2
Baker, Syracuse	.945	105	65	210	16	18	LoGrande, Charleston	.667	1	1	1	1	0
Booker, Toledo	.889	5	1	7	1	0	Machemer, Toledo	.925	53	36	87	10	11
Chapman, Tidewater	.813	7	4	9	3	0	Mankowski, Tidewater	.990	45	29	68	1	5
Christensen, Toledo	.912	44	29	85	11	10	Manrique, Syracuse	.833	17	6	29	7	4
Cubbage, Tidewater	1.000	5	2	0	0	0	Murray, Charleston	1.000	1	0	3	0	0
Curry, Richmond	.667	2	1	1	1	1	Nandin, Syracuse	.938	8	8	7	1	1
Davis, Tidewater	.935	93	62	138	14	15	Norrid, Charleston	.887	24	19	36	7	4
Dempsey, Syracuse	.898	28	13	40	6	7	Rhomberg, Charleston	.500	1	1	1	2	1
Doyle, Charleston	.933	20	14	42	4	5	Rosello, Charleston	.941	97	46	176	14	15
Evans, Columbus	1.000	7	7	23	0	0	Ruiz, Richmond	.875	3	2	5	1	0
Fitzgerald, Tidewater	1.000	1	0	1	0	0	Schmitz, Columbus	1.000	1	0	2	0	0
Graham, Rochester	1.000	4	2	6	0	0	Sodders, Toledo	.925	36	18	68	7	3
Gulliver, Rochester	.950	79	75	152	12	17	Sofield, Toledo	1.000	1	1	1	0	1
Hernandez, Rochester	.955	45	32	95	6	6	Stegman, Columbus	.950	6	7	12	1	1
Hobson, Columbus	.917	5	1	10	1	0	Stimac, Charleston	1.000	4	1	1	0	0
Howard, Tidewater	1.000	3	2	2	0	1	Ullger, Toledo	.938	14	12	18	2	0
Jacoby, Richmond	.943	131	83	229	19	22	Walker, Pawtucket	.833	9	0	5	1	0
Johnson, Richmond	.923	4	5	7	1	1	Wilson, Pawtucket	.944	71	67	135	12	16
Jurak, Pawtucket	.934	71	42	156	14	19							

SHORTSTOPS

Player and Club	Pct.	G.	PO.	A.	E.	DP.	Player and Club	Pct.	G.	PO.	A.	E.	DP.
Booker, Toledo	.930	78	137	211	26	55	Jurak, Pawtucket	.914	11	11	21	3	9
Bustabad, Pawtucket	.944	131	211	384	35	84	Manrique, Syracuse	.935	6	11	18	2	5
Chapman, Tidewater	1.000	4	5	7	0	2	McMullen, Tidewater	.909	5	10	20	3	3
Davis, Tidewater	.933	12	15	27	3	4	Mesa, Toledo	.956	45	65	110	8	25
DeLeon, Charleston	.943	101	179	320	30	77	Nixon, Columbus	.903	17	32	33	7	8
Dempsey, Syracuse	.929	3	6	7	1	3	Oquendo, Tidewater	.954	113	186	337	25	76
Doyle, Charleston	1.000	1	2	1	0	0	Pacho, Charleston	1.000	3	7	9	0	2
Dybzinski, Charleston	.957	30	71	107	8	29	Robertson, Columbus*	.957	55	106	137	11	34
Evans, Columbus	.977	38	76	94	4	24	Rosello, Charleston	1.000	6	20	21	0	5
FERNANDEZ, Syracuse	.964	132	246	364	23	84	Ruiz, Richmond	.892	9	10	23	4	4
Giles, Tidewater	.968	17	37	53	3	13	Schmitz, Columbus	.971	22	40	60	3	12
Gulliver, Rochester	.833	4	0	5	1	0	Ric. Scott, Columbus	.941	5	8	8	1	3
Howard, Tidewater	1.000	5	1	2	0	0	Rod. Scott, Columbus	.956	11	20	23	2	4
Jimenez, Toledo	.972	37	54	122	5	25	Stimac, Charleston	.933	3	4	10	1	1
Johnson, Richmond	1.000	2	4	1	0	0	Wilson, Pawtucket	1.000	3	1	1	0	0
Jones, Rochester	.959	139	221	440	28	101	Zuvella, Richmond	.963	132	245	335	22	78

OUTFIELDERS

Player and Club	Pct.	G.	PO.	A.	E.	DP.	Player and Club	Pct.	G.	PO.	A.	E.	DP.
Adams, Syracuse	.958	14	23	0	1	0	Bonaparte, Toledo*	.940	106	190	14	13	3
R. Baker, Charleston	.943	49	93	7	6	1	Bonds, Columbus	.919	19	34	0	3	0
Beamon, Syracuse*	.875	11	7	0	1	0	Bourjos, Rochester	.985	48	64	3	1	2
Bell, Syracuse	.987	36	72	3	1	0	Bowen, 54 Paw.-14 Char	.970	68	121	9	4	0
Beltre, Tidewater	1.000	13	22	1	0	0	Brooks, Pawtucket	.936	34	44	0	3	0

OUTFIELDERS—Continued

Player and Club	Pct.	G.	PO.	A.	E.	DP.
Burns, Pawtucket	1.000	1	1	0	0	0
Bush, Toledo*	.986	44	68	0	1	0
Butler, Richmond*	.990	40	101	2	1	0
Cannon, Syracuse	.968	28	58	3	2	0
Castillo, Charleston	.939	68	159	10	11	1
Chapman, Tidewater	1.000	22	28	1	0	0
Charboneau, Charleston	.976	19	40	1	1	0
Christensen, Toledo	1.000	6	11	1	0	0
David, Toledo*	.931	13	26	1	2	0
Davis, Tidewater	1.000	7	14	0	0	0
Dempsey, Syracuse	.948	46	66	7	4	2
Engle, Toledo	1.000	9	15	4	0	0
Fitzgerald, Tidewater	1.000	8	8	0	0	0
Flores, Tidewater	.957	67	107	5	5	1
Gentile, Pawtucket*	1.000	18	20	3	0	2
Graham, Pawtucket*	.967	122	284	5	10	2
Hall, Richmond	.977	128	297	6	7	1
Hammond, Richmond	1.000	4	4	0	0	0
Hancock, Pawtucket*	.981	87	147	7	3	4
Harer, Columbus*	.983	49	115	2	2	0
Harper, Richmond	.988	37	77	8	1	2
Hart, 28 Roch-48 Col	.956	76	103	5	5	0
L. Hernandez, Rochester	1.000	3	9	2	0	1
P. Hernandez, Syracuse	1.000	43	82	8	0	0
Howard, Tidewater	.983	93	159	10	3	2
Komminsk, Richmond	1.000	3	10	0	0	0
Landis, Richmond	.969	18	30	1	1	0
Lickert, Pawtucket	1.000	3	7	0	0	0
Lisi, Rochester	1.000	61	101	5	0	2
Littleton, 70 Char-61 Toledo	.985	131	262	6	4	2
Lora, Syracuse	.867	6	12	1	2	0
Machemer, Toledo	.943	20	32	1	2	0
Mattingly, Columbus*	.977	120	199	13	5	1
Mitchell, Toledo*	.957	12	44	1	2	0
Norrid, Charleston	.900	28	51	3	6	1
Pagel, Charleston	.974	24	37	1	1	0
Patterson, Columbus	.961	92	190	5	8	3
Poe, Tidewater*	.917	9	9	2	1	0
Porter, Richmond*	.979	68	133	8	3	4
Rhomberg, Charleston	1.000	22	32	2	0	0
Rivera, Charleston	.950	89	148	5	8	0
Rosello, Charleston	1.000	5	14	1	0	0
Ruiz, Charleston	1.000	5	8	0	0	0
Scott, Columbus	1.000	2	4	1	0	0
Shelby, Rochester	.977	133	331	13	8	3
G. Smith, Columbus*	1.000	26	64	2	0	1
K. Smith, Richmond	.967	23	27	2	1	0
Sofield, Toledo	.949	80	122	7	7	2
Stegman, Columbus	.986	109	199	17	3	4
Stimac, Charleston	.923	14	22	2	2	0
Tarver, Tidewater*	.800	2	4	0	1	0
Taylor, Charleston	.955	36	63	0	3	0
Tevlin, Syracuse	.991	128	195	14	2	2
Thompson, Richmond	1.000	3	4	0	0	0
Tillman, Tidewater	.982	95	156	10	3	1
Ullger, Toledo	.990	92	182	9	2	1
Valle, Rochester	.960	22	22	2	1	2
Vargas, Richmond	.945	108	161	10	10	2
Walker, Pawtucket	.958	118	192	11	9	3
WEBSTER, Syracuse	.995	137	367	16	2	5
Wells, Toledo	1.000	2	5	1	0	0
Wilson, Pawtucket	1.000	20	26	1	0	0
Wynne, Tidewater*	.961	128	283	13	12	0
Young, Rochester	.964	136	291	7	11	2

CATCHERS

Player and Club	Pct.	G.	PO.	A.	E.	DP.	PB.
BOCHY, Tidewater	.9898	77	427	57	5	9	5
Bockhorn, Richmond	1.000	2	9	0	0	0	0
Callahan, Columbus	.971	27	146	19	5	3	5
Colbern, Richmond	.947	6	34	2	2	0	1
Derryberry, Rochester	.993	23	121	12	1	1	1
Duff, Tidewater	1.000	7	30	4	0	0	1
Espino, Columbus	.983	52	264	34	5	4	1
Fitzgerald, Tidewater	.987	63	361	27	5	2	5
Foote, Columbus	1.000	4	25	2	0	0	0
Gaudet, Syracuse	1.000	3	14	0	0	0	0
Graham, Rochester	.966	81	342	54	14	6	17
Keller, Richmond	.981	9	48	3	1	1	2
Laudner, Toledo	1.000	20	121	9	0	2	0
Lickert, Pawtucket	.981	98	526	78	12	8	6
Lora, Syracuse	1.000	1	3	0	0	0	0
Nahorodny, Charleston	.980	14	82	14	2	2	1
Norrid, Charleston	.989	16	81	9	1	0	3
Owen, Richmond	.981	56	265	37	6	5	5
Petralli, Syracuse	.974	117	633	86	19	10	3
Plante, Columbus	1.000	1	3	0	0	0	0
Ramos, Charleston	.983	61	313	31	6	4	1
Rey, Charleston	.988	45	223	26	3	1	5
Robinson, Columbus	.964	14	48	5	2	0	2
Royster, Rochester	.975	48	254	23	7	1	6
Saferight, Toledo	.971	38	124	10	4	1	4
Schmidt, Pawtucket	.962	51	222	28	10	6	6
Simunic, Charleston	1.000	3	12	2	0	0	1
Sinatro, Richmond	.9896	72	423	53	5	8	6
Smith, Toledo	.979	89	449	59	11	8	4
Stimac, Charleston	.981	73	350	58	8	7	7
Sullivan, Pawtucket	.958	4	19	4	1	1	2
Westmoreland, Toledo	.964	5	24	3	1	1	2
Whitmer, Syracuse	.992	30	112	15	1	4	0

PITCHERS

Player and Club	Pct.	G.	PO.	A.	E.	DP.
Alexander, Columbus	1.000	1	0	1	0	0
Alvarez, Richmond	.966	36	9	19	1	1
K. Anderson, Charleston	1.000	11	3	9	0	0
R. Anderson, Tidewater	.909	31	4	16	2	2
Baker, Syracuse	1.000	11	8	9	0	2
Barlow, Syracuse*	.929	53	8	18	2	0
Biercevicz, Tidewater	.958	22	8	15	1	1
Boddicker, Rochester	.981	20	15	37	1	7
Boggs, Richmond	.500	3	1	1	2	0
Bohnet, Charleston*	1.000	9	7	10	0	1
Bomback, Syracuse	1.000	9	8	7	0	0
Boris, Toledo	1.000	17	0	2	0	0
Brizzolara, Richmond	.955	32	16	26	2	1
Brown, Rochester	1.000	3	1	0	0	0
Bruhert, Columbus	.800	29	4	4	2	1
Burns, Pawtucket	.972	28	13	22	1	0
Burtt, Pawtucket	.860	25	11	26	6	1
Camacho, Rochester	1.000	8	0	3	0	1
Cerutti, Syracuse*	1.000	6	1	4	0	0
Christenson, Charleston*	1.000	13	2	13	0	1
Cochran, Columbus	.968	25	12	18	1	1
Cole, Richmond*	1.000	23	5	14	0	1
Combe, Charleston	1.000	23	1	3	0	0
Cooper, Toledo	.939	28	17	29	3	2
Cowley, Richmond	1.000	9	4	6	0	1
Crawford, Pawtucket	1.000	10	2	6	0	1
D'Acquisto, Richmond	.833	17	3	7	2	0
Darling, Tidewater	.905	26	12	26	4	4
Davis, Rochester	1.000	4	0	9	0	1
Dayley, Richmond*	.941	13	4	12	1	1
Denman, Pawtucket	1.000	20	2	18	0	1
Diaz, Richmond*	1.000	31	1	5	0	0
Dixon, 15 Syr.-7 Tide	.913	22	7	20	0	1
Dooner, Toledo	.913	54	6	15	2	1
Dorsey, Pawtucket	.813	22	5	8	3	0
Dye, Tidewater	1.000	20	2	3	0	0
Eichhorn, Syracuse	.974	27	12	26	1	1
Fidrych, Pawtucket	1.000	20	5	16	0	1
Field, Richmond	1.000	1	0	1	0	0
Filson, 5 Col-18 Toledo	.929	23	1	25	2	0
Flinn, Rochester	1.000	39	2	6	0	1
Ford, Rochester	.938	20	5	10	1	1
Fore, Richmond	.923	15	2	10	1	1
Fregin, Toledo	1.000	5	2	8	0	0
Gaff, Tidewater	.968	23	10	20	1	1
Garvin, Syracuse*	1.000	4	0	1	0	0
Geisel, Charleston	.900	21	2	7	1	0
Gibson, Richmond*	1.000	13	0	1	0	0
Glaser, Charleston	.974	32	12	26	1	0
Glynn, Charleston*	1.000	7	3	0	0	0
Gorman, Tidewater*	1.000	4	0	1	0	0
Grimsley, Rochester*	1.000	6	0	1	0	0
Heaton, Charleston*	.889	29	5	27	4	3
Hernaiz, Columbus	1.000	4	0	1	0	0
Hodge, Toledo*	1.000	5	1	2	0	0
Holman, Pawtucket	.950	24	10	28	2	2
Howell, Columbus	.857	5	3	3	1	0
Hrynko, Charleston	.962	41	3	22	1	2
Jackson, Toledo*	.500	4	0	2	2	0
Johnson, Pawtucket*	.889	29	3	5	1	0
Jones, Richmond	1.000	2	0	0	0	0
Kaufman, Columbus	1.000	55	8	9	0	2
King, Pawtucket	1.000	16	1	1	0	0
Korczyk, Toledo	.970	39	8	24	1	4
Kromy, Toledo	.938	10	5	10	1	1
LaRoche, Columbus*	1.000	17	3	5	0	1
Leach, Tidewater	1.000	30	2	20	0	2
Lewallyn, Charleston	.946	41	11	24	2	0
Lewis, Columbus	.980	32	21	27	1	3
Little, Toledo*	.857	25	5	7	2	1

PITCHERS—Continued

Player and Club	Pct.	G.	PO.	A.	E.	DP.
Littlefield, Syracuse	1.000	14	5	8	0	1
MacPherson, Rochester	1.000	6	0	5	0	0
MacWhorter, Pawtucket	.853	40	11	18	5	2
Mapel, Toledo	1.000	3	2	1	0	0
Martinez, Charleston	.833	4	4	1	1	0
McGlothen, Columbus	.929	22	4	9	1	1
McMurtry, Richmond	.938	32	26	35	4	3
Minetto, Rochester*	.867	55	4	9	2	1
Moloney, Pawtucket*	1.000	53	5	22	0	3
Moore, Richmond	.867	36	7	6	2	1
Mulligan, Toledo*	1.000	11	2	11	0	0
Munninghoff, Charleston	1.000	4	1	3	0	0
Nuismer, Charleston	.908	30	20	39	6	5
O'Connor, Toledo*	1.000	12	0	4	0	0
O'Keeffe, Syracuse*	.889	14	0	8	1	2
Ownbey, Tidewater	.917	23	6	27	3	3
Pacella, Columbus	1.000	6	1	1	0	0
Parks, Pawtucket	.972	28	11	24	1	1
Patterson, 2 Rich-27 Col	.971	29	14	20	1	1
Perez, Richmond	.889	5	3	5	1	0
Pietroburgo, Charleston*	.917	62	8	14	2	1
Ramirez, Rochester	1.000	24	8	15	0	0
Ratzer, Tidewater	1.000	47	12	17	0	3
Riccelli, Syracuse*	1.000	3	0	2	0	0
Righetti, Columbus*	1.000	4	1	3	0	1
Rowe, Rochester	1.000	5	1	3	0	1
Schneider, Syracuse*	1.000	34	5	12	0	1
Schoppee, Pawtucket	1.000	54	4	11	0	1
Schrom, Syracuse	.943	27	13	20	2	0

Player and Club	Pct.	G.	PO.	A.	E.	DP.
Searage, Charleston*	.870	38	8	12	3	0
Senteney, Syracuse	1.000	44	12	17	0	4
Serum, Columbus	1.000	36	6	16	0	1
Mi. Smith, Richmond	1.000	10	0	2	0	1
Snell, Rochester	.944	37	2	15	1	4
Speck, Rochester	.968	31	14	16	1	0
Stanhouse, Rochester	1.000	15	3	13	0	2
Stoddard, Rochester	1.000	5	1	1	0	0
SWAGGERTY, Rochester	1.000	29	12	20	0	2
Sykes, Columbus	1.000	15	4	6	0	0
Terrell, Tidewater	.972	21	17	18	1	1
Todd, Syracuse	.977	28	17	25	1	1
Torrez, Rochester*	1.000	5	0	2	0	0
Twitty, Richmond*	1.000	9	4	1	0	0
Verhoeven, 18 Paw.-25 Syr	.955	43	3	18	1	1
Veselic, Toledo	.933	15	1	13	1	0
Viola, Toledo*	.952	8	3	17	1	1
Von Ohlen, Tidewater*	.938	36	3	12	1	3
Walters, Toledo	.962	41	5	20	1	2
Weaver, Richmond	.970	29	6	26	1	2
Wehrmeister, Columbus	.933	36	9	19	2	1
Welchel, Rochester	1.000	30	12	18	0	1
Werly, Columbus	.000	25	15	12	0	1
Wihtol, Charleston	1.000	26	2	9	0	0
A. Williams, Toledo	1.000	3	2	2	0	1
R. Williams, Toledo	.970	18	11	21	1	0
Wilson, Syracuse	1.000	5	0	3	0	1
Wirth, Rochester	1.000	10	1	1	0	0
Young, Toledo	.923	15	6	18	2	1

The following players do not have any recorded accepted chances at the positions indicated and therefore, are not listed in the fielding averages for those particular positions: D. Baker, of; Bonner, ss; Browning, p; Burns, 1b; Dugas, ss; Hart, p; Hausman, p; Lickert, 1b; Mac-Whorter, of; May, p; Moloney, 1b; Petralli, 3b; Pettaway, p; Ramos, 3b; Saferight, of; Schmidt, p; Schoppee, 1b; G. Smith, p; Ma. Smith, p; Walker, ss; Westmoreland, of; Wright, p.

CLUB PITCHING

Club	ERA.	G.	CG.	ShO.	Sv.	IP.	H.	R.	ER.	HR.	HB.	BB.	Int. BB.	SO.	WP.	Bk.
Tidewater	3.42	137	27	10	28	1197.2	1124	530	455	92	18	594	39	776	36	5
Charleston	4.14	140	21	6	21	1225.1	1349	673	563	102	26	519	37	714	76	10
Rochester	4327	140	22	12	31	1204.1	1216	660	572	115	24	309	39	685	56	2
Richmond	4.35	139	28	9	40	1198.2	1258	632	580	103	31	586	12	735	69	4
Toledo	4.65	140	27	3	27	1190	1326	720	615	128	35	464	29	678	54	8
Syracuse	4.69	140	23	9	31	1186.2	1235	696	618	145	37	567	37	706	64	10
Columbus	4.70	140	20	5	36	1216.2	1239	732	635	118	28	599	40	772	71	5
Pawtucket	4.75	138	21	6	33	1175.1	1287	704	620	146	35	605	54	723	55	8

PITCHERS' RECORDS
(Leading Qualifiers for Earned-Run Average Leadership — 112 or More Innings)

*Throws lefthanded.

Pitcher—Club	W.	L.	Pct.	ERA.	G.	GS.	CG.	GF.	ShO.	Sv.	IP.	H.	R.	ER.	HR.	HB.	BB.	Int. BB.	SO.	WP.
Lewis, Columbus	12	6	.667	2.60	32	22	5	6	0	5	166	139	61	48	14	2	64	6	107	13
Biercevicz, Tidewater	6	4	.600	2.64	22	11	4	8	2	1	119.1	101	40	35	8	3	54	5	82	2
Hrynko, Charleston	10	7	.588	2.86	41	10	2	14	1	2	116.1	126	46	37	5	7	44	6	46	6
Ownbey, Tidewater	8	7	.533	3.35	23	23	4	0	1	0	150.1	107	64	56	10	0	112	0	122	6
Holman, Tidewater	10	8	.556	3.43	24	24	3	0	1	0	141.2	125	61	54	9	2	95	1	67	6
Speck, Rochester	8	10	.444	3.45	31	19	1	5	1	2	156.2	148	77	60	16	3	72	3	88	8
Boddicker, Rochester	10	5	.667	3.58	20	19	5	1	1	0	133.1	121	59	53	12	4	36	2	82	2
Darling, Tidewater	7	9	.438	3.73	26	26	6	0	2	0	152	143	76	63	18	5	95	4	114	12
Dixon, Tidewater	8	9	.471	3.79	22	19	2	1	0	0	118.2	108	63	50	12	4	47	4	92	5
McMurtry, Richmond	17	9	.654	3.81	32	32	8	0	1	0	210	198	98	89	12	4	107	1	96	7

Departmental Leaders: G—Pietroburgo, 62; GS—Brizzolara, McMurtry, 32; CG—Filson, 11; GF—Schoppee, 38; ShO—Ford, 3; W—McMurtry, 17; L—Todd, 15; Pct.—Flinn, .750; Sv—Schoppee, 15; IP—McMurtry, 210; H—Brizzolara, 231; R—Brizzolara, 119; ER—Brizzolara, 108; HR—Todd, 29; HB—MacWhorter, 9; BB—Ramirez, 117; IBB—Burtt, Schoppee, Terrell, 9; SO—Cooper, 125; WP—Searage, 14.

(All Pitchers—Listed Alphabetically)

Pitcher—Club	W.	L.	Pct.	ERA.	G.	GS.	CG.	GF.	ShO.	Sv.	IP.	H.	R.	ER.	HR.	HB.	BB.	Int. BB.	SO.	WP.
Alexander, Columbus	0	0	.000	9.82	1	0	0	0	0	0	3.2	5	4	4	0	0	2	0	1	1
Alvarez, Richmond	5	5	.500	3.97	36	7	1	13	0	6	111	111	54	49	6	4	50	3	91	5
K. Anderson, Charleston	1	5	.167	3.68	11	11	3	0	0	0	73.1	81	40	30	7	1	39	2	60	5
R. Anderson, Tidewater	4	2	.667	3.26	31	0	0	17	0	2	80	84	35	29	6	0	23	2	49	2
Baker, Syracuse	3	7	.300	3.90	11	11	3	0	1	0	60	73	34	26	7	4	24	0	23	5
Barlow, Syracuse*	9	4	.692	3.48	53	3	0	36	0	8	108.2	117	52	42	8	5	40	8	59	3
Biercevicz, Tidewater	6	4	.600	2.64	22	11	4	8	2	1	119.1	101	40	35	8	3	54	5	82	2
Boddicker, Rochester	10	5	.667	3.58	20	19	5	1	1	0	133.1	121	59	53	12	4	36	2	82	2
Boggs, Richmond	1	1	.500	1.50	3	3	0	0	0	0	12	9	5	2	0	0	3	0	13	2
Bohnet, Charleston*	2	4	.333	3.18	9	9	2	0	0	0	56.2	45	24	20	8	0	26	0	29	1
Bomback, Syracuse	3	2	.600	3.70	9	9	0	0	0	0	56	55	25	23	4	4	19	0	30	2
Boris, Toledo	0	3	.000	3.47	17	0	0	9	0	6	23.1	21	11	9	4	0	15	0	25	0
Brizzolara, Richmond	15	11	.577	5.04	32	32	5	0	2	0	193	231	119	108	24	3	75	0	102	6
Brown, Rochester	1	0	1.000	1.42	3	0	0	2	0	1	6.1	5	1	1	0	2	0	0	5	0
Browning, Columbus	0	0	.000	8.31	4	0	0	1	0	0	4.1	5	4	4	2	0	2	1	4	0
Bruhert, Columbus	5	4	.556	4.35	29	5	0	12	0	2	62	74	41	30	7	1	34	3	17	2
Burns, Pawtucket	5	3	.625	4.77	28	5	1	5	0	0	88.2	74	55	47	10	2	55	3	48	4
Burtt, Pawtucket	13	7	.650	4.79	25	25	4	0	1	0	150.1	163	96	80	25	5	98	9	79	5
Camacho, Rochester	0	1	.000	2.04	8	0	0	3	0	0	17.2	16	7	4	1	4	10	0	11	2
Cerutti, Syracuse*	0	3	.000	6.60	6	6	0	0	0	0	30	42	25	22	6	1	16	0	20	1
Christenson, Charleston*	2	8	.200	6.20	13	13	2	0	1	0	61	79	43	42	11	1	21	1	37	2

Pitcher—Club	W.	L.	Pct.	ERA.	G.	GS.	CG.	GF.	ShO.	Sv.	IP.	H.	R.	ER.	HR.	HB.	BB.	Int. BB.	SO.	WP.
Cochran, Columbus	8	10	.444	7.04	25	21	1	3	1	0	122.2	161	105	96	14	1	54	2	47	5
Cole, Richmond°	5	5	.500	6.77	23	15	2	3	0	0	97	119	77	73	18	5	80	0	52	5
Combe, Charleston	3	2	.600	4.80	23	0	0	14	0	1	30	34	19	16	6	0	10	3	21	5
Cooper, Toledo	12	10	.545	4.64	28	28	4	0	1	0	176.2	196	105	91	19	3	69	2	125	9
Cowley, Richmond	4	2	.667	4.03	9	9	0	0	0	0	51.1	46	24	23	4	2	30	0	33	2
Crawford, Pawtucket	1	4	.200	4.11	10	10	1	0	0	0	46	55	25	21	4	0	15	2	20	2
D'Acquisto, Richmond	3	6	.333	9.15	17	8	1	4	0	0	61	80	67	62	5	5	66	0	36	8
Darling, Tidewater	7	9	.438	3.73	26	26	6	0	2	0	152	143	76	63	18	5	95	4	114	12
Davis, Rochester	2	1	.667	3.71	4	4	0	0	0	0	26.2	25	13	11	1	0	7	0	27	1
Dayley, Richmond°	8	3	.727	3.11	13	13	6	0	0	0	98.1	89	43	34	6	1	47	0	79	4
Denman, Pawtucket	7	4	.636	5.05	20	16	3	3	2	0	92.2	120	56	52	13	3	30	3	41	5
Diaz, Richmond°	3	4	.429	2.70	31	0	0	23	0	9	53.1	52	21	16	5	1	17	1	52	4
Dixon, 15 Syr-7 Tide	8	9	.471	3.79	22	19	2	1	0	0	118.2	108	63	50	12	4	47	4	92	5
Dooner, Toledo	3	5	.375	4.75	54	2	0	34	0	5	113.2	140	68	60	11	6	24	6	46	3
Dorsey, Pawtucket	5	7	.417	4.36	22	13	2	2	0	0	97	115	52	47	10	2	50	2	81	4
Dye, Tidewater	3	2	.600	1.64	20	0	0	15	0	6	38.1	29	8	7	0	0	16	1	27	0
Eichhorn, Syracuse	10	11	.476	4.54	27	27	6	0	1	0	156.2	158	92	79	18	7	83	5	71	8
Fidrych, Pawtucket	6	8	.429	4.98	20	19	2	0	0	0	123	139	71	68	12	3	59	1	51	6
Field, Richmond	0	0	.000	4.50	1	0	0	1	0	0	2	3	1	1	0	1	0	0	0	0
Filson, 5 Col-18 Tol°	8	10	.444	4.60	23	23	11	0	1	0	150.2	168	87	77	16	2	53	0	84	5
Flinn, Rochester	9	3	.750	3.61	39	2	0	24	0	10	87.1	92	45	35	8	2	34	8	59	6
Ford, Rochester	5	5	.500	3.93	20	16	4	0	3	0	100.2	99	51	44	16	1	32	1	52	3
Fore, Richmond	2	3	.400	3.80	15	4	1	9	1	4	45	44	19	19	5	1	17	1	26	4
Fregin, Toledo	0	3	.000	10.93	5	4	0	1	0	0	14	27	24	17	4	0	4	0	2	1
Gaff, Tidewater	9	8	.529	4.02	23	20	5	1	2	1	132	142	63	59	9	3	41	3	83	1
Garvin, Syracuse°	2	1	.667	4.15	4	3	0	1	0	0	17.1	17	10	8	3	0	7	0	19	0
Geisel, Syracuse°	4	2	.667	3.90	21	10	3	3	1	1	80.2	74	38	35	11	1	38	1	43	1
Gibson, Richmond°	1	1	.500	2.31	13	0	0	7	0	4	11.2	7	4	3	0	0	8	0	9	1
Glaser, Charleston	5	12	.294	3.95	32	20	3	9	1	1	139	172	77	61	9	4	39	3	38	6
Glynn, Charleston°	3	1	.750	4.66	7	0	0	5	0	1	9.2	7	5	5	1	1	2	0	17	1
Gorman, Tidewater°	1	1	.500	6.35	4	1	0	1	0	0	11.1	12	8	8	2	0	4	0	6	0
Grimsley, Rochester°	1	0	1.000	8.71	6	0	0	2	0	0	10.1	13	11	10	2	0	10	0	1	3
Hart, Columbus	0	0	.000	15.00	1	0	0	1	0	0	3	4	5	5	1	0	3	0	0	0
Hausman, Tidewater	0	0	.000	9.00	3	0	0	2	0	0	3	3	2	2	1	0	1	0	2	0
Heaton, Charleston°	10	5	.667	4.01	29	29	5	0	2	0	172.2	194	97	77	16	4	66	1	105	7
Hernaiz, Columbus	0	0	.000	7.20	4	2	0	1	0	0	10	14	9	8	2	0	6	0	7	1
Hodge, Toledo°	1	3	.250	8.50	5	3	0	0	0	0	18	23	17	17	5	0	13	1	20	2
Holman, Tidewater	10	8	.556	3.43	24	24	3	0	1	0	141.2	125	61	54	9	2	95	1	67	6
Howell, Columbus	2	1	.667	2.41	5	5	2	0	1	0	37.1	18	13	10	1	1	19	1	33	1
Hrynko, Charleston	10	7	.588	2.86	41	10	2	14	1	2	116.1	126	46	37	5	7	44	6	46	6
Jackson, Toledo°	1	3	.250	7.00	4	4	0	0	0	0	18	24	18	14	2	1	12	0	11	1
Johnson, Pawtucket°	3	1	.750	4.04	29	0	0	11	0	1	42.1	37	21	19	5	0	23	5	45	1
Jones, Richmond	0	1	.000	8.64	2	2	0	0	0	0	8.1	12	11	8	0	1	4	0	1	2
Kaufman, Columbus	6	3	.667	3.46	55	0	0	35	0	10	91	76	40	35	6	0	47	2	103	11
King, Pawtucket	1	4	.200	6.34	16	6	0	7	0	3	49.2	60	46	35	12	2	38	1	43	2
Korczyk, Toledo	6	3	.667	4.05	39	1	0	17	0	2	95.2	96	53	43	9	5	47	6	38	3
Kromy, Toledo	3	3	.500	4.77	10	9	2	0	0	0	60.1	68	33	32	5	2	33	0	32	6
LaRoche, Columbus°	3	1	.750	3.77	17	0	0	9	0	4	31	27	17	13	2	1	14	3	20	1
Leach, Tidewater	4	1	.800	2.96	30	0	0	18	0	5	48.2	48	20	16	2	2	19	1	34	0
Lewallyn, Charleston	1	5	.167	4.24	41	2	1	26	0	7	93.1	95	51	44	6	1	28	3	55	3
Lewis, Columbus	12	6	.667	2.60	32	22	5	6	0	5	166	139	61	48	14	2	64	6	107	13
Little, Toledo°	2	2	.500	1.76	25	0	0	15	0	3	41	21	12	8	1	0	21	0	40	6
Littlefield, Syracuse	0	3	.000	7.49	14	3	0	2	0	0	39.2	58	38	33	11	2	20	2	17	3
MacPherson, Rochester	1	1	.500	10.24	6	0	0	3	0	1	9.2	17	11	11	3	1	7	4	4	1
MacWhorter, Pawtucket	6	11	.353	4.62	40	17	5	15	0	5	156	176	90	80	14	9	73	6	95	9
Mapel, Toledo	0	0	.000	3.38	3	0	0	0	0	0	8	7	3	3	0	1	0	0	4	0
Martinez, Charleston	1	1	.500	6.06	4	4	0	0	0	0	16.1	22	12	11	3	0	10	0	8	1
May, Columbus°	0	0	.000	4.91	1	1	0	0	0	0	3.2	1	2	2	1	0	4	0	5	1
McGlothen, Columbus	7	2	.778	3.98	22	7	1	12	0	0	63.1	57	29	28	5	1	29	2	42	2
McMurtry, Richmond	17	9	.654	3.81	32	32	8	0	1	0	210	198	98	89	12	4	107	1	96	7
Minetto, Rochester°	4	5	.444	3.27	55	0	0	31	0	11	71.2	65	31	26	5	1	32	2	67	3
Moloney, Pawtucket°	2	3	.400	3.72	53	0	0	25	0	6	72.2	61	35	30	8	0	32	6	56	2
Moore, Richmond	5	3	.625	2.29	36	0	0	27	0	12	55	51	17	14	3	0	18	4	45	7
Mulligan, Toledo°	4	5	.444	5.50	11	9	1	1	0	0	54	65	37	33	6	0	20	1	28	1
Munninghoff, Charleston	0	0	.000	3.95	4	0	0	2	0	1	13.2	10	6	6	0	0	7	0	5	1
Nuismer, Charleston	11	13	.458	4.76	30	30	3	0	0	0	170	204	109	90	9	4	71	3	88	9
O'Connor, Toledo°	3	3	.500	3.40	12	6	1	2	0	1	42.1	42	22	16	4	0	17	1	42	0
O'Keeffe, Syracuse°	2	3	.400	7.64	14	10	0	2	0	0	50.2	74	45	43	11	1	27	0	19	6
Ownbey, Tidewater	8	7	.533	3.35	23	23	4	0	1	0	150.1	107	64	56	10	0	112	0	122	6
Pacella, Columbus	0	2	.000	6.75	6	0	0	2	0	1	5.1	6	9	4	1	1	12	1	2	1
Parks, Pawtucket	11	12	.478	5.48	28	27	3	0	1	0	159.1	183	109	97	23	7	95	5	103	11
Patterson, 2 Rich-27 Col	7	12	.368	5.50	29	26	2	0	0	0	155.1	163	106	95	18	5	85	4	104	5
Perez, Richmond	5	0	1.000	1.26	5	5	4	0	2	0	43	32	7	6	1	1	8	0	27	2
Pettaway, Richmond	1	0	1.000	1.59	3	0	0	2	0	0	5.2	3	1	1	0	1	0	4	4	0
Pietroburgo, Charleston°	4	7	.364	3.44	62	3	0	29	0	5	91.2	102	42	35	8	0	32	5	66	9
Ramirez, Rochester	6	10	.375	4.86	24	24	1	0	1	0	124	111	77	67	9	2	117	2	85	8
Ratzer, Tidewater	11	7	.611	3.08	47	1	0	37	0	10	87.2	98	38	30	5	0	28	7	52	1
Riccelli, Syracuse°	0	2	.000	6.08	3	3	0	0	0	0	13.1	16	10	9	2	0	15	0	7	0
Righetti, Columbus°	1	0	1.000	2.81	4	4	1	0	0	0	25.2	22	11	8	0	0	12	0	33	1
Rowe, Rochester	1	2	.333	7.36	5	5	1	0	0	0	25.2	32	22	21	3	1	10	0	11	2
Schmidt, Pawtucket	0	0	.000	0.00	1	0	1	0	0	1	1	0	0	0	0	0	0	0	0	0
Schneider, Syracuse°	2	3	.400	4.00	34	2	1	16	0	8	54	43	27	24	8	0	31	1	45	4
Schoppee, Pawtucket	4	6	.400	3.26	54	0	0	38	0	15	66.1	67	28	24	4	2	27	9	34	4
Schrom, Syracuse	4	5	.444	5.14	27	8	1	6	0	0	98	102	61	56	10	3	41	4	49	6
Searage, Charleston°	2	7	.222	4.89	38	9	0	12	0	3	114	112	73	62	9	2	87	4	87	14
Senteney, Syracuse	4	8	.333	2.44	44	0	0	34	0	13	96	73	32	26	5	1	42	7	98	6
Serum, Columbus	6	1	.857	5.14	36	1	0	17	0	6	77	85	52	44	9	2	34	4	37	0
G. Smith, Columbus°	0	0	.000	0.00	2	0	0	2	0	0	2	2	0	0	0	0	1	0	1	0
Ma. Smith, Rochester	0	0	.000	2.45	2	0	0	0	0	0	3.2	2	1	1	0	0	6	0	3	1
Mi. Smith, Richmond	0	1	.000	2.95	10	0	0	5	0	0	21.1	23	8	7	1	2	11	0	10	3
Snell, Rochester	4	6	.400	3.67	37	0	0	27	0	5	83.1	83	40	34	7	0	26	8	31	4
Speck, Rochester	8	10	.444	3.45	31	19	1	5	1	2	156.2	148	77	60	16	3	72	3	88	8

Pitcher—Club	W.	L.	Pct.	ERA.	G.	GS.	CG.	GF.	ShO.	Sv.	IP.	H.	R.	ER.	HR.	HB.	BB.	Int. BB.	SO.	WP.
Stanhouse, Rochester	2	3	.400	4.12	15	10	1	0	0	0	59	59	32	27	3	0	41	3	26	1
Stoddard, Rochester	0	0	.000	1.50	5	0	0	3	0	0	6	2	1	1	0	0	2	0	6	0
Swaggerty, Rochester	6	5	.545	5.38	29	14	3	10	1	1	92	111	63	55	10	0	59	0	27	5
Sykes, Columbus°	1	2	.333	8.03	15	0	0	7	0	2	37	44	34	33	3	2	23	2	15	2
Terrell, Tidewater	7	8	.467	3.96	21	20	3	1	0	0	138.2	130	69	61	13	1	72	1	74	5
Todd, Syracuse	10	15	.400	5.74	28	28	8	0	1	0	160	164	109	102	29	3	78	1	99	8
Torrez, Rochester°	0	1	.000	17.61	5	2	0	1	0	0	7.2	17	15	15	3	2	13	1	2	0
Twitty, Richmond°	0	1	.000	6.32	9	0	0	6	0	1	15.2	17	12	11	5	0	4	0	7	0
Verhoeven, 18 Paw-25 Syr	5	3	.625	5.42	43	0	0	24	0	4	84.2	103	55	51	8	1	33	7	50	4
Veselic, Toledo	1	5	.167	6.68	15	12	1	1	0	0	63.1	79	53	47	9	4	42	1	34	4
Viola, Toledo°	2	3	.400	3.88	8	8	2	0	0	0	58	61	27	25	3	2	18	1	34	4
Von Ohlen, Tidewater	4	1	.800	2.80	36	6	1	9	0	3	64.1	64	22	20	4	0	25	3	44	0
Walters, Toledo	4	4	.500	3.82	41	0	0	33	0	10	66	72	31	28	6	3	22	6	22	1
Weaver, Richmond	6	0	1.000	4.48	29	7	0	11	0	4	92.1	119	55	46	5	1	35	2	44	7
Wehrmeister, Columbus	10	7	.588	4.57	36	19	2	10	1	4	151.2	162	85	77	16	7	74	6	96	13
Welchel, Rochester	12	7	.632	4.64	30	25	6	1	2	0	163	180	91	84	11	2	82	5	82	5
Werly, Columbus	9	10	.474	5.44	25	24	5	1	0	0	144	158	101	87	15	4	63	3	90	11
Wihtol, Charleston	4	4	.500	3.59	26	0	0	8	0	0	67.2	66	29	27	4	1	37	6	52	6
A. Williams, Toledo	3	0	1.000	2.14	3	3	1	0	0	0	21	13	5	5	2	1	7	0	14	0
R. Williams, Toledo	4	11	.267	4.73	18	18	1	0	0	0	104.2	120	70	55	14	4	36	3	52	4
Wilson, Syracuse	1	1	.500	10.43	5	3	0	0	0	0	14.2	25	17	17	2	0	14	0	3	1
Wirth, Rochester	0	3	.000	5.49	10	0	0	5	0	0	19.2	18	12	12	4	1	11	0	16	1
Wright, Syracuse	0	0	.000	6.75	5	0	0	3	0	0	9.1	7	7	7	1	2	10	0	9	2
Young, Toledo	6	5	.545	4.61	15	15	4	0	0	0	93.2	111	57	48	10	2	31	1	41	4

BALKS—Filson, 8; Eichhorn, Ownbey, 3 each; Christenson, Geisel, King, MacWhorter, Nuismer, Schrom, Von Ohlen, Weaver, 2 each; Boddicker, Bohnet, Boris, Burns, Burtt, Combe, D'Acquisto, Heaton, Kaufman, Lewallyn, Littlefield, McGlothen, O'Keeffe, Parks, Perez, Pietroburgo, Schneider, Schoppee, Searage, Stanhouse, Werly, R. Williams, 1 each.

COMBINATION SHUTOUTS—Bohnet-Lewallyn, Charleston; Lewis-Kaufman-Serum, Columbus; Parks-Moloney-Verhoeven, Dorsey-King-Schoppee, Pawtucket; Alvarez-Diaz, McMurtry-Alvarez, Cowley-Diaz, Richmond; Speck-Minetto, Speck-Wirth, Boddicker-Minetto, Rochester; Dixon-Senteney 2, Dixon-Barlow, Dixon-Schneider-Barlow, Schrom-Barlow, Syracuse; Holman-Von Ohlen-Ratzer, Von Ohlen-Dye, Tidewater; O'Connor-Dooner, A. Williams-Walters, Toledo.

NO-HIT GAME—None.

Mexican League

CLASS AAA

CHAMPIONSHIP WINNERS IN PREVIOUS YEARS

1955—Mexico City Tigers* .... .539	1967—Jalisco .... .607	1976—Mexico City Reds x .... .543
1956—Mexico City Reds .... .692	1968—Mexico City Reds .... .586	Union Laguna.......................... .547
1957—Yucatan .... .567	1969—Reynosa .... .591	1977—Mexico City Reds .... .623
Mex. C. Reds (2nd)† .... .550	1970—Aguila§................................. .580	Nuevo Laredo x...................... .507
1958—Nuevo Laredo .... .625	Mexico City Reds .... .607	1978—Aguascalientes x .... .589
1959—Poza Rica .... .575	1971—Jalisco§................................. .558	Union Laguna.......................... .523
Mex. C. Reds (3rd)† .... .507	Saltillo .... .593	1979—Saltillo.................................. .704
1960—Mexico City Tigers .... .538	1972—Saltillo.................................. .636	Puebla x.................................. .628
1961—Veracruz................................ .575	Cordoba§............................... .541	1980—No champion y
1962—Monterrey .... .592	1973—Saltillo.................................. .656	1981—Mexico City Reds .... .615
1963—Puebla .... .606	Mexico City Reds .... .590	Reynosa .... .492
1964—Mexico City Reds .... .586	1974—Jalisco.................................. .627	
1965—Mexico City Tigers .... .590	Mexico City Reds x .... .551	
1966—Mexico City Tigers‡............... .614	1975—Tampico x.............................. .541	
Mexico City Reds .... .571	Cordoba .... .649	

*Defeated Nuevo Laredo, two games to none, in playoff for pennant. †Won four-team playoff. ‡Won split-season playoff. §League divided into Northern, Southern divisions; won two-team playoff. xLeague divided into Northern, Southern zones; sub-divided into Eastern, Western divisions, won eight-team playoff. yA players strike on July 1 forced the cancellation of the regular season and playoff schedule.

STANDING OF CLUBS AT CLOSE OF SEASON
NORTHERN ZONE
EASTERN DIVISION

Club	Ctz.	Mt.	Ver.	Tab.	CJ	Sal.	Mva.	Chi.	NL	Rey.	Ags.	Mon.	W.	L.	T.	Pct.	G.B.
Nuevo Laredo	6	2	4	6	5	6	14	10	.....	6	10	9	78	53	1	.595	....
Reynosa.....................................	3	3	0	7	7	6	9	9	8	.....	9	9	70	61	1	.534	8
Aguascalientes	3	5	5	5	3	8	7	10	4	5	.....	11	66	63	0	.512	11
Monterrey..................................	1	2	5	4	3	6	4	9	5	7	2	.....	48	81	2	.372	29

WESTERN DIVISION

Club	PR	Yuc.	MR	Cam.	CJ	Sal.	Mon.	Chic	NL	Rey.	Ags.	Mon.	W.	L.	T.	Pct.	G.B.
Ciudad Juarez...........................	5	3	3	5	.....	5	7	8	9	7	10	11	73	55	1	.570	....
Saltillo......................................	3	6	3	2	8	.....	6	11	8	8	8	7	70	58	2	.547	3
Monclova..................................	3	5	4	5	7	8	.....	7	2	5	7	9	62	68	1	.477	12
Chihuahua.................................	2	0	3	3	7	3	7	.....	4	5	4	5	43	87	0	.331	31

SOUTHERN ZONE
EASTERN DIVISION

Club	Ctz.	MT.	Ver.	Tab.	PR	Yuc.	MR	Cam.	CJ	Sal.	Mva.	Chi.	W.	L.	T.	Pct.	G.B.
Poza Rica...................................	5	7	11	12	.....	11	7	9	3	5	5	6	81	49	0	.623	....
Yucatan.....................................	9	9	11	9	3	.....	7	8	4	2	2	8	72	56	2	.563	8
Mexico City Reds......................	8	9	7	5	7	7	.....	8	5	4	4	5	69	61	0	.531	12
Campeche	2	6	6	9	5	6	6	.....	3	5	3	4	55	70	2	.440	23½

WESTERN DIVISION

Club	Ctz.	MT	Ver.	Tab.	PR	Yuc.	MT	Cam.	NL	Rey.	Ags.	Mon.	W.	L.	T.	Pct.	G.B.
Coatzacoalcos	.....	9	8	8	7	5	6	12	2	5	4	7	73	54	2	.575	....
Mexico City Tigers	5	.....	8	7	7	5	7	7	5	5	3	6	65	63	1	.508	8½
Veracruz....................................	6	5	.....	10	5	3	7	6	4	7	3	3	59	69	1	.461	14½
Tabasco	6	6	4	.....	2	5	8	5	2	1	3	4	46	82	2	.359	27½

Arano Ready for 25th M. L. Season

Ramon Arano, a righthanded pitcher for the Mexico City Diablos Rojos (Red Devils), will be celebrating his silver anniversary in the Mexican League in 1983.

Arano, who will be 44 in July, surpassed the coveted 300-victory total in 1982. He had a 9-9 record with a 3.87 ERA last season.

Through 24 years in the Mexican League, Arano has won 302 games and lost 216. Arano started his Mexican League career in 1959 with Poza Rica, compiling an 8-9 record.

Ironically, Arano has never had a 20-victory season. He won 19 games each in 1978 and 1979 for Cordoba at the age of 39 and 40. Ten times he has won 15 or more games.

Arano has pitched more than 4,000 innings and struck out more than 2,000 batters. His lifetime ERA is 3.30.

Playoffs—Ciudad Juarez defeated Saltillo, four games to none, in North Zone finals; Mexico City Tigers defeated Coatzacoalcos, four games to none, in South Zone finals; Ciudad Juarez defeated Mexico City Tigers, four games to none, for League Championship.

Regular-Season Attendance—Aguascalientes, 180,000; Campeche, 150,000; Chihuahua, 100,000; Ciudad Juarez, 130,000; Coatzacoalcos, 182,000; Mexico City Reds, 130,000; Monclova, 140,000; Monterrey, 90,000; Nuevo Laredo, 110,000; Poza Rica, 240,000; Reynosa, 110,000; Saltillo, 190,000; Tabasco, 120,000; Mexico City Tigers, 150,000; Veracruz, 100,000; Yucatan, 560,000. Total, 2,762,000.

Managers—Aguascalientes, Moises Camacho; Campeche, Juan Ramon Benhart; Chihuahua, Arnoldo Castro; Ciudad Juarez, Jose Guerrero; Coatzacoalcos, Benjamin Reyes; Mexico City Reds, Winston Llenas; Monclova, Felipe Hernandez; Monterrey, Gregorio Juque; Nuevo Laredo, Victor Ramirez; Poza Rica, David Garcia; Reynosa, Benjamin Valenzuela; Saltillo, Marcelo Juarez, Gerardo Gutierrez; Tabasco, Raul Cano; Mexico City Tigers, Fernando Remes; Veracruz, Lee Sigman; Yucatan, Wilfredo Calvino, Jose Luis Garcia, Carlos Paz.

All-Star Team—1B—Scott, Poza Rica; 2B—Navarrete, Saltillo; 3B—Sommers, Tabasco; SS—Blanks, Coatzacoalcos; LF—Mora, Nuevo Laredo; CF—B. Smith, Ciudad Juarez; RF—Dyes, Monclova; C—Ruiz, Saltillo; DH—Lopez Felix, Ciudad Juarez; RHP—Hernaiz, Coatzacoalcos; LHP—Sandate, Poza Rica; Manager—Garcia, Poza Rica.

(Compiled by Ana Luisa Perea de Silva, League Statistician, Mexico, D.F.)

CLUB BATTING

Club	Pct.	G.	AB.	R.	OR.	H.	TB.	2B.	3B.	HR.	RBI.	GW.	SH.	SF.	HP.	BB.	Int. BB.	SO.	SB.	CS.	LOB.
Ciudad Juarez	.288	129	4060	558	495	1171	1510	149	41	36	488	63	59	32	27	428	34	483	161	51	900
Saltillo	.284	130	3982	515	479	1130	1465	166	23	41	465	60	76	36	31	451	44	450	66	42	881
Aguascalientes	.280	129	4074	542	531	1140	1573	162	29	71	487	63	53	38	37	416	27	549	88	55	883
Mexico City Tigers	.279	129	4047	509	502	1129	1457	147	41	33	439	59	74	35	19	353	36	485	102	80	828
Mexico City Reds	.273	130	4096	556	487	1117	1515	148	53	48	520	66	58	48	28	537	38	533	99	73	963
Nuevo Laredo	.273	132	4105	566	464	1119	1616	159	19	100	509	66	73	31	35	422	32	570	105	61	869
Poza Rica	.270	130	3961	509	423	1068	1353	139	37	24	449	70	90	36	26	459	31	528	65	50	878
Coatzacoalcos	.269	129	4067	535	425	1095	1433	166	32	36	455	59	49	33	31	446	28	517	113	79	854
Chihuahua	.265	130	4054	476	710	1074	1397	139	35	38	413	36	54	39	44	296	25	482	64	37	793
Reynosa	.263	132	4105	515	451	1079	1498	163	29	66	464	61	64	23	38	470	35	539	100	28	898
Yucatan	.262	130	4175	461	253	1095	1375	126	41	24	417	57	71	40	26	392	42	539	102	67	934
Campeche	.258	127	3943	392	421	1018	1284	125	27	29	336	48	100	23	32	369	46	439	67	48	912
Monclova	.252	131	3956	458	506	998	1354	123	22	63	404	50	75	25	31	388	32	695	102	48	816
Veracruz	.252	129	3920	402	436	986	1212	113	19	25	330	46	65	30	26	455	37	543	83	66	870
Monterrey	.247	131	4027	416	568	993	1313	137	36	37	365	38	68	31	32	418	41	599	100	57	865
Tabasco	.243	130	4013	366	506	977	1228	136	17	27	325	45	89	22	27	357	32	563	78	46	846

INDIVIDUAL BATTING
(Leading Qualifiers for Batting Championship—356 or More Plate Appearances)

°Bats lefthanded.   †Switch-hitter.

Player and Club	Pct.	G.	AB.	R.	H.	TB.	2B.	3B.	HR.	RBI.	GW.	SH.	SF.	HP.	BB.	Int. BB.	SO.	SB.	CS.
Smith, Robert, Ciudad Juarez°	.357	122	459	70	164	212	24	6	4	48	6	1	3	2	48	8	41	26	19
Navarrete, Juan, Saltillo°	.343	110	397	70	136	162	13	2	3	33	2	15	1	4	40	2	9	18	7
Scott, George, Poza Rica	.333	105	330	40	110	147	12	2	7	66	13	0	2	4	63	8	51	1	3
Dyes, Andy, Monclova	.328	100	332	62	109	189	12	4	20	53	4	0	3	4	40	14	72	4	2
Cervantes, Eduardo, Aguascalientes	.325	125	421	72	137	169	14	6	2	43	7	11	3	3	82	1	71	7	3
Cossey, Donald, 27 Tab-71 Sal	.325	98	335	46	109	147	20	6	2	31	3	4	2	3	25	5	41	7	4
Cox, Ted, Mexico City Reds	.324	94	306	50	99	133	18	2	4	47	4	0	2	2	60	2	44	4	8
Collins, James, Coatzacoalcos°	.322	108	397	66	128	153	19	3	0	49	8	1	2	6	34	4	41	15	8
Blanks, Larvell, Coatzacoalcos	.319	126	452	55	144	196	21	8	5	68	8	6	6	1	29	1	37	10	10
Lopez, Felix Jaime, Ciudad Juarez°..	.316	99	342	41	108	128	13	2	1	34	4	4	4	0	15	2	16	4	0
Lee, Terry, Ciudad Juarez°	.315	105	356	54	112	169	24	6	7	52	12	1	3	2	28	2	55	4	1
Cruz, Henry, Reynosa	.312	119	394	64	123	199	27	2	15	58	6	1	2	2	72	10	32	13	4
Monasterio, Juan, Poza Rica	.311	129	489	72	152	205	25	5	6	70	12	5	5	1	24	3	32	3	6
Howard, Wilbur, Yucatan	.310	125	467	68	145	175	15	6	1	45	4	5	2	1	39	11	37	17	15
Castro, Anthony, Mexico City Tigers°	.310	124	422	60	131	158	14	5	1	51	5	11	4	0	54	8	39	8	8
Bellacetin, Juan Jose, Agua°	.310	128	426	77	132	162	17	5	1	30	1	8	4	9	92	3	32	5	10
Castillo, Anthony, Mexico City Tigers.	.310	129	436	61	135	207	26	2	14	78	11	7	7	11	50	1	62	0	5

Departmental Leaders: G—Rivero, 132; AB—Monasterio, 489; R—Alston, 98; H—Smith, 164; TB—Mora, 214; 2B—Batista, Cruz, Santana, 27; 3B—Rodriguez, 11; HR—Mora, 25; RBI—Mora, 80; GWRBI—Santana, 15; SH—Gomez, Ortiz, Rodriguez, 20; SF—Duncan, Llenas, 10; HP—Roys, 14; BB—Bellacetin, 92; IBB—Obradovich, 18; SO—Batista, 95; SB—Briones, 60; CS—Alexander, Alston, 23.

(All Players—Listed Alphabetically)

Player and Club	Pct.	G.	AB.	R.	H.	TB.	2B.	3B.	HR.	RBI.	GW.	SH.	SF.	HP.	BB.	Int. BB.	SO.	SB.	CS.
Abarca, David, Campeche	.000	1	0	1	0	0	0	0	0	0	0	0	0	0	0	0	0	0	0
Aceves, Alfredo, Yucatan	.228	40	92	5	21	27	2	2	0	7	1	3	0	0	13	0	25	0	0
Acuna, Clemente, Campeche	.200	5	15	1	3	3	0	0	0	2	0	1	0	0	0	0	1	0	1
Aguilar, Enrique, Aguascalientes	.265	128	471	62	125	181	20	3	10	65	6	3	4	4	24	3	43	33	9
Aispuro, Javier, Chihuahua	.164	34	55	5	9	10	1	0	0	3	1	0	0	1	5	0	22	0	0
Alexander, Gary, Yucatan	.264	48	159	13	42	63	2	2	5	22	3	0	3	2	31	2	31	1	4
Alexander, Matt, Mexico City Tigers°	.271	106	388	65	105	134	12	7	1	23	0	10	1	0	51	3	46	36	23
Almeida, Reynaldo, Reynosa	.100	46	30	13	3	4	1	0	0	1	0	0	0	0	5	0	9	1	1
Alston, Wendell, Coatzacoalcos	.290	117	424	98	123	177	25	10	3	40	3	4	3	1	83	5	37	52	23
Alvarado, Natanael, Coatzacoalcos....	.270	111	400	69	108	125	12	1	1	28	5	11	2	0	67	0	68	8	13
Alvarez, John, Mexico City Tigers	.261	127	433	53	113	158	15	3	8	56	8	8	9	0	38	8	46	3	3
Alvarez, Jorge, Mexico City Reds	.188	12	16	3	3	4	1	0	0	1	0	0	1	0	0	0	4	0	0
Alvarez, Juan Carlos, Yucatan	.244	109	344	34	84	96	5	2	1	30	2	8	1	1	31	4	88	6	3
Alvarez, Manuel, Coatzacoalcos°	.232	63	164	16	38	53	7	1	2	24	1	2	4	3	42	6	29	3	2
Alvarez, Orlando, Aguascalientes	.260	26	96	12	25	38	5	1	2	12	2	0	1	0	7	1	21	1	0
Alvarez, Raymundo, Monclova	.165	52	85	13	14	14	0	0	0	4	2	5	0	1	6	0	26	1	0
Arzate, Martin, Veracruz	.185	16	54	3	10	12	2	0	0	2	1	1	0	0	3	0	7	2	1
Ault, Douglas, Mexico City Tigers	.200	9	20	0	4	4	0	0	0	0	0	0	0	0	0	0	1	0	0
Avina, Fco. Javier, 4 Sal-19 Cam	.089	23	45	2	4	5	1	0	0	1	0	2	0	0	6	0	4	2	0
Barrera, Nelson, Nuevo Laredo	.281	114	391	53	110	163	23	0	10	52	10	7	0	3	38	7	64	5	6
Batista, Rafael, Monclova°	.271	118	410	59	111	191	27	1	17	69	9	0	3	3	54	7	95	1	0
Beck, Romel, Tabasco	.280	7	25	3	7	8	1	0	0	1	0	1	0	0	1	0	6	3	2
Bellacetin, Juan, Aguascalientes°....	.310	128	426	77	132	162	17	5	1	30	1	8	4	9	92	3	32	5	10
Beltre, Sergio, Aguascalientes	.292	107	346	38	101	147	10	6	9	40	6	4	1	2	43	0	60	21	17
Benitez, Jose Luis, Saltillo	.219	66	137	9	30	39	7	1	0	14	3	3	2	1	16	0	34	0	0
Benitez, Julio Cesar, Nuevo Laredo	.288	83	212	24	61	82	13	1	2	32	6	2	1	1	16	2	31	2	1
Bernal, Cosme, Aguascalientes	.191	35	68	10	13	19	3	0	1	2	1	0	0	1	10	0	21	0	1
Bernhardt, Juan Ramon, Campeche ...	.272	65	239	23	65	82	12	1	1	21	1	4	2	3	14	5	13	1	1
Beswick, James, Yucatan	.256	82	285	31	73	108	15	1	6	39	3	1	3	1	32	5	40	4	3

Player and Club	Pct.	G.	AB.	R.	H.	TB.	2B.	3B.	HR.	RBI.	GW.	SH.	SF.	HP.	BB.	Int. BB.	SO.	SB.	CS.
Bigini, Gregory, Ciudad Juarez†	.294	99	343	51	101	137	15	3	5	49	5	0	3	1	46	7	59	9	0
Blanks, Larvell, Coatzacoalcos	.319	126	452	55	144	196	21	8	5	68	8	6	6	1	29	1	37	10	10
Bobadilla, Manuel, Ciudad Juarez	.248	99	282	44	70	82	8	2	0	33	7	6	2	1	35	2	36	7	5
Bojorquez, Jose, Mexico City Tigers	.181	80	238	16	43	56	6	2	1	20	4	6	5	1	23	4	37	2	1
Briones, Antonio, Ciudad Juarez	.276	122	399	58	110	121	5	3	0	37	4	11	2	0	49	1	22	60	9
Bryant, Dereck, Mexico City Tigers	.293	105	358	53	105	144	22	4	3	41	8	7	2	0	36	5	45	13	10
Burke, Norberto Reynosa	.241	129	378	46	91	128	17	1	6	39	5	5	4	8	77	1	62	7	1
Cain, Aaron, Campeche	.387	20	62	15	24	29	5	0	0	6	1	5	1	2	8	1	9	1	2
Camaoho, Sergio, Aguascalientes	.300	4	10	1	3	3	0	0	0	0	0	0	0	0	1	0	2	0	0
Campaneris, D'berto, 67 Vera-37 PR	.277	104	350	44	97	122	11	4	2	37	2	10	2	3	45	2	49	12	7
Canedo, Donald, Mexico City Reds	.295	105	292	42	86	105	8	4	1	36	3	5	4	0	44	2	44	6	7
Cano, Javier, Saltillo⁰	.148	47	54	7	8	8	0	0	0	4	1	1	0	1	7	0	24	1	3
Carbo, Bernie, Veracruz⁰	.278	105	306	36	85	123	20	0	6	47	6	1	3	2	91	12	61	0	1
Carrillo, Matias, Poza Rica	.309	99	301	59	93	112	9	5	0	29	4	3	2	2	39	3	54	17	6
Castelan, Miguel Angel, Campeche⁰	.252	91	286	33	72	98	11	3	3	24	4	3	2	1	33	0	52	6	6
Castillo, Anthony, Mexico City Tigers	.310	129	436	61	135	207	26	2	14	78	11	7	7	11	50	1	62	0	5
Castro, Anthony, Mexico City Tigers⁰	.310	124	422	60	131	158	14	5	1	51	5	11	4	0	54	8	39	8	8
Castro, Efren, Tabasco	.071	16	14	1	1	1	0	0	0	0	0	0	0	0	1	0	5	0	0
Castro, Jose Antonio, Veracruz	.222	89	243	23	54	62	8	0	0	16	4	5	1	3	15	1	51	8	5
Cazarez, Jose, Yucatan	.198	97	298	27	59	68	9	0	0	16	0	6	2	1	23	1	32	4	4
Cerda, Benjamin, Veracruz	.252	79	242	13	61	63	2	0	0	16	2	1	2	2	19	3	21	1	1
Cervantes, Eduardo, Aguascalientes	.325	125	421	72	137	169	14	6	2	43	7	11	3	3	82	1	71	7	3
Chaidez, Jose Antonio, Tabasco	.250	10	20	1	5	7	2	0	0	4	0	2	0	0	1	0	1	0	0
Chappas, Harry, Monterrey†	.197	24	76	12	15	19	2	1	0	3	0	5	0	1	18	0	8	3	2
Chavarria, Miguel Angel, Monclova	.184	101	267	30	49	73	7	4	3	26	2	6	4	7	42	0	72	7	4
Chavez, Baeza, Guadalupe, Saltillo⁰	.222	82	216	16	48	54	6	0	0	16	1	6	4	3	27	1	4	2	0
Chavez, Jose Santos, Nuevo Laredo	.216	76	148	24	32	43	4	2	1	16	3	5	2	0	32	0	26	1	3
Chavez, Juan de Dios, Chihuahua	.173	76	225	16	39	50	3	1	2	17	1	11	1	4	14	1	30	0	0
Chavez, Ricardo, Mexico City Tigers	.167	4	6	1	1	1	0	0	0	0	0	0	0	0	0	0	1	0	0
Chavez, Soto, Guadalupe, Monclova	.000	4	1	1	0	0	0	0	0	0	0	0	0	0	0	0	0	0	0
Collins, James, Coatzacoalcos⁰	.322	108	397	66	128	153	19	3	0	49	8	1	2	6	34	4	41	15	8
Collins, Silvester, Coatzacoalcos⁰	.167	2	6	1	1	1	0	0	0	1	0	0	0	0	1	0	1	0	0
Contreras, Juan Carlos, Monclova	.258	117	392	40	101	116	5	5	0	24	5	17	1	2	28	0	63	8	3
Contreras, Rafael, Saltillo	.304	21	69	5	21	25	2	1	0	11	2	4	0	0	9	0	6	1	3
Cossey, Donald R., 27 Tab-71 Sal⁰	.325	98	335	46	109	147	20	6	2	31	3	4	3	5	25	5	41	7	4
Cota, Mario Alberto, Monterrey	.252	49	111	11	28	28	0	0	0	5	0	4	0	1	4	0	12	2	2
Cotes, Eugenio, Monterrey	.357	86	283	51	101	158	16	7	9	39	3	2	3	3	26	5	43	25	7
Cox, Ted, Mexico City Reds	.324	94	306	50	99	133	18	2	4	47	4	0	2	2	60	2	44	4	8
Crug, Gary, Monterrey	.203	21	64	3	13	15	2	0	0	2	0	0	1	0	6	1	12	0	1
Cruz, Domingo, Yucatan	.245	105	359	35	88	110	11	4	1	46	8	6	4	5	27	1	41	4	3
Cruz, Henry, Reynosa	.312	119	394	64	123	199	27	2	15	58	6	1	2	2	72	10	32	13	4
Cuataneconzy, Guillermo, Campeche	.000	4	2	0	0	0	0	0	0	0	0	0	0	0	0	0	1	0	0
Daut, Manuel, Monterrey	.250	34	84	8	21	27	2	2	0	8	1	4	0	2	12	2	21	0	2
Davila, Luis Alberto, Monterrey	.266	87	252	22	67	83	5	4	1	29	2	6	0	5	23	4	44	4	4
DeFreites, Arturo, Tabasco	.278	129	486	44	135	174	19	1	6	58	10	3	8	1	23	2	69	13	5
Deliza, Juan Ernesto, Monclova	.267	120	449	53	120	151	16	3	3	44	8	4	4	2	13	2	55	6	2
De Los Santos, Ramon, Monclova	.000	3	3	0	0	0	0	0	0	0	0	0	0	0	0	0	1	0	0
Diaz, Albino, 47 Chi-31 Yuc	.219	78	233	36	51	61	3	2	1	12	2	8	0	2	31	0	34	8	2
Diaz, Jesus, Reynosa	.141	45	85	10	12	18	4	1	0	6	1	0	0	0	11	0	13	0	0
Dominguez, Raul, Campeche	.125	17	8	1	1	1	0	0	0	0	0	0	0	0	1	0	3	0	0
Douglas, Lester, Poza Rica	.000	6	8	0	0	0	0	0	0	1	0	0	0	0	1	0	3	0	0
Duncan, Taylor, Coatzacoalcos	.306	124	447	57	137	198	23	1	12	78	10	1	10	1	43	4	29	7	2
Duran, Danny, Nuevo Laredo	.268	96	321	44	86	125	15	0	8	33	6	8	5	5	31	0	32	5	1
Duran, Ricardo, Ciudad Juarez	.279	110	373	51	104	148	14	0	10	61	5	2	5	3	52	6	39	4	2
Dyes, Andy, Monclova	.328	100	332	62	109	189	12	4	20	53	4	0	3	4	40	14	72	4	2
Early, William, Tabasco	1.000	1	1	0	1	1	0	0	0	1	0	0	0	0	0	0	0	0	0
Edwards, Mike, 2 Mex-71 PR	.304	73	257	30	78	98	5	6	1	25	2	9	4	2	10	0	24	8	8
Elizondo, Fernando, Veracruz	.235	119	379	30	89	102	11	1	0	31	1	12	5	1	19	2	44	3	6
Ellis, Robert, Mexico City Reds	.211	7	19	0	4	5	1	0	0	1	0	0	1	0	3	0	7	0	0
Esparza, Julio, Poza Rica	.150	33	60	4	9	13	0	2	0	3	1	2	1	0	3	0	6	0	0
Espino, Hector, Monterrey	.270	70	233	16	63	88	11	1	4	41	6	2	5	0	22	5	13	1	4
Espinosa Ramos, Ern., MC Tigers⁰	.268	35	71	11	19	25	0	3	0	3	1	1	0	0	2	0	15	0	0
Estes, Frank, Yucatan	.289	122	436	52	126	153	12	6	1	63	10	6	7	0	53	7	28	17	7
Estrada, Francisco, Campeche	.249	119	362	27	90	105	7	1	2	39	5	10	3	5	48	7	18	6	1
Fabela, Lorenzo, Saltillo	.238	31	42	8	10	10	0	0	0	5	0	0	0	0	7	0	5	1	2
Felix, Victor Manuel, 7 Mva-83 MCR	.251	90	271	36	68	91	9	4	2	25	1	6	2	2	31	0	40	2	5
Ferrer, Sergio, 13 Ta-40 Ca-31 PR	.260	84	285	30	74	84	10	0	0	19	5	6	1	1	43	2	22	9	6
Figueroa, Jesus Maria, Campeche	.324	67	225	32	73	90	13	2	0	13	2	6	0	1	26	2	15	10	3
Figueroa, Leobardo, Juarez	.257	89	276	36	71	89	10	1	2	34	3	3	1	7	47	1	33	21	6
Firova, Dan, Nuevo Laredo	.256	72	215	18	55	63	5	0	1	15	1	5	1	0	17	0	41	1	3
Ford, Theodore, 6 Rey-37 Sal	.248	43	129	15	32	44	4	1	2	9	0	0	1	3	31	2	18	1	0
Gamundi, Timoteo, Poza Rica	.293	124	420	59	123	142	11	4	0	43	9	14	3	2	49	2	69	12	10
Garcia, Danny, Mexico City Tigers⁰	.424	26	92	15	39	46	7	0	0	17	2	1	0	1	11	0	7	4	2
Garcia, Pedro, Mexico City Reds	.270	21	74	5	20	24	2	1	0	5	1	1	0	0	4	0	7	3	2
Gates, Joseph, Mexico City Reds	.304	7	23	1	7	8	1	0	0	1	0	0	0	0	5	2	2	2	2
Gomez, Alejandro, Nuevo Laredo	.233	129	416	51	97	115	10	1	2	32	3	20	2	5	23	0	47	15	8
Gomez, Graciano, Chihuahua	.303	128	475	57	144	174	16	7	0	39	3	8	2	6	18	1	41	12	7
Gonzalez, Alonso, Tabasco	.000	1	2	0	0	0	0	0	0	0	0	0	0	0	0	0	1	0	0
Gonzalez, Arturo, Chihuahua	.170	73	165	12	28	33	5	0	0	11	1	3	0	2	16	0	34	0	3
Gonzalez, Efrain, Monclova	.175	60	126	8	22	29	1	0	2	8	0	7	0	1	5	1	24	0	0
Gonzalez, Fernando, 47 PR-53 MCR	.292	100	359	38	105	138	26	2	1	50	10	3	7	1	30	1	29	10	3
Gonzalez, Jaime, Veracruz	.194	18	31	1	6	6	0	0	0	1	1	1	0	1	0	0	6	0	0
Gonzalez, Jesus, Coatzacoalcos	.273	126	444	37	121	147	16	2	2	37	6	2	1	5	20	1	54	2	6
Gonzalez Mata Arturo, Monterrey	.000	1	1	0	0	0	0	0	0	0	0	0	0	0	0	0	0	0	0
Gonzalez, Noe, Mexico City Tigers	.200	8	10	1	2	3	1	0	0	0	0	0	0	0	1	0	1	0	0
Gonzalez, Ricardo, Ciudad Juarez	.285	56	137	21	39	52	7	0	2	15	2	2	0	2	13	0	25	2	2
Greene, Altar, Coatzacoalcos⁰	.240	127	404	57	97	146	17	4	8	65	10	3	4	5	85	4	60	10	5
Guerra, Ricardo, Nuevo Laredo	.295	118	396	62	117	183	21	0	15	65	6	7	4	1	62	0	54	16	3
Guerrero, Leobardo, Yucatan	.278	117	418	56	116	140	20	2	0	30	7	15	4	3	41	1	35	17	12
Gutierrez, Gerardo, 1-Lar-1 Sal	.000	2	4	0	0	0	0	0	0	0	0	0	0	0	1	0	2	0	0
Guzman, Andres, Coatzacoalcos	.207	84	261	20	54	64	7	0	1	20	2	5	0	2	18	1	39	1	1
Guzman, Marco Antonio, MC Reds	.194	102	310	20	60	74	10	2	0	31	6	8	3	1	28	2	55	5	2

Player and Club	Pct.	G.	AB.	R.	H.	TB.	2B.	3B.	HR.	RBI.	GW.	SH.	SF.	HP.	BB.	Int. BB.	SO.	SB.	CS.
Heras, Roberto, 18 Tig-67 Mon	.235	85	285	23	67	87	6	4	2	23	4	2	0	2	14	5	52	3	2
Heredia, Hector, Monterrey	.000	1	1	0	0	0	0	0	0	0	0	0	0	0	0	0	0	0	0
Heredia, Ubaldo, Veracruz	.000	1	0	0	0	0	0	0	0	0	0	1	0	0	0	0	0	0	0
Hernandez, Eduardo, Veracruz	.192	21	26	2	5	5	0	0	0	1	0	0	0	0	3	0	4	1	3
Hernandez, Gustavo, MC Reds	.278	12	8	1	5	5	0	0	0	0	0	0	0	0	4	0	4	0	2
Hernandez, Jorge Luis, Campeche	.199	51	151	13	30	32	0	1	0	7	1	9	0	7	6	1	22	1	1
Hernandez, Juan, Monclova	.257	121	417	42	107	129	11	1	3	32	1	10	4	0	38	0	93	32	13
Hernandez, Miguel, Coatzacoalcos	.233	80	232	23	54	63	7	1	0	17	2	5	1	2	23	1	26	4	4
Hernandez, Pedro, Chihuahua	.229	82	240	25	55	70	8	2	1	17	1	2	1	5	15	0	17	0	2
Herrera, Ricardo, 6 MCR-89 Vera	.255	95	286	41	73	85	8	2	0	18	2	2	2	1	43	1	33	11	7
Herring, Paul, Tabasco	.289	49	173	31	50	71	12	0	3	18	2	5	0	0	30	2	21	8	4
Hicks, Joseph, Tabasco	.263	72	224	19	59	72	9	2	0	10	5	4	0	0	39	4	49	7	2
Hilton, John Dave, Mexcio City Reds	.256	44	160	19	41	50	9	0	0	15	2	0	0	2	19	3	21	1	2
Howard, Wilbur, Yucatan	.310	125	467	68	145	175	15	6	1	45	4	5	2	1	39	11	37	17	15
James, Arthur, Chihuahua°	.305	118	383	57	117	156	18	3	5	43	2	2	4	1	59	12	31	7	4
Javier, Ignacio Alfredo, Tabasco	.182	18	55	6	10	11	1	0	0	1	0	1	0	3	4	0	8	1	0
Jimenez, Leopoldo, Campeche	.214	78	220	10	47	59	7	1	0	13	1	4	0	2	10	1	45	1	4
Jimenez, Sergio, Tabasco	.000	7	5	2	0	0	0	0	0	0	0	0	0	0	1	0	2	0	0
Johnson, Larry Don, Veracruz	.226	115	368	35	83	118	7	2	8	36	4	3	7	4	49	7	40	5	7
Johnson, Lorenzo, Nuevo Laredo	.204	27	49	9	10	15	2	0	1	4	0	0	1	3	1	0	10	1	0
Joshua, Von Everett, Yucatan°	.272	114	423	42	115	145	12	3	4	57	7	3	8	3	34	3	69	4	5
Juarez, Esteban, Chihuahua	.000	1	4	0	0	0	0	0	0	0	0	0	0	0	0	0	1	0	0
Juarez, Marcelo, Saltillo	.000	10	18	3	0	0	0	0	0	0	0	0	0	0	1	0	1	0	0
Lara, Francisco, 14 Ags-61 Mva	.237	75	219	19	52	55	3	0	0	13	2	8	0	2	11	1	10	1	1
Leal, Jose Guadalupe, Reynosa°	.199	100	251	29	50	85	6	4	7	26	5	4	0	4	26	4	64	4	2
Lee, Terry, Ciudad Juarez°	.315	105	356	54	112	169	24	6	7	52	12	1	3	2	28	2	55	4	1
Lentine, James, Monterrey	.280	98	343	58	96	134	20	3	4	35	4	9	1	0	48	5	37	23	6
Leon, Juan Carlos, Yucatan	.081	21	37	3	3	4	1	0	0	0	0	0	0	1	1	0	8	0	0
Leonard, Bernard, Aguascalientes	.309	21	81	12	25	32	4	0	1	10	1	0	1	1	8	0	10	2	1
Limon, Arturo, Mexico City Reds	.133	21	45	5	6	8	2	0	0	4	0	1	1	0	0	0	4	0	0
Lizarraga, Alejandro, 92 Tab-24 Yuc	.237	116	418	37	99	120	12	0	3	31	4	14	3	0	25	4	38	4	9
Llanes, Ernesto Ramon, Aguas.	.196	25	51	8	10	11	1	0	0	2	0	0	0	1	0	3	0	1	1
Llenas, Winston, Mexico City Reds	.268	127	452	64	121	181	20	2	12	75	10	5	10	8	46	3	59	7	5
Lopez, Carlos, Tabasco	.263	126	429	42	113	153	14	1	8	45	5	2	3	9	32	7	54	8	6
Lopez, Felix Jaime, Ciudad Juarez°	.316	99	342	41	108	128	13	2	1	34	2	4	4	0	15	2	16	4	0
Lopez, Raul Armando, Ciudad Juarez	.222	7	9	2	2	2	0	0	0	0	0	0	0	0	4	1	1	0	0
Lopez, Victor Manuel, Chihuahua	.234	104	338	35	79	104	12	2	3	48	1	5	8	0	29	1	44	1	1
Lora, Ramon, Mexico City Tigers	.313	75	268	42	84	105	8	2	3	32	3	4	1	0	32	3	20	15	5
Lugo, Gabriel, Reynosa	.191	90	277	29	53	70	8	0	3	34	6	4	1	3	22	2	37	1	0
Luna, Jose Luis, Monterrey	.197	81	229	18	45	61	7	3	1	17	0	1	1	0	14	0	59	0	0
Madero, Carlos, Poza Rica	.179	50	112	6	20	23	0	0	1	12	0	6	1	0	13	0	23	0	2
Mapel, Steve, Reynosa	.000	1	2	0	0	0	0	0	0	0	0	0	0	0	0	0	1	0	0
Martinez, Alonso, Monclova	.148	19	27	0	4	4	0	0	0	0	0	0	0	0	0	0	3	0	0
Martinez, Enrico, Coatzacoalcos	.000	3	2	0	0	0	0	0	0	0	0	0	0	0	1	0	1	0	0
Marquez, Francisco, Aguascalientes	.235	105	353	32	83	109	8	0	6	36	3	1	2	6	17	2	48	3	2
Martinez, Reynaldo, Veracruz	.260	85	265	20	69	78	4	1	1	25	5	7	3	1	20	0	40	10	5
Martinez, Teodoro, Campeche	.301	119	432	36	130	166	17	5	3	41	8	8	3	2	18	5	30	9	7
Maza, Celerio, Ciudad Juarez	.250	27	12	5	3	3	0	0	0	1	0	1	0	0	1	0	3	1	0
Medina, Elpidio, Chihuahua	.070	21	43	2	3	5	0	1	0	3	0	1	0	1	0	0	10	0	0
Mejias, Samuel, Campeche	.258	105	372	30	96	124	9	2	5	32	5	12	3	2	27	3	51	5	2
Mendez, Roberto, Veracruz	.218	60	133	16	29	37	4	2	0	12	2	2	0	1	39	1	20	1	4
Mendoza, Margarito, Ciudad Juarez	.100	9	20	0	2	3	1	0	0	2	0	1	0	3	0	0	2	0	1
Mendoza, Mario, Mexico City Reds	.240	34	100	6	24	26	2	0	0	7	2	0	0	0	9	0	12	2	4
Mendoza, Porfirio, 10 Tig-62 Cam	.209	72	187	19	39	47	1	2	1	10	2	14	1	0	26	0	26	2	6
Mendoza, Saul, Poza Rica	.261	116	375	54	98	118	17	0	1	42	5	12	3	2	70	3	45	4	3
Molina, Jose Maria, Veracruz	.173	22	52	3	9	12	0	0	1	6	2	0	0	1	2	0	9	0	1
Monasterio, Juan, Poza Rica	.311	129	489	72	152	205	25	5	6	70	12	5	5	1	24	3	32	3	6
Monroy, Victor Hugo, Chihuahua	.230	57	152	13	35	45	6	2	0	8	1	3	3	0	8	0	26	0	1
Moore, Alvin, Reynosa	.270	84	300	31	81	113	12	4	4	38	5	0	2	1	34	2	28	4	2
Mora, Andres, 9 Sal-117 Lar	.288	126	413	72	119	214	16	2	25	80	12	0	6	3	56	6	40	12	8
Morales, Luis, Reynosa	.143	7	7	1	1	1	0	0	0	0	0	0	0	0	2	0	5	0	0
Morales, Manuel, Mexico City Tigers	.261	122	371	43	97	104	5	1	0	30	9	9	1	1	19	0	43	8	9
Moreno, Jesus, Veracruz	.000	1	0	1	0	0	0	0	0	0	0	0	0	0	0	0	0	0	0
Munoz, Eduardo, Reynosa	.266	130	477	70	127	181	20	2	10	34	3	9	1	3	69	7	73	16	1
Murrell, Ivan, Saltillo	.326	69	242	37	79	118	15	0	8	41	4	1	3	2	10	2	40	3	0
Navarrete, Carlos, Campeche	.202	48	114	6	23	23	0	0	0	10	0	5	2	1	7	1	10	0	0
Navarrete, Juan, Saltillo°	.343	110	397	70	136	162	13	2	3	33	2	15	1	4	40	2	9	18	7
Negron, Miguel Angel, Nuevo Laredo°	.301	105	399	48	120	152	1	3	5	39	6	4	2	2	27	1	44	29	9
Nettles, Morris, 29 Chi-45 Cam°	.247	74	255	36	63	75	6	3	0	11	0	2	1	0	38	0	38	8	6
Norwood, Willie, Reynosa	.289	71	242	36	70	104	8	1	8	39	2	3	1	3	23	3	44	8	3
Novelo, Jaime, Tabasco	.219	97	229	16	50	56	1	1	1	18	3	9	1	1	15	1	27	5	2
Obradovich, James, Campeche°	.278	124	417	54	116	176	21	3	11	56	8	7	3	1	63	18	60	8	0
Olivares, Oswaldo, Mexico City Reds°.	.317	72	252	47	80	103	4	5	3	27	2	4	4	3	41	7	26	22	9
Orozco, Arturo, Tabasco	.250	55	112	7	28	35	5	1	0	11	1	0	0	1	15	2	22	2	1
Ortiz, Alejandro, Nuevo Laredo	.260	97	311	38	81	114	10	4	5	29	2	5	4	3	23	2	58	3	9
Ortiz, Alfredo°	.150	16	15	0	3	3	0	0	0	0	0	0	0	0	5	1	1	0	1
Ortiz, Jose Manuel, Tabasco	.233	123	424	30	99	124	15	2	2	43	4	20	6	0	18	0	48	3	1
Ortiz, Leopoldo, Tabasco	.235	7	17	2	4	4	0	0	0	0	0	0	0	0	0	0	3	1	0
Otero, Pedro, Yucatan	.261	11	23	2	6	6	0	0	0	1	0	0	0	0	2	0	4	0	0
Pactwa, Joseph, Reynosa	.000	2	3	0	0	0	0	0	0	0	0	0	0	0	1	0	1	0	0
Paredes, Jesus, Nuevo Laredo	.215	20	65	5	14	14	0	0	0	4	0	1	1	1	6	0	14	1	1
Paredes, Raul, Campeche	.221	82	231	25	51	60	5	2	0	13	3	3	1	1	10	0	31	5	6
Pasillas, Andy, 19 Reds-69 Tigers	.276	88	268	24	74	101	14	2	3	34	4	4	3	4	12	2	42	0	2
Perera, Mario, Tabasco	.151	48	86	12	13	14	1	0	0	2	0	2	0	0	12	0	7	0	1
Perez, Alfredo, Ciudad Juarez	.219	45	114	14	25	32	3	0	2	9	1	6	0	0	17	0	24	2	1
Perez, Jose Luis, Aguascalientes°	.292	121	421	55	123	186	16	4	13	61	10	1	2	5	30	5	58	8	3
Perry, Kenneth, Nuevo Laredo	.271	94	332	51	90	131	16	5	5	43	3	7	2	3	55	4	38	12	8
Pierce, Jack, Aguascalientes°	.269	123	438	65	118	195	22	2	17	74	10	2	6	2	51	11	66	1	1
Posadas, Rafael, Poza Rica	.000	1	0	1	0	0	0	0	0	0	0	0	0	0	0	0	0	0	0
Prieto, Ricardo, Mexico City Reds	.231	50	130	11	30	39	2	2	1	18	6	3	1	0	10	0	12	2	1
Quintero, Victor, Saltillo	.244	99	312	32	76	91	11	2	0	23	1	3	2	5	24	0	21	4	4
Quinonez, Ventura, Monterrey	.290	14	31	1	9	11	0	1	0	0	0	1	0	1	1	0	5	0	0

Player and Club	Pct.	G.	AB.	R.	H.	TB.	2B.	3B.	HR.	RBI.	GW.	SH.	SF.	HP.	BB.	Int. BB.	SO.	SB.	CS.
Quiroz, Julian, Mexico City Reds	.167	7	18	0	3	3	0	0	0	0	0	1	0	0	0	0	5	1	0
Ramirez, Manuel, Chihuahua	.286	130	479	66	137	181	14	6	6	59	9	2	6	4	34	3	42	12	4
Ramirez, Orlando, Chihuahua	.301	124	449	56	135	170	16	5	3	59	8	6	7	4	33	3	49	4	4
Raymundo, Oscar, Yucatan	.133	16	15	4	2	4	0	1	0	0	0	0	1	0	0	0	2	0	0
Rendon, Josue, Aguascalientes	.256	103	301	36	77	114	12	2	7	45	7	7	4	1	20	0	65	3	2
Rios, Carlos, Mexico City Tigers	.280	128	460	41	129	150	11	5	0	48	6	3	3	3	13	1	45	11	5
Rivera, Carlos, Yucatan	.258	118	396	34	102	138	11	5	5	32	6	8	5	5	22	5	61	9	1
Rivera, Eduardo, 1 Chi.-92 CJ	.260	93	273	33	71	83	7	1	1	22	2	13	2	2	26	2	25	2	0
Rivero, Gener, Reynosa	.260	132	384	36	100	116	5	4	1	20	3	10	1	4	40	0	25	14	6
Robles, Eduardo, Tabasco	.000	1	1	0	0	0	0	0	0	0	0	0	0	0	0	0	1	0	0
Robles, Humberto, Monterrey	.118	21	51	2	6	7	1	0	0	2	0	1	1	0	4	0	12	0	0
Robles, Sergio, Mexico City Reds	.188	24	80	8	15	15	0	0	0	3	0	0	0	0	3	0	13	0	1
Rodriguez, Clayton Leonardo, Sal.†	.280	127	432	70	121	169	12	3	10	50	8	6	1	1	67	6	70	19	6
Rodriguez, Eliseo, Monclova	.234	104	290	18	68	96	13	0	5	51	5	3	4	7	54	3	38	0	0
Rodriguez, I. Francisco, Ags.	.300	126	470	55	141	175	25	0	3	56	9	12	9	6	23	1	34	3	4
Rodriguez, Guillermo, Coatzacoalcos	.220	100	313	22	69	84	12	0	1	23	3	6	0	4	5	1	62	1	4
Rodriguez, Jaime, Mex. City Tigers	.214	8	14	1	3	3	0	0	0	1	0	0	0	0	0	0	1	1	1
Rodriguez, Jose, Poza Rica	.198	94	232	23	46	56	2	4	0	11	1	10	1	4	9	0	43	2	4
Rodriguez, Juan Francisco, Reynosa	.299	125	462	69	138	155	15	1	0	38	6	20	4	3	40	0	25	26	4
Rodriguez, Roberto, MC Reds⚬	.300	128	467	75	140	176	14	11	0	49	5	5	2	0	80	8	33	12	15
Rodriguez, Rodolfo, Saltillo⚬	.287	130	422	49	121	146	17	1	2	48	7	11	2	1	70	7	31	3	5
Rojas, Omar, Monterrey	.091	38	55	3	5	7	2	0	0	1	0	1	0	1	0	1	14	0	0
Rojo, Gonzalo, Reynosa	.000	1	1	0	0	0	0	0	0	0	0	0	0	0	0	0	0	0	0
Romo, Jose Maria, Poza Rica	.251	63	195	27	49	77	11	1	5	22	3	2	2	3	37	3	37	4	1
Ron, Arnold 12 Cam.-12 NL	.284	24	74	12	21	30	3	0	2	10	3	1	0	1	11	0	3	1	2
Rosado, Luis, Poza Rica	.250	120	368	30	92	114	15	2	1	43	4	10	4	2	41	1	35	1	1
Rosales, Arturo, Ciudad Juarez	.303	115	380	50	115	158	13	9	4	54	6	2	2	7	12	1	58	16	5
Rosario, Angel, Saltillo⚬	.277	123	386	60	107	172	19	5	12	63	7	5	9	0	79	15	48	3	4
Rosas, Clemente, ⚬Reynosa	.236	109	369	29	87	130	18	2	7	56	8	2	4	1	18	4	62	1	0
Roys, Luis, Chihuahua	.307	123	460	57	141	189	20	2	8	44	6	2	4	14	11	2	50	17	9
Rubio, Arturo, Tabasco	.264	72	159	14	42	50	2	3	0	9	1	8	0	4	16	0	18	6	3
Ruiz, Porfirio, Saltillo	.294	102	286	33	84	99	9	0	2	36	4	8	3	2	22	3	30	2	2
Saiz, Francisco, Poza Rico⚬	.253	76	166	25	42	56	5	3	1	22	7	1	1	0	24	4	20	2	1
Salazar, Ronaldo, Monclova	.292	116	367	53	107	160	24	1	9	48	7	5	1	1	55	4	34	15	7
Salcido, Teodoro, Veracruz	.251	98	319	44	80	99	13	0	2	21	4	2	1	3	36	1	64	10	6
Sanchez, Armando, Mexico City Reds	.299	80	251	33	75	96	5	8	0	27	6	6	2	0	31	0	21	6	5
Sanchez, Felipe, Nuevo Laredo	.500	1	2	0	1	1	0	0	0	0	0	0	0	0	0	0	1	0	0
Sanchez, Juan, Mexico City Reds	.000	3	6	0	0	0	0	0	0	0	0	0	0	0	0	0	2	0	0
Sandate, Ricardo, Poza Rico⚬	.000	1	1	0	0	0	0	0	0	0	0	0	0	0	0	0	1	0	0
Sanguillen, Manny, Reynosa	.357	58	224	24	80	112	12	4	4	45	4	3	1	1	7	0	14	2	0
Santana, Blas, Saltillo	.291	124	457	50	133	168	27	4	0	68	15	8	6	4	20	2	52	5	2
Sarabia, Antonio, Veracruz	.280	94	271	38	76	102	11	3	3	22	2	7	2	0	34	0	49	11	6
Sauceda, Ramiro, Mex. City Tigers	.000	4	0	3	0	0	0	0	0	0	0	0	0	0	0	0	0	0	0
Sauceda, Victor, 36 Sal.-11 Mva.	.253	47	154	15	39	44	5	0	0	17	3	2	0	1	7	0	22	0	1
Scott, George, Poza Rico	.333	105	330	40	110	147	12	2	7	66	13	0	2	4	63	8	51	1	3
Scott, John, Campeche	.161	8	31	2	5	5	0	0	0	0	0	1	0	0	0	0	6	1	0
Segui, Diego, Reynosa	.000	1	0	0	0	0	0	0	0	0	0	0	0	0	1	0	0	0	0
Serna, Joel, Monterrey	.193	123	383	31	74	103	16	2	3	32	8	7	3	5	48	2	72	6	4
Serratos, Javier, Monclova	.000	3	1	2	0	0	0	0	0	0	0	0	0	0	0	0	0	0	0
Serratos, Miguel, Coatzacoalcos	.175	52	120	14	21	26	0	1	1	5	1	3	0	0	5	0	33	0	1
Smith, Robert, Ciudad Juarez⚬	.357	122	459	70	164	212	24	6	4	48	6	1	3	2	48	8	41	26	19
Sommers, Jesus, Tabasco	.278	121	399	36	111	144	20	2	3	41	9	3	0	0	51	3	41	7	2
Sotelo, Emilio, Reynosa	.000	3	3	0	0	0	0	0	0	0	0	0	0	0	1	0	1	0	0
Soto, Carlos, Nuevo Laredo	.285	119	421	63	120	192	13	1	19	65	7	3	1	6	29	10	69	2	1
Soto, Gregorio, Tabasco	.254	86	232	21	59	68	7	1	0	13	0	8	1	5	18	0	36	2	6
Stenholm, Richard, Mex. City Reds	.274	107	369	59	101	184	10	5	21	72	8	3	4	3	63	7	58	3	3
Stennett, Renaldo, Reynosa	.326	24	92	15	30	43	6	2	1	18	5	1	2	1	6	1	12	1	1
Suarez, Miguel, 5 Tigers-105 Vera.	.271	110	413	42	112	133	11	2	2	29	4	13	0	4	18	3	17	3	4
Sutton, John, Nuevo Laredo	.000	1	2	0	0	0	0	0	0	0	0	0	0	0	0	0	1	0	0
Tiburcio, Zeferino, Poza Rica	.185	19	54	5	10	13	3	0	0	4	1	3	1	0	5	0	12	0	0
Tisdale, Alfred, Veracruz	.304	60	214	22	65	70	3	1	0	19	4	1	3	1	22	3	23	4	1
Torres, Antonio, Monclova	.255	120	377	40	96	103	5	1	0	19	2	7	0	2	32	0	63	21	12
Torres, Nemesio Jaime, Monterrey	.232	112	341	36	79	99	6	4	2	24	2	10	4	3	35	0	40	5	4
Torres, Raymundo, Mexico City Reds	.311	66	212	41	66	97	17	4	2	31	2	5	4	3	37	1	36	13	0
Torres, Rosendo, Monterrey	.283	65	212	34	60	93	13	1	6	23	1	3	4	1	38	3	41	5	5
Trevino, Ted, Tabasco	.170	119	341	23	58	74	13	0	1	15	2	11	0	1	29	3	68	0	0
Uzcanga, Hernan, Veracruz	.179	10	28	0	5	7	0	1	0	2	0	0	0	0	1	1	0	0	0
Valdez, Baltazar, Chihuahua	.268	104	314	34	84	129	14	2	9	49	1	1	2	2	16	2	50	1	1
Valenzuela, Horacio, Mex. City Tigers	.000	1	2	2	0	0	0	0	0	0	0	0	0	0	0	0	0	0	0
Valle, Guadalupe, Ciudad Juarez	.258	104	287	28	74	91	5	6	0	37	8	7	4	0	32	1	44	3	0
Vargas, Antonio, Mex. City Tigers	.269	12	26	4	7	11	2	1	0	0	0	1	0	0	1	0	7	1	0
Vazquez, Nicolas, 12-Tig.-70 Cam.	.273	82	264	25	72	87	7	1	2	30	2	3	2	1	23	2	18	0	2
Vazquez, Rafael, Poza Rica	.000	2	2	0	0	0	0	0	0	0	0	0	0	0	0	0	2	0	0
Vega, Abelardo, Monterrey	.237	87	279	19	66	72	3	0	1	26	0	1	5	4	24	2	35	5	3
Vega, Jesus, Reynosa	.000	6	2	1	0	0	0	0	0	0	0	0	0	0	0	0	0	0	0
Vega, Ramon, Aguascalientes	.224	41	85	3	19	22	3	0	0	11	0	3	1	1	5	0	14	1	0
Vega, Valenoiano, Monterrey	.213	41	108	9	23	24	1	0	0	3	2	3	2	0	13	0	12	2	0
Velarde, Roman, Tabasco	.277	24	47	4	13	1	0	0	0	2	1	0	0	0	1	0	6	0	0
Vergara, Salvador, Veracruz	.188	62	96	7	18	21	1	1	0	7	0	2	0	1	8	0	24	4	4
Villaescusa, Fernando, Yucatan	.309	75	269	36	83	106	9	7	0	19	2	3	0	1	28	2	16	18	5
Villalobos, Juan Enrique, Reynosa	.288	47	104	10	30	36	4	1	0	12	2	2	0	4	8	1	30	2	1
Villarreal, Viterbo, Reynosa	.000	8	3	1	0	0	0	0	0	0	0	0	0	0	0	0	2	0	0
Villela, Carlos, Monclova	.220	56	177	21	39	47	1	2	1	10	1	4	0	0	12	0	38	6	4
Villela, Rigoberto, Monterrey	.239	124	397	34	95	129	23	1	3	39	4	5	2	3	32	4	40	6	6
Wallis, Joseph, Tabasco	.111	16	45	7	5	5	0	0	0	1	0	0	1	0	12	1	15	0	0
Washington, Larve, Poza Rica	.286	11	28	5	8	11	0	0	1	4	1	0	1	0	5	0	6	3	0
Westmoreland, Claude, Monterrey	.225	16	49	7	11	14	0	0	1	6	0	0	1	6	3	1	12	1	1
Yepez, Francisco, Poza Rica	.193	84	181	26	35	43	4	2	0	13	2	4	2	1	28	1	29	1	1
Zambrano, Rosario, Monterrey	.295	77	217	23	64	73	1	4	0	12	2	1	0	0	20	0	22	9	4
Zamora, Roberto, Mex. City Tigers	.161	42	87	8	14	23	3	3	0	5	0	3	0	0	4	1	22	0	0
Zuniga, Rafael, Coatzacoalcos	.000	1	1	0	0	0	0	0	0	0	0	0	0	0	0	0	0	0	0

MORE THAN ONE CLUB—Avina, Fco. Javier (4 Saltillo, 19 Campeche); Campaneris, Dagoberto (67 Veracruz, 37 Poza Rica); Cossey, Donald Ray (27 Tabasco, 71 Saltillo); Diaz, Albino (47 Chihuahua, 31 Yucatan); Edwards, Mike (2 Mexico City Reds, 71 Poza Rica); Felix, Victor Manuel (7 Monclova, 83 Mexico City Reds); Ferrer, Sergio (13 Tabasco, 40 Campeche, 31 Poza Rica); Ford, Theodore (6 Reynosa, 37 Saltillo); Gonzalez, Fernando (47 Poza Rica, 53 Mexico City Reds); Gutierrez, Gerardo (1 Nuevo Laredo, 1 Saltillo); Heras, Roberto (18 Mexico City Tigers, 67 Monterrey); Herrera, Ricardo (6 Mexico City Reds, 89 Veracruz); Lara, Francisco (14 Aguascalientes, 61 Monclova); Lizarraga, Alejandro (92 Tabasco, 24 Yucatan); Mendoza, Porfirio (10 Mexico City Tigers, 62 Campeche); Mora, Andres (9 Saltillo, 117 Nuevo Laredo); Nettles, Morris (29 Chihuahua, 45 Campeche); Pasillas, Andy (19 Mexico City Reds, 69 Mexico City Tigers); Rivera, Eduardo (1 Chihuahua, 92 Ciudad Juarez); Ron, Arnold (12 Campeche, 12 Nuevo Laredo); Sauceda, Victor (36 Saltillo, 11 Monclova); Suarez, Miguel (5 Mexico City Tigers, 105 Veracruz); Vazquez, Nicolas (12 Mexico City Tigers, 70 Campeche).

GRAND SLAM HOME RUNS—E. Rodriguez, 2; Alvarez, Barrera, Blanks, Burke, A. Castillo, Duran, Dyes, Herring, Joshua, Lee, Llenas, V. M. Lopez, Monasterio, Obradovich, Perry, Salazar, Soto, Valdez, 1 each.

AWARDED FIRST BASE ON CATCHER'S INTERFERENCE—C. Lopez 7 (A. Guzman, Madero, M. A. Guzman, M. Hernandez, Heras, Vega, Sarabia); Trevino (Heras); Mendoza (Trevino); Beswick (M. Hernandez), 1 each.

CLUB FIELDING

Club	Pct.	G.	PO.	A.	E.	DP.	PB.	Club	Pct.	G.	PO.	A.	E.	DP.	PB.
Aguascalientes	.979	129	3200	1525	101	132	10	Nuevo Laredo	.972	132	3268	1435	133	118	17
Saltillo	.979	130	3184	1530	102	125	11	Yucatan	.972	130	3338	1502	137	90	19
Reynosa	.977	132	3298	1483	113	90	6	Mexico City Reds	.970	130	3287	1644	150	113	5
Coatzacoalcos	.976	129	3253	1490	116	98	5	Monclova	.970	131	3208	1451	146	116	22
Mexico City Tigers	.976	129	3214	1496	117	112	8	Poza Rica	.968	130	3193	1390	150	82	11
Veracruz	.975	129	3206	1523	120	102	8	Chihuahua	.966	130	3144	1516	165	133	11
Campeche	.975	127	3176	1384	118	99	15	Tabasco	.964	130	3219	1399	170	115	12
Ciudad Juarez	.975	129	3170	1427	119	108	21	Monterrey	.963	131	3258	1389	181	124	25

Triple Plays—Mexico City Tigers, Saltillo.

INDIVIDUAL FIELDING

FIRST BASEMEN

*Throws lefthanded.

Player and Club	Pct.	G.	PO.	A.	E.	DP.	Player and Club	Pct.	G.	PO.	A.	E.	DP.
Cox, Mexico City Reds	1.000	18	170	7	0	13	Herring, Tabasco	.991	14	90	16	1	6
Navarrete, Campeche	1.000	13	127	8	0	6	L. Clayton, Saltillo*	.991	126	1090	71	11	120
Serna, Monterrey	1.000	13	78	3	0	5	J. Rodriguez, Poza Rica	.990	13	96	7	1	6
Batista, Monclova*	.997	69	630	45	2	65	J. Lopez Felix, Ciudad Juarez*	.990	11	94	5	1	9
Bojorquez, Mexico City Tigers	.997	72	623	32	2	56	J. Hicks, Tabasco	.990	34	280	9	3	29
Valdez, Chihuahua	.996	58	527	35	2	49	R. Salazar, Monclova	.989	33	250	12	3	18
Espino, Monterrey	.996	57	499	33	2	46	Lugo, Reynosa	.988	56	454	27	6	36
H. Cruz, Reynosa*	.996	28	219	14	1	13	Lara, Monclova	.988	31	222	17	3	24
Llenas, Mexico City Reds	.995	60	618	34	3	58	A. Mora, Nuevo Laredo	.987	17	153	4	2	15
Aceves, Yucatan	.995	22	198	7	1	19	DeFreites, Tabasco	.987	85	728	47	10	65
R. DURAN, Ciudad Juarez*	.995	106	940	58	5	82	Obradovich, Campeche*	.986	86	679	42	10	56
Rosado, Poza Rica	.995	23	180	16	1	11	Sanguillen, Reynosa	.986	25	269	12	4	17
Cerda, Veracruz	.994	55	485	18	3	33	A. Castillo, Mexico City Tigers	.986	61	586	33	9	52
Pierce, Aguascalientes	.994	118	1102	68	7	105	Scott, Poza Rica	.986	79	708	41	11	39
Heras, Monterrey	.993	46	402	20	3	41	Tisdale, Veracruz	.984	55	536	26	9	43
Estes, Yucatan	.993	109	1071	54	8	68	Villalobos, Reynosa	.983	34	221	12	4	22
D. Duran, Nuevo Laredo*	.993	91	783	57	6	64	Bernhardt, Campeche	.982	27	261	12	5	28
R. Rodriguez, Mexico City Reds	.992	26	248	4	2	20	Stenholm, Mexico City Reds	.982	21	200	18	4	8
G. Rodriguez, Coatzacoalcos	.992	68	590	33	5	48	Vergara, Veracruz	.982	23	105	3	2	5
V.M. Lopez, Chihuahua	.992	67	559	40	5	60	L. Johnson, Veracruz	.981	13	96	8	2	7
Prieto, Mexico City Reds	.991	13	106	7	1	10	Soto, Nuevo Laredo	.981	14	98	5	2	5
Alvarez, Coatzacoalcos	.991	47	417	24	4	27	Robles, Monterrey	.980	13	98	2	2	4
Biagini, Ciudad Juarez	.991	17	101	5	1	8	Saiz, Poza Rica*	.965	21	129	8	5	12

(Fewer Than Ten Games)

Player and Club	Pct.	G.	PO.	A.	E.	DP.	Player and Club	Pct.	G.	PO.	A.	E.	DP.
A. Guzman, Coatzacoalcos	1.000	6	60	3	0	4	R. Lopez, Ciudad Juarez	1.000	1	6	0	0	1
Soto, Tabasco	1.000	8	40	2	0	3	Aispuro, Chihuahua	1.000	1	5	0	0	0
Cossey, Saltillo	1.000	4	39	2	0	0	Ault, Mexico City Tigers	1.000	1	1	0	0	0
Carrillo, Poza Rica	1.000	7	21	3	0	2	Barrera, Nuevo Laredo	.989	9	80	7	1	9
Alexander, Yucatan	1.000	2	18	4	0	1	Duncan, Coatzacoalcos	.986	8	66	7	1	8
Zamora, Mexico City Tigers	1.000	4	15	0	0	1	Rendon, Aguascalientes	.983	7	57	2	1	9
Deliza, Monclova	1.000	2	15	0	0	2	Collins, Coatzacoalcos*	.982	7	52	4	1	1
Tiburcio, Poza Rica	1.000	2	14	0	0	0	J. Perez, Aguascalientes*	.981	6	49	2	1	7
Juarez, Chihuahua	1.000	1	13	1	0	1	Crug, Monterrey	.974	4	35	2	1	5
Contreras, Monclova	1.000	2	13	1	0	1	Guerra, Nuevo Laredo	.973	8	63	10	2	1
Alston, Coatzacoalcos*	1.000	1	13	1	0	0	Stennett, Reynosa	.967	4	29	0	1	2
Westmoreland, Saltillo	1.000	1	9	1	0	2	James, Chihuahua*	.953	7	38	3	2	0
DeLos Santos, Monclova*	1.000	3	8	0	0	0	Carbo, Veracruz	.952	2	20	0	1	1
Pactwa, Reynosa	1.000	1	8	0	0	0	N. Vazquez, Campeche	.947	4	18	0	1	0
Lee, Ciudad Juarez	1.000	1	8	0	0	0	Villaescusa, Yucatan	.889	1	8	0	1	0
A. Ortiz, Tabasco*	1.000	2	6	0	0	1	Moore, Reynosa	.846	2	11	0	2	0
H. Valenzuela, MC Tigers	1.000	1	6	0	0	0							

Triple Plays—Cossey, Bojorquez.

SECOND BASEMEN

Player and Club	Pct.	G.	PO.	A.	E.	DP.	Player and Club	Pct.	G.	PO.	A.	E.	DP.
Quintero, Saltillo	1.000	22	61	48	0	12	Mendez, Veracruz	.980	57	123	168	6	26
Avina, Campeche	1.000	12	20	34	0	6	Barrera, Nuevo Laredo	.979	26	67	76	3	15
Limon, Mexico City Reds	1.000	10	21	19	0	4	Contreras, Monclova	.978	47	112	115	5	21
T. Martinez, Campeche	.992	75	203	168	3	36	Buerrero, Yucatan	.976	105	248	287	13	49
J. L. Hernandez, Campeche	.991	42	93	125	2	32	J. M. Ortiz, Tabasco	.976	120	317	328	16	70
J. F. RODRIGUEZ, Reynosa	.990	125	340	414	8	67	Cazares, Yucatan	.975	23	53	66	3	13
N. J. Torres, Monterrey	.986	33	69	77	2	22	P. Garcia, Mexico City Reds	.974	21	45	66	3	12
Cervantes, Aguascalientes	.986	125	290	339	9	86	Serna, Monterrey	.968	83	207	218	14	45
Sanchez, Mexico City Reds	.985	66	163	225	6	58	Herrera, 1 Reds-79 Veracruz	.968	80	187	207	13	44
Edwards, Poza Rica	.984	39	88	101	3	18	Villela, Monclova	.967	51	112	123	8	32
Navarrete, Saltillo	.984	109	307	321	10	83	J. J. Rodriguez, Poza Rica	.965	63	158	174	12	26
J. Gonzalez, Coatzacoalcos	.984	125	326	359	11	69	Chavez, Chihuahua	.965	73	169	214	14	60
Briones, Nuevo Laredo	.982	121	295	370	12	82	Leon, Yucatan	.959	16	21	26	2	5
Rios, Mexico City Tigers	.980	124	317	331	13	74	A. Gonzalez, Chihuahua	.958	60	127	149	12	25

SECOND BASEMEN—Continued

Player and Club	Pct.	G.	PO.	A.	E.	DP.	Player and Club	Pct.	G.	PO.	A.	E.	DP.
Perry, Nuevo Laredo	.958	93	214	219	19	47	F. Gonzalez, 29 PR-27 Reds	.948	56	121	152	15	21
Deliza, Monclova	.957	38	96	126	10	29	Johnson, Nuevo Laredo	.945	12	28	24	3	10
Hilton, Mexico City Reds	.952	13	37	43	4	1	Cota, Monterrey	.933	25	53	45	7	12

(Fewer Than Ten Games)

Player and Club	Pct.	G.	PO.	A.	E.	DP.	Player and Club	Pct.	G.	PO.	A.	E.	DP.
Llanes, Aguascalientes	1.000	9	14	22	0	4	Esparza, Poza Rica	1.000	2	1	5	0	0
Perera, Tabasco	1.000	6	11	19	0	2	Rubio, Tabasco	1.000	2	2	1	0	0
N. Gonzalez, Mexico City Tigers	1.000	8	8	21	0	4	Stennett, Reynosa	1.000	1	1	2	0	1
Bohadilla, Ciudad Juarez	1.000	5	5	12	0	5	Sommers, Tabasco	1.000	1	1	1	0	1
P. Mendoza, Campeche	1.000	2	8	3	0	1	Villaescusa, Yucatan	1.000	2	1	0	0	0
Chavez, Mexico City Tigers	1.000	3	6	5	0	2	J. Alvarez, Mexico City Tigers	1.000	1	1	0	0	0
Almeida, Reynosa	1.000	3	4	7	0	1	Moore, Reynosa	.977	8	15	27	1	3
Fabela, Saltillo	1.000	5	3	5	0	1	R. Gonzalez, Ciudad Juarez	.950	7	6	13	1	1
V.M. Lopez, Chihuahua	1.000	3	0	7	0	0	Velarde, Tabasco	.938	4	7	8	1	1
Acuna, Campeche	1.000	1	4	2	0	1	Serratos, Coatzacoalcos	.935	6	15	14	2	0
Guerra, Nuevo Laredo	1.000	3	4	2	0	0	Castro, Veracruz	.875	7	8	6	2	0
Salazar, Monclova	1.000	1	3	3	0	1	Yepez, Poza Rica	.800	5	5	3	2	0

Triple Play—Navarrete.

THIRD BASEMEN

Player and Club	Pct.	G.	PO.	A.	E.	DP.	Player and Club	Pct.	G.	PO.	A.	E.	DP.
Herrera, 2 Reds-8 Vera	1.000	10	5	17	0	1	Sommers, Tabasco	.943	103	101	180	17	29
F. Gonzalez, 12 PR-27 Reds	.974	39	29	82	3	9	Barrera, Nuevo Laredo	.942	81	59	169	14	10
S. Mendoza, Poza Rica	.971	60	52	114	5	14	Campaneris, Veracruz	.942	50	32	97	10	8
Ortiz, Nuevo Laredo	.973	57	57	126	5	10	T. Martinez, Campeche	.941	34	34	78	7	6
RIVERA, Yucatan	.971	117	96	301	12	22	Serna, Monterrey	.938	32	28	62	6	3
B. Santana, Saltillo	.969	122	119	318	14	39	M. Ramirez, Chihuahua	.937	127	109	277	26	25
Deliza, Monclova	.968	53	45	137	6	7	Vega, Monterrey	.936	84	73	148	15	20
J. Castro, Veracruz	.966	78	65	162	8	10	Hilton, Mexico City Reds	.929	31	25	79	8	4
J. Alvarez, Mexico City Tigers	.958	127	120	295	18	15	Jimenez, Campeche	.923	68	48	120	14	6
Duncan, Coatzacoalcos	.958	108	74	221	13	16	Bobadilla, Ciudad Juarez	.921	58	40	89	11	5
Contreras, Monclova	.956	50	37	94	6	7	Yepez, Poza Rica	.918	48	39	87	11	5
Cox, Mexico City Reds	.956	45	24	105	6	9	Serratos, Coatzacoalcos	.917	26	19	36	5	2
Edwards, 1 Reds-10 PR	.955	11	5	16	1	1	DeFreites, Tabasco	.914	28	19	45	6	4
Aguilar, Aguascalientes	.953	122	104	285	19	22	Bernhardt, Campeche	.908	23	21	38	6	3
Llenas, Mexico City Reds	.951	24	19	39	3	0	Salazar, Monclova	.894	30	21	38	7	4
N.J. Torres, Monterrey	.949	21	15	41	3	3	Guerrero, Yucatan	.878	14	10	26	5	2
Burke, Reynosa	.946	129	109	256	21	15	Zamora, Mexico City Tigers	.857	10	4	14	3	4
Lee, Ciudad Juarez	.945	91	60	147	12	12							

(Fewer Than Ten Games)

Player and Club	Pct.	G.	PO.	A.	E.	DP.	Player and Club	Pct.	G.	PO.	A.	E.	DP.
Quintero, Saltillo	1.000	8	2	14	0	0	N. Gonzalez, Mexico City Tigers	1.000	1	1	1	0	0
Chaidez, Tabasco	1.000	7	3	13	0	0	Vega, Monterrey	1.000	1	0	2	0	0
Valdez, Chihuahua	1.000	5	3	7	0	0	Villaescusa, Yucatan	1.000	1	0	2	0	0
Velarde, Tabasco	1.000	4	1	7	0	1	Maza, Ciudad Juarez	1.000	3	0	1	0	0
Elizondo, Veracruz	1.000	3	2	6	0	0	M. Mendoza, Mexico City Reds	.938	4	8	7	1	1
Esparza, Poza Rica	1.000	6	2	5	0	1	Rendon, Aguascalientes	.916	8	10	23	3	2
Moore, Reynosa	1.000	2	3	4	0	0	Paredes, Campeche	.917	5	3	8	1	0
Avina, Campeche	1.000	3	4	2	0	1	Johnson, Nuevo Laredo	.889	4	3	5	1	0
Limon, Mexico City Reds	1.000	3	2	3	0	0	Cerda, Veracruz	.875	6	4	10	2	0
Fabela, Saltillo	1.000	3	2	2	0	0	Villalobos, Reynosa	.875	4	3	4	1	0
R. Gonzalez, Ciudad Juarez	1.000	2	0	3	0	1	Murrell, Saltillo	.867	4	8	5	2	2
Llanes, Aguascalientes	1.000	1	0	3	0	1	J.J. Rodriguez, Poza Rica	.857	7	4	2	1	0
G. Rodriguez, Coatzacoalcos	1.000	1	2	0	0	0	Hicks, Tabasco	.714	1	0	5	2	0
Alvarez, Coatzacoalcos	1.000	1	2	0	0	0	Acuna, Campeche	.500	1	0	4	4	0
Stennett, Reynosa	1.000	1	1	1	0	0	Almeida, Reynosa	.500	3	0	1	1	1

Triple Play—Murrell.

SHORTSTOPS

Player and Club	Pct.	G.	PO.	A.	E.	DP.	Player and Club	Pct.	G.	PO.	A.	E.	DP.
A. Sanchez, Mexico City Reds	1.000	18	22	45	0	6	M. Mendoza, Mexico City Reds	.952	29	38	121	8	22
F. RODRIGUEZ, Aguascalientes	.984	125	191	438	10	70	Canedo, Mexico City Reds	.949	91	163	318	26	59
Valle, Ciudad Juarez	.984	103	149	318	8	68	S. Mendoza, Poza Rica	.949	44	64	121	10	15
T. Martinez, Campeche	.981	12	16	37	1	5	Cazares, Yucatan	.946	66	114	183	17	32
Cota, Monterrey	.979	10	18	28	1	4	Campaneris, 13 Vera-36 PR	.945	49	90	151	14	27
Rivero, Reynosa	.977	132	223	424	15	60	Esparza, Poza Rica	.944	10	14	20	2	0
J.L. Hernandez, Campeche	.974	10	6	31	1	4	Ferrer, 13 Tab-41 Cam-31 PR	.943	85	160	284	27	48
Quintero, Saltillo	.970	65	86	207	9	33	Deliza, Monclova	.943	21	49	66	7	16
Elizondo, Veracruz	.968	115	177	399	19	58	Perera, Tabasco	.942	40	49	98	9	17
A. Gomez, Nuevo Laredo	.967	131	225	425	22	70	Chavez, Saltillo	.942	61	71	203	17	35
Blanks, Coatzacoalcos	.965	126	211	420	23	65	J. Hernandez, Monclova	.939	109	186	340	34	65
Bobadilla, Ciudad Juarez	.963	40	61	96	6	11	Chappis, Monterrey	.926	24	43	83	10	11
M. Morales, Mexico City Tigers	.963	121	181	444	24	67	Vega, Monterrey	.923	40	68	123	16	22
R. Ramirez, Chihuahua	.961	123	218	429	26	68	Velarde, Tabasco	.914	16	12	20	3	2
P. Mendoza, 9 Tig-60 Cam	.957	69	115	197	14	34	Novelo, Tabasco	.914	95	118	223	32	36
Torres, Monterrey	.956	52	95	166	12	29	Washington, Poza Rica	.878	11	12	31	6	2
Fabela, Saltillo	.956	11	18	25	2	8	Quinonez, Monterrey	.862	13	18	32	8	5
Villaescusa, Yucatan	.953	72	106	221	16	39							

(Fewer Than Ten Games)

Player and Club	Pct.	G.	PO.	A.	E.	DP.	Player and Club	Pct.	G.	PO.	A.	E.	DP.
Jimenez, Campeche	1.000	5	5	7	0	0	J.M. Ortiz, Tabasco	1.000	2	0	1	0	0
A. Ortiz, Nuevo Laredo	1.000	3	2	8	0	0	R. Herrera, Veracruz	1.000	2	0	1	0	0
Avina, Campeche	1.000	3	4	6	0	1	A. Gonzalez, Chihuahua	.967	5	13	16	1	2
Contreras, Monclova	1.000	2	3	5	0	1	Aguilar, Aguascalientes	.923	2	3	9	1	1
Limon, Mexico City Reds	1.000	3	4	3	0	0	Llanes, Aguascalientes	.920	6	8	15	2	3
Rios, Mexico City Tigers	1.000	2	2	5	0	1	M. Ramirez, Chihuahua	.917	3	4	7	1	0

SHORTSTOPS—Continued

Player and Club	Pct.	G.	PO.	A.	E.	DP.	Player and Club	Pct.	G.	PO.	A.	E.	DP.
Sommers, Tabasco	.833	2	1	4	1	1	Almeida, Reynosa	.778	7	1	6	2	0
Yepez, Poza Rica	.833	1	1	4	1	1	Acuna, Campeche	.750	2	2	4	2	2
Serratos, Coatzacoalcos	.778	4	8	6	4	3							

Triple Play—M. Morales.

OUTFIELDERS

Player and Club	Pct.	G.	PO.	A.	E.	DP.	Player and Club	Pct.	G.	PO.	A.	E.	DP.
A. MORA, 5 Sal-92 NL	1.000	97	188	9	0	2	G. Rodriguez, Coatzacoalcos	.971	19	32	1	1	0
Sauceda, 32 Sal-8 Mva	1.000	40	101	2	0	1	A. Torres, Monclova	.970	119	239	19	8	3
A. Ortiz, Nuevo Laredo	1.000	35	58	4	0	0	Salcido, Veracruz	.968	97	226	14	8	1
R. Alvarez, Monclova*	1.000	38	56	1	0	0	Beswick, Yucatan	.967	80	175	3	6	0
Arnold, 11 Cam-11 NL	1.000	22	47	3	0	1	Lizarraga, 90 Tab-24 Yuc	.967	114	240	21	9	3
Cain, Campeche	1.000	20	46	1	0	0	Joshua, Yucatan*	.966	82	137	5	5	0
Vergara, Veracruz	1.000	34	39	3	0	0	Guerra, Nuevo Laredo	.965	96	183	9	7	2
Cox, Mexico City Reds	1.000	15	28	3	0	1	Soto, Tabasco	.965	68	130	7	5	2
Arzate, Veracruz	1.000	15	26	0	0	0	Rubio, Tabasco	.963	47	74	5	3	2
J. Gonzalez, Veracruz	1.000	17	23	0	0	0	Mejias, Campeche	.962	84	169	9	7	1
Estes, Yucatan	1.000	11	20	2	0	0	Negron, Nuevo Laredo*	.962	101	195	7	8	2
M. Hernandez, Coatzacoalcos	1.000	15	18	2	0	0	Murrell, Saltillo	.959	60	91	3	4	0
Ford, 6 Rey-9 Sal	1.000	15	17	2	0	0	G. Gomez, Chihuahua	.959	128	264	17	12	3
Espinosa, Mexico City Tigers*	1.000	19	17	0	0	0	Howard, Yucatan	.959	125	243	12	11	1
E. Hernandez, Veracruz	1.000	11	9	0	0	0	Carrillo, Poza Rica	.959	77	129	10	6	1
Saiz, Poza Rica*	1.000	10	6	1	0	0	R. Lora, Mexico City Tigers	.958	10	22	1	1	0
Alexander, Mexico City Tigers*	.995	80	186	8	1	0	Lentine, Monterrey	.958	97	171	10	8	1
J.L. Perez, Aguascalientes*	.995	109	173	12	1	2	Wallis, Tabasco	.957	16	41	4	2	0
Rod. Rodriguez, Saltillo*	.994	94	167	4	1	3	Chavez, Nuevo Laredo*	.956	62	78	8	4	2
Figueroa, Campeche	.993	62	136	9	1	2	Romo, Poza Rica	.955	54	123	4	6	0
H. Cruz, Reynosa	.993	88	131	2	1	0	Suarez, 5 Tig-97 Vera	.954	102	176	13	5	4
Bryant, Mexico City Tigers	.991	103	217	10	2	1	Contreras, Saltillo	.953	21	41	0	2	0
Rosario, Saltillo	.991	102	203	7	2	4	Smith, Ciudad Juarez*	.953	121	212	10	11	2
Cossey, 21 Tab-57 Sal*	.989	78	173	4	2	0	Ray. Torres, Mexico City Reds	.952	66	133	5	7	1
D. Cruz, Yucatan	.986	39	69	1	1	0	DeFreites, Tabasco	.951	25	55	3	3	1
Alvarado, Coatzacoalcos	.984	105	175	14	3	0	Stenholm, Mexico City Reds*	.950	77	123	11	7	2
Beltre, Aguascalientes	.982	106	252	19	5	4	C. Lopez, Tabasco	.950	94	138	15	8	6
E. Munoz, Reynosa	.981	130	255	6	5	1	Norwood, Reynosa	.950	27	37	1	2	0
Javier, Tabasco	.981	17	51	1	1	0	Rendon, Aguascalientes	.949	43	69	5	4	1
Paredes, Campeche	.981	67	97	6	2	2	Rosales, Ciudad Juarez	.948	106	170	13	10	2
Ros. Torres, Monterrey	.979	63	134	6	3	3	Moore, Reynosa	.948	60	70	3	4	0
Monasterio, Poza Rica	.978	126	297	21	7	0	Cotes, Monterrey	.947	64	84	6	5	1
Biagini, Ciudad Juarez	.978	74	124	12	3	2	Olivares, Mexico City Reds*	.944	72	144	7	9	2
Aispuro, Chihuahua	.978	29	39	6	1	0	Chavarria, Monterrey	.943	97	138	10	9	2
A. Castro, Mexico City Tigers*	.978	123	214	10	5	2	Zambrano, Monterrey*	.942	64	94	3	6	1
Greene, Coatzacoalcos*	.978	72	124	7	3	0	Nettles, 29 Chi-33 Cam*	.941	62	106	6	7	0
Gamundi, Poza Rica	.977	123	236	15	6	1	Paredes, Nuevo Laredo	.941	20	30	2	2	0
Collins, Coatzacoalcos*	.976	81	116	8	3	1	Roys, Chihuahua	.941	121	203	20	14	4
Carbo, Veracruz	.976	30	39	2	1	0	Davila, Monterrey	.937	47	71	3	5	0
Bellacetin, Aguascalientes*	.976	110	198	5	5	2	Figueroa, Ciudad Juarez	.935	61	97	4	7	0
Dues, Monclova	.976	99	153	8	4	2	Lara, 4 Ags-23 Mva	.931	27	21	6	2	0
A. Perez, Ciudad Juarez	.976	29	39	1	1	0	Cano, Saltillo*	.931	24	25	2	2	1
N. Vazquez, 11 Tig-30 Cam	.975	41	76	3	2	1	Medina, Chihuahua	.931	19	27	0	2	0
Rob. Rodriguez, M C Reds	.975	65	115	2	3	0	Herring, Tabasco	.930	18	37	3	3	0
Diaz, 44 Chi-24 Yuc	.974	68	102	11	3	4	James, Chihuahua*	.930	34	63	3	5	1
Castelan, Campeche*	.974	77	143	6	4	2	Alexander, Yucatan	.923	13	20	4	2	0
R. Martinez, Veracruz	.974	70	146	3	4	1	D. Garcia, Mexico City Tigers	.920	25	44	2	4	0
Felix, 6 Mva-78 Reds	.974	84	139	9	4	1	Leonard, Aguascalientes	.908	21	52	7	6	2
Alston, Coatzacoalcos	.972	100	167	5	5	0	Salazar, Monclova	.902	24	34	3	4	1
Sarabia, Veracruz	.971	50	66	2	2	0	Prieto, Mexico City Reds	.900	20	27	0	3	0
Leal, Reynosa*	.971	87	125	10	4	1	Bernal, Aguascalientes	.875	12	13	1	2	0
Villela, Monterrey	.971	78	128	6	4	2	J. Hernandez, Monclova	.846	10	18	4	4	0

(Fewer Than Ten Games)

Player and Club	Pct.	G.	PO.	A.	E.	DP.	Player and Club	Pct.	G.	PO.	A.	E.	DP.
Beck, Tabasco	1.000	7	20	0	0	0	Sanguillen, Reynosa	1.000	2	3	0	0	0
D. Duran, Nuevo Laredo*	1.000	8	18	0	0	0	Clayton, Saltillo*	1.000	3	2	1	0	0
Uzcanga, Veracruz	1.000	6	10	1	0	0	Johnson, Veracruz	1.000	2	2	1	0	0
Quiroz, Mexico City Reds	1.000	6	9	1	0	0	Dominguez, Campeche	1.000	6	2	0	0	0
Scott, Campeche	1.000	8	9	0	0	0	Bojorquez, Mexico City Tigers	1.000	4	2	0	0	0
Yepez, Poza Rica	1.000	6	6	2	0	1	Quintero, Saltillo	1.000	1	2	0	0	0
Almeida, Reynosa	1.000	5	6	2	0	1	Tisdale, Veracruz	1.000	2	2	0	0	0
Zamora, Mexico City Tigers	1.000	5	6	0	0	0	Jimenez, Tabasco	1.000	2	2	0	0	0
J. Rodriguez, Mexico City Tigers	1.000	3	5	0	0	0	A Castillo, Mexico City Tigers	1.000	1	1	0	0	0
Maza, Cidad Juarez	1.000	2	5	0	0	0	Fabela, Saltillo	1.000	1	1	0	0	0
Juarez, Saltillo	1.000	5	4	0	0	0	Sotelo, Reynosa	1.000	1	1	0	0	0
R. Gonzalez, Ciudad Juarez	1.000	4	3	1	0	0	O. Alvarez, Aguascalientes*	1.000	1	0	1	0	0
L. Morales, Reynosa	1.000	7	3	0	0	0	G. Hernandez, Mexico City Reds	.833	9	10	0	2	0
Ellis, Mexico City Reds	1.000	3	3	0	0	0	Vargas, Mexico City Tigers	.813	9	13	0	3	0
Robles, Monterrey	1.000	2	3	0	0	0	Stennett, Reynosa	.765	7	13	0	4	0
							Hicks, Tabasco	.750	3	3	0	1	0

CATCHERS

Player and Club	Pct.	G.	PO.	A.	E.	DP.	PB.	Player and Club	Pct.	G.	PO.	A.	E.	DP.	PB.
E. Castro, Tabasco	1.000	16	21	6	0	0	0	Rosas, Reynosa	.989	104	554	75	7	7	6
J. Alvarez, Mexico City Reds	1.000	10	18	2	0	0	0	Pasillas, 17 Reds-36 Tig	.988	53	207	30	3	1	2
Raymundo, Yucatan	1.000	13	20	0	0	0	0	Johnson, Veracruz	.986	82	358	66	6	8	4
R. Gonzalez, Ciudad Juarez	.995	41	157	27	1	1	6	J.C. Alvarez, Yucatan	.986	109	493	67	8	1	17
P. RUIZ, Saltillo	.993	65	344	81	3	7	6	Marquez, Aguascalientes	.983	100	438	75	9	12	8
Estrada, Campeche	.991	109	551	79	6	8	11	E. Gonzalez, Monclova	.982	33	138	26	3	2	1
Robles, Mexico City Reds	.990	23	91	13	1	2	0	Benitez, Nuevo Laredo	.982	35	145	16	3	2	6
E. Rodriguez, Monclova	.990	103	507	63	6	7	20	Rosado, Poza Rica	.981	98	399	65	9	3	5

CATCHERS—Continued

Player and Club	Pct.	G.	PO.	A.	E.	DP.	PB.
J. Diaz, Reynosa	.980	34	89	10	2	0	0
A. Gunzman, Coatzacoalcos ...	.980	77	428	60	10	3	2
Trevino, Tabasco	.979	118	487	78	12	10	11
Rojas, Monterrey	.978	32	81	8	2	1	5
Rivera, 1 Chi-93 CJ	.978	94	514	60	13	4	12
Sarabia, Veracruz	.976	38	132	29	4	3	3
Soto, Nuevo Laredo	.975	40	212	24	6	3	1
Firova, Nuevo Laredo	.975	67	257	51	8	6	10
R. Vega, Aguascalientes	.973	40	117	26	4	1	2
P. Hernandez, Chihuahua	.971	70	287	48	10	13	4
Molina, Veracruz	.971	16	59	9	2	0	1
M. Hernandez, Coatzacoalcos	.971	64	297	40	10	0	3
Luna, Monterrey	.971	81	375	54	13	2	14
A. Castillo, MC Tigers	.969	47	205	45	8	6	5
R. Lora, Mexico City Tigers ...	.967	49	201	30	8	4	1
Monroy, Chihuahua	.966	47	199	29	8	4	3
M.A. Guzman, MC Reds	.965	96	333	85	15	9	5
Benitez, Saltillo	.963	66	207	29	9	5	4
Daut, Monterrey	.962	32	147	31	7	4	2
Madero, Poza Rica	.958	45	157	27	8	2	6
Valdez, Chihuahua	.958	19	74	18	4	2	4
Alezander, Yucatan	.953	15	53	8	3	0	0
Otero, Yucatan	.951	11	33	6	2	0	2
Heras, 3 Tig-10 Mon	.935	13	64	8	5	0	1
Navarrete, Campeche	.933	26	84	13	7	1	4
A. Martinez, Monclova	.929	11	10	3	1	0	1

(Fewer Than Ten Games)

Player and Club	Pct.	G.	PO.	A.	E.	DP.	PB.
Sanguillen, Reynosa	1.000	7	24	5	0	0	0
Camacho, Aguascalientes	1.000	3	15	5	0	0	0
Roys, Chihuahua	1.000	2	10	3	0	0	0
Fabela, Saltillo	1.000	1	1	0	0	1	1
Rojo, Reynosa	1.000	1	1	0	0	0	0
M. Mendoza, Ciudad Juarez....	.973	9	31	5	1	0	3
L. Ortiz, Tabasco	.973	6	31	5	1	1	1
Westmoreland, Monterrey	.966	8	52	5	2	0	3
Orozco, Tabasco	.956	9	37	6	2	0	0
Villalobos, Reynosa	.938	8	27	3	2	0	0
J. Sanchez, Mexico City Reds	.818	2	9	0	2	0	0

PITCHERS

Player and Club	Pct.	G.	PO.	A.	E.	DP.
R. Vazquez, Poza Rica	1.000	28	15	45	0	2
Orozco, Campeche	1.000	28	12	42	0	4
Jimenez, Campeche	1.000	29	8	44	0	3
Rasmussen, Yucatan	1.000	22	8	41	0	1
Higueras, Ciudad Juarez	1.000	24	7	35	0	2
E. Beltran, Monclova	1.000	25	8	24	0	1
Cordova, Veracruz	1.000	28	4	25	0	1
Montague, 4 Tigers-17 Ags.	1.000	21	8	21	0	2
Carranza, Campeche°	1.000	25	4	24	0	2
Morales, Veracruz	1.000	34	7	18	0	1
Arano, Mexico City Reds	1.000	29	2	23	0	0
Aguilar, Monterrey	1.000	35	6	18	0	1
Drago, Mexico City Tigers	1.000	17	7	16	0	0
Murillo, Mexico City Reds	1.000	33	5	17	0	1
D. Vazquez, Mexico City Tigers	1.000	29	2	19	0	4
McLaughlin, Nuevo Laredo	1.000	28	8	13	0	1
Divison, Saltillo	1.000	48	4	16	0	2
R. Guzman, Monclova	1.000	45	7	13	0	1
Heredia, Monterrey	1.000	28	4	16	0	1
Segui, Reynosa	1.000	26	4	10	0	0
Lance, Monterrey	1.000	25	8	12	0	1
Lacey, Saltillo	1.000	14	3	15	0	1
Pulido, 36 Cam.-9 Tig.	1.000	45	4	13	0	0
L.F. Guzman, Chihuahua	1.000	37	6	11	0	0
Rivera, 4 Yuc.-20 Juarez	1.000	24	3	14	0	0
J.L. Garcia, Tabasco	1.000	24	2	15	0	1
Low, Aguascalientes	1.000	23	1	16	0	0
M. Martinez, Yucatan	1.000	17	6	11	0	2
Abarca, Campeche	1.000	16	2	15	0	1
Silva, Nuevo Laredo	1.000	16	6	11	0	4
H. Lopez, Mexico City Tigers	1.000	36	3	13	0	2
Casas, 1 Tig.-29 Ags.	1.000	30	3	13	0	0
J. Pena, Ciudad Juarez	1.000	22	3	13	0	0
Pulido, Mexico City Reds°	1.000	43	3	12	0	0
Purata, Poza Rica°	1.000	23	4	11	0	1
Contreras, Monclova	1.000	22	6	9	0	0
F.M. Hernandez, Lar.°	1.000	24	2	12	0	0
Sauceda, Mexico City Tigers	1.000	33	1	10	0	1
Palacios, Tabasco	1.000	23	2	9	0	0
Duran, Chihuahua	1.000	11	1	10	0	1
R. Rodriguez, Poza Rica	1.000	28	4	6	0	1
Zamudio, Veracruz	1.000	22	1	9	0	0
J. Ochoa, Campeche	1.000	14	3	7	0	0
Rog. Garcia, Saltillo	1.000	22	4	5	0	1
I. Gonzalez, Monterrey	1.000	21	4	5	0	0
Arceo, Yucatan	1.000	12	2	7	0	0
Batista, 8 Chi.-1 Mva.-2 Rey.	1.000	11	0	9	0	1
J.R. Guzman, Veracruz	1.000	41	1	7	0	0
Baruch, Poza Rica	1.000	28	1	7	0	0
H. Madrigal, Tabasco	1.000	22	3	5	0	0
J. Moreno, Veracruz	1.000	19	1	7	0	1
D. Ochoa, Coatzacoalcos	1.000	36	0	7	0	1
M. Villegas, 3 Chi.-10 Ags.	1.000	13	0	7	0	1
Pole, 8 Tigers-2 Lar.	1.000	11	0	7	0	0
M. Beltran, Mexico City Reds.	1.000	10	0	7	0	0
F. Sanchez, 4 Tigers-17 Lar.	1.000	21	3	3	0	0
F. Munoz, Tabasco	1.000	18	3	3	0	1
Delfin, Campeche	1.000	14	4	2	0	0
Armienta, Chihuahua	1.000	12	1	5	0	0
Figueroa, Veracruz	1.000	12	1	5	0	1
R. Rios, Coatzacoalcos	1.000	19	0	5	0	1
Aguilar, Mexico City Tigers°	1.000	15	1	4	0	0
Montenegro, Ciudad Juarez.	1.000	11	0	5	0	1
Delgadillo, Aguascalientes	1.000	19	1	3	0	1
Tejeda, Coatzacoalcos°	1.000	18	1	3	0	0
M. Pena, Chihuahua°	1.000	27	1	2	0	0
Inzunza, Reynosa	1.000	20	0	3	0	0
R. Ruiz, Monterrey	1.000	18	0	3	0	0
Gamez, Campeche	1.000	15	3	0	0	0
Canedo, Aguascalientes	1.000	13	1	2	0	0
J. Espinosa, Aguascalientes	1.000	17	0	2	0	0
R. Martinez, Saltillo	1.000	12	0	2	0	0
Santiago, Tabasco	1.000	11	0	2	0	0
Glekel, Yucatan°	.980	27	4	44	1	4
Rogers, Tabasco	.977	27	11	32	1	1
Colorado, Coatzacoalcos	.976	23	6	35	1	4
Juarez, Chihuahua	.975	27	10	29	1	1
Paul, Mexico City Reds°	.974	25	3	35	1	0
Camper, Chihuahua	.974	30	12	25	1	0
Kuk Lee, Poza Rica	.973	17	4	32	1	2
Hernaiz, Coatzacoalcos	.982	25	15	40	1	2
Villanueva, Coatzacoalcos°	.980	24	3	46	1	3
Dominguez, Campeche°	.970	25	3	29	1	0
C. Diaz, Mexico City Reds	.968	29	7	23	1	4
Quiroz, Veracruz	.967	25	4	54	2	3
Leon, Mexico City Reds	.966	25	11	45	2	4
Alicea, Ciudad Juarez	.964	42	7	20	1	0
P. Rodriguez, Yucatan	.963	51	6	20	1	1
R. Villegas, Mexico City Tigers	.962	26	4	21	1	3
M. Solis, Saltillo	.958	28	7	39	2	2
Sutton, Nuevo Laredo	.958	18	8	38	2	3
G. Valenzuela, Reynosa	.958	27	3	20	1	0
Peralta, Coatzacoalcos°	.958	22	1	22	1	2
De Los Santos, Monclova°	.957	25	9	35	2	4
Tiant, Tabasco	.957	18	10	12	1	1
A. Diaz, Coatzacoalcos	.957	16	3	19	1	1
Early, Tabasco	.957	14	3	19	1	2
Polloronia, Saltillo	.952	27	13	27	2	3
Cuellar, Nuevo Laredo	.952	37	4	16	1	1
C. Moreno, 11 Ags.-16 Sal.	.952	27	3	17	1	3
H. Rios, Reynosa	.944	28	10	24	2	0
Feola, 3 Lar.-24 Ags.	.944	27	2	15	1	1
Prieto, 5 Tigers-22 Reds	.944	27	3	14	1	1
J. Urrea, 7 Vera-8 PR	.944	15	2	15	1	0
Matus, Reynosa	.943	30	11	39	3	2
Soto, Yucatan	.943	27	8	25	2	1
Esquer, Monterrey°	.943	26	5	28	2	1
Brunet, Veracruz°	.941	25	2	30	2	3
Salas, Veracruz	.941	24	7	25	2	3
Preciado, Campeche	.941	30	5	11	1	1
Raf. Garcia, Ciudad Juarez	.939	28	12	34	3	1
A. Rodriguez, Reynosa	.938	45	6	9	1	0
Nunez, Mexico City Tigers	.938	34	2	13	1	1
Mata, Monterrey	.936	31	6	38	3	3
Sandate, Poza Rica°	.936	23	9	35	3	1
G. Martinez, Chihuahua	.935	32	7	36	3	1
Sosa, Monclova	.935	28	9	34	3	1
Ortiz, Tabasco°	.935	27	7	36	3	2
L. Garcia, Nuevo Laredo	.933	29	9	19	2	1
Moya, Saltillo	.933	22	4	10	1	2
J. Vazquez, Monterrey	.933	17	4	10	1	3
C. Perez, Tabasco°	.931	20	3	24	2	0
J. Madrigal, Poza Rica	.929	26	8	18	2	1
Arratia, Monclova	.929	10	4	9	1	1
Gutierrez, Ciudad Juarez	.923	27	5	19	2	0
M.A. Madrigal, Chihuahua	.923	27	13	11	2	0
Moran, 5 Chi.-18 Tigers	.923	23	8	16	2	1
Ako, Aguascalientes	.921	24	6	29	3	2
Villegas, Campeche	.920	33	8	25	3	0
Soto, Monclova	.920	31	6	17	2	0

PITCHERS—Continued

Player and Club	Pct.	G.	PO.	A.	E.	DP.
Montano, 3 Reds-17 Tigers	.920	20	5	18	2	1
Salinas, Mexico City Reds	.919	27	6	28	3	2
Arroyo, Aguascalientes*	.917	26	8	25	3	2
P. Ruiz, Chihuahua*	.917	28	2	9	1	1
Ma. Vazquez, Ciudad Juarez	.917	19	3	8	1	0
Branch, Nuevo Laredo	.917	12	4	7	1	1
Moret, 2 Ags.-20 Mva.*	.913	22	3	18	2	1
Menendez, Saltillo	.907	31	11	28	4	2
Rincon, Yucatan	.906	27	8	21	3	3
Pruneda, Chihuahua	.905	36	6	13	2	1
Dominguez, Tabasco	.905	35	3	16	2	1
Rondon, 12 Sal.-2 Tab.-5 Vera	.903	19	7	21	3	3
Mendoza, Yucatan	.900	22	8	28	4	5
A. Hernandez, Monclova	.900	42	4	14	2	1
J. Solis, Nuevo Laredo	.889	43	2	14	2	0
Mapel, 2 Tigers-13 Rey.	.889	15	4	12	2	1
Castillejos, 3 Tig.-30 Ags.	.889	33	2	6	1	0
Bresnen, Aguascalientes*	.882	17	6	9	2	0
Acosta, Poza Rica	.880	23	7	15	3	0
Quinonez, Ciudad Juarez	.868	26	11	22	5	1
E. Rodriguez, Monclova	.867	22	3	10	2	0
Bernal, Monterrey	.867	21	4	9	2	0
F. Franco, Poza Rico	.867	17	3	10	2	1
Williams, Nuevo Laredo*	.864	19	3	16	3	2
Wiltbank, Mexico City Tigers	.857	12	2	10	2	1
Maytorena, 10 Mva.-15 Sal.	.857	25	1	5	1	0
R. Solis, Coatzacoalcos	.850	15	2	15	3	1
Esquivel, 4 Yuc.-29 Vera	.846	33	2	9	2	0
Jefferson, Nuevo Laredo	.846	12	2	9	2	0
Gaxiola, Monterrey	.833	21	6	19	5	0
C.J. Perez, Ciudad Juarez	.833	21	3	12	3	1
Camacho, Mexico City Reds	.833	15	3	2	1	0
Mundo, Chihuahua	.813	20	4	9	3	1
Vidana, Reynosa	.800	32	4	12	4	0
Miranda, Coatzacoalcos	.800	34	0	8	2	0
Luna, Mexico City Tigers	.750	11	1	2	1	0
J. Beltran, Yucatan	.714	11	3	7	4	0
Alcala, Monterrey	.667	28	4	8	6	0
Enyart, Reynosa*	.667	20	2	0	1	0
Castaneda, Saltillo*	.600	13	0	3	2	1
Meza, Nuevo Laredo	.500	10	0	1	1	0
Navarro, Mexico City Reds	.000	10	0	0	1	0

(Fewer Than Ten Games)

Player and Club	Pct.	G.	PO.	A.	E.	DP.
Christiansen, Aguascalientes*	1.000	9	2	6	0	0
L. Urrea, Saltillo	1.000	9	3	5	0	1
Ibarra, Reynosa	1.000	9	1	7	0	1
Prevost, Veracruz	1.000	5	1	7	0	0
J.L. Martinez, Monterrey	1.000	7	2	4	0	0
O. Acosta, Tabasco	1.000	3	1	4	0	1
Wardlow, Monclova	1.000	5	2	2	0	0
Gallegos, Coatzacoalcos*	1.000	5	1	3	0	0
E. Lopez, Poza Rica	1.000	5	1	3	0	0
Angulo, Reynosa*	1.000	8	0	4	0	1
Hidalgo, Coatzacoalcos	1.000	5	0	4	0	0
Hopkins, Reynosa	1.000	5	0	3	0	0
U. Heredia, Veracruz	1.000	5	0	3	0	0
Quintero, Coatzacoalcos	1.000	1	0	3	0	0
Myerchin, Mexico City Tigers	1.000	2	0	3	0	0
L.T. Castillo, Nuevo Laredo	1.000	6	1	2	0	0
Escarrega, Mexico City Reds	1.000	1	1	2	0	0
F. Martinez, Aguascalientes	1.000	6	1	1	0	0
Valencia, Poza Rica	1.000	3	1	1	0	0
Kobel, Ciudad Juarez	1.000	1	1	1	0	0
Armas, Coatzacoalcos	1.000	1	0	2	0	0
Manriquez, Tabasco	1.000	5	0	2	0	0
A. Valenzuela, Aguascalientes*	1.000	5	0	1	0	0
Orea, Veracruz	1.000	4	0	1	0	0
Franco, Nuevo Laredo	1.000	5	1	0	0	0
Romo, Coatzacoalcos	.944	8	5	12	1	1
Calderon, Mexico City Tigers	.889	7	1	7	1	0
V. Garcia, Nuevo Laredo	.875	7	2	5	1	0
Velazquez, 3 Mva.-5 Tigers	.750	8	1	2	1	0
James, Chihuahua*	.750	3	0	3	1	0
Fosas, Tabasco	.750	3	0	3	1	0
Wirth, Mexico City Tigers	.667	3	1	1	1	0
Pactwa, Reynosa	.667	2	1	1	1	0
Belman, Coatzacoalcos	.500	1	0	1	1	0
Posadas, Poza Rica	.333	2	0	1	2	0
Pickert, Mexico City Tigers	.000	2	0	0	1	0

Triple play—Villegas.

CLUB PITCHING

Club	ERA.	G.	CG.	ShO.	Sv.	IP.	H.	R.	ER.	HR.	HB.	BB.	Int. BB.	SO.	WP.	Bk.
Yucatan	2.84	130	58	25	19	1112.2	947	352	285	13	25	337	26	528	41	1
Coatzacoalcos	2.88	129	56	20	17	1084.1	1023	425	347	31	16	414	16	657	28	4
Poza Rica	2.91	130	69	14	8	1064.1	1050	420	344	35	37	419	42	465	25	5
Campeche	3.09	127	45	21	6	1058.2	973	421	363	51	19	447	51	528	25	7
Nuevo Laredo	3.21	132	46	13	22	1089.1	1018	464	388	59	38	432	40	552	44	3
Veracruz	3.23	129	37	14	24	1068.2	1007	456	384	37	33	416	27	472	43	5
Mexico City Reds	3.34	130	50	14	11	1095.2	1176	487	406	38	24	304	27	421	40	6
Ciudad Juarez	3.36	129	56	10	20	1056.2	1030	495	395	37	31	476	28	611	34	0
Tabasco	3.41	130	52	17	10	1073	1099	506	407	26	37	376	48	498	40	0
Reynosa	3.43	132	45	15	21	1099.1	1057	451	419	51	30	396	40	611	35	1
Monclova	3.54	131	31	7	19	1069.1	1056	506	421	38	47	457	32	594	35	2
Mexico City Tigers	3.64	129	29	9	17	1071.1	1090	502	433	41	28	408	38	494	48	7
Saltillo	3.71	130	34	6	25	1061.1	1108	479	438	69	32	358	29	450	39	2
Monterrey	3.79	131	43	8	5	1086	1153	568	457	41	44	448	37	664	28	2
Aguascalientes	3.86	129	43	10	14	1066.2	1174	531	457	46	34	423	34	497	46	8
Chihuahua	4.95	130	44	3	11	1048	1228	710	576	65	39	546	45	472	70	4

PITCHERS' RECORDS
(Leading Qualifiers for Earned-Run Average Leadership — 106 or More Innings)

*Throws lefthanded.

Pitcher—Club	W.	L.	Pct.	ERA.	G.	GS.	CG.	GF.	ShO.	Sv.	IP.	H.	R.	ER.	HR.	HB.	BB.	Int. BB.	SO.	WP.
Cordova, Veracruz	8	10	.444	1.58	28	19	6	3	2	1	147.2	130	35	26	2	1	32	5	42	1
Glekel, Yucatan	11	9	.550	1.68	27	26	16	1	5	0	193	142	47	36	0	2	60	4	89	8
Hernaiz, Coatzacoalcos	18	6	.750	1.72	25	25	18	0	5	0	204.1	164	44	39	3	1	51	1	131	4
Quiroz, Veracruz	12	11	.522	1.94	25	25	15	0	3	0	199	161	55	43	5	7	54	1	99	1
Kuk Lee, Poza Rica	7	4	.636	1.98	17	15	9	2	1	0	109.1	103	35	24	3	6	36	4	29	2
Orozco, Campeche	13	8	.619	2.10	28	28	16	0	5	0	222.1	185	58	52	7	3	58	8	136	6
Soto, Yucatan	6	6	.500	2.12	27	16	6	7	3	1	127.1	116	37	30	1	5	31	4	45	5
Sutton, Nuevo Laredo	8	8	.500	2.21	18	18	10	0	3	0	134.1	115	45	33	4	10	38	4	39	4
Paul, Mexico City Reds*	9	11	.450	2.22	25	25	12	0	2	0	178	176	57	44	3	3	35	1	81	4
Matus, Reynosa	16	8	.667	2.24	30	22	8	4	0	0	189	150	51	47	6	4	52	8	81	4
Rincon, Yucatan	15	10	.600	2.24	27	27	10	0	4	0	197	154	60	49	4	4	64	2	107	3
Jimenez, Campeche	11	10	.524	2.25	29	24	8	3	5	1	164.1	157	47	41	3	4	61	3	74	1
Rasmussen, Yucatan	10	8	.556	2.26	22	22	14	0	6	0	163.1	131	44	41	1	2	35	3	92	4
R. Garcia, Ciudad Juarez	19	8	.704	2.29	28	27	21	1	6	1	208.1	165	70	53	8	8	52	2	177	6

Departmental Leaders: G—P. Rodriguez, 51; GS—A. Gonzalez, 29; CG—R. Garcia, 21; GF—P. Rodriguez, 47; ShO—R. Garcia, A. Ortiz, E. Rasmussen, 6; W—R. Garcia, 19; L—Camper, Rogers, 17; Sv.—Divison, 23; Pct.—J. Pena, .909; IP—Orozco, 222.1; H—Camper, 233; R—Camper, 109; ER—Camper, 92; HR—Pollorena, 15; BB—Quinonez, 109; IBB—Vidana, 11; HB—Moreno, 16; SO—Alcala, 192; WP—Brunet, 12.

(All Pitchers—Listed Alphabetically)

Pitcher—Club	W.	L.	Pct.	ERA.	G.	GS.	CG.	GF.	ShO.	Sv.	IP.	H.	R.	ER.	HR.	HB.	BB.	Int. BB.	SO.	WP.
Abarca, Campeche	6	6	.500	3.31	16	13	2	1	1	0	73.1	67	33	27	4	0	43	4	25	3
C. Acosta, Poza Rica	11	9	.550	2.57	23	23	12	0	4	0	147.1	138	52	42	5	11	43	5	47	3
O. Acosta, Tabasco	0	3	.000	6.75	3	2	0	0	0	0	13.1	12	12	10	1	0	13	1	5	1
M. Aguilar, Mexico City Tigers	0	5	.000	4.06	15	11	0	4	0	0	31	32	19	14	2	0	14	0	14	0
R. Aguilar, Monterrey	2	11	.154	4.07	35	5	0	21	0	1	95	108	57	43	4	8	33	10	44	4
Ako, Aguascalientes	12	7	.632	3.16	24	22	9	2	2	0	159.1	186	65	56	8	5	33	9	71	5
Alcala, Monterrey	9	15	.375	2.92	28	26	12	2	1	1	194	186	80	63	4	9	62	4	192	1
Alicea, Ciudad Juarez	7	2	.778	1.67	42	1	1	38	0	15	70	45	14	13	1	0	20	1	22	4
Angulo, Reynosa	1	1	.500	3.60	8	1	0	4	0	1	15	15	6	6	2	1	5	0	11	0
Alvarado, Coatzacoalcos	0	0	.000	0.00	1	0	0	0	0	0	1	1	0	0	0	0	0	0	0	0
Arano, Mexico City Reds	9	9	.500	3.87	29	24	8	3	3	1	155.2	194	80	67	6	1	33	3	38	6
Armas, Coatzacoalcos	0	0	.000	9.00	1	0	0	0	0	0	2	1	2	2	1	0	2	0	0	0
Arceo, Yucatan	1	1	.500	2.03	12	1	0	4	0	0	31	34	9	7	1	0	11	2	14	2
Armienta, Chihuahua	0	0	.000	7.56	12	0	0	4	0	0	16.2	25	15	14	1	3	9	0	5	1
Arratia, Monclova	1	3	.250	2.89	10	8	0	0	0	0	53	52	19	17	1	1	19	1	22	1
Arroyo, Aguascalientes°	10	6	.625	2.85	26	25	7	0	2	0	151.1	155	63	48	1	3	59	1	56	3
Baruch, Poza Rica	6	3	.667	3.16	28	0	0	19	0	4	57	49	25	20	3	0	32	5	36	1
Barrera, Nuevo Laredo	0	0	.000	0.00	1	0	0	1	0	0	0.1	0	0	0	0	0	0	0	0	0
Batista, 8 Chi.-1 Mva.-2 Rey.	2	6	.250	5.54	11	9	1	1	0	0	39	43	27	24	1	1	32	0	33	8
Belman, Coatzacoalcos	0	0	.000	2.46	1	0	0	0	0	0	3.2	4	3	1	0	0	3	0	0	0
E. Beltran, Monclova	10	8	.556	2.95	25	24	5	0	0	0	131	113	54	43	8	7	55	2	62	2
J. Beltran, Yucatan	3	2	.600	4.10	11	6	1	3	0	0	41.2	39	25	19	1	1	24	0	18	2
M. Beltran, Mexico City Reds	2	0	1.000	3.86	10	1	1	2	0	0	30.1	39	13	13	1	0	13	0	13	2
Bernal, Monterrey	1	5	.167	5.49	21	6	0	7	0	0	60.2	82	42	37	4	2	18	1	23	2
Bobadilla, Ciudad Juarez	0	0	.000	0.00	1	0	0	1	0	0	0.1	0	0	0	0	1	0	0	0	0
Branch, Nuevo Laredo	7	3	.700	3.25	12	12	5	0	0	0	72	80	38	26	1	2	18	0	37	1
Bresnen, Aguascalientes°	2	2	.500	5.31	17	2	0	11	0	1	39	49	28	23	3	2	18	1	16	2
Brunet, Veracruz°	14	9	.609	2.67	25	25	6	0	2	0	168.2	163	62	50	5	2	67	1	108	12
Calderon, Mexico City Tigers	1	4	.200	5.45	7	7	3	0	0	0	39.2	40	28	24	1	2	20	0	17	6
Camacho, Mexico City Reds	3	1	.750	5.31	15	0	0	9	0	4	20.1	21	12	12	0	1	6	0	15	3
Camper, Chihuahua	11	17	.393	4.25	30	28	16	2	2	1	195	233	109	92	10	8	60	5	80	8
Canedo, Aguascalientes	1	1	.500	6.25	13	2	0	6	0	0	31.2	46	23	22	0	2	27	0	11	0
Carranza, Campeche°	6	8	.429	2.78	25	25	6	0	3	0	142.1	121	69	44	9	0	70	4	58	4
Casas, 1 Tigers-29 Ags.	1	4	.200	5.80	30	3	0	17	0	5	59	83	41	38	3	3	23	7	34	3
Castillejos, 3 Tigers-30 Ags.	7	4	.636	3.96	33	4	1	19	0	5	77.1	88	36	34	6	0	12	4	31	5
Castillo, Nuevo Laredo	1	1	.500	3.94	6	0	0	2	0	0	32	29	16	14	0	1	14	0	16	2
Castaneda, Saltillo	0	0	.000	4.19	13	0	0	5	0	0	19.1	20	10	9	2	1	17	2	8	2
Chavez Soto, Monclova	6	6	.500	3.27	31	8	3	11	0	0	121	119	52	44	6	3	54	5	65	6
Churchill, Tabasco	1	0	1.000	2.35	5	0	0	3	0	0	7.2	8	5	2	0	0	3	2	1	1
Colorado, Coatzacoalcos	12	7	.632	2.83	23	23	15	0	3	0	172	173	70	54	4	1	42	1	95	1
Collins, Poza Rica	0	0	.000	9.00	2	0	0	0	0	0	4	8	5	4	0	0	1	1	5	0
Contreras, Monclova	6	7	.462	5.17	22	13	2	4	0	0	76.2	83	50	44	9	1	26	3	35	6
Cordova, Veracruz	8	10	.444	1.58	28	19	6	3	2	1	147.2	130	35	26	2	1	32	5	42	1
Christiansen, Aguascalientes	4	3	.571	4.23	9	7	1	1	0	0	44.2	48	24	21	2	1	17	0	21	4
J. Cruz, Yucatan	0	0	.000	5.63	4	0	0	3	0	1	8	8	5	5	0	1	4	0	3	0
Cuellar, Nuevo Laredo	3	2	.600	2.45	17	1	0	29	0	11	51.1	55	17	14	4	1	22	7	24	2
Delfin, Campeche	1	2	.333	3.04	14	0	0	9	0	0	15.2	17	14	14	1	0	12	4	10	0
Delgadillo, Aguascalientes	1	1	.500	2.82	19	0	0	8	0	1	44.2	46	22	14	3	0	30	1	21	4
De Los Santos, Monclova°	12	8	.600	2.82	25	25	11	0	1	0	182	152	67	59	9	3	78	3	141	5
A. Diaz, Coatzacoalcos	6	5	.545	3.10	16	12	5	1	1	0	81.1	87	36	28	2	0	31	0	27	5
C. Diaz, Mexico City Reds	7	11	.389	3.95	29	21	6	5	2	2	130	143	73	57	11	5	54	3	43	4
Divison, Saltillo	3	6	.333	3.64	48	0	0	40	0	23	81.2	77	39	33	5	5	36	6	64	3
H. Dominguez, Campeche	8	10	.444	2.83	25	21	8	3	4	0	140	125	53	44	7	2	56	2	76	2
M. Dominguez, Tabasco	4	6	.400	3.60	35	4	0	19	0	3	80	77	38	32	2	2	45	8	39	6
Duran, Chihuahua	0	8	.000	5.79	11	9	4	2	0	0	56	73	44	36	4	3	17	5	20	6
Drago, Mexico City Tigers	8	5	.615	3.50	17	16	5	0	0	0	113	122	55	44	3	5	36	4	43	3
Early, Tabasco	4	4	.500	2.09	14	13	4	1	3	1	77.2	63	22	18	1	4	26	0	43	1
Enyart, Reynosa°	0	1	.000	5.40	20	0	0	13	0	4	21.2	21	14	13	2	0	16	1	18	0
Escarrega, Mexico City Reds	0	1	.000	0.00	1	1	1	0	0	0	9	6	1	0	0	0	2	0	4	0
A. Espinosa, Mexico City Tigers	0	0	.000	7.71	1	1	0	0	0	0	4.2	7	5	4	0	0	2	0	1	0
J. Espinosa, Aguascalientes	1	2	.333	6.75	17	1	0	7	0	0	25.1	38	19	19	1	0	12	1	13	2
Esquer, Monterrey°	6	11	.353	3.85	26	25	8	0	2	0	154.1	152	79	66	7	11	66	4	119	3
Esquivel, 4 Yuc.-29 Vera.	3	1	.750	3.90	33	0	0	24	0	7	60	59	26	26	3	4	13	3	21	0
Feola, 3 Lar.-24 Ags.	6	8	.429	3.47	27	14	6	6	0	1	103.2	98	46	40	1	4	56	2	67	5
Figueroa, Veracruz	0	0	.000	7.16	12	0	0	6	0	0	16.1	24	16	13	0	1	20	1	7	0
Fosas, Tabasco	0	3	.000	5.56	3	3	0	0	0	0	11.1	15	14	7	0	1	10	0	6	1
D. Franco, Nuevo Laredo	0	0	.000	9.82	5	0	0	1	0	0	7.1	11	8	8	3	0	3	0	1	0
F. Franco, Poza Rica	6	6	.500	3.18	17	10	3	6	0	1	70.2	74	35	25	7	3	34	3	21	3
Gallegos, Coatzacoalcos°	2	3	.600	3.91	6	3	0	0	0	0	23	20	12	10	2	2	16	0	13	1
Gamez, Campeche	0	1	.000	4.43	15	3	0	11	0	0	22.1	27	16	11	1	2	23	1	7	1
J.L. Garcia, Tabasco	3	3	.500	4.67	24	4	0	10	0	0	54	63	33	28	3	1	33	9	28	5
L. Garcia, Nuevo Laredo	15	6	.714	2.71	29	25	14	3	3	0	169.1	144	58	51	10	2	65	0	117	6
Raf. Garcia, Ciudad Juarez	19	8	.704	2.29	28	27	21	1	6	1	208.1	165	70	53	8	8	52	2	177	6
Rog. Garcia, Saltillo	4	4	.500	6.92	22	7	0	8	0	0	53.1	73	43	41	10	3	27	4	20	3
V. Garcia, Nuevo Laredo	3	2	.600	2.21	7	6	1	0	0	0	40.2	33	12	10	4	0	19	0	10	1
Gaxiola, Monterrey	5	9	.357	3.81	21	17	4	2	1	0	106.1	113	62	45	6	6	52	1	51	3
Ma. Gonzalez, Monterrey	13	12	.520	2.81	31	29	15	1	3	0	214.1	203	89	67	3	4	80	4	118	2
I. Gonzalez, Monterrey	3	0	1.000	5.86	21	0	0	20	0	0	35.1	37	24	23	4	1	22	2	25	2
Gutierrez, Ciudad Juarez	8	7	.533	3.56	27	18	5	2	0	0	116.1	116	58	46	2	4	60	5	66	5
J. R. Guzman, Veracruz	1	4	.200	3.64	41	1	0	20	0	6	59.1	48	27	24	1	0	35	2	31	1
R. Guzman, Monclova	6	5	.545	2.75	45	0	0	34	0	12	68.2	52	25	21	4	1	25	2	50	1
Glekel, Yucatan°	11	9	.550	1.68	27	26	16	1	5	0	193	143	47	36	0	2	60	4	89	8
Hernaiz, Coatzacoalcos	18	6	.750	1.72	25	25	18	0	5	0	204.1	164	44	39	3	1	51	1	131	4
A. Hernandez, Monclova	7	6	.538	4.65	42	2	0	29	0	55	69.2	83	37	36	4	0	24	4	34	0
H. Heredia, Monterrey	0	4	.000	4.42	28	3	1	13	0	1	79.1	92	45	39	4	1	35	1	24	4
U. Heredia, Veracruz	0	1	.000	2.31	5	2	0	2	0	1	11.2	8	4	3	0	1	6	1	8	0
Hidalgo, Coatzacoalcos	0	2	.000	15.92	5	5	0	0	0	0	13	14	26	23	0	1	33	0	10	7
Higueras, Ciudad Juarez	9	12	.429	4.05	24	24	8	0	0	0	142.1	163	77	64	5	1	53	2	74	2
Hopkins, Reynosa	1	2	.333	6.75	5	5	0	0	0	0	18.2	25	16	14	1	4	16	0	7	4
Ibarra, Reynosa	6	1	.857	2.15	9	6	4	3	1	2	50.1	40	14	12	1	0	11	0	41	2
Inzunza, Reynosa	0	2	.000	7.27	20	1	0	6	0	0	17.1	20	16	14	1	0	22	2	12	2

Pitcher—Club	W.	L.	Pct.	ERA.	G.	GS.	CG.	GF.	ShO.	Sv.	IP.	H.	R.	ER.	HR.	HB.	BB.	Int. BB.	SO.	WP.
James, Chihuahua*	0	1	.000	1.86	3	1	0	1	0	0	9.2	9	6	2	0	0	10	1	5	2
Jefferson, Nuevo Laredo	5	3	.625	3.27	12	9	5	0	1	0	63.1	61	30	23	4	3	30	0	30	6
Jimenez, Campeche	11	10	.524	2.25	29	24	8	3	5	1	164.1	157	47	41	3	4	61	3	74	1
Juarez, Chihuahua	8	11	.421	3.74	27	23	10	3	1	2	156.1	187	90	65	9	1	44	7	55	6
Kobel, Ciudad Juarez	0	1	.000	9.00	1	1	0	0	0	0	4	9	6	4	0	0	1	0	0	1
Kuk Lee, Poza Rica	7	4	.636	1.98	17	15	9	2	1	0	109.1	103	35	24	3	6	36	4	29	1
Lacey, Saltillo	8	4	.667	2.73	14	13	5	0	1	0	92.1	94	32	28	2	1	28	0	43	6
Lance, Monterrey	5	6	.455	5.03	25	5	0	15	0	2	53.2	64	39	30	1	1	37	6	26	3
Leon, Mexico City Reds	13	8	.619	2.87	25	25	11	0	1	0	175.1	174	66	56	5	4	24	3	51	4
E. Lopez, Poza Rica	0	1	.000	7.94	5	1	0	1	0	0	11.1	15	10	10	1	2	2	0	1	0
H. Lopez, Mexico City Tigers	8	3	.727	2.59	36	0	0	24	0	6	73	62	26	21	6	2	31	7	26	1
Low, Aguascalientes	5	8	.385	3.05	23	13	2	6	1	1	85.2	81	35	29	4	2	45	4	48	2
Luna, Mexico City Tigers	1	2	.333	6.87	11	0	0	3	0	0	18.1	22	16	14	3	0	17	0	8	1
H. Madrigal, Tabasco	1	8	.111	4.87	22	11	2	8	0	2	81.1	98	59	44	0	3	19	4	34	1
J. Madrigal, Poza Rica	10	6	.625	2.25	26	13	7	9	1	0	111	101	40	29	2	3	41	3	55	3
Manriquez, Tabasco	0	1	.000	14.53	5	3	0	2	0	0	4.1	11	7	7	0	0	8	0	1	2
Mapel, 2 Tigers-13 Rey.	6	4	.600	3.39	15	15	3	0	0	0	87.2	90	33	23	4	4	33	3	44	1
Matus, Reynosa	16	8	.667	2.24	30	22	8	4	0	0	189	150	51	47	6	4	52	8	81	4
F. H. Martinez, Nuevo Laredo*	4	3	.571	4.44	24	6	0	6	0	0	52.2	63	29	26	2	0	25	5	13	2
F. Martinez, Aguascalientes	1	4	.200	5.40	6	5	2	0	0	0	31.2	33	21	19	2	1	20	0	14	0
G. Martinez, Chihuahua	7	11	.389	5.42	32	16	3	13	0	1	116.1	136	87	70	6	7	79	8	40	5
J. L. Martinez, Monterrey	0	5	.000	6.21	7	6	1	0	0	0	33.1	42	27	23	1	0	19	2	19	2
M. Martinez, Yucatan	3	4	.429	2.97	17	8	1	3	0	0	78.2	87	29	26	2	2	28	1	31	2
R. Martinez, Saltillo	1	1	.500	3.60	12	1	0	7	0	0	30	26	14	12	1	0	14	0	9	1
Maytorena, 10 Mva.-15 Sal.	3	2	.600	3.52	25	1	0	12	0	2	38.1	36	17	15	5	1	12	0	23	1
McLaughlin, Nuevo Laredo	12	6	.667	3.22	28	24	7	3	1	1	162.1	135	69	58	10	4	51	1	123	6
Myerchin, Mexico City Tigers	0	0	.000	4.76	2	0	0	0	0	0	5.2	8	3	3	1	0	1	0	4	1
Mendez, Chihuahua	3	1	.750	4.39	37	2	0	18	0	1	80	76	49	39	8	2	55	2	45	3
Mendoza, Yucatan	9	10	.474	2.72	22	20	9	2	2	1	132.1	119	57	40	2	4	44	4	71	9
Menendez, Saltillo	15	12	.556	3.91	31	27	8	0	0	0	175	195	87	76	13	2	62	2	60	4
Meza, Nuevo Laredo	1	2	.333	4.32	10	0	0	6	0	1	16.2	21	10	8	2	0	7	2	2	1
Miranda, Coatzacoalcos	3	4	.429	3.62	34	3	0	16	0	3	59.2	51	25	24	4	3	44	2	47	2
Montague, 4 Tigers-17 Ags.	10	6	.625	3.10	21	17	11	1	2	0	124.2	128	46	43	4	2	26	0	44	6
Montano, 3 Reds-17 Tigers	6	2	.750	2.99	20	12	1	2	0	0	87.1	90	32	29	1	1	33	1	32	2
Montenegro, Ciudad Juarez	0	0	.000	5.87	11	0	0	9	0	0	23	24	18	15	4	1	10	0	4	2
Montijo, Tabasco	0	0	.000	8.31	3	0	0	1	0	0	4.1	6	4	4	0	1	3	0	1	0
Morales, Veracruz	3	6	.333	3.75	34	6	1	18	0	5	86.1	89	42	36	8	0	33	4	27	3
Moran, 5 Chi.-18 Tigers	7	7	.500	3.58	23	20	8	2	1	1	133.2	136	62	53	6	3	43	6	48	1
C. Moreno, 11 Ags.-16 Sal.	7	7	.500	4.79	27	21	4	6	0	0	109	107	66	58	7	16	64	4	53	6
J. Moreno, Veracruz	3	2	.600	2.67	19	0	0	13	0	4	33.2	23	11	10	1	1	12	3	13	3
Moret, 2 Ags.-20 Monclova*	4	13	.235	4.40	22	19	4	2	0	1	110.1	128	70	54	6	1	53	1	54	5
Moya, Saltillo	2	6	.250	4.53	22	2	0	11	0	1	53.2	59	29	27	5	2	24	1	14	1
Mundo, Chihuahua	0	5	.000	5.67	20	7	2	4	0	0	73	88	55	46	8	2	41	5	23	6
E. Munoz, Nuevo Laredo	0	0	.000	11.57	2	0	0	1	0	0	2.1	3	3	3	0	0	4	0	1	1
F. Munoz, Tabasco	1	2	.333	4.96	18	3	1	10	0	0	45.1	50	30	25	3	2	32	3	9	5
Murillo, Mexico City Reds	8	4	.667	3.61	33	11	5	13	3	1	104.2	104	46	42	1	9	48	7	65	5
Navarro, Mexico City Reds	0	1	.000	4.42	10	2	0	6	0	0	18.1	20	12	9	1	0	8	0	9	2
Nieblas, Coatzacoalcos	0	0	.000	27.00	1	0	0	0	0	0	0.2	2	2	2	0	0	2	0	0	1
Nunez, Mexico City Tigers	6	4	.600	3.52	34	1	1	23	0	5	79.1	65	37	31	3	5	41	8	46	6
D. Ochoa, Coatzacoalcos	4	7	.364	1.35	36	0	0	34	0	12	60	50	14	9	4	1	15	5	31	1
J. Ochoa, Campeche	1	1	.500	5.53	14	0	0	8	0	1	27.2	37	19	17	3	1	6	3	6	1
Orea, Veracruz	0	3	.000	18.78	4	0	0	0	0	0	7.2	26	16	16	1	0	2	0	3	1
Orozco, Campeche	13	8	.619	2.10	28	28	16	0	5	0	222.1	185	58	52	7	3	58	8	36	6
Ortiz, Tabasco*	9	11	.450	2.84	27	24	17	1	6	0	177.2	186	74	56	6	3	37	5	49	3
Pactwa, Reynosa	0	1	.000	45.00	2	2	0	0	0	0	1	1	5	5	1	2	4	0	1	1
Palacios, Tabasco	0	3	.000	5.26	23	1	0	14	0	2	37.2	48	27	22	0	3	23	6	15	3
Paul, Mexico City Reds*	9	11	.450	2.22	25	25	12	0	2	0	178	176	57	44	3	3	35	1	81	4
J. Pena, Ciudad Juarez	10	1	.909	3.19	22	10	4	3	0	0	118.1	134	57	42	3	3	49	4	54	7
M. Pena, Chihuahua*	1	0	1.000	9.59	27	0	0	6	0	0	25.1	44	34	27	2	2	16	0	12	4
Peralta, Coatzacoalcos	7	4	.636	3.36	22	17	3	3	1	1	104.1	89	50	39	3	5	70	0	83	2
C. J. Perez, Ciudad Juarez	4	8	.333	4.58	21	12	2	4	0	1	78.2	82	50	40	5	2	50	0	46	3
C. Perez, Tabasco	8	6	.571	2.50	20	18	5	0	2	0	147.2	141	57	41	5	5	43	3	72	4
Pickert, Mexico City Tigers	0	1	.000	3.52	2	2	0	0	0	0	7.2	6	3	3	0	1	3	0	6	0
Pole, 8 Tigers-2 Lar.	2	8	.200	5.80	10	10	0	0	0	0	45	65	33	29	0	0	15	2	15	4
Pollorena, Saltillo	11	9	.550	3.51	27	27	11	0	3	0	184.2	193	75	72	15	3	41	3	87	7
Posadas, Poza Rica	1	0	1.000	3.12	2	0	0	1	0	0	8.2	7	4	3	0	0	3	0	2	0
Alf. Pulido, Mexico City Reds	8	8	.500	2.41	43	1	1	25	1	2	93.1	94	34	25	5	0	31	7	50	3
Ant. Pulido, 36 Cam.-9 Tigers	4	10	.286	4.10	45	4	1	30	0	9	79	82	40	36	4	0	44	7	61	1
Purata, Poza Rica*	4	4	.500	3.51	23	11	2	4	0	0	74.1	88	34	29	2	2	39	3	22	5
Preciado, Campeche	2	3	.400	3.32	30	1	0	14	0	0	86.2	73	36	32	3	1	40	6	32	2
Prevost, Veracruz	2	1	.667	2.74	5	5	0	0	0	0	23	14	7	7	2	0	19	0	14	0
Prieto, 5 Tigers-22 Reds	4	1	.800	2.85	27	0	0	14	0	1	60	59	27	19	0	0	17	0	21	8
Pruneda, Chihuahua	5	9	.357	5.71	36	12	1	17	0	3	86.2	104	65	55	3	4	60	6	51	6
Quintero, Coatzacoalcos	0	1	.000	54.00	1	1	0	0	0	0	0.2	3	4	4	0	0	2	0	0	1
Quinonez, Ciudad Juarez	14	8	.636	2.78	26	24	14	1	0	0	184.2	161	68	57	4	5	109	6	116	3
Quiroz, Veracruz	12	11	.522	1.94	25	25	15	0	3	0	199	161	55	43	5	7	54	1	99	4
Ramirez, Reynosa	0	0	.000	9.53	1	0	0	0	0	0	5.2	9	6	6	0	0	4	0	1	0
Rasmussen, Yucatan	10	8	.556	2.26	22	22	14	0	6	0	163.1	131	44	41	1	2	35	3	92	4
H. Rios, Reynosa	10	12	.455	3.98	29	28	8	0	3	0	176.1	193	83	78	6	5	50	6	95	4
R. Rios, Coatzacoalcos	3	0	1.000	2.96	19	1	0	7	0	0	48.2	54	18	16	2	0	22	4	16	1
Rincon, Reynosa	15	10	.600	2.24	27	27	10	0	4	0	197	154	60	49	4	4	64	2	107	3
Rivera, 4 Yuc.-20 Juarez	2	4	.333	4.96	24	7	1	8	0	1	69	89	48	38	6	6	35	5	29	4
A. Rodriguez, Reynosa	3	4	.429	2.55	45	0	0	25	0	9	81.1	61	23	23	4	4	38	4	54	5
E. Rodriguez, Monclova	1	0	1.000	4.56	22	1	1	15	0	0	51.1	70	32	26	5	2	30	4	17	1
Ma. Rodriguez, Chihuahua	4	11	.267	3.71	27	14	5	5	0	2	121.1	115	65	50	5	1	71	2	52	6
P. Rodriguez, Yucatan	13	5	.722	1.48	51	0	0	47	0	16	104.1	72	20	17	1	1	27	6	49	4
R. Rodriguez, Poza Rica	4	2	.667	4.53	28	0	0	15	0	3	51.2	62	34	26	1	1	32	9	35	3
Rogers, Veracruz	8	17	.320	2.97	27	23	14	4	2	2	173	173	60	57	1	11	30	5	71	3
Romo, Coatzacoalcos	7	0	1.000	1.54	8	8	4	0	2	0	58.1	41	12	10	0	0	12	0	63	0
Rondon, 12 Sal.-2 Tab.-5 Vera.	7	10	.412	4.54	19	19	6	0	0	0	123	139	71	62	4	3	43	3	42	3
P. Ruiz, Chihuahua*	1	6	.143	6.75	28	9	1	8	0	0	65.1	78	52	49	6	4	58	4	49	4
R. Ruiz, Reynosa	1	1	.500	4.77	18	1	0	11	0	0	28.1	38	16	15	1	3	15	1	8	3

Pitcher—Club	W.	L.	Pct.	ERA.	G.	GS.	CG.	GF.	ShO.	Sv.	IP.	H.	R.	ER.	HR.	HB.	BB.	Int. BB.	SO.	WP.
Salas, Veracruz	7	10	.412	4.41	24	24	3	0	1	0	134.2	155	76	66	4	11	58	3	48	3
Salinas, Mexico City Reds	7	6	.538	4.55	27	19	5	3	1	0	122.2	151	69	62	5	1	36	3	33	1
Sanchez, 4 Tigers-17 Lar.	5	1	.833	2.37	21	2	0	9	0	0	64.2	53	19	17	2	2	31	3	29	4
Sandate, Poza Rica*	13	5	.722	2.47	23	23	14	0	4	0	160.1	165	48	44	4	0	54	4	79	4
Santiago, Tabasco	1	4	.200	4.91	11	1	0	5	0	0	22	25	12	12	0	0	16	1	15	2
Sauceda, Mexico City Tigers	6	4	.600	4.32	33	0	0	21	0	1	58.1	54	29	28	4	2	25	3	32	8
Segui, Reynosa	12	10	.545	2.57	26	25	19	1	4	1	196.1	171	60	56	4	1	42	2	131	4
Silva, Nuevo Laredo	4	4	.500	6.59	16	11	0	3	0	0	56	70	48	41	8	5	32	5	22	3
J. Solis, Nuevo Laredo	4	5	.444	2.87	43	1	0	20	0	5	84.2	75	31	27	4	6	36	10	19	1
M. Solis, Saltillo	15	6	.714	2.86	28	28	8	0	1	0	198.1	198	66	63	8	4	37	4	56	4
R. Solis, Coatzacoalcos	1	5	.167	3.33	15	5	2	3	0	0	54	56	27	20	3	0	18	1	28	1
Sosa, Monclova	9	10	.474	3.15	28	28	6	0	3	0	171.1	172	82	60	3	4	76	7	102	9
Soto, Yucatan	6	6	.500	2.12	27	16	6	7	3	1	127.1	116	37	30	1	5	31	4	45	5
Sutton, Nuevo Laredo	8	8	.500	2.21	18	18	10	0	3	0	134.1	115	45	33	4	10	38	4	39	4
Tejeda, Coatzacoalcos*	0	2	.000	3.68	18	1	0	8	0	0	44	46	20	18	2	0	11	1	32	0
Tiant, Tabasco	6	10	.375	2.34	18	18	9	0	2	0	119.1	98	41	31	3	1	29	0	103	2
J. Urrea, 7 Vera.-8 PR	4	4	.500	5.09	15	14	4	0	1	0	86.2	75	52	49	4	7	51	3	46	5
L. Urrea, Saltillo	0	1	.000	4.91	9	2	0	6	0	0	18.1	25	11	10	2	0	4	0	13	1
Valencia, Poza Rica	0	1	.000	5.40	3	1	0	2	0	0	10	16	8	6	1	0	5	0	8	0
A. Valenzuela, Aguascalientes*	0	1	.000	7.07	5	1	0	2	0	0	14	21	13	11	5	0	7	0	9	3
G. Valenzuela, Reynosa	6	9	.400	4.39	27	19	3	5	1	1	127	130	65	62	13	1	52	2	69	5
D. Vazquez, Mexico City Tigers ..	5	5	.500	3.95	29	10	1	10	0	0	95.2	115	47	42	3	0	33	3	55	3
J. Vazquez, Monterrey	4	3	.571	3.17	17	9	2	7	1	0	59.2	74	24	21	3	1	24	2	23	2
Ma. Vazquez, Ciudad Juarez	1	5	.167	4.66	19	9	1	6	0	2	63.2	70	43	33	5	3	45	3	29	0
R. Vazquez, Poza Rica	16	7	.696	2.64	28	25	19	2	1	0	194.1	178	67	57	4	6	66	3	100	2
Velazquez, 3 Mva.-5 Tigers	0	0	.000	6.57	8	0	0	2	0	0	12.1	17	10	9	1	1	8	0	7	2
Vidana, Reynosa	8	5	.615	3.64	32	7	0	15	0	3	81.2	91	41	33	5	1	36	11	34	0
Villanueva, Coatzacoalcos*	10	8	.556	2.81	24	23	9	0	2	0	153.2	168	60	48	1	2	40	1	81	2
D. Villegas, Campeche	3	11	.214	4.35	33	8	4	13	1	0	97.1	91	58	47	9	6	39	9	49	4
M. Villegas, 3 Chi.-10 Ags.	3	1	.750	3.15	13	1	1	4	0	0	40	42	16	14	0	1	15	4	26	4
R. Villegas, Mexico City Tigers	10	10	.500	2.58	26	25	7	0	3	0	163.2	160	54	47	6	3	27	4	65	2
Wardlow, Monclova	0	2	.000	6.28	5	4	0	1	0	0	14.1	15	13	10	0	1	12	0	4	0
Wiltbank, Mexico City Tigers	4	3	.571	2.99	12	12	4	0	2	0	69.1	53	28	23	0	3	39	0	62	4
Williams, Nuevo Laredo*	5	5	.500	2.85	19	10	4	5	2	4	79	65	28	25	3	2	35	2	70	2
Wirth, Mexico City Tigers	0	2	.000	13.09	3	3	0	0	0	0	11	19	16	16	0	1	5	0	5	1
Zamudio, Veracruz	3	5	.375	4.00	22	7	2	8	1	0	69.2	61	39	31	3	1	31	2	27	10

BALKS—Ako, 3; M. Aguilar, Kuk Lee, Montano, Morales, Moya, Orozco, Preciado, 2 each; Abarca, C. Acosta, E. Beltran, M. Beltran, Bresnen, Brunet, Calderon, Carranza, Christiansen, Delgadillo, De Los Santos, A. Diaz, C. Diaz, J. Espinosa, Esquer, L. Garcia, I. Gonzalez, Hernaiz, Ibarra, James, Jimenez, Juarez, E. Lopez, H. Lopez, M. Martinez, Moran, Moret, Murillo, Navarro, Nunez, Paul, Peralta, Pruneda, Quiroz, M.A. Rodriguez, Silva, J. Solis, Valencia, Villanueva, Zamudio.

NO-HIT GAMES—Dominguez, Campeche, defeated Mexico City Tigers, 2-0, May 6 (seven innings); Soto, Yucatan, defeated Veracruz, 2-0, July 3 (seven innings); Jefferson, Nuevo Laredo, defeated Chihuahua, 9-0, July 7 (seven innings); Hernaiz, Coatzacoalcos, defeated Yucatan, 11-0, July 15; L. Garcia, Nuevo Laredo, defeated Reynosa, 5-0, July 18 (seven innings).

PERFECT GAME—R. Garcia, Ciudad Juarez, defeated Mexico City Reds, 2-0, May 19 (eight innings).

Pacific Coast League

CLASS AAA

Leading Batter
MICHAEL WILSON
Albuquerque

League President
BILL CUTLER

Leading Pitcher
CHRIS CODIROLI
Tacoma

CHAMPIONSHIP WINNERS IN PREVIOUS YEARS

1903—Los Angeles	.630
1904—Tacoma	.589
Tacoma§	.571
Los Angeles§	.571
1905—Tacoma	.583
Los Angeles*	.604
1906—Portland	.657
1907—Los Angeles	.608
1908—Los Angeles	.585
1909—San Francisco	.623
1910—Portland	.567
1911—Portland	.589
1912—Oakland	.591
1913—Portland	.559
1914—Portland	.574
1915—San Francisco	.570
1916—Los Angeles	.601
1917—San Francisco	.561
1918—Vernon	.569
Los Angeles (2nd) x	.548
1919—Vernon	.613
1920—Vernon	.556
1921—Los Angeles	.574
1922—San Francisco	.638
1923—San Francisco	.617
1924—Seattle	.545
1925—San Francisco	.643
1926—Los Angeles	.599
1927—Oakland	.615
1928—San Francisco*	.630
Sacramento§§	.626
San Francisco§§	.626
1929—Mission	.643
Hollywood*	.592
1930—Los Angeles	.576
Hollywood*	.650
1931—Hollywood	.626
San Francisco*	.608
1932—Portland	.587
1933—Los Angeles	.610

1934—Los Angeles z	.786
Los Angeles z	.689
1935—Los Angeles	.648
San Francisco*	.608
1936—Portland‡	.549
1937—Sacramento	.573
San Diego (3rd)†	.545
1938—Los Angeles	.590
Sacramento (3rd)†	.537
1939—Seattle	.589
Sacramento (4th)†	.500
1940—Seattle‡	.629
1941—Seattle‡	.598
1942—Sacramento	.590
Seattle (3rd)†	.539
1943—Los Angeles	.710
S. Francisco (2nd)†	.574
1944—Los Angeles	.586
S. Francisco (3rd)†	.509
1945—Portland	.622
S. Francisco (4th)†	.525
1946—San Francisco‡	.628
1947—Los Angeles††	.567
1948—Oakland‡	.606
1949—Hollywood‡	.583
1950—Oakland	.590
1951—Seattle‡	.593
1952—Hollywood	.606
1953—Hollywood	.589
1954—San Diego y	.604
1955—Seattle	.552
1956—Los Angeles	.637
1957—San Francisco	.601
1958—Phoenix	.578
1959—Salt Lake City	.552
1960—Spokane	.601
1961—Tacoma	.630
1962—San Diego	.604

1963—Spokane	.620
Oklahoma City a	.632
1964—Arkansas	.609
San Diego a	.576
1965—Oklahoma City a	.628
Portland	.547
1966—Seattle a	.561
Tulsa	.578
1967—San Diego a	.574
Spokane	.541
1968—Tulsa a	.642
Spokane	.586
1969—Tacoma a	.589
Eugene	.603
1970—Spokane a	.644
Hawaii	.671
1971—Salt Lake City	.534
Tacoma	.545
1972—Albuquerque	.622
Eugene	.534
1973—Tucson	.583
Spokane a	.563
1974—Spokane a	.549
Albuqerque	.535
1975—Salt Lake City	.556
Hawaii a	.611
1976—Salt Lake City	.625
Hawaii a	.531
1977—Phoenix a	.579
Hawaii	.541
1978—Tacoma b	.584
Albuquerque b	.557
1979—Albuquerque	.581
Salt Lake City c	.541
1980—Albuquerque*	.578
Hawaii	.539
1981—Albuquerque*	.712
Tacoma	.561

*Won split-season playoff. †Won four-team playoff. ‡Won pennant and four-team playoff. §Tied for second-half title with Tacoma winning playoff. §§Tied for second-half title, with Sacramento winning playoff. ††Ended regular season in tie with San Francisco and won one-game playoff for pennant, then won four-club playoff. xWon playoff from first place Vernon and awarded championship. yDefeated Hollywood in one-game playoff for pennant. zWon both halves, no playoff. aLeague was divided into Northern, Southern divisions in 1963, 1969-70-71, and Eastern, Western divisions in 1964 through 1968 and 1972 through 1977, won two-team playoff. bLeague divided into Eastern and Western divisions, Tacoma and Albuquerque declared co-champions following cancellation of four-team playoff due to continuing rain and wet grounds. cWon second-half title and defeated Hawaii in four-team playoff.

STANDING OF CLUBS AT CLOSE OF FIRST HALF, JUNE 21

NORTHERN DIVISION

Club	W.	L.	T.	Pct.	G.B.
Tacoma (A's)	42	28	0	.600	......
Vancouver (Brewers)	38	33	0	.535	4½
Edmonton (White Sox)	35	36	0	.493	7½
Spokane (Angels)	35	36	0	.493	7½
Portland (Pirates)	32	39	0	.451	10½

SOUTHERN DIVISION

Club	W.	L.	T.	Pct.	G.B.
Albuquerque (Dodgers)	46	25	0	.648	......
Hawaii (Padres)	36	35	0	.507	10
Salt Lake City (Mariners)	33	37	0	.471	12½
Phoenix (Giants)	30	41	0	.423	16
Tucson (Astros)	27	44	0	.380	19

STANDING OF CLUBS AT CLOSE OF SECOND HALF, SEPTEMBER 1

NORTHERN DIVISION

Club	W.	L.	T.	Pct.	G.B.
Spokane (Angels)	43	29	0	.597	......
Tacoma (A's)	42	31	0	.575	1½
Edmonton (White Sox)	35	38	0	.479	8½
Vancouver (Brewers)	34	39	0	.466	9½
Portland (Pirates)	33	40	0	.452	10½

SOUTHERN DIVISION

Club	W.	L.	T.	Pct.	G.B.
Salt Lake City (Mariners)	40	33	0	.548	......
Albuquerque (Dodgers)	39	33	0	.542	½
Hawaii (Padres)	37	36	0	.507	3
Tucson (Astros)	32	39	0	.451	7
Phoenix (Giants)	28	45	0	.384	12

COMPOSITE STANDING OF CLUBS AT CLOSE OF SEASON, SEPTEMBER 1

NORTHERN DIVISION

Club	Tac.	Spo.	Van.	Edm.	Port.	Ab.	SLC	Haw.	Tuc.	Phx.	W.	L.	T.	Pct.	G.B.
Tacoma (A's)	....	10	9	12	9	7	8	10	9	10	84	59	0	.587	......
Spokane (Angels)	6	....	9	4	12	7	8	9	11	12	78	65	0	.545	6
Vancouver (Brewers)	7	7	....	9	10	5	7	6	11	10	72	72	0	.500	12½
Edmonton (White Sox)	4	12	7	....	8	8	8	8	6	9	70	74	0	.486	14½
Portland (Pirates)	7	4	6	8	....	6	6	8	10	10	65	79	0	.451	19½

SOUTHERN DIVISION

Club	Tac.	Spo.	Van.	Edm.	Port.	Ab.	SLC	Haw.	Tuc.	Phx.	W.	L.	T.	Pct.	G.B.
Albuquerque (Dodgers)	9	9	11	8	10	....	8	9	11	10	85	58	0	.594	......
Salt Lake City (Mariners)	7	8	9	8	10	8	....	6	7	10	73	70	0	.510	12
Hawaii (Padres)	6	7	10	8	8	7	10	....	8	9	73	71	0	.507	12½
Tucson (Astros)	7	4	5	10	6	4	9	8	....	6	59	83	0	.415	25½
Phoenix (Giants)	6	4	6	7	6	6	6	7	10	....	58	86	0	.403	27½

Hawaii club represented Honolulu, Hawaii.

Major league affiliations in parentheses.

Playoffs—Albuquerque defeated Salt Lake City, two games to none; Spokane defeated Tacoma, two games to one; Albuquerque defeated Spokane, four games to two, for league championship.

Regular-Season Attendance—Albuquerque, 290,249; Edmonton, 233,044; Hawaii, 136,676; Phoenix, 244,570; Portland, 272,781; Salt Lake City, 255,671; Spokane, 221,526; Tacoma, 223,289; Tucson, 196,009; Vancouver, 158,767. Total, 2,232,552.

Managers: Albuquerque, Del Crandall; Edmonton, Gordy Lund; Hawaii, Doug Rader; Phoenix, Rocky Bridges; Portland, Tom Trebelhorn; Salt Lake City, Bobby Floyd; Spokane, Moose Stubing; Tacoma, Ed Nottle; Tucson, Jimmy Johnson; Vancouver, Dick Phillips.

All-Star Team: 1B—Brock, Albuquerque; 2B—Doran, Tucson; 3B—Lubratich, Spokane; SS—Anderson, Albuquerque; OF—Kittle, Edmonton; Gray, Edmonton; Davis, Tacoma; C—Rabb, Phoenix; DH—Wilson, Albuquerque; RHP—Baker, Tacoma; LHP—DiPino, Vancouver; Manager—Stubing, Spokane.

(Compiled by William J. Weiss, League Statistician, San Mateo, Calif.)

CLUB BATTING

Club	Pct.	G.	AB.	R.	OR.	H.	TB.	2B.	3B.	HR.	RBI.	GW.	SH.	SF.	HP.	BB.	Int. BB.	SO.	SB.	CS.	LOB.
Albuquerque	.313	143	4898	956	811	1534	2312	263	49	139	869	74	65	52	43	691	31	767	184	108	1116
Edmonton	.295	144	4945	886	902	1458	2313	263	53	162	815	62	36	40	40	632	25	780	167	72	1124
Salt Lake City	.292	143	4835	794	850	1411	2095	234	53	115	719	66	44	39	32	584	31	653	107	71	1018
Tucson	.288	142	4859	788	877	1401	2035	267	56	85	715	50	38	50	37	584	30	735	180	54	1115
Spokane	.286	143	4853	785	737	1390	2113	300	62	100	721	71	32	44	35	516	35	685	142	75	1025
Phoenix	.286	144	4750	769	866	1357	2111	266	70	116	703	49	23	53	36	495	24	720	155	80	962
Tacoma	.280	143	4737	749	668	1327	1939	215	47	101	681	72	60	45	34	551	29	812	230	104	983
Portland	.277	144	4801	729	729	1331	2046	233	52	126	677	56	26	38	40	526	28	739	138	79	1002
Vancouver	.269	144	4795	647	686	1288	1926	208	47	112	599	67	61	44	26	523	45	819	158	92	1036
Hawaii	.259	144	4662	697	672	1209	1825	235	53	91	629	67	53	42	40	569	21	746	153	67	1016

INDIVIDUAL BATTING

(Leading Qualifiers for Batting Championship—389 or More Plate Appearances)

°Bats lefthanded.   †Switch-hitter.

Player and Club	Pct.	G.	AB.	R.	H.	TB.	2B.	3B.	HR.	RBI.	GW.	SH.	SF.	HP.	BB.	Int. BB.	SO.	SB.	CS.
Wilson, Michael, Albuquerque	.378	99	368	77	139	182	25	6	2	56	0	5	2	6	48	1	27	25	17
Gray, Lorenzo, Edmonton	.358	124	481	97	172	263	33	5	16	79	5	4	3	7	38	1	54	20	10
Pate, Robert, Tucson	.347	94	329	76	114	168	23	8	5	59	5	2	5	3	57	1	33	26	5
Kittle, Ronald, Edmonton	.345	127	472	121	163	355	22	10	50	144	12	0	3	10	74	9	109	5	3
Anderson, David, Albuquerque	.343	132	507	100	174	222	19	7	5	76	5	6	5	0	54	0	65	43	12
Lubratich, Steven, Spokane	.338	132	535	92	181	263	43	6	9	88	13	9	2	10	41	0	29	7	4
Nyman, Christopher, Edmonton	.335	118	465	96	156	236	28	5	14	92	12	1	8	8	62	0	40	31	8
Sconiers, Daryl, Spokane°	.329	98	383	64	126	194	33	10	5	73	9	0	6	0	31	11	28	4	4
Gwynn, Anthony, Hawaii°	.328	93	366	65	120	162	23	2	5	46	6	5	3	1	18	2	18	14	5
Wellman, Brad, Phoenix	.324	102	339	64	110	155	19	7	4	42	5	3	3	5	26	0	41	9	6

Departmental Leaders: G—Doran, 142; AB—T. Davis, 571; R—Kittle, 121; H—Lubratich, 181; TB—Kittle, 355; 2B—Lubratich, 43; 3B—Pettis, 14; HR—Kittle, 50; RBI—Kittle, 144; GWRBI—Schroeder, 15; SH—Allen, 11; SF—Barrios, Bradley, 10; HP—Kittle, Lubratich, 10; BB—Brock, 105; IBB—Brock, 15; SO—Schroeder, 136; SB—Pettis, 53; CS—T. Davis, 22.

(All Players—Listed Alphabetically)

Player and Club	Pct.	G.	AB.	R.	H.	TB.	2B.	3B.	HR.	RBI.	GW.	SH.	SF.	HP.	BB.	Int. BB.	SO.	SB.	CS.
Adams, Ricky, Spokane	.310	71	248	42	77	111	10	3	6	33	3	4	2	6	16	2	29	18	8
Allen, James, Salt Lake City	.280	135	496	73	139	180	22	5	3	65	2	11	5	3	51	2	70	9	4
Allen, Roderick, Salt Lake City	.323	117	436	82	141	215	25	2	15	75	6	2	2	5	44	2	62	15	6
Amelung, Edward, Albuquerque°	.222	2	9	1	2	2	0	0	0	2	1	0	0	0	0	0	4	0	0
Anderson, David, Albuquerque	.343	132	507	100	174	222	19	7	5	76	5	6	5	0	54	0	65	43	12

Player and Club	Pct.	G.	AB.	R.	H.	TB.	2B.	3B.	HR.	RBI.	GW.	SH.	SF.	HP.	BB.	Int. BB.	SO.	SB.	CS.
Atherton, Keith, Tacoma	.000	28	1	0	0	0	0	0	0	0	0	0	0	0	0	0	1	0	0
Augustine, David, Portland	.213	30	80	15	17	33	3	2	3	13	3	1	1	2	7	0	6	2	0
Babitt, Mack, Tacoma	.290	47	169	25	49	56	5	1	0	16	1	3	2	0	16	0	10	11	6
Baker, Steven, Tacoma	.000	23	0	0	0	0	0	0	0	0	0	1	0	0	0	0	0	0	0
Barnes, Richard, Edmonton	.000	22	0	1	0	0	0	0	0	0	0	0	0	0	0	0	0	0	0
Barrios, Jose, Phoenix	.273	116	436	62	119	208	19	8	18	90	6	1	10	3	42	3	94	3	3
Bass, Kevin, Vancouver	.315	102	413	70	130	218	23	7	17	65	5	1	2	2	44	8	44	23	16
Bell, Kevin, Tacoma	.225	106	360	45	81	125	11	3	9	47	4	6	6	0	65	1	112	1	1
Benson, Steve, Tucson	.275	53	138	20	38	47	6	0	1	16	0	2	4	1	13	0	18	8	4
Bertoni, Jeffrey, Spokane	.254	42	122	23	31	52	10	1	3	19	2	2	0	0	16	0	29	3	2
Bishop, Michael, Spokane	.267	107	345	66	92	164	26	5	12	49	3	3	5	1	62	3	60	1	4
Bordi, Richard, Salt Lake City	1.000	25	1	0	1	1	0	0	0	0	0	0	0	0	0	0	0	0	0
Bosetti, Richard, Tacoma	.322	101	342	58	110	159	22	3	7	56	7	6	1	3	22	0	51	21	9
Bosley, Thaddis, Salt Lake City°	.298	22	84	15	25	40	2	2	3	9	0	0	1	0	11	1	11	2	2
Boyland, Dorian, Phoenix°	.259	107	371	51	96	152	19	8	7	52	2	1	5	1	38	7	73	8	5
Bradley, Mark, Albuquerque	.317	139	523	112	166	255	31	11	12	101	6	7	10	6	90	1	103	50	18
Bream, Sidney, Albuquerque°	.375	3	8	3	3	7	1	0	1	2	0	0	0	0	0	0	2	0	0
Brewer, Anthony, Albuquerque	.333	2	6	2	2	2	0	0	0	3	0	0	0	0	0	0	1	0	0
Brock, Gregory, Albuquerque°	.310	135	480	118	149	318	21	8	44	138	14	2	7	3	105	15	81	4	6
Brouhard, Mark, Vancouver	.282	17	71	12	20	31	1	2	2	8	0	0	0	3	1	0	15	0	0
Brown, Darrell, Tacoma	.288	140	534	75	154	205	26	5	5	65	5	3	4	0	24	3	51	28	11
Brown, Michael, Spokane	.284	134	476	74	135	212	30	7	11	73	7	2	5	1	47	0	70	5	6
Brown, Rogers, Salt Lake City†	.250	22	84	12	21	30	2	2	1	9	1	0	2	0	7	2	6	8	2
Brunansky, Thomas, Spokane	.205	25	88	12	18	29	6	1	1	6	1	0	1	0	15	0	19	4	4
Cacek, Craig, Spokane	.274	64	212	29	58	78	11	0	3	29	1	0	3	0	34	0	15	1	0
Cain, Aaron, Hawaii	.214	30	84	13	18	23	3	1	0	10	2	1	1	1	14	1	13	12	1
Carnes, Scott, Spokane	.245	101	286	41	70	98	13	0	5	31	3	6	2	3	27	0	53	4	4
Castro, Jose, Edmonton	.263	129	487	74	128	196	30	4	10	80	2	2	5	4	42	1	71	5	6
Caughey, Wayne, Portland°	.352	35	128	34	45	57	8	2	0	14	1	1	1	0	27	0	6	4	3
Chambers, Albert, Salt Lake City°	.280	97	343	57	96	158	28	5	8	50	6	1	2	0	47	5	75	12	6
Chappas, Harry, Edmonton†	.324	44	145	30	47	73	12	4	2	19	4	3	1	0	27	0	19	9	3
Cias, Darryl, Tacoma	.316	47	117	20	37	47	4	0	2	13	2	0	1	2	16	0	15	0	0
Clark, Roy, Salt Lake City	.291	125	475	85	138	188	25	5	5	50	10	6	6	4	62	3	36	13	11
Clements, Wesley, Tucson	.284	48	176	29	50	82	10	2	6	25	1	1	0	2	19	0	51	0	0
Cliburn, Stanley, Portland	.176	27	68	5	12	19	2	1	1	6	0	1	0	0	10	1	12	1	1
Crow, Donald, Albuquerque	.273	67	227	45	62	88	17	0	3	35	5	7	1	0	26	0	25	1	2
Cypret, Gregory, Tucson	.288	136	517	81	149	203	23	2	9	73	4	4	3	2	54	3	60	6	0
Dade, Paul, Portland	.405	22	37	7	15	20	3	1	0	6	0	0	0	0	13	0	6	1	0
Davis, Gerald, Hawaii	.269	41	145	26	39	56	8	0	3	19	2	1	1	3	21	1	25	3	1
Davis, Michael, Tacoma°	.316	100	374	71	118	183	23	3	12	68	13	3	3	2	45	4	53	40	10
Davis, Stanley, Vancouver°	.288	126	451	63	130	194	30	2	10	51	5	4	4	1	43	9	73	11	7
Davis, Trench, Portland°	.268	141	571	80	153	185	16	5	2	46	2	4	2	0	45	1	78	42	22
DeSimone, Gerald, Hawaii†	.273	136	487	91	133	183	27	7	3	41	4	9	4	0	87	1	58	12	6
Diaz, Mario, Salt Lake City	.368	5	19	2	7	8	1	0	0	2	1	1	0	0	0	0	1	1	0
Dillard, Stephen, Edmonton	.313	124	482	88	151	226	31	7	10	68	4	1	4	0	44	1	64	14	9
Doran, William, Tucson†	.302	142	559	100	169	218	32	7	1	65	5	2	2	0	87	4	63	48	10
Drumright, Keith, Tacoma°	.329	81	277	36	91	103	6	3	0	29	3	6	5	0	21	2	18	10	9
Edwards, Marshall, Vancouver°	.347	18	75	16	26	33	3	2	0	11	2	1	1	1	5	0	2	4	2
Essian, James, Salt Lake City	.226	10	31	1	7	8	1	0	0	1	0	1	0	2	0	0	4	0	0
Estrada, Manuel, Salt Lake City	.458	5	24	6	11	14	3	0	0	3	0	2	0	1	1	0	2	1	0
Evans, Johnny, 24 Van.-7 Tacoma	.220	31	82	11	18	26	5	0	1	10	1	0	1	3	17	1	11	0	1
Fobbs, Larry, Albuquerque	.281	118	405	69	114	144	22	1	2	54	9	8	6	1	64	1	47	14	11
Foley, Rickey, Spokane	.000	23	0	1	0	0	0	0	0	0	0	0	0	0	0	0	0	0	0
Frobel, Douglas, Portland°	.261	135	472	76	123	236	38	3	23	75	6	0	4	4	50	4	134	21	6
Fucci, Dominic, Edmonton°	.311	94	299	57	93	170	22	2	17	62	6	6	1	6	49	3	80	5	3
Gallego, Michael, Tacoma	.221	44	136	12	30	35	3	1	0	11	1	8	1	0	7	0	12	4	2
Gates, Joseph, Portland°	.271	29	70	13	19	24	2	0	1	3	0	0	0	1	5	0	11	2	0
Gausepohl, Daniel, Hawaii	.226	64	208	40	47	75	8	4	4	24	1	4	2	3	30	0	36	4	7
Gerber, Craig, Spokane°	.625	2	8	2	5	7	2	0	0	0	0	0	0	1	0	0	0	0	0
Gladden, Daniel, Phoenix†	.308	130	503	93	155	235	40	5	10	74	8	2	8	5	44	0	69	41	8
Gonzalez, Denio, Portland	.226	51	164	23	37	53	4	6	0	9	0	2	0	1	19	1	34	2	4
Goodwin, Danny, Tacoma°	.301	89	306	41	92	163	20	9	11	58	8	0	3	4	58	7	63	9	6
Grandas, Robert, Tacoma	.241	107	361	55	87	130	14	4	7	44	5	4	1	8	32	0	42	14	8
Gray, Gary, Salt Lake City	.303	39	145	25	44	70	5	0	7	26	1	0	0	3	15	0	32	1	1
Gray, Lorenzo, Edmonton	.358	124	481	97	172	263	33	5	16	79	5	4	3	7	38	1	54	20	10
Greer, Brian, Hawaii	.186	37	118	17	22	48	8	3	4	19	3	2	1	0	29	1	57	2	1
Gwosdz, Douglas, Hawaii	.186	29	86	11	16	27	5	0	2	12	0	3	2	3	11	1	22	0	1
Gwynn, Anthony, Hawaii°	.328	93	366	65	120	162	23	2	5	46	6	5	3	1	18	2	18	14	5
Hamm, Timothy, Hawaii	.000	3	3	0	0	0	0	0	0	0	0	0	0	0	0	0	2	0	0
Harper, Brian, Portland	.284	101	395	71	112	208	29	8	17	73	8	1	6	8	25	2	29	3	2
Harris, John, Spokane°	.221	98	331	35	73	114	15	1	8	61	5	0	7	0	28	2	50	1	0
Hart, Michael, Salt Lake City°	.269	134	472	86	127	184	15	6	10	74	11	4	2	3	89	4	70	8	10
Herz, Steven, 1 Spokane-64 Van.	.233	65	202	24	47	76	13	2	4	21	0	4	0	0	25	3	23	0	1
Hogg, David, Edmonton	.245	92	253	30	62	96	9	2	7	36	2	6	2	0	49	0	58	2	1
Holman, Dale, Albuquerque°	.284	103	299	39	85	111	12	4	2	44	4	3	3	1	43	2	61	3	3
Holton, Brian, Albuquerque	.500	32	2	0	1	1	0	0	0	0	0	0	0	0	0	0	0	0	0
Horton, William, Portland	.275	119	440	61	121	200	11	1	22	82	9	0	6	3	48	5	71	2	2
Hosley, Timothy, Tacoma	1.000	2	1	0	1	1	0	0	0	0	0	0	0	0	1	0	0	0	0
Irvine, Edward, Vancouver	.275	127	459	64	126	166	16	6	4	33	1	8	2	2	32	1	65	27	17
Jackson, Ronnie, Spokane	.300	7	30	5	9	12	1	1	0	2	1	0	0	1	3	2	4	1	0
Johnson, Jerry, Hawaii	.279	67	219	30	61	95	13	0	7	35	2	0	0	2	20	0	31	6	3
Jones, Christopher, Tucson°	.226	36	115	17	26	36	6	2	0	9	0	2	1	1	16	0	20	7	4
Jones, Ross, Albuquerque	.288	128	459	84	132	184	19	3	9	74	6	10	5	2	61	1	87	7	5
Kearney, Robert, Tacoma	.253	115	388	41	98	138	13	3	7	55	2	8	4	4	26	0	57	10	9
Kennedy, Kevin, Albuquerque	.285	51	137	17	39	53	5	0	3	23	3	6	0	2	10	1	22	3	3
Kittle, Ronald, Edmonton	.345	127	472	121	163	355	22	10	50	144	12	0	3	10	74	9	109	5	3
Kuntz, Russell, Edmonton	.269	69	193	35	52	88	11	2	7	34	2	3	3	0	50	1	54	7	11
Lake, Steven, Tucson	.265	112	378	42	100	132	15	4	3	45	3	7	5	1	17	2	28	5	2
Lamonde, Lawrence, Portland	.000	13	0	1	0	0	0	0	0	0	0	0	0	0	0	0	0	0	0
Lancellotti, Richard, Hawaii°	.272	136	500	76	136	235	31	4	20	95	9	0	6	7	61	7	81	3	5
Lansford, Joseph, Hawaii	.237	116	417	54	99	160	18	2	13	75	11	2	7	3	42	0	81	6	5
Lefebvre, Joseph, Hawaii°	.344	8	32	7	11	16	3	1	0	5	0	0	1	0	4	1	5	1	0

Player and Club	Pct.	G.	AB.	R.	H.	TB.	2B.	3B.	HR.	RBI.	GW.	SH.	SF.	HP.	BB.	Int. BB.	SO.	SB.	CS.
Leonard, Jeffrey, Phoenix	.356	17	59	14	21	38	5	0	4	12	0	0	0	6	1	10	2	4
Loman, Douglas, Vancouver°	.258	118	411	57	106	179	19	6	14	64	8	7	6	3	53	1	54	10	4
Long, Robert, Portland	.000	32	1	0	0	0	0	0	0	0	0	1	0	0	0	0	0	0	1
Loucks, Scott, Tucson	.265	74	310	48	82	107	12	5	1	21	2	3	2	4	28	0	48	43	6
Loviglio, John, Edmonton	.257	111	451	72	116	147	16	3	3	38	4	4	2	0	53	2	39	34	5
Lozado, William, Vancouver	.242	136	463	53	112	138	8	3	4	48	3	7	3	2	50	0	69	29	14
Lubratich, Steven, Spokane	.338	132	535	92	181	263	43	6	9	88	13	9	2	10	41	0	29	7	4
Madison, Scotti, Albuquerque†	.222	11	36	5	8	9	1	0	0	2	0	0	0	0	4	0	5	0	0
Maldonado, Candido, Albuquerque	.301	138	541	91	163	275	28	6	24	96	6	6	5	4	48	4	89	4	18
Maler, James, Salt Lake City	.336	63	253	51	85	129	18	4	6	53	2	0	2	3	26	1	25	7	4
Mangual, Jose, Spokane	.235	50	81	20	19	31	4	1	2	9	3	0	0	2	17	0	17	9	2
Manuel, Jerry, Hawaii	.196	26	92	8	18	23	3	1	0	7	1	1	0	0	11	0	12	2	2
Marshall, Michael, Albuquerque	.388	66	255	74	99	163	20	1	14	58	7	0	2	6	46	3	58	11	2
McDonald, James, Tucson°	.286	59	189	21	54	83	12	1	5	41	4	0	5	0	11	2	17	0	1
McHenry, Vance, Salt Lake City	.292	97	325	49	95	128	11	5	4	39	3	6	1	2	37	0	51	14	8
Mercado, Orlando, Salt Lake City	.280	90	321	43	90	161	19	2	16	66	5	4	4	0	22	0	59	2	1
Mitchell, Robert, Portland°	.262	133	454	49	119	156	17	7	2	57	3	6	2	2	45	3	42	26	17
Mize, Paul, Tacoma	.225	76	213	32	48	57	7	1	0	17	3	2	1	3	23	0	40	2	3
Moore, Kelvin, Tacoma	.264	113	421	77	111	201	19	4	21	82	6	0	6	2	60	6	133	15	5
Moreno, Jose, Spokane†	.302	68	248	44	75	113	16	5	4	30	1	2	1	1	25	4	31	28	12
Mullins, Francis, Edmonton	.282	98	309	55	87	148	15	2	14	57	1	3	3	2	48	0	71	2	2
Narron, Jerry, Spokane°	.311	110	408	60	127	191	24	2	12	61	8	1	5	2	47	5	45	0	1
Nettles, James, Tacoma°	.500	5	10	3	5	6	1	0	0	3	1	0	0	0	0	0	1	0	0
Norman, Nelson, Portland†	.270	134	445	58	120	138	7	4	1	52	4	4	3	2	76	3	27	9	11
Nyman, Christopher, Edmonton	.335	118	465	96	156	236	28	5	14	92	12	1	8	8	62	0	40	31	8
O'Malley, Thomas, Phoenix°	.448	26	96	23	43	65	11	1	3	15	2	0	0	0	11	1	9	0	1
Ortiz, Adalberto, Portland	.292	124	449	46	131	171	22	0	6	57	5	2	3	5	34	2	61	4	4
Page, Mitchell, Tacoma°	.305	85	295	62	90	154	18	2	14	59	7	0	2	4	46	5	72	25	9
Pankovits, James, Hawaii	.267	139	494	84	132	216	25	7	15	77	10	6	3	5	67	3	72	22	10
Parsons, Casey, Salt Lake City°	.285	96	323	47	92	124	11	3	5	35	3	1	2	1	59	6	35	8	7
Pate, Robert, Tucson	.347	94	329	76	114	168	23	8	5	59	5	2	5	3	57	1	33	26	5
Pearsey, Leslie, Spokane	.268	130	488	63	131	219	29	4	17	85	6	1	4	5	36	2	86	2	3
Pena, Adalberto, Tucson	.215	97	362	53	78	120	17	5	5	33	0	4	3	5	32	1	75	13	8
Pettini, Joseph, Phoenix	.325	80	305	51	99	153	21	3	9	46	0	0	1	4	34	1	27	16	11
Pettis, Gary, Spokane†	.288	133	528	108	152	205	22	14	1	59	5	4	1	1	78	4	107	53	18
Phillips, Anthony, Tacoma†	.297	86	300	76	89	129	18	5	4	47	4	7	3	1	73	1	63	29	12
Pittman, Joseph, Tucson	.400	8	30	6	12	14	2	0	0	4	0	2	0	1	0	1	3	2	—
Pruitt, Ronald, Phoenix	.320	73	225	38	72	122	16	2	10	37	1	1	5	2	29	1	30	3	2
Purpura, Daniel, Hawaii	.250	7	20	4	5	6	1	0	0	0	0	0	0	3	0	2	0	0	—
Pyburn, Jeffrey, Hawaii	.270	77	241	24	65	81	11	1	1	29	2	6	4	0	33	0	29	12	6
Rabb, John, Phoenix	.278	119	413	66	115	212	27	2	22	73	5	0	3	9	41	2	81	4	4
Ramirez, Mario, Hawaii	.257	22	70	14	18	27	6	0	1	9	0	0	1	0	8	0	17	2	0
Ramos, Domingo, Salt Lake City	.314	112	427	75	134	187	19	8	6	56	5	4	3	4	39	0	32	5	2
Ray, Larry, Tucson°	.294	107	391	57	115	196	22	7	15	79	5	1	3	8	40	4	94	4	5
Rex, Michael, Phoenix	.242	61	190	30	46	67	10	1	3	23	0	1	1	1	15	0	14	2	1
Richards, David, Hawaii	.150	8	20	1	3	3	0	0	0	1	0	0	0	0	1	0	3	1	0
Rodriguez, Jose, Portland	.265	32	98	14	26	47	8	2	3	19	1	0	1	1	11	0	31	3	1
Roenicke, Ronald, Albuquerque†	.308	23	78	18	24	43	5	1	4	15	1	0	0	1	20	0	11	3	2
Runnells, Thomas, Phoenix†	.268	108	347	52	93	123	8	11	0	48	4	4	4	0	43	3	23	15	4
Rush, Lawrence, Vancouver	.262	131	477	58	125	197	29	2	13	70	9	7	4	1	31	3	104	14	8
Sax, David, Albuquerque	.317	117	417	71	132	199	29	1	12	75	7	2	6	7	51	2	54	10	6
Schofield, Richard, Spokane	.300	7	30	4	9	18	4	1	1	12	1	0	0	3	0	6	0	0	—
Schroeder, William, Vancouver	.266	116	425	66	113	201	16	3	22	77	15	4	6	7	34	2	136	2	0
Schultz, Greg, Albuquerque	.329	26	73	15	24	34	4	0	2	10	1	0	0	2	10	0	12	1	3
Schuster, Mark, Vancouver°	.191	53	162	14	31	53	2	1	6	19	2	2	1	1	26	3	40	0	0
Sconiers, Daryl, Spokane°	.329	98	383	64	126	194	33	10	5	73	9	0	6	0	31	11	28	4	4
Seilheimer, Ricky, Edmonton°	.237	88	274	34	65	95	10	1	6	34	1	2	1	1	24	2	33	0	0
Sexton, Jimmy, Tacoma	.310	24	100	20	31	41	4	0	2	6	2	1	1	0	13	0	9	9	4
Sherow, Dennis, Tacoma	.231	3	13	0	3	4	1	0	0	2	0	0	0	0	0	0	4	1	0
Shoebridge, Terence, Vancouver°	.000	3	3	0	0	0	0	0	0	1	0	0	1	0	0	0	1	0	0
Skorochocki, John, Vancouver°	.262	90	260	32	68	90	9	5	1	25	3	4	6	1	35	1	28	5	7
Skube, Robert, Vancouver°	.279	130	433	55	121	190	26	2	13	61	7	3	3	1	67	12	78	13	7
Smith, Kelly, Phoenix	.235	76	187	25	44	52	6	1	0	16	3	2	0	0	21	0	30	3	1
Smith, Steven, Hawaii	.232	120	422	40	98	125	17	2	2	53	7	6	4	5	30	0	29	7	9
Spilman, Harry, Tucson°	.332	53	190	34	63	103	16	3	6	33	3	0	6	2	24	1	27	1	0
Steels, James, Hawaii°	.250	52	196	33	49	83	10	6	4	26	1	1	0	5	14	2	42	12	2
Stroughter, Stephen, Salt Lake City°	.333	54	192	34	64	118	11	2	13	48	4	0	1	1	32	5	26	1	2
Sularz, Guy, Phoenix	.436	9	39	8	17	22	0	1	1	7	2	0	0	1	4	1	0	1	2
Sutherland, Leonardo, Edmonton°	.241	121	489	72	118	147	13	5	2	55	4	2	4	2	43	0	64	33	10
Swiacki, William, Tacoma	.000	29	0	0	0	0	0	0	0	0	0	1	0	0	0	0	0	0	0
Szymarek, Paul, Phoenix	.255	82	251	47	64	121	12	3	13	42	2	2	2	1	50	0	66	5	6
Taveras, Alejandro, Albuquerque	.269	24	67	14	18	22	4	0	0	7	1	2	0	2	11	0	12	3	0
Thomas, Franklin, Vancouver	.271	125	425	52	115	134	8	4	1	37	5	8	5	2	62	0	74	20	10
Thurmond, Mark, Hawaii°	.000	28	3	0	0	0	0	0	0	0	0	0	0	0	0	0	3	0	0
Tingley, Ronald, Hawaii	.262	115	362	45	95	142	13	8	6	42	6	5	2	2	56	0	103	11	6
Tolman, Timothy, Tucson°	.302	125	473	93	143	231	31	6	15	82	10	4	5	2	77	4	50	10	3
Torres, Raymundo, Edmonton	.233	10	30	5	7	15	3	1	1	5	0	0	0	4	0	6	0	0	—
Tracy, James, Tucson°	.318	133	481	85	153	230	35	3	12	100	5	0	4	1	81	9	83	5	2
Turgeon, Michael, Phoenix†	.269	126	469	71	126	194	32	3	10	66	6	2	8	1	42	4	74	8	6
Valle, David, Salt Lake City	.209	75	234	28	49	74	11	1	4	28	4	1	2	1	26	0	26	0	2
Vargas, Hediberto, Portland	.311	124	440	87	137	252	27	2	28	80	7	1	4	5	55	2	108	3	1
Venable, McKinley, Phoenix°	.250	8	32	5	8	13	1	2	0	3	0	0	0	0	4	0	2	1	0
Vessey, Thomas, Tucson	.189	51	122	14	23	29	3	0	1	13	1	3	1	3	14	0	36	0	1
Walker, Gregory, Edmonton°	.350	35	117	18	41	58	8	0	3	12	3	0	0	0	25	4	14	0	1
Walker, Glen, Salt Lake City°	.303	44	142	23	43	78	6	1	9	30	2	1	2	2	13	0	28	0	2
Walton, Reginald, Portland°	.302	95	344	62	104	181	31	2	14	59	5	0	6	2	37	3	52	10	5
Wellman, Brad, Phoenix	.324	102	339	64	110	155	19	7	4	42	5	3	3	5	26	0	41	9	6
Wherry, Clifton, Tucson†	.392	16	51	7	20	24	4	0	0	13	2	1	0	2	9	0	11	2	1
Wiedenbauer, Thomas, Tucson	.245	25	49	4	12	14	0	1	0	5	0	0	1	0	4	0	15	0	1
Wiggins, Alan, Hawaii†	.312	19	77	14	24	37	2	4	1	4	0	1	0	0	9	0	5	21	1
Wilborn, Thaddeus, Phoenix†	.257	132	501	69	129	179	20	12	2	58	0	5	3	3	46	0	62	34	17
Wilson, Michael, Albuquerque	.378	99	368	77	139	182	25	6	2	56	0	5	2	6	48	1	27	25	17

Player and Club	Pct.	G.	AB.	R.	H.	TB.	2B.	3B.	HR.	RBI.	GW.	SH.	SF.	HP.	BB.	Int. BB.	SO.	SB.	CS.
Wotus, Ronald, Portland	.290	42	145	27	42	67	6	5	3	23	2	2	1	0	17	1	19	3	0
Wright, Richard, Albuquerque*	.000	18	1	1	0	0	0	0	0	0	0	0	0	0	0	0	0	0	0

The following pitchers, listed alphabetically by club, with games in parentheses, had no plate appearances, primarily through use of designated hitters:

ALBUQUERQUE—Beckwith, Joseph (26); Fernandez, Sidney (13); Franco, John (5); Geiger, Burwell (45); Hershiser, Orel (48); Moore, David (13); Niedenfuer, Thomas (4); Pena, Alejandro (16); Power, Ted (15); Rennicke, Dean (1); Rodas, Richard (29); Shirley, Steven (34); White, Larry (28); Wise, Brett (1).

EDMONTON—Agosto, Juan (50); Arroyo, Fernando (18); Bradley, Leonard (33); Camacho, Ernie (7); Capilla, Douglas (21); Combe, Geoffrey (33); Contreras, Arnaldo (1); Desjarlais, Keith (7); Edwards, Larry (5); Escarrega, Ernesto (2); Hardy, John (1); Hoffman, Guy (29); Ibarra, Carlos (16); Johnson, Charles (14); Maitland, Michael (6); Patterson, Reginald (31); Schattinger, Jeffrey (31); Siwy, James (26).

HAWAII—Coffman, James (23); Couchee, Michael (11); Dravecky, David (16); Fireovid, Stephen (25); Hawkins, Andrew (18); Kuhaulua, Fred (17); Meredith, Ronald (37); Miggins, Mark (27); Seaman, Kim (11); Stablein, George (24); Tellmann, Thomas (41).

PHOENIX—Calvert, Mark (6); Chamberlain, Craig (31); Chris, Michael (17); Cornell, Jeffery (25); Dempsey, Mark (27); Fowlkes, Alan (13); Hammaker, Atlee (1); Hargesheimer, Alan (29); Hinrichs, Phillip (38); Laskey, William (2); Martin, Renie (3); McGaffigan, Andrew (18); Rowland, Michael (28); Schatzeder, Daniel (1); Stember, Jeffrey (28); Tucker, Michael (37).

PORTLAND—Alcala, Santo (2); DeLeon, Jose (24); Edge, Claude (35); Esquer, Mercedes (7); Guante, Cecilio (21); Jones, Odell (28); Kobel, Kevin (7); Lee, Mark (27); Miscik, Dennis (32); Moskau, Paul (4); Neuenschwander, Douglas (1); Niemann, Randy (8); Perez, Pascual (19); Sarmiento, Manuel (6); Tunnell, Lee (28).

SALT LAKE CITY—Abbott, Glenn (2); Allard, Brian (5); Andersen, Larry (5); Clark, Bryan (4); Decker, George (8); Finch, Steven (42); Harris, Tracy (27); Moore, Michael (1); Musselman, Ronald (51); Nelson, Eugene (5); Nunez, Edwin (11); Snyder, Brian (51); Stoddard, Robert (24); Thomas, Roy (33); Welborn, Sammye (46); Young, Matthew (29).

SPOKANE—Braun, Barton (2); Brown, Curtis (50); Brown, Steven (27); Cliburn, Stewart (8); Coleman, Joseph (13); Corbett, Douglas (8); Eaton, James (55); Mahler, Michael (20); McLaughlin, Byron (6); Moreno, Angel (22); Quiros, Gustavo (6); Rasmussen, Dennis (27); Sanchez, Luis (2); Schneider, Jeffrey (18); Steirer, Ricky (30); Walters, Michael (10).

TACOMA—Beard, David (1); Bradley, Bert (17); Buice, DeWayne (19); Castro, William (12); Codiroli, Christopher (16); Comstock, Keith (5); D'Acquisto, John (4); Figueroa, Eduardo (2); Fowler, Don (18); Heaverlo, David (2); Heimueller, Gorman (5); Jones, Jeffrey (8); Kingman, Brian (9); Kinney, Dennis (47); McLaughlin, Michael (23); Mustad, Eric (25); Patterson, David (35).

TUCSON—Boone, Daniel (25); Cappuzzello, George (15); Keeton, Rickey (41); Leatherwood, Delrick (3); Lysander, Richard (42); Mathis, Ronald (14); Moffitt, Randall (7); Morris, Jeffrey (9); Paris, Zacarias (28); Pladson, Gordon (24); Richard, James (6); Roberge, Bertrand (34); Ross, Mark (43); Smith, Billy (28); Sprowl, Robert (10).

VANCOUVER—Anderson, Michael (30); Cocanower, James (14); Cook, Timothy (27); DiPino, Frank (26); Gibson, Robert (6); Jones, Douglas (23); Kranitz, Richard (35); Ladd, Peter (34); Madden, Michael (20); Martinez, Alfredo (21); Olsen, Richard (21); Porter, Charles (25); Robinson, Dewey (21); Uhey, Jackie (3); Valley, Charles (38).

GRAND-SLAM HOME RUNS—R. Allen, Brock, Mercado, Szymarek, 2 each; Bertoni, Bosetti, M. Brown, Fucci, Grandas, Horton, Lozado, Maldonado, Maler, Page, Parsons, Pate, Pearsey, Rush, Schofield, Schroeder, Skube, Tingley, Tolman, Tracy, Vargas, Walton, 1 each.

AWARDED FIRST BASE ON CATCHER'S INTERFERENCE—Harris 4 (Crow, Essian, Kearney, Rabb); Bertoni 3 (Ortiz 2, Mercado); M. Brown 2 (Kearney, Ortiz), S. Davis 2 (Mercado, Rabb); McDonald (Essian); Pyburn (Cias); Rabb (Schroeder); Runnells (Crow); Wilson (Pruitt).

CLUB FIELDING

Club	Pct.	G.	PO.	A.	E.	DP.	PB.	Club	Pct.	G.	PO.	A.	E.	DP.	PB.
Spokane	.970	143	3694	1533	164	116	16	Edmonton	.966	144	3681	1731	188	153	23
Vancouver	.968	144	3751	1610	176	140	23	Salt Lake City	.966	143	3715	1587	185	129	19
Phoenix	.968	144	3604	1458	167	129	16	Tacoma	.966	143	3739	1624	188	100	7
Albuquerque	.967	143	3720	1591	179	132	22	Tucson	.965	142	3628	1622	192	162	15
Hawaii	.967	144	3646	1693	181	134	17	Portland	.964	144	3678	1409	190	100	11

INDIVIDUAL FIELDING
FIRST BASEMEN

*Throws lefthanded

Player and Club	Pct.	G.	PO.	A.	E.	DP.	Player and Club	Pct.	G.	PO.	A.	E.	DP.
Augustine, Portland	1.000	4	17	3	0	0	Marshall, Albuquerque	.971	4	34	0	1	4
Barrios, Phoenix	.987	99	795	63	11	79	McDonald, Tucson*	.917	4	21	1	2	1
Bishop, Spokane	1.000	1	6	0	0	1	Mercado, Salt Lake City	1.000	2	24	0	0	1
Bosetti, Tacoma	.967	3	27	2	1	1	Moore, Tacoma*	.991	104	889	73	9	59
Boyland, Phoenix*	.983	45	340	16	6	32	NYMAN, Edmonton	.994	108	1022	76	7	94
Bream, Albuquerque*	1.000	1	11	0	0	0	Ortiz, Portland	1.000	2	1	0	0	0
Brock, Albuquerque	.983	130	1076	106	20	106	Parsons, Salt Lake City	.968	18	169	14	6	17
Cacek, Spokane	1.000	12	114	14	0	7	Pearsey, Spokane	.974	4	37	1	1	3
Clements, Tucson	.984	38	333	35	6	35	Rush, Vancouver	1.000	1	9	0	0	0
Davis, Tacoma*	1.000	1	2	0	0	0	Sax, Albuquerque	1.000	14	104	4	0	8
Davis, Vancouver	.991	67	596	32	6	61	Schuster, Vancouver*	.981	52	385	31	8	37
Dillard, Edmonton	1.000	6	60	1	0	8	Sconiers, Spokane*	.988	96	842	32	11	69
Evans, Vancouver-Tacoma	.994	16	150	11	1	12	Skorochocki, Vancouver	.971	4	30	4	1	2
Fucci, Edmonton*	.976	23	187	19	5	27	Skube, Vancouver*	.951	17	70	8	4	15
Goodwin, Tacoma	.987	32	288	22	4	18	Smith, Phoenix	1.000	2	4	0	0	0
Gray, Salt Lake City	.992	37	342	27	3	27	Spilman, Tucson	.991	35	307	13	3	38
Gray, Edmonton	1.000	1	10	4	0	0	Steels, Hawaii*	.882	3	14	1	2	1
Harris, Spokane*	.991	29	203	23	2	18	Stroughter, Salt Lake City	.987	25	210	16	3	16
Hogg, Edmonton	1.000	1	7	0	0	1	Tolman, Tucson	.979	51	440	40	12	43
Holman, Albuquerque	.889	1	8	0	1	0	Tracy, Tucson	.987	23	213	9	3	27
Horton, Portland	.936	5	41	3	3	2	Turgeon, Phoenix	1.000	5	27	1	0	2
Jackson, Spokane	.987	7	67	8	1	7	Valle, Salt Lake City	1.000	1	12	2	0	1
Lancellotti, Hawaii*	.987	31	286	15	4	27	Vargas, Portland	.988	122	1016	64	13	69
Lansford, Hawaii	.987	111	1057	66	15	96	Walker, Edmonton	1.000	10	94	11	0	7
Maler, Salt Lake City	.990	62	557	58	6	55	Walton, Portland	.979	18	130	8	3	9

SECOND BASEMEN

Player and Club	Pct.	G.	PO.	A.	E.	DP.	Player and Club	Pct.	G.	PO.	A.	E.	DP.
Adams, Spokane	.976	51	120	121	6	26	Dade, Portland	.885	8	7	16	3	0
Babitt, Tacoma	.968	41	82	102	6	15	DeSimone, Hawaii	.959	11	21	26	2	10
Bertoni, Spokane	1.000	4	3	3	0	0	Dillard, Edmonton	.976	39	100	102	5	26
Bosetti, Tacoma	.923	4	6	6	1	1	Doran, Tucson	.972	142	361	424	23	123
Carnes, Spokane	1.000	4	2	2	0	0	Drumright, Tacoma	.962	54	121	129	10	29
Clark, Salt Lake City	.965	106	206	321	19	67	Fobbs, Albuquerque	.920	8	11	12	2	1

SECOND BASEMEN—Continued

Player and Club	Pct.	G.	PO.	A.	E.	DP.
Gallego, Tacoma	.985	27	60	69	2	11
Gates, Portland	.970	22	29	35	2	5
Gerber, Spokane	1.000	1	2	3	0	1
Gonzalez, Portland	.921	49	104	130	20	22
Gray, Edmonton	.935	8	12	17	2	4
Jones, Albuquerque	.966	123	265	331	21	76
LOVIGLIO, Edmonton	.980	103	244	291	11	69
Lubratich, Spokane	.972	90	185	237	12	53
McHenry, Salt Lake City	.962	39	68	111	7	18
Mitchell, Portland	.933	43	77	91	12	19
Mize, Tacoma	.971	38	78	92	5	11
J. Moreno, Spokane	.964	7	9	18	1	4
Norman, Portland	1.000	1	0	1	0	0
Pankovits, Hawaii	.979	38	99	90	4	20
Pettini, Phoenix	1.000	3	7	15	0	1
Purpura, Hawaii	1.000	2	5	2	0	1
Rex, Phoenix	.943	33	59	74	8	15
Runnells, Phoenix	.973	14	30	41	2	10
Schultz, Albuquerque	.974	10	13	24	1	5
Sexton, Tacoma	1.000	4	6	13	0	1
Skorochocki, Vancouver	.972	35	57	83	4	17
Smith, Hawaii	.973	97	208	299	14	55
Taveras, Albuquerque	.963	6	8	18	1	6
Thomas, Vancouver	.973	120	290	334	17	72
Wellman, Phoenix	.970	102	201	254	14	64
Wilborn, Phoenix	.933	4	7	7	1	2
Wilson, Albuquerque	.952	4	10	10	1	3
Wotus, Portland	.978	36	57	74	3	20

THIRD BASEMEN

Player and Club	Pct.	G.	PO.	A.	E.	DP.
J. Allen, Salt Lake City	.928	135	104	271	29	25
Augustine, Portland	.913	16	17	25	4	1
Barrios, Phoenix	1.000	1	1	1	0	0
Bell, Tacoma	.928	106	87	249	26	15
Benson, Tucson	.833	3	0	5	1	1
Bertoni, Spokane	1.000	5	4	3	0	1
Bishop, Spokane	1.000	3	0	2	0	0
Bosetti, Tacoma	.762	8	3	13	5	1
Castro, Edmonton	.932	61	49	142	14	18
Caughey, Portland	.960	31	25	70	4	10
CYPRET, Tucson	.945	133	93	299	23	33
Dade, Portland	.786	9	4	7	3	0
DeSimone, Hawaii	.908	22	15	44	6	2
Dillard, Edmonton	.905	43	31	93	13	11
Drumright, Tacoma	.976	25	33	49	2	4
Fobbs, Albuquerque	.941	112	54	247	19	16
Gallego, Tacoma	.891	13	11	30	5	2
Gerber, Spokane	1.000	1	2	3	0	1
Gonzalez, Portland	1.000	1	2	3	0	1
Gray, Edmonton	.934	40	27	100	9	12
Harper, Portland	.971	13	7	26	1	1
Johnson, Hawaii	.886	32	11	67	10	9
Lefebvre, Hawaii	.875	3	1	6	1	0
Lubratich, Spokane	.961	48	41	105	6	9
McHenry, Salt Lake City	.810	8	3	14	4	1
Mercado, Salt Lake City	1.000	2	0	1	0	0
Mitchell, Portland	.915	78	62	122	17	11
Nyman, Edmonton	.907	12	15	34	5	7
O'Malley, Phoenix	.903	26	12	44	6	4
Pankovits, Hawaii	.925	76	49	172	18	12
Pearsey, Spokane	.944	97	77	212	17	23
Pettini, Phoenix	.867	3	3	10	2	1
Pittman, Tucson	.867	5	3	10	2	0
Purpura, Hawaii	1.000	2	2	3	0	0
Rex, Phoenix	.895	9	6	11	2	0
Runnells, Phoenix	.959	20	12	35	2	4
Rush, Vancouver	.931	125	113	265	28	30
Sax, Albuquerque	.929	20	7	32	3	4
Schofield, Spokane	1.000	4	1	8	0	0
Schultz, Albuquerque	.966	14	5	23	1	1
Skorochocki, Vancouver	.975	25	27	52	2	7
Smith, Hawaii	.962	15	12	38	2	3
Sularz, Phoenix	1.000	6	2	12	0	0
Taveras, Albuquerque	.833	6	3	7	2	0
Tolman, Tucson	1.000	3	1	1	0	0
Turgeon, Phoenix	.942	84	79	166	15	23
Walton, Portland	.843	18	22	21	8	2
Wellman, Phoenix	1.000	2	0	3	0	0

SHORTSTOPS

Player and Club	Pct.	G.	PO.	A.	E.	DP.
Adams, Spokane	.979	24	35	60	2	12
J. Allen, Salt Lake City	1.000	1	2	0	0	0
Anderson, Albuquerque	.948	129	223	397	34	81
Babitt, Tacoma	1.000	1	3	2	0	1
Benson, Tucson	.947	35	45	98	8	16
Bertoni, Spokane	.930	35	56	90	11	13
Carnes, Spokane	.937	94	105	235	23	32
Caughey, Portland	1.000	4	3	7	0	1
Chappas, Edmonton	.923	33	51	81	11	21
Cypret, Tucson	1.000	2	4	9	0	1
DeSimone, Hawaii	.937	92	147	347	33	60
Diaz, Salt Lake City	.950	4	4	15	1	0
Dillard, Edmonton	.942	33	41	106	9	16
Fobbs, Albuquerque	1.000	1	3	5	0	2
Gallego, Tacoma	.933	5	2	12	1	2
Jones, Albuquerque	.900	5	8	19	3	2
Lozado, Vancouver	.959	136	255	418	29	79
Manuel, Hawaii	.991	25	41	73	1	12
McHenry, Salt Lake City	.933	45	67	127	14	26
Mitchell, Portland	.714	3	1	4	2	0
Mize, Tacoma	.942	38	58	120	11	20
Mullins, Edmonton	.938	93	135	305	29	57
NORMAN, Portland	.968	134	224	342	19	50
Pena, Tucson	.939	96	181	299	31	63
Pettini, Phoenix	.958	75	127	218	15	36
Phillips, Tacoma	.926	86	138	236	30	32
Purpura, Hawaii	1.000	3	1	2	0	0
Ramirez, Spokane	.949	20	29	64	5	12
Ramos, Salt Lake City	.960	98	174	288	19	55
Runnells, Phoenix	.941	75	121	183	19	33
Schofield, Spokane	1.000	4	6	12	0	4
Sexton, Tacoma	.942	20	41	57	6	13
Skorochocki, Vancouver	.625	6	4	6	6	2
Smith, Hawaii	.886	7	13	18	4	4
Sularz, Phoenix	1.000	3	9	11	0	4
Taveras, Albuquerque	1.000	13	27	43	0	3
Thomas, Vancouver	.967	8	8	21	1	1
Wherry, Tucson	.927	16	19	57	6	14
Wotus, Portland	.957	7	8	14	1	0

OUTFIELDERS

Player and Club	Pct.	G.	PO.	A.	E.	DP.
Adams, Spokane	.000	1	0	0	1	0
R. Allen, Salt Lake City	.969	96	178	8	6	1
Amelung, Albuquerque°	1.000	3	5	0	0	0
Augustine, Portland	1.000	2	2	0	0	0
Babitt, Tacoma	1.000	6	8	0	0	0
Bass, Vancouver	.955	100	199	15	10	3
Bertoni, Spokane	1.000	2	7	0	0	0
Bishop, Spokane	1.000	3	5	1	0	0
Bosetti, Tacoma	.980	82	191	10	4	2
Bosley, Salt Lake City°	1.000	13	24	2	0	0
Bradley, Albuquerque	.975	133	255	13	7	5
Brewer, Albuquerque	1.000	1	3	0	0	0
Brouhard, Vancouver	.971	13	30	3	1	0
Brown, Tacoma	.983	136	261	20	5	4
M. Brown, Spokane	.957	132	230	14	11	1
Brown, Salt Lake City	.979	22	44	2	1	0
Brunansky, Spokane	.981	24	44	7	1	1
Cacek, Spokane	.857	5	6	0	1	0
Cain, Hawaii	.951	28	37	3	3	0
Castro, Edmonton	.978	53	82	9	2	1
Chambers, Salt Lake City°	.971	93	165	3	5	0
Chappas, Edmonton	.833	3	5	0	1	0
Cliburn, Portland	1.000	1	1	0	0	0
Davis, Hawaii	.919	41	68	11	7	1
Davis, Tacoma°	.959	96	195	13	9	2
Davis, Portland°	.961	141	333	16	14	3
Edwards, Vancouver°	.917	15	21	1	2	0
Frobel, Portland	.956	134	229	11	11	3
Fucci, Edmonton°	.905	14	18	1	2	0
Gausepohl, Hawaii	.990	62	96	6	1	1
Gladden, Phoenix	.976	129	264	16	7	5
Goodwin, Tacoma	.925	32	60	2	5	1
Grandas, Tacoma	.945	91	145	9	9	1
Gray, Edmonton	.970	78	158	5	5	0
Greer, Hawaii	1.000	21	54	2	0	1
Gwosdz, Hawaii	1.000	1	1	0	0	0
Gwynn, Hawaii°	.982	92	208	11	4	5
Harper, Portland	.959	88	134	7	6	1
Harris, Spokane°	.964	28	27	0	1	0
Hart, Salt Lake City°	.982	126	268	10	5	2

OUTFIELDERS—Continued

Player and Club	Pct.	G.	PO.	A.	E.	DP.
Holman, Albuquerque	.975	77	110	5	3	2
Irvine, Vancouver	.980	123	279	9	6	2
Johnson, Hawaii	1.000	18	26	1	0	0
Jones, Tucson	.967	31	58	1	2	0
Kittle, Edmonton	.953	122	148	15	8	1
Kuntz, Edmonton	.965	59	134	3	5	0
Lancellotti, Hawaii*	1.000	13	18	1	0	0
Lefebvre, Hawaii	1.000	5	13	0	0	0
Leonard, Phoenix	1.000	4	5	0	0	0
Loman, Vancouver*	.959	93	176	12	8	3
Loucks, Tucson	.968	73	173	6	6	1
Maldonado, Albuquerque	.970	135	303	15	10	3
Mangual, Spokane	.952	33	37	3	2	1
Marshall, Albuquerque	.965	52	79	3	3	2
McDonald, Tucson*	.960	22	24	0	1	0
McHenry, Salt Lake City	1.000	2	3	0	0	0
Mercado, Salt Lake City	.800	6	4	0	1	0
Mitchell, Portland	.909	5	10	0	1	0
J. Moreno, Spokane	.943	60	97	3	6	0
Nettles, Tacoma*	1.000	4	7	0	0	0
Ortiz, Portland	1.000	2	6	0	0	0
Page, Tacoma	1.000	5	5	0	0	0
Pankovits, Hawaii	1.000	22	44	0	0	0
Parsons, Salt Lake City	.966	53	81	4	3	0
Pate, Tucson	.951	87	168	6	9	3
Pearsey, Spokane	1.000	32	36	2	0	0
Pena, Tucson	.500	1	1	0	1	0
PETTIS, Spokane	.983	132	345	9	6	3
Pittman, Tucson	1.000	3	4	0	0	0
Pruitt, Phoenix	1.000	13	28	0	0	0
Pyburn, Hawaii	.960	77	140	4	6	2
Rabb, Phoenix	.857	5	6	0	1	0
Ray, Tucson	.950	102	183	9	10	0
Rodriguez, Portland	.984	32	57	4	1	0
Roenicke, Albuquerque*	1.000	13	14	1	0	0
Runnells, Phoenix	1.000	2	1	0	0	0
Sax, Albuquerque	.950	14	19	0	1	0
Schultz, Albuquerque	1.000	1	4	0	0	0
Sherow, Tacoma	1.000	3	8	0	0	0
Skorochocki, Vancouver	1.000	3	3	0	0	0
Skube, Vancouver	.957	105	192	9	9	6
Smith, Phoenix	.980	71	140	9	3	5
Steels, Hawaii*	.978	50	89	1	2	0
Sutherland, Edmonton*	.975	118	259	12	7	3
Szymarek, Phoenix	.977	77	160	8	4	1
Tolman, Tucson	.967	54	84	5	3	0
Torres, Edmonton	1.000	10	19	1	0	0
Tracy, Tucson	.989	51	81	5	1	1
Turgeon, Phoenix	.950	25	37	1	2	0
Venable, Phoenix	1.000	8	16	0	0	0
Vessey, Tucson	1.000	1	2	1	0	0
Walker, Salt Lake City	.915	34	52	2	5	2
Walton, Portland	.986	46	67	4	1	1
Wiedenbauer, Tucson	1.000	23	45	1	0	0
Wiggins, Hawaii	1.000	19	33	4	0	1
Wilborn, Phoenix	.970	128	283	6	9	1
Wilson, Albuquerque	.963	32	51	1	2	0

CATCHERS

Player and Club	Pct.	G.	PO.	A.	E.	DP.	PB.
Bishop, Spokane	.975	74	411	48	12	4	11
Cias, Tacoma	.972	39	163	13	5	2	2
Cliburn, Portland	.988	26	157	10	2	1	0
Crow, Albuquerque	.984	64	400	43	7	3	8
Essian, Salt Lake City	.968	10	53	8	2	0	0
Gwosdz, Hawaii	.974	26	132	16	4	0	3
Harper, Portland	.963	6	23	3	1	0	1
Herz, Spokane-Vancouver	.983	43	209	23	4	3	8
Hogg, Edmonton	.979	85	359	52	9	9	18
Hosley, Tacoma	1.000	1	3	0	0	0	0
Johnson, Hawaii	1.000	2	5	0	0	0	0
Kearney, Tacoma	.987	114	589	93	9	6	5
Kennedy, Albuquerque	.971	49	217	21	7	4	3
Kittle, Edmonton	1.000	1	1	0	0	0	0
Lake, Tucson	.980	112	504	91	12	3	9
Madison, Albuquerque	1.000	1	6	0	0	0	0
Mercado, Salt Lake City	.977	73	469	42	12	5	8
Narron, Spokane	.976	74	446	46	12	2	5
Ortiz, Portland	.978	120	744	110	19	17	10
Pruitt, Phoenix	.978	37	193	31	5	2	2
Rabb, Phoenix	.976	109	546	55	15	10	14
Rex, Phoenix	.875	3	7	0	1	0	0
Richards, Hawaii	.974	8	31	2	1	1	0
Sax, Albuquerque	.974	47	273	21	8	0	1
SCHROEDER, Vancouver	.989	106	569	77	7	9	15
Seilheimer, Edmonton	.984	77	337	37	6	6	5
Shoebridge, Vancouver	1.000	2	9	0	0	0	0
Tingley, Hawaii	.981	114	540	77	12	8	13
Valle, Salt Lake City	.972	70	335	47	11	2	11
Vessey, Tucson	.971	50	208	23	7	6	6

PITCHERS

Player and Club	Pct.	G.	PO.	A.	E.	DP.
Abbott, Salt Lake City	1.000	2	0	1	0	0
Agosto, Edmonton*	.885	50	9	14	3	0
Allard, Salt Lake City	.667	5	2	0	1	0
Andersen, Salt Lake City	.750	5	2	1	1	0
Anderson, Vancouver*	.960	30	8	16	1	3
Arroyo, Tacoma-Edmonton	.933	18	7	7	1	1
Atherton, Tacoma	.897	28	11	24	4	1
Baker, Tacoma	.893	23	12	13	3	1
Barnes, Edmonton*	.923	19	7	17	2	0
Beard, Tacoma	1.000	1	0	1	0	0
Beckwith, Albuquerque	.885	26	10	13	3	2
Boone, Tucson*	1.000	25	1	5	0	2
Bordi, Salt Lake City	.971	25	12	22	1	0
Bradley, Tacoma	1.000	17	2	4	0	0
Bradley, Edmonton	.913	33	6	15	2	0
Braun, Spokane	1.000	2	1	4	0	1
C. Brown, Spokane	.933	50	4	10	1	0
S. Brown, Spokane	.902	27	13	33	5	6
Buice, Tacoma	1.000	19	3	3	0	1
Calvert, Phoenix	1.000	6	2	1	0	1
Camacho, Edmonton	1.000	7	2	1	0	0
Capilla, Edmonton*	1.000	21	0	7	0	0
Cappuzzello, Tucson*	.857	15	0	6	1	0
Castro, Tacoma	.833	12	1	4	1	1
Chamberlain, Phoenix	.895	31	6	11	2	1
Chappas, Edmonton	1.000	1	1	0	0	0
Chris, Phoenix*	.920	17	2	21	2	0
B. Clark, Salt Lake City*	1.000	4	0	1	0	0
Cliburn, Spokane	.818	8	2	7	2	0
Cocanower, Vancouver	.778	14	5	16	6	1
Codiroli, Tacoma	1.000	16	18	20	0	3
Coffman, Hawaii	.857	23	4	2	1	2
Coleman, Spokane	1.000	13	3	7	0	1
Combe, Edmonton	.909	33	3	7	1	1
Comstock, Tacoma*	1.000	5	1	7	0	0
Cook, Vancouver	.824	26	13	15	6	0
Corbett, Spokane	1.000	8	1	1	0	0
Cornell, Phoenix	.875	25	2	5	1	1
Couchee, Hawaii	1.000	11	0	5	0	1
Decker, Salt Lake City	1.000	8	0	1	0	0
DeLeon, Portland	.867	24	4	9	2	0
Dempsey, Phoenix	.955	27	9	12	1	1
Desjarlais, Edmonton	1.000	7	3	5	0	0
DiPino, Vancouver*	.912	26	7	24	3	1
Dravecky, Hawaii*	1.000	16	0	8	0	0
Eaton, Spokane	.931	35	11	16	2	0
Edge, Portland	.857	35	5	7	2	1
Edwards, Edmonton*	1.000	5	3	2	0	0
Escarrega, Edmonton	1.000	2	1	2	0	0
Esquer, Portland*	1.000	7	0	3	0	0
Fernandez, Albuquerque*	.917	13	3	8	1	0
Figueroa, Tacoma	1.000	2	0	1	0	0
Finch, Salt Lake City	1.000	42	6	17	0	6
Fireovid, Hawaii	1.000	25	12	22	0	4
Foley, Spokane	.974	22	10	28	1	1
Fowler, Tacoma	.889	18	9	15	3	0
Fowlkes, Phoenix	1.000	13	4	14	0	2
Franco, Albuquerque*	1.000	5	1	7	0	1
Geiger, Albuquerque	.897	45	10	16	3	3
Gibson, Vancouver	1.000	6	0	1	0	0
Guante, Portland	1.000	21	0	4	0	0
Hamm, Hawaii	.866	28	16	42	9	3
Hardy, Edmonton	1.000	1	0	1	0	0
Hargesheimer, Phoenix	.939	29	5	26	2	0
Harris, Salt Lake City	.936	27	19	25	3	1
Hawkins, Hawaii	.947	18	6	12	1	0
Heimueller, Tacoma*	1.000	5	1	7	0	0
Hershiser, Albuquerque	.941	47	14	18	2	2
Hinrichs, Phoenix	.938	38	5	10	1	0
Hoffman, Edmonton*	.941	28	8	24	2	2
Holton, Albuquerque	.940	32	17	30	3	7
Ibarra, Edmonton	.889	16	5	3	1	0
Johnson, Edmonton	.889	14	4	12	2	2
Jones, Vancouver	.920	23	6	17	2	1
Jones, Tacoma	1.000	8	1	0	0	0
Jones, Portland	.881	28	10	27	5	1
Keeton, Tucson	.917	40	11	33	4	4
Kennedy, Albuquerque	1.000	1	0	1	0	0

PITCHERS—Continued

Player and Club	Pct.	G.	PO.	A.	E.	DP.	Player and Club	Pct.	G.	PO.	A.	E.	DP.
Kingman, Tacoma	.889	8	4	4	1	0	Pena, Albuquerque	.909	16	4	6	1	0
Kinney, Tacoma*	1.000	47	3	7	0	0	Perez, Portland	1.000	19	4	20	0	2
Kobel, Portland*	.750	7	0	3	1	0	Pladson, Tucson	.903	24	8	20	3	1
Kranitz, Vancouver	.857	35	4	20	4	0	Porter, Vancouver	.980	25	15	33	1	2
Kuhaulua, Hawaii*	.813	17	2	11	3	1	Power, Albuquerque	1.000	14	4	6	0	0
Ladd, Vancouver	1.000	34	3	5	0	1	Quiros, Spokane	1.000	6	1	3	0	0
Lamonde, Portland	.958	12	5	18	1	0	Rasmussen, Spokane*	.935	27	1	28	2	2
Laskey, Phoenix	1.000	2	2	3	0	0	Richard, Tucson	.750	6	2	1	1	0
Leatherwood, Tucson	1.000	3	1	1	0	0	Roberge, Tucson	1.000	34	2	4	0	0
Lee, Portland	.857	27	1	5	1	0	Robinson, Port.-Vancouver	.889	21	1	7	1	0
Long, Portland	.974	31	11	26	1	0	Rodas, Albuquerque*	.944	29	15	36	3	0
Lysander, Tucson	.974	42	11	27	1	2	Ross, Tucson	.955	43	6	15	1	0
Madden, Vancouver*	1.000	18	1	18	0	1	Rowland, Phoenix	.905	28	13	25	4	0
Mahler, Spokane*	.969	20	4	27	1	1	Sanchez, Spokane	.000	2	0	0	1	0
Maitland, Edmonton*	1.000	6	1	8	0	1	Sarmiento, Portland	1.000	6	1	1	0	0
Martin, Phoenix	1.000	3	1	9	0	1	Schattinger, Edmonton	.929	31	2	11	1	0
Martinez, Spokane-Vancouver	.947	21	2	16	1	1	Schatzeder, Phoenix*	.800	1	1	3	1	0
Mathis, Tucson	.929	14	6	7	1	1	Schneider, Spokane*	1.000	18	4	5	0	0
McGaffigan, Phoenix	.917	18	6	5	1	1	Seaman, Hawaii*	1.000	11	1	4	0	0
McLaughlin, Spokane	1.000	6	1	6	0	1	Shirley, Albuquerque*	.889	34	3	5	1	0
McLaughlin, Tacoma	1.000	23	3	3	0	0	Siwy, Edmonton	.940	26	7	40	3	5
Meredith, Hawaii*	.923	37	5	19	2	3	Smith, Tucson	.938	28	5	10	1	0
Miggins, Tucson-Hawaii*	.895	27	7	27	4	1	Snyder, Salt Lake City*	1.000	51	3	4	0	2
Miscik, Portland*	1.000	32	3	9	0	0	Sprowl, Tucson*	1.000	10	0	5	0	0
Moffitt, Tucson	.000	7	0	0	1	0	Stablein, Hawaii	1.000	24	5	17	0	0
Moore, Albuquerque	1.000	13	5	7	0	0	Steirer, Spokane	1.000	30	5	11	0	1
Moore, Salt Lake City	1.000	1	0	2	0	0	Stember, Phoenix	.889	28	1	7	1	1
A. Moreno, Spokane*	1.000	22	0	7	0	0	STODDARD, Salt Lake City	1.000	24	16	30	0	1
Morris, Tucson*	.944	9	2	15	1	0	Swiacki, Tacoma	.952	29	15	44	3	1
Moskau, Portland	1.000	4	0	1	0	0	Tellmann, Hawaii	.926	41	3	22	2	2
Musselman, Salt Lake City	.895	51	2	15	2	3	Thomas, Salt Lake City	.889	33	11	21	4	0
Mustad, Tacoma	1.000	24	3	12	0	0	Thurmond, Hawaii*	.976	28	5	36	1	2
Nelson, Salt Lake City	.923	5	6	6	1	0	Tucker, Phoenix	.964	37	9	18	1	0
Neuenschwander, Portland	1.000	1	0	1	0	0	Tunnell, Portland	.941	28	9	39	3	1
Niedenfuer, Albuquerque	1.000	4	0	1	0	0	Uhey, Vancouver	1.000	3	0	1	0	0
Niemann, Portland*	.800	8	1	3	1	0	Valley, Vancouver*	1.000	38	4	10	0	0
Nunez, Salt Lake City	1.000	11	4	8	0	1	Walters, Spokane	1.000	10	2	9	0	1
Olsen, Vancouver	.952	21	6	14	1	0	Welborn, Salt Lake City	.846	46	2	9	2	1
Paris, Tucson	.891	28	11	30	5	3	White, Albuquerque	.896	28	16	27	5	2
Patterson, Tacoma	.962	35	9	16	1	0	Wright, Albuquerque*	.929	15	3	10	1	0
Patterson, Edmonton	.933	29	11	31	3	4	Young, Salt Lake City*	.813	29	9	30	9	0

The following players do not have any recorded accepted chances at the positions indicated; therefore, are not listed in the fielding averages for those particular positions: Alcala, p; Benson, of; Bosetti, p; Contreras, p; D'Acquisto, p; Drumright, ss; Hammaker, p; Heaverlo, p; Hosley, of; Hoss, p; Johnson, p; Lancellotti, p; Marshall, 3b; Parsons, p; Rennicke, p; Rex, p; Skorochocki, c; Spilman, 3b; Stroughter, of; Wiedenbauer, p; Wise, p.

CLUB PITCHING

Club	ERA.	G.	CG.	ShO.	Sv.	IP.	H.	R.	ER.	HR.	HB.	BB.	Int. BB.	SO.	WP.	Bk.
Tacoma	4.00	143	41	10	25	1246.1	1345	668	554	124	27	417	31	693	39	3
Vancouver	4.19	144	39	9	19	1250.1	1257	686	582	97	28	538	29	740	59	2
Hawaii	4.21	144	42	11	17	1215.1	1287	672	569	111	20	438	12	674	86	6
Portland	4.64	144	39	3	23	1226	1219	729	632	115	46	614	39	861	68	9
Spokane	4.82	143	28	7	32	1231.1	1352	737	660	95	39	546	20	816	65	4
Albuquerque	5.05	143	33	6	29	1240	1377	811	696	116	31	608	30	864	76	5
Salt Lake City	5.36	143	31	4	27	1238.1	1435	850	738	117	45	603	42	806	105	5
Tucson	5.48	142	18	3	26	1209.1	1499	877	736	74	39	608	35	684	64	8
Phoenix	5.58	144	35	4	22	1201.1	1472	866	745	141	39	577	31	683	57	5
Edmonton	5.78	144	28	3	27	1227	1463	902	788	157	50	622	29	631	80	8

PITCHERS' RECORDS
(Leading Qualifiers for Earned-Run Average Leadership — 115 or More Innings)

*Throws lefthanded.

Pitcher — Club	W.	L.	Pct.	ERA.	G.	GS.	CG.	GF.	ShO.	Sv.	IP.	H.	R.	ER.	HR.	HB.	BB.	Int. BB.	SO.	WP.
Codiroli, Tacoma	10	3	.769	1.90	16	16	10	0	2	0	123.1	100	36	26	15	1	21	0	85	0
Hawkins, Hawaii	9	7	.563	2.17	18	18	10	0	6	0	132.2	108	49	32	7	2	47	1	91	9
Baker, Tacoma	13	5	.722	2.48	23	22	9	0	3	0	163	147	65	45	6	5	68	3	79	2
Tunnell, Portland	12	9	.591	3.46	28	27	9	1	2	0	189.2	182	93	73	9	7	91	3	112	8
Eaton, Spokane	9	3	.750	3.53	35	12	1	12	0	3	135	131	61	53	10	2	39	5	60	5
Thurmond, Hawaii*	12	10	.545	3.57	28	28	9	0	2	0	194.1	202	88	77	13	1	58	2	106	8
Hershiser, Albuquerque	9	6	.600	3.71	47	7	2	20	0	4	123.2	121	73	51	10	4	63	6	93	12
S. Brown, Spokane	14	11	.560	3.88	27	27	12	0	3	0	185.2	206	96	80	12	2	53	0	117	3
Porter, Vancouver	8	12	.400	3.98	25	25	12	0	1	0	183.1	196	98	81	15	5	59	4	102	2
DiPino, Spokane	13	9	.591	4.03	26	26	11	0	3	0	189.2	187	102	85	17	0	86	3	115	7

Departmental Leaders: G—Musselman, Snyder, 51; GS—Patterson, 29; CG—S. Brown, Hamm, Porter, 12; GF—Musselman, 44; ShO—Hawkins, 6; W—O. Jones, 16; L—Hamm, Hoffman, 14; Pct.—Codiroli, .769; Sv.—C. Brown, 15; IP—Atherton, 200; H—Rodas, 223; R—Hargesheimer, 136; ER—Paris, 114; HR—Rowland, 30; HB—Kranitz, Siwy, Thomas, 10; BB—Rasmussen, 113; IBB—Snyder, 11; SO—O. Jones, 172; WP—Thomas, 27.

(All Pitchers—Listed Alphabetically)

Pitcher — Club	W.	L.	Pct.	ERA.	G.	GS.	CG.	GF.	ShO.	Sv.	IP.	H.	R.	ER.	HR.	HB.	BB.	Int. BB.	SO.	WP.
Abbott, Salt Lake City	1	1	.500	8.10	2	2	0	0	0	0	10	15	10	9	2	0	3	0	3	0
Agosto, Edmonton*	3	4	.429	5.00	50	2	1	27	0	11	95.1	101	63	53	7	5	49	1	39	10
Alcala, Portland	0	0	.000	5.40	2	0	0	1	0	0	3.1	3	2	2	1	0	1	0	0	0
Allard, Salt Lake City	1	2	.333	9.12	5	5	0	0	0	0	24.2	31	26	25	9	1	11	0	10	3
Andersen, Salt Lake City	1	0	1.000	0.00	5	0	0	5	0	4	6.2	2	0	0	0	0	3	0	8	1
Anderson, Vancouver*	5	5	.500	3.29	30	6	1	11	0	0	101.1	92	47	37	3	1	64	1	61	10

Pitcher—Club	W.	L.	Pct.	ERA.	G.	GS.	CG.	GF.	ShO.	Sv.	IP.	H.	R.	ER.	HR.	HB.	BB.	Int. BB.	SO.	WP.
Arroyo, 4 Tacoma-14 Edm.	2	3	.400	3.94	18	2	0	11	0	4	48	57	31	21	5	2	17	3	22	1
Atherton, Tacoma	12	9	.571	4.37	28	28	6	0	1	0	200	214	108	97	26	2	54	3	128	3
Baker, Tacoma	13	5	.722	2.48	23	22	9	0	3	0	163	147	65	45	6	5	68	3	79	2
Barnes, Edmonton°	10	6	.625	5.52	19	18	8	1	1	0	117.1	125	79	72	12	4	59	1	56	10
Beard, Tacoma	0	0	.000	0.00	1	0	0	1	0	1	1	0	0	0	0	0	0	0	1	0
Beckwith, Albuquerque	5	6	.455	6.68	26	12	2	8	1	2	102.1	138	90	76	5	7	55	0	80	11
Boone, Tucson°	5	4	.556	3.31	25	1	0	15	0	1	49	51	19	18	4	2	13	3	43	4
Bordi, Salt Lake City	12	9	.571	4.49	25	25	8	0	0	0	168.1	212	105	84	19	2	31	1	118	5
Bosetti, Tacoma	0	0	.000	9.00	1	0	0	0	0	0	1	2	1	1	0	0	1	0	0	0
B. Bradley, Tacoma	1	1	.500	3.80	17	0	0	12	0	4	23.2	25	12	10	1	0	13	3	13	2
L. Bradley, Edmonton	4	9	.308	7.54	33	10	1	11	0	0	105	141	97	88	24	4	60	3	59	7
Braun, Spokane	0	1	.000	9.75	2	2	0	0	0	0	12	22	17	13	2	0	4	0	4	0
C. Brown, Spokane	3	4	.429	4.46	50	0	0	38	0	15	72.2	85	40	36	9	2	23	5	36	2
S. Brown, Spokane	14	11	.560	3.88	27	27	12	0	3	0	185.2	206	96	80	12	2	53	0	117	3
Buice, Tacoma	4	2	.667	4.17	19	5	1	8	0	1	41	51	22	19	3	0	19	0	36	2
Calvert, Phoenix	0	2	.000	7.04	6	0	0	3	0	1	7.2	9	7	6	0	1	8	1	1	0
Camacho, Edmonton	0	0	.000	3.20	7	0	0	1	0	1	19.2	10	8	7	1	1	16	0	18	3
Capilla, Edmonton°	4	3	.571	5.53	21	1	0	9	0	0	55.1	58	37	34	11	3	34	1	38	3
Cappuzzello, Tucson°	5	0	1.000	2.16	15	0	0	4	0	0	33.1	31	15	8	0	0	20	0	22	0
Castro, Tacoma	2	0	1.000	3.00	12	2	1	8	1	1	30	34	11	10	3	2	5	0	15	1
Chamberlain, Phoenix	2	13	.133	6.91	31	16	3	6	0	0	125	156	110	96	19	6	83	1	70	12
Chappas, Edmonton	0	0	.000	4.50	1	0	0	1	0	0	4	3	2	2	0	0	0	0	0	0
Chris, Phoenix°	11	4	.733	3.94	17	17	4	0	0	0	109.2	107	54	48	9	1	71	1	62	3
Clark, Salt Lake City°	1	1	.500	10.13	4	0	0	3	0	0	5.1	5	6	6	0	1	5	1	2	1
Cliburn, Spokane	1	6	.143	7.68	8	6	0	2	0	0	38.2	51	37	33	1	3	17	0	28	3
Cocanower, Vancouver	4	3	.571	4.86	14	12	1	0	0	0	74	81	49	40	3	2	59	1	32	8
Codiroli, Tacoma	10	3	.769	1.90	16	16	10	0	2	0	123.1	100	36	26	15	1	21	0	85	0
Coffman, Hawaii	2	0	1.000	3.35	23	0	0	17	0	0	37.2	49	16	14	1	0	12	0	20	2
Coleman, Spokane	2	2	.500	4.04	13	1	0	8	0	1	35.2	42	19	16	3	1	7	0	25	2
Combe, Edmonton	3	2	.600	2.93	33	0	0	27	0	6	46	43	19	15	2	3	21	2	34	6
Comstock, Tacoma°	1	2	.333	7.16	5	5	0	0	0	0	27.2	34	24	22	4	1	12	1	22	0
Contreras, Edmonton	0	0	.000	0.00	1	0	0	0	0	0	1	0	0	0	0	0	1	0	3	0
Cook, Vancouver	7	9	.438	4.18	26	20	3	4	1	0	129.1	138	72	60	16	0	48	2	68	6
Corbett, Spokane	1	0	1.000	3.79	8	1	0	5	0	2	19	16	11	8	0	1	4	0	19	2
Cornell, Phoenix	2	4	.333	5.01	25	0	0	24	0	6	41.1	42	26	23	2	0	28	2	33	4
Couchee, Hawaii	3	1	.750	2.12	11	0	0	11	0	3	17	11	4	4	1	0	3	0	11	3
D'Acquisto, Tacoma	0	0	.000	0.00	4	0	0	1	0	0	6	5	0	0	0	0	3	0	2	1
Decker, Salt Lake City	2	0	1.000	6.57	8	0	0	2	0	0	12.1	16	9	9	4	0	9	0	8	1
DeLeon, Portland	10	7	.588	5.97	24	23	3	0	0	0	119	138	81	79	15	5	65	0	94	3
Dempsey, Phoenix	10	10	.500	5.01	27	22	9	2	1	0	156.1	167	95	87	21	2	72	4	118	4
Desjarlais, Edmonton	2	3	.400	6.91	7	7	0	0	0	0	28.2	42	25	22	3	1	20	0	8	5
DiPino, Vancouver°	13	9	.591	4.03	26	26	11	0	3	0	189.2	187	100	85	17	0	86	3	115	7
Dravecky, Hawaii°	4	1	.800	2.48	16	1	0	8	0	1	36.1	28	15	10	2	1	14	0	26	3
Eaton, Spokane	9	3	.750	3.53	35	12	1	12	0	3	135	131	61	53	10	2	39	5	60	5
Edge, Portland	4	6	.400	4.80	35	11	1	10	0	1	114.1	118	70	61	13	5	64	3	82	11
Edwards, Edmonton°	0	0	.000	13.89	5	0	0	1	0	1	11.2	24	20	18	3	3	8	2	5	1
Escarrega, Edmonton	0	0	.000	6.39	2	2	0	0	0	0	12.2	11	10	9	4	0	5	0	5	0
Esquer, Portland°	0	2	.000	5.30	7	3	0	1	0	0	37.1	38	24	22	4	2	17	3	26	2
Fernandez, Albuquerque°	6	5	.545	5.42	13	13	5	0	0	0	88	76	54	53	13	5	52	2	86	4
Figueroa, Tacoma	2	2	.000	6.75	2	2	0	0	0	0	9.1	14	8	7	2	0	6	0	3	1
Finch, Salt Lake City	6	1	.857	6.75	42	0	0	19	0	0	78.2	110	65	59	8	5	42	4	59	3
Fireovid, Hawaii	10	8	.556	5.37	25	23	5	2	0	0	135.2	171	87	81	13	3	39	1	56	8
Foley, Spokane	6	9	.400	6.50	22	21	3	0	0	0	126	177	98	91	11	5	69	1	68	10
Fowler, Tacoma	8	1	.889	4.46	18	18	2	0	0	0	107	127	64	53	10	1	36	3	37	5
Fowlkes, Phoenix	6	3	.667	2.70	13	8	7	3	0	1	73.1	78	26	22	2	1	14	1	31	3
Franco, Albuquerque°	1	2	.333	7.24	5	5	0	0	0	0	27.1	41	22	22	3	0	15	1	24	1
Geiger, Albuquerque	6	7	.462	4.64	45	1	0	22	0	5	114.1	136	76	59	8	2	54	6	70	9
Gibson, Vancouver	1	1	.500	1.13	6	0	0	4	0	2	8	3	2	1	0	0	10	2	6	0
Guante, Portland	3	2	.600	3.86	21	0	0	20	0	7	35	34	17	15	3	1	26	5	29	3
Hamm, Hawaii	9	14	.391	4.21	28	28	12	0	0	0	198.2	207	110	93	15	2	40	0	106	5
Hammaker, Phoenix°	0	1	.000	6.35	1	1	0	0	0	0	5.2	13	5	4	0	0	2	0	6	0
Hardy, Edmonton	0	0	.000	15.00	1	1	0	0	0	0	3	7	5	5	0	1	0	0	1	0
Hargesheimer, Phoenix	6	12	.333	6.54	29	27	3	0	1	0	152.2	214	136	111	16	4	95	5	89	8
Harris, Salt Lake City	7	10	.412	6.63	27	23	2	2	0	1	135.2	167	114	100	13	3	83	4	47	13
Hawkins, Hawaii	9	7	.563	2.17	18	18	10	0	6	0	132.2	108	49	32	7	2	47	1	91	9
Heaverlo, Tacoma	0	0	.000	0.00	1	0	0	1	0	1	1.2	0	0	0	0	0	1	0	1	0
Heimueller, Tacoma°	1	1	.500	7.27	5	3	0	1	0	0	17.1	16	16	14	2	1	9	0	9	0
Hershiser, Albuquerque	9	6	.600	3.71	47	7	2	20	0	4	123.2	121	73	51	10	4	63	6	93	12
Hinrichs, Phoenix°	1	6	.143	3.75	38	0	0	32	0	9	60	64	38	25	6	1	19	2	30	1
Hoffman, Edmonton°	8	14	.364	6.90	28	24	3	3	0	1	138.1	186	129	106	20	1	67	2	72	7
Hogg, Edmonton	0	0	.000	0.00	2	0	0	2	0	0	2.2	0	0	0	0	0	3	0	3	0
Holton, Albuquerque	12	8	.600	5.13	32	22	7	6	1	3	161.1	191	102	92	15	4	60	2	76	6
Ibarra, Edmonton	1	6	.143	10.13	16	6	0	7	0	0	40	59	45	45	6	2	34	2	19	5
C. Johnson, Edmonton	5	6	.455	7.28	14	13	1	0	0	0	68	98	61	55	11	2	30	2	40	2
J. Johnson, Hawaii	0	0	.000	0.00	2	0	0	2	0	0	2	0	0	0	0	0	1	0	1	0
D. Jones, Vancouver	5	8	.385	2.97	23	9	4	10	2	2	106	109	48	35	9	1	31	4	60	2
J. Jones, Tacoma	1	1	.500	8.71	8	1	0	5	0	1	10.1	17	10	10	1	0	7	2	6	2
O. Jones, Portland	16	9	.640	4.26	28	28	9	0	0	0	190.1	162	103	90	13	7	94	2	172	15
Keeton, Tucson°	7	13	.350	5.19	40	15	3	14	0	2	161.1	199	106	93	13	3	68	4	72	3
Kennedy, Albuquerque	0	0	.000	9.00	1	0	0	1	0	0	1	2	1	1	0	0	0	0	0	0
Kingman, Albuquerque	5	1	.833	3.54	8	8	1	0	0	0	53.1	59	28	21	5	1	20	0	27	2
Kinney, Tacoma°	5	6	.455	4.50	47	0	0	28	0	6	60	63	35	30	7	2	20	3	49	3
Kobel, Portland°	0	1	.000	5.21	7	1	0	2	0	1	19	28	15	11	5	0	4	1	9	2
Kranitz, Vancouver	4	5	.444	5.13	35	5	1	17	1	2	108.2	95	64	62	10	10	89	1	85	7
Kuhaulua, Hawaii°	3	3	.500	5.87	17	11	0	1	0	1	69	81	57	45	9	1	40	0	32	13
Ladd, Vancouver	10	2	.833	2.91	34	0	0	30	0	8	55.2	42	19	18	5	2	18	3	63	4
Lamonde, Portland	5	5	.500	3.30	12	12	4	0	1	0	79	72	44	29	1	2	39	1	52	2
Lancellotti, Hawaii°	0	0	.000	9.00	1	0	0	1	0	0	1	1	1	1	0	0	3	0	2	0
Laskey, Phoenix	1	0	1.000	1.29	2	2	0	0	0	0	14	12	5	2	1	0	2	0	10	0
Leatherwood, Tucson	0	2	.000	9.00	3	3	0	0	0	0	8	11	10	8	0	3	9	0	5	0
Lee, Portland	0	5	.000	4.19	27	0	0	23	0	8	34.1	36	21	16	0	2	22	7	20	3
Long, Portland	5	13	.278	5.78	31	18	7	5	0	0	157.1	146	110	101	26	8	73	3	91	4

Pitcher—Club	W.	L.	Pct.	ERA.	G.	GS.	CG.	GF.	ShO.	Sv.	IP.	H.	R.	ER.	HR.	HB.	BB.	Int. BB.	SO.	WP.
Lysander, Tucson	10	7	.588	4.05	42	13	2	17	0	5	162.1	203	95	73	7	2	49	7	99	6
Madden, Vancouver°	3	8	.273	7.03	18	18	1	0	0	0	80.2	92	69	63	3	1	60	0	41	8
Mahler, Spokane°	9	7	.563	5.68	20	20	2	0	0	0	134.2	156	90	85	13	6	75	0	116	21
Maitland, Edmonton°	1	1	.500	4.65	6	6	1	0	0	0	31	36	17	16	6	0	17	0	9	2
Martin, Phoenix	1	2	.333	4.74	3	3	1	0	0	0	19	25	12	10	2	0	2	0	12	0
Martinez, 15 Spokane-6 Van.	8	7	.533	5.37	21	21	5	0	1	0	120.2	136	77	72	11	6	64	1	62	2
Mathis, Tucson	4	8	.333	4.48	14	14	4	0	1	0	84.1	90	50	42	7	2	42	0	79	1
McGaffigan, Phoenix	1	6	.143	6.00	18	15	2	1	0	0	96	115	72	64	6	7	51	6	64	9
B. McLaughlin, Spokane	1	0	1.000	1.26	6	1	0	0	0	0	14.1	10	6	2	0	0	5	0	9	0
M. McLaughlin, Tacoma	1	3	.250	5.20	23	1	0	12	0	6	36.1	39	23	21	2	2	15	2	24	2
Meredith, Hawaii°	6	2	.750	3.80	37	4	1	16	0	1	111.1	105	53	47	14	2	41	1	68	8
Miggins, 16 Tucson-11 Hawaii°..	5	10	.333	6.25	27	13	3	10	0	0	116.2	149	94	81	11	5	57	2	67	14
Miscik, Portland°	2	3	.400	3.78	32	0	0	22	0	2	50	41	27	21	6	0	24	3	38	4
Moffitt, Tucson	0	1	.000	4.32	7	0	0	3	0	2	8.1	11	6	4	0	0	0	0	7	0
D. Moore, Albuquerque	2	1	.667	5.63	13	3	1	2	0	0	48	53	31	30	7	1	18	0	21	0
M. Moore, Salt Lake City	0	0	.000	4.50	1	1	0	0	0	0	8	9	4	4	1	0	5	0	6	0
Moreno, Spokane°	5	0	1.000	5.73	22	2	0	13	0	1	44	54	28	28	6	0	30	1	35	1
Morris, Tucson°	2	2	.500	4.76	9	8	0	0	0	0	51	56	31	27	3	2	22	1	25	1
Moskau, Portland	0	4	.000	10.32	4	4	0	0	0	0	11.1	17	13	13	2	0	11	0	10	2
Musselman, Salt Lake City	5	4	.556	3.28	51	0	0	44	0	14	68.2	68	25	25	4	1	19	6	40	5
Mustad, Tacoma	3	4	.429	5.52	24	1	0	10	0	2	45.2	66	39	28	5	2	18	4	22	4
Nelson, Salt Lake City	1	3	.250	3.35	5	5	2	0	0	0	37.2	36	18	14	1	1	28	2	22	0
Neuenschwander, Portland	0	0	.000	108.00	1	0	0	0	0	0	.1	3	5	4	1	0	2	0	0	0
Niedenfuer, Albuquerque	2	0	1.000	0.00	4	0	0	3	0	1	10.2	6	0	0	0	0	2	0	15	0
Niemann, Portland°	3	2	.600	3.83	8	6	2	2	0	0	44.2	41	22	19	4	1	26	1	28	5
Nunez, Salt Lake City	4	3	.571	3.42	11	8	1	1	0	0	55.1	40	26	21	5	3	23	2	42	4
Olsen, Vancouver	5	5	.500	3.56	21	16	3	0	1	0	101	101	49	40	6	3	54	1	52	1
Paris, Tucson	6	8	.429	6.19	28	28	3	0	0	0	165.2	209	131	114	14	8	104	4	85	16
Parsons, Salt Lake City	0	0	.000	10.80	1	0	0	1	0	0	1.2	3	2	2	0	0	1	0	1	1
D. Patterson, Tacoma	5	5	.500	3.30	35	2	0	14	0	3	92.2	93	41	34	9	1	28	5	63	1
R. Patterson, Edmonton	14	10	.583	4.87	29	29	5	0	1	0	186.2	212	125	101	19	6	89	6	109	8
Pena, Albuquerque	1	1	.500	5.34	16	0	0	14	0	5	28.2	37	18	17	3	0	10	2	27	3
Perez, Portland	4	9	.308	4.82	19	10	4	8	0	0	106.1	111	59	57	8	5	37	5	59	2
Pladson, Tucson	4	12	.250	5.96	24	22	2	0	0	0	131.1	153	101	87	3	2	88	3	80	10
Porter, Vancouver	8	12	.400	3.98	25	25	12	0	1	0	183.1	196	98	81	15	5	59	4	102	2
Power, Albuquerque	5	4	.556	5.18	14	14	2	0	2	0	73	77	51	42	5	1	49	1	54	7
Quiros, Spokane	1	0	1.000	0.00	6	0	0	5	0	0	17	6	0	0	0	1	2	1	6	0
Rasmussen, Spokane°	11	8	.579	5.03	27	27	4	0	2	0	171.2	166	110	96	15	8	113	0	162	12
Rennicke, Albuquerque	0	0	.000	0.00	1	0	0	0	0	0	2	1	0	0	0	0	0	0	1	0
Rex, Phoenix	0	0	.000	0.00	2	0	0	2	0	0	1.1	1	0	0	0	0	0	0	0	0
Richard, Tucson	0	2	.000	13.68	6	6	0	0	0	0	24.1	35	45	37	1	1	27	0	13	10
Roberge, Tucson	4	4	.500	3.28	34	0	0	33	0	9	46.2	49	21	17	2	3	23	6	31	0
Robinson, 14 Portland-7 Van.	1	2	.333	5.06	21	1	0	9	0	2	48	52	32	27	7	1	29	4	41	1
Rodas, Albuquerque°	14	8	.636	5.28	29	28	8	1	0	0	187.2	223	125	110	26	1	78	3	103	11
Ross, Tucson	4	3	.571	4.88	43	1	0	26	0	7	83	106	55	45	5	3	32	5	35	2
Rowland, Phoenix	9	13	.409	5.78	28	25	5	2	0	0	162	203	125	104	30	6	52	0	76	3
Sanchez, Spokane	0	1	.000	9.31	2	2	0	0	0	0	9.2	13	13	10	1	0	8	0	5	1
Sarmiento, Portland	1	0	1.000	1.00	6	0	0	5	0	3	9	10	2	1	0	0	4	0	3	0
Schattinger, Edmonton	1	1	.500	8.36	31	0	0	16	0	3	56	91	60	52	8	2	42	1	20	6
Schatzeder, Phoenix°	0	0	.000	12.27	1	1	0	0	0	0	3.2	10	6	5	1	0	3	0	1	0
Schneider, Spokane°	1	2	.333	4.13	18	0	0	6	0	0	24	19	11	11	0	0	19	0	6	3
Seaman, Hawaii°	3	2	.600	0.64	11	0	0	8	0	1	14	12	2	1	0	0	7	0	14	1
Shirley, Albuquerque°	6	2	.750	4.53	34	0	0	27	0	7	45.2	44	28	23	4	0	32	6	43	2
Siwy, Edmonton	12	8	.600	4.04	26	25	8	0	1	0	171.2	184	84	77	17	10	58	3	79	4
Smith, Spokane°	4	8	.333	7.15	28	19	2	1	0	0	113.1	183	108	90	7	3	47	2	35	8
Snyder, Salt Lake City°	4	3	.571	4.71	51	0	0	20	0	5	57.1	64	32	30	6	3	45	11	56	4
Sprowl, Tucson°	0	3	.000	12.00	10	3	0	4	0	0	21	29	31	28	1	2	31	0	14	0
Stablein, Hawaii	4	12	.250	6.85	24	20	4	2	0	0	110.1	133	93	84	17	3	70	2	58	10
Steirer, Spokane	6	6	.500	3.51	30	5	3	20	0	10	92.1	92	41	36	3	4	30	4	66	0
Stember, Phoenix	2	3	.400	7.43	28	4	1	16	0	3	72.2	103	66	60	13	4	43	3	35	8
Stoddard, Salt Lake City	7	11	.389	5.20	24	23	8	0	0	0	147	158	91	85	12	3	65	0	86	5
Swiacki, Tacoma	12	11	.522	4.72	29	27	11	0	1	0	181	214	111	95	21	7	56	2	63	8
Tellmann, Hawaii	7	7	.500	3.81	41	7	2	28	1	10	104	113	56	44	11	2	36	4	55	6
Thomas, Salt Lake City	8	9	.471	5.63	33	23	2	1	0	0	156.2	195	112	98	7	10	84	6	96	27
Thurmond, Hawaii°	12	10	.545	3.57	28	28	9	0	2	0	194.1	202	88	77	13	1	58	2	106	8
Tucker, Phoenix	6	7	.462	6.95	37	3	0	18	0	2	101	153	84	78	13	5	33	5	45	2
Tunnell, Portland	12	9	.571	3.46	28	27	9	1	2	0	189.2	182	93	73	9	7	91	3	112	8
Uhey, Vancouver	0	0	.000	6.43	3	0	0	1	0	1	7	6	5	5	2	0	1	0	1	0
Valley, Vancouver°	4	3	.571	5.15	38	1	0	24	0	3	50.2	58	31	29	5	1	15	3	27	3
Walters, Spokane	2	0	1.000	1.20	10	0	0	6	0	0	15	12	2	2	0	0	8	3	4	0
Welborn, Salt Lake City	1	3	.250	7.98	46	2	0	13	0	2	88	113	92	78	16	6	71	4	84	11
White, Albuquerque	12	5	.706	4.42	28	26	5	2	0	0	165	168	93	81	11	4	81	1	114	6
Wiedenbauer, Tucson	0	0	.000	0.00	1	0	0	1	0	0	1	0	0	0	0	0	3	0	0	0
Wise, Albuquerque	0	0	.000	0.00	1	0	0	0	0	0	3	0	0	0	0	0	3	0	0	0
Wright, Albuquerque°	4	3	.571	5.67	15	12	1	3	0	2	60.1	63	45	38	5	0	36	0	57	4
Young, Salt Lake City°	12	10	.545	4.65	29	26	8	1	4	1	176	192	113	91	10	3	75	1	118	22

BALKS—Hamm, 5; R. Patterson, Tunnell, 4 each; Agosto, 3; Hargesheimer, 2; Alcala, Baker, Bordi, S. Brown, Camacho, Cappuzzello, Cliburn, Cocanower, Codiroli, Coleman, Dempsey, Edge, Esquer, Finch, Franco, Harris, Hawkins, Hershiser, Keeton, Kennedy, Leatherwood, Lysander, Madden, Mahler, Mathis, McGaffigan, Miggins, Miscik, Mustad, Niemann, Nunez, Paris, Rodas, Shirley, Sprowl, Stember, Swiacki, White, Young, 1 each.

COMBINATION SHUTOUTS—White-Shirley, Wright-White, Albuquerque; Stablein-Coffman-Meredith, Stablein-Tellmann, Hawaii; Dempsey-Hinrichs, Rowland-Hinrichs, Phoenix; S. Brown-Moreno, Spokane; Codiroli-D'Acquisto, Fowler-D'Acquisto-McLaughlin, Tacoma; Lysander-Roberge, Mathis-Ross, Tucson.

NO-HIT GAME—None.

Eastern League

CLASS AA

Leading Batter
PHILIP KLIMAS
Glens Falls

League President
CHARLES ESHBACH

Leading Pitcher
JAY BALLER
Reading

CHAMPIONSHIP WINNERS IN PREVIOUS YEARS

Year	Team	Pct.
1923	Williamsport	.661
1924	Williamsport	.654
1925	York§	.583
	Williamsport§	.583
1926	Scranton	.627
1927	Harrisburg	.630
1928	Harrisburg	.603
1929	Binghamton	.597
1930	Wilkes-Barre	.572
1931	Harrisburg	.597
1932	Wilkes-Barre	.561
1933	Binghamton	.690
1934	Binghamton	.694
	Williamsport°	.603
1935	Scranton	.657
	Binghamton°	.580
1936	Scranton°	.609
	Elmira	.629
1937	Elmira†	.622
1938	Binghamton	.622
	Elmira (3rd)‡	.522
1939	Scranton†	.571
1940	Scranton	.568
	Binghamton (2nd)‡	.554
1941	Wilkes-Barre	.630
	Elmira (3rd)‡	.514
1942	Albany	.600
	Scranton (2nd)‡	.593
1943	Scranton	.630
	Elmira (2nd)‡	.568
1944	Hartford	.723
	Binghamton (4th)‡	.474

Year	Team	Pct.
1945	Utica	.615
	Albany (3rd)‡	.564
1946	Scranton†	.691
1947	Utica†	.652
1948	Scranton†	.636
1949	Albany	.664
	Binghamton (4th)‡	.500
1950	Wilkes-Barre‡	.652
1951	Wilkes-Barre	.612
	Scranton (2nd)†	.562
1952	Albany	.603
	Binghamton (2nd)‡	.562
1953	Reading	.682
	Binghamton (2nd)‡	.636
1954	Wilkes-Barre	.576
	Albany (3rd)‡	.540
1955	Reading	.613
	Allentown (2nd)‡	.565
1956	Schenectady†	.609
1957	Binghamton	.607
	Reading (3rd)‡	.529
1958	Lancaster x	.568
	Binghamton (6th)‡	.493
1959	Springfield†	.607
1960	Williamsport y	.551
	Springfield (3rd)y	.496
1961	Springfield	.612
1962	Williamsport	.593
	Elmira (2nd)‡	.514
1963	Charleston	.593
1964	Elmira	.586
1965	Pittsfield	.607

Year	Team	Pct.
1966	Elmira	.633
1967	Binghamton z	.586
	Elmira	.532
1968	Pittsfield	.604
	Reading (2nd)‡	.579
1969	York	.640
1970	Waterbury a	.560
	Reading a	.553
1971	Three Rivers	.569
	Elmira b	.561
1972	West Haven b	.600
	Three Rivers	.559
1973	Reading b	.551
	Pittsfield	.551
1974	Thetford Mines (2nd)c	.536
	Pittsfield (2nd)	.496
1975	Reading	.613
	Bristol°	.587
1976	Three Rivers	.601
	West Haven d	.576
1977	West Haven e	.623
	Three Rivers	.551
1978	Reading	.642
	Bristol°	.580
1979	West Haven f	.597
1980	Holyoke°	.561
	Waterbury	.540
1981	Glens Falls	.615
	Bristol°	.577

°Won split-season playoff. †Won championship and four-team playoff. ‡Won four-team playoff. §Tied for pennant, York winning playoff. xLeague was divided into Northern, Southern divisions and played a split season; Lancaster over-all season leader. yPlayoff finals canceled after one game because of rain with Williamsport and Springfield declared playoff co-champions. zLeague was divided into Eastern, Western divisions; Binghamton won playoff. aTied for pennant, Waterbury winning playoff. bLeague was divided into American, National divisions; won playoff. cLeague was divided into American and National divisions; won four-team playoff. dLeague was divided into Northern, Southern divisions, won playoff. eLeague was divided into New England and Canadian-American divisions; won playoff. fWon both halves of split season (no playoffs).

STANDING OF CLUBS AT CLOSE OF FIRST HALF, JUNE 21

NORTHERN DIVISION						SOUTHERN DIVISION					
Club	W.	L.	T.	Pct.	G.B.	Club	W.	L.	T.	Pct.	G.B.
Glens Falls (White Sox)	36	29	0	.554	......	West Haven (A's)	42	21	0	.667	......
Lynn (Mariners)	30	30	0	.500	3½	Bristol (Red Sox)	34	30	0	.531	8½
Holyoke (Angels)	29	39	0	.426	8½	Reading (Phillies)	33	31	0	.516	9½
Buffalo (Pirates)	25	43	0	.368	12½	Waterbury (Reds)	29	35	0	.453	13½

STANDING OF CLUBS AT CLOSE OF SECOND HALF, AUGUST 31

NORTHERN DIVISION						SOUTHERN DIVISION					
Club	W.	L.	T.	Pct.	G.B.	Club	W.	L.	T.	Pct.	G.B.
Lynn (Mariners)	52	27	0	.658	......	West Haven (A's)	44	33	0	.571	......
Glens Falls (White Sox)	41	34	0	.547	9	Bristol (Red Sox)	41	35	0	.539	2½
Holyoke (Angels)	34	38	0	.472	14½	Reading (Phillies)	30	44	0	.405	12½
Buffalo (Pirates)	30	41	0	.423	18	Waterbury (Reds)	27	47	0	.365	15½

COMPOSITE STANDING OF CLUBS AT CLOSE OF SEASON, AUGUST 31

Club	W.H.	Lynn	G.F.	Bris.	Read.	Holy.	Wat.	Buff.	W.	L.	T.	Pct.	G.B.
West Haven (Athletics)	....	12	10	11	13	12	14	14	86	54	0	.614	......
Lynn (Mariners)	8	....	11	11	14	11	16	11	82	57	0	.590	3½
Glens Falls (White Sox)	10	9	....	10	10	12	11	15	77	63	0	.550	9
Bristol (Red Sox)	9	9	10	....	12	13	9	13	75	65	0	.536	11
Reading (Phillies)	7	5	10	8	....	12	10	11	63	75	0	.457	22
Holyoke (Angels)	8	9	8	7	8	....	12	11	63	77	0	.450	23
Waterbury (Reds)	6	4	9	11	9	8	....	9	56	82	0	.406	29
Buffalo (Pirates)	6	9	5	7	9	9	10	....	55	84	0	.396	30½

Major league affiliations in parentheses.

Playoffs—Lynn defeated Glens Falls, two games to none; West Haven defeated Lynn, three games to none, to win league championship.

Regular-Season Attendance—Bristol, 67,564; Buffalo, 77,077; Glens Falls, 93,428; Holyoke, 54,291; Lynn, 23,791; Reading, 81,875; Waterbury, 54,757; West Haven, 51,791. Total, 504,574. Playoffs, 2,803. No all-star games.

Managers—Bristol, Tony Torchia; Buffalo, Tommy Sandt; Glens Falls, Jim Maloney; Holyoke, Jack Hiatt; Lynn, Mickey Bowers; Reading, John Felske; Waterbury, Jim Lett; West Haven, Bob Didier.

All-Star Team; 1B—Whittemore, Bristol; 2B—Hulett, Glens Falls; 3B—Barnes, Waterbury; SS—Gutierrez, Bristol; OF—Bennett, West Haven; Moses, Lynn; Yobs, Glens Falls; C—Skinner, Glens Falls; DH—Torres, Buffalo; RHP—Boyd, Bristol; LHP—Krueger, West Haven; Manager—Bowers, Lynn.

(Compiled by Howe News Bureau, Boston, Mass.)

CLUB BATTING

Club	Pct.	G.	AB.	R.	OR.	H.	TB.	2B.	3B.	HR.	RBI.	GW.	SH.	SF.	HP.	BB.	Int. BB.	SO.	SB.	CS.	LOB.
West Haven	.273	140	4299	722	597	1173	1773	193	28	117	648	76	61	38	35	582	27	779	232	124	852
Glens Falls	.271	140	4596	752	669	1247	1986	215	40	148	704	73	25	34	31	647	26	936	50	32	1069
Buffalo	.261	139	4412	628	706	1153	1773	181	29	127	560	45	40	26	26	440	8	899	108	63	863
Lynn	.261	139	4243	642	615	1109	1656	190	39	93	568	71	53	35	31	631	31	757	212	106	945
Reading	.256	138	4472	621	661	1144	1668	185	51	79	542	56	37	34	35	477	34	982	104	63	923
Holyoke	.255	140	4550	619	674	1158	1679	199	38	82	549	56	48	32	34	535	19	935	75	56	997
Waterbury	.252	138	4395	558	690	1106	1565	169	37	72	513	50	72	30	23	514	31	950	160	54	979
Bristol	.248	140	4425	639	569	1099	1564	212	20	71	530	59	49	40	38	577	31	936	173	76	955

INDIVIDUAL BATTING

(Leading Qualifiers for Batting Championship—378 or More Plate Appearances)

*Bats lefthanded.   †Switch-hitter.

Player and Club	Pct.	G.	AB.	R.	H.	TB.	2B.	3B.	HR.	RBI.	GW.	SH.	SF.	HP.	BB.	Int. BB.	SO.	SB.	CS.
Klimas, Philip, Glens Falls	.311	139	527	88	164	280	32	6	24	95	10	2	7	8	54	2	82	2	2
McNealy, Robert, West Haven*	.310	130	390	80	121	155	11	4	5	41	8	5	2	2	74	3	64	39	17
Barnes, William, Waterbury	.306	112	418	67	128	200	24	6	12	72	8	5	2	1	44	5	32	31	9
Sherow, Dennis, West Haven	.304	108	382	55	116	144	11	7	1	53	6	12	4	3	22	0	76	31	8
Garrett, Lynn, West Haven	.302	104	321	74	97	168	25	2	14	60	8	5	4	5	45	0	61	13	10
Gilbert, Mark, Waterbury†	.300	109	380	65	114	148	17	1	5	41	3	4	2	3	64	1	78	41	10
Yobs, David, Glens Falls*	.297	119	441	72	131	234	26	1	25	93	10	1	4	1	54	10	76	2	5
Whittemore, Reginald, Bristol	.296	128	426	88	126	215	34	2	17	78	11	0	5	5	84	1	120	8	10
Nanni, Tito, Lynn*	.293	134	475	71	139	222	25	5	16	77	13	0	5	4	59	11	113	32	10
Burgess, Gus, Bristol*	.289	133	477	71	138	206	25	5	11	62	11	2	5	2	35	6	102	42	11
Clark, Christopher, Holyoke*	.289	132	471	48	136	200	25	3	11	67	3	8	2	2	53	1	72	4	3

Departmental Leaders: G—Bienek, Hulett, 140; AB—Hulett, 536; R—Hulett, 113; H—Klimas, 164; TB—Klimas, 280; 2B—Whittemore, 34; 3B—Miller, 10; HR—Bennett, 29; RBI—Bennett, 115; GWRBI—Presley, 16; SH—Sherow, 12; SF—Fryer, Hill, 8; HP—Klimas, 8; BB—Williams, 103; IBB—Nanni, 11; SO—Little, 142; SB—Woodard, 54; CS—Reynolds, 20.

(All Players—Listed Alphabetically)

Player and Club	Pct.	G.	AB.	R.	H.	TB.	2B.	3B.	HR.	RBI.	GW.	SH.	SF.	HP.	BB.	Int. BB.	SO.	SB.	CS.
Adams, Ricky, Holyoke	.304	60	227	37	69	98	9	4	4	28	4	1	2	3	17	0	30	11	5
Baez, Jesse, Lynn	.214	79	215	29	46	60	6	1	2	19	3	2	0	3	40	2	28	1	4
Barnes, William, Waterbury	.306	112	418	67	128	200	24	6	12	72	8	5	2	1	44	5	32	31	9
Bathe, William, West Haven	.281	128	370	57	104	177	22	0	17	57	6	8	1	2	43	1	86	4	5
Belliard, Rafael, Buffalo†	.274	40	124	14	34	37	1	1	0	19	4	3	0	0	8	0	16	6	4
Bennett, James, West Haven*	.278	133	446	81	124	237	22	2	29	115	14	0	6	6	53	5	78	24	8
Beswick, James, Holyoke†	.278	57	209	26	58	79	10	1	3	20	2	1	0	0	25	5	42	4	4
Bienek, Vincent, Glens Falls	.275	140	513	72	141	210	24	0	15	78	10	0	3	4	64	2	91	3	5
Bohnet, Robert, Holyoke	.208	116	361	49	75	106	13	3	4	45	6	3	3	3	56	1	76	4	2
Borucki, Raymond, Reading†	.288	106	375	49	108	146	26	3	2	47	4	5	5	2	42	1	26	9	2
Bradley, Bert, West Haven†	.000	39	1	0	0	0	0	0	0	0	0	0	0	0	0	0	0	0	0
Brown, Jeffrey, Glens Falls	.220	70	236	35	52	70	11	2	1	21	1	7	0	1	25	0	45	4	2
Brown, Samuel, Buffalo	.063	7	16	1	1	1	0	0	0	1	0	1	0	1	0	1	7	0	0
Bruno, Joseph, Reading*	.362	27	105	18	38	49	6	1	1	16	2	1	0	0	11	3	7	7	3
Bryant, Erwin, Bristol	.243	67	202	27	49	54	5	0	0	7	1	9	2	0	26	0	27	11	2
Buchanan, Robert, Waterbury*	.140	27	57	2	8	11	3	0	0	5	2	5	1	0	0	0	17	1	0

Player and Club	Pct.	G.	AB.	R.	H.	TB.	2B.	3B.	HR.	RBI.	GW.	SH.	SF.	HP.	BB.	Int. BB.	SO.	SB.	CS.
Buckle, Lawrence, Waterbury	.065	27	46	2	3	3	0	0	0	2	0	3	0	0	7	0	27	0	0
Burgess, Gus, Bristol°	.289	133	477	71	138	206	25	5	11	62	11	2	5	2	35	6	102	42	11
Cato, J. Keefe, Waterbury	.091	18	11	0	1	1	0	0	0	0	0	1	0	1	1	0	3	0	0
Chappas, Harry, Glens Falls†	.258	34	132	27	34	59	3	8	2	11	2	2	0	0	20	0	31	2	0
Cipot, Edwin, Glens Falls°	.226	31	93	12	21	34	4	0	3	15	1	1	3	1	17	1	15	1	0
Clark, Christopher, Holyoke°	.289	132	471	48	136	200	25	3	11	67	3	8	2	2	53	1	72	4	3
Colbert, Richard, Bristol	.167	98	252	27	42	63	12	0	3	18	4	5	0	6	33	0	79	9	5
Corbett, Raymond, Waterbury	.283	98	269	38	76	104	13	3	3	38	9	6	3	2	40	0	58	3	3
Crist, Clark, Lynn	.171	11	35	3	6	7	1	0	0	2	1	2	0	0	4	0	3	0	1
Crone, William, Lynn	.231	109	316	57	73	110	14	7	3	40	2	4	0	1	67	1	63	23	8
Davis, Alvin, Lynn°	.284	74	225	37	64	112	10	1	12	56	5	3	7	4	53	4	38	1	1
DeLaRosa, Bienvenido, Buffalo°°	.225	20	71	7	16	25	3	0	2	5	1	0	0	0	4	0	11	1	0
Dempsey, Patrick, West Haven	.237	72	177	23	42	67	10	0	5	27	2	0	3	1	12	2	31	3	7
Diaz, Enrique, Lynn	.204	38	113	14	23	27	4	0	0	5	1	0	0	0	12	0	30	6	3
Diaz, Mario, Lynn	.216	53	162	19	35	47	7	1	1	13	1	5	1	1	19	0	24	2	1
Donofrio, Larry, Glens Falls°	.295	43	95	20	28	45	5	0	4	9	2	0	1	0	17	0	38	1	0
Ender, Scot, Waterbury	.296	18	27	2	8	11	0	0	1	3	0	3	0	0	0	0	10	0	0
Enos, David, Reading†	.163	16	43	9	7	9	0	1	0	2	0	0	0	0	12	2	14	0	1
Estepa, Ramon, Lynn	.217	132	420	60	91	142	12	6	9	46	3	4	2	5	68	2	80	9	10
Evans, Johnny, West Haven	.274	97	266	36	73	125	11	1	13	57	4	0	5	6	41	1	41	4	3
Fallon, Robert, Glens Falls°	.000	28	1	0	0	0	0	0	0	0	0	0	0	0	0	0	0	0	0
Fick, Charles, West Haven	.286	42	63	11	18	25	4	0	1	6	2	2	1	0	4	0	18	0	1
Fiorillo, Nickolas, Waterbury°	.333	13	21	0	7	7	0	0	0	3	0	3	1	0	0	0	4	0	0
Flammang, J. Christopher, Lynn°	.223	48	139	17	31	41	10	0	0	6	1	4	0	0	16	0	24	0	2
Francis, Harry, Holyoke	.223	114	358	48	80	103	8	3	3	33	3	6	5	4	39	1	80	7	7
Franklin, Glen, Waterbury°	.293	109	259	38	76	97	10	1	3	31	3	3	2	2	25	0	29	13	3
Fredlund, Jay, Bristol	.000	15	1	0	0	0	0	0	0	0	0	0	0	0	0	0	0	0	0
Freeman, Clements, Waterbury°	.333	32	6	0	2	2	0	0	0	0	0	0	0	0	1	0	3	0	0
Fryer, Paul, Reading	.268	129	474	66	127	205	29	8	11	65	10	1	8	5	28	0	137	6	7
Gallego, Michael, West Haven	.180	54	139	17	25	26	1	0	0	5	0	1	0	1	13	0	25	3	5
Garcia, Daniel, Buffalo°	.378	57	193	32	73	100	7	1	6	31	4	1	1	3	26	2	21	5	10
Garrett, Lynn, West Haven	.302	104	321	74	97	168	25	2	14	60	8	5	4	5	45	0	61	13	10
Gause, Ernest, Waterbury°	.250	29	4	0	1	1	0	0	0	0	0	0	0	0	0	0	0	0	0
Gelfarb, Stephen, West Haven°	.250	105	280	39	70	96	11	0	5	36	4	0	0	3	46	7	47	2	5
Gilbert, Dennis, Holyoke	.247	127	434	48	107	175	21	1	15	59	4	3	2	2	42	1	129	4	4
Gilbert, Mark, Waterbury†	.300	109	380	65	114	148	17	1	5	41	3	4	2	3	64	1	78	41	10
Gonzalez, Denio, Buffalo	.278	68	252	28	70	92	5	4	3	21	3	3	1	1	28	0	62	11	7
Gutierrez, Joaquin, Bristol	.278	138	468	64	130	157	20	2	1	44	2	4	2	1	54	1	40	19	15
Hall, Jeffrey, Bristol	.225	125	462	54	104	148	24	1	6	59	4	3	5	3	19	3	94	9	2
Harvey, Steven, Reading	.284	55	194	16	55	74	10	0	3	18	3	0	1	0	8	0	43	0	4
Hearn, Edward, Reading	.274	43	135	16	37	56	6	2	3	27	2	1	1	1	9	0	20	0	0
Herring, Paul, Waterbury	.175	27	80	12	14	26	3	0	3	10	0	1	2	0	13	2	12	4	1
Hill, Donald, West Haven†	.254	132	405	66	103	160	21	3	10	59	9	3	8	2	49	4	54	15	13
Hobbs, Rodney, West Haven	.270	57	122	25	33	56	4	2	5	19	2	3	1	0	22	0	37	7	6
Holland, John, Buffalo	.224	109	366	52	82	130	17	2	9	42	6	3	6	3	37	1	95	1	0
Houston, Kevin, Buffalo°	.261	50	176	18	46	66	8	0	4	22	0	1	0	2	6	0	27	1	4
Hulett, Timothy, Glens Falls	.271	140	536	113	145	249	28	5	22	87	8	1	6	3	95	1	135	1	8
Hundhammer, Paul, Bristol†	.272	111	382	69	104	141	18	2	5	51	3	5	4	5	77	2	76	20	10
Hunt, Ronald, Holyoke	.182	14	44	6	8	11	3	0	0	4	0	0	1	4	1	9	0	9	0
Hunter, Marion, Holyoke	.198	27	91	8	18	21	3	0	0	4	0	4	0	2	9	0	15	3	2
Ibarra, Miguel, Reading	.263	97	342	50	90	125	11	3	6	35	3	1	2	2	45	5	55	4	3
Incaviglia, Tony, Buffalo	.252	102	313	44	79	131	13	3	11	45	1	1	1	1	46	0	81	3	8
Jeltz, Larry, Reading†	.242	126	380	61	92	129	10	3	7	28	3	7	0	3	65	0	104	12	4
Jones, Kenneth, Waterbury	.227	38	22	1	5	8	1	1	0	1	0	4	0	0	1	0	4	1	0
Keedy, C. Patrick, Holyoke	.247	125	437	68	108	196	19	6	19	73	9	2	2	3	56	1	131	9	6
Kepshire, Kurt, Waterbury°	.200	30	5	0	1	1	0	0	0	0	0	0	0	0	0	0	2	0	0
Kirsch, Paul, Waterbury°	.275	79	291	27	80	106	15	1	3	33	4	1	2	2	17	5	26	6	5
Klimas, Philip, Glens Falls	.311	139	527	88	164	280	32	6	24	95	10	2	7	8	54	2	82	2	2
Krauss, Timothy, Holyoke	.267	129	498	76	133	183	28	2	6	44	5	6	3	3	55	5	79	3	8
Kripner, Michael, Waterbury°	.203	90	251	30	51	67	8	1	2	22	1	2	3	1	42	8	63	1	4
Landrum, T. William, Waterbury	.130	58	23	2	3	4	1	0	0	2	0	2	0	0	1	0	12	0	0
Liddle, Steven, Holyoke	.300	45	150	13	45	56	8	0	1	16	2	0	3	0	11	0	14	0	0
Lindsey, Jon, Reading°	.233	43	159	24	37	57	5	0	5	26	0	2	2	2	12	1	34	0	2
Little, Ronald, Waterbury°	.282	128	444	50	125	191	16	7	12	51	6	3	3	1	33	2	142	11	2
Lochner, David, Waterbury°	.000	7	5	1	0	0	0	0	0	0	0	0	0	0	0	0	0	0	0
Lyons, Stephen, Bristol°	.243	135	460	86	112	180	23	3	13	58	4	6	3	2	81	7	119	35	9
MacAuley, J. Andrew, Buffalo†	.213	19	47	7	10	15	2	0	1	4	0	1	0	0	4	0	12	0	1
Mahlberg, Gregory, Lynn°	.000	2	4	0	0	0	0	0	0	0	0	0	0	0	1	0	0	0	0
McAbee, Monte, West Haven°	.167	6	12	0	2	2	0	0	0	0	0	0	0	0	3	0	2	1	1
McDonald, Manuel, Reading	.263	25	95	15	25	36	6	1	1	11	1	1	0	0	10	0	10	1	0
McGehee, C. Connor, Buffalo°	.282	117	418	79	118	177	18	4	11	36	4	6	1	2	58	2	103	33	8
McNealy, Robert, West Haven°	.310	130	390	80	121	155	11	4	5	41	8	5	2	2	74	3	64	39	17
Miller, Darrell, Holyoke	.262	119	450	76	118	196	25	0	11	60	8	3	2	4	52	1	104	12	6
Miscik, Robert, Buffalo	.257	131	420	74	108	174	19	1	15	51	3	5	4	4	53	0	68	2	3
Mize, Paul, West Haven	.200	20	40	7	8	9	1	0	0	7	1	4	0	0	8	0	14	3	0
Morse, Michael, Glens Falls	.246	62	256	40	63	93	9	0	7	19	3	3	0	1	24	0	47	5	4
Moses, John, Lynn†	.285	128	466	87	133	188	25	6	6	52	6	10	4	0	67	3	69	50	18
Murray, Jed, Lynn	.000	42	0	0	0	0	0	0	0	0	0	0	0	0	0	0	0	0	0
Nanni, Tito, Lynn°	.293	134	475	71	139	222	25	5	16	77	13	0	5	4	59	11	113	32	10
Nelson, James, Lynn	.285	111	316	48	90	137	15	4	8	42	7	1	5	2	75	3	35	8	7
Nemeth, Joseph, Reading°	.215	110	335	37	72	104	8	6	4	47	1	2	4	3	36	5	108	4	3
Nixon, R. Donell, Lynn	.292	6	24	5	7	11	2	1	0	1	0	1	0	1	2	0	4	3	0
Orensky, Herbert, Reading°	.286	20	63	8	18	33	4	1	3	18	4	1	1	0	8	3	12	0	0
Owen, Spike, Lynn†	.266	78	241	32	64	80	9	2	1	27	1	7	0	1	44	1	33	18	8
Palmer, Robert, Holyoke	.224	73	201	28	45	57	7	1	1	26	1	4	3	1	33	0	49	1	1
Pastors, Gregory, Buffalo	.193	114	347	34	67	99	11	0	7	39	3	8	3	2	32	0	69	6	4
Patterson, Larry, Holyoke	.308	86	279	55	86	106	10	2	2	36	7	4	3	4	63	2	54	5	3
Pautt, Jan, Bristol	.269	110	353	41	95	122	16	1	3	46	5	3	5	1	54	2	77	6	4
Peltz, Peter, Glens Falls	.267	88	255	38	68	99	11	4	4	36	3	2	3	4	46	0	38	8	2
Polidor, Gustavo, Holyoke	.226	56	208	17	47	60	7	0	2	23	1	2	1	1	5	0	23	2	5
Pratt, Crestwell, Waterbury	.209	44	129	20	27	48	3	0	6	28	1	1	1	0	23	0	53	2	1
Presley, James, Lynn	.266	133	462	65	123	213	24	0	22	79	16	1	4	4	38	1	119	12	9

Player and Club	Pct.	G.	AB.	R.	H.	TB.	2B.	3B.	HR.	RBI.	GW.	SH.	SF.	HP.	BB.	Int. BB.	SO.	SB.	CS.
Pruitt, Lee, Bristol°	.228	104	303	44	69	112	19	0	8	47	6	3	4	6	50	6	61	6	1
Pyle, Scot, West Haven	.255	89	184	29	47	67	7	2	3	24	3	4	1	0	46	9	40	10	13
Pyznarski, Timothy, West Haven	.262	108	294	54	77	124	18	4	7	34	3	5	0	2	46	3	61	14	8
Ramos, Wolfgangh, Bristol	.204	90	270	37	55	76	8	2	3	27	3	3	3	4	21	0	49	5	3
Reynolds, Harold, Lynn†	.272	102	375	58	102	130	14	4	2	48	7	8	3	3	36	1	41	39	20
Riley, Michael, Waterbury	.000	2	2	0	0	0	0	0	0	0	0	0	0	0	0	0	2	0	0
Robbins, Michael, Glens Falls°	.230	62	178	32	41	60	10	0	3	28	3	0	0	2	41	1	53	5	0
Robinson, Ronald, Waterbury	.053	32	57	4	3	3	0	0	0	2	0	4	0	0	7	0	25	0	0
Rodriquez, Jose, Buffalo	.254	99	342	55	87	155	16	5	14	52	3	2	0	3	45	1	112	26	8
Rodriguez, Luis, Reading	.251	77	263	40	66	95	10	5	3	31	5	2	1	1	31	0	51	9	5
Rojas, Luis, West Haven	.000	1	2	0	0	0	0	0	0	0	0	0	0	0	0	0	0	0	0
Rowe, Peter, Buffalo	.103	11	29	1	3	6	0	0	1	5	0	0	0	0	2	0	3	0	0
Russell, Jeffrey, Waterbury	.269	16	26	4	7	12	2	1	7	5	0	5	0	1	0	0	8	0	0
Russell, John, Reading	.202	77	263	26	53	91	10	5	6	30	2	2	3	4	23	3	84	3	2
Salava, Randy, Reading°	.210	114	386	58	81	138	19	4	10	43	5	0	2	5	55	6	123	13	5
Scarpace, Kenneth, Waterbury°	.253	126	423	42	107	139	17	6	1	41	5	6	2	3	39	2	56	3	3
Schaive, John, Buffalo	.268	134	482	63	129	187	29	1	9	51	3	5	3	1	26	0	48	4	1
Scherrer, William, Waterbury°	.182	5	11	0	2	2	0	0	0	2	0	0	0	0	0	0	4	0	0
Sherow, Dennis, West Haven	.304	108	382	55	116	144	11	7	1	53	6	12	4	3	22	0	76	31	8
Skinner, Joel, Glens Falls	.254	120	422	49	107	151	11	6	7	65	7	2	3	1	38	0	115	1	0
Sproesser, Mark, Holyoke	.189	46	132	16	25	32	3	2	0	11	1	1	1	1	15	0	28	6	0
Sullivan, Marc, Bristol	.203	117	369	31	75	90	8	2	1	33	5	6	2	3	42	3	92	3	4
Tartabull, Danilo, Waterbury	.227	126	409	64	93	167	17	3	17	63	4	1	3	2	89	5	120	12	5
Thibodeaux, Keith, Buffalo	.000	13	0	0	0	0	0	0	0	0	0	0	0	0	0	0	1	1	0
Thomas, Vernon, Glens Falls	.267	129	453	62	121	179	20	7	8	59	3	3	1	2	49	2	88	12	4
Torres, Alfredo, Buffalo	.271	135	494	69	134	237	19	3	26	97	5	0	3	2	33	2	110	4	2
Velasquez, Alfredo, Reading†	.145	20	76	7	11	18	4	0	1	7	1	0	1	1	2	0	25	0	0
Viltz, Eskimilo, Waterbury†	.254	129	481	59	122	146	13	4	1	36	3	7	3	4	35	1	89	22	7
Walker, Glen, Lynn	.322	68	255	40	82	129	12	1	11	55	4	1	4	2	30	2	53	8	3
Walker, Tony, Waterbury	.176	85	238	28	42	60	6	3	2	20	1	2	0	1	32	0	71	9	1
Washington, Keith, Reading†	.288	136	503	78	145	173	11	7	1	40	5	11	3	2	42	2	81	35	19
Wheeler, Timothy, Buffalo	.000	20	1	0	0	0	0	0	0	0	0	0	0	0	0	0	1	0	0
Whittemore, Reginald, Bristol	.296	128	426	88	126	215	34	2	17	78	11	0	5	5	84	1	120	8	10
Willard, Gerald, Reading°	.292	81	281	43	82	130	10	1	12	51	5	0	2	4	38	3	48	1	3
Williams, Daniel, Glens Falls°	.286	128	458	92	131	223	21	1	23	88	10	1	3	3	103	7	82	3	0
Woodard, Michael, West Haven°	.273	104	348	55	95	113	13	1	1	43	4	4	2	2	35	1	31	54	13
Wotus, Ronald, Buffalo	.299	86	321	50	96	141	13	4	8	39	5	1	1	2	31	0	53	4	3
Yobs, David, Glens Falls°	.297	119	441	72	131	234	26	1	25	93	10	1	4	1	54	10	76	2	5
Young, Selwyn, West Haven	.316	29	57	13	18	22	1	0	1	5	0	0	0	0	20	0	13	5	1

The following pitchers, listed alphabetically by club, with games in parentheses, had no plate appearances, primarily through use of designated hitters:

BRISTOL—Birrell, Robert (24); Boyd, Dennis (27); Brown, Michael (16); Burns, Michael (9); Denman, Brian (5); Goff, Wallace (21); Johnson, Clinton (46); King, Jerome (8); Nipper, Albert (19); Rivas, Martin (28); Shields, Stephen (29); Tyler, David (17); Woody, Harley (48).

BUFFALO—Barez, Angel (5); Bielecki, Michael (25); Burke, Timothy (25); Cuen, Eleno (22); Farr, Steven (25); Green, Christopher (13); Keenan, Kerry (9); Krawczyk, Raymond (38); Leggatt, Richard (15); Mohorcic, Dale (44); Peterson, Eric (2); Pippin, Craig (23); Ray, Arthur (6); Wiltbank, Benjamin (6); Winn, James (3); Zamba, Michael (4).

GLENS FALLS—Atkinson, William (56); Desjarlais, Keith (7); Edwards, Larry (14); Esser, Mark (9); Flannery, Kevin (26); Hardy, John (28); Howard, Fred (14); Johnson, Charles (14); Lackey, John (27); Maitland, Michael (10); McKeon, Joel (7); Mullen, Tom (3); Schattinger, Jeffrey (6); Teutsch, Mark (48); Withrow, Michael (25).

HOLYOKE—Barba, Michael (37); Boxburger, Rodney (28); Buckley, Brian (42); Cliburn, Stewart (22); Conner, Jeffrey (30); Dugger, Lawrence (1); Duran, David (2); Kibbe, Jay (23); Mooneyham, William (8); Morrison, Perry (12); Romanick, Ronald (16); Smith, David A. (50); Smith, David W. (39); Venezia, Michael (23).

LYNN—Adair, Richard (27); Best, Karl (21); Dukes, Kevin (34); Georger, Joseph (34); Gleaton, Jerry Don (24); Hudson, Robert (23); Krueger, Steven (31); Stottlemyre, Jeffrey (32); Stranski, Scott (24); Welborn, Sammye (1).

READING—Baller, Jay (50); Burroughs, Darren (8); Carman, Donald (20); Faulk, Kelly (40); Gross, Kevin (26); Money, Kyle (26); Palmieri, John (21); Prior, Daniel (26); Rasmussen, James (6); Riley, George (37); Smith, Leroy (26); Thomas, Dennis (26); Wortham, Richard (24); Wright, James (4).

WEST HAVEN—Abraham, Brian (55); Buice, DeWayne (8); Codiroli, Christopher (12); Comstock, Keith (24); Hallgren, Tim (5); Heimueller, Gorman (23); Hensley, Charles (37); Krueger, William (28); Marietta, Louis (35); Moore, Robert (16); Ontiveros, Steve (16); Smith, Jack (53).

GRAND SLAM HOME RUNS—Williams, 3; Hill, Hulett, Pratt, Yobs, 2 each; Barnes, Clark, Colbert, Garrett, Gilbert, Hundhammer, Houston, Klimas, Miscik, Moses, Russell, Walker, Willard, Woodard, 1 each.

AWARDED FIRST BASE ON CATCHER'S INTERFERENCE—Herring 2 (Bathe 2); Barnes (Colbert); Cipot (Willard); Gelfarb (Baez); Krauss (Sullivan).

CLUB FIELDING

Club	Pct.	G.	PO.	A.	E.	DP.	PB.	Club	Pct.	G.	PO.	A.	E.	DP.	PB.
Lynn	.969	139	3443	1449	156	114	18	Bristol	.961	140	3547	1442	203	113	17
Glens Falls	.967	140	3526	1510	174	148	8	West Haven	.961	140	3475	1394	200	106	12
Buffalo	.967	139	3413	1350	175	114	19	Holyoke	.960	140	3565	1590	217	115	25
Reading	.964	138	3505	1383	184	132	20	Waterbury	.960	138	3470	1418	202	103	26

Triple Plays—Holyoke 2, Bristol.

°Throws lefthanded.

INDIVIDUAL FIELDING
FIRST BASEMEN

Player and Club	Pct.	G.	PO.	A.	E.	DP.	Player and Club	Pct.	G.	PO.	A.	E.	DP.
Adams, Holyoke	1.000	1	8	0	0	1	Enos, Reading	1.000	4	32	0	0	0
Baez, Lynn	1.000	1	1	1	0	0	Estepa, Lynn	.977	16	119	10	3	12
Barnes, Waterbury	.983	22	167	9	3	14	Evans, West Haven	.997	49	316	23	1	28
Bohnet, Holyoke	.989	111	956	58	11	74	Fick, West Haven	1.000	5	19	1	0	0
Borucki, Reading	1.000	10	72	6	0	7	Francis, Holyoke	.987	19	141	12	2	7
Cipot, Glens Falls°	.984	29	233	21	4	31	Garcia, Buffalo°	1.000	3	30	2	0	4
Colbert, Bristol	1.000	5	41	1	0	3	Gelfarb, West Haven°	.985	96	696	41	11	54
Crone, Lynn	1.000	1	2	0	0	0	Hearn, Reading	.979	28	172	15	4	17
Davis, Lynn	.991	74	579	51	6	51	Herring, Waterbury	.982	23	207	12	4	11
Dempsey, West Haven	.976	20	115	9	3	7	Hunt, Holyoke	1.000	3	24	1	0	1
Diaz, Lynn	.980	37	309	29	7	25	Kirsch, Waterbury°	.984	77	640	43	11	54

FIRST BASEMEN—Continued

Player and Club	Pct.	G.	PO.	A.	E.	DP.
Klimas, Glens Falls	.984	19	178	11	3	23
Kripner, Waterbury	1.000	1	4	1	0	0
Liddle, Holyoke	.964	4	26	1	1	2
McDonald, Reading	.923	4	23	1	2	4
Nelson, Lynn	.988	21	145	14	2	15
Nemeth, Reading*	.987	107	752	66	11	88
Patterson, Holyoke	.988	17	157	7	2	11
Peltz, Glens Falls	.982	7	50	4	1	3
Pratt, Waterbury	.983	21	162	10	3	13
Pruitt, Bristol	.986	16	127	12	2	9
Pyznarski, West Haven	1.000	1	1	0	0	0
Russell, Reading	1.000	1	6	0	0	0
SCHAIVE, Buffalo	.993	129	1027	82	8	91
Sullivan, Bristol	1.000	1	6	0	0	0
Torres, Buffalo	.957	6	39	5	2	6
Whittemore, Bristol	.982	122	977	87	19	82
Williams, Glens Falls*	.995	87	765	62	4	73
Wotus, Buffalo	1.000	2	13	1	0	2

Triple Plays—Bohnet 2, Whittemore.

SECOND BASEMEN

Player and Club	Pct.	G.	PO.	A.	E.	DP.
Adams, Holyoke	.991	39	85	128	2	18
Borucki, Reading	.984	41	91	92	3	25
Brown, Glens Falls	.846	5	12	10	4	4
Bryant, Bristol	.959	55	87	125	9	19
Colbert, Bristol	1.000	2	1	3	0	0
Crist, Lynn	1.000	2	5	6	0	1
Crone, Lynn	.981	53	123	136	5	30
Enos, Reading	.920	4	11	12	2	5
Francis, Holyoke	.909	2	5	5	1	0
Franklin, Waterbury	.919	13	15	19	3	4
Gallego, West Haven	.979	47	78	107	4	17
Garrett, West Haven	1.000	1	1	0	0	0
Gilbert, Waterbury	.967	6	16	13	1	3
Gonzalez, Buffalo	.966	66	137	176	11	39
HULETT, Glens Falls	.975	135	343	386	19	95
Hundhammer, Bristol	.960	79	186	203	16	46
Incaviglia, Buffalo	1.000	2	2	4	0	0
Jeltz, Reading	.960	98	211	225	18	58
Krauss, Holyoke	.973	99	191	282	13	46
MacAuley, Buffalo	.962	13	22	28	2	2
Miscik, Buffalo	.714	1	3	2	2	1
Pastors, Buffalo	.964	13	26	27	2	4
Pyle, West Haven	.944	7	8	9	1	2
Ramos, Bristol	.944	14	24	27	3	7
Reynolds, Lynn	.958	87	202	232	19	56
Sproesser, Holyoke	.900	3	4	5	1	1
Tartabull, Waterbury	.944	123	237	306	32	61
Woodard, West Haven	.969	84	190	190	12	51
Wotus, Buffalo	.956	48	94	146	11	27
Young, West Haven	.933	21	41	43	6	14

Triple Plays—Bryant, Krauss

THIRD BASEMEN

Player and Club	Pct.	G.	PO.	A.	E.	DP.
BARNES, Waterbury	.947	94	85	183	15	9
Bohnet, Holyoke	1.000	4	0	3	0	0
Borucki, Reading	1.000	10	4	20	0	1
Brown, Glens Falls	1.000	3	1	4	0	0
Colbert, Bristol	.869	35	21	52	11	3
Crist, Lynn	1.000	3	1	8	0	1
Crone, Lynn	1.000	3	2	2	0	1
Enos, Reading	.900	3	3	6	1	1
Estepa, Lynn	1.000	1	2	0	0	0
Evans, West Haven	1.000	3	0	1	0	0
Francis, Holyoke	.896	58	35	112	17	11
Franklin, Waterbury	.843	39	26	60	16	3
Fryer, Reading	.927	128	100	231	26	32
Hill, West Haven	1.000	2	0	3	0	0
Hundhammer, Bristol	.865	31	9	55	10	2
Incaviglia, Buffalo	.889	18	14	26	5	5
Jeltz, Reading	1.000	1	0	2	0	0
Keedy, Holyoke	.918	89	45	191	21	20
Klimas, Glens Falls	.932	93	56	231	21	30
Krauss, Holyoke	1.000	2	1	0	0	0
Kripner, Waterbury	.871	13	10	17	4	3
Miscik, Buffalo	.935	127	81	219	21	18
Mize, West Haven	.857	3	1	5	1	1
Nelson, Lynn	1.000	1	0	2	0	0
Nixon, Lynn	1.000	1	0	2	0	0
Pastors, Buffalo	1.000	1	0	3	0	0
Patterson, Holyoke	1.000	1	0	1	0	0
Peltz, Glens Falls	.951	46	34	83	6	10
Presley, Lynn	.904	131	83	247	35	16
Pruitt, Bristol	.966	40	17	67	3	10
Pyle, West Haven	.882	60	33	101	18	10
Pyznarski, West Haven	.883	98	65	168	31	13
Ramos, Bristol	.882	57	29	91	16	11
Thomas, Glens Falls	.750	1	0	3	1	0
Woodard, West Haven	.963	17	8	18	1	2
Wotus, Buffalo	.857	2	2	4	1	2

Triple Plays—Francis, Keedy,

SHORTSTOPS

Player and Club	Pct.	G.	PO.	A.	E.	DP.
Adams, Holyoke	.965	16	24	59	3	11
Barnes, Waterbury	.000	1	0	0	1	0
Belliard, Buffalo	.966	40	56	87	5	18
Borucki, Reading	.953	50	69	133	10	20
Brown, Glens Falls	.962	48	56	119	7	23
Chappas, Glens Falls	.977	31	42	84	3	16
Colbert, Bristol	.667	2	0	2	1	0
Crist, Lynn	.939	5	14	17	2	3
Crone, Lynn	1.000	9	9	22	0	4
Diaz, Lynn	.952	53	75	143	11	25
Enos, Reading	1.000	1	3	3	0	1
Francis, Holyoke	.875	3	4	3	1	2
Franklin, Waterbury	.942	13	22	27	3	5
Gallego, West Haven	1.000	3	7	4	0	0
GUTIERREZ, Bristol	.939	138	199	368	37	58
Hill, West Haven	.938	118	141	298	29	48
Hulett, Glens Falls	.913	4	9	12	2	2
Peltz, Reading	.965	26	40	70	4	16
Keedy, Holyoke	.937	36	46	88	9	12
Lindsey, Reading	.909	37	61	98	16	30
Lyons, Bristol	1.000	1	0	1	0	0
McDonald, Reading	.917	3	2	9	1	0
Miscik, Buffalo	1.000	1	0	1	0	0
Mize, West Haven	.956	16	13	30	2	3
Morse, Glens Falls	.913	62	79	193	26	42
Owen, Lynn	.972	76	106	207	9	40
Pastors, Buffalo	.955	91	134	208	16	46
Polidor, Holyoke	.914	55	74	149	21	23
Pyle, West Haven	.933	18	15	41	4	7
Ramos, Bristol	1.000	6	3	8	0	0
Rodriguez, Reading	.903	25	33	51	9	7
Sproesser, Holyoke	.886	42	41	106	19	11
Viltz, Waterbury	.936	128	187	379	39	65
Wotus, Buffalo	.913	10	21	21	4	5
Young, West Haven	1.000	2	0	1	0	0

Triple Plays—Adams, Gutierrez.

OUTFIELDERS

Player and Club	Pct.	G.	PO.	A.	E.	DP.
Adams, Holyoke	.667	1	2	0	1	0
Baez, Lynn	.833	3	5	0	1	0
Bennett, West Haven*	.953	114	164	17	9	1
Beswick, Holyoke	.986	56	137	4	2	1
Benek, Glens Falls*	.958	139	241	8	11	3
Bohnet, Holyoke	1.000	2	4	0	0	0
Brown, Glens Falls	.905	11	19	0	2	0
Brown, Buffalo	1.000	7	14	0	0	0
Bruno, Reading*	.968	27	55	5	2	0
Burgess, Bristol*	.938	126	198	12	14	2
Spot, Glens Falls*	1.000	2	1	1	0	0
Clark, Holyoke*	.945	90	142	12	9	1
Colbert, Bristol	.912	20	29	2	3	0
Crone, Lynn	.500	2	1	0	1	0
DeLaRosa, Buffalo*	.919	20	34	0	3	0
Dempsey, West Haven	1.000	1	1	0	0	0
Donofrio, Glens Falls	1.000	3	5	0	0	0
Enos, Reading	.667	3	2	0	1	0
Estepa, Lynn	.978	101	171	6	4	0
Flammang, Lynn*	.974	22	37	0	1	0
Francis, Holyoke	.935	29	41	2	3	0
Garcia, Buffalo*	.973	49	66	7	2	2
Garrett, West Haven	.917	56	73	4	7	1
Gelfarb, West Haven*	1.000	7	10	0	0	0

OUTFIELDERS—Continued

Player and Club	Pct.	G.	PO.	A.	E.	DP.
D. Gilbert, Holyoke	.928	122	178	14	15	5
M. Gilbert, Waterbury	.987	99	133	14	2	1
Hall, Bristol	.968	115	175	7	6	2
Harvey, Reading	.968	43	58	3	2	0
Hobbs, West Haven	.985	50	63	4	1	1
Houston, Buffalo°	.907	44	76	2	8	0
Hunter, Holyoke	.895	26	49	2	6	0
Incaviglia, Buffalo	.939	65	84	9	6	1
Little, Waterbury	.960	124	258	6	11	2
Lyons, Bristol	.969	133	275	10	9	2
McAbee, West Haven°	1.000	1	6	0	0	0
McDonald, Reading	.941	19	31	1	2	0
McGehee, Buffalo°	.922	113	163	3	14	0
McNealy, West Haven°	.968	125	232	10	8	1
Miller, Holyoke	.961	105	187	8	8	1
MOSES, Lynn°	1.000	128	259	20	0	6
Nanni, Lynn°	.910	129	165	6	17	3
Nelson, Lynn	1.000	6	8	1	0	0
Pastors, Buffalo	1.000	3	1	0	0	0
Patterson, Holyoke	1.000	1	3	0	0	0
Pautt, Bristol	.918	42	62	5	6	1
Pratt, Waterbury	.909	19	26	4	3	0
Presley, Lynn	1.000	1	1	3	0	0
Robbins, Glens Falls°	.968	37	55	6	2	1
J. Rodriguez, Buffalo	.956	99	212	4	10	0
L. Rodriguez, Reading	.967	53	81	8	3	0
Rojas, West Haven	1.000	1	1	1	0	0
Russell, Reading	.973	36	65	6	2	1
Salava, Reading	.963	114	198	13	8	5
Scarpace, Waterbury°	.977	116	199	11	5	2
Sherow, West Haven	.908	104	118	11	13	1
Thomas, Glens Falls	.950	129	253	12	14	2
Torres, Glens Falls	1.000	3	8	1	0	0
G. Walker, Lynn	1.000	34	43	1	0	1
T. Walker, Waterbury	.970	73	121	8	4	5
Washington, Reading	.957	136	295	17	14	2
Williams, Glens Falls°	.913	12	21	0	2	0
Wotus, Buffalo	.977	26	41	2	1	0
Yobs, Glens Falls°	.970	102	158	6	5	1

CATCHERS

Player and Club	Pct.	G.	PO.	A.	E.	DP.	PB.
Baez, Lynn	.984	71	391	34	7	3	7
BATHE, West Haven	.989	114	763	55	9	8	11
Colbert, Bristol	.968	41	269	30	10	2	4
Corbett, Waterbury	.973	80	493	50	15	5	14
Dempsey, West Haven	.993	30	135	15	1	1	1
Donofrio, Glens Falls	.967	23	105	12	4	1	3
Fick, West Haven	.975	36	102	13	3	0	0
Hall, Bristol	1.000	1	2	1	0	0	0
Hearn, Reading	.917	5	32	1	3	0	2
Holland, Buffalo	.986	92	638	58	10	6	9
Ibarra, Reading	1.000	1	6	1	0	0	0
Kripner, Waterbury	.985	68	407	49	7	6	12
Liddle, Holyoke	.970	36	222	35	8	6	5
Mahlberg, Lynn	1.000	2	3	0	0	0	0
Nelson, Lynn	.980	86	510	43	11	2	11
Orensky, Reading	.976	18	112	8	3	2	3
Palmer, Holyoke	.986	69	388	46	6	7	8
Pastors, Buffalo	1.000	1	2	0	0	1	0
Patterson, Holyoke	.984	50	274	32	5	2	12
Pruitt, Bristol	1.000	2	4	0	0	0	0
Rowe, Buffalo	.941	8	56	8	4	2	1
Russell, Reading	.970	48	283	38	10	2	3
Skinner, Glens Falls	.985	119	726	80	12	11	5
Sullivan, Bristol	.984	110	722	89	13	13	13
Torres, Buffalo	.980	40	250	46	6	1	9
Velasquez, Reading	1.000	1	6	1	0	0	0
Willard, Reading	.979	74	534	64	13	5	12

Triple Plays—Liddle, Patterson.

PITCHERS

Player and Club	Pct.	G.	PO.	A.	E.	DP.
Abraham, West Haven°	.895	55	5	12	2	0
Adair, Lynn°	.875	26	8	41	7	0
Atkinson, Glens Falls	.862	56	9	16	4	2
Baller, Reading	.844	50	8	19	5	3
Barba, Holyoke	.926	37	2	23	2	1
Barez, Buffalo	.333	5	0	1	2	0
Best, Lynn	.926	21	9	16	2	1
Bielecki, Buffalo	.900	25	6	21	3	5
Birrell, Bistol°	.958	24	7	16	1	0
Bohnet, Holyoke	1.000	2	1	0	0	0
Boxburger, Holyoke	.974	28	8	30	1	3
Boyd, Bristol	.939	27	20	26	3	1
Bradley, West Haven	.923	39	3	9	1	0
Brown, Bristol	.955	16	2	19	1	0
Buchanan, Waterbury°	.956	27	7	36	2	3
Buckle, Waterbury	.886	27	11	28	5	3
Buckley, Holyoke	.952	42	6	14	1	2
Buice, West Haven	1.000	8	3	2	0	0
Burke, Buffalo	.975	25	13	26	1	3
Burns, Bristol	1.000	9	4	1	0	0
Burroughs, Reading°	.889	8	3	5	1	0
Carman, Waterbury°	1.000	20	2	18	0	1
Cato, Waterbury	1.000	18	6	9	0	1
Cliburn, Holyoke	.935	22	9	20	2	4
Codiroli, West Haven	1.000	12	3	7	0	0
Comstock, West Haven°	1.000	24	5	17	0	1
Conner, Holyoke°	.949	30	7	30	2	3
Cuen, Buffalo	.857	22	9	15	4	1
Denman, Bristol	.895	5	4	13	2	1
Desjarlais, Glens Falls	1.000	7	3	6	0	0
Dukes, Lynn°	1.000	34	1	17	0	0
Edwards, Glens Falls	.857	14	2	4	1	0
Ender, Waterbury	1.000	14	1	15	0	1
Esser, Glens Falls°	1.000	9	1	3	0	0
Fallon, Glens Falls°	.915	28	18	25	4	4
Farr, Buffalo	.733	25	2	9	4	1
Faulk, Reading	1.000	40	2	12	0	1
Fiorillo, Waterbury°	.867	13	1	12	2	0
Flannery, Glens Falls	1.000	26	5	11	0	2
Fredlund, Bristol	.923	15	4	8	1	1
Freeman, Waterbury°	.917	32	2	9	1	0
Gause, Waterbury°	1.000	29	5	5	0	1
Gelfarb, West Haven°	1.000	2	0	1	0	0
Georger, Lynn	.958	34	6	17	1	1
Gleaton, Lynn°	.976	24	11	29	1	3
Goff, 6 Reading-15 Bristol	.933	21	4	10	1	0
Green, Buffalo°	1.000	13	2	17	0	0
Gross, Reading	.964	26	7	20	1	3
Hallgren, West Haven	1.000	5	2	1	0	0
Hardy, Glens Falls	.947	28	13	23	2	2
Heimueller, West Haven°	.750	23	5	13	6	2
Hensley, West Haven°	.825	37	6	27	7	0
Hudson, Lynn	.975	23	14	25	1	1
Ch. Johnson, Glens Falls	.952	14	5	15	1	0
Cl. Johnson, Bristol	1.000	46	3	9	0	2
Jones, Waterbury	.941	36	2	14	1	0
Keenan, Buffalo	.857	9	2	4	1	0
Kepshire, Waterbury	.875	30	1	6	1	0
Kibbe, Holyoke	.864	23	4	15	3	1
King, Bristol	1.000	8	1	6	0	0
Krawczyk, Buffalo	.893	38	4	21	3	1
S. Krueger, Lynn°	.833	31	1	4	1	1
W. Krueger, West Haven°	.939	28	6	25	2	2
Lackey, Glens Falls	.971	27	12	22	1	1
Landrum, Waterbury	.917	58	8	14	2	0
Leggatt, Buffalo	1.000	15	7	4	0	0
Lochner, Waterbury°	1.000	7	0	2	0	0
Maitland, Glens Falls°	1.000	10	0	2	0	0
Marietta, West Haven	.974	35	12	25	1	2
McKeon, Glens Falls°	1.000	7	2	3	0	0
Mohorcic, Buffalo	1.000	44	5	5	0	1
Money, Reading	.906	26	16	32	5	5
Mooneyham, Holyoke	.692	8	4	5	4	0
Moore, West Haven	.889	16	2	6	1	1
Morrison, Holyoke	.875	12	2	5	1	1
Mullen, Glens Falls	1.000	3	2	4	0	2
Murray, Lynn	.909	42	5	5	1	1
NIPPER, Bristol	1.000	19	17	31	0	3
Ontiveros, West Haven	.714	16	1	4	2	0
Palmieri, Reading°	1.000	21	3	19	0	2
Peterson, Buffalo	1.000	2	0	4	0	0
Pippin, Buffalo	.909	23	1	9	1	0
Prior, Reading	1.000	26	1	3	0	1
Rasmussen, Reading	1.000	6	1	5	0	0
Ray, Buffalo	.500	6	1	0	1	0
G. Riley, Reading°	1.000	37	3	8	0	2
M. Riley, Waterbury	1.000	2	2	1	0	0
Rivas, Bristol	1.000	28	2	4	0	0
Robinson, Waterbury	.964	32	5	22	1	0
Romanick, Holyoke	.864	16	3	16	3	2
Russell, Waterbury	.952	14	2	18	1	0
Schattinger, Glens Falls	1.000	6	0	2	0	0
Scherrer, Waterbury°	.667	5	2	6	4	0
Shields, Bristol	.838	29	10	21	6	3
D.A. Smith, Holyoke	.943	50	8	25	2	1
D.W. Smith, Holyoke	.839	39	14	33	9	3

PITCHERS—Continued

Player and Club	Pct.	G.	PO.	A.	E.	DP.	Player and Club	Pct.	G.	PO.	A.	E.	DP.
J. Smith, West Haven	.903	52	6	22	3	2	Venezia, Holyoke	1.000	23	3	8	0	0
L. Smith, Reading	.958	26	9	14	1	1	Wheeler, Buffalo	.966	20	6	22	1	2
Stottlemyre, Lynn	1.000	32	5	19	0	1	Winn, Buffalo	1.000	3	1	1	0	0
Stranski, Lynn	.978	24	12	33	1	1	Withrow, Glens Falls	.765	25	7	19	8	1
Teutsch, Glens Falls	1.000	48	5	7	0	0	Woody, Bristol°	1.000	48	5	17	0	1
Thibodeaux, Buffalo	1.000	12	8	8	0	1	Wortham, Reading°	1.000	24	2	7	0	0
Thomas, Reading	.950	26	4	15	1	0	Wright, Reading	1.000	4	1	0	0	0
Tyler, Bristol	1.000	17	1	3	0	0	Zamba, Buffalo	1.000	4	0	1	0	0

The following players do not have any recorded accepted chances at the positions indicated; therefore, are not listed in the fielding averages for those particular positions: Bryant, 3b; Donofrio, 1b; Dugger, p; Duran, p; Garrett, 3b; Houston, p; Howard, p; Ibarra, 1b, 2b; Nemeth, 3b; Pratt, ss; Welborn, p; Young, 3b.

CLUB PITCHING

Club	ERA.	G.	CG.	ShO.	Sv.	IP.	H.	R.	ER.	HR.	HB.	BB.	Int. BB.	SO.	WP.	Bk.
Bristol	3.55	140	46	12	19	1182.1	1147	569	467	84	25	496	38	971	48	10
West Haven	3.72	140	26	10	27	1158.1	1110	597	479	91	40	519	20	984	53	10
Lynn	4.00	139	57	13	15	1147.2	1125	615	510	81	32	517	10	874	43	12
Holyoke	4.14	140	18	3	27	1188.1	1195	674	547	71	29	601	33	840	65	7
Reading	4.26	138	26	9	24	1168.1	1107	661	553	83	38	653	29	923	106	8
Glens Falls	4.30	140	29	7	32	1175.1	1196	669	561	128	28	494	24	792	49	6
Waterbury	4.38	138	21	7	24	1156.2	1149	690	563	95	24	610	30	862	78	9
Buffalo	4.82	139	32	6	21	1137.2	1160	706	609	156	37	548	23	928	51	7

PITCHERS' RECORDS
(Leading Qualifiers for Earned-Run Average Leadership — 112 or More Innings)

°Throws lefthanded.

Pitcher—Club	W.	L.	Pct.	ERA.	G.	GS.	CG.	GF.	ShO.	Sv.	IP.	H.	R.	ER.	HR.	HB.	BB.	Int. BB.	SO.	WP.
Baller, Reading	9	8	.529	2.68	50	15	4	30	2	8	151.1	110	64	45	7	12	85	7	155	14
Gleaton, Lynn°	15	7	.682	2.72	24	24	13	0	2	0	182	175	71	55	16	3	54	0	132	7
Boyd, Bristol	14	8	.636	2.81	27	27	13	0	2	0	205	190	71	64	18	3	49	4	191	4
W. Krueger, West Haven°	15	9	.625	2.83	28	27	7	1	3	0	181	160	69	57	7	6	81	3	163	10
Atkinson, Glens Falls	6	9	.400	2.85	56	2	1	35	0	11	142.1	135	55	45	19	3	49	6	111	3
Comstock, West Haven°	9	5	.643	3.02	24	18	4	2	2	0	125	99	48	42	11	3	69	1	132	8
Robinson, Waterbury	13	7	.650	3.28	32	23	6	2	2	1	178.1	166	78	65	18	2	65	0	149	4
Marietta, West Haven	11	6	.647	3.31	35	24	3	3	1	1	168.1	162	76	62	14	9	77	5	96	3
Stranski, Lynn	14	6	.700	3.34	24	23	10	0	2	0	156.1	141	66	58	14	3	65	2	124	2
D.W. Smith, Holyoke	4	9	.308	3.41	39	16	1	9	0	3	142.2	154	80	54	7	5	70	5	104	7

Departmental Leaders: G—Landrum, 58; GS—Boyd, Fallon, Krueger, Lackey, 27; CG—Boyd, Gleaton, Shields, 13; GF—D.A. Smith, 43; ShO—Adair, Krueger, Shields, 3; W—Lackey, 16; L—Buckle, 17; Pct.—Abraham, .750; Sv.—D.A. Smith, 13; IP—Boyd, 205; H—Lackey, 199; R—Buckle, 104; ER—Bielecki, Lackey, 85; HR—Bielecki, Cuen, 24; HB—Baller, 12; BB—Jones, 110; IBB—D.A. Smith, 11; SO—Boyd, 191; WP—Jones, 18.

(All Pitchers—Listed Alphabetically)

Pitcher—Club	W.	L.	Pct.	ERA.	G.	GS.	CG.	GF.	ShO.	Sv.	IP.	H.	R.	ER.	HR.	HB.	BB.	Int. BB.	SO.	WP.
Abraham, West Haven°	12	4	.750	2.81	55	3	0	38	0	6	89.2	91	40	28	7	5	33	4	77	0
Adair, Lynn°	7	9	.438	4.30	26	25	7	0	3	0	138	140	86	66	9	2	70	0	95	4
Atkinson, Glens Falls	6	9	.400	2.85	56	2	1	35	0	11	142.1	135	55	45	19	3	49	6	111	3
Baller, Reading	9	8	.529	2.68	50	15	4	30	2	8	151.1	110	64	45	7	12	85	7	155	14
Barba, Holyoke	4	12	.250	6.48	37	10	0	13	0	3	91.2	110	79	66	11	3	58	2	87	8
Barez, Buffalo	0	0	.000	7.00	5	1	0	1	0	0	9	11	8	7	1	1	5	1	9	0
Best, Lynn	9	4	.692	3.45	21	21	9	0	2	0	138.1	104	63	53	8	4	90	2	125	6
Bielecki, Buffalo	7	12	.368	5.85	25	24	4	0	0	0	157.1	165	96	85	24	3	75	3	135	7
Birrell, Bristol°	9	9	.500	4.23	24	22	1	1	0	1	121.1	115	73	57	14	1	58	1	112	4
Bohnet, Holyoke	0	0	.000	0.00	2	0	0	2	0	0	4	2	0	0	0	1	0	1	0	1
Boxburger, Holyoke	5	9	.357	3.78	28	19	5	5	1	0	140.1	125	71	59	7	1	81	2	75	10
Boyd, Bristol	14	8	.636	2.81	27	27	13	0	2	0	205	190	71	64	18	3	49	4	191	4
Bradley, West Haven	6	3	.667	2.43	39	1	0	21	0	6	59.1	47	23	16	3	1	32	3	48	2
Brown, Bristol	9	6	.600	2.45	16	15	5	1	2	0	110	92	39	30	3	1	35	4	113	3
Buchanan, Waterbury°	10	8	.556	3.86	27	26	4	1	2	0	165.1	174	90	71	12	1	68	1	78	11
Buckle, Waterbury	4	17	.190	5.17	27	26	2	2	0	0	146.1	147	104	84	10	2	91	2	111	16
Buckley, Holyoke	6	11	.353	4.97	42	10	1	29	0	8	96	97	68	53	8	5	90	1	87	5
Buice, West Haven	1	1	.500	3.42	8	2	0	3	0	1	23.2	18	11	9	2	0	8	0	40	0
Burke, Buffalo	7	10	.412	5.19	25	21	4	1	0	0	144	162	93	83	23	2	57	1	93	8
Burns, Bristol	3	0	1.000	2.78	9	0	0	7	0	1	22.2	22	7	7	0	1	7	1	11	0
Burroughs, Reading°	1	2	.333	1.73	8	5	1	1	0	0	36.1	33	13	7	1	0	15	0	34	2
Carman, Reading°	6	7	.462	4.16	20	15	0	4	0	0	97.1	99	58	45	9	5	62	3	81	13
Cato, Waterbury	2	0	1.000	2.50	18	3	0	9	0	2	50.1	43	15	14	2	0	15	0	42	0
Cliburn, Holyoke	5	3	.625	3.56	22	12	2	2	0	0	103.2	91	48	41	4	4	42	3	78	5
Codiroli, West Haven	6	1	.857	2.40	12	6	3	5	1	2	45	37	14	12	1	1	19	0	45	6
Comstock, West Haven°	9	5	.643	3.02	24	18	4	2	2	0	125	99	48	42	11	3	69	1	132	8
Conner, Holyoke°	6	7	.462	3.67	30	20	2	3	0	0	125	135	62	51	10	3	55	2	76	7
Cuen, Buffalo	5	13	.278	5.33	22	20	5	1	1	0	123.1	125	86	73	24	6	31	0	77	4
Denman, Bristol	3	0	1.000	2.11	5	4	3	1	1	0	38.1	26	11	9	2	0	15	0	21	2
Desjarlais, Glens Falls	2	3	.400	7.71	7	7	0	0	0	0	28	32	25	24	3	2	22	1	15	5
Dugger, Holyoke	0	1	.000	13.50	1	1	0	0	0	0	3.1	6	5	5	2	0	2	0	1	0
Dukes, Lynn°	4	5	.444	4.40	34	8	1	11	0	1	90	87	53	44	4	4	71	0	63	10
Duran, Holyoke	0	0	.000	6.75	2	0	0	1	0	0	4	5	3	3	0	0	1	0	5	0
Edwards, Glens Falls°	0	1	.000	10.13	14	0	0	2	0	0	21.1	35	28	24	5	2	20	0	23	3
Ender, Waterbury	1	9	.100	5.50	14	14	1	0	0	0	75.1	81	57	46	15	5	35	1	60	7
Esser, Glens Falls°	1	1	.500	6.51	9	6	0	3	0	0	27.2	20	23	20	4	0	30	1	13	3
Fallon, Glens Falls°	9	9	.500	4.75	28	27	3	0	1	0	147.2	142	90	78	16	8	87	1	119	5
Farr, Buffalo	5	8	.385	4.01	25	7	2	13	0	5	76.1	72	40	34	10	3	38	2	84	4
Faulk, Reading	3	9	.250	2.63	40	0	0	29	0	11	65	46	22	19	1	0	35	10	52	8
Fiorillo, Waterbury°	3	4	.429	4.24	13	12	0	1	0	0	68	67	43	32	7	3	31	0	57	6
Flannery, Glens Falls	5	2	.714	3.22	26	0	0	15	0	7	72.2	68	27	26	6	0	16	2	36	0
redlund, Bristol	1	3	.250	6.55	15	12	0	2	0	0	57.2	72	48	42	7	3	50	0	34	1
reeman, Waterbury°	2	5	.286	3.19	32	0	0	19	0	4	42.1	49	26	15	5	0	20	4	24	1

Pitcher—Club	W.	L.	Pct.	ERA.	G.	GS.	CG.	GF.	ShO.	Sv.	IP.	H.	R.	ER.	HR.	HB.	BB.	Int. BB.	SO.	WP.
Gause, Waterbury°	2	2	.500	3.20	29	1	0	14	0	1	45	40	22	16	1	2	25	6	38	0
Gelfarb, West Haven°	0	0	.000	4.50	2	0	0	2	0	0	2	1	1	1	0	0	0	0	1	0
Georger, Lynn	6	3	.667	4.47	34	6	2	12	1	2	90.2	95	54	45	5	2	44	0	68	4
Gleaton, Lynn°	15	7	.682	2.72	24	24	13	0	2	0	182	175	71	55	16	3	54	0	132	7
Goff, 6 Read-15 Bris°	1	3	.250	4.95	21	9	0	7	0	0	60	66	39	33	6	2	39	0	51	10
Green, Buffalo°	7	5	.583	3.26	13	13	5	0	2	0	99.1	71	41	36	6	3	52	1	82	2
Gross, Reading	10	15	.400	4.23	26	24	8	1	2	0	151	138	81	71	9	4	89	3	136	12
Hallgren, West Haven	1	1	.500	7.23	5	4	0	1	0	0	18.2	20	16	15	6	0	15	0	10	0
Hardy, Glens Falls	11	8	.579	3.57	28	18	6	6	0	0	146.1	140	85	58	10	3	32	2	96	3
Heimueller, West Haven	7	9	.438	5.08	23	17	4	3	0	0	118.2	124	75	67	12	2	54	1	99	8
Hensley, West Haven°	10	4	.714	3.91	37	20	4	5	1	3	145	149	82	63	8	5	49	2	108	6
Houston, Buffalo	0	0	.000	108.00	1	0	0	0	0	0	0.1	2	4	4	0	0	2	0	1	1
Howard, Glens Falls	1	1	.500	3.00	2	2	0	0	0	0	9	13	6	3	2	0	3	0	4	0
Hudson, Lynn	8	10	.444	4.20	23	23	12	0	0	0	156.1	151	85	73	9	9	46	3	118	4
Ch. Johnson, Glens Falls	6	3	.667	4.13	14	14	4	0	0	0	96	95	46	44	11	2	28	3	74	2
Cl. Johnson, Bristol	7	5	.583	3.33	46	0	0	30	0	6	78.1	75	37	29	6	2	36	8	76	2
Jones, Waterbury	1	10	.091	7.95	36	10	2	9	0	1	94	110	96	83	6	2	110	1	47	18
Keenan, Buffalo	0	1	.000	4.64	9	0	0	3	0	0	21.1	20	15	11	2	2	13	0	15	3
Kepshire, Waterbury	1	4	.200	4.08	30	0	0	26	0	9	46.1	35	22	21	1	4	22	6	31	2
Kibbe, Holyoke	12	6	.667	4.01	23	20	4	1	1	0	143.2	127	74	64	8	1	62	2	115	11
King, Bristol	2	2	.500	2.96	8	7	4	0	1	0	48.2	48	20	16	1	2	17	0	49	4
Krawczyk, Buffalo	3	5	.375	4.71	38	8	2	23	0	7	101.1	93	59	53	10	4	59	2	102	5
S. Krueger, Lynn°	4	4	.500	5.82	31	0	0	16	0	4	34	41	26	22	6	2	18	1	24	0
W. Krueger, West Haven°	15	9	.625	2.83	28	27	7	1	3	0	181	160	69	57	7	6	81	3	163	10
Lackey, Glens Falls	16	8	.667	4.42	27	27	12	0	1	0	173	199	94	85	16	0	46	2	116	5
Landrum, Waterbury	10	6	.625	4.09	58	2	1	32	0	6	112.1	109	63	51	4	3	65	8	104	4
Leggatt, Glens Falls	0	4	.000	5.93	15	2	0	6	0	0	41	58	32	27	6	1	18	0	28	0
Lochner, Waterbury°	0	2	.000	16.88	7	3	0	0	0	0	13.1	21	26	25	3	0	23	0	4	4
Maitland, Glens Falls°	0	2	.000	7.59	10	2	0	4	0	0	21.1	24	20	18	7	2	10	0	12	2
Marietta, West Haven	11	6	.647	3.31	35	24	3	3	1	1	168.1	162	76	62	14	9	77	5	96	3
McKeon, Glens Falls°	5	2	.714	3.00	7	7	1	0	0	0	45	44	19	15	1	0	15	0	23	3
Mohorcic, Buffalo	2	8	.200	4.99	44	0	0	40	0	6	57.2	71	41	32	9	4	23	2	40	1
Money, Reading	12	5	.706	4.38	26	26	5	0	1	0	166.1	178	97	81	14	4	58	0	84	6
Mooneyham, Holyoke	2	3	.400	4.22	8	8	1	0	0	0	49	44	26	23	1	2	24	0	46	2
Moore, West Haven	1	3	.250	5.89	16	6	1	3	0	1	47.1	55	41	31	6	0	24	0	34	4
Morrison, Holyoke	1	3	.250	5.44	12	6	1	2	0	0	49.2	61	36	30	2	0	19	2	30	1
Mullen, Glens Falls	0	0	.000	6.75	3	1	0	2	0	0	9.1	13	9	7	2	0	2	0	5	0
Murray, Lynn	5	4	.556	4.14	42	1	0	30	0	6	58.2	61	34	27	3	0	26	1	61	3
Nipper, Bristol	6	7	.462	3.68	19	18	6	1	1	0	115	108	50	47	3	1	45	1	66	6
Ontiveros, West Haven	2	2	.500	6.33	16	2	0	5	0	0	27	34	26	19	4	3	12	0	28	1
Palmieri, Reading°	4	7	.364	5.19	21	18	3	1	0	0	93.2	83	60	54	5	6	71	0	71	9
Peterson, Buffalo	0	0	.000	1.17	2	1	0	1	0	0	7.2	8	5	1	0	0	1	0	6	0
Pippin, Buffalo	0	4	.000	2.82	23	2	0	14	0	3	51	52	24	16	6	2	34	4	53	8
Prior, Reading	1	3	.250	9.09	26	0	0	13	0	2	33.2	57	38	34	6	1	20	2	21	1
Rasmussen, Reading	1	2	.333	3.38	6	6	1	0	0	0	34.2	30	20	13	5	0	14	0	42	2
Ray, Buffalo	1	3	.250	10.89	6	6	1	0	0	0	20.2	35	27	25	3	0	14	0	18	1
G. Riley, Reading°	2	3	.400	3.53	37	0	0	15	0	1	58.2	56	27	23	1	2	25	1	46	6
M. Riley, Waterbury	0	1	.000	6.00	2	1	0	1	0	0	9	10	6	6	1	0	2	0	11	2
Rivas, Bristol	3	0	1.000	2.68	28	0	0	21	0	5	47	42	14	14	5	1	16	4	37	0
Robinson, Waterbury	13	7	.650	3.28	32	23	6	2	2	1	178.1	166	78	65	18	2	65	0	149	4
Romanick, Holyoke	6	3	.667	4.26	16	16	1	0	1	0	86.2	104	52	41	2	2	26	0	62	3
Russell, Waterbury	6	4	.600	2.37	14	12	2	1	1	0	79.2	67	27	21	8	0	23	1	88	3
Schattinger, Glens Falls	0	0	.000	2.63	6	1	0	5	0	3	13.2	13	4	4	0	0	8	0	9	0
Scherrer, Waterbury°	1	3	.250	3.77	5	5	3	0	1	0	31	30	15	13	2	0	15	0	18	0
Shields, Bristol	10	13	.435	3.54	29	23	13	1	3	0	170.1	172	100	67	11	5	71	4	125	13
D.A. Smith, Holyoke	9	7	.563	1.94	50	0	0	43	0	13	88.1	67	26	19	3	3	44	11	57	2
D.W. Smith, Holyoke	4	9	.308	3.41	39	16	1	9	0	3	142.2	154	80	54	7	5	70	5	104	7
J. Smith, West Haven	5	6	.455	4.76	52	10	0	22	0	7	107.2	113	75	57	9	5	46	1	103	5
L. Smith, Reading	10	8	.556	3.85	26	26	4	0	0	0	166	141	81	71	15	4	82	1	122	12
Stottlemyre, Reading	10	5	.667	5.72	32	8	3	12	2	2	102.1	129	75	65	7	3	31	0	63	3
Stranski, Lynn	14	6	.700	3.34	24	23	10	0	2	0	156.1	141	66	58	14	3	65	2	124	2
Teutsch, Glens Falls	6	5	.545	4.56	48	1	0	38	0	11	79	86	51	40	10	2	33	6	45	4
Thibodeaux, Buffalo	7	1	.875	4.02	12	12	3	0	0	0	71.2	52	36	32	7	3	39	0	66	1
Thomas, Reading	4	1	.800	3.50	26	0	0	6	0	1	61.2	65	27	24	5	0	23	2	38	3
Tyler, Bristol	2	1	.667	3.25	17	1	0	9	0	2	36	33	14	13	2	2	14	3	31	2
Venezia, Holyoke	3	3	.500	5.67	23	2	0	12	0	6	60.1	67	44	38	6	0	26	3	16	4
Welborn, Lynn	0	0	.000	18.00	1	0	0	1	0	0	1	3	2	2	0	0	2	1	0	0
Wheeler, Buffalo	10	5	.667	4.60	20	19	6	0	0	0	125.1	129	70	64	16	1	61	6	92	5
Williams, Glens Falls	0	0	.000	0.00	1	0	0	1	0	0	2	2	0	0	0	0	1	0	4	1
Wiltbank, Buffalo	1	0	1.000	3.68	6	0	0	2	0	0	14.2	8	6	6	2	0	18	0	13	1
Winn, Buffalo	0	2	.000	5.40	3	2	0	1	0	0	6.2	6	7	4	2	0	5	0	7	0
Withrow, Glens Falls	9	9	.500	4.47	25	25	2	0	0	0	141	135	87	70	16	4	57	0	87	10
Woody, Bristol°	5	8	.385	5.12	48	2	1	16	0	4	82.2	98	56	47	8	1	51	8	63	0
Wortham, Holyoke°	0	5	.000	11.54	24	3	0	9	0	1	36.2	47	51	47	2	0	58	0	27	14
Wright, Reading	0	0	.000	20.25	4	0	0	0	0	0	5.1	12	12	12	1	0	9	0	5	1
Zamba, Buffalo	0	3	.000	16.00	4	0	0	1	0	0	9	20	16	16	5	2	3	1	7	0

BALKS—Hudson, 4; Abraham, Gross, Marietta, Romanick, 3 each; Boyd, Buckle, Farr, Fiorillo, Flannery, Hensley, S. Krueger, Money, Robinson, Stottlemyre, Wheeler, Withrow, Woody, 2 each; Bielecki, Birrell, Brown, Buchanan, Buckley, Carman, Cato, Conner, Desjarlais, Dukes, Georger, Gleaton, Goff, Green, Cl. Johnson, King, W. Krueger, Lackey, Landrum, Mooneyham, Nipper, Pippin, D. A. Smith, J. Smith, L. Smith, Stranski, Thomas, 1 each.

COMBINATION SHUTOUTS—Birrell-Rivas, Goff-M. Johnson, Bristol; Thibodeaux-Krawczyk, Bielecki-Krawczyk, Wheeler-Wiltbank-Pippin, Buffalo; Withrow-Teutsch 2, Withrow-Atkinson, Withrow-Flannery, Esser-Atkinson, Glens Falls; Stottlemyre-Dukes, Lynn; Gross-Thomas-Faulk, Smith-Faulk, Smith-Baller, Smith-Riley-Baller, Reading; Ender-Landrum-Kepshire, Waterbury; W. Krueger-Marietta-Abraham, Codoroli-Bradley-Abraham-Buice, West Haven.

NO-HIT GAMES—Romanick, Holyoke, defeated Buffalo, 1-0, April 27; Esser and Atkinson, Glens Falls, defeated Reading, 1-0, August 2; Wheeler, Wiltbank and Pippin, Buffalo, defeated West Haven, 1-0, August 27.

Southern League

CLASS AA

**Leading Batter
KENNETH BAKER
Birmingham**

**League President
JIMMY BRAGAN**

**Leading Pitcher
STEFAN WEVER
Nashville**

CHAMPIONSHIP WINNERS IN PREVIOUS YEARS

1904—Macon	.598
1905—Macon	.625
1906—Savannah	.637
1907—Charleston	.620
1908—Jacksonville	.694
1909—Chattanooga*	.738
Augusta	.702
1910—Columbus	.588
1911—Columbus*	.681
Columbia	.710
1912—Jacksonville*	.679
Columbus	.632
1913—Savannah	.754
Savannah	.593
1914—Savannah*	.667
Albany	.650
1915—Macon	.588
Columbus*	.686
1916—Augusta*	.617
Columbia	.631
1917—Charleston	.741
Columbia*	.667
1918—Did not operate.	
1919—Columbia	.585
1920—Columbia	.633
1921—Columbia	.642
1922—Charleston	.625
1923—Charlotte*	.653
Macon	.580
1924—Augusta	.612
1925—Spartanburg	.620
1926—Greenville	.662
1927—Greenville	.622
1928—Asheville	.664
1929—Asheville	.605
Knoxville*	.634
1930—Greenville*	.620
Macon	.643

1931-35—Did not operate.	
1936—Jacksonville	.652
Columbus*	.650
1937—Columbus	.572
Savannah (3rd)†	.565
1938—Savannah	.574
Macon (2nd)†	.570
1939—Columbus	.601
Augusta (2nd)†	.597
1940—Savannah	.627
Columbus (2nd)†	.583
1941—Macon	.643
Columbia (2nd)†	.636
1942—Charleston	.620
Macon (2nd)†	.585
1943-45—Did not operate.	
1946—Columbus	.568
Augusta (4th)†	.547
1947—Columbus	.575
Savannah (2nd)†	.563
1948—Charleston	.572
Greenville (3rd)†	.549
1949—Macon‡	.623
1950—Macon‡	.588
1951—Montgomery	.607
1952—Columbia	.649
Montgomery (3rd)†	.558
1953—Jacksonville	.679
Savannah (2nd)†	.571
1954—Jacksonville	.593
Savannah (2nd)†	.571
1955—Columbia	.636
Augusta (3rd)†	.543
1956—Jacksonville‡	.621
1957—Augusta	.636
Charlotte (2nd)†	.562
1958—Augusta	.550
Macon (3rd)†	.500

1959—Knoxville	.557
Gastonia (4th)†	.504
1960—Columbia	.597
Savannah (3rd)†	.561
1961—Asheville	.635
1962—Savannah	.662
Macon (3rd)†	.576
1963—Augusta*	.661
Lynchburg	.662
1964—Lynchburg	.579
1965—Columbus	.572
1966—Mobile	.629
1967—Birmingham	.604
1968—Asheville	.614
1969—Charlotte	.579
1970—Columbus	.569
1971—Did not operate as league—clubs were members of Dixie Association.	
1972—Asheville	.583
Montgomery§	.561
1973—Montgomery§	.580
Jacksonville	.559
1974—Jacksonville	.565
Knoxville§	.533
1975—Orlando	.587
Montgomery§	.545
1976—Montgomery x	.591
Orlando	.540
1977—Montgomery x	.628
Jacksonville	.522
1978—Knoxville x	.611
Savannah	.500
1979—Columbus	.587
Nashville x	.576
1980—Memphis	.576
Charlotte x	.500
1981—Nashville	.566
Orlando x	.556

*Won split-season playoff. †Won four-club playoff. ‡Won championship and four-club playoff. §League was divided into Eastern and Western divisions; won playoff. xLeague was divided into Eastern and Western divisions and played split-season; won playoff.

STANDING OF CLUBS AT CLOSE OF FIRST HALF, JUNE 19

EASTERN DIVISION						WESTERN DIVISION					
Club	W.	L.	T.	Pct.	G.B.	Club	W.	L.	T.	Pct.	G.B.
Jacksonville (Royals)	41	31	0	.569	......	Knoxville (Blue Jays)	38	33	0	.535	......
Charlotte (Orioles)	37	32	0	.536	2½	Memphis (Expos)	37	35	0	.514	1½
Savannah (Braves)	37	34	0	.521	3½	Chattanooga (Indians)	34	38	0	.472	4½
Columbus (Astros)	36	36	0	.500	5	Nashville (Yankees)	32	38	0	.457	5½
Orlando (Twins)	31	38	0	.449	8½	Birmingham (Tigers)	32	40	0	.444	6½

STANDING OF CLUBS AT CLOSE OF SECOND HALF, AUGUST 31

EASTERN DIVISION						WESTERN DIVISION					
Club	W.	L.	T.	Pct.	G.B.	Club	W.	L.	T.	Pct.	G.B.
Jacksonville (Royals)	42	30	0	.583	......	Nashville (Yankees)	45	29	0	.608	......
Orlando (Twins)	43	32	0	.573	½	Birmingham (Tigers)	37	34	0	.521	6½
Columbus (Astros)	38	33	0	.535	3½	Knoxville (Blue Jays)	35	38	0	.479	9½
Savannah (Braves)	32	41	0	.438	10½	Memphis (Expos)	33	39	0	.458	11
Charlotte (Orioles)	29	45	0	.392	14	Chattanooga (Indians)	29	42	0	.408	14½

COMPOSITE STANDING OF CLUBS AT CLOSE OF SEASON, AUGUST 31

Club	Jax.	Nash.	Col.	Orl.	Knox.	Mem.	Birm.	Sav.	Char.	Chat.	W.	L.	T.	Pct.	G.B.
Jacksonville (Royals)	....	5	9	17	5	5	8	16	12	4	83	61	0	.576	......
Nashville (Yankees)	7	....	8	5	9	14	7	7	9	11	77	67	0	.535	6
Columbus (Astros)	3	12	....	6	12	7	11	6	8	9	74	69	0	.517	8½
Orlando (Twins)	7	7	6	....	6	7	8	13	14	6	74	70	0	.514	9
Knoxville (Blue Jays)	5	11	8	6	....	8	9	7	8	11	73	71	0	.507	10
Memphis (Expos)	7	6	13	5	8	....	9	6	6	10	70	74	0	.486	13
Birmingham (Tigers)	4	9	9	4	11	11	....	4	6	11	69	74	0	.483	13½
Savannah (Braves)	8	5	6	11	5	6	8	....	12	8	69	75	0	.479	14
Charlotte (Orioles)	12	3	4	10	4	6	5	12	....	10	66	77	0	.462	16½
Chattanooga (Indians)	8	9	6	6	9	10	9	4	2	....	63	80	0	.441	19½

Major league affiliations in parentheses.

Playoffs—Jacksonville defeated Columbus, three games to one; Nashville defeated Knoxville, three games to one; Nashville defeated Jacksonville, three games to one, to win league championship.

Regular-Season Attendance—Birmingham, 231,294; Charlotte, 148,973; Chattanooga, 157,948; Columbus, 159,266; Jacksonville, 125,645; Knoxville, 84,451; Memphis, 315,628; Nashville, 507,907; Orlando, 66,505; Savannah, 111,910. Total, 1,909,527. Playoffs, 34,851. All-star game, 11,511.

Managers—Birmingham, Ed Brinkman; Charlotte, Mark Wiley; Chattanooga, Al Gallagher; Columbus, Matt Galante; Jacksonville, Gene Lamont; Knoxville, Larry Hardy; Memphis, Rick Renick; Nashville, Johnny Oates; Orlando, Tom Kelly; Savannah, Andy Gilbert.

All-Star Team: 1B—Thompson, Knoxville; 2B—Teufel, Orlando; 3B—Reynolds, Knoxville; SS—Alfaro, Charlotte; OF—Baker, Birmingham; Dayett, Nashville; Fuentes, Memphis; C—(tie) Mizerock, Columbus, and Stephens, Jacksonville; DH—Garbey, Birmingham; RHP—Wever, Nashville; LHP—Gibson, Birmingham; Manager—Lamont, Jacksonville.

(Compiled by Howe News Bureau, Boston, Mass.)

CLUB BATTING

Club	Pct.	G.	AB.	R.	OR.	H.	TB.	2B.	3B.	HR.	RBI.	GW.	SH.	SF.	HP.	BB.	Int. BB.	SO.	SB.	CS.	LOB.
Memphis	.265	144	4784	701	729	1266	1888	201	29	121	632	58	84	36	43	611	31	743	140	58	1120
Columbus	.264	143	4690	667	667	1237	1805	213	29	99	594	67	60	32	43	536	33	780	143	74	1007
Nashville	.263	144	4836	672	619	1271	1911	210	38	118	604	69	56	38	44	583	15	783	102	51	1125
Orlando	.263	144	4577	690	677	1202	1780	191	39	103	622	60	61	59	47	610	21	695	121	65	1034
Birmingham	.256	143	4659	626	619	1192	1729	171	36	98	565	64	56	35	45	540	18	868	103	50	1087
Knoxville	.256	144	4594	618	1183	1770	211	44	96	527	62	61	45	39	428	19	903	178	65	965	
Charlotte	.253	143	4519	690	687	1144	1908	206	33	164	626	58	52	33	36	631	18	948	149	71	1006
Chattanooga	.250	143	4619	594	668	1153	1727	191	37	103	538	51	55	51	23	548	32	916	162	60	1000
Jacksonville	.246	144	4691	593	527	1152	1645	163	30	90	518	68	48	30	25	478	21	823	156	60	1002
Savannah	.239	144	4456	622	638	1063	1695	153	37	135	565	63	31	33	55	573	15	1043	118	44	981

INDIVIDUAL BATTING

(Leading Qualifiers for Batting Championship—389 or More Plate Appearances)

*Bats lefthanded.   †Switch-hitter.

Player and Club	Pct.	G.	AB.	R.	H.	TB.	2B.	3B.	HR.	RBI.	GW.	SH.	SF.	HP.	BB.	Int. BB.	SO.	SB.	CS.
Baker, Kenneth, Birmingham*	.342	112	409	67	140	213	24	5	13	70	8	5	2	2	64	4	37	9	7
Nealeigh, Rodney, Memphis*	.305	137	475	66	145	203	24	2	10	52	2	3	1	5	54	9	62	10	4
Foster, Kenneth, Orlando	.302	128	430	64	130	179	18	2	9	64	6	5	4	4	45	1	44	6	3
Alfaro, Jesus, Charlotte	.301	137	501	86	151	213	23	0	13	71	6	6	3	4	86	0	61	8	6
Peterson, Erik, Nashville	.301	114	409	64	123	›196	25	3	14	62	3	4	1	3	41	3	51	1	2
Garbey, Barbaro, Birmingham	.298	120	480	69	143	234	32	4	17	99	9	3	7	7	25	1	47	5	5
Robles, Rubén, Columbus	.297	125	445	70	132	184	13	3	11	55	6	2	0	10	21	0	96	36	10
Showalter, W. Nathan, Nashville*	.294	132	517	66	152	196	29	3	3	46	3	14	4	0	61	2	42	2	5
Csefalvay, John, Columbus*	.294	113	361	70	106	184	23	2	17	65	6	1	1	1	65	4	37	5	6
Leeper, David, Jacksonville*	.293	132	502	59	147	189	23	5	3	50	8	4	2	3	31	4	60	24	3

Departmental Leaders: G—Dayett, Thompson, 144; AB—Fuentes, 539; R—Fuentes, 105; H—Showalter, 152; TB—Dayett, 285; 2B—Hoeksema, 33; 3B—Denman, 10; HR—Fuentes, 37; RBI—Fuentes, 115; GWRBI—Dayett, 15; SH—Newman, 18; SF—Saavedra, 12; HP—Croft, 14; BB—Hazewood, 95; IBB—Mizerock, 12; SO—Denman, 173; SB—Thompson, 68; CS—Thompson, 19.

(All Players—Listed Alphabetically)

Player and Club	Pct.	G.	AB.	R.	H.	TB.	2B.	3B.	HR.	RBI.	GW.	SH.	SF.	HP.	BB.	Int. BB.	SO.	SB.	CS.
Adams, W. Craig, Chattanooga	.240	96	254	33	61	83	10	0	4	27	2	4·	2	1	30	0	55	8	6
Alfaro, Jesus, Charlotte	.301	137	501	86	151	213	23	0	13	71	6	6	3	4	86	0	61	8	6
Ashmore, W. Mitchell, Jacksonville	.182	23	66	2	12	15	3	0	0	9	1	1	1	0	9	0	19	0	0
Atkinson, James, Jacksonville*	.266	110	383	51	102	165	21	3	12	47	7	1	1	1	0	46	4	53	6	6
Austin, Richard, Orlando	.230	109	317	37	73	104	16	0	5	39	5	7	3	2	41	1	50	8	7
Auten, James, Memphis	.266	119	410	58	109	180	19	2	16	70	6	5	2	1	51	1	70	1	4
Bailey, Welby, Savannah	.214	6	14	2	3	7	1	0	1	3	1	0	0	0	4	0	3	0	0
Baker, Douglas, Birmingham†	.225	70	213	28	48	62	3	4	1	21	3	7	1	1	38	0	42	5	2
Baker, Kenneth, Birmingham*	.342	112	409	67	140	213	24	5	13	70	8	5	2	2	64	4	37	9	7

Player and Club	Pct.	G.	AB.	R.	H.	TB.	2B.	3B.	HR.	RBI.	GW.	SH.	SF.	HP.	BB.	Int. BB.	SO.	SB.	CS.
Baker, Ricky, Chattanooga†	.254	43	134	17	34	45	7	2	0	7	1	0	0	2	19	0	33	16	6
Banes, David, Nashville	.191	17	47	6	9	19	1	0	3	9	1	1	0	1	2	0	13	0	0
Belue, Benjamin, Memphis	.200	10	35	5	7	8	1	0	0	3	0	0	0	0	2	0	4	0	0
Benson, Steven, Columbus	.282	67	245	37	69	98	15	1	4	31	6	5	3	2	42	1	37	17	5
Bockhorn, Glen, Savannah	.207	82	246	28	51	83	6	1	8	23	5	1	1	0	28	0	57	0	0
Bodie, Keith, Columbus	.257	54	171	24	44	59	9	3	0	28	1	2	3	1	20	1	31	4	2
Bonaparte, Elijah, Orlando°	.426	12	54	15	23	29	1	1	1	2	1	0	1	0	4	3	8	6	1
Bonine, Eddie, Columbus	.500	33	2	1	1	2	1	0	0	0	0	0	0	1	1	0	0	0	0
Borges, George, Memphis	.500	2	4	1	2	2	0	0	0	0	0	0	0	1	1	0	2	1	0
Bourjos, Christopher, Charlotte	.319	40	160	30	51	103	10	6	10	41	2	0	3	2	16	0	16	6	1
Bowman, Donald, Charlotte	.257	97	358	68	92	176	18	3	20	61	8	4	4	5	44	1	69	4	3
Brackenridge, Lyle, Orlando	.259	11	27	8	7	7	0	0	0	8	0	0	0	0	10	0	5	0	0
Bradley, Scott, Nashville°	.105	5	19	2	2	3	1	0	0	0	1	0	1	0	1	0	0	0	0
Brewer, Michael, Jacksonville	.249	121	438	74	109	192	15	4	20	68	7	0	1	5	56	0	80	34	5
Broersma, Eric, Orlando	.000	43	1	0	0	0	0	0	0	1	0	0	0	0	0	0	0	0	0
Brunson, Eddie, Charlotte	.252	37	127	15	32	48	5	1	3	11	1	2	1	1	11	1	22	3	4
Bullock, Eric, Columbus°	.303	18	66	6	20	27	1	0	2	13	2	0	1	1	7	2	10	5	1
Butterfield, Brian, Nashville†	.133	11	30	3	4	4	0	0	0	3	0	0	1	2	0	4	0	0	0
Cadahia, Aurelio, Orlando	.226	57	155	17	35	50	3	0	4	24	2	5	2	0	18	0	12	0	1
Callahan, Patrick, Nashville	.206	53	170	15	35	50	2	2	3	22	2	4	2	0	14	0	25	2	0
Cannon, Joseph J., Knoxville°	.266	86	331	40	88	137	14	7	7	46	4	0	2	2	16	0	71	25	4
Carl, Jeffrey, Memphis	.172	45	157	22	27	55	2	1	8	26	1	0	4	3	18	0	51	2	2
Carrasquel, Emilio, Birmingham	.295	18	61	4	18	20	0	1	0	8	2	2	0	0	8	1	4	0	0
Carrion, Leonel, Memphis	.290	102	362	70	105	173	20	3	14	62	8	6	6	2	70	1	49	6	1
Carter, Don, Memphis°	.172	12	29	2	5	5	0	0	0	0	0	0	0	1	0	1	4	0	2
Cecchetti, George, Chattanooga°	.229	131	415	52	95	154	18	1	13	50	4	3	2	5	65	10	100	11	3
Chapman, Nathan, Nashville°	.287	126	509	69	146	220	27	7	11	77	6	2	9	4	23	1	68	7	8
Charboneau, Joseph, Chattanooga	.207	13	29	4	6	10	1	0	1	2	0	0	1	1	0	5	1	0
Clements, Wesley, Columbus	.313	67	252	46	79	141	18	1	14	52	3	0	3	2	39	0	79	4	1
Colbern, Michael, Savannah	.235	87	293	36	69	101	8	0	8	34	3	4	2	6	15	0	56	1	0
Corey, Mark, Charlotte	.253	48	162	26	41	79	8	0	10	26	3	1	1	5	25	1	46	4	2
Craig, R. Dean, Nashville†	.189	31	95	13	18	28	4	0	2	7	1	0	1	0	15	0	18	0	0
Croft, Paul, Savannah	.213	114	376	64	80	162	9	8	19	57	5	2	2	14	49	0	150	13	7
Cruz, Jose, Memphis°	.266	122	473	70	126	157	16	3	3	47	3	5	0	5	57	5	70	7	5
Csefalvay, John, Columbus°	.294	113	361	70	106	184	23	2	17	65	6	1	1	1	65	4	37	5	6
Cuervo, Edward, Columbus†	.216	35	74	8	16	17	1	0	0	3	1	2	0	0	2	0	13	6	2
Curry, Stephen, Savannah	.257	142	470	81	121	196	19	1	18	66	5	3	8	6	95	1	108	8	4
David, Andre, Orlando°	.279	107	366	61	102	148	17	7	5	49	5	4	6	7	42	3	30	8	5
Davis, Glenn, Columbus	.247	26	97	14	24	44	6	1	4	8	0	1	0	1	5	1	26	0	0
Davis, Odie, Birmingham	.268	12	41	4	11	12	1	0	0	5	0	2	0	0	5	0	5	1	1
Davis, Wallace, Jacksonville	.256	122	450	64	115	171	18	4	10	57	6	3	3	3	46	1	101	17	9
Dayett, Brian, Nashville	.280	144	536	89	150	285	29	2	34	96	15	0	5	6	80	3	87	2	0
Dees, Gregory, Charlotte°	.153	20	59	3	9	10	1	0	0	2	1	0	1	0	5	0	13	0	0
Dempsey, Peter, Knoxville	.366	26	93	19	34	47	8	1	1	10	2	0	0	2	14	0	12	5	0
Denman, John, Charlotte	.249	136	506	93	126	229	23	10	20	57	7	4	2	2	75	1	173	58	17
Dennis, Eduardo, Knoxville	.251	123	423	42	106	128	13	3	1	38	3	7	6	1	13	0	51	26	13
Derryberry, Timothy, Charlotte°	.250	6	24	7	6	13	1	0	2	10	1	0	1	0	9	2	9	1	0
Dewey, Duane, Jacksonville	.301	32	93	15	28	44	1	0	5	21	1	4	0	1	19	0	28	3	2
Djakonow, Powel, Birmingham	.220	55	173	25	38	72	10	0	8	23	1	1	3	4	18	0	55	2	0
Dodd, Thomas, 94 Nash.-29 Knox.	.235	123	387	49	91	167	20	7	14	51	7	1	1	5	61	0	127	2	3
Doerr, Jeffrey, Charlotte	.200	2	5	1	1	2	1	0	0	0	0	0	0	0	0	0	2	0	0
Douglas, Stephen, Orlando	.270	45	115	19	31	45	6	1	2	13	1	2	1	1	15	0	22	8	3
Dugas, Shanie, Chattanooga°	.288	89	309	54	89	155	15	6	13	45	8	1	2	3	41	5	86	12	3
Ferris, Robert, Jacksonville	.238	122	399	54	95	168	26	1	15	56	14	2	2	2	62	4	121	5	2
Fields, Bruce, Birmingham°	.228	43	162	26	37	44	3	2	0	14	2	2	2	1	19	0	29	10	2
Flannery, John, Birmingham	.203	37	79	5	16	17	1	0	0	5	0	3	0	3	7	0	8	0	1
Followell, Vernon, Birmingham†	.316	11	38	7	12	15	3	0	0	5	0	0	2	0	6	1	4	0	0
Foster, Kenneth, Orlando	.302	128	430	64	100	179	18	2	9	64	6	5	4	4	45	1	44	6	3
Foussianes, George, Birmingham	.256	34	121	24	31	50	3	2	4	15	3	3	1	7	19	0	37	0	1
Fuentes, Michael, Memphis	.267	142	539	104	144	283	24	2	37	115	9	2	5	2	91	6	143	18	6
Funderburk, Mark, Orlando	.264	121	402	80	106	200	23	1	23	85	11	4	8	7	54	5	71	9	3
Gagne, Gregory, Orlando	.232	136	504	73	117	183	23	5	11	57	5	4	7	5	57	1	100	8	9
Gainey, Telmanich, Columbus°	.293	16	58	9	17	25	5	0	1	5	2	0	0	0	6	0	9	3	2
Gallagher, David, Chattanooga	.222	15	54	10	12	16	2	1	0	4	1	0	0	0	5	0	8	2	0
Garbey, Barbaro, Birmingham	.298	120	480	69	143	234	32	4	17	99	9	3	7	7	25	1	47	5	5
Garcia, Michael, Savannah	.181	47	160	13	29	36	4	0	1	15	3	1	0	2	15	1	15	1	1
Garcia, Steven, Columbus°	.259	8	27	4	7	8	1	0	0	3	0	0	0	0	4	0	1	1	1
Gardner, Vassie, Knoxville	.248	96	319	40	79	115	5	8	5	30	3	3	5	0	22	1	70	22	7
Gates, Eddie, Birmingham	.164	29	73	17	12	21	3	0	2	10	2	1	0	1	32	2	21	0	0
Gayden, Huey, Nashville°	.176	10	34	3	6	6	0	0	0	1	0	0	0	0	5	0	5	2	0
Glass, Timothy, Chattanooga	.265	137	480	68	127	218	21	5	20	88	9	2	4	1	77	0	133	1	0
Glynn, Eugene, Memphis	.240	96	300	50	72	94	12	2	2	25	3	15	1	4	45	0	36	16	10
Gonzales, Rene, Memphis	.213	56	183	10	39	47	3	1	1	11	1	5	0	3	9	0	44	2	3
Grace, Michael, Columbus	.257	134	470	68	121	174	16	2	11	60	11	4	2	4	57	0	85	2	7
Grout, Ronald, Savannah	.246	141	491	58	121	220	31	1	22	97	12	0	7	6	61	7	117	0	2
Gruber, Kelly, Chattanooga	.243	128	441	53	107	172	18	4	13	54	4	4	7	3	21	1	89	11	6
Hampton, Raphael, Birmingham°	.248	84	318	54	79	113	11	1	7	23	3	5	1	4	41	0	75	18	9
Harvey, Randall, Birmingham°	.183	36	115	9	21	26	3	1	0	9	1	0	1	0	14	1	38	0	0
Hayes, Thomas, Savannah	.238	100	320	41	76	97	6	0	5	16	1	3	2	4	30	0	66	4	0
Hazewood, Drungo, Charlotte	.226	136	451	75	102	159	16	4	11	49	5	0	2	0	98	1	143	28	9
Hegman, Robert, Jacksonville	.210	87	262	36	55	56	1	0	0	15	2	5	1	1	28	0	41	11	4
Hench, R. William, Nashville	.226	14	53	5	12	15	1	1	0	4	1	1	0	0	3	0	3	1	1
Hernandez, Leonard, Charlotte	.289	68	270	46	78	160	18	2	20	62	6	2	2	4	7	2	40	13	4
Hernandez, Tobias, Knoxville	.256	84	273	20	70	92	13	0	3	25	3	11	3	1	7	2	46	2	1
Herrick, Neal, Charlotte	.000	4	13	2	0	0	0	0	0	1	0	1	0	0	2	0	3	1	0
Hinson, Gary, Birmingham	.271	78	247	30	67	78	6	1	1	20	2	3	0	4	51	0	30	1	2
Hodgson, Paul, Knoxville	.236	69	174	11	41	50	6	0	1	9	0	2	0	2	35	0	47	0	0
Hoeksema, David, Memphis	.280	121	460	56	129	198	33	3	10	64	9	12	5	4	35	0	50	1	0
Holmes, Stanley, Orlando	.250	31	80	7	20	31	2	0	3	12	2	2	2	1	12	0	23	2	0
Hough, Stanley, Columbus	.233	36	86	5	20	22	2	0	0	8	2	4	1	2	8	0	9	0	0
Hudler, Rex, Nashville	.237	89	299	27	71	87	14	1	0	24	5	4	0	5	9	1	51	9	2
Huppert, David, Charlotte	.223	83	220	28	49	70	9	0	4	24	1	5	1	1	33	1	44	0	0

Player and Club	Pct.	G.	AB.	R.	H.	TB.	2B.	3B.	HR.	RBI.	GW.	SH.	SF.	HP.	BB.	Int. BB.	SO.	SB.	CS.
Ingle, Randy, Savannah	.221	100	340	33	75	106	4	6	5	33	4	2	3	0	13	1	72	0	1
Jabalera, Francisco, Columbus*	.249	128	446	71	111	150	21	6	2	35	3	15	1	4	76	6	62	39	16
Jacobson, Kevin, Charlotte	.200	13	50	8	10	12	2	0	0	2	0	1	0	0	3	0	8	0	0
Johnson, Rondin, Jacksonville†	.221	128	494	59	109	126	8	3	1	28	3	11	3	0	34	0	65	14	5
Kelly, D. Patrick, Savannah	.234	18	64	6	15	26	1	2	2	11	2	0	0	0	15	0	15	1	0
Kneuer, Frank, Nashville	.286	8	14	4	4	6	2	0	0	0	0	0	0	0	3	0	1	0	1
Knight, Timothy, Nashville*	.276	134	442	75	122	191	23	5	12	57	6	2	3	6	74	2	87	4	6
Komminsk, Brad, Savannah*	.273	133	454	88	124	234	18	7	26	78	6	1	1	4	72	3	114	14	3
Landis, Craig, Savannah	.278	89	291	46	81	131	13	2	11	54	5	3	2	10	59	0	46	2	1
Laurie, Robert, Birmingham	.207	35	116	7	24	28	1	0	1	11	3	3	1	1	6	0	34	0	1
Leeper, David, Jacksonville*	.293	132	502	59	147	189	23	5	3	50	8	4	4	2	31	4	60	24	3
Lepel, Joel, Memphis*	.213	41	136	8	29	37	5	0	1	11	0	2	0	0	11	0	12	0	0
Lulay, Douglas, Columbus	.000	3	4	0	0	0	0	0	0	0	0	0	0	1	0	0	1	0	0
Martin, Sam, Chattanooga†	.000	1	3	0	0	0	0	0	0	0	0	0	0	0	0	0	0	0	0
Maxwell, James, Birmingham*	.188	6	13	3	3	6	0	0	1	2	0	0	1	0	2	0	6	0	0
McCain, Michael, Orlando*	.269	134	454	70	122	185	23	5	10	64	3	9	5	1	79	5	53	2	8
McCann, Francis, 29 Birm-8 Mem	.175	37	114	13	20	23	3	0	0	10	3	1	3	1	14	1	29	3	0
McDonald, James, Columbus*	.270	47	163	11	44	58	8	0	2	21	4	0	1	1	13	4	12	0	1
McLaughlin, Colin, Knoxville	.000	20	2	0	0	0	0	0	0	0	0	0	0	0	0	0	1	0	0
Meier, David, Orlando	.287	134	474	71	136	193	19	7	8	63	7	3	5	1	65	0	77	4	6
Melvin, Robert, Birmingham	.236	98	364	33	86	139	12	1	13	52	4	1	1	0	24	2	70	1	0
Mesa, Ivan, Orlando	.266	33	109	16	29	33	4	0	0	11	0	3	0	2	17	0	5	8	1
Methven, Marlin, Chattanooga†	.138	27	80	8	11	18	2	1	1	9	1	1	0	0	10	0	20	0	2
Miller, Michael, Savannah	.189	80	228	23	43	48	3	1	0	16	0	6	1	0	26	0	58	3	4
Milner, Brian, Knoxville	.148	37	115	8	17	19	2	0	0	11	0	1	3	2	11	0	38	0	0
Mizerock, John, Columbus*	.229	128	420	46	96	148	14	1	12	48	5	4	3	3	50	12	73	1	6
Montague, James, Charlotte	.000	4	0	0	0	0	0	0	0	0	0	0	0	0	0	0	0	0	0
Moronko, Jeffrey, Chattanooga	.253	132	471	52	119	156	16	3	5	50	5	6	6	3	30	1	62	16	8
Naehring, Mark, Chattanooga	.281	72	231	27	65	86	10	1	3	31	3	2	2	0	49	0	43	1	0
Narleski, Steven, Chattanooga	.000	50	1	0	0	0	0	0	0	0	0	0	0	0	0	0	1	0	0
Nealeigh, Rodney, Memphis*	.305	137	475	66	145	203	24	2	10	52	2	3	1	5	54	9	62	10	4
Newman, Albert, Memphis†	.275	142	494	85	136	171	16	8	1	41	5	18	3	6	64	2	45	63	17
Nixon, Otis, Nashville†	.283	72	283	47	80	87	3	2	0	20	3	3	0	1	59	0	56	61	17
Oliveras, Francisco, Charlotte	.000	24	4	0	0	0	0	0	0	0	0	0	0	0	0	0	2	0	0
Pacho, Juan, Chattanooga	.237	71	173	16	41	46	5	0	0	15	1	12	1	1	13	0	22	1	1
Pasley, Kevin, Birmingham	.257	20	74	5	19	21	2	0	0	12	2	0	1	1	5	0	5	0	0
Perez, Julio, Charlotte*	.238	56	168	22	40	64	7	1	5	14	1	2	0	0	14	2	23	0	2
Peterson, Erik, Nashville	.301	114	409	64	123	196	25	3	14	62	3	4	1	3	41	3	51	1	2
Pilla, Anthony, Orlando	.163	33	80	6	13	16	0	0	1	8	1	1	2	1	17	0	21	2	1
Pirruccello, Mark, Jacksonville*	.000	2	6	1	0	0	0	0	0	0	0	0	0	0	1	0	1	0	0
Poldberg, Brian, Nashville	.229	49	140	18	32	52	5	0	5	17	2	1	1	5	24	0	20	1	0
Poole, Stine, Birmingham	.256	95	351	46	90	165	17	2	18	60	8	3	2	2	33	3	87	0	0
Pulley, Martin, Knoxville	.154	6	13	0	2	2	0	0	0	1	0	0	0	0	1	0	3	0	0
Quinones, Rene, Memphis†	.235	9	17	4	4	4	0	0	0	0	0	0	1	0	2	0	3	0	0
Ramie, Vernon, Knoxville*	.285	119	347	58	99	178	22	3	17	68	10	1	8	1	66	6	67	3	3
Rende, Salvatore, Chattanooga*	.214	124	393	41	84	147	22	1	13	52	3	6	10	0	61	6	75	2	1
Rey, Everett, Chattanooga	.176	49	148	11	26	33	7	0	0	7	1	1	1	0	18	0	32	0	0
Reynolds, Jeff, 26 Nash-106 Knox	.242	132	471	71	114	210	30	3	20	63	8	1	5	8	41	5	113	1	2
Reynolds, Michael, Savannah	.235	51	183	20	43	64	10	1	3	17	5	1	1	0	15	0	21	3	2
Richards, David, Memphis	.244	75	254	20	62	75	7	0	2	37	3	6	4	3	31	1	37	5	2
Rios, Carlos, Knoxville	.285	125	463	67	132	161	24	1	1	38	5	17	3	3	39	0	39	23	9
Robles, Ruben, Columbus	.297	125	445	70	132	184	13	3	11	55	6	2	0	10	21	0	96	36	10
Rodriguez, Edwin, Nashville	.206	10	34	4	7	9	0	1	0	3	1	3	0	0	6	0	7	2	0
Rodriguez, Victor, Charlotte	.291	47	165	17	48	70	13	0	3	18	3	1	2	1	14	2	14	0	1
Rollin, Rondal, Birmingham	.243	121	419	51	102	163	14	7	11	37	6	2	3	2	41	1	117	4	2
Rosario, Simon, Columbus	.280	134	532	62	149	190	24	4	3	69	7	1	3	0	35	1	58	3	4
Saavedra, Edwin, Chattanooga	.279	126	469	66	131	182	21	3	8	57	5	0	12	1	37	2	47	28	6
Salas, Mark, Nashville*	.255	43	137	19	35	60	7	0	6	20	0	4	1	2	11	2	15	0	0
Schaefer, Jeffrey, Charlotte	.251	106	331	35	83	107	15	0	3	32	0	17	1	3	32	0	35	16	13
Schmitz, Daniel, Nashville*	.271	60	203	29	55	63	4	2	0	26	2	6	2	0	35	0	19	1	2
Scranton, James, Jacksonville	.235	128	413	44	97	112	7	4	0	41	4	5	3	2	36	0	68	10	11
Sheperd, Ronald, Knoxville	.247	136	482	62	119	199	19	8	15	65	13	5	5	2	40	2	125	31	8
Shines, A. Raymond, Memphis†	.280	122	432	67	121	191	18	2	16	66	7	3	4	6	65	6	58	7	2
Showalter, W. Nathaniel, Nashville*	.294	132	517	66	152	196	29	3	3	46	3	14	4	0	61	2	42	2	5
Simcox, Larry, Columbus	.211	19	71	6	15	20	3	1	0	7	2	1	2	0	4	0	12	0	0
Simmons, Nelson, Birmingham†	.200	8	30	2	6	6	0	0	0	4	0	0	0	2	0	0	14	0	0
Simunic, Douglas, 12 Jax-84 Chat	.266	96	323	36	86	137	17	2	10	42	5	0	4	2	62	4	66	0	1
Smith, Garry, Nashville	.235	55	166	17	39	59	3	1	5	19	2	2	2	2	17	0	29	0	1
Smith, P. Keith, Nashville†	.000	4	12	0	0	0	0	0	0	0	0	0	0	0	2	0	6	0	0
Sodders, Michael, Orlando	.251	61	207	28	52	91	13	1	8	30	2	2	1	4	22	0	54	9	3
Soriano, Hilario, Knoxville*	.283	18	60	1	17	22	3	1	0	6	0	1	1	0	0	0	14	0	0
Stefero, John, Charlotte*	.230	115	357	45	82	146	9	2	17	60	4	1	4	4	49	4	85	0	2
Stephans, Russell, Jacksonville	.263	120	384	47	101	145	14	0	10	42	6	3	3	2	43	4	43	10	6
Strucher, Mark, Nashville	.227	45	141	21	32	66	7	0	9	30	1	1	1	2	15	0	25	1	0
Taylor, Dwight, Chattooga*	.289	110	426	71	123	157	10	9	2	33	2	12	0	0	57	0	74	50	17
Taylor, Michael, Chattooga*	.188	5	16	3	3	4	1	0	0	1	0	1	0	0	2	0	5	2	0
Teufel, Timothy, Orlando	.282	100	340	52	96	143	12	4	9	56	6	5	9	3	67	1	51	16	5
Thomas, James, Columbus†	.222	23	63	8	14	18	1	0	1	10	1	5	1	0	10	0	6	1	1
Thompson, Milton, Savannah*	.251	144	526	83	132	184	20	7	6	45	6	4	3	4	87	2	145	68	19
Thompson, Richard, Chattooga	.000	50	1	0	0	0	0	0	0	0	0	0	0	0	0	0	0	0	0
Thompson, Timothy, Knoxville*	.282	133	471	81	133	224	31	3	18	73	6	0	3	9	55	5	105	3	1
Turner, Ira, Jacksonville	.220	102	341	47	75	108	9	3	6	25	2	3	5	2	29	1	97	22	5
Tutt, Johnny, Charlotte	.314	8	35	6	11	15	2	1	0	5	0	0	0	0	7	4	0	0	
Tyner, Matthew, Charlotte	.221	93	290	49	64	141	15	1	20	46	6	2	4	5	53	0	88	2	6
Villaman, Rafael, Nashville†	.211	70	204	23	43	52	3	0	2	18	4	1	1	2	5	0	30	7	4
Wever, Stefan, Nashville	.000	29	0	0	0	0	0	0	0	0	0	0	0	0	0	0	0	0	0
Wheeler, Ralph, Knoxville	.276	12	29	9	8	13	2	0	1	4	1	1	0	0	3	0	4	2	0
Wherry, Clifton, Columbus	.251	121	422	63	106	153	21	4	6	39	4	11	5	7	47	1	83	14	8
Whitfield, Robert, Charlotte	.107	10	28	1	3	5	0	1	0	3	0	0	0	0	3	0	2	0	1
Whitmer, Daniel, Knoxville	.256	13	39	7	10	17	1	0	2	5	0	1	1	0	6	0	10	0	0
Wiedenbauer, Thomas, Columbus	.189	23	74	17	14	17	3	0	0	6	0	1	1	0	9	0	15	1	1
Wihtol, Alexander, Chattanooga	.500	10	2	0	1	1	0	0	0	0	0	0	0	0	0	0	0	0	0

Player and Club	Pct.	G.	AB.	R.	H.	TB.	2B.	3B.	HR.	RBI.	GW.	SH.	SF.	HP.	BB.	Int. BB.	SO.	SB.	CS.
Wilkerson, Martin, Jacksonville*	.233	121	417	36	97	139	14	2	8	49	6	6	6	2	34	3	37	0	2
Williams, Kevin, Orlando	.242	129	455	67	110	143	11	5	4	36	3	5	4	5	45	1	69	25	9
Wilson, James, Chattanooga	.175	11	40	3	7	8	1	0	0	5	0	2	0	0	3	0	12	1	0
Winters, Matthew, Nashville*	.303	29	99	22	30	51	5	2	4	17	5	1	2	0	29	0	23	0	0
Wood, Andre, Knoxville	.235	134	506	61	119	161	20	5	4	40	4	11	4	3	59	1	83	33	16
Woodard, Darrell, Birmingham	.232	133	435	55	101	112	8	0	1	23	1	8	3	3	47	0	54	30	11
Younger, Stanley, Birmingham*	.308	61	234	44	72	94	12	5	0	29	2	2	2	0	26	1	23	15	6

The following pitchers, listed alphabetically by club, with games in parentheses, had no plate appearances, primarily through use of designated hitters:

BIRMINGHAM—Bass, Jerry (30); Beecroft, Michael (7); Cary, Charles (28); Gibson, Paul (44); Gumpert, David (42); Heinkel, Donald (9); Kelly, Bryan (16); Moncrief, Homer (29); Nail, Charles (24); Nutter, Gary (7); O'Neal, Randall (27); Quealey, Steven (4); Tabor, Scott (1); Williams, Mark (22); Wirth, Alan (2).

CHARLOTTE—Arias, Juan (26); Arnold, Tony (15); Boyd, Randy (20); Brown, Mark (19); Cabassa, Carlos (31); Dixon, Kenneth (14); Hoke, Leon (26); Hook, Edwin (20); Kucharski, Joseph (4); MacPherson, Bruce (11); Maples, Timothy (14); McCullock, Alec (6); Nastu, Philip (6); Norris, Timothy (3); Pensiero, Russell (17); Rowe, Thomas (25); Sadey, Richard (3); Sczesnak, Marc (3); Smith, Mark (26).

CHATTANOOGA—Anthony, Dane (1); Borchers, Rickey (19); Fuson, Robin (30); Jeffcoat, Michael (18); Lintz, Rickey (4); Munninghoff, Scott (26); Owens, Thomas (20); Puryear, Nathaniel (21); Roche, Stephen (7); Romero, Ramon (20); Schwarber, Michael (26); Silvas, Brian (1); Willis, Alan (3).

COLUMBUS—Calhoun, Jeffrey (7); Dunnegan, Steven (5); Gardner, Scott (11); Heathcock, Jeffrey (29); Leatherwood, Delrick (4); Ledduck, Daniel (19); MacDonald, James (24); Mathis, Ronald (12); Meckes, Timothy (52); Morris, Jeffrey (14); Penate, Miguel (13); Perry, Patrick (22); Sarmiento, Walfredo (14); Snyder, Benjamin (12); Sprowl, Robert (22); Williams, Richard (10).

JACKSONVILLE—Alvarez, Evelio (24); Botelho, Derek (9); Ferreira, Anthony (6); Harsh, Nicholas (8); Huffman, Phillip (8); Huismann, Mark (36); Jackson, Danny (14); Parrott, Michael (6); Pickert, Gary (36); Potestio, Douglas (4); Raine, Steven (6); Ray, Glenn (28); Shaw, Theodore (20); St. Clair, Daniel (51); Vanderbush, Walter (28); Williams, Larry (5); Wyatt, Reginald (4); Yuhas, Vincent (14).

KNOXVILLE—Baker, James (17); Cerutti, John (4); Clarke, Stanley (11); Cuellar, Miguel (4); Elam, Scott (29); Ford, Randy (26); Howard, Dennis (30); Lukish, Thomas (54); O'Keeffe, Richard (2); Stemberger, Brian (43); Walker, Keith (33); Williams, Matthew (28); Wilson, Gary (4).

MEMPHIS—Abone, Joseph (23); Bargar, Gregory (16); Barnicle, Theodore (2); Capilla, Doug (2); Chapin, Peter (10); Chesser, Brandon (20); Dilks, Darren (27); Dues, Hal (16); Engle, Ricky (11); Glasscock, Larry (39); Goldetsky, Larry (1); Horn, Larry (20); Palmer, David (9); Ramos, Richard (5); Schuler, Mark (44); Shimp, Tommy Joe (19); Simond, Robert (6); Taylor, Jeffrey (23); Waymire, Ronald (1); Westray, Kenneth (5); Yanus, Raymond (44).

NASHVILLE—Bersano, Mark (1); Browning, Michael (35); Callahan, Benjamin (30); Christiansen, Clay (29); Elston, Guy (31); Fontenot, Ray (14); Garland, Wayne (6); Guerra, Randall (3); Lein, Christopher (32); Ricci, Frank (39); Scott, Kelly (6); Serum, Gary (10); Slagle, Roger (9); Smith, Kenneth (23); Sykes, Robert (23).

ORLANDO—Angulo, Samuel (24); Belanger, Lee (41); Everett, Conrad (24); Flores, James (1); Fregin, Douglas (10); Hobbs, Jack (52); Hodge, Eddie (39); Konopa, Robert (20); Kromy, Ted (25); Little, Jeffrey (9); May, Larry (8); Mulligan, Robert (18); Oelkers, Bryan (3); Pettibone, Jay (5); Veselic, Robert (12).

SAVANNAH—Acker, James (26); Behenna, Richard (28); Clay, David (7); Coatney, Ricky (12); Field, Gregory (29); Fore, Charles (18); Gibson, James (22); Johnson, Joseph (6); Jones, Craig (22); North, Roy (4); Pettaway, Felix (36); Santana, Rafael (9); Shields, Michael (19); Smith, Michael (4); Twitty, Jeffrey (2); West, Matthew (22).

GRAND SLAM HOME RUNS—Stefero, 3; Brewer, Fuentes, Landis, Melvin, Ramie, 2 each; Auten, Benson, Cadahia, Cecchetti, Clements, David, Djakonow, Funderbunk, Grace, Hayes, Hazewood, Poldberg, Poole, Rende, Salas, Sodders, Thompson, Tyner, 1 each.

AWARDED FIRST BASE ON CATCHER'S INTERFERENCE—Atkinson 3 (Callahan, Mizerock, Siminuc); Scranton 3 (Mizerock, Poole, Shines); Winters 2 (Melvin, Mizerock); Cruz (Ashmore); Cuervo (Stephans); Fuentes (Stephans); Gates (Cadahia); Miller (Stephans); Perez (Salas); Turner (Stefero), 1 each.

CLUB FIELDING

Club	Pct.	G.	PO.	A.	E.	DP.	PB.	Club	Pct.	G.	PO.	A.	E.	DP.	PB.
Orlando	.968	144	3620	1452	165	116	19	Chattanooga	.965	143	3671	1542	189	129	24
Knoxville	.967	144	3631	1582	177	118	21	Savannah	.965	144	3537	1429	182	120	30
Memphis	.967	144	3738	1513	178	132	25	Charlotte	.964	143	3566	1476	191	119	16
Jacksonville	.966	144	3712	1448	179	133	15	Columbus	.964	143	3699	1620	198	135	17
Birmingham	.965	143	3620	1510	187	130	10	Nashville	.961	144	3777	1657	223	135	25

Triple Play—Nashville.

INDIVIDUAL FIELDING

*Throws lefthanded.

.FIRST BASEMEN

Player and Club	Pct.	G.	PO.	A.	E.	DP.	Player and Club	Pct.	G.	PO.	A.	E.	DP.
Atkinson, Jacksonville	.974	7	36	2	1	2	Hoeksema, Memphis	1.000	2	12	0	0	1
Auten, Memphis	1.000	2	6	0	0	0	Hough, Columbus	1.000	1	2	1	0	0
Bockhorn, Savannah	1.000	4	30	1	0	2	Huppert, Charlotte	.900	1	9	0	1	0
Bodie, Columbus	.985	7	64	6	1	5	McCann, 13 Birm-1 Memphis	.984	14	116	10	2	8
Bowman, Charlotte	.984	91	765	48	13	75	McDonald, Columbus*	.987	39	371	8	5	34
Brunson, Charlotte	.965	6	50	5	2	2	Melvin, Birmingham	1.000	10	92	4	0	9
Cecchetti, Chattanooga*	.981	29	248	11	5	19	Mizerock, Columbus	.958	3	23	0	1	1
Clements, Columbus	.981	67	586	41	12	60	Naehring, Charlotte	.985	15	124	7	2	8
Craig, Nashville	.987	18	137	12	2	12	Nealeigh, Memphis*	.987	102	831	51	12	86
Csefalvay, Columbus*	1.000	3	17	4	0	0	Pasley, Birmingham	.960	4	23	1	1	2
David, Orlando*	1.000	3	10	1	0	2	Peterson, Nashville	1.000	8	42	3	0	2
Davis, Columbus	.993	26	257	11	2	26	Poole, Birmingham	.994	68	621	54	4	60
Dees, Charlotte	.986	20	132	8	2	10	Ramie, Knoxville	1.000	1	7	0	0	1
Djakonow, Birmingham	.982	8	48	6	1	7	Rende, Chattanooga*	.988	108	940	63	12	91
Ferris, Jacksonville	.989	110	889	72	11	89	Shines, Memphis	.979	46	343	29	8	28
Foster, Orlando	.988	126	1045	70	14	79	Showalter, Nashville*	.990	120	1281	51	13	101
Foussianes, Birmingham	.955	2	20	1	1	1	Simunic, 1 Jax-6 Chattanooga ..	.971	7	67	1	2	4
Funderburk, Orlando	.976	21	151	10	4	16	Smith, Nashville*	.957	4	41	3	2	4
Garbey, Birmingham	.937	9	64	10	5	4	Sodders, Orlando	1.000	2	2	0	0	1
Glass, Chattanooga	.973	5	35	1	1	2	Stephans, Jacksonville	1.000	2	2	0	0	1
GROUT, Savannah	.993	140	1225	60	9	109	Thompson, Knoxville*	.992	132	1207	65	10	92
Harvey, Birmingham*	.989	32	257	15	3	25	Turner, Jacksonville	.989	32	256	14	3	25
Hernandez, Charlotte	.973	12	102	7	3	13	Wilson, Chattanooga	.968	4	29	1	1	1
Hodgson, Knoxville	.972	15	99	6	3	10							

Triple Play—Showalter.

SECOND BASEMEN

Player and Club	Pct.	G.	PO.	A.	E.	DP.	Player and Club	Pct.	G.	PO.	A.	E.	DP.
Benson, Columbus	.960	55	146	145	12	42	Meier, Orlando	1.000	2	1	0	0	0
Bockhorn, Savannah	1.000	1	0	1	0	0	Mesa, Orlando	1.000	13	26	32	0	6
Butterfield, Nashville	.955	10	17	25	2	1	Methven, Chattanooga	.957	26	52	59	5	13
Cuervo, Columbus	.945	24	42	62	6	7	Moronko, Chattanooga	.941	21	43	52	6	16
Curry, Savannah	.955	27	50	76	6	15	Naehring, Charlotte	1.000	4	7	13	0	3
Dennis, Knoxville	.967	13	31	28	2	6	Newman, Memphis	.959	142	356	388	32	94
Djakonow, Birmingham	1.000	1	1	0	0	0	Nixon, Nashville	.984	34	74	105	3	22
Dugas, Chattanooga	.975	87	178	244	11	53	Pacho, Chattanooga	.964	26	38	43	3	8
Flannery, Birmingham	.982	15	23	31	1	9	Perez, Charlotte	.972	12	16	19	1	3
Gagne, Orlando	1.000	3	1	0	0	0	Pilla, Orlando	1.000	2	2	2	0	0
M. Garcia, Savannah	.984	23	56	71	2	11	Quinones, Memphis	1.000	2	4	0	0	0
S. Garcia, Columbus	.953	8	17	24	2	4	Rios, Knoxville	.833	1	2	3	1	0
Glynn, Memphis	.944	4	7	10	1	3	Rodriguez, Charlotte	.955	47	95	116	10	16
Grace, Columbus	.975	43	104	128	6	32	Schaefer, Charlotte	.949	66	179	172	19	43
Hegman, Jacksonville	.957	23	46	64	5	15	Schmitz, Nashville	.969	21	36	57	3	11
Hernandez, Charlotte	1.000	2	4	3	0	2	Teufel, Orlando	.965	85	231	185	15	54
Hinson, Birmingham	1.000	1	0	1	0	0	Thomas, Columbus	.975	23	53	62	3	15
Hudler, Columbus	.945	73	131	214	20	50	Villaman, Nashville	.981	10	23	28	1	3
Ingle, Savannah	.964	95	179	270	17	51	Wheeler, Knoxville	1.000	1	1	2	0	0
Jacobson, Charlotte	.947	11	29	25	3	6	Whitfield, Charlotte	.923	8	20	16	3	5
JOHNSON, Jacksonville	.985	125	268	315	9	79	Wood, Knoxville	.982	133	298	371	12	81
Martin, Chattanooga	1.000	1	4	3	0	2	Woodard, Birmingham	.981	133	271	388	13	83
McCain, Orlando	.948	48	90	93	10	22							

THIRD BASEMEN

Player and Club	Pct.	G.	PO.	A.	E.	DP.	Player and Club	Pct.	G.	PO.	A.	E.	DP.
Adams, Chattanooga	.925	28	8	41	4	5	McCain, Orlando	.920	51	43	106	13	14
Atkinson, Jacksonville	1.000	4	2	3	0	0	McCann, 11 Birm-7 Memphis	.909	18	16	34	5	3
Benson, Columbus	.895	7	4	13	2	0	Meier, Orlando	.913	7	5	16	2	2
Bockhorn, Savannah	1.000	3	1	3	0	0	Melvin, Birmingham	.500	1	1	0	1	0
Bodie, Columbus	1.000	2	0	6	0	0	Mesa, Orlando	.958	19	9	37	2	1
Carl, Memphis	.911	45	25	88	11	6	Mizerock, Columbus	1.000	2	1	2	0	0
Cuervo, Columbus	.750	6	2	4	2	1	MORONKO, Chattanooga	.946	114	88	247	19	29
Curry, Savannah	.870	38	24	70	14	6	Naehring, Charlotte	.957	42	30	104	6	8
David, Orlando°	1.000	1	0	1	0	0	Pacho, Chattanooga	.923	12	9	27	3	2
Dempsey, Knoxville	.922	26	14	57	6	5	Perez, Charlotte	.931	28	16	51	5	2
Dennis, Knoxville	.846	7	6	16	4	2	Peterson, Nashville	.926	103	64	251	25	19
Djakonow, Birmingham	.906	27	14	63	8	6	Pilla, Orlando	.954	21	19	43	3	8
Doerr, Charlotte	1.000	2	1	0	0	0	Quinones, Memphis	1.000	2	2	0	0	0
Flannery, Birmingham	.733	8	4	7	4	2	J. Reynolds, 26 Nash-105 Knox	.917	131	91	294	35	31
Foussianes, Birmingham	.924	32	25	60	7	4	M. Reynolds, Savannah	.800	4	0	4	1	1
M. Garcia, Savannah	.889	6	3	13	2	2	Robles, Columbus	1.000	1	0	1	0	1
Glynn, Memphis	.891	27	11	38	6	3	Schaefer, Charlotte	.967	24	16	42	2	6
Grace, Columbus	.913	91	65	228	28	31	Shines, Memphis	1.000	3	1	4	0	0
Gruber, Chattanooga	.933	8	4	10	1	1	Sodders, Orlando	.952	61	41	138	9	6
Hayes, Savannah	.914	98	77	167	23	17	Stefero, Charlotte	.875	7	3	4	1	1
Hegman, Jacksonville	.908	39	17	62	8	6	Strucher, Columbus	.898	45	23	118	16	6
Hench, Nashville	1.000	14	11	27	0	2	Villaman, Nashville	1.000	10	2	4	0	0
Hernandez, Charlotte	.947	47	48	94	8	9	Wheeler, Knoxville	.870	6	6	14	3	3
Hinson, Birmingham	.919	69	50	120	15	13	Whitfield, Charlotte	1.000	1	0	1	0	0
Hoeksema, Memphis	.949	76	56	132	10	8	Wilkerson, Jacksonville	.912	116	78	193	26	17

SHORTSTOPS

Player and Club	Pct.	G.	PO.	A.	E.	DP.	Player and Club	Pct.	G.	PO.	A.	E.	DP.
Alfaro, Charlotte	.943	137	181	413	36	70	Meier, Orlando	1.000	1	5	0	0	0
Baker, Birmingham	.956	70	115	190	14	40	Mesa, Orlando	.923	7	2	10	1	0
Banes, Nashville	.877	14	21	43	9	5	Miller, Savannah	.937	79	109	203	21	35
Benson, Columbus	1.000	4	5	10	0	0	Moronko, Chattanooga	.900	8	5	13	2	4
Cuervo, Columbus	.750	3	0	3	1	0	Nixon, Nashville	.888	38	52	106	20	19
Curry, Savannah	.951	64	68	166	12	29	Pacho, Chattanooga	.935	34	44	85	9	16
Davis, Birmingham	.846	12	10	45	10	6	Pilla, Orlando	1.000	7	8	10	0	2
Dennis, Knoxville	.905	23	24	52	8	6	Quinones, Memphis	1.000	2	0	1	0	0
Flannery, Birmingham	.943	11	9	24	2	7	Reynolds, Savannah	.968	7	14	16	1	3
Followell, Birmingham	.957	11	17	28	2	7	Rios, Knoxville	.926	120	166	363	42	60
Gagne, Orlando	.938	134	184	403	39	62	Rodriguez, Nashville	.934	10	19	38	4	11
Glynn, Memphis	.919	55	82	145	20	26	Schaefer, Charlotte	.972	8	18	17	1	4
Gonzales, Memphis	.949	55	77	183	14	37	Schmitz, Nashville	.944	41	35	150	11	15
Gruber, Chattanooga	.918	114	157	323	43	53	SCRANTON, Jacksonville	.957	128	210	364	26	76
Hegman, Jacksonville	.968	15	19	41	2	9	Simcox, Columbus	.910	19	26	65	9	14
Hinson, Birmingham	.918	10	10	35	4	7	Smith, Nashville	.944	4	4	13	1	2
Hoeksema, Memphis	.904	43	35	115	16	18	Villaman, Nashville	.890	41	75	136	26	20
Hudler, Nashville	1.000	6	1	5	0	1	Wheeler, Knoxville	1.000	3	3	6	0	0
Ingle, Savannah	.700	3	1	6	3	2	Wherry, Columbus	.956	121	168	378	25	72
Laurie, Birmingham	.888	35	53	89	18	14	Wilkerson, Jacksonville	.833	1	2	3	1	1
McCain, Orlando	1.000	3	1	5	0	0	Wood, Knoxville	1.000	1	1	6	0	0

Triple Play—Rodriguez.

OUTFIELDERS

Player and Club	Pct.	G.	PO.	A.	E.	DP.	Player and Club	Pct.	G.	PO.	A.	E.	DP.
Adams, Chattanooga	.934	53	80	5	6	1	Bockhorn, Savannah	1.000	4	6	0	0	0
Atkinson, Jacksonville	1.000	8	6	0	0	0	Bodie, Columbus	.965	35	54	1	2	0
Auten, Memphis	.983	107	218	13	4	4	Bonaparte, Orlando°	.895	11	15	2	2	0
K. Baker, Birmingham°	.959	105	182	4	8	0	Bourjos, Charlotte	.962	31	47	4	2	1
R. Baker, Chattanooga	.938	30	30	0	2	0	Bowman, Charlotte	1.000	2	4	0	0	0
Belue, Memphis	1.000	9	30	1	0	0	Brackenridge, Orlando	1.000	9	9	3	0	0
Benson, Columbus	1.000	2	2	0	0	0	Brewer, Jacksonville	.962	120	269	13	11	4

OUTFIELDERS—Continued

Player and Club	Pct.	G.	PO.	A.	E.	DP.
Brunson, Charlotte	.964	31	51	3	2	1
Bullock, Columbus*	1.000	15	21	1	0	0
Cannon, Knoxville	.987	85	142	9	2	3
Carrion, Memphis	.977	93	204	8	5	3
Carter, Memphis	1.000	11	18	1	0	0
Cecchetti, Chattanooga*	.979	104	174	13	4	2
Chapman, Nashville*	.961	124	237	8	10	2
Charboneau, Chattanooga	.900	10	9	0	1	0
Corey, Charlotte	.983	40	55	3	1	1
Croft, Savannah	.983	87	169	1	3	1
Cruz, Memphis*	.974	63	106	8	3	1
Csefalvay, Columbus*	1.000	94	125	7	0	1
David, Orlando*	.965	97	185	7	7	1
Davis, Jacksonville	.992	116	231	7	2	2
Dayett, Nashville	.946	140	201	9	12	2
Denman, Charlotte	.976	125	277	7	7	0
Dennis, Knoxville	.971	80	124	10	4	2
Dewey, Jacksonville	1.000	2	1	0	0	0
Djakonow, Birmingham	1.000	2	3	1	0	0
Dodd, 77 Nash-27 Knox	.969	104	174	12	6	5
Douglas, Orlando	1.000	22	34	0	0	0
Fields, Birmingham	.944	42	102	0	6	0
Flannery, Birmingham	1.000	2	1	0	0	0
Fuentes, Memphis	.984	138	284	22	5	2
Funderburk, Orlando	.988	53	73	9	1	0
Gainey, Columbus	1.000	13	19	1	0	0
Gallagher, Chattanooga	1.000	15	32	1	0	0
Garbey, Birmingham	.963	80	142	12	6	5
Gardner, Knoxville	.967	90	139	9	5	1
Gayden, Nashville*	.875	2	7	0	1	0
Glynn, Memphis	1.000	5	9	0	0	0
Hampton, Birmingham	.959	81	175	11	8	1
Hazewood, Charlotte	.976	130	268	11	7	2
Hegman, Jacksonville	1.000	10	8	0	0	0
Hernandez, Charlotte	1.000	3	5	0	0	0
Herrick, Charlotte	.750	3	3	0	1	0
Hodgson, Knoxville	1.000	23	32	0	0	0
Holmes, Orlando	1.000	12	21	0	0	0
Hudler, Nashville	1.000	2	4	0	0	0
Jabalera, Columbus*	.929	121	190	6	15	1
Knight, Nashville*	.924	33	59	2	5	1
Komminsk, Savannah	.943	112	158	6	10	2
Landis, Savannah	.974	61	103	10	3	3
Leeper, Jacksonville*	.956	132	210	8	10	1
McCain, Orlando	1.000	3	1	1	0	0
McDonald, Columbus*	.833	4	5	0	1	0
Meier, Orlando	.984	126	243	11	4	5
Nealeigh, Memphis*	1.000	17	21	3	0	0
Ramie, Knoxville	1.000	2	1	0	0	0
Reynolds, Savannah	.938	26	41	4	3	1
Robles, Columbus	.972	124	265	13	8	0
Rollin, Birmingham	.934	68	111	3	8	2
Rosario, Columbus	1.000	18	32	0	0	0
SAAVEDRA, Chattanooga	.996	123	212	14	1	3
Schaeffer, Charlotte	1.000	8	18	1	0	0
Shepherd, Knoxville	.967	136	260	4	9	1
Showalter, Nashville*	1.000	2	1	0	0	0
Simmons, Birmingham	1.000	6	11	0	0	0
Smith, Nashville*	.983	34	53	5	1	0
Stefero, Charlotte	.973	18	36	0	1	0
Taylor, D., Chattanooga*	.950	109	256	9	14	3
Taylor, M., Chattanooga	.833	5	5	0	1	0
Thompson, Savannah	.958	143	312	10	14	3
Turner, Jacksonville	.921	61	110	7	10	3
Tutt, Charlotte	.813	8	13	0	3	0
Tyner, Charlotte	.974	37	71	4	2	2
Wiedenbauer, Columbus	.962	21	49	1	2	0
Williams, Orlando	.982	126	268	7	5	1
Winters, Nashville	1.000	29	40	3	0	1
Younger, Birmingham*	.963	49	74	4	3	0

CATCHERS

Player and Club	Pct.	G.	PO.	A.	E.	DP.	PB.
Ashmore, Jacksonville	.933	8	40	2	3	0	4
Austin, Orlando	.977	106	565	61	15	6	10
Bailey, Savannah	.976	6	40	1	1	1	1
Bockhorn, Savannah	.980	53	272	25	6	2	17
Borges, Memphis	1.000	2	15	1	0	0	2
Bradley, Nashville	.958	5	44	2	2	0	1
Cadahia, Orlando	.987	53	281	23	4	1	9
Callahan, Nashville	.964	53	288	32	12	3	8
Carrasquel, Birmingham	1.000	17	101	10	0	0	1
Colbern, Savannah	.977	74	430	33	11	2	10
Derryberry, Charlotte	.950	2	19	0	1	0	1
Dewey, Jacksonville	.985	27	174	17	3	1	2
Dodd, Nashville	.933	2	12	2	1	0	0
Glass, Chattanooga	.967	43	227	6	8	3	7
Hernandez, Knoxville	.976	83	461	64	13	8	14
Hough, Columbus	.974	29	141	7	4	0	3
Huppert, Charlotte	.985	76	390	61	7	5	4
Kelly, D. Savannah	.959	18	112	6	5	2	2
Kneuer, Nashville	.967	8	27	2	1	1	1
Lepel, Memphis	.986	39	258	16	4	6	5
MELVIN, Birmingham	.987	86	545	50	8	6	4
Milner, Knoxville	.983	33	201	29	4	0	5
Mizerock, Columbus	.982	122	762	87	16	7	14
Pasley, Birmingham	.990	15	92	5	1	1	1
Pirruccello, Jacksonville	1.000	2	10	0	0	0	0
Poldberg, Nashville	.991	47	278	37	3	4	6
Poole, Birmingham	.988	26	149	20	2	1	4
Pulley, Knoxville	.929	6	24	2	2	0	0
Rey, Chattanooga	.991	48	291	35	3	2	7
Richards, Memphis	.981	71	419	51	9	4	9
Salas, Nashville	.977	40	267	24	7	0	9
Shines, Memphis	.977	40	229	30	6	6	9
Simunic, 1 Jax-61 Chat	.987	62	353	36	5	4	11
Soriano, Knoxville	.985	17	117	11	2	1	2
Stefero, Charlotte	.967	78	396	47	15	2	11
Stephans, Jacksonville	.977	112	728	64	19	4	8
Whitmer, Knoxville	.962	13	68	7	3	1	0
Wilkerson, Jacksonville	1.000	3	6	0	0	0	0

PITCHERS

Player and Club	Pct.	G.	PO.	A.	E.	DP.
Abone, Memphis	.900	23	3	6	1	0
Acker, Savannah	.939	26	8	23	2	0
Alvarez, Jacksonville	.864	24	3	16	3	1
Angulo, Orlando*	1.000	6	0	6	0	0
Anthony, Chattanooga	1.000	1	1	0	0	0
Arias, Charlotte	.938	26	6	9	1	1
Arnold, Charlotte	1.000	15	7	11	0	0
Arrington, Orlando	.947	24	4	14	1	0
Baker, Knoxville	.960	17	3	21	1	0
Bargar, Memphis	.950	16	4	15	1	0
Barnicle, Memphis*	1.000	2	0	1	0	1
Bass, Birmingham	.909	30	8	12	2	2
Beecroft, Birmingham	.857	7	2	4	1	0
Behenna, Savannah	.886	28	7	32	5	0
Belanger, Orlando*	.958	41	1	22	1	1
Bersano, Nashville	1.000	1	0	1	0	0
Bonine, Columbus	.781	33	5	20	7	2
Borchers, Chattanooga*	.909	19	4	6	1	1
Botelho, Jacksonville	.900	9	1	8	1	0
Boyd, Charlotte*	1.000	20	3	1	0	1
Broersma, Orlando	.958	43	10	13	1	2
Brown, Charlotte	.938	19	4	11	1	3
Browning, Nashville	1.000	35	3	8	0	1
Cabassa, Charlotte*	.800	31	3	9	3	1
Calhoun, Columbus*	.833	7	1	4	1	0
Callahan, Nashville	1.000	29	9	21	0	1
Capilla, Memphis*	.000	2	0	0	1	0
CARY, Birmingham*	1.000	28	13	33	0	3
Cerutti, Knoxville*	1.000	4	2	5	0	0
Chapin, Memphis	1.000	10	0	5	0	0
Chesser, Memphis	1.000	20	10	17	0	2
CHRISTIANSEN, Nashville	1.000	29	6	40	0	1
Clarke, Knoxville*	1.000	11	1	3	0	1
Clay, Savannah	.882	7	9	6	2	2
Coatney, Savannah	.909	12	2	8	1	0
Cuellar, Knoxville	1.000	4	0	1	0	0
Dilks, Memphis*	.938	27	8	22	2	1
Dixon, Charlotte	.941	13	4	12	1	1
Dues, Memphis	.938	16	2	13	1	1
Dunnegan, Columbus	.857	5	2	4	1	0
Elam, Knoxville	.960	29	13	35	2	1
Elston, Nashville	1.000	31	3	4	0	1
Engle, Memphis*	1.000	10	0	5	0	0
Everett, Orlando	1.000	24	3	4	0	0
Ferreira, Jacksonville*	1.000	6	1	13	0	2
Field, Savannah	.938	29	4	11	1	0
Fontenot, Nashville*	.941	14	1	15	1	0
Ford, Knoxville*	1.000	26	7	5	0	0
Fore, Savannah	.976	18	15	26	1	3
Fregin, Orlando	1.000	10	2	4	0	3
Fuson, Chattanooga	.920	30	32	37	6	2
Gardner, Columbus	.909	11	1	9	1	1
Garland, Nashville	.800	6	2	6	2	1
J. Gibson, Savannah	1.000	22	0	7	0	1
P. Gibson, Birmingham*	.952	44	4	16	1	2
Glasscock, Birmingham*	.933	39	5	9	1	0
Gumpert, Birmingham	.957	42	3	19	1	0
Harsh, Jacksonville	.882	8	4	11	2	1
Heathcock, Columbus	.957	29	12	32	2	1
Heinkel, Birmingham	1.000	9	1	11	0	0

PITCHERS—Continued

Player and Club	Pct.	G.	PO.	A.	E.	DP.	Player and Club	Pct.	G.	PO.	A.	E.	DP.
Hobbs, Orlando*	.963	51	5	21	1	2	Potestio, Jacksonville	1.000	4	0	3	0	0
Hodge, Orlando*	1.000	39	8	11	0	0	Puryear, Chattanooga	1.000	21	5	18	0	1
Hoke, Charlotte	1.000	26	3	4	0	0	Quealey, Birmingham	1.000	4	1	0	0	0
Hook, Charlotte	.931	20	8	19	2	3	Raine, Jacksonville	1.000	6	1	2	0	0
Horn, Memphis	.895	20	7	10	2	0	Ramos, Memphis	1.000	5	3	3	0	0
Howard, Knoxville	.907	30	6	33	4	2	Ray, Jacksonville	.972	28	15	20	1	2
Huffman, Jacksonville	.900	8	4	5	1	0	Ricci, Nashville	.950	38	4	15	1	1
Huismann, Jacksonville	.900	36	4	5	1	0	Roche, Chattanooga	1.000	7	1	3	0	0
Jackson, Jacksonville*	.897	14	6	20	3	1	Romero, Chattanooga*	.917	20	2	9	1	0
Jeffcoat, Chattanooga*	1.000	18	3	24	0	1	Rowe, Charlotte	.911	24	9	32	4	4
Johnson, Savannah	1.000	6	0	3	0	1	Sadey, Charlotte	.500	3	0	1	1	0
Jones, Savannah	.944	22	6	28	2	2	Santana, Savannah	1.000	9	0	6	0	0
Kelly, Birmingham	.815	16	6	16	5	1	Sarmiento, Columbus	1.000	13	1	5	0	0
Konopa, Orlando*	.870	20	3	17	3	1	Schuler, Memphis	1.000	44	4	9	0	0
Kromy, Orlando	1.000	24	5	15	0	1	Schwarber, Chattanooga	1.000	26	7	0	0	0
Kucharski, Charlotte	.833	4	1	4	1	0	Scott, Nashville	1.000	6	3	5	0	0
Leatherwood, Columbus	1.000	4	3	2	0	0	Sczesnak, Charlotte*	1.000	3	1	1	0	0
Ledduke, Columbus	1.000	19	3	6	0	1	Serum, Nashville	1.000	10	3	7	0	0
Lein, Nashville	.879	32	8	21	4	2	Shaw, Jacksonville	.897	20	7	19	3	1
Lintz, Chattanooga	1.000	4	1	2	0	0	Shields, Savannah	.909	19	1	9	1	0
Little, Orlando*	1.000	9	0	1	0	0	Shimp, Memphis	1.000	19	6	10	0	0
Lukish, Knoxville	1.000	54	3	17	0	2	Simond, Memphis*	1.000	6	0	3	0	0
MacDonald, Columbus	.952	24	3	17	1	1	Slagle, Savannah	1.000	9	3	3	0	0
MacPherson, Charlotte	1.000	11	0	3	0	0	K. Smith, Nashville	1.000	23	3	7	0	0
Maples, Charlotte	.857	14	4	8	2	1	Ma. Smith, Charlotte	.867	26	3	10	2	0
Mathis, 2 Birm-10 Col	.857	12	3	3	1	0	Mi. Smith, Savannah	1.000	4	0	1	0	0
May, Orlando	1.000	8	0	6	0	0	Snyder, Columbus	.923	12	8	16	2	1
McCulloch, Charlotte	1.000	6	0	2	0	0	Sprowl, Columbus*	1.000	22	3	9	0	1
McLaughlin, Knoxville	.862	20	4	21	4	0	St. Clair, Jacksonville	.667	51	4	4	4	0
Meckes, Columbus	1.000	52	5	13	0	0	Stemberger, Knoxville	1.000	43	3	13	0	1
Moncrief, Birmingham	.880	29	9	13	3	0	Sykes, Nashville*	1.000	23	1	5	0	2
Morris, Columbus*	1.000	14	4	20	0	0	Tabor, Birmingham	1.000	1	0	1	0	0
Mulligan, Orlando*	.962	18	3	22	1	0	Taylor, Memphis*	.889	23	4	4	1	0
Munninghoff, Chattanooga	.944	26	5	29	2	3	Thompson, Chattanooga	.895	50	4	13	2	0
Nail, Birmingham	.889	24	8	8	2	1	Twitty, Savannah*	1.000	2	0	1	0	0
Narleski, Chattanooga	.958	50	3	20	1	0	Vanderbush, Jacksonville	.911	28	12	39	5	4
Nastu, Charlotte*	1.000	5	1	2	0	0	Veselic, Orlando	.765	12	4	9	4	0
Norris, Charlotte	1.000	3	1	0	0	0	Walker, Knoxville*	.941	33	6	26	2	1
North, Savannah	1.000	4	0	5	0	0	Waymire, Memphis	1.000	1	0	2	0	0
Nutter, Birmingham	1.000	7	1	3	0	0	West, Savannah	1.000	22	5	26	0	1
O'Keeffe, Knoxville*	1.000	2	0	1	0	0	Westray, Memphis*	.500	5	0	1	1	0
O'Neal, Birmingham	.979	27	12	35	1	2	Wever, Nashville	.915	29	9	34	4	3
Oelkers, Orlando*	1.000	3	0	1	0	0	Wihtol, Chattanooga	.800	10	0	4	1	0
Oliveras, Charlotte	.850	24	7	27	6	1	L. Williams, Jacksonville	1.000	5	2	4	0	0
Owens, Chattanooga	.824	20	2	12	3	2	Mark Williams, Birmingham	.971	22	15	18	1	3
Palmer, Memphis	1.000	9	7	6	0	0	Matt Williams, Knoxville	.980	28	19	29	1	1
Parrott, Jacksonville	.833	6	2	3	1	0	R. Williams, Columbus	1.000	10	0	5	0	0
Penate, Columbus	.833	13	1	4	1	1	Willis, Chattanooga	1.000	3	1	2	0	0
Pensiero, Charlotte	1.000	17	3	4	0	2	Wilson, Knoxville	.000	4	0	0	1	0
Perry, Columbus*	1.000	22	3	7	0	1	Wirth, Birmingham	1.000	2	1	1	0	0
Pettaway, Savannah	1.000	36	0	14	0	0	Yanus, Memphis	1.000	44	5	16	0	2
Pettibone, Orlando	.250	5	1	0	3	0	Yuhas, Jacksonville	.880	14	8	14	3	0
Pickert, Jacksonville*	.929	36	2	11	1	0							

The following players do not have any recorded accepted chances at the positions indicated; therefore, are not listed in the fielding averages for those particular positions: Adams, 1b; Benson, p; Cadahia, p; Curry, of; Dayett, 3b; Dugas, of; Flannery, p; Goldetsky, of; Guerra, p; Harvey, p; Ingle, 3b; McCann, of; Pacho, of; Peterson, 2b; Rowe, 3b; Schmitz, 3b; Silvas, p; Simunic, of; Sodders, of; Strucher, 1b; Wyatt, p.

CLUB PITCHING

Club	ERA.	G.	CG.	ShO.	Sv.	IP.	H.	R.	ER.	HR.	HB.	BB.	Int. BB.	SO.	WP.	Bk.
Jacksonville	3.13	144	37	15	29	1237.1	1031	527	430	111	40	549	21	922	54	3
Nashville	3.64	144	38	10	21	1259	1241	619	509	100	41	467	33	902	54	7
Knoxville	3.80	144	49	13	29	1210.1	1106	618	511	73	36	630	15	851	113	6
Birmingham	3.89	143	29	12	30	1206.2	1156	619	522	123	30	502	20	848	47	10
Savannah	3.95	144	57	9	14	1179	1082	638	517	100	39	607	12	815	75	8
Columbus	3.98	143	36	8	27	1233	1272	667	545	128	54	462	26	855	57	6
Chattanooga	4.03	143	33	6	21	1223.2	1237	668	548	97	39	584	21	836	81	9
Orlando	4.32	144	26	6	29	1206.2	1276	677	579	147	34	509	33	837	62	6
Charlotte	4.38	143	46	9	21	1188.2	1171	687	579	118	37	594	19	769	92	11
Memphis	4.41	144	21	3	25	1246	1291	729	611	130	50	634	23	867	69	8

PITCHERS' RECORDS

(Leading Qualifiers for Earned-Run Average Leadership — 115 or More Innings)

*Throws lefthanded.

Pitcher—Club	W.	L.	Pct.	ERA.	G.	GS.	CG.	GF.	ShO.	Sv.	IP.	H.	R.	ER.	HR.	HB.	BB.	Int. BB.	SO.	WP.
Wever, Nashville	16	6	.727	2.78	29	29	10	0	2	0	214	176	75	66	9	6	80	2	191	7
Shaw, Jacksonville	7	5	.583	2.80	20	20	5	0	2	0	128.2	80	53	40	18	7	79	0	114	9
Walker, Knoxville*	8	6	.571	2.82	33	13	5	1	2	0	127.2	113	49	40	12	0	51	1	61	7
Jeffcoat, Chattanooga*	8	8	.500	2.88	18	18	6	0	2	0	128.1	122	49	41	3	4	51	1	107	7
Christiansen, Nashville	16	8	.667	3.07	29	29	13	0	2	0	214.1	214	102	73	11	9	80	2	157	17
MacDonald, Columbus	11	7	.611	3.23	24	20	10	3	3	1	153.1	160	70	55	12	5	38	2	81	3
Nail, Birmingham	9	6	.600	3.34	24	24	4	0	1	0	143	139	64	53	14	1	46	3	109	3
Narleski, Chattanooga	9	10	.474	3.34	50	5	0	36	0	7	137.1	119	64	51	9	3	39	5	98	4
Fore, Savannah	8	6	.571	3.36	18	18	9	0	1	0	128.2	109	61	48	16	5	44	2	67	5
O'Neal, Birmingham	11	7	.611	3.41	27	27	8	0	1	0	185	169	83	70	21	1	71	2	105	5

Departmental Leaders: G—Lukish, 54; GS—Fuson, 30; CG—Fuson, 15; GF—Lukish, 51; ShO—Ray, 4; W—Christiansen, Wever, 16; L—Elam, 16; Pct.—Brown, .800; Sv—Lukish, 20; IP—Fuson, 222.1; H—Fuson, 232; R—Heathcock, 119; ER—Heathcock, 101; HR—Heathcock, 26; HB—Bonine, 12; BB—Elam, 146; IBB—Yanus, 9; SO—Wever, 191; WP—M. Williams, 31.

(All Pitchers—Listed Alphabetically)

Pitcher—Club	W.	L.	Pct.	ERA.	G.	GS.	CG.	GF.	ShO.	Sv.	IP.	H.	R.	ER.	HR.	HB.	BB.	Int. BB.	SO.	WP.
Abone, Memphis	4	3	.571	4.08	23	2	0	13	0	1	57.1	67	34	26	1	1	23	3	40	1
Acker, Savannah	9	14	.391	4.44	26	24	7	2	1	1	142	120	96	70	12	6	86	2	96	7
Alvarez, Jacksonville	9	0	1.000	2.34	24	5	2	14	0	4	92.1	80	31	24	8	4	19	3	53	2
Angulo, Orlando*	3	3	.500	7.23	6	5	0	0	0	0	23.2	29	22	19	1	0	18	1	14	1
Anthony, Chattanooga	0	0	.000	13.50	1	0	0	1	0	0	2.2	8	4	4	0	0	1	0	0	0
Arias, Charlotte	1	4	.200	6.28	26	2	0	13	0	5	67.1	76	51	47	9	2	31	1	49	7
Arnold, Charlotte	5	6	.455	5.22	15	15	5	0	1	0	88	103	55	51	11	2	29	1	49	1
Arrington, Orlando	8	8	.500	5.68	24	22	1	2	0	1	117.1	133	85	74	15	7	50	2	65	7
Baker, Knoxville	10	6	.625	3.86	17	17	7	0	2	0	116.2	127	55	50	8	4	34	2	60	7
Bargar, Memphis	5	6	.455	4.10	16	16	5	0	0	0	118.2	100	61	54	12	11	63	0	124	5
Barnicle, Memphis*	0	0	.000	17.18	2	0	0	1	0	0	3.2	8	8	7	1	1	6	0	2	1
Bass, Birmingham	6	6	.500	4.29	30	3	1	17	0	1	94.1	100	53	45	8	4	29	3	77	1
Beecroft, Birmingham	1	4	.200	9.45	7	5	0	0	0	0	20	33	25	21	2	2	14	0	5	3
Behenna, Savannah	13	10	.565	3.71	28	28	11	0	2	0	201.1	195	97	83	10	5	97	3	153	13
Belanger, Orlando*	5	11	.313	4.13	41	14	4	19	2	4	126.1	132	62	58	15	4	44	3	73	6
Benson, Columbus	0	0	.000	0.00	1	0	0	0	0	0	1	0	0	0	0	0	0	0	0	0
Bersano, Nashville	1	0	1.000	0.00	1	0	0	1	0	0	2	1	0	0	0	0	1	1	2	0
Bonine, Columbus	11	13	.458	4.03	33	26	7	5	2	2	185.1	177	100	83	22	12	70	5	183	9
Borchers, Chattanooga*	2	1	.667	4.00	19	1	0	10	0	0	45	45	24	20	5	1	23	1	24	4
Botelho, Jacksonville	3	4	.429	4.57	9	9	3	0	1	0	65	54	35	33	10	1	25	0	35	1
Boyd, Charlotte*	2	3	.400	3.75	20	0	0	7	0	1	36	38	19	15	4	0	27	2	40	7
Broersma, Orlando	7	5	.583	4.02	43	14	0	14	0	3	152.1	151	76	68	17	6	73	6	137	6
Brown, Charlotte	8	2	.800	2.09	19	5	2	11	1	3	73.1	46	20	17	4	2	44	2	57	3
Browning, Nashville	2	3	.400	3.68	35	0	0	24	0	4	51.1	54	24	21	1	1	22	6	38	6
Cabassa, Charlotte*	4	7	.364	3.73	31	6	1	9	0	0	72.1	70	41	30	8	1	39	0	47	9
Cadahia, Orlando	0	0	.000	0.00	1	0	0	1	0	0	1	0	0	0	0	0	0	0	0	0
Calhoun, Columbus*	1	3	.250	5.71	7	7	0	0	0	0	34.2	44	35	22	5	1	28	1	32	4
Callahan, Nashville	13	13	.500	4.75	29	29	6	0	2	0	180	190	109	95	19	7	72	4	120	8
Capilla, Memphis*	0	1	.000	43.20	2	0	0	0	0	0	1.2	7	12	8	1	1	5	0	3	0
Cary, Birmingham*	8	14	.364	4.17	28	28	5	0	1	0	166	162	93	77	19	5	64	1	125	8
Cerutti, Knoxville*	4	0	1.000	1.11	4	4	1	0	1	0	32.1	18	4	4	0	2	10	0	17	2
Chapin, Memphis	0	2	.000	7.06	10	0	0	3	0	0	29.1	37	24	23	3	2	19	1	16	7
Chesser, Memphis	3	9	.250	4.40	20	15	1	2	0	0	104.1	120	62	51	13	2	49	2	62	5
Christiansen, Nashville	16	8	.667	3.07	29	29	13	0	2	0	214.1	214	102	73	11	9	80	2	157	17
Clarke, Knoxville*	0	1	.000	1.69	11	0	0	6	0	2	16	11	3	3	0	2	3	0	12	3
Clay, Savannah	3	4	.429	3.35	7	7	4	0	1	0	45.2	38	22	17	2	3	22	1	12	1
Coatney, Savannah	3	6	.333	4.87	12	11	3	1	1	0	64.2	58	43	35	5	0	52	0	43	10
Cuellar, Knoxville	0	0	.000	11.37	4	0	0	1	0	0	6.1	9	8	8	0	1	6	0	3	0
Dilks, Memphis*	9	9	.500	4.89	27	27	3	0	0	0	158.1	153	98	86	25	10	79	0	99	10
Dixon, Charlotte	3	8	.273	4.58	13	12	3	1	1	0	76.2	72	44	39	7	1	42	0	61	7
Dues, Memphis	4	4	.500	4.85	16	10	2	2	0	2	89	96	59	48	6	3	39	1	61	1
Dunnegan, Columbus	1	1	.500	3.81	5	5	0	0	0	0	26	25	18	11	2	1	18	1	15	1
Elam, Knoxville	6	16	.273	4.23	29	29	9	0	1	0	187.1	158	118	88	9	4	146	0	147	27
Elston, Nashville	4	1	.800	1.40	31	0	0	21	0	7	45	24	7	7	0	1	25	1	51	1
Engle, Memphis*	1	1	.500	3.52	10	3	0	4	0	1	30.2	31	13	12	4	1	16	0	15	1
Everett, Orlando	4	1	.800	3.26	24	0	0	17	0	4	38.2	36	20	14	7	2	15	2	24	5
Ferreira, Jacksonville*	2	4	.333	4.10	6	6	0	0	0	0	37.1	38	20	17	3	0	14	0	30	0
Field, Savannah	8	3	.727	2.72	29	5	3	15	0	3	102.2	86	35	31	8	4	37	2	73	2
Flannery, Birmingham*	0	0	.000	27.00	1	0	0	1	0	0	0.2	3	2	2	0	0	0	0	1	0
Fontenot, Nashville*	5	6	.455	2.17	14	14	4	0	1	0	91.1	85	34	22	6	3	17	1	69	1
Ford, Knoxville*	2	4	.333	5.67	26	4	0	8	0	1	60.1	69	46	38	4	2	34	1	51	1
Fore, Savannah	8	6	.571	3.36	18	18	9	0	1	0	128.2	109	61	48	16	5	44	2	67	5
Fregin, Orlando	1	4	.200	4.01	10	5	1	1	0	0	33.2	28	16	15	3	0	19	3	17	1
Fuson, Chattanooga	14	12	.538	3.44	30	30	15	0	1	0	222.1	232	112	85	18	5	72	2	151	6
Gardner, Columbus	1	2	.333	6.25	11	6	1	2	0	0	44.2	72	35	31	10	0	12	0	27	3
Garland, Nashville	1	3	.250	7.48	6	6	0	0	0	0	27.2	36	27	23	3	0	15	0	15	1
J. Gibson, Savannah*	0	2	.000	4.15	22	0	0	11	0	1	30.1	46	20	14	3	0	18	0	20	0
P. Gibson, Birmingham*	3	3	.500	2.68	44	0	0	33	0	12	77.1	60	25	23	6	3	39	2	71	2
Glasscock, Memphis*	3	3	.500	4.50	39	0	0	25	0	0	54	50	31	27	8	4	36	3	39	3
Guerra, Nashville*	0	0	.000	17.18	3	0	0	2	0	0	3.2	9	7	7	0	0	4	0	3	0
Gumpert, Birmingham	9	6	.600	2.17	42	0	0	40	0	14	70.2	56	20	17	3	0	23	4	52	1
Harsh, Jacksonville	4	2	.667	3.00	8	8	3	0	2	0	51	47	20	17	3	2	14	0	20	2
Harvey, Birmingham*	0	0	.000	0.00	1	0	0	1	0	0	2	2	0	0	0	0	0	0	1	0
Heathcock, Columbus	13	13	.500	4.76	29	29	10	0	1	0	191	216	119	101	26	8	56	4	108	6
Heinkel, Birmingham	4	5	.444	2.81	9	9	3	0	0	0	64	59	25	20	7	1	15	0	44	4
Hobbs, Orlando*	8	4	.667	3.97	51	4	2	20	0	4	131.1	122	70	58	19	1	63	2	87	5
Hodge, Orlando	6	9	.400	4.90	39	6	1	27	1	6	79	91	49	43	14	3	39	7	77	6
Hoke, Charlotte	3	2	.600	5.21	26	0	0	17	0	5	38	43	30	22	3	2	23	1	25	6
Hook, Charlotte	4	9	.308	4.60	20	20	4	0	1	0	109.2	130	75	56	11	2	54	2	49	16
Horn, Memphis	6	7	.462	3.80	20	17	2	1	0	0	94.2	107	53	40	9	0	40	0	45	8
Howard, Knoxville	13	13	.500	4.07	30	28	13	0	3	1	194.2	181	96	88	15	6	85	2	150	10
Huffman, Jacksonville	3	3	.500	3.99	8	8	1	0	0	0	49.2	47	24	22	6	2	22	0	41	2
Huismann, Jacksonville	4	4	.500	2.14	36	0	0	24	0	9	54.2	52	18	13	5	3	15	4	60	3
Jackson, Jacksonville*	7	2	.778	2.39	14	14	3	0	1	0	98	78	30	26	4	1	42	1	74	1
Jeffcoat, Chattanooga*	8	8	.500	2.88	18	18	6	0	2	0	128.1	122	49	41	3	4	51	1	107	7
Johnson, Savannah	2	1	.667	3.77	6	3	2	3	1	0	28.2	32	14	12	3	0	10	0	15	0
Jones, Savannah	8	13	.381	3.93	22	22	11	0	1	0	151	156	84	66	17	4	51	1	110	4
Kelly, Birmingham	8	3	.727	3.59	16	16	2	0	1	0	95.1	78	44	38	7	0	74	0	91	7
Konopa, Orlando*	9	4	.692	3.85	20	18	5	0	0	0	110	112	59	47	14	0	42	1	92	8
Kromy, Orlando*	5	9	.357	4.70	24	14	4	8	1	0	107.1	120	70	56	13	4	43	0	68	4
Kucharski, Charlotte	2	2	.500	2.70	4	4	2	0	0	0	30	20	10	9	1	0	6	0	21	0
Leatherwood, Columbus	0	1	.000	4.22	4	4	0	0	0	0	21.1	23	16	10	2	0	5	0	9	1
Ledduke, Columbus	2	3	.400	4.08	19	2	0	10	0	3	57.1	73	29	26	8	0	21	4	28	5
Lein, Nashville	7	10	.412	3.97	32	20	5	10	3	2	143	155	79	63	13	3	34	1	58	3
Lintz, Chattanooga	0	0	.000	5.06	4	0	0	3	0	0	5.1	9	3	3	0	0	5	0	1	0
Little, Orlando*	1	2	.333	1.33	9	0	0	6	0	3	20.1	15	6	3	0	0	7	1	29	3
Lukish, Knoxville	4	5	.444	2.71	54	0	0	51	0	20	66.1	62	29	20	2	3	26	6	47	6
MacDonald, Columbus	11	7	.611	3.23	24	20	10	3	3	1	153.1	160	70	55	12	5	38	2	81	3
MacPherson, Charlotte	0	0	.000	8.38	11	0	0	6	0	1	19.1	31	21	18	3	0	11	1	18	2
Maples, Charlotte	5	3	.625	5.78	14	13	3	0	0	0	62.1	58	43	40	8	6	62	1	46	7
Mathis, 2 Birm-10 Colum	6	2	.750	3.28	12	9	2	1	0	0	71.1	59	26	26	8	3	29	0	69	2

Pitcher—Club	W.	L.	Pct.	ERA	G.	GS.	CG.	GF.	ShO.	Sv.	IP	H.	R.	ER.	HR.	HB.	BB.	Int. BB.	SO.	WP.
May, Orlando	0	1	.000	6.95	8	5	0	2	0	1	33.2	46	28	26	4	1	14	0	18	2
McCullock, Charlotte	1	0	1.000	1.59	6	1	0	4	0	1	11.1	4	2	2	1	1	7	0	12	0
McLaughlin, Knoxville	8	7	.533	3.42	20	20	4	0	2	0	123.2	104	60	47	4	3	89	1	103	18
Meckes, Columbus	5	7	.417	3.90	52	0	0	42	0	12	92.1	88	46	40	5	5	38	4	86	7
Moncrief, Birmingham	4	8	.333	4.34	29	13	2	12	0	3	124.1	122	75	60	9	5	72	5	84	7
Morris, Columbus*	6	3	.667	3.06	14	12	3	1	0	0	82.1	81	39	28	5	2	26	0	53	2
Mulligan, Orlando*	8	3	.727	3.97	18	17	4	1	0	1	113.1	128	55	50	17	4	33	2	58	4
Munninghoff, Chattanooga	4	8	.333	3.88	26	15	3	2	1	0	123	130	62	53	8	6	51	0	31	6
Nail, Birmingham	9	6	.600	3.34	24	24	4	0	1	0	143	139	64	53	14	1	46	3	109	3
Narleski, Chattanooga	9	10	.474	3.34	50	5	0	36	0	7	137.1	119	64	51	9	3	39	5	98	4
Nastu, Charlotte*	0	0	.000	7.59	5	0	0	3	0	0	10.2	9	9	9	4	0	5	0	3	0
Norris, Charlotte	2	0	1.000	0.56	3	2	1	0	0	0	16	7	2	1	0	0	4	0	11	0
North, Savannah	1	1	.500	9.00	4	3	0	0	0	0	15	20	18	15	1	0	17	0	14	5
Nutter, Birmingham	0	1	.000	9.78	7	1	0	4	0	0	19.1	31	21	21	6	1	9	0	12	3
O'Keeffe, Knoxville*	0	0	.000	1.59	2	0	0	1	0	0	5.2	2	1	1	0	0	2	0	3	0
O'Neal, Birmingham	11	7	.611	3.41	27	27	8	0	1	0	185	169	83	70	21	1	71	2	105	5
Oelkers, Orlando*	1	0	1.000	1.44	3	3	0	0	0	0	25	16	6	4	1	0	9	0	14	0
Oliveras, Charlotte	10	9	.526	3.55	24	24	10	0	2	0	162.1	132	71	64	17	6	64	2	97	10
Owens, Chattanooga	3	12	.200	4.37	20	20	4	0	1	0	129.2	139	80	63	16	3	61	0	80	9
Palmer, Memphis	3	2	.600	3.51	9	9	1	0	1	0	51.1	38	21	20	5	2	33	1	44	2
Parrott, Jacksonville	2	0	1.000	1.57	6	3	0	1	0	0	23	12	5	4	1	3	12	1	17	1
Penate, Columbus	1	1	.500	4.29	13	0	0	7	0	0	35.2	38	23	17	4	3	11	2	17	2
Pensiero, Charlotte	0	1	.000	4.03	17	0	0	10	0	5	29	38	17	13	4	1	9	1	17	3
Perry, Columbus*	4	0	1.000	4.06	22	0	0	11	0	3	37.2	32	19	17	1	2	18	1	28	3
Pettaway, Savannah	3	4	.429	2.79	36	0	0	30	0	8	67.2	39	24	21	7	3	33	0	64	4
Pettibone, Orlando	0	3	.000	10.57	5	5	0	0	0	0	15.1	26	19	18	4	0	10	1	11	1
Pickert, Jacksonville*	3	3	.500	4.29	36	1	0	12	0	1	42	34	23	20	6	0	20	4	35	4
Potestio, Jacksonville	1	0	1.000	5.23	4	0	0	2	0	0	10.1	11	13	6	1	1	5	2	2	2
Puryear, Chattanooga	4	2	.667	5.32	21	12	0	5	0	0	71	62	55	42	5	3	70	0	59	14
Quealey, Birmingham	0	1	.000	3.72	4	0	0	2	0	0	9.2	10	6	4	0	1	7	0	9	0
Raine, Jacksonville	0	3	.000	4.76	6	4	0	1	0	0	22.2	23	14	12	3	1	22	1	16	2
Ramos, Memphis	4	0	1.000	3.93	5	4	2	1	0	0	34.1	45	16	15	3	0	5	0	16	0
Ray, Jacksonville	10	9	.526	3.49	28	24	7	2	4	0	170	148	76	66	13	1	90	2	84	7
Ricci, Nashville	6	4	.600	3.40	38	4	0	15	0	1	103.1	90	48	39	10	1	56	3	83	3
Roche, Chattanooga	0	3	.000	9.15	7	3	0	3	0	0	19.2	29	22	20	2	2	15	2	10	2
Romero, Chattanooga*	5	5	.500	3.94	20	11	2	2	0	0	89	87	49	39	5	5	55	0	75	13
Rowe, Charlotte	10	12	.455	4.15	24	24	14	0	1	0	173.1	182	101	80	12	7	69	3	93	5
Sadey, Charlotte	0	1	.000	2.00	3	0	0	2	0	0	9	3	3	2	0	2	4	1	0	1
Santana, Savannah	1	0	1.000	4.73	9	1	1	6	0	1	32.1	35	18	17	2	0	15	0	28	5
Sarmiento, Columbus	0	5	.000	7.53	13	3	0	8	0	2	28.2	37	27	24	6	2	16	1	22	1
Schuler, Memphis	10	5	.667	2.61	44	0	0	37	0	14	76	71	29	22	6	2	25	2	52	5
Schwarber, Chattanooga	7	11	.389	4.20	26	25	3	1	1	0	139.1	133	75	65	12	1	90	2	127	9
Scott, Nashville	0	2	.000	7.50	6	6	0	0	0	0	30	38	28	25	4	3	13	1	20	2
Sczesnak, Charlotte*	0	0	.000	7.36	3	0	0	0	0	0	3.2	8	3	3	0	0	4	0	2	1
Serum, Nashville	3	0	1.000	2.48	10	0	0	6	0	0	29	28	9	8	0	0	13	1	18	1
Shaw, Nashville	7	5	.583	2.80	20	20	5	0	1	0	128.2	80	53	40	18	7	79	0	114	9
Shields, Savannah	3	3	.500	5.52	19	0	0	13	0	4	44	46	34	27	3	6	30	1	24	4
Shimp, Memphis	4	6	.400	3.84	19	12	4	4	0	1	100.2	100	52	43	10	5	50	1	62	5
Silvas, Chattanooga	0	0	.000	0.00	1	0	0	0	0	0	2	2	2	0	0	0	0	0	0	0
Simond, Memphis*	0	0	.000	4.09	6	0	0	5	0	0	11	12	9	5	2	0	2	0	7	1
Slagle, Nashville	1	5	.167	6.08	9	7	0	2	0	0	40	43	32	27	11	3	17	1	25	2
K. Smith, Nashville	0	5	.000	4.47	23	0	0	14	0	1	48.1	65	29	24	8	1	19	8	38	2
Ma. Smith, Charlotte	6	8	.429	5.56	26	15	1	11	0	0	100.1	101	70	62	11	2	60	1	72	7
Mi. Smith, Savannah	1	0	1.000	0.00	4	0	0	4	0	0	4.1	1	0	0	0	3	3	0	5	2
Snyder, Columbus	5	5	.500	4.03	12	11	2	1	0	0	73.2	70	38	33	8	6	23	0	32	4
Sprowl, Columbus*	5	3	.625	2.79	22	8	1	10	0	3	71	58	26	22	4	5	48	0	55	3
St. Clair, Jacksonville	9	4	.692	1.53	51	0	0	48	0	14	70.2	48	17	12	4	4	23	1	73	2
Stemberger, Knoxville	7	0	1.000	3.31	43	1	0	22	0	5	73.1	74	36	27	6	1	31	1	33	0
Sykes, Nashville*	2	1	.667	2.25	23	0	0	11	0	3	36	33	9	9	3	0	4	1	14	0
Tabor, Birmingham	0	1	.000	54.00	1	1	0	0	0	0	1	6	6	6	2	0	2	0	0	0
Taylor, Memphis*	6	9	.400	6.24	23	23	1	0	0	0	102.1	101	77	71	12	2	93	0	94	10
Thompson, Chattanooga	7	6	.538	4.04	50	0	0	42	0	12	78	69	39	35	10	4	36	7	55	6
Twitty, Savannah*	0	0	.000	3.60	2	0	0	0	0	0	5	4	2	2	0	1	0	0	4	1
Vanderbush, Jacksonville	13	12	.520	3.45	28	28	8	0	2	0	193	162	88	74	9	9	100	2	161	13
Veselic, Orlando	8	3	.727	2.95	12	12	4	0	1	0	79.1	90	34	26	3	2	30	2	53	3
Walker, Knoxville*	8	6	.571	2.82	33	13	5	1	2	0	127.2	113	49	40	12	0	51	1	61	7
Waymire, Memphis	1	0	1.000	4.50	1	0	0	1	0	0	2	3	1	1	0	0	0	0	2	0
West, Savannah	6	8	.429	4.59	22	22	6	0	0	0	115.2	97	70	59	9	3	91	0	91	13
Westray, Memphis*	0	3	.000	6.75	5	0	0	0	0	0	10.2	13	14	8	0	2	18	0	10	0
Wever, Nashville	16	6	.727	2.78	29	29	10	0	6	0	214	176	75	66	9	6	80	2	191	7
Wihtol, Chattanooga	0	0	.000	4.50	10	0	0	5	0	2	22	28	14	11	2	1	10	1	12	1
L. Williams, Jacksonville	0	0	.000	5.71	5	0	0	1	0	1	17.1	17	12	11	6	1	7	0	9	1
Mark Williams, Birmingham	4	7	.364	4.61	22	12	2	4	1	0	113.1	108	70	58	18	4	33	0	49	2
Matt Williams, Knoxville	11	13	.458	4.28	28	28	10	0	1	0	193.1	173	106	92	13	5	107	1	157	31
R. Williams, Columbus	3	1	.750	1.08	10	3	0	5	0	1	33.1	30	6	4	1	0	9	1	14	2
Willis, Chattanooga	0	2	.000	11.45	3	3	0	0	0	0	11	23	14	14	2	1	5	0	6	0
Wilson, Knoxville	0	0	.000	6.75	4	0	0	3	0	0	6.2	5	7	5	0	3	6	0	7	1
Wirth, Birmingham	1	1	.500	1.38	2	2	2	0	1	0	13	7	2	2	0	2	0	0	8	0
Wyatt, Jacksonville*	0	0	.000	10.80	4	0	0	2	0	0	6.2	10	8	8	1	0	10	0	4	1
Yanus, Memphis	7	4	.636	3.57	44	1	0	24	0	6	116	132	55	46	9	1	33	9	74	4
Yuhas, Jacksonville	7	5	.583	2.14	14	14	5	0	1	0	105	90	40	25	10	0	30	0	94	1

BALKS—Cary, Fuson, Hook, West, 3 each; Bonine, Callahan, Christiansen, Dilks, Dixon, Elam, Lukish, Moncrief, Narleski, O'Neal, Owens, Snyder, Wever, 2 each; Abone, Arias, Behenna, Boyd, Broersma, Browning, Coatney, Dues, Everett, Fregin, P. Gibson, Gumpert, Heinkel, Hobbs, Hodge, Howard, Huismann, Jeffcoat, Jones, Leatherwood, MacPherson, Maples, Morris, Mulligan, Oliveras, Palmer, Puryear, Ramos, Ray, Rowe, Santana, Shaw, Shields, Shimp, Matt Williams, Yanus, 1 each.

COMBINATION SHUTOUTS—Mathis-Beecroft-Gibson, O'Neal-Gibson, Nail-Gibson, O'Neal-Gumpert, Kelly-Gibson, Kelly-Moncrief, Birmingham; M. Smith-Arias, Brown-Penserio, Charlotte; Williams-Meckes, Williams-Ledduke, Columbus; Jackson-St. Clair, Ferreira-Alvarez, Jacksonville; Baker-Lukish, Knoxville; Taylor-Yanus 2, Memphis; Arrington-Belanger, Orlando; Acker-Pettaway, Savannah.

NO-HIT GAME—West, Savannah, lost to Jacksonville, 1-0, May 21.

Texas League

CLASS AA

Leading Batter
RANDY READY
El Paso

League President
CARL SAWATSKI

Leading Pitcher
DOUGLAS SISK
Jackson

CHAMPIONSHIP WINNERS IN PREVIOUS YEARS

1888—Dallas .671	1925—Fort Worth .711	1958—Fort Worth .582
1889—Houston .551	Fort Worth y .653	Cor. Christi (3rd)§ .507
1890—Galveston .705	1926—Dallas .574	1959—Victoria .589
1892—Houston .741	1927—Wichita Falls .654	Austin (2nd)§ .548
Houston .613	1928—Houston* .679	1960—Rio Grande Valley .590
1895—Dallas .754	Wichita Falls .731	Tulsa (3rd) .528
Fort Worth* .750	1929—Dallas* .588	1961—Amarillo .643
1896—Fort Worth .757	Wichita Falls .620	San Antonio (3rd)§ .532
Houston* .679	1930—Wichita Falls .697	1962—El Paso .571
Galveston .548	Fort Worth* .632	Tulsa (2nd)§ .550
1897—San Antonio† .657	1931—Houston a .625	1963—San Antonio .564
Galveston† .717	Houston .734	Tulsa (3rd)§ .529
1898—League disbanded.	1932—Beaumont* .640	1964—San Antonio‡ .607
1899—Galveston .632	Dallas .727	1965—Tulsa .574
Galveston .762	1933—Houston .623	Albuquerque b .550
1900-01—Did not operate.	San Antonio (4th)§ .523	1966—Arkansas .579
1902—Corsicana .866	1934—Galveston‡ .579	1967—Albuquerque .557
Corsicana .682	1935—Oklahoma City‡ .590	1968—Arkansas .586
1903—Paris-Waco .615	1936—Dallas .604	El Paso b .562
Dallas* .648	Tulsa (3rd)§ .519	1969—Amarillo .593
1904—Corsicana* .615	1937—Oklahoma City .635	Memphis b .504
Fort Worth .800	Fort Worth (3rd)§ .535	1970—Albuquerque a .615
1905—Fort Worth .545	1938—Beaumont .635	Memphis .507
1906—Fort Worth .677	1939—Houston .606	1971—Did not operate as league— clubs
Cleburne x .609	Fort Worth (4th)§ .540	were members of Dixie Associa-
1907—Austin .629	1940—Houston‡ .652	tion.
1908—San Antonio .664	1941—Houston .673	1972—Alexandria .600
1909—Houston .601	Dallas (4th)§ .519	El Paso b .557
1910—Dallas† .586	1942—Beaumont .605	1973—San Antonio .590
Houston† .586	Shreveport (2nd)§ .576	Memphis b .558
1911—Austin .575	1943-44-45—Did not operate.	1974—Victoria b .581
1912—Houston .626	1946—Fort Worth .656	El Paso .555
1913—Houston .620	Dallas (2nd)§ .591	1975—Lafayette c .558
1914—Houston† .671	1947—Houston‡ .623	Midland c .604
Waco† .671	1948—Fort Worth‡ .601	1976—Amarillo b .600
1915—Waco .592	1949—Fort Worth .649	Shreveport .515
1916—Waco .587	Tulsa (2nd)§ .584	1977—El Paso .600
1917—Dallas .600	1950—Beaumont .595	Arkansas d .485
1918—Dallas .584	San Antonio (4th)§ .513	1978—El Paso d .593
1919—Shreveport* .677	1951—Houston‡ .619	Jackson .567
Fort Worth .651	1952—Dallas .571	1979—Arkansas d .571
1920—Fort Worth .703	Shreveport (3rd)§ .522	Midland .563
Fort Worth .750	1953—Dallas‡ .571	1980—Arkansas d .596
1921—Fort Worth .691	1954—Shreveport .559	San Antonio .544
Fort Worth .662	Houston (2nd)§ .553	1981—San Antonio .571
1922—Fort Worth .694	1955—Dallas .581	Jackson d .507
Fort Worth .711	Shreveport (3rd)§ .540	
1923—Fort Worth .632	1956—Houston‡ .623	
1924—Fort Worth .689	1957—Dallas .662	
Houston .763	Houston (2nd)§ .630	

*Won split-season playoff. †No playoff for title. ‡Finished first and won four-club playoff. §Won four-club playoff. xTitle to Cleburne by default. yTied with Dallas in second half and won playoff for championship. zFort Worth disbanded. aTied with Beaumont at end of first half and won title in best-of-five series played as part of second half schedule. bLeague divided into Eastern, Western divisions; won two-team playoff. cLeague divided into Eastern, Western divisions; declared co-champions when playoffs were not completed. dLeague divided into Eastern and Western divisions and played split-season; won playoffs. **NOTE**—Championship awarded to winner of four-team playoff, 1933-51; first-place team and playoff winner co-champions, 1952-64.

STANDING OF CLUBS AT CLOSE OF FIRST HALF, JUNE 19

EASTERN DIVISION

Club	W.	L.	T.	Pct.	G.B.
Jackson (Mets)	39	29	1	.574	....
Shreveport (Giants)	33	34	0	.493	5½
Arkansas (Cardinals)	30	37	0	.448	8½
Tulsa (Rangers)	24	43	0	.358	14½

WESTERN DIVISION

Club	W.	L.	T.	Pct.	G.B.
El Paso (Brewers)	42	23	0	.646	....
San Antonio (Dodgers)	39	29	2	.574	4½
Midland (Cubs)	30	35	0	.462	12
Amarillo (Padres)	30	37	1	.448	13

STANDING OF CLUBS AT CLOSE OF SECOND HALF, SEPTEMBER 1

EASTERN DIVISION

Club	W.	L.	T.	Pct.	G.B.
Tulsa (Rangers)	46	23	0	.667	....
Arkansas (Cardinals)	38	31	0	.551	8
Jackson (Mets)	29	36	0	.446	15
Shreveport (Giants)	29	39	1	.426	16½

WESTERN DIVISION

Club	W.	L.	T.	Pct.	G.B.
Midland (Cubs)	37	31	1	.544	....
El Paso (Brewers)	34	37	0	.479	4½
Amarillo (Padres)	31	37	0	.456	6
San Antonio (Dodgers)	29	39	0	.426	8

COMPOSITE STANDING OF CLUBS AT CLOSE OF SEASON, SEPTEMBER 1

EASTERN DIVISION

Club	Tul.	Jack.	Ark.	Shrv.	Amar.	EIP.	Mid.	S.A.	W.	L.	T.	Pct.	G.B.
Tulsa (Rangers)	.....	11	18	21	6	3	4	7	70	66	0	.515	....
Jackson (Mets)	21	.....	12	17	5	6	3	4	68	65	1	.511	½
Arkansas (Cardinals)	14	20	.....	15	6	1	5	7	68	68	0	.500	2
Shreveport (Giants)	11	15	17	.....	4	3	7	5	62	73	1	.459	7½

WESTERN DIVISION

Club	EIP.	Mid.	S.A.	Amar.	Ark.	Jack.	Shrv.	Tul.	W.	L.	T.	Pct.	G.B.
El Paso (Brewers)	.....	17	14	18	9	4	7	7	76	60	0	.559	....
Midland (Cubs)	15	.....	14	20	5	4	6	7	67	66	0	.504	7½
San Antonio (Dodgers)	18	18	.....	15	3	6	5	3	68	68	2	.500	8
Amarillo (Padres)	14	12	17	.....	4	5	5	4	61	74	1	.452	14½

Arkansas club represented Little Rock, Ark.

Major league affiliations in parentheses.

Playoffs—Tulsa defeated Jackson, two games to one; El Paso defeated Midland, two games to none; and Tulsa defeated El Paso, three games to none, to win league championship.

Regular-Season Attendance—Amarillo, 51,812; Arkansas, 213,566; El Paso, 326,084; Jackson, 103,535; Midland, 114,045; San Antonio, 138,024; Shreveport, 46,920; Tulsa, 128,668. Total, 1,122,654. Playoffs, 17,235. All-Star Game, 4,821.

Managers: Amarillo, Glenn Ezell; Arkansas, Gaylen Pitts and Nick Leyva; El Paso, Tony Muser; Jackson, Gene Dusan; Midland, Brian Murphy; San Antonio, Don (Ducky) LeJohn; Shreveport, Jack Mull; Tulsa, Tom Burgess.

All-Star Team: 1B—Torve, Shreveport; 2B—Koenigfeld, El Paso; 3B—Ready, El Paso; SS—Davidsmeier, El Paso; OF—Strawberry, Jackson; Greer, Amarillo; Dunbar, Tulsa; C-Foley, El Paso, and Bilardello, San Antonio; DH—Carter, Midland; P—Couchee, Amarillo; Bittiger, Jackson; Rennicke, San Antonio; Voigt, San Antonio; Hagen, Arkansas; Brecht, Shreveport; Mengwasser, Tulsa; Manager—Don (Ducky) LeJohn, San Antonio.

(Compiled by Ed Williams, League Statistician, Shawnee, Okla.)

CLUB BATTING

Club	Pct.	G.	AB.	R.	OR.	H.	TB.	2B.	3B.	HR.	RBI.	GW.	SH.	SF.	HP.	BB.	Int. BB.	SO.	SB.	CS.	LOB.
El Paso	.303	136	4684	928	832	1420	2271	292	38	161	861	66	43	56	44	572	27	782	74	43	1009
Midland	.296	136	4455	739	730	1317	2030	191	51	140	667	58	30	37	22	518	14	693	126	52	990
Amarillo	.291	136	4662	814	861	1357	2035	205	43	129	735	55	33	57	55	533	14	789	77	53	1068
San Antonio	.287	138	4651	689	741	1335	2030	225	37	132	631	64	33	30	28	432	31	507	98	52	956
Tulsa	.263	136	4391	633	666	1153	1746	217	44	96	574	60	63	28	39	530	34	738	93	49	958
Arkansas	.258	136	4242	637	557	1095	1653	203	50	85	573	64	34	33	38	500	24	725	113	67	865
Shreveport	.254	136	4220	591	638	1073	1611	217	27	89	532	53	32	39	28	522	32	774	84	48	919
Jackson	.252	134	4279	577	583	1078	1614	188	30	96	522	60	32	39	41	487	33	828	182	98	873

INDIVIDUAL BATTING

(Leading Qualifiers for Batting Championship—367 or More Plate Appearances)

*Bats lefthanded.   †Switch-hitter.

Player and Club	Pct.	G.	AB.	R.	H.	TB.	2B.	3B.	HR.	RBI.	GW.	SH.	SF.	HP.	BB.	Int. BB.	SO.	SB.	CS.
Ready, Randy, El Paso	.375	132	475	122	178	281	33	5	20	99	7	3	7	4	92	3	48	13	4
Davis, Gerald, Amarillo	.353	95	365	78	129	191	18	1	14	67	5	1	3	8	62	0	54	7	4
Michael, Steven, El Paso*	.345	121	435	92	150	246	35	2	19	89	4	2	6	2	63	4	81	9	5
Martinez, Carmelo, Midland	.334	131	467	100	156	280	35	4	27	93	12	0	6	1	85	2	78	1	5
Ronk, Jeffrey, Amarillo	.326	132	488	87	159	225	26	5	10	77	7	3	6	8	57	3	41	10	7
Dunbar, Thomas, Tulsa*	.323	131	461	93	149	249	44	4	16	85	10	0	3	0	78	2	96	15	7
James, Dion, El Paso*	.322	106	422	103	136	194	25	3	9	72	8	1	7	1	62	2	46	16	4
Carter, Joseph, Midland	.319	110	427	84	136	249	22	8	25	98	10	3	7	4	26	1	51	15	4
Steels, James, Amarillo*	.318	86	371	61	118	168	16	8	6	57	4	2	5	4	23	2	49	8	6
Owen, Dave, Midland†	.316	125	427	59	135	177	12	9	4	40	1	4	4	1	56	1	71	15	4

Departmental Leaders: G—L. Miller, 138; AB—L. Miller, 570; R—Ready, 122; H—Ready, 178; TB—Ready, 281; 2B—Dunbar, 44; 3B—Van Slyke, 11; HR—Strawberry, 34; RBI—Foley, 106; GWRBI—Adduci, 14; SH—Koenigsfeld, Wilkerson, 11; SF—Cummings, Torve, 9; HP—M. Johnston, R. Reynolds, 10; BB—Strawberry, 100; IBB—Torve, 11; SO—Deer, 177; SB—Cotto, 52; CS—Strawberry, 22.

(All Players—Listed Alphabetically)

Player and Club	Pct.	G.	AB.	R.	H.	TB.	2B.	3B.	HR.	RBI.	GW.	SH.	SF.	HP.	BB.	Int. BB.	SO.	SB.	CS.
Adduci, James, Arkansas*	.298	121	392	64	117	221	28	5	22	92	14	2	4	2	59	3	109	3	2
Aguayo, Carmelo, Tulsa	.284	32	109	17	31	45	6	1	2	24	2	1	1	1	7	1	9	2	0
Amelung, Edward, San Antonio*	.302	135	529	96	160	271	27	6	24	91	11	6	4	0	27	5	83	10	5
Anicich, Michael, Jackson	.251	96	327	54	82	163	15	0	22	72	8	1	4	4	70	2	75	1	3
Ayer, Jonathan, Arkansas	.262	125	442	68	116	165	23	1	8	55	2	5	7	5	41	4	75	8	10
Baker, Gregory, Shreveport	.246	120	402	50	99	149	18	4	8	50	3	1	3	1	40	1	81	3	5
Ball, Robert, Tulsa	.272	46	151	18	41	59	12	3	0	21	1	1	0	1	20	0	28	7	4
Beane, William, Jackson†	.211	126	418	39	88	124	13	4	5	36	3	2	1	2	27	3	136	12	12

Player and Club	Pct.	G.	AB.	R.	H.	TB.	2B.	3B.	HR.	RBI.	GW.	SH.	SF.	HP.	BB.	Int. BB.	SO.	SB.	CS.
Beltre, Sergio, Jackson	.444	6	18	5	8	12	2	1	0	2	0	0	0	1	4	0	3	2	0
Benza, Brett, Tulsa	.226	60	186	17	42	56	5	3	1	21	2	9	2	2	16	0	29	6	5
Beyers, Tom, San Antonio°	.306	122	474	67	145	216	23	9	10	64	6	1	7	1	31	4	31	3	4
Bilardello, Dann, San Antonio	.285	103	347	49	99	168	14	2	17	48	2	1	3	2	27	3	40	2	2
Blocker, Terry, Jackson°	.260	118	438	69	114	153	20	2	5	38	6	5	4	3	40	1	80	40	19
Bream, Sidney, San Antonio°	.320	70	259	43	83	125	18	0	8	50	5	1	2	1	34	3	41	1	2
Brewer, Anthony, San Antonio	.292	135	496	88	145	256	35	5	22	88	8	1	3	2	64	2	61	5	6
Brown, Chris, Shreveport	.265	58	185	26	49	66	14	0	1	21	0	0	1	0	30	1	39	9	2
Brunson, Eddie, El Paso	.276	9	29	5	8	14	3	0	1	7	0	0	0	0	2	0	5	0	0
Buechele, Steven, Tulsa	.296	62	213	21	63	94	12	2	5	33	4	1	2	7	18	2	42	2	2
Carter, Joseph, Midland	.319	110	427	84	136	249	22	8	25	98	10	3	7	4	26	1	51	15	4
Casey, Patrick, Amarillo	.275	46	167	28	46	76	10	1	6	27	2	0	1	2	21	1	29	3	1
Chaney, Bruce, Midland	.237	85	232	45	55	97	12	0	10	37	5	3	0	0	41	0	47	5	1
Chavez, Christopher, San Antonio†	.143	7	14	1	2	2	0	0	0	0	0	0	0	0	5	0	4	0	0
Clark, Randall, Midland	.000	23	0	1	0	0	0	0	0	0	0	0	0	0	0	0	0	0	0
Coffman, James, Amarillo	.000	14	2	1	0	0	0	0	0	0	0	0	0	0	1	0	0	0	0
Colletti, Manuel, Arkansas†	.230	77	196	31	45	46	1	0	0	14	2	6	2	0	46	0	22	3	1
Connally, Fritzie, Midland	.290	123	428	75	124	225	23	3	24	91	6	0	4	9	66	4	50	0	1
Corey, Mark, El Paso	.345	36	139	19	48	80	13	2	5	35	0	0	2	2	6	0	27	0	3
Cotto, Henry, Midland	.307	130	524	103	161	186	12	5	1	36	2	6	1	1	59	2	79	52	16
Cowger, Tracy, Tulsa	.258	67	233	36	60	89	13	2	4	22	0	3	2	1	13	1	39	2	3
Cox, Larry, Midland	.143	13	49	1	7	7	0	0	0	3	1	0	1	0	1	0	8	3	0
Cummings, Robert, Shreveport	.261	112	364	62	95	159	25	3	11	62	9	2	9	1	62	0	73	2	2
Davidsmeier, David, El Paso	.272	136	489	85	133	198	27	4	10	69	2	7	6	3	57	3	73	4	1
Davis, Gerald, Amarillo	.353	95	365	78	129	191	18	1	14	67	5	1	3	8	62	0	54	7	4
Deer, Robert, Shreveport	.207	128	410	58	85	192	26	0	27	73	6	0	2	9	53	4	177	6	2
Diaz, Michael, Midland	.289	121	443	54	128	225	23	4	22	75	5	0	3	4	32	2	85	8	7
Dillard, Ronald, Tulsa	.217	9	23	1	5	5	0	0	0	0	0	1	0	0	4	0	7	0	0
Duff, David, Jackson	.231	69	221	19	51	71	11	0	3	25	3	1	2	0	21	0	39	2	2
Dunbar, Thomas, Tulsa°	.323	131	461	93	149	249	44	4	16	85	12	0	3	0	78	2	96	15	7
Fierro, Javier, Midland	.291	86	309	38	90	127	4	3	9	42	2	3	3	1	31	1	32	4	0
Foley, William, El Paso	.308	108	415	76	128	223	26	0	23	106	13	1	6	4	27	1	100	0	1
Gauntlett, Gordon, San Antonio	.305	49	154	15	47	60	10	0	1	22	2	2	1	4	7	0	13	0	1
Gausepohl, Daniel, Amarillo	.229	16	48	6	11	13	2	0	0	3	0	2	0	0	12	0	14	0	1
Gibbons, John, Jackson	.278	6	18	1	5	7	0	1	0	3	1	2	0	0	1	1	5	0	0
Gillaspie, Mark, Amarillo†	.250	29	112	21	28	49	9	0	4	18	0	0	1	2	7	2	19	0	1
Gomez, Randall, Shreveport	.263	84	274	33	72	95	15	1	2	25	3	2	0	1	19	1	29	0	1
Gonzalez, Jose, Arkansas†	.247	123	465	73	115	146	17	7	0	41	4	0	3	1	40	2	65	16	9
Gonzalez, Luis, Tulsa	.212	21	66	7	14	16	2	0	0	4	0	1	0	0	11	0	16	0	0
Gooch, Ronald, Tulsa	.149	13	47	2	7	9	2	0	0	2	0	0	1	0	6	0	5	1	1
Greer, Brian, Amarillo	.275	94	334	69	92	194	17	2	27	80	6	2	2	4	74	0	145	7	5
Guin, Greg, Arkansas°	.249	116	366	43	91	142	22	4	7	63	5	4	4	7	27	2	49	1	3
Gutierrez, Julian, Arkansas	.224	26	85	11	19	24	3	1	0	7	0	0	0	0	7	0	18	3	4
Hagen, Kevin, Arkansas	.000	28	0	1	0	0	0	0	0	0	0	0	0	0	0	0	0	0	0
Hansen, Jon, El Paso	.263	99	357	63	94	172	18	3	18	69	3	3	4	3	28	1	75	5	7
Heimach, William, Shreveport	.224	54	156	22	35	40	3	1	0	12	2	5	3	1	18	0	17	2	2
Hernandez, Leonardo, San Antonio	.320	19	75	8	24	39	4	1	3	14	1	2	0	0	3	2	3	0	1
Hinshaw, George, Amarillo	.297	129	519	90	154	238	24	3	18	89	6	4	6	4	37	1	93	9	6
Hyman, Donald, Midland	.278	45	133	16	37	51	8	0	2	19	2	1	3	0	13	0	32	1	2
Jamerson, Daniel, Shreveport°	.200	37	5	0	1	1	0	0	0	0	0	0	0	0	0	0	1	0	0
James, Dion, El Paso°	.322	106	422	103	136	194	25	3	9	72	8	1	7	1	62	2	46	16	4
Jirschele, Michael, Tulsa	.226	95	340	52	77	112	15	4	4	23	1	6	1	7	42	0	66	9	1
Johnston, Mark, El Paso°	.237	81	253	41	60	93	17	2	4	40	6	5	3	10	29	1	48	3	3
Kaczmarski, Randy, Amarillo	.264	80	292	37	77	113	14	2	6	37	4	6	4	3	30	0	36	0	2
Kastelic, Bruce, Jackson°	.227	69	198	23	45	62	9	4	0	17	1	3	2	1	21	2	44	4	7
Kelley, Michael, Midland°	.309	117	459	80	142	183	21	7	2	57	5	5	4	0	42	0	23	11	5
Kingsolver, Kurtis, El Paso	.256	104	348	43	89	146	16	1	13	47	4	5	0	5	35	0	81	6	2
Koenigsfeld, Ronald, El Paso	.298	128	477	98	142	193	23	5	6	57	4	11	4	6	61	2	61	3	1
Kornacher, Dean, Shreveport	.218	21	55	7	12	14	2	0	0	6	0	3	2	1	8	0	8	0	0
Kutcher, Randy, Shreveport	.247	116	397	56	98	129	18	2	3	31	2	5	5	1	25	1	67	30	12
Lezcano, Carlos, Midland	.278	125	453	70	126	197	16	8	13	64	6	5	0	1	47	1	108	10	7
Long, Dennis, Tulsa	.000	43	1	0	0	0	0	0	0	0	0	0	0	0	0	0	1	0	0
Lulay, Douglas, Amarillo	.460	13	50	14	23	29	1	1	1	8	0	0	0	4	0	0	4	1	0
Lyons, William, Arkansas	.304	26	79	18	24	35	3	1	2	10	0	1	0	1	14	0	11	7	1
Madison, Scott, San Antonio†	.235	88	294	39	69	105	11	2	7	35	5	1	1	0	54	4	27	4	0
Martin, Jared, Midland°	.200	5	20	2	4	4	0	0	0	0	0	0	0	0	1	0	3	0	0
Martin, Joseph, Amarillo°	.271	110	373	67	101	152	14	2	11	63	3	2	1	6	62	5	56	2	2
Martinez, Carmelo, Midland	.334	131	467	100	156	280	35	4	27	93	12	0	6	1	85	2	78	1	5
Maxwell, James, Tulsa°	.161	18	62	8	10	12	2	0	0	0	0	0	0	1	12	0	15	1	0
Mazzilli, Donald, Shreveport°	.249	59	197	21	49	72	11	0	4	23	1	0	1	1	21	1	34	1	1
McMullen, Ricky, Jackson	.291	106	388	51	113	139	21	1	1	40	8	1	3	5	43	1	31	31	9
McReynolds, Kevin, Amarillo	.352	40	162	30	57	86	8	3	5	39	3	0	1	0	12	1	34	4	1
Mejia, Oscar, Tulsa	.222	57	203	21	45	62	8	3	1	15	1	4	1	3	15	0	14	0	5
Michael, Steven, El Paso°	.345	121	435	92	150	246	35	2	19	89	4	2	6	2	63	5	81	9	5
Miller, Lemmie, San Antonio	.279	138	570	88	159	210	21	3	8	51	9	5	2	2	56	2	59	45	19
Moore, Donald, Arkansas†	.249	107	349	56	87	153	18	3	14	63	8	2	3	3	59	1	64	2	1
Moore, Steven, Tulsa†	.271	125	479	69	130	175	24	3	5	48	5	7	1	2	59	6	66	24	11
Morales, Julio, Midland	.400	7	25	3	10	13	3	0	0	7	1	0	0	0	3	0	4	0	0
Murphy, Daniel, Tulsa°	.241	123	435	51	105	171	13	7	13	68	8	5	3	3	40	8	70	4	3
Neufang, Gerald, Tulsa	.237	49	139	19	33	45	6	0	2	16	3	6	3	1	26	2	18	0	0
Nieto, Thomas, Arkansas	.242	96	298	33	72	104	11	3	5	31	4	1	1	6	29	0	82	1	3
Ojeda, Luis, Arkansas	.269	96	335	41	90	127	17	4	4	47	3	2	3	2	22	2	39	6	4
Owen, Dave, Midland†	.316	125	427	59	135	177	12	9	4	40	1	4	4	1	56	1	71	15	4
Pagel, David, Midland°	.286	3	7	3	2	5	0	0	1	2	0	0	0	0	2	0	2	0	0
Parent, Mark, Amarillo	.191	26	89	12	17	25	3	1	1	13	0	0	0	1	11	1	13	2	0
Payne, James, Midland	.098	18	51	4	5	5	0	0	0	3	0	0	0	0	12	0	17	1	0
Pedrique, Alfredo, Jackson	.219	121	392	38	86	109	13	2	2	36	4	5	6		22	1	41	9	2
Perdue, Doran, Shreveport°	.279	113	384	54	107	130	19	2	0	35	2	6	2	2	58	5	64	13	8
Perlman, Jonathan, Midland°	.000	27	0	1	0	0	0	0	0	0	0	0	0	0	0	0	0	0	0
Peyton, Eric, El Paso°	.284	129	524	104	149	246	34	6	17	91	7	4	6	3	63	6	74	14	9
Poe, Richard, Jackson°	.295	107	366	46	108	157	24	2	7	66	8	2	6	0	30	7	50	3	4
Purpura, Daniel, Amarillo	.272	109	390	71	106	124	7	4	1	33	0	3	0	2	75	0	76	10	7

Player and Club	Pct.	G.	AB.	R.	H.	TB.	2B.	3B.	HR.	RBI.	GW.	SH.	SF.	HP.	BB.	Int. BB.	SO.	SB.	CS.
Quinones, Luis, Amarillo	.292	95	411	69	120	186	19	7	11	60	9	4	2	0	39	2	53	8	3
Ransom, Jeffrey, Shreveport†	.235	76	238	33	56	97	7	2	10	36	5	0	1	2	38	1	58	4	0
Ready, Randy, El Paso	.375	132	475	122	178	281	33	5	20	99	7	3	7	4	92	3	48	13	4
Reynolds, Larry, Arkansas	.241	105	316	46	76	95	15	2	0	19	1	8	0	2	47	0	27	16	13
Reynolds, R. J., San Antonio	.167	3	12	3	2	5	0	0	1	2	0	0	0	0	1	0	1	2	0
Reynolds, Ronn, Jackson	.255	123	431	50	110	155	13	1	10	42	4	4	3	10	50	6	66	9	5
Rittweger, William, Jackson	.240	38	121	14	29	35	3	0	1	3	1	2	0	1	18	0	23	2	2
Rivera, German, San Antonio	.289	136	474	63	137	207	17	4	15	60	4	3	4	4	37	2	61	8	2
Ronk, Jeffrey, Amarillo	.326	132	488	87	159	225	26	5	10	77	7	3	6	8	57	3	41	10	7
Rubel, Michael, Tulsa	.271	63	221	43	60	114	11	2	13	43	7	0	0	1	41	3	70	0	0
Salas, Mark, Arkansas°	.224	27	76	4	17	21	4	0	0	5	0	0	0	3	1	5	1	0	
Sanchez, Jose, Arkansas	.250	7	12	2	3	3	0	0	0	1	0	0	0	0	0	0	2	0	0
Sanford, Edmund, Arkansas	.000	14	2	0	0	0	0	0	0	0	0	0	0	0	0	0	1	0	0
Sayler, Barry, Arkansas	.289	67	201	28	58	95	13	6	4	28	4	1	0	6	18	2	36	1	1
Scherger, Joseph, Amarillo	.218	62	188	32	41	69	8	1	6	31	2	1	1	5	34	3	46	4	1
Schultz, Greg, San Antonio	.246	40	118	16	29	51	8	1	4	11	2	2	0	2	11	0	11	1	1
Schuster, Mark, El Paso°	.331	73	281	70	93	166	20	4	15	71	6	1	5	1	44	3	59	1	2
Scott, Donald, Tulsa†	.283	108	367	55	104	165	19	3	12	61	5	3	1	1	57	5	71	1	0
Sheehy, Mark, San Antonio	.275	111	444	51	122	145	13	2	2	42	3	4	1	5	26	3	34	9	6
Smith, Gregory, San Antonio	.221	44	136	16	30	51	4	1	5	16	3	1	1	7	0	17	2	2	
Steels, James, Amarillo°	.318	86	371	61	118	168	16	8	6	57	4	2	5	4	23	2	49	8	6
Stevenson, John, 35 Ama-11 Shr	.267	46	165	25	44	53	7	1	0	13	0	1	1	3	19	0	19	1	4
Stockstill, David, Tulsa°	.288	90	323	65	93	160	16	3	15	68	7	0	7	2	45	3	29	5	4
Strawberry, Darryl, Jackson	.283	129	435	93	123	262	19	9	34	97	8	1	6	6	100	6	145	45	22
Tabor, Gregory, Tulsa	.197	23	66	6	13	19	1	1	1	6	0	4	0	0	5	0	16	2	0
Tarver, LaSchelle, Jackson°	.203	24	74	15	15	17	2	0	0	8	0	1	1	1	12	1	12	12	3
Taveras, Alejandro, San Antonio	.328	73	250	45	82	119	20	1	5	37	3	3	1	4	41	1	20	6	1
Thomas, Jimmy, Amarillo	.238	54	172	19	41	54	5	1	2	22	4	2	2	4	16	0	41	1	2
Thompson, Michael, Midland°	.000	37	2	0	0	0	0	0	0	0	0	0	0	0	1	0	1	0	0
Thurberg, Thomas, Arkansas	1.000	31	1	0	1	1	0	0	0	1	1	0	0	0	0	0	0	0	0
Toener, Sean, Shreveport	.296	52	169	26	50	74	14	2	2	24	3	3	1	2	21	0	33	1	2
Torve, Kelvin, Shreveport°	.305	127	449	66	137	225	29	7	15	84	9	3	9	2	43	11	47	9	1
Van Slyke, Andrew, Arkansas°	.279	123	416	83	116	199	13	11	16	70	12	1	3	1	61	7	85	37	8
Voigt, Paul, San Antonio	.000	28	5	1	0	0	0	0	0	0	0	0	0	0	1	0	1	0	0
Wabeke, Douglas, Shreveport	.274	104	361	55	99	127	12	2	4	35	5	1	0	3	55	3	28	2	6
Whiting, Don, El Paso°	.333	12	39	7	13	20	2	1	1	9	0	0	0	3	0	4	0	1	
Wickensheimer, Clint, 23 SA-10 EIP	.000	33	1	0	0	0	0	0	0	0	0	1	0	0	0	0	0	0	0
Wiggins, David, Shreveport°	.111	7	18	5	2	8	0	0	2	4	0	0	0	1	9	1	3	1	0
Wilkerson, Curtis, Tulsa†	.267	72	266	32	71	89	6	3	2	14	2	11	0	6	15	1	31	12	3
Wojcik, James, Shreveport°	.167	36	120	14	20	23	1	1	0	7	2	1	0	0	19	2	12	1	4
Wolters, Michael, Arkansas	.224	63	210	35	47	75	15	3	2	26	2	1	4	2	27	0	36	8	7
Woodward, James, Jackson	.233	122	434	54	101	148	23	3	6	37	5	5	1	2	28	2	78	10	8

The following pitchers, listed alphabetically by club, with games in parentheses, had no plate appearances, primarily through use of designated hitters:

AMARILLO—Biko, Thomas (49); Brown, Lawrence (37); Bryant, Neil (27); Cacciatore, Paul (8); Couchee, Michael (51); Hardwick, Willie (28); Kain, Martin (25); Long, William (27); Macias, Robert (10); Oberbruner, James (3); Oliver, Bruce (16); Plesac, Joseph (5); Smith, Wesley (1); Stone, Steven (15); White, John (33).

ARKANSAS—Adams, John (14); Arigoni, Scott (13); Horton, Ricky (16); Johnson, Jerry (16); Keener, Jeffrey (24); Kinnunen, Michael (18); Neely, Alex (14); Perry, Gerald (34); Pimental, Rafael (30); Riggins, Mark (27); Schultz, Charles (7); Seiple, Dennis (2); Winfield, Steven (8).

EL PASO—Beene, Andrew (16); Burns, Daniel (25); Cocanower, James (9); Gallo, Raymond (10); Gibson, Robert (47); Gonzalez, Arturo (6); Grier, David (34); Jenkins, Jerry (41); Koontz, James (24); Manderfield, Steven (3); Parrott, Stephen (17); Schroeck, Robert (31); Swift, Weldon (9); Tatsuno, Derek (39); Uhey, Jackie (20); Vasquez, Jesse (12).

JACKSON—Bittiger, Jeffrey (25); Bullinger, Matthews (45); Davis, Ted (23); Dye, Scott (16); Ibarguen, Stephen (18); Johnston, Jody (7); Kolbe, Brian (23); Miller, Thomas (4); Myles, Rick (10); Rodriguez, Jose (37); Semprini, John (43); Sisk, Douglas (44); Tibbs, Jay (1); Violette, John (20).

MIDLAND—Blyth, Robert (24); Gerlach, James (15); Gil, Carlos (24); King, Michael (25); Millner, Timothy (30); Moore, Edmund (5); Pryce, Kenneth (26); Smith, Thomas (24); Spino, Thomas (4); Welenc, Douglas (25).

SAN ANTONIO—Dente, Frank (5); Franco, John (17); Hammond, Shayne (4); Klawitter, Thomas (28); Madden, Morris (4); Malden, Christopher (21); McDonald, Russell (21); Nobles, James (28); Perry, Steven (19); Rennicke, Dean (24); Wise, Brett (42).

SHREVEPORT—Brecht, Michael (34); Chue, Jose (3); Cornell, Jeffrey (21); Dunn, James (23); Garrelts, Scott (27); Gendron, Robert (14); Hinrichs, Phillip (9); Lusted, Charles (14); McKenna, Kevin (12); Pisel, Ronald (12); Ronan, Kernan (16); Williams, Frank (27); Williams, Larry (19).

TULSA—Babcock, Robert (9); Gideon, James (25); Henke, Thomas (52); Henry, Timothy (30); Lachowicz, Allen (25); Lazorko, Jack (15); Leach, Martin (27); Mason, Michael (26); McEnaney, William (5); McLane, Larry (6); Mengwasser, Bradley (37); Mercer, Mark (5); Richards, Kevin (29); Smith, Daryl (9).

GRAND SLAM HOME RUNS—Greer, Lezcano, Poe, 3 each; Foley, Hansen, Hinshaw, Torve, 2 each; Aguayo, Baker, Blocker, Brewer, Bream, Chaney, Deer, Diaz, Dunbar, Fierro, Guin, Hernandez, James, Michael, D. Moore, S. Moore, Murphy, Schuster, Scott, Steels, Stockstill, VanSlyke, Woodward, 1 each.

AWARDED FIRST BASE ON CATCHER'S INTERFERENCE—Chaney 8 (Kingsolver 3, Bilardello, Gomez, Madison, Martin, Reynolds); Casey 2 (Gauntlett, Kingsolver); Schuster 2 (Bilardello, Martin); VanSlyke 2 (D. Scott 2); Guin (Gomez); Lezcano (D. Scott); Poe (D. Scott); Quinones (Sayler); Ransom (Reynolds); Sheehy (Kingsolver), 1 each.

CLUB FIELDING

Club	Pct.	G.	PO.	A.	E.	DP.	PB.	Club	Pct.	G.	PO.	A.	E.	DP.	PB.
Jackson	.971	134	3427	1480	149	130	9	Shreveport	.965	136	3325	1359	165	104	25
Arkansas	.970	136	3344	1444	147	140	15	El Paso	.965	136	3483	1575	185	137	24
Midland	.967	134	3356	1383	162	128	15	Amarillo	.957	136	3484	1498	222	142	12
Tulsa	.965	136	3468	1530	176	131	26	San Antonio	.957	138	3519	1476	225	127	23

Triple Play—Tulsa.

INDIVIDUAL FIELDING
FIRST BASEMEN

°Throws lefthanded.

Player and Club	Pct.	G.	PO.	A.	E.	DP.	Player and Club	Pct.	G.	PO.	A.	E.	DP.
Anicich, Jackson	.989	52	488	40	6	42	Casey, Amarillo	.986	37	330	33	5	32
Beyers, San Antonio°	.976	27	224	20	6	22	Connally, Midland	1.000	8	54	5	0	6
Bream, San Antonio°	.982	70	621	40	12	60	Deer, Shreveport	1.000	1	1	0	0	0

FIRST BASEMEN—Continued

Player and Club	Pct.	G.	PO.	A.	E.	DP.
Duff, Jackson	.988	10	74	11	1	6
Gauntlett, San Antonio	1.000	1	5	1	0	0
L. Gonzalez, Tulsa*	.988	16	152	11	2	20
GUIN, Arkansas*	.993	101	821	72	6	82
Hernandez, San Antonio	1.000	2	17	0	0	2
Kastelic, Jackson	1.000	1	2	0	0	0
Lezcano, Midland	.923	3	20	4	2	4
Lulay, Amarillo	.958	2	22	1	1	4
Martinez, Midland	.986	127	1087	77	16	102
Michael, El Paso*	.969	65	530	34	18	68
D. Moore, Arkansas	.991	39	323	14	3	35
Murphy, Tulsa*	.970	19	154	8	5	16
Poe, Jackson*	.989	77	643	54	8	62
Rittweger, Jackson	1.000	3	25	4	0	2
Rubel, Tulsa	.990	63	567	40	6	48
Sayler, Arkansas	.949	6	35	2	2	2
Schuster, El Paso	.991	70	649	46	6	62
G. Smith, San Antonio	.981	42	297	18	6	22
Steels, Amarillo*	.977	86	789	61	20	81
Stockstill, Tulsa	.987	41	345	32	5	35
Thomas, Amarillo	.979	11	91	4	2	10
Torve, Shreveport	.985	126	1040	96	17	85
Wabeke, Shreveport	.988	10	81	2	1	4
Whiting, El Paso*	.909	2	9	1	1	0
Wiggins, Shreveport	1.000	1	8	0	0	0

SECOND BASEMEN

Player and Club	Pct.	G.	PO.	A.	E.	DP.
Aguayo, Tulsa	1.000	4	7	12	0	5
C. Brown, Shreveport	1.000	4	11	9	0	1
Buechele, Tulsa	.980	47	95	150	5	28
Chaney, Midland	.962	58	117	139	10	31
Chavez, San Antonio	1.000	7	16	14	0	3
Colletti, Arkansas	.973	71	142	188	9	57
Dillard, Tulsa	.971	8	11	22	1	2
Fierro, Midland	.972	69	130	185	9	44
Gooch, Tulsa	.961	13	34	39	3	7
Gutierrez, Arkansas	.959	26	50	68	5	11
Heimach, Shreveport	.965	50	79	140	8	22
Jirschele, Tulsa	.982	12	26	29	1	12
M. Johnston, El Paso	.959	17	33	38	3	7
Kaczmarski, Amarillo	.984	30	71	109	3	23
Kastelic, Jackson	.989	20	40	49	1	12
Koenigsfeld, El Paso	.968	127	338	365	23	93
Madison, San Antonio	1.000	2	5	2	0	2
McMULLEN, Jackson	.974	98	217	277	13	56
Mejia, Tulsa	.938	34	75	106	12	25
Payne, Midland	.947	15	32	39	4	5
Perdue, Shreveport	.974	59	116	150	7	29
Purpura, Amarillo	.960	107	238	337	24	84
L. Reynolds, Arkansas	.950	9	18	20	2	5
Rittweger, Jackson	.978	23	36	54	2	5
Sanchez, Arkansas	1.000	4	6	7	0	2
G. Schultz, San Antonio	.927	19	44	45	7	7
Sheehy, San Antonio	.967	110	275	289	19	77
Tabor, Tulsa	.957	22	38	50	4	6
Taveras, San Antonio	1.000	9	16	23	0	8
Toener, Shreveport	.889	10	12	20	4	5
Wabeke, Shreveport	.956	25	27	60	4	8
Wolters, Arkansas	.949	34	64	84	8	20
Woodward, Jackson	.733	2	5	6	4	1

Triple Play—Buechele.

THIRD BASEMEN

Player and Club	Pct.	G.	PO.	A.	E.	DP.
Ayer, Arkansas	.882	7	6	9	2	2
Brewer, San Antonio	.813	7	4	9	3	0
C. Brown, Shreveport	.926	46	40	73	9	8
Buechele, Tulsa	.930	16	16	24	3	0
Chaney, Midland	.727	5	3	5	3	1
CONNALLY, Midland	.948	115	108	238	19	25
Cowger, Tulsa	.912	50	36	98	13	16
Duff, Jackson	1.000	1	0	1	0	0
Fierro, Midland	.949	19	20	36	3	4
Gauntlett, San Antonio	.927	18	12	26	3	2
Gomez, Shreveport	.889	7	3	5	1	1
Heimach, Shreveport	.667	2	2	2	2	1
Hernandez, San Antonio	.905	18	22	35	6	5
Hinshaw, Amarillo	1.000	1	0	1	0	0
Jirschele, Tulsa	.958	31	28	64	4	4
M. Johnston, El Paso	1.000	4	4	7	0	1
Kaczmarski, Amarillo	.909	5	6	4	1	0
Kastelic, Jackson	.957	12	9	36	2	3
Kornacher, Shreveport	.925	21	15	34	4	3
Lezcano, Midland	1.000	1	0	1	0	0
Lyons, Arkansas	.903	15	7	21	3	1
Madison, San Antonio	.872	27	20	55	11	3
Maxwell, Tulsa	.920	18	15	31	4	5
Mejia, Tulsa	.950	13	12	26	2	5
Ojeda, Arkansas	.917	91	65	166	21	19
Owen, Midland	1.000	1	1	4	0	1
Pagel, Midland	1.000	1	1	1	0	0
Perdue, Shreveport	.941	12	5	11	1	2
Ransom, Shreveport	.889	9	4	12	2	2
Ready, El Paso	.936	132	115	312	29	27
Ron Reynolds, Jackson	.800	3	2	2	1	0
Rittweger, Jackson	.857	4	1	5	1	1
Rivera, San Antonio	.882	64	59	157	29	21
Ronk, Amarillo	.929	132	110	256	28	22
G. Schultz, San Antonio	.979	15	12	34	1	3
Scott, Tulsa	1.000	2	0	1	0	0
Stockstill, Tulsa	.800	13	7	21	7	1
Wabeke, Shreveport	.950	46	36	60	5	3
Wolters, Arkansas	.948	31	30	61	5	8
Woodward, Jackson	.939	120	84	237	21	19

Triple Play—Jirschele.

SHORTSTOPS

Player and Club	Pct.	G.	PO.	A.	E.	DP.
Chaney, Midland	.917	15	27	50	7	8
Colletti, Arkansas	.889	2	0	8	1	0
Connally, Midland	1.000	1	0	1	0	0
Davidsmeier, El Paso	.951	136	268	445	37	87
J. Gonzalez, Arkansas	.941	123	185	385	36	88
Jirschele, Tulsa	.936	54	88	162	17	38
M. Johnston, El Paso	1.000	1	1	4	0	1
Kaczmarski, Amarillo	.900	8	15	21	4	3
Kastelic, Jackson	.880	17	22	44	9	8
Koenigsfeld, El Paso	1.000	5	3	3	0	1
Kutcher, Shreveport	.939	58	93	137	15	24
Lyons, Arkansas	.920	11	22	24	4	5
Mejia, Tulsa	.962	11	18	32	2	5
Owen, Midland	.944	121	182	305	29	65
PEDRIQUE, Jackson	.960	119	189	370	23	71
Perdue, Shreveport	.938	32	54	68	8	12
Quinones, Amarillo	.936	94	164	288	31	69
Rivera, San Antonio	.903	78	112	185	32	33
Stevenson, 35 Am-11 Shr	.918	46	82	108	17	33
Tabor, Tulsa	.857	2	3	3	1	0
Taveras, San Antonio	.946	67	91	189	16	37
Toener, Shreveport	.931	42	68	108	13	16
Wabeke, Shreveport	.875	7	4	10	2	2
Wilkerson, Tulsa	.948	72	102	225	18	40

Triple Play—Wilkerson.

CATCHERS

Player and Club	Pct.	G.	PO.	A.	E.	DP.	PB.
Bilardello, San Antonio	.977	96	546	80	15	15	17
Cowger, Tulsa	.963	9	44	8	2	9	3
Cox, Midland	1.000	10	44	11	0	4	0
Cummings, Shreveport	.987	41	264	29	4	3	14
Diaz, Midland	.968	91	417	42	15	6	13
Duff, Jackson	.990	34	163	28	2	4	6
Foley, El Paso	.990	55	262	22	3	1	11
Gauntlett, San Antonio	.993	26	126	13	1	1	3
Gibbons, Jackson	1.000	3	21	1	0	0	0
Gomez, Shreveport	.979	63	377	53	9	4	6
Hyman, Midland	.990	38	173	18	2	2	2
Kingsolver, El Paso	.976	89	424	68	12	3	13
Madison, San Antonio	.970	23	142	18	5	1	3
Martin, Amarillo	.982	99	505	53	10	9	7
Neufang, Tulsa	.990	45	279	29	3	3	2
NIETO, Arkansas	.994	84	466	58	3	4	12
Parent, Amarillo	.981	20	100	6	2	1	3
Ransom, Shreveport	.993	36	257	30	2	6	5
Reynolds, Jackson	.980	102	583	55	13	8	3
Salas, Arkansas	.990	17	88	15	1	4	0
Sayler, Arkansas	.984	44	227	27	4	2	3
Scott, Tulsa	.967	90	537	74	21	5	21
Thomas, Amarillo	.970	23	82	16	3	2	2

OUTFIELDERS

Player and Club	Pct.	G.	PO.	A.	E.	DP.
Adduci, Arkansas*	.984	105	178	6	3	0
Aguayo, Tulsa	1.000	2	1	0	0	0
Amelung, San Antonio*	.978	128	301	17	7	3
Ayer, Arkansas	.984	118	171	9	3	0
Baker, Shreveport	.947	120	188	9	11	1
Ball, Tulsa	.936	41	71	2	5	1
Beane, Jackson	.954	122	200	6	10	2
Beltre, Jackson	1.000	5	8	1	0	0
Benza, Tulsa	.992	60	129	3	1	0
Beyers, San Antonio	.964	57	100	6	4	1
Bilardello, San Antonio	1.000	1	1	0	0	0
BLOCKER, Jackson*	.988	114	248	7	3	1
Brewer, San Antonio	.941	93	150	10	10	1
Brunson, El Paso	1.000	5	10	0	0	0
Carter, Midland	.974	87	182	6	5	2
Casey, Amarillo	.917	9	11	0	1	0
Corey, El Paso	.960	28	45	3	2	1
Cotto, Midland	.979	123	310	16	7	4
G. Davis, Amarillo	.942	84	158	4	10	0
Deer, Shreveport	.946	124	183	10	11	2
Duff, Jackson	.800	1	3	1	1	1
Dunbar, Tulsa*	.967	124	201	5	7	1
Gausepohl, Amarillo	.971	16	32	1	1	0
Gillaspie, Amarillo	1.000	27	49	4	0	0
Greer, Amarillo	.950	78	185	6	10	2
Guin, Arkansas*	.833	5	4	1	1	0
Hansen, El Paso	.983	88	167	5	3	2
Heimach, Shreveport	1.000	1	1	0	0	0
Hinshaw, Amarillo	.939	125	246	16	17	2
Hyman, Midland	1.000	1	1	0	0	0
Jamerson, Shreveport	.800	3	4	0	1	0
James, El Paso*	.972	106	237	9	7	1
M. Johnston, El Paso	.975	23	37	2	1	0
Kastelic, Jackson	.929	19	24	2	2	0
Kelley, Midland*	.980	77	139	6	3	0
Kutcher, Shreveport	.969	55	90	5	3	0
Lezcano, Midland	.969	108	198	19	7	6
Lulay, Amarillo	1.000	3	4	0	0	0
J. Martin, Midland*	1.000	1	1	0	0	0
Martinez, Midland	.923	5	11	1	1	1
Mazzilli, Shreveport*	.931	58	76	5	6	0
McReynolds, Amarillo	.975	39	76	3	2	0
Michael, El Paso	.915	37	49	5	5	0
L. Miller, San Antonio	.964	135	228	13	9	2
S. Moore, Tulsa	.966	99	135	9	5	1
Morales, Midland	1.000	4	8	0	0	0
Murphy, Tulsa*	.968	59	85	6	3	1
Pagel, Midland	1.000	1	2	0	0	0
Perdue, Shreveport	1.000	18	25	2	0	0
Peyton, El Paso*	.937	127	228	26	17	1
Poe, Jackson*	1.000	15	16	1	0	0
Ransom, Shreveport	.971	19	30	3	1	0
L. Reynolds, Arkansas	.982	82	106	5	2	1
R. J. Reynolds, San Antonio	1.000	3	10	1	0	0
Rittweger, Jackson	1.000	9	3	0	0	0
Scherger, Amarillo	.952	32	54	6	3	0
Stockstill, Tulsa	1.000	34	42	4	0	0
Strawberry, Jackson*	.961	124	211	8	9	3
Tarver, Jackson*	1.000	12	18	0	0	0
Van Slyke, Arkansas	.976	119	266	17	7	3
Whiting, El Paso*	1.000	3	3	1	0	0
Wojcik, Shreveport	.938	26	28	2	2	0

PITCHERS

Player and Club	Pct.	G.	PO.	A.	E.	DP.
Adams, Arkansas	.929	14	2	11	1	1
Arigoni, Arkansas*	.933	13	3	11	1	0
Babcock, Tulsa	1.000	9	1	4	0	1
Beene, El Paso	.944	16	6	11	1	0
Biko, Amarillo*	.941	49	5	11	1	0
Bittiger, Jackson	.846	25	9	24	6	0
Blyth, Midland	.900	24	4	5	1	0
Brecht, Shreveport*	1.000	34	9	20	0	1
L. Brown, Amarillo	.939	37	8	23	2	0
Bryant, Amarillo*	.833	27	9	21	6	1
Bullinger, Jackson*	1.000	45	3	17	0	1
Burns, El Paso	1.000	25	6	13	0	1
Cacciatore, Amarillo	1.000	8	0	1	0	0
Chaney, Midland	.000	1	0	0	0	0
Clark, Midland	.846	22	5	17	4	0
Cocanower, El Paso	.850	9	6	11	3	2
Coffman, Amarillo	1.000	14	2	2	0	0
Cornell, Shreveport	1.000	21	5	2	0	1
Couchee, Amarillo	.870	51	7	13	3	2
T. Davis, Jackson	.974	23	14	23	1	4
Dente, San Antonio	1.000	5	0	4	0	0
Dunn, Shreveport	.974	23	12	26	1	1
Dye, Jackson	.958	16	9	14	1	2
Franco, San Antonio*	.867	17	1	12	2	0
Garrelts, Shreveport	.939	27	10	21	2	1
Gendron, Shreveport	1.000	14	3	7	0	0
Gerlach, Midland	1.000	15	2	4	0	0
Gibson, El Paso	.833	47	3	2	1	0
Gideon, Tulsa	.923	25	7	17	2	1
Gil, Midland	.957	24	9	13	1	1
A. Gonzalez, El Paso	1.000	6	1	2	0	0
GRIER, El Paso	1.000	34	7	33	0	1
Hagen, Arkansas	.927	27	13	38	4	9
Hammond, San Antonio*	1.000	30	1	10	0	0
Hardwick, Amarillo	.864	28	5	14	3	0
Henke, El Paso	.941	52	6	10	1	1
Henry, Tulsa*	.962	30	5	20	1	4
Hinrichs, Shreveport	1.000	9	2	3	0	0
Horton, Arkansas*	.964	16	6	21	1	1
Ibarguen, Jackson	.769	18	5	5	3	1
Jamerson, Shreveport	.958	34	7	16	1	0
Jenkins, El Paso	.929	41	4	9	1	0
Johnson, Arkansas	.933	16	7	21	2	0
J. Johnston, Jackson	1.000	7	6	5	0	1
Kain, Amarillo	.861	25	9	22	5	1
Keener, Arkansas	.714	24	0	5	2	0
King, Midland*	.818	25	12	15	6	1
Kinnunen, Arkansas*	.778	18	2	5	2	0
Klawitter, San Antonio*	.847	28	8	42	9	1
Kolbe, Jackson	1.000	23	7	13	0	0
Koontz, El Paso	.947	24	6	12	1	2
Lachowicz, Tulsa	.953	25	14	27	2	1
Lazorko, Tulsa	1.000	15	9	7	0	1
Leach, Tulsa	.947	27	13	23	2	1
D. Long, Tulsa	1.000	43	9	11	0	2
W. Long, Amarillo	.962	27	16	35	2	2
Lusted, Shreveport	.917	14	7	15	2	3
Macias, Amarillo	1.000	10	1	5	0	1
Madden, San Antonio*	.800	4	0	4	1	0
Malden, San Antonio	.950	21	5	14	1	1
Manderfield, El Paso	.750	3	0	3	1	0
Mason, Tulsa*	.978	26	20	25	1	2
McDonald, San Antonio	1.000	21	1	3	0	0
McKenna, Shreveport	.933	12	3	11	1	2
McLane, Tulsa	.900	6	3	6	1	0
Mengwasser, Tulsa	.941	37	15	33	3	1
Mercer, Tulsa*	1.000	5	0	2	0	0
T. Miller, Jackson*	1.000	4	2	5	0	0
Millner, Midland	.941	30	4	12	1	1
E. Moore, Midland	1.000	5	2	4	0	2
Myles, Midland*	.933	10	2	12	1	0
Neely, Arkansas	1.000	14	1	1	0	0
Nobles, San Antonio*	.875	28	1	6	1	0
Oberbruner, Amarillo	.800	3	0	4	1	0
Oliver, Amarillo	1.000	16	4	4	0	1
Parrott, Tulsa	1.000	16	3	15	0	1
Perlman, Midland	.912	26	15	37	5	1
G. Perry, Arkansas	.957	34	7	15	1	0
S. Perry, San Antonio	1.000	19	2	8	0	0
Pimentel, Arkansas	1.000	30	2	7	0	0
Pisel, Shreveport	.964	12	8	19	1	1
Plesac, Amarillo	.889	5	4	4	1	0
Pryce, Midland	.958	26	3	20	1	1
Rennicke, San Antonio	.960	24	19	29	2	4
Richards, Tulsa	1.000	29	9	16	0	0
Riggins, Arkansas*	.974	27	15	23	1	2
Rodriguez, Jackson*	1.000	37	5	13	0	0
Ronan, Shreveport	1.000	16	4	4	0	0
Sanford, Arkansas	.909	13	1	9	1	2
Schroeck, Jackson*	.930	31	10	30	3	3
Semprini, Jackson	.938	43	4	11	1	1
Sisk, Arkansas	.941	44	18	30	3	1
D. Smith, Tulsa	.875	9	4	3	1	0
T. Smith, Midland	1.000	24	3	9	0	0
Spino, Arkansas*	.875	4	0	7	0	0
Stone, Amarillo	.818	15	2	7	2	0
Swift, Tulsa	.857	9	5	7	2	1
Tatsuno, El Paso*	.905	39	3	16	2	4
Thompson, Midland*	1.000	37	6	6	0	0
Thurberg, Arkansas	1.000	30	2	10	0	1
Tibbs, Jackson	1.000	1	1	0	0	0
Uhey, El Paso	.941	20	4	12	1	0
Vasquez, El Paso	1.000	12	1	2	0	0
Violette, Tulsa	1.000	20	6	8	0	1
Voigt, San Antonio	.950	28	15	23	2	0
Welenc, Midland	.974	25	15	23	1	3
White, Amarillo	.966	33	9	19	1	3
Wickensheimer, 23SA-10EIP	.800	33	8	12	5	0
F. Williams, Shreveport	.896	27	12	31	5	3
L. Williams, Shreveport	1.000	19	4	14	0	3
Winfield, Arkansas	1.000	8	1	1	0	1
Wise, San Antonio	.938	42	5	10	1	4

The following players do not have any recorded accepted chances at the positions indicated; therefore, are not listed in the fielding averages for those particular positions: Chue, p; Fierro, of; Gallo, p; Gauntlett, 2b; M. Johnston, 1b, p; Kingsolver, of; Kutcher, 3b; Madison, of; McEnaney, p; McMullen, ss; D. Moore, 2b; Neufang, of; Ronn Reynolds, of; Sanchez, of; C. Schultz, p; G. Schultz, 1b; Seiple, p; Sheehy, ss; W. Smith, p.

CLUB PITCHING

Club	ERA.	G.	CG.	ShO.	Sv.	IP.	H.	R.	ER.	HR.	HB.	BB.	Int. BB.	SO.	WP.	Bk.
Arkansas	3.75	136	34	10	18	1114.2	1051	557	464	85	39	501	36	753	49	12
Jackson	3.98	134	22	8	31	1142.1	1092	583	505	97	30	547	41	728	42	4
Tulsa	4.33	136	13	10	36	1156	1136	666	556	96	49	503	13	845	73	10
Shreveport	4.39	136	33	7	26	1108.1	1117	638	541	109	41	537	14	856	70	18
San Antonio	4.65	138	36	5	27	1173	1328	741	606	117	35	514	27	770	65	11
Midland	5.06	134	38	4	22	1118.2	1301	730	629	136	44	454	32	591	53	8
El Paso	5.46	136	24	3	34	1161	1415	832	704	162	30	550	19	640	98	6
Amarillo	5.49	136	19	3	35	1161.1	1388	861	708	126	27	548	34	653	63	10

PITCHERS' RECORDS
(Leading Qualifiers for Earned-Run Average Leadership — 109 or More Innings)

°Throws lefthanded.

Pitcher—Club	W.	L.	Pct.	ERA.	G.	GS.	CG.	GF.	ShO.	Sv.	IP.	H.	R.	ER.	HR.	HB.	BB.	Int. BB.	SO.	WP.
Sisk, Jackson	11	7	.611	2.67	44	9	6	22	0	5	138	136	59	41	3	5	58	7	53	8
Bittiger, Jackson	12	5	.706	2.96	25	25	3	0	1	0	164	106	59	54	14	3	94	0	190	5
Pryce, Midland	6	5	.545	3.18	26	10	6	10	1	4	124.2	127	53	44	11	3	28	2	80	2
T. Davis, Jackson	12	8	.600	3.49	23	23	6	0	2	0	152	136	65	59	15	3	55	5	70	3
Brecht, Shreveport°	10	5	.667	3.50	34	13	4	17	0	4	131	126	55	51	12	2	47	0	103	7
Hagen, Arkansas	11	10	.524	3.61	27	27	6	0	1	0	189.2	176	88	76	7	10	75	1	102	8
Perlman, Midland	13	7	.650	3.66	26	26	8	0	0	0	184.1	196	89	75	15	13	50	1	81	7
Burns, El Paso	10	4	.714	3.78	25	14	3	6	1	0	116.2	128	56	49	9	1	29	1	63	5
Garrelts, Shreveport	9	10	.474	3.81	27	27	8	0	1	0	151.1	131	76	64	7	7	90	2	159	14
Lachowicz, Tulsa	12	8	.600	3.88	25	25	5	0	1	0	146	137	69	63	10	2	53	1	109	7

Departmental Leaders: G—Henke, 52; GS—Voigt, 28; CG—Rennicke, Welenc, 12; GF—Couchee, 49; ShO—Voigt, 3; W—Mengwasser, Perlman, Welenc, 13; L—Klawitter, 14; Pct.—Burns, .714; Sv—Couchee, 19; IP—W. Long, 198⅓; H—W. Long, 222; R—Klawitter, 122; ER—Schroeck, 102; HR—Welenc, 27; HB—Perlman, F. Williams, 13; BB—Bryant, 101; IBB—Couchee, 13; SO—Bittiger, 190; WP—Schroeck, 15.

(All-Pitchers—Listed Alphabetically)

Pitcher—Club	W.	L.	Pct.	ERA.	G.	GS.	CG.	GF.	ShO.	Sv.	IP.	H.	R.	ER.	HR.	HB.	BB.	Int. BB.	SO.	WP.
Adams, Arkansas	7	4	.636	3.32	14	13	3	1	1	0	81.1	78	36	30	7	1	30	1	61	4
Arigoni, Arkansas°	0	3	.000	4.12	13	5	0	4	0	1	43.2	47	29	20	4	0	25	2	22	1
Babcock, Tulsa	0	1	.000	6.19	9	0	0	7	0	2	16	16	12	11	2	1	7	1	12	2
Beene, El Paso	8	2	.800	4.15	16	12	1	1	0	0	80.1	73	45	37	10	3	51	2	62	11
Biko, Amarillo°	3	2	.600	4.27	49	0	0	17	0	3	71.2	72	38	34	5	2	38	3	49	4
Bittiger, Jackson	12	5	.706	2.96	25	25	3	0	1	0	164	106	59	54	14	3	94	0	190	5
Blyth, Midland	1	2	.333	5.57	24	1	0	17	0	2	32.1	37	26	20	9	3	19	2	27	4
Brecht, Shreveport°	10	5	.667	3.50	34	13	4	17	0	4	131	126	55	51	12	2	47	0	103	7
Brown, Amarillo	5	10	.333	4.98	37	9	0	15	0	6	103	116	71	57	8	5	49	2	72	6
Bryant, Amarillo°	7	8	.467	6.05	27	23	2	1	0	0	132.1	159	118	89	14	1	101	0	75	12
Bullinger, Jackson°	6	3	.667	3.08	45	0	0	31	0	10	84.2	67	32	29	5	1	48	6	70	5
Burns, El Paso	10	4	.714	3.78	25	14	3	6	1	0	116.2	128	56	49	9	1	29	1	63	5
Cacciatore, Amarillo	0	1	.000	11.37	8	0	0	2	0	0	19	29	35	24	6	0	22	1	10	2
Chaney, Midland	0	0	.000	36.00	1	0	0	1	0	0	1	4	4	4	0	0	2	0	0	0
Chue, Shreveport	1	0	1.000	18.00	3	0	0	1	0	0	5	13	11	10	2	0	9	0	6	0
Clark, Midland	3	6	.333	6.44	22	13	1	4	0	3	95	132	79	68	12	4	35	2	36	9
Cocanower, El Paso	3	1	.750	3.32	9	9	3	0	0	0	62.1	73	36	23	2	3	30	0	29	8
Coffman, Amarillo	2	0	1.000	1.83	14	0	0	6	0	0	19.2	13	8	4	0	0	21	0	9	2
Cornell, Shreveport	3	2	.600	1.84	21	0	0	17	0	10	44	24	10	9	1	0	14	0	38	3
Couchee, Shreveport	7	5	.583	2.48	51	0	0	49	0	19	87	87	35	24	4	1	29	13	52	1
T. Davis, Jackson	12	8	.600	3.49	23	23	6	0	2	0	152	136	65	59	15	3	55	5	70	3
Dente, San Antonio	1	1	.500	5.95	5	0	0	4	0	0	19.2	30	15	13	1	0	15	3	12	4
Dunn, Shreveport	7	11	.389	5.08	23	21	5	2	1	0	127.2	132	84	72	15	1	70	1	96	7
Dye, Jackson	7	5	.583	3.17	16	16	3	0	1	0	105	105	41	37	10	0	30	1	53	1
Franco, San Antonio°	10	5	.667	4.96	17	17	3	0	0	0	105.1	137	70	58	11	1	46	1	76	3
Gallo, El Paso°	1	0	1.000	8.49	10	0	0	3	0	1	11.2	15	12	11	3	0	11	1	7	3
Garrelts, Shreveport	9	10	.474	3.81	27	27	8	0	1	0	151.1	131	76	64	7	7	90	2	159	14
Gendron, Shreveport	5	3	.625	4.81	14	1	0	11	0	2	43	44	26	23	7	2	13	0	24	2
Gerlach, Midland	1	2	.333	4.08	15	0	0	10	0	5	17.2	15	8	8	3	0	8	2	9	0
Gibson, El Paso	6	2	.750	2.17	47	0	0	40	0	18	66.1	55	23	16	4	2	39	1	66	7
Gideon, Tulsa	2	5	.286	6.35	25	11	0	4	0	2	89.1	108	72	63	8	6	41	0	54	5
Gil, Midland	9	6	.600	5.99	24	19	3	3	1	0	118.2	145	87	79	17	3	55	3	69	5
A. Gonzalez, El Paso	3	2	.600	4.63	6	6	1	0	0	0	35	51	19	18	2	0	7	1	16	0
Grier, El Paso	9	9	.500	6.46	34	17	3	4	0	1	140.2	198	121	101	21	0	38	2	40	4
Hagen, Arkansas	11	10	.524	3.61	27	27	6	0	1	0	189.2	176	88	76	7	10	75	1	102	8
Hammond, San Antonio°	1	3	.250	4.83	30	0	0	13	0	3	54	57	31	29	5	3	38	7	50	6
Hardwick, Amarillo	0	6	.000	5.84	28	7	0	9	0	4	69.1	71	52	45	10	7	57	3	57	11
Henke, Tulsa	3	6	.333	2.67	52	1	0	42	0	14	87.2	69	35	26	8	3	40	2	100	5
Henry, Tulsa°	5	5	.500	4.27	30	11	2	9	1	1	86.1	72	44	41	10	2	66	2	74	12
Hinrichs, Shreveport	1	2	.333	3.05	9	0	0	8	0	2	20.2	22	8	7	2	0	5	1	9	1
Horton, Arkansas°	9	6	.600	3.15	16	16	5	0	2	0	108.2	83	45	38	6	2	52	1	90	6
Ibarguen, Jackson	4	6	.400	5.72	18	16	0	1	0	0	91.1	112	71	58	6	0	54	2	33	4
Jamerson, Shreveport	1	7	.125	5.26	34	8	2	20	0	3	119.2	131	79	70	17	5	61	3	68	10
Jenkins, El Paso	4	5	.444	4.48	41	1	0	15	0	3	98.1	110	59	49	17	2	36	2	57	9
Johnson, Arkansas	5	7	.417	3.14	16	16	8	0	1	0	106	90	40	37	11	3	26	2	60	1
J. Johnston, Jackson	2	5	.286	6.42	7	7	0	0	0	0	33.2	44	26	24	5	2	19	0	18	1
M. Johnston, El Paso	0	0	.000	36.00	1	0	0	1	0	0	2	6	9	8	3	1	3	0	0	1
Kain, Amarillo	10	8	.556	5.74	25	18	4	1	0	0	125.1	171	93	80	23	1	24	2	64	4
Keener, Arkansas	4	3	.571	2.37	24	0	0	22	0	6	38	29	11	10	3	0	14	4	39	0
King, Midland°	8	12	.400	6.29	25	25	6	0	2	0	133	154	104	93	10	2	83	2	71	13
Kinnunen, Arkansas°	4	2	.667	1.76	18	0	0	15	0	5	30.2	28	6	6	2	2	17	2	18	2
Klawitter, San Antonio°	9	14	.391	5.30	28	26	5	2	1	0	163	189	122	96	22	1	93	1	83	7

Pitcher—Club	W.	L.	Pct.	ERA.	G.	GS.	CG.	GF.	ShO.	Sv.	IP.	H.	R.	ER.	HR.	HB.	BB.	Int. BB.	SO.	WP.
Kolbe, Jackson	3	3	.500	5.01	23	8	0	6	0	1	82.2	71	48	46	11	7	39	2	69	3
Koontz, El Paso	4	8	.333	6.75	24	18	3	5	0	0	113.1	164	97	85	21	0	57	1	60	8
Lachowicz, Tulsa	12	8	.600	3.88	25	25	5	0	1	0	146	137	69	63	10	2	53	1	109	7
Lazorko, Tulsa	2	2	.500	2.04	15	3	1	8	1	2	39.2	27	9	9	1	0	7	1	40	0
Leach, Tulsa	6	9	.400	5.20	27	19	0	2	0	1	119.1	138	91	69	10	7	50	1	63	8
D. Long, Tulsa	6	1	.857	3.73	43	1	0	27	0	10	94	89	49	39	9	4	25	1	66	2
W. Long, Amarillo	12	10	.545	4.40	27	27	9	0	1	0	198.1	222	116	97	9	1	53	3	117	4
Lusted, Shreveport	2	6	.250	5.24	14	14	1	0	0	0	80.2	93	54	47	15	5	28	3	70	3
Macias, Amarillo	0	3	.000	9.59	10	4	0	3	0	1	25.1	42	34	27	4	0	15	1	14	1
Madden, San Antonio°	1	1	.500	8.53	4	4	0	0	0	0	19	26	19	18	3	0	15	1	18	7
Malden, San Antonio	6	7	.462	4.86	21	17	3	4	0	1	113	110	75	61	14	3	45	0	77	8
Manderfield, El Paso°	0	1	.000	10.38	3	3	0	0	0	0	8.2	10	14	10	2	2	14	0	7	2
Mason, Tulsa°	10	9	.526	3.89	26	26	3	0	2	0	155	153	84	67	11	5	46	1	111	5
McDonald, San Antonio	4	1	.800	3.90	21	0	0	14	0	3	30	30	16	13	3	0	9	2	30	0
McEnaney, Tulsa°	1	0	1.000	1.29	5	0	0	5	0	1	7	4	1	1	0	0	1	0	5	0
McKenna, Shreveport	4	4	.500	2.76	12	3	2	7	1	1	42.1	46	16	13	2	1	9	1	21	1
McLane, Tulsa°	3	2	.600	1.82	6	4	0	0	0	0	29.2	21	13	6	1	1	11	0	16	0
Mengwasser, Tulsa	13	6	.684	4.34	37	14	2	14	2	3	137	114	75	66	11	12	68	1	105	12
Mercer, Tulsa°	1	2	.333	8.05	5	5	0	0	0	0	19	28	19	17	2	1	9	0	18	0
Miller, Jackson°	1	3	.250	6.86	4	4	1	0	0	0	19.2	31	18	15	3	0	9	0	13	0
Millner, Midland	2	4	.333	5.79	30	0	0	20	0	3	70	88	49	45	9	2	42	9	39	3
Moore, Midland	2	0	1.000	5.40	5	4	0	1	0	0	18.1	26	12	11	3	0	9	0	4	0
Myles, Jackson°	2	4	.333	7.34	10	10	0	0	0	0	41.2	47	40	34	5	1	39	1	18	2
Neely, Arkansas	0	1	.000	6.11	14	0	0	11	0	1	17.2	23	13	12	0	0	7	1	12	1
Nobles, San Antonio°	4	3	.571	4.83	28	6	1	13	1	4	87.2	90	55	47	8	5	44	2	79	7
Oberbruner, Amarillo	1	1	.500	4.64	3	2	0	1	0	0	21.1	20	12	11	2	0	7	0	11	0
Oliver, Amarillo	2	2	.500	7.08	16	3	0	8	0	1	34.1	44	29	27	4	4	16	1	10	2
Parrott, El Paso	4	5	.444	7.51	16	16	1	0	0	0	80.1	111	76	67	17	2	51	1	26	4
Perlman, Midland	13	7	.650	3.66	26	26	8	0	0	0	184.1	196	89	75	15	13	50	1	81	7
G. Perry, Arkansas	6	8	.429	4.68	34	14	2	10	1	0	100	94	60	52	11	5	52	6	56	3
S. Perry, San Antonio	3	6	.333	5.29	19	11	3	4	0	1	80	90	53	47	8	2	36	1	43	7
Pimentel, Arkansas	5	2	.714	2.45	30	4	0	12	0	2	73.1	65	24	20	4	4	47	2	68	3
Pisel, Shreveport	6	3	.667	5.31	12	12	0	0	0	0	62.2	86	44	37	4	1	46	0	35	8
Plesac, Amarillo	1	2	.333	6.91	5	5	1	0	0	0	28.2	38	26	22	1	3	18	0	7	3
Pryce, Midland	6	5	.545	3.18	26	10	6	10	1	4	124.2	127	53	44	11	3	28	2	80	2
Rennicke, San Antonio	12	8	.600	4.11	24	24	12	0	0	0	188.1	211	102	86	18	2	43	4	94	4
Richards, Tulsa	4	5	.444	4.68	29	9	0	5	0	0	92.1	109	58	48	9	0	55	2	54	10
Riggins, Arkansas°	10	8	.556	3.93	27	26	7	0	1	0	165	180	93	72	15	5	54	3	86	7
Rodriguez, Jackson°	2	8	.200	4.45	37	8	2	15	1	8	93	103	51	46	6	0	52	9	60	3
Ronan, Shreveport	0	3	.000	6.67	16	0	0	14	0	3	28.1	34	26	21	4	2	11	1	20	4
Sanford, Arkansas	0	5	.000	6.39	13	7	0	3	0	0	49.1	61	41	35	7	3	21	2	28	3
Schroeck, El Paso°	10	12	.455	6.24	31	25	7	4	1	2	147	184	114	102	20	4	67	2	89	15
Schultz, Arkansas°	0	1	.000	6.10	7	0	0	4	0	0	10.1	12	7	7	2	1	6	1	8	2
Seiple, Arkansas°	0	0	.000	72.00	2	0	0	0	0	0	1	5	8	8	0	0	5	0	1	1
Semprini, Jackson	4	2	.667	3.22	43	0	0	31	0	7	67	56	26	24	3	5	33	7	55	5
Sisk, Jackson	11	7	.611	2.67	44	9	6	22	0	5	138	136	54	41	3	5	58	7	53	8
D. Smith, Tulsa	2	5	.286	7.17	9	7	0	0	0	0	37.2	51	35	30	4	5	24	0	18	5
T. Smith, Midland	4	5	.444	5.48	24	6	2	5	0	1	69	94	50	42	8	4	40	1	21	3
W. Smith, Amarillo	0	1	.000	67.50	1	1	0	0	0	0	0.2	7	5	5	0	0	2	0	0	0
Spino, Midland°	1	1	.500	6.38	4	4	0	0	0	0	18.1	22	23	13	3	1	14	0	9	4
Stone, Amarillo	4	8	.333	8.72	15	15	2	0	0	0	74.1	103	77	72	17	0	41	1	50	6
Swift, El Paso	3	2	.600	4.84	9	9	0	0	0	0	48.1	53	31	26	3	0	40	0	27	12
Tatsuno, El Paso°	7	2	.778	6.42	39	2	1	16	0	3	54.2	62	42	39	6	4	44	4	39	4
Thompson, Midland°	4	6	.400	6.39	37	1	0	25	0	4	56.1	64	43	40	9	1	25	6	41	2
Thurberg, Arkansas	5	8	.385	3.93	30	8	3	14	0	3	89.1	71	53	39	6	2	62	5	98	6
Tibbs, Jackson	0	0	.000	0.00	1	0	0	0	0	0	3.1	2	1	0	0	0	1	0	3	0
Uhey, El Paso	3	2	.600	4.78	20	3	1	7	0	2	52.2	73	46	28	5	1	18	3	24	3
Vasquez, El Paso	1	0	1.000	6.75	12	0	0	5	0	2	14.2	17	13	11	3	0	8	0	10	0
Violette, Jackson	2	6	.250	5.29	20	8	1	6	0	0	66.1	76	46	39	11	3	16	1	23	2
Voigt, San Antonio	12	13	.480	3.98	28	28	8	0	3	0	187.2	208	102	83	13	10	68	0	129	6
Welenc, Midland	13	10	.565	4.60	25	25	12	0	1	0	180	197	103	92	27	8	44	2	104	1
White, Amarillo	7	7	.500	5.36	33	22	1	5	0	1	151	195	112	90	19	2	55	4	56	5
Wickensheimer, 23 SA-10 EIP	1	7	.125	5.20	33	6	1	16	0	3	90	128	80	52	11	9	54	4	51	6
F. Williams, Shreveport	11	9	.550	3.93	27	26	8	1	2	0	169.2	143	96	74	15	13	99	1	145	5
L. Williams, Shreveport	2	8	.200	4.70	19	11	3	5	0	1	82.1	92	53	43	6	2	35	1	62	5
Winfield, Arkansas	2	0	1.000	1.69	8	0	0	6	0	0	16	9	3	2	0	1	8	3	4	1
Wise, San Antonio	4	2	.667	2.28	42	0	0	37	0	14	59.1	48	21	15	6	1	24	1	46	3

BALKS—Brecht, Dunn, Franco, Hagen, King, Mason, 4 each; Gideon, Klawitter, Perlman, 3 each; Brown, Hinrichs, Jamerson, Jenkins, W. Long, Lusted, Rodriguez, Schultz, Voigt, White, 2 each; Adams, Beene, Bittiger, Bryant, Bullinger, Cacciatore, Couchee, Gallo, Garrelts, Henke, Johnson, Lachowicz, Leach, Nobles, Oliver, G. Perry, S. Perry, Pimental, Pisel, Riggins, Ronan, Tatsuno, Thompson, Thurberg, Uhey, F. Williams, 1 each.

COMBINATION SHUTOUTS—Hardwick-Macias, Stone-Macias, Amarillo; Thurberg-Perry, Johnson-Neely, Hagen-Kinnunen, Arkansas; Beene-Jenkins, El Paso; Bittiger-Semprini-Rodriguez, Dye-Bullinger, Bittiger-Rodriguez, Jackson; Pisel-Brecht, Garrelts-Cornell, Shreveport; Lachowicz-Henry-Henke, Long-Henry-Mengwasser, Mason-Long, Tulsa.

NO-HIT GAMES—Rodriguez, Jackson, defeated San Antonio, 5-0, May 24 (seven innings); Henry, Tulsa, defeated Arkansas, 1-0, August 8 (seven innings).

California League

CLASS A

CHAMPIONSHIP WINNERS IN PREVIOUS YEARS

1914—Fresno	.571
1915—Modesto	.857
1916-40—Did not operate.	
1941—Fresno	.643
S. Barbara (2nd)*	.597
1942—Santa Barbara†	.642
1943-44-45—Did not operate.	
1946—Stockton‡	.600
1947—Stockton‡	.679
1948—Fresno	.607
S. Barbara (3rd)*	.529
1949—Bakersfield	.612
San Jose (4th)*	.543
1950—Ventura	.607
Modesto (2nd)*	.586
1951—Santa Barbara‡	.599
1952—Fresno‡	.629
1953—San Jose‡	.664
1954—Modesto‡	.623
1955—Stockton	.733
Fresno§	.718
1956—Fresno‡	.650
1957—Visalia x	.622
Salinas (4th)*	.504

1958—Fresno*	.639
Bakersfield	.672
1959—Bakersfield	.592
Modesto§	.643
1960—Reno	.614
Reno	.657
1961—Reno	.743
Reno	.643
1962—San Jose§	.686
Reno	.587
1963—Modesto	.589
Stockton§	.687
1964—Fresno	.638
Fresno	.600
1965—San Jose	.586
Stockton§	.614
1966—Modesto	.577
Modesto	.671
1967—San Jose§	.676
Modesto	.586
1968—San Jose	.629
Fresno§	.623
1969—Stockton§	.600
Visalia	.614

1970—Bakersfield	.667
Bakersfield	.671
1971—Visalia§	.583
Fresno	.500
1972—Modesto§	.547
Bakersfield	.629
1973—Lodi§	.657
Bakersfield	.571
1974—Fresno§	.607
San Jose	.579
1975—Reno	.614
Reno	.614
1976—Salinas	.650
Reno§	.547
1977—Salinas	.564
Lodi§	.579
1978—Visalia§	.698
Lodi	.607
1979—San Jose§	.636
Reno	.525
1980—Stockton§	.638
Visalia	.507
1981—Visalia	.621
Lodi§	.521

*Won four-club playoff. †League disbanded June 28. ‡Won championship and four-club playoff. §Won split-season playoff. xWon both halves of split-season.

STANDING OF CLUBS AT CLOSE OF FIRST HALF, JUNE 20

NORTHERN DIVISION

Club	W.	L.	T.	Pct.	G.B.
Modesto (A's)	45	25	0	.643	......
Stockton (Brewers)	38	30	0	.559	6
Redwood (Angels)	37	33	0	.529	8
Reno (Padres)	29	39	0	.426	15
Lodi (Dodgers)	29	42	0	.408	16½

SOUTHERN DIVISION

Club	W.	L.	T.	Pct.	G.B.
Visalia (Twins)	41	29	0	.586	......
Bakersfield (Mariners)	36	34	0	.514	5
San Jose (Expos)	36	34	0	.514	5
Salinas (Cubs)	33	38	0	.465	8½
Fresno (Giants)	25	45	0	.357	16

STANDING OF CLUBS AT CLOSE OF SECOND HALF, AUGUST 29

NORTHERN DIVISION

Club	W.	L.	T.	Pct.	G.B.
Modesto (A's)	49	21	0	.700	......
Stockton (Brewers)	43	27	0	.614	6
Reno (Padres)	41	29	0	.586	8
Lodi (Dodgers)	29	40	0	.420	19½
Redwood (Angels)	28	42	0	.400	21

SOUTHERN DIVISION

Club	W.	L.	T.	Pct.	G.B.
Visalia (Twins)	41	29	0	.586	......
Salinas (Cubs)	35	34	0	.507	5½
San Jose (Expos)	30	40	0	.429	11
Bakersfield (Mariners)	28	42	0	.400	13
Fresno (Giants)	25	45	0	.357	16

COMPOSITE STANDING OF CLUBS AT CLOSE OF SEASON, AUGUST 29

NORTHERN DIVISION

Club	Mod.	Sto.	Reno.	Red.	Lodi.	Vis.	Sal.	SJ.	Bak.	Fr.	W.	L.	T.	Pct.	G.B.
Modesto (A's)	....	12	13	12	16	8	7	9	9	8	94	46	0	.671	......
Stockton (Brewers)	8	....	13	13	13	5	6	6	8	9	81	57	0	.587	12
Reno (Padres)	7	5	....	10	12	6	6	7	8	9	70	68	0	.507	23
Redwood (Angels)	8	7	10	....	12	6	6	5	7	4	65	75	0	.464	29
Lodi (Dodgers)	4	7	8	8	....	3	9	4	7	8	58	82	0	.414	36

SOUTHERN DIVISION

Club	Mod.	Sto.	Reno.	Red.	Lodi.	Vis.	Sal.	SJ.	Bak.	Fr.	W.	L.	T.	Pct.	G.B.
Visalia (Twins)	4	7	6	6	9	....	15	14	11	10	82	58	0	.586	......
Salinas (Cubs)	5	6	6	6	3	5	....	15	8	14	68	72	0	.486	14
San Jose (Expos)	3	6	5	7	8	6	5	....	11	15	66	74	0	.471	16
Bakersfield (Mariners)	3	4	4	5	5	9	12	9	....	13	64	76	0	.457	18
Fresno (Giants)	4	3	3	8	4	10	6	5	7	....	50	90	0	.357	32

Major league affiliations in parentheses.

Playoffs—Modesto defeated Visalia, four games to two, for League Championship.

Regular-Season Attendance—Bakersfield, 82,745; Fresno, 77,286; Lodi, 62,530; Modesto, 83,651; Redwood, 82,119; Reno, 54,750; Salinas, 51,693; San Jose, 66,221; Stockton, 117,561; Visalia, 43,845. Total, 712,401. Playoffs, 8,704. No All-Star Game.

Managers: Bakersfield—Ken Pape; Fresno—Jim Maloney; Lodi—Rick Ollar; Modesto—Pete Whisenant; Redwood—Chris Cannizzaro; Reno—Jack Maloof; Salinas—Richard Morales; San Jose—Tommy Thompson; Stockton—Duane Espy; Visalia—Phil Roof.

All-Star Team: 1B—Reid, Fresno; Stephens, Redwood; 2B—Etchebarren, Reno; 3B—Debus, Lodi; SS—Guillen, Reno; OF—Bradley, Bakersfield; Hudgens, Modesto; Nelson, Bakersfield; C—Reed, Visalia; DH—McReynolds, Reno; P—Conroy, Modesto; Ferguson, Modesto; Sylvia, Redwood; Warren, Stockton; Manager—Whisenant, Modesto.

(Compiled by William J. Weiss, League Statistician, San Mateo, Calif.)

CLUB BATTING

Club	Pct.	G.	AB.	R.	OR.	H.	TB.	2B.	3B.	HR.	RBI.	GW.	SH.	SF.	HP.	BB.	Int. BB.	SO.	SB.	CS.	LOB.
Reno	.288	138	4607	779	760	1325	1910	219	48	90	665	62	58	58	44	495	23	790	149	59	1030
Visalia	.277	140	4647	732	588	1287	1754	210	28	67	653	71	50	44	42	570	30	709	234	76	1055
Bakersfield	.271	140	4579	660	666	1239	1707	211	19	73	580	51	50	44	37	561	12	620	245	87	1048
Lodi	.269	140	4537	611	709	1221	1668	183	21	74	534	45	34	38	31	464	14	766	139	68	962
Stockton	.262	138	4344	619	538	1140	1553	166	56	45	519	67	56	59	25	504	19	729	310	99	908
Modesto	.260	140	4380	637	482	1139	1643	200	29	82	541	80	64	41	44	615	19	695	196	116	977
Fresno	.258	140	4482	623	859	1146	1558	176	32	54	539	37	63	46	40	616	19	766	111	57	1062
Salinas	.258	140	4500	600	617	1159	1538	148	42	49	517	48	43	50	31	508	18	881	234	95	1000
Redwood	.257	140	4457	556	578	1146	1535	189	37	42	484	49	54	36	44	444	15	669	177	112	897
San Jose	.252	140	4601	614	634	1158	1526	171	25	49	544	58	31	46	49	587	16	824	211	86	1107

INDIVIDUAL BATTING

(Leading Qualifiers for Batting Championship—378 or More Plate Appearances)

*Bats lefthanded.　†Switch-hitter.

Player and Club	Pct.	G.	AB.	R.	H.	TB.	2B.	3B.	HR.	RBI.	GW.	SH.	SF.	HP.	BB.	Int. BB.	SO.	SB.	CS.
McReynolds, Kevin, Reno	.376	90	338	83	127	238	17	5	28	98	5	0	6	0	36	6	50	0	0
Guillen, Oswaldo, Reno	.347	130	528	103	183	224	33	1	2	54	6	14	6	2	16	1	53	25	14
Levi, Stanley, Stockton*	.336	121	422	77	142	178	12	9	2	51	6	11	3	1	41	3	37	57	12
Bradley, Philip, Bakersfield	.331	109	405	98	134	171	17	10	0	37	0	6	2	9	82	0	39	58	13
Reed, Jeffrey, Visalia*	.329	125	395	69	130	168	19	2	5	54	3	4	4	7	78	3	32	1	2
Debus, Jon, Lodi	.325	138	498	73	162	245	23	6	16	94	5	0	8	2	69	2	84	10	5
Reynolds, Robert, Lodi†	.313	108	403	67	126	169	19	3	6	35	3	1	1	0	36	2	68	25	11
Hatcher, William, Salinas	.311	138	549	92	171	229	18	8	8	59	5	4	5	9	40	0	47	84	18
Kruk, John, Reno*	.311	125	441	82	137	216	30	8	11	92	14	4	11	1	72	4	55	17	5
Palica, John, Visalia†	.309	130	485	72	150	199	30	2	5	73	8	2	5	1	44	3	55	24	8

Departmental Leaders: G—Nelson, 140; AB—Nelson, 566; R—Guillen, 103; H—Guillen, 183; TB—Debus, Nelson 245; 2B—Nelson, 36; 3B—Ponce, 13; HR—McReynolds, 28; RBI—Nelson, 101; GWRBI—Nelson, Ponce, 15; SH—Gomez, Guillen, 14; SF—T. Johnson, Ponce, 12; HP—DeJesus, 12; BB—Riles, 84; IBB—Weaver, 11; SO—Cataline, 166; SB—Felder, 92; CS—Carter, Gerber, 20.

(All Players—Listed Alphabetically)

Player and Club	Pct.	G.	AB.	R.	H.	TB.	2B.	3B.	HR.	RBI.	GW.	SH.	SF.	HP.	BB.	Int. BB.	SO.	SB.	CS.
Adams, Jeffrey, Fresno	.207	17	58	4	12	12	0	0	0	7	0	0	2	0	3	0	18	0	0
Aponte, Edwin, Bakersfield	.261	139	499	45	130	167	26	1	3	62	4	6	5	5	42	1	26	23	10
Austin, Terry, Salinas	.252	125	441	71	111	132	12	3	1	39	3	7	4	2	57	1	90	43	18
Bailey, Robert, Lodi	.237	57	169	18	40	47	4	0	1	16	2	0	1	1	12	0	24	0	1
Bass, Ricki, Stockton	.247	95	255	40	63	74	6	1	1	25	2	2	3	3	40	1	34	34	6
Baughn, Stanley, Fresno†	.229	66	236	20	54	62	6	1	0	19	1	4	0	0	18	0	42	14	3
Bazan, Pedro, Salinas*	.248	106	355	31	88	112	18	3	0	46	6	2	8	6	37	5	35	2	1
Bradley, Philip, Bakersfield	.331	109	405	98	134	171	17	10	0	37	0	6	2	9	82	0	39	58	13
Brennan, Thomas, Bakersfield*	.667	45	3	1	2	2	0	0	0	0	0	0	0	0	1	0	1	0	0
Bridges, Cory, Fresno	.228	70	215	30	49	60	8	0	1	16	2	7	0	4	27	0	28	0	0
Brooks, Fred, Salinas	.254	135	480	65	122	151	20	3	1	48	2	0	7	3	77	1	70	12	10
Brooks, Michael, Redwood	.212	68	170	20	36	52	7	0	3	17	2	1	1	0	11	0	47	2	1
Brown, Christopher, Fresno	.293	41	133	22	39	62	9	1	4	31	2	0	1	3	25	3	15	4	0
Brunson, Eddie, Stockton	.256	65	223	23	57	75	7	1	3	30	3	0	3	3	16	1	35	12	5
Buckley, Michael, Salinas	.223	106	301	17	67	72	5	0	0	23	1	9	1	1	16	0	70	1	4
Burden, John, Bakersfield	.000	9	2	0	0	0	0	0	0	0	0	0	0	0	0	0	1	0	0
Byrum, Terry, Modesto*	.000	1	3	0	0	0	0	0	0	0	0	0	0	0	0	0	0	0	0
Camacho, James, Modesto	.246	124	406	66	100	135	14	3	5	40	8	7	4	4	67	0	63	35	12
Campbell, Steven, Bakersfield	.235	39	119	5	28	33	5	0	0	7	0	0	3	10	10	0	21	1	1
Carl, Jeffrey, San Jose	.223	86	300	46	67	120	12	1	13	46	6	0	2		52	2	76	14	4
Carroll, Carson, Visalia	.233	102	339	51	79	98	4	3	3	39	3	6	1	1	41	2	71	21	4
Carter, Don, San Jose*	.302	105	434	73	131	141	5	1	1	43	0	11	2	3	39	1	70	71	20
Cartwright, Alan, Stockton*	.228	57	167	19	38	46	8	0	0	13	3	0	2	0	17	0	32	4	4
Castillo, Juan, Stockton†	.269	134	483	60	130	155	9	8	0	42	7	12	5	4	50	0	84	36	18
Cataline, Daniel, Salinas	.246	135	488	74	120	217	21	11	18	79	10	2	5	3	53	2	166	11	7
Cecchini, James, San Jose	.258	64	240	26	62	89	12	0	5	32	2	0	1	4	21	0	41	1	1
Chavez, Christopher, Lodi†	.246	82	207	40	51	58	5	1	0	22	1	4	0	0	66	0	43	10	5
Chelette, Mark, Bakersfield*	.500	13	22	8	11	12	1	0	0	4	1	1	1	0	2	0	1	3	0
Chinn, Gregory, Lodi	.274	120	416	61	114	178	22	3	12	53	10	3	7	1	44	1	95	21	4
Codiroli, Michael, Bakersfield	.245	27	102	18	25	36	8	0	1	8	1	1	0	0	16	0	19	6	1
Cole, Michael, Visalia*	.289	114	381	86	110	136	15	4	1	40	4	2	1	7	49	3	43	71	14
Coles, Darnell, Bakersfield	.303	136	482	91	146	211	24	4	11	55	7	8	9	6	68	0	61	27	16
Contreras, Henry, Stockton	.183	52	131	16	24	27	3	0	0	14	1	3	2	2	25	0	29	5	1
Copeland, Thomas, Modesto*	.255	119	369	40	94	122	16	3	2	31	4	3	0	1	52	4	28	21	12
Coughlon, Kevin, Modesto	.226	8	31	5	7	12	2	0	1	3	1	0	0	0	3	0	9	0	0
Cruz, Juan, Modesto	.231	97	225	31	52	60	8	0	0	14	4	12	2	4	24	0	42	9	7
Culbert, Aurdie, Modesto	.274	94	285	33	78	118	16	0	8	40	3	8	4	1	25	0	61	2	3
Davenport, Gary, Fresno	.260	127	466	52	121	168	18	4	7	61	3	2	9	4	45	0	101	7	7
Dawes, Stephen, San Jose	.205	78	268	28	55	65	8	1	0	30	2	0	1	1	23	0	39	3	1
Dawson, Gary, Modesto	.230	88	304	37	70	101	9	5	4	35	3	3	3	5	26	0	75	19	18
Debus, Jon, Lodi	.325	138	498	73	162	245	23	6	16	94	5	0	8	2	69	2	84	10	5
DeJesus, Alejandro, San Jose	.249	104	353	45	88	122	18	2	4	45	6	0	3	12	46	1	69	2	3
Delany, Dennis, San Jose	.284	92	327	45	93	115	16	0	2	47	9	5	4	1	44	1	37	7	2
Doerrer, Robert, San Jose	.248	137	504	74	125	156	17	1	4	60	6	2	6	3	92	5	61	38	11
Durrmann, James, Modesto*	.266	84	241	26	64	88	15	0	3	26	1	1	0	2	32	2	12	3	4
Eakes, Steven, Redwood	.262	116	362	36	95	124	12	4	3	39	5	8	3	4	30	1	44	9	6
Etchebarren, Raymond, Reno	.285	132	505	80	144	202	31	0	9	68	8	5	4	3	42	1	45	10	7
Faulconer, Randall, Bakersfield	.250	2	4	0	1	1	0	0	0	0	0	0	0	0	0	0	3	0	0
Favata, Salvatore, Stockton	.250	25	44	8	11	17	3	0	1	3	0	0	0	0	6	0	12	2	2
Felder, Michael, Stockton†	.263	137	524	102	138	199	18	11	7	47	10	5	6	2	62	0	79	92	14
Felix, Paul, Visalia†	.245	95	322	50	79	117	13	2	7	49	5	4	2	3	40	1	97	5	9
Fettig, Thomas, San Jose	.248	109	379	45	94	122	17	1	3	47	4	1	3	3	58	0	82	5	9
Firova, Daniel, Bakersfield	.231	11	39	3	9	11	2	0	0	5	1	1	0	0	2	0	7	0	0
Flores, Michael, Visalia*	.177	34	62	10	11	11	0	0	0	5	0	1	0	0	14	0	9	1	1
Franko, Philip, Visalia†	.278	32	90	8	25	26	1	0	0	9	1	3	0	1	15	1	15	2	1
Gatewood, Henry, Lodi	.205	13	39	5	8	10	2	0	0	4	0	2	0	0	1	0	6	0	1

Player and Club	Pct.	G.	AB.	R.	H.	TB.	2B.	3B.	HR.	RBI.	GW.	SH.	SF.	HP.	BB.	Int. BB.	SO.	SB.	CS.
Gauntlett, Todd, Lodi	.253	43	162	16	41	53	9	0	1	16	4	1	1	2	13	0	15	2	2
Gavilan, Pedro, Reno	.219	64	210	27	46	62	11	1	1	14	1	4	0	4	10	0	25	2	1
Gerber, Craig, Redwood°	.294	131	493	71	145	178	21	6	0	39	1	11	0	6	40	0	36	36	20
Giordano, Michael, Visalia	.000	51	1	0	0	0	0	0	0	0	0	0	0	0	0	0	1	0	0
Gomez, Ernesto, Bakersfield	.237	129	443	48	105	117	5	2	1	40	2	14	4	3	54	0	64	15	12
Gomez, Jose, Reno°	.246	49	171	23	42	64	7	3	3	26	0	0	0	0	23	4	47	0	0
Gonzalez, Joaquin, Visalia	.245	22	49	6	12	15	0	0	1	6	2	0	0	0	6	0	10	0	1
Gonzalez, Orlando, Stockton	.174	69	219	24	38	50	7	1	1	15	1	8	2	0	6	1	40	4	1
Gregory, John, Lodi°	.200	48	145	14	29	37	8	0	0	10	0	2	1	0	12	1	31	0	1
Guillen, Oswaldo, Reno†	.347	130	528	103	183	224	33	1	2	54	6	14	6	2	16	1	53	25	14
Gutierrez, Felipe, Lodi	.272	61	202	28	55	75	11	0	3	27	0	3	4	3	16	0	30	2	1
Guzman, Hector, Lodi†	.216	61	204	30	44	58	5	3	1	14	2	2	1	2	11	0	50	11	6
Harper, Therron, 11-Mod-69-Red....	.234	80	235	22	55	74	10	3	1	32	3	3	5	0	21	0	22	3	5
Harrigan, David, Salinas	.206	87	253	28	52	94	10	1	10	38	6	4	4	0	21	2	83	0	2
Hatcher, William, Salinas	.311	138	549	92	171	229	18	8	8	59	5	4	5	9	40	0	47	84	18
Heimach, William, Fresno†	.234	39	137	26	32	34	2	0	0	13	0	4	3	3	32	1	10	2	2
Henry, Chris, Bakersfield°	.242	111	396	45	96	141	18	0	9	49	6	2	5	1	38	2	35	2	3
Hertzler, Paul, San Jose°	.281	130	474	65	133	190	26	8	5	63	10	2	5	11	56	3	59	19	16
Hill, Clay, Bakersfield°	.298	107	329	50	98	125	21	0	2	33	3	3	4	3	64	0	48	8	5
Hobbs, Rodney, Modesto	.111	4	9	0	1	1	0	0	0	1	0	1	1	4	1	3	1	0	
Hotchkiss, John, Modesto	.271	134	435	71	118	163	20	2	7	52	4	2	8	9	51	0	97	18	9
Howe, Gregory, Visalia	.236	47	148	19	35	43	3	1	1	15	1	3	1	3	14	0	29	8	3
Hudgens, David, Modesto°	.301	132	435	75	131	240	27	5	24	82	11	0	5	5	50	6	80	7	8
Hudson, Lance, Lodi†	.276	55	134	18	37	42	2	0	1	15	1	1	0	3	7	1	22	3	4
Hunger, Christopher, Bakersfield	.000	29	1	1	0	0	0	0	0	0	0	0	0	0	0	0	1	0	
Hunt, Ronald, Redwood	.220	68	200	14	44	47	3	0	0	15	1	2	2	4	18	2	23	6	7
Hunter, Marion, Redwood	.259	67	266	44	69	85	8	4	0	17	2	6	2	1	21	0	30	25	9
Ireland, Billy, Reno	.291	90	299	31	87	108	17	2	0	47	3	5	5	1	25	1	35	1	1
Jacobson, Kevin, Redwood	.241	81	257	30	62	81	14	1	1	27	4	3	3	1	25	0	51	4	4
Johnnson, James, Fresno	.268	70	250	56	67	87	12	4	0	19	2	6	3	1	38	0	51	33	9
Johnson, Kevin, Reno	.252	45	119	12	30	41	6	1	1	16	1	1	0	1	11	1	32	3	0
Johnson, Steven, Reno	.259	132	482	80	125	164	8	5	7	51	6	5	4	8	67	1	112	46	14
Johnson, Thomas, Salinas	.268	135	477	75	128	168	18	2	6	81	6	1	12	1	75	2	120	44	11
Keeney, Steven, Fresno°	.241	60	174	22	42	48	2	2	0	8	1	6	0	0	25	3	23	5	4
King, Kevin, Bakersfield†	.251	133	499	74	125	203	18	0	20	81	6	1	2	0	59	4	128	27	3
Kornacker, Dean, Fresno	.191	42	136	14	26	32	3	0	1	14	1	0	0	2	19	0	24	0	2
Krueger, Kirby, Visalia	.000	43	1	0	0	0	0	0	0	0	0	0	0	0	0	0	1	0	
Kruk, John, Reno°	.311	125	441	82	137	216	30	8	11	92	14	4	11	1	72	4	55	17	5
Kubit, Joseph, Visalia	.283	99	360	47	102	144	22	7	2	52	6	5	2	7	31	1	65	0	3
Kwiecinski, Michael, San Jose	.223	99	319	36	71	90	6	2	3	36	3	5	6	3	37	0	67	7	8
Lachemann, William, Fresno°	.000	1	0	0	0	0	0	0	0	0	0	0	0	0	0	0	0	0	0
Langie, Louis, Reno	.232	57	151	28	35	52	6	4	1	13	3	4	2	0	19	0	48	4	1
Langston, Mark, Bakersfield	1.000	27	1	1	1	2	1	0	0	0	0	0	0	0	0	0	0	0	0
Levi, Stanley, Stockton°	.336	121	422	77	142	178	12	9	2	51	6	11	3	1	41	3	37	57	12
Liddle, Steven, Redwood	.234	55	158	14	37	53	7	0	3	19	1	4	3	2	17	0	21	1	3
Littmann, Jerome, Fresno°	.266	111	365	60	97	119	13	3	1	32	2	8	2	3	76	1	51	8	7
Lomastro, Gerardo, Visalia	.301	133	501	84	151	243	31	2	19	91	11	2	7	6	56	2	70	10	6
Lombardozzi, Stephen, Visalia	.297	122	441	81	131	175	24	1	6	67	8	5	10	1	64	3	41	14	4
Lulay, Douglas, Reno	.300	98	363	67	109	160	11	8	8	51	5	2	5	8	32	1	60	12	4
Martin, Jared, Salinas°	.260	31	77	10	20	26	4	1	0	6	0	2	0	0	7	0	10	3	1
Martin, Victor, Bakersfield°	1.000	48	1	1	1	1	0	0	0	0	0	0	0	0	1	0	1	0	
Max, William, Stockton	.303	60	198	40	60	111	16	1	11	38	5	3	4	2	32	2	53	6	2
Mazzilli, Donald, Fresno°	.280	65	232	36	65	92	9	3	4	42	2	0	5	1	38	1	32	4	1
McDaniel, Kevin, San Jose	.111	5	9	1	1	1	0	0	0	0	0	0	0	1	0	2	0	0	
McReynolds, Kevin, Reno	.376	90	338	83	127	238	17	5	28	98	5	0	6	0	36	6	50	0	0
Montanari, David A., Salinas°	.296	13	27	6	8	9	1	0	0	2	0	1	0	6	0	7	0	0	
Moore, Michael, Lodi	.213	27	75	6	16	19	1	1	0	11	2	0	0	2	6	0	10	0	0
Moore, Robert, Modesto	1.000	7	1	0	1	1	0	0	0	0	0	0	0	0	0	0	0	0	0
Moreno, Jaime, Reno	.232	33	95	11	22	23	1	0	0	11	0	7	0	1	8	0	23	1	1
Morris, David, Redwood	.289	26	38	6	11	15	2	1	0	3	0	0	0	0	6	0	16	1	0
Myers, David, Bakersfield	.147	40	109	22	16	23	4	0	1	13	0	3	0	2	26	0	23	2	0
Morrison, Perry, Redwood	.000	16	0	1	0	0	0	0	0	0	0	0	0	0	0	0	0	0	0
Murphy, Roderick, Modesto	.235	90	213	27	50	62	5	2	1	25	5	5	2	0	49	0	40	12	6
Murray, Steven, Reno	.233	99	317	72	74	115	12	4	7	34	4	2	5	6	63	0	81	12	6
Nago, Garrett, Stockton†	.140	24	43	5	6	7	1	0	0	5	1	0	0	5	0	13	0	0	
Nay, Len, San Jose°	.218	33	87	10	19	28	2	2	1	13	2	2	1	0	15	3	21	6	0
Nelson, Ricky, Bakersfield°	.307	140	566	65	174	245	36	1	11	101	15	2	7	4	32	3	60	43	15
Nieves, Tito, San Jose	.231	107	325	55	75	104	10	2	5	25	2	2	4	1	66	0	86	21	6
Noce, Paul, Reno	.259	56	185	23	48	71	7	5	2	20	0	3	2	19	1	51	6	2	
O'Brien, Charles, Modesto	.300	41	140	23	42	57	6	0	3	32	7	2	2	2	20	0	19	7	3
Ornest, Maury, Stockton†	.185	61	184	29	34	49	7	1	2	22	0	2	4	3	31	2	34	10	2
Pagel, David, Salinas°	.250	57	172	19	43	52	7	1	0	19	5	4	1	0	23	3	22	3	2
Palica, John, Visalia°	.309	130	485	72	150	199	30	2	5	73	8	2	5	1	44	3	55	24	8
Paskiewicz, Larry, Bakersfield†	.224	61	201	23	45	56	5	0	2	25	1	0	3	1	15	0	31	9	2
Payne, James, Salinas	.280	73	236	31	66	77	5	3	0	22	2	1	0	3	41	0	65	21	8
Perkins, Harold, Lodi†	.262	34	122	13	32	38	6	0	0	11	1	0	1	0	19	0	16	7	2
Piatnik, Michael, Visalia	.176	32	74	8	13	18	5	0	0	11	0	2	0	0	5	0	16	2	0
Piggott, Russell, Salinas	.261	82	299	40	78	105	7	4	4	33	0	1	2	0	28	0	42	5	5
Ponce, Carlos, Stockton	.286	132	489	59	140	215	31	13	6	79	15	4	12	4	40	2	84	17	6
Rammpen, Frank, Visalia	.246	115	374	60	92	114	16	0	2	38	4	8	5	2	35	1	71	14	7
Randall, James, Redwood†	.274	135	504	64	138	206	27	4	11	74	7	1	4	5	46	5	86	28	15
Reece, Thad, Modesto°	.275	80	182	28	50	64	10	2	0	16	1	5	1	0	35	1	18	3	3
Reed, Jeffrey, Visalia°	.329	125	395	69	130	168	19	2	5	54	3	4	4	7	78	3	32	1	2
Reid, Jessie, Fresno°	.292	127	476	78	139	187	20	5	6	73	6	2	7	0	67	5	80	20	12
Reyes, Gilberto, Lodi	.281	127	424	65	119	184	18	1	15	55	3	5	3	2	39	0	74	5	6
Reynolds, Robert, Lodi†	.313	108	403	67	126	169	19	3	6	35	3	1	1	0	36	2	68	25	11
Riles, Earnest, Stockton°	.286	138	447	60	128	169	23	6	2	56	5	3	5	3	84	3	53	21	15
Rivera, Luis, San Jose	.258	130	476	53	123	158	20	3	3	49	5	1	7	4	27	0	94	12	4
Robertson, Gary, Reno°	.364	19	66	14	24	44	2	0	6	24	2	1	0	2	8	1	11	1	0
Romero, Albert, Redwood	.276	137	490	78	135	203	24	4	12	76	11	2	7	4	41	2	70	16	9
Rosenhahn, David, Salinas	.225	62	222	24	50	59	2	2	1	15	1	0	0	1	23	1	37	3	3
Rossi, Joseph, Lodi	.243	110	362	42	88	117	11	0	6	32	2	6	3	7	35	0	75	21	8

Player and Club	Pct.	G.	AB.	R.	H.	TB.	2B.	3B.	HR.	RBI.	GW.	SH.	SF.	HP.	BB.	Int. BB.	SO.	SB.	CS.
Rudolph, Wayne, Modesto†	.261	106	326	41	85	107	12	2	2	35	4	11	2	2	40	1	23	20	8
Saatzer, Michael, Redwood°	.000	23	1	0	0	0	0	0	0	0	0	0	0	0	0	0	1	0	0
Schofield, Richard, Redwood	.245	33	102	15	25	37	3	3	1	8	0	1	0	0	17	0	20	6	4
Skeens, George, Visalia	.147	14	34	1	5	7	2	0	0	1	0	1	0	0	1	0	5	0	0
Smelko, Mark, Redwood†	.167	28	84	6	14	20	4	1	0	12	2	0	0	0	12	0	8	0	3
Smith, Brick, Bakersfield	.259	96	348	59	90	148	20	1	12	58	3	1	2	0	47	0	53	16	5
Smith, Gregory, Lodi°	.270	72	263	39	71	113	13	1	9	41	3	0	2	2	20	3	35	5	2
Smith, Jeffrey, Redwood	.000	39	0	1	0	0	0	0	0	0	0	0	0	0	0	0	0	0	0
Snyder, Bryan, Fresno°	.304	133	483	68	147	216	25	7	10	75	7	6	5	7	48	2	69	7	6
Soprano, Joseph, Modesto	.239	69	176	30	42	74	6	1	8	30	8	1	1	1	24	0	41	4	1
Soriano, Hilario, San Jose	.143	7	21	0	3	4	1	0	0	1	0	0	0	0	0	0	7	0	0
Spiroff, George, Fresno	.231	74	234	30	54	80	11	0	5	32	4	6	1	4	21	1	27	2	1
Sproesser, Mark, Redwood	.198	48	116	12	23	30	4	0	1	14	2	0	2	1	14	0	16	9	3
Spurlin, Robert, Fresno	.217	73	212	24	46	48	2	0	0	19	1	8	0	3	43	0	32	1	1
Stanicek, Stephen, Fresno	.246	22	69	9	17	29	3	0	3	6	0	0	1	7	0	21	0	0	
Stassi, James, Fresno	.270	52	159	22	43	53	7	0	1	15	1	3	3	1	23	0	21	2	2
Steger, Kevin, Bakersfield°	.250	46	4	1	1	1	0	0	0	1	0	0	0	0	1	0	1	0	0
Stein, Raymond, Visalia°	.235	44	136	12	32	36	4	0	0	16	1	0	0	3	7	0	13	2	1
Stephens, Darryl, Redwood°	.278	127	414	51	115	152	23	1	4	50	4	3	3	7	42	4	43	6	5
Stephenson, Phillip, Modesto°	.283	64	212	39	60	93	14	2	5	26	6	0	2	0	28	1	25	18	12
Stromer, Richard, Redwood	.253	33	83	11	21	35	8	0	2	9	1	0	0	1	21	1	18	0	1
Su'a, Murphy, Stockton	.231	109	368	43	85	126	10	2	9	58	4	2	7	1	34	4	97	10	10
Sundberg, Richard, Redwood	.203	32	64	2	13	14	1	0	0	5	0	1	1	1	11	0	15	0	3
Tarnow, Greg, Salinas	.222	5	9	1	2	2	0	0	0	1	0	0	0	1	0	0	2	0	0
Tenney, Mickey, Salinas	.281	57	114	15	32	32	0	0	0	6	0	1	6	0	1	4	1	15	2	4
Tettleton, Mickey, Modesto†	.249	88	253	44	63	105	18	0	8	37	8	0	2	2	63	3	46	4	4
Thomas, Jimmy, Reno	.185	19	65	2	12	19	1	0	2	10	2	0	2	0	6	0	11	0	1
Thompson, Craig, Lodi	.123	23	57	4	7	7	0	0	0	5	1	1	0	0	9	1	10	1	0
Vavra, Joseph, Lodi°	.242	49	149	19	36	44	5	0	1	10	0	2	1	0	16	2	17	2	3
Ward, Randall, Fresno°	.257	92	300	40	77	140	26	2	11	44	2	1	5	4	47	2	80	1	0
Wasinger, Mark, Reno	.318	60	220	36	70	94	18	0	2	32	2	2	4	3	34	1	32	7	2
Watanabe, Curt, Stockton	.313	45	144	14	45	54	5	2	0	21	4	1	1	0	20	0	18	1	1
Weaver, James, Visalia°	.286	125	454	68	130	204	21	4	15	86	14	0	6	0	70	11	65	60	19
White, William, Lodi	.243	11	37	3	9	13	2	1	0	8	1	0	1	2	6	0	12	0	0
Wiggins, Kevin, Reno°	.192	16	52	5	10	13	1	1	0	6	0	0	1	1	5	0	18	1	0
Williams, Brian, Lodi†	.290	127	469	49	136	161	17	1	2	55	4	1	3	1	28	1	49	14	6
Wilson, David, Fresno	.196	48	148	10	29	30	1	0	0	13	0	0	1	0	13	0	42	1	0
Wood, Johnson, Stockton°	.333	21	3	0	1	1	0	0	0	0	0	0	0	0	0	0	1	0	0
Woods, Victor, Modesto	.000	9	17	1	0	0	0	0	0	0	0	0	0	0	2	0	9	0	0
Wren, Franklin, San Jose	.212	24	85	12	18	21	1	1	0	7	1	0	0	1	10	0	13	5	1
Wright, Paul, Redwood	.258	125	383	56	99	112	9	2	0	27	2	7	0	6	48	0	91	18	9
Young, Curtis, Modesto	1.000	28	1	0	1	1	0	0	0	0	0	0	0	0	0	0	0	0	0
Young, Selwyn, Modesto†	.267	43	86	16	23	30	2	1	1	12	1	3	3	4	18	0	5	13	4
Zambrana, Luis, Redwood	.232	40	69	5	16	26	2	4	0	5	2	2	0	0	6	0	16	4	5

The following pitchers, listed alphabetically by club, with games in parentheses, had no plate appearances, primarily through use of designated hitters:

BAKERSFIELD—Cahill, Mark (25); Crisler, Joel (1); Guetterman, Lee (26); Pedersen, Mark (49); Randolph, Robert (15); Spicer, Kevin (24).

FRESNO—Biagini, Robert (28); Bordley, William (13); Buckmier, James (28); Chue, Jose (27); Gallo, Bernard (31); Maloney, James (1); Mathiesen, Marty (27); McSparran, Gregory (35); Patterson, Gilbert (4); Ronan, Kernan (10); Schafer, Dennis (35); Trax, Jeffrey (19); Wilhelmi, David (25); Winters, Mark (26).

LODI—Anderson, David (16); Beard, Charles (36); Beuder, Michael (17); Bryant, Franklin (11); Carne, Gregory (17); deLeon, Orlando (5); Dente, Frank (21); Innis, Brian (13); Madden, Morris (12); Montalvo, Rafael (39); Moscaret, Jeffrey (50); Piper, Brian (13); Reade, Curtis (34); Reeves, Mathew (3); Smith, Don (21); Sylvia, John (2); Thorp, Bradley (9); Vucsko, Kirk (12).

MODESTO—Anderson, Scott (1); Conroy, Timothy (27); Ferguson, Mark (26); Figueroa, Eduardo (3); Hallgren, Tim (9); Hampton, Timothy (1); Herron, Anthony (15); Josephson, Paul (42); Lynes, Michael (22); Odekirk, Richard (4); Palica, Wayne (3); Powers, Michael (20, SJ 12-Mod 8); Retzer, Edwin (17); Rodriguez, Ricardo (15); Van Marter, Donald (7); Warren, Michael (28, Sto 6-Mod 22).

REDWOOD—Bankowski, Kris (18); Bastian, Robert (29); Braun, Barton (15); Clapham, Mark (9); Fisher, Glenn (15); Halicki, Kevin (9); Jones, Lee (53); Kammeyer, Timothy (25); Kibbe, Jay (8); Oliver, Scott (18); Roen, Thomas (1); Ruzek, Don (10); Sylvia, Ronald.(57); Venezia, Michael (11).

RENO—Booker, Gregory (27); Brown, Lawrence (10); Christy, Mark (10); Cota, Francisco (24); Fiechtner, Jeff (33); Gerhardt, William (15); Goodchild, Christopher (8); Harris, Craig (2); Kutsukos, Peter (37); Leopold, James (18); Macias, Robert (19); Oliver, Bruce (19); Oroz, Felix (30); Patterson, Robert (4); Ruiz, Cecilio (3); Schefsky, Steven (26); Stadler, Jeffrey (9); Williamson, Mark (26).

SALINAS—Adanczak, James (7); Andrews, Jeffrey (33); Bachmeier, Ronald (1); Giacomazzi, James (3); Hardy, Bryan (24); Housey, Joseph (25); Johnson, Scott (8); Kyles, Stanley (26); Lockie, Randall (17); Nowlin, Mark (22); Pantaleo, Joseph (12); Schilling, Robert (34); Schulze, Donald (24); Soff, Raymond (43); Swaggerty, Glenn (25); Vaji, Mark (3).

SAN JOSE—Branam, Barry (36); Budd, Randy (2); Cates, Timothy (27); Edwards, Derek (17); Fadhel, Antonio (15); Flores, David (17); Gilbreath, Ronald (11); Grapenthin, Richard (27); Groves, Larry (15); Huber, Randolph (40); Johnson, Gregory (15); Maria, Alan (11); McIntosh, James (6); St. Claire, Randy (9); Staffon, Gregory (6); Tenenini, Robert (10); Torres, Miguel (15); Vega, Randolph (7); Westray, Kenneth (11).

STOCKTON—Biggus, Bengie (21); Burns, Daniel (9); Crews, Timothy (19); Dinkins, Charles (13); Effrig, Mark (34); Ember, Richard (14); Gallo, Raymond (32); Manderfield, Steven (12); Mignano, Brian (15); Parrott, Stephen (8); Pone, Vincent (4); Roberts, Scott (24); Swift, Weldon (17); Tatsuno, Derek (7); Teahan, James (8); Vasquez, Jesse (1).

VISALIA—Angulo, Kenneth (11); Fregin, Doug (11); Guerrero, Anthony (17); Oelkers, Bryan (5); Pena, Manuel (25); Pettibone, Harry (11); Snider, Eric (17); Suarez, Luis (5); Wardle, Curtis (28); Weibel, Randy (28); Yett, Richard (27).

GRAND SLAM HOME RUNS—Carl, Debus, Hudgens, 2 each; Delany, Etchebarren, Felder, Hatcher, Kwiecinski, McReynolds, Ornest, Palica, Randall, Robertson, Randolph, B. Smith, G. Smith, Snyder, Spiroff, Ward, 1 each.

AWARDED FIRST BASE ON CATCHER'S INTERFERENCE—Stephenson 3 (Moore, Romero, Su'a); Piggott 2 (Hill 2); Durrman (Su'a); T. Johnson (Adams); Payne (Stassi); Soprano (Ireland).

CLUB FIELDING

Club	Pct.	G.	PO.	A.	E.	DP.	PB.	Club	Pct.	G.	PO.	A.	E.	DP.	PB.
Modesto	.972	140	3602	1436	145	96	22	San Jose	.960	140	3586	1452	209	123	24
Redwood	.965	140	3572	1583	189	121	23	Salinas	.960	140	3525	1510	210	100	23
Stockton	.964	138	3496	1510	185	126	27	Bakersfield	.956	140	3547	1618	239	125	45
Visalia	.961	140	3590	1555	208	112	15	Fresno	.953	140	3503	1506	246	105	22
Reno	.960	138	3461	1500	205	124	21	Lodi	.950	140	3500	1445	262	112	31

Triple Plays—Modesto, San Jose.

INDIVIDUAL FIELDING

*Throws lefthanded.

FIRST BASEMEN

Player and Club	Pct.	G.	PO.	A.	E.	DP.	Player and Club	Pct.	G.	PO.	A.	E.	DP.
Austin, Salinas	1.000	2	16	0	0	2	Johnson, Salinas	.983	135	1215	78	23	74
Bailey, Lodi	1.000	17	100	9	0	12	Kruk, Reno*	1.000	2	21	0	0	3
Brennan, Bakersfield*	1.000	1	6	0	0	1	Kubit, Visalia	.987	79	655	54	16	49
Brooks, Redwood	1.000	2	11	0	0	1	Levi, Stockton*	.962	8	47	3	2	1
Brown, Fresno	1.000	3	11	2	0	0	Lulay, Reno	.985	72	632	34	10	48
Carroll, Visalia	1.000	5	8	0	0	0	Mazzilli, Fresno*	.985	8	63	3	1	6
Chinn, Lodi	1.000	5	23	3	0	3	Myers, Bakersfield	1.000	1	1	1	0	0
Culbert, Modesto	.997	74	563	45	2	38	Murphy, Modesto	1.000	5	25	2	0	1
Dawes, San Jose	1.000	1	7	0	0	0	Paskiewicz, Bakersfield	.992	26	251	9	2	13
deJesus, San Jose	.991	65	520	40	5	50	Piatnik, Visalia	1.000	1	1	0	0	0
Felix, Visalia	.991	60	505	29	5	42	Ponce, Stockton	.986	132	1225	78	19	112
Franko, Visalia	.967	6	53	5	2	5	Reid, Fresno*	.973	27	238	14	7	22
Gauntlett, Lodi	.992	14	111	16	1	10	Robertson, Reno	.989	16	161	16	2	12
Gomez, Reno*	.979	42	363	14	8	39	Smelko, Redwood	1.000	2	9	1	0	2
Gregory, Lodi*	.983	45	370	27	7	36	Smith, Bakersfield	.987	96	911	83	13	85
Harper, 4 Mod-22 Red	.991	26	206	14	2	14	G. Smith, Lodi	.987	68	662	42	9	31
Harrigan, Salinas	1.000	4	43	3	0	5	Stanicek, Fresno	.985	13	119	9	2	6
Henry, Bakersfield	1.000	2	12	3	0	2	STEPHENS, Redwood*	.990	125	1053	81	11	87
Hertzler, San Jose*	.981	84	635	38	13	61	Stephenson, Modesto*	.992	55	436	39	4	30
Hill, Bakersfield	.970	16	152	10	5	12	Su'a, Stockton	1.000	1	5	1	0	0
Hudgens, Modesto*	.991	17	105	8	1	9	Sundberg, Redwood	1.000	2	4	0	0	0
Hunt, Redwood	1.000	9	32	3	0	8	Ward, Fresno	.972	65	558	41	17	41
Ireland, Reno	1.000	9	83	4	0	8	White, Lodi	1.000	3	31	3	0	2
Johnson, Fresno	.986	28	267	14	4	17	Woods, Modesto	.909	2	18	2	2	1

Triple Plays—deJesus.

SECOND BASEMEN

Player and Club	Pct.	G.	PO.	A.	E.	DP.	Player and Club	Pct.	G.	PO.	A.	E.	DP.
Bailey, Lodi	1.000	1	0	1	0	0	Gomez, Bakersfield	.939	127	269	346	40	67
Baughn, Fresno	.959	53	87	148	10	19	Gonzalez, Stockton	.950	8	12	7	1	2
Brooks, Salinas	.967	128	244	424	23	64	Gutierrez, Lodi	.950	53	120	164	15	39
Brooks, Redwood	.955	15	17	25	2	8	Guzman, Lodi	.917	38	75	79	14	14
Burden, Bakersfield	1.000	1	1	0	0	0	Heimach, Fresno	.977	39	85	124	5	19
Camacho, Modesto	1.000	7	6	13	0	0	Hudson, Lodi	.964	16	34	20	2	5
Carroll, Visalia	.969	81	178	194	12	37	Johnson, Fresno	.833	2	2	3	1	0
Castillo, Stockton	.968	134	273	428	23	88	Langie, Reno	.921	49	81	129	18	27
Chavez, Lodi	.949	14	20	36	3	5	Littmann, Fresno	.925	29	56	79	11	16
Chelette, Bakersfield	.935	8	12	17	2	2	Montanari, Salinas	1.000	3	3	4	0	1
Cole, Visalia	.940	61	125	156	18	42	Myers, Bakersfield	.957	6	7	15	1	3
CRUZ, Modesto	.975	96	181	206	10	36	Payne, Salinas	.857	3	4	8	2	1
Davenport, Fresno	.921	22	49	56	9	8	Perkins, Lodi	.920	33	62	88	13	11
Dawes, San Jose	1.000	6	11	15	0	4	Piatnik, Visalia	.900	2	4	5	1	0
Doerrer, San Jose	.968	137	315	387	23	69	Piggott, Salinas	.941	9	16	16	2	1
Eakes, Redwood	.968	95	198	293	16	48	Reece, Modesto	.971	56	102	98	6	22
Etchebarren, Reno	.964	43	69	119	7	18	Sproesser, Redwood	.954	20	26	36	3	8
Favata, Stockton	1.000	2	0	2	0	0	Vavra, Lodi	1.000	1	1	3	0	0
Flores, Visalia	.955	14	22	20	2	4	Wasinger, Reno	.970	56	108	184	9	28
Franko, Visalia	1.000	1	0	1	0	0	S. Young, Modesto	.949	18	29	46	4	7
Gerber, Redwood	.989	29	68	113	2	24							

Triple Play—Cruz.

THIRD BASEMEN

Player and Club	Pct.	G.	PO.	A.	E.	DP.	Player and Club	Pct.	G.	PO.	A.	E.	DP.
Aponte, Bakersfield	.942	138	97	329	26	33	Kornacker, Fresno	.895	14	14	20	4	2
Bachemeier, Salinas	1.000	1	0	1	0	0	Littmann, Fresno	.864	40	29	79	17	8
Bailey, Lodi	.700	4	3	4	3	1	Lulay, Reno	.813	6	6	7	3	0
Bridges, Fresno	.857	26	15	39	9	2	Martin, Bakersfield	1.000	1	1	0	0	0
Brooks, Redwood	.924	27	20	41	5	6	Max, Stockton	.933	57	43	110	11	5
Brown, Fresno	.967	36	26	62	3	3	Murphy, Modesto	1.000	4	1	3	0	1
Camacho, Modesto	.667	1	1	1	1	0	Myers, Bakersfield	.667	3	2	2	2	0
Carroll, Visalia	.848	13	10	18	5	1	Nago, Stockton	.333	2	0	1	2	0
Chavez, Lodi	.857	3	1	5	1	0	Pagel, Salinas	.930	18	9	31	3	3
Davenport, Fresno	.911	31	32	70	10	4	Payne, Salinas	.600	3	0	3	2	0
Dawes, San Jose	.910	52	32	79	11	4	Piatnik, Visalia	.880	11	3	19	3	2
Debus, Lodi	.870	133	101	219	48	21	Ramppen, Visalia	.900	113	69	174	27	20
Etchebarren, Reno	.934	87	67	131	14	11	Reece, Modesto	.944	11	5	12	1	1
Fettig, San Jose	.863	91	69	120	30	8	Reyes, Lodi	1.000	1	1	0	0	0
Flores, Visalia	1.000	5	0	3	0	0	Rosenhahn, Salinas	.889	57	27	93	15	2
Franko, Visalia	.923	15	13	23	3	1	Sproesser, Redwood	.833	2	4	1	1	0
Gauntlett, Lodi	1.000	2	0	1	0	0	Stanicek, Fresno	1.000	3	3	2	0	0
Gerber, Redwood	.922	25	20	39	5	5	Stromer, Redwood	.878	31	23	42	9	5
Gonzalez, Stockton	.910	63	55	106	16	8	Su'a, Stockton	.667	3	0	2	1	0
HOTCHKISS, Modesto	.962	133	98	230	13	13	Tenney, Salinas	.940	47	57	101	10	15
Noce, Reno	.915	11	12	31	4	5	Watanabe, Stockton	.870	17	4	36	6	1
Ireland, Reno	.917	10	5	6	1	1	Woods, Modesto	1.000	1	0	1	0	0
Jocobson, Redwood	.931	67	47	101	11	5							

SHORTSTOPS

Player and Club	Pct.	G.	PO.	A.	E.	DP.	Player and Club	Pct.	G.	PO.	A.	E.	DP.
Brown, Fresno	.786	2	4	7	3	0	Eakes, Redwood	.880	24	37	58	13	11
Buckley, Salinas	.922	106	147	290	37	57	Flores, Visalia	.909	11	7	13	2	2
Camacho, Modesto	.910	91	121	193	31	29	Franko, Visalia	1.000	6	10	21	0	3
Chavez, Lodi	.950	66	94	194	15	31	Gerber, Redwood	.953	79	88	233	16	41
Chelette, Bakersfield	1.000	2	3	6	0	1	Gomez, Bakersfield	1.000	2	1	5	0	1
Coles, Bakersfield	.895	136	200	419	73	72	Guillen, Reno	.940	129	240	399	41	71
Cruz, Modesto	1.000	1	0	1	0	0	Guzman, Lodi	.833	20	26	44	14	10
Davenport, Fresno	.940	75	120	240	23	32	Hudson, Lodi	.841	24	38	52	17	12
Dawes, San Jose	.981	11	20	33	1	10	Kornacker, Fresno	.880	22	31	64	13	11

SHORTSTOPS—Continued

Player and Club	Pct.	G.	PO.	A.	E.	DP.	Player and Club	Pct.	G.	PO.	A.	E.	DP.
Langie, Reno	.923	6	2	10	1	1	Piatnik, Visalia	.870	19	28	52	12	8
Littmann, Fresno	.733	3	3	8	4	0	Riles, Stockton	.9465	138	204	451	37	95
LOMBARDOZZI, Visalia	.9474	119	183	393	32	57	Rivera, San Jose	.918	130	226	389	55	76
Murphy, Modesto	.938	69	101	187	19	30	Schofield, Redwood	.979	32	35	103	3	19
Myers, Bakersfield	.900	3	4	5	1	1	Sproesser, Redwood	.911	12	18	23	4	4
Noce, Reno	.915	11	12	31	4	5	Tenney, Salinas	.940	47	57	101	10	15
Pagel, Salinas	.960	7	8	16	1	0	Vavra, Lodi	.898	47	66	101	19	16
Payne, Salinas	.600	3	0	3	2	0	Wilson, Fresno	.911	48	54	131	18	22

Triple Plays—Camacho, Rivera.

OUTFIELDERS

Player and Club	Pct.	G.	PO.	A.	E.	DP.	Player and Club	Pct.	G.	PO.	A.	E.	DP.
Austin, Salinas	.959	120	251	4	11	0	Levi, Stockton°	.978	117	167	8	4	0
Bass, Stockton	.961	56	71	2	3	0	Littmann, Fresno	1.000	9	19	0	0	0
Baughn, Fresno	.947	14	18	0	1	0	Lomastro, Visalia	.970	121	188	7	6	2
Bradley, Bakersfield	.976	109	226	13	6	5	Lombardozzi, Visalia	1.000	1	2	0	0	0
Bridges, Fresno	.981	36	49	3	1	0	Lulay, Reno	.500	2	2	0	2	0
Brooks, Redwood	.917	15	10	1	1	1	Martin, Salinas°	.889	6	8	0	1	0
Brunson, Stockton	.923	12	24	0	2	0	Mazzilli, Reno°	.978	57	89	2	2	0
Camacho, Modesto	.985	33	63	4	1	0	McReynolds, Reno	.952	42	52	7	3	0
Campbell, Bakersfield	.947	28	34	2	2	0	Morris, Redwood°	.926	23	24	1	2	0
Carl, San Jose	.975	67	112	7	3	1	Murray, Reno	.969	92	175	10	6	1
Carroll, Visalia	1.000	2	7	0	0	0	Myers, Bakersfield	1.000	3	4	0	0	0
CARTER, San Jose	.996	105	231	2	1	1	Nay, San Jose	.965	26	52	3	2	1
Cartwright, Stockton°	.990	54	94	9	1	1	Nelson, Bakersfield	.959	137	197	13	9	3
Cataline, Salinas	.962	131	230	23	10	4	Nieves, San Jose	.967	89	168	8	6	2
Chavez, Lodi	1.000	1	1	0	0	0	Ornest, Stockton	.956	52	99	9	5	5
Chinn, Lodi	.968	103	136	13	5	6	Pagel, Salinas	1.000	13	15	0	0	0
Codiroli, Bakersfield°	.935	27	71	1	5	0	Palica, Visalia°	.976	110	231	8	6	1
Cole, Visalia	1.000	7	14	0	0	0	Paskiewicz, Bakersfield	1.000	26	28	1	0	0
Copeland, Modesto°	.980	116	183	16	4	4	Payne, Salinas	1.000	1	1	0	0	0
Coughlon, Modesto	1.000	8	12	4	0	1	Piggott, Salinas	1.000	16	33	2	0	0
Dawson, Modesto	.960	87	205	9	9	3	Randall, Redwood°	.942	131	187	23	13	6
Doerrer, San Jose	1.000	2	2	0	0	0	Reece, Modesto	1.000	2	3	0	0	0
Favata, Stockton	1.000	11	24	1	0	0	Reid, Fresno	.958	88	147	13	7	2
Felder, Stockton	.970	137	314	9	10	2	Reynolds, Lodi	.974	99	212	12	6	2
Gerber, Redwood	1.000	1	2	0	0	0	Romero, Redwood	.953	25	39	2	2	1
Harper, 12 Mod-1 Red	.929	13	13	0	1	0	Rossi, Lodi	.964	101	226	13	9	1
Hatcher, Salinas	.953	138	235	10	12	0	Rudolph, Modesto°	.988	102	149	10	2	2
Hertzler, San Jose°	.960	45	71	1	3	1	Smelko, Redwood	1.000	7	7	1	0	1
Hill, Bakersfield	1.000	3	1	0	0	0	Snyder, Fresno°	.978	133	344	9	8	1
Hobbs, Modesto	1.000	4	3	0	0	0	Soprano, Modesto	.981	61	101	2	2	1
Hotchkiss, Modesto	1.000	1	1	0	0	0	Spiroff, Fresno	1.000	6	7	0	0	0
Howe, Visalia	.977	44	126	3	3	0	Sproesser, Redwood	1.000	3	3	0	0	0
Hudgens, Modesto°	1.000	46	63	3	0	1	Stein, Visalia°	.977	27	41	1	1	0
Hunt, Redwood	.914	36	31	1	3	1	Tettleton, Modesto	.500	2	1	0	1	0
Hunter, Redwood	.972	67	169	5	5	1	Thompson, Lodi	1.000	22	26	2	0	0
Ireland, Reno	1.000	12	14	1	0	0	Weaver, Visalia°	.967	119	261	6	9	0
Johnson, Fresno	.979	34	46	0	1	0	White, Lodi	1.000	3	4	0	0	0
K. Johnson, Reno	.909	20	17	3	2	0	Wiggins, Reno°	.974	16	36	2	1	0
S. Johnson, Reno	.991	128	336	12	3	3	Williams, Lodi	.960	109	186	6	8	1
Keeney, Fresno	.989	59	86	4	1	2	Woods, Modesto	1.000	4	1	0	0	0
King, Bakersfield°	.915	97	101	7	10	0	Wren, San Jose	.983	24	53	4	1	1
Kruk, Reno°	.972	120	232	11	7	2	Wright, Redwood	.973	123	234	19	7	2
Kubit, Visalia	1.000	4	10	3	0	0	S. Young, Modesto	1.000	11	18	2	0	1
Kwiecinski, San Jose	.959	80	149	15	7	5	Zambrana, Redwood	1.000	35	36	5	0	0

CATCHERS

Player and Club	Pct.	G.	PO.	A.	E.	DP.	PB.	Player and Club	Pct.	G.	PO.	A.	E.	DP.	PB.
Adams, Fresno	.942	12	59	6	4	1	2	Lachemann, Fresno	1.000	1	1	0	0	0	0
Bailey, Lodi	.944	13	48	3	3	0	4	Liddle, Redwood	.968	46	265	35	10	5	5
Bazan, Salinas	.981	81	504	62	11	9	11	Moore, Lodi	.974	23	107	4	3	0	3
Cecchini, San Jose	.980	49	295	47	7	2	12	Moreno, Reno	.981	33	144	15	3	1	3
Contreras, Stockton	.980	48	211	32	5	1	4	Nieves, San Jose	.714	1	5	0	2	0	0
Culbert, Modesto	1.000	1	1	0	0	0	1	O'Brien, Modesto	.983	41	239	44	5	5	7
Delaney, San Jose	.975	91	508	85	15	8	10	Reed, Visalia	.9868	118	642	106	10	9	13
Durrman, Modesto	.992	42	234	27	2	2	5	Reyes, Lodi	.968	97	492	106	20	9	22
Faulconer, Bakersfield	.800	1	4	0	1	0	1	Romero, Redwood	.962	88	432	93	21	4	12
Felix, Visalia	1.000	1	1	0	0	0	0	Skeens, Visalia	1.000	12	52	4	0	0	2
Firova, Bakersfield	.949	11	48	8	3	1	3	Soriano, San Jose	1.000	5	23	2	0	0	2
Gatewood, Lodi	.971	12	60	8	2	1	1	Spiroff, Fresno	.952	21	106	12	6	1	5
Gauntlett, Lodi	.983	9	49	9	1	1	1	Spurlin, Modesto	.970	68	330	53	12	6	12
Gavillan, Reno	.970	64	306	50	11	3	9	Stassi, Fresno	.967	48	260	33	10	3	3
Gonzalez, Visalia	.945	21	67	19	5	0	2	SU'A, Stockton	.9874	96	559	68	8	6	23
Harper, Redwood	.750	3	2	1	1	0	0	Sundberg, Redwood	.977	22	112	14	3	1	6
Harrigan, Salinas	.977	59	304	33	8	0	11	Tarnow, Salinas	.950	5	18	1	1	0	1
Henry, Fresno	.989	64	414	34	5	4	19	Tettleton, Modesto	.983	64	423	36	8	2	9
Hill, Bakersfield	.971	68	323	51	11	4	22	Thomas, Reno	.978	15	76	13	2	2	2
Ireland, Reno	.967	35	132	16	5	2	7								

PITCHERS

Player and Club	Pct.	G.	PO.	A.	E.	DP.	Player and Club	Pct.	G.	PO.	A.	E.	DP.
Adamczak, Salinas	1.000	7	1	3	0	0	Beuder, Lodi°	.840	17	1	20	4	1
Anderson, Lodi	.933	16	2	12	1	1	Biagini, Fresno	.957	28	12	10	1	0
Andrews, Salinas	.923	33	3	9	1	1	Biggus, Stockton	.917	21	10	12	2	2
Angulo, Visalia°	.857	11	3	3	1	0	Booker, Reno	.921	27	7	28	3	2
Bankowski, Redwood°	1.000	18	0	3	0	0	Bordley, Fresno°	.857	13	2	16	3	0
Bastian, Redwood	.970	29	7	25	1	3	Branam, San Jose	.923	36	4	20	2	1
Beard, Lodi	.913	36	14	28	4	2	Braun, Redwood	1.000	15	2	8	0	1

PITCHERS—Continued

Player and Club	Pct.	G.	PO.	A.	E.	DP.
Brennan, Bakersfield°	.818	44	2	7	2	1
Brown, Reno	1.000	10	0	1	0	0
Bryant, Lodi	1.000	11	4	2	0	1
Buckmier, Fresno	.839	28	8	18	5	1
Budd, San Jose	.750	2	2	1	1	0
Burden, Bakersfield	1.000	8	7	2	0	0
Burns, Stockton	1.000	9	0	3	0	0
Cahill, Bakersfield	.962	25	15	35	2	1
Carne, Lodi°	1.000	17	5	10	0	1
Carroll, Visalia	1.000	1	0	2	0	0
Cates, San Jose	.868	27	12	21	5	1
Christy, Reno	1.000	10	0	2	0	0
Chue, Fresno	.952	27	6	14	1	1
Clapham, Redwood	1.000	9	1	5	0	0
Conroy, Modesto°	.879	27	6	23	4	1
Cota, Reno	.792	24	8	11	5	0
Crews, Stockton	.810	19	11	6	4	0
Crisler, Bakersfield	1.000	1	1	0	0	0
deLeon, Lodi	1.000	5	3	4	0	0
Dente, Lodi	.926	21	10	15	2	0
Dinkins, Stockton°	1.000	13	0	4	0	0
Edwards, San Jose	1.000	17	4	4	0	0
Effrig, Stockton	.923	34	3	9	1	0
Embser, Stockton°	.833	14	2	8	2	0
Fadhel, San Jose	.909	15	4	6	1	0
FERGUSON, Modesto	1.000	26	3	28	0	2
Fiechtner, Reno	.875	33	0	7	1	1
Figueroa, Modesto	1.000	3	1	1	0	0
Fisher, Redwood	.800	15	5	7	3	0
Flores, San Jose	.938	17	5	10	1	1
Franko, Visalia	1.000	1	0	1	0	0
Fregin, Visalia	.944	11	4	13	1	2
Gallo, Fresno	1.000	31	0	11	0	0
Gallo, Stockton°	1.000	32	0	7	0	0
Gerhardt, Reno	.800	15	2	2	1	1
Giacomazzi, Salinas	1.000	3	1	3	0	0
Gilbreath, San Jose	.893	11	5	20	3	2
Giordano, Visalia	.923	50	4	8	1	0
Goodchild, Reno	1.000	8	0	2	0	0
Grapenthin, San Jose	1.000	27	4	4	0	1
Groves, San Jose	.889	15	3	13	2	1
Guerrero, Visalia°	.944	17	1	16	1	0
Guetterman, Bakersfield°	.949	26	15	41	3	4
Halicki, Redwood	.895	9	3	14	2	0
Hallgren, Modesto	1.000	9	1	7	0	0
Hardy, Salinas°	1.000	24	3	15	0	2
Harris, Reno	1.000	2	0	1	0	0
Herron, Modesto°	.941	15	4	12	1	0
Housey, Salinas	.950	25	15	23	2	1
Huber, San Jose	1.000	40	6	3	0	1
Hunger, Bakersfield	.952	26	11	29	2	1
Innis, Lodi	.882	13	5	10	2	0
Johnson, San Jose	1.000	15	3	7	0	2
S. Johnson, Salinas°	1.000	8	0	3	0	0
Jones, Redwood	.897	53	9	17	3	1
Josephson, Modesto	.920	42	9	14	2	2
Kammeyer, Redwood	.909	25	17	13	3	0
Kibbe, Redwood	.929	8	5	8	1	1
Krueger, Visalia	.846	42	7	15	4	1
Kutsukos, Reno	.938	37	6	9	1	3
Kyles, Salinas	.851	26	18	39	10	4
Langston, Bakersfield°	.942	26	17	48	4	1
Leopold, Reno	.864	18	5	14	3	1
Lockie, Salinas	1.000	17	3	2	0	1
Lombardozzi, Visalia	.000	1	0	0	1	0
Lynes, Modesto°	1.000	22	6	12	0	1
Macias, Reno	.762	19	3	13	5	1
Madden, San Jose	.900	12	4	14	2	0
Manderfield, Stockton°	.733	12	0	11	4	0
Maria, San Jose°	.920	11	7	16	2	1
Martin, Bakersfield	.950	47	7	12	1	2
Mathiesen, Fresno	.857	27	3	9	2	0
McIntosh, San Jose	1.000	6	1	1	0	0
McSparran, Fresno	.963	34	10	16	1	2
Mignano, Stockton	1.000	15	0	4	0	1
Montalvo, Lodi	1.000	39	7	10	0	0
Moore, Modesto	1.000	7	0	3	0	0
Morrison, Redwood	1.000	15	6	8	0	0
Moscaret, Lodi°	.778	50	2	12	4	1
Nago, Stockton	1.000	9	3	8	0	0
Nowlin, Salinas	.943	22	11	22	2	1
Odekirk, Modesto°	1.000	4	1	1	0	0
Oelkers, Visalia°	.833	5	3	7	2	1
Oliver, Reno	1.000	19	1	7	0	3
Oliver, Redwood	.938	18	8	22	2	1
Oroz, Reno°	.923	30	6	42	4	3
Palica, Modesto	1.000	3	0	2	0	0
Pantaleo, Salinas	1.000	12	0	2	0	0
Parrott, Stockton	1.000	8	4	8	0	0
Patterson, Fresno	.750	4	4	2	2	0
Patterson, Reno	1.000	4	1	4	0	0
Pedersen, Bakersfield	.917	49	8	14	2	2
Pena, Visalia°	.966	25	6	22	1	0
Pettibone, Visalia	.900	11	4	5	1	0
Piper, Lodi	.900	13	3	6	1	0
Pone, Stockton	1.000	4	0	1	0	0
Powers, Modesto	.947	20	5	13	1	1
Randolph, Bakersfield	1.000	15	5	8	0	0
Reade, Lodi	.889	34	4	4	1	0
Reeves, Lodi°	1.000	3	1	0	0	0
Retzer, Modesto	.875	17	5	2	1	0
Roberts, Stockton	.784	24	8	21	8	0
Rodriguez, Modesto	.957	15	9	13	1	1
Ronan, Fresno	1.000	10	3	0	0	0
Ruiz, Reno°	1.000	3	0	2	0	0
Ruzek, Redwood	1.000	10	1	2	0	0
Saatzer, Redwood	1.00	22	11	16	0	1
St. Claire, San Jose	.941	9	6	10	1	0
Schafer, Fresno	.826	35	6	13	4	1
Schefsky, Reno	.821	26	10	22	7	0
Schilling, Salinas	.967	34	9	20	1	1
Schulze, Salinas	.979	24	14	32	1	5
D. Smith, Lodi	.778	21	2	5	2	0
Smith, Redwood	.875	38	2	12	2	0
Snider, Visalia	.667	17	6	6	6	1
Soff, Salinas	.818	43	5	13	4	2
Spicer, Bakersfield°	.966	24	2	26	1	0
Stadler, Reno	.000	9	0	0	1	0
Staffon, San Jose	.500	6	1	1	2	0
Steger, Bakersfield	.821	45	10	13	5	1
Suarez, Visalia	.800	5	4	0	1	0
Swaggerty, Salinas	.842	25	3	13	3	0
Swift, Stockton	.967	17	12	17	1	3
Sylvia, Lodi	.667	2	0	2	1	0
Sylvia, Redwood	.824	57	5	9	3	1
Tatsuno, Stockton°	1.000	7	0	1	0	0
Teahan, Stockton	1.000	8	4	6	0	1
Tenenini, San Jose	1.000	10	1	4	0	0
Thorp, Lodi	1.000	9	2	4	0	0
Torres, San Jose	.923	15	10	14	2	1
Trax, Fresno	.882	19	5	10	2	1
Vaji, Salinas°	.750	3	1	2	1	0
Vega, San Jose	.875	7	2	5	1	0
Venezia, Redwood	1.000	11	6	6	0	0
Vucsko, Lodi	1.000	12	5	11	0	0
Wardle, Visalia°	.947	28	5	13	1	0
Warren, Modesto	.900	28	7	20	3	0
Weibel, Visalia	.940	28	13	34	3	3
Westray, San Jose°	1.000	11	5	11	0	0
Wilhelmi, Fresno	.969	25	14	17	1	2
Williamson, Reno	.889	26	1	7	1	0
Winters, Fresno°	1.000	26	1	18	0	0
Wood, Stockton	.917	18	4	18	2	1
Yett, Visalia	.879	27	9	20	4	1
C. Young, Modesto°	.953	28	17	44	3	3

The following players do not have any recorded accepted chances at the positions indicated; therefore, are not listed in the fielding averages for those particular positions: Anderson, p; Brooks, ss; Carroll, ss; Chinn, 3b; Contreras, 1b, 3b; Dawes, p; Durrman, 3b; Favata, 3b; Felix, p; Flores, 1b; Franko, p; J. Gonzalez, p; O. Gonzalez, ss; Gregory, p; Hampton, p; Hunger, 2b; Maloney, p; Martin, p; McDaniel, ss; Montanari, ss; Murphy, 2b, of; Nago, c; Piatnik, p; Roen, p; Stephenson, of; Sundberg, p; VanMarter, p; Vasquez, p.

CLUB PITCHING

Club	ERA.	G.	CG.	ShO.	Sv.	IP.	H.	R.	ER.	HR.	HB.	BB.	Int. BB.	SO.	WP.	Bk.
Modesto	3.08	140	65	23	19	1200.2	1092	482	411	49	36	464	7	852	73	5
Stockton	3.28	138	42	11	28	1165.1	1086	538	425	53	24	483	8	745	55	13
Redwood	3.51	140	19	7	36	1190.2	1145	578	464	43	39	516	57	759	56	7
Visalia	3.68	140	39	5	36	1196.2	1160	588	489	71	25	528	15	737	65	15
Salinas	3.70	140	29	5	26	1175	1198	617	483	67	37	397	18	770	65	3
San Jose	3.87	140	38	11	23	1195.1	1146	634	514	53	41	661	31	791	82	5
Bakersfield	3.92	140	33	10	21	1182.1	1183	666	515	63	53	561	2	800	83	10
Lodi	4.19	140	26	6	24	1166.2	1234	709	543	72	61	555	12	720	99	12
Reno	4.75	138	28	2	18	1153.2	1287	760	609	80	32	636	19	589	63	20
Fresno	5.29	140	20	4	17	1167.2	1439	859	686	74	39	563	16	686	66	16

PITCHERS' RECORDS
(Leading Qualifiers for Earned-Run Average Leadership — 112 or More Innings)

°Throws lefthanded.

Pitcher—Club	W.	L.	Pct.	ERA.	G.	GS.	CG.	GF.	ShO.	Sv.	IP.	H.	R.	ER.	HR.	HB.	BB.	Int. BB.	SO.	WP.
Ferguson, Modesto	17	6	.739	1.77	26	25	20	1	8	0	198	154	48	39	5	1	52	0	124	3
Conroy, Modesto°	15	4	.789	2.25	27	25	9	1	3	0	171.2	139	59	43	7	5	62	0	184	12
Kyles, Salinas	11	5	.688	2.51	26	26	5	0	2	0	172	160	71	48	4	5	66	1	118	15
Roberts, Stockton	14	6	.700	2.53	24	24	9	0	4	0	174.1	151	65	49	9	3	41	1	137	5
Langston, Bakersfield°	12	7	.632	2.54	26	26	7	0	3	0	177.1	143	71	50	7	8	102	1	161	13
Schilling, Salinas	11	9	.550	2.59	34	15	4	18	0	4	125	120	49	36	11	1	22	4	100	6
Schulze, Salinas	13	7	.650	2.84	24	24	9	0	1	0	165	150	61	52	3	6	59	4	122	10
Warren, Stockton	19	4	.826	3.00	28	27	13	0	5	0	195	160	76	65	11	9	83	0	154	8
Bastian, Redwood	9	7	.563	3.05	29	26	5	0	0	0	168.1	158	66	57	4	3	49	3	103	2
Jones, Redwood	8	8	.500	3.14	53	0	0	31	0	7	114.2	96	55	40	2	4	59	12	83	10

Departmental Leaders: G—R. Sylvia, 57; GS—Young, 28; CG—Ferguson, 20; GF—R. Sylvia, 51; ShO—Ferguson, 8; Sv—R. Sylvia, 25; IP—Young, 205; W—Warren, 19; L—Booker, 13; Pct.—Warren, .826; H—Weibel, 208; R—Booker, 133; ER—Booker, 114; HR—Winters, 16; HB—Reade, 10; BB—Booker, 157; IBB—R. Sylvia, 15; SO—Conroy, 184; WP—Booker, 20.

(All Pitchers—Listed Alphabetically)

Pitcher—Club	W.	L.	Pct.	ERA.	G.	GS.	CG.	GF.	ShO.	Sv.	IP.	H.	R.	ER.	HR.	HB.	BB.	Int. BB.	SO.	WP.
Adamczak, Salinas	0	1	.000	6.87	7	1	0	4	0	0	18.1	23	15	14	1	0	7	0	4	1
D. Anderson, Lodi	2	9	.182	5.29	16	16	3	0	0	0	95.1	101	66	56	7	7	34	0	70	8
S. Anderson, Modesto	0	1	.000	20.25	1	1	0	0	0	0	1.1	3	3	3	0	0	1	0	0	1
Andrews, Salinas	3	4	.429	3.56	33	0	0	15	0	5	68.1	68	31	27	5	2	25	2	39	4
Angulo, Visalia°	2	3	.400	3.53	11	3	1	7	0	2	43.1	35	22	17	4	0	25	0	47	3
Bankowski, Redwood°	0	1	.000	3.00	18	0	0	8	0	0	18	19	7	6	2	0	14	1	19	4
Bastian, Redwood	9	7	.563	3.05	29	26	5	0	0	0	168.1	158	66	57	4	3	49	3	103	2
Beard, Lodi	8	6	.571	4.10	36	11	4	12	0	0	151.1	188	96	69	13	6	44	3	55	12
Beuder, Lodi°	2	8	.200	4.11	17	12	1	3	0	1	72.1	65	44	33	5	7	40	1	60	13
Biagini, Fresno	7	10	.412	4.78	28	20	7	6	1	0	148.2	167	103	79	10	2	60	1	92	8
Biggus, Stockton	5	3	.625	3.21	21	7	4	7	1	0	81.1	88	35	29	2	1	26	0	31	3
Booker, Reno	8	13	.381	6.35	27	27	4	0	0	0	161.2	160	133	114	15	3	157	1	81	20
Bordley, Fresno°	5	5	.500	4.71	13	13	0	0	0	0	70.2	82	49	37	4	0	32	1	32	5
Branam, San Jose	2	4	.333	2.64	36	0	0	22	0	6	78.1	65	27	23	5	2	56	8	67	9
Braun, Redwood	2	2	.500	1.27	15	3	2	7	1	2	42.2	42	11	6	2	0	12	1	17	3
Brennan, Bakersfield	3	6	.333	3.29	44	0	0	27	0	2	54.2	54	25	20	2	3	26	0	38	4
Brown, Reno	1	2	.333	5.29	10	0	0	9	0	3	17	19	12	10	1	1	11	0	13	2
Bryant, Lodi	0	1	.000	6.04	11	0	0	5	0	1	25.1	36	20	17	1	0	16	0	18	4
Buckmier, Fresno	5	11	.313	6.15	28	18	1	9	0	0	105.1	125	94	72	5	6	69	1	61	9
Budd, San Jose	0	1	.000	17.18	2	1	0	1	0	0	3.2	8	8	7	0	1	5	0	1	0
Burden, Bakersfield	1	3	.250	2.58	8	5	3	3	1	0	38.1	31	12	11	1	3	16	0	26	0
Burns, Stockton	2	0	1.000	1.59	18	1	1	8	0	4	22.2	13	5	4	0	1	6	0	14	0
Cahill, Bakersfield	12	7	.632	3.72	25	25	9	0	0	0	172	174	91	71	1	3	59	0	69	4
Carne, Lodi°	4	7	.364	4.43	17	17	2	0	1	0	89.1	94	60	44	7	2	66	3	54	5
Carroll, Visalia	0	0	.000	13.50	1	0	0	0	0	0	2	3	3	3	0	0	1	0	1	2
Cates, San Jose	12	10	.545	3.64	27	26	13	0	3	0	188	165	85	76	11	7	99	2	142	4
Christy, Reno	0	2	.000	5.74	10	5	0	0	0	0	31.1	38	30	20	4	1	29	0	13	6
Chue, Fresno	4	6	.400	4.57	27	2	0	17	0	0	65	76	40	33	2	3	24	1	51	2
Clapham, Redwood	0	0	.000	2.95	9	2	0	2	0	0	21.1	26	10	7	2	1	8	2	8	1
Conroy, Modesto°	15	4	.789	2.25	27	25	9	1	3	0	171.2	139	59	43	7	5	62	0	184	12
Cota, Reno	7	5	.583	4.88	24	24	3	0	0	0	142	168	94	77	11	3	51	2	48	1
Crews, Stockton	10	4	.714	3.37	19	19	8	0	1	0	139	151	66	52	9	0	28	0	83	6
Crisler, Bakersfield	0	1	.000	22.50	1	1	0	0	0	0	2	5	5	5	1	0	2	0	0	0
Dawes, San Jose	0	0	.000	0.00	1	0	0	1	0	0	2	0	0	0	0	0	0	0	1	0
DeLeon, Lodi	0	1	.000	3.06	5	2	0	1	0	0	17.2	22	7	6	3	0	7	0	7	0
Dente, Lodi	4	7	.364	5.33	21	16	4	2	0	1	99.2	109	75	59	6	5	50	1	38	5
Dinkins, Stockton	0	0	.000	2.94	13	1	0	6	0	0	33.2	28	24	11	1	2	27	0	13	4
Edwards, San Jose	4	7	.364	2.70	17	11	3	2	1	0	70	66	28	21	0	6	30	0	60	2
Effrig, Stockton	6	7	.462	3.33	34	5	3	27	0	8	83.2	78	41	31	6	3	33	3	56	7
Embser, Stockton°	6	5	.545	4.36	14	14	2	0	0	0	76.1	74	46	37	3	2	54	0	50	4
Fadhel, San Jose	3	3	.500	6.29	15	8	2	2	0	0	48.2	64	43	34	4	6	32	0	22	6
Felix, Visalia	0	0	.000	0.00	1	1	0	0	0	0	2	3	0	0	0	0	0	0	1	0
Ferguson, Modesto	17	6	.739	1.77	26	25	20	1	8	0	198	154	48	39	5	1	52	0	124	3
Fiechtner, Reno	4	3	.571	4.06	33	4	0	14	0	3	71	78	35	32	4	1	27	1	35	5
Figueroa, Modesto	0	1	.000	54.00	3	3	0	0	0	0	3	14	18	18	0	1	10	0	2	3
Fisher, Redwood	3	3	.500	4.67	15	8	0	0	0	0	52	52	32	27	0	4	27	1	40	6
Flores, San Jose	4	2	.667	4.70	17	6	2	4	1	0	51.2	64	35	27	2	7	20	1	28	4
Franko, Visalia	0	0	.000	0.00	1	0	0	0	0	0	1	0	0	0	0	0	0	0	0	0
Fregin, Visalia	8	1	.889	2.25	11	8	3	2	0	1	68	61	21	17	3	0	25	0	25	1
B. Gallo, Fresno°	0	4	.000	7.14	31	0	0	18	0	0	74.1	85	65	59	6	0	76	0	64	3
R. Gallo, Stockton°	6	2	.751	1.81	32	0	0	25	0	8	44.2	37	11	9	3	1	22	1	39	0
Gerhardt, Reno	0	1	.000	3.00	15	0	0	7	0	0	30	25	13	10	3	1	10	1	19	0
Giacomazzi, Salinas	0	2	.000	12.27	3	2	0	1	0	0	7.1	13	11	10	1	0	4	0	0	0
Gilbreath, San Jose	3	5	.375	4.54	11	11	4	0	1	0	77.1	88	49	39	6	3	31	1	39	3
Giordano, Visalia	6	6	.500	1.66	50	0	0	41	0	20	92.1	52	22	17	3	1	26	2	57	4
Gonzalez, Visalia	0	0	.000	9.00	1	0	0	1	0	0	1	1	1	1	0	0	3	0	0	1
Goodchild, Fresno	0	2	.000	9.56	8	1	0	3	0	0	16	27	19	17	2	1	6	0	5	1
Grapenthin, San Jose	2	1	.667	0.80	27	0	0	24	0	9	45	41	7	4	0	0	19	6	39	3
Gregory, Lodi°	0	0	.000	6.75	1	0	0	1	0	0	1.1	1	1	1	0	0	2	0	1	0
Groves, Salinas	5	5	.500	3.92	15	15	2	0	1	0	85	88	44	37	5	2	37	0	42	6
Guerrero, Visalia°	6	3	.667	2.96	17	14	1	2	1	0	82	72	36	27	4	2	39	0	58	2
Guetterman, Bakersfield°	7	11	.389	4.44	26	26	4	0	1	0	154	172	100	76	8	6	69	0	82	8
Halicki, Redwood	0	3	.000	3.71	9	9	1	0	0	0	53.1	53	34	22	2	2	23	2	27	2
Hallgren, Modesto	1	1	.000	4.67	9	2	1	4	0	0	27	28	16	14	3	2	13	0	11	1
Hampton, Modesto	0	0	.000	9.00	1	1	0	0	0	0	3	7	3	3	1	0	2	0	4	0
Hardy, Salinas	5	6	.455	3.60	24	16	4	3	2	0	110	118	60	44	3	2	23	0	74	2
Harris, Reno	0	1	.000	12.00	2	2	0	0	0	0	6	10	10	8	0	1	9	0	1	1
Herron, Modesto°	3	3	.500	3.88	15	7	1	3	1	1	53.1	57	30	23	3	0	27	0	27	8
Housey, Salinas	6	11	.353	4.50	25	21	4	1	0	1	140	162	86	70	4	7	42	0	79	8
Huber, San Jose	5	9	.357	3.49	40	0	0	25	0	4	77.1	66	47	30	0	0	59	6	65	6
Hunger, Bakersfield	6	11	.353	3.65	26	25	6	0	1	0	145.2	150	73	59	6	6	54	0	69	5

Pitcher—Club	W.	L.	Pct.	ERA.	G.	GS.	CG.	GF.	ShO.	Sv.	IP.	H.	R.	ER.	HR.	HB.	BB.	Int. BB.	SO.	WP.
Innis, Lodi	5	5	.500	3.18	13	12	3	0	2	0	73.2	76	32	26	1	2	47	0	45	1
G. Johnson, San Jose	3	2	.600	2.86	15	5	0	2	0	0	56.2	48	25	18	1	1	35	0	31	3
S. Johnson, Salinas*	1	2	.333	6.17	8	0	0	4	0	0	11.2	19	11	8	2	1	6	0	11	0
Jones, Redwood	8	8	.500	3.14	53	0	0	31	0	7	114.2	96	55	40	2	4	59	12	83	10
Josephson, Modesto	7	6	.538	1.92	42	0	0	37	0	13	84.1	71	24	18	2	3	29	1	66	1
Kammeyer, Redwood	5	9	.357	4.05	25	23	2	0	0	0	135.2	132	83	61	6	7	61	3	120	6
Kibbe, Redwood	4	2	.667	3.83	8	7	1	0	0	0	49.1	44	25	21	3	1	16	0	28	3
Krueger, Visalia	5	4	.556	3.83	42	1	0	30	0	11	96.1	98	49	41	4	4	36	2	63	6
Kutsukos, Reno	4	1	.800	4.91	37	0	0	25	0	0	51.1	52	32	28	3	2	27	1	22	2
Kyles, Salinas	11	5	.688	2.51	26	26	5	0	2	0	172	160	71	48	4	5	66	1	118	15
Langston, Bakersfield*	12	7	.632	2.54	26	26	7	0	3	0	177.1	143	71	50	7	8	102	1	161	13
Leopold, Reno	8	8	.500	4.90	18	18	4	0	0	0	104.2	127	73	57	7	5	57	1	48	3
Lockie, Salinas	0	1	.000	3.00	17	2	0	10	0	0	39	38	20	13	1	2	10	0	20	3
Lombardozzi, Visalia	0	1	.000	36.00	1	0	0	0	0	0	1	5	4	4	0	0	0	0	2	1
Lynes, Modesto*	9	3	.750	2.73	22	10	4	8	2	4	92.1	89	32	28	5	1	20	2	39	2
Macias, Reno	7	5	.583	3.66	19	17	6	0	1	0	123	138	64	50	6	2	36	0	69	3
Madden, Lodi*	3	7	.300	2.60	12	12	3	0	0	0	72.2	67	32	21	0	4	36	0	47	7
Maloney, Fresno	0	1	.000	20.25	1	1	0	0	0	0	1.1	3	4	3	0	0	0	0	1	2
Manderfield, Stockton*	2	3	.400	4.03	12	11	0	0	0	0	60.1	70	35	27	2	1	45	0	32	3
Maria, San Jose*	2	3	.400	3.29	11	9	2	1	1	0	65.2	58	28	24	1	1	27	1	42	1
J. Martin, Salinas*	0	0	.000	9.00	2	0	0	2	0	0	2	3	2	2	0	0	1	0	0	0
V. Martin, Bakersfield	4	4	.500	3.05	47	1	0	34	0	13	79.2	63	35	27	3	0	29	1	86	6
Mathiesen, Fresno	1	10	.091	6.00	27	7	3	13	0	4	78	117	72	52	4	2	32	0	54	5
McIntosh, San Jose	1	0	1.000	2.65	6	0	0	4	0	0	17	17	7	5	0	0	10	1	15	0
McSparran, Fresno	1	6	.143	4.34	34	9	0	15	0	2	120.1	131	66	58	8	4	59	3	71	5
Mignano, Stockton	1	4	.200	2.89	15	0	0	10	0	2	28	21	12	9	1	0	13	3	14	2
Montalvo, Lodi	3	3	.500	3.44	39	0	0	28	0	3	70.2	68	31	27	3	6	33	2	38	9
Moore, Modesto	3	1	.750	0.64	7	0	0	6	0	0	14	11	2	1	0	0	4	0	8	0
Morrison, Redwood	4	5	.444	4.00	15	13	2	1	1	0	90	86	42	40	7	1	38	2	53	3
Moscaret, Lodi*	6	7	.462	3.50	50	7	1	34	0	12	87.1	79	48	34	2	5	47	2	88	12
Nago, Stockton	1	0	1.000	2.59	9	1	0	5	0	1	24.1	23	8	7	1	0	4	0	10	0
Nowlin, Salinas	4	8	.333	4.50	22	21	2	0	0	0	114	125	81	57	15	4	48	2	61	4
Odekirk, Modesto*	0	1	.000	3.72	4	1	0	3	0	0	9.2	10	4	4	0	2	4	0	2	1
Oelkers, Visalia*	2	2	.500	3.55	5	5	0	0	0	0	33	27	15	13	2	1	17	1	17	1
B. Oliver, Reno	4	2	.667	2.43	19	0	0	14	0	2	29.2	26	13	8	1	1	11	1	14	2
S. Oliver, Redwood	3	10	.231	4.67	18	16	1	1	0	0	90.2	106	58	47	3	2	30	2	44	6
Oroz, Reno*	7	5	.583	5.29	30	11	4	8	0	1	100.1	135	69	59	8	1	55	2	59	5
Palica, Modesto	0	0	.000	13.50	3	0	0	1	0	0	3.1	5	5	5	0	2	1	0	1	0
Pantaleo, Salinas	2	1	.667	2.39	12	0	0	8	0	3	26.1	19	8	7	1	0	6	1	18	0
Parrott, Stockton	6	0	1.000	2.09	8	8	5	0	1	0	60.1	44	17	14	2	1	11	0	32	0
G. Patterson, Fresno	1	1	.500	1.33	4	4	1	0	0	0	27	28	12	4	0	0	11	0	8	3
R. Patterson, Reno*	1	0	1.000	3.55	4	4	1	0	0	0	25.1	28	11	10	0	0	5	1	10	0
Pedersen, Bakersfield	4	6	.400	5.51	49	1	0	31	0	5	78.1	97	68	48	9	3	36	0	66	11
Pena, Visalia	12	5	.706	3.18	25	23	9	1	1	1	164	140	65	58	10	1	63	2	105	9
Pettibone, Visalia	8	1	.889	2.44	11	10	2	0	1	0	66.1	61	23	18	3	2	20	0	51	1
Piatnik, Visalia	0	0	.000	0.00	1	0	0	1	0	0	1	1	1	0	0	0	2	0	1	0
Piper, Lodi	4	5	.444	4.47	13	11	2	0	0	0	52.1	45	31	26	2	2	36	0	40	4
Pone, Stockton	0	2	.000	8.31	4	2	0	0	0	0	8.2	16	9	8	0	0	11	0	5	3
Powers, 12 SJ-8 Mod	7	2	.778	4.81	20	7	0	5	0	0	67.1	68	38	36	5	3	44	1	30	4
Randolph, Bakersfield	3	5	.375	5.97	15	15	1	0	0	0	66.1	89	57	44	9	5	34	0	31	3
Reade, Lodi	8	3	.727	4.59	34	0	0	10	0	2	80.1	102	53	41	4	10	28	0	58	8
Reeves, Lodi*	0	1	.000	6.89	3	3	0	0	0	0	15.2	20	15	12	4	1	9	0	16	0
Retzer, Modesto	1	3	.250	7.12	17	1	0	5	0	1	43	47	35	34	4	2	34	1	31	3
Roberts, Stockton	14	6	.700	2.53	24	24	9	0	4	0	174.1	151	65	49	9	3	41	1	137	5
Rodriguez, Modesto	8	2	.800	2.73	15	15	5	0	1	0	105.2	100	38	32	2	1	41	0	70	12
Roen, Redwood*	0	0	.000	....	1	0	0	0	0	0	0	1	0	0	0	0	1	0	0	0
Ronan, Fresno	2	2	.500	2.91	10	0	0	9	0	3	21.2	24	9	7	0	2	12	2	15	3
Ruiz, Reno*	0	1	.000	3.24	3	2	1	1	0	0	16.2	14	7	6	1	0	12	0	10	0
Ruzek, Redwood	0	0	.000	3.75	10	0	0	4	0	0	12	11	6	5	0	1	8	1	10	0
Saatzer, Redwood	13	8	.619	3.38	22	22	5	0	2	0	141	121	59	53	7	5	65	0	89	4
St. Claire, San Jose	2	5	.286	4.13	9	8	2	1	0	0	61	58	32	28	1	1	20	1	44	3
Schafer, Fresno	8	10	.444	4.44	35	13	2	21	0	6	127.2	160	72	63	10	5	31	3	57	2
Schefsky, Reno	11	11	.500	3.88	26	26	5	0	0	0	174	190	108	75	8	7	107	6	107	4
Schilling, Salinas	11	9	.550	2.59	34	15	4	18	0	4	125	120	49	36	11	1	22	4	100	6
Schulze, Salinas	13	7	.650	2.84	24	9	9	0	1	0	165	150	61	52	3	6	59	4	122	10
D. Smith, Lodi	2	2	.500	3.32	21	0	0	17	0	4	40.2	41	21	15	4	0	11	0	33	2
J. Smith, Redwood	4	5	.444	3.90	38	1	0	14	0	2	60	56	30	26	0	2	27	10	35	2
Snider, Visalia	1	4	.200	5.95	17	6	1	7	0	0	62	67	48	41	8	4	41	1	25	4
Soff, Visalia	10	7	.588	3.16	43	0	0	37	0	11	82.2	74	36	29	5	4	30	2	80	3
Spicer, Bakersfield*	6	9	.400	4.35	24	15	3	2	0	0	99.1	100	56	48	10	6	74	0	62	18
Stadler, Reno	1	1	.500	5.68	9	1	0	6	0	0	12.2	18	12	8	2	1	8	1	6	4
Staffon, San Jose	0	1	.000	11.12	6	1	0	2	0	0	11.1	17	16	14	0	0	16	0	10	3
Steger, Bakersfield	6	6	.500	4.32	45	0	0	10	0	0	114.2	105	70	55	8	8	60	0	99	11
Suarez, Redwood	1	3	.250	4.28	5	5	1	0	0	0	27.1	27	19	13	0	1	11	1	16	5
Sundberg, Redwood	0	0	.000	36.00	1	0	0	1	0	0	1	6	4	4	0	0	0	0	1	0
Swaggerty, Salinas	2	7	.222	6.34	25	9	1	8	0	2	82.1	94	64	58	10	2	41	2	34	8
Swift, Stockton	5	9	.357	4.26	17	17	5	0	1	0	112	101	61	53	4	0	66	0	89	10
J. Sylvia, Lodi	0	0	.000	5.14	2	1	0	1	0	0	7	8	6	4	0	0	8	0	4	2
R. Sylvia, Redwood	3	9	.250	2.63	57	0	0	51	0	25	82	72	29	24	2	2	54	15	61	2
Tatsuno, Stockton*	0	3	.000	4.15	7	0	0	6	0	4	8.2	10	6	4	0	0	8	0	7	2
Teahan, Stockton	1	4	.200	4.38	8	5	0	1	0	0	39	37	24	19	1	1	18	0	17	1
Tenenini, San Jose	1	0	1.000	0.50	10	0	0	9	0	1	18	13	1	1	0	1	5	1	8	1
Thorp, Lodi	4	4	.500	4.75	9	8	1	0	0	0	41.2	59	33	22	3	1	20	0	22	3
Torres, San Jose	8	3	.727	3.93	15	15	6	0	3	0	100.2	83	52	44	4	1	63	0	59	9
Trax, Fresno	4	3	.571	6.90	19	11	3	6	0	1	75.2	102	69	58	6	4	38	0	38	7
Vaji, Salinas*	0	1	.000	6.55	3	3	0	0	0	1	11	12	10	8	1	1	7	0	10	1
Van Marter, Modesto	0	2	.000	6.75	7	0	0	2	0	0	13.1	17	10	10	1	2	9	1	5	0
Vasquez, Stockton	0	0	.000	0.00	1	0	0	0	0	0	2	2	0	0	0	0	0	0	2	0
Vega, San Jose	2	3	.400	4.99	7	6	1	0	0	0	30.2	28	25	17	3	0	12	0	10	1
Venezia, Redwood	7	3	.700	2.61	11	10	1	0	0	0	58.2	58	25	17	0	4	24	2	21	2
Vucsko, Lodi	3	6	.333	4.23	12	12	2	0	0	0	72.1	73	38	34	7	2	21	0	26	6
Wardle, Visalia*	3	4	.429	6.69	28	10	1	9	0	1	79.1	114	66	59	11	2	56	2	42	4

Pitcher—Club	W.	L.	Pct.	ERA.	G.	GS.	CG.	GF.	ShO.	Sv.	IP.	H.	R.	ER.	HR.	HB.	BB.	Int. BB.	SO.	WP.
Warren, Stockton	19	4	.826	3.00	28	27	13	0	5	0	195	160	76	65	11	9	83	0	154	8
Weibel, Visalia	12	12	.500	4.04	28	27	9	0	1	0	178	208	95	80	10	1	66	2	105	9
Westray, San Jose*	1	8	.111	5.49	11	11	1	0	0	0	60.2	60	45	37	4	1	50	2	47	4
Wilhelmi, Fresno	7	10	.412	4.48	25	24	3	1	0	0	142.2	181	95	71	3	9	68	2	68	9
Williamson, Reno	7	5	.583	4.39	26	0	0	23	0	9	41	34	24	20	4	1	18	2	30	4
Winters, Fresno*	5	11	.313	7.41	26	18	1	4	0	0	109.1	157	109	90	16	2	51	2	74	3
Wood, Stockton	12	5	.706	3.38	18	17	5	1	2	1	122.1	108	54	46	6	3	51	0	68	2
Yett, Visalia	16	9	.640	3.66	27	27	11	0	0	0	196.2	183	98	80	9	6	97	2	121	13
Young, Modesto*	15	8	.652	3.47	28	28	12	0	1	0	205	189	90	79	7	9	81	2	162	19

BALKS—Oroz, 5; Biagini, Pena, Schafer, Schefsky, Weibel, 4 each; Booker, Cahill, Crews, Manderfield, Randolph, Ruiz, 3 each; Bastian, Dente, B. Gallo, Jones, Leopold, Madden, Montalvo, Pedersen, St. Claire, Suarez, Swift, Trax, Warren, Young, 2 each; D. Anderson, Angulo, Beard, Biggus, Bordley, Carne, Chue, Cota, Effrig, Fregin, R. Gallo, Guetterman, Halicki, S. Johnson, Josephson, Krueger, Kyles, Lombardozzi, Macias, V. Martin, Mathiesen, Moscaret, Nowlin, Odekirk, R. Patterson, Reade, D. Smith, J. Smith, Snider, Staffon, Vega, Venezia, Wilhelmi, Winters, Wood, 1 each.

COMBINATION SHUTOUTS—Hunger-Martin, Hunger-Pedersen, Bakersfield; Buckmier-Schafer, Buckmier-Mathiesen, Trax-Ronan, Fresno; Piper-Innis-Smith, Thorp-Moscaret, Vucsko-Smith, Lodi; Herron-Josephson, Young-Retzer-Lynes, Modesto; Kammeyer-Sylvia, Saatzer-Bankowski, Saatzer-Sylvia, Redwood; Edwards-Huber, San Jose; Manderfield-Mignano, Stockton; Pettibone-Giordano, Visalia.

NO-HIT GAMES—Kammeyer (3)-Sylvia (3), Redwood defeated Bakersfield, 1-0, May 6 (six innings); Innis, Lodi, defeated Visalia, 5-0, July 21.

Carolina League

CLASS A

CHAMPIONSHIP WINNERS IN PREVIOUS YEARS

1945—Danville .681	1960—Greensboro‡ .636	1959—Raleigh .600
1946—Greensboro .599	Burlington .586	Wilson (2nd)† .550
Raleigh (2nd)† .563	1961—Wilson .594	1970—Winston-Salem‡ .586
1947—Burlington .613	1962—Durham .636	Burlington .597
Raleigh (3rd)† .574	Wilson .600	1971—Peninsula‡ .647
1948—Raleigh .592	Kinston (2nd)† .593	Kinston .623
Martinsville (2nd)† .570	1963—Kinston§ .538	1972—Salem‡ .657
1949—Danville .601	Greensboro§ .590	Burlington .632
Burlington (4th)† .500	Wilson (2nd)† .535	1973—Lynchburg .588
1950—Winston-Salem* .693	1964—Kinston§ .572	Winston-Salem‡ .557
1951—Durham .600	Winston-Salem§† .590	1974—Salem .671
Wins-Salem (2nd)† .583	1965—Peninsula§ .597	Salem .582
1952—Raleigh .581	Durham§ .580	1975—Rocky Mount .667
Reidsville (4th)† .536	Tidewater† .528	Rocky Mount .614
1953—Raleigh .593	1966—Kinston§ .547	1976—Winston-Salem .618
Danville (2nd)† .572	Winston-Salem§ .586	Winston-Salem .551
1954—Fayetteville* .628	Rocky Mount† .533	1977—Lynchburg .591
1955—HP-Thomasville .580	1967—Durham x (West.) .536	Peninsula‡ .556
Danville (2nd)† .533	Raleigh (East.) .542	1978—Peninsula .696
1956—HP-Thomasville .591	1968—Salem (West.) .607	Lynchburg‡ .614
Fayetteville (4th)† .523	Ral-Dur (East.) .597	1979—Winston-Salem a .607
1957—Durham .632	HP-Thom. y (W.) .493	1980—Peninsula‡ .714
HP-Thomasville .622	1969—Rocky M (East.) .569	Durham .600
1958—Danville .576	Salem (West.) .542	1981—Peninsula .522
Burlington (4th)† .511	Ral-Dur z (East.) .560	Hagerstown‡ .507

*Won championship and four-club playoff. †Won four-club playoff. ‡Won split-season playoff. §League was divided into Eastern, Western divisions. xWon eight-club, two-division playoff. yWon eight-club, two-division playoff against Raleigh-Durham. zWon eight-club, two-division playoff against Burlington. aWon both halves of split-season (no playoffs).

STANDING OF CLUBS AT CLOSE OF FIRST HALF, JUNE 17

NORTHERN DIVISION

Club	W.	L.	T.	Pct.	G.B.
Alexandria (Pirates)	45	20	1	.692	....
Hagerstown (Orioles)	38	29	0	.567	8
Lynchburg (Mets)	29	37	1	.439	16½
Salem (Padres)	22	48	0	.314	25½

SOUTHERN DIVISION

Club	W.	L.	T.	Pct.	G.B.
Durham (Braves)	43	25	0	.632	....
Peninsula (Phillies)	41	27	0	.603	2
Kinston (Blue Jays)	34	33	0	.507	8½
Winston-Salem (Red Sox)	18	51	0	.261	25½

STANDING OF CLUBS AT CLOSE OF SECOND HALF, AUGUST 31

NORTHERN DIVISION

Club	W.	L.	T.	Pct.	G.B.
Lynchburg (Mets)	36	34	0	.514	....
Alexandria (Pirates)	35	34	0	.507	½
Hagerstown (Orioles)	33	36	0	.478	2½
Salem (Padres)	17	53	0	.243	19

SOUTHERN DIVISION

Club	W.	L.	T.	Pct.	G.B.
Peninsula (Phillies)	49	20	1	.710	....
Kinston (Blue Jays)	42	26	0	.618	6½
Durham (Braves)	37	31	0	.544	11½
Winston-Salem (Red Sox)	27	42	1	.391	22

COMPOSITE STANDING OF CLUBS AT CLOSE OF SEASON, AUGUST 31

Club	Pen.	Alex.	Dur.	Kin.	Hag.	Lyn.	W-S	Sal.	W.	L.	T.	Pct.	G.B.
Peninsula (Phillies)	....	13	10	14	12	13	14	14	90	47	1	.657	....
Alexandria (Pirates)	6	....	7	10	11	13	15	18	80	54	1	.597	8½
Durham (Braves)	9	13	....	8	7	9	15	19	80	56	0	.588	9½
Kinston (Blue Jays)	6	10	10	....	14	12	13	11	76	59	0	.563	13
Hagerstown (Orioles)	8	8	12	4	....	10	13	16	71	65	0	.522	18½
Lynchburg (Mets)	7	3	11	8	10	....	13	13	65	71	1	.478	24½
Winston-Salem (Red Sox)	5	5	5	6	7	7	....	10	45	93	1	.326	45½
Salem (Padres)	6	2	1	9	4	7	10	....	39	101	0	.279	52½

Major league affiliations in parentheses.

Peninsula represented Hampton, Va.

Playoffs—Alexandria defeated Lynchburg, one game to none; Durham defeated Peninsula, one game to none; Alexandria defeated Durham, three games to none, to win league championship.

Regular-Season Attendance—Alexandria, 44,306; Durham, 157,325; Hagerstown, 135,336; Kinston, 41,861; Lynchburg, 49,539; Peninsula, 42,145; Salem, 47,202; Winston-Salem, 46,430. Total, 564,144. Playoffs, 9,724. All-Star Game, 1,817.

Managers: Alexandria, John Lipon; Durham, Bobby Dews; Hagerstown, Grady Little; Kinston, John McLaren; Lynchburg, Danny Monzon; Peninsula, Bill Darcy; Salem, Jim Zerilla; Winston-Salem, Rac Slider.

All-Star Team: 1B—Hagman, Durham; 2B—Samuel, Peninsula; 3B—Dumouchelle, Hagerstown; SS—Sosa, Durham; OF—Gillaspie, Salem; Stone, Peninsula; (tie) Orsulak, Alexandria, and Tarver, Lynchburg; C—Malpeso, Winston-Salem; DH—Renteria, Alexandria; RHP—Hudson, Peninsula; LHP—(tie) Green, Alexandria, and Griffin, Peninsula; Manager—Darcy, Peninsula.

(Compiled by Howe News Bureau, Boston, Mass.)

CLUB BATTING

Club	Pct.	G.	AB.	R.	OR.	H.	TB.	2B.	3B.	HR.	RBI.	GW.	SH.	SF.	HP.	BB.	Int. BB.	SO.	SB.	CS.	LOB.
Peninsula	.269	138	4502	718	542	1210	1816	205	43	105	633	73	53	57	50	514	23	890	247	89	941
Alexandria	.265	135	4275	675	575	1131	1689	197	29	101	592	67	53	44	31	532	26	841	130	68	927
Hagerstown	.262	136	4481	674	668	1176	1802	205	41	113	595	38	30	37	40	504	27	855	140	71	947

CLUB BATTING

Club	Pct.	G	AB	R	OR	H	TB	2B	3B	HR	RBI	GW	SH	SF	HP	BB	Int. BB	SO	SB	CS	LOB
Kinston	.255	135	4327	548	540	1104	1537	185	25	66	499	60	40	40	39	455	23	839	155	52	978
Durham	.254	136	4509	598	538	1145	1653	172	21	98	530	64	53	42	35	583	24	759	104	45	1075
Lynchburg	.254	137	4504	653	613	1143	1575	170	29	68	571	47	45	33	33	525	18	918	247	71	966
Salem	.235	140	4507	609	834	1059	1616	150	31	115	532	31	39	30	48	486	19	1055	103	56	934
Winston-Salem	.232	139	4593	567	732	1065	1608	190	19	105	500	36	37	33	37	511	12	1115	78	41	1003

INDIVIDUAL BATTING

(Leading Qualifiers for Batting Championship—378 or More Plate Appearances)

°Bats lefthanded.   †Switch-hitter.

Player and Club	Pct.	G	AB	R	H	TB	2B	3B	HR	RBI	GW	SH	SF	HP	BB	Int. BB	SO	SB	CS
Renteria, Richard, Alexandria	.331	127	508	80	168	244	24	5	14	100	8	3	7	4	24	2	54	12	9
Samuel, Juan, Peninsula	.320	135	494	111	158	283	29	6	28	94	10	0	7	15	31	1	124	64	17
Malpeso, David, Winston-Salem	.317	116	441	68	140	253	24	1	29	91	6	3	3	4	22	1	76	0	1
Tarver, Laschelle, Lynchburg°	.308	99	399	75	123	144	14	2	1	34	2	6	1	2	45	2	54	56	16
Hagman, Keith, Durham°	.303	122	449	59	136	192	25	2	9	67	9	2	3	1	67	5	38	2	1
Ford, Kenneth, Alexandria	.300	115	393	67	118	216	22	2	24	96	14	0	2	3	33	3	68	10	5
Dumouchelle, Patrick, Hagerstown	.298	127	450	78	134	205	25	5	12	73	5	3	3	2	59	1	58	19	9
Stone, Jeffrey, Alexandria°	.297	137	559	110	166	216	18	13	2	50	9	10	7	9	34	1	102	94	15
Garcia, Steven, Salem°	.296	125	510	84	151	189	21	4	3	35	2	5	4	1	32	0	62	28	9
Winningham, Herman, Lynchburg°	.295	120	430	65	127	175	20	5	6	61	7	1	4	0	64	2	106	50	9

Departmental Leaders: G—J. Stone, 137; AB—J. Stone, 559; R—Samuel, 111; H—Renteria, 168; TB—Samuel, 283; 2B—Melendez, 33; 3B—J. Stone, 13; HR—Malpeso, 29; RBI—Renteria, 100; GWRBI—Ford, 14; SH—Quade, 13; SF—Dowell, Felt, 9; HP—Gillaspie, Samuel, 15; BB—Clack, 92; IBB—Gillaspie, 8; SO—Schroeder, 172; SB—J. Stone, 94; CS—Clack, 18.

(All Players—Listed Alphabetically)

Player and Club	Pct.	G	AB	R	H	TB	2B	3B	HR	RBI	GW	SH	SF	HP	BB	Int. BB	SO	SB	CS
Ackley, John, Winston-Salem	.252	109	357	51	90	162	23	2	15	58	4	1	4	2	61	0	90	2	1
Adamiak, Mark, Peninsula	.202	36	89	6	18	18	0	0	0	6	1	2	1	2	8	0	13	5	1
Aitcheson, J. Kevin, Kinston°	.268	128	433	45	116	156	20	1	6	55	7	7	6	1	32	4	55	9	5
Arfstrom, Joseph, Winston-Salem†	.240	96	308	24	74	92	14	2	0	27	1	4	2	2	29	1	79	6	6
Bailey, Welby, Durham	.171	15	35	3	6	6	0	0	0	1	0	0	1	0	6	0	6	0	0
Banner, Thomas, Hagerstown†	.300	11	30	4	9	12	1	1	0	3	0	0	0	0	3	0	2	0	0
Beal, Anthony, Winston-Salem	.255	114	423	62	108	159	16	4	9	39	1	3	3	7	47	0	116	38	10
Benzinger, Todd, Winston-Salem†	.219	121	443	54	97	133	19	1	5	46	1	4	6	3	41	2	71	4	1
Bertucio, Charles, Hagerstown†	.194	29	72	8	14	19	0	1	1	6	0	1	1	0	6	0	19	0	1
Brassil, Thomas, Salem	.248	66	250	31	62	65	3	0	0	17	0	5	2	1	22	0	31	5	7
Brown, Mark, Hagerstown	.000	15	1	0	0	0	0	0	0	0	0	0	0	0	0	0	0	0	0
Butler, William, Hagerstown	.216	13	37	11	8	9	1	0	0	4	0	0	0	0	1	0	6	1	0
Cannon, Thomas, Salem	.167	4	6	1	1	1	0	0	0	0	0	0	0	0	0	0	1	0	0
Cannon, Timothy, Salem†	.213	120	376	49	80	132	16	6	8	38	6	5	3	4	49	0	135	3	7
Carpenter, William, Winston-Salem	.141	41	128	12	18	21	1	1	0	2	1	0	0	1	11	0	37	0	2
Casey, Patrick, Salem	.258	76	252	42	65	135	8	1	20	60	3	2	3	2	51	5	68	15	3
Castaneda, Nick, Alexandria	.255	120	380	55	97	165	21	1	15	62	6	2	6	2	51	0	96	1	1
Cerutti, John, Kinston°	.000	17	0	1	0	0	0	0	0	0	0	0	0	0	0	0	0	0	0
Chmil, Stephen, Durham	.231	114	376	49	87	111	10	1	4	32	5	7	2	6	52	1	68	16	4
Christensen, John, Lynchburg	.323	8	31	7	10	13	1	1	0	4	0	0	0	2	2	0	2	3	0
Christianson, David, Salem°	.198	103	328	46	65	120	11	1	14	49	1	0	2	3	58	3	107	0	0
Churchill, James, Alexandria	.250	12	20	4	5	6	1	0	0	1	0	0	0	0	4	0	2	0	0
Clack, Marvin, Alexandria†	.236	126	419	73	99	119	5	6	1	37	5	12	4	2	92	1	121	21	18
Clow, Dennis, Durham	.125	12	24	1	3	6	0	0	1	2	0	1	0	2	0	0	11	0	0
Coleman, Ricky, Salem	.265	30	98	10	26	31	2	0	1	5	0	2	0	0	12	0	16	12	3
Corman, David, Hagerstown	.291	125	388	61	113	147	12	11	0	34	1	4	1	4	58	1	64	14	9
Currier, William, Peninsula°	.143	34	105	11	15	22	5	1	0	7	1	0	0	0	8	0	35	0	2
Cusack, David, Hagerstown	.190	80	258	27	49	96	12	1	11	32	4	2	1	8	24	1	93	2	1
Daniels, Samuel, Salem	.000	13	0	0	0	0	0	0	0	0	0	0	0	0	1	0	0	0	0
Darkis, William, Peninsula	.240	90	304	49	73	152	9	2	22	60	5	0	1	4	33	1	105	4	5
Daulton, Darren, Peninsula°	.241	110	324	65	78	136	21	2	11	44	6	2	1	1	89	3	51	17	6
Dees, Gregory, Hagerstown	.224	90	281	35	63	107	10	2	10	46	3	1	2	4	27	3	87	0	2
De La Rosa, Bienvenido, Alexandria°.	.195	32	87	10	17	19	2	0	0	5	2	1	0	2	8	0	20	8	1
DeLaRosa, Nelson, Alexandria°	.198	34	116	15	23	37	3	1	3	14	1	0	1	1	8	0	26	5	2
DelMonte, John, Lynchburg°	.196	51	143	16	28	40	10	1	0	14	1	1	0	0	13	0	42	7	3
Denby, Darryl, Lynchburg	.200	72	200	15	40	51	8	0	1	19	0	3	3	1	7	0	58	5	4
Devalk, Brian, Alexandria	.206	25	63	13	13	22	2	2	1	7	0	1	0	1	9	2	22	3	0
Dowell, Kenneth, Peninsula	.220	114	381	55	84	102	14	2	0	35	4	8	9	2	72	0	50	12	11
Dumouchelle, Patrick, Hagerstown	.298	127	450	78	134	205	25	5	12	73	5	3	3	2	59	1	58	19	9
Enos, David, Peninsula†	.357	14	42	10	15	15	0	0	0	11	1	0	0	0	10	2	5	1	0
Erickson, Steven, Kinston	.000	27	36	0	0	0	0	0	0	0	1	0	0	0	6	0	19	0	0
Escobar, Jose, Kinston	.240	84	225	30	54	63	9	0	0	16	0	4	0	4	25	0	39	2	5
Estrada, Craig, Salem	.208	26	77	7	16	18	2	0	0	1	0	0	1	4	0	14	0	2	
Evans, Duane, Lynchburg°	.209	104	320	41	67	115	10	1	12	40	4	1	1	4	40	1	102	3	4
Falcone, David, Hagerstown°	.278	104	360	61	100	190	22	1	22	68	6	0	1	2	56	3	80	6	3
Felt, James, Alexandria	.251	128	426	55	107	158	24	3	7	53	7	4	9	1	40	3	95	17	4
Fisher, Charles, Winston-Salem	.210	83	262	30	55	89	14	1	6	31	6	1	0	3	45	0	98	1	2
Ford, Kenneth, Alexandria	.300	115	393	67	118	216	22	2	24	96	14	0	2	3	33	3	68	10	5
Frash, Roger, Lynchburg°	.225	124	431	51	97	169	24	3	14	79	6	0	6	3	30	2	74	23	9
Fultz, William, Lynchburg	.000	27	1	0	0	0	0	0	0	0	0	0	0	0	0	0	0	0	0
Garcia, Michael, Durham	.273	83	330	46	90	126	16	4	4	48	5	4	0	3	39	1	50	8	5
Garcia, Steven, Salem°	.296	125	510	84	151	189	21	4	3	35	2	5	4	1	32	0	62	28	9
Garnett, Bradley, Alexandria°	.210	103	309	35	65	109	14	0	10	38	6	1	2	6	44	5	87	14	5
Gillaspie, Mark, Salem†	.292	110	353	83	103	209	20	4	26	88	4	2	6	15	87	8	90	13	4
Gilles, Robert, Lynchburg°	.183	30	93	13	17	37	5	0	5	17	0	0	1	15	0	39	3	1	
Goldthorn, Burk, Alexandria°	.251	96	287	39	72	98	20	0	2	33	3	0	2	3	55	4	49	2	4
Gonzalez, Julian, Hagerstown°	.000	30	1	0	0	0	0	0	0	0	0	0	0	0	0	0	0	1	0
Gordon, Timothy, Winston-Salem°	.143	57	182	13	26	38	6	0	2	11	1	9	1	0	13	0	52	2	1
Granger, Lee Randle, Hagerstown†	.221	30	77	16	17	27	1	0	3	8	0	1	3	12	1	26	9	3	
Guerrero, Inocencio, Durham	.000	1	3	0	0	0	0	0	0	0	0	0	0	0	0	0	0	0	0
Hagman, Keith, Durham°	.303	122	449	59	136	192	25	2	9	67	9	2	3	1	67	5	38	2	1
Harris, Gerry, Kinston	.235	93	341	38	80	117	12	2	7	44	11	1	5	2	21	2	70	24	2
Harvey, Steven, Peninsula	.175	28	97	7	17	24	2	1	1	7	0	3	1	1	7	0	27	4	2
Hearn, Edward, Peninsula	.329	21	76	15	25	45	2	0	6	14	2	0	1	0	5	0	24	1	2

Player and Club	Pct.	G.	AB.	R.	H.	TB.	2B.	3B.	HR.	RBI.	GW.	SH.	SF.	HP.	BB.	Int. BB.	SO.	SB.	CS.
Heiser, Bruce, Durham	.250	38	92	17	23	30	2	1	1	14	3	2	1	0	17	0	17	2	2
Hernandez, Tobias, Kinston	.182	8	22	2	4	7	1	1	0	1	0	0	0	1	3	0	5	0	1
Herrick, Neal, Hagerstown°	.213	65	221	23	47	70	11	0	4	15	1	1	0	1	18	1	42	2	4
Holmes, J. Christopher, Hagerstown°.	.000	2	5	0	0	0	0	0	0	0	0	0	0	0	1	0	5	0	0
Hood, Scott, Durham°	.220	106	332	42	73	86	8	1	1	23	4	4	2	0	46	3	66	3	5
Houston, Kevin, Alexandria°	.250	3	4	0	1	1	0	0	0	1	0	0	0	0	1	0	1	0	0
Howard, J. Christopher, Win.-Sal.†	.195	41	133	20	26	33	4	0	1	8	1	3	0	0	18	0	37	0	1
Hunter, Jeffrey, Winston-Salem°	.244	118	394	44	96	163	22	3	13	61	5	1	6	1	60	5	107	1	4
Huyck, Paul, Salem	.000	26	0	1	0	0	0	0	0	0	0	0	0	0	0	0	0	0	0
Kastelic, Bruce, Lynchburg°	.202	25	84	13	17	27	3	2	1	8	0	0	1	0	8	0	26	5	0
Keiser, Kent, Peninsula°	.231	5	13	2	3	3	0	0	0	3	0	0	1	0	2	0	1	1	1
Kelly, D. Patrick, Durham	.231	7	13	1	3	4	1	0	0	1	0	0	0	0	1	0	4	0	0
Krzanik, Andrew, Salem	.000	26	0	0	0	0	0	0	0	0	0	0	0	0	1	0	0	0	0
Lavalliere, Michael, Peninsula°	.275	66	178	20	49	63	4	2	2	23	2	1	4	0	26	2	20	3	3
Leboeuf, Alan, Peninsula°	.263	116	392	61	103	168	21	1	14	78	7	2	5	3	46	6	55	5	1
Ledbetter, Jeffrey, Winston-Salem°.	.238	62	223	30	53	88	12	1	7	28	4	0	1	5	24	1	47	1	0
Legg, Gregory, Peninsula	.343	44	134	20	46	55	9	0	0	20	4	1	3	1	14	0	8	2	3
Lewis, Herman, Kinston	.233	96	227	37	53	65	2	2	2	25	3	4	3	7	34	0	41	32	5
Lindsey, Jon, Peninsula°	.234	64	209	32	49	72	6	1	5	21	1	3	1	1	17	1	37	6	2
Lorenz, Jerome, Durham	.259	71	201	20	52	70	7	1	3	27	5	4	3	1	27	0	35	1	2
Luzon, Robert, Durham	.211	38	57	14	12	13	1	0	0	0	0	2	0	0	16	0	18	1	2
Malpeso, David, Winston-Salem	.317	116	441	68	140	253	24	1	29	91	6	3	3	4	22	1	76	0	1
Mann, Daniel, Durham	.232	61	125	16	29	39	7	0	1	6	0	2	1	2	8	1	29	2	1
Marcano, Jose, Lynchburg	.265	110	351	55	93	104	11	0	0	30	6	11	2	5	48	0	60	10	6
McClendon, Lloyd, Lynchburg	.273	108	384	61	105	186	25	1	18	78	8	0	3	2	55	2	65	4	3
McInerny, Dan, Hagerstown°	.241	12	29	6	7	7	0	0	0	3	0	0	1	0	7	1	7	1	2
McNair, Robert, Kinston°	.265	134	480	60	127	199	26	2	14	71	7	0	3	1	42	5	91	2	2
Melendez, Francisco, Peninsula°	.292	118	424	54	124	175	33	3	4	69	13	4	6	5	42	3	76	6	4
Meleski, Mark, Winston-Salem°	.185	71	227	28	42	48	4	1	0	13	1	1	2	1	35	0	40	4	3
Mesh, Michael, Winston-Salem	.236	69	263	38	62	69	5	1	0	16	0	1	0	1	29	1	45	16	2
Miller-Jones, Gary, Winston-Salem†..	.292	59	236	40	69	90	10	1	3	19	1	5	2	0	24	0	35	2	2
Milligan, Randy, Lynchburg	.269	118	420	63	113	150	10	6	5	55	4	1	1	4	54	0	101	25	3
Mitchell, Kevin, Lynchburg	.318	29	85	19	27	37	5	1	1	16	2	0	2	0	13	0	25	0	0
Moreno, Jaime, Salem	.176	28	91	12	16	24	3	1	1	7	0	1	0	1	9	0	23	1	1
Morrison, Bruce, Lynchburg	.235	10	34	7	8	12	1	0	1	6	1	0	1	0	5	0	11	0	0
Nandin, Robert, Kinston†	.300	83	323	44	97	111	9	1	1	28	3	4	2	4	22	0	25	28	6
Neal, Bryan, Durham°	.251	61	191	27	48	79	12	2	5	24	4	1	0	1	25	0	45	1	0
Neal, Earl, Hagerstown	.182	13	44	7	8	15	1	0	2	8	0	0	1	1	6	1	12	1	1
Noce, Paul, Salem	.196	59	204	16	40	60	2	3	4	19	1	1	1	3	17	0	73	2	0
Norris, Timothy, Hagerstown	.000	25	1	0	0	0	0	0	0	0	0	0	0	0	1	0	1	0	0
Olsen, Greg, Lynchburg	.264	32	91	10	24	25	1	0	0	5	0	2	0	2	12	1	5	1	1
Orsulak, Joseph, Alexandria°	.289	129	463	92	134	202	18	4	14	65	4	8	6	6	47	2	46	28	11
Pardo, Alberto, Hagerstown†	.289	130	492	76	142	225	24	4	17	86	5	3	6	1	38	3	79	5	3
Parent, Mark, Salem	.225	99	360	39	81	118	15	2	6	41	3	1	3	0	32	0	58	2	1
Parsons, Scott, Salem	.167	26	24	2	4	4	0	0	0	3	0	1	0	1	1	0	3	0	0
Paulino, Jose, Kinston	.299	58	201	34	60	85	9	5	2	28	3	1	1	4	20	1	34	20	2
Pena, Jorge, Salem	.225	45	142	14	32	44	9	0	1	10	2	2	0	2	12	0	44	0	5
Perez, Benjamin, Kinston	.245	83	229	26	56	66	8	1	0	24	3	4	5	4	20	2	25	11	3
Perez, George, Salem°	.217	84	249	26	54	71	12	1	1	25	0	2	2	1	22	0	52	5	4
Pinkham, William, Kinston	.263	133	471	55	124	184	28	1	10	59	6	0	3	1	36	2	97	3	1
Poston, Mark, Salem	.000	17	1	0	0	0	0	0	0	0	0	0	0	0	0	0	0	0	0
Quade, Michael, Alexandria	.263	104	315	69	83	104	13	4	0	22	4	13	1	0	75	1	53	9	4
Quinones, Luis, Salem†	.277	41	173	32	48	72	1	4	5	28	5	2	1	1	9	1	21	6	1
Raeside, John, Lynchburg	.281	73	228	32	64	77	6	2	1	22	3	1	0	1	33	2	41	11	3
Raley, Terry, Kinston†	.280	113	371	46	104	142	26	3	2	36	3	2	1	1	50	4	58	6	3
Rembielak, Richard, Hagerstown	.095	17	42	4	4	5	1	0	0	4	0	0	1	0	3	0	8	0	0
Renteria, Richard, Alexandria	.331	127	508	80	168	244	24	5	14	100	8	3	7	4	24	2	54	12	9
Reynolds, Leonardo, Peninsula	.293	40	133	11	39	53	6	1	2	22	0	4	3	0	1	0	23	5	2
Rowe, Peter, Alexandria	.315	61	181	25	57	82	14	1	3	28	4	3	1	0	9	1	16	0	0
Samuel, Juan, Peninsula	.320	135	494	111	158	283	29	6	28	94	10	0	7	15	31	3	124	64	17
Scanlon, Kenneth, Durham	.241	62	166	24	40	47	7	0	0	7	0	4	1	1	20	1	28	6	2
Schaefer, Jeffrey, Hagerstown	.100	18	60	4	6	6	0	0	0	7	0	0	1	0	8	0	16	1	1
Scheller, David, Winston-Salem°	.126	30	103	6	13	19	3	0	1	8	0	0	2	1	8	0	24	1	0
Schmidt, August, Kinston	.297	50	182	31	54	75	10	1	3	22	3	5	2	1	24	1	31	7	2
Schnoor, Charles, Lynchburg	.217	119	304	44	66	84	8	2	2	37	0	7	4	5	53	1	45	13	1
Schroeder, Jay, Kinston	.218	132	435	59	95	159	17	1	15	55	5	5	4	7	65	1	172	6	7
Sheets, Larry, Hagerstown°	.296	88	324	46	96	171	21	0	18	59	4	0	1	4	27	3	66	1	1
Shipanoff, David, Kinston	.000	63	1	0	0	0	0	0	0	0	0	0	0	0	0	0	0	0	0
Siebert, Barry, Peninsula	.270	56	159	31	43	59	7	3	1	14	1	5	2	1	35	1	42	8	3
Siriano, Rick, Durham°	.228	131	413	46	94	129	19	2	4	38	5	3	3	10	63	1	66	12	8
Smith, Wesley, Salem	.000	34	1	0	0	0	0	0	0	0	0	0	0	0	0	0	1	0	0
Snaith, Andrew, Alexandria	.237	106	304	43	72	107	14	0	7	30	3	5	2	1	32	2	85	0	4
Sosa, Miguel, Durham	.288	132	507	77	146	247	18	4	25	69	9	4	4	3	37	1	101	35	5
Stefanski, James, Durham	.259	25	58	6	15	20	2	0	1	6	0	0	0	1	4	1	7	1	0
Stone, Jeffrey, Peninsula°	.297	137	559	110	166	216	18	13	2	50	9	10	7	9	34	1	102	94	15
Styons, Raymond, Salem	.201	109	363	52	73	141	10	2	18	47	1	2	1	9	37	2	112	0	4
Sunderlage, Jeffrey, Lynchburg°	.000	37	2	0	0	0	0	0	0	0	0	0	0	0	0	0	2	0	0
Sutton, Ricardo, Kinston	.160	28	75	15	12	19	1	0	2	4	0	0	1	0	14	0	21	1	3
Tarver, Laschelle, Lynchburg°	.308	99	399	75	123	144	14	2	1	34	2	6	1	2	45	2	54	56	16
Teller, Jeems, Winston-Salem	.211	6	19	2	4	4	0	0	0	1	0	0	0	0	5	0	11	0	0
Thompson, Scott, Salem	.265	95	332	38	88	121	11	2	6	39	3	4	1	3	19	0	71	10	1
Thompson, Tommy, Durham°	.247	114	360	41	89	148	8	0	17	57	9	4	5	3	68	4	41	0	0
Tiburcio, Frederick, Durham°	.257	127	487	72	125	160	17	3	4	55	3	6	1	5	31	1	82	14	7
Tiefenthaler, Dennis, Hagerstown	.270	11	37	9	10	14	1	0	1	3	0	1	1	0	3	0	10	1	1
Timko, Andrew, Hagerstown°	.292	129	480	80	140	176	26	2	2	60	5	6	6	3	54	3	55	15	5
Tippin, Richard, Lynchburg	.114	23	44	3	5	6	1	0	0	2	0	0	0	0	4	0	21	0	0
Traber, James, Hagerstown°	.346	7	26	1	9	11	2	0	0	2	0	0	0	0	2	0	3	0	1
Tumpane, Robert, Durham°	.255	95	290	37	74	140	12	0	18	53	3	2	6	2	37	4	45	0	1
Tutt, Johnny, Hagerstown	.266	108	365	47	97	135	16	8	2	30	1	2	3	4	43	1	63	30	17
Ubri, Fermin, Lynchburg	.261	115	429	63	112	123	7	1	0	44	3	11	4	3	24	2	40	28	8
Vanderburg, Michael, Hagerstown°.	.240	7	25	8	6	7	1	0	0	1	0	0	1	0	4	0	6	3	1
Wahlig, James, Kinston	.247	100	275	24	68	89	7	4	2	30	6	2	5	1	41	1	56	4	5
Warner, Harold, Peninsula°	.232	54	112	11	26	40	6	4	0	11	2	1	2	3	10	0	35	3	2

Player and Club	Pct.	G.	AB.	R.	H.	TB.	2B.	3B.	HR.	RBI.	GW.	SH.	SF.	HP.	BB.	Int. BB.	SO.	SB.	CS.
Waynick, Edward, Winston-Salem	.239	84	289	32	69	113	8	0	12	31	1	0	1	3	32	0	100	0	4
Williams, Jeffrey, Hagerstown°	.259	109	375	61	97	148	17	5	8	46	3	5	6	2	42	4	88	32	5
Williams, Melvin, Peninsula.............	.285	87	277	37	79	115	13	1	7	44	4	7	2	2	24	0	58	6	7
Wilson, Gary, Kinston.....................	.000	8	0	1	0	0	0	0	0	0	0	0	0	0	0	0	0	0	0
Wilson, J. Parker, Winston-Salem	.142	49	162	13	23	34	5	0	2	10	2	1	1	2	7	1	50	0	1
Winningham, Herman, Lynchburg°	.295	120	430	65	127	175	20	5	6	61	7	1	4	0	64	2	106	50	9
Wood, Joseph, Salem°	.170	104	317	24	54	61	4	0	1	20	0	1	1	0	11	0	72	1	4

The following pitchers, listed alphabetically by club, with games in parentheses, had no plate appearances, primarily through use of designated hitters:

ALEXANDRIA—Barez, Angel (5); Cordoba, Wilfrido (43); Dodd, Lance (5); Gonzales, Fernando (24); Green, Alexander (14); Horne, Jeffrey (25); Krawczyk, Raymond (6); Lamonde, Lawrence (15); Leggatt, Richard (11); Marcheskie, Lee (33); Ray, Arthur (24); Taylor, Johnny (30); Warthen, Daniel (17); Wheeler, Timothy (6); Winn, James (7); Zamba, Michael (22); Zaske, Jeffrey (48).

DURHAM—Clay, David (22); Coatney, Ricky (15); Dedmon, Jeffrey (31); Fisher, Brian (18); Fuller, Timothy (4); Hatcher, Richard (40); Mortillaro, John (4); North, Roy (21); Payne, Michael (21); Reiter, Gary (61); Santana, Rafael (2); Sears, Hubert (1); Smith, Michael (4); Treadway, Andre (25); Twitty, Jeffrey (22); Waddell, Thomas (42).

HAGERSTOWN—Arnold, Tony (12); Dixon, Kenneth (15); Gilbert, Jeffrey (3); Gold, Bret (7); Guinn, Charles (25); Habyan, John (1); Hoke, Leon (22); Kucharski, Joseph (17); Maples, Timothy (9); McCullock, Alec (24); McDonough, Brian (9); Mitcheltree, John (43); Rooney, James (26); Sczesnak, Marc (26); Stewart, Samuel (2); Summers, Jeffrey (23); Willsher, Christopher (13); Wilson, Randall (6).

KINSTON—Blackmon, Thomas (36); Holton, Mark (7); Layton, Thomas (25); Leal, Carlos (23); Lychak, Perry (5); McKnight, Jonathan (26); Phillips, Christopher (11); Reish, Stephan (1); Rodgers, Timothy (31); Terry, Glenn (34).

LYNCHBURG—Ballard, Byron (31); Begue, Roger (47); Bettendorf, Jeffrey (4); Johnston, Jody (18); McDowell, Roger (5); Miller, Thomas (22); Myles, Rick (10); Rech, Edward (29); Tibbs, Jay (7); Vaughn, DeWayne (20); Webster, Richard (22); Wilmet, Paul (29).

PENINSULA—Bartholow, Foster (42); Darnell, Jimmy (16); Dorin, Matthew (12); Gaynor, Richard (34); Ghelfi, Anthony (25); Goff, Wallace (6); Griffin, Frankie (42); Hudson, Charles (27); Johnson, William (50); Richardson, Ronald (22); True, Steven (26); Wojna, Edward (27).

SALEM—Cacciatore, Paul (15); Gerhardt, William (14); Klusacek, Robert (16); Lovekamp, Scott (5); McClain, Michael (13); Oberbruner, James (30); Ochal, Mark (15); Solomon, William (32); Stone, Steven (11); Warner, Frank (18).

WINSTON-SALEM—Bowlin, Allan (28); Clinton, Kevin (37); Dale, Charles (38); Fredlund, Jay (9); Garrett, Steven (36); Gering, Scott (36); Grubbs, Kevin (32); Hulbert, Alvin (10); Kane, Kevin (25); McCarthy, Thomas (30); Mecerod, George (25); Plainte, Brandon (31); Valdez, Miguel (26).

GRAND SLAM HOME RUNS—Gillaspie, 4; Ackley, Ford, Gilles, McClendon, 2 each; Christianson, Fisher, Garcia, Ledbetter, Lewis, Malpeso, Melendez, Noce, Pardo, Quinones, Renteria, Styons, 1 each.

AWARDED FIRST BASE ON CATCHER'S INTERFERENCE—Mann 6 (Falcone 2, Lavalliere 2, Ackley, Goldthorn); Case 2 (Ackley 2).

CLUB FIELDING

Club	Pct.	G.	PO.	A.	E.	DP.	PB.	Club	Pct.	G.	PO.	A.	E.	DP.	PB.
Durham	.966	136	3582	1460	178	122	15	Hagerstown	.959	136	3485	1347	205	106	16
Kinston	.960	135	3402	1293	196	92	23	Peninsula	.956	138	3575	1580	238	124	24
Lynchburg	.960	137	3517	1466	209	98	17	Salem	.952	140	3485	1406	249	109	29
Alexandria.................	.959	135	3363	1304	201	100	21	Winston-Salem	.952	139	3573	1537	256	133	36

Triple Play—Kinston.

INDIVIDUAL FIELDING
FIRST BASEMEN

°Throws lefthanded.

Player and Club	Pct.	G.	PO.	A.	E.	DP.	Player and Club	Pct.	G.	PO.	A.	E.	DP.
Bailey, Durham	1.000	1	4	0	0	0	Malpeso, Winston-Salem	.994	16	150	7	1	14
Benzinger, Winston-Salem	.992	41	343	17	3	26	McNair, Kinston°	.987	131	1020	79	14	78
Bertucio, Hagerstown°	1.000	2	8	2	0	1	Melendez, Peninsula°	.987	85	739	75	11	65
Casey, Salem	.989	22	160	22	2	18	Milligan, Lynchburg	.967	26	225	10	8	13
Castaneda, Alexandria	.987	92	705	55	10	59	Noce, Salem	1.000	1	3	1	0	0
Christianson, Salem°	.981	84	662	61	14	48	Orsulak, Alexandria°	.980	8	46	2	1	1
Churchill, Alexandria	1.000	4	21	0	0	0	Pardo, Hagerstown	1.000	9	52	10	0	3
Clow, Durham	1.000	5	39	6	0	0	Parent, Salem	1.000	1	5	0	0	1
Daulton, Peninsula	1.000	2	6	0	0	0	Pinkham, Kinston	1.000	1	5	1	0	0
Dees, Hagerstown	.981	37	284	22	6	24	Raeside, Lynchburg	.986	15	135	8	2	10
Dumouchelle, Hagerstown	.990	14	82	14	1	2	Scheller, Winston-Salem°	.970	21	208	15	7	18
Evans, Lynchburg°	.983	66	540	32	10	33	Snaith, Alexandria	1.000	3	23	2	0	4
Falcone, Alexandria	.978	84	639	64	16	57	Stefanski, Durham	1.000	2	18	0	0	1
Frash, Lynchburg°	.983	40	314	32	6	29	Styons, Salem	.976	33	265	17	7	21
Garnett, Alexandria°	.968	41	311	21	11	18	Thompson, Durham	.988	10	79	1	1	7
HAGMAN, Durham°	.990	104	875	83	10	78	Traber, Hagerstown°	1.000	1	5	0	0	0
Hearn, Peninsula	.949	4	36	1	2	2	Tumpane, Durham°	.996	23	209	21	1	20
Herrick, Hagerstown	.909	4	7	3	1	1	Wahlig, Kinston	.980	10	47	2	1	0
Hunter, Winston-Salem	.991	68	593	36	6	56	Wood, Salem	.974	5	35	2	1	4
Leboeuf, Peninsula	.989	57	497	36	6	36							

Triple Play—McNair.

SECOND BASEMEN

Player and Club	Pct.	G.	PO.	A.	E.	DP.	Player and Club	Pct.	G.	PO.	A.	E.	DP.
Adamiak, Peninsula	1.000	4	6	11	0	1	Marcano, Lynchburg	.967	26	54	64	4	8
Banner, Hagerstown	.500	1	1	0	1	0	Meleski, Winston-Salem	.945	46	65	142	12	16
Butler, Hagerstown	.938	4	7	8	1	1	Miller-Jones, Winston-Salem	.951	59	125	204	17	46
Chmil, Durham	.977	10	14	28	1	7	Nandin, Kinston	.971	20	40	60	3	14
Corman, Hagerstown	.943	114	219	261	29	50	Noce, Salem	1.000	4	6	6	0	2
Dowell, Peninsula	1.000	6	13	13	0	3	Pena, Kinston	.940	44	75	113	12	15
Dumouchelle, Hagerstown	1.000	8	16	16	0	3	Perez, Kinston	.950	24	29	47	4	9
Escobar, Kinston	1.000	4	4	4	0	1	Quade, Alexandria	.964	17	27	26	2	2
M. Garcia, Durham	.971	75	110	196	9	33	Raeside, Lynchburg	.973	23	43	65	3	6
S. Garcia, Salem	.9655	97	217	287	18	53	Raley, Kinston	.908	16	28	31	6	4
Harris, Kinston	.937	84	151	205	24	30	Renteria, Alexandria	.951	124	196	346	28	57
Heiser, Durham	.920	17	11	35	4	7	Samuel, Peninsula	.951	134	244	442	35	82
Howard, Winston-Salem	.927	40	64	127	15	20	Scanlon, Durham	.959	50	79	154	10	25
Kastelic, Lynchburg	.933	3	3	11	1	1	Schaefer, Hagerstown	.964	17	39	41	3	7
Lorenz, Durham	1.000	1	0	2	0	0	UBRI, Lynchburg	.9658	95	159	265	15	47

THIRD BASEMEN

Player and Club	Pct.	G.	PO.	A.	E.	DP.	Player and Club	Pct.	G.	PO.	A.	E.	DP.
Adamiak, Peninsula	.920	25	14	32	4	5	McClendon, Lynchburg	.941	17	9	23	2	1
Banner, Hagerstown	.905	10	6	13	2	1	Meleski, Winston-Salem	.857	6	1	11	2	2
Butler, Hagerstown	1.000	7	4	13	0	1	Mitchell, Lynchburg	.815	25	11	33	10	0
CHMIL, Durham	.931	105	87	171	19	13	Nandin, Kinston	.905	44	37	68	11	5
Corman, Hagerstown	.857	5	2	4	1	0	Noce, Salem	.929	35	27	51	6	3
Cusack, Hagerstown	.829	28	8	26	7	3	Olsen, Lynchburg	.900	7	4	14	2	3
Dees, Hagerstown	.938	33	15	46	4	6	Perez, Kinston	.939	20	12	19	2	1
Dowell, Peninsula	.917	45	28	83	10	8	Quade, Alexandria	.876	50	33	59	13	4
Dumouchelle, Hagerstown	.911	56	41	72	11	7	Raeside, Lynchburg	.778	9	6	8	4	0
Enos, Peninsula	.971	14	10	23	1	4	Raley, Kinston	.909	82	65	94	16	5
M. Garcia, Durham	.857	12	6	12	3	2	Rembielak, Hagerstown	.962	13	9	16	1	1
S. Garcia, Salem	.929	23	20	45	5	5	Schnoor, Lynchburg	.961	66	43	106	6	7
Gordon, Winston-Salem	.883	53	45	76	16	3	Snaith, Alexandria	.922	102	71	130	17	12
Heiser, Durham	.688	7	2	9	5	0	Thompson, Durham	.955	9	7	14	1	3
Hunter, Winston-Salem	.924	30	25	48	6	4	Tiefenthaler, Hagerstown	1.000	11	5	16	0	0
Kastelic, Lynchburg	.906	19	15	33	5	1	Ubri, Lynchburg	.984	27	15	48	1	3
Lavalliere, Peninsula	1.000	1	0	1	0	1	Wahlig, Kinston	.667	3	1	1	1	0
Leboeuf, Peninsula	.769	10	3	7	3	1	Waynick, Winston-Salem	.835	32	27	44	14	8
Lindsey, Peninsula	.823	59	44	77	26	6	Wilson, Winston-Salem	.840	28	27	41	13	3
Lorenz, Durham	.825	22	10	23	7	0	Wood, Salem	.906	93	91	131	23	14

SHORTSTOPS

Player and Club	Pct.	G.	PO.	A.	E.	DP.	Player and Club	Pct.	G.	PO.	A.	E.	DP.
Brassil, Salem	.875	62	97	141	34	20	Marcano, Lynchburg	.934	84	131	223	25	31
Carpenter, Winston-Salem	.914	39	68	103	16	23	Meleski, Winston-Salem	.979	14	18	29	1	3
Chmil, Durham	.750	4	5	7	4	2	Mesh, Winston-Salem	.940	68	118	198	20	44
Clack, Alexandria	.919	125	196	290	43	57	Nandin, Kinston	.918	26	19	37	5	4
Corman, Hagerstown	1.000	1	0	4	0	0	Noce, Salem	.964	14	17	36	2	9
Dowell, Peninsula	.930	63	85	209	22	42	Quade, Alexandria	.938	12	25	20	3	4
Dumouchelle, Hagerstown	1.000	10	10	28	0	2	Quinones, Salem	.903	41	41	99	15	17
Escobar, Kinston	.938	77	85	171	17	32	Rembielak, Hagerstown	.800	5	3	5	2	0
Estrada, Salem	.940	25	42	68	7	15	Reynolds, Peninsula	.855	38	46	102	25	20
Garcia, Salem	1.000	1	2	2	0	1	Schmidt, Kinston	.946	48	70	142	12	22
Gordon, Winston-Salem	1.000	5	11	12	0	5	Schnoor, Lynchburg	.897	59	80	137	25	34
Heiser, Durham	.867	5	2	11	2	2	Sosa, Durham	.942	129	185	354	33	83
Kastelic, Lynchburg	.941	6	10	22	2	3	TIMKO, Hagerstown	.947	127	223	326	31	64
Legg, Peninsula	.925	44	56	130	15	21	Wilson, Winston-Salem	.830	21	36	47	17	10
Lindsey, Peninsula	1.000	2	1	1	0	1	Wood, Salem	1.000	2	3	4	0	0

Triple Play—Escobar.

OUTFIELDERS

Player and Club	Pct.	G.	PO.	A.	E.	DP.	Player and Club	Pct.	G.	PO.	A.	E.	DP.
Ackley, Winston-Salem	.923	26	32	4	3	2	Luzon, Durham	.917	38	30	3	3	1
Aitcheson, Kinston	.963	126	222	12	9	2	Malpeso, Winston-Salem	.952	23	39	1	2	0
Arfstrom, Winston-Salem	.946	93	131	10	8	3	Mann, Durham	.928	57	60	4	5	2
Beal, Winston-Salem	.930	113	197	15	16	2	McInerny, Hagerstown°	1.000	5	3	0	0	0
Benzinger, Winston-Salem	.955	82	95	11	5	1	Milligan, Lynchburg	.975	68	116	2	3	1
Bertucio, Hagerstown°	.947	24	36	0	2	0	B. Neal, Durham	.970	31	30	2	1	0
Cannon, Salem	.976	118	276	14	7	2	E. Neal, Hagerstown	.867	11	12	1	2	0
Casey, Salem	.963	50	73	5	3	0	Noce, Salem	1.000	2	2	0	0	0
Christensen, Lynchburg	.923	8	11	1	1	0	Orsulak, Alexandria°	.965	124	240	5	9	0
Coleman, Salem	.955	30	62	2	3	1	Paulino, Kinston	.913	56	90	5	9	0
Currier, Peninsula	.905	32	35	3	4	1	G. Perez, Salem°	.936	45	70	3	5	1
Cusack, Hagerstown	.920	13	22	1	2	0	Quade, Alexandria	.960	35	48	0	2	0
Darkis, Peninsula	.923	72	105	3	9	0	Schroeder, Kinston	.929	125	178	17	15	5
De La Rosa, Alexandria°	.963	26	49	3	2	0	Sheets, Hagerstown	.955	72	123	5	6	1
DeLaRosa, Alexandria°	.947	33	48	6	3	1	Siebert, Peninsula	.966	52	82	2	3	1
DelMonte, Lynchburg°	.972	42	66	3	2	2	Siriano, Durham°	.963	128	173	8	7	2
Denby, Lynchburg	.976	65	116	5	3	2	Stefanski, Durham	.000	1	0	0	2	0
Devalk, Alexandria	.941	8	15	1	1	0	Stone, Peninsula	.973	127	276	9	8	3
Dumouchelle, Hagerstown	1.000	18	39	3	0	1	Sutton, Durham	1.000	8	14	1	0	0
FELT, Alexandria	.982	126	199	23	4	10	Tarver, Lynchburg°	.947	88	140	3	8	1
Fisher, Winston-Salem	.930	55	78	2	6	0	Teller, Winston-Salem	1.000	4	1	1	0	0
Ford, Alexandria	.926	74	108	5	9	1	S. Thompson, Salem	.928	86	166	1	13	0
Frash, Lynchburg°	.989	53	82	7	1	1	Tiburcio, Durham°	.953	124	236	6	12	1
Gillaspie, Salem	.914	108	172	19	18	5	Traber, Hagerstown°	1.000	6	7	0	0	0
Granger, Hagerstown	.969	24	29	2	1	0	Tumpane, Durham°	.922	46	56	3	5	0
Hagman, Durham°	1.000	9	5	1	0	0	Tutt, Durham	.949	106	197	6	11	2
Harvey, Peninsula	.816	27	31	0	7	0	Vanderburg, Hagerstown	1.000	7	14	0	0	0
Herrick, Hagerstown	.969	56	82	12	3	2	Wahlig, Kinston	.966	43	54	2	2	0
Hunter, Winston-Salem	.333	2	1	0	2	0	Warner, Peninsula°	.927	37	44	7	4	1
Keiser, Peninsula	1.000	5	4	0	0	0	J. Williams, Hagerstown°	.957	105	205	15	10	3
Ledbetter, Winston-Salem°	.954	41	80	3	4	0	M. Williams, Peninsula	.950	82	104	9	6	1
Lewis, Kinston	.957	82	196	4	9	2	Winningham, Lynchburg	.980	110	235	6	5	1
Lorenz, Durham	1.000	50	42	3	0	2							

CATCHERS

Player and Club	Pct.	G.	PO.	A.	E.	DP.	PB.	Player and Club	Pct.	G.	PO.	A.	E.	DP.	PB.
Ackley, Winston-Salem	.974	76	501	59	15	6	15	HOOD, Durham	.9883	102	772	75	10	6	14
Bailey, Durham	1.000	14	79	5	0	0	0	Lavalliere, Peninsula	.983	46	306	34	6	4	10
Churchill, Alexandria	1.000	5	20	3	0	0	1	Malpeso, Winston-Salem	.978	71	420	73	11	8	21
Daulton, Peninsula	.9875	95	648	63	9	10	14	McClendon, Lynchburg	.977	85	483	64	13	5	10
Dumouchelle, Hagerstown	.964	32	193	24	8	5	4	Moreno, Salem	.968	25	159	21	6	2	11
Erickson, Kinston	.973	26	105	2	3	0	3	Olsen, Lynchburg	.975	25	145	12	4	0	2
Escobar, Kinston	1.000	1	1	0	0	0	0	Pardo, Hagerstown	.984	99	633	64	11	5	11
Falcone, Hagerstown	.962	21	111	16	5	3	1	Parent, Salem	.978	87	470	64	12	8	12
Gilles, Lynchburg	.968	24	166	17	6	2	3	Pinkham, Kinston	.982	120	783	98	16	11	19
Goldthorn, Alexandria	.975	89	607	60	17	11	13	Rowe, Alexandria	.988	53	302	34	4	10	7
Hearn, Peninsula	1.000	5	33	1	0	0	0	Styons, Salem	.976	29	182	18	5	0	6
Hernandez, Kinston	.985	8	59	7	1	2	1	Thompson, Durham	.993	31	256	27	2	2	1
Holmes, Hagerstown	1.000	1	0	2	0	0	0	Tippin, Lynchburg	.947	19	85	5	5	0	2

PITCHERS

Player and Club	Pct.	G.	PO.	A.	E.	DP.
Arnold, Hagerstown	.941	12	5	11	1	1
Ballard, Lynchburg	1.000	31	4	10	0	0
Barez, Alexandria	1.000	5	0	2	0	0
Bartholow, Peninsula	.923	42	5	7	1	1
Begue, Lynchburg	.952	47	7	13	1	0
Bettendorf, Lynchburg	1.000	4	3	4	0	1
Blackmon, Kinston	.862	35	5	20	4	0
Bowlin, Winston-Salem*	.947	28	2	16	1	1
Brown, Hagerstown	1.000	14	3	4	0	0
Cacciatore, Salem	.842	15	5	11	3	0
Cerutti, Kinston*	.967	16	7	22	1	0
Clay, Durham	.978	22	18	27	1	4
Clinton, Winston-Salem	1.000	37	11	31	0	1
Coatney, Durham	.880	15	5	17	3	0
Cordoba, Alexandria	.957	43	3	19	1	1
Dale, Winston-Salem	.929	38	5	8	1	0
Daniels, Salem	.667	13	4	2	3	0
Darnell, Peninsula	.900	15	3	6	1	0
Dedmon, Durham	.955	31	12	30	2	3
DelMonte, Lynchburg*	1.000	4	0	3	0	0
Dixon, Hagerstown	.947	15	5	13	1	0
Dorin, Peninsula	1.000	12	0	3	0	0
Fisher, Durham	.800	18	3	9	3	0
Fredlund, Winston-Salem	1.000	9	3	8	0	1
Fultz, Lynchburg	.887	27	19	28	6	3
Garrett, Winston-Salem	.952	36	4	16	1	3
Gaynor, Peninsula	1.000	34	7	22	0	1
Gerhardt, Salem	1.000	14	8	4	0	0
Gering, Winston-Salem	.880	36	5	17	3	0
Ghelfi, Peninsula	.891	25	21	28	6	0
Gilbert, Hagerstown	1.000	3	3	4	0	1
Goff, Peninsula*	1.000	6	0	3	0	0
Gold, Hagerstown	1.000	7	5	2	0	0
GONZALES, Alexandria	1.000	24	12	34	0	2
Gonzalez, Hagerstown*	.944	30	3	14	1	0
Green, Alexandria*	.909	14	2	18	2	1
Griffin, Peninsula*	1.000	41	3	6	0	1
Grubbs, Winston-Salem	.882	32	11	19	4	4
Guinn, Hagerstown	.870	25	11	9	3	0
Habyan, Hagerstown	1.000	1	1	0	0	1
Hatcher, Durham	.920	40	12	34	4	3
Herrick, Hagerstown	1.000	1	2	0	0	0
Hoke, Hagerstown	.917	22	4	7	1	1
Holton, Kinston	1.000	7	2	0	0	0
Horne, Alexandria	.893	25	7	18	3	1
Hudson, Peninsula	1.000	27	10	25	0	1
Hulbert, Winston-Salem	1.000	10	2	0	0	0
Huyck, Salem*	.897	25	7	19	3	1
Johnson, Peninsula	.917	50	4	18	2	0
Johnston, Lynchburg	.955	18	5	16	1	1
Kane, Winston-Salem	.941	25	3	13	1	3
Klusacek, Salem*	1.000	16	1	3	0	0
Krawczyk, Alexandria	.857	6	1	5	1	1
Krzanik, Salem	1.000	26	3	16	0	1
Kucharski, Hagerstown	.933	7	4	10	1	0
Lamonde, Alexandria	1.000	15	7	19	0	1
Layton, Kinston	.955	25	8	13	1	0
Leal, Kinston	.966	23	9	19	1	2
Leggatt, Alexandria	1.000	11	1	11	0	2
Lovekamp, Salem	.909	5	2	8	1	0
Lychak, Kinston*	1.000	5	0	4	0	1

Player and Club	Pct.	G.	PO.	A.	E.	DP.
Maples, Hagerstown	.500	9	2	2	4	0
Marcheskie, Alexandria	.914	33	9	23	3	4
McCarthy, Winston-Salem	1.000	30	8	26	0	1
McClain, Salem	.938	13	2	13	1	0
McCullock, Hagerstown	1.000	24	1	6	0	0
McDonough, Hagerstown	1.000	9	9	7	0	0
McDowell, Lynchburg	1.000	4	2	7	0	0
McKnight, Kinston	.978	26	14	31	1	3
Mecerod, Winston-Salem	.912	25	8	23	3	0
Miller, Lynchburg*	.900	22	3	15	2	0
Mitcheltree, Hagerstown	.950	43	9	29	2	0
Mortillaro, Durham*	1.000	4	0	4	0	0
Myles, Lynchburg*	.950	10	2	17	1	2
Norris, Hagerstown	.786	25	3	8	3	0
North, Durham	.938	21	8	7	1	3
Oberbruner, Salem	.923	30	7	17	2	2
Ochal, Salem	.912	15	11	20	3	0
Parsons, Salem	.886	19	13	18	4	0
Payne, Durham	.907	21	11	28	4	4
Phillips, Kinston	.905	11	8	11	2	2
Plainte, Winston-Salem*	.914	31	11	21	3	2
Poston, Salem	.800	17	3	5	2	0
Ray, Alexandria	.900	24	8	10	2	0
Rech, Lynchburg*	.912	29	4	27	3	0
Reish, Kinston	1.000	1	2	2	0	0
Reiter, Durham*	.867	61	6	7	2	2
Richardson, Peninsula	.783	22	7	11	5	0
Rodgers, Kinston	.926	31	22	28	4	2
Rooney, Hagerstown*	.953	26	13	28	2	2
Santana, Durham	1.000	2	1	0	0	0
Sczesnak, Hagerstown*	.769	26	2	8	3	1
Shipanoff, Kinston	1.000	63	2	15	0	1
W. Smith, Salem	.889	34	3	5	1	1
Solomon, Salem	.789	32	3	12	4	1
Stewart, Hagerstown	1.000	2	0	2	0	0
Stone, Salem	.727	11	4	4	3	1
Summers, Alexandria	.895	23	7	10	2	0
Sunderlage, Lynchburg*	.842	37	9	23	6	1
Taylor, Alexandria	.958	30	5	18	1	1
Terry, Kinston*	1.000	34	4	8	0	0
Tibbs, Lynchburg	1.000	7	2	11	0	0
Treadway, Durham	1.000	25	16	16	0	3
True, Peninsula*	.944	26	4	30	2	2
Twitty, Durham*	1.000	22	2	10	0	0
Valdez, Winston-Salem.	.800	26	1	3	1	0
Vaughn, Lynchburg	1.000	20	2	6	0	0
Waddell, Durham	.938	42	7	8	1	1
F. Warner, Salem	.960	18	8	16	1	0
H. Warner, Peninsula*	1.000	16	2	7	0	0
Warthen, Alexandria*	1.000	17	0	5	0	0
Webster, Lynchburg	.917	22	10	23	3	2
Wheeler, Alexandria	.842	6	7	9	3	1
Willsher, Hagerstown	.846	13	1	10	2	1
Wilmet, Lynchburg	.636	29	3	4	4	0
G. Wilson, Kinston	.882	7	4	11	2	1
R. Wilson, Hagerstown	.750	6	1	2	1	0
Winn, Alexandria	.875	7	4	3	1	0
Wojna, Peninsula	.914	27	13	40	5	2
Wood, Salem	1.000	3	1	0	0	0
Zamba, Alexandria	.923	22	3	9	1	1
Zaske, Alexandria	.778	48	4	10	4	1

The following players had no recorded accepted chances at the positions indicated; therefore, are not listed in the fielding averages for those particular positions: Adamiak, of; Cannon, 3b; Clow, 3b; Dodd, p; Dumouchelle, p; Estrada, 2b; Fuller, p; Heiser, p; Herrick, 2b; Malpeso, 3b; Pardo, of; B. Perez, of; Rowe, 1b; Sears, p; M. Smith, p; Styons, of; T. Thompson, of; Winningham, 2b.

CLUB PITCHING

Club	ERA.	G.	CG.	ShO.	Sv.	IP.	H.	R.	ER.	HR.	HB.	BB.	Int. BB.	SO.	WP.	Bk.
Peninsula	3.10	138	21	14	37	1191.2	1040	542	411	74	37	512	11	969	77	10
Durham	3.28	136	21	8	37	1194.0	1046	538	435	107	37	474	13	1089	63	1
Kinston	3.35	135	31	10	34	1134.0	1017	540	422	79	30	531	32	921	57	3
Lynchburg	3.59	137	43	14	16	1172.1	1074	613	468	88	50	502	9	855	80	8
Alexandria	3.64	135	16	6	37	1121.0	1031	575	453	88	54	530	21	881	68	13
Hagerstown	4.28	136	23	9	17	1161.2	1174	668	552	113	37	527	39	891	74	13
Winston-Salem	4.31	139	10	5	18	1191.0	1297	732	571	87	37	506	27	891	99	4
Salem	5.10	140	29	6	8	1161.2	1354	834	658	135	31	528	20	775	75	5

PITCHERS' RECORDS

*Throws lefthanded.   (Leading Qualifiers for Earned-Run Average Leadership—112 or More Innings)

Pitcher—Club	W.	L.	Pct.	ERA.	G.	GS.	CG.	GF.	ShO.	Sv.	IP.	H.	R.	ER.	HR.	HB.	BB.	Int. BB.	SO.	WP.
Hudson, Peninsula	15	5	.750	1.85	27	26	7	1	3	0	185	143	56	38	10	0	64	0	147	4
Ghelfi, Peninsula	12	6	.667	2.64	25	24	4	1	2	1	160.1	147	70	47	8	7	60	1	162	8
Dedmon, Durham	5	6	.455	2.74	31	14	4	7	1	2	121.1	113	57	37	11	4	54	1	102	9
Blackmon, Kinston	11	6	.647	2.79	35	12	2	14	0	3	113	101	51	35	4	1	54	3	81	7
Wojna, Peninsula	12	8	.600	2.90	27	26	4	1	2	1	176.2	156	79	57	3	9	49	1	116	9
Layton, Kinston	7	9	.438	2.91	25	18	6	2	0	0	151.1	147	61	49	10	1	53	2	94	8
Clay, Durham	9	5	.643	3.11	22	21	4	0	1	0	139	122	54	48	9	5	61	0	88	4
Johnston, Lynchburg	12	3	.800	3.12	18	18	5	0	3	0	121.1	102	49	42	9	2	49	1	103	7
Cerutti, Kinston*	10	5	.667	3.19	16	16	5	0	1	0	113	88	47	40	9	2	49	1	136	5
Rodgers, Kinston	11	8	.579	3.23	31	22	6	2	2	1	172.2	159	79	62	14	3	50	4	138	5

Departmental Leaders: G—Shipanoff, 63; GS—Rech, 28; CG—Fultz, 12; GF—Shipanoff, 56; ShO—Hudson, Johnston, 3; W—Hudson, McKnight, 15; L—Rech, 14; Pct.—Green, .900; Sv—Shipanoff, 30; IP—Fultz, 188.1; H—Fultz, 181; R—Rech, 101; ER—Fultz, 77; HR—Treadway, 20; HB—Lamonde, Taylor, 11; BB—McKnight, True, 87; IBB—Norris, 12; SO—Ghelfi, 162; WP—Plainte, 20.

(All Pitchers—Listed Alphabetically)

Pitcher—Club	W.	L.	Pct.	ERA.	G.	GS.	CG.	GF.	ShO.	Sv.	IP.	H.	R.	ER.	HR.	HB.	BB.	Int. BB.	SO.	WP.
Arnold, Hagerstown	8	2	.800	3.81	12	12	3	0	1	0	80.1	78	38	34	16	3	16	0	48	1
Ballard, Lynchburg	4	4	.500	1.56	31	2	1	21	0	6	57.2	35	16	10	3	0	22	0	56	5
Barez, Alexandria	1	0	1.000	6.48	5	0	0	1	0	0	8.1	9	6	6	1	1	7	0	7	4
Bartholow, Peninsula	5	4	.556	4.37	42	2	0	22	0	4	78.1	75	47	38	7	0	28	2	63	4
Begue, Lynchburg	2	8	.200	3.00	47	0	0	33	0	7	72	73	35	24	3	5	22	1	53	2
Bettendorf, Lynchburg	0	1	.000	6.53	4	4	0	0	0	0	20.2	20	19	15	1	0	18	1	8	4
Blackmon, Kinston	11	6	.647	2.79	35	12	2	14	0	3	113	101	51	35	4	1	54	3	81	7
Bowlin, Winston-Salem°	5	4	.556	2.61	28	11	0	4	0	0	86.1	84	31	25	3	5	33	1	75	3
Brown, Hagerstown	0	0	.000	3.10	14	0	0	8	0	0	20.1	23	9	7	0	0	6	2	16	2
Cacciatore, Salem	3	3	.500	5.80	15	10	2	2	1	1	59	57	45	38	6	6	33	1	37	11
Cerutti, Kinston°	10	5	.667	3.19	16	16	5	0	1	0	113	88	47	40	9	2	49	1	136	5
Clay, Durham	9	5	.643	3.11	22	21	4	0	1	0	139	122	54	48	9	5	61	0	88	4
Clinton, Winston-Salem	5	9	.357	5.17	37	15	1	18	0	3	125.1	129	82	72	9	3	80	1	108	17
Coatney, Durham	6	3	.667	3.21	15	15	1	0	0	0	87	79	45	31	9	6	46	0	87	9
Cordoba, Alexandria	5	5	.500	3.51	43	0	0	33	0	10	59	40	28	23	5	6	39	6	64	2
Dale, Winston-Salem	4	7	.364	2.39	38	3	2	28	0	4	83	71	32	22	7	2	15	3	63	5
Daniels, Salem	0	2	.000	6.67	13	2	0	5	0	1	29.2	35	32	22	3	1	27	1	15	2
Darnell, Peninsula	4	2	.667	6.82	15	5	0	9	0	3	30.1	39	25	23	4	2	12	0	22	0
Dedmon, Durham	5	6	.455	2.74	31	14	4	7	1	2	121.1	113	57	37	11	4	54	1	102	9
Delmonte, Lynchburg°	0	1	.000	9.95	4	1	0	2	0	0	6.1	4	8	7	3	0	6	0	1	0
Dixon, Hagerstown	7	8	.467	4.61	15	15	5	0	2	0	97.2	97	59	50	11	1	50	1	71	7
Dodd, Alexandria°	0	0	.000	11.81	5	0	0	2	0	1	5.1	6	8	7	1	0	9	0	2	0
Dorin, Peninsula	1	0	1.000	2.78	12	0	0	6	0	3	22.2	27	9	7	0	0	9	0	11	0
Dumouchelle, Hagerstown	0	0	.000	0.00	1	0	0	1	0	0	2.2	2	1	0	0	1	0	0	4	2
Fisher, Durham	6	6	.500	2.77	18	18	3	0	0	0	104	72	43	32	12	1	43	1	129	3
Fredlund, Winston-Salem	3	5	.375	7.48	9	8	0	1	0	0	43.1	63	41	36	4	2	23	0	17	1
Fuller, Durham	0	0	.000	7.94	4	0	0	3	0	1	5.2	7	5	5	1	0	6	0	4	0
Fultz, Lynchburg	9	12	.429	3.68	27	27	12	0	2	0	188.1	181	89	77	18	6	46	0	121	10
Garrett, Winston-Salem	2	5	.286	3.97	36	2	0	17	0	2	70.1	68	42	31	7	3	26	1	47	3
Gaynor, Peninsula	11	4	.733	3.31	34	9	1	8	0	2	111.1	99	47	41	13	3	46	0	96	4
Gerhardt, Salem	1	3	.250	4.77	14	5	0	3	0	0	54.2	65	38	29	6	2	28	3	25	2
Gering, Winston-Salem	6	10	.375	3.76	36	18	2	16	0	3	127	136	66	53	11	5	44	3	113	6
Ghelfi, Peninsula	12	6	.667	2.64	25	24	4	1	2	1	160.1	147	70	47	8	7	60	1	162	8
Gilbert, Hagerstown	2	0	1.000	3.94	3	1	0	1	0	0	16	12	7	7	1	0	7	0	13	0
Goff, Peninsula°	0	1	.000	2.79	6	0	0	5	0	1	9.2	1	4	3	0	0	4	0	16	3
Gold, Hagerstown	0	0	.000	19.29	7	0	0	1	0	0	9.1	18	22	20	1	1	8	0	4	3
Gonzales, Alexandria	13	8	.619	3.99	24	24	6	0	2	0	155.2	162	75	69	17	2	47	0	116	6
Gonzalez, Hagerstown°	7	6	.538	3.42	30	11	0	10	0	3	102.2	82	48	39	9	6	70	1	117	9
Green, Alexandria°	9	1	.900	2.50	14	14	1	0	0	0	86.1	76	29	24	5	1	33	1	84	4
Griffin, Peninsula°	7	2	.778	1.66	41	0	0	22	0	8	48.2	20	15	9	4	2	32	0	47	6
Grubbs, Winston-Salem	1	9	.100	3.84	32	15	1	5	0	1	133.2	153	81	57	13	2	44	5	80	5
Guinn, Hagerstown	8	6	.571	4.18	25	11	3	2	1	0	97	99	55	45	9	2	36	2	54	3
Habyan, Hagerstown	0	0	.000	67.50	1	1	0	0	0	0	0.2	5	5	5	2	0	2	0	1	0
Hatcher, Durham	10	5	.667	3.46	40	3	1	20	1	2	119.2	116	56	46	10	0	30	0	98	1
Heiser, Durham	0	0	.000	0.00	1	0	0	1	0	0	1	0	0	0	0	0	0	0	2	0
Herrick, Hagerstown	0	0	.000	10.13	1	0	0	1	0	0	2.2	4	3	3	1	0	2	0	2	0
Hoke, Hagerstown	0	2	.000	2.83	22	0	0	21	0	5	28.2	25	11	9	5	0	9	3	21	3
Holton, Kinston	0	0	.000	4.38	7	0	0	2	0	0	12.1	10	6	6	1	2	8	0	19	2
Horne, Alexandria	6	11	.353	4.10	25	18	1	4	0	3	101	108	74	46	7	4	68	0	67	10
Hudson, Peninsula	15	5	.750	1.85	27	26	7	1	3	0	185	143	56	38	10	0	64	0	147	4
Hulbert, Winston-Salem	0	2	.000	9.47	10	0	0	3	0	0	19	24	23	20	2	1	17	0	13	4
Huyck, Salem°	3	9	.250	4.88	25	15	1	4	0	0	114.1	127	79	62	15	0	62	1	56	7
Johnson, Peninsula	8	3	.727	1.81	50	0	0	34	0	13	89.2	69	26	18	3	4	39	5	54	10
Johnston, Lynchburg	12	3	.800	3.12	18	18	5	0	3	0	121.1	102	49	42	9	2	49	1	103	7
Kane, Winston-Salem	5	10	.333	3.96	25	20	3	3	0	0	129.2	143	70	57	10	3	34	2	94	8
Klusacek, Salem°	0	2	.000	6.57	16	2	1	9	0	0	37	48	30	27	6	3	25	1	24	3
Krawczyk, Alexandria	1	0	1.000	0.48	6	1	0	3	0	1	18.2	10	1	1	0	0	13	0	25	1
Krzanik, Salem	4	6	.400	5.47	26	12	3	8	1	1	100.1	121	74	61	10	1	46	0	101	8
Kucharski, Hagerstown	3	2	.600	3.35	7	5	1	1	0	0	37.2	43	17	14	3	2	20	3	27	0
Lamonde, Alexandria	7	1	.875	3.36	15	15	3	0	0	0	88.1	69	41	33	5	11	52	0	66	8
Layton, Kinston	7	9	.438	2.91	25	18	6	2	0	0	151.1	147	61	49	10	1	53	2	94	8
Leal, Kinston	5	10	.333	4.68	23	18	2	2	0	0	100.2	112	65	48	7	1	57	2	72	5
Leggatt, Alexandria	7	4	.636	4.68	11	11	1	0	1	0	65.1	63	40	34	5	2	31	2	50	4
Lovekamp, Salem	1	4	.200	4.66	5	5	2	0	0	0	29	31	21	15	4	1	12	1	16	2
Lychak, Salem°	2	2	.500	2.51	5	5	0	0	0	0	28.2	26	12	8	1	3	21	1	27	6
Maples, Hagerstown	3	4	.429	6.40	9	6	0	2	0	0	32.1	30	26	23	2	3	22	1	22	2
Marcheskie, Alexandria	9	3	.750	3.87	33	3	1	15	0	3	79	84	38	34	7	6	28	3	31	6
McCarthy, Winston-Salem	3	11	.214	6.53	30	15	1	9	0	1	103.1	128	95	75	7	2	65	1	75	15
McClain, Salem	1	4	.200	7.05	13	6	1	2	0	0	60	80	52	47	6	0	31	1	43	4
McCullock, Salem	0	1	.000	2.63	24	0	0	17	0	2	24	23	13	7	0	2	9	0	26	7
McDonough, Hagerstown	3	0	1.000	4.19	9	6	0	0	0	0	38.2	43	26	18	4	1	19	2	13	6
McDowell, Lynchburg	2	0	1.000	2.15	4	4	2	0	1	0	29.1	26	12	7	0	1	11	0	23	0
McKnight, Kinston	15	6	.714	3.44	26	25	6	1	1	0	167.2	149	78	64	11	9	87	6	124	6
Mecerod, Winston-Salem	4	11	.267	3.86	25	21	0	3	0	1	128.1	141	71	55	9	8	47	1	88	6
Miller, Lynchburg°	6	5	.545	3.63	22	11	4	6	1	0	89.1	82	48	36	7	3	36	0	73	9
Mitcheltree, Hagerstown	5	10	.333	4.59	43	9	1	16	0	3	127.1	147	85	65	11	2	45	5	101	5
Mortillaro, Durham°	0	2	.000	5.68	4	3	0	1	0	0	19	20	12	12	4	1	10	0	19	1
Myles, Lynchburg°	3	0	1.000	1.87	10	7	3	1	2	0	62.2	39	15	13	3	3	32	0	54	5
Norris, Hagerstown	2	5	.286	4.97	25	2	0	12	0	1	54.1	59	38	30	4	2	43	12	37	5
North, Durham	6	4	.600	4.67	21	16	2	2	0	0	96.1	103	57	50	10	3	46	0	79	9
Oberbruner, Salem	7	13	.350	4.68	30	8	1	18	0	0	100	116	62	52	6	3	35	3	79	4
Ochal, Salem	2	10	.167	5.72	15	15	4	0	0	0	89.2	114	75	57	12	2	35	0	49	2
Parsons, Salem	4	10	.286	4.86	19	18	6	0	1	0	111	116	76	60	14	4	37	1	85	6
Payne, Durham	8	7	.533	4.07	21	21	0	0	0	0	126	127	66	57	7	2	55	0	88	6
Phillips, Kinston	3	6	.333	4.46	11	11	2	0	0	0	78.2	66	47	39	8	2	39	2	37	4
Plainte, Winston-Salem°	5	5	.500	4.65	31	17	1	5	0	0	110.1	127	76	57	4	1	62	3	79	20
Poston, Salem	0	4	.000	4.39	17	0	0	14	0	4	26.2	38	18	13	1	1	12	4	10	2

Pitcher—Club	W.	L.	Pct.	ERA.	G.	GS.	CG.	GF.	ShO.	Sv.	IP.	H.	R.	ER.	HR.	HB.	BB.	Int. BB.	SO.	WP.
Ray, Alexandria	7	6	.538	3.82	24	13	1	5	0	2	96.2	91	51	41	8	2	51	1	71	4
Rech, Lynchburg°	6	14	.300	4.02	29	28	5	0	0	0	154.2	157	101	69	13	8	76	3	100	8
Reish, Kinston	0	1	.000	2.57	1	1	1	0	0	0	7	5	3	2	0	1	1	0	8	0
Reiter, Durham°	9	7	.563	2.94	61	0	0	39	0	16	67.1	53	29	22	2	2	33	5	77	3
Richardson, Peninsula	7	8	.467	3.95	22	22	4	0	1	0	127.2	131	73	56	7	7	71	0	108	11
Rodgers, Kinston	11	8	.579	3.23	31	22	6	2	2	1	172.2	159	79	62	14	3	50	4	138	5
Rooney, Hagerstown°	8	8	.500	3.51	26	26	5	0	1	0	156.1	152	70	61	14	5	51	2	108	1
Santana, Durham	1	0	1.000	2.57	2	0	0	1	0	0	7	3	2	2	1	0	6	0	6	0
Sczesnak, Hagerstown	4	0	1.000	4.67	26	0	0	17	0	2	27	24	17	14	2	1	31	3	24	4
Sears, Durham	0	0	.000	0.00	1	0	0	1	0	0	1.2	0	0	0	0	1	2	0	2	0
Shipanoff, Kinston	7	3	.700	1.94	63	0	0	56	0	30	92.2	57	22	20	5	0	46	9	105	1
M. Smith, Durham	0	0	.000	0.00	4	0	0	2	0	1	4.2	2	0	0	0	0	3	0	4	2
W. Smith, Salem	5	9	.357	4.69	34	10	2	21	1	1	94	101	61	49	12	3	37	0	98	6
Solomon, Salem	3	8	.273	4.54	32	12	1	16	0	0	101	119	72	51	11	2	55	1	59	10
Stewart, Hagerstown	0	0	.000	2.25	2	2	0	0	0	0	8	8	2	2	0	0	1	0	6	0
Stone, Salem	2	9	.182	4.81	11	11	5	0	0	0	73	94	52	39	18	2	22	2	53	1
Summers, Hagerstown	9	6	.600	4.49	23	18	2	1	1	0	118.1	127	70	59	12	3	38	0	96	9
Sunderlage, Lynchburg°	8	3	.727	2.74	37	4	1	9	0	1	85.1	70	39	26	4	6	35	1	32	8
Taylor, Alexandria	0	5	.000	4.52	30	7	0	5	0	2	93.2	74	60	47	10	11	63	1	80	5
Terry, Kinston°	3	0	1.000	4.71	34	0	0	25	0	0	57.1	58	44	30	4	4	42	2	60	5
Tibbs, Lynchburg	2	4	.333	5.63	7	7	1	0	1	0	38.1	42	28	24	2	0	23	0	31	4
Treadway, Durham	11	8	.579	3.39	25	25	6	0	1	0	169.2	126	70	64	20	10	51	0	158	10
True, Peninsula°	4	4	.500	4.87	26	20	1	3	0	0	114.2	101	78	62	13	3	87	0	98	15
Twitty, Durham°	4	0	1.000	3.22	22	0	0	12	0	4	50.1	59	22	18	2	1	7	0	44	3
Valdez, Winston-Salem	2	5	.286	3.16	26	0	0	17	0	3	31.1	30	22	11	1	0	16	6	39	6
Vaughn, Lynchburg	1	5	.167	5.16	20	2	0	8	0	2	45.1	52	34	26	4	0	30	0	36	2
Waddell, Durham	5	3	.625	1.45	42	0	0	26	0	11	74.1	44	20	12	7	1	26	6	102	2
F. Warner, Salem	3	5	.375	3.94	18	9	0	6	0	0	77.2	86	44	34	5	0	25	0	25	3
H. Warner, Peninsula°	4	0	1.000	2.95	16	4	0	5	0	1	36.2	32	13	12	2	0	13	0	36	3
Warthen, Alexandria°	0	0	.000	0.75	17	0	0	13	0	0	24	18	5	2	0	1	8	1	20	2
Webster, Lynchburg	8	8	.500	3.49	22	22	9	0	2	0	147	126	74	57	12	6	68	0	116	11
Wheeler, Alexandria	4	1	.800	1.95	6	6	0	0	0	0	37	26	13	8	2	0	11	0	38	2
Willsher, Hagerstown	2	5	.286	4.52	13	11	3	0	0	0	69.2	64	41	35	5	3	37	2	73	5
Wilmet, Lynchburg	2	3	.400	5.83	29	0	0	14	0	0	54	65	46	35	6	10	28	2	48	5
G. Wilson, Kinston	2	3	.400	4.38	7	7	1	0	0	0	39	39	25	19	5	1	24	0	20	3
R. Wilson, Hagerstown	0	0	.000	4.50	6	0	0	2	0	0	10	9	5	5	1	0	5	0	7	0
Winn, Alexandria	1	2	.333	3.86	7	7	0	0	0	0	28	31	14	12	2	2	11	0	20	4
Wojna, Peninsula	12	8	.600	2.90	27	26	4	1	2	1	176.2	156	79	57	3	9	49	1	116	9
Wood, Salem	0	0	.000	3.86	3	0	0	3	0	0	4.2	6	3	2	0	0	6	0	2	2
Zamba, Alexandria	3	3	.500	3.78	22	16	2	2	0	1	100	101	59	42	9	1	30	0	56	2
Zaske, Alexandria	7	4	.636	2.89	48	0	0	36	0	14	74.2	63	30	24	4	4	29	6	84	4

BALKS—Green, 4; Gonzales, Guinn, Rech, Taylor, 3 each; Clinton, Fultz, Gaynor, Gonzalez, Horne, Hudson, Ochal, Summers, Willsher, Wojna, 2 each; Bartholow, Cacciatore, Cerutti, Daniels, Fisher, Gering, Ghelfi, Johnston, Kane, Kucharski, Lamonde, Leal, McClain, Mitcheltree, Myles, Richardson, Rodgers, Rooney, Sczesnak, True, Webster, 1 each.

COMBINATION SHUTOUTS—Ray-Marcheskie, Green-Taylor-Zaske-Warthen, Green-Ray, Alexandria; Fisher-Fuller, Coatney-Reiter, Payne-Waddell, Dedmon-Waddell, Durham; Arnold-Norris, Guinn-Mitcheltree, Guinn-Hoke, Hagerstown; Lychak-Shipanoff 2, Leal-Shipanoff 2, McKnight-Shipanoff, Layton-Shipanoff, Kinston; Myles-Begue, Miller-Ballard, Lynchburg; Darnell-Bartholow, Ghelfi-Gaynor-Warner, Ghelfi-Johnson, Hudson-Griffin, Richardson-Dorin-Griffin, Gaynor-Johnson, Peninsula; Ochal-W. Smith, Warner-Poston, Salem; Mecerod-Bowlin, Grubbs-Bowlin-Garrett, Mecerod-Bowlin-Valdez, Bowlin-Garrett, Clinton-Dale, Winston-Salem.

PERFECT GAME—Hatcher, Durham, defeated Salem, 3-0, August 13 (seven innings).

NO-HIT GAME—Gonzales, Alexandria, defeated Winston-Salem, 3-0, August 13.

Florida State League

CLASS A

CHAMPIONSHIP WINNERS IN PREVIOUS YEARS

1919—Sanford°	.605
Orlando°	.703
1920—Tampa	.654
Tampa	.722
1921—Orlando	.635
1922—St. Petersburg	.503
St. Petersburg	.618
1923—Orlando	.667
Orlando	.678
1924—Lakeland	.695
Lakeland	.683
1925—St. Petersburg	.667
Tampa†	.696
1926—Sanford	.647
Sanford	.623
1927—Orlando†	.600
Miami	.661
1928-35—Did not operate.	
1936—Gainesville	.542
St. Augustine (4th)†	.492
1937—Gainesville§	.616
1938—Leesburg	.626
Gainesville (2nd)‡	.615
1939—Sanford§	.787
1940—Daytona Beach	.619
Orlando (4th)‡	.507
1941—St. Augustine	.659
Leesburg (4th)‡	.488
1942-45—Did not operate.	
1946—Orlando§	.681
1947—St. Augustine	.625
Gainesville (2nd)‡	.584

1948—Orlando	.643
Daytona Beach (2nd)‡	.616
1949—Gainesville	.635
St. Augustine (3rd)‡	.556
1950—Orlando	.629
DeLand (3rd)‡	.590
1951—DeLand§	.643
1952—DeLand x	.704
Palatka (3rd)‡	.569
1953—Daytona Beach†	.657
DeLand	.703
1954—Jacksonville Beach	.629
Lakeland†	.594
1955—Orlando	.671
Orlando	.643
1956—Cocoa	.614
Cocoa	.629
1957—Palatka	.671
Tampa†	.681
1958—St. Petersburg	.732
St. Petersburg	.681
1959—Tampa	.591
St. Petersburg†	.612
1960—Lakeland	.731
Palatka†	.614
1961—Tampa†	.710
Sarasota	.696
1962—Sarasota	.689
Fort Lauderdale†	.623
1963—Sarasota	.645
Sarasota	.667
1964—Fort Lauderdale†	.629
St. Petersburg	.594
1965—Fort Lauderdale	.627
Fort Lauderdale	.634

1966—Leesburg†	.781
St. Petersburg	.700
1967—St. Petersburg y	.691
Orlando	.638
1968—Miami	.613
Orlando z	.579
1969—Miami a	.606
Orlando	.606
1970—Miami b	.662
St. Petersburg	.600
1971—Miami b	.667
Daytona Beach	.586
1972—Miami c	.562
Daytona Beach	.606
1973—St. Petersburg d	.575
West Palm Beach	.580
1974—West Palm Beach d	.598
Ft. Lauderdale	.626
1975—St. Petersburg d	.652
Miami	.581
1976—Tampa	.559
Lakeland d	.536
1977—Lakeland d	.616
West Palm Beach	.583
1978—Lakeland	.565
Miami§	.539
1979—Ft. Lauderdale	.643
Winter Haven e	.577
1980—Daytona Beach	.628
Ft. Lauderdale d	.606
1981—Fort Myers	.554
Daytona Beach f	.504

°Split-season playoff abandoned after each team won three games. †Won split-season playoff. ‡Won four-club playoff. §Won championship and four-club playoff. xWon both halves of split season. yLeague divided into Eastern and Western divisions with split season. St. Petersburg and Orlando won both halves of split season; St. Petersburg won playoff. zLeague divided into Eastern and Western divisions. Miami won regular-season pennant on basis of highest won-lost percentage. Orlando won four-club playoff involving first two teams in each division. aLeague divided into Southern and Central divisions. Miami won playoff between division leaders. (NOTE—Pennant awarded to playoff winner in 1936.) bLeague divided into Eastern and Western divisions. Miami won regular-season pennant on basis of highest won-loss percentage, and also won four-club playoff involving first two teams in each division. cLeague divided into Eastern and Western divisions. Won four-club playoff involving first two teams in each division. dLeague divided into Northern and Southern divisions. Won four-club playoff involving first two teams in each division. eLeague divided into Northern and Southern divisions. Same two clubs won both halves; won playoffs. fWon split-season playoff.

STANDING OF CLUBS AT CLOSE OF FIRST HALF, JUNE 15

NORTHERN DIVISION

Club	W.	L.	T.	Pct.	G.B.
Tampa (Reds)	36	32	0	.529	......
St. Petersburg (Cardinals)	34	34	0	.500	2
Daytona Beach (Astros)	35	35	0	.500	2
Lakeland (Tigers)	29	37	2	.439	6
Winter Haven (Red Sox)	30	39	0	.435	6½

SOUTHERN DIVISION

Club	W.	L.	T.	Pct.	G.B.
Fort Lauderdale (Yankees)	47	21	2	.691	......
Vero Beach (Dodgers)	38	31	0	.551	9½
West Palm Beach (Expos)	33	34	0	.493	13½
Fort Myers (Royals)	34	36	0	.486	14
Miami (Independent)	26	43	0	.377	21½

STANDING OF CLUBS AT CLOSE OF SECOND HALF, AUGUST 26

NORTHERN DIVISION

Club	W.	L.	T.	Pct.	G.B.
Tampa (Reds)	35	27	1	.565	......
St. Petersburg (Cardinals)	35	30	1	.538	1½
Lakeland (Tigers)	36	31	3	.537	1½
Daytona Beach (Astros)	31	33	1	.484	5
Winter Haven (Red Sox)	29	35	0	.453	7

SOUTHERN DIVISION

Club	W.	L.	T.	Pct.	G.B.
Vero Beach (Dodgers)	42	22	1	.656	......
Fort Lauderdale (Yankees)	35	29	1	.547	7
Fort Myers (Royals)	35	32	0	.522	8½
Miami (Independent)	27	41	0	.397	17
West Palm Beach (Expos)	21	46	0	.313	22½

COMPOSITE STANDING OF CLUBS AT CLOSE OF SEASON, AUGUST 26

Club	Ft.L.	VeB.	Tam.	St.P.	Ft.M.	Day.	Lak.	Wi.H.	WPB	Mia.	W.	L.	T.	Pct.	G.B.
Fort Lauderdale (Yankees)	..	9	5	4	15	6	5	6	18	14	82	50	3	.621	......
Vero Beach (Dodgers)	13	..	7	6	14	4	5	3	13	15	80	53	1	.602	2½
Tampa (Reds)	3	2	..	11	5	14	12	14	4	6	71	59	1	.546	10
St. Petersburg (Cardinals)	5	4	11	..	6	7	12	12	6	6	69	64	1	.519	13½
Fort Myers (Royals)	7	8	4	4	..	6	6	8	13	13	69	68	0	.504	15½
Daytona Beach (Astros)	4	4	8	13	4	..	10	12	4	7	66	68	1	.493	17
Lakeland (Tigers)	3	4	10	9	4	12	..	11	7	5	65	68	5	.489	17½
Winter Haven (Red Sox)	3	7	6	10	2	10	10	..	5	6	59	74	0	.444	23½
West Palm Beach (Expos)	4	9	4	3	9	6	3	4	..	12	54	80	0	.403	29
Miami (Independent)	8	6	4	4	4	9	3	5	4	10	53	84	0	.387	31½

Major league affiliations in parentheses.

Playoffs—Fort Lauderdale defeated Vero Beach, two games to one; Fort Lauderdale defeated Tampa, three games to two, to win league championship.

Regular-Season Attendance—Daytona Beach, 97,037; Fort Lauderdale, 62,686; Fort Myers, 101,597; Lakeland, 47,774; Miami, 44,774; St. Petersburg, 132,629; Tampa, 61,950; Vero Beach, 70,798; West Palm Beach, 143,840; Winter Haven, 23,000. Total, 785,486. Playoffs, 7,133. All-Star Game, 1,657.

Managers: Daytona Beach, Eric Swanson; Fort Lauderdale, Carl Merrill; Fort Myers, Rick Mathews; Lakeland, Bruce Kimm; Miami, Jose Arcia, Oscar Zamora, John Tamargo; St. Petersburg, Nick Leyva; Tampa, Jim Hoff; Vero Beach, Terry Collins; West Palm Beach, Junior Minor; Winter Haven, Tom Kotchman.

All-Star Team: Northern Division: 1B—Dodson, Winter Haven; 2B—Earl, Lakeland; 3B—Foussianes, Lakeland; SS—Meacham, St. Petersburg; OF—Gainey, Daytona Beach; Ciampa, Winter Haven; Bullock, Daytona Beach; Simmons, Lakeland; C—Padia, Tampa, and Lowry, Lakeland; DH—Davis, Daytona Beach; RHP—Ferrante, Daytona Beach, and Gnacinski, Winter Haven; LHP—Bolton, Winter Haven, and Cherry, St. Petersburg; Manager—Hoff, Tampa. Southern Division: 1B—Demeter, Fort Lauderdale; 2B—Damon, West Palm Beach; 3B—Weislak, West Palm Beach; SS—Salazar, West Palm Beach; OF—Pederson, Vero Beach; Espy, Vero Beach; Tovar, Miami; Jordan, Fort Lauderdale; C—Fimple, Vero Beach, and Bradley, Fort Lauderdale; DH—Bryant, Vero Beach; RHP—Alexander, Vero Beach, and Tewksbury, Fort Lauderdale; LHP—George, Miami, and Ferreira, Fort Myers; Manager—Collins, Vero Beach.

(Compiled by Howe News Bureau, Boston, Mass.)

CLUB BATTING

Club	Pct.	G.	AB.	R.	OR.	H.	TB.	2B.	3B.	HR.	RBI.	GW.	SH.	SF.	HP.	BB.	Int. BB.	SO.	SB.	CS.	LOB.
Daytona Beach	.278	135	4479	707	663	1247	1741	196	47	68	604	53	51	43	46	526	27	696	177	78	995
Vero Beach	.272	134	4360	669	500	1185	1684	169	63	68	588	70	48	40	55	528	34	732	188	62	994
West Palm Beach	.264	134	4318	557	659	1141	1490	176	28	39	479	46	35	38	32	490	19	573	119	47	1015
Fort Lauderdale	.261	135	4196	554	427	1095	1482	189	33	44	494	72	65	53	40	550	34	628	91	46	1018
Lakeland	.255	138	4246	558	593	1081	1518	159	37	68	483	57	42	32	22	521	39	719	102	48	969
St. Petersburg	.253	134	4059	486	475	1027	1290	150	22	23	415	61	56	32	27	474	29	612	143	76	899
Winter Haven	.248	133	4197	535	629	1041	1389	138	30	50	463	52	64	35	31	526	27	720	124	56	969
Miami	.247	137	4283	477	690	1056	1363	172	36	21	414	48	40	31	48	499	21	668	157	69	969
Tampa	.244	131	4084	481	427	995	1328	157	37	34	401	63	72	30	31	453	56	674	130	46	942
Fort Myers	.236	137	4264	540	501	1008	1377	148	40	47	467	61	35	31	34	534	25	719	191	63	940

INDIVIDUAL BATTING

(Leading Qualifiers for Batting Championship—373 or More Plate Appearances)

°Bats lefthanded.   †Switch-hitter.

Player and Club	Pct.	G.	AB.	R.	H.	TB.	2B.	3B.	HR.	RBI.	GW.	SH.	SF.	HP.	BB.	Int. BB.	SO.	SB.	CS.
Gainey, Telmanch, Daytona Beach°	.341	106	425	92	145	217	20	11	10	58	7	1	1	6	38	7	74	45	16
Bullock, Eric, Daytona Beach°	.339	117	442	90	150	211	24	11	5	85	8	2	2	5	44	5	55	45	8
Pederson, Stuart, Vero Beach°	.336	134	464	95	156	229	16	18	7	79	8	2	9	8	79	8	61	16	5
Espy, Cecil, Vero Beach†	.317	131	523	100	166	197	14	7	1	34	3	3	0	1	58	4	70	74	15
Ciampa, Michael, Winter Haven°	.316	121	434	81	137	163	11	6	1	36	3	10	1	1	91	5	34	54	16
Davis, Glenn, Daytona Beach	.315	103	378	70	119	210	28	3	19	79	4	2	4	6	44	4	77	1	2
Bryant, Ralph, Vero Beach°	.306	122	409	71	125	188	22	7	9	71	6	2	2	6	42	7	104	20	6
Campbell, Mark, Daytona Beach	.303	114	393	74	119	154	24	1	3	48	7	7	3	4	45	1	38	10	6
Tovar, Raul, Miami	.302	112	394	48	119	146	14	5	1	52	6	0	1	4	32	4	43	10	5
Bradley, Scott, Fort Lauderdale°	.296	121	439	52	130	175	28	4	3	66	13	2	6	8	26	5	13	5	4
Simons, Neil, Daytona Beach°	.296	130	419	64	124	155	17	4	2	68	3	5	9	1	96	2	50	10	14

Departmental Leaders: G—Earl, 136; AB—Espy, 523; R—Espy, 100; H—Espy, 166; TB—Pederson, 229; 2B—See, 29; 3B—Pederson, 18; HR—Davis, Strucher, 19; RBI—Bullock, See, 85; GWRBI—Bradley, Smith, 13; SH—Allen, 15; SF—Helsom, 10; HP—Guzman, 10; BB—Simons, 96; IBB—Simmons, 13; SO—Bryant, 104; SB—Espy, 74; CS—Beltran, 20.

(All Players—Listed Alphabetically)

Player and Club	Pct.	G.	AB.	R.	H.	TB.	2B.	3B.	HR.	RBI.	GW.	SH.	SF.	HP.	BB.	Int. BB.	SO.	SB.	CS.
Albino, William, Tampa	.091	21	22	1	2	2	0	0	0	0	0	0	0	0	5	0	11	0	1
Allen, Robert, Vero Beach	.237	116	355	34	84	120	15	6	3	36	5	15	3	0	33	0	35	6	7
Alvarez, Carmelo, Vero Beach†	.197	24	61	7	12	14	0	1	0	3	0	2	0	0	3	0	9	3	0
Alvarez, Roberto, Miami	.240	135	466	54	112	143	14	4	3	55	5	6	6	3	49	4	62	10	6
Arce, Lorenzo, Lakeland	.375	3	8	0	3	4	1	0	0	0	0	0	0	0	0	0	1	0	0
Arfstrom, Joseph, Winter Haven†	.500	6	28	7	14	19	2	0	1	1	0	0	0	0	0	0	3	0	0
Arroyo, Hector, Fort Myers°	.160	9	25	2	4	4	0	0	0	1	0	0	0	1	1	0	5	1	1
Baker, Derrell, West Palm Beach	.288	130	434	65	125	170	21	3	6	68	5	4	4	6	85	4	36	10	3
Banes, Jeffrey, Fort Lauderdale	.222	23	72	8	16	28	6	0	2	8	1	0	0	2	7	0	17	0	1
Bard, Paul, 26 Vero-47 Miami	.231	73	199	18	46	69	11	0	4	27	0	2	2	6	23	0	38	2	0
Beltran, Julio, Miami†	.237	111	376	58	89	107	11	2	1	19	1	3	1	0	48	1	54	62	20
Belue, Benjamin, West Palm Beach	.262	56	195	15	51	63	8	2	0	17	0	1	3	0	9	0	27	6	1
Bendorf, Jerry, Vero Beach	.265	117	419	57	111	134	13	2	2	38	4	5	3	8	47	2	49	12	2
Benza, Brett, St. Petersburg	.270	57	185	19	50	56	4	1	0	20	5	0	2	1	33	2	19	11	5
Best, William, Fort Myers°	.294	57	197	32	58	82	5	5	3	21	2	0	1	3	30	4	19	27	5
Boddy, William, Tampa	.216	70	125	12	27	35	5	0	1	18	1	2	2	1	15	1	20	5	1
Bodie, Keith, Daytona Beach	.272	42	147	16	40	60	10	2	2	19	2	1	2	0	13	0	24	11	2
Boncore, Steven, Vero Beach	.160	42	106	7	17	22	2	0	1	8	1	2	1	1	11	0	18	0	1
Borges, George, West Palm Beach	.174	21	46	5	8	9	1	0	0	4	0	0	2	1	4	0	6	0	0
Botkin, Michael, Daytona Beach°	.175	14	40	5	7	7	0	0	0	3	0	0	1	1	6	0	8	1	2
Boyce, Robert, Miami	.234	64	201	27	47	64	15	1	0	16	3	1	0	1	36	1	48	2	0
Bradley, Scott, Fort Lauderdale°	.296	121	439	52	130	175	28	4	3	66	13	2	6	8	26	5	13	5	4
Bream, Sidney, Vero Beach°	.310	63	226	41	70	105	13	5	4	43	9	0	1	2	32	2	25	6	4
Bruno, Michael, Miami	.167	4	6	0	1	1	0	0	0	1	0	0	0	1	0	0	0	0	0
Bryant, Ralph, Vero Beach°	.306	122	409	71	125	188	22	7	9	71	6	2	2	6	42	7	104	20	6
Bullock, Eric, Daytona Beach°	.339	117	442	90	150	211	24	11	5	85	8	2	2	5	44	5	55	45	8
Burns, James, St. Petersburg°	.130	39	54	1	7	9	2	0	0	3	1	3	1	1	3	0	22	0	0
Burrell, Kevin, Winter Haven	.233	26	73	9	17	25	5	0	1	6	3	2	0	2	3	0	11	0	0
Butler, William, Miami	.250	2	4	1	1	1	0	0	0	0	0	0	0	1	0	0	1	0	0
Butterfield, Brian, Fort Lauderdale†	.259	70	247	42	64	79	10	1	1	29	1	6	4	0	48	3	32	7	5
Cadahia, C. Benito, Fort Myers	.239	71	197	21	47	59	12	0	0	32	7	3	2	3	49	2	31	4	2
Campbell, Mark, Daytona Beach	.303	114	393	74	119	154	24	1	3	48	7	7	3	4	45	1	38	10	6
Canseco, Jose, Miami°	.111	6	9	0	1	2	1	0	0	0	0	0	0	0	0	0	3	0	0
Cardieri, Ronald, Miami°	.147	17	34	3	5	8	3	0	0	2	0	1	0	0	7	0	5	0	0
Carpenter, Glenn, Daytona Beach	.213	18	47	4	10	15	1	2	0	3	1	0	0	1	11	0	14	0	0
Carrasquel, Emilio, Lakeland	.167	37	102	4	17	22	2	0	1	6	1	1	1	1	6	0	7	0	0
Casasnovas, Roberto, Lakeland°	.182	67	154	16	28	45	5	0	4	12	1	2	3	4	21	1	48	3	1
Castiglia, Patrick, Winter Haven°	.222	94	288	32	64	84	8	0	4	33	2	5	2	1	35	1	45	2	1

Player and Club	Pct.	G.	AB.	R.	H.	TB.	2B.	3B.	HR.	RBI.	GW.	SH.	SF.	HP.	BB.	Int. BB.	SO.	SB.	CS.
Castro, Edgar, Miami*	.234	83	256	28	60	79	10	0	3	34	5	0	4	6	64	2	62	1	3
Castro, Guillermo, Daytona Beach*	.000	52	2	0	0	0	0	0	0	0	0	0	0	0	0	0	0	0	0
Chavez, Pedro, Lakeland	.268	83	254	27	68	87	11	1	2	29	4	5	2	2	10	0	28	8	4
Ciampa, Michael, Winter Haven*	.316	121	434	81	137	163	11	6	1	36	3	10	1	1	91	5	34	54	16
Cimorelli, Bruce, Tampa	.091	14	11	0	1	2	1	0	0	0	0	1	0	1	2	0	7	0	0
Colclough, Charles, Tampa*	.252	127	425	46	107	128	19	1	0	47	7	4	7	2	40	10	59	9	0
Coleman, Jerome, West Palm Beach*	.276	99	294	40	81	89	8	0	0	22	0	3	1	3	35	0	31	23	12
Contreras, Francisco, Miami*	.236	64	199	20	47	64	11	3	0	27	3	3	1	5	17	2	35	8	4
Cooley, Willie, West Palm Beach	.240	115	388	49	93	116	18	1	1	37	4	5	3	2	37	1	57	14	9
Crisp, Hughes, Miami	.208	15	53	1	11	13	0	1	0	5	1	2	0	0	1	0	16	1	1
Curbelo, Jorge, Miami	.250	99	300	24	75	110	23	0	4	29	5	3	1	5	35	1	45	4	1
D'Onofrio, Gary, Daytona Beach	.250	32	96	11	24	32	6	1	0	9	0	2	1	0	14	1	17	1	0
Damon, John, West Palm Beach	.277	134	499	84	138	174	21	6	1	49	10	4	3	1	73	1	60	27	13
Davis, Glenn, Daytona Beach	.315	103	378	70	119	210	28	3	19	79	4	2	4	6	44	4	77	1	2
Day, Dexter, Tampa	.249	118	297	39	74	111	8	4	7	34	6	2	2	0	43	5	64	10	3
Deaza, Manuel, St. Petersburg	.248	105	315	34	78	100	11	1	3	34	4	8	4	1	18	2	46	19	11
DeLeon, Orlando, Miami	.000	27	0	1	0	0	0	0	0	0	0	0	0	0	0	0	0	0	0
Demeter, Todd, Fort Lauderdale	.284	125	408	63	116	180	24	2	12	63	9	2	8	5	69	3	83	2	4
Diehl, John, Vero Beach*	.156	22	45	5	7	9	0	1	0	1	0	1	0	0	9	0	11	1	0
Dodson, Patrick, Winter Haven*	.252	104	345	50	87	148	16	0	15	69	5	2	4	2	55	5	65	1	2
Dotson, William, West Palm Beach*	.222	14	36	2	8	8	0	0	0	1	0	0	0	0	3	0	5	0	1
Duncan, Timothy, Winter Haven	.235	80	243	23	57	66	7	1	0	18	3	12	0	1	23	0	43	6	5
Earl, William, Lakeland	.287	136	464	86	133	196	17	5	12	47	5	5	3	4	69	3	69	34	8
Ender, Scot, Tampa	.200	13	30	2	6	6	0	0	0	1	0	2	0	0	1	0	5	0	0
Espy, Cecil, Vero Beach†	.317	131	523	100	166	197	14	7	1	34	3	3	0	1	58	4	70	74	15
Filkins, Randy, Fort Lauderdale	.242	22	33	7	8	13	2	0	1	4	2	0	2	2	6	0	6	0	0
Fimple, John, Vero Beach	.281	111	359	53	101	152	14	5	9	54	8	4	4	4	48	1	60	1	1
Ford, Curtis, St. Petersburg*	.275	133	447	59	123	160	18	8	1	49	11	6	4	4	60	1	46	18	8
Foussianes, George, Lakeland	.231	98	308	50	71	121	10	5	10	51	7	3	4	3	77	1	55	2	2
Funk, Bryan, Tampa	.389	43	18	2	7	8	1	0	0	1	0	1	0	0	3	0	1	0	0
Gagne, Gregory, Fort Lauderdale	.333	1	3	0	1	1	0	0	0	0	0	0	0	0	1	0	1	0	0
Gainey, Telmanch, Daytona Beach*	.341	106	425	92	145	217	20	11	10	58	7	1	1	6	38	7	74	45	16
Galarraga, Andres, West Palm Beach	.281	105	338	39	95	161	20	2	14	51	7	0	2	9	34	5	77	2	1
Garcia, Frank, St. Petersburg	.243	126	400	46	97	138	21	1	6	40	8	5	2	0	41	0	49	6	9
Gause, Ernest, Tampa*	.222	27	9	0	2	2	0	0	0	1	1	0	0	0	0	0	2	0	0
Gayden, Huey, Fort Lauderdale*	.206	47	102	13	21	25	4	0	0	12	1	3	0	0	18	1	14	5	3
George, William, Miami*	1.000	31	1	0	1	1	0	0	0	0	0	0	0	0	0	0	0	0	0
Geren, Robert, St. Petersburg	.244	110	352	38	86	115	24	1	1	45	7	3	3	5	29	5	68	3	1
Gilcrease, Douglas, Fort Myers	.215	64	209	34	45	75	3	3	7	33	2	2	2	4	17	0	35	5	3
Gilles, Robert, St. Petersburg	.179	46	106	8	19	30	2	0	3	14	1	3	0	1	22	0	28	0	2
Gleissner, James, Fort Myers	.285	40	123	15	35	43	8	0	0	10	1	2	0	0	10	0	21	0	0
Glenn, James, Winter Haven	.231	63	199	29	46	51	3	1	0	15	2	1	3	2	29	0	33	16	2
Glinatsis, Michael, Miami	.000	37	0	1	0	0	0	0	0	0	0	0	0	0	0	0	0	0	0
Gonzalez, Marcos, Miami	.000	29	2	0	0	0	0	0	0	0	0	0	0	0	0	0	1	0	0
Goodyear, Chris, 10 Lake-10 Mia	.250	20	44	3	11	14	1	1	0	6	0	0	0		9	0	6	2	0
Gotay, Ruben, St. Petersburg	.000	29	0	2	0	0	0	0	0	0	0	0	0	0	0	0	0	0	0
Granger, Lee Randle, Miami†	.297	49	172	21	51	66	7	4	0	20	2	1	1	3	15	0	30	29	10
Griggs, David, Miami†	.161	21	62	2	10	10	0	0	0	5	0	1	0	0	7	0	8	0	2
Guzman, Hector, Vero Beach†	.182	4	11	1	2	2	0	0	0	0	1	0	0	0	0	0	3	0	0
Guzman, Ruben, Tampa	.260	123	427	50	111	166	19	9	6	50	4	5	3	10	50	7	95	17	7
Haas, Stanley, St. Petersburg	.257	32	74	7	19	27	5	0	1	10	1	0	1	0	12	0	15	0	1
Harvey, Randall, Lakeland*	.263	50	137	15	36	54	5	2	3	16	2	0	0	0	21	2	33	0	1
Hatcher, Harold, Fort Myers	.257	109	404	45	104	161	24	3	9	70	12	0	6	3	29	1	66	7	0
Hawkins, Johnny, Fort Lauderdale†	.000	2	4	1	0	0	0	0	0	0	0	0	0	0	0	0	4	0	0
Haynes, Kennie, Lakeland	.186	31	70	8	13	14	1	0	0	2	0	0	0	0	4	0	27	1	0
Helsom, Robert, Fort Lauderdale*	.295	103	281	28	83	117	24	2	2	41	7	3	10	1	45	3	26	1	4
Hench, R. William, Fort Lauderdale	.277	32	112	9	31	38	5	1	0	16	4	2	3	1	7	1	10	0	0
Hocutt, Michael, West Palm Beach*	.286	24	77	10	22	37	2	2	3	15	2	0	3	1	6	0	17	1	0
Hollenbach, Charlton, Tampa	.133	19	15	3	2	2	0	0	0	1	0	7	0	0	3	0	9	0	0
Holt, David, Winter Haven*	.253	94	304	33	77	97	13	2	1	46	7	2	5	1	49	2	45	1	0
Hood, Michael, Tampa	.000	2	1	0	0	0	0	0	0	0	0	0	.0	0	2	0	0	0	0
Hoyt, David, St. Petersburg	.242	28	91	8	22	26	4	0	0	6	1	1	0		11	1	15	3	2
Hudler, Rex, Fort Lauderdale	.250	9	32	2	8	12	1	0	1	6	0	0	0		4	0	5	0	1
Hughes, John, Fort Lauderdale*	.154	6	13	0	2	2	0	0	0	0	0	0	0		1	0	4	0	0
Jennings, Charles, Tampa	.245	82	151	20	37	42	3	1	0	10	3	5	0		18	0	40	6	4
Jonson, Greg, Fort Myers*	.237	118	405	42	96	123	9	3	4	44	3	2	4		43	5	43	3	2
Jordan, Timothy, Fort Lauderdale*	.263	120	395	62	104	148	11	6	7	49	9	6	2		36	3	59	24	3
Kempton, Gary, Fort Lauderdale	.260	59	146	22	38	55	5	3	2	13	2	4	0		20	1	37	0	2
Klosicki, Daniel, Tampa	.000	9	9	0	0	0	0	0	0	0	0	1	0	0	0	0	0	0	0
Knox, Michael, Tampa	.043	28	23	0	1	1	0	0	0	0	0	0	0		3	0	3	0	0
Krupa, Thomas, West Palm Beach*	.220	12	41	4	9	15	1	1	1	7	0	0	0		2	0	10	0	0
Kutner, Michael, Miami*	.240	111	366	57	88	116	14	7	0	31	1	3	2	8	58	2	41	11	5
Lachowetz, Anthony, Vero Beach	.242	117	393	63	95	169	19	5	15	79	9	4	7	6	54	3	101	26	8
Lane, Ira, Daytona Beach	.093	41	54	6	5	5	0	0	0	2	0	0	0		7	0	25	2	1
Laurie, Robert, Lakeland	.273	27	88	11	24	28	4	0	0	8	1	0	0		8	0	15	5	0
Lepel, Joel, West Palm Beach*	.293	56	191	19	56	65	9	0	0	16	2	2	1		22	0	8	1	0
Leppert, Stephen, Tampa†	.217	102	212	25	46	58	10	1	0	17	4	2	2		41	3	40	11	1
Lewis, Amos, St. Petersburg	.238	46	126	15	30	41	5	0	2	16	2	1	0		29	0	40	2	2
Llano, Jorge, Miami	.240	50	129	15	31	34	3	0	0	13	2	1	0		24	0	34	0	2
Lowry, Dwight, Lakeland*	.277	93	278	33	77	113	11	2	7	28	1	5	1		28	6	31	0	1
Maloney, Joseph, Lakeland	.253	108	308	43	78	118	16	3	6	42	4	3	3		67	3	67	5	6
Manfre, Michael, Tampa	.252	99	258	33	65	99	15	2	5	34	6	2	3		21	2	57	6	4
Marchand, Rene, West Palm Beach	.232	70	203	22	47	55	4	2	0	18	1	0	1		22	1	28	2	0
Mariano, Robert, Fort Lauderdale*	.252	109	286	28	72	90	8	2	2	25	3	11	4		42	3	32	4	3
Martin, Steven, Vero Beach	.500	3	2	0	1	1	0	0	0	0	0	0	0	0	0	0	0	0	0
Matamoros, Carlos, Miami	.161	13	31	3	5	5	0	0	0	3	0	3	0	0	0	0	4	0	1
Maxwell, James, Lakeland*	.229	12	35	4	8	10	2	0	0	2	0	0	0	0	3	0	9	0	0
McCorkle, Robert, Daytona Beach	.185	55	130	13	24	26	2	0	0	11	2	4	0	2	9	0	39	1	1
McKnight, James, Daytona Beach	.233	57	86	8	20	20	0	0	0	9	0	3	1	0	7	0	9	1	0
McNealy, Derwin, Fort Lauderdale*	.261	121	322	61	84	104	12	4	0	16	1	5	0	0	60	0	60	20	2
Meacham, Robert, St. Petersburg	.259	120	421	57	109	132	15	4	0	37	6	5	2	6	43	4	62	21	8
Medina, Valentin, Daytona Beach	.265	106	373	40	99	126	15	3	2	46	2	4	6	4	19	3	65	11	3

Player and Club	Pct.	G.	AB.	R.	H.	TB.	2B.	3B.	HR.	RBI.	GW.	SH.	SF.	HP.	BB.	Int. BB.	SO.	SB.	CS.
Miley, David, Tampa*	.204	30	93	11	19	33	8	3	0	10	2	0	1	0	11	4	9	1	0
Moreno, Carlos, Miami	.167	36	24	2	4	4	0	0	0	2	1	1	0	1	0	6	0	0
Morris, John, Fort Myers*	.285	45	137	21	39	56	7	2	2	17	1	0	1	1	33	3	27	11	3
Neal, Willie, Fort Myers	.225	54	200	25	45	61	8	1	2	26	2	1	0	1	14	0	46	15	6
Newman, Mark, Fort Myers	.206	90	243	22	50	56	6	0	0	17	4	2	2	1	21	0	61	11	1
Norman, Greg, 25 Lake-75 St. Pete .	.295	100	285	47	84	126	21	0	7	52	4	2	3	2	59	3	45	4	3
Oliver, Warren, Fort Myers	.177	86	231	19	41	42	1	0	0	11	0	9	1	2	40	0	74	5	2
Padia, Steven, Tampa*	.319	75	204	28	65	100	15	1	6	23	2	1	0	0	30	5	27	1	1
Palmer, Michael, Fort Myers†	.223	99	314	41	70	107	9	5	6	33	8	2	1	4	44	3	44	20	3
Pate, Brian, Winter Haven	.239	71	209	22	50	77	8	5	3	18	0	3	1	1	21	1	39	1	0
Pecota, William, Fort Myers	.239	135	482	71	115	155	16	6	4	49	8	4	3	1	79	4	72	39	16
Pederson, Stuart, Vero Beach*	.336	134	464	95	156	229	16	18	7	79	8	2	9	8	79	8	61	16	5
Pendleton, Terry, St. Petersburg†	.261	20	69	4	18	25	2	1	1	7	1	0	0	0	2	0	18	1	2
Perkins, Harold, Vero Beach†	.198	59	172	19	34	40	4	1	0	17	1	0	0	3	11	1	27	10	1
Pirrucello, Mark, Fort Myers*	.300	30	90	7	27	37	7	0	1	6	0	2	0	0	7	0	19	0	0
Plante, Daniel, Fort Lauderdale	.180	30	50	1	9	10	1	0	0	6	1	0	1	0	6	0	12	0	1
Plautz, Richard, Fort Myers	.245	77	274	47	67	95	11	7	1	21	2	2	2	0	28	1	54	18	5
Pope, Gregory, West Palm Beach	.000	30	1	0	0	0	0	0	0	0	0	0	0	0	0	0	0	0	0
Portes, Carlos, Tampa	.277	108	303	32	84	115	15	5	2	38	6	1	1	3	22	8	35	5	4
Pratt, Crestwell, Tampa	.098	19	51	5	5	9	1	0	1	7	3	0	2	0	6	0	20	0	0
Quinones, Rene, West Palm Beach†	.234	48	137	11	32	38	6	0	0	18	3	1	1	0	10	0	21	3	1
Raines, Michael, Tampa	.125	38	16	1	2	2	0	0	0	1	0	0	0	0	1	0	5	0	0
Ramsey, Michael, Tampa	.188	29	48	7	9	9	0	0	0	3	0	2	0	0	3	0	7	4	0
Rembielak, Richard, Miami	.257	112	373	41	96	129	19	4	2	33	5	3	9	2	49	3	47	5	3
Riche, Timothy, Miami*	.200	22	60	5	12	14	2	0	0	2	0	0	1	0	10	1	6	3	1
Riley, Thomas, Tampa	.250	28	44	4	11	14	3	0	0	5	1	0	0	0	2	0	10	1	0
Rincones, Hector, Tampa	.236	127	441	45	104	129	15	2	2	44	6	10	3	5	40	6	40	7	2
Rivera, Hector, West Palm Beach	.188	14	32	4	6	6	0	0	0	0	0	0	0	0	0	0	1	1	0
Rizzo, Richard, Fort Myers	.248	124	452	63	112	145	15	3	4	50	5	3	3	5	50	1	49	23	13
Robertson, Glenn, Fort Lauderdale	.244	96	287	19	70	83	10	0	1	36	3	6	6	2	20	1	26	1	1
Roman, Luis, St Petersburg*	.284	116	405	42	115	132	11	3	0	29	5	4	3	1	23	5	29	14	8
Romine, Kevin, Winter Haven	.254	55	201	24	51	72	4	4	3	22	3	3	2	0	16	0	29	8	4
Ross, James, Lakeland	.000	46	1	0	0	0	0	0	0	0	0	0	0	0	0	0	0	0	0
Roth, John, Winter Haven	.236	67	144	22	34	47	2	1	3	20	1	5	1	1	14	0	52	4	4
Ruiz, Benny, Lakeland	.299	31	77	10	23	24	1	0	0	6	1	0	0	0	13	0	6	1	1
Salazar, Argenis, West Palm Beach ...	.267	112	408	63	109	134	15	2	2	36	2	4	4	5	27	0	54	25	6
Salazar, Roberto, Miami*	.154	18	52	4	8	11	1	1	0	4	1	1	0	1	4	0	4	0	0
Santovenia, Nelson, W.P. Beach	.246	40	118	8	29	36	4	0	1	12	3	1	3	0	14	0	12	0	0
Sayler, Barry, St. Petersburg	.270	34	115	11	31	34	3	0	0	11	2	2	2	3	14	0	24	1	2
Scherrer, William, Tampa*	.154	7	13	0	2	2	0	0	0	0	0	4	0	0	1	0	5	0	1
Schoeller, Michael, Miami*	.300	7	20	1	6	7	1	0	0	2	0	0	0	0	2	0	2	0	0
Scott, Richard, Fort Lauderdale	.187	90	235	26	44	63	6	2	3	24	0	7	1	2	37	0	56	4	2
Scott, T. Kelly, Fort Lauderdale	.000	18	1	0	0	0	0	0	0	0	0	0	0	0	0	0	0	0	0
Seats, Dennis, Tampa	.227	103	269	39	61	80	7	3	2	24	4	2	2	2	26	1	23	5	5
See, R. Laurence, Vero Beach	.264	132	455	74	120	187	29	1	12	85	12	4	8	9	57	4	66	6	6
Seiple, Dennis, St. Petersburg*	.000	8	1	0	0	0	0	0	0	0	0	0	0	0	0	0	1	0	0
Seymour, Robert, 23 Vero-52 Mia	.162	75	204	10	33	44	2	0	3	16	4	2	1	2	13	0	58	1	3
Sheaffer, Danny, Winter Haven	.250	82	260	20	65	84	4	0	5	25	4	4	3	1	18	2	37	2	2
Silva, Albert, Lakeland	.000	7	7	0	0	0	0	0	0	1	1	0	1	0	0	0	3	0	0
Silverio, Virgilio, Lakeland*	.242	124	455	59	110	137	11	5	2	39	1	9	1	1	50	2	79	28	11
Simcox, Larry, Daytona Beach	.271	112	413	59	112	128	9	2	1	39	3	6	5	3	41	2	34	9	7
Simmons, Nelson, Lakeland†	.293	133	491	68	144	211	24	8	9	61	7	0	1	0	48	13	73	2	3
Simons, Neil, Daytona Beach*	.296	130	419	64	124	155	17	4	2	68	3	5	9	1	96	2	50	10	14
Smith, Mark, Lakeland	.290	122	434	58	126	162	15	3	5	62	13	3	7	3	25	1	56	6	3
Smith, Mark, Tampa	.250	48	8	0	2	4	2	0	0	3	1	2	1	1	0	0	6	0	0
Smith, P. Keith, Fort Lauderdale	.219	94	178	26	39	47	8	0	0	11	3	4	1	4	31	1	31	6	3
Smith, Philander, Daytona Beach	.251	122	387	59	97	110	5	4	0	29	3	5	5	3	41	0	35	20	9
Spears, Kenneth, St. Petersburg*	.228	109	303	44	69	75	4	1	0	27	2	4	3	1	43	5	37	17	7
Stacheit, Glen, West Palm Beach	.215	52	186	22	40	54	4	2	2	20	2	0	0	1	18	1	34	2	0
Straker, Lester, Tampa	.128	25	39	1	5	6	1	0	0	2	0	6	0	1	3	0	14	0	0
Strucher, Mark, Daytona Beach	.263	92	312	54	82	163	18	3	19	64	9	0	6	8	49	1	72	6	2
Stubbs, Franklin, Vero Beach*	.204	16	54	6	11	23	1	1	3	5	1	0	0	0	6	1	13	2	1
Sullivan, Michael, Tampa	.091	23	22	2	2	2	0	0	0	3	0	1	0	0	4	0	6	0	1
Teegarden, Robert, Fort Lauderdale .	.277	122	397	58	110	149	13	4	6	55	8	2	3	4	72	7	74	8	5
Thomas, Reginald, Lakeland*	.191	20	68	8	13	19	1	1	1	7	1	2	2	0	7	1	22	2	2
Thompson, Craig, Vero Beach	.154	10	13	2	2	2	0	0	0	1	0	0	0	1	3	0	3	0	1
Thompson, Thomas, Fort Myers	.196	63	204	25	40	59	6	2	3	21	3	0	3	2	32	0	35	2	0
Threatt, Anthony, Tampa	.000	1	1	0	0	0	0	0	0	0	0	0	0	0	0	0	0	0	0
Tovar, Raul, Miami	.302	112	394	48	119	146	14	5	1	52	6	0	1	4	32	4	43	10	5
Townley, Robin, Fort Myers	.056	6	18	0	1	1	0	0	0	0	0	0	0	0	0	0	5	0	0
Turco, Steve, St. Petersburg*	.232	124	366	54	85	95	5	1	1	26	1	9	2	2	43	1	65	23	6
Valdez, Angel, Miami	.284	107	352	38	100	121	10	4	1	22	3	5	1	3	7	0	42	8	3
Vaughn, Michael, West Palm Beach*..	.284	72	222	33	63	78	9	3	0	22	3	3	2	0	20	2	28	0	0
Vazquez, Francisco, Winter Haven	.251	121	430	68	108	141	13	4	4	46	6	6	2	3	49	1	81	14	9
Ventura, Jose, Vero Beach*	.120	14	25	1	3	3	0	0	0	2	0	1	0	1	1	0	8	0	0
Waag, William, Fort Myers	.200	1	5	0	1	1	0	0	0	1	0	0	0	0	0	0	1	0	0
Walck, Craig, Winter Haven	.240	114	379	52	91	128	20	1	5	44	8	2	5	5	57	6	54	1	3
Walker, Anthony, Tampa†	.273	128	499	73	136	161	9	5	2	28	6	4	1	2	57	4	54	42	12
Walker, Stephen, Winter Haven	.226	79	217	23	49	59	5	1	1	19	3	6	2	2	22	0	39	10	4
Weems, William, Daytona Beach*	.286	21	56	7	16	20	4	0	0	2	0	3	0	0	17	0	3	1	2
Weislak, Kenneth, West Palm Beach..	.273	133	472	62	129	182	25	2	8	66	2	5	6	2	67	4	61	2	0
Weppner, Daniel, Winter Haven	.214	43	70	6	15	18	1	1	0	8	2	1	0	0	6	0	13	0	0
White, William, Vero Beach	.316	45	158	22	50	65	6	3	1	22	3	1	2	2	21	1	35	3	3
Wiedenbauer, Thomas, Day. Beach	.000	18	1	2	0	0	0	0	0	0	0	0	0	1	0	0	0	0	0
Wieser, Daniel, Fort Myers	.204	21	54	8	11	15	1	0	1	4	1	1	0	0	7	1	12	0	1
Williams, Jamie, Daytona Beach	.194	91	278	33	54	82	13	0	5	30	0	2	6	2	24	1	57	2	5
Williams, Michael, Lakeland	.226	102	318	34	72	90	12	0	2	38	3	2	2	0	38	3	59	2	2
Willman, Timothy, St. Petersburg	.500	2	4	0	2	2	0	0	0	1	0	0	0	0	0	0	0	0	0
Zanini, Louis, Miami	.357	9	14	3	5	5	0	0	0	3	0	0	0	0	1	0	0	0	0
Zell, Brian, Winter Haven*	.212	118	373	44	79	110	16	3	3	37	1	1	4	7	38	4	97	4	4
Zunino, Gregory, Fort Lauderdale	.292	70	154	25	45	63	11	2	1	14	2	2	2	2	33	2	30	4	1
Zureich, Jonathan, Lakeland*	.160	49	119	14	19	27	3	1	1	11	2	1	0	1	10	3	16	3	1

The following pitchers had no plate appearances, primarily through use of designated hitters, listed alphabetically by club, games in parentheses:

DAYTONA BEACH—Britt, Douglas (14); Calhoun, Jeffrey (21); Coplon, Mitchell (37); Dunnegan, Steven (22); Ferrante, Joseph (37); Gardner, Scott (14); Hernandez, Manuel (21); Kasprzak, Michael (5); Knudson, Mark (12); Ledduke, Daniel (3); Penate, Miguel (22); Perez, Virgilio (6); Regalado, Uvaldo (7); Richard, James Rodney (6); Schmipf, Rex (7); Snyder, Benjamin (14); Strasser, Richard (2); Yan, Roberto (27).

FORT LAUDERDALE—Alexander, Doyle (2); Andrews, Sheldon (25); Brown, Rory (1); Browning, Michael (14); Cartwright, Mark (18); Fauland, Herbert (33); Fontenot, Ray (13); Hernandez, Carlo (18); Mendez, Mark (2); Olwine, Edward (39); Smith, Kenneth (13); Tewksbury, Robert (24); Wex, Gary (20); Williams, Stanley (22); Woodworth, David (1).

FORT MYERS—Albright, David (5); Alvarez, Evelio (6); Cone, David (10); Cutty, Francis (23); Ferreira, Anthony (22); Gladden, Jeffrey (23); Gubicza, Mark (11); Harsh, Nicholas (15); Huismann, Mark (14); Leonard, Dennis (1); Martinez, Arthur (11); Miner, James (19); Olson, Michael (25); Prior, Daniel (7); Strode, Lester (24); Wong, David (49); Wyatt, Reginald (22).

LAKELAND—Beecroft, Michael (18); Cook, Kerry (5); Furman, Kevin (16); Garner, Walter (17); Heinkel, Donald (4); Jacob, Mark (2); Kelly, Bryan (11); Langfield, Paul (15); Lockenmeyer, Mark (25); Mason, Roger (22); Moller, John (39); Nutter, Gary (28); O'Connor, Nickolas (31); Tabor, Scott (13); Trevel, Ralph (17); Ward, Colin (11); Williams, Mark (5).

MIAMI—Ballard, Byron (3); Caballero, Jose (14); Escribano, Eddie (4); Gilbert, Jeffrey (3); Gonzalez, James (5); Karjalainen, Robert (10); Marlow, Stephen (9); McArthur, Gregory (8); McDonough, Brian (18); Pina, Elvin (15); Pyfrom, Joel (29); Thorpe, Bradley (2); Wadley, Anthony (23); Zamora, Oscar (16).

ST. PETERSBURG—Adams, John (13); Carrasco, Ernest (9); Cherry, Paul (27); Clark, Terry (58); Fulgham, John (8); Martin, John (10); Ortega, Jose (2); Pierce, Walter (24); Rhodes, Michael (48); Robbins, Robin (27); Sanford, Edmund (12); Silkwood, Joseph (10); Thomas, William (23).

TAMPA—Moore, Mark (5).

VERO BEACH—Alexander, Roberto (26); Beuder, Michael (9); Borbon, Ernesto (49); Cozzolino, Paul (36); Daniel, David (36); Felt, Richard (14); Fernandez, Sid (12); Howell, Kenneth (11); Kenyon, Robert (26); Mosher, Peyton (40); Reeves, Mathew (7); Slezak, Robert (25).

WEST PALM BEACH—Branham, Barry (14); Budd, Randy (9); Chesser, Brandon (8); Gilbreath, Ronald (12); Hesketh, Joseph (8); Johnson, Gregory (10); Kinns, Glenn (9); Maria, Alan (19); Mendon, Kevin (12); Nurthen, John (30); Schuler, Mark (4); Scott, Charles (28); Simond, Robert (8); St. Clair, Randy (19); St. John, William (31); Tenenini, Robert (6); Torres, Miguel (6); Waymire, Ronald (12); Westray, Kenneth (8); Yenser, Steven (23).

WINTER HAVEN—Araujo, Anazario (26); Baum, Mark (24); Bolton, Thomas (28); Cappadona, Anthony (27); Davis, Charles (26); Gnacinski, Paul (46); Greco, George (47); Johnson, Mitchell (34); McKay, Karl (5); Rivas, Martin (9); Weinbrecht, Mark (18); Weston, William (27); Woodward, Robert (27).

GRAND SLAM HOME RUNS—Gilcrease, Lachowetz, 2 each; Bradley, Bryant, Campbell, Castiglia, Castro, Earl, Fimple, Gilles, Padia, Rizzo, Scott, 1 each.

AWARDED FIRST BASE ON CATCHER'S INTERFERENCE—Vaughn 6 (Fimple 2, Williams 2, Curbelo, Padia); See 3 (Borges, Carrasquel, Gleissner); Alvarez (Gilles); Baker (Padia); Colclough (Holt); Ender (Kempton); Gleissner (Gotay); Rizzo (Griggs); Simons (Gilles); White (Griggs).

CLUB FIELDING

Club	Pct.	G.	PO.	A.	E.	DP.	PB.	Club	Pct.	G.	PO.	A.	E.	DP.	PB.
Fort Lauderdale	.969	135	3368	1504	156	125	13	St. Petersburg	.963	134	3291	1374	177	109	14
Fort Myers	.966	137	3406	1560	177	107	28	Winter Haven	.961	133	3351	1472	198	119	10
Lakeland	.966	138	3337	1469	171	141	16	Tampa	.960	131	3243	1385	193	122	19
West Palm Beach	.966	134	3315	1503	170	114	21	Daytona Beach	.958	135	3436	1561	217	120	28
Vero Beach	.964	134	3414	1408	179	116	19	Miami	.958	137	3408	1518	218	115	9

Triple Plays—St. Petersburg, Vero Beach, West Palm Beach.

INDIVIDUAL FIELDING

*Throws lefthanded.

FIRST BASEMEN

Player and Club	Pct.	G.	PO.	A.	E.	DP.	Player and Club	Pct.	G.	PO.	A.	E.	DP.
Banes, Fort Lauderdale	1.000	3	17	1	0	4	Holt, Winter Haven	1.000	3	5	0	0	0
Bard, Miami	1.000	2	2	0	0	1	Hughes, Fort Lauderdale	1.000	1	2	0	0	0
Bodie, Daytona Beach	.913	3	20	1	2	1	Jonson, Fort Myers	.984	14	119	7	2	6
Boyce, Miami	.986	30	264	14	4	28	Jordan, Fort Lauderdale*	1.000	8	45	2	0	5
Bradley, Fort Lauderdale	1.000	3	18	3	0	1	Krupa, West Palm Beach	.991	11	103	7	1	12
Bream, Vero Beach*	.991	63	523	40	5	44	Lewis, St. Petersburg	.978	41	301	13	7	25
Burns, St. Petersburg*	.995	38	169	20	1	15	Llano, Miami	1.000	24	178	18	0	16
Campbell, Daytona Beach	1.000	9	55	3	0	6	Manfre, Tampa	.958	14	62	7	3	5
Carpenter, Daytona Beach*	.993	18	142	7	1	10	Marchand, West Palm Beach	.988	64	558	33	7	39
Castiglia, Winter Haven*	.985	49	357	41	6	27	McKnight, Daytona Beach	1.000	2	10	1	0	2
Castro, Miami*	.991	78	735	43	7	51	Norman, 23 Lake-60 St. Pete	.986	83	740	42	11	56
Colclough, Tampa	.9878	125	955	103	13	99	Perkins, Vero Beach	1.000	3	23	1	0	1
Contreras, Miami*	1.000	2	4	0	0	0	Pratt, Tampa	.976	7	38	2	1	3
Curbelo, Miami	1.000	5	30	1	0	5	Robertson, Fort Lauderdale	1.000	2	18	3	0	2
D'Onofrio, Daytona Beach	1.000	1	2	0	0	0	Salazar, Miami*	1.000	1	4	1	0	0
Davis, Daytona Beach	.988	83	750	59	10	67	Sayler, St. Petersburg	1.000	1	1	0	0	0
DEMETER, Fort Lauderdale	.9883	124	1119	67	14	90	Schoeller, Miami*	1.000	4	33	3	0	6
Dodson, Winter Haven*	.993	88	786	54	6	73	K. Smith, Fort Lauderdale	1.000	2	21	3	0	2
Fimple, Vero Beach	.960	12	68	4	3	11	M. Smith, Lakeland	.974	15	104	9	3	16
Foussianes, Lakeland	1.000	2	13	0	0	3	Strucher, Daytona Beach	.987	37	275	22	4	16
Galarraga, W Palm Beach	.981	55	443	34	9	47	Stubbs, Vero Beach*	.979	16	134	3	3	13
Geren, St. Petersburg	1.000	1	2	0	0	1	Thompson, Fort Myers	.975	31	257	15	7	18
Gilles, St. Petersburg	1.000	2	3	0	0	0	White, Vero Beach	.984	45	396	34	7	37
Haas, St. Petersburg	1.000	5	24	4	0	2	Wieser, Fort Myers	1.000	2	5	1	0	0
Harvey, Lakeland*	.992	33	233	23	2	23	Williams, Lakeland	.989	50	405	25	5	36
Hatcher, Fort Myers	.976	93	840	51	22	60	Zureich, Lakeland*	.994	47	310	27	2	41
Hocutt, West Palm Beach	.966	18	132	9	5	10							

Triple Plays—Fimple, Lewis, Marchand.

SECOND BASEMEN

Player and Club	Pct.	G.	PO.	A.	E.	DP.	Player and Club	Pct.	G.	PO.	A.	E.	DP.
Alvarez, Miami	1.000	2	6	1	0	0	Campbell, Daytona Beach	.949	21	41	70	6	13
Arce, Lakeland	.917	2	3	8	1	2	Curbelo, Miami	1.000	1	3	1	0	1
Arroyo, Fort Myers	.860	6	8	29	6	3	D'Onofrio, Daytona Beach	.981	9	23	30	1	6
Baker, West Palm Beach	1.000	1	3	0	0	0	Damon, West Palm Beach	.960	134	250	428	28	71
Banes, Fort Lauderdale	1.000	1	1	1	0	0	Deaza, St. Petersburg	.867	3	6	7	2	0
Beltran, Miami	.940	13	15	32	3	4	Duncan, Winter Haven	.917	4	10	1	1	2
BENDORF, Vero Beach	.969	108	199	307	16	51	Earl, Lakeland	.966	136	298	419	25	96
Butterfield, Fort Lauderdale	.975	70	162	193	9	45	Ford, St. Petersburg	.965	109	261	291	20	58

SECOND BASEMEN—Continued

Player and Club	Pct.	G.	PO.	A.	E.	DP.
Garcia, St. Petersburg	1.000	1	0	1	0	0
Gilcrease, Fort Myers	.981	63	128	184	6	31
Goodyear, 1 Lake-10 Miami	.941	11	24	24	3	4
Hudler, Fort Lauderdale	.960	9	23	25	2	8
Jennings, Tampa	.945	52	80	91	10	24
Jonson, Fort Myers	.986	43	78	135	3	18
Laurie, Lakeland	1.000	2	3	4	0	0
Leppert, Tampa	.962	10	27	23	2	6
Llano, Miami	1.000	1	1	3	0	1
Manfre, Tampa	1.000	1	1	0	0	0
Mariano, Fort Lauderdale	1.000	1	2	2	0	0
Matamoros, Miami	.951	10	20	38	3	7
McKnight, Daytona Beach	.929	8	10	16	2	1
Newman, Fort Myers	1.000	22	46	75	0	14
Pendleton, St. Petersburg	.979	20	41	51	2	9
Perkins, Vero Beach	.941	33	72	71	9	16
Portes, Tampa	.964	99	160	216	14	48
Quinones, West Palm Beach	1.000	1	0	1	0	0
Rembielak, Miami	.941	2	3	13	1	0
Robertson, Fort Lauderdale	.964	45	72	115	7	26
K. Smith, Fort Lauderdale	.944	33	43	58	6	14
P. Smith, Daytona Beach	.965	110	252	330	21	64
Turco, St. Petersburg	.923	3	6	6	1	0
Valdez, Miami	.957	105	240	314	25	64
Vazquez, Winter Haven	.961	60	131	165	12	38
Ventura, Vero Beach	1.000	9	14	35	0	9
Waag, Fort Myers	.875	1	4	3	1	0
Walck, Winter Haven	.979	21	41	53	2	7
Walker, Winter Haven	.960	59	97	144	10	29
Wieser, Fort Myers	.933	7	10	18	2	6
Zanini, Miami	.800	2	5	3	2	1

Triple Plays—Damon, Ford.

THIRD BASEMEN

Player and Club	Pct.	G.	PO.	A.	E.	DP.
Allen, Vero Beach	.875	4	1	6	1	1
Alvarez, Miami	.874	125	97	229	47	21
Beltran, Miami	.500	2	0	1	1	1
Bodie, Daytona Beach	.500	2	0	2	2	1
Boyce, Miami	.882	6	2	13	2	2
Bradley, Fort Lauderdale	.833	2	2	3	1	0
Burns, St. Petersburg°	1.000	1	1	0	0	1
Canseco, Miami	.800	5	3	1	1	0
Chavez, Lakeland	.854	16	8	27	6	5
Curbelo, Miami	1.000	1	0	1	0	0
D'Onofrio, Daytona Beach	.833	3	2	3	1	0
Davis, Daytona Beach	.769	9	9	11	6	0
Deaza, St. Petersburg	.811	20	11	32	10	2
Filkins, Fort Lauderdale	1.000	1	1	0	0	0
Foussianes, Lakeland	.937	98	76	176	17	21
Garcia, St. Petersburg	.937	121	90	238	22	27
Goodyear, Lakeland	.833	8	1	4	1	3
Guzman, Vero Beach	1.000	1	0	3	0	0
Harvey, Lakeland°	1.000	1	1	0	0	0
Hench, Fort Lauderdale	.943	29	25	57	5	4
Hocutt, West Palm Beach	.500	1	1	0	1	0
Jonson, Fort Myers	.600	2	0	3	2	0
Laurie, Lakeland	1.000	1	1	2	0	0
Leppert, Tampa	.909	71	32	78	11	9
Llano, Miami	.000	2	0	0	1	0
Maloney, Lakeland	.932	22	10	31	3	0
Manfre, Tampa	.879	69	44	101	20	10
MARIANO, Fort Lauderdale	.964	101	56	208	10	23
Maxwell, Lakeland	1.000	9	7	18	0	2
McKnight, Daytona Beach	.757	26	9	19	9	1
Medina, Daytona Beach	.886	71	54	156	27	19
Moreno, Miami	.870	8	7	13	3	0
Pate, Winter Haven	.920	43	30	74	9	4
Pecota, Fort Myers	.959	134	109	243	15	18
Perkins, Vero Beach	1.000	1	2	0	0	0
Riley, Tampa	.500	5	0	2	2	0
Robertson, Fort Lauderdale	.897	19	12	23	4	0
Seats, Tampa	.848	38	17	50	12	6
See, Vero Beach	.906	131	118	228	36	21
Sheaffer, Winter Haven	.905	6	5	14	2	1
Smith, Fort Lauderdale	.895	9	4	13	2	1
Strucher, Daytona Beach	.889	45	27	109	17	17
Vazquez, Winter Haven	.917	3	5	6	1	0
Walck, Winter Haven	.903	93	80	172	27	19
Weems, Daytona Beach	.875	4	0	7	1	0
Weislak, West Palm Beach	.953	133	114	274	19	20
Williams, Lakeland	1.000	2	1	2	0	0

SHORTSTOPS

Player and Club	Pct.	G.	PO.	A.	E.	DP.
Allen, Vero Beach	.955	110	159	305	22	52
C. Alvarez, Vero Beach	.924	23	29	56	7	12
R. Alvarez, Miami	.950	7	13	25	2	3
Banes, Fort Lauderdale	1.000	10	18	28	0	3
Beltran, Miami	.922	23	21	62	7	7
Bendorf, Vero Beach	.875	7	9	19	4	4
Butler, Miami	.833	2	2	3	1	1
Campbell, Daytona Beach	.909	4	4	6	1	0
Chavez, Lakeland	.929	67	63	147	16	36
D'Onofrio, Daytona Beach	.929	19	28	50	6	7
Duncan, Winter Haven	.920	76	114	206	28	37
Gagne, Fort Lauderdale	1.000	1	3	5	0	2
Guzman, Vero Beach	.778	2	3	4	2	1
Haynes, Lakeland	.861	28	34	59	15	13
Jennings, Tampa	1.000	1	0	1	0	1
Laurie, Lakeland	.983	26	50	65	2	19
Maloney, Lakeland	1.000	4	2	1	0	1
McKnight, Daytona Beach	.878	14	18	18	5	4
Meacham, St. Petersburg	.915	111	201	306	47	54
Newman, Fort Myers	.944	61	92	160	15	23
Oliver, Fort Myers	.930	86	141	217	27	45
Quinones, West Palm Beach	.933	29	25	73	7	8
Rembielak, Miami	.941	110	174	340	32	60
Riley, RTampa	.918	14	17	28	4	6
Rincones, Tampa	.954	126	230	332	27	68
Robertson, Fort Lauderdale	.938	16	20	41	4	9
Ruiz, Lakeland	.929	31	43	87	10	19
Salazar, West Palm Beach	.939	111	176	364	35	65
Scott, Fort Lauderdale	.914	89	114	238	33	47
SIMCOX, Daytona Beach	.965	111	183	336	19	56
Smith, Fort Lauderdale	.972	56	62	110	5	20
Turco, St. Petersburg	.922	25	31	63	8	10
Vazquez, Winter Haven	.925	64	104	181	23	38
Ventura, Vero Beach	.778	4	3	4	2	0
Zanini, Miami	.923	3	4	8	1	3

Triple Plays—Bendorf, Quinones.

OUTFIELDERS

Player and Club	Pct.	G.	PO.	A.	E.	DP.
Albino, Tampa	1.000	13	7	1	0	0
Arfstrom, Winter Haven	1.000	6	13	1	0	0
Baker, West Palm Beach	.974	120	216	7	6	2
Banes, Fort Lauderdale	1.000	8	3	0	0	0
Beltran, Miami	.929	60	138	5	11	0
Belue, West Palm Beach	.962	56	93	7	4	1
Benza, St. Petersburg	.979	52	87	5	2	1
Best, Fort Myers	.944	51	65	3	4	0
Bodie, Daytona Beach	.981	23	48	4	1	0
Botkin, Daytona Beach	.958	14	21	2	1	1
Bryant, Vero Beach	.951	56	91	6	5	1
Bullock, Daytona Beach°	.974	111	180	11	5	3
Campbell, Daytona Beach	.936	25	42	2	3	1
Casasnovas, Lakeland	.981	41	48	3	1	1
Ciampa, Winter Haven°	.978	121	299	11	7	4
Coleman, West Palm Beach°	.990	64	94	3	1	1
Contreras, Miami°	.962	49	72	3	3	0
Cooley, West Palm Beach	.961	111	234	10	10	1
Crisp, Miami	.962	13	25	0	1	0
Day, Tampa	.981	114	151	8	3	1
Deaza, St. Petersburg	.945	55	69	0	4	0
Diehl, Vero Beach°	1.000	9	9	0	0	0
Dotson, West Palm Beach°	1.000	11	15	0	0	0
Espy, Vero Beach	.966	120	275	9	10	4
Filkins, Fort Lauderdale	1.000	3	2	1	0	0
Ford, St. Petersburg	.944	17	31	3	2	1
Gainey, Daytona Beach	.949	91	161	6	9	1
Galarraga, West Palm Beach	1.000	16	19	2	0	0
Gayden, Fort Lauderdale°	.982	43	49	5	1	0
Geren, St. Petersburg°	1.000	1	2	0	0	0
Glenn, Winter Haven	.963	50	74	5	3	1
Granger, Miami	.962	38	75	1	3	0
Guzman, Tampa	.957	120	215	5	10	2
Haas, St. Petersburg	1.000	7	11	1	0	0
Helsom, St. Petersburg	.976	60	79	3	2	2
Hoyt, St. Petersburg	.983	21	55	3	1	1
Jordan, Fort Lauderdale°	.978	97	173	6	4	2
Kutner, Miami	.975	99	185	9	5	0
Lachowetz, Vero Beach	.984	96	175	13	3	5
Lane, Daytona Beach	.846	30	21	1	4	0
Leppert, Tampa	1.000	5	6	0	0	0
Maloney, Lakeland	.988	84	159	7	2	1
Manfre, Tampa	1.000	3	0	1	0	0
McKnight, Daytona Beach	1.000	4	3	0	0	0

OUTFIELDERS—Continued

Player and Club	Pct.	G.	PO.	A.	E.	DP.
McNealy, Fort Lauderdale°	.977	114	204	9	5	2
Medina, Daytona Beach	1.000	5	4	1	0	0
Moreno, Miami	1.000	1	1	0	0	0
Morris, Fort Myers°	.971	38	64	2	2	0
Neal, Fort Myers	.947	54	83	7	5	1
Palmer, Fort Myers°	.968	85	142	9	5	3
Pate, Winter Haven	.900	8	8	1	1	0
Pederson, Vero Beach°	.974	129	211	14	6	3
Perkins, Vero Beach	1.000	1	1	0	0	0
Plautz, Fort Myers	.939	59	85	7	6	1
Pratt, Tampa	1.000	8	4	0	0	0
Riche, Miami°	.968	20	28	2	1	1
Rizzo, Fort Myers	.975	122	253	16	7	7
Roman, St. Petersburg°	.970	110	181	16	6	4
Romine, Winter Haven	.972	55	97	6	3	1
Roth, Winter Haven	.969	60	89	6	3	0
Salazar, Miami°	.867	9	12	1	2	0
Seats, Tampa	.959	56	88	5	4	1
Seymour, 12 Vero-46 Miami	.982	58	102	5	2	0
Silverio, Lakeland°	.967	86	169	6	6	2
Simmons, Lakeland	.939	123	178	7	12	3
Simons, Daytona Beach°	.976	128	272	7	7	3
M. SMITH, Lakeland	.988	92	153	12	2	5
P. Smith, Daytona Beach	1.000	4	4	0	0	0
Spears, St. Petersburg°	1.000	82	127	8	0	1
Stacheit, West Palm Beach	.952	47	73	7	4	1
Strucher, Daytona Beach	1.000	2	2	0	0	0
Teegarden, Fort Lauderdale	.970	115	182	12	6	1
Thomas, Lakeland°	.950	17	19	0	1	0
Thompson, Vero Beach	.857	7	6	0	1	0
Tovar, Miami	.961	106	224	23	10	3
Townley, Fort Myers	1.000	6	10	1	0	0
Turco, St. Petersburg	.985	90	192	8	3	3
Vaughn, West Palm Beach	1.000	2	2	0	0	0
Walker, Tampa	.962	128	277	23	12	5
Weems, Daytona Beach	.857	6	6	0	1	0
Weppner, Winter Haven°	.941	24	29	3	2	1
Wieser, Fort Myers	.857	5	5	1	1	0
J. Williams, Daytona Beach	1.000	1	1	0	0	0
Zell, Winter Haven	.959	112	178	8	8	2
Zunino, Fort Lauderdale	1.000	31	39	1	0	0

Triple Play—Turco.

CATCHERS

Player and Club	Pct.	G.	PO.	A.	E.	DP.	PB.
Bard, 18 Vero-36 Miami	.975	54	241	35	7	2	8
Boddy, Tampa	.979	68	237	38	6	4	3
Boncore, Vero Beach	.960	42	175	15	8	3	4
Borges, West Palm Beach	.965	18	99	10	4	2	1
Bradley, Fort Lauderdale	.980	75	387	51	9	5	5
Bruno, Miami	1.000	4	10	0	0	0	0
Burrell, Winter Haven	.956	16	82	5	4	1	2
Cadahia, Fort Myers	.977	71	389	44	10	4	11
Campbell, Daytona Beach	.992	28	117	9	1	2	6
Cardieri, Miami	.974	10	34	4	1	1	1
Carrasquel, Lakeland	.977	32	156	17	4	4	1
Curbelo, Miami	.965	63	272	34	11	2	2
Fimple, Vero Beach	.987	90	542	54	8	1	11
Geren, St. Petersburg	.983	96	496	72	10	6	9
Gilles, St. Petersburg	.966	29	149	20	6	0	3
Gleissner, Fort Myers	.977	33	196	19	5	3	8
Griggs, Miami	.965	18	75	8	3	0	1
Haas, St. Petersburg	.971	9	31	2	1	1	1
Hatcher, Fort Myers	1.000	10	47	6	0	0	1
Hawkins, Fort Lauderdale	1.000	2	10	2	0	0	0
Holt, Winter Haven	.976	62	327	46	9	5	4
Hood, Tampa	1.000	2	6	0	0	0	0
Hughes, Fort Lauderdale	.000	1	0	0	0	0	1
Kempton, Fort Lauderdale	.976	52	256	25	7	5	6
Lepel, West Palm Beach	.987	42	203	27	3	1	6
Leppert, Tampa	1.000	9	15	1	0	1	1
Llano, Miami	.977	22	63	23	2	1	1
LOWRY, Lakeland	.993	81	350	53	3	8	7
Mariano, Fort Lauderdale	1.000	1	0	1	0	0	0
McCorkle, Daytona Beach	.990	51	190	13	2	0	6
Miley, Tampa	.987	30	207	23	3	5	7
Padia, Miami	.970	66	289	34	10	5	8
Pirruccello, Fort Myers	.979	30	171	15	4	3	8
Plante, Fort Lauderdale	.973	20	61	11	2	0	1
Rivera, West Palm Beach	.970	14	59	6	2	0	2
Santovenia, WP Beach	.967	29	127	21	5	1	5
Sayler, St. Petersburg	1.000	14	74	15	0	4	1
Sheaffer, Winter Haven	.961	64	311	37	14	2	4
Silva, Lakeland	.952	6	15	5	1	0	2
Valdez, Miami	1.000	1	1	0	0	0	0
Vaughn, West Palm Beach	.987	48	201	27	3	1	7
J. Williams, Daytona Beach	.969	88	370	40	13	1	16
M. Williams, Lakeland	.973	35	196	24	6	1	6
Willman, St. Petersburg	1.000	1	1	0	0	0	0

Triple Play—Boncore.

PITCHERS

Player and Club	Pct.	G.	PO.	A.	E.	DP.
Adams, St. Petersburg	.700	13	1	6	3	0
Albright, Fort Myers°	1.000	5	0	2	0	0
D. Alexander, Fort Lauderdale	1.000	2	1	2	0	0
R. Alexander, Vero Beach	.880	26	18	26	6	0
Alvarez, Fort Myers	1.000	6	2	9	0	1
Andrews, Fort Lauderdale	.806	25	6	19	6	0
Araujo, Winter Haven	.868	26	15	18	5	2
Ballard, Miami	1.000	3	2	4	0	0
Baum, Winter Haven	.933	24	4	10	1	2
Beecroft, Lakeland	.750	18	1	2	1	1
Beuder, Vero Beach°	.875	9	2	5	1	0
Bodie, Daytona Beach	1.000	1	1	1	0	0
BOLTON, Winter Haven°	1.000	28	9	40	0	0
Borbon, Vero Beach°	.800	49	2	6	2	0
Branham, West Palm Beach	.818	14	5	4	2	1
Britt, Daytona Beach°	.857	14	2	4	1	0
Browning, Fort Lauderdale	1.000	14	1	1	0	0
Budd, West Palm Beach	1.000	9	1	3	0	0
Caballero, Miami	1.000	14	3	1	0	0
Calhoun, Daytona Beach	.952	21	5	15	1	1
Cappadona, Winter Haven°	.929	27	5	8	1	2
Carrasco, St. Petersburg	1.000	9	0	3	0	0
Cartwright, Fort Lauderdale	.913	18	6	15	2	2
Castro, Daytona Beach°	.778	52	1	13	4	1
Cherry, St. Petersburg°	1.000	27	8	21	0	0
Chesser, West Palm Beach	1.000	8	4	7	0	0
Cimorelli, Tampa°	.895	14	6	11	2	0
Clark, St. Petersburg	.900	58	5	13	2	2
Cone, Fort Myers	.941	10	3	13	1	1
Cook, Lakeland	.636	5	1	6	4	1
Coplon, Daytona Beach	.964	37	9	18	1	0
Cozzolino, Vero Beach	.909	36	5	5	1	0
Cutty, Fort Myers	.957	23	5	17	1	0
Daniel, Vero Beach	.952	36	3	17	1	2
Davis, Winter Haven	.962	26	7	43	2	2
DeLeon, Miami	1.000	24	1	7	0	1
Dunnegan, Daytona Beach	.922	22	19	28	4	3
Ender, Tampa	.885	13	10	13	3	1
Escribano, Miami°	.333	4	0	1	2	0
Fauland, Fort Lauderdale	1.000	33	2	7	0	0
Felt, Vero Beach°	.957	14	2	20	1	2
Fernandez, Vero Beach°	1.000	12	2	5	0	0
Ferrante, Daytona Beach	.879	37	7	22	4	0
Ferreira, Fort Myers°	.898	22	6	38	5	1
Fontenot, Fort Lauderdale°	1.000	12	4	8	0	1
Fulgham, St. Petersburg	1.000	8	3	4	0	0
Funk, Tampa	.923	43	8	16	2	1
Furman, Lakeland	.786	16	3	8	3	1
Gardner, Daytona Beach	.943	14	5	28	2	2
Garner, Lakeland	1.000	17	1	10	0	1
Gause, Tampa°	1.000	26	7	9	0	0
George, Miami°	1.000	30	15	33	0	3
Gilbert, Miami	1.000	3	2	1	0	0
Gilbreath, West Palm Beach	1.000	12	2	4	0	1
Gladden, Fort Myers	1.000	23	6	16	0	0
Glinatsis, Miami	1.000	34	7	22	0	1
Gnacinski, Winter Haven	1.000	46	5	19	0	3
J. Gonzalez, Miami°	.000	5	0	0	1	0
M. Gonzalez, Miami	.951	29	11	28	2	2
Gotay, St. Petersburg	1.000	27	4	19	0	0
Greco, Winter Haven	.900	47	3	24	3	0
Gubicza, Fort Myers	.909	11	5	15	2	0
Harsh, Fort Myers	.943	15	9	24	2	0
Harvey, Lakeland°	1.000	7	0	3	0	2
Heinkel, Lakeland	.875	4	1	6	1	0
C. Hernandez, Fort Lauderdale	.943	18	8	25	2	1
M. Hernandez, Daytona Beach	.909	21	4	16	2	0
Hesketh, West Palm Beach°	.889	8	4	12	2	0
Hollenbach, Tampa°	.920	19	4	19	2	0
Howell, Vero Beach	.889	14	2	14	2	1
Huismann, Fort Myers	1.000	14	1	8	0	0
Jacob, Lakeland	.500	2	0	1	1	0
G. Johnson, West Palm Beach	1.000	10	1	8	0	1
M. Johnson, Winter Haven	.958	34	3	20	1	1
Karjalainen, Miami°	1.000	10	0	1	0	0
Kasprzak, Daytona Beach	1.000	5	0	4	0	0
Kelly, Lakeland	.950	11	6	13	1	1
Kenyon, Vero Beach	1.000	26	9	10	0	1
Kinns, Miami	.500	9	0	1	1	0
Klosicki, Tampa	.667	9	1	3	2	0
Knox, Tampa	1.000	28	7	22	0	2
Knudson, Daytona Beach	.900	12	4	14	2	0
Langfield, Lakeland	1.000	15	0	6	0	1
Ledduke, Daytona Beach	.667	3	0	2	1	0
Leonard, Fort Myers	1.000	1	0	2	0	0
Leppert, Tampa	1.000	2	1	0	0	0

PITCHERS—Continued

Player and Club	Pct.	G.	PO.	A.	E.	DP.
Lockenmeyer, Lakeland	.943	25	9	24	2	3
Maria, West Palm Beach°	1.000	19	1	9	0	2
Marlow, Miami	1.000	9	1	3	0	0
J. Martin, St. Petersburg	1.000	10	1	3	0	0
S. Martin, Vero Beach	.929	29	12	27	3	3
Martinez, Fort Myers	.000	11	0	0	1	0
Mason, Lakeland	.941	22	14	18	2	0
McArthur, Miami	1.000	8	0	3	0	0
McDonough, Miami	.943	18	7	26	2	2
McKay, Winter Haven	1.000	5	1	2	0	0
McKnight, Daytona Beach	1.000	1	1	1	0	0
Mendez, Fort Lauderdale	.833	2	0	5	1	0
Mendon, West Palm Beach	.909	12	3	7	1	0
Miner, Fort Myers	1.000	19	1	14	0	0
Moller, Lakeland	1.000	39	1	16	0	2
Moore, Tampa°	.000	5	0	0	1	0
Moreno, Miami	.917	27	5	6	1	1
Mosher, Vero Beach	.952	40	6	14	1	1
Nurthen, West Palm Beach	.826	30	10	9	4	1
Nutter, Lakeland	.889	28	4	4	1	0
O'Connor, Lakeland	.920	31	7	16	2	1
Olson, Fort Myers	.951	25	12	27	2	4
Olwine, Fort Lauderdale°	.842	39	2	14	3	0
Ortega, St. Petersburg	1.000	2	0	2	0	1
Penate, Daytona Beach	1.000	22	1	3	0	0
Perez, Daytona Beach°	1.000	6	1	0	0	0
Pierce, St. Petersburg	.919	24	7	27	3	1
Pina, Miami	.750	15	1	5	2	0
Pope, West Palm Beach	.955	30	9	12	1	0
Prior, Fort Myers	1.000	7	0	11	0	0
Pyfrom, Miami	1.000	29	2	8	0	1
Raines, Tampa	.947	38	2	16	1	1
Ramsey, Tampa°	.871	24	6	21	4	3
Reeves, Vero Beach°	1.000	7	1	7	0	0
Regalado, Daytona Beach	.917	7	1	10	1	0
Rhodes, St. Petersburg°	1.000	48	3	14	0	2
Richard, Daytona Beach	1.000	6	1	4	0	0
Rivas, Winter Haven	1.000	9	0	1	0	0
Robbins, St. Petersburg	.947	27	9	9	1	0
Ross, Lakeland	.875	46	4	10	2	1
Sanford, St. Petersburg	.947	12	7	11	1	0
Scherrer, Tampa°	.889	7	1	15	2	0
Schmipf, Daytona Beach	.714	7	4	1	2	0
Schuler, West Palm Beach	1.000	4	1	2	0	0
C. Scott, West Palm Beach	.971	28	15	18	1	1
K. Scott, Fort Lauderdale	.967	16	10	19	1	0
Seiple, St. Petersburg°	1.000	8	0	2	0	0
Silkwood, St. Petersburg	1.000	10	1	11	0	1
Simond, West Palm Beach°	1.000	8	1	2	0	0
Slezak, Vero Beach	.941	25	3	13	1	0
K. Smith, Fort Lauderdale	1.000	13	2	4	0	1
M. Smith, Tampa	.909	48	6	14	2	1
Snyder, Daytona Beach	.955	14	5	16	1	2
St. Clair, West Palm Beach	1.000	19	2	11	0	1
St. John, West Palm Beach°	1.000	31	2	7	0	1
Straker, Tampa	.925	25	12	37	4	1
Strode, Fort Myers°	.902	24	4	33	4	0
Sullivan, Tampa	.957	21	7	15	1	1
Tabor, Lakeland	.967	13	11	18	1	1
Tenenini, West Palm Beach	.750	6	0	3	1	0
Tewksbury, Fort Lauderdale	.958	24	15	31	2	2
Thomas, St. Petersburg	.875	23	5	9	2	0
Threatt, Tampa	1.000	1	0	1	0	1
Torres, West Palm Beach	.900	6	2	7	1	0
Treuel, Lakeland	1.000	17	2	6	0	0
Wadley, Miami	.952	22	9	11	1	0
Ward, Lakeland	.913	11	2	19	2	1
Waymire, West Palm Beach	.667	12	1	1	1	0
Weinbrecht, Winter Haven°	.917	18	5	6	1	0
Weppner, Winter Haven°	1.000	13	3	4	0	1
Weston, Winter Haven	1.000	27	7	19	0	1
Westray, West Palm Beach°	.833	8	1	4	1	1
Wex, Fort Lauderdale	1.000	20	0	10	0	0
Wiedenbauer, Daytona Beach	.867	12	6	7	2	0
M. Williams, Lakeland	.889	5	2	6	1	1
S. Williams, Fort Lauderdale	.957	22	6	16	1	0
Wong, Fort Myers	.944	49	3	31	2	1
Woodward, Winter Haven	.909	27	12	18	3	2
Woodworth, Fort Lauderdale°	1.000	1	0	2	0	1
Wyatt, Fort Myers°	1.000	22	2	29	0	2
Yan, Daytona Beach	.833	27	3	2	1	1
Yenser, West Palm Beach	1.000	23	10	22	0	1
Zamora, Miami	.933	16	5	9	1	0

The following players do not have any recorded accepted chances at the positions indicated; therefore, are not listed in the fielding averages for those particular positions: Allen, c; Banes, p; Brown, p; Casasnovas, ss; Curbelo, p; Dodson, p; Hocutt, 2b, of; Jennings, 3b; Leppert, ss; Llano, of; Martin, 1b; Miley, of; Newman, of; Palmer, p; Plante, p; Portes, 3b; Quinones, 3b; Robertson, of; Seymour, 1b; K. Smith, of; Strasser, p; Thorpe, p; Weems, 2b; Wiedenbauer, of; Wieser, 3b; M. Williams, of.

CLUB PITCHING

Club	ERA.	G.	CG.	ShO.	Sv.	IP.	H.	R.	ER.	HR.	HB.	BB.	Int. BB.	SO.	WP.	Bk.
Tampa	2.66	131	18	15	38	1081	939	427	320	41	30	477	34	686	44	12
Fort Lauderdale	2.83	135	47	16	25	1122.2	1010	427	353	45	29	394	30	685	65	8
Vero Beach	3.08	134	22	9	23	1138	983	500	389	37	37	555	15	750	73	15
St. Petersburg	3.11	134	26	12	23	1097	1038	475	379	26	26	454	57	672	64	8
Fort Myers	3.19	137	39	9	28	1135.1	1070	501	402	46	46	521	6	766	59	10
Lakeland	3.92	138	35	9	23	1112.1	1085	593	485	59	32	536	37	676	75	15
Daytona Beach	4.09	135	28	8	17	1145.1	1195	663	521	42	45	570	52	644	104	15
Winter Haven	4.27	133	14	9	21	1117	1160	629	530	52	36	558	27	661	83	15
Miami	4.41	137	34	5	17	1136	1248	690	557	60	49	522	39	553	73	13
West Palm Beach	4.53	134	43	8	9	1105	1148	659	556	74	36	514	14	648	88	16

PITCHERS' RECORDS
(Leading Qualifiers for Earned-Run Average Leadership — 110 or More Innings)

°Throws lefthanded.

Pitcher—Club	W.	L.	Pct.	ERA.	G.	GS.	CG.	GF.	ShO.	Sv.	IP.	H.	R.	ER.	HR.	HB.	BB.	Int. BB.	SO.	WP.
Tewksbury, Ft. Lauderdale	15	4	.789	1.88	24	23	13	1	5	1	182.1	146	46	38	6	5	47	0	92	11
Kenyon, Vero Beach	11	3	.786	2.41	26	15	4	3	2	0	130.2	108	43	35	6	1	28	1	75	5
Alexander, Vero Beach	12	8	.600	2.54	26	26	5	0	0	0	173.2	156	71	49	3	9	78	2	91	13
Straker, Tampa	9	9	.500	2.57	25	25	3	0	2	0	154.1	137	58	44	3	3	60	4	99	10
Slezak, Vero Beach	13	7	.650	2.61	25	25	3	0	0	0	158.2	118	51	46	3	2	106	1	108	11
Scott, Fort Lauderdale	10	3	.769	2.61	16	16	8	0	1	0	117.1	115	44	34	6	2	21	2	54	5
Pierce, St. Petersburg	10	9	.526	2.78	24	24	7	0	1	0	152.1	143	61	47	3	6	60	7	67	6
Andrews, Fort Lauderdale	12	7	.632	2.83	25	25	4	0	1	0	171.2	159	75	54	5	5	64	2	105	6
Ferreira, Fort Myers	12	7	.632	2.87	22	22	6	0	1	0	150.1	144	64	48	1	1	66	0	120	6
Cartwright, Fort Lauderdale	6	7	.462	2.95	18	17	6	1	1	0	125	111	45	41	8	2	41	0	55	5
Lockenmeyer, Lakeland	7	10	.412	2.97	25	24	9	1	1	0	157.2	161	61	52	9	1	37	1	68	10

Departmental Leaders: G—Clark, 58; GS—George, 29; CG—George, Tewksbury, 13; GF—Clark, 51; ShO—Tewksbury, 5; W—Tewksbury, 15; L—C. Scott, 15; Pct.—Tabor, .800; Sv—M. Smith, 21; IP—George, 208.2; H—George, 217; R—George, 104; ER—C. Scott, 86; HR—George, 15; HB—Wong, 13; BB—Slezak, 106; IBB—Fauland, 13; SO—Fernandez, 137; WP—Calhoun, 17.

(All Pitchers—Listed Alphabetically)

Pitcher—Club	W.	L.	Pct.	ERA.	G.	GS.	CG.	GF.	ShO.	Sv.	IP.	H.	R.	ER.	HR.	HB.	BB.	Int. BB.	SO.	WP.
Adams, St. Petersburg	7	3	.700	3.24	13	13	4	0	0	0	86	85	40	31	4	0	25	2	73	6
Albright, Fort Myers°	0	0	.000	3.00	5	0	0	2	0	0	3	6	1	1	0	0	2	2	0	0
D. Alexander, Fort Lauderdale	0	0	.000	4.09	2	2	1	0	0	0	11	5	5	0	0	2	0	4	0	
R. Alexander, Vero Beach	12	8	.600	2.54	26	26	5	0	0	0	173.2	156	71	49	3	9	78	2	91	13
Alvarez, Fort Myers	1	3	.250	3.09	6	1	1	0	0	0	23.1	18	9	8	1	3	7	0	9	1
Andrews, Fort Lauderdale	12	7	.632	2.83	25	25	4	0	1	0	171.2	159	75	54	5	5	64	2	105	6
Araujo, Winter Haven	4	4	.500	3.77	26	16	1	6	1	0	102.2	129	52	43	5	3	37	2	49	6

Pitcher—Club	W.	L.	Pct.	ERA	G.	GS.	CG.	GF.	ShO.	Sv.	IP.	H.	R.	ER.	HR.	HB.	BB.	Int. BB.	SO.	WP.
Ballard, Miami	1	1	.500	3.54	3	2	1	1	0	0	20.1	20	10	8	1	2	12	1	8	2
Banes, Fort Lauderdale	0	0	.000	27.00	1	0	0	1	0	0	1	5	3	3	0	0	0	0	2	0
Baum, Winter Haven	2	5	.286	7.00	24	9	1	11	1	1	63	53	51	49	4	12	68	1	50	9
Beecroft, Lakeland	1	2	.333	4.67	18	2	0	6	0	3	27	25	21	14	0	3	24	2	20	1
Beuder, Vero Beach*	3	3	.500	4.89	9	8	1	1	1	0	42.1	44	28	23	4	1	18	0	15	0
Bodie, Daytona Beach	0	0	.000	9.00	1	0	0	1	0	0	2	1	2	2	0	1	0	0	0	0
Bolton, Winter Haven*	9	8	.529	2.99	28	25	4	1	0	0	162.2	161	67	54	3	2	63	3	77	7
Borbon, Vero Beach*	1	4	.200	2.64	49	0	0	34	0	13	61.1	50	24	18	2	2	30	3	40	2
Branham, West Palm Beach	1	1	.500	5.82	14	0	0	7	0	1	21.2	20	16	14	3	1	18	1	22	7
Britt, Daytona Beach*	3	1	.750	2.98	14	9	1	2	0	1	45.1	34	18	15	0	5	36	2	34	3
Brown, Fort Lauderdale*	0	0	.000	0.00	1	0	0	1	0	0	2	1	1	0	0	0	1	1	3	1
Browning, Fort Lauderdale	0	1	.000	2.95	14	0	0	12	0	9	18.1	18	6	6	0	1	6	0	17	1
Budd, West Palm Beach	2	2	.500	3.86	9	3	1	2	0	0	28	27	13	12	2	1	17	0	17	4
Caballero, Miami	1	2	.333	5.85	14	1	0	10	0	1	32.1	42	23	21	0	0	12	0	24	5
Calhoun, Daytona Beach*	9	6	.600	4.64	21	19	5	1	2	1	116.1	126	71	60	5	3	55	4	62	17
Cappadona, Winter Haven*	2	4	.333	4.70	27	5	0	10	0	0	59.1	69	34	31	2	2	24	0	44	3
Carrasco, St. Petersburg	1	1	.500	4.30	9	1	0	3	0	1	23	29	17	11	0	0	10	2	10	1
Cartwright, Fort Lauderdale	6	7	.462	2.95	18	17	6	1	1	0	125	111	45	41	8	2	41	0	55	5
Castro, Daytona Beach*	6	7	.462	2.49	52	0	0	37	0	7	86.2	81	25	24	5	1	45	3	63	2
Cherry, St. Petersburg*	7	9	.438	3.17	27	26	4	0	1	0	159	156	63	56	5	1	54	8	77	4
Chesser, West Palm Beach	4	3	.571	4.05	8	8	3	0	0	0	53.1	48	30	24	6	1	27	1	38	3
Cimorelli, Tampa*	3	1	.750	2.50	14	11	0	1	0	0	50.1	52	20	14	0	1	22	1	17	3
Clark, St. Petersburg	10	7	.588	2.55	58	0	0	51	0	19	88.1	81	32	25	1	3	34	8	61	6
Cone, Fort Myers	7	1	.875	2.12	10	9	6	1	1	0	72.1	56	21	17	1	3	25	0	57	1
Cook, Lakeland	3	1	.750	2.86	5	5	0	0	0	0	22	26	13	7	3	0	8	0	6	3
Coplon, Daytona Beach	4	3	.571	3.72	37	4	1	9	0	0	84.2	82	47	35	2	4	51	4	73	14
Cozzolino, Vero Beach	3	4	.429	3.55	36	2	0	16	0	3	76	66	43	30	2	7	49	3	63	5
Curbelo, Miami	0	0	.000	0.00	1	0	0	1	0	0	1	0	0	0	0	1	0	0	0	0
Cutty, Fort Myers	5	2	.714	2.93	23	6	3	6	0	0	73.2	81	32	24	1	1	43	0	39	3
Daniel, Vero Beach	3	2	.600	4.24	36	3	0	18	0	1	68	71	37	32	1	3	36	2	25	6
Davis, Winter Haven	8	11	.421	4.34	26	24	4	0	2	0	141	140	82	68	9	3	56	0	87	6
DeLeon, Miami	4	0	1.000	0.75	24	0	0	20	0	6	36	22	7	3	0	1	14	5	28	0
Dunnegan, Daytona Beach	4	9	.308	4.68	22	20	3	0	0	0	115.1	138	78	60	7	5	62	7	63	14
Ender, Tampa	6	4	.600	2.00	13	13	4	0	0	0	90	67	25	20	2	1	27	1	65	6
Escribano, Miami	2	2	.500	7.02	4	4	1	0	0	0	16.2	18	15	13	2	2	9	0	2	0
Fauland, Fort Lauderdale*	5	3	.625	2.05	33	0	0	25	0	6	44	45	12	10	1	1	25	13	38	6
Felt, Vero Beach*	5	2	.714	4.26	14	14	2	0	1	0	76	74	41	36	3	1	40	0	39	11
Fernandez, Vero Beach*	8	1	.889	1.91	12	12	5	0	4	0	84.2	38	19	18	3	5	38	0	137	1
Ferrante, Daytona Beach	7	4	.636	4.79	37	2	0	12	0	2	97.2	106	64	52	4	5	41	4	38	8
Ferreira, Fort Myers*	12	7	.632	2.87	22	22	6	0	1	0	150.1	144	64	48	1	1	66	0	120	8
Fontenot, Fort Lauderdale*	6	5	.545	2.92	12	10	4	2	1	0	74	57	29	24	2	2	31	2	72	6
Fulgham, St. Petersburg	4	2	.667	2.45	8	7	3	1	1	0	47.2	40	20	13	0	0	11	0	31	4
Funk, Tampa	7	3	.700	1.88	43	2	0	25	0	6	100.1	83	39	21	2	4	30	5	48	3
Furman, Lakeland	4	3	.571	2.79	16	3	0	5	0	2	42	32	23	13	0	1	21	3	37	5
Gardner, Daytona Beach	6	4	.600	1.95	14	13	6	0	2	0	101.2	86	31	22	2	5	28	5	54	2
Garner, Lakeland	1	2	.333	6.14	17	4	1	5	0	0	55.2	61	48	38	9	2	27	3	31	4
Gause, Tampa*	4	4	.500	3.40	26	1	0	18	0	8	39.2	42	19	15	0	0	19	4	24	1
George, Miami*	12	14	.462	3.54	31	29	13	0	2	0	208.2	217	104	82	15	2	81	9	95	10
Gilbert, Miami*	2	0	1.000	1.74	3	1	0	1	0	0	10.1	1	4	2	1	0	7	0	10	0
Gilbreath, West Palm Beach	1	3	.250	7.39	12	4	1	5	0	0	28	35	26	23	1	2	12	0	8	0
Gladden, Fort Myers	0	3	.000	3.58	23	2	1	8	0	4	55.1	59	24	22	0	2	26	1	42	3
Glinatsis, Miami	4	10	.286	4.02	34	14	4	14	0	3	132	141	71	59	8	3	61	8	89	11
Gnacinski, Winter Haven	8	3	.727	2.93	46	1	0	30	0	9	95.1	87	34	31	2	0	40	8	82	8
J. Gonzalez, Miami*	0	0	.000	11.81	5	0	0	3	0	0	5.1	7	8	7	0	1	8	0	3	3
M. Gonzalez, Miami	8	13	.381	3.84	29	22	6	3	2	0	152.1	181	93	65	6	3	53	7	92	5
Gotay, St. Petersburg	8	11	.421	3.31	27	26	3	1	2	0	155	126	73	57	4	6	80	6	134	8
Greco, Winter Haven*	7	5	.583	3.18	47	0	0	28	0	7	76.1	83	36	27	4	0	34	2	53	4
Gubicza, Fort Myers	2	5	.286	4.13	11	11	0	0	0	0	48	49	33	22	1	0	25	0	36	5
Harsh, Fort Myers	6	7	.462	3.49	15	15	7	0	1	0	105.2	116	49	41	2	5	29	0	52	9
Harvey, Lakeland*	1	0	1.000	3.09	7	1	0	4	0	2	11.2	5	5	4	1	1	4	1	8	0
Heinkel, Lakeland	3	0	1.000	1.71	4	4	1	0	0	0	31.2	27	7	6	0	2	12	1	14	2
C. Hernandez, Fort Lauderdale*	6	9	.400	3.83	18	18	4	0	2	0	115	99	55	49	9	3	64	1	58	6
M. Hernandez, Daytona Beach	6	6	.500	4.98	21	17	3	0	0	0	99.1	114	70	55	7	5	52	4	50	6
Hesketh, West Palm Beach	3	2	.600	2.76	8	8	2	0	1	0	45.2	41	16	14	2	0	16	0	24	1
Hollenbach, Tampa*	2	6	.250	4.48	19	17	1	0	0	0	82.1	72	50	41	6	3	56	2	40	1
Howell, Vero Beach	5	4	.556	4.22	11	11	0	0	0	0	59.2	58	40	28	3	0	36	0	37	4
Huismann, Fort Myers	3	1	.750	0.39	14	0	0	14	0	3	23	16	1	1	0	1	4	1	21	1
Jacob, Lakeland	0	2	.000	11.57	2	2	0	0	0	0	2.1	5	6	3	0	0	3	0	2	0
G. Johnson, West Palm Beach	1	2	.333	4.91	10	4	0	4	0	0	33	25	21	18	3	3	25	1	21	2
M. Johnson, Winter Haven	9	4	.692	4.72	34	13	1	9	0	2	118.1	122	70	62	3	4	65	2	65	8
Karjalainen, Miami*	0	1	.000	10.22	10	1	0	5	0	0	12.1	23	17	14	0	0	10	1	10	0
Kasprzak, Daytona Beach	2	0	1.000	0.93	5	3	1	1	0	0	19.1	14	4	2	0	1	10	1	10	1
Kelly, Lakeland	5	6	.455	4.22	11	11	3	0	1	0	64	55	36	30	0	2	51	1	39	2
Kenyon, Vero Beach	11	3	.786	2.41	26	15	4	3	2	0	130.2	108	43	35	6	1	28	1	75	5
Kinns, West Palm Beach	0	0	.000	5.65	9	0	0	3	0	0	14.1	16	12	9	1	3	9	0	8	0
Klosicki, Tampa	4	2	.667	2.81	9	4	0	3	0	0	32	31	17	10	1	3	17	1	17	1
Knox, Tampa	7	9	.438	2.92	28	12	1	5	1	0	95.2	99	40	31	3	2	24	2	32	3
Knudson, Daytona Beach	2	6	.250	4.77	12	11	2	0	1	0	60.1	75	35	32	0	0	23	5	15	3
Langfield, Lakeland	1	5	.167	6.69	15	6	0	2	0	0	39	51	34	29	1	0	33	0	33	3
Ledduke, Daytona Beach	2	0	1.000	2.84	3	0	0	3	0	0	6.1	4	2	2	0	0	5	2	5	1
Leonard, Fort Myers	0	0	.000	0.00	1	1	0	0	0	0	5	4	0	0	0	2	0	1	4	1
Leppert, Tampa	0	0	.000	0.00	2	0	0	2	0	0	3	3	4	0	0	0	5	2	5	1
Lockenmeyer, Lakeland	7	10	.412	2.97	25	24	9	1	1	0	157.2	161	61	52	9	1	37	1	68	10
Maria, West Palm Beach*	2	3	.400	4.00	19	0	0	11	0	2	36	38	19	16	2	1	16	2	27	3
Marlow, Miami	0	2	.000	7.62	9	3	0	0	0	0	28.1	34	29	24	2	2	24	0	14	1
J. Martin, St. Petersburg	1	4	.200	4.64	10	6	1	3	0	1	42.2	46	23	22	2	0	13	1	18	2
S. Martin, Vero Beach	5	6	.455	3.90	29	14	1	9	0	1	99.1	98	63	43	5	2	56	0	53	14
Martinez, Fort Myers	2	0	1.000	0.47	11	0	0	11	0	3	19.1	9	1	1	0	0	2	0	20	0
Mason, Lakeland	7	7	.500	3.46	22	22	5	0	0	0	132.2	124	60	51	9	6	52	2	72	7
McArthur, Miami	1	3	.250	7.36	8	6	0	0	0	0	25.2	23	24	21	9	3	37	1	19	6
McDonough, Miami	5	11	.313	4.89	18	18	4	0	1	0	108.2	130	73	59	6	4	35	4	38	6
McKay, Winter Haven	0	0	.000	5.19	5	0	0	1	0	0	8.2	6	6	5	0	0	6	1	5	2
McKnight, Daytona Beach	0	0	.000	4.50	1	0	0	1	0	0	2	3	1	1	0	0	1	0	0	0

Pitcher—Club	W.	L.	Pct.	ERA.	G.	GS.	CG.	GF.	ShO.	Sv.	IP.	H.	R.	ER.	HR.	HB.	BB.	Int. BB.	SO.	WP.
Mendez, Fort Lauderdale	0	0	.000	3.46	2	2	0	0	0	0	13	12	5	5	0	1	5	0	7	1
Mendon, West Palm Beach	2	0	1.000	3.24	12	6	0	3	0	1	33.1	27	16	12	1	5	25	0	24	1
Miner, Fort Myers	3	1	.750	5.36	19	1	0	6	0	2	47	51	30	28	2	1	20	0	15	1
Moller, Lakeland*	5	4	.556	3.96	39	8	1	7	1	1	91	89	49	40	1	1	65	3	80	10
Moore, Tampa*	0	0	.000	3.60	5	1	0	1	0	0	5	4	3	2	0	0	5	0	2	0
Moreno, Miami	3	3	.500	4.10	26	6	1	9	0	1	83.1	90	44	38	5	3	37	0	30	6
Mosher, Vero Beach	10	6	.625	1.77	40	1	0	31	0	5	81.1	77	25	16	1	3	26	2	56	1
Nurthen, West Palm Beach	7	7	.500	3.73	30	11	7	11	2	1	115.2	108	59	48	5	3	33	2	63	7
Nutter, Lakeland	3	6	.333	4.53	28	3	0	22	0	5	55.2	54	29	28	6	1	19	2	35	8
O'Connor, Lakeland	3	8	.273	6.83	31	15	2	8	1	0	88.1	99	76	67	6	3	70	5	75	6
Olson, Fort Myers	7	10	.412	3.81	25	25	5	0	0	0	144	148	73	61	6	6	65	0	67	12
Olwine, Fort Lauderdale*	5	4	.556	3.33	39	1	0	24	0	6	67.2	70	32	25	0	3	21	4	48	7
Ortega, St. Petersburg	0	0	.000	8.53	2	0	0	2	0	0	6.1	12	6	6	0	0	3	0	1	1
Palmer, Fort Myers	0	0	.000	9.00	2	0	0	2	0	0	5	2	2	0	0	0	0	0	0	1
Penate, Daytona Beach	0	4	.000	4.61	22	0	0	15	0	4	27.1	30	16	14	2	1	11	2	14	1
Perez, Daytona Beach*	0	0	.000	6.43	6	0	0	1	0	0	14	16	10	10	0	1	9	0	12	0
Pierce, St. Petersburg	10	9	.526	2.78	24	24	7	0	1	0	152.1	143	61	47	3	3	60	7	67	6
Pina, Miami	0	0	.000	8.69	15	0	0	4	0	0	29	44	31	28	1	6	17	0	10	3
Plante, Fort Lauderdale	0	0	.000	0.00	2	0	0	2	0	0	2	0	0	0	0	0	0	0	0	0
Pope, West Palm Beach	5	10	.333	5.19	30	16	5	4	1	0	128.1	132	87	74	12	3	75	3	91	13
Prior, Fort Myers	2	2	.500	3.74	7	6	2	0	1	0	33.2	31	17	14	1	2	18	0	15	0
Pyfrom, Miami	2	5	.286	4.88	29	1	0	21	0	5	51.2	56	38	28	4	4	34	2	12	6
Raines, Tampa	5	4	.556	2.77	38	0	0	15	0	3	74.2	72	35	23	3	3	45	6	47	1
Ramsey, Tampa*	7	9	.438	2.98	24	21	4	0	2	0	129.2	94	48	43	11	3	77	1	115	7
Reeves, Vero Beach*	1	3	.250	5.13	7	3	1	0	1	0	26.1	25	15	15	1	1	14	1	11	0
Regaldo, Daytona Beach	1	4	.200	3.68	7	6	0	1	0	0	29.1	36	30	12	1	0	11	2	17	2
Rhodes, St. Petersburg*	5	5	.500	3.10	48	5	0	12	0	0	93	79	40	32	0	6	58	8	70	7
Richard, Daytona Beach	3	1	.750	2.79	6	6	2	0	0	0	42	36	14	13	0	1	15	0	28	5
Rivas, Winter Haven	1	3	.250	3.38	9	0	0	8	0	1	16	14	12	6	1	1	4	2	17	0
Robbins, St. Petersburg	5	1	.833	2.38	27	0	0	21	0	1	45.1	39	16	12	0	2	32	7	29	9
Ross, Lakeland	5	3	.625	3.14	46	0	0	34	0	9	83	85	38	29	3	4	34	6	50	4
Sanford, St. Petersburg	5	4	.556	2.58	12	12	2	0	0	0	73.1	76	28	21	2	2	24	1	33	4
Scherrer, Tampa*	3	2	.600	2.28	7	6	2	1	0	0	47.1	37	13	12	3	1	18	0	45	0
Schmipf, Daytona Beach	1	3	.250	11.05	7	6	0	0	0	0	22	37	38	27	1	1	18	0	14	2
Schuler, West Palm Beach	1	1	.500	1.64	4	0	0	3	0	1	11	7	3	2	0	0	3	0	5	0
C. Scott, West Palm Beach	5	15	.250	5.33	28	22	6	4	0	0	145.1	172	94	86	14	4	49	1	78	13
K. Scott, Fort Lauderdale	10	3	.769	2.61	16	16	8	0	1	0	117.1	115	44	34	6	2	21	2	54	5
Seiple, St. Petersburg	1	0	1.000	4.91	8	0	0	6	0	0	14.2	11	8	8	1	3	14	0	5	0
Silkwood, St. Petersburg	3	2	.600	2.96	10	9	1	1	1	0	51.2	49	20	17	0	0	16	3	34	1
Simond, West Palm Beach*	0	1	.000	5.17	8	1	0	4	0	0	15.2	18	9	9	1	0	4	0	8	1
Slezak, Vero Beach	13	7	.650	2.61	25	25	3	0	0	0	158.2	118	51	46	3	2	106	1	108	11
K. Smith, Fort Lauderdale	4	1	.800	3.77	13	2	2	6	1	0	28.2	33	13	12	4	0	3	1	17	0
M. Smith, Tampa	7	1	.875	1.23	48	0	0	39	0	21	80.1	55	17	11	0	2	42	4	80	4
Snyder, Daytona Beach	7	4	.636	2.90	14	14	4	0	1	0	93	87	42	30	0	5	39	3	47	12
St. Clair, West Palm Beach	3	8	.273	5.26	19	5	2	8	0	2	65	74	41	38	3	2	17	0	38	4
St. John, West Palm Beach*	2	5	.286	4.91	31	12	3	11	1	0	91.2	106	56	50	4	2	58	1	66	10
Straker, Tampa	9	9	.500	2.57	25	25	3	0	2	0	154.1	137	58	44	3	3	60	4	99	10
Strasser, Daytona Beach	0	0	.000	7.94	2	1	0	0	0	0	5.2	8	5	5	1	0	4	0	3	1
Strode, Fort Myers*	8	11	.421	3.55	24	24	5	0	1	0	144.1	131	74	57	5	5	79	1	109	8
Sullivan, Tampa	7	5	.583	3.05	21	17	3	3	0	0	94.1	89	38	32	6	4	30	3	54	4
Tabor, Lakeland	8	2	.800	2.12	13	11	7	0	2	0	80.2	66	22	19	1	0	15	1	42	3
Tenenini, West Palm Beach	1	1	.500	2.92	6	0	0	5	0	1	12.1	12	5	4	1	0	8	1	6	1
Tewksbury, Fort Lauderdale	15	4	.789	1.88	24	23	13	1	5	1	182.1	146	46	38	6	5	47	0	92	11
Thomas, St. Petersburg	1	6	.143	3.22	23	5	1	7	0	1	58.2	66	28	21	3	0	20	4	29	5
Thorpe, Miami	0	1	.000	13.50	2	1	0	1	0	0	0.2	2	1	1	0	0	2	0	1	1
Threatt, Tampa	0	0	.000	4.50	1	1	0	0	0	0	2	2	1	1	0	0	1	0	0	0
Torres, West Palm Beach	1	4	.200	4.99	6	6	2	0	1	0	30.2	38	19	17	2	1	18	0	8	3
Treuel, Lakeland	3	3	.500	4.59	17	2	0	8	0	1	33.1	36	21	17	3	1	10	2	11	4
Wadley, Miami	4	12	.250	4.76	22	22	3	0	0	0	113.1	127	71	60	2	6	57	1	39	8
Ward, Lakeland*	2	2	.500	3.43	11	10	4	1	0	0	63	55	29	24	5	1	44	4	37	3
Waymire, West Palm Beach	2	0	1.000	5.23	12	0	0	5	0	0	20.2	24	18	12	2	0	14	0	11	2
Weinbrecht, Winter Haven*	2	2	.500	5.44	18	6	0	3	0	0	44.2	42	34	27	2	2	43	0	26	9
Weppner, Winter Haven*	0	1	.000	4.05	13	1	0	6	0	1	20	26	13	9	2	1	8	1	11	4
Weston, Winter Haven	3	10	.231	5.03	27	10	0	5	0	0	82.1	91	53	46	6	2	48	4	45	8
Westray, West Palm Beach*	2	3	.400	5.46	8	5	2	1	0	0	31.1	36	27	19	3	1	20	0	24	4
Wex, Fort Lauderdale	7	1	.875	2.44	20	8	1	7	0	3	59	46	18	16	1	2	29	1	61	7
Wiedenbauer, Daytona Beach	1	3	.250	6.45	12	4	0	6	0	0	37.2	44	33	27	1	0	31	2	15	5
M. Williams, Lakeland	3	2	.600	3.98	5	5	2	0	1	0	31.2	29	15	14	2	3	7	0	16	0
S. Williams, Fort Lauderdale	5	4	.556	3.33	22	10	4	6	1	0	83.2	78	38	31	3	2	34	3	44	3
Wong, Fort Myers	4	8	.333	1.79	49	0	0	43	0	15	85.1	68	23	17	1	13	49	3	78	4
Woodward, Winter Haven	7	9	.438	5.12	27	23	3	1	2	0	126.2	140	85	72	9	4	62	1	50	9
Woodworth, Fort Lauderdale*	1	0	1.000	0.00	1	1	0	0	0	0	7	3	0	0	0	0	0	0	8	0
Wyatt, Fort Myers*	7	7	.500	3.42	22	14	3	5	1	1	100	78	47	38	4	3	59	0	81	2
Yan, Daytona Beach	2	3	.400	5.06	27	0	0	17	0	1	37.1	37	27	21	3	2	22	2	27	5
Yenser, West Palm Beach	9	9	.500	3.44	23	23	9	0	1	0	144	144	72	55	6	3	46	1	65	9
Zamora, Miami	4	3	.571	3.18	16	6	1	10	0	1	68	70	26	24	4	1	11	0	29	0

BALKS—Bolton, Davis, Garner, M. Gonzalez, St. Clair, 4 each; R. Alexander, Cozzolino, Knudson, S. Martin, Rhodes, Snyder, St. John, Straker, 3 each; Cartwright, Cherry, Cook, Cutty, Furman, Gause, George, Gladden, Gnacinski, C. Hernandez, Hollenbach, G. Johnson, M. Johnson, Kelly, Maria, O'Connor, Reeves, Silkwood, Strode, Wadley, Wyatt, 2 each; Beecroft, Cappadona, Cone, Coplon, Dunnegan, Ender, Felt, Ferreira, Fontenot, Gardner, Gilbreath, Glinatsis, Gotay, Heinkel, Howell, Kenyon, Leppert, McDonough, Mendez, Moreno, Nurthen, Penate, Perez, Pope, Pyfrom, Raines, Regaldo, Richard, C. Scott, Slezak, M. Smith, Sullivan, Tewksbury, Ward, Weinbrecht, Weston, Wex, Wiedenbauer, Yan, Yenser, Zamora, 1 each.

COMBINATION SHUTOUTS—Gardner-Ferrante-Castro, Richard-Ferrante-Castro, Daytona Beach; Alexander-Fontenot, Tewksbury-Smith-Olwine, Woodworth-Williams-Olwine, Fort Lauderdale; Olson-Huismann, Ferreira-Wong, Strode-Miner, Fort Myers; Lockenmeyer-Ross, Mason-Beecroft-Ross-Harvey, Lakeland; Pierce-Clark, Adams-Rhodes-Clark, Cherry-Rhodes-Robbins, Sanford-Rhodes-Clark, Cherry-Clark, Sanford-Clark, St. Petersburg; Straker-Ramsey-Gause, Sullivan-Gause, Ender-Funk, Straker-Gause, Ender-Smith, Knox-Gause, Sullivan-Hollenbach-Funk, Staker-Raines-Smith, Cimorelli-Smith, Sullivan-Funk-Smith, Tampa; Torres-Nurthen, West Palm Beach; Bolton-Gnacinski, Weston-Cappadona, Davis-Greco, Winter Haven.

NO-HIT GAMES—Fernandez, Vero Beach, defeated Winter Haven, 5-0, April 24; Kenyon, Vero Beach, defeated Fort Myers, 3-0, May 23; Fernandez, Vero Beach, defeated Fort Lauderdale, 1-0, June 8; Straker, Tampa, defeated Winter Haven, 4-0, July 17; Chesser, West Palm Beach, defeated Tampa, 3-1, July 26 (second game); Moller, Lakeland, defeated Fort Myers, 4-0, August 6 (second game); Pierce, St. Petersburg, defeated Miami, 2-0, August 9 (first game).

Midwest League

CLASS A

CHAMPIONSHIP WINNERS IN PREVIOUS YEARS

1947—Belleville	.667
Belleville	.672
1948—West Frankfort*	.708
1949—Centralia	.627
Paducah (4th)†	.454
1950—Centralia‡	.675
1951—Paris§	.700
Danville (4th)†	.432
1952—Danville x	.685
Decatur (3rd)†	.584
1953—Decatur*	.576
1954—Decatur	.587
Danville (2nd)‡	.528
1955—Dubuque*	.587
1956—Paris y	.656
Dubuque	.603
1957—Decatur y	.683
Clinton	.623
1958—Michigan City	.623
Waterloo z	.613
1959—Waterloo	.613
Waterloo	.613
1960—Waterloo	.629
Waterloo	.677
1961—Waterloo	.613
Quincy z	.594
1962—Dubuque z	.667
Waterloo	.625
1963—Clinton	.710
Clinton	.629
1964—Clinton	.667
Fox Cities z	.667
1965—Burlington	.667
Burlington	.677
1966—Fox Cities z	.689
Cedar Rapids	.762
1967—Wisconsin Rapids	.685
Appleton z	.587
1968—Decatur	.656
Quad Cities z	.648
1969—Appleton	.648
Appleton	.690
1970—Quincy z	.691
Quad Cities	.581
1971—Appleton	.642
Quad Cities a	.548
1972—Appleton	.598
Danville a	.584
1973—Wisconsin Rapids a	.562
Danville	.537
1974—Appleton	.593
Danville a	.517
1975—Waterloo a	.727
Quad Cities	.624
1976—Waterloo a	.600
Cedar Rapids	.595
1977—Waterloo	.580
Burlington a	.511
1978—Appleton a	.708
Burlington	.500
1979—Waterloo	.600
Quad Cities a	.579
1980—Waterloo a	.610
Quad Cities	.532
1981—Wausau a	.636
Quad Cities	.570

*Won championship and four-club playoff. †Won four-club playoff. ‡Playoff finals canceled because of bad weather. §Won both halves of split-season. xWon first half of split-season and tied Paris for second-half title. yWon first-half title and four-team playoff. zWon split-season playoff. aLeague divided into Northern and Southern divisions and played split-season. Playoff winner. (NOTE—Known as Illinois State League in 1947-48 and Mississippi-Ohio Valley League from 1949 through 1955.)

STANDING OF CLUBS AT CLOSE OF SEASON, AUGUST 31

NORTHERN DIVISION

Club	W.	L.	T.	Pct.	G.B.
Madison (A's)	87	52	0	.626	....
Appleton (White Sox)	81	59	0	.579	6½
Wisconsin Rapids (Twins)	56	82	0	.406	30½
Wausau (Mariners)	55	84	0	.396	32

CENTRAL DIVISION

Club	W.	L.	T.	Pct.	G.B.
Springfield (Cardinals)	83	53	0	.610	....
Beloit (Brewers)	71	68	0	.511	13½
Clinton (Giants)	63	75	0	.457	21
Danville (Angels)	57	80	0	.416	26½

SOUTHERN DIVISION

Club	W.	L.	T.	Pct.	G.B.
Quad Cities (Cubs)	79	60	0	.568	....
Waterloo (Indians)	75	64	0	.540	4
Burlington (Rangers)	63	75	0	.457	15½
Cedar Rapids (Reds)	61	79	0	.436	18½

COMPOSITE STANDING OF CLUBS AT CLOSE OF SEASON, AUGUST 31

Club	Mad.	Spr.	Apl.	QC	Wat.	Bel.	Cln.	Bur.	C.R.	Dan.	WR	Wau.	W.	L.	T.	Pct.	G.B.
Madison (Athletics)	.....	7	6	8	8	9	8	8	7	9	9	8	87	52	0	.626	....
Springfield (Cardinals)	4	....	4	3	9	10	11	10	7	7	6	12	83	53	0	.610	2½
Appleton (White Sox)	6	8	....	7	6	4	6	7	9	7	9	12	81	59	0	.579	6½
Quad Cities (Cubs)	4	9	5	....	8	5	6	10	8	9	8	7	79	60	0	.568	8
Waterloo (Indians)	4	3	6	8	....	6	6	11	8	10	3	10	75	64	0	.540	12
Beloit (Brewers)	3	6	8	7	6	....	5	4	8	7	9	8	71	68	0	.511	16
Clinton (Giants)	4	4	6	6	6	7	....	3	9	7	7	4	63	75	0	.457	23½
Burlington (Rangers)	4	2	5	2	4	8	9	....	8	7	7	7	63	75	0	.457	23½
Cedar Rapids (Reds)	5	5	3	8	4	4	3	8	....	8	7	6	61	79	0	.436	26½
Danville (Angels)	3	3	5	3	2	8	9	5	4	....	10	5	57	80	0	.416	29
Wisconsin Rapids (Twins)	7	6	7	3	9	3	4	5	5	2	....	5	56	82	0	.406	30½
Wausau (Mariners)	8	0	4	5	2	4	8	4	6	7	7	....	55	84	0	.396	32

Quad Cities represented Davenport and Bettendorf, Ia., and Moline and Rock Island, Ill.

Major league affiliations in parentheses.

Playoffs—Appleton defeated Springfield, two games to none; Madison defeated Quad Cities, two games to one; Appleton defeated Madison, two games to one, to win league championship.

Regular-Season Attendance—Appleton, 81,970; Beloit, 81,512; Burlington, 59,292; Cedar Rapids, 101,096; Clinton, 89,352; Danville, 44,105; Madison, 127,639; Quad Cities, 157,960; Springfield, 108,182; Waterloo, 73,597; Wausau, 43,077; Wisconsin Rapids, 37,748. Total, 1,005,530. Playoffs, 8,775. All-Star Game, 3,214.

Managers: Appleton, Adrian Garrett; Beloit, Terry Bevington; Burlington, Marty Scott; Cedar Rapids, Randy Davidson; Clinton, Wendell Kim; Danville, Gus Gil and Aurelio Monteagudo; Madison, Brad Fischer; Quad Cities, George Enright; Springfield, Dave Bialas; Waterloo, Gomer Hodge; Wausau, R.J. Harrison; Wisconsin Rapids, Ken Staples.

All-Star Team: 1B—Henderson, Quad Cities; 2B—Carrasco, Danville; 3B—(tie) Nixon, Wausau, and Rowdon, Appleton; SS—Schofield, Danville; OF—Boston, Appleton; Buckley, Burlington; Calderon, Wausau; Jones, Cedar Rapids; Romano, Madison; C—Hunt, Springfield; DH—McAbee, Madison; RHP—Grant, Clinton; LHP—Tanzi, Appleton; Manager—Enright, Quad Cities.

(Compiled by Howe News Bureau, Boston, Mass.)

CLUB BATTING

Club	Pct.	G.	AB.	R.	OR.	H.	TB.	2B.	3B.	HR.	RBI.	GW.	SH.	SF.	HP.	BB.	Int. BB.	SO.	SB.	CS.	LOB.
Springfield	.265	136	4475	709	604	1185	1789	181	30	121	635	74	33	38	40	520	26	763	122	57	970
Wausau	.264	139	4357	658	797	1151	1708	173	24	112	581	46	45	26	47	488	18	852	232	109	875
Madison	.263	139	4327	704	588	1140	1690	193	24	103	594	73	84	50	30	596	28	813	305	128	921
Cedar Rapids	.261	140	4453	664	724	1162	1786	191	32	123	586	53	65	34	32	550	21	1019	158	58	982
Waterloo	.258	139	4436	680	626	1144	1695	199	35	94	555	43	98	35	40	512	20	871	219	63	946
Appleton	.251	140	4377	638	550	1099	1597	177	45	77	577	74	43	31	33	596	21	1002	128	54	998
Quad Cities	.250	139	4442	668	643	1112	1542	161	34	67	576	63	33	42	49	575	25	920	191	71	969
Beloit	.249	139	4416	613	646	1099	1580	182	25	83	524	61	62	35	55	495	19	940	166	91	906
Burlington	.249	138	4323	616	618	1078	1633	176	26	109	525	50	49	41	44	493	21	858	277	105	877
Danville	.248	137	4422	677	803	1098	1659	192	45	93	582	47	35	41	43	610	25	992	205	73	992
Clinton	.247	138	4304	582	573	1061	1429	173	27	47	486	49	60	32	44	574	28	749	195	97	945
Wisconsin Rapids	.240	138	4217	586	623	1012	1421	144	20	75	516	52	73	35	45	564	10	905	117	41	941

INDIVIDUAL BATTING

(Leading Qualifiers for Batting Championship—389 or More Plate Appearances)

°Bats lefthanded.   †Switch-hitter.

Player and Club	Pct.	G.	AB.	R.	H.	TB.	2B.	3B.	HR.	RBI.	GW.	SH.	SF.	HP.	BB.	Int. BB.	SO.	SB.	CS.
Schofield, Richard, Danville	.360	92	308	80	111	188	21	10	12	53	6	2	4	3	70	5	66	17	4
Romano, Thomas, Madison	.340	128	485	102	165	283	32	4	26	98	11	1	1	3	47	2	86	66	23
Nixon, R. Donell, Wausau	.338	116	461	102	156	221	18	7	11	56	5	1	1	4	41	1	75	85	13
Batista, Francisco, Springfield	.310	130	538	90	167	256	29	6	16	75	8	4	7	8	33	2	98	24	9
O'Connor, Robert, Clinton	.309	130	472	83	146	194	29	2	5	56	9	6	4	2	62	1	55	28	9
Jones, Jeffrey, Cedar Rapids	.301	135	432	111	130	286	26	2	42	101	9	0	4	6	91	5	151	22	6
McAbee, Monte, Madison°	.301	119	386	62	116	182	20	2	14	57	5	12	5	5	75	6	71	17	2
Erdahl, Jay, Wausau°	.301	109	359	55	108	178	22	3	14	73	5	4	3	2	51	3	66	6	10
Hunsinger, Alan, Springfield	.298	130	459	94	137	234	22	0	25	102	14	1	5	4	52	3	77	0	1
Reed, Curtis, Appleton°	.293	105	331	63	97	150	20	3	9	56	12	2	3	3	72	3	75	8	0
Henderson, Wendell, Quad Cities	.290	133	472	79	137	181	14	0	10	66	9	0	3	4	67	4	51	2	4

Departmental Leaders: G—Boston, 139; AB—Carrasco, 553; R— Carrasco, 115; H—Batista, 167; TB—Jones, 286; 2B—Carrasco, 34; 3B—Schofield, 10; HR—Jones, 42; RBI—Hunsinger, 102; GWRBI—Hunsinger, Hunt, Ovellette, 14; SH—Gallagher, 21; SF—Conklin, 9; HP—Dekraai, 20; BB—Miller, 92; IBB—Ashman, Bonner, Malkin, McAbee, Montanari, Ovellette, 6; SO—Jones, 151; SB—Nixon, 85; CS—Romano, 23.

(All Players—Listed Alphabetically)

Player and Club	Pct.	G.	AB.	R.	H.	TB.	2B.	3B.	HR.	RBI.	GW.	SH.	SF.	HP.	BB.	Int. BB.	SO.	SB.	CS.
Adams, Patrick, Appleton	.189	112	333	36	63	98	13	2	6	44	3	0	4	6	60	2	99	2	2
Allen, James, Quad Cities†	.167	38	120	14	20	27	3	2	0	9	0	3	1	0	16	2	14	0	1
Alpert, Geoge, Waterloo°	.219	93	297	44	65	94	11	3	4	29	1	2	1	0	25	0	70	9	5
Amador, Bruce, Madison†	.260	104	285	48	74	88	8	3	0	26	3	9	0	1	52	2	52	11	17
Antunez, Martin, Beloit°	.000	36	1	0	0	0	0	0	0	0	0	0	0	0	0	0	0	0	0
Aragon, Steven, Wisconsin Rapids	.243	136	489	73	119	187	21	4	13	75	9	7	7	4	60	1	70	12	4
Arnerich, Kenneth, Quad Cities	.130	22	69	5	9	15	1	1	1	4	0	0	1	1	7	0	40	3	1
Ashman, Michael, Madison°	.274	134	489	83	134	207	21	2	16	86	9	5	7	3	71	6	71	16	10
Babcock, William, Appleton°	.000	19	0	0	0	0	0	0	0	0	0	0	0	1	0	0	0	0	1
Baier, Martin, Clinton°	.073	19	55	0	4	4	0	0	0	5	0	0	0	5	14	0	0	0	0
Ball, Robert, Burlington†	.236	40	140	25	33	43	5	1	1	6	0	3	1	0	18	2	24	22	7
Barros, Eleazar, Danville	.075	14	40	5	3	4	1	0	0	1	0	0	0	1	6	0	20	0	2
Batista, Francisco, Springfield	.310	130	538	90	167	256	29	6	16	75	8	4	7	8	33	2	98	24	9
Bennett, Bradley, Springfield°	.230	100	313	50	72	104	7	2	7	43	6	2	1	1	45	2	70	17	9
Bialas, David, Springfield	.309	33	68	10	21	32	5	0	2	10	1	0	0	0	11	1	7	2	0
Bingham, Mark, Danville°	.268	32	97	10	26	33	5	1	0	10	0	0	1	0	10	1	19	2	3
Boddy, William, Cedar Rapids	.147	11	34	5	5	8	0	0	1	5	2	1	0	1	5	0	10	2	0
Boni, Joel, Madison†	.225	65	142	28	32	39	3	2	0	10	1	6	2	1	17	0	42	16	8
Bonner, Mark, Danville	.254	134	484	87	123	230	27	4	24	91	11	2	3	3	79	6	112	9	6
Borowsky, Erez, Wisconsin Rapids	.243	67	189	22	46	56	4	0	2	19	1	6	2	0	34	0	26	1	0
Borriello, Sebastian, Wis. Rapids	.182	45	132	19	24	33	1	1	2	9	1	6	0	2	34	0	32	2	0
Boston, Daryl, Appleton°	.279	139	512	86	143	225	19	9	15	77	8	9	4	2	44	2	147	28	13
Brown, Renard, Wausau	.296	63	189	24	56	68	4	1	2	13	5	2	1	2	23	0	18	21	7
Bucci, Michael, Wausau	.225	18	40	6	9	12	0	0	1	5	0	1	0	2	12	0	9	3	3
Buckley, Kevin, Burlington	.287	123	418	76	120	225	16	1	29	93	9	0	7	4	59	4	105	10	5
Buggs, Michael, Appleton	.208	86	245	30	51	78	3	6	4	35	5	0	2	0	41	2	82	7	2
Burley, Anthony, Cedar Rapids	.226	89	252	37	57	83	8	6	2	24	0	1	0	4	38	0	31	16	5
Calderon, Ivan, Wausau	.286	126	461	91	132	236	22	5	24	89	9	4	2	3	45	4	90	26	15
Canady, Chuckie, Burlington	.266	138	473	90	126	221	25	5	20	75	9	2	8	7	80	4	94	51	14
Carrasco, Norman, Danville	.278	136	553	115	154	222	34	2	10	51	4	2	4	6	52	0	82	72	19
Carraway, Rodney, Waterloo	.249	123	386	47	96	137	16	2	7	54	5	6	5	7	53	2	72	13	5
Carter, Herbert, Wisconsin Rapids	.217	48	166	14	36	47	4	2	1	20	2	2	1	1	16	1	49	6	3
Cartwright, Alan, Beloit°	.000	1	4	0	0	0	0	0	0	0	0	0	0	0	0	0	1	0	0
Christy, Alexander, Beloit	.149	16	47	6	7	12	2	0	1	2	1	0	0	0	4	0	17	1	0
Clayton, Kenneth, Beloit	.216	47	167	13	36	56	8	0	4	28	3	2	2	1	9	0	40	0	0
Conklin, Graham, Wausau	.252	124	409	58	103	168	25	2	12	46	2	5	9	4	42	2	103	9	10
Cordova, Anthony, Quad Cities	.252	108	404	56	102	153	14	8	7	62	8	2	4	16	22	4	84	10	12
Coughlon, Kevin, Madison	.266	115	394	41	105	151	16	3	8	57	8	3	7	1	37	3	66	3	4
Crawford, Jack, Danville	.153	64	176	19	27	35	3	1	1	10	0	5	0	0	4	0	34	8	6
Crum, George, Burlington	.266	55	139	20	37	43	4	1	0	8	0	4	0	1	20	0	21	15	6
Dale, Wayne, Waterloo	.167	7	18	0	3	4	1	0	0	1	0	0	0	0	4	0	4	0	0
David, Brian, Wausau	.253	72	233	29	59	70	9	1	0	21	1	6	2	0	33	0	26	14	7
Davidson, Mark, Wisconsin Rapids	.300	79	247	54	74	115	11	0	10	41	3	5	3	4	47	0	74	12	2
Davis, Douglas, Burlington	.285	88	291	45	83	142	19	2	12	51	5	4	4	1	29	1	52	8	2
Davis, Eric, Cedar Rapids	.276	111	434	80	120	195	20	5	15	56	5	3	2	2	51	2	103	53	12
DeCosta, Robert, Wisconsin Rapids	.256	73	246	30	63	84	6	0	5	34	6	5	1	3	16	0	28	3	1
Dekraai, Bradley, Beloit	.243	106	354	49	86	119	15	0	6	35	6	2	2	20	19	1	71	8	3
DeSantis, Frank, Quad Cities	.212	32	99	8	21	33	4	1	2	15	0	1	0	0	12	0	13	2	1
Diaz, Mario, Wausau	.262	56	187	15	49	62	8	1	1	23	1	0	1	7	0	23	3	3	
Dillard, Ronald, Burlington	.230	37	100	16	23	27	2	1	0	6	3	0	0	15	1	15	23	3	
Dunn, Michael, Clinton	.278	83	273	35	76	103	7	1	6	28	4	3	4	24	4	51	12	5	
Duquette, Bryan, Beloit°	.000	2	1	0	0	0	0	0	0	0	0	0	0	0	0	0	0	0	
Ebersberger, Randolph, Clinton	.206	72	223	22	46	62	4	0	6	20	1	3	2	1	24	0	57	10	1
Echols, Tracy, Waterloo	.264	59	159	13	42	47	3	1	0	10	1	2	1	0	6	0	21	2	2

Player and Club	Pct.	G.	AB.	R.	H.	TB.	2B.	3B.	HR.	RBI.	GW.	SH.	SF.	HP.	BB.	Int. BB.	SO.	SB.	CS.
Edmonds, J. Stanley, Wausau°	.255	125	455	58	116	181	12	1	17	84	6	1	6	2	39	2	95	23	13
Embser, Richard, Beloit°	.000	9	1	0	0	0	0	0	0	0	0	0	0	0	0	0	1	0	0
Emmert, Kenneth, Quad Cities	.193	17	57	4	11	14	1	1	0	5	0	1	0	4	0	0	12	3	0
Epperson, Charles, Appleton†	.248	44	109	15	27	42	4	1	3	23	2	1	1	0	17	0	24	0	2
Erdahl, Jay, Wausau°	.301	109	359	55	108	178	22	3	14	73	5	4	3	2	51	3	66	6	10
Espinal, Feliz, Clinton	.118	6	17	1	2	2	0	0	0	0	0	0	0	0	2	0	6	0	1
Espinoza, Alvaro, Wisconsin Rapids	.266	112	379	41	101	125	9	0	5	29	3	10	2	2	16	1	66	9	3
Evans, Anthony, Cedar Rapids	.200	54	140	9	28	35	7	0	0	12	0	0	2	1	18	0	35	1	0
Evans, Gary, Beloit	.000	27	2	0	0	0	0	0	0	0	0	0	0	0	0	0	0	0	0
Faulconer, Randall, Wausau	.099	27	71	5	7	10	0	0	1	6	0	0	0	0	11	0	24	0	0
Feliz, Adolfo, Cedar Rapids	.268	129	410	55	110	144	26	1	2	36	3	3	6	4	51	3	60	7	5
Ferguson, Michael, Cedar Rapids	.190	36	42	2	8	8	0	0	0	0	0	7	0	0	1	0	25	0	0
Ficklin, Winston, Waterloo†	.239	113	330	53	79	121	11	2	9	42	2	8	4	6	37	1	78	33	4
Finley, Brian, Beloit°	.230	72	222	37	51	66	7	1	2	16	2	1	1	7	34	1	34	12	11
Fleming, Paul, Wisconsin Rapids	.000	5	7	0	0	0	0	0	0	0	0	0	0	0	0	0	7	0	0
Fonseca, Angel, Wausau	.242	40	128	17	31	37	3	0	1	15	0	3	0	3	21	0	19	2	4
Franco, Phillip, Wisconsin Rapids°	.136	17	44	6	6	6	0	0	0	4	0	0	0	0	8	0	11	0	0
Freeburg, Larry, Cedar Rapids	.130	18	23	4	3	4	1	0	0	1	0	3	0	1	2	0	15	0	0
Gallagher, David, Waterloo°	.289	110	409	61	118	175	25	7	6	47	5	21	4	2	41	0	57	19	2
Garcia, Leonardo, Appleton°	.264	117	435	56	115	150	17	6	2	37	4	6	2	0	25	1	59	30	8
Garza, Lonnie, Danville†	.106	25	66	8	7	7	0	0	0	1	0	0	1	0	17	0	24	2	2
Gayden, Huey, Springfield°	.271	37	118	24	32	36	2	1	0	10	2	2	2	2	19	0	14	10	3
George, Leo, Quad Cities	.225	73	213	26	48	91	13	3	8	38	2	0	2	0	31	0	59	3	2
Gertz, Michael, Waterloo°	.233	54	180	23	42	51	6	0	1	10	0	2	1	4	17	1	52	6	4
Gibbons, John, Beloit°	.273	79	216	33	59	77	10	1	2	17	0	4	2	3	25	1	30	14	8
Gil, Jose, Wisconsin Rapids	.243	44	136	18	33	45	7	1	1	15	1	4	0	2	2	1	17	0	1
Gilmartin, Daniel, Beloit	.000	22	1	0	0	0	0	0	0	0	0	0	0	0	0	0	1	0	1
Gomez, George, Burlington	.270	110	348	49	94	157	20	2	13	57	4	3	3	2	52	0	72	14	7
Gomez, Marcos, Beloit	.280	106	361	54	101	155	28	4	6	58	8	3	5	3	19	1	67	6	8
Gonzales, Joaquin, Wisconsin Rapids	.203	18	59	9	12	20	2	0	2	8	0	0	1	0	3	0	16	1	1
Gonzalez, Luis, Burlington	.267	82	243	35	65	109	12	1	10	34	5	0	4	0	31	2	51	6	3
Gonzalez, Otto, Burlington	.265	82	268	26	71	110	14	2	7	43	2	2	1	1	24	3	52	5	6
Graham, Everett, Clinton°	.273	125	417	74	114	144	21	3	1	42	1	8	2	8	64	1	65	37	22
Hall, David, Cedar Rapids	.256	135	464	75	119	194	17	2	18	71	11	1	5	2	72	3	97	7	4
Harris, Michael, Springfield†	.230	128	444	51	102	138	17	5	3	43	4	8	0	3	30	1	86	11	6
Harrison, Ronald, Madison°	.280	127	447	59	125	177	20	4	8	64	7	10	5	4	24	4	55	29	9
Harry, Whitney, Burlington	.220	77	186	27	41	75	8	1	8	29	1	1	1	7	23	0	67	7	2
Hartsock, Brian, Danville°	.244	117	397	57	97	138	19	5	4	62	7	3	4	2	64	2	79	16	7
Heidenreich, Curtis, Danville	.173	25	52	5	9	14	2	0	1	4	0	6	0	0	3	0	20	0	0
Henderson, Craig, Wisconsin Rapids	.000	25	2	0	0	0	0	0	0	0	0	0	0	0	0	0	1	0	0
Henderson, Joseph, Beloit°	.230	59	161	31	37	57	6	1	4	15	1	1	1	1	22	1	42	3	2
Henderson, Wendell, Quad Cities	.290	133	472	79	137	181	14	0	10	66	9	0	3	4	67	4	51	2	4
Hennessey, Michael, Cedar Rapids	.200	27	5	1	1	1	0	0	0	0	0	3	0	0	1	0	1	0	0
Hennessy, Brendan, Burlington	.148	29	61	5	9	9	0	0	0	1	0	0	2	0	5	1	21	0	1
Hicks, Robert, Springfield	.256	124	453	60	116	191	19	1	18	71	6	1	6	6	30	2	93	7	2
Hines, Bruce, Madison†	.167	4	6	2	1	1	0	0	0	0	0	0	0	0	1	0	4	2	0
Hodde, Rodney, Burlington°	.232	22	56	8	13	15	2	0	0	3	0	0	0	9	0	0	11	4	0
Hooker, Elton, Madison†	.200	6	10	2	2	2	0	0	0	1	0	0	0	1	0	0	3	0	1
Houston, Barry, Wisconsin Rapids°	.182	32	88	13	16	21	2	0	1	8	0	2	0	0	13	0	33	5	0
Howe, Gregory, Wisconsin Rapids	.258	11	31	8	8	9	1	0	0	6	0	0	1	1	4	0	10	3	0
Hoyt, David, Wisconsin Rapids	.253	67	249	37	63	95	11	0	7	35	2	1	3	3	29	0	57	6	4
Hunsinger, Alan, Springfield	.298	130	459	94	137	234	22	0	25	102	14	1	5	4	52	3	77	0	1
Hunt, Randy, Springfield	.289	134	494	72	143	211	17	3	15	79	14	1	4	5	72	3	94	9	8
Hyman, Donald, Quad Cities	.242	10	33	8	8	18	1	0	3	11	2	0	2	0	7	0	6	1	0
Jackson, Darrin, Quad Cities	.276	132	529	86	146	194	23	5	5	48	1	7	3	4	47	0	106	58	17
James, Dewey, Beloit†	.136	35	110	10	15	23	2	0	2	10	1	1	1	3	9	1	38	9	7
Jeffries, James, Burlington	.206	14	34	5	7	11	1	0	1	2	0	0	0	0	5	0	10	2	1
Jones, Glenn, Clinton	.268	129	436	51	117	175	22	6	8	62	8	6	4	12	40	2	79	20	13
Jones, Jeffrey, Cedar Rapids	.301	135	432	111	130	286	26	2	42	101	9	0	4	6	91	5	151	22	6
Jones, Keith, Burlington†	.220	100	345	46	76	89	7	3	0	20	2	5	1	3	21	0	47	42	12
Jones, Michael, Clinton°	.238	93	269	47	64	85	16	1	1	35	3	4	3	6	68	5	55	25	12
Junker, Lance, Danville	.272	55	191	36	52	79	11	2	4	32	1	2	1	3	30	0	26	5	1
Kennedy, Jeffrey, Danville†	.196	43	138	27	27	37	1	3	1	7	0	0	5	0	30	1	47	27	5
Kent, Wesley, Appleton°	.239	37	142	20	34	67	8	2	7	29	4	0	1	1	14	0	57	0	0
Kepshire, Kurt, Cedar Rapids°	.250	21	8	2	2	2	0	0	0	0	0	0	0	0	1	0	3	0	0
Kiefer, Steven, Madison	.234	124	415	72	97	168	24	1	15	58	2	3	5	6	44	2	105	36	10
Kirby, Charles, Beloit	.222	116	415	54	92	111	9	5	0	37	7	3	4	3	38	1	88	45	18
Kirsch, Paul, Cedar Rapids°	.353	60	224	40	79	121	17	2	7	46	2	1	5	3	15	2	17	6	3
Klipstein, David, Beloit	.273	47	154	33	42	52	5	1	1	15	1	1	0	0	15	3	23	15	2
Koch, Donald, Appleton	.260	85	273	35	71	99	13	3	3	31	7	1	0	3	44	2	46	1	1
Lamar, Daniel, Cedar Rapids	.305	45	131	22	40	61	7	1	4	21	3	1	1	1	18	0	26	0	1
Lowery, Steven, Cedar Rapids	.000	51	11	0	0	0	0	0	0	0	0	1	0	0	0	0	6	0	0
Lyons, Williams, Springfield	.332	55	205	56	68	104	5	2	9	31	2	1	1	2	46	3	20	25	3
Machuca, Freddy, Danville	.143	12	21	4	3	3	0	0	0	0	0	0	0	0	0	0	10	0	0
Mackie, Bart, Wausau	.208	35	96	12	20	30	4	0	2	7	0	2	0	2	10	2	19	2	1
Malespin, Gustavo, Springfield	.264	127	454	74	120	205	20	4	19	76	7	3	5	4	59	3	45	3	3
Malkin, John, Waterloo	.265	112	392	63	104	188	22	1	20	72	12	2	4	4	44	6	97	5	1
Martin, Sam, 35 W'loo-57 Spring†	.191	92	262	31	50	56	2	2	0	19	4	6	0	4	15	0	32	17	4
Martinez, Ray, Waterloo°	.233	48	133	22	31	54	6	1	5	20	2	2	0	0	9	1	30	3	1
Matos, Carlos, Danville	.212	73	165	9	35	41	4	1	0	14	0	2	0	0	14	0	69	8	2
Matzen, Mark, Cedar Rapids°	.198	67	177	13	35	41	4	1	0	20	1	1	2	2	26	4	37	0	0
Max, William, Beloit	.333	54	189	31	63	100	8	4	7	37	5	2	1	0	31	1	50	5	4
McAbee, Monte, Madison°	.301	119	386	62	116	182	20	2	14	57	5	12	5	5	75	6	71	17	2
McAfee, Bret, Wausau	.241	90	270	52	65	91	5	0	7	29	4	4	0	4	34	0	65	11	2
McCulla, Henry, Springfield	.233	87	257	36	60	88	13	3	3	32	1	5	4	0	49	4	63	1	4
Meier, Randal, Wausau	.258	75	264	37	68	83	10	1	1	27	2	6	2	4	27	0	40	13	5
Meier, Scott, Appleton	.186	71	188	26	35	43	6	1	0	18	1	3	2	2	47	0	41	3	4
Mejia, Oscar, Burlington	.240	53	154	17	37	43	6	0	0	17	0	1	4	0	12	0	14	4	3
Methven, Marlin, Waterloo	.259	92	321	63	83	120	17	4	4	38	1	12	5	3	58	3	73	18	4
Metil, William, Cedar Rapids°	.338	101	328	44	111	125	10	2	0	11	0	10	2	1	35	0	30	14	10
Miles, Edward, Appleton	.196	51	158	18	31	47	5	1	3	13	4	0	2	1	21	2	50	2	0
Miller, Gerald, Beloit	.225	46	169	28	38	60	7	0	5	29	0	3	3	3	22	0	38	4	2
Miller, Scott, Quad Cities°	.264	125	394	74	104	131	15	0	4	52	6	6	3	2	92	2	92	14	7

Player and Club	Pct.	G.	AB.	R.	H.	TB.	2B.	3B.	HR.	RBI.	GW.	SH.	SF.	HP.	BB.	Int. BB.	SO.	SB.	CS.
Mitchell, Scot, Madison†	.230	76	213	36	49	77	10	0	6	30	5	1	2	1	52	0	55	6	6
Montanari, David, Quad Cities*	.260	90	308	42	80	102	17	1	1	37	3	1	4	2	43	6	54	9	5
Morales, Joe, Beloit†	.254	99	252	37	64	80	7	3	1	27	2	7	1	0	31	2	47	6	3
Morris, Angel, Beloit	.248	47	105	6	26	38	7	1	1	4	1	3	0	0	8	0	26	0	2
Morris, David, Danville	.214	74	252	29	54	78	7	4	3	25	1	4	3	7	36	1	58	4	0
Murphy, Robert, Cedar Rapids*	.120	31	25	1	3	3	0	0	0	0	0	1	0	0	0	0	17	0	0
Nalley, Jerry, Waterloo	.254	90	299	37	76	116	17	1	7	48	3	4	1	4	17	1	49	7	2
Nix, David, Appleton*	.287	131	477	63	137	194	26	2	9	64	12	4	4	5	50	1	59	21	7
Nixon, Donell, Wausau	.338	116	461	102	156	221	18	7	11	56	5	1	1	4	41	1	75	85	13
Noboa, Milciades, Waterloo	.249	121	385	69	96	118	12	5	0	23	1	19	3	2	62	1	61	44	12
Nokes, Matthew, Clinton*	.215	82	247	19	53	74	12	0	3	23	2	3	1	3	15	1	44	1	2
O'Connor, Robert, Clinton	.309	130	472	83	146	194	29	2	5	56	9	6	4	2	62	1	55	28	9
O'Neill, Paul, Cedar Rapids*	.272	116	386	50	105	152	19	2	8	71	9	0	4	1	21	0	79	12	5
Ornest, Maury, Beloit†	.257	46	152	25	39	64	8	1	5	19	2	0	2	0	25	0	42	9	6
Ouellette, Phillip, Clinton†	.274	109	351	59	96	155	18	1	13	74	14	4	5	2	69	6	50	3	2
Pacho, Juan, Waterloo	.333	4	12	3	4	6	2	0	0	1	0	0	0	1	0	1	0	1
Paciorek, James, Beloit	.324	85	312	38	101	131	16	1	4	37	2	0	0	1	37	1	37	6	3
Paglino, Joseph, Appleton	.149	56	161	16	24	26	2	0	0	21	3	1	0	2	21	0	51	3	1
Pellant, Gary, Wausau†	.276	21	58	12	16	30	2	0	4	13	1	0	0	1	16	1	16	3	1
Perkins, Ted, Wisconsin Rapids	.223	58	179	22	40	53	2	1	3	17	2	4	0	1	25	0	58	7	2
Perna, Robert, Clinton	.178	41	129	13	23	23	0	0	0	7	0	2	1	1	16	0	30	3	1
Pettibone, James, Cedar Rapids	.091	26	33	3	3	4	1	0	0	1	0	5	0	0	4	0	14	0	0
Peyton, Byron, Cedar Rapids	.220	16	41	7	9	10	1	0	0	3	0	4	0	0	16	1	6	0	0
Pierce, Donald, Wausau	.197	39	117	17	23	27	1	0	1	8	0	3	0	1	12	0	26	1	8
Pilla, Anthony, Wisconsin Rapids	.220	70	209	38	46	73	2	2	7	24	3	5	2	6	42	0	44	4	0
Porter, Eric, Wisconsin Rapids	.165	25	85	12	14	23	1	1	2	13	2	1	2	0	13	0	35	1	0
Portugal, Mark, Wisconsin Rapids	.500	36	2	1	1	1	0	0	0	1	0	0	0	0	0	0	0	0	0
Pratt, Crestwell, Cedar Rapids	.262	48	164	22	43	73	5	2	7	27	2	0	0	0	22	1	47	0	0
Ransom, H. Eugene, Madison	.185	64	151	26	28	36	8	0	0	8	1	3	3	1	23	0	37	23	7
Reed, Curtis, Appleton*	.293	105	331	63	97	150	20	3	9	56	12	2	3	3	72	3	75	8	0
Rehbaum, Christopher, Waterloo*	.261	85	226	39	59	84	10	0	5	20	0	5	2	1	27	1	43	8	5
Remo, Jeffrey, Quad Cities	.176	65	216	20	38	60	7	0	5	29	4	1	3	3	24	2	65	0	0
Riley, Michael, Cedar Rapids	.214	29	14	2	3	6	0	0	1	3	0	0	0	1	0	0	4	0	0
Rodriguez, Ivan, Beloit	.171	29	82	3	14	18	1	0	1	7	1	4	1	1	5	0	13	2	1
Romano, Michael, Cedar Rapids	.164	41	128	9	21	34	2	1	3	11	0	3	1	0	8	0	46	0	1
Romano, Thomas, Madison	.340	128	485	102	165	283	32	4	26	98	11	1	1	3	47	2	86	66	23
Romero, Ramon, Appleton†	.275	119	440	78	121	152	17	1	4	38	3	10	1	4	62	3	77	11	7
Roomes, Rolando, Quad Cities	.150	31	80	11	12	22	1	0	3	8	1	0	0	1	7	1	42	7	2
Rosenhahn, David, Quad Cities	.273	67	220	35	60	80	8	3	2	32	1	2	3	3	25	0	29	6	0
Rothey, Mark, Cedar Rapids*	.118	38	17	2	2	2	0	0	0	0	0	3	0	0	3	0	2	0	0
Rowdon, Wade, Appleton	.284	126	433	75	123	194	19	8	12	79	5	3	5	4	55	3	101	5	5
Rupe, Brian, Wisconsin Rapids*	.204	72	235	37	48	64	7	3	1	16	2	1	2	1	47	2	54	12	3
Rutledge, Jeffrey, Quad Cities	.285	118	417	66	119	154	17	3	4	56	7	8	4	1	54	2	88	18	6
Salery, John, Wisconsin Rapids	.314	57	207	37	65	96	13	3	4	28	1	4	2	2	26	0	32	12	6
Samuel, Michael, Beloit	.163	81	208	21	34	38	2	1	0	17	2	19	1	0	29	1	76	11	3
Sanchez, Jose, Springfield	.148	12	27	4	4	6	2	0	0	1	1	0	0	0	2	0	2	0	0
Saunier, Randall, Clinton	.152	68	178	13	27	30	3	0	0	11	0	5	0	1	11	0	33	4	5
Saverino, Michael, Danville	.195	67	159	16	31	39	2	3	0	17	1	5	1	1	33	1	33	7	3
Scheetz, Ricky, Wisconsin Rapids	.268	65	198	35	53	80	13	1	4	41	5	1	3	5	57	2	46	8	5
Schofield, Richard, Danville	.360	92	308	80	111	188	21	10	12	53	6	2	4	3	70	5	66	17	4
Sedar, Edward, Appleton	.152	16	46	7	7	8	1	0	0	3	0	0	0	1	11	0	19	3	0
Sharp, Gary, Burlington	.098	18	41	0	4	5	1	0	0	4	1	0	1	0	3	0	11	0	1
Skoglund, Brad, Wisconsin Rapids*	.215	50	144	8	31	34	3	0	0	14	3	5	2	4	14	0	32	5	2
Smajstrla, Craig, Appleton†	.241	8	29	5	7	9	2	0	0	2	0	0	0	3	0	2	4	1
Smith, John, Madison	.245	54	110	15	27	38	8	0	1	19	4	3	4	0	28	0	24	0	1
Smoot, Allen, Clinton	.252	90	309	29	78	100	13	0	3	44	4	3	4	2	43	1	58	3	5
Soprano, Joseph, Madison	.067	5	15	1	1	1	0	0	0	1	0	1	0	1	4	0	5	0	0
Sorce, Samuel, Burlington	.297	14	37	9	11	12	1	0	0	1	0	0	0	2	2	0	10	0	0
Sowards, Van, Clinton	.336	34	122	15	41	46	3	1	0	12	0	1	1	0	13	2	11	5	4
Stalp, Joseph, Cedar Rapids	.094	17	32	0	3	5	0	1	0	1	1	3	0	0	1	0	13	0	0
Stewart, Eric, Wausau*	.163	15	43	3	7	9	2	0	0	3	0	0	0	2	0	12	0	1
Stewart, James, Wisconsin Rapids	.239	33	113	9	27	41	8	0	2	15	1	0	1	0	8	0	26	0	1
Stout, Timothy, Cedar Rapids	.254	36	71	7	18	19	1	0	0	4	1	1	0	0	6	0	13	3	0
Strom, Phillip, Madison	.136	5	22	3	3	3	0	0	0	2	1	0	0	2	0	6	0	0
Stromer, Richard, Danville	.301	76	236	40	71	119	14	2	10	54	3	1	8	2	64	2	38	4	2
Stryffeler, Daniel, Springfield*	.243	87	251	38	61	86	12	2	3	32	3	1	1	1	41	2	31	2	4
Suarez, Luis, Wisconsin Rapids	.000	11	0	1	0	0	0	0	0	0	0	0	0	0	0	0	0	0	1
Swenson, Michael, Clinton	.182	101	324	33	59	83	11	2	3	27	1	5	0	1	46	2	68	8	5
Tabor, Greg, Burlington	.248	98	326	58	81	109	12	5	2	21	3	12	2	6	35	1	52	30	12
Tanabe, Collin, Beloit	.279	111	365	49	102	147	15	0	10	51	8	1	5	4	40	1	40	6	3
Tanner, Edwin, Waterloo†	.140	21	50	4	7	10	1	1	0	4	0	0	1	0	6	0	5	0	2
Taylor, Dwight, Waterloo*	.267	27	101	28	27	33	4	1	0	6	0	3	0	0	24	1	20	20	5
Taylor, Johnny, Appleton	.200	29	65	9	13	15	2	0	0	7	1	3	0	0	13	0	13	0	0
Taylor, Michael, Waterloo*	.291	34	127	19	37	55	3	0	5	29	3	1	1	1	15	0	30	14	3
Terry, Scott, Cedar Rapids	.254	108	335	50	85	143	16	3	12	54	4	2	2	3	34	0	102	13	6
Thomas, Deron, Springfield†	.228	70	232	32	53	67	9	1	1	18	2	2	1	1	24	0	42	1	2
Tipton, Jeffrey, Madison	.240	85	254	35	61	86	8	1	5	33	6	5	5	2	38	0	63	6	7
Toliver, Freddie, Cedar Rapids	.250	29	40	6	10	13	1	1	0	3	0	1	0	0	6	0	9	2	0
Tramble, Otis, Quad Cities†	.211	66	218	26	46	48	2	0	0	11	1	0	0	0	23	0	49	17	5
Triplett, Antonio, Burlington	.189	82	244	23	46	61	7	1	2	22	2	2	2	4	22	1	63	5	4
Tryon, Michael, Wisconsin Rapids	.248	49	145	16	36	50	9	1	1	14	1	2	0	1	21	0	33	5	1
Turner, Rick, Danville	.253	76	241	26	61	71	5	1	1	30	2	2	2	3	15	1	43	4	3
VanBurkleo, Tyler, Beloit*	.240	129	412	61	99	188	21	1	22	65	9	5	3	5	77	4	135	5	4
VanKrevelen, Ronn, Wis. Rapids*	.199	51	151	18	30	40	4	0	2	20	2	0	1	1	24	2	29	3	1
Varsho, Gary, Quad Cities*	.251	76	271	52	68	94	9	4	3	40	5	2	7	5	49	0	50	30	5
Venner, W. Gary, Burlington*	.231	83	221	18	51	71	8	0	4	22	4	4	2	1	13	1	33	8	6
Waller, Kevin, Madison*	.209	54	91	13	19	27	1	2	1	6	3	3	0	0	16	1	13	6	1
Walsh, James, Quad Cities	.258	96	322	56	83	125	11	2	9	53	13	0	1	7	45	2	66	8	3
Washington, Randy, Waterloo	.171	18	41	6	7	9	2	0	0	8	1	0	2	0	15	0	12	1	0
Whisman, Rhett, Wisconsin Rapids	.235	23	85	8	20	23	3	0	0	10	2	1	0	1	5	0	19	0	0
White, Devon, Danville†	.215	57	186	21	40	51	6	1	1	11	2	1	0	1	10	0	45	11	0
White, William, Danville	.232	83	267	22	62	88	11	3	3	32	4	3	5	1	30	1	67	3	6

Player and Club	Pct.	G.	AB.	R.	H.	TB.	2B.	3B.	HR.	RBI.	GW.	SH.	SF.	HP.	BB.	Int. BB.	SO.	SB.	CS.
Wilkerson, Curtis, Burlington	.253	56	198	18	50	56	6	0	0	13	3	3	0	3	15	0	33	21	10
Wilkinson, Ron, Madison	.250	113	400	75	100	123	14	0	3	39	7	18	3	2	60	2	50	67	22
Wilson, James, Waterloo	.358	55	204	40	73	134	17	1	14	48	3	0	0	4	23	2	47	0	1
Wilson, Phillip, Waterloo	.278	93	266	33	74	114	13	3	7	38	2	4	1	1	30	0	38	10	3
Wilson, Ricky, Wausau	.221	111	340	40	75	121	19	0	9	49	2	2	0	6	39	1	72	4	4
Wishnefski, Michael, Wausau*	.290	59	176	25	51	74	7	2	4	14	3	0	1	1	23	2	54	6	3
Woods, Victor, Madison	.083	5	12	1	1	1	0	0	0	0	0	0	0	0	4	0	5	1	0
Worden, William, Danville	.269	113	398	60	107	184	19	2	18	79	4	1	5	5	41	4	103	5	2
Zacher, Todd, Clinton*	.239	134	482	88	115	149	14	4	4	40	2	7	3	1	71	3	73	36	12

The following pitchers had no plate appearances, primarily through use of designated hitters; listed alphabetically by club, games in parentheses:

APPLETON—Anderson, Jesse (24); Flannery, Kevin (16); Gibson, Scott (14); Heath, Allan (6); Jones, Alfornia (26); Maitland, Michael (4); Niemann, Arthur (21); Noworyta, Steven (12); Pastrovich, Steven (37); Schneider, Paul (14); Schuckert, Wayne (21); Skinner, John (5); Solomon, Eddie (4); Sutton, James (25); Tanzi, Michael (24).

BELOIT—Clutterbuck, Bryan (26); Derksen, Robert (18); Fedor, Christian (55); Hoban, John (9); Myerchin, Michael (17); Pallas, Theodore (2); Scarpetta, Dan (2); Sullivan, Robert (16); Walker, Cameron, (21); Watson, Bret (15); Wegman, William (25); Wood, Johnson (7).

BURLINGTON—Bass, Barry (4); Benes, Joseph (25); Brosious, Frank (12); Cook, Glenn (18); Fossas, Anthony (25); Gammage, Mark (37); Hartman, Albert (27); Henry, Dwayne (4); Henry, Timothy (3); Hudson, Anthony (43); Maki, Timothy (13); McLane, Larry (21); Schmid, Michael (41); Schulte, Todd (15); Smith, Daryl (19); Taylor, William (37); Warren, Raymond (22); Zwolensky, Mitchell (26).

CLINTON—Barling, Glenn (23); Bautista, Ramon (28); Cline, Steven (1); Crews, Lawrence (28); Erickson, Donald (8); Grant, Mark (27); Lambert, Gene (29); Murtha, Brian (27); Nenad, David (27); Ronan, Kernan (6); Swenson, Mark (23); Weir, James (6); Wilcox, Steven (28); Wilhelmi, David (1).

DANVILLE—Ahern, Jeffrey (26); Bryden, Thomas (22); Dowies, Thomas (15); King, Joseph (37); Lindsey, Douglas (10); Lora, Alejandro (5); Lugo, Rafel (10); McKenzie, Douglas (13); Oliver, Scott (15); Price, Kevin (27); Rosenbaum, Dwayne (12); Salazar, Jeffrey (11); Schumacher, Roy (22); Williams, Willie (23); Wright, Mark (20).

MADISON—Anderson, Scott (18); Cary, Jeff (23); Edwards, Allen (29); Feeley, James (2); Fellows, Mark (28); Finn, Michael (17); Hallgren, Tom (4); Harris, Frank (2); Heckman, Thomas (1); Herron, Anthony (8); Jarrett, Mark (28); Kobernus, Jeffrey (43); Kolotka, Charles (49); McDonald, Mark (15); Moore, Robert (9); Olshane, Scott (8); Retzer, Edwin (12); Vavrock, Robert (30); Weatherman, David (3).

QUAD CITIES—Banks, Darryl (31); Boudreau, James (16); Brahms, Russell (41); Buonantony, Richard (26); Carpio, Jorge (30); Clarke, Timothy (25); Fruge, Jeffrey (11); Johnson, Scott (19); Kaufman, Ronald (53); Lovelace, Vance (21); Shuleeta, Michael (8); Smith, Scott (30); Viskas, Steven (2); Weissman, Craig (11).

SPRINGFIELD—Arigoni, Scott (26); Boever, Joseph (3); Collins, Donald (25); Cox, Daniel (15); Dozier, Thomas (26); Droschak, David (14); Dunn, Gregory (27); Epple, Thomas (28); Kish, Robert (11); Mason, Martin (53); Neely, Alex (33); Pittman, Michael (9); Reed, George (8); Silva, Freddie (24); Winfield, Steven (22).

WATERLOO—Anthony, Dane (16); Cushing, Stephen (8); Doyle, Richard (21); Elpin, Ralph (11); Jeffcoat, Michael (9); Johnson, Wayne (20); Lintz, Rickey (37); Long, Edelano (27); McDonald, Rodney (26); Miglio, John (43); Owens, Thomas (7); Roche, Stephen (20); Roman, Jose (24); Romero, Ramon (7); Silvas, Brian (4); Wick, David (17); Willis, Alan (11).

WAUSAU—Bartley, Gregory (25); Castillo, Luis (11); Dixon, Ronn (33); Enriquez, Martin (13); Evans, Michael (35); Hayes, Terry (28); Holland, Donald (12); Johnson, Michael (30); Kinley, Wayne (5); Kouba, Curtis (14); Parent, Eric (9); Ramirez, Randolph (15); Schassler, Jeffrey (5); Sismondo, Ronald (14); Whitmer, Joseph (13).

WISCONSIN RAPIDS—Arney, Jeffrey (16); Eufemia, Frank (27); Flores, Wilfredo (6); Foster, John (6); Gross, David (3); Henkemeyer, Richard (27); Higgins, Kiel (8); Klump, Kenneth (15); Larcom, Mark (16); Malascewski, Joseph (6); Mancuso, Paul (17); McMahon, John (19); Mikesell, Lawrence (13); Page, Marc (4); Weiermueller, Mike (24).

GRAND SLAM HOME RUNS—Aragon, Bennett, Bonner, Junker, Terry, VanBurkleo, 2 each; Adams, Boston, Buckley, Davidson, Davis, Gomez, Hall, Hicks, Hunsinger, Kent, Kiefer, Mackie, Nalley, Pierce, Pratt, Romano, Stryffeler, Triplett, VanKrevelen, J. Wilson, P. Wilson, Worden, 1 each.

AWARDED FIRST BASE ON CATCHER'S INTERFERENCE—Ficklin (Worden); George (Worden); Jones (Henderson); Meier (Gonzalez); Miller (R. Wilson); Mitchell (Matzen); Porter (Malkin); Rehbaum (Bonner); Romano (P. Wilson).

CLUB FIELDING

Club	Pct.	G.	PO.	A.	E.	DP.	PB.	Club	Pct.	G.	PO.	A.	E.	DP.	PB.
Appleton	.966	140	3469	1447	172	108	20	Springfield	.961	136	3474	1511	201	125	30
Beloit	.962	139	3547	1344	192	111	34	Burlington	.959	138	3436	1595	214	123	12
Clinton	.962	138	3479	1329	191	84	12	Waterloo	.958	139	3514	1419	214	106	34
Madison	.962	139	3512	1527	199	113	25	Cedar Rapids	.949	140	3453	1327	256	78	42
Quad Cities	.962	139	3537	1499	201	124	21	Danville	.946	137	3443	1454	281	117	18
Wisconsin Rapids	.962	138	3382	1428	190	103	23	Wausau	.945	139	3390	1383	277	99	35

Triple Plays—Clinton 2.

*Throws lefthanded.

INDIVIDUAL FIELDING

FIRST BASEMEN

Player and Club	Pct.	G.	PO.	A.	E.	DP.	Player and Club	Pct.	G.	PO.	A.	E.	DP.
Adams, Appleton	.990	106	859	68	9	64	HENDERSON, Quad Cities	.991	131	1153	91	11	98
Allen, Quad Cities	1.000	4	32	1	0	3	Hodde, Burlington*	.988	18	145	16	2	10
Ashman, Madison	.992	55	473	26	4	34	Houston, Wisconsin Rapids*	1.000	12	78	8	0	2
Bingham, Danville	.973	22	172	11	5	22	Hunsinger, Springfield	.990	129	1169	53	12	109
Bonner, Danville	.982	73	614	47	12	50	Jones, Cedar Rapids	.980	44	329	15	7	21
Bucci, Wausau	1.000	4	13	2	0	4	Kent, Appleton	.981	31	248	14	5	26
Buckley, Burlington	.981	10	100	3	2	8	Kirsch, Cedar Rapids*	.982	60	453	32	9	29
Calderon, Wausau	1.000	1	3	0	0	1	Koch, Appleton	1.000	1	6	0	0	1
Clayton, Beloit	1.000	13	112	11	0	13	Malespin, Springfield	.974	8	71	4	2	5
Conklin, Wausau	.986	79	596	59	9	51	Malkin, Waterloo	.993	20	144	7	1	10
Dunn, Clinton	.983	72	545	40	10	31	Martinez, Waterloo*	.979	43	312	17	7	19
Epperson, Appleton	1.000	5	22	1	0	4	McAbee, Madison*	.992	86	788	48	7	58
Espinoza, Wisconsin Rapids	.941	16	100	12	7	9	McAfee, Wausau	.973	41	268	18	8	21
George, Quad Cities	1.000	3	14	0	0	1	McCulla, Springfield	1.000	3	24	3	0	1
Gertz, Waterloo*	.993	53	409	14	3	33	Meier, Wausau	.981	8	49	2	1	4
L. Gonzalez, Burlington*	.979	65	522	32	12	54	Miller, Quad Cities	1.000	5	26	0	0	3
O. Gonzalez, Burlington	1.000	5	41	2	0	5	Montanari, Quad Cities	1.000	1	8	0	0	1
Harry, Burlington	.993	59	416	27	3	33	Nalley, Waterloo	.980	43	272	21	6	27
Hartsock, Danville	1.000	3	25	1	0	1	O'Connor, Clinton	1.000	5	21	1	0	1

FIRST BASEMEN—Continued

Player and Club	Pct.	G.	PO.	A.	E.	DP.
Pacioreck, Beloit	.938	3	15	0	1	0
Pellant, Wausau	.974	8	70	5	2	2
Perkins, Wisconsin Rapids	.978	58	472	19	11	37
Porter, Wisconsin Rapids	.985	23	186	13	3	16
Pratt, Cedar Rapids	.975	36	284	22	8	17
Reed, Appleton	1.000	2	10	1	0	1
Saverino, Danville	1.000	1	1	0	0	1
Scheetz, Wisconsin Rapids	.990	23	183	9	2	16
Sharp, Burlington	1.000	1	3	0	0	0
Skoglund, Wisconsin Rapids°	1.000	11	72	7	0	9
Smith, Madison	1.000	1	1	0	0	1
Smoot, Clinton	.987	67	551	36	8	41
Strom, Madison	1.000	1	8	0	0	1
Stromer, Danville	.990	22	188	11	2	19
VanBurkleo, Beloit°	.980	127	1036	64	23	81
J. Wilson, Waterloo	1.000	1	5	0	0	0
P. Wilson, Waterloo	1.000	4	7	0	0	0
R. Wilson, Wausau	.977	11	72	13	2	4
Woods, Madison	.750	1	3	0	1	0
Worden, Danville	.995	24	192	7	1	15

SECOND BASEMEN

Player and Club	Pct.	G.	PO.	A.	E.	DP.
Allen, Quad Cities	.923	2	7	5	1	1
Amador, Madison	.964	103	182	252	16	43
ARAGON, Wisconsin Rapids	.986	135	290	334	9	68
Boni, Madison	.978	27	59	75	3	20
Bucci, Wausau	1.000	2	2	1	0	0
Burley, Cedar Rapids	.953	47	104	119	11	19
Carrasco, Danville	.961	136	313	379	28	85
Crum, Burlington	.898	16	27	26	6	4
David, Wausau	.940	70	119	131	16	27
Dillard, Burlington	.971	33	78	90	5	19
Echols, Waterloo	.947	23	39	32	4	6
Emmert, Quad Cities	.917	17	32	56	8	11
Feliz, Cedar Rapids	.933	29	63	63	9	10
Ficklin, Waterloo	.951	28	55	61	6	11
Fonseca, Wausau	.944	39	77	75	9	16
Garza, Danville	1.000	2	1	5	0	0
Hines, Madison	1.000	2	2	6	0	0
Kirby, Beloit	.973	115	253	278	15	65
Lyons, Springfield	.965	17	34	48	3	10
Malespin, Springfield	.909	5	5	5	1	0
Martin, 33 Wloo-54 Spring.	.966	87	168	198	13	50
McAfee, Wausau	.970	33	63	65	4	8
Mejia, Burlington	1.000	2	2	2	0	0
Methven, Waterloo	.968	73	145	190	11	34
Metil, Cedar Rapids	.945	68	128	132	15	14
Montanari, Quad Cities	.924	23	46	51	8	13
Morales, Beloit	.983	27	59	57	2	11
Nix, Appleton	.948	129	272	315	32	74
Paglino, Appleton	.970	9	18	14	1	5
Pellant, Wausau	1.000	2	2	5	0	1
Peyton, Cedar Rapids	1.000	2	4	2	0	0
Pilla, Wisconsin Rapids	.938	4	11	4	1	2
Ransom, Madison	.942	15	35	46	5	4
Rutledge, Quad Cities	.965	24	46	64	4	17
Sanchez, Springfield	1.000	6	1	12	0	1
Saunier, Clinton	.974	13	18	19	1	3
Saverino, Danville	1.000	2	0	2	0	1
Smajstrla, Appleton	.929	6	5	8	1	2
Swenson, Clinton	.946	87	144	192	19	38
Tabor, Burlington	.963	95	226	249	18	50
Thomas, Springfield	.967	70	172	208	13	48
Varsho, Quad Cities	.964	76	190	180	14	48
Wilkerson, Burlington	1.000	6	11	10	0	2
Wilkinson, Madison	.933	4	7	7	1	1
Zacher, Clinton	.926	44	85	78	13	15

THIRD BASEMEN

Player and Club	Pct.	G.	PO.	A.	E.	DP.
Allen, Quad Cities	.884	31	18	43	8	4
Arnerich, Quad Cities	.880	22	7	37	6	1
Ashman, Madison	.667	1	0	2	1	0
Batista, Springfield	.727	6	3	5	3	0
Bialas, Springfield	.800	1	1	3	1	0
Boni, Madison	1.000	2	2	1	0	0
Buckley, Burlington	.875	4	1	6	1	1
Burley, Cedar Rapids	.837	15	19	22	8	3
Calderon, Wausau	1.000	5	2	6	0	1
Carraway, Waterloo	.901	121	74	209	31	21
Conklin, Wausau	.878	37	22	57	11	2
Cordova, Quad Cities	1.000	1	1	1	0	0
DeCosta, Wisconsin Rapids	.905	61	56	135	20	16
Dekraai, Beloit	.938	104	78	147	15	9
Dillard, Burlington	1.000	1	2	0	0	0
Ebersberger, Clinton	.917	40	28	71	9	5
Espinoza, Wisconsin Rapids	.910	25	24	57	8	4
Franco, Wisconsin Rapids	1.000	4	3	7	0	2
Gomez, Burlington	.927	71	53	163	17	13
Hall, Cedar Rapids	.887	109	66	153	28	12
Henderson, Beloit	.893	11	11	14	3	1
Hennessy, Burlington	.915	25	19	46	6	6
Klipstein, Beloit	.833	3	2	3	1	0
Lyons, Springfield	.967	35	27	60	3	5
Malespin, Springfield	.912	104	75	173	24	16
Malkin, Waterloo	1.000	3	1	5	0	0
Max, Beloit	.833	14	9	21	6	1
Mejia, Burlington	.875	4	3	11	2	1
Methven, Waterloo	1.000	4	2	9	0	1
Metil, Cedar Rapids	.873	17	11	37	7	2
Montanari, Quad Cities	.952	19	18	41	3	4
Morales, Beloit	.939	19	13	18	2	4
Nixon, Wausau	.848	100	87	187	49	15
O'Connor, Clinton	.919	79	43	160	18	11
Paglino, Appleton	.881	17	7	30	5	1
Pilla, Wisconsin Rapids	1.000	2	0	3	0	0
Ransom, Madison	.939	35	20	73	6	7
Rosenhahn, Quad Cities	.942	67	54	140	12	15
ROWDON, Appleton	.953	125	81	264	17	24
Saunier, Clinton	.826	20	13	25	8	0
Saverino, Danville	.885	32	14	63	10	3
Scheetz, Wisconsin Rapids	.903	36	31	62	10	3
Sharp, Burlington	.750	15	3	9	4	0
Stromer, Danville	.912	34	41	62	10	4
Tanner, Waterloo	.917	3	7	4	1	0
Triplett, Burlington	.878	34	19	67	12	2
Whisman, Wisconsin Rapids	.925	13	9	28	3	0
White, Danville	.864	74	73	112	29	13
Wilkinson, Madison	.940	110	69	180	16	11
Wilson, Wausau	.837	17	9	32	8	0
Worden, Danville	.762	6	6	10	5	0
Zacher, Clinton	.818	4	2	7	2	0

SHORTSTOPS

Player and Club	Pct.	G.	PO.	A.	E.	DP.
Boni, Madison	.928	24	21	56	6	9
Bucci, Wausau	.960	5	7	17	1	2
Calderon, Wausau	.893	69	124	192	38	36
Carraway, Waterloo	1.000	2	3	5	0	1
Conklin, Wausau	.900	2	1	8	1	1
DeCosta, Wisconsin Rapids	.854	10	16	19	6	4
Dekraai, Beloit	1.000	1	1	2	0	0
Diaz, Wausau	.934	56	78	148	16	26
Ebersberger, Clinton	.821	6	7	16	5	3
Espinal, Clinton	.750	3	1	2	1	0
Espinoza, Wisconsin Rapids	.941	73	113	172	18	30
Evans, Cedar Rapids	.876	36	36	77	16	12
Feliz, Cedar Rapids	.911	90	101	217	31	32
Franco, Wisconsin Rapids	.893	11	11	14	3	5
Garza, Danville	.898	22	30	58	10	8
Harris, Springfield	.921	128	178	414	51	75
Kiefer, Madison	.928	122	173	395	44	69
Lyons, Springfield	.950	9	17	21	2	3
Martin, 3 Waterloo-5 Spring	.833	8	6	14	4	3
McAfee, Wausau	.938	8	11	19	2	5
Mejia, Burlington	.949	47	57	148	11	19
Methven, Waterloo	1.000	5	5	10	0	2
Morales, Beloit	.888	51	40	95	17	19
Noboa, Waterloo	.918	119	207	306	46	48
O'Connor, Clinton	1.000	1	3	6	0	1
Pacho, Waterloo	1.000	4	5	5	0	2
Paglino, Appleton	.967	24	28	60	3	11
Perna, Clinton	.949	41	52	97	8	14
Peyton, Cedar Rapids	.895	15	28	40	8	4
Pilla, Wisconsin Rapids	.938	53	56	141	13	19
Ransom, Madison	1.000	2	1	6	0	0
Rodriguez, Beloit	.881	29	29	60	12	11
ROMERO, Appleton	.941	119	180	331	32	52
Rutledge, Quad Cities	.938	95	128	310	29	54
Samuel, Beloit	.945	81	105	206	18	45
Saunier, Clinton	.800	5	3	9	3	0
Saverino, Danville	.864	28	33	56	14	12
Schofield, Danville	.943	90	129	249	23	51
Tabor, Burlington	.955	2	12	9	1	3
Tanner, Waterloo	.896	15	23	46	8	7
Thomas, Springfield	1.000	1	0	1	0	0
Tramble, Quad Cities	.921	47	66	120	16	22
Triplett, Burlington	.908	50	65	132	20	24
White, Danville	.947	8	11	25	2	4
Wilkerson, Burlington	.931	53	67	149	16	30
Wilkinson, Madison	.750	1	0	3	1	0
Zacher, Clinton	.938	83	127	221	23	32

Triple Plays—Zacher 2

OUTFIELDERS

Player and Club	Pct.	G.	PO.	A.	E.	DP.	Player and Club	Pct.	G.	PO.	A.	E.	DP.
Alpert, Waterloo*	.949	86	109	3	6	1	M. Jones, Clinton*	.979	89	137	6	3	1
Baier, Clinton*	1.000	13	18	2	0	0	Junker, Danville	.971	52	97	3	3	1
Ball, Burlington	.987	38	76	2	1	0	Kennedy, Danville*	.965	38	78	4	3	1
Barros, Danville	.958	15	21	2	1	0	Klipstein, Beloit	.970	37	61	3	2	1
Batista, Springfield	.941	124	197	11	13	3	Machuca, Danville	.750	8	9	0	3	0
Bennett, Springfield*	.980	96	185	8	4	2	Malespin, Springfield	1.000	15	21	1	0	0
Bonner, Danville	.955	13	21	0	1	0	Martinez, Waterloo*	1.000	1	1	0	0	0
Boston, Appleton*	.968	139	293	9	10	2	Matos, Danville	.882	64	88	9	13	1
Brown, Wausau	.957	47	65	1	3	0	Max, Beloit	.872	27	27	7	5	0
Bucci, Wausau	1.000	5	3	1	0	0	McAfee, Wausau	1.000	2	1	0	0	0
Buckley, Burlington	.917	102	131	13	13	2	Meier, Wausau	.962	66	98	4	4	2
Buggs, Appleton	.949	78	106	5	6	1	Miles, Appleton	.962	50	73	3	3	0
Calderon, Wausau	.928	44	86	4	7	2	G. Miller, Beloit	.963	45	77	1	3	0
Canady, Burlington	.964	128	178	10	7	3	S. Miller, Quad Cities	.973	119	211	8	6	1
Carter, Wisconsin Rapids	.936	33	67	6	5	2	Morales, Beloit	.750	4	2	1	1	0
Cartwright, Beloit*	1.000	1	2	0	0	0	Morris, Danville*	.954	73	117	8	6	0
Christy, Danville	.848	15	25	3	5	0	Nalley, Waterloo*	1.000	3	3	0	0	0
Cordova, Quad Cities	.925	69	94	17	9	2	O'Connor, Clinton	.985	36	65	1	1	1
Coughlon, Madison	.977	114	197	14	5	3	O'Neill, Cedar Rapids	.947	101	137	7	8	2
Crawford, Danville	.946	55	85	3	5	1	Ornest, Beloit	.500	2	1	0	1	0
Crum, Burlington	.929	30	26	0	2	0	Paciorek, Beloit	.980	83	140	8	3	3
Davidson, Wisconcin Rapids	.973	77	166	13	5	5	Pierce, Wausau	.960	39	70	2	3	0
D. Davis, Burlington	.929	10	12	1	1	0	Pratt, Cedar Rapids	1.000	9	7	1	0	0
E. Davis, Cedar Rapids	.965	109	239	9	9	1	Reed, Appleton	.952	39	39	1	2	0
Dunn, Clinton	1.000	5	4	0	0	0	Rehbaum, Waterloo*	.899	69	81	8	10	0
Ebersberger, Clinton	.962	15	23	2	1	0	Romano, Madison	.928	126	179	13	15	1
Echols, Waterloo	.949	37	36	1	2	0	Roomes, Quad Cities	.944	28	50	1	3	0
Edmonds, Wausau	.963	122	199	11	8	1	Rupe, Wisconsin Rapids*	.971	66	96	5	3	0
Erdahl, Wausau	.925	74	117	6	10	0	Salery, Wisconsin Rapids	.955	55	99	6	5	1
Ficklin, Waterloo	.980	81	142	5	3	0	Sanchez, Springfield	1.000	5	2	0	0	0
Finley, Beloit*	.965	64	129	10	5	4	Saunier, Clinton	1.000	8	9	2	0	0
Fleming, Wisconsin Rapids	1.000	3	4	0	0	0	Sedar, Appleton	.962	16	25	0	1	0
GALLAGHER, Waterloo	.984	110	232	15	4	2	Skoglund, Winconsin Rapids*	.976	32	38	3	1	0
Garcia, Appleton*	.957	116	207	15	10	3	Smith, Madison	.960	21	21	3	1	0
Gayden, Springfield*	.962	36	75	1	3	0	Soprano, Madison	1.000	5	6	0	0	0
Gibbons, Beloit*	.967	64	113	4	4	1	Sorce, Burlington	.857	8	6	0	1	0
Gil, Wisconsin Rapids	1.000	19	37	2	0	1	Sowards, Burlington	.960	28	45	3	2	1
G. Gomez, Burlington	1.000	22	24	2	0	1	Stewart, Wisconsin Rapids	.933	19	25	3	2	0
M. Gomez, Beloit	.956	83	128	3	6	0	Stout, Cedar Rapids	.920	17	21	2	2	0
Graham, Clinton*	.980	117	237	13	5	0	Stryffeler, Springfield*	.921	36	34	1	3	0
Hall, Cedar Rapids	1.000	20	32	2	0	0	D. Taylor, Waterloo*	.981	27	49	3	1	1
Harrison, Madison	.955	126	238	15	12	6	M. Taylor, Waterloo	.980	26	45	3	1	0
Hartsock, Danville	.887	78	109	9	15	0	Terry, Cedar Rapids	.954	90	156	10	8	3
Hicks, Springfield	.980	117	181	17	4	1	Triplett, Burlington	1.000	3	2	0	0	0
Hooker, Madison*	1.000	3	3	1	0	0	Tryon, Wisconsin Rapids	.920	18	23	0	2	0
Houston, Wisconsin Rapids*	.958	18	21	2	1	1	Vankrevelen, Wisconsin Rapids*	.968	21	29	1	1	0
Howe, Wisconsin Rapids	.909	9	10	0	1	0	Waller, Madison	.942	45	61	4	4	1
Hoyt, Wisconsin Rapids	.943	64	95	4	6	0	Walsh, Quad Cities	.959	80	88	5	4	0
Jackson, Quad Cities	.972	132	266	9	8	2	Washington, Waterloo	.840	15	20	1	4	0
James, Beloit	.933	33	68	2	5	1	White, Danville	.920	50	89	3	8	0
Jeffries, Burlington	1.000	10	11	0	0	0	Wilson, Waterloo	1.000	4	3	0	0	0
G. Jones, Clinton	.955	124	179	10	9	2	Wishnefski, Wausau*	.930	33	38	2	3	0
J. Jones, Cedar Rapids	.977	83	124	5	3	1	Woods, Madison	1.000	1	1	0	0	0
K. Jones, Burlington	.960	96	184	10	8	2	Worden, Danville	.500	1	1	0	1	0

Triple Plays—Graham, M. Jones.

CATCHERS

Player and Club	Pct.	G.	PO.	A.	E.	DP.	PB.	Player and Club	Pct.	G.	PO.	A.	E.	DP.	PB.
Ashman, Madison	1.000	1	1	0	0	0	0	Matzen, Cedar Rapids	.971	60	396	38	13	4	13
Boddy, Cedar Rapids	.978	11	77	11	2	1	4	McCulla, Springfield	.966	54	283	27	11	1	7
Bonner, Danville	.966	26	152	20	6	0	5	Meier, Appleton	.989	65	391	57	5	9	8
Borowsky, Wisconsin Rapids	.991	63	374	60	4	6	8	Mitchell, Madison	.971	74	436	61	15	8	17
Borriello, Wisconsin Rapids	.990	38	281	27	3	2	6	Morris, Beloit	.978	27	120	11	3	1	5
Dale, Waterloo	1.000	7	21	5	0	1	0	Nokes, Clinton	.969	59	363	41	13	2	6
Davis, Burlington	.992	17	116	12	1	1	2	QUELLETTE, Clinton	.992	90	681	65	6	8	6
DeSantis, Quad Cities	.986	31	186	20	3	4	3	Porter, Wisconsin Rapids	1.000	2	15	3	0	0	1
Faulconer, Wausau	.986	23	135	9	2	0	11	Remo, Quad Cities	.975	64	430	46	12	4	12
George, Quad Cities	.987	44	271	24	4	6	6	Romano, Cedar Rapids	.961	39	280	38	13	4	19
Gil, Wisconsin Rapids	1.000	3	2	0	0	0	1	Sorce, Burlington	1.000	2	7	1	0	0	0
Gonzales, Wisconsin Rapids	.962	15	128	22	6	1	5	Stewart, Wausau	.957	12	88	2	4	0	6
Gonzalez, Burlington	.975	65	400	62	12	5	7	Tanabe, Beloit	.982	104	695	110	15	8	19
Hartsock, Danville	1.000	1	4	1	0	0	0	Taylor, Appleton	.977	29	148	19	4	2	6
Henderson, Beloit	.984	32	162	18	3	4	10	Tipton, Madison	.989	70	473	54	6	4	8
Hunt, Springfield	.973	86	557	90	18	8	23	Tryon, Wisconsin Rapids	.992	24	111	15	1	1	2
Hyman, Quad Cities	.929	3	10	3	1	0	0	Turner, Danville	.980	74	393	39	9	5	7
Koch, Appleton	.988	55	379	30	5	2	6	Venner, Burlington	.980	69	340	50	8	3	3
Lamar, Cedar Rapids	.963	37	292	45	13	1	6	P. Wilson, Waterloo	.988	63	348	65	5	6	11
Mackie, Wausau	.934	19	106	8	8	0	3	R. Wilson, Wausau	.974	95	640	85	19	4	15
Malkin, Waterloo	.978	85	592	88	15	10	23	Worden, Danville	.944	50	259	47	18	2	6

PITCHERS

Player and Club	Pct.	G.	PO.	A.	E.	DP.	Player and Club	Pct.	G.	PO.	A.	E.	DP.
Adams, Appleton	1.000	1	0	1	0	0	Babcock, Appleton*	.933	19	4	24	2	0
Ahern, Danville*	.839	26	6	46	10	0	Banks, Quad Cities	.889	31	16	40	7	3
J. Anderson, Appleton	.886	24	10	21	4	0	Barling, Clinton	.833	22	1	24	5	1
S. Anderson, Madison	.882	18	1	14	2	0	Bartley, Wausau	1.000	25	6	8	0	1
Anthony, Waterloo	1.000	16	9	22	0	1	Bass, Burlington	.909	4	2	8	1	0
Antunez, Beloit*	1.000	36	3	12	0	1	Bautista, Clinton	.786	28	4	7	3	0
Arigoni, Springfield*	1.000	26	0	13	0	0	Benes, 20 Wau-5 Burl*	.917	25	3	19	2	1
Arney, Wisconsin Rapids	.833	16	5	15	4	0	Boever, Springfield	1.000	3	0	1	0	0

PITCHERS—Continued

Player and Club	Pct.	G.	PO.	A.	E.	DP.	Player and Club	Pct.	G.	PO.	A.	E.	DP.
Boudreau, Quad Cities°	1.000	16	4	10	0	1	Lowery, Cedar Rapids	.970	51	5	27	1	0
Brahms, Quad Cities°	.917	41	3	8	1	2	Lugo, Danville	.889	10	1	7	1	1
Brosious, Burlington	1.000	12	6	17	0	1	Maki, Burlington	.875	13	1	13	2	2
Bryden, Danville	.939	22	7	24	2	3	Malascewski, Wisconsin Rapids..	.857	6	2	4	1	0
Buonantony, Quad Cities	.976	26	15	26	1	0	Mancuso, Wisconsin Rapids°	1.000	17	3	15	0	0
Carpio, Quad Cities	.846	30	5	17	4	1	Mason, Springfield	.867	53	3	10	2	0
Cary, Madison	.857	23	1	5	1	0	M. McDonald, Madison	.700	15	2	5	3	0
Castillo, Wausau°	.727	11	3	5	3	0	R. McDonald, Waterloo	.862	26	5	20	4	2
Clarke, Quad Cities	.907	26	16	33	5	1	McKenzie, Danville	.700	13	2	5	3	0
Clutterbuck, Beloit	.957	26	10	34	2	0	McLane, Burlington°	.939	21	8	38	3	2
Collins, Springfield	.929	25	4	22	2	2	McMahon, Wisconsin Rapids	.964	19	1	26	1	1
Cook, Burlington	.909	18	2	8	1	1	Miglio, Waterloo°	.842	43	2	14	3	0
Cox, Springfield	.880	15	8	14	3	1	Mikesell, Wisconsin Rapids°	.857	13	4	8	2	0
Crews, Clinton	.920	28	15	54	6	4	Moore, Madison	.889	9	1	7	1	2
Cushing, Waterloo°	.500	8	0	1	1	0	Murphy, Cedar Rapids°	.905	31	3	16	2	1
Derksen, Beloit	1.000	18	3	7	0	0	Murtha, Clinton	.952	27	4	16	1	1
Dixon, Wausau°	.814	33	7	41	11	0	Myerchin, Beloit°	1.000	17	1	2	0	0
Dowies, Danville	.938	15	5	10	1	0	Neely, Springfield	1.000	33	1	5	0	0
Doyle, Waterloo	.958	21	3	20	1	0	Nenad, Clinton	.920	27	10	13	2	0
Dozier, Springfield	1.000	26	5	23	0	0	Niemann, Appleton	.857	21	11	13	4	2
Droschak, Springfield	1.000	14	1	16	0	1	Noworyta, Appleton	1.000	12	4	12	0	1
Dunn, Springfield	.868	27	3	30	5	1	Oliver, Danville	.800	15	1	7	2	0
Duquette, Beloit°	.786	22	0	11	3	0	Olshane, Madison	1.000	8	0	1	0	1
Edwards, Madison°	.842	29	10	22	6	1	Owens, Waterloo	.833	7	3	12	3	1
Elpin, Waterloo	.750	11	2	4	2	0	Pallas, Beloit	.000	2	0	1	0	0
Embser, Beloit°	.800	9	0	4	1	0	Parent, Wausau	.867	9	3	10	2	0
Enriquez, Wausau	1.000	13	4	6	0	1	Pastrovich, Appleton	.926	37	9	16	2	0
Epperson, Appleton	1.000	1	0	1	0	0	Pettibone, Cedar Rapids	.824	26	8	20	6	2
Epple, Springfield°	1.000	28	10	10	0	0	Pittman, Springfield°	.750	9	1	2	1	0
Erickson, Clinton	1.000	8	2	3	0	0	Portugal, Wisconsin Rapids	.806	36	7	18	6	1
Eufemia, Wisconsin Rapids	1.000	27	3	13	0	1	Price, Danville	.911	27	11	30	4	1
G. Evans, Beloit	.867	27	2	11	2	1	Ramirez, Wausau	.905	15	3	16	2	0
M. Evans, Wausau°	.905	35	5	14	2	0	Reed, Springfield°	.000	8	0	0	1	0
Fedor, Beloit	.885	55	5	18	3	2	Retzer, Wausau	.889	12	1	7	1	0
Fellows, Madison	.845	28	11	38	9	4	Riley, Cedar Rapids	.900	29	4	5	1	0
Ferguson, Cedar Rapids	.966	35	4	24	1	1	Roche, Waterloo	1.000	20	5	12	0	1
Flannery, Appleton	1.000	16	1	10	0	1	Roman, Waterloo	.833	24	1	9	2	1
Flinn, 8 Beloit-9 Mad°	.917	17	5	17	2	3	Romero, Waterloo°	.500	7	0	2	2	0
Flores, Wisconsin Rapids	1.000	6	1	2	0	0	Ronan, Clinton	1.000	6	1	5	0	1
Fossas, Burlington°	.926	25	3	22	2	3	Rosenbaum, Danville	.800	12	2	6	2	1
Foster, Wisconsin Rapids°	1.000	6	1	5	0	0	Rothey, Cedar Rapids°	.875	38	4	17	3	0
Freeburg, Cedar Rapids	1.000	18	3	9	0	1	Salazar, Danville	1.000	11	0	9	0	0
Fruge, Quad Cities	.938	11	4	11	1	1	Scarpetta Beloit°	1.000	2	0	1	0	0
Gammage, Burlington	.933	37	3	11	1	1	Schassler, Wausau	.750	5	2	4	2	0
Gibson, Appleton	.909	14	2	8	1	0	Schmid, Burlington°	.900	41	1	17	2	0
Gilmartin, Beloit	1.000	20	5	4	0	1	Schneider, Appleton	.667	14	0	2	1	0
Grant, Clinton	.947	27	19	17	2	0	Schuckert, Appleton°	.952	21	7	13	1	0
Gross, Wisconsin Rapids	.500	3	0	1	1	0	Schulte, Burlington°	1.000	4	1	1	0	0
Hallgren, Madison	.800	6	1	3	1	0	Schumacher, Danville	.857	22	4	8	2	1
Harris, Madison	1.000	2	0	1	0	0	Shuleeta, Quad Cities°	.900	8	4	5	1	0
Hartman, Burlington	.912	27	5	26	3	2	Silva, Springfield	.902	24	9	28	4	2
Hayes, Wausau°	.877	28	7	43	7	2	Silvas, Waterloo	1.000	4	0	5	0	1
Heath, Appleton°	1.000	6	1	4	0	0	Sismondo, Wausau°	1.000	14	3	17	0	0
Heidenreich, Cedar Rapids	.909	25	13	37	5	2	Skinner, Appleton	1.000	5	0	3	0	0
Henderson, Wisconsin Rapids°	.774	24	1	23	7	2	D. Smith, Burlington	.897	19	5	21	3	2
Henkemeyer, Wisconsin Rapids	.923	26	4	20	2	1	S. Smith, Quad Cities	.800	30	7	17	5	2
Hennessey, Cedar Rapids	.944	27	5	12	1	0	Solomon, Appleton	.833	4	1	4	1	0
D. Henry, Burlington	.833	4	1	4	1	0	Sorce, Burlington	1.000	1	1	0	0	0
T. Henry, Burlington°	.000	3	0	0	1	0	Stalp, Cedar Rapids	.932	17	11	30	3	1
Herron, Madison	1.000	8	0	1	0	0	Suarez, Wisconsin Rapids	1.000	9	2	6	0	0
Higgins, Wisconsin Rapids	.929	8	4	9	1	1	Sullivan, Beloit	1.000	16	1	0	0	0
Hoban, Beloit	.944	9	5	12	1	0	Sutton, Appleton	1.000	25	7	26	0	1
Holland, Wausau	.905	12	6	13	2	1	Swenson, Clinton°	.964	23	3	24	1	1
Hudson, Burlington	.938	43	4	11	1	4	Tanzi, Appleton°	.896	24	11	32	5	1
JARRETT, Madison	1.000	28	6	35	0	1	Taylor, 19 Wausau-19 Burl	.955	37	4	17	1	1
Jeffcoat, Waterloo°	1.000	9	0	4	0	0	Toliver, Cedar Rapids	.853	23	6	23	5	1
M. Johnson, Wausau	.909	30	11	9	2	2	Vavrock, Madison	.969	30	7	24	1	1
S. Johnson, Quad Cities°	.950	19	3	16	1	0	Walker, Beloit	.960	21	5	19	1	0
W. Johnson, Waterloo°	.909	20	4	16	2	0	Waller, Madison	1.000	2	0	1	0	0
Jones, Appleton	1.000	26	4	12	0	0	Warren, Burlington°	1.000	22	5	21	0	0
Kaufman, Quad Cities	1.000	53	2	13	0	0	Watson, Beloit	.909	15	2	8	1	0
Kepshire, Cedar Rapids	1.000	21	0	8	0	0	Weatherman, Madison	1.000	3	0	1	0	1
King, Danville	.938	37	2	13	1	1	Wegman, Beloit	.918	25	13	32	4	2
Kinley, Wausau	1.000	5	2	0	0	0	Weiermiller, Wisconsin Rapids°..	.953	24	5	36	2	4
Kish, Springfield	.963	11	6	20	1	2	Weir, Clinton	.800	6	1	3	1	0
Klump, Wisconsin Rapids	.813	15	6	7	3	0	Weissman, Quad Cities	1.000	11	1	3	0	0
Kobernus, Madison°	1.000	43	6	10	0	0	Whitmer, Wausau	.957	13	5	17	1	0
Kolotka, Madison	.692	49	3	6	4	0	Wick, Waterloo°	1.000	17	3	7	0	0
Kouba, Wausau°	1.000	14	3	6	0	.0	Wilcox, Clinton	.941	28	10	22	2	1
Lambert, Clinton°	1.000	29	5	15	0	1	Wilhelmi, Clinton	1.000	1	0	1	0	0
Larcom, Wisconsin Rapids°	1.000	16	1	1	0	0	Williams, Danville	.957	23	4	18	1	1
Lindsey, Danville°	1.000	10	1	4	0	1	Willis, Waterloo	.900	11	2	7	1	0
Lintz, Waterloo	.952	37	3	17	1	2	Winfield, Springfield	1.000	22	1	7	0	0
Long, 12 Danville-15 Water	.808	27	3	18	5	1	Wood, Beloit	.800	7	1	3	1	0
Lora, Danville	1.000	5	1	4	0	0	Wright, 5 Wis. Rap.-15 Dan	.857	20	4	8	2	0
Lovelace, Quad Cities°	.889	21	5	27	4	2	Zwolinski, 23 Wausau-3 Burl..	.933	26	4	10	1	2

The following players do not have any recorded accepted chances at the positions indicated; therefore, are not listed in the fielding averages for those particular positions: Adams, 3b; Ashman, of; Boni, of; Borowsky, of; p; Carrasco, ss; Carraway, of; Cline, p; Conklin, of; Epperson, 3b; Espinosa, of; Feeley, p; George, of; Gomez, p; Gonzales, of; Harry, of; Heckman, p; Hunt, of; Maitland, p; McCulla, of; Meier, 2b; Metil, of; Nixon, 1b; Page, p; Pellant, of; Scheetz, of; Sorce, 3b; Viskas, p.

CLUB PITCHING

Club	ERA.	G.	CG.	ShO.	Sv.	IP.	H.	R.	ER.	HR.	HB.	BB.	Int. BB.	SO.	WP.	Bk.
Appleton	3.39	140	39	18	30	1156.1	1033	550	435	70	37	506	6	888	77	5
Clinton	3.42	138	48	10	16	1159.2	1071	573	441	73	32	432	11	1000	42	10
Madison	3.67	139	30	8	27	1170.2	1127	588	478	98	29	429	17	877	58	8
Springfield	3.74	136	21	10	32	1158	1074	604	481	97	40	524	41	812	91	5
Burlington	3.89	138	28	11	23	1145.1	1066	618	495	85	51	539	21	821	85	12
Waterloo	3.91	139	44	7	17	1171.1	1125	626	509	90	52	544	35	922	90	14
Wisconsin Rapids	3.94	138	46	8	18	1127.1	1063	623	493	120	30	611	28	883	89	14
Beloit	3.95	139	34	11	27	1182.1	1158	646	519	85	30	517	41	948	88	16
Quad Cities	4.01	139	28	8	28	1179	1126	643	525	87	44	569	5	852	97	10
Cedar Rapids	4.36	140	24	3	20	1151	1124	724	558	89	59	614	23	1003	98	6
Wausau	4.58	139	33	9	17	1130	1129	797	575	123	40	684	19	935	95	11
Danville	4.96	137	43	14	18	1147.2	1245	803	632	87	58	604	15	743	72	22

PITCHERS' RECORDS
(Leading Qualifiers for Earned-Run Average Leadership — 115 or More Innings)

✽Throws lefthanded.

Pitcher — Club	W.	L.	Pct.	ERA.	G.	GS.	CG.	GF.	ShO.	Sv.	IP.	H.	R.	ER.	HR.	HB.	BB.	Int. BB.	SO.	WP.
Tanzi, Appleton✽	14	6	.700	2.22	24	17	12	4	4	0	166	123	55	41	7	6	64	1	142	9
Grant, Clinton	16	5	.762	2.36	27	27	12	0	4	0	198.2	139	65	52	8	2	60	0	243	2
Crews, Clinton	12	12	.500	2.68	28	28	16	0	1	0	188	171	78	56	10	3	40	0	145	9
Wegman, Beloit	12	6	.667	2.81	25	25	10	0	1	0	179.2	176	77	56	11	3	38	3	129	7
Clarke, Quad Cities	11	7	.611	2.91	25	23	9	0	1	0	164	155	70	53	13	9	42	0	81	4
R. McDonald, Waterloo	11	5	.688	2.98	26	20	9	4	2	1	142	114	59	47	5	9	68	3	68	4
Fossas, Burlington✽	8	9	.471	3.08	25	18	10	1	1	0	146.1	121	63	50	9	7	33	1	115	4
McLane, Burlington✽	10	6	.625	3.11	21	20	8	1	3	0	121.2	116	52	42	3	5	43	1	76	4
Edwards, Madison✽	12	4	.750	3.21	29	22	8	2	0	0	168.1	164	77	60	11	2	52	2	159	18
Wilcox, Clinton	8	11	.421	3.22	28	25	9	1	1	0	162	142	77	58	6	4	43	1	168	8

Departmental Leaders: G—Fedor, 55; GS—Vavrock, 29; CG—Crews, 16; GF—Kaufman, 43; ShO—Clutterbuck, Grant, Tanzi, 4; W—Grant, 16; L—Price, 16; Pct.—Grant, .762; Sv—Kaufman, 17; IP—Grant, 198.2; H—Jarrett, 207; R—Price, 119; ER—Price, 97; HR—Vavrock, 22; HB—Bryden, 15; BB—Long, 114; IBB—Lintz, 10; SO—Grant, 243; WP—Long, 26.

(All Pitchers—Listed Alphabetically)

Pitcher — Club	W.	L.	Pct.	ERA.	G.	GS.	CG.	GF.	ShO.	Sv.	IP.	H.	R.	ER.	HR.	HB.	BB.	Int. BB.	SO.	WP.
Adams, Appleton	0	0	.000	27.00	1	0	0	0	0	0	1.1	3	4	4	1	0	3	0	1	0
Ahern, Danville✽	9	9	.500	4.11	26	26	13	0	1	0	181.2	181	106	83	17	4	99	2	138	9
J. Anderson, Appleton	12	7	.632	3.40	24	24	8	0	0	0	156	149	74	59	13	3	67	0	132	14
S. Anderson, Madison	3	2	.600	1.88	18	6	0	4	0	1	52.2	42	13	11	3	3	26	2	32	0
Anthony, Waterloo	10	4	.714	3.19	16	12	9	2	1	0	101.2	104	43	36	6	5	33	1	49	3
Antunez, Beloit✽	9	7	.563	3.26	36	9	2	20	1	8	88.1	73	35	32	5	0	41	5	77	6
Arigoni, Springfield✽	4	2	.667	5.43	26	3	1	10	0	1	63	80	40	38	4	3	34	5	40	3
Arney, Wisconsin Rapids	6	4	.600	2.47	16	16	5	0	0	0	98.1	84	38	27	16	1	33	0	98	0
Babcock, Appleton	7	7	.500	3.53	19	19	5	0	2	0	109.2	108	54	43	7	2	24	0	86	4
Banks, Quad Cities	13	6	.684	3.26	31	19	6	5	1	1	162.2	154	79	59	9	4	75	0	137	18
Barling, Clinton	5	8	.385	3.69	22	19	4	3	0	0	129.1	120	74	53	12	7	90	0	132	9
Bartley, Wausau	4	3	.571	2.60	25	1	0	15	0	4	45	42	29	13	6	1	28	2	27	4
Bass, Burlington	0	4	.000	4.10	4	4	1	0	0	0	26.1	23	18	12	3	0	10	1	15	0
Bautista, Clinton	3	8	.273	6.08	28	2	0	19	0	2	53.1	59	51	36	5	3	40	5	25	1
Benes, 20 Wausau-5 Burl.✽	6	11	.353	5.60	25	23	2	1	0	1	128.2	139	108	80	14	3	91	1	92	6
Boever, Springfield	0	0	.000	2.25	3	0	0	1	0	0	4	3	1	1	0	0	2	0	7	0
Borowsky, Quad Cities	0	0	.000	0.00	1	0	0	1	0	0	1	1	0	0	0	0	0	0	1	0
Boudreau, Quad Cities✽	4	0	1.000	2.18	16	1	1	10	0	1	53.2	48	13	13	1	1	11	0	32	3
Brahms, Quad Cities✽	6	3	.667	2.52	41	0	0	34	0	6	53.2	39	16	15	4	3	11	0	48	4
Brosious, Burlington	1	8	.111	4.64	12	12	0	0	0	0	66	60	41	34	9	3	35	0	35	5
Bryden, Danville	10	9	.526	4.38	22	22	6	0	3	0	135.2	125	87	66	4	15	79	1	101	11
Buonantony, Quad Cities	12	4	.750	3.91	26	26	5	0	3	0	161	151	79	70	9	6	79	0	103	15
Carpio, Quad Cities	7	4	.636	3.48	30	10	4	8	1	2	101	101	52	39	7	5	60	1	70	3
Cary, Madison	4	4	.500	5.40	23	1	0	4	0	1	43.1	47	29	26	7	2	27	0	39	1
Castillo, Wausau	1	3	.250	7.82	11	7	1	0	0	0	35.2	61	43	31	6	0	23	0	18	5
Clarke, Quad Cities	11	7	.611	2.91	25	23	9	0	1	0	164	155	70	53	13	9	42	0	81	4
Cline, Clinton	0	0	.000	0.00	1	0	0	1	0	0	0.2	0	0	0	0	0	1	0	1	0
Clutterbuck, Beloit	13	6	.684	3.63	26	26	8	0	4	0	173.2	165	84	70	14	2	56	3	138	9
Collins, Springfield	10	8	.556	3.85	25	25	2	0	0	0	145	136	86	62	12	3	71	2	81	13
Cook, Burlington	2	3	.400	4.22	18	2	0	9	0	3	42.2	47	30	20	1	1	15	1	37	6
Cox, Springfield	5	3	.625	2.56	15	13	2	2	0	0	84.1	82	46	24	7	4	29	1	68	8
Crews, Clinton	12	12	.500	2.68	28	28	16	0	1	0	188	171	78	56	10	3	40	0	145	9
Cushing, Waterloo✽	0	1	.000	9.50	8	3	0	2	0	0	18	29	26	19	2	2	21	0	9	4
Derksen, Beloit	3	3	.500	1.79	18	5	2	7	0	1	55.1	39	18	11	2	0	16	2	48	2
Dixon, Wausau✽	1	8	.111	6.66	33	10	1	11	0	0	102.2	114	99	76	17	5	96	2	65	17
Dowies, Burlington✽	3	3	.500	6.44	15	4	2	8	0	1	43.1	57	35	31	5	3	33	0	29	1
Doyle, Waterloo	7	6	.538	3.94	21	20	2	1	0	0	121	113	61	53	9	7	55	1	124	7
Dozier, Springfield	11	6	.647	4.20	26	18	3	4	1	1	133	131	74	62	10	8	52	4	87	14
Droschak, Springfield	4	3	.571	2.08	14	7	2	5	1	0	52	37	17	12	3	3	27	2	36	4
Dunn, Springfield	12	7	.632	4.32	27	27	4	0	1	0	162.2	149	92	78	21	3	90	6	116	11
Duquette, Beloit✽	3	4	.429	3.99	22	5	1	10	0	2	56.1	52	32	25	2	1	28	3	59	6
Edwards, Madison✽	12	4	.750	3.21	29	22	8	2	0	0	168.1	164	77	60	11	2	52	2	159	18
Elpin, Waterloo	2	3	.400	8.13	11	3	0	5	0	0	27.2	37	29	25	6	1	12	1	18	0
Embser, Beloit	1	5	.167	3.80	9	8	2	0	0	0	47.1	58	29	20	3	1	20	1	51	7
Enriquez, Wausau	0	1	.000	12.10	13	0	0	4	0	0	19.1	32	31	26	3	1	24	1	18	4
Epperson, Appleton	0	0	.000	27.00	1	0	0	1	0	0	1	1	3	3	0	2	2	0	0	1
Epple, Springfield✽	6	3	.667	4.65	28	9	0	6	0	1	69.2	67	37	36	10	4	30	4	54	6
Erickson, Clinton✽	0	0	.000	6.97	8	4	0	2	0	0	20.2	17	20	16	2	4	23	0	19	2
Eufemia, Wisconsin Rapids	2	1	.667	1.71	27	0	0	20	0	9	58	47	18	11	3	1	17	3	36	1
G. Evans, Beloit	3	8	.273	4.16	27	10	3	4	0	0	101.2	111	57	47	8	2	47	5	67	5
M. Evans, Wausau✽	6	7	.462	2.83	35	0	0	32	0	12	60.1	51	26	19	7	2	17	2	73	1
Fedor, Beloit	6	7	.462	5.00	55	0	0	34	0	14	77.1	67	57	43	6	4	65	7	79	16
Feeley, Madison	0	0	.000	6.00	2	0	0	2	0	0	3	3	2	2	0	2	2	0	2	2
Fellows, Madison	12	7	.632	3.29	28	25	5	1	2	0	175	156	84	64	6	5	81	3	107	5
Ferguson, Cedar Rapids	7	9	.438	3.67	35	17	5	8	1	1	142.1	128	77	58	15	3	72	3	128	10

Pitcher—Club	W.	L.	Pct.	ERA.	G.	GS.	CG.	GF.	ShO.	Sv.	IP.	H.	R.	ER.	HR.	HB.	BB.	Int. BB.	SO.	WP.
Flannery, Appleton	2	0	1.000	1.42	16	0	0	16	0	10	19	20	3	3	1	0	3	1	17	1
Flinn, 8 Beloit-9 Madison°	4	4	.500	6.41	17	11	1	2	0	0	66	77	56	47	16	3	29	0	48	4
Flores, Wisconsin Rapids	0	3	.000	7.32	6	3	0	1	0	0	19.2	25	18	16	6	0	18	1	20	3
Fossas, Burlington	8	9	.471	3.08	25	18	10	1	1	0	146.1	121	63	50	7		33	1	115	4
Foster, Wisconsin Rapids°	0	0	.000	5.00	6	0	0	1	0	0	18	23	12	10	3	0	8	1	11	0
Freeburg, Cedar Rapids	3	6	.333	5.81	18	15	3	1	1	0	88.1	96	64	57	9	7	49	1	65	7
Fruge, Quad Cities	3	5	.375	4.50	11	11	0	0	0	0	58	55	32	29	4	1	45	0	32	5
Gammage, Burlington	3	7	.300	6.69	37	2	1	20	0	3	78	79	63	58	14	5	68	4	77	8
Gibson, Appleton	4	7	.364	4.38	14	14	1	0	0	0	72	66	46	35	5	2	53	1	37	13
Gilmartin, Beloit	1	0	1.000	6.23	20	2	0	7	0	0	34.2	40	30	24	1	2	29	1	12	6
Gomez, Burlington	0	0	.000	0.00	1	0	0	1	0	0	1	0	0	0	0	0	0	0	1	0
Grant, Clinton	16	5	.762	2.36	27	27	12	0	4	0	198.2	139	65	52	8	2	60	0	243	2
Gross, Wisconsin Rapids	0	1	.000	0.00	3	0	0	1	0	0	3.2	5	3	0	1	1	5	0	1	0
Hallgren, Madison	0	0	.000	4.91	6	1	0	0	0	0	11	10	8	6	1	0	9	0	11	0
Harris, Madison	0	1	.000	10.13	2	1	0	1	0	0	5.1	8	7	6	3	0	4	0	1	1
Hartman, Burlington	10	5	.667	4.52	27	26	1	0	0	0	141.1	143	89	71	10	11	84	0	101	11
Hayes, Wausau	7	7	.500	3.65	28	19	7	2	2	1	148	145	90	60	10	2	72	2	133	10
Heath, Appleton°	1	1	.500	3.86	6	6	0	0	0	0	25.2	25	13	11	1	1	25	0	19	1
Heckman, Madison	0	0	.000	54.00	1	0	0	0	0	0	0.1	3	3	2	0	0	0	0	0	0
Heidenreich, Cedar Rapids	11	9	.550	3.29	25	25	8	0	0	0	166.2	143	77	61	7	11	65	1	168	17
Henderson, Wisconsin Rapids°	8	11	.421	3.89	24	24	8	0	3	0	152.2	133	85	66	17	4	78	2	154	9
Henkemeyer, Wisconsin Rapids°.	4	7	.364	4.71	26	15	3	6	0	0	116.2	108	74	61	12	6	85	3	76	10
Hennessey, Cedar Rapids	4	4	.500	8.48	27	1	0	12	0	2	40.1	63	43	38	4	2	19	3	27	5
D. Henry, Burlington	2	0	1.000	0.00	4	4	0	0	0	0	18.2	6	0	0	0	1	6	0	25	0
T. Henry, Burlington°	0	1	.000	10.13	3	0	0	2	0	1	2.2	2	3	3	0	0	6	1	5	1
Herron, Madison	0	1	.000	0.93	8	0	0	4	0	2	19.1	7	2	2	0	0	5	2	20	4
Higgins, Wisconsin Rapids	4	4	.500	3.35	8	8	5	0	0	0	48.1	48	22	18	2	0	11	3	16	1
Hoban, Beloit	2	4	.333	5.92	9	9	0	0	0	0	48.2	61	38	32	5	0	16	1	37	1
Holland, Wausau	4	5	.444	3.61	12	12	4	0	2	0	67.1	58	44	27	9	0	45	0	58	8
Hudson, Burlington	6	1	.857	1.92	43	0	0	36	0	10	70.1	55	21	15	4	0	23	6	39	6
Jarrett, Madison	14	8	.636	4.29	28	28	6	0	1	0	189	207	100	90	11	2	46	0	121	7
Jeffcoat, Waterloo°	5	4	.556	4.06	9	9	3	0	0	0	62	58	29	28	9	1	15	1	68	0
M. Johnson, Wausau	9	7	.563	5.01	30	17	2	7	1	0	106	97	77	59	9	9	76	1	103	10
S. Johnson, Quad Cities	5	9	.357	4.98	19	15	3	0	0	0	99.1	111	66	55	5	1	36	0	72	5
W. Johnson, Waterloo°	8	7	.533	3.14	20	18	6	0	1	0	109	103	53	38	7	2	42	2	100	19
Jones, Appleton	2	4	.333	3.32	26	1	0	13	0	1	57	53	27	21	2	2	34	1	64	6
Kaufman, Quad Cities	10	5	.667	3.58	53	0	0	43	0	17	75.1	62	34	30	8	0	23	4	73	7
Kepshire, Cedar Rapids	3	1	.750	2.18	21	0	0	17	0	7	33	23	11	8	2	1	10	1	29	1
King, Danville	4	5	.444	5.35	37	0	0	26	0	3	74	87	56	44	6	4	41	1	34	5
Kinley, Wausau	0	0	.000	8.74	5	1	0	1	0	0	11.1	9	12	11	1	1	6	0	4	1
Kish, Springfield	4	4	.500	4.19	11	10	2	1	1	0	58	47	39	27	2	5	31	2	50	5
Klump, Wisconsin Rapids	1	6	.143	4.13	15	7	4	6	0	0	52.1	49	36	24	4	2	36	0	32	3
Kobernus, Madison°	7	2	.778	1.72	43	1	0	34	0	13	52.1	35	11	10	0	2	13	1	59	1
Kolotka, Madison	9	3	.750	3.50	49	0	0	42	0	8	54	54	24	21	3	5	22	6	47	2
Kouba, Wausau°	1	1	.500	6.41	14	3	0	6	0	1	39.1	47	29	28	7	4	16	0	23	2
Lambert, Clinton°	3	6	.333	2.52	29	2	0	19	0	5	71.1	52	20	20	7	0	24	1	64	1
Larcom, Wisconsin Rapids°	3	3	.500	4.01	16	1	0	9	0	2	33.2	38	21	15	4	2	20	3	24	2
Lindsey, Danville°	0	1	.000	6.39	10	1	1	4	0	0	25.1	33	26	18	4	5	18	0	14	2
Lintz, Waterloo	5	5	.500	3.86	37	1	0	25	0	5	74.2	73	39	32	6	2	35	10	58	4
Long, 12 Danville-15 Waterloo ..	8	7	.533	5.20	27	23	5	1	1	0	138.1	107	90	80	11	10	114	2	125	26
Lora, Danville	0	0	.000	4.74	5	2	0	2	0	0	19	20	10	10	1	0	8	1	8	0
Lovelace, Quad Cities°	4	6	.400	4.98	21	20	0	0	0	0	94	62	67	52	8	6	94	0	107	20
Lowery, Cedar Rapids	8	5	.615	3.82	51	1	1	36	0	3	92	90	52	39	4	6	35	5	78	3
Lugo, Danville	0	2	.000	10.13	10	0	0	3	0	0	24	35	30	27	3	1	16	1	13	5
Maitland, Appleton°	4	0	1.000	1.93	4	4	2	0	0	0	28	15	6	6	3	0	8	0	21	3
Maki, Burlington	2	7	.222	4.04	13	13	2	0	0	0	69	62	42	31	5	1	36	1	38	11
Malascewski, Wisconsin Rapids...	0	2	.000	5.40	6	3	1	2	0	1	25	27	20	15	2	2	14	3	14	3
Mancuso, Wisconsin Rapids°	2	4	.333	3.40	17	1	1	12	0	3	47.2	49	22	18	6	0	27	4	43	1
Mason, Springfield	10	5	.667	2.39	53	0	0	35	0	10	98	77	34	26	9	1	33	6	82	6
M. McDonald, Madison	1	1	.500	6.07	15	0	0	5	0	1	29.2	26	26	20	5	3	17	0	16	3
R. McDonald, Waterloo	11	5	.688	2.98	26	20	9	4	2	1	142	114	59	47	5	9	68	3	68	4
McKenzie, Danville	2	1	.667	3.27	13	4	2	9	0	7	44	41	24	16	2	0	15	0	24	0
McLane, Burlington°	10	6	.625	3.11	21	20	8	1	3	0	121.2	116	52	42	3	5	43	1	76	4
McMahon, Wisconsin Rapids	6	9	.400	4.50	19	17	6	2	2	0	102	95	60	51	10	2	67	0	63	9
Miglio, Waterloo°	3	7	.300	4.00	43	4	0	28	0	4	99	95	52	44	11	6	47	7	101	4
Mikesell, Wisconsin Rapids°	1	4	.200	2.70	13	1	0	8	0	1	30	27	15	9	2	0	16	1	22	1
Moore, Madison	3	5	.375	4.30	9	9	3	0	0	0	52.1	47	34	25	7	0	29	0	41	3
Murphy, Cedar Rapids°	3	7	.300	4.04	31	9	0	11	0	2	89	92	62	40	2	1	61	2	96	6
Murtha, Clinton°	5	12	.294	4.32	27	9	2	14	1	4	110.1	114	65	53	12	3	35	1	64	5
Myerchin, Beloit°	3	1	.750	5.73	17	1	0	8	0	0	37.2	34	29	24	7	1	24	1	28	1
Neely, Springfield	2	4	.333	3.76	33	0	0	26	0	12	55	43	31	23	5	3	21	5	38	5
Nenad, Clinton	4	6	.400	2.34	27	6	3	19	0	4	84.2	92	37	22	2	1	29	1	51	2
Niemann, Appleton	7	3	.700	2.97	21	9	2	6	2	1	88	69	39	29	1	6	38	0	68	6
Noworyta, Appleton	6	2	.750	3.45	12	12	2	0	1	0	75.2	66	35	29	4	1	32	0	41	1
Oliver, Danville	4	1	.800	3.00	15	0	0	13	0	4	21	27	13	7	0	1	10	4	15	2
Olshane, Madison	0	1	.000	2.57	8	0	0	7	0	1	7	8	3	2	1	1	6	1	5	0
Owens, Waterloo	5	2	.714	2.92	7	7	6	0	1	0	61.2	44	23	20	2	2	21	0	58	6
Page, Wisconsin Rapids°	0	0	.000	6.75	4	0	0	4	0	0	4	4	3	3	0	0	5	0	2	2
Pallas, Beloit	1	0	1.000	0.90	2	1	0	0	0	0	10	5	2	1	0	0	4	0	6	1
Parent, Wausau	0	6	.000	7.19	9	9	0	0	0	0	41.1	50	46	33	4	3	40	1	27	12
Pastrovich, Appleton	1	3	.250	1.49	37	0	0	32	0	13	78.2	65	19	13	3	2	21	2	68	4
Pettibone, Cedar Rapids	3	14	.176	5.88	26	26	2	0	0	0	127	115	105	83	15	14	101	0	92	21
Pittman, Springfield°	0	0	.000	7.41	9	0	0	2	0	0	17	29	15	14	3	0	10	1	18	4
Portugal, Wisconsin Rapids	9	8	.529	4.01	36	15	4	15	1	2	119	110	62	53	13	3	62	1	95	21
Price, Danville	10	16	.385	4.98	27	27	7	0	0	0	175.1	197	119	97	14	4	67	0	111	10
Ramirez, Wausau	7	1	.875	2.16	15	10	7	3	2	0	95.2	62	33	23	8	1	28	1	90	3
Reed, Springfield°	0	1	.000	7.71	8	0	0	6	0	0	14	21	16	12	1	0	15	1	4	1
Retzer, Madison	6	4	.600	2.52	12	11	2	0	1	0	75	60	31	21	6	0	18	0	62	2
Riley, Cedar Rapids	5	5	.500	6.03	29	8	0	11	0	0	65.2	74	54	44	9	3	51	4	67	6
Roche, Waterloo	6	5	.545	3.73	20	14	5	5	1	1	103.2	121	57	43	10	5	28	2	60	3
Roman, Waterloo	2	5	.286	5.15	24	5	1	12	0	2	57.2	64	42	33	5	0	37	5	56	13
Romero, Waterloo°	3	1	.750	2.03	7	4	1	1	0	1	31	22	11	7	2	1	21	0	30	0

Pitcher—Club	W.	L.	Pct.	ERA.	G.	GS.	CG.	GF.	ShO.	Sv.	IP.	H.	R.	ER.	HR.	HB.	BB.	Int. BB.	SO.	WP.
Ronan, Clinton	0	2	.000	7.50	6	0	0	4	0	0	12	15	11	10	0	1	5	0	10	0
Rosenbaum, Danville	2	6	.250	5.63	12	5	2	5	0	0	48	66	45	30	5	2	15	1	19	4
Rothey, Cedar Rapids*	5	3	.625	3.16	38	1	0	20	0	5	82.2	72	41	29	6	2	40	2	75	7
Salazer, Danville	3	3	.500	2.74	11	9	2	1	2	0	65.2	64	30	20	2	2	26	0	36	1
Scarpetta, Beloit*	0	2	.000	7.45	2	2	0	0	0	0	9.2	17	8	8	3	1	1	0	8	0
Schassler, Wausau	1	3	.250	4.78	5	5	0	0	0	0	26.1	22	18	14	2	1	16	0	15	1
Schmid, Burlington*	3	7	.300	4.06	41	3	2	18	0	3	71	76	40	32	7	2	30	4	67	6
Schneider, Appleton	1	3	.250	2.61	14	0	0	13	0	4	20.2	18	8	6	3	0	11	0	21	2
Schuckert, Appleton*	11	8	.579	4.56	21	21	3	0	3	0	128.1	123	74	65	8	4	64	0	91	4
Schulte, Burlington*	0	1	.000	9.95	4	0	0	2	0	1	6.1	8	8	7	0	0	2	0	6	0
Schumacher, Danville	2	4	.333	5.60	22	4	2	11	2	1	62.2	73	48	39	6	1	40	3	41	3
Shuleeta, Quad Cities*	0	4	.000	9.82	8	5	0	2	0	0	29.1	49	36	32	5	0	10	0	16	3
Silva, Springfield	10	7	.588	3.59	24	24	5	0	0	0	163	148	74	65	10	3	72	2	102	11
Silvas, Waterloo	2	0	1.000	2.70	4	3	0	0	0	0	23.1	17	7	7	1	1	13	0	12	1
Sismondo, Wausau*	2	8	.200	3.97	14	12	1	1	1	0	68	77	42	30	12	2	32	2	55	2
Skinner, Appleton	0	2	.000	11.40	5	2	0	3	0	0	15	20	21	19	3	1	15	0	3	1
D. Smith, Burlington	3	5	.375	3.35	19	10	0	6	0	0	80.2	78	40	30	5	7	40	1	32	7
S. Smith, Quad Cities	3	5	.375	5.40	30	4	0	9	0	1	93.1	103	64	56	11	4	46	0	57	4
Solomon, Appleton	3	1	.750	4.38	4	4	1	0	0	0	24.2	24	12	12	3	3	6	0	22	1
Sorce, Burlington	0	0	.000	0.00	1	0	0	1	0	0	2	1	0	0	0	3	0	0	0	0
Stalp, Cedar Rapids	3	9	.250	3.88	17	17	4	0	0	0	109	114	61	47	8	4	45	1	61	9
Suarez, Wisconsin Rapids	1	3	.250	7.11	9	3	0	2	0	0	25.1	31	22	20	4	2	18	1	17	8
Sullivan, Beloit	1	1	.500	6.48	16	1	0	9	0	1	25	29	22	18	1	3	17	2	15	1
Sutton, Appleton	6	5	.545	3.61	25	7	3	12	0	1	89.2	85	57	36	5	2	36	0	55	6
Swenson, Clinton*	7	5	.583	4.24	23	16	2	3	0	1	116.2	136	63	55	7	3	32	2	68	2
Tanzi, Appleton*	14	6	.700	2.22	24	17	12	5	4	0	166	123	55	41	7	6	64	1	142	9
Taylor, 19 Wausau-18 Burl	7	9	.438	4.18	37	9	2	14	0	3	112	100	64	52	8	6	63	1	95	8
Toliver, Cedar Rapids	6	7	.462	4.23	23	20	1	0	0	0	115	114	77	54	8	5	66	0	117	6
Vavrock, Madison	12	7	.632	3.72	30	29	6	0	1	0	193.1	203	97	80	22	1	49	0	127	4
Viskas, Quad Cities	0	0	.000	1.50	2	2	0	0	0	0	6	5	1	1	0	0	5	0	3	1
Walker, Beloit	8	6	.571	3.28	21	18	4	1	1	0	123.1	114	55	45	6	6	56	4	89	10
Waller, Madison	0	0	.000	0.00	2	0	0	1	0	0	2.2	0	0	0	0	0	3	0	0	1
Warren, Burlington*	5	6	.455	4.15	22	9	1	7	0	1	82.1	86	47	38	4	1	45	0	65	7
Watson, Beloit	2	6	.250	4.12	15	11	1	2	1	0	63.1	61	33	29	3	1	42	1	54	7
Weatherman, Madison	1	0	1.000	6.23	3	0	0	0	0	0	4.1	7	5	3	1	0	2	0	3	0
Wegman, Beloit	12	6	.667	2.81	25	25	10	0	1	0	179.2	176	77	56	11	3	38	3	129	7
Weiermiller, Wisconsin Rapids*	8	11	.421	3.62	24	23	9	1	2	0	159	140	79	64	14	4	82	2	147	10
Weir, Clinton	0	0	.000	9.00	6	0	0	4	0	0	9	13	11	9	2	1	9	0	6	1
Weissman, Quad Cities	1	2	.333	6.83	11	3	0	0	0	0	27.2	31	34	21	3	4	32	0	21	5
Whitmer, Wausau	5	6	.455	3.10	13	13	7	0	0	0	90	86	44	31	6	3	39	0	88	7
Wick, Waterloo*	0	5	.000	7.07	17	2	0	6	0	1	35.2	48	33	28	2	3	19	0	29	5
Wilcox, Clinton	8	11	.421	3.22	28	25	9	1	1	0	162	142	77	58	6	4	43	1	168	8
Wilhelmi, Clinton	0	0	.000	3.00	1	0	0	1	0	0	3	1	1	1	0	0	1	0	4	0
Williams, Danville	5	12	.294	5.70	23	20	3	2	1	0	120	133	96	76	6	9	76	0	79	8
Willis, Waterloo	0	2	.000	6.43	11	2	0	3	0	2	28	35	27	20	3	0	12	0	21	2
Winfield, Springfield	5	0	1.000	0.23	22	0	0	17	0	7	39.1	24	2	1	0	0	6	0	29	0
Wood, Beloit	1	0	1.000	7.41	7	0	0	3	0	1	17	19	16	14	3	1	6	2	28	3
Wright, 5 Wis. Rap.-15 Dan.	2	3	.400	4.50	20	3	0	11	0	2	58	66	35	29	6	3	21	1	28	5
Zwolensky, 23 Wausau-3 Burl	2	3	.400	2.42	26	3	1	15	0	0	52	40	23	14	5	0	25	3	38	3

BALKS—Price, 7; Wegman, 6; Barling, Doyle, Hayes, Portugal, D. Smith, 4 each; J. Anderson, Henkemeyer, Jeffcoat, 3 each; Benes, Bryden, Castillo, Dowies, Flinn, S. Johnson, Kolotka, Larcom, Lovelace, Lugo, Maki, Myerchin, Oliver, Warren, Weiermiller, Wick, Wilcox, Williams, 2 each; Ahern, S. Anderson, Antunez, Banks, Bartley, Bautista, Buonantony, Carpio, Clarke, Clutterbuck, Collins, Cox, Dixon, Dozier, G. Evans, Fellows, Ferguson, Gammage, Gibson, Gilmartin, Grant, Henderson, D. Henry, Higgins, W. Johnson, Jones, Long, Lowery, Mason, M. McDonald, R. McDonald, McKenzie, McMahon, Moore, Murphy, Nenad, Owens, Parent, Ramirez, Reed, Riley, Roche, Roman, Salazer, Schumacher, Shuleeta, S. Smith, Stalp, Swenson, Taylor, Toliver, Walker, Waller, Watson, Wood, 1 each.

COMBINATION SHUTOUTS—Heath-Niemann, Anderson-Jones-Sutton, Heath-Tanzi, Babcock-Sutton-Flannery, Maitland-Jones, Schuckert-Pastrovich, Appleton; Pallas-Antunez, Walker-Antunez-Sullivan, Embser-Fedor, Beloit; McLane-Gammage, D. Henry-Cook, D. Henry-Schmid, McLane-Warren-Hudson, Warren-Fossas-Cook, Cook-Schmid-Hudson, Smith-Hudson, Burlington; Heidenreich-Riley, Cedar Rapids; Murtha-Swenson, Grant-Lambert, Bautista-Lambert, Clinton; Price-McKenzie 2, Williams-Oliver, Ahern-Lora, Danville; Vavrock-Kolotka, Fellows-Edwards-Kolotka, Jarrett-Kobernus, Madison; Lovelace-Boudreau, Banks-Kaufman, Quad Cities; Cox-Neely, Collins-Neely, Silva-Winfield, Epple-Mason, Droschak-Neely, Epple-Cox, Springfield; Silvas-Lintz, Waterloo; Whitmer-Evans, Wausau.

NO-HIT GAME—Grant, Clinton, defeated Danville, 9-0, August 12.

NY-Pennsylvania League

CLASS A

CHAMPIONSHIP WINNERS IN PREVIOUS YEARS

1939—Olean*	.631	1954—Corning*	.621	1968—Auburn	.645
1940—Olean*	.625	1955—Hamilton*	.656	Oneonta (2nd)*	.558
1941—Jamestown	.618	1956—Wellsville*	.617	1969—Oneonta	.662
Bradford (2nd)†	.549	1957—Wellsville	.632	1970—Auburn	.623
1942—Jamestown*	.672	Erie (2nd)†	.598	1971—Oneonta	.662
1943—Lockport	.591	1958—Wellsville	.556	1972—Niagara Falls	.686
Wellsville (3rd)†	.532	Geneva (2nd)†	.548	1973—Auburn	.667
1944—Lockport	.608	1959—Wellsville†	.635	1974—Oneonta	.768
Jamestown (2nd)†	.565	1960—Erie	.643	1975—Newark	.688
1945—Batavia*	.677	Wellsville (2nd)†	.535	Newark	.714
1946—Jamestown‡	.672	1961—Geneva	.616	1976—Elmira	.727
Batavia‡	.672	Olean (4th)†	.512	Elmira	.703
1947—Jamestown*	.690	1962—Jamestown	.580	1977—Oneonta y	.671
1948—Lockport*	.603	Auburn (3rd)†	.521	Batavia	.600
1949—Bradford*	.635	1963—Auburn	.585	1978—Oneonta	.729
1950—Hornell	.653	Batavia (3rd)†	.485	Geneva z	.718
Olean (2nd)†	.568	1964—Auburn§	.622	1979—Geneva	.725
1951—Olean	.622	1965—Binghamton	.677	Oneonta z	.618
Hornell (3rd)†	.568	Binghamton	.607	1980—Oneonta y	.662
1952—Hamilton	.659	1966—Auburn x	.620	Geneva	.649
Jamestown (2nd)†	.643	Binghamton	.646	1981—Oneonta y	.658
1953—Jamestown*	.704	1967—Auburn	.667	Jamestown	.649

*Won championship and four-club playoff. †Won four-club playoff. ‡Jamestown and Batavia declared co-champions; Batavia defeated Jamestown in final of four-club playoff. §Won championship and two-club playoff. xWon split-season playoff. yLeague divided into Eastern and Western Divisions; won playoff. zLeague divided into Wrigley and Yawkey Divisions; won playoff. (NOTE—Known as Pennsylvania-Ontario-New York League from 1939 through 1956.)

STANDING OF CLUBS AT CLOSE OF SEASON, SEPTEMBER 2

EASTERN DIVISION

Club	W.	L.	T.	Pct.	G.B.
Oneonta (Yankees)	43	33	0	.566	....
Utica (Independent)	41	34	0	.547	1½
Little Falls (Mets)	38	38	0	.500	5
Auburn (Astros)	35	39	0	.473	7
Elmira (Red Sox)	34	40	1	.459	8

WESTERN DIVISION

Club	W.	L.	T.	Pct.	G.B.
Niagara Falls (White Sox)	42	34	0	.553	....
Jamestown (Expos)	36	38	1	.486	5
Geneva (Cubs)	36	39	0	.480	5½
Erie (Cardinals)	35	38	0	.479	5½
Batavia (Indians)	33	40	0	.452	7½

COMPOSITE STANDINGS OF CLUBS AT CLOSE OF SEASON, SEPTEMBER 2

Club	Ont.	N.F.	Utica	L.F.	Jmt.	Gen.	Erie	Aub.	Elm.	Bat.	W.	L.	T.	Pct.	G.B.
Oneonta (Yankees)	....	2	5	7	4	5	3	6	7	4	43	33	0	.566	....
Niagara Falls (White Sox)	2	....	1	3	7	5	6	7	4	7	42	34	0	.553	1
Utica (Independent)	7	3	....	11	2	5	1	1	7	4	41	34	0	.547	1½
Little Falls (Mets)	5	1	5	....	3	3	4	5	7	5	38	38	0	.500	5
Jamestown (Expos)	0	5	2	1	....	5	8	3	5	8	36	38	1	.486	6
Geneva (Cubs)	5	7	3	5	3	....	2	4	5	2	36	39	0	.480	6½
Erie (Cardinals)	1	6	3	0	8	6	....	2	5	4	35	38	0	.479	6½
Auburn (Astros)	4	1	6	5	3	5	6	....	1	4	35	39	0	.473	7
Elmira (Red Sox)	5	4	5	3	4	3	3	5	....	2	34	40	1	.459	8
Batavia (Indians)	4	5	4	3	4	2	5	4	2	....	33	40	0	.452	8½

Major league affiliations in parentheses.

Playoff—Niagara Falls defeated Oneonta, two games to one, to win league championship.

Regular-Season Attendance—Auburn, 38,075; Batavia, 26,378; Elmira, 50,189; Erie, 48,138; Geneva, 23,341; Jamestown, 38,139; Little Falls, 21,918; Niagara Falls, 29,883; Oneonta, 40,155; Utica, 34,014. Total, 350,230. Playoffs, 3,042. No all-star game.

Managers: Auburn, Bob Hartsfield; Batavia, Dave Oliver; Elmira, Dick Berardino; Erie, Joe Rigoli; Geneva, Tony Franklin; Jamestown, Moby Benedict; Little Falls, Sam Perlozzo; Niagara Falls, Fred Nelson; Oneonta, Ken Berry; Utica, Jim Gattis.

All-Star Team: 1B—Hennell, Utica; 2B—Alcala, Oneonta; 3B—Cochran, Little Falls; SS—Clements, Erie; OF—Alonzo, Utica; Felice, Little Falls; Lemon, Jamestown; C—Packer, Erie, and Rivera, Jamestown; RHP—Moretti, Utica, and Trujillo, Niagara Falls; LHP—Deshaies, Oneonta, and Tomaselli, Oneonta; DH—Horn, Elmira; Manager—Nelson, Niagara Falls.

(Compiled by Howe News Bureau, Boston, Mass.)

CLUB BATTING

Club	Pct.	G.	AB.	R.	OR.	H.	TB.	2B.	3B.	HR.	RBI.	GW.	SH.	SF.	HP.	BB.	Int. BB.	SO.	SB.	CS.	LOB.
Utica	.290	76	2545	498	437	739	1241	116	13	120	439	37	17	19	26	356	11	485	119	30	546
Jamestown	.273	75	2490	375	387	680	929	95	26	34	322	31	19	15	34	278	13	406	41	15	575
Elmira	.272	75	2558	429	429	697	1016	132	11	55	370	30	43	18	21	291	10	567	64	10	591
Little Falls	.264	76	2594	454	477	684	1106	114	16	92	390	31	20	14	26	326	17	690	89	30	561
Oneonta	.261	76	2527	424	359	659	944	103	28	42	363	35	30	34	23	370	15	561	125	19	575
Niagara Falls	.258	76	2490	414	355	643	992	103	36	58	361	36	42	20	19	315	16	509	100	22	562
Auburn	.254	75	2618	428	422	666	1048	115	24	73	356	29	21	17	15	317	17	581	70	21	550
Batavia	.249	73	2328	311	416	580	881	86	13	63	268	27	31	16	23	206	9	563	63	24	487
Erie	.248	73	2404	367	375	595	918	110	15	61	303	31	21	14	25	295	12	556	50	26	501
Geneva	.242	75	2436	381	424	589	915	97	17	65	336	32	18	16	25	307	6	707	161	48	493

INDIVIDUAL BATTING
(Leading Qualifiers for Batting Championship—205 or More Plate Appearances)

*Bats lefthanded.　†Switch-hitter.

Player and Club	Pct.	G.	AB.	R.	H.	TB.	2B.	3B.	HR.	RBI.	GW.	SH.	SF.	HP.	BB.	Int. BB.	SO.	SB.	CS.
Alonzo, Raymond, Utica*	.340	70	250	58	85	145	9	3	15	56	5	3	1	2	37	2	21	40	6
Hennell, John, Utica*	.337	76	270	68	91	178	18	0	23	69	4	0	3	1	56	5	49	2	1
Rivera, Hector, Jamestown*	.335	56	215	32	72	114	12	3	8	47	9	0	1	1	17	1	23	0	0
Lemon, Ricky, Jamestown*	.330	70	276	50	91	120	14	6	1	41	3	1	1	2	15	1	35	13	4
Stellern, Michael, Auburn	.329	52	210	30	69	109	9	2	9	43	4	3	2	1	16	1	39	6	1
Oliva, David, Elmira	.324	67	250	43	81	101	15	1	1	20	1	3	0	3	21	1	46	11	2
Wolfe, Ed, Utica	.321	74	277	63	89	137	16	1	10	48	7	2	2	4	29	0	40	9	1
Roomes, Rolondo, Geneva	.319	65	251	57	80	163	11	3	22	59	6	1	2	2	24	2	110	27	6
Hendershot, Robert, Utica	.314	71	261	59	82	136	10	1	14	42	3	1	3	1	32	0	47	17	2
Nattile, Samuel, Elmira*	.313	72	275	58	86	144	20	1	12	57	6	5	8	1	20	2	41	1	1

Departmental Leaders: G—Cangelosi, Hennell, Kinsel, 76; AB—Dotson, 307; R—Hennell, 68; H—Hennell, Lemon, 91; TB—Hennell, 178; 2B—Kent, Nattile, 20; 3B—Smajstrla, 10; HR—Hennell, 23; RBI—Hennell, 69; GWRBI—Rivera, 9; SH—Pedraza, 8; SF—Nattile, 8; HP—Alcala, Lumpe, Turgeon, 6; BB—Cangelosi, Hennell, Doggett, 56; IBB—Cochran, 7; SO—Cochran, 117; SB—Doggett, 66; CS—Doggett, 13.

(All Players—Listed Alphabetically)

Player and Club	Pct.	G.	AB.	R.	H.	TB.	2B.	3B.	HR.	RBI.	GW.	SH.	SF.	HP.	BB.	Int. BB.	SO.	SB.	CS.
Abone, Tony, Jamestown	.279	14	43	5	12	13	1	0	0	3	0	0	0	0	7	0	9	1	0
Adams, Peter, Oneonta	.282	39	103	17	29	41	4	1	2	17	2	3	0	0	9	0	28	5	0
Alcala, Jesus, Oneonta	.297	64	229	45	68	90	9	5	1	28	6	2	2	6	27	1	37	11	3
Allen, James, Geneva†	.242	75	260	30	63	106	15	2	8	44	3	3	6	2	35	1	31	2	3
Allen, Shane, Auburn	.234	45	167	24	39	68	6	1	7	22	1	4	1	0	14	2	34	4	0
Alomar, Luis V., Elmira*	.311	37	103	15	32	51	8	1	3	22	2	3	1	0	4	1	21	2	0
Alonzo, Raymond, Utica*	.340	70	250	58	85	145	9	3	15	56	5	3	1	2	37	2	21	40	6
Anderson, Eric, Auburn*	.125	6	8	3	1	1	0	0	0	3	0	0	0	0	7	0	2	0	0
Arnerich, Kenneth, Geneva	.171	44	123	18	21	27	4	1	0	10	0	1	0	4	21	0	54	7	3
Bailey, Mark J., Auburn†	.300	65	230	46	69	114	10	1	11	40	5	0	2	2	43	6	40	6	2
Barbagelata, Mark, Batavia	.221	52	131	13	29	42	7	0	2	8	1	1	0	0	12	0	32	4	3
Barton, Shawn, Geneva	.216	50	134	27	29	30	1	0	0	13	1	5	2	1	21	0	12	1	1
Bernstine, Nehames, Batavia	.312	71	263	48	82	105	13	2	2	18	1	6	0	2	32	1	41	31	11
Berroa, Eduardo, Elmira	.364	3	11	1	4	4	0	0	0	0	0	0	0	0	1	0	1	0	0
Biagini, Robert J., Elmira	.000	1	2	0	0	0	0	0	0	0	0	0	0	0	0	0	2	0	0
Bielawski, David, Utica	.231	41	117	10	27	31	4	0	0	10	0	1	2	1	15	0	19	1	1
Bonk, Thomas, Elmira*	.276	60	192	26	53	82	10	2	5	36	1	2	2	1	24	0	28	0	1
Brito, Bernardo, Batavia	.236	41	123	10	29	43	2	0	4	15	1	1	2	2	8	0	34	1	0
Burns, Christopher J., Erie*	.254	64	181	23	46	65	6	2	3	25	3	0	1	2	26	2	55	4	1
Burrell, Kevin, Geneva*	.207	47	140	14	29	40	8	0	1	10	0	2	1	2	7	1	30	0	0
Burton, Steven, Geneva*	.210	43	143	13	26	34	5	0	1	7	1	0	3	10	0	47	4	2	
Cangelosi, John, Niagara*	.289	76	277	60	80	118	15	4	5	38	4	7	2	4	56	4	51	45	7
Caraballo, Wilmer, Little Falls	.207	57	184	17	38	42	2	1	0	11	1	4	2	0	5	0	31	7	2
Castoria, Bruce Richard, Auburn	.218	58	220	30	48	97	16	0	11	41	3	1	2	0	26	2	74	2	1
Cawthon, Christopher D., Batavia*	.280	69	246	47	69	130	11	4	14	49	4	1	0	3	21	4	57	1	0
Champion, Randall Keith, Erie†	.370	12	27	6	10	11	1	0	0	3	1	0	1	0	4	0	1	0	0
Christensen, Kerry, Utica*	.149	30	74	14	11	19	2	0	2	11	1	0	2	0	19	0	21	1	1
Clements, David, Erie	.254	66	264	47	67	139	17	2	17	52	6	0	1	3	22	1	39	1	0
Cochran, Arnold, Batavia	.113	22	53	6	6	7	1	0	0	2	0	1	0	2	6	0	26	1	0
Cochrane, David, Little Falls†	.301	70	269	51	81	167	16	2	22	62	6	0	1	0	39	7	117	3	0
Coleman, Moses, Batavia†	.186	37	97	13	18	31	2	1	3	13	1	0	2	2	22	0	41	0	0
Cordner, Steven, Geneva	.269	73	275	42	74	116	10	4	8	45	3	1	0	0	36	0	76	5	3
Coyle, Rocky, Utica	.322	37	143	25	46	74	8	1	6	21	1	0	1	3	11	1	17	7	4
Dale, Wayne C., Batavia	.250	27	76	10	19	27	2	0	2	10	2	2	0	0	7	0	20	0	1
Datz, Jeffrey, Auburn	.224	36	116	15	26	42	4	0	4	15	3	0	1	0	15	0	24	1	1
DeJesus, Jose E., Niagara	.219	44	128	13	28	35	4	0	1	14	0	4	1	0	8	0	28	1	1
DeMatties, Stephen, Utica*	.289	59	149	34	43	94	7	1	14	32	3	1	0	2	36	0	37	2	0
Destrade, Orestes, Oneonta†	.232	64	194	44	45	71	12	1	4	30	3	0	4	3	38	4	56	11	2
Diaz, Carlos, Batavia	.220	40	118	10	26	40	5	0	3	10	0	2	0	0	3	0	28	0	0
Dishman, Curtis, Jamestown*	.229	73	249	30	57	79	9	2	3	32	4	2	4	2	36	3	43	1	0
Doggett, Geoff, Geneva†	.283	75	283	67	80	85	5	0	0	19	1	2	1	1	56	2	65	66	13
Dophied, W. Tracy, Auburn*	.282	48	170	28	48	80	8	3	6	25	0	3	0	0	18	1	29	8	0
Dotson, W. Hardy, Jamestown*	.261	74	307	56	80	98	9	3	1	28	2	3	1	35	3	37	11	3	
Dreizler, Robin, Utica	.234	50	145	18	34	57	2	0	7	20	2	1	0	0	16	0	34	1	1
Echols, Tracy, Batavia	.091	4	11	1	1	4	0	0	1	1	0	0	0	0	1	0	2	0	0
Elway, John, Oneonta*	.318	42	151	26	48	70	6	2	4	25	1	0	2	4	28	0	25	13	3
Emmert, Kenneth, Geneva	.242	56	186	29	45	77	9	4	5	33	6	0	3	0	22	1	35	7	4
Fagan, Mark, Batavia	.000	10	1	0	0	0	0	0	0	0	0	0	0	0	0	0	0	0	0
Fagan, Pat, Utica*	.000	28	4	0	0	0	0	0	0	0	0	0	0	0	0	0	2	0	0
Farmar, Damon, Geneva†	.197	57	183	27	36	51	7	1	2	20	1	4	0	0	29	0	70	21	3
Felice, Jason J., Little Falls	.301	75	292	63	88	164	13	3	19	64	6	0	3	1	42	1	52	23	3
Fennell, Michael, Oneonta*	.246	65	203	29	50	83	7	4	6	33	3	3	1	0	53	2	56	5	1
Ferguson, James, Oneonta	.305	36	118	23	36	57	9	3	2	17	1	5	3	2	14	0	21	3	0
Flores, Edison, Niagara Falls	.132	15	38	1	5	5	0	0	0	4	1	3	0	0	2	0	9	0	0
Garrett, Augie, Utica	.188	28	85	9	16	29	1	0	4	15	2	0	0	0	7	0	22	1	3
Gasparino, Daniel, Oneonta	.212	30	66	9	14	22	3	1	1	5	0	0	1	0	11	0	17	1	0
Gatlin, Michael, Oneonta*	.246	20	61	9	15	17	2	0	0	7	1	0	1	3	6	0	10	1	1
Gattis, James, Utica	.429	8	7	2	3	6	0	0	1	4	1	0	0	0	1	0	1	0	0
Gayton, William, Niagara Falls*	.243	66	222	35	54	76	9	2	3	31	3	4	0	1	31	4	27	2	0
Geels, Robbie, Elmira*	.239	49	142	19	34	46	5	2	1	18	1	2	0	2	23	2	23	2	1
Gill, Gary, Erie	.160	44	125	14	20	21	1	0	0	4	1	0	0	0	12	1	37	4	2
Giordano, Donald, Oneonta	.254	20	59	8	15	21	3	0	1	3	2	1	1	3	10	0	14	1	1
Gjesdal, Brent, Oneonta	.269	64	201	34	54	73	7	3	2	30	2	0	3	0	38	1	50	16	3
Greenwell, Michael, Elmira*	.269	72	268	57	72	102	10	1	6	36	5	4	3	3	37	0	37	5	1
Hall, Mark, Jamestown	.209	21	43	7	9	9	0	0	0	3	0	1	1	2	4	1	12	0	1
Hartshorn, Ronald, Little Falls	.000	14	0	1	0	0	0	0	0	0	0	0	0	0	0	0	0	0	0
Hawkins, Johnny, Oneonta†	.248	42	137	19	34	43	3	0	2	21	0	2	7	1	0	18	3	28	1	0
Hayner, Kenneth, Utica	.253	56	190	31	48	71	9	1	4	21	2	4	1	3	12	0	49	5	1
Hendershot, Robert, Utica	.314	71	261	59	82	136	10	1	14	42	3	1	3	1	32	0	47	17	2
Henley, Michael, Niagara Falls*	.273	64	205	41	56	103	15	1	10	43	7	0	4	1	23	4	54	1	0
Hennell, John, Utica*	.337	76	270	68	91	178	18	0	23	69	4	0	3	1	56	5	49	2	1
Hines, Bruce, Utica†	.258	52	163	29	42	59	6	1	3	12	2	0	0	1	30	2	44	13	3

Player and Club	Pct.	G.	AB.	R.	H.	TB.	2B.	3B.	HR.	RBI.	GW.	SH.	SF.	HP.	BB.	Int. BB.	SO.	SB.	CS.
Hinson, Bobby Joe, Auburn	.292	42	130	33	38	47	5	2	0	12	1	0	0	1	23	1	12	7	2
Hocutt, Michael, Jamestown°	.323	35	127	28	41	88	5	3	12	39	3	1	0	4	14	0	19	2	0
Holecek, Joseph, Geneva	.189	10	37	1	7	10	3	0	0	1	0	0	0	1	1	0	15	0	0
Holliday, Scot, Little Falls	.231	66	208	35	48	85	8	1	9	31	2	1	4	2	37	2	85	1	2
Holmes, Andre, Batavia	.091	11	11	2	1	1	0	0	0	0	0	0	0	0	1	0	5	0	0
Horn, Samuel, Elmira°	.300	61	213	47	64	112	13	1	11	48	3	0	0	1	40	2	59	2	0
Howard, J. Christopher, Elmira†	.196	53	163	21	32	41	6	0	1	13	3	3	0	2	23	1	51	3	1
Howroyd, Richard, Batavia	.214	15	28	2	6	6	0	0	0	2	1	0	0	0	2	0	8	0	0
Hurst, Dale A., 3 Batavia-11 Erie	1.000	14	1	1	1	1	0	0	0	0	0	0	0	0	0	0	0	0	0
Jacobson, Jeffrey, Auburn	.205	39	127	20	26	44	6	0	4	17	2	1	1	7	22	1	23	1	0
Jacoby, Donald, Utica°	.350	43	143	26	50	83	10	1	7	25	0	0	3	24	1	25	3	4	
Jelks, Patrick, Elmira	.287	57	157	19	45	63	13	1	1	23	0	1	1	1	17	0	35	2	0
Jones, Gary, Geneva°	.200	2	5	1	1	4	0	0	1	1	0	0	0	0	1	0	1	0	0
Jongewaard, Steven, Elmira	.265	58	185	31	49	60	8	0	1	18	1	4	1	3	19	0	50	1	0
Jose, Manuel, Elmira†	.265	40	113	17	30	35	5	0	0	13	1	4	0	0	14	0	32	6	1
Keeton, Garry, Niagara Falls	.250	6	20	4	5	7	0	1	0	1	0	0	0	0	2	0	4	1	0
Kent, Wesley, Niagara Falls	.277	75	282	48	78	164	20	3	20	64	7	0	2	3	20	3	91	0	3
Kiesling, Lawrence, Auburn	.207	48	164	25	34	62	5	1	7	26	3	2	3	2	22	0	48	3	0
King, Reginald, Jamestown°	.271	17	48	4	13	17	2	1	0	4	1	0	0	1	5	0	12	0	0
Kinsel, David, Niagara Falls	.267	76	251	37	67	79	8	2	0	34	3	4	3	2	50	1	32	2	2
Kordeck, David, Utica	.074	16	27	4	2	3	1	0	0	1	0	1	0	0	2	0	21	1	0
Lajszky, Werner, Little Falls	.182	4	11	2	2	3	1	0	0	0	0	0	0	3	0	0	2	1	0
LaTorre, Pedro, Erie	.268	67	246	45	66	89	13	2	2	20	1	2	2	0	40	0	33	15	4
Lauck, Jeffrey, Erie†	.257	51	109	23	28	49	7	1	4	17	1	2	0	2	38	1	32	5	3
Lauziere, Michael, Jamestown°	.253	32	91	8	23	35	4	1	2	10	2	0	1	1	10	0	23	0	0
Leggitt, Eric W., Jamestown°	.242	54	190	25	46	65	6	2	3	27	1	2	1	3	14	0	42	1	0
Lemon, Ricky, Jamestown°	.330	70	276	50	91	120	14	6	1	41	3	1	1	2	15	1	35	13	4
Liska, Anthony, Little Falls	.255	23	51	9	13	15	2	0	0	4	0	1	0	0	6	0	16	0	1
Lumpe, James, Jamestown°	.242	57	186	28	45	54	4	1	1	15	2	2	1	6	22	0	19	1	0
Madison, Dwight, Batavia	.261	17	23	4	6	7	1	0	0	2	0	0	1	1	4	0	10	2	0
Maggio, Douglas, Batavia	.080	11	25	1	2	2	0	0	0	0	0	0	0	2	0	0	5	0	0
Martinez, Ray, Batavia°	.533	5	15	3	8	14	0	0	2	3	1	0	0	2	0	3	0	0	
Maynor, Howard, Oneonta	.259	9	27	8	7	13	3	0	1	7	1	0	0	0	3	0	12	0	0
McIver, Lawrence, Auburn	.256	39	129	23	33	71	8	6	6	27	0	1	0	2	13	1	47	1	1
McPhail, Marlin, Little Falls	.270	22	74	12	20	29	3	0	2	11	0	0	1	0	11	1	16	3	0
Medina, Pedro, Oneonta†	.266	60	214	33	57	68	6	1	1	32	2	1	5	0	10	0	43	10	0
Merritt, Kenneth, Little Falls	.258	64	217	30	56	79	11	0	4	18	0	1	0	2	9	0	49	6	3
Metasavage, John, Little Falls°	.258	64	217	32	56	83	9	0	6	24	0	4	0	2	31	3	55	6	1
Minor, Bruster, Elmira	.000	19	1	0	0	0	0	0	0	0	0	0	0	0	0	0	0	0	0
Mitchell, Charles, Batavia	.236	60	216	29	51	82	7	0	8	34	4	2	4	2	17	0	29	13	3
Mitchell, William, Erie	.000	21	1	0	0	0	0	0	0	0	0	0	0	0	0	0	1	0	0
Morander, Ronald, Erie	.188	47	144	24	27	29	2	0	0	13	1	1	1	1	22	1	49	1	2
Moss, Barry, Utica°	.317	47	164	31	52	96	11	3	9	44	3	1	3	1	23	0	18	8	1
Nattile, Samuel, Elmira°	.313	72	275	58	86	144	20	1	12	57	6	5	8	1	20	2	41	1	1
Nichting, Timothy, Jamestown	.130	26	69	9	9	10	1	0	0	6	1	1	0	3	17	1	15	0	0
Nittoli, Michael, Niagara Falls	.294	27	68	11	20	25	3	1	0	7	1	0	0	0	4	0	25	0	0
O'Regan, Daniel, Oneonta°	.149	40	114	17	17	27	2	1	2	10	1	0	0	0	23	2	38	7	0
Oliva, David, Elmira	.324	67	250	43	81	101	15	1	1	20	1	3	0	3	21	1	46	11	2
Packer, William, Erie	.257	63	226	31	58	103	14	2	9	32	5	0	1	2	26	1	68	2	0
Parker, Marvin, Little Falls°	.277	24	65	11	18	25	1	0	2	8	1	0	2	1	15	0	14	1	2
Pasqua, Daniel, Oneonta°	.294	4	17	3	5	12	1	0	2	4	0	0	0	2	0	3	1	0	
Pasquale, Jeffrey, Erie	.215	58	191	28	41	61	8	0	4	19	2	3	0	1	23	2	54	2	2
Pedraza, Nelson, Batavia	.200	57	170	14	34	48	5	0	3	10	0	8	0	2	3	0	45	1	0
Perez, Edgar, Niagara Falls	.197	54	142	15	28	46	2	5	2	18	2	5	3	1	20	0	40	3	0
Peters, Rodney, Batavia	.281	53	178	29	50	70	6	4	2	14	2	2	0	3	12	0	47	6	2
Phillips, Stephen, Little Falls°	.249	65	209	37	52	70	11	2	1	26	3	5	0	4	27	2	52	3	4
Picchioni, Joseph, Utica	.237	41	76	17	18	23	2	0	1	8	1	2	1	4	6	0	18	8	1
Redfield, Joseph, Little Falls	.286	54	206	44	59	107	14	5	8	57	7	0	1	2	31	0	46	11	1
Reyes, Rafael J., Batavia	.000	2	5	0	0	0	0	0	0	0	0	0	0	0	0	0	1	0	0
Richardson, Billy Joe, Elmira	.262	47	122	13	32	44	1	1	3	23	1	3	0	0	11	0	35	0	0
Riggs, James, Oneonta°	.309	72	272	45	84	122	16	2	6	44	4	1	5	0	35	1	32	9	1
Rivera, Hector, Jamestown	.335	56	215	32	72	114	12	3	8	47	9	0	1	1	17	1	23	0	0
Rivera, Ricardo, Auburn†	.290	51	193	27	56	66	5	1	1	14	0	2	2	1	20	1	27	18	7
Roarke, Thomas, Auburn	.360	27	100	19	36	51	3	0	4	18	0	0	0	0	12	0	25	2	0
Roath, Steven, Erie°	.235	55	162	17	38	48	3	2	1	13	2	1	1	3	10	0	29	2	3
Roe, Michael, Jamestown	.231	5	13	1	3	3	0	0	0	2	0	0	0	0	2	0	4	0	0
Roehner, Mark, Jamestown	.229	10	35	2	8	11	3	0	0	3	0	0	0	0	6	0	10	0	0
Roman, Miguel, Batavia	.295	59	200	21	59	90	9	2	6	27	2	4	3	1	4	1	36	1	0
Roomes, Rolondo, Geneva	.319	65	251	57	80	163	11	3	22	59	6	1	2	2	24	2	110	27	6
Rossi, Thomas, Erie	.239	69	243	30	58	86	16	0	4	30	2	4	1	2	23	0	38	2	2
Ruffner, William, Oneonta	.193	59	171	28	33	50	4	2	3	22	3	4	4	1	19	1	53	6	1
Russell, Anthony, Oneonta	.281	30	121	15	34	49	5	2	2	15	1	1	1	1	12	0	22	20	2
Saccoccio, Michael, Jamestown	.288	18	52	5	15	16	1	0	0	2	0	1	0	1	7	1	13	0	0
Sanchez, Miguel, Little Falls	.227	7	22	4	5	8	0	0	1	2	0	0	0	0	2	0	5	0	0
Sedar, Edward, Niagara Falls	.287	61	202	48	58	101	9	5	8	30	1	1	0	5	28	0	54	17	4
Shirley, Gregory, Little Falls	.116	24	43	5	5	10	2	0	1	1	0	0	0	2	12	0	21	0	0
Skripko, Scott J., Elmira	.244	65	221	48	54	91	10	0	9	33	5	7	1	2	30	0	76	29	2
Smajstrla, Craig, Niagara Falls†	.304	63	270	38	82	116	11	10	1	29	4	6	2	1	14	0	21	19	3
Smith, Derick, Geneva	.248	53	161	27	40	53	4	0	3	19	1	3	0	4	21	0	30	0	1
Springer, Steven, Little Falls	.246	67	244	49	60	104	11	0	11	38	2	2	0	3	34	1	56	9	3
Stacheit, Glen, Jamestown	.250	9	36	8	9	14	2	0	1	7	1	0	1	0	5	0	5	0	0
Stellern, Michael, Auburn	.329	52	210	30	69	109	9	2	9	43	4	3	2	1	16	1	39	6	1
Stewart, Charles, Geneva	.198	32	96	9	19	33	5	0	3	13	1	0	0	1	5	0	25	3	1
Stovall, Kelvin, Batavia	.000	1	0	0	0	0	0	0	0	0	0	0	0	0	0	0	0	0	0
Swain, Steven, Auburn	.203	74	237	28	48	76	9	5	3	24	3	0	1	0	16	0	86	4	3
Szajko, Daniel, Jamestown	.290	65	238	41	69	81	7	1	1	17	0	3	0	4	34	0	36	9	3
Tarnow, Greg, Geneva	.139	54	165	15	23	40	8	0	3	20	2	1	0	4	12	0	73	1	1
Thiessen, Timothy, Jamestown	.287	75	272	36	78	102	15	3	1	37	2	2	1	4	28	2	49	2	4
Thomas, James, Auburn†	.264	30	129	27	34	45	9	1	0	8	2	0	1	0	18	0	10	3	1
Thompson, Richard, Auburn	.212	73	288	50	61	75	12	1	0	21	0	2	4	2	47	0	61	4	2
Thornton, John, Batavia	.193	26	57	8	11	15	1	0	1	2	0	0	0	0	14	0	19	0	0
Toothman, Michael, Niagara Falls	.232	62	211	32	49	83	6	2	8	30	2	3	1	0	34	0	54	8	1

Player and Club	Pct.	G.	AB.	R.	H.	TB.	2B.	3B.	HR.	RBI.	GW.	SH.	SF.	HP.	BB.	Int. BB.	SO.	SB.	CS.
Turgeon, Stephen, Erie	.305	70	262	49	80	146	18	3	14	50	4	0	4	6	31	3	58	10	5
Valera, Alcadio, Batavia†	.131	28	61	9	8	10	2	0	0	2	0	1	0	2	9	0	27	0	0
Walker, Steven, Little Falls	.000	15	0	1	0	0	0	0	0	0	0	0	0	0	0	0	0	0	0
Wallace, Patrick, Erie	.292	45	96	16	28	37	4	1	1	11	1	3	0	2	7	0	15	1	2
Washington, Randy, Batavia	.289	65	225	31	65	107	12	0	10	46	7	0	4	1	23	3	48	2	5
Willman, Timothy, Erie	.232	32	99	12	23	29	0	0	2	12	1	2	2	0	10	0	38	0	0
Wilson, John, Little Falls*	.294	69	282	51	83	115	10	2	6	33	3	2	0	4	25	0	73	15	8
Wolfe, Ed, Utica	.321	74	277	63	89	137	16	1	10	48	7	2	2	4	29	0	40	9	1
Woodcock, Robert, Oneonta	.173	33	52	9	9	9	0	0	0	6	0	2	0	0	12	0	10	2	1
Woods, Tony, Geneva	.262	73	282	45	74	116	11	2	9	45	7	2	4	3	34	0	74	18	8
Worrell, Todd, Erie	.148	17	27	1	4	4	0	0	0	2	0	2	0	0	1	0	10	0	0
Wright, Ronald, Oneonta	.294	8	17	2	5	6	1	0	0	2	0	0	0	0	2	0	6	2	0
Ybarra, Troy, Niagara Falls*	.100	18	40	4	4	4	0	0	0	5	0	0	0	0	2	0	7	0	0

The following pitchers, listed alphabetically by club, with games in parentheses, had no plate appearances, primarily through use of designated hitters:

AUBURN—Blas, William (7); Bombard, Richard (17); Callahan, Michael (14); Cerefin, Michael (4); Hogan, Michael (10); Kasprzak, Michael (13); Kizer, Craig (18); Meadows, Geoffrey (17); Perkins, Ray (29); Polemir, Miguel (10); Riewerts, Thomas (22); Schimpf, Rex (16); Shoupee, Jamey (3).

BATAVIA—Barkley, Jeffrey (15); Beck, Paul (1); Clark, Edward (8); Connolly, Michael (7); Conroy, Steven (23); Cushing, Stephen (2); Elpin, Ralph (1); Emmons, Edward (15); Figueroa, Carlos (3); Filippo, Richard (15); Keeler, Jeffrey (24); Ortiz, Andrew (7); Pierorazio, Wesley (13); Poindexter, Michael (18); Snyder, Mark (2); Wick, David (14).

ELMIRA—Diez, Scott (14); Hill, Ronnie (15); Key, John (16); Lockhart, Bruce (18); Mitchell, Charles (23); Rochford, Michael (16); Rodriguez, Carlos (17); Sellers, Jeffrey (17); Silva, Jesus (14).

ERIE—Boever, Joseph (19); Carrasco, Ernest (14); Carson, Henry (15); Donathan, William (15); Dunn, Bruce (17); Farley, Brian (14); Maldonado, Ovidio (1); Mills, Kenneth (23); Shade, Michael (13); Suggs, Tyris (3); Young, John (10).

GENEVA—Adamczak, James (16); Blevins, Brad (20); Cook, Mitchell (15); Fruge, Jeffrey (14); Isgett, David (20); Lockie, Randolph (9); Pantaleo, Joe (10); Serafini, Rudolph (16); Shulleeta, Michael (10); Tuller, Brian (8); Weissman, Craig (14).

JAMESTOWN—Baldrick, Robert (14); Dopson, John (15); Kinns, Glenn (14); McIntosh, James (5); Miller, Richard (12); Mitchell, Frederick (10); Ratliff, Daniel (5); Roy, Jacques (16); Schulte, Michael (13); Skorupa, Elliot (7); Valliant, Robert (11); Waymire, Ronald (22).

LITTLE FALLS—Arnold, Gail (22); Boyles, John (19); Foulks, Stuart (16); Gardner, Wesley (23); Gooden, Dwight (2); Jensen, David (17); Paul, Rick (16); Pruitt, Edwin (26); Robair, Michael (1); Teate, Kevin (14); Weston, Michael (17); Wyatt, David (1).

NIAGARA FALLS—Cruz, Gregorio (12); Devincenzo, Richard (1); Gibson, Scott (11); Guzman, Pedro (22); Heath, Allan (14); Moses, John (29); Noworyta, Steven (1); Schneider, Paul (17); Skinner, John (14); Sunde, Bjerne (15); Trujillo, Michael (12).

ONEONTA—Bailey, Boyce (3); Bailey, Kirk (13); Birtsas, Timothy (6); Bone, Patrick (11); Bryant, John (5); Byron, Timothy (12); Compagno, Steven (3); Corsi, James (15); Deshaies, James (15); Doty, Paul (16); Ferrin, Trent (15); Graham, Randy (22); Lindsey, Edward (1); Morgan, Stacy (14); Seidel, Richard (4); Tomaselli, Charles (15); White, Randall (13).

UTICA—Green, Jeffrey (19); Jones, Bob (3); Livesay, Michael (9); Merlach, Scott (14); Moretti, Roy (42); Naughton, Timothy (5); Norton, Randy (14); Perrino, Dominic (15); Peterson, Brian (26); Thomas, David (17); Weatherman, David (4); Zmudosky, Thomas (17).

GRAND SLAM HOME RUNS—Dematties, 2; Allen, Cochrane, Coleman, Dreizler, Gattis, Lauck, Maynor, McPhail, Moss, Redfield, Richardson, Rossi, Springer, 1 each.

AWARDED FIRST BASE ON CATCHER'S INTERFERENCE—Burton (Diaz); Peters (Willman).

CLUB FIELDING

Club	Pct.	G.	PO.	A.	E.	DP.	PB.	Club	Pct.	G.	PO.	A.	E.	DP.	PB.
Jamestown	.969	75	1882	779	84	45	19	Batavia	.954	73	1791	784	125	83	16
Niagara Falls	.957	76	1913	804	123	66	25	Auburn	.952	75	2000	809	142	59	19
Utica	.957	76	1933	801	123	41	19	Geneva	.950	75	1931	712	138	58	21
Erie	.956	73	1892	757	121	59	17	Little Falls	.949	76	1962	709	145	50	35
Oneonta	.956	76	1996	790	128	62	10	Elmira	.936	75	1913	785	183	49	11

INDIVIDUAL FIELDING

*Throws lefthanded.

FIRST BASEMEN

Player and Club	Pct.	G.	PO.	A.	E.	DP.	Player and Club	Pct.	G.	PO.	A.	E.	DP.
Adams, Oneonta	1.000	1	2	0	0	0	Gayton, Niagara Falls	.980	7	49	1	1	4
J. Allen, Geneva	1.000	15	102	4	0	5	Gill, Erie	.990	29	194	10	2	18
S. Allen, Auburn	1.000	3	9	2	0	2	Henley, Utica*	1.000	1	3	1	0	0
Bailey, Auburn	1.000	20	184	16	0	19	Hennell, Utica*	.986	75	634	51	10	32
Biagini, Elmira	1.000	1	9	0	0	0	Holliday, Little Falls	.973	44	314	16	9	26
Bonk, Elmira	.991	24	204	14	2	10	Horn, Elmira*	.973	47	368	29	11	21
Burns, Erie*	.975	62	433	31	12	32	Jacoby, Utica	1.000	1	3	0	0	0
Castoria, Auburn	.978	54	491	40	12	33	Kent, Niagara Falls	.985	71	612	32	10	55
Cawthon, Batavia	.978	63	541	25	13	68	Lauziere, Jamestown	1.000	2	12	2	0	0
Coleman, Batavia*	.979	7	44	3	1	2	Martinez, Batavia*	.956	5	42	1	2	1
Cordner, Geneva	.975	43	322	27	9	25	Metasavage, Little Falls	.993	35	260	21	2	20
Destrade, Oneonta	.971	41	298	33	10	24	Richardson, Elmira	.962	11	50	1	2	6
DISHMAN, Jamestown	.988	73	625	29	8	35	Ruffner, Oneonta	1.000	1	1	0	0	0
Fagan, Utica*	1.000	1	9	0	0	2	Smith, Geneva	.983	19	159	15	3	14
Felice, Little Falls	1.000	1	8	0	0	0	Thornton, Batavia	1.000	2	18	4	0	1
Fennell, Oneonta	.974	41	312	29	9	31							

SECOND BASEMEN

Player and Club	Pct.	G.	PO.	A.	E.	DP.	Player and Club	Pct.	G.	PO.	A.	E.	DP.
Adams, Oneonta	1.000	1	1	0	0	1	Hinson, Auburn	.965	13	19	36	2	4
Alcala, Oneonta	.964	62	115	151	10	32	Howard, Elmira	.922	45	85	117	17	23
Allen, Geneva	.942	23	49	64	7	13	Jacoby, Utica	.951	38	71	103	9	16
Bernstine, Elmira	1.000	8	15	26	0	7	Jose, Elmira	.803	17	23	26	12	3
Caraballo, Little Falls	.950	46	83	109	10	17	Keeton, Niagara Falls	.967	6	9	20	1	4
Echols, Batavia	1.000	3	6	6	0	1	Latorre, Erie	.948	66	113	180	16	37
Emmert, Geneva	.937	53	88	134	15	24	Lumpe, Jamestown	.961	57	102	147	10	23
Greenwell, Elmira	.949	24	51	61	6	8	McPhail, Little Falls	1.000	2	2	6	0	1
Hall, Jamestown	.935	14	27	31	4	6	Medina, Oneonta	1.000	4	5	13	0	3
Hayner, Utica	1.000	6	10	13	0	2	MITCHELL, Batavia	.974	58	150	181	9	50
Hines, Utica	.928	34	57	84	11	16	Morander, Erie	.959	10	22	25	2	10

SECOND BASEMEN—Continued

Player and Club	Pct.	G.	PO.	A.	E.	DP.
Perez, Niagara Falls	.854	8	13	22	6	3
Peters, Batavia	.913	5	11	10	2	2
Phillips, Little Falls	.937	37	64	100	11	10
Picchioni, Utica	.900	2	7	2	1	0
Rivera, Auburn	.933	35	56	110	12	13
Smajstrla, Niagara Falls	.952	62	129	185	16	42
Szajko, Jamestown	1.000	6	13	14	0	4
Thomas, Auburn	.955	30	50	77	6	18
Woodcock, Oneonta	.987	23	37	41	1	9

THIRD BASEMEN

Player and Club	Pct.	G.	PO.	A.	E.	DP.
Abone, Jamestown	.857	7	5	7	2	0
Adams, Oneonta	1.000	6	2	4	0	0
J. Allen, Geneva	.948	39	35	56	5	2
S. Allen, Auburn	.842	34	21	64	16	2
Anderson, Auburn	.667	4	2	8	5	0
Arnerich, Geneva	.865	39	36	54	14	5
Bailey, Auburn	.808	10	8	13	5	0
Bielawski, Utica	1.000	1	0	2	0	0
Clements, Erie	.938	14	6	24	2	0
Cochran, Batavia	.875	18	8	27	5	1
Cochrane, Little Falls	.846	63	49	110	29	7
Greenwell, Elmira	.844	48	45	90	25	10
Hines, Utica	1.000	2	1	0	0	0
Hinson, Auburn	.897	21	18	34	6	3
Hocutt, Jamestown	.895	35	25	77	12	5
KINSEL, Niagara Falls	.931	76	55	135	14	13
Maynor, Oneonta	.800	7	7	9	4	0
Medina, Oneonta	.667	1	0	2	1	0
Metasavage, Little Falls	.917	3	1	10	1	1
Morander, Erie	.889	11	6	18	3	1
Nattile, Elmira	.909	32	22	48	7	3
Pasquale, Erie	.924	50	38	95	11	11
Peters, Batavia	.898	45	24	90	13	5
Picchioni, Utica	1.000	1	3	3	0	0
Redfield, Little Falls	.889	4	5	11	2	2
Riggs, Oneonta	.903	69	45	113	17	10
Rivera, Auburn	.917	11	4	7	1	0
Roman, Batavia	.889	19	11	37	6	2
Ruffner, Oneonta	1.000	1	1	2	0	1
Springer, Little Falls	.913	7	10	11	2	1
Szajko, Jamestown	.966	34	32	82	4	6
Tarnow, Geneva	.667	1	0	2	1	0
Wolfe, Utica	.912	74	35	121	15	11

SHORTSTOPS

Player and Club	Pct.	G.	PO.	A.	E.	DP.
Adams, Oneonta	.966	28	44	69	4	16
Alcala, Oneonta	1.000	2	0	5	0	0
Arnerich, Geneva	1.000	4	3	6	0	0
Barton, Niagara Falls	.930	45	52	121	13	19
Bielawski, Utica	.883	38	38	98	18	7
Clements, Erie	.888	51	74	139	27	24
Cordner, Geneva	1.000	1	7	0	0	0
Hayner, Utica	.920	47	63	120	16	14
Howard, Elmira	.906	8	12	17	3	1
Jongewaard, Elmira	.865	58	83	147	36	25
Jose, Elmira	.768	18	14	39	16	5
Medina, Oneonta	.924	53	66	153	18	27
Morander, Erie	.841	26	27	63	17	11
Pedraza, Batavia	.936	57	99	165	18	42
Perez, Niagara Falls	.911	40	48	96	14	21
Phillips, Little Falls	.897	28	39	66	12	12
Redfield, Little Falls	.899	50	95	119	24	25
Rivera, Auburn	.800	2	5	11	4	2
Ruffner, Oneonta	1.000	1	0	1	0	0
THIESSEN, Jamestown	.941	75	89	215	19	25
Thompson, Auburn	.931	73	122	188	23	34
Valera, Batavia	.904	26	34	51	9	16
Woodcock, Oneonta	1.000	2	0	1	0	1
Woods, Geneva	.912	73	112	197	30	40

OUTFIELDERS

Player and Club	Pct.	G.	PO.	A.	E.	DP.
Alomar, Elmira	.946	33	29	6	2	0
Alonzo, Utica*	.937	37	58	1	4	0
Bailey, Auburn	1.000	2	3	0	0	0
Barbagelata, Batavia	.970	51	61	4	2	3
Barton, Niagara Falls	1.000	3	2	0	0	0
Bernstine, Batavia	.967	40	59	0	2	0
Berroa, Elmira	1.000	1	2	0	0	0
Brito, Batavia	.870	35	40	0	6	0
Burton, Geneva*	.778	17	20	1	1	1
Cangelosi, Niagara*	.969	61	118	5	4	1
Cawthon, Batavia	.875	5	7	0	1	0
Christensen, Utica	1.000	26	25	2	0	0
Cordner, Geneva	1.000	20	24	2	0	0
Coyle, Utica	.981	37	48	3	1	0
Dematties, Utica	.000	1	0	0	1	0
Doggett, Geneva	.970	75	190	7	6	3
Dophied, Auburn	.959	43	65	6	3	1
Dotson, Jamestown*	.9838	74	172	11	3	1
Elway, Oneonta	1.000	41	69	8	0	1
Farmar, Geneva	.942	53	77	4	5	2
Felice, Little Falls	.946	73	96	9	6	1
Ferguson, Oneonta	1.000	34	61	4	0	1
Garrett, Utica	.913	21	20	1	2	0
Gatlin, Oneonta	.875	15	20	1	3	0
Gayton, Niagara Falls	.956	33	40	3	2	0
Gjesdal, Oneonta	.911	47	51	0	5	0
Hayner, Utica	1.000	1	1	0	0	0
Hendershot, Utica	.942	64	92	5	6	0
Henley, Niagara Falls	1.000	31	34	0	0	0
Hines, Utica	1.000	9	11	0	0	0
Holmes, Batavia	.800	7	3	1	1	0
Jelks, Elmira	.946	53	85	3	5	0
Kiesling, Auburn	.921	45	61	9	6	3
Lauck, Erie	.878	38	41	2	6	0
Lauziere, Jamestown	1.000	10	9	2	0	0
Leggitt, Jamestown	.967	46	83	4	3	1
Lemon, Jamestown*	.944	70	92	9	6	1
Madison, Batavia	.800	9	4	0	1	0
McIver, Auburn	.949	32	36	1	2	0
McPhail, Little Falls	.944	13	17	0	1	0
Metasavage, Little Falls	1.000	7	7	1	0	0
Moss, Utica	.894	34	41	1	5	0
Nattile, Elmira	.948	40	66	7	4	0
O'Regan, Oneonta	.907	28	39	0	4	0
Oliva, Elmira	.953	67	117	5	6	1
Parker, Little Falls	.978	20	44	1	1	0
Pasqua, Oneonta*	.750	3	2	1	1	0
Picchioni, Utica	.864	26	19	0	3	0
Roath, Erie*	.968	29	29	1	1	0
Roe, Jamestown	1.000	2	2	0	0	0
Roman, Batavia	.982	41	53	2	1	1
Roomes, Geneva	.945	64	129	8	8	4
Rossi, Erie	.982	67	103	4	2	2
Ruffner, Oneonta	.913	48	62	1	6	0
Russell, Oneonta	.945	27	51	1	3	0
Saccoccio, Jamestown	.917	6	11	0	1	0
Sanchez, Little Falls	.857	4	6	0	1	0
Sedar, Niagara Falls	.963	50	74	5	3	1
Shirley, Little Falls	1.000	3	1	0	0	0
Skripko, Elmira	.964	63	102	6	4	0
Springer, Little Falls	.933	52	80	3	6	0
Stacheit, Jamestown	1.000	9	14	1	0	0
Stellern, Auburn	.931	49	89	6	7	0
Swain, Auburn	.891	61	111	4	14	0
Szajko, Jamestown	1.000	13	19	1	0	1
Toothman, Niagara Falls	.950	58	71	5	4	2
TURGEON, Erie	.9841	69	109	15	2	2
Wallace, Erie	1.000	41	62	3	0	0
Washington, Batavia	.949	63	89	5	5	1
Wilson, Little Falls	.949	64	107	5	6	0
Ybarra, Niagara Falls	.750	3	3	0	1	0

CATCHERS

Player and Club	Pct.	G.	PO.	A.	E.	DP.	PB.
Adams, Oneonta	1.000	1	2	0	0	0	0
Bonk, Elmira	1.000	1	3	0	0	0	0
Burrell, Elmira	.974	34	211	13	6	2	4
Champion, Erie	1.000	11	61	6	0	2	1
Cordner, Geneva	1.000	1	4	0	0	0	2
Dale, Batavia	.977	27	151	19	4	2	5
Datz, Auburn	.990	36	260	27	3	3	8
DeJesus, Niagara Falls	.978	44	271	35	7	2	20
DeMatties, Utica	.989	39	252	26	3	3	10
Diaz, Batavia	.955	40	197	17	10	1	9
Dreizler, Utica	.987	49	352	37	5	0	7
Fennell, Oneonta	.961	23	179	18	8	1	7

CATCHERS—Continued

Player and Club	Pct.	G.	PO.	A.	E.	DP.	PB.	Player and Club	Pct.	G.	PO.	A.	E.	DP.	PB.
Flores, Niagara Falls	.966	15	72	13	3	1	2	Nittoli, Niagara Falls	.976	26	151	11	4	1	3
Gasparino, Oneonta	.963	27	146	11	6	1	1	Packer, Erie	.983	39	333	22	6	1	9
Geels, Elmira	.974	40	221	38	7	2	5	Richardson, Elmira	.956	17	73	14	4	0	2
Giordano, Oneonta	1.000	4	15	2	0	0	0	RIVERA, Jamestown	.995	48	345	35	2	2	7
Hawkins, Oneonta	.980	39	314	30	7	2	2	Roarke, Auburn	.976	6	37	3	1	0	6
Holecek, Geneva	1.000	2	21	0	0	0	2	Roehner, Jamestown	1.000	4	26	1	0	0	9
Howroyd, Batavia	.980	10	43	5	1	0	2	Shirley, Little Falls	.963	6	26	0	1	0	3
Jacobson, Auburn	.988	39	309	30	4	4	5	Stewart, Geneva	.980	28	176	23	4	5	8
Kordeck, Utica	1.000	8	38	4	0	0	2	Tarnow, Geneva	.976	51	337	31	9	3	9
Liska, Little Falls	1.000	23	151	12	0	0	13	Willman, Erie	.991	29	202	11	2	0	7
Maggio, Batavia	1.000	11	53	4	0	1	0	Wright, Oneonta	1.000	4	8	1	0	0	0
Merritt, Little Falls	.986	59	474	36	7	3	19	Ybarra, Niagara Falls	.988	13	73	8	1	1	0
Nichting, Jamestown	.977	26	147	20	4	2	3								

PITCHERS

Player and Club	Pct.	G.	PO.	A.	E.	DP.	Player and Club	Pct.	G.	PO.	A.	E.	DP.
Adamczak, Geneva	.931	15	6	21	2	0	Meadows, Auburn	1.000	17	2	12	0	0
Arnold, Little Falls	.667	22	1	1	1	0	Merlach, Utica	.900	14	2	7	1	0
Baldrick, Jamestown°	.955	14	4	17	1	2	Miller, Jamestown	1.000	12	5	8	0	0
Barkley, Batavia	1.000	15	4	11	0	1	Mills, Erie°	1.000	23	0	5	0	1
Birtsas, Oneonta°	.000	6	0	0	1	0	Minor, Elmira	.846	19	3	8	2	0
Blas, Auburn	1.000	7	0	2	0	0	C. MITCHELL, Elmira	1.000	23	3	21	0	1
Blevins, Geneva	1.000	20	2	4	0	0	F. Mitchell, Jamestown	1.000	10	1	2	0	0
Boever, Erie	.750	19	0	3	1	0	W. Mitchell, Erie	1.000	21	1	1	0	0
Bombard, Auburn	1.000	17	5	17	0	1	Moretti, Utica	.941	42	4	12	1	1
Bone, Oneonta	1.000	11	2	6	0	0	Morgan, Oneonta	1.000	13	4	7	0	0
Boyles, Little Falls	.667	19	1	9	5	0	MOSES, Niagara Falls°	1.000	29	7	17	0	3
Bryant, Oneonta	1.000	5	0	1	0	0	Naughton, Utica°	1.000	4	0	1	0	0
Byron, Oneonta	1.000	12	3	13	0	1	Norton, Utica	.778	14	3	4	2	0
Callahan, Auburn	.857	14	4	8	2	0	Noworyta, Niagara Falls	.800	1	1	3	1	0
Carrasco, Erie	.913	14	10	32	4	0	Ortiz, Batavia°	.833	7	0	5	1	0
Carson, Erie	.941	15	8	8	1	2	Pantaleo, Geneva	.800	10	1	3	1	1
Cerefin, Auburn	.000	4	0	0	1	0	Paul, Little Falls	.600	16	0	3	2	0
Conroy, Batavia°	1.000	23	2	4	0	0	Perkins, Auburn	1.000	29	5	10	0	1
Cook, Geneva	.875	15	8	6	2	0	Perrino, Utica°	.955	15	7	14	1	0
Cruz, Niagara Falls	.778	12	1	6	2	0	Peterson, Utica	1.000	26	3	12	0	0
Cushing, Batavia°	1.000	2	1	2	0	0	Pierorazio, Batavia°	.867	13	4	22	4	2
Deshaies, Oneonta°	1.000	15	7	13	0	0	Poindexter, Batavia	.950	18	6	13	1	0
DeVincenzo, Niagara Falls°	1.000	1	0	1	0	0	Polemir, Auburn	.875	10	4	10	2	0
Diez, Elmira°	1.000	14	0	3	0	0	Pruitt, Little Falls°	.833	26	1	4	1	0
Donathan, Erie	1.000	15	2	12	0	1	Ratliff, Jamestown	1.000	5	1	4	0	0
Dopson, Jamestown	.875	15	6	15	3	0	Riewerts, Auburn°	1.000	22	0	3	0	0
Doty, Oneonta	.846	16	12	10	4	0	Robair, Little Falls	1.000	1	0	1	0	1
Dunn, Erie	1.000	17	3	8	0	0	Rochford, Elmira°	1.000	16	5	15	0	1
Emmons, Batavia	.846	15	2	9	2	2	Rodriguez, Elmira	.714	17	0	5	2	0
M. Fagan, Batavia	1.000	9	2	4	0	1	Roy, Jamestown	.923	16	2	10	1	0
P. Fagan, Utica°	.944	27	6	11	1	1	Schimpf, Auburn	.917	15	8	25	3	3
Farley, Erie	.933	14	4	10	1	1	Schneider, Niagara Falls	1.000	7	1	2	0	0
Ferrin, Oneonta	.938	15	5	10	1	0	Schulte, Jamestown	1.000	13	3	9	0	0
Figueroa, Oneonta	.000	3	0	0	2	0	Sedar, Niagara Falls	1.000	3	2	0	0	0
Filippo, Batavia°	.857	15	1	11	2	1	Seidel, Oneonta	1.000	4	1	0	0	0
Foulks, Little Falls	.818	16	2	7	2	1	Sellers, Elmira	.905	17	6	13	2	0
Fruge, Geneva	.882	14	3	12	2	0	Serafini, Geneva°	.909	16	4	6	1	0
Gardner, Little Falls	.882	23	2	13	2	1	Shade, Erie	1.000	13	2	6	0	0
Gibson, Niagara Falls	.750	11	2	7	3	0	Shoupee, Auburn°	1.000	3	2	3	0	0
Gooden, Little Falls	1.000	2	0	2	0	0	Shulleeta, Geneva	.875	10	2	5	1	0
Graham, Oneonta	.889	22	1	7	1	1	Silva, Elmira	1.000	14	3	10	0	0
Green, Utica	.667	19	2	4	3	0	Skinner, Niagara Falls	.870	14	5	15	3	0
Guzman, Niagara Falls	1.000	22	4	10	0	1	Skorupa, Jamestown	1.000	7	2	1	0	0
Hartshorn, Little Falls	1.000	13	2	2	0	0	Snyder, Batavia	1.000	2	2	0	0	0
Heath, Niagara Falls°	.778	14	4	10	4	0	SUNDE, Niagara Falls	1.000	15	4	20	0	2
Henley, Niagara Falls	.778	19	1	6	2	0	Teate, Little Falls	1.000	14	5	2	0	0
Hill, Elmira°	.952	15	10	10	1	0	Thomas, Utica	.889	17	7	9	2	1
Hogan, Auburn	.944	10	4	13	1	0	Tomaselli, Oneonta°	.875	15	5	16	3	1
Hurst, 3 Bat-11 Erie	.917	14	3	8	1	0	Trujillo, Niagara Falls	.733	12	2	9	4	1
Isgett, Geneva	.714	20	3	2	2	0	Tuller, Geneva	1.000	8	0	1	0	0
Jensen, Little Falls°	1.000	17	3	8	0	1	Valliant, Jamestown°	.909	11	2	8	1	0
Jones, Oneonta	1.000	3	1	0	0	0	Walker, Little Falls	1.000	12	1	3	0	0
Kasprzak, Auburn	1.000	13	5	12	0	1	Waymire, Jamestown	1.000	22	1	8	0	0
Keeler, Batavia	1.000	24	1	11	0	0	Weatherman, Utica	1.000	4	3	3	0	0
Key, Elmira	1.000	16	5	6	0	0	Weissman, Geneva	.750	14	7	8	5	1
Kinns, Jamestown	1.000	14	5	8	0	0	Weston, Little Falls	.929	17	5	8	1	1
Kizer, Auburn	.750	18	1	2	1	0	White, Oneonta°	.800	13	1	3	1	0
Livesey, Utica°	1.000	9	1	14	0	0	Wick, Batavia°	1.000	14	1	6	0	0
Lockhart, Elmira°	.941	18	3	13	1	0	Worrell, Erie	.857	9	6	12	3	1
Lockie, Geneva	1.000	9	4	9	0	0	Young, Erie°	1.000	9	2	6	0	1
McIntosh, Jamestown	1.000	5	0	1	0	0	Zmudosky, Utica	.951	17	6	33	2	1

The following players had no recorded accepted chances at the positions indicated; therefore, are not listed in the fielding averages for those particular positions: Adams, of; B. Bailey, p; Beck, p; K. Bailey, p; Burton, 1b; Caraballo, 3b, ss; Clark, p; Coleman, of; Compagno, p; Connolly, p; Corsi, p; Geels, of; Giordano, of; Gjesdal, 1b; Hayner, 3b; Henley, 3b; Jacoby, ss; Kinsel, p; Lindsey, p; Maldonado, p; Maynor, of; Moretti, of; Pasquale, ss; Perez, of; Phillips, 3b; Stovall, of; Suggs, p; Tarnow, of, p; Wyatt, p.

CLUB PITCHING

Club	ERA.	G.	CG.	ShO.	Sv.	IP.	H.	R.	ER.	HR.	HB.	BB.	Int. BB.	SO.	WP.	Bk.
Oneonta	3.91	76	20	3	17	665.1	629	359	289	49	17	300	26	641	59	4
Niagara Falls	3.94	76	16	5	17	637.2	586	355	279	33	25	314	3	573	49	4
Erie	4.30	73	7	2	15	630.2	632	375	301	66	38	249	18	589	67	6
Elmira	4.33	75	5	5	13	637.2	697	429	307	68	21	339	28	499	41	3

Club	ERA.	G.	CG.	ShO.	Sv.	IP.	H.	R.	ER.	HR.	HB.	BB.	Int. BB.	SO.	WP.	Bk.
Auburn	4.35	75	8	6	14	666.2	672	422	322	62	35	295	20	586	45	3
Jamestown	4.59	75	20	5	14	627.1	647	387	320	55	20	299	6	496	49	4
Geneva	4.78	75	16	2	13	643.2	640	424	342	67	19	332	12	526	51	2
Utica	4.85	76	7	1	8	644.1	695	437	347	86	17	312	3	641	54	9
Batavia	4.85	73	11	4	13	597	638	416	322	76	22	303	2	436	69	7
Little Falls	5.19	76	10	4	15	654	696	477	377	101	23	318	8	638	39	5

PITCHERS' RECORDS
(Leading Qualifiers for Earned-Run Average Leadership — 61 or More Innings)

*Throws lefthanded.

Pitcher — Club	W.	L.	Pct.	ERA.	G.	GS.	CG.	GF.	ShO.	Sv.	IP.	H.	R.	ER.	HR.	HB.	BB.	Int. BB.	SO.	WP.
Hogan, Auburn	5	2	.714	1.82	10	10	3	0	1	0	74.1	56	26	15	6	5	19	1	69	3
Kinns, Jamestown	7	3	.700	2.21	14	13	7	0	2	0	97.2	77	35	24	3	4	44	1	88	12
Trujillo, Niagara Falls	5	4	.556	2.39	12	12	3	0	1	0	79	54	33	21	5	3	25	0	100	5
Doty, Oneonta	7	3	.700	2.68	16	15	5	1	0	1	107.1	97	46	32	4	4	42	3	92	7
Schimpf, Auburn	7	2	.778	2.85	15	15	2	0	1	0	91.2	87	43	29	6	4	28	1	76	3
Tomaselli, Oneonta*	7	4	.636	2.88	15	15	6	0	1	0	109.1	96	44	35	6	1	40	1	111	10
Moretti, Utica	9	3	.750	2.99	42	0	0	39	0	7	69.1	54	30	23	10	3	32	1	115	4
Sellers, Elmira	1	4	.200	3.06	17	8	1	8	0	1	61.2	55	31	21	3	1	39	5	45	5
Pierorazio, Batavia*	4	6	.400	3.19	13	12	0	0	0	0	73.1	80	40	26	8	4	43	0	41	7
Deshaies, Oneonta*	6	5	.545	3.32	15	14	6	0	1	0	108.1	93	50	40	10	3	40	1	137	3

Departmental Leaders: G—Moretti, 42; GS—Zmudosky, 17; CG—Barkley, Kinns, 7; GF—Moretti, 39; ShO—Barkley, Jensen, 3; W—Moretti, 9; L—Dopson, Skinner, 8; Pct.—Baldrick, Schimpf, .778; Sv.—Moses, 10; IP—Zmudosky, 110.1; H—Zmudosky, 122; R—Foulks 70; ER—Fruge, 57; HR—Jensen, 18; HB—Carrasco, 14; BB—Heath, 63; IBB—Boever, Graham, Kasprzak, Lockhart, Sellers, 5; SO—Deshaies, 137; WP—Carrasco, 13.

(All Pitchers—Listed Alphabetically)

Pitcher — Club	W.	L.	Pct.	ERA.	G.	GS.	CG.	GF.	ShO.	Sv.	IP.	H.	R.	ER.	HR.	HB.	BB.	Int. BB.	SO.	WP.
Adamczak, Geneva	7	5	.583	3.99	15	15	4	0	0	0	106	108	62	47	4	4	41	2	72	6
Arnold, Little Falls	5	4	.556	2.97	22	0	0	15	0	3	36.1	32	17	12	2	1	27	1	42	0
B. Bailey, Oneonta	0	1	.000	16.88	3	1	0	2	0	0	2.2	5	5	5	3	0	3	0	4	0
K. Bailey, Oneonta	3	0	1.000	3.92	13	0	0	7	0	2	39	34	18	17	2	1	19	4	42	6
Baldrick, Jamestown*	7	2	.778	3.54	14	11	3	2	1	1	86.1	83	36	34	8	2	27	0	85	4
Barkley, Batavia	5	6	.455	4.08	15	14	7	0	3	0	90.1	81	44	41	9	0	34	0	82	4
Beck, Batavia	0	0	.000	3.00	1	0	0	0	0	0	3	4	1	1	0	0	1	0	1	2
Birtsas, Oneonta*	1	1	.500	3.86	6	5	0	1	0	1	16.1	19	13	7	2	0	17	0	24	4
Blas, Auburn	2	2	.500	5.09	20	0	0	18	0	5	35.1	31	24	20	5	0	21	1	39	7
Blevins, Geneva	2	2	.500	4.15	7	0	0	5	0	0	17.1	15	10	8	2	0	6	1	26	7
Boever, Erie	2	3	.400	1.93	19	0	0	19	0	9	32.2	20	8	7	0	1	12	5	63	0
Bombard, Auburn	3	6	.333	3.96	17	9	1	5	0	1	86.1	96	57	38	8	2	22	3	80	4
Bone, Oneonta	0	2	.000	9.74	11	1	0	5	0	1	20.1	28	30	22	3	1	20	2	18	4
Boyles, Little Falls	1	1	.500	5.98	19	4	0	6	0	0	46.2	51	39	31	6	0	33	2	51	4
Bryant, Oneonta	0	1	.000	11.12	5	1	0	0	0	0	5.2	7	7	7	1	0	9	0	4	1
Byron, Oneonta	3	5	.375	4.84	12	11	0	0	0	0	57.2	53	38	31	2	2	34	2	37	11
Callahan, Auburn	4	5	.444	5.94	14	14	1	0	0	0	77.1	98	66	51	9	4	39	0	49	6
Carrasco, Erie	3	7	.300	5.03	14	14	1	0	0	0	87.2	85	61	49	8	14	35	1	56	13
Carson, Erie	8	5	.615	4.26	15	14	3	0	0	0	88.2	92	49	42	11	1	25	0	62	6
Cerefin, Auburn	0	4	.000	22.00	4	4	0	0	0	0	9	14	23	22	1	2	21	0	5	1
Clark, Batavia	0	0	.000	13.50	8	0	0	6	0	0	12	22	22	18	1	2	16	0	8	6
Compagno, Oneonta*	0	0	.000	7.71	3	0	0	2	0	1	2.1	2	2	2	0	0	2	0	4	0
Connolly, Batavia	0	0	.000	14.40	7	0	0	2	0	0	10	22	17	16	0	2	10	0	7	1
Conroy, Batavia*	0	2	.000	3.74	23	0	0	17	0	3	33.2	25	18	14	4	2	18	0	36	5
Cook, Geneva	5	6	.455	4.11	15	15	5	0	1	0	92	90	58	42	11	1	47	0	70	6
Corsi, Oneonta	0	0	.000	10.80	1	0	0	0	0	0	3.1	5	4	4	0	0	6	0	6	0
Cruz, Niagara Falls	2	0	1.000	3.21	12	1	1	7	0	1	28	21	12	10	1	1	13	0	27	1
Cushing, Batavia*	0	1	.000	1.42	2	0	0	0	0	0	6.1	5	4	1	0	0	5	0	5	1
Deshaies, Oneonta*	6	5	.545	3.32	15	14	6	0	1	0	108.1	93	50	40	10	3	40	1	137	3
DeVincenzo, Niagara Falls*	1	0	1.000	0.00	1	1	0	0	0	0	5	3	0	0	0	0	7	0	6	1
Diez, Elmira*	4	3	.571	3.66	14	6	1	4	0	2	51.2	51	30	21	5	4	35	0	41	5
Donathan, Erie	3	5	.375	4.87	15	10	1	2	1	0	61	75	45	33	10	2	19	1	46	7
Dopson, Jamestown	6	8	.429	3.97	15	15	6	0	1	0	106.2	117	58	47	4	2	34	3	62	8
Doty, Oneonta	7	3	.700	2.68	16	15	5	1	0	1	107.1	97	46	32	4	4	42	3	92	7
Dunn, Erie	1	0	1.000	5.08	17	2	0	3	0	0	39	52	31	22	5	0	22	2	22	4
Elpin, Batavia	0	1	.000	15.00	1	1	0	0	0	0	3	6	5	5	3	0	1	0	2	0
Emmons, Batavia	4	4	.500	4.11	15	7	0	5	0	1	57	57	33	26	7	4	20	0	31	9
M. Fagan, Batavia	2	2	.500	2.29	9	4	1	5	1	0	35.1	22	15	9	2	1	16	0	24	1
P. Fagan, Utica*	3	0	1.000	3.77	27	2	0	6	0	0	57.1	56	35	24	5	4	23	0	61	6
Farley, Erie	3	4	.429	3.87	14	13	2	1	0	0	86	88	49	37	12	6	30	2	71	7
Ferrin, Oneonta	5	5	.500	3.86	15	9	2	5	0	1	74.2	73	38	32	5	3	20	3	48	6
Figueroa, Batavia	0	2	.000	8.44	3	2	0	0	0	0	5.1	11	16	5	1	0	5	0	6	0
Filippo, Batavia*	2	3	.400	4.34	15	11	0	2	0	1	64.1	70	47	31	10	2	27	0	37	9
Foulks, Little Falls	0	5	.000	8.32	16	8	0	3	0	0	57.1	92	70	53	11	1	31	0	54	3
Fruge, Geneva	4	7	.364	6.81	14	11	1	0	0	0	75.1	90	65	57	16	0	45	1	52	8
Gardner, Little Falls	3	6	.333	3.71	23	7	2	14	0	6	77.2	73	48	32	7	3	29	0	77	1
Gibson, Niagara Falls	6	3	.667	3.50	11	10	5	0	1	0	74.2	66	35	29	0	1	33	0	60	3
Gooden, Little Falls	0	1	.000	4.15	2	2	0	0	0	0	13	11	6	6	2	1	3	0	18	0
Graham, Oneonta	6	0	1.000	3.06	22	0	0	19	0	8	35.1	33	13	12	3	0	15	5	74	5
Green, Utica	2	1	.667	5.27	19	5	0	9	0	1	42.2	49	30	25	6	0	28	0	51	4
Guzman, Niagara Falls	5	3	.625	5.14	22	4	1	11	0	2	77	76	56	44	7	10	47	0	65	5
Hartshorn, Little Falls	5	2	.714	6.83	13	9	2	1	0	0	54	65	53	41	15	3	30	1	52	3
Heath, Niagara Falls*	3	6	.333	5.40	14	14	0	0	0	0	73.1	63	54	44	5	3	63	0	57	7
Henley, Niagara Falls	3	3	.500	3.95	19	0	0	14	0	2	43.1	38	21	19	3	0	22	1	54	4
Hill, Elmira*	3	6	.333	4.68	15	14	0	1	0	1	73	83	60	38	10	4	45	3	41	6
Hogan, Auburn	5	2	.714	1.82	10	10	3	0	1	0	74.1	56	26	15	6	5	19	1	69	3
Hurst, 3 Bat-11 Erie	2	2	.500	5.36	14	3	0	6	0	1	48.2	52	32	29	7	2	18	0	48	4
Isgett, Geneva	1	3	.250	5.16	20	0	0	18	0	4	29.2	31	26	17	2	2	22	3	26	2
Jensen, Little Falls*	6	6	.500	4.55	17	15	4	2	3	1	95	92	59	48	18	1	27	0	110	5

Pitcher—Club	W.	L.	Pct.	ERA.	G.	GS.	CG.	GF.	ShO.	Sv.	IP.	H.	R.	ER.	HR.	HB.	BB.	Int. BB.	SO.	WP.
Jones, Utica	0	0	.000	16.20	3	0	0	0	0	0	3.1	7	6	6	2	0	3	0	3	1
Kasprzak, Auburn	1	0	1.000	3.43	13	3	0	6	0	1	60.1	62	30	23	5	2	22	5	47	1
Keeler, Batavia	6	4	.600	4.09	24	2	0	20	0	8	44	50	26	20	4	1	16	1	43	4
Key, Elmira	7	4	.636	3.42	16	15	1	1	0	0	84.1	81	43	32	6	0	51	1	78	5
Kinns, Jamestown	7	3	.700	2.21	14	13	7	0	2	0	97.2	77	35	24	3	4	44	1	88	12
Kinsel, Niagara Falls	0	0	.000	9.00	1	0	0	1	0	0	1	3	1	1	0	0	0	0	1	0
Kizer, Auburn	1	2	.333	4.96	18	0	0	13	0	1	32.2	36	25	18	4	1	24	3	35	3
Lindsey, Oneonta*	0	0	.000	27.00	1	0	0	1	0	0	1	1	3	3	1	0	1	0	2	0
Livesey, Utica*	1	2	.333	5.74	9	3	0	2	0	0	31.1	29	28	20	6	1	32	0	19	5
Lockhart, Elmira*	3	4	.429	5.79	18	6	0	9	0	0	56	74	46	36	6	1	27	5	44	3
Lockie, Geneva	3	2	.600	4.53	9	7	3	1	0	0	59.2	64	32	30	6	1	18	1	49	0
Maldonado, Erie	0	0	.000	16.20	1	0	0	1	0	0	1.2	3	3	3	0	0	2	1	1	0
McIntosh, Jamestown	1	3	.250	7.20	5	5	1	0	0	0	25	35	20	20	4	1	4	0	15	1
Meadows, Auburn	2	5	.286	5.49	17	7	0	3	0	0	57.1	54	39	35	7	3	43	0	43	6
Merlach, Utica	2	3	.400	6.59	14	6	0	3	0	0	42.1	48	40	31	2	1	27	1	46	4
Miller, Jamestown	2	5	.286	6.83	12	10	1	1	0	0	59.1	69	52	45	7	1	42	0	54	9
Mills, Erie*	1	1	.500	2.67	23	0	0	12	0	2	30.1	30	9	9	1	0	13	4	15	6
Minor, Elmira	2	4	.333	5.87	19	1	0	13	0	0	46	53	37	30	7	4	34	1	36	7
C. Mitchell, Elmira	4	3	.571	3.53	23	0	0	17	0	9	66.1	70	34	26	5	1	14	4	45	2
F. Mitchell, Jamestown	3	0	1.000	4.91	10	0	0	8	0	1	33	30	22	18	3	1	14	0	25	4
W. Mitchell, Erie	1	3	.250	6.00	21	0	0	15	0	3	30	25	24	20	4	4	21	1	46	4
Moretti, Utica	9	3	.750	2.99	42	0	0	39	0	7	69.1	54	30	23	10	3	32	1	115	4
Morgan, Oneonta	2	5	.286	5.56	13	2	1	5	0	0	43.2	49	35	27	5	1	18	3	33	1
Moses, Niagara Falls*	8	4	.667	3.53	29	5	2	20	0	10	79	73	34	31	1	1	24	1	60	4
Naughton, Utica*	0	1	.000	7.27	4	0	0	0	0	0	8.2	7	9	7	1	0	7	0	4	2
Norton, Utica	4	5	.444	5.72	14	13	2	0	0	0	61.1	77	53	39	12	1	30	0	53	10
Noworyta, Niagara Falls	1	0	1.000	1.00	1	1	1	0	0	0	9	4	1	1	1	0	5	0	5	0
Ortiz, Batavia*	1	4	.200	8.13	7	7	0	0	0	0	34.1	49	38	31	6	0	21	0	27	7
Pantaleo, Geneva	2	2	.500	3.86	10	0	0	8	0	3	14	14	9	6	2	0	6	1	19	3
Paul, Little Falls	1	1	.500	6.39	16	1	0	6	0	1	38	43	32	27	7	0	21	1	41	2
Perkins, Auburn	5	6	.455	4.14	29	0	0	23	0	8	45.2	40	24	21	3	3	20	3	43	3
Perrino, Auburn	6	5	.545	4.14	15	14	2	0	0	0	78.1	91	44	36	5	1	27	0	73	10
Peterson, Utica	3	3	.500	4.08	26	1	0	8	0	0	53	56	26	24	7	1	13	1	48	0
Pierorazio, Batavia*	4	6	.400	3.19	13	12	0	0	0	0	73.1	80	40	26	8	4	43	0	41	7
Poindexter, Batavia	6	2	.750	4.34	18	8	3	1	0	0	74.2	74	43	36	11	3	46	1	52	8
Polemir, Auburn	2	3	.400	6.83	10	10	0	0	0	0	55.1	60	52	42	8	7	33	3	46	6
Pruitt, Little Falls*	2	2	.500	2.51	26	0	0	12	0	4	32.1	29	12	9	4	2	10	3	46	4
Ratliff, Jamestown	0	1	.000	9.20	5	2	0	3	0	0	14.2	20	16	15	1	0	9	0	5	0
Riewerts, Auburn*	1	2	.333	4.86	22	0	0	12	0	3	33.1	42	24	18	2	1	13	0	38	2
Robair, Little Falls	1	0	1.000	3.60	1	1	0	0	0	0	5	2	3	2	0	0	4	0	1	0
Rochford, Elmira*	6	4	.600	4.20	16	14	2	2	2	0	85.2	99	53	40	9	3	26	2	66	4
Rodriguez, Elmira	1	4	.200	4.99	17	1	0	13	0	0	48.2	58	52	27	3	2	40	3	41	3
Roy, Jamestown	3	3	.500	4.40	16	6	1	9	0	1	59.1	69	38	29	5	3	21	0	35	2
Schimpf, Auburn	7	2	.778	2.85	15	15	2	0	1	0	91.2	87	43	29	6	4	28	1	76	3
Schneider, Niagara Falls	0	1	.000	6.00	7	0	0	5	0	2	9	12	7	6	0	0	6	1	5	2
Schulte, Jamestown*	3	2	.600	4.99	13	4	0	5	0	1	48.2	47	29	27	4	3	42	2	40	4
Sedar, Niagara Falls	0	0	.000	3.86	3	0	0	2	0	0	7	5	4	3	0	0	7	0	9	1
Seidel, Oneonta	1	1	.500	5.14	4	1	0	2	0	1	7	7	4	4	1	0	4	1	11	0
Sellers, Elmira	1	4	.200	3.06	17	8	1	8	0	1	61.2	55	31	21	3	1	39	5	45	5
Serafini, Geneva*	4	2	.667	4.43	16	0	0	11	0	1	40.2	35	27	20	5	3	32	1	28	2
Shade, Erie	3	4	.429	3.97	13	4	0	4	0	0	45.1	38	24	20	5	5	16	1	63	3
Shoupee, Auburn*	2	0	1.000	0.69	3	3	1	0	1	0	26	12	3	2	1	5	0	0	29	0
Shulleeta, Geneva	3	2	.600	5.66	10	8	0	0	0	0	49.1	49	33	31	4	3	23	0	30	6
Silva, Elmira	3	4	.429	5.04	14	10	0	2	0	0	64.1	73	43	36	14	1	28	4	62	1
Skinner, Niagara Falls	2	8	.200	4.93	14	14	1	0	0	0	69.1	77	55	38	5	1	34	0	72	12
Skorupa, Jamestown	0	0	.000	7.63	7	0	0	4	0	1	15.1	19	16	13	3	2	9	0	17	2
Snyder, Batavia	0	0	.000	3.00	2	2	0	0	0	0	6	3	2	2	1	0	4	0	2	1
Suggs, Erie	0	0	.000	10.80	3	0	0	3	0	0	5	5	11	6	0	1	6	0	6	4
Sunde, Niagara Falls	6	2	.750	3.47	15	14	2	0	0	0	83	91	42	32	5	5	28	0	52	4
Tarnow, Geneva	0	0	.000	0.00	1	0	0	1	0	0	1	1	0	0	0	0	0	0	1	0
Teate, Little Falls	4	2	.667	5.96	14	7	0	4	0	0	54.1	65	43	36	7	3	41	0	36	6
Thomas, Utica	4	2	.667	5.45	17	11	0	2	0	0	66	72	52	40	13	1	49	0	72	2
Tomaselli, Oneonta*	7	4	.636	2.88	15	15	6	0	1	0	109.1	96	44	35	6	1	40	1	111	10
Trujillo, Niagara Falls	5	4	.556	2.39	12	12	3	0	1	0	79	54	33	21	5	3	25	0	100	5
Tuller, Geneva	1	2	.333	5.01	8	5	0	2	0	0	41.1	37	27	23	6	0	26	1	39	1
Valliant, Jamestown*	2	7	.222	5.37	11	9	1	1	0	0	55.1	54	45	33	9	0	42	0	44	3
Walker, Little Falls	3	2	.600	4.97	12	9	0	1	0	0	50.2	36	32	28	6	4	38	0	41	11
Waymire, Jamestown	2	4	.333	5.19	22	0	0	22	0	9	26	27	20	15	4	1	11	0	26	0
Weatherman, Utica	0	3	.000	7.52	4	4	0	0	0	0	20.1	27	18	17	6	2	7	0	21	1
Weissman, Geneva	4	6	.400	4.44	14	14	3	0	0	0	99.1	90	61	49	6	5	51	1	101	10
Weston, Little Falls	7	6	.538	5.07	17	13	2	2	0	0	92.1	105	63	52	16	4	22	0	67	0
White, Oneonta*	2	0	1.000	2.59	13	1	0	6	0	1	31.1	27	9	9	1	1	14	1	34	1
Wick, Batavia*	3	3	.500	7.29	14	1	0	4	0	0	33.1	37	31	27	6	1	14	0	24	3
Worrell, Erie	4	1	.800	3.31	9	8	0	0	0	0	51.2	52	23	19	5	2	15	0	57	7
Wyatt, Little Falls*	0	0	.000	0.00	1	0	0	0	0	0	2	0	0	0	0	0	2	0	2	0
Young, Erie*	4	3	.571	4.76	9	7	0	0	0	0	34	35	20	18	1	0	21	0	41	3
Zmudosky, Utica	7	6	.538	4.49	17	17	3	0	1	0	110.1	122	66	55	11	2	34	0	75	5

BALKS—Barkley, 4; Heath, 3; Carrasco, Livesey, Norton, Paul, Shulleeta, Tomaselli, Zmudosky, 2 each; Arnold, Baldrick, Carson, Compagno, Dunn, Fagan, Farley, Filippo, Gardner, Hill, Hogan, Kizer, Meadows, Miller, C. Mitchell, Moretti, Pierorazio, Poindexter, Pruitt, Rodriguez, Roy, Schulte, Sunde, Thomas, White, Young, 1 each.

COMBINATION SHUTOUTS—Meadows-Perkins-Riewerts, Hogan-Riewerts, Schimpf-Perkins, Auburn; Key-Sellers, Rochford-Lockhart, Hill-Silva, Elmira; Young-Dunn-Mitchell, Erie; Shulleeta-Isgett-Serafini-Blevins, Geneva; Kinns-Mitchell, Jamestown; Walker-Weston-Jensen, Little Falls; Trujillo-Cruz, Skinner-Moses, Trujillo-Cruz-Moses, Niagara Falls; Byron-Graham, Oneonta.

NO-HIT GAME—None.

Northwest League

CLASS A

CHAMPIONSHIP WINNERS IN PREVIOUS YEARS

1901—Portland .675	1941—Spokane .669	1964—Eugene. .636
1902—Butte .608	1942—Vancouver .594	Yakima* .611
1903—Butte .578	1943-45—Did not operate.	1965—Lewiston .667
1904—Boise .625	1946—Wenatchee .622	Tri-City* .681
1905—Vancouver .586	1947—Vancouver .566	1966—Tri-City .679
Everett* .667	1948—Spokane .614	1967—Medford .607
1906—Tacoma .600	1949—Yakima .660	1968—Tri-City .600
1907—Aberdeen .625	Vancouver (2nd)† .615	1969—Rogue Valley .633
1908—Vancouver .578	1950—Yakima .613	1970—Lewiston a .538
1909—Seattle .653	1951—Spokane .655	Coos Bay-No. Bend .563
1910—Spokane .596	1952—Victoria .631	1971—Tri-City a .625
1911—Vancouver .628	1953—Salem. .635	Bend .538
1912—Seattle .600	Spokane* .590	1972—Lewiston a .675
1913—Vancouver .600	1954—Vancouver* .636	Walla Walla .513
1914—Vancouver .632	Lewiston .629	1973—Walla Walla b .638
1915—Seattle .564	1955—Salem. .646	Portland .563
1916—Spokane .622	Eugene* .639	1974—Bellingham .619
1917—Great Falls .592	1956—Yakima .691	Eugene c .571
1918—Seattle .588	Yakima .619	1975—Portland .545
1919—Seattle .590	1957—Eugene. .576	Eugene d .684
1920—Victoria .600	Wenatchee* .647	1976—Portland .556
1921—Yakima .710	1958—Lewiston .621	Walla Walla d .639
Yakima .660	Yakima* .594	1977—Bellingham e .618
1922—Calgary† .600	1959—Salem. .623	Portland .667
1923-36—Did not operate.	Yakima* .563	1978—Grays Harbor f .671
1937—Wenatchee .603	1960—Yakima .638	Eugene. .514
Tacoma* .627	Yakima .562	1979—Central Oregon d .606
1938—Yakima .583	1961—Lewiston* .621	Walla Walla .571
Bellingham (2nd)† .511	Yakima .600	1980—Bellingham g .643
1939—Wenatchee .601	1962—Wenatchee* .574	Eugene g .529
Tacoma (2nd)† .533	Tri-City .580	1981—Medford d .600
1940—Spokane .587	1963—Lewiston .594	Bellingham .557
Tacoma (4th)† .500	Yakima* .613	

*Won split-season playoff. †Won four-club playoff. §League disbanded June 18. aLeague divided into Northern and Southern divisions, declared champion under league rules. bLeague divided into Eastern and Western divisions, declared champion under league rules. cLeague divided into Eastern and Western divisions; won two-team playoff. dLeague divided into Northern and Southern divisions; won two-team playoff. eLeague divided into Affiliate and Independent divisions; won two-team playoff. fDeclared league champion after winning one-game playoff. Balance of playoff canceled due to rain and wet grounds. gDeclared co-champion after winning one game. Balance of playoff canceled due to rain and wet grounds. (NOTE—Known as Pacific Northwest League 1901-02, Pacific National League 1903-04, Northwestern League 1905-18, Pacific Coast International League 1919-22 and Western International League 1937-54.)

STANDING OF CLUBS AT CLOSE OF SEASON, SEPTEMBER 2
NORTHERN DIVISION

Club	Sal.	Bell.	W.W.	Med.	Bend	Eug.	W.	L.	T.	Pct.	G.B.
Salem (Angels)	....	7	8	4	7	8	34	36	0	.486	......
Bellingham (Mariners)	7	....	7	3	7	9	33	37	0	.471	1
Walla Walla (Padres)	6	7	....	2	8	9	32	38	0	.457	2

SOUTHERN DIVISION

Club	Sal.	Bell.	W.W.	Med.	Bend	Eug.	W.	L.	T.	Pct.	G.B.
Medford (A's)	10	11	12	....	11	9	53	17	0	.757	......
Bend (Phillies)	7	7	6	3	....	7	30	40	0	.429	23
Eugene (Reds)	6	5	5	5	7	....	28	42	0	.400	25

Bend represented Bend, Ore.

Major league affiliations in parentheses.

Playoff—Salem defeated Medford, two games to none.

Regular-Season Attendance—Bellingham, 17,211; Bend, 28,334; Eugene, 55,273; Medford, 58,053; Salem, 37,392; Walla Walla, 18,771. Total, 215,034. Playoffs, 2,443. All-Star Game, 1,911.

Managers: Bellingham, Jeff Scott; Bend, Rolando Jesus de Armas; Eugene, Jim Stewart; Medford, Dennis Rogers; Salem, Joe Maddon; Walla Walla, Jim Skaalen.

All-Star Team: 1B—Eppard, Medford; 2B—Graham, Medford; 3B—James, Bend; SS—Thoma, Medford; OF—Laurenzi, Medford; Key, Salem; Hill, Bellingham; DH—Strom, Medford; C—McGriff, Eugene; P—Barry, Medford; Myers, Medford; Manager—Maddon, Salem.

(Compiled by William J. Weiss, League Statistician, San Mateo, Calif.)

CLUB BATTING

Club	Pct.	G.	AB.	R.	OR.	H.	TB.	2B.	3B.	HR.	RBI.	GW.	SH.	SF.	HP.	BB.	Int. BB.	SO.	SB.	CS.	LOB.
Medford	.283	70	2346	499	337	653	992	94	19	69	413	34	32	19	19	415	14	424	140	42	533
Walla Walla	.245	70	2302	349	431	564	760	97	18	21	282	27	22	17	15	391	15	539	137	58	565
Bend	.245	70	2364	396	403	579	921	107	20	65	339	21	13	15	27	342	8	584	92	33	545
Salem	.241	70	2301	373	372	554	751	74	27	23	294	30	20	22	29	399	10	498	148	44	577
Eugene	.240	70	2257	349	433	542	781	101	18	34	286	21	25	14	23	407	19	588	114	27	568
Bellingham	.228	70	2281	366	356	520	704	74	7	32	287	28	27	26	23	451	13	456	117	45	599

INDIVIDUAL BATTING
(Leading Qualifiers for Batting Championship—189 or More Plate Appearances)

*Bats lefthanded.   †Switch-hitter.

Player and Club	Pct.	G.	AB.	R.	H.	TB.	2B.	3B.	HR.	RBI.	GW.	SH.	SF.	HP.	BB.	Int. BB.	SO.	SB.	CS.
Eppard, James, Medford*	.376	64	242	58	91	111	13	2	1	41	3	0	2	1	50	1	15	6	3
Laurenzi, Anthony, Medford	.362	58	199	58	72	110	10	2	8	38	2	4	0	2	40	0	35	20	4
Gomez, Jose, Walla Walla*	.352	64	196	42	69	111	16	1	8	39	5	0	1	1	73	8	55	2	3
Radloff, Scott, Eugene*	.335	61	191	37	64	88	10	4	2	30	2	0	2	0	56	5	29	5	2
Key, Gregory, Salem	.327	69	263	40	86	138	14	7	8	51	3	1	6	1	38	0	39	28	7
James, Chris, Bend	.317	63	227	47	72	133	19	3	12	50	3	1	1	4	20	0	56	10	4
Brown, Anthony, Bend*	.312	51	189	27	59	104	11	5	8	26	2	1	1	0	14	2	33	10	3
Strom, Phillip, Medford	.310	65	226	49	70	133	16	1	15	71	9	1	2	3	46	1	53	1	0
Hill, Roger, Bellingham*	.305	61	203	34	62	92	5	2	7	36	3	1	2	1	41	4	25	16	6
McLemore, Mark, Salem†	.297	55	165	42	49	59	6	2	0	25	4	1	3	2	39	0	38	14	6

Departmental Leaders: G—Duggan, Smith, 70; AB—Duggan, 283; R—Madril, 61; H—Eppard, 91; TB—Key, 138; 2B—James, 19; 3B—Key, 7; HR—Strom, 15; RBI—Strom, 71; GWRBI—Strom, 9; SH—Good, Stout, Thoma, 6; SF—Key, Smith, 6; HP—Madril, 10; BB—Vollmer, 94; IBB—Gomez, 8; SO—Culver, 71; SB—Madril, 45; CS—Freeman, Vollmer, 10.

(All Players—Listed Alphabetically)

Player and Club	Pct.	G.	AB.	R.	H.	TB.	2B.	3B.	HR.	RBI.	GW.	SH.	SF.	HP.	BB.	Int. BB.	SO.	SB.	CS.
Adamiak, Mark, Bend	.255	54	212	32	54	74	10	2	2	23	1	4	3	2	24	0	38	11	6
Adams, Bert, Salem	.182	24	66	12	12	12	0	0	0	5	0	0	0	2	9	0	28	5	1
Allinger, Robert, Walla Walla	.205	48	151	21	31	40	6	0	1	11	0	0	0	0	13	2	46	6	4
Anderson, Willie, Walla Walla	.217	55	198	17	43	57	7	2	1	24	2	4	3	0	27	0	67	6	5
Bailey, Vincent, Medford	.274	45	124	20	34	42	6	1	0	19	0	4	0	1	19	1	13	8	2
Bathe, Robert, Medford	.288	64	215	43	62	105	10	3	9	41	5	0	1	5	51	1	24	12	4
Bender, Kenneth, Walla Walla*	.195	31	87	7	17	20	1	1	0	6	0	3	1	0	12	1	27	1	2
Berry, Troy, Bend†	.167	28	66	19	11	13	2	0	0	4	0	0	0	0	18	0	14	6	0
Bickers, Darrell, Bellingham†	.042	13	24	0	1	1	0	0	0	0	0	0	0	0	8	0	17	0	0
Blume, David, Bellingham*	.000	6	4	0	0	0	0	0	0	2	0	1	0	1	2	1	2	0	0
Brady, David, Salem*	.174	38	115	11	20	22	0	1	0	4	0	5	0	1	19	2	31	3	0
Briggs, Kenneth, Bellingham	.193	63	202	31	39	49	4	0	2	11	0	1	4	1	31	0	48	14	4
Brown, Anthony, Bend*	.312	51	189	27	59	104	11	5	8	26	2	1	1	0	14	2	33	10	3
Chavous, Joel, Bend	.143	22	56	7	8	14	3	0	1	4	0	0	1	0	13	0	19	0	3
Choate, Milo, Bend	.188	40	112	24	21	36	3	0	4	18	0	0	1	1	35	1	47	4	0
Colburn, Thomas, Medford†	.314	16	35	13	11	27	0	2	4	13	0	0	0	1	12	1	12	1	0
Creel, Leland, Bend	.248	32	105	13	26	47	6	0	5	18	1	0	1	1	17	2	31	0	0
Crump, Paul, Bend	.286	5	14	0	4	4	0	0	0	0	0	0	0	0	3	0	3	2	0
Cruz, Eduardo, Bellingham	.212	12	33	3	7	7	0	0	0	5	1	4	1	0	5	0	8	0	0
Culver, Lanell, Eugene†	.188	52	165	26	31	56	7	0	6	21	2	1	0	4	33	1	71	10	3
Davis, Kevin, Salem	.247	58	198	24	49	61	6	3	0	19	5	1	1	1	15	1	38	10	4
Day, Randall, Bend	.239	58	205	41	49	75	14	0	4	30	2	1	2	2	29	0	30	8	0
DeLaCruz, Francisco, Salem	.200	4	5	0	1	2	1	0	0	0	0	0	0	0	1	0	2	0	0
Dodd, Timothy, Eugene	.148	16	27	2	4	4	0	0	0	1	0	4	1	0	0	0	9	1	0
Duggan, Thomas, Bellingham	.233	70	283	34	66	89	11	0	4	37	4	5	4	1	33	0	52	3	6
Duncan, John, Bellingham	.160	33	106	9	17	23	6	0	0	15	1	1	0	0	17	0	16	6	0
Dye, Mark, Medford	.045	12	22	5	1	1	0	0	0	0	0	1	0	0	7	0	4	2	0
Eppard, James, Medford*	.376	64	242	58	91	111	13	2	1	41	3	0	2	1	50	1	15	6	3
Fenton, Donald, Eugene	.125	18	8	0	1	1	0	0	0	1	0	1	0	0	0	0	3	0	0
Findeisen, Guy, Eugene	.000	6	7	0	0	0	0	0	0	0	0	0	0	0	0	0	3	0	0
Fonseca, Angel, Bellingham	.235	58	170	34	40	44	4	0	0	15	3	3	0	3	38	0	24	7	5
Freeman, Donald, Walla Walla	.178	66	230	30	41	57	4	3	2	30	2	1	3	0	44	1	49	18	10
Frierson, John, Walla Walla	.000	2	4	1	0	0	0	0	0	0	0	0	0	0	1	0	3	0	0
George, Thomas, Bend	.191	41	141	30	27	43	3	2	3	10	0	2	1	4	30	0	48	5	4
Glick, David, Medford	.223	36	103	22	23	29	3	0	1	15	1	1	2	1	25	1	22	8	0
Gomez, Jose, Walla Walla*	.352	64	196	42	69	111	16	1	8	39	5	0	1	1	73	8	55	2	3
Good, James, Medford	.252	50	127	24	32	52	5	0	5	18	3	6	2	1	12	0	26	1	1
Govea, David, Salem*	.250	62	224	27	56	72	9	2	1	42	1	2	4	0	42	1	36	5	6
Graham, Brian, Medford	.250	60	236	57	59	87	11	4	3	28	4	4	2	2	37	0	28	25	6
Haberle, David, Eugene*	.317	52	142	17	45	65	8	3	2	21	0	0	1	3	29	0	31	14	2
Harms, Duane, Eugene	.042	17	24	1	1	1	0	0	0	1	0	0	0	0	2	0	14	1	0
Hennessy, Michael, Eugene†	.200	8	15	4	3	5	2	0	0	2	0	1	0	0	2	0	9	0	0
Herrera, Cesar, Bellingham	.219	28	96	10	21	25	4	0	0	8	0	3	1	0	10	0	9	1	1
Hill, Orsino, Eugene*	.250	54	136	30	34	65	8	1	7	28	2	0	1	3	49	4	44	8	1
Hill, Roger, Bellingham*	.305	61	203	34	62	92	5	2	7	36	3	1	2	1	41	4	25	16	6
Hooker, Elton, Medford†	.222	29	81	13	18	21	1	1	0	8	0	1	0	0	17	0	22	12	3
Hoskins, Osbe, Walla Walla	.243	68	268	53	65	83	15	0	1	21	0	2	2	2	50	0	43	37	9
Hughes, Keith, Bend*	.257	55	179	29	46	69	10	2	3	26	1	1	2	1	30	1	42	2	0
Hume, Timothy, Eugene†	.173	39	81	18	14	18	2	1	0	7	0	1	0	3	18	1	32	6	2
James, Chris, Bend	.317	63	227	47	72	133	19	3	12	50	3	1	1	4	20	0	56	10	4
Jelks, Gregory, Bend	.179	42	140	18	25	51	3	1	7	30	2	0	0	1	28	2	52	3	1
Jimenez, Ramon, Salem	.215	50	158	13	34	43	4	1	1	20	1	1	0	3	23	0	24	1	0
Johns, Richard, Eugene	.375	26	8	2	3	4	1	0	0	2	0	1	0	0	2	0	3	0	0
Jones, Daniel, Walla Walla	.243	62	206	29	50	70	4	5	2	35	4	0	1	4	27	0	34	12	5
Jones, Kenneth, Bend	.288	56	212	23	61	78	4	2	3	30	2	1	0	0	5	0	55	12	5
Kanter, John, Bend†	.227	53	172	32	39	67	9	2	5	21	3	2	1	4	24	0	49	9	3
Key, Gregory, Salem	.327	69	263	40	86	138	14	7	8	51	3	1	6	1	38	0	39	28	7
Kline, Kris, Salem	.257	69	268	41	69	97	11	1	5	38	5	0	3	4	40	2	51	14	8
Laurenzi, Anthony, Medford	.362	58	199	58	72	110	10	2	8	38	2	4	0	2	40	0	35	20	4
Lee, Terry, Eugene	.256	32	117	23	30	53	5	3	4	21	2	0	1	0	20	0	27	4	2
Lewis, Jay, Salem	.220	49	159	30	35	58	7	2	4	25	4	1	1	1	29	0	46	8	3
Longa, Ramon, Salem	.183	43	131	25	24	30	1	1	1	17	4	3	2	2	29	0	28	5	1
Mack, Tony, Salem	.000	14	0	1	0	0	0	0	0	0	0	0	0	0	0	0	0	0	0
Mackie, Bart, Bellingham	.133	11	30	1	4	4	0	0	0	1	0	0	0	0	2	0	6	0	0
Madril, Michael, Salem†	.246	69	260	61	64	82	4	4	2	21	0	3	1	10	56	2	59	45	8
Matos, Rafael, Bellingham	.000	4	6	0	0	0	0	0	0	0	0	0	0	0	1	0	4	0	0
McGriff, Terence, Eugene	.242	53	190	23	46	72	10	2	4	31	4	0	3	0	26	0	47	1	0
McLemore, Mark, Salem†	.297	55	165	42	49	59	6	2	0	25	4	1	3	2	39	0	38	14	6
Minyard, John, Eugene	.000	13	22	0	0	0	0	0	0	0	0	2	0	0	2	0	8	0	0
Mitchell, Donald, Eugene	.197	43	122	20	24	34	4	0	2	13	0	1	0	3	14	0	29	5	1

Player and Club	Pct.	G.	AB.	R.	H.	TB.	2B.	3B.	HR.	RBI.	GW.	SH.	SF.	HP.	BB.	Int. BB.	SO.	SB.	CS.
Morris, Manuel, Bellingham	.184	18	38	6	7	7	0	0	0	3	0	0	0	0	2	0	10	2	0
Munson, Jay, Eugene	.230	57	213	36	49	55	6	0	0	21	0	1	1	1	41	0	42	17	3
Myers, David, Bellingham	.281	59	221	42	62	74	10	1	0	34	4	2	4	5	34	0	21	14	2
O'Brien, Charles, Medford	.283	17	60	11	17	29	3	0	3	14	1	0	1	1	10	1	10	0	1
O'Connor, Curtis, Eugene*	.169	27	65	12	11	22	3	1	2	8	1	1	1	2	4	0	23	2	0
O'Hara, Patrick, Medford	.193	35	88	13	17	33	1	0	5	21	2	1	2	0	11	0	40	0	1
Perez, Paul, Bend	.219	50	128	17	28	34	3	0	1	16	1	0	0	1	17	0	21	0	2
Peterson, David, Medford*	.224	53	161	25	36	49	4	0	3	23	1	0	2	0	16	2	35	6	5
Pott, Lawrence, Walla Walla	.234	55	167	27	39	46	7	0	0	22	4	1	0	4	34	0	27	9	4
Proctor, John, Bend	.143	6	14	1	2	5	0	0	1	1	0	0	0	0	2	0	5	2	0
Radloff, Scott, Eugene*	.335	61	191	37	64	88	10	4	2	30	2	0	2	0	56	5	29	5	2
Rhoads, Kevin, Walla Walla	.000	18	1	0	1	1	0	0	0	0	0	0	0	0	0	0	0	0	0
Rhodes, Jeffrey, Eugene	.215	44	107	11	23	41	7	1	3	17	1	0	0	2	13	0	37	1	0
Riley, Thomas, Eugene	.280	64	243	34	68	79	9	1	0	21	3	0	1	1	28	3	21	7	3
Ritchie, Robert, Salem*	.173	28	75	10	13	19	2	2	0	7	2	0	1	1	14	1	28	2	0
Rizzo, Michael, Salem	.235	40	132	13	31	37	6	0	0	13	1	1	0	1	20	0	23	4	0
Rodriguez, David, Bellingham	.140	34	100	10	14	25	2	0	3	9	1	0	0	0	14	0	47	1	0
Rodriguez, Rigo, Walla Walla	.240	68	258	43	62	91	13	2	4	31	2	4	2	2	26	1	53	10	6
Roebuck, Scott, Bellingham	.243	66	230	45	56	86	7	1	7	40	5	2	1	6	50	0	54	13	6
Rojas, Luis, Medford	.246	65	199	51	49	78	4	2	7	33	5	3	1	0	37	2	47	27	6
Salgueiro, Miguel, Eugene	.000	4	1	0	0	0	0	0	0	0	0	0	0	0	0	0	0	0	0
Segura, Americo, Salem	.100	6	10	0	1	1	0	0	0	0	0	0	0	0	2	0	3	1	0
Seibert, Gibson, Bend	.100	4	10	4	1	1	0	0	0	0	0	0	0	0	5	0	3	3	0
Simmons, Allison, Walla Walla†	.283	63	244	40	69	80	6	1	1	25	3	4	0	0	24	0	51	24	8
Smith, David, Bellingham*	.254	70	244	44	62	103	10	2	9	44	2	0	6	2	64	4	52	10	4
Stout, Steven, Eugene	.231	18	26	2	6	6	0	0	0	4	1	6	0	0	2	0	13	0	0
Stout, Timothy, Eugene	.224	39	67	12	15	19	4	0	0	4	0	0	0	0	18	0	17	5	1
Strichek, James, Eugene	.000	27	10	1	0	0	0	0	0	0	0	3	0	0	3	0	5	0	0
Strom, Phillip, Medford	.310	65	226	49	70	133	16	1	15	71	9	1	2	3	46	1	53	1	0
Thoma, Raymond, Medford	.268	58	228	37	61	85	7	1	5	30	4	6	2	2	25	3	38	11	6
Vernon, David, Bend	.178	24	45	5	8	10	2	0	0	5	0	0	4	7	0	14	1	0
Vest, James, Bend	.277	46	137	27	38	63	5	1	6	27	3	0	1	2	21	0	24	4	2
Vollmer, Robert, Bellingham*	.220	65	214	53	47	58	9	1	0	22	3	1	4	0	94	4	40	29	10
Walker, Thomas, Eugene	.210	34	62	8	13	15	2	0	0	5	1	0	1	1	11	1	13	1	1
Watson, Steven, Eugene	.200	27	10	1	2	2	0	0	0	0	1	0	0	0	0	0	3	0	1
Westmoreland, John, Walla Walla*	.247	44	146	18	36	53	12	1	1	23	3	1	1	1	33	2	57	3	0
Wiesler, William, Salem†	.139	34	72	18	10	18	3	1	1	7	0	1	0	2	23	1	24	3	0
Wiggins, Kevin, Walla Walla*	.281	40	146	21	41	51	6	2	0	15	2	2	3	1	27	0	27	9	2
Yeampierre, Eddie, Bellingham	.195	23	77	10	15	17	2	0	0	5	1	4	1	1	5	0	21	1	1
Young, Delwyn, Eugene†	.278	62	198	29	55	76	13	1	2	27	2	1	1	0	32	4	55	26	6

The following pitchers, listed alphabetically by club, with games in parentheses, had no plate appearances, primarily through use of designated hitters:

BELLINGHAM—Barnhouse, Scott (19); Bergendahl, Wray (15); Eldridge, Jeffrey (15); Enriquez, Martin (14); Kinley, Wayne (11); McDonald, Jeffrey (11); Newman, Randall (22); Parent, Eric (8); Richard, Todd (7); Roy, Kevin (9); Schassler, Jeffrey (8); Taylor, Terry (14); Towey, Curtis (19).

BEND—Brewer, Stanley (19); Burgess, Kirk (17); Maddux, Michael (11); Miller, Todd (24); Morel, Nelson (14); Olson, James (12); Rasnick, James (1); Robertson, Michael (12); Robinson, Paul (19); Scarpetta, Dennis (11); Segura, Jose (24); Witt, Stephen (14).

MEDFORD—Bailey, James (5); Barry, Eric (15); Feeley, James (5); Godwin, Glenn (16); Gonsalves, Dennis (28); Gorman, Michael (16); Jackson, Milton (12); Kaiser, Jeffrey (15); Mine, Gregory (2); Myers, Edward (31); Ontiveros, Steven (4); Perez, Jose (2); Vela, John (12).

SALEM—Cedeno, Vinicio (2); Glanz, Scott (9); Gonzalez, Julian (10); Groh, Donald (28); Hudson, John (9); Kilmer, Robert (17); Kipper, Robert (13); Knowles, Kirk (10); Lora, Alejandro (1); Lugo, Rafael (14); McCaskill, Kirk (11); McKenzie, Douglas (5); Suehr, Scott (25); Timberlake, Donald (11); Valdez, Jose (1).

WALLA WALLA—Crabb, Gregory (14); Dean, Jeffrey (20); Jones, James (14); Lloyd, Richard (16); Mutz, Jack (10); Odom, Craig (23); Plesac, Joseph (7); Steffanich, Gregory (22); Towers, Kevin (6); Walter, Gene (17); Williams, Mitchell (12).

GRAND SLAM HOME RUNS—Good, Key, Lee, O'Brien, O'Hara, Peterson, R. Rodriguez, Rojas, Simmons, Strom, 1 each.

AWARDED FIRST BASE ON CATCHER'S INTERFERENCE—Day 3 (Segura, Westmoreland, Yeampierre); Perez 2 (Good, Mitchell); Simmons 2 (O'Hara, Perez); Smith 2 (Good, Segura); Glick (O'Connor); Lewis (Yeampierre); Hennessy (Yeampierre); Lewis (Yeampierre); Pott (Chavous); Rojas (Jimenez); Westmoreland (Duncan).

CLUB FIELDING

Club	Pct.	G.	PO.	A.	E.	DP.	PB.	Club	Pct.	G.	PO.	A.	E.	DP.	PB.
Bellingham	.954	70	1838	766	126	45	30	Bend	.946	70	1811	806	149	64	14
Medford	.948	70	1853	708	140	44	15	Eugene	.944	70	1789	744	150	53	14
Salem	.946	70	1820	738	145	57	15	Walla Walla	.942	70	1829	792	162	66	31

Triple Play—Walla Walla.

INDIVIDUAL FIELDING

FIRST BASEMEN

*Throws lefthanded.

Player and Club	Pct.	G.	PO.	A.	E.	DP.	Player and Club	Pct.	G.	PO.	A.	E.	DP.
Bathe, Medford	1.000	2	3	0	0	0	Lee, Eugene	1.000	14	102	5	0	5
Creel, Bend	.993	30	245	14	2	25	Proctor, Bend	.800	2	8	0	2	0
Day, Bend	.982	6	55	1	1	1	Radloff, Eugene*	.982	58	458	35	9	41
Eppard, Medford*	.980	59	459	38	10	33	Ritchie, Salem*	1.000	21	178	4	0	12
Gomez, Walla Walla*	.980	60	511	31	11	48	Rizzo, Salem	.714	1	4	1	2	1
Govea, Salem*	.977	53	434	31	11	37	SMITH, Bellingham*	.991	70	650	28	6	40
Haberle, Eugene	1.000	1	1	0	0	0	Strom, Medford	.954	12	96	7	5	5
Jelks, Bend	.975	36	341	13	9	30	Walker, Eugene	.933	7	38	4	3	2
D. Jones, Walla Walla	1.000	7	57	3	0	7	Wiggins, Walla Walla*	.959	6	46	1	2	2

Triple Play—Gomez.

SECOND BASEMEN

Player and Club	Pct.	G.	PO.	A.	E.	DP.	Player and Club	Pct.	G.	PO.	A.	E.	DP.
V. Bailey, Medford	1.000	1	0	1	0	0	D. Jones, Walla Walla	1.000	1	1	0	0	1
Berry, Bend	.974	24	48	66	3	12	Kanter, Bend	.946	53	94	149	14	31
Cruz, Bellingham	1.000	7	11	22	0	2	Key, Salem	.912	28	59	76	13	16
DeLaCruz, Salem	1.000	3	1	2	0	0	Kline, Salem	.900	2	4	5	1	2
Dye, Medford	.929	8	13	13	2	1	Matos, Bellingham	1.000	2	0	1	0	0
Fonseca, Bellingham	.932	50	85	106	14	20	McLemore, Salem	.957	39	74	106	8	18
Freeman, Walla Walla	.967	14	27	31	2	11	Mitchell, Eugene	1.000	3	1	0	0	0
George, Bend	.938	4	5	10	1	2	Rizzo, Salem	1.000	2	5	0	0	0
Glick, Medford	.922	35	54	65	10	12	Rodriguez, Bellingham	.934	22	24	47	5	6
Graham, Medford	.969	36	81	75	5	15	Simmons, Walla Walla	.946	57	122	157	16	36
Hume, Eugene	.947	20	42	30	4	7	YOUNG, Eugene	.949	61	129	150	15	25

Triple Play—Freeman.

THIRD BASEMEN

Player and Club	Pct.	G.	PO.	A.	E.	DP.	Player and Club	Pct.	G.	PO.	A.	E.	DP.
Bathe, Medford	.874	61	45	122	24	7	Hume, Eugene	1.000	1	2	2	0	0
Choate, Bend	.841	39	21	69	17	1	James, Bend	.901	32	24	49	8	4
Davis, Salem	.500	1	0	1	1	0	D. Jones. Walla Walla	.833	29	18	42	12	0
DUGGAN, Bellingham	.924	70	39	144	15	7	Kline, Salem	.879	54	50	103	21	8
Freeman, Walla Walla	.824	43	29	97	27	10	Mitchell, Eugene	.926	36	28	60	7	4
George, Bend	.833	7	4	16	4	3	Rizzo, Salem	1.000	2	5	0	0	0
Graham, Medford	.818	6	2	7	2	1	Simmons, Walla Walla	1.000	1	1	4	0	0
Haberle, Eugene	.789	44	31	55	23	6	Strom, Medford	.867	6	5	8	2	0

SHORTSTOPS

Player and Club	Pct.	G.	PO.	A.	E.	DP.	Player and Club	Pct.	G.	PO.	A.	E.	DP.
Adamiak, Bend	.902	44	65	138	22	26	Glick, Medford	1.000	1	0	1	0	0
Bickers, Bellingham	.333	1	0	1	2	0	Graham, Medford	.877	14	25	32	8	8
Choate, Bend	1.000	1	0	2	0	1	Hume, Eugene	.833	14	12	28	8	3
Cruz, Bellingham	.778	5	4	10	4	0	Kline, Salem	.960	12	18	30	2	4
Davis, Salem	.904	52	88	156	26	27	McLemore, Salem	.897	7	7	19	3	1
DeLaCruz, Salem	1.000	1	0	1	0	0	Myers, Bellingham	.930	59	110	170	21	25
Fonseca, Bellingham	.926	8	7	18	2	1	Riley, Eugene	.924	63	96	195	24	27
Freeman, Walla Walla	1.000	3	6	10	0	3	Rodriguez, Walla Walla	.929	68	120	244	28	46
George, Bend	.956	29	35	95	6	15	THOMA, Medford	.937	58	91	161	17	20

OUTFIELDERS

Player and Club	Pct.	G.	PO.	A.	E.	DP.	Player and Club	Pct.	G.	PO.	A.	E.	DP.
Adams, Salem	1.000	17	23	2	0	0	Lee, Eugene	.958	23	21	2	1	1
Allinger, Walla Walla	.892	46	64	2	8	2	Lewis, Salem	.966	46	52	4	2	1
Anderson, Walla Walla	.893	50	64	3	8	0	Longa, Salem	.936	25	43	1	3	0
V. Bailey, Medford	.943	36	49	1	3	0	Madril, Salem	.935	69	124	6	9	0
Bender, Walla Walla*	1.000	24	25	1	0	0	Morris, Bellingham	.750	7	3	0	1	0
Briggs, Bellingham	.897	53	64	6	8	1	MUNSON, Eugene	.980	57	98	1	2	0
Brown, Bend	.902	32	34	3	4	1	O'Hara, Medford	.818	7	9	0	2	0
Culver, Eugene*	.961	49	118	4	5	0	Peterson, Medford*	.917	51	51	4	5	0
Day, Bend	.934	40	52	5	4	1	Rizzo, Salem	1.000	2	2	0	0	0
Graham, Medford	1.000	9	13	3	0	0	Rhodes, Bellingham	.897	30	25	1	3	0
Hill, Eugene	.924	47	56	5	5	1	Roebuck, Bellingham	.937	43	57	2	4	0
Hill, Bellingham	.968	52	83	9	3	0	Rojas, Medford	.967	60	112	4	4	0
Hooker, Medford*	.919	26	33	1	3	0	Seibert, Bend	1.000	4	3	0	0	0
Hoskins, Walla Walla	.933	68	141	12	11	1	T. Stout, Eugene	.870	23	19	1	3	0
Hughes, Bend*	.950	51	90	6	5	2	Vest, Bend	.939	33	44	2	3	0
James, Bend	.974	31	69	5	2	0	Vollmer, Bellingham	.934	62	97	2	7	0
D. Jones, Walla Walla	.889	7	8	0	1	0	Walker, Eugene	1.000	15	12	1	0	0
Jones, Bend	.930	40	50	3	4	1	Wiesler, Salem	.967	27	28	1	1	0
Key, Salem	.852	36	48	4	9	1	Wiggins, Walla Walla*	.936	26	40	4	3	0
Laurenzi, Medford	.963	52	74	4	3	1	Young, Eugene	.667	1	2	0	1	0

CATCHERS

Player and Club	Pct.	G.	PO.	A.	E.	DP.	PB.	Player and Club	Pct.	G.	PO.	A.	E.	DP.	PB.
Brady, Salem	.966	28	178	18	7	2	7	Mitchell, Eugene	.971	7	30	3	1	0	1
Chavous, Bend	.943	21	109	6	7	0	5	O'Brien, Medford	.971	16	116	18	4	2	2
Colburn, Medford	.991	14	107	6	1	0	1	O'Connor, Eugene	.938	23	105	15	8	1	8
Crump, Bend	1.000	5	38	3	0	0	0	O'Hara, Medford	.950	13	51	6	3	0	1
Duncan, Bellingham	.960	31	218	25	10	2	14	Perez, Bend	.974	49	267	37	8	2	7
Frierson, Walla Walla	1.000	1	1	0	0	0	0	POTT, Walla Walla	.983	36	251	39	5	1	13
Good, Medford	.969	47	331	39	12	3	11	Segura, Salem	.893	5	21	4	3	0	3
Herrera, Bellingham	.995	25	183	19	1	0	13	Vernon, Bend	.965	17	74	9	3	1	2
Jimenez, Salem	.973	45	335	29	10	5	5	Westmoreland, Walla Walla	.949	37	269	30	16	2	18
Mackie, Bellingham	.905	3	17	2	2	0	2	Yeampierre, Bellingham	.958	22	162	20	8	0	1
McGriff, Eugene	.978	53	320	43	8	0	5								

PITCHERS

Player and Club	Pct.	G.	PO.	A.	E.	DP.	Player and Club	Pct.	G.	PO.	A.	E.	DP.
J. Bailey, Medford	1.000	5	0	2	0	0	Enriquez, Bellingham	1.000	14	1	13	0	0
Barnhouse, Bellingham	.889	19	3	13	2	0	Fenton, Eugene	1.000	18	2	7	0	0
Barry, Medford*	.971	15	4	30	1	3	Findeisen, Eugene	.875	6	2	5	1	1
Bergendahl, Bellingham	.792	15	3	16	5	1	Glanz, Salem	.917	9	1	10	1	1
Brewer, Bend	.750	19	2	1	1	0	Godwin, Medford*	.643	16	9	9	10	0
Burgess, Bend	.615	17	1	7	5	0	Gonsalves, Medford	1.000	28	2	4	0	0
Cedeno, Salem	1.000	2	1	0	0	0	Gonzalez, Salem	.900	10	3	6	1	1
Crabb, Walla Walla	1.000	14	5	14	0	1	Gorman, Medford	1.000	16	5	16	0	0
Dean, Walla Walla	.818	20	5	4	2	0	Groh, Salem*	.944	28	4	13	1	1
Dodd, Eugene	.882	16	6	9	2	0	Harms, Eugene	.818	15	8	19	6	0
Eldridge, Bellingham	1.000	15	1	4	0	1	Hennessy, Eugene	.833	8	2	8	2	0

PITCHERS—Continued

Player and Club	Pct.	G.	PO.	A.	E.	DP.	Player and Club	Pct.	G.	PO.	A.	E.	DP.
Hudson, Salem	1.000	9	0	3	0	0	Parent, Bellingham	1.000	8	0	10	0	0
Jackson, Medford	.667	12	0	4	2	0	Plesac, Walla Walla	1.000	7	1	4	0	0
Johns, Eugene	.769	26	4	6	3	0	Rasnick, Bend	1.000	1	0	1	0	0
J. Jones, Walla Walla	.950	14	3	6	1	1	Rhoads, Walla Walla	.800	18	1	3	1	0
Kaiser, Medford°	1.000	15	6	14	0	0	Richard, Bellingham°	1.000	7	0	2	0	0
Kilmer, Salem	1.000	17	0	2	0	0	Robertson, Bend°	1.000	12	4	0	0	0
Kinley, Bellingham	1.000	11	1	4	0	1	Robinson, Bend	.933	19	4	10	1	0
Kipper, Salem°	.889	13	3	13	2	0	Roy, Bellingham	1.000	9	3	10	0	1
Knowles, Salem	1.000	10	0	2	0	0	Salgueiro, Eugene	.800	4	1	3	1	0
Lloyd, Walla Walla	.846	16	1	10	2	0	Scarpetta, Bend	1.000	11	4	11	0	0
LUGO, Salem	1.000	14	8	26	0	3	Schassler, Bellingham	1.000	8	0	5	0	0
Mack, Salem	.947	13	7	11	1	0	Segura, Bend	.667	24	3	3	3	0
Maddux, Bend	.875	11	2	12	2	1	Steffanich, Walla Walla°	.700	22	2	5	3	0
McCaskill, Salem	.833	11	4	6	2	0	S. Stout, Eugene	.857	18	5	13	3	1
McDonald, Bellingham	.944	11	4	13	1	0	Strichek, Eugene	.846	27	3	8	2	0
McKenzie, Salem	1.000	5	0	1	0	0	Suehr, Salem	.889	25	1	7	1	1
Miller, Bend	1.000	24	2	10	0	0	Taylor, Bellingham	.850	14	4	13	3	1
Minyard, Eugene	1.000	13	4	11	0	0	Timberlake, Salem	.950	11	4	15	1	0
Morel, Bend°	.857	14	2	16	3	1	Towers, Walla Walla	1.000	6	1	2	0	0
Mutz, Walla Walla	1.000	10	0	1	0	0	Towey, Bellingham	1.000	19	0	4	0	0
Myers, Medford	1.000	31	5	4	0	1	Vela, Medford°	.889	12	2	6	1	0
Newman, Bellingham°	.939	22	4	27	2	0	Walter, Walla Walla°	1.000	17	2	13	0	1
Odom, Walla Walla	.667	13	2	0	1	0	Watson, Eugene	1.000	27	6	15	0	1
Olson, Bend	.867	12	1	12	2	0	Williams, Walla Walla°	.875	12	5	9	2	0
Ontiveros, Medford	1.000	4	0	3	0	0	Witt, Bend	.889	14	2	22	3	2

The following players do not have any recorded accepted chances at the positions indicated; therefore, are not listed in the fielding averages for those particular positions: Bathe, of; Dye, 3b; Eppard, of; Feeley, p; Hume, p; Longa, 1b; Lora, p; Mine, p; Perez, p; Pott, of; Rhodes, 3b; T. Stout, 3b, p; Strom, 2b, of; Valdez, p.

CLUB PITCHING

Club	ERA.	G.	CG.	ShO.	Sv.	IP.	H.	R.	ER.	HR.	HB.	BB.	Int. BB.	SO.	WP.	Bk.
Medford	3.80	70	16	3	16	617.2	558	337	261	37	23	364	0	586	60	6
Bellingham	3.92	70	12	5	11	612.2	528	356	267	42	25	418	18	560	67	10
Salem	4.21	70	9	3	13	606.2	569	372	284	34	24	401	17	503	50	10
Bend	4.61	70	8	2	8	603.2	617	403	309	44	12	356	7	468	62	4
Walla Walla	4.77	70	11	0	12	609.2	599	431	323	45	28	411	12	528	62	6
Eugene	5.01	70	12	3	8	596.1	541	433	332	42	24	455	25	444	54	3

PITCHERS' RECORDS
(Leading Qualifiers for Earned-Run Average Leadership — 56 or More Innings)

°Throws lefthanded.

Pitcher—Club	W.	L.	Pct.	ERA.	G.	GS.	CG.	GF.	ShO.	Sv.	IP.	H.	R.	ER.	HR.	HB.	BB.	Int. BB.	SO.	WP.
Newman, Bellingham°	3	5	.375	1.88	22	6	2	14	0	4	71.2	48	27	15	4	1	39	5	73	4
Barry, Medford°	13	2	.867	2.40	15	15	9	0	2	0	124	108	44	33	8	4	43	0	106	3
McDonald, Bellingham	5	4	.556	2.47	11	10	3	0	0	0	73	59	30	20	2	2	37	1	69	5
Lugo, Salem	7	3	.700	2.88	14	13	3	0	0	0	90.2	74	45	29	1	4	61	3	62	6
Gorman, Medford	11	3	.786	3.11	16	16	5	0	0	0	121.2	107	52	42	8	4	57	0	103	5
Jones, Walla Walla	4	6	.400	3.22	14	14	2	0	0	0	78.1	64	49	28	4	1	71	0	78	7
Dodd, Eugene	6	3	.667	3.25	16	13	2	0	1	0	88.2	78	47	32	6	4	52	2	66	6
Harms, Eugene	2	4	.333	3.72	15	9	1	3	0	0	72.2	58	42	30	2	1	39	1	37	2
Crabb, Walla Walla	9	3	.750	3.73	14	14	5	0	0	0	94	92	47	39	6	5	36	2	70	7
Strichek, Eugene	3	7	.300	3.76	27	3	0	11	0	2	67	52	37	28	5	5	50	5	89	2

Departmental Leaders: G—Myers, 31; GS—Gorman, 16; CG—Barry, 9; GF—Myers, 27; ShO—Barry, 2; W—Barry, 13; L—Mack, 8; Pct.—Kaiser, .889; Sv—Myers, 12; IP—Barry, 124; H—Barry, 108; R—Godwin, 64; ER—Minyard, 51; HR—Witt, 11; HB—Bergendahl, 6; BB—Williams, 72; IBB—Watson, 6; SO—Barry, 106; WP—Johns, Parent, 15.

(All Pitchers—Listed Alphabetically)

Pitcher—Club	W.	L.	Pct.	ERA.	G.	GS.	CG.	GF.	ShO.	Sv.	IP.	H.	R.	ER.	HR.	HB.	BB.	Int. BB.	SO.	WP.
Bailey, Medford	0	0	.000	9.53	5	0	0	2	0	0	5.2	5	6	6	0	1	9	0	6	3
Barnhouse, Bellingham	5	2	.714	2.68	19	0	0	13	0	3	40.1	21	16	12	1	2	48	2	57	3
Barry, Medford°	13	2	.867	2.40	15	15	9	0	2	0	124	108	44	33	8	4	43	0	106	3
Bergendahl, Bellingham	4	7	.364	5.40	15	10	0	3	0	0	83.1	86	55	50	6	6	57	1	60	7
Brewer, Bend	2	4	.333	4.88	19	2	0	5	0	1	51.2	57	34	28	3	2	25	1	63	4
Burgess, Bend	1	4	.200	4.79	17	6	0	5	0	2	47	39	37	25	1	0	40	1	35	5
Cedeno, Salem	0	0	.000	4.50	2	0	0	1	0	0	4	3	3	2	0	1	7	0	3	2
Crabb, Walla Walla	9	3	.750	3.73	14	14	5	0	0	0	94	92	47	39	6	5	36	2	70	7
Dean, Walla Walla	4	7	.364	5.02	20	9	2	9	0	3	71.2	70	52	40	6	2	36	3	42	6
Dodd, Eugene	6	3	.667	3.25	16	13	2	0	1	0	88.2	78	47	32	6	4	52	2	66	6
Eldridge, Bellingham	0	1	.000	3.86	15	1	0	3	0	0	28	24	26	12	0	4	36	0	30	10
Enriquez, Bellingham	3	3	.500	6.34	14	9	2	2	0	0	61	58	47	43	8	3	43	0	53	4
Feeley, Medford	0	0	.000	12.27	5	2	0	0	0	0	7.1	6	12	10	1	4	11	0	4	1
Fenton, Eugene	1	4	.200	8.33	18	4	0	8	0	0	35.2	40	42	33	3	2	60	2	28	11
Findeisen, Eugene	0	3	.000	5.40	6	4	1	1	0	0	26.2	25	22	16	4	0	13	0	10	3
Glanz, Salem	2	5	.286	7.25	9	8	1	0	0	0	36	44	39	29	3	3	32	1	37	4
Godwin, Medford°	6	4	.600	4.42	16	15	1	0	0	0	97.2	97	64	48	8	1	50	0	92	8
Gonsalves, Medford	3	2	.600	4.76	28	0	0	17	0	4	45.1	41	27	24	5	2	29	0	55	3
Gonzalez, Salem	0	1	.000	8.27	10	1	0	4	0	0	16.1	17	18	15	1	2	19	2	6	1
Gorman, Medford	11	3	.786	3.11	16	16	5	0	0	0	121.2	107	52	42	8	4	57	0	103	5
Groh, Salem°	2	1	.667	1.99	28	0	0	23	0	9	45.1	41	13	10	3	1	16	1	41	5
Harms, Eugene	2	4	.333	3.72	15	9	1	3	0	0	72.2	58	42	30	2	1	39	1	37	2
Hennessy, Eugene	4	4	.500	6.08	18	7	0	5	0	0	47.1	53	45	32	4	2	24	2	32	3
Hudson, Salem	0	0	.000	6.48	9	0	0	4	0	0	16.2	21	12	12	0	0	14	1	12	2
Hume, Eugene	0	0	.000	0.00	3	0	0	3	0	0	3	0	1	0	0	0	3	0	7	1
Jackson, Medford	4	0	1.000	3.63	12	0	0	2	0	0	22.1	20	15	9	1	3	21	0	15	5
Johns, Eugene	0	2	.000	5.98	26	2	1	9	0	0	46.2	39	51	31	1	5	59	2	32	15

Pitcher—Club	W.	L.	Pct.	ERA.	G.	GS.	CG.	GF.	ShO.	Sv.	IP.	H.	R.	ER.	HR.	HB.	BB.	Int. BB.	SO.	WP.
Jones, Walla Walla	4	6	.400	3.22	14	14	2	0	0	0	78.1	64	49	28	4	1	71	0	78	7
Kaiser, Medford°	8	1	.889	5.31	15	15	1	0	0	0	78	91	56	46	5	2	57	0	69	12
Kilmer, Salem	1	0	1.000	5.23	17	0	0	13	0	2	20.2	21	13	12	0	2	21	2	15	2
Kinley, Bellingham	1	1	.500	3.15	11	0	0	5	0	0	20	23	9	7	1	0	17	0	16	4
Kipper, Salem°	6	5	.545	4.46	13	13	1	0	1	0	76.2	62	46	38	8	0	52	2	65	3
Knowles, Salem	0	1	.000	9.75	10	0	0	1	0	0	12	22	15	13	0	1	13	0	11	1
Lloyd, Walla Walla	0	2	.000	4.91	16	0	0	6	0	1	33	42	24	18	5	1	20	0	24	6
Lora, Salem	0	0	.000	4.91	1	0	0	0	0	0	3.2	5	2	2	0	0	2	0	0	0
Lugo, Salem	7	3	.700	2.88	14	13	3	0	0	0	90.2	74	45	29	1	4	61	3	62	6
Mack, Salem	3	8	.273	4.23	13	13	3	0	1	0	87.1	92	56	41	3	2	50	1	70	9
Maddux, Bend	3	6	.333	3.99	11	10	3	1	0	0	65.1	68	35	29	4	0	26	0	59	7
McCaskill, Salem	5	5	.500	4.29	11	11	1	0	0	0	71.1	63	43	34	6	5	51	1	87	6
McDonald, Bellingham	5	4	.556	2.47	11	10	3	0	0	0	73	59	30	20	2	2	37	1	69	5
McKenzie, Salem	0	1	.000	2.79	5	0	0	4	0	2	9.2	7	3	3	2	0	7	1	13	3
Miller, Bend	2	3	.400	4.58	24	0	0	20	0	2	39.1	45	30	20	0	0	24	3	28	6
Mine, Medford	0	1	.000	18.00	2	0	0	0	0	0	3	11	11	6	0	0	2	0	1	0
Minyard, Eugene	1	4	.200	7.21	13	11	1	0	1	0	63.2	56	54	51	6	1	59	3	45	4
Morel, Bend°	2	5	.286	5.14	14	14	2	0	0	0	75.1	79	52	43	6	3	48	0	47	5
Mutz, Walla Walla	0	0	.000	6.88	10	0	0	7	0	0	17	17	17	13	0	1	15	0	16	2
Myers, Medford	6	2	.750	1.63	31	0	0	27	0	12	49.2	24	12	9	0	0	29	0	81	8
Newman, Bellingham°	3	5	.375	1.88	22	6	2	14	0	4	71.2	48	27	15	4	1	39	5	73	4
Odom, Walla Walla	1	2	.333	6.69	23	0	0	12	0	2	39	51	36	29	7	3	18	1	41	5
Olson, Bend	3	6	.333	4.62	12	12	0	0	0	0	62.1	53	44	32	4	1	52	0	71	6
Ontiveros, Medford	1	0	1.000	0.00	4	0	0	3	0	0	8	3	0	0	0	0	4	0	9	0
Parent, Bellingham	1	5	.167	6.50	8	8	0	0	0	0	45.2	55	47	33	9	2	31	0	45	15
Perez, Medford°	0	0	.000	13.50	2	0	0	1	0	0	1.1	4	2	2	0	0	0	0	1	0
Plesac, Walla Walla	1	3	.250	4.38	7	6	0	0	0	0	37	35	24	18	2	4	23	0	25	4
Rasnick, Bend	0	0	.000	9.00	1	0	0	1	0	0	2	4	2	2	0	0	1	0	3	0
Rhoads, Walla Walla	1	2	.333	4.25	18	0	0	12	0	5	29.2	31	20	14	2	0	21	1	32	2
Richard, Bellingham°	1	0	1.000	0.00	7	0	0	6	0	2	8	4	0	0	0	0	1	1	11	0
Robertson, Bend°	0	0	.000	7.65	12	0	0	5	0	0	20	26	22	17	3	2	22	0	8	4
Robinson, Bend	4	2	.667	4.72	19	1	0	5	0	0	55.1	70	37	29	7	0	20	1	32	2
Roy, Bellingham	2	3	.400	4.66	9	9	1	0	0	0	46.1	51	33	24	3	1	16	1	35	4
Salgueiro, Eugene	0	2	.000	11.00	4	2	0	0	0	0	9	11	13	11	1	0	11	1	5	1
Scarpetta, Bend	3	1	.750	5.17	11	11	0	0	0	0	55.2	60	37	32	4	0	27	0	34	6
Schassler, Bellingham	1	0	1.000	0.48	8	0	0	3	0	0	18.2	5	1	1	0	0	13	1	29	0
Segura, Bend	4	4	.500	1.72	24	0	0	20	0	3	36.2	27	16	7	1	0	28	1	43	9
Steffanich, Walla Walla°	4	1	.800	7.46	22	0	0	12	0	1	41	53	41	34	5	2	26	2	43	6
S. Stout, Eugene	5	4	.556	4.64	18	12	3	1	0	0	85.1	82	50	44	8	3	49	1	58	4
T. Stout, Eugene	0	0	.000	36.00	1	0	0	1	0	0	1	2	4	4	0	0	5	0	1	1
Strichek, Eugene	3	7	.300	3.76	27	3	0	11	0	2	67	52	37	28	5	5	50	5	89	2
Suehr, Salem	3	2	.600	2.80	25	0	0	10	0	0	45	34	27	14	3	3	20	2	28	1
Taylor, Bellingham	6	4	.600	4.36	14	14	0	1	0	0	86.2	75	53	42	6	1	54	1	61	6
Timberlake, Salem	5	4	.556	3.88	11	11	1	0	0	0	69.2	63	37	30	4	0	35	0	52	4
Towers, Walla Walla	1	4	.200	4.74	6	6	0	0	0	0	38	34	29	20	2	4	27	1	30	3
Towey, Bellingham	1	2	.333	2.40	19	0	0	12	0	2	30	19	12	8	2	3	26	5	21	5
Valdez, Salem	0	0	.000	0.00	1	0	0	1	0	0	1.2	0	0	0	0	0	1	0	1	1
Vela, Medford°	1	2	.333	4.36	12	7	0	2	0	0	53.2	41	36	26	1	2	52	0	44	12
Walter, Walla Walla°	4	4	.500	4.83	17	9	2	3	0	0	72.2	73	55	39	5	1	46	0	61	10
Watson, Eugene	6	5	.545	3.62	27	2	0	21	0	6	49.2	45	25	20	2	1	31	6	34	1
Williams, Walla Walla°	3	4	.429	4.78	12	12	0	0	0	0	58.1	37	37	31	1	4	72	2	66	4
Witt, Bend	6	5	.545	4.35	14	14	3	0	1	0	93	89	57	45	11	4	43	0	45	8

BALKS—Newman, 4; Myers, Timberlake, 3 each; Dean, Gonzalez, Harms, Kipper, Parent, 2 each; Bergendahl, Burgess, Crabb, Findeisen, Gorman, Groh, Jackson, Jones, Kaiser, Lugo, Mack, Maddux, McDonald, Olson, Roy, Schassler, Segura, Steffanich, Towers, 1 each.

COMBINATION SHUTOUTS—McDonald-Barnhouse 2, McDonald-Towey, Newman-Kinley, Bellingham; Scarpetta-Maddux, Bend; Barry-Myers-Ontiveros, Medford; Timberlake-Knowles-Suehr, Salem.

NO-HIT GAME—None.

South Atlantic League

CLASS A

CHAMPIONSHIP WINNERS IN PREVIOUS YEARS

1948—Lincolnton°	.627	1964—Rock Hill	.672	1973—Spartanburg‡	.646
1949—Newton-Conover	.667	Salisbury‡	.631	Gastonia	.619
Ruth'ford Co. (2nd)†	.627	1965—Salisbury	.641	1974—Gastonia	.606
1950—Newton-Conover	.627	Rock Hill‡	.603	Gastonia	.672
Lenoir (2nd)†	.626	1966—Spartanburg	.682	1975—Spartanburg	.543
1951—Morganton	.645	Spartanburg	.767	Spartanburg	.614
Shelby (2nd)†	.604	1967—Spartanburg	.730	1976—Asheville	.544
1952—Lincolnton	.649	Spartanburg	.567	Greenwood‡	.600
Shelby (2nd)†	.645	1968—Spartanburg	.597	1977—Greenwood	.557
1953-59—League inactive.		Greenwood‡	.597	Gastonia‡	.590
1960—Lexington	.707	1969—Greenwood‡	.587	1978—Greenwood	.614
Salisbury (2nd)†	.650	Shelby	.565	Greenwood	.565
1961—Salisbury	.627	1970—Greenville	.576	1979—Greenwood‡	.565
Shelby (4th)†	.481	Greenville	.619	Spartanburg	.525
1962—Statesville	.563	1971—Greenwood	.631	1980—Greensboro	.590
Statesville	.700	Greenwood	.759	Charleston	.561
1963—Greenville†	.576	1972—Spartanburg‡	.788	1981—Greensboro‡	.695
Salisbury	.631	Greenville	.652	Greenwood	.549

°Won championship and four-club playoff. †Won four-club playoff. ‡Won split-season playoff. (NOTE—Known as Western Carolina League from 1948 through 1962 and known as Western Carolinas League through 1979.)

STANDING OF CLUBS AT CLOSE OF FIRST HALF, JUNE 19

NORTHERN DIVISION						SOUTHERN DIVISION					
Club	W.	L.	T.	Pct.	G.B.	Club	W.	L.	T.	Pct.	G.B.
Greensboro (Yankees)	45	25	0	.643	....	Charleston (Royals)	43	27	0	.614	....
Shelby (Mets)	37	34	0	.521	8½	Anderson (Braves)	39	33	0	.542	5
Gastonia (Cardinals)	35	36	0	.493	10½	Florence (Blue Jays)	37	32	0	.536	5½
Spartanburg (Phillies)	34	36	0	.486	11	Macon (Tigers)	30	40	0	.429	13
Asheville (Astros)	28	42	0	.400	17	Greenwood (Pirates)	23	46	0	.333	19½

STANDING OF CLUBS AT CLOSE OF SECOND HALF, AUGUST 31

NORTHERN DIVISION						SOUTHERN DIVISION					
Club	W.	L.	T.	Pct.	G.B.	Club	W.	L.	T.	Pct.	G.B.
Greensboro (Yankees)	51	20	0	.718	....	Florence (Blue Jays)	40	32	0	.556	....
Shelby (Mets)	40	29	0	.580	10	Macon (Tigers)	36	32	0	.529	2
Asheville (Astros)	37	34	0	.521	14	Anderson (Braves)	33	37	0	.471	6
Spartanburg (Phillies)	35	35	0	.500	15½	Charleston (Royals)	31	39	0	.443	8
Gastonia (Cardinals)	19	53	0	.264	32½	Greenwood (Pirates)	29	40	0	.420	9½

COMPOSITE STANDING OF CLUBS AT CLOSE OF SEASON, AUGUST 31

Club	Gbr.	Shel.	Flo.	Char.	And.	Spar.	Mac.	Ash.	Gas.	Gwd.	W.	L.	T.	Pct.	G.B.
Greensboro (Yankees)	....	13	7	7	14	13	8	12	15	7	96	45	0	.681	....
Shelby (Mets)	7	....	6	7	11	9	6	14	12	5	77	63	0	.550	18½
Florence (Blue Jays)	4	6	....	11	7	8	15	5	7	14	77	64	0	.546	19
Charleston (Royals)	4	5	12	....	7	6	13	5	8	14	74	66	0	.529	21½
Anderson (Braves)	6	9	5	5	....	10	6	10	12	9	72	70	0	.507	24½
Spartanburg (Phillies)	2	11	3	5	10	....	9	10	11	8	69	71	0	.493	26½
Macon (Tigers)	4	4	9	11	4	3	....	8	7	16	66	72	0	.478	28½
Asheville (Astros)	8	6	7	7	6	10	3	....	12	6	65	76	0	.461	31
Gastonia (Cardinals)	5	4	5	4	8	9	5	7	....	7	54	89	0	.378	43
Greenwood (Pirates)	5	5	10	9	3	3	7	5	5	....	52	86	0	.377	42½

Major league affiliations in parentheses.

Playoffs—Florence defeated Charleston, two games to one; Greensboro defeated Florence, three games to two, for league championship.

Regular-Season Attendance—Anderson, 35,023; Asheville, 55,228; Charleston, 114,859; Florence, 54,446; Gastonia, 51,025; Greensboro, 224,107; Greenwood, 21,019; Macon, 66,467; Shelby, 11,784; Spartanburg, 40,288. Total, 674,246. Playoffs, 12,949. All-star game, 2,342.

Managers: Anderson, Brian Snitker; Asheville, Dave Cripe; Charleston, Roy Tanner; Florence, Dennis Holmberg; Gastonia, Lloyd Merritt; Greensboro, Doug Holmquist; Greenwood, Joe Frisina; Macon, Ted Brazell; Shelby, Rick Miller; Spartanburg, Tony Taylor and P.J. Carey.

All-Star Team: 1B—Carpenter, Asheville; 2B—E. Rodriguez, Greensboro; 3B—Pastornicky, Charleston; SS—Lowery, Spartanburg; OF—Carreon, Shelby; Mata, Greensboro; Winters, Greensboro; C—Hansen, Charleston; DH—Guerrero, Anderson; RHP—Szymczak, Greensboro; LHP—Shiflett, Greensboro; Manager—Brazell, Macon.

(Compiled by Howe News Bureau, Boston, Mass.)

CLUB BATTING

Club	Pct.	G.	AB.	R.	OR.	H.	TB.	2B.	3B.	HR.	RBI.	GW.	SH.	SF.	HP.	BB.	Int. BB.	SO.	SB.	CS.	LOB.
Greensboro	.280	141	4846	857	645	1356	1998	238	25	118	751	81	35	42	39	803	34	804	101	47	123
Asheville	.279	141	4695	809	779	1312	1994	240	32	126	699	50	33	39	34	590	22	891	148	38	100
Shelby	.275	141	4609	843	736	1266	1872	206	38	108	706	65	23	45	45	648	18	690	239	58	99
Charleston	.268	140	4572	731	657	1225	1780	197	36	94	634	63	28	45	40	562	23	720	161	51	99
Spartanburg	.268	140	4380	733	703	1173	1730	234	34	85	606	57	16	46	29	567	9	873	253	109	85
Florence	.259	142	4524	750	677	1172	1677	168	38	87	618	61	42	42	34	704	22	887	280	59	103
Macon	.244	140	4448	658	734	1096	1559	166	21	85	596	58	69	35	36	666	13	807	143	50	106
Anderson	.243	142	4451	654	759	1080	1557	180	48	67	559	64	17	30	22	636	24	843	113	35	103
Greenwood	.242	138	4507	583	742	1091	1503	168	32	60	482	43	25	29	25	505	20	981	152	68	95
Gastonia	.241	143	4564	523	709	1099	1387	153	15	35	429	43	27	35	33	549	22	782	112	48	106

INDIVIDUAL BATTING

(Leading Qualifiers for Batting Championship—389 or More Plate Appearances)

°Bats lefthanded.   †Switch-hitter.

Player and Club	Pct.	G.	AB.	R.	H.	TB.	2B.	3B.	HR.	RBI.	GW.	SH.	SF.	HP.	BB.	Int. BB.	SO.	SB.	CS.
Pastornicky, Clifford, Charleston	.343	135	530	98	182	269	36	6	13	92	8	1	7	0	38	6	27	26	7
Christensen, John, Shelby	.334	125	440	100	147	241	24	2	22	97	7	0	4	7	75	2	53	21	5
Carreon, Mark, Shelby	.329	133	486	120	160	207	29	6	2	79	12	2	7	2	78	3	37	33	8
Delgado, Juan, Asheville	.328	123	464	77	152	235	33	4	14	68	4	1	1	3	48	1	78	5	2
Winters, Matthew, Greensboro°	.325	104	326	76	106	190	20	2	20	93	12	0	4	3	118	5	65	1	3
Carpenter, Glenn, Asheville	.323	105	384	76	124	195	24	4	13	81	7	1	2	1	56	3	91	2	2
Kingery, Michael, Charleston°	.318	140	513	65	163	214	19	4	8	75	8	1	8	2	62	4	77	25	12
Mata, Victor, Greensboro	.314	123	481	89	151	201	25	5	5	64	5	4	5	7	32	1	52	8	2
Olander, James, Spartanburg	.305	121	423	77	129	202	25	6	12	63	4	0	2	5	61	0	86	12	12
Keiser, Kent, Spartanburg°	.299	123	445	90	133	182	30	5	3	54	8	2	6	0	54	1	48	28	9

Departmental Leaders: G—Luther, 142; AB—Pastornicky, 530; R—Carreon, 120; H—Pastornicky, 182; TB—Pastornicky, 269; 2B—Pastornicky, 36; 3B—Clark, Distefano, Kinnard, Plautz, 8; HR—Braun, 23; RBI—Christensen, 97; GWRBI—Carreon, Winters, 12; SH—Arce, 13; SF—Hansen, 12; HP—McNutt, 19; BB—Winters, 118; IBB—Braun, 10; SO—Penigar, 142; SB—Tatis, 83; CS—Tatis, 18.

(All Players—Listed Alphabetically)

Player and Club	Pct.	G.	AB.	R.	H.	TB.	2B.	3B.	HR.	RBI.	GW.	SH.	SF.	HP.	BB.	Int. BB.	SO.	SB.	CS.
Aaron, Lawrence, Anderson°	.059	10	17	2	1	1	0	0	0	1	0	1	0	0	0	0	3	0	1
Agapay, Felix, Spartanburg°	.222	6	18	2	4	5	1	0	0	2	0	1	0		4	0	5	0	1
Alexander, Tommy, Macon	.000	46	1	0	0	0	0	0	0	0	0	0	0	0	0	0	0	0	0
Arce, Lorenzo, Macon	.261	96	283	44	74	109	17	0	6	34	7	13	5	6	24	3	37	9	2
Ashmore, W. Mitchell, Charleston	.285	70	239	42	68	92	8	2	4	30	3	2	2	1	41	0	69	6	4
Aubin, D. Gerard, Greenwood	.252	42	151	29	38	64	8	0	6	19	3	0	1	2	19	2	44	1	3
Bagwell, T. Jacin, Greenwood	.176	39	102	10	18	22	2	1	0	5	2	1	1	0	15	1	29	2	0
Bailey, David, Charleston	.000	1	1	1	0	0	0	0	0	0	0	0	0	0	0	0	0	0	0
Baker, Christopher, Macon	.221	116	376	50	83	134	15	0	12	53	5	0	6	2	42	0	62	0	1
Baker, Kerry, Greenwood†	.231	8	26	0	6	6	0	0	0	3	0	1	0		3	0	9	0	1
Barker, Stanley, Macon°	.230	57	165	20	38	54	7	3	1	16	1	1	1	1	31	0	34	16	2
Barragan, Gerardo, Macon†	.208	25	72	9	15	18	1	1	0	4	1	2	0		5	0	14	2	1
Berger, Michael, Greenwood	.270	85	259	31	70	110	14	1	8	37	4	3	1	3	33	0	59	1	1
Berti, Donald, Asheville	.266	88	259	39	69	118	11	1	12	50	5	3	2	3	48	0	41	4	0
Bettendorf, Jeffrey, Shelby	.000	20	1	0	0	0	0	0	0	0	0	0	0	0	0	0	0	0	0
Bishop, James, Florence	.286	141	503	78	144	220	19	6	15	71	8	3	2	0	71	3	80	10	4
Blaser, Mark, Greensboro	.314	80	239	42	75	107	15	1	5	33	3	3	0	2	35	1	33	1	0
Bomerito, Robert, Shelby°	.260	110	377	51	98	122	11	2	3	48	7	1	5	0	50	3	52	12	3
Braun, Randall, Asheville°	.296	97	348	46	103	197	21	4	23	72	8	0	2	6	68	10	69	7	1
Brill, Clint, Anderson	.236	79	246	29	58	82	7	1	5	32	5	1	2	1	45	1	42	3	0
Brown, Brian, Gastonia	1.000	27	1	0	1	1	0	0	0	0	0	0	0	0	0	0	0	0	0
Brown, Samuel, Greenwood	.259	126	463	55	120	149	17	0	4	64	5	1	5	6	36	1	113	32	12
Bryeans, Christian, Charleston°	.240	120	408	59	98	151	15	4	10	55	9	6	2	1	36	1	65	17	3
Burge, Kevin, Greenwood°	.267	6	15	4	4	4	0	0	0	1	0	0	0		5	0	3	0	0
Burke, Curtis, Asheville	.278	132	503	95	140	229	22	5	19	81	6	1	4	6	57	0	105	22	4
Carpenter, Glenn, Asheville	.323	105	384	76	124	195	24	4	13	81	7	1	2	1	56	3	91	2	2
Carreon, Mark, Shelby	.329	133	486	120	160	207	29	6	2	79	12	2	7	2	78	3	37	33	8
Casasnovas, Roberto, Macon°	.138	27	80	17	11	20	1	1	2	6	0	1	0	2	26	2	36	4	0
Champion, Keith, Gastonia	.152	18	46	1	7	7	0	0	0	4	1	0	0	0	9	1	6	0	0
Ching, Mauricio, Greensboro°	.206	35	102	14	21	37	4	0	4	16	3	0	0	1	17	0	35	0	2
Chmil, Stephen, Anderson	.364	5	22	3	8	10	2	0	0	6	0	0	0	1	0	1	0	1	0
Christensen, John, Shelby	.334	125	440	100	147	241	24	2	22	97	7	0	4	7	75	2	53	21	5
Churchill, James, Greenwood	.245	16	49	9	12	14	2	0	0	2	1	0	0		12	0	15	1	2
Cipolloni, Joseph, Spartanburg	.257	73	230	33	59	81	16	0	2	29	3	4	1	3	21	0	49	10	5
Clark, Henry, Asheville	.278	99	338	56	94	135	22	2	5	53	0	3	9	0	22	3	42	3	1
Clark, T. Kennedy, Anderson	.208	126	424	49	88	120	13	8	1	43	5	4	2	3	43	0	88	25	4
Clow, Dennis, Anderson	.239	57	180	36	43	87	14	0	10	36	4	0	1	0	29	2	41	1	0
Cormack, Terry, Anderson°	.249	67	213	25	53	67	11	0	1	33	1	0	2	2	22	1	30	0	0
Crump, Adolph, Spartanburg	.169	23	59	5	10	12	2	0	0	7	0	0	1	1	12	0	7	4	1
Cunningham, Charles, Greenwood	.174	26	92	6	16	20	4	0	0	6	0	0	1		4	1	34	0	0
Currier, William, Spartanburg°	.270	62	211	41	57	96	8	2	9	37	2	0	2	1	17	1	62	2	2
Czeszewski, Larry, Shelby	.190	23	58	4	11	16	5	0	0	7	0	0	0	0	7	0	7	0	0
D'Onofrio, Gary L., Asheville	.303	29	89	11	27	33	1	1	1	10	0	3	1		13	0	13	2	1
Dalena, Peter, Greensboro°	.285	71	281	27	80	125	15	0	10	43	4	0	2	0	24	5	49	0	0
Davisson, Robert, Spartanburg	.000	28	1	0	0	0	0	0	0	0	0	0	0	0	0	0	0	0	0
Delarosa, Nelson, Greenwood°	.255	88	333	50	85	117	18	1	4	36	4	3	3	1	28	2	64	19	6
Delgado, Juan, Asheville	.328	123	464	77	152	235	33	4	14	68	4	1	1	3	48	1	78	5	2
Delgado, Rumaldo, Greenwood°	.222	64	212	21	47	63	6	5	0	13	0	0	1	0	26	2	61	7	6
Denby, Darryl, Shelby	.297	40	138	30	41	75	4	0	10	29	3	1	3	2	16	0	31	12	3
Destrade, Orestes, Greensboro†	.180	43	122	9	22	31	4	1	1	14	2	1	4	0	27	0	42	1	1
Devalk, Brian, Greenwood	.310	12	42	5	13	21	2	0	2	3	0	0	0	0	6	1	9	1	0
Diaz, Angel, Florence	.318	10	22	5	7	7	0	0	0	3	0	0	2		1	0	6	0	0
Diaz, Richard, Shelby	.180	16	50	5	9	13	1	0	1	8	0	0	1	0	4	0	7	2	1
Digioia, John, Gastonia	.205	75	219	24	45	68	8	0	5	29	3	0	1	1	46	1	94	1	0
Distefano, Benito, Greenwood°	.289	136	477	74	138	222	23	8	15	89	6	1	2	1	85	8	58	11	4
Dorin, Matthew, Spartanburg	.000	8	1	0	0	0	0	0	0	0	0	0	0	0	0	0	1	0	0
Dykstra, Leonard, Shelby°	.291	120	413	95	120	156	13	7	3	38	3	4	0	2	95	3	40	77	11
Eaton, Coleman, Anderson	.244	75	217	31	53	88	10	2	7	30	5	0	1	2	29	3	62	15	2
Ereu, William, Macon	.200	4	10	1	2	5	0	0	1	1	0	1	0		0	0	2	0	0
Espinal, Nelson, Anderson	.216	13	37	7	8	9	1	0	0	3	0	0	0	0	6	0	13	0	1
Falls, Robert, Asheville†	.236	128	423	63	100	130	13	1	5	48	3	3	1	0	41	0	116	15	5
Faucette, Charles, Florence	.000	4	7	0	0	0	0	0	0	0	0	0	0	0	0	0	1	0	0
Fields, Bruce, Macon°	.337	80	312	61	105	142	13	3	6	38	2	3	0	3	34	0	39	28	15
Filkins, Randy, Greensboro	.311	29	103	23	32	45	5	1	2	11	0	2	0	1	29	0	26	3	2
Fincher, Steve, Greensboro	.000	26	1	0	0	0	0	0	0	0	0	0	0	0	0	0	1	0	0
Fink, Billy, Gastonia°	.228	112	347	53	79	102	7	2	4	30	4	0	1	3	63	1	68	19	7
Fisher, Keith, Macon	.191	74	220	19	42	65	6	1	5	24	2	4	2	0	42	0	42	3	0
Foley, John, Gastonia°	.275	125	432	71	119	148	21	1	2	27	3	5	1	6	51	3	74	16	7
Forchee, Mark, Gastonia†	.000	23	1	0	0	0	0	0	0	0	0	0	0	0	0	0	1	0	0
Fredrick, David, Greenwood°	.288	35	111	20	32	50	4	1	4	25	0	1	1	1	13	0	44	7	1
Frishman, Mark, Spartanburg	.261	87	307	51	80	108	11	1	5	42	5	0	3	8	33	0	37	10	10

Player and Club	Pct.	G.	AB.	R.	H.	TB.	2B.	3B.	HR.	RBI.	GW.	SH.	SF.	HP.	BB.	Int. BB.	SO.	SB.	CS.
Gallegos, Matthew, Greensboro†	.268	109	358	68	96	112	10	3	0	26	4	10	4	5	79	4	34	24	9
Gambeski, Michael, Gastonia	.231	131	468	57	108	153	21	0	8	71	11	2	9	1	47	2	101	4	2
Garcia, Agustin, Shelby	.190	109	353	57	67	106	9	3	8	23	2	3	2	1	45	0	87	12	3
Garcia, Ramon, Asheville	.214	45	145	23	31	37	6	0	0	11	0	0	0	0	8	0	26	6	0
Gauci, Bob, Macon	.289	26	76	7	22	26	1	0	1	9	1	0	1	0	12	0	12	0	0
Gaunce, David, Charleston	.226	33	93	14	21	24	3	0	0	14	1	1	2	0	16	0	28	0	1
Giansanti, Ralph, Anderson	.238	54	172	18	41	51	5	1	1	23	2	3	2	3	20	0	22	1	2
Gibbons, John, Shelby	.265	99	321	60	85	138	13	2	12	67	8	2	3	5	58	3	65	6	4
Gjesdal, Brent, Greensboro	.000	9	15	1	0	0	0	0	0	1	0	1	1	0	2	0	11	0	0
Goodin, Craig, Charleston	.169	63	160	21	27	37	6	2	0	9	1	4	1	1	28	2	37	7	2
Goodyear, Christopher, Macon	.240	64	192	24	46	50	4	0	0	19	1	11	1	4	40	0	36	11	4
Graves, Joseph, Shelby	.333	47	3	0	1	1	0	0	0	1	0	0	0	0	0	0	0	0	0
Graziano, Thomas, Greenwood°	.258	57	182	21	47	56	6	0	1	28	3	0	4	0	31	0	25	1	2
Grove, Trent, Greensboro°	.250	95	300	44	75	88	6	2	1	27	2	3	2	1	15	1	44	3	1
Guerrero, Inocencio, Anderson	.288	131	441	70	127	202	25	4	14	81	10	0	4	1	83	6	80	1	0
Haas, Stanley, Gastonia	.273	49	150	15	41	56	6	0	3	16	1	3	3	0	25	0	35	1	1
Hansen, Roger, Charleston	.293	137	505	78	148	227	34	0	15	94	7	0	12	10	55	2	60	10	1
Harris, Kenneth, Shelby	.353	9	34	7	12	16	4	0	0	6	0	0	1	0	4	0	1	0	0
Hatcher, Johnny, Anderson	.271	53	207	44	56	82	8	3	4	16	3	0	0	1	14	0	39	10	0
Heiser, Bruce, Anderson	.254	45	173	27	44	50	4	1	0	16	0	0	0	0	27	0	31	3	1
Heller, John, Shelby°	.207	86	261	45	54	79	6	2	5	25	4	2	0	0	34	1	32	6	2
Hibner, David, Macon	.125	15	32	7	4	4	0	0	0	2	0	0	0	0	15	0	11	1	1
Hinson, Gary, Macon	.308	49	172	36	53	82	13	2	4	24	5	0	2	0	29	0	24	6	4
Hodge, Patrick, Anderson°	.267	124	438	91	117	182	26	6	9	62	6	1	4	1	95	4	95	15	6
Hoppie, Bryan, Spartanburg†	.268	110	388	52	104	132	16	3	2	35	2	2	2	0	55	0	58	41	15
Howard, Bernardo, Spartanburg†	.237	75	232	33	55	79	15	0	3	35	5	0	3	1	32	1	74	14	4
Hubbard, Tyson, Gastonia	.000	23	1	0	0	0	0	0	0	0	0	0	0	0	0	0	1	0	0
Hughes, John, Greensboro°	.264	51	140	27	37	47	5	1	1	21	3	2	2	1	34	1	17	0	0
Irvin, Otis, Macon	.218	50	147	17	32	36	4	0	0	14	1	5	1	2	9	0	27	6	1
Isaac, Johnny, Asheville	.237	67	236	22	56	74	10	1	2	24	2	0	3	1	13	0	61	6	1
Jackson, Reginald, Shelby	.000	31	2	0	0	0	0	0	0	0	0	0	0	0	0	0	0	0	0
James, Richard, Gastonia	.296	136	510	58	151	177	9	4	3	54	3	0	2	2	57	4	38	12	3
Janssen, Henry, Asheville	.260	62	177	40	46	80	16	0	6	37	1	0	3	3	52	1	29	3	0
Johnson, Duane, Macon†	.246	121	411	66	101	123	14	1	2	41	4	10	2	0	72	1	70	15	3
Jones, Thomas, Greensboro°	.247	87	300	50	74	98	16	4	0	25	3	5	1	1	39	0	52	12	5
Keiser, Kent, Spartanburg°	.299	123	445	90	133	182	30	5	3	54	8	2	6	0	54	1	48	28	9
Kelly, Ronald, Macon°	.265	113	343	51	91	151	18	0	14	66	9	3	3	3	86	4	60	2	1
Khalifa, Sammy, Greenwood	.305	48	177	29	54	62	6	1	0	19	3	0	0	0	24	0	20	5	3
Kingery, Michael, Charleston°	.318	140	513	65	163	214	19	4	8	75	8	1	8	2	62	4	77	25	12
Kinnard, Kenneth, Florence	.263	138	524	101	138	188	10	8	8	67	5	2	5	·0	87	0	124	70	11
Kneuer, Frank, Greensboro	.304	36	112	18	34	46	9	0	1	18	2	2	0	0	14	0	11	0	0
Kowalski, Stephen, Greenwood†	.176	7	17	4	3	3	0	0	0	0	0	0	0	0	4	0	7	0	1
Kuntz, Eric, Shelby	.000	25	2	1	0	0	0	0	0	0	0	0	0	0	1	0	1	0	0
Latham, William, Shelby°	1.000	24	1	1	1	1	0	0	0	1	0	0	0	0	0	0	0	0	0
Laurie, Robert, Macon	.229	44	140	26	32	41	4	1	1	10	1	3	0	0	18	0	29	4	2
Lebo, Michael, Greensboro°	.298	87	255	36	76	146	14	1	18	63	8	0	5	0	40	3	65	1	1
Lindsey, William, Greensboro	.271	102	336	55	91	126	20	0	5	47	5	0	1	6	49	3	39	4	3
Llewellyn, Paul, Anderson	.205	49	161	20	33	46	1	6	0	15	1	0	0	0	24	0	57	3	0
Lowery, Edward, Spartanburg	.246	133	427	65	105	171	22	1	14	63	5	3	5	4	55	1	73	10	12
Lucas, William, Anderson	.195	33	82	12	16	21	3	1	0	8	1	0	0	0	20	0	12	5	2
Luther, Bradley, Gastonia	.202	142	485	46	98	120	17	1	1	27	2	3	3	3	56	1	84	4	4
Luzon, Robert, Anderson	.317	22	60	10	19	26	3	2	0	4	2	0	0	0	8	1	14	2	3
Lyons, Barry, Shelby	.280	45	164	23	46	70	12	0	4	46	3	1	2	1	24	1	10	0	0
Malave, Omar, Florence	.176	64	142	16	25	30	5	0	0	8	1	1	2	0	21	0	26	6	1
Mann, Daniel, Anderson	.243	51	185	32	45	63	10	1	2	26	5	0	2	3	21	1	36	10	2
Maris, Kevin, Gastonia	.121	26	66	4	8	8	0	0	0	4	0	3	0	0	11	0	21	2	0
Marte, Alexis, Florence°	.254	83	264	47	67	84	8	3	1	22	6	3	4	0	39	2	34	47	6
Martinez, Z. Tomas, Greenwood	.247	109	381	61	94	120	11	3	3	28	2	2	3	1	44	0	59	22	4
Martino, Martin, Charleston°	.426	20	61	10	26	35	7	1	0	12	1	0	1	0	2	0	8	0	0
Mata, Victor, Greensboro	.314	123	481	89	151	201	25	5	5	64	5	4	5	7	32	1	52	8	2
Maxwell, James, Macon°	.208	30	101	12	21	31	3	2	1	18	1	1	1	0	13	0	22	1	0
McAllister, Steven, Asheville†	.248	127	467	65	116	152	22	1	4	42	4	6	6	2	58	1	80	21	12
McCardell, Michael, Greenwood	.178	16	45	5	8	9	1	0	0	6	0	0	1	1	6	0	4	0	1
McHugh, Thomas, Charleston°	.191	114	361	44	69	86	10	2	1	35	6	6	1	4	64	2	62	6	3
McNutt, Lawrence, Shelby	.270	109	348	70	94	153	15	4	12	58	3	1	3	19	53	1	67	22	4
Meadows, Mike, Asheville°	.316	66	228	43	72	113	9	1	10	41	5	1	1	5	39	2	43	21	2
Mena, Cesar, Greenwood	.193	30	83	7	16	19	1	1	0	7	1	0	0	0	3	0	15	1	0
Menzhuber, Charles, Gastonia†	.260	135	519	67	135	167	28	2	0	42	2	3	5	0	43	4	60	17	6
Morrison, Bruce, Shelby	.299	94	328	55	98	174	24	2	16	73	5	0	4	1	42	1	57	3	1
Moscat, Fernando, Shelby	.286	84	276	39	79	95	11	1	1	31	2	4	5	1	21	0	49	10	3
Moser, Larry, Anderson†	.133	29	105	14	14	16	2	0	0	4	0	1	0	1	16	0	20	1	2
Neal, Willie, Charleston	.278	63	241	41	67	110	14	1	9	40	3	0	1	1	23	1	47	14	3
Nelson, Mitchell, Anderson	.000	9	15	2	0	0	0	0	0	0	0	0	0	0	6	0	10	0	1
Nichols, Carl, Macon	.214	84	257	33	55	69	10	2	0	30	6	1	3	2	27	0	50	7	1
O'Shea, Shane, Greensboro†	.199	53	136	23	27	38	5	0	2	25	2	3	1	0	21	1	23	2	0
Olander, James, Spartanburg	.305	121	423	77	129	202	25	6	12	63	4	0	2	5	61	0	86	12	12
Opie, James, Greenwood	.243	58	214	34	52	83	9	2	6	26	1	1	0	2	23	1	37	8	5
Oruna, Roland, Charleston	.239	118	419	73	100	155	17	4	10	57	2	3	3	8	78	4	100	20	4
Pagliarulo, Michael, Greensboro†	.280	123	403	79	113	201	22	0	22	79	5	0	0	2	83	6	76	7	1
Palma, Gerald Jay, Anderson	.220	131	454	52	100	120	10	2	2	52	6	1	4	1	33	1	53	9	4
Pastornicky, Clifford, Charleston	.343	135	530	98	182	269	36	6	13	92	8	1	7	0	38	6	27	26	7
Patterson, Kenneth, Charleston†	.162	12	37	3	6	7	1	0	0	4	0	1	0	0	2	0	6	4	0
Payano, Vidal, Anderson	.263	37	133	15	35	45	4	3	0	9	1	4	2	0	4	0	20	2	2
Penigar, Charles L., Spartanburg†	.259	133	455	95	118	164	17	7	5	53	4	1	2	4	92	3	142	65	17
Perdomo, Felix, Shelby	.260	121	465	69	121	178	21	6	8	61	5	2	5	3	31	0	79	22	8
Perez, Onesimo, Florence°	.242	70	198	27	48	59	4	2	1	17	4	0	1	2	23	1	39	1	2
Pettis, Stacey, Greenwood°	.207	36	135	12	28	38	1	3	1	6	1	2	0	0	11	0	57	8	5
Pickett, Richard, Shelby°	.200	50	5	0	1	1	0	0	0	0	0	0	0	0	0	0	2	0	0
Pittaro, Christopher, Macon†	.229	68	218	25	50	62	6	0	2	25	2	6	2	2	26	0	45	7	1
Pittman, Michael, Gastonia°	.000	22	1	0	0	0	0	0	0	0	0	0	0	0	0	0	1	0	0
Plautz, Richard, Charleston	.276	53	214	42	59	95	8	8	4	26	3	0	1	1	16	0	30	3	1
Pleis, W. Scott, Florence	.198	52	116	16	23	30	4	0	1	12	0	0	0	0	14	0	25	1	0

Player and Club	Pct.	G.	AB.	R.	H.	TB.	2B.	3B.	HR.	RBI.	GW.	SH.	SF.	HP.	BB.	Int. BB.	SO.	SB.	CS.
Poole, Mark, Florence	.262	106	355	54	93	133	19	0	7	43	5	2	4	4	28	0	47	2	0
Powell, H. Lee, Spartanburg	.241	47	141	18	34	57	10	2	3	26	1	0	4	0	13	0	19	4	3
Pulley, Martin, Florence	.259	82	266	32	69	82	7	0	2	40	1	8	1	3	27	1	41	0	1
Raeside, John, Shelby	.256	23	82	11	21	30	4	1	1	9	1	0	0	1	9	0	13	1	2
Reddish, Michael, Greensboro	.293	121	409	88	120	193	20	1	17	83	10	0	5	4	80	2	51	9	6
Rice, A. Cepeda, Greenwood	.170	70	182	17	31	59	7	3	5	17	1	2	0	2	24	0	65	8	4
Rivas, Rafael, Florence†	.256	124	379	63	97	145	16	7	6	63	5	3	3	4	61	1	77	7	1
Rivera, Ricardo, Asheville†	.225	62	231	33	52	64	6	3	0	19	1	6	1	2	20	0	36	11	4
Roberts, Leon, Greenwood†	.215	33	107	15	23	28	3	1	0	6	0	3	1	1	15	0	18	10	3
Rodriguez, D. Ruben, Greenwood	.248	69	218	26	54	70	13	0	1	15	2	4	3	2	11	0	54	0	2
Rodriguez, Edwin, Greensboro	.296	115	425	88	126	167	23	3	4	62	6	1	4	5	65	1	78	25	11
Rodriguez, Jose, Gastonia	.284	96	338	38	96	111	10	1	1	18	3	0	2	5	14	0	37	18	11
Sanchez, Jose, Gastonia	.253	32	99	2	25	26	1	0	0	7	0	0	0	4	0	6	0	4	
Sanford, B. Kyle, Anderson°	.241	99	340	51	82	115	15	3	4	33	4	0	3	3	71	2	41	3	2
Santos, Edward, Florence	.268	140	489	88	131	212	22	1	19	94	10	1	9	3	90	6	88	7	1
Sarmiento, Ramon, Florence	.240	113	334	54	80	146	17	5	13	60	5	2	2	5	64	1	113	12	5
Schu, Rick, Spartanburg	.273	125	429	78	117	183	28	1	12	60	7	0	5	1	55	1	66	37	12
Sharperson, Mike, Florence	.255	111	326	51	83	110	16	1	3	33	3	6	3	6	59	1	59	28	7
Sherman, James, Asheville	.354	46	195	49	69	124	16	3	11	32	2	3	0	0	17	0	42	4	1
Shiflett, Mark, Greensboro	.000	32	1	0	0	0	0	0	0	0	0	0	0	0	0	0	0	0	0
Silva, Albert, Macon	.500	5	8	0	4	4	0	0	0	2	1	0	0	0	5	0	2	0	0
Siwiec, Michael, Greensboro	.000	36	1	0	0	0	0	0	0	0	0	0	0	0	0	0	1	0	0
Smith, Daniel, Greenwood	.199	64	206	16	41	47	6	0	0	11	0	0	1	0	16	0	43	6	2
Smith, Donald, Gastonia	.174	110	311	30	54	70	10	0	2	32	3	6	4	2	36	0	62	5	2
Soreca, Vincent, Spartanburg	.143	38	42	3	6	7	1	0	0	1	0	0	0	3	0	14	1	0	
Sorel, Michael, Charleston	.280	33	125	23	35	41	3	0	1	13	4	0	0	1	17	1	23	7	2
Sottile, Louis, Macon°	.243	52	152	22	37	56	4	0	5	14	1	0	0	1	20	1	33	4	1
Southern, Mitchell, Gastonia°	.239	35	113	14	27	30	3	0	0	11	1	0	0	2	11	1	20	4	1
Street, P. Keith, Anderson°	.283	50	166	21	47	83	7	4	7	29	3	1	1	0	25	2	47	3	1
Suarez, Brian, Spartanburg	.287	133	474	76	136	210	28	5	12	83	10	2	7	1	48	1	103	9	2
Tatis, Bernardo, Florence°	.260	117	381	75	99	127	9	5	3	38	3	7	0	2	86	3	98	83	18
Thomas, Reginald, Macon°	.266	95	290	54	77	104	9	3	4	35	0	1	1	1	49	1	62	12	7
Thompson, Thomas, Charleston	.233	39	129	23	30	57	3	0	8	23	3	0	1	1	22	0	27	1	1
Villa, Boris, Greenwood	.164	50	171	14	28	33	3	1	0	7	0	0	1	0	4	1	22	1	0
Vitato, Richard, Charleston°	.221	113	393	70	87	134	8	3	11	46	3	2	3	7	44	0	43	6	3
Watson, J. Andrew, Greenwood	.228	16	57	8	13	14	1	0	0	3	0	1	0	0	4	0	13	0	0
Weems, C. Richard, Gastonia	.244	92	291	29	71	99	8	4	4	36	5	0	2	5	44	3	51	7	0
Weems, William, Asheville°	.310	51	171	34	53	69	7	3	1	27	2	2	2	1	24	1	6	16	1
West, Reginald, Charleston°	.273	43	143	24	39	46	5	1	0	9	1	1	0	2	18	0	11	9	4
Wheeler, Ralph, Florence	.312	59	218	43	68	104	12	0	8	48	5	4	5	3	31	3	27	6	2
Whiting, Donald, Macon°	.238	113	361	49	86	149	15	0	16	60	6	2	3	3	42	0	40	2	1
Winters, Matthew, Greensboro°	.325	104	326	76	106	190	20	2	20	93	12	0	4	3	118	5	65	1	3
Wirth, Mike, Gastonia°	.205	61	166	14	34	44	4	0	2	21	1	2	2	3	32	1	23	2	0
Wyatt, David, Shelby°	.000	11	1	0	0	0	0	0	0	0	0	0	0	0	0	0	0	0	0
Young, Kevin, Macon°	.231	28	65	8	15	24	1	1	2	11	1	0	2	2	14	1	17	3	2
Ysambert, Sergio, Spartanburg	.268	35	97	14	26	41	4	1	3	16	1	2	2	0	12	0	28	6	4

The following pitchers, listed alphabetically by club, with games in parentheses, had no plate appearances, primarily through use of designated hitters:

ANDERSON—Baker, John (8); Fuller, Timothy (10); Klaus, Leonard (27); Lance, Mark (13); Lee, John (32); Lubert, Dennis (15); Rymer, Carlos (5); Sears, Hubert (46); Seitz, John (16); Smith, Mark (26); Smith, Zane (12); Sperto, Carmine (23); Torres, Rudy (12); Vargas, Ramon (27); Waddell, Thomas (4); Walker, Alan (6); Ward, Duane (5); Willerson, Thomas (16).

ASHEVILLE—Ambrose, James (13); Blas, William (5); Callahan, Michael (5); Corniel, Rafael (9); DePaula, Elvido (25); Espinosa, Ernesto (16); Godwin, Roger (54); Koenig, Kalvin (25); Malloy, David (15); Mize, Gregory (6); Regalado, Uvaldo (24); Reilly, Edward (27); Riewerts, Thomas (22); Robertson, Charles (49); Shoupe, Jamey (11); Solano, Julio (28); Turner, Mark (5); Yan, Roberto (10).

CHARLESTON—Ballard, Timothy (43); Bryant, John (25); Cone, David (16); Cook, Douglas (12); Evans, Richard (16); Jackson, Danny (13); Johnson, Bert (20); Kennedy, Robert (20); Krauss, Ronald (17); Miner, James (12); Psaltis, Spiro (27); Swank, Kenneth (25); Swanson, Perry (38); Undenstock, Robert (20); Walsh, James (5).

FLORENCE—Alba, Gibson (32); Clarke, Stanley (50); Cullen, Michael (28); Gallagher, Glenn (14); Harper, Devallon (31); Key, James (9); Malave, Benito (4); Moore, Gregory (26); Phillips, Christopher (16); Pursell, Joe (63); Reish, Stephan (33); Romagna, Randy (23); Ruetter, Derrick (5); Rusch, Robin (31).

GASTONIA—Bear, David (41); Kincannon, William (24); Milligan, Brent (14); Mills, Kenneth (13); Mitchell, William (11); Morelock, Allen (13); North, Jay (27); Parmenter, Walter (34); Silkwood, Joseph (1); Thomas, William (2); Young, Scott (18).

GREENSBORO—Bailey, Boyce (3); Baldwin, Johnny (4); Elston, Guy (18); Mendez, Mark (17); Niemiec, David (6); Peltola, William (40); Raftice, Robert (30); Silva, Mark (30); Swope, Andrew (24); Szymczak, David (30); Woodworth, David (20).

GREENWOOD—Acker, Larry (26); Azcona, Manuel (7); Baez, Miguel (13); Bailes, Scott (3); Downs, Dorley (20); Estrella, Orlando (2); Giron, Tomas (33); Hall, Joseph (10); Johnson, Dave (16); Manzanillo, Ravelo (27); Marty, Charles (10); Mott, Richard (15); Padgett, Glenn (3); Pellien, Kenneth (12); Stinnett, James (4); Storm, Luis (18); Susce, Steven (21); Taylor, Donald (27); Taylor, Ronald (15).

MACON—Anderson, Kirk (16); Barlow, Ricky (13); Butler, Mark (25); Charley, Tandy (17); Conte, Randall (17); Cratch, Richard (26); Culver, William (13); Edgell, Thor (12); Faber, Walter (11); Hosick, Steven (17); Jacob, Mark (25); McFadden, Robert (3); Moya, Ernest (18); O'Connor, Donald (43); Sadey, Richard (14).

SHELBY—Buttles, David (10); Collins, Joseph (19); Kreymborg, Michael (3); Leach, Ron (12); McDowell, Roger (12); Oates, Malcolm (13); Pina, Elvin (13); Ray, Steven (24); Robair, Michael (9); Stenquist, Steven (4); Teate, Kevin (7).

SPARTANBURG—Arnold, Jerry (15); Childress, Rodney (46); Hunter, Brian (25); Irions, Billy (18); Knight, Larry (10); Machin, John (9); Nye, Scott (23); Reilly, Jim (16); Rodriguez, Yonis (24); Rubio, Frank (14); Segura, Jose (20); Seiler, David (28); Surhoff, Richard (21).

GRAND SLAM HOME RUNS—Reddish, 3; Braun, Gibbons, 2 each; Berti, Bryeans, Burke, Distefano, Eaton, Fisher, Gambeski, Graziano, Hansen, Janssen, Lebo, Lowery, Morrison, Neal, Opie, Pagliarulo, Powell, E. Rodriguez, Suarez, Wheeler, Winters, 1 each.

AWARDED FIRST BASE ON CATCHER'S INTERFERENCE—Foley 4 (Garcia, Gibbons, Lebo, Poole); Pastornicky 3 (Cormack, Janssen, Poole); Baker 2 (Cormack 2); Ashmore (Cormack); Berger (Crump); Burke (Gibbons); Delgado (Poole); Distefano (Brill); Mann (Crump); R. Rodriguez (Brill); M. Smith (Gibbons).

CLUB FIELDING

Club	Pct.	G.	PO.	A.	E.	DP.	PB.
Gastonia	.962	143	3576	1571	201	149	47
Macon	.961	140	3564	1421	202	105	31
Greensboro	.959	141	3724	1614	231	133	30
Charleston	.957	140	3549	1501	226	130	27
Asheville	.955	141	3560	1713	249	149	37

Triple Play—Charleston.

CLUB FIELDING—Continued

Club	Pct.	G.	PO.	A.	E.	DP.	PB.	Club	Pct.	G.	PO.	A.	E.	DP.	PB.
Anderson	.954	142	3470	1498	241	106	40	Greenwood	.949	138	3499	1550	271	125	43
Florence	.952	142	3578	1409	254	102	32	Spartanburg	.947	140	3455	1504	277	117	17
Shelby	.950	141	3554	1477	265	115	35								

INDIVIDUAL FIELDING

*Throws lefthanded.

FIRST BASEMEN

Player and Club	Pct.	G.	PO.	A.	E.	DP.	Player and Club	Pct.	G.	PO.	A.	E.	DP.
Baker, Macon	1.000	1	9	1	0	0	Janssen, Asheville	1.000	6	53	3	0	3
Berger, Greenwood	.900	1	7	2	1	0	Kelly, Macon*	.992	72	574	45	5	47
Bomerito, Shelby	.977	5	39	3	1	1	Lindsey, Greensboro	.984	30	232	22	4	23
Braun, Asheville	.986	36	348	11	5	28	Lyons, Shelby	.948	9	67	6	4	5
Carpenter, Asheville*	.992	93	919	52	8	90	McHugh, Charleston	.985	106	896	62	15	83
Ching, Greensboro*	.983	8	55	3	1	4	McNutt, Shelby	.984	51	415	22	7	35
Churchill, Greenwood	1.000	1	12	0	0	3	Morrison, Shelby	.979	71	623	31	14	51
Clark, Asheville	1.000	9	57	6	0	7	Nichols, Macon	1.000	5	33	4	0	4
Clow, Anderson	.991	49	399	23	4	31	Perez, Florence*	.970	34	210	13	7	11
Crump, Spartanburg	1.000	1	4	0	0	0	Raeside, Shelby	.968	13	86	5	3	6
Dalena, Greensboro	.989	62	574	44	7	54	Rivas, Florence	.980	122	970	66	21	71
Destrade, Greensboro	.989	40	359	15	4	24	SANFORD, Anderson*	.991	96	874	54	8	65
Distefano, Greenwood*	.985	133	1184	104	19	102	Santos, Florence	.833	1	5	0	1	1
Foley, Gastonia*	.987	125	1058	93	15	115	Southern, Gastonia*	1.000	1	6	2	0	1
Gambeski, Gastonia	.980	6	49	1	1	10	Suarez, Spartanburg	.980	130	1079	73	24	98
Gibbons, Shelby	1.000	1	2	0	0	0	Thompson, Charleston	.988	20	160	10	2	14
Graziano, Greenwood*	.974	4	33	4	1	3	Vitato, Charleston	.967	5	28	1	1	3
Haas, Gastonia	.980	10	91	7	2	9	Wheeler, Florence	.920	3	22	1	2	3
Hansen, Charleston	.991	12	99	6	1	12	Whiting, Macon*	.993	71	557	30	4	42
Howard, Spartanburg	.981	11	100	4	2	5	Winters, Greensboro	1.000	1	4	0	0	0
Hughes, Greensboro	.978	18	132	4	3	14	Wirth, Gastonia*	.984	8	59	2	1	3

Triple Play—McHugh.

SECOND BASEMEN

Player and Club	Pct.	G.	PO.	A.	E.	DP.	Player and Club	Pct.	G.	PO.	A.	E.	DP.
Arce, Macon	974	75	149	186	9	26	Maris, Gastonia	.924	26	40	82	10	14
Bagwell, Greenwood	.935	34	58	72	9	15	Martinez, Greenwood	1.000	3	6	4	0	3
Barragan, Macon	1.000	1	2	0	0	0	Mata, Greensboro	.944	8	19	15	2	4
Bomerito, Shelby	1.000	1	2	1	0	1	Mena, Greenwood	.956	25	47	61	5	8
Bryeans, Charleston	.951	118	259	324	30	78	Menzhuber, Gastonia	.942	22	33	48	5	9
D'Onofrio, Asheville	.942	16	21	44	4	8	Moscat, Shelby	.991	22	47	66	1	12
Diaz, Shelby	.821	6	11	12	5	0	O'Shea, Greensboro	1.000	8	12	18	0	1
Ereu, Macon	1.000	3	10	5	0	2	Payano, Anderson	.949	36	77	72	8	17
Espinal, Asheville	.962	13	18	32	2	4	Perdomo, Shelby	.952	111	217	314	27	71
Falls, Asheville	.953	120	239	408	32	99	Pleis, Florence	.967	36	59	86	5	18
Fink, Gastonia	.667	1	1	1	1	1	Raeside, Shelby	.914	7	15	17	3	3
Gallegos, Greensboro	1.000	1	0	1	0	0	Roberts, Greenwood	.950	32	52	82	7	18
Giansanti, Anderson	.948	54	107	166	15	30	E. Rodriguez, Greensboro	.956	113	227	320	25	73
Goodyear, Macon	.966	30	70	72	5	16	Sanchez, Gastonia	.853	11	8	21	5	4
Grove, Greensboro	.950	33	58	75	7	17	Schu, Spartanburg	.950	37	91	101	10	20
Heiser, Anderson	.967	42	90	118	7	17	Dan Smith, Greenwood	.954	12	23	39	3	10
Heller, Shelby	1.000	2	1	1	0	0	DON SMITH, Gastonia	.957	101	229	309	24	74
Hinson, Macon	1.000	4	7	19	0	7	Tatis, Florence	.937	93	174	229	27	38
Hoppie, Spartanburg	.952	105	249	283	27	64	Villa, Greenwood	.955	44	94	118	10	28
Howard, Spartanburg	1.000	4	7	10	0	1	Vitato, Charleston	.982	24	50	59	2	6
Keiser, Spartanburg	1.000	1	4	1	0	0	Watson, Greenwood	.887	8	13	34	6	3
Laurie, Macon	.949	37	88	98	10	26	Wheeler, Florence	.966	24	36	48	3	7
Lucas, Anderson	.955	13	21	42	3	10							

THIRD BASEMEN

Player and Club	Pct.	G.	PO.	A.	E.	DP.	Player and Club	Pct.	G.	PO.	A.	E.	DP.
Arce, Macon	..846	9	5	17	4	3	Martinez, Greenwood	.877	57	47	110	22	17
Bishop, Florence	.884	137	107	237	45	14	Mata, Greensboro	.667	2	0	2	1	0
Blaser, Greensboro	.909	12	8	12	2	2	Maxwell, Macon	.907	27	28	40	7	5
Bomerito, Shelby	.895	97	73	182	30	23	McCardell, Greenwood	1.000	1	0	2	0	0
Chmil, Anderson	.923	5	3	9	1	0	Moscat, Shelby	.857	30	20	46	11	4
Churchill, Greenwood	1.000	4	4	8	0	1	O'Shea, Greensboro	.905	31	14	43	6	4
Cipolloni, Spartanburg	1.000	2	0	2	0	0	Opie, Greenwood	.936	58	39	136	12	9
Clark, Asheville	.912	48	42	93	13	12	Pagliarulo, Greensboro	.929	118	73	278	27	24
Cunningham, Greenwood	.848	18	13	26	7	2	Palma, Anderson	.927	128	114	269	30	27
D'Onofrio, Asheville	1.000	5	1	10	0	3	PASTORNICKY, Charleston	.935	134	133	258	27	26
Delgado, Asheville	.884	92	59	162	29	14	Pleis, Florence	.333	3	0	1	2	0
Diaz, Shelby	.778	10	7	14	6	2	Powell, Spartanburg	.667	1	2	0	1	0
Eaton, Anderson	.926	9	5	20	2	1	Raeside, Shelby	.846	4	5	6	2	0
Frishman, Spartanburg	.890	67	53	133	23	14	Rivera, Asheville	.800	1	3	1	1	0
Gambeski, Gastonia	.905	108	74	145	23	15	Schu, Spartanburg	.859	62	48	117	27	6
Goodyear, Macon	.966	25	19	37	2	1	Sharperson, Florence	.667	1	0	2	1	0
Harris, Shelby	.813	7	3	10	3	0	Smith, Gastonia	1.000	2	2	7	0	0
Heller, Shelby	.750	3	1	2	1	0	Sottile, Macon	.909	44	29	71	10	5
Hinson, Macon	.899	44	51	56	12	3	Villa, Greenwood	.800	1	3	1	1	0
Howard, Spartanburg	.828	12	6	18	5	0	Vitato, Charleston	.950	9	5	14	1	1
James, Gastonia	.895	35	23	62	10	3	Wheeler, Florence	1.000	3	6	4	0	0
Lucas, Anderson	.778	5	1	6	2	0							

Triple Play—Pastornicky.

SHORTSTOPS

Player and Club	Pct.	G.	PO.	A.	E.	DP.
Bagwell, Greenwood	.923	4	3	9	1	3
Barragan, Macon	.918	25	32	69	9	11
Bomerito, Shelby	.857	1	1	5	1	0
Clark, Anderson	.916	126	164	359	48	54
D'Onofrio, Asheville	.929	10	12	27	3	5
Falls, Asheville	.972	8	10	25	1	3
Gallegos, Greensboro	.931	102	141	307	33	54
Garcia, Shelby	.907	107	153	296	46	43
Goodin, Charleston	.888	59	92	139	29	26
Goodyear, Macon	.786	5	3	8	3	0
Grove, Greensboro	.932	65	70	163	17	28
Heiser, Anderson	1.000	2	3	8	0	1
Hoppie, Spartanburg	1.000	1	1	2	1	0
Hughes, Greensboro	1.000	1	1	0	0	0
Irvin, Macon	.907	48	67	127	20	18
Khalifa, Greenwood	.915	48	69	136	19	26
Kowalski, Greenwood	.852	5	9	14	4	1
Laurie, Macon	.957	5	8	14	1	3
Lowery, Spartanburg	.921	129	192	371	48	70
Lucas, Anderson	.891	14	22	27	6	7
LUTHER, Gastonia	.953	142	242	468	35	110
Malave, Florence	.873	33	44	80	18	18
Martinez, Greenwood	.881	25	47	64	15	15
McAllister, Asheville	.943	127	213	438	39	92
Moscat, Shelby	.939	31	43	80	8	18
Payano, Anderson	1.000	1	0	2	0	1
Perdomo, Shelby	.862	8	9	16	4	3
Pittaro, Macon	.928	68	99	212	24	44
Rivera, Asheville	1.000	3	3	8	0	1
Schu, Spartanburg	.877	13	18	39	8	6
Sharperson, Florence	.925	102	136	259	32	41
Dan Smith, Greensboro	.900	51	66	149	24	22
Don Smith, Gastonia	.952	5	6	14	1	3
Sorel, Charleston	.946	32	44	95	8	23
Villa, Greenwood	.925	9	17	20	3	5
Vitato, Charleston	.937	63	64	173	16	30
Watson, Greenwood	.857	6	7	17	4	2
Wheeler, Florence	.938	18	30	46	5	5

OUTFIELDERS

Player and Club	Pct.	G.	PO.	A.	E.	DP.
Aaron, Anderson	1.000	7	6	0	0	0
Agapay, Spartanburg	.667	3	2	0	1	0
Aubin, Greenwood	.913	26	38	4	4	1
Baker, Macon	.968	55	88	4	3	0
Barker, Macon	.940	51	75	4	5	1
Blaser, Greensboro	.893	25	24	1	3	0
Braun, Anderson	.950	18	37	1	2	0
Brown, Greenwood	.972	124	198	7	6	0
Burge, Greenwood°	.875	4	6	1	1	0
Burke, Asheville	.940	129	222	14	15	2
Carreon, Greenwood	.974	125	183	8	5	0
Casasnovas, Macon	.972	27	33	2	1	2
Ching, Greensboro°	.938	10	14	1	1	0
Christensen, Shelby	.988	98	156	9	2	2
Clark, Asheville	.980	33	47	3	1	0
Currier, Spartanburg	.974	33	37	1	1	0
Delarosa, Greenwood°	.947	82	172	7	10	2
J. Delgado, Asheville	1.000	2	2	0	0	0
R. Delgado, Greenwood°	.957	44	80	8	4	3
Denby, Shelby	.958	36	62	6	3	0
Devalk, Greenwood	.957	12	22	0	1	0
Digioia, Gastonia	.938	18	15	0	1	0
Dykstra, Shelby°	.947	115	239	11	14	1
Eaton, Anderson	.935	57	93	7	7	2
Faucette, Florence	.750	4	3	0	1	0
Fields, Macon	.982	79	162	4	3	0
Filkins, Greensboro	.974	27	35	2	1	0
FINK, Gastonia	.994	105	165	7	1	1
Frederick, Greenwood	.965	32	54	1	2	0
Gallegos, Greensboro	1.000	6	7	0	0	0
Garcia, Shelby	1.000	3	5	1	0	0
Gjesdal, Greensboro	1.000	3	1	0	0	0
Graziano, Greenwood°	.959	29	44	3	2	1
Haas, Gastonia	1.000	2	1	0	0	0
Harris, Shelby	.667	2	2	0	1	0
Hatcher, Anderson	.971	53	98	3	3	1
Heller, Shelby	.944	19	32	2	2	0
Hibner, Macon	.950	14	18	1	1	0
Hodge, Anderson	.946	124	240	4	14	1
Howard, Spartanburg	1.000	12	11	0	0	0
Isaac, Asheville	.857	61	65	7	12	1
James, Gastonia	.962	50	73	3	3	0
Johnson, Macon	.981	121	248	10	5	0
Jones, Greensboro	.853	63	79	2	14	1
Keiser, Spartanburg	.912	104	149	17	16	2
Kingery, Charleston°	.975	140	250	21	7	5
Kinnard, Florence	.950	126	205	5	11	2
Llewellyn, Anderson	.907	49	75	3	8	0
Luzon, Anderson	.938	19	28	2	2	0
Malave, Florence	.938	24	15	0	1	0
Mann, Anderson	.964	51	74	7	3	0
Marte, Florence°	.964	68	102	4	4	2
Martinez, Greenwood	.667	1	2	0	1	0
Martino, Charleston	1.000	17	28	3	0	1
Mata, Greensboro	.960	119	259	7	11	4
McNutt, Shelby	.906	37	46	2	5	0
Meadows, Asheville	.875	58	87	4	13	1
Menzhuber, Gastonia	.950	117	203	27	12	4
Moser, Anderson°	.988	29	76	4	1	0
Neal, Charleston	.915	56	94	3	9	0
Nelson, Anderson	1.000	4	3	0	0	0
Nichols, Macon	1.000	6	5	0	0	0
Olander, Spartanburg	.972	121	227	16	7	4
Oruna, Charleston	.957	114	255	12	12	5
Patterson, Charleston	.750	11	15	0	5	0
Penigar, Spartanburg	.912	130	202	15	21	3
Perdomo, Shelby	1.000	2	2	0	0	0
Perez, Florence°	1.000	5	5	0	0	0
Pettis, Greenwood	.975	34	75	4	2	1
Plautz, Charleston	.971	46	63	3	2	1
Reddish, Greensboro	.951	112	130	5	7	0
Rice, Greenwood	.954	42	81	2	4	0
Rivera, Asheville	.869	52	67	6	11	0
Rodriguez, Gastonia	.980	94	228	11	5	2
Sanchez, Greensboro	.800	5	4	0	1	0
Santos, Florence	.941	132	199	8	13	0
Sarmiento, Florence	.912	83	76	7	8	1
Sherman, Asheville	.929	46	86	5	7	0
Southern, Gastonia°	.981	33	49	3	1	1
Street, Anderson	.954	49	95	8	5	3
Thomas, Macon°	.949	89	152	14	9	0
Vitato, Charleston	1.000	2	6	0	0	0
Weems, Asheville	1.000	36	52	4	0	0
West, Charleston	.968	36	60	0	2	0
Wheeler, Florence	.938	13	14	1	1	0
Winters, Greensboro	.982	98	159	3	3	0
Wirth, Gastonia°	.984	39	58	3	1	0
Young, Macon	.966	19	28	0	1	0
Ysambert, Spartanburg	.981	34	47	5	1	1

CATCHERS

Player and Club	Pct.	G.	PO.	A.	E.	DP.	PB.
Ashmore, Charleston	.968	22	133	16	5	3	10
Baker, Greenwood	.985	8	62	2	1	0	1
Berger, Greenwood	.979	54	289	34	7	3	19
BERTI, Asheville	.987	86	450	66	7	4	16
Blaser, Greensboro	.950	11	36	2	2	0	3
Brill, Anderson	.958	79	425	75	22	5	18
Champion, Gastonia	.953	17	93	9	5	0	6
Churchill, Greenwood	.976	6	37	3	1	0	4
Cipolloni, Spartanburg	.976	69	422	62	12	5	8
Clow, Anderson	.857	2	10	2	2	0	0
Cormack, Anderson	.956	67	306	42	16	4	22
Crump, Spartanburg	.966	23	124	17	5	1	3
Czeszewski, Shelby	.975	17	74	4	2	0	2
Diaz, Florence	1.000	3	8	0	0	0	0
Digioia, Gastonia	.934	22	95	4	7	1	8
Fisher, Macon	.984	68	372	50	7	3	11
Garcia, Asheville	.982	45	227	47	5	4	13
Gauci, Anderson	.974	18	101	11	3	0	8
Gaunce, Charleston	.985	32	168	23	3	3	8
Gibbons, Shelby	.974	84	557	72	17	8	20
Haas, Gastonia	.984	32	161	27	3	1	10
Hansen, Charleston	.977	89	578	56	15	5	9
Heller, Shelby	.988	25	139	20	2	1	6
Howard, Spartanburg	1.000	2	2	0	0	0	0
Hughes, Greensboro	.958	5	23	0	1	0	1
Janssen, Asheville	.978	27	157	18	4	2	8
Kneuer, Greensboro	.983	33	209	17	4	1	3
Lebo, Greensboro	.959	60	378	22	17	3	10
Lindsey, Greensboro	.986	59	320	36	5	2	13
Lyons, Shelby	.978	24	159	15	4	1	7
Martinez, Greenwood	.982	9	48	7	1	0	2
Nichols, Macon	.950	65	353	45	21	1	10
Poole, Florence	.982	98	757	47	15	5	20
Powell, Spartanburg	.954	41	226	24	12	0	3
Pulley, Florence	.975	50	314	44	9	7	12
Rodriguez, Greenwood	.956	69	351	60	19	4	17
Silva, Macon	1.000	4	20	0	0	0	2
Soreca, Spartanburg	.981	14	89	13	2	3	3
Weems, Gastonia	.977	80	405	60	11	6	23

OFFICIAL BASEBALL GUIDE

PITCHERS

Player and Club	Pct.	G.	PO.	A.	E.	DP.
Acker, Greenwood°	.889	26	13	35	6	2
Alba, Florence°	.917	32	3	8	1	0
Alexander, Macon	.929	46	2	11	1	0
Ambrose, Asheville	1.000	13	4	3	0	1
Anderson, Macon	.923	16	5	7	1	0
Arnold, Spartanburg°	.857	15	1	5	1	0
Azcona, Greenwood	1.000	7	1	2	0	0
Baez, Greenwood°	.667	13	2	2	2	1
Bailes, Greenwood	1.000	3	1	2	0	0
Bailey, Greensboro	1.000	3	1	1	0	0
Baker, Anderson°	.923	8	3	9	1	0
Baldwin, Greensboro	1.000	4	2	1	0	1
Ballard, Charleston	1.000	43	5	18	0	1
Barlow, Macon	1.000	13	5	16	0	0
Bear, Gastonia	.850	41	4	13	3	1
Bettendorf, Shelby	.885	20	8	15	3	2
Blas, Asheville	1.000	5	0	3	0	0
Brown, Gastonia	.897	26	12	14	3	1
Bryant, Charleston	.833	25	7	28	7	3
Butler, Macon°	.972	25	8	27	1	1
Buttles, Shelby	1.000	10	3	7	0	0
Callahan, Asheville	.500	5	1	0	1	0
Charley, Macon°	.900	17	3	6	1	0
Childress, Spartanburg	.826	46	2	17	4	2
Clarke, Florence°	.857	50	5	7	2	1
Collins, Shelby	.900	19	1	8	1	0
Cone, Charleston	.885	16	6	17	3	1
Conte, Macon	.833	17	1	4	1	0
Cook, Charleston	.968	12	9	21	1	0
Corniel, Asheville	1.000	9	0	1	0	0
Cratch, Macon	.862	26	5	20	4	1
Cullen, Florence	.857	28	1	5	1	0
Culver, Macon	.769	13	4	6	3	0
Davisson, Spartanburg	.945	27	20	32	3	2
Depaula, Asheville	.960	25	6	18	1	1
Dorin, Spartanburg	.800	8	2	2	1	0
Downs, Greenwood	.875	20	5	9	2	0
Edgell, Macon	.667	12	0	6	3	0
Elston, Greensboro	1.000	18	2	0	0	0
Espinoza, Asheville	.750	16	0	9	3	3
Estrella, Greenwood	1.000	2	0	2	0	0
Evans, Charleston°	1.000	16	5	15	0	0
Faber, Macon°	1.000	11	0	7	0	0
Fincher, Greensboro°	.813	25	6	20	6	0
Forchee, Gastonia	.903	23	14	14	3	0
Fuller, Anderson	.750	10	1	2	1	0
Gallagher, Florence	.786	14	1	10	3	2
Giron, Greenwood	.870	33	9	11	3	0
Godwin, Asheville	.963	54	6	20	1	1
Graves, Shelby	.786	47	4	7	3	1
Hall, Greenwood°	.750	10	1	2	1	0
Harper, Florence	.938	31	19	26	3	1
Hosick, Macon°	1.000	17	4	5	0	0
Hubbard, Gastonia	.943	23	13	20	2	1
Hunter, Spartanburg	.921	25	9	26	3	2
Irions, Spartanburg°	.875	18	4	17	3	0
D. Jackson, Charleston°	.914	13	8	24	3	0
R. Jackson, Shelby	.875	31	8	27	5	2
Jacob, Macon	1.000	25	10	10	0	1
B. Johnson, Charleston°	1.000	20	2	4	0	0
D. Johnson, Greenwood	.933	16	9	5	1	0
Kennedy, Charleston	.857	20	1	11	2	0
Key, Florence°	.909	9	7	13	2	0
Kincannon, Gastonia	.964	24	10	17	1	1
Klaus, Anderson	.824	27	4	10	3	0
Knight, Spartanburg	1.000	10	1	2	0	0
Koenig, 6 Anderson-19 Ashe°	.923	25	0	12	1	0
Krauss, Charleston°	.813	17	3	10	3	0
Kreymborg, Shelby	1.000	3	0	1	0	0
Kuntz, Shelby	.789	25	5	25	8	0
Lance, Anderson°	1.000	13	2	14	0	1
Latham, Shelby°	.974	24	5	32	1	5
Leach, Shelby	.750	12	1	2	1	0
Lee, Anderson	.784	32	11	18	8	2
Lubert, Anderson°	1.000	15	5	8	0	2
Machin, Spartanburg°	.857	9	1	5	1	0
Malave, Florence	.750	4	0	3	1	0
Malloy, Asheville°	.971	15	9	24	1	1
Manzanillo, Greenwood°	.896	27	9	34	5	1
Marty, Greenwood	.870	10	9	11	3	0
McDowell, Shelby	.905	12	9	10	2	1
McFadden, Macon.	1.000	3	0	1	0	0
Mendez, Greensboro	.975	17	10	29	1	3
Milligan, Gastonia°	.947	14	8	10	1	0
Mills, Gastonia°	1.000	13	2	0	0	0
Miner, Charleston	.875	12	3	11	2	0
Mitchell, Gastonia	1.000	11	2	2	0	0
Mize, Asheville	1.000	6	2	0	0	0
Moore, Florence	.958	26	8	15	1	1
Morelock, Gastonia	.938	13	3	12	1	2
Mott, Greenwood	.700	15	0	7	3	1
Moya, Macon	.938	18	9	21	2	2
Niemiec, Greensboro	1.000	6	0	1	0	0
North, Gastonia	.925	27	18	19	3	3
Nye, Spartanburg	.900	23	1	8	1	0
O'Connor, Macon	1.000	43	10	17	0	0
Oates, Shelby°	.889	13	0	8	1	1
Padgett, Greenwood	.500	3	0	1	1	0
Parmenter, Gastonia	1.000	34	5	12	0	0
Pellien, Greenwood°	1.000	12	2	2	0	0
Peltola, Greensboro	.857	40	5	7	2	0
Phillips, Florence	.920	16	4	19	2	2
Pickett, Shelby°	1.000	50	2	17	0	0
Pina, Shelby	.875	13	0	7	1	2
Pittman, Gastonia°	1.000	22	0	5	0	1
Pleis, Florence	1.000	1	0	1	0	0
Psaltis, Charleston°	.871	27	7	20	4	1
Pursell, Florence	.929	63	6	33	3	3
Raftice, Greensboro°	.750	30	3	3	2	0
Ray, Shelby°	.880	24	7	15	3	1
Regalado, Asheville	.816	24	6	25	7	1
E. Reilly, Asheville	.863	27	11	33	7	2
J. Reilly, Spartanburg	.900	16	2	7	1	2
Reish, Florence	.977	33	9	33	1	4
Rice, Greewood	.875	14	2	5	1	0
Riewerts, Asheville°	.833	22	7	8	3	1
Robair, Shelby	.875	9	4	3	1	0
Robertson, Asheville	.885	49	1	22	3	0
Rodriguez, Spartanburg	.929	24	8	18	2	0
Romagna, Florence	.977	23	14	29	1	3
Rubio, Spartanburg	1.000	14	3	7	0	0
Ruetter, Florence°	1.000	5	2	4	0	0
Rusch, Florence°	.944	31	2	15	1	0
Rymer, Anderson	1.000	5	0	1	0	0
Sadey, Macon	.667	14	1	1	1	0
Sanford, Anderson°	1.000	2	1	2	0	1
Sears, Anderson	.857	46	3	9	2	0
Segura, Spartanburg	1.000	20	0	8	0	0
Seiler, Spartanburg°	.882	28	3	12	2	0
Seitz, Anderson	1.000	16	1	6	0	0
Shiflett, Greensboro°	.919	31	12	45	5	1
Shoupee, Asheville°	.857	11	1	11	2	1
Silva, Greensboro	.956	30	13	30	2	2
Siwiec, Greensboro	1.000	36	1	13	0	0
M. Smith, Anderson	.879	26	9	20	4	2
Z. Smith, Anderson°	1.000	12	6	17	0	3
Solano, Asheville	.949	28	7	30	2	1
Soreca, Spartanburg	.875	25	2	5	1	0
Sperto, Anderson	.875	23	2	5	1	0
Stenquist, Shelby	1.000	4	0	2	0	0
Storm, Greenwood	1.000	18	6	12	0	0
Surhoff, Spartanburg	.929	21	3	10	1	0
Susce, Greenwood	1.000	21	6	19	0	1
Swank, Charleston°	.941	25	4	12	1	2
Swanson, Charleston	.722	38	3	10	5	0
Swope, Greensboro	.846	24	7	4	2	0
Szymczak, Greensboro	.933	30	9	33	3	5
D. Taylor, Greenwood	.957	27	14	31	2	2
R. Taylor, Greenwood	.333	15	0	1	2	1
Teate, Shelby	1.000	7	1	4	0	0
Thomas, Gastonia	1.000	2	3	1	0	0
Torres, Anderson	.636	12	3	4	4	0
Turner, Asheville°	.500	5	1	0	1	0
Undenstock, Charleston	.923	20	6	18	2	1
VARGAS, Anderson	1.000	27	8	23	0	2
Waddell, Anderson	1.000	4	0	1	0	0
Walker, Anderson°	1.000	6	1	4	0	1
Walsh, Charleston	.800	5	0	4	1	0
Ward, Anderson	1.000	5	0	3	0	0
Whiting, Macon°	1.000	4	2	0	0	0
Willerson, Anderson	1.000	16	1	9	0	0
Woodworth, Greensboro°	1.000	20	0	7	0	0
Wyatt, Shelby°	.667	11	0	2	1	0
Yan, Asheville	.333	10	1	0	2	0
S. Young, Gastonia	1.000	18	11	16	0	2

Triple Play—Evans.

The following players do not have any recorded accepted chances at the positions indicated; therefore, are not listed in the fielding averages for those particular positions: Arce, of; Ashmore, of; Bailey, of; Barlow, of; Gallegos, p; Gibbons, of; Goodyear, of; Heller, ss; Hughes, of; Keiser, 3b; Kelly, of; Luther, p; Malave, 3b; Marte, 1b; Menzhuber, p; Moscat, of; O'Shea, ss; Pulley, 3b; J. Rodriguez, 2b; Silkwood, p; D. Smith, c; Stinnett, p; Tatis, of; Weems, 2b; Wirth, p; K. Young, p.

CLUB PITCHING

Club	ERA.	G.	CG.	ShO.	Sv.	IP.	H.	R.	ER.	HR.	HB.	BB.	Int. BB.	SO.	WP.	Bk.
Greensboro	3.49	141	36	7	31	1241.1	1164	645	482	74	28	571	25	934	88	14
Florence	3.78	142	14	7	34	1192.2	1133	677	501	86	31	600	8	1032	73	12
Charleston	3.98	140	24	9	25	1183	1163	657	523	80	40	607	8	826	70	14
Greenwood	4.31	138	34	11	18	1166.1	1148	742	559	82	27	674	32	763	88	21
Spartanburg	4.42	140	27	8	19	1151.2	1222	703	566	86	32	556	32	824	86	6
Shelby	4.44	141	32	10	24	1184.2	1135	736	585	80	37	679	28	884	60	14
Gastonia	4.50	143	46	9	11	1192	1156	709	596	101	27	642	15	721	105	17
Asheville	4.73	141	20	9	20	1186.2	1304	779	624	114	45	627	27	790	73	20
Anderson	4.78	142	30	9	32	1156.2	1235	759	614	94	28	638	9	724	101	12
Macon	4.82	140	27	4	16	1188	1210	734	636	68	42	636	23	780	74	13

PITCHERS' RECORDS
(Leading Qualifiers for Earned-Run Average Leadership — 115 or More Innings)

*Throws lefthanded.

Pitcher — Club	W.	L.	Pct.	ERA.	G.	GS.	CG.	GF.	ShO.	Sv.	IP.	H.	R.	ER.	HR.	HB.	BB.	Int. BB.	SO.	WP.
D. Taylor, Greenwood	9	8	.529	2.30	27	24	9	3	2	2	164.2	128	57	42	6	1	92	3	133	16
Shiflett, Greensboro*	14	5	.737	2.42	31	16	6	3	1	0	156	129	57	42	5	2	61	2	123	4
Harper, Florence	9	9	.500	2.84	31	24	5	3	2	0	174	145	74	55	12	3	79	1	196	12
S. Young, Gastonia	8	9	.471	2.85	18	16	8	2	2	0	123	104	47	39	7	1	38	2	69	12
Silva, Greensboro	14	7	.667	2.92	30	27	12	3	0	0	184.2	161	87	60	10	3	82	3	140	11
Hunter, Spartanburg	12	7	.632	3.17	25	25	5	0	3	0	144.2	124	63	51	7	1	75	5	93	11
Szymczak, Greensboro	14	2	.875	3.19	30	23	5	5	0	1	175	174	84	62	9	1	55	3	63	11
Reish, Florence	12	6	.667	3.28	33	13	1	6	1	2	137	133	67	50	8	1	39	1	97	3
Mendez, Greensboro	9	5	.643	3.35	17	17	6	0	0	0	126.1	126	66	47	4	3	53	2	89	4
Hubbard, Gastonia	8	9	.471	3.50	23	20	9	1	0	0	138.2	139	70	54	10	3	37	2	88	8

Departmental Leaders: G—Pursell, 63; GS—Davisson, Silva, Solano, 27; CG—Davisson, 14; GF—Pursell, 46; ShO—Hunter, Solano, 3; W—Shiflett, Silva, Szymczak, 14; L—Acker, Forchee, 15; Pct.—D. Jackson, .909; Sv—Purcell, 18; IP—Davisson, 186.2; H—Davisson, 185; R—Manzanillo, North, 108; ER—North, 94; HR—Davisson, 18; HB—Solano, 11; BB—Ray, 127; IBB—Godwin, 11; SO—Harper, 196; WP—Fincher, 21.

(All Pitchers — Listed Alphabetically)

Pitcher — Club	W.	L.	Pct.	ERA.	G.	GS.	CG.	GF.	ShO.	Sv.	IP.	H.	R.	ER.	HR.	HB.	BB.	Int. BB.	SO.	WP.
Acker, Greenwood*	7	15	.318	3.62	26	26	5	0	0	0	181.1	177	101	73	14	1	72	3	115	8
Alba, Florence*	6	9	.400	5.13	32	19	0	4	0	0	114	117	86	65	9	3	98	0	107	12
Alexander, Macon	9	8	.529	4.84	46	0	0	33	0	4	102.1	94	62	55	2	1	80	4	80	5
Ambrose, Asheville	4	1	.800	4.30	13	2	0	6	0	0	37.2	56	24	18	3	0	15	0	22	3
Anderson, Macon	1	1	.500	9.37	16	1	0	3	0	0	32.2	39	36	34	3	6	43	1	10	10
Arnold, Spartanburg*	0	0	.000	6.45	15	5	0	5	0	0	37.2	57	39	27	3	1	18	1	24	1
Azcona, Greenwood	0	0	.000	6.75	7	0	0	5	0	0	12	11	16	9	1	1	17	0	9	2
Baez, Greenwood*	2	2	.500	3.91	13	0	0	7	0	2	23	22	17	10	0	3	16	2	7	3
Bailes, Greenwood*	0	1	.000	7.24	3	1	1	1	0	0	13.2	17	12	11	4	0	6	0	8	0
Bailey, Greensboro	0	0	.000	10.38	3	0	0	0	0	0	4.1	7	5	5	0	2	4	0	3	1
Baker, Anderson*	4	2	.667	5.29	8	5	0	1	0	1	34	36	25	20	4	2	26	0	29	3
Baldwin, Greenwood*	0	0	.000	1.74	4	0	0	1	0	0	10.1	8	4	2	1	0	7	0	9	0
Ballard, Charleston	8	5	.615	4.24	43	0	0	30	0	4	91.1	118	57	43	4	2	28	2	32	5
Barlow, Macon	2	4	.333	5.46	13	13	1	1	0	0	64.1	64	41	39	3	4	49	2	36	5
Bear, Gastonia	4	4	.500	4.10	41	0	0	31	0	4	59.1	45	29	27	3	2	37	3	26	2
Bettendorf, Shelby	9	5	.643	4.28	20	19	4	0	0	0	117.2	111	69	56	9	5	62	0	86	5
Blas, Asheville	0	0	.000	5.40	5	0	0	1	0	0	8.1	11	6	5	0	0	5	0	6	2
Brown, Gastonia	5	12	.294	4.76	26	22	7	3	1	0	157	145	96	83	13	0	108	1	101	12
Bryant, Charleston	6	7	.462	4.71	25	22	2	1	0	1	126	113	79	66	7	6	100	1	94	9
Butler, Macon*	7	11	.389	4.17	25	18	6	2	0	0	131.2	157	76	61	13	0	27	1	39	3
Buttles, Shelby	4	2	.667	3.83	10	10	0	0	0	0	40	38	25	17	4	4	19	0	23	1
Callahan, Asheville	1	2	.333	7.23	5	5	0	0	0	0	23.2	28	25	19	1	5	22	0	15	3
Charley, Macon*	4	3	.571	2.45	17	1	1	9	0	1	55	47	17	15	1	0	23	3	34	3
Childress, Spartanburg	4	4	.500	4.01	46	0	0	32	0	6	92	101	53	41	5	0	44	9	54	9
Clarke, Florence*	6	4	.600	1.89	50	0	0	30	0	13	95	60	26	20	2	2	52	2	136	3
Collins, Shelby	0	1	.000	7.25	19	1	0	7	0	4	36	38	32	29	2	0	17	2	26	1
Cone, Charleston	9	2	.818	2.06	16	16	1	0	1	0	104.2	84	38	24	4	4	47	0	87	9
Conte, Macon	3	3	.500	5.32	17	1	0	9	0	1	44	45	30	26	1	4	34	1	25	6
Cook, Charleston	2	7	.222	3.46	12	12	3	0	2	0	75.1	58	35	29	5	1	36	0	53	3
Corniel, Asheville	0	0	.000	16.76	9	0	0	3	0	0	9.2	22	19	18	3	1	6	0	5	0
Cratch, Macon	13	9	.591	4.36	26	26	4	0	0	0	154.2	170	81	75	10	1	44	3	89	3
Cullen, Florence	0	1	.000	4.83	28	4	0	18	0	0	31.2	20	22	17	1	2	52	0	49	6
Culver, Macon	2	5	.286	5.57	13	12	1	0	0	0	64.2	76	45	40	4	1	24	1	27	5
Davisson, Spartanburg	11	10	.524	3.76	27	27	14	0	1	0	186.2	185	92	78	18	3	54	2	115	5
DePaula, Greenwood	7	8	.467	5.54	25	18	2	2	1	0	115.1	138	92	71	17	2	50	1	56	8
Dorin, Spartanburg	3	2	.600	3.98	8	4	1	2	0	0	31.2	44	26	14	3	2	10	0	14	3
Downs, Greenwood	3	6	.333	4.50	20	7	3	10	0	2	76	83	56	38	8	1	34	5	64	3
Edgell, Macon	2	4	.333	5.03	12	12	0	0	0	0	48.1	48	41	27	4	3	41	1	31	8
Elston, Greensboro	3	0	1.000	0.68	18	0	0	15	0	10	26.2	13	2	2	1	1	10	2	44	3
Espinoza, Asheville	1	1	.500	6.88	16	0	0	10	0	0	34	42	30	26	2	2	19	1	12	3
Estrella, Greenwood	0	0	.000	7.36	2	0	0	1	0	0	3.2	6	3	3	1	0	5	1	2	0
Evans, Charleston*	8	4	.667	2.53	16	11	6	3	1	1	92.1	96	37	26	3	2	29	0	56	6
Faber, Macon*	2	6	.250	6.23	11	9	1	1	0	0	43.1	34	35	30	2	5	45	0	50	8
Fincher, Greensboro*	10	7	.588	4.28	25	24	3	1	2	0	134.2	132	97	64	9	0	85	2	100	21
Forchee, Gastonia	7	15	.318	5.30	23	23	3	0	1	0	132.1	137	93	78	11	5	82	1	47	16
Fuller, Anderson	1	1	.500	5.59	10	2	0	1	0	1	19.1	21	13	12	1	0	14	0	5	3
Gallagher, Florence	2	4	.333	4.28	14	11	0	1	0	0	48.1	52	34	23	7	0	35	0	30	2
Gallegos, Greensboro	0	0	.000	3.00	2	0	0	2	0	0	3	1	1	1	1	0	2	0	2	0
Giron, Greenwood	6	7	.462	4.13	33	8	1	22	0	4	96	105	65	44	8	0	35	1	44	5
Godwin, Asheville	6	8	.429	3.70	54	1	0	41	0	7	80.1	84	47	33	7	5	38	11	57	4
Graves, Shelby	8	7	.533	4.62	47	2	0	28	0	6	87.2	80	52	45	4	4	63	4	61	1
Hall, Greenwood*	0	1	.000	5.12	10	0	0	7	0	1	19.1	21	17	11	1	1	21	2	9	6
Harper, Florence	9	9	.500	2.84	31	24	5	3	2	0	174	145	74	55	12	3	79	1	196	12
Hosick, Macon*	1	1	.500	6.26	17	3	0	4	0	2	46	44	33	32	4	2	33	0	53	2
Hubbard, Gastonia	8	9	.471	3.50	23	20	9	1	0	0	138.2	139	70	54	10	3	37	2	88	8

Pitcher—Club	W.	L.	Pct.	ERA.	G.	GS.	CG.	GF.	ShO.	Sv.	IP.	H.	R.	ER.	HR.	HB.	BB.	Int. BB.	SO.	WP.
Hunter, Spartanburg	12	7	.632	3.17	25	25	5	0	3	0	144.2	124	63	51	7	1	75	5	93	11
Irions, Spartanburg°	3	7	.300	3.66	18	11	1	5	1	0	76.1	81	40	31	3	1	43	0	65	8
D. Jackson, Charleston°	10	1	.909	2.62	13	13	3	0	0	0	96.1	80	37	28	6	3	39	1	62	4
R. Jackson, Shelby	10	10	.500	4.42	31	19	7	7	1	0	163	156	100	80	14	2	72	4	138	12
Jacob, Macon	7	3	.700	4.92	25	22	4	2	1	0	133.2	117	78	73	11	2	73	1	124	3
B. Johnson, Charleston°	2	2	.500	5.12	20	10	0	7	0	0	58	64	43	33	4	5	32	0	40	5
D. Johnson, Greenwood	4	4	.500	3.86	16	6	1	7	1	0	58.1	50	32	25	2	0	41	1	41	7
Kennedy, Charleston	4	3	.571	5.37	20	15	0	3	0	0	68.2	67	53	41	3	6	67	0	40	12
Key, Florence°	5	2	.714	3.72	9	9	0	0	0	0	58	59	33	24	10	4	18	0	49	2
Kincannon, Gastonia	10	10	.500	4.61	24	22	7	2	1	0	146.1	138	87	75	17	5	69	0	88	6
Klaus, Anderson	4	2	.667	4.14	27	0	0	20	0	5	45.2	50	25	21	2	1	22	1	36	3
Knight, Spartanburg	1	2	.333	5.68	10	2	0	4	0	1	31.2	49	26	20	2	1	18	1	29	1
Koenig, 6 Anderson-19 Ashe.°	3	1	.750	4.98	25	3	1	9	1	1	59.2	63	43	33	5	0	42	2	52	5
Krauss, Charleston°	2	5	.286	8.04	17	9	1	4	0	0	56	68	54	50	8	3	36	0	38	2
Kreymborg, Shelby	0	0	.000	12.27	3	0	0	2	0	0	3.2	6	5	5	0	0	3	0	3	3
Kuntz, Shelby	6	7	.462	5.20	25	18	3	2	1	0	128	144	106	74	6	9	79	5	84	7
Lance, Anderson°	4	7	.364	5.43	13	13	2	0	1	0	71.1	96	55	43	6	3	41	0	32	7
Latham, Shelby°	9	7	.563	4.40	24	22	7	2	1	0	143.1	145	81	70	13	3	53	3	114	2
Leach, Shelby	2	0	1.000	2.87	12	0	0	7	0	0	15.2	8	6	5	1	0	8	0	6	1
Lee, Anderson	10	9	.526	4.18	32	18	7	8	0	1	153	160	86	71	12	5	89	3	77	8
Lubert, Anderson°	4	5	.444	3.21	15	12	3	2	2	1	81.1	64	42	29	6	1	32	0	52	4
Luther, Gastonia	0	0	.000	54.00	1	0	0	1	0	0	1	7	6	6	1	0	0	0	2	2
Machin, Spartanburg°	3	1	.750	3.04	9	8	0	1	0	1	50.1	34	18	17	4	0	18	1	66	2
Malave, Florence	0	0	.000	11.57	4	0	0	0	0	0	7	9	13	9	2	0	6	0	6	2
Malloy, Asheville°	7	6	.538	3.78	15	15	3	0	2	0	102.1	105	50	43	10	8	29	0	62	2
Manzanillo, Greenwood°	9	9	.500	4.97	27	25	7	1	2	1	157.2	156	108	87	15	1	109	3	93	6
Marty, Greenwood	0	5	.000	5.89	10	10	0	0	0	0	55	63	49	36	2	2	36	1	25	2
McDowell, Shelby	6	4	.600	3.28	12	11	4	0	0	0	71.1	61	34	26	1	1	30	1	40	3
McFadden, Macon	0	1	.000	19.29	3	1	0	1	0	0	7	14	15	15	0	1	10	0	8	2
Mendez, Greensboro	9	5	.643	3.35	17	17	6	0	0	0	126.1	126	66	47	4	3	53	2	89	4
Menzhuber, Gastonia	0	0	.000	0.00	1	0	0	1	0	0	2	1	0	0	0	0	0	0	2	2
Milligan, Gastonia°	3	4	.429	5.92	14	9	1	3	0	0	62.1	72	46	41	5	3	37	0	25	5
Mills, Gastonia°	0	0	.000	5.18	13	0	0	4	0	0	24.1	26	16	14	0	0	17	1	22	1
Miner, Charleston	3	2	.600	1.01	12	0	0	10	0	3	44.2	33	9	5	2	1	13	0	30	1
Mitchell, Gastonia	0	1	.000	6.08	11	0	0	8	0	0	23.2	19	18	16	5	0	26	0	19	4
Mize, Asheville	2	2	.500	6.85	6	4	0	0	0	0	22.1	28	19	17	4	0	15	0	26	3
Moore, Florence	6	7	.462	5.59	26	16	2	2	1	1	95	105	80	59	4	3	63	0	57	15
Morelock, Gastonia	2	4	.333	4.14	13	4	3	4	0	1	54.1	58	31	25	6	0	15	2	57	4
Mott, Greenwood	1	3	.250	4.63	15	0	0	10	0	4	35	37	23	18	2	1	23	5	15	3
Moya, Macon	6	7	.462	3.49	18	18	5	0	0	0	113.1	112	56	44	1	5	47	1	85	0
Niemiec, Greensboro	1	0	1.000	7.20	6	0	0	1	0	0	10	11	10	8	0	1	8	0	7	3
North, Gastonia	6	14	.300	5.13	27	24	6	2	2	0	165	174	108	94	13	3	101	1	89	19
Nye, Spartanburg	0	2	.000	3.72	23	0	0	12	0	0	46	56	26	19	2	1	17	1	31	3
O'Connor, Macon	6	5	.545	3.73	43	1	0	35	0	8	101.1	104	52	42	8	3	29	4	53	5
Oates, Shelby°	0	1	.000	5.59	13	2	0	2	0	1	29	28	21	18	2	1	25	0	24	2
Padgett, Greensboro	0	1	.000	4.50	3	0	0	1	0	0	4	6	3	2	0	0	4	1	3	1
Parmenter, Gastonia	1	5	.167	3.96	34	2	1	19	0	5	63.2	60	44	28	6	2	39	0	40	6
Pellien, Greenwood°	0	1	.000	10.13	12	0	0	5	0	0	21.1	27	27	24	2	1	18	1	11	2
Peltola, Greensboro	5	1	.833	3.27	40	0	0	22	0	8	71.2	73	31	26	6	4	21	2	50	3
Phillips, Florence	10	2	.833	2.61	16	16	1	0	0	0	96.2	68	37	28	4	4	50	0	68	6
Pickett, Shelby°	6	3	.667	2.98	50	0	0	34	0	11	93.2	81	39	31	6	3	34	4	78	2
Pina, Shelby	1	1	.500	2.41	13	0	0	8	0	0	18.2	15	10	5	0	0	21	0	10	3
Pittman, Gastonia°	0	1	.000	4.81	22	0	0	15	0	1	24.1	24	14	13	4	3	25	2	34	7
Pleis, Florence	0	0	.000	0.00	1	0	0	1	0	0	1	0	0	0	0	0	1	0	1	0
Psaltis, Charleston°	8	10	.444	4.10	27	18	5	6	1	1	153.2	165	81	70	16	2	51	0	130	4
Pursell, Florence	10	8	.556	2.65	63	0	0	46	0	18	105.1	106	45	31	5	4	26	2	80	4
Raftice, Greensboro°	8	4	.667	3.89	30	10	1	18	0	8	85.2	72	49	37	7	3	56	3	103	9
Ray, Shelby°	10	9	.526	5.39	24	23	4	0	2	0	123.2	106	95	74	11	4	127	2	119	11
Regalado, Asheville°	5	7	.417	5.28	24	17	2	4	1	1	109	126	70	64	13	4	41	1	44	8
E. Reilly, Asheville	6	10	.375	3.61	27	22	4	2	0	0	152	144	88	61	14	4	73	1	90	6
J. Reilly, Spartanburg	2	3	.400	5.40	16	3	0	4	0	0	43.1	51	28	26	3	2	29	2	22	7
Reish, Florence	12	6	.667	3.28	33	13	1	6	1	2	137	133	67	50	8	1	39	1	97	3
Rice, Greenwood	3	2	.600	4.63	14	4	0	5	0	0	44.2	36	25	23	2	1	39	0	43	9
Riewerts, Asheville°	2	8	.200	6.44	22	10	0	7	0	0	64.1	93	59	46	6	1	35	2	41	10
Robair, Shelby	5	1	.833	2.36	9	8	3	0	2	0	53.1	35	16	14	1	0	34	0	46	2
Robertson, Asheville	9	6	.600	3.67	49	7	1	30	1	9	117.2	107	61	48	10	1	63	2	99	6
Rodriguez, Spartanburg	8	5	.615	4.33	24	17	1	2	0	0	112.1	120	73	54	9	3	50	0	77	5
Romagna, Florence	9	6	.600	4.21	23	17	5	4	0	0	115.1	131	67	54	9	1	29	1	85	3
Rubio, Spartanburg	2	7	.222	7.32	14	10	1	2	0	0	51.2	66	48	42	4	4	29	3	36	5
Ruetter, Florence°	0	0	.000	6.23	5	0	0	4	0	0	8.2	11	12	6	1	0	8	0	4	1
Rusch, Florence°	2	6	.250	5.11	31	13	0	9	0	0	105.2	117	81	60	12	4	45	1	67	2
Rymer, Anderson	0	0	.000	15.75	5	0	0	3	0	0	8	8	16	14	0	1	16	0	10	7
Sadey, Macon	0	1	.000	6.43	14	2	0	8	0	0	35	35	29	25	0	4	30	0	29	6
Sanford, Anderson°	1	0	1.000	9.00	2	1	0	1	0	0	7	11	7	7	2	0	5	0	4	0
Sears, Anderson	4	2	.667	3.94	46	0	0	39	0	17	75.1	76	41	33	4	4	33	1	54	5
Segura, Spartanburg	2	2	.500	7.76	20	2	0	12	0	4	29	32	28	25	2	4	18	1	17	6
Seiler, Spartanburg°	9	12	.429	6.18	28	25	3	1	1	0	126.2	141	102	87	16	7	83	2	107	14
Seitz, Anderson	4	1	.800	3.59	16	2	2	8	0	2	42.2	48	21	17	4	0	9	0	32	1
Shiflett, Greensboro°	14	5	.737	2.42	31	16	6	3	1	0	156	129	57	42	5	2	61	2	123	4
Shoupee, Asheville°	2	6	.250	5.31	11	10	0	0	0	0	57.2	65	41	34	9	0	41	1	33	1
Silkwood, Gastonia	0	0	.000	0.00	1	0	0	0	0	0	1.2	0	0	0	0	0	2	0	4	1
Silva, Greensboro	14	7	.667	2.92	30	27	12	3	0	0	184.2	161	87	60	10	3	82	3	140	11
Siwiec, Greensboro	10	6	.625	3.36	36	8	2	18	1	2	101.2	74	48	38	7	3	52	3	86	7
M. Smith, Anderson	12	12	.500	3.89	26	26	11	0	4	0	173.1	181	97	75	16	4	69	2	101	15
Z. Smith, Anderson°	5	3	.625	6.86	12	10	1	1	1	1	63	65	53	48	8	1	34	1	32	5
Solano, Asheville	10	7	.588	3.54	28	27	7	0	3	0	178	165	89	70	8	11	116	2	163	9
Soreca, Spartanburg	5	5	.500	3.83	25	1	1	12	0	1	56.1	50	28	24	5	0	36	1	53	4
Sperto, Anderson	1	0	1.000	6.80	23	0	0	11	0	1	42.1	41	39	32	5	4	40	0	44	1
Stenquist, Shelby	0	1	.000	8.68	4	0	0	1	0	0	9.1	17	11	9	3	1	7	0	3	1
Stinnett, Greenwood	0	2	.000	9.00	4	0	0	1	0	0	5	4	6	5	0	1	9	2	2	1
Storm, Greenwood	3	6	.333	4.38	18	14	1	3	0	0	74	74	47	36	6	3	30	0	48	6
Surhoff, Spartanburg	4	2	.667	2.55	21	0	0	19	0	6	35.1	31	13	10	0	2	14	3	21	2

Pitcher—Club	W.	L.	Pct.	ERA.	G.	GS.	CG.	GF.	ShO.	Sv.	IP.	H.	R.	ER.	HR.	HB.	BB.	Int. BB.	SO.	WP.
Susce, Greenwood	5	9	.357	4.51	21	13	6	3	1	1	101.2	108	65	51	5	9	44	0	77	6
Swank, Charleston*	2	6	.250	5.58	25	1	0	11	0	2	61.1	75	46	38	4	2	31	0	56	0
Swanson, Charleston	3	7	.300	3.47	38	0	0	32	0	12	57	46	28	22	4	1	32	3	49	6
Swope, Greensboro	6	5	.545	4.58	24	12	1	7	0	1	94.1	108	61	48	9	5	48	0	64	6
Szymczak, Greensboro	14	2	.875	3.19	30	23	5	5	0	1	175	174	84	62	9	1	55	3	63	11
D. Taylor, Greenwood	9	8	.529	2.30	27	24	9	3	2	2	164.2	128	57	42	6	1	92	3	133	16
R. Taylor, Greenwood	0	4	.000	4.95	15	0	0	12	0	1	20	17	13	11	3	0	23	1	15	3
Teate, Shelby	0	4	.000	7.48	7	4	0	1	0	0	27.2	37	28	23	3	0	14	1	10	3
Thomas, Gastonia	0	1	.000	2.25	2	1	1	0	0	0	12	6	4	3	0	0	8	0	6	2
Torres, Anderson	3	4	.429	4.32	12	11	1	1	0	0	66.2	65	46	32	2	0	50	0	51	6
Turner, Asheville*	0	0	.000	22.50	5	0	0	2	0	0	6	18	15	15	2	1	8	0	3	1
Undenstock, Charleston	5	5	.500	4.48	20	12	3	5	0	1	86.1	88	54	43	9	2	53	1	48	3
Vargas, Anderson	10	11	.476	5.39	27	26	3	0	1	0	147	166	101	88	10	0	87	1	61	18
Waddell, Anderson	0	0	.000	4.82	4	0	0	3	0	0	9.1	9	5	5	1	0	6	0	13	1
Walker, Anderson*	0	2	.000	7.36	6	1	0	3	0	0	14.2	24	12	12	1	0	14	0	14	4
Walsh, Charleston	2	0	1.000	3.97	5	1	0	4	0	0	11.1	8	6	5	1	0	13	0	11	1
Ward, Anderson	1	2	.333	5.32	5	4	0	1	0	0	23.2	24	16	14	0	1	15	0	18	4
Whiting, Macon*	1	0	1.000	2.70	4	0	0	4	0	0	10	9	6	3	0	0	3	0	7	0
Willerson, Anderson	3	7	.300	4.67	16	10	0	6	0	2	71.1	83	51	37	10	1	30	0	53	5
Wirth, Gastonia*	0	0	.000	0.00	1	0	0	1	0	0	1	1	0	0	0	0	1	0	2	0
Woodworth, Greensboro*	2	3	.400	6.32	20	4	0	9	0	1	57	75	43	40	5	0	28	3	51	5
Wyatt, Shelby*	1	0	1.000	1.57	11	0	0	8	0	2	23	28	6	4	0	0	11	1	13	0
Yan, Asheville	1	3	.250	4.96	10	0	0	7	0	0	16.1	16	9	9	0	0	15	3	10	0
K. Young, Macon	0	0	.000	0.00	1	0	0	1	0	0	0.2	1	1	0	0	0	1	0	0	0
S. Young, Gastonia	8	9	.471	2.85	18	16	8	2	2	0	123	104	47	39	7	1	38	2	69	12

BALKS—Butler, 5; Fincher, Forchee, R. Jackson, Kincannon, Lee, Malloy, Susce, 4 each; Acker, Bryant, Harper, Kuntz, E. Reilly, Reish, Swope, 3 each; Bailey, Blas, Brown, Charley, Downs, Edgell, Evans, Kennedy, Klaus, Marty, McDowell, Parmenter, Raftice, Ray, Regalado, Rice, Rodriguez, Rusch, Silva, Storm, R. Taylor, Vargas, 2 each; Alba, Baldwin, Ballard, Bear, Clarke, Cone, Conte, Cook, Corniel, Culver, Davisson, DePaula, Godwin, Hosick, Hubbard, D. Jackson, D. Johnson, Key, Krauss, Lance, Latham, Manzanillo, Milligan, Miner, Moore, Moya, Pellien, Pickett, Pittman, J. Reilly, Riewerts, Robair, Robertson, Rubio, Seitz, Shoupee, M. Smith, Solano, Soreca, D. Taylor, Torres, Turner, Undenstock, Yan, S. Young, 1 each.

COMBINATION SHUTOUTS—Vargas-Sears, Torres-Klaus, Torres-Sears, Vargas-Lee-Klaus, Anderson; Jackson-Miner, Johnson-Ballard, Bryant-Psaltis, Cone-Swank, Charleston; Cullen-Clarke, Key-Rusch, Rusch-Pursell, Florence; Young-Bear 2, Gastonia; Fincher-Peltola, Fincher-Siwiec, Shiflett-Raftice, Greensboro; Storm-Mott, Acker-D. Taylor, D. Taylor-Downs, D. Taylor-Rice, Rice-Susce, Greenwood; Barlow-Alexander, Cratch-O'Connor, Macon; Bettendorf-Pickett, Buttles-Wyatt, Latham-Graves-Wyatt, Shelby; Hunter-Soreca, Seiler-Childress, Spartanburg.

NO-HIT GAME—Brown, Gastonia, defeated Macon, 3-0, May 9.

Appalachian League

SUMMER CLASS A CLASSIFICATION

CHAMPIONSHIP WINNERS IN PREVIOUS YEARS

1921—Greenville .608	1946—New River‡ .675	1965—Salem .614
Johnson City° .627	1947—Pulaski .648	1966—Marion .623
1922—Bristol .557	New River (3rd)† .516	1967—Bluefield .627
1923—Knoxville .635	1948—Pulaski‡ .680	1968—Marion .583
1924—Knoxville° .642	1949—Bluefield‡ .721	1969—Pulaski a .576
Bristol .607	1950—Bluefield .600	Johnson City .544
1925—Greenville .667	Bluefield z .745	1970—Bluefield .638
1926-36—Did not operate.	1951—Kingsport‡ .659	1971—Bluefield a .609
1937—Elizabethton .559	1952—Johnson City .595	Kingsport .559
Pennington Gap° .580	Welch (3rd)† .509	1972—Bristol a .588
1938—Elizabethton .664	1953—Welch° .705	Covington .586
Greenville (3rd)† .571	Johnson City .672	1973—Kingsport .757
1939—Elizabethton‡ .597	1954—Bluefield‡ .619	1974—Bristol a .754
1940—Johnson City§ .726	1955—Salem°° .689	Bluefield .536
Elizabethton .750	1956—Did not operate.	1975—Bluefield .515
1941—Johnson City .614	1957—Bluefield .701	Johnson City a .603
Elizabethton° .661	1958—Johnson City .662	1976—Johnson City a .714
1942—Bristol .667	1959—Morristown .603	Bluefield .600
Bristol x .660	1960—Wytheville .614	1977—Kingsport .623
1943—Bristol .755	1961—Middlesboro .591	1978—Elizabethton .594
Bristol y .617	1962—Bluefield .671	1979—Paintsville .800
1944—Kingsport‡ .575	1963—Bluefield .652	1980—Paintsville .657
1945—Kingsport‡ .670	1964—Johnson City .662	1981—Paintsville .657

°Won split-season playoff. †Won four-team playoff. ‡Won championship and four-team playoff. §Johnson City, first-half winner, won playoff involving six clubs. xWon both halves and defeated second-place Elizabethton in playoff. yWon both halves, but Erwin won four-team playoff. zWon both halves, but Bristol won two-club playoff. °°Salem and Johnson City declared playoff co-champions when weather forced cancellation of final series. aLeague was divided into Northern, Southern divisions; declared league champion, based on highest won-lost percentage.

STANDING OF CLUBS AT CLOSE OF SEASON, AUGUST 30

NORTHERN DIVISION

Club	W.	L.	T.	Pct.	G.B.
Bluefield (Orioles)	47	22	0	.681	....
Paintsville (Yankees)	43	27	0	.614	4½
Pulaski (Braves)	36	33	0	.522	11
Pikeville (Brewers)	25	42	0	.373	21

SOUTHERN DIVISION

Club	W.	L.	T.	Pct.	G.B.
Johnson City (Cardinals)	32	35	0	.478	....
Elizabethton (Twins)	32	36	0	.471	½
Bristol (Tigers)	28	36	0	.438	2½
Kingsport (Mets)	28	40	0	.412	4½

COMPOSITE STANDING OF CLUBS AT CLOSE OF SEASON, AUGUST 30

Club	Blu.	Pvl.	Pula.	JC	Eliz.	Bri.	Kpt.	Pike.	W.	L.	T.	Pct.	G.B.
Bluefield (Orioles)	....	7	5	3	10	6	8	8	47	22	0	.681	....
Paintsville (Yankees)	3	....	6	7	7	5	7	8	43	27	0	.614	4½
Pulaski (Braves)	4	4	....	4	6	7	5	6	36	33	0	.522	11
Johnson City (Cardinals)	7	3	6	....	4	5	1	6	32	35	0	.478	14
Elizabethton (Twins)	0	3	4	5	....	5	7	8	32	36	0	.471	14½
Bristol (Tigers)	4	5	3	3	5	....	5	3	28	36	0	.438	16½
Kingsport (Mets)	2	3	5	9	2	4	....	3	28	40	0	.412	18½
Pikeville (Brewers)	2	2	4	4	2	4	7	....	25	42	0	.373	21

Major league affiliations in parentheses.

Playoffs—None.

Regular-Season Attendance—Bluefield, 28,837; Bristol, 7,835; Elizabethton, 10,912; Johnson City, 21,619; Kingsport, 13,522; Paintsville, 12,973; Pikeville, 13,441; Pulaski, 31,009. Total, 140,148. No playoffs. No all-star game.

Managers: Bluefield, John Hart; Bristol, Boots Day; Elizabethton, Fred Waters; Johnson City, Rich Hacker; Kingsport, Ed Olsen; Paintsville, Mike Notaro; Pikeville, Tim Nordbrook; Pulaski, Rick Albert.

All-Star Team: 1B—Traber, Bluefield; 2B—Diaz, Kingsport; 3B—Doerr, Bluefield; SS—Moreno, Elizabethton; OF—Javier, Johnson City; Pasqua, Paintsville; Puckett, Elizabethton; C—Wallace, Johnson City; DH—Cash, Pulaski; RHP—Gooden, Kingsport; LHP—Charley, Bluefield; Manager—Hart, Bluefield.

(Compiled by Howe News Bureau, Boston, Mass.)

CLUB BATTING

Club	Pct.	G.	AB.	R.	OR.	H.	TB.	2B.	3B.	HR.	RBI.	GW.	SH.	SF.	HP.	BB.	Int. BB.	SO.	SB.	CS.	LOB.
Elizabethton	.285	68	2256	393	328	644	831	100	12	21	339	25	8	25	18	298	5	355	102	12	547
Bluefield	.273	69	2258	442	285	616	916	102	15	56	372	36	21	28	17	343	10	426	183	43	497
Paintsville	.269	70	2289	381	268	615	844	99	11	36	335	34	39	22	17	328	8	385	45	25	555
Pulaski	.255	69	2163	353	391	552	774	95	17	31	294	27	21	18	24	297	7	407	79	17	495
Kingsport	.254	68	2251	337	453	571	812	97	15	38	291	21	21	16	34	290	3	452	68	25	525
Johnson City	.244	67	2173	293	362	530	731	85	13	30	252	21	14	14	249		7	464	114	20	479
Pikeville	.244	67	2106	310	354	514	704	93	11	25	267	20	19	23	14	290	10	468	107	24	463
Bristol	.232	64	1979	253	321	459	608	43	14	26	205	24	21	15	10	245	4	327	82	45	419

INDIVIDUAL BATTING
(Leading Qualifiers for Batting Championship—189 or More Plate Appearances)

°Bats lefthanded.　　†Switch-hitter.

Player and Club	Pct.	G.	AB.	R.	H.	TB.	2B.	3B.	HR.	RBI.	GW.	SH.	SF.	HP.	BB.	Int. BB.	SO.	SB.	CS.
Puckett, Kirby, Elizabethton	.382	65	275	65	105	135	15	3	3	35	1	1	1	3	25	0	27	43	4
Barrett, Thomas, Paintsville†	.364	61	231	59	84	93	5	2	0	21	3	4	2	1	42	0	17	20	8
Whisman, Rhett, Elizabethton	.342	63	219	44	75	97	10	3	2	37	2	1	3	1	41	1	30	8	0
Diaz, Richard, Kingsport	.328	63	259	42	85	125	19	0	7	50	3	3	0	3	22	0	43	3	3
Reynolds, Thomas, Pulaski°	.325	62	209	43	68	102	14	1	6	42	3	2	2	1	28	2	24	2	1
Lawrence, Andy, Kingsport	.323	66	263	42	85	117	8	0	8	43	6	1	1	1	15	0	44	0	1
Traber, James, Bluefield°	.323	61	235	41	76	127	18	3	9	63	10	0	2	4	20	1	31	22	4
Moreno, Michael, Elizabethton	.321	66	246	54	79	104	10	0	5	59	6	1	2	3	43	0	33	19	2
Pendleton, Terry, Johnson City†	.320	43	181	38	58	92	14	4	4	27	6	0	2	0	12	1	28	13	2
Sokolowski, Paul, Bristol†	.312	56	186	33	58	82	7	1	5	34	2	1	2	0	31	2	14	5	7
Lesieur, Paul, Paintsville	.304	60	217	31	66	81	13	1	0	35	4	9	2	1	16	1	25	4	1

Departmental Leaders: G—Kubacki, 70; AB—Puckett, 275; R—Puckett, 65; H—Puckett, 105; TB—Puckett, 135; 2B—R. Diaz, 19; 3B—Javier, Pendleton, 4; HR—Pasqua, 16; RBI—Pasqua, Traber, 63; GWRBI—Traber, 10; SH—Lesieur, 9; SF—Gerhart, 8; HP—Hollis, Thompson, Young, 6; BB—Wallace, 53; IBB—James, Vanderburg, 3; SO—Doerr, 66; SB—Coleman, Puckett, 43; CS—Barrett, Moriarty, 8.

(All Players—Listed Alphabetically)

Player and Club	Pct.	G.	AB.	R.	H.	TB.	2B.	3B.	HR.	RBI.	GW.	SH.	SF.	HP.	BB.	Int. BB.	SO.	SB.	CS.
Andujar, Jose, Kingsport	.111	6	9	1	1	1	0	0	0	1	0	0	0	0	0	0	4	0	0
Anglin, Russell, Pulaski	.308	23	65	9	20	27	2	1	1	13	1	2	0	0	8	0	13	1	0
Aviles, Luis, Elizabethton	.100	8	30	4	3	4	1	0	0	4	0	0	0	0	4	1	7	0	0
Barker, Stanley, Bristol°	.220	39	109	14	24	35	2	0	3	17	5	1	1	1	8	0	15	9	5
Barragan, Gerardo, Bluefield†	.282	51	149	23	42	50	3	1	1	22	2	6	0	0	12	0	14	1	3
Barrett, Thomas, Paintsville†	.364	61	231	59	84	93	5	2	0	21	3	4	2	1	42	0	17	20	8
Bertucio, Charles, Bluefield†	.265	39	102	17	27	36	6	0	1	12	0	2	1	1	22	0	27	1	2
Beucher, Gregory, Bluefield	.250	9	16	2	4	5	1	0	0	2	0	0	0	0	0	0	7	0	0
Bocock, Thomas, Johnson City	.249	66	237	33	59	74	6	0	3	38	3	0	4	2	23	1	31	5	0
Bodle, Kennith, Kingsport	.279	65	240	36	67	94	14	2	3	33	1	1	6	1	35	0	48	10	4
Boroski, Stanley, Pikeville	.288	30	66	5	19	22	3	0	0	7	0	4	0	0	7	0	16	2	1
Brazoban, Luis, Pikeville	.227	28	44	11	10	14	2	1	0	3	0	0	0	1	5	0	11	12	1
Butters, David, Elizabethton	.160	10	25	2	4	4	0	0	0	1	0	0	0	0	0	0	10	0	0
Cain, Michael, Bluefield	.280	64	236	55	66	89	8	3	3	22	1	2	1	0	38	0	34	41	7
Candelaria, Albert, Pulaski°	.000	10	1	0	0	0	0	0	0	0	0	0	0	0	0	0	0	0	0
Carmichael, Alan, Pulaski°	.175	35	114	17	20	24	4	0	0	7	1	2	0	2	16	0	23	1	2
Carter, Herbert, Elizabethton	.267	61	221	35	59	75	6	2	2	24	1	0	2	3	23	0	52	6	1
Carvajal, Luis, Johnson City	.122	28	41	3	5	7	2	0	0	6	0	0	2	2	7	1	13	0	0
Cash, A. Preston, Pulaski°	.254	49	142	36	36	83	12	1	11	34	6	1	3	2	48	0	40	6	2
Chatham, Dale, Pulaski°	.000	13	0	1	0	0	0	0	0	0	0	0	0	0	0	0	0	0	0
Childress, Willie, Pulaski°	.244	65	225	36	55	76	6	3	3	25	0	2	3	1	25	2	30	11	0
Ching, Mauricio, Paintsville°	.271	65	240	33	65	101	18	0	6	43	8	0	0	1	36	2	62	0	2
Cichon, Thomas, Elizabethton°	.172	17	58	10	10	12	2	0	0	7	0	0	0	0	8	0	21	0	0
Coleman, Vincent, Johnson City	.250	58	212	40	53	57	2	1	0	16	2	2	0	3	29	0	49	43	3
Cowgill, William, Bluefield	.154	9	13	2	2	2	0	0	0	2	0	1	0	0	0	0	8	0	0
Crisp, Hughes, Bluefield	.242	31	95	11	23	34	1	2	2	12	1	0	0	0	13	1	23	1	1
Cruz, Luis, Elizabethton°	.375	10	8	2	3	3	0	0	0	0	0	0	0	0	0	0	0	0	0
Darling, Edward, Paintsville†	.155	33	71	9	11	18	4	0	1	8	1	1	1	0	22	1	27	0	1
Detmer, Tom, Johnson City	.275	34	102	9	28	36	5	0	1	5	0	3	0	1	9	0	11	6	2
Diaz, Edgar, Pikeville	.083	15	24	4	2	2	0	0	0	0	0	0	0	1	5	0	5	0	0
Diaz, Richard, Kingsport	.328	63	259	42	85	125	19	0	7	50	3	3	0	3	22	0	43	3	3
Diguardi, Scott, Pulaski°	.067	7	15	1	1	2	1	0	0	0	0	1	0	1	0	0	3	0	0
Doerr, Jeffrey, Bluefield	.289	57	187	51	54	110	12	1	14	39	5	1	3	3	44	2	66	1	0
Dudek, Gene, Bluefield	.217	10	23	5	5	7	2	0	0	2	0	1	0	0	3	0	3	0	0
Ferro, Robert, Elizabethton	.221	29	77	15	17	24	1	0	2	14	1	1	4	1	19	0	20	1	1
Fitzgerald, Francis, Bluefield	.238	22	63	10	15	24	4	1	1	11	1	1	0	0	4	0	10	1	0
Fleming, Stephen, Johnson City	.266	54	154	22	41	70	13	2	4	30	3	0	0	0	23	0	55	3	0
Frey, John, Johnson City°	.000	16	1	0	0	0	0	0	0	0	0	0	0	0	0	0	1	0	0
Geren, Gregory, Kingsport	.238	49	168	20	40	53	6	2	1	20	2	2	6	4	20	1	32	2	0
Gerhart, H. Kenneth, Bluefield	.259	66	228	57	59	108	13	0	12	43	3	2	8	2	37	1	57	36	4
Gil, Jose, Elizabethton	.273	10	33	7	9	16	4	0	1	7	0	0	0	1	4	1	8	0	0
Gooden, Dwight, Kingsport	.000	10	1	0	0	0	0	0	0	0	0	0	0	0	0	0	0	0	0
Goodyear, Christopher, Bristol	.237	12	38	5	9	14	0	1	1	5	1	2	1	0	2	0	5	3	1
Granger, Lee Randle, Bluefield†	.237	23	93	15	22	36	2	0	4	16	3	0	1	1	7	0	19	13	6
Graupman, Timothy, Elizabethton	.214	32	98	8	21	25	1	0	1	9	0	1	1	1	13	0	11	2	0
Griggs, David, Bluefield†	.111	10	27	3	3	4	1	0	0	1	0	0	0	0	9	0	7	0	0
Grissom, Jon, Bluefield°	.000	4	1	0	0	0	0	0	0	0	0	0	0	0	0	0	1	0	0
Gutierrez, Isidro, Johnson City	.235	57	196	14	46	53	7	0	0	15	0	2	4	1	13	0	18	4	3
Hall, Gary, Pulaski	.209	44	139	18	29	41	7	1	1	18	2	4	1	4	15	1	45	4	2
Harris, Carlton, Johnson City†	.273	5	11	1	3	3	0	0	0	0	0	0	0	0	1	0	4	0	0
Harris, Kenneth, Kingsport	.282	59	209	31	59	73	10	2	0	27	1	1	1	2	37	1	17	18	2
Hatley, Larry, Elizabethton°	.400	2	5	0	2	3	1	0	0	2	0	1	0	0	0	0	1	0	0
Hawkins, Eugene, Kingsport	.203	23	64	12	13	14	1	0	0	4	1	0	0	0	15	0	20	2	1
Haynes, Kennie, Bristol	.200	21	50	7	10	12	0	1	0	3	0	3	0	1	6	0	7	4	1
Hendricks, Hector, Johnson City	.074	21	27	2	2	2	0	0	0	0	0	1	0	0	1	0	17	1	0
Heredia, Cesar, Pikeville	.136	30	59	3	8	8	0	0	0	1	0	0	0	0	6	0	4	3	0
Hollis, Carl, Kingsport	.289	54	187	40	54	93	11	2	8	26	1	2	0	6	42	0	46	6	3
Holmes, J. Christopher, Bluefield°	.000	2	1	0	0	0	0	0	0	0	0	0	0	0	0	0	2	0	0
Irwin, James, Bristol	.235	45	153	16	36	46	4	0	2	18	3	0	0	0	16	0	24	2	3
Isherwood, James, Paintsville	.182	35	110	12	20	26	2	0	0	10	1	3	3	1	13	0	20	0	2
Jackson, Larry, Pikeville°	.262	39	84	11	22	26	2	1	0	8	0	2	1	1	10	0	10	8	3
James, Dewey, Pikeville°	.263	64	213	38	56	92	14	2	6	27	1	0	3	0	34	3	55	22	3
Javier, Stanley, Johnson City†	.276	57	185	45	51	86	3	4	8	36	3	1	3	0	42	2	55	11	3
Knox, Michael, Pulaski	.275	68	255	44	70	87	8	3	1	22	1	2	2	0	40	0	39	20	5
Krynitsky, Mark, Pikeville	.213	52	122	21	26	30	1	0	1	11	0	1	0	0	22	0	36	3	2
Kubacki, Timothy, Paintsville	.236	70	246	35	58	74	13	0	1	32	2	5	4	1	34	0	43	3	0
Lance, Mark, Pulaski	.000	18	1	0	0	0	0	0	0	0	0	0	0	0	0	0	0	0	0
Landers, Harold, Pikeville	.286	57	189	36	54	82	9	2	5	36	3	0	2	3	30	2	39	7	0
Lawrence, Andy, Kingsport	.323	66	263	42	85	117	8	0	8	43	6	1	1	1	15	0	44	0	1

Player and Club	Pct.	G.	AB.	R.	H.	TB.	2B.	3B.	HR.	RBI.	GW.	SH.	SF.	HP.	BB.	Int. BB.	SO.	SB.	CS.
Lawrence, V. Scott, Bluefield	.167	8	12	3	2	5	0	0	1	1	0	0	0	0	1	0	1	1	1
Lee, Manuel, Kingsport	.222	16	54	2	12	13	1	0	0	3	0	2	0	0	3	0	12	1	1
Lesieur, Paul, Paintsville	.304	60	217	31	66	81	13	1	0	35	4	9	2	1	16	1	25	4	1
Lesnak, Andrew, Elizabethton	.250	21	64	7	16	18	2	0	0	5	0	0	1		9	0	14	1	1
Llewellyn, Paul, Pulaski	.256	47	156	23	40	57	6	1	3	19	1	1	3	2	13	0	45	7	0
Lombardi, Phillip, Paintsville	.250	50	180	26	45	53	8	0	0	14	1	3	0	1	16	0	23	3	0
Long, Anthony, Bristol	.275	46	131	19	36	36	0	0	0	8	0	1	2	1	17	0	20	14	4
Lucido, John, Paintsville	.267	8	15	1	4	4	0	0	0	3	0	0	0		1	0	2	0	0
Lynch, Robyn, Pulaski°	.221	48	154	12	34	43	6	0	1	19	1	0	1	2	11	1	32	0	0
Lyon, Bruce, Kingsport	.283	18	60	8	17	27	1	0	3	9	0	0	0	1	7	1	15	0	0
Maris, Kevin, Johnson City	.000	7	6	1	0	0	0	0	0	0	0	0	0	0	3	0	2	0	0
Maull, Oliver, Bluefield°	.136	12	22	1	3	3	0	0	0	4	0	0	1	1	5	0	3	1	0
Maynor, Howard, Paintsville	.253	28	87	18	22	30	5	0	1	12	1	1	1	0	23	1	12	0	0
McCarver, M. Rodney, Elizabethton°	.195	45	164	17	32	43	9	1	0	35	2	0	6	0	12	0	28	0	0
McManus, Robert, Bristol	.245	60	216	26	53	71	8	2	2	23	2	2	0	1	24	0	38	7	0
McPhail, Marlin, Kingsport	.182	4	11	1	2	2	0	0	0	0	0	0	0	0	1	0	0	0	0
Melillo, Gerry, Bluefield	.252	35	111	17	28	42	6	1	2	26	0	1	1	0	11	1	17	0	1
Metski, Raymond, Bristol	.176	9	17	1	3	3	0	0	0	0	0	0	0	0	0	0	6	0	1
Meyer, Michael, Bristol	.218	59	197	28	43	54	4	2	1	16	2	5	3	2	20	0	29	16	5
Milligen, Brent, Johnson City	.000	9	1	0	0	0	0	0	0	0	0	0	0	0	1	0	1	0	0
Miranda, Manuel, Bluefield	.262	41	84	16	22	24	2	0	0	9	1	0	0	0	14	0	13	9	2
Mitchell, John, Pikeville°	.223	37	94	20	21	28	5	1	0	7	0	1	0	1	16	1	23	7	0
Montague, James, Bluefield	.154	15	26	5	4	4	0	0	0	5	0	1	2	1	8	0	4	0	1
Moreno, Michael, Elizabethton	.321	66	246	54	79	104	10	0	5	59	6	1	2	3	43	0	33	19	2
Moriarty, James, Bristol	.291	59	237	25	69	78	2	2	1	20	3	2	0	1	12	0	28	13	8
Moser, Larry, Pulaski†	.246	52	175	30	43	57	10	2	0	21	1	1	0	1	37	0	29	11	2
Murray, Kevin, Pikeville	.161	41	124	6	20	27	7	0	0	12	0	1	2	0	5	0	39	6	1
Neuendorff, Tony, Pulaski	.270	32	111	14	30	31	1	0	0	13	2	0	0	0	11	0	13	1	0
Nunez, Mauricio, Johnson City	.165	60	206	17	34	45	5	0	2	8	2	3	1	0	8	0	52	5	3
O'Shea, Shane, Paintsville†	.259	37	116	17	30	37	4	0	1	14	2	1	0	1	13	0	11	1	0
Orrick, Russell, Kingsport°	.236	17	55	7	13	26	2	1	3	11	1	0	2		10	0	10	4	3
Ortega, Jose, Johnson City	.000	26	1	0	0	0	0	0	0	0	0	0	0	0	1	0	1	0	0
Ortiz, Hector, Elizabethton	.262	31	103	7	27	33	6	0	0	11	1	0	0	0	2	0	15	1	0
Oxendine, Forace, Pikeville	.269	21	67	9	18	28	4	0	2	21	0	0	1	0	10	0	25	0	1
Page, George, Bluefield	.250	33	72	15	18	21	0	0	1	14	0	0	2	2	10	0	15	4	1
Pasqua, Daniel, Paintsville	.301	60	239	43	72	134	10	2	16	63	5	0	4	1	22	2	42	1	2
Peer, Paul, Paintsville°	.298	57	181	29	54	73	4	3	3	31	3	3	3	2	13	0	29	4	5
Pendleton, Terry, Johnson City†	.320	43	181	38	58	92	14	4	4	27	6	0	2	0	12	1	28	13	2
Pevey, Marty, Elizabethton	.284	24	81	9	23	32	6	0	1	13	0	1	0	1	8	0	10	0	0
Post, E. Peter, Paintsville°	.265	38	98	13	26	43	6	1	3	16	1	1	1	0	13	1	22	0	0
Priessman, Kraig, Bristol	.068	17	44	1	3	6	0	0	1	7	1	0	2	0	1	0	12	0	0
Puckett, Kirby, Elizabethton	.382	65	275	65	105	135	15	3	3	35	1	1	1	3	25	0	27	43	6
Quinones, Hector, Pikeville	.222	8	18	2	4	4	0	0	0	0	0	0	0	0	5	0	3	1	0
Ragsdale, Jerry, Pulaski	.267	4	15	5	4	9	0	1	1	2	0	0	0	1	4	1	4	0	0
Reynolds, Thomas, Pulaski°	.325	62	209	43	68	102	14	1	6	42	3	2	2	1	28	2	24	2	1
Ripken, William, Bluefield	.244	27	45	8	11	12	1	0	0	4	0	0	0	0	8	0	6	0	0
Rivera, Juan, Elizabethton	.306	23	62	13	19	24	3	1	0	10	2	0	1	0	3	0	13	0	0
Robidoux, William J., Pikeville°	.287	54	167	28	48	60	10	1	0	13	2	1	2	1	28	1	29	2	0
Robinson, Dana, Bristol	.053	12	19	3	1	3	0	1	0	2	0	1	0	0	5	0	12	1	0
Rodriguez, Claudio, Johnson City°	.248	51	149	20	37	56	8	1	3	19	0	0	1	0	8	0	36	3	0
Russell, Paul, Johnson City	.054	20	37	1	2	3	1	0	0	1	0	0	0	1	1	0	20	1	0
Russomagno, Vincent, Johnson City	.265	59	204	12	54	68	6	1	2	24	1	1	0	3	15	1	23	8	2
Rymer, Victor, Kingsport	.038	11	26	1	1	1	0	0	0	1	0	0	1	1	5	0	13	0	0
Sanchez, Miguel, Kingsport	.186	31	97	18	18	26	4	2	0	12	0	1	0	0	12	0	24	3	2
Scheer, Ronald, Elizabethton	.247	45	146	22	36	51	7	1	2	23	2	0	1	0	23	1	22	1	0
Silva, Albert, Bristol	.183	37	104	13	19	24	3	1	0	7	1	0	1	1	13	0	21	0	4
Simmons, John, Pulaski	.125	16	40	1	5	5	0	0	0	1	0	1	0	0	4	0	11	0	1
Sokolowski, Paul, Bristol†	.312	56	186	33	58	82	7	1	5	34	2	1	2	0	31	2	14	5	7
Sottile, Louis, Bristol°	.237	12	38	4	9	14	2	0	1	4	0	0	2	0	8	0	2	1	0
Spalt, Steven, Bluefield	.353	20	34	8	12	13	1	0	0	2	0	0	0	0	5	0	6	2	1
Springer, Gary, Bristol°	.251	58	179	37	45	58	4	3	1	17	2	3	1	0	48	1	22	13	6
Stewart, James, Elizabethton	.302	26	96	18	29	42	7	0	2	14	3	0	1	1	8	0	16	2	0
Sveum, Dale, Pikeville	.233	58	223	29	52	73	13	1	2	21	4	3	2	2	20	0	50	6	3
Szczecinski, Jeffrey, Elizabethton°	.357	43	143	38	51	59	6	1	0	14	2	1	1	1	36	1	7	16	3
Thompson, Richard, Pulaski	.246	62	207	41	51	72	10	1	3	31	5	1	1	6	31	0	54	11	3
Thornton, Louis, Kingsport°	.210	57	210	29	44	72	9	2	5	29	3	1	4	1	14	0	36	12	1
Tiefenthaler, Dennis, Bluefield	.336	42	122	29	41	56	10	1	1	18	2	3	1	2	24	1	21	5	2
Traber, James, Bluefield°	.323	61	235	41	76	127	18	3	9	63	10	0	2	4	20	1	31	22	4
Traylor, Keith, Bristol	.186	47	140	10	26	34	2	0	2	11	1	5	1	0	8	0	23	3	0
Utecht, Timothy, Pikeville	.259	61	185	23	48	76	10	0	6	45	2	0	4	1	36	2	49	5	2
Van Horn, David, Pulaski	.261	67	253	39	66	82	12	2	0	34	4	3	2	3	22	0	25	5	1
Vanderburg, Michael, Bluefield°	.301	60	226	43	68	95	11	2	4	40	6	0	3	0	41	3	29	42	5
Vargas, Antonio, Pikeville	.000	4	9	0	0	0	0	0	0	0	0	0	0	1	2	0	6	0	0
Wallace, Timothy, Johnson City	.257	66	222	35	57	79	13	0	3	27	1	1	1	1	53	1	47	11	3
Washington, Marc, Bristol	.181	32	83	8	15	17	2	0	0	5	0	0	1	0	5	0	27	3	2
Weatherford, Joel, Pikeville°	.289	63	211	35	61	76	9	0	2	38	6	1	3	0	28	1	37	7	2
Weller, John, Paintsville°	.259	58	170	37	44	62	6	0	4	28	1	6	1	3	48	0	36	6	3
Whaley, Gary, Bristol°	.189	19	37	2	7	7	0	0	0	5	0	0	1		6	1	6	1	1
Whisman, Rhett, Elizabethton°	.342	63	219	44	75	97	10	3	2	37	2	1	3	1	41	1	30	8	0
Wiley, Jeffrey, Paintsville	.159	37	88	18	14	15	1	0	0	5	1	2	0	4	16	0	14	3	1
Williams, Fred, Pikeville	.200	6	10	1	2	2	0	0	0	1	0	0	0	0	1	0	2	0	0
Williams, Leon, Kingsport	.185	9	27	3	5	8	1	1	0	0	0	0	0	1	3	0	13	0	0
Williamson, Robert, Bristol°	.214	36	103	15	22	41	6	2	3	10	1	0	0	0	14	0	25	0	1
Wilson, Jeffrey, Elizabethton°	.229	12	35	6	8	9	1	0	0	5	0	1	0	0	6	0	4	1	0
Young, Gerald, Kingsport	.178	59	197	27	35	43	6	1	0	15	1	5	0	6	33	0	52	7	2
Young, John, Bristol°	.147	40	95	14	14	27	1	0	4	9	2	0	0	2	21	0	20	3	1
Zanini, Louis, Bluefield	.257	16	35	5	9	9	0	0	2	1	0	0	0	0	7	0	3	2	0
Zappala, Alberto, Elizabethton	.239	19	67	10	16	18	2	0	0	10	2	1	1	0	9	0	7	1	0

The following pitchers, listed alphabetically by club, with games in parentheses, had no plate appearances, primarily through use of designated hitters:

BLUEFIELD—Anderson, Joel (16); Bell, Eric (11); Charley, Tandy (13); Concepcion, Carlos (21); Crumley, Herbert (11); Habyan, John

(12); Krsnich, Nicholas (9); Lackey, Jeffrey (10); Leiter, Kurt (9); Leonard, John (3); Mason, Victor (11); Mulcahy, Timothy (22); Sczesnak, Marc, (9); Wilson, Roger (12).

BRISTOL—Barlow, Ricky (10); Cook, Kerry (4); Cooper, William (11); Diez, Mark (6); Edgell, Thor (9); Gordon, Donald (22); Granger, William (16); Heinkel, Donald (1); Hobbie, Glen (15); Legumina, Gary (12); Miquel, George (2); Monteleone, Richard (12); Raubolt, Arthur (12); Whitmore, Ronnie (11).

ELIZABETHTON—Burnos, James (11); Castelono, Carlos (2); Delacruz, Sixto (3); Everett, Albert (11); Gross, David (6); Hesting, Martin (7); Hulett, Randall (8); Kindred, Curtis (11); Larcom, Mark (10); Maack, Mike (19); Parham, Terrill (12); Sanders, Archie (4); Sawyer, Theodore (9); Smith, Douglas (23).

JOHNSON CITY—Blunt, Bradley (10); Caito, Steven (12); Finnegan, William (13); Hartley, Michael (8); Maldonado, Ovidio (17); Mejia, Ramon (20); Moon, Kevin (7); Sanchez, Carlos (13); Suggs, Tyris (8); Turnbull, Keith (13).

KINGSPORT—Adams, Scott (14); Allen, Robert (14); Bautista, Jose (14); Brandt, Nicholas (21); Fitts, Matthew (12); Gay, Steven (11); Martinez, Manuel (9); Moody, Anthony (8); Myers, Randall (13); Pimentel, Jose (12); Tirado, Aristarco (13); Youmans, Floyd (10).

PAINTSVILLE—Bersano, Mark (11); Brown, Rory (14); Compagno, Steven (2); Corsi, James (8); Easley, Logan (13); George, Stephen (13); Gumbert, Richard (10); Inman, Ronald (6); Lewis, Larry (6); Niemiec, David (10); Plunk, Eric (12); Rijo, Jose (13); Unger, Gregory (22).

PIKEVILLE—Aldrich, Jay (11); Artemenko, William (5); Bosio, Christopher (13); Crim, Charles (11); Downs, Delrin (12); Gyarmati, Jeffrey (3); Koch, Barry (13); Nordbrook, Timothy (1); Pena, Hipilito (7); Ream, Gary (14); Rice, Woolsey (14); Scarpetta, Daniel (12); Shamblin, Archie (6); Sullivan, Robert (1); Watson, Bret (2); Williams, Bruce (11); Williams, Scott (8).

PULASKI—Green, Jeffrey (10); Hentz, Peter (13); Lynn, Kenneth (12); Mehalko, Andrew (4); Moody, Kurt (13); Page, Marc (7); Rivera, James (23); Sperto, Carmine (17); Torres, Rudy (10); Van Gennep, John (3); Winters, Joe (10).

GRAND SLAM HOME RUNS—Diaz, 2; Cain, Ferro, Hall, Irwin, Melillo, Moreno, Oxedine, Reynolds, Traber, Thornton, Utecht, Vanderburg, 1 each.

AWARDED FIRST BASE ON INTERFERENCE—Aviles (Wallace); Bertucio (Pevey); Candelaria (Graupman); Gerhart (Vargas); James (Ragsdale); Maynor (Pevey); Melillo (Vargas); Metski (Montague); Vargas (Graupman).

CLUB FIELDING

Club	Pct.	G.	PO.	A.	E.	DP.	PB.	Club	Pct.	G.	PO.	A.	E.	DP.	PB.
Paintsville	.966	70	1784	739	89	47	8	Bristol	.951	64	1587	683	117	32	10
Bluefield	.959	69	1763	743	107	55	11	Elizabethton	.946	68	1661	711	135	42	13
Pulaski	.955	69	1673	696	111	42	15	Pikeville	.943	67	1671	665	142	45	18
Johnson City	.954	67	1688	701	116	64	15	Kingsport	.937	68	1733	725	166	47	16

Triple Play—Bristol.

INDIVIDUAL FIELDING
FIRST BASEMEN

*Throws lefthanded.

Player and Club	Pct.	G.	PO.	A.	E.	DP.	Player and Club	Pct.	G.	PO.	A.	E.	DP.
Barragan, Bluefield	1.000	2	10	2	0	1	Reynolds, Pulaski	.977	45	358	16	9	20
Bertucio, Bluefield*	.971	5	32	2	1	4	Robidoux, Pikeville	.953	5	41	0	2	4
Bocock, Johnson City	1.000	1	3	1	0	0	Rodriguez, Johnson City*	.961	14	96	2	4	11
Ching, Paintsville*	.969	31	266	18	9	17	Russell, Johnson City	1.000	3	15	0	0	1
Cichon, Elizabethton	.964	13	105	2	4	8	Russomagno, Johnson City	.988	52	476	23	6	43
Darling, Paintsville	.989	25	179	8	2	9	Rymer, Kingsport	1.000	4	11	0	0	2
Detmer, Johnson City	.966	3	25	3	1	0	Silva, Bristol	1.000	5	49	1	0	1
Doerr, Bluefield	1.000	2	17	3	0	1	SOKOLOWSKI, Bristol	.991	54	503	25	5	24
Landers, Pikeville	.917	7	20	2	2	0	Thornton, Kingsport	.959	9	90	4	4	6
Lawrence, Kingsport	.983	58	506	20	9	33	Traber, Bluefield*	.988	59	540	34	7	44
Lesieur, Paintsville	.987	20	149	5	2	11	Utecht, Pikeville	.977	52	402	20	10	31
Lynch, Pulaski	.991	28	209	13	2	13	Weatherford, Pikeville*	1.000	1	5	3	0	0
Maris, Johnson City	1.000	1	1	0	0	0	Weller, Paintsville*	1.000	1	3	0	0	1
McCarver, Elizabethton*	.974	40	346	28	10	23	Whaley, Bristol*	1.000	1	4	0	0	1
Melillo, Bluefield	1.000	3	15	0	0	1	Whisman, Elizabethton	.981	17	146	9	3	7
Oxendine, Pikeville	1.000	10	69	5	0	5	Williamson, Bristol	1.000	4	41	2	0	1

Triple play—Sokolowski.

SECOND BASEMEN

Player and Club	Pct.	G.	PO.	A.	E.	DP.	Player and Club	Pct.	G.	PO.	A.	E.	DP.
Barragan, Bluefield	.857	2	3	3	1	1	Meyer, Pikeville	.943	58	111	152	16	25
BARRETT, Paintsville	.986	61	134	138	4	19	Miranda, Bluefield	.867	17	17	22	6	2
Bocock, Johnson City	.955	11	30	33	3	5	Moreno, Elizabethton	.976	21	37	45	2	8
Brazoban, Pikeville	1.000	2	1	1	0	0	Nunez, Johnson City	1.000	1	1	1	0	1
Cain, Bluefield	.937	55	102	135	16	27	Pendelton, Johnson City	.915	32	79	105	17	25
Childress, Pulaski	.833	2	3	2	1	0	Quinones, Pikeville	.909	2	4	6	1	0
Detmer, Johnson City	.965	13	26	29	2	6	Ripken, Bluefield	1.000	1	2	0	0	0
Diaz, Kingsport	.955	50	81	129	10	22	Springer, Bristol	.944	17	23	44	4	6
Dudek, Bluefield	.966	6	14	14	1	4	Van Horn, Pulaski	.943	67	162	169	20	31
Ferro, Elizabethton	1.000	1	0	5	0	0	Wallace, Johnson City	1.000	2	4	7	0	2
Goodyear, Bristol	.945	12	23	29	3	3	Whisman, Elizabethton	.957	10	18	26	2	6
Gutierrez, Johnson City	.980	12	21	28	1	7	Wiley, Paintsville	.905	18	17	21	4	5
Heredia, Pikeville	1.000	9	11	15	0	4	Williams, Pikeville	.913	4	12	9	2	2
Hollis, Kingsport	.959	11	21	26	2	4	Wilson, Elizabethton	.957	11	17	27	2	4
Lee, Kingsport	.974	9	20	17	1	4	Young, Kingsport	.909	2	3	7	1	0
Lesnak, Elizabethton	.950	9	13	25	2	2	Zanini, Bluefield	1.000	1	3	3	0	2
Long, Bristol	.952	42	90	88	9	9	Zappala, Elizabethton	.926	19	37	38	6	6
Lucido, Paintsville	1.000	3	1	1	0	0							

Triple play—Long.

THIRD BASEMEN

Player and Club	Pct.	G.	PO.	A.	E.	DP.	Player and Club	Pct.	G.	PO.	A.	E.	DP.
Barker, Bristol	1.000	1	0	5	0	0	Hollis, Kingsport	.929	15	18	34	4	5
Bocock, Johnson City	.939	32	33	74	7	8	Landers, Pikeville	1.000	4	2	0	0	1
Brazoban, Pikeville	.895	8	5	12	2	1	Lesnak, Elizabethton	.882	10	12	18	4	1
CHILDRESS, Pulaski	.9264	57	58	131	15	6	Lucido, Paintsville	1.000	1	1	1	0	0
Detmer, Johnson City	.892	16	10	23	4	0	Maynor, Paintsville	.918	28	21	46	6	3
Diaz, Kingsport	.837	15	13	28	8	3	McManus, Bristol	.9263	54	45	106	12	6
Doerr, Bluefield	.903	44	41	108	16	9	Moreno, Elizabethton	1.000	3	1	5	0	0
Harris, Kingsport	.835	39	17	64	16	3	Nunez, Johnson City	.923	20	11	25	3	1
Heredia, Pikeville	.875	19	7	21	4	2	O'Shea, Paintsville	.961	34	26	72	4	3

THIRD BASEMEN—Continued

Player and Club	Pct.	G.	PO.	A.	E.	DP.
Quinones, Pikesville	.750	2	1	2	1	0
Reynolds, Pulaski	.853	15	10	19	5	1
Ripken, Bluefield	1.000	6	5	6	0	1
Robidoux, Pikesville	.843	42	16	54	13	6
Rymer, Kingsport	1.000	2	3	2	0	0
Sottile, Bristol	.889	9	7	17	3	0
Spalt, Bluefield	1.000	2	2	5	0	0
Stewart, Elizabethton	.900	25	14	40	6	2
Sveum, Pikeville	1.000	2	2	4	0	0
Thornton, Kingsport	1.000	1	1	0	0	0
Tiefenthaler, Bluefield	1.000	20	15	50	0	1
Utecht, Pikeville	.923	5	2	10	1	0
Wallace, Johnson City	.500	4	1	0	1	0
Whisman, Elizabethton	.866	31	29	55	13	2
Wiley, Paintsville	.947	14	9	9	1	0
Young, Kingsport	1.000	2	1	1	0	0

Triple Play—McManus.

SHORTSTOPS

Player and Club	Pct.	G.	PO.	A.	E.	DP.
Barragan, Bluefield	.935	46	58	130	13	17
Beucher, Bluefield	.000	3	0	0	3	0
Bocock, Johnson City	.935	23	36	65	7	12
Childress, Pulaski	1.000	2	7	8	0	2
Detmer, Johnson City	1.000	3	1	5	0	0
Diaz, Pikeville	.933	12	12	30	3	7
Ferro, Elizabethton	.866	26	28	75	16	6
Gutierrez, Johnson City	.961	45	66	132	8	22
Haynes, Bristol	.844	20	37	39	14	6
Hollis, Kingsport	.875	12	18	31	7	7
Knox, Pulaski	.917	68	91	198	26	24
KUBACKI, Paintsville	.941	70	109	227	21	35
Lee, Kingsport	.861	6	14	17	5	2
Lesnak, Elizabethton	1.000	1	0	6	0	0
Moreno, Elizabethton	.921	42	63	136	17	20
Quinones, Pikeville	.909	4	6	4	1	0
Ripken, Bluefield	.864	12	8	11	3	2
Robinson, Bristol	.862	9	11	14	4	1
Spalt, Bluefield	.939	15	14	17	2	1
Springer, Bristol	.934	44	48	150	14	13
Sveum, Pikeville	.868	56	82	154	36	20
Tiefenthaler, Bluefield	.800	1	1	3	1	0
Young, Kingsport	.862	54	75	162	38	19
Zanini, Bluefield	.915	13	16	27	4	7

OUTFIELDERS

Player and Club	Pct.	G.	PO.	A.	E.	DP.
Andujar, Kingsport	.833	5	5	0	1	0
Aviles, Elizabethton	.909	8	8	2	1	0
Barker, Bristol	.955	33	60	4	3	1
Bertucio, Bluefield°	.946	27	34	1	2	1
Bodle, Kingsport	.963	61	100	3	4	1
Cain, Bluefield	.929	4	12	1	1	1
Carter, Elizabethton	.947	60	117	8	7	4
Cash, Pulaski°	.926	13	24	1	2	0
Childress, Pulaski	1.000	3	6	2	0	0
Cichon, Elizabethton	1.000	2	6	0	0	0
Coleman, Johnson City	.942	58	123	7	8	3
Crisp, Bluefield	.914	26	30	2	3	0
Cruz, Elizabethton°	1.000	1	3	0	0	0
Detmer, Johnson City	1.000	1	1	0	0	0
Fleming, Johnson City	.935	41	53	5	4	1
Geren, Kingsport	.977	48	79	5	2	1
Gerhart, Bluefield	.9818	60	105	3	2	1
Gil, Elizabethton	1.000	7	11	0	0	0
Granger, Bluefield	.951	21	38	1	2	0
Hall, Pulaski	.975	40	74	3	2	0
Harris, Kingsport	.800	6	8	0	2	0
Hatley, Elizabethton°	.500	2	1	0	1	0
Hendricks, Johnson City	.875	16	7	0	1	0
Hollis, Kingsport	.905	10	19	0	2	0
Irwin, Bristol	.842	30	32	0	6	0
Jackson, Pikeville°	.964	26	24	3	1	0
James, Pikeville	.9818	61	102	6	2	2
Javier, Johnson City	.962	54	94	8	4	1
Landers, Pikeville	.900	43	61	2	7	0
Lawrence, Bluefield	1.000	5	3	0	0	0
Lesieur, Paintsville	1.000	40	54	4	0	0
Llewellyn, Pulaski	.959	43	67	4	3	0
McManus, Bristol	.917	4	7	4	1	0
Metski, Bristol	.857	7	5	1	1	0
Mitchell, Pikeville	.980	28	45	3	1	2
Moriarty, Bristol	.951	58	108	9	6	1
MOSER, Pulaski°	.9819	50	99	10	2	2
Murray, Kingsport	.917	12	11	0	1	0
Nunez, Johnson City	.970	40	60	4	2	0
Orrick, Kingsport°	.842	14	16	0	3	0
Ortiz, Elizabethton	.900	23	17	1	2	0
Page, Bluefield	1.000	15	12	1	0	0
Pasqua, Paintsville	.967	59	114	4	4	0
Peer, Paintsville°	.933	51	66	4	5	0
Post, Paintsville	.968	22	29	1	1	0
Puckett, Elizabethton	.966	65	133	11	5	1
Rodriguez, Johnson City°	.938	11	14	1	1	0
Russomagno, Johnson City	1.000	3	5	0	0	0
Sanchez, Kingsport	.929	23	51	1	4	0
Scheer, Elizabethton	.954	44	79	4	4	0
Thompson, Pulaski	.926	60	95	5	8	1
Thornton, Kingsport	.913	44	91	3	9	0
Tiefenthaler, Bluefield	.818	6	9	0	2	0
Traylor, Bristol	.907	40	37	2	4	0
Utecht, Pikeville	1.000	1	2	0	0	0
Vanderburg, Bluefield	.980	59	145	5	3	1
Wallace, Johnson City	.500	3	1	0	1	0
Washington, Bristol	.887	31	45	2	6	0
Weatherford, Pikeville°	.947	51	65	6	4	0
Weller, Paintsville°	.966	54	81	5	3	1
Whaley, Bristol°	1.000	9	15	0	0	0
Williams, Kingsport	.889	4	7	1	1	0

CATCHERS

Player and Club	Pct.	G.	PO.	A.	E.	DP.	PB.
Anglin, Pulaski	.986	21	123	18	2	1	3
Boroski, Pikeville	.971	30	158	12	5	1	8
Butters, Elizabethton	.943	10	29	4	2	0	1
Carmichael, Kingsport	.964	34	218	25	9	2	10
Carvajal, Johnson City	.974	14	37	1	1	0	2
Diguardi, Pulaski	1.000	6	14	0	0	0	1
Fitzgerald, Bluefield	.981	21	88	16	2	1	4
Gil, Elizabethton	.917	2	10	1	1	0	0
Graupman, Elizabethton	.952	26	127	12	7	0	5
Griggs, Bluefield	1.000	10	52	6	0	4	1
Harris, Johnson City	1.000	2	1	0	0	0	1
Hawkins, Kingsport	.962	23	133	17	6	0	4
Holmes, Bluefield	1.000	1	1	0	0	0	0
Isherwood, Paintsville	.989	25	166	21	2	4	2
KRYNITSKY, Pikeville	.982	52	345	32	7	2	8
Lawrence, Bluefield	.500	1	1	0	1	0	0
Lombardi, Paintsville	.979	47	323	50	8	2	6
Lyon, Kingsport	.958	14	86	6	4	1	1
Maull, Bluefield	.972	6	30	5	1	1	3
McPhail, Kingsport	1.000	1	1	0	0	0	1
Melillo, Bluefield	.996	31	198	28	1	3	2
Montague, Bluefield	.958	12	59	9	3	1	1
Neuendorff, Pulaski	.995	32	183	17	1	0	6
Pevey, Elizabethton	.967	21	108	8	4	1	1
Priessman, Bristol	.971	13	62	5	2	0	2
Ragsdale, Pulaski	.944	4	32	2	2	0	1
Rivera, Elizabethton	.974	21	102	9	3	0	6
Russell, Johnson City	1.000	5	16	1	0	0	2
Silva, Bristol	.972	23	127	11	4	0	3
Simmons, Pulaski	.939	12	45	1	3	0	4
Vargas, Pikeville	.920	3	20	3	2	0	0
Wallace, Johnson City	.967	62	313	39	12	5	10
Williamson, Bristol	.923	4	10	2	1	0	0
Young, Bristol	.960	35	164	27	8	2	5

PITCHERS

Player and Club	Pct.	G.	PO.	A.	E.	DP.
Adams, Kingsport	.867	14	3	10	2	2
Aldrich, Pikeville	.909	11	5	5	1	0
Allen, Kingsport°	.842	14	2	14	3	0
Anderson, Bluefield	1.000	16	0	4	0	0
Artemenko, Pikeville	1.000	5	0	3	0	0
Barlow, Bristol	1.000	10	2	10	0	0
Bautista, Kinsport	.778	14	3	4	2	0
Bell, Bluefield	.923	11	2	10	1	0
Bersano, Paintsville	1.000	11	2	3	0	2
Blunt, Johnson City	.923	10	4	8	1	0
Bosio, Pikeville	.909	13	3	7	1	1
Brandt, Kingsport°	1.000	21	2	12	0	0

PITCHERS—Continued

Player and Club	Pct.	G.	PO.	A.	E.	DP.
Brown, Paintsville°	1.000	14	4	17	0	2
Burnos, Elizabethton	1.000	11	7	13	0	1
Caito, 5 Bristol-7 John. City	1.000	12	2	4	0	0
Candalaria, Pulaski°	.667	10	0	4	2	0
Castelono, Elizabethton°	1.000	2	0	1	0	0
Charley, Bluefield°	1.000	13	6	10	0	0
Chatham, Pulaski°	.909	12	1	9	1	0
Compagno, Paintsville°	1.000	2	1	1	0	0
Concepcion, Bluefield	.800	21	1	7	2	0
Cook, Bristol	1.000	4	2	8	0	0
Cooper, Bristol	.750	11	3	6	3	0
Corsi, Paintsville	1.000	8	3	8	0	0
Crim, Pikeville	.813	11	4	9	3	0
Crumley, Bluefield	.909	11	5	5	1	2
Cruz, Elizabethton°	.667	8	0	2	1	0
Diez, Bristol	1.000	6	2	2	0	0
Downs, Pikeville	.750	12	3	3	2	0
Easley, Paintsville	.895	13	5	12	2	1
Edgell, Bristol	.857	9	2	4	1	0
Everett, Elizabethton	.818	11	3	6	2	1
Finnegan, Johnson City	.696	13	3	13	7	1
Fitts, Kingsport	.947	12	4	14	1	0
Frey, Johnson City°	1.000	16	0	4	0	0
Gay, Kingsport	.938	11	2	13	1	2
George, Paintsville°	.833	13	4	6	2	0
Gooden, Kingsport	.955	9	3	18	1	0
Gordon, Bristol	.969	22	6	25	1	1
Granger, Bristol	1.000	16	2	4	0	0
Green, Pulaski	1.000	10	2	8	0	0
Gross, Elizabethton	1.000	6	6	5	0	0
Gumbert, Paintsville	.833	10	0	5	1	0
Gyarmati, Pikeville	1.000	3	0	2	0	0
Habyan, Bluefield	1.000	12	6	11	0	2
Hartley, Johnson City	1.000	8	3	5	0	1
Heinkel, Bristol	1.000	1	1	3	0	0
Hentz, Pulaski	.857	13	2	4	1	2
Hesting, Elizabethton°	1.000	7	1	3	0	0
Hobbie, Bristol	.900	15	1	8	1	0
Hulette, Elizabethton	1.000	8	2	2	0	0
Inman, Paintsville°	.800	6	3	1	1	0
Kindred, Elizabethton	.786	11	0	11	3	0
Koch, Pikeville	1.000	13	1	6	0	0
Krsnich, Bluefield	1.000	9	0	4	0	0
Lackie, Bluefield°	.833	10	1	9	2	0
Lance, Pulaski°	.889	18	2	6	1	0
Larcom, Elizabethton°	.958	10	4	19	1	0
Legumina, Bristol°	1.000	12	2	7	0	0
Leiter, Bluefield	.882	9	7	8	2	0
Lewis, Paintsville	.833	6	1	4	1	0
Lynn, Pulaski	.909	12	1	9	1	0
Maack, Elizabethton°	.905	19	9	10	2	1
Maldonado, Johnson City	.769	17	3	7	3	1
Martinez, Kingsport	1.000	9	0	1	0	0
Mason, Bluefield	1.000	11	0	5	0	1
Mehalko, Pulaski°	1.000	4	0	5	0	0
Mejia, Johnson City	.909	20	2	8	1	1
Milligen, Johnson City°	1.000	9	2	7	0	1
Miquel, Bristol°	1.000	2	4	0	0	0
Monteleone, Bristol	.938	12	2	13	1	1
A. Moody, Kingsport	.833	8	1	4	1	0
K. Moody, Pulaski°	1.000	13	0	18	0	1
Moon, Johnson City	1.000	7	0	2	0	0
Mulcahy, Bluefield°	.857	22	1	5	1	0
Myers, Kingsport°	.938	13	2	13	1	1
Niemiec, Paintsville	.800	10	1	3	1	0
Ortega, Johnson City	.929	26	4	9	1	0
Page, 6 Eliza.-1 Pulaski	1.000	7	0	6	0	1
Parham, Elizabethton°	1.000	12	7	18	0	0
Pena, Pikeville°	.875	7	0	7	1	0
Pimentel, Kingsport	1.000	12	1	4	0	0
Plunk, Paintsville	.882	12	9	6	2	1
Raubolt, Bristol	1.000	12	5	1	0	0
Ream, Pikeville	.786	14	1	10	3	1
Rice, Pikeville	.933	14	3	11	1	0
RIJO, Paintsville	1.000	13	3	24	0	1
Rivera, Pulaski	1.000	23	1	6	0	0
Sanchez, Johnson City	.818	13	3	6	2	2
Sanders, Elizabethton	1.000	4	1	1	0	0
Sawyer, Elizabethton	.750	9	3	3	2	0
Scarpetta, Pikeville°	.900	12	2	16	2	1
Sczesnak, Bluefield°	1.000	9	1	3	0	0
Shamblin, Pikeville	1.000	6	1	4	0	1
Smith, Elizabethton	1.000	23	1	11	0	0
Sperto, Pulaski	.600	17	2	1	2	1
Suggs, Johnson City	.000	7	0	0	1	0
Sullivan, Pikeville	.500	1	0	1	1	1
Tirado, Kingsport	1.000	13	1	7	0	1
Torres, Pulaski	1.000	9	0	5	0	0
Turnbull, Johnson City	.800	13	2	6	2	1
Unger, Paintsville°	.824	22	0	14	3	0
Watson, Pulaski	1.000	2	2	0	0	0
Whitmore, Bristol	1.000	11	0	5	0	0
B. Williams, Pikeville	.846	11	2	9	2	0
S. Williams, Pikeville	.500	8	0	1	1	0
Wilson, Bluefield°	.909	12	1	9	1	0
Winters, Pulaski°	1.000	10	2	2	0	0
Youmans, Kingsport	.846	10	3	8	2	1

The following players do not have any recorded accepted chances at the positions indicated; therefore, are not listed in the fielding averages for those particular positions: Beucher, p; Bocock, p; Brazoban, of; Childress, p; Cowgill, of; Delacruz, p; Grissom, p; Hendricks, p; Heredin, ss; Leonard, p; Lynch, 3b, p; Maris, 2b; Maull, of; Montague, 1b; Nordbrook, p; Ripken, of; Van Gennep, p; Wiley, of; F. Williams, 3b; Zanini, 3b.

CLUB PITCHING

Club	ERA.	G.	CG.	ShO.	Sv.	IP.	H.	R.	ER.	HR.	HB.	BB.	Int. BB.	SO.	WP.	Bk.
Paintsville	3.21	70	23	9	10	594.2	566	268	212	23	11	235	1	494	62	11
Bluefield	3.55	69	13	2	15	587.2	526	285	232	23	19	299	5	425	47	12
Elizabethton	4.02	68	16	5	11	553.2	531	328	247	39	16	287	12	363	48	5
Pikeville	4.17	67	20	5	4	557	515	354	258	37	31	311	11	498	62	8
Bristol	4.54	64	10	3	14	529	525	321	267	28	19	268	3	352	44	8
Johnson City	4.65	67	9	5	14	562.2	618	362	291	31	20	313	12	351	46	6
Kingsport	5.03	68	10	4	10	577.2	629	453	323	39	16	323	2	426	66	9
Pulaski	5.25	69	15	2	9	557.2	591	391	325	43	16	304	8	375	52	4

PITCHERS' RECORDS
(Leading Qualifiers for Earned-Run Average Leadership — 56 or More Innings)

°Throws lefthanded.

Pitcher—Club	W.	L.	Pct.	ERA.	G.	GS.	CG.	GF.	ShO.	Sv.	IP.	H.	R.	ER.	HR.	HB.	Int. BB.	SO.	WP.
Ortega, Johnson City	7	1	.875	1.55	26	0	0	24	0	10	58	43	10	10	2	0	12	39	2
Turnbull, Johnson City	9	4	.692	2.05	13	13	5	0	2	0	92.1	74	26	21	2	1	30	86	1
Gordon, Bristol	4	4	.500	2.19	22	0	0	21	0	8	65.2	48	17	16	4	2	14	42	0
Charley, Bluefield°	8	1	.889	2.22	13	13	3	0	1	0	81	69	23	20	3	2	32	53	7
Brown, Paintsville°	7	4	.636	2.47	14	12	6	2	2	0	87.1	78	30	24	2	1	35	77	10
Gooden, Kingsport	5	4	.556	2.47	9	9	4	0	2	0	65.2	53	34	18	1	1	25	66	2
Rijo, Paintsville	8	4	.667	2.50	13	12	6	1	3	0	79.1	76	33	22	6	0	22	66	6
Easley, Paintsville	7	4	.636	2.56	13	12	4	1	1	0	84.1	77	31	24	3	2	28	59	5
Crim, Pikeville	4	6	.400	2.56	11	11	8	0	1	0	77.1	62	32	22	3	1	18	76	6
Kindred, Elizabethton	8	2	.800	2.79	11	11	1	0	0	0	71	59	29	22	4	1	30	34	3

Departmental Leaders: G—Ortega, 26; GS—Charley, Finnegan, K. Moody, Myers, Turnbull, 13; CG—Crim, 8; GF—Ortega, 24; ShO—Maack, Rijo, 3; W—Habyan, Turnbull, 9; L—Smith, 7; Pct.—Charley, .889; Sv—Ortega, 10; IP—Turnbull, 92.1; H—Fitts, 89; R—Fitts, 61; ER—Fitts, 47; HR—Monteleone, 8; HB—B. Williams, 8; BB—Finnegan, 72; IBB—Smith, 5; SO—Myers, Turnbull, 86; WP—Blunt, 17.

(All Pitchers—Listed Alphabetically)

Pitcher—Club	W.	L.	Pct.	ERA.	G.	GS.	CG.	GF.	ShO.	Sv.	IP.	H.	R.	ER.	HR.	HB.	BB.	Int. BB.	SO.	WP.
Adams, Kingsport	2	3	.400	3.69	14	6	0	6	0	1	46.1	43	35	19	1	2	32	0	37	5
Aldrich, Pikeville	1	2	.333	4.19	11	8	1	3	1	1	53.2	44	33	25	5	2	28	0	37	5
Allen, Kingsport°	3	1	.750	3.38	14	3	2	7	0	2	56	51	29	21	4	0	9	0	33	4
Anderson, Bluefield	0	0	.000	4.61	16	0	0	6	0	2	27.1	32	21	14	1	0	11	0	18	0
Artemenko, Pikeville	1	0	1.000	1.00	5	0	0	4	0	0	9	8	3	1	0	1	8	1	8	0
Barlow, Bristol	4	4	.500	3.75	10	10	2	0	1	0	57.2	46	31	24	0	4	37	0	56	8
Bautista, Kingsport	0	4	.000	8.92	14	4	0	5	0	0	38.1	61	44	38	3	0	19	0	13	3
Bell, Bluefield°	4	1	.800	2.10	11	9	0	2	0	0	51.1	42	19	12	2	2	36	0	30	2
Bersano, Paintsville	3	0	1.000	0.96	11	0	0	11	0	6	18.2	11	2	2	1	0	4	0	23	1
Beucher, Bluefield	0	0	.000	0.00	1	0	0	1	0	0	1.2	1	0	0	0	1	0	4	0
Blunt, Johnson City	1	6	.143	7.60	10	8	0	0	0	0	45	55	46	38	2	3	38	3	25	17
Bocock, Johnson City	0	0	.000	0.00	1	0	0	1	0	0	1	0	0	0	0	0	0	0	1	0
Bosio, Pikeville	3	2	.600	4.91	13	3	2	6	1	1	51.1	60	31	28	2	6	17	3	53	9
Brandt, Kingsport°	0	4	.000	4.30	21	0	0	15	0	3	37.2	44	31	18	4	1	22	1	25	5
Brown, Paintsville°	7	4	.636	2.47	14	12	6	2	2	0	87.1	78	30	24	2	1	35	0	77	10
Burnos, Elizabethton	2	3	.400	4.42	11	4	2	4	1	0	38.2	33	28	19	3	1	18	1	22	4
Caito, 5 Bristol-7 John. City	0	5	.000	9.22	12	3	1	3	0	0	27.1	46	36	28	1	1	30	1	15	5
Candalaria, Pulaski°	6	1	.857	3.69	10	10	4	0	1	0	61	53	34	25	2	0	32	0	53	5
Castelono, Elizabethton°	0	0	.000	6.75	2	0	0	2	0	0	4	5	3	3	0	1	5	0	3	2
Charley, Bluefield°	8	1	.889	2.22	13	13	3	0	1	0	81	69	23	20	3	2	32	2	53	7
Chatham, Pulaski°	4	5	.444	5.05	12	10	2	2	0	1	62.1	68	39	35	5	1	26	0	36	7
Childress, Pulaski	0	0	.000	20.25	2	0	0	1	0	0	2.2	6	6	6	2	0	2	0	1	0
Compagno, Paintsville°	0	0	.000	0.00	2	0	0	2	0	0	3	0	0	0	0	3	0	3	0
Concepcion, Bluefield	2	1	.667	4.25	21	0	0	12	0	1	36	28	19	17	0	6	22	0	26	3
Cook, Bristol	0	2	.000	5.60	4	2	1	1	0	0	17.2	18	12	11	2	0	8	0	7	1
Cooper, Bristol	3	2	.600	3.77	11	8	0	2	0	0	57.1	55	30	24	6	1	26	1	29	3
Corsi, Paintsville	0	2	.000	2.90	8	4	0	1	0	0	31	32	11	10	0	0	13	0	20	2
Crim, Pikeville	4	6	.400	2.56	11	11	8	0	1	0	77.1	62	32	22	3	1	18	0	76	6
Crumley, Bluefield	4	5	.444	3.77	11	10	1	0	0	0	57.1	53	33	24	2	2	33	0	37	6
Cruz, Elizabethton°	2	1	.667	8.22	8	0	0	1	0	0	15.1	17	17	14	1	0	12	0	13	3
Delacruz, Elizabethton°	0	0	.000	8.10	3	0	0	3	0	0	3.1	4	3	3	0	0	8	0	2	1
Diez, Bristol	0	1	.000	17.72	6	1	0	1	0	0	10.2	25	24	21	1	0	15	0	4	1
Downs, Pikeville	1	4	.200	3.63	12	1	0	10	0	2	22.1	23	16	9	0	1	14	2	26	3
Easley, Paintsville	7	4	.636	2.56	13	12	4	1	1	0	84.1	77	31	24	3	2	28	0	59	5
Edgell, Bristol	0	5	.000	4.93	9	8	0	1	0	0	34.2	34	22	19	2	3	21	0	15	7
Everett, Elizabethton	1	6	.143	4.72	11	11	2	0	0	0	55.1	55	37	29	4	2	45	0	33	12
Finnegan, Johnson City	3	4	.429	5.32	13	13	1	0	0	0	69.1	74	54	41	2	1	72	1	27	10
Fitts, Kingsport	3	6	.333	6.82	12	11	1	1	1	0	62	89	61	47	6	1	27	0	25	6
Frey, Johnson City°	0	3	.000	8.27	16	0	0	8	0	1	32.2	48	37	30	3	4	26	4	23	1
Gay, Kingsport	3	5	.375	5.90	11	9	0	1	0	0	58	70	48	38	6	0	21	1	30	1
George, Paintsville°	3	4	.429	4.97	13	7	2	3	0	1	63.1	62	45	35	2	0	38	0	64	12
Gooden, Kingsport	5	4	.556	2.47	9	9	4	0	2	0	65.2	53	34	18	1	1	25	0	66	2
Gordon, Bristol	4	4	.500	2.19	22	0	0	21	0	8	65.2	48	17	16	4	2	14	0	42	0
Granger, Bristol	2	3	.400	4.82	16	0	0	9	0	2	28	25	16	15	0	1	18	1	9	4
Green, Pulaski	1	1	.500	6.75	10	4	0	2	0	0	30.2	30	31	23	4	4	24	0	11	2
Grissom, Bluefield°	0	2	.000	14.54	4	0	0	3	0	0	4.1	4	9	7	0	0	9	0	5	2
Gross, Elizabethton	1	3	.250	2.49	6	6	3	0	0	0	43.1	30	16	12	4	2	12	1	28	3
Gumbert, Paintsville	1	0	1.000	3.94	10	6	1	2	1	0	48	49	26	21	3	1	18	0	32	2
Gyarmati, Pikeville	0	2	.000	3.75	3	1	0	2	0	0	12	11	8	5	1	2	6	0	10	3
Habyan, Bluefield	9	2	.818	3.54	12	12	2	0	1	0	81.1	68	35	32	3	1	24	1	55	4
Hartley, Johnson City	3	1	.750	2.79	8	5	0	0	0	0	29	32	12	9	1	1	8	0	13	3
Heinkel, Bristol	1	0	1.000	0.00	1	1	1	0	0	0	9	2	1	0	0	1	0	0	11	1
Hendricks, Johnson City	0	0	.000	36.00	1	0	0	1	0	0	1	4	4	4	1	0	1	0	1	1
Hentz, Pulaski	2	5	.286	4.91	13	8	1	0	0	0	58.2	60	38	32	4	2	36	1	49	6
Hesting, Elizabethton°	1	1	.500	5.95	7	3	1	2	1	0	19.2	22	16	13	1	0	16	1	9	2
Hobbie, Bristol	1	2	.333	6.62	15	0	0	8	0	3	35.1	50	29	26	1	0	30	0	26	6
Hulette, Elizabethton	1	0	1.000	4.74	8	1	0	2	0	1	19	22	12	10	1	0	8	0	11	0
Inman, Paintsville°	1	0	1.000	5.28	6	1	0	5	0	1	15.1	23	12	9	0	0	6	0	6	3
Kindred, Elizabethton	8	2	.800	2.79	11	11	1	0	0	0	71	59	29	22	4	1	30	2	34	3
Koch, Pikeville	2	5	.286	4.75	13	6	1	6	0	0	41.2	46	31	22	0	0	14	1	35	1
Krsnich, Bluefield	3	0	1.000	5.40	9	0	0	7	0	2	11.2	12	7	7	0	2	5	2	3	1
Lackie, Bluefield°	1	2	.333	5.53	10	10	0	0	0	0	40.2	38	28	25	1	1	41	0	28	8
Lance, Pulaski°	5	4	.556	5.27	18	3	1	9	0	1	42.2	44	34	25	5	0	23	2	32	4
Larcom, Elizabethton°	4	4	.500	4.53	10	10	2	0	0	0	59.2	60	41	30	5	0	30	0	32	2
Legumina, Bristol°	7	2	.778	3.25	12	11	3	1	0	0	69.1	72	31	25	2	0	17	0	44	1
Leiter, Bluefield	4	5	.444	3.81	9	9	4	0	0	0	59	59	28	25	1	3	21	0	33	5
Leonard, Bluefield	1	1	.500	4.70	3	1	0	0	0	0	7.2	6	5	4	0	0	7	0	8	1
Lewis, Paintsville	1	3	.250	4.55	6	6	0	0	0	0	27.2	25	16	14	3	1	13	0	17	0
Lynch, Pulaski	0	0	.000	4.50	1	0	0	1	0	0	2	2	1	1	0	0	2	0	2	0
Lynn, Pulaski	2	3	.400	4.73	12	12	2	0	0	0	59	67	38	31	3	1	31	1	42	5
Maack, Elizabethton°	3	4	.429	2.83	19	4	4	9	3	3	60.1	55	25	19	4	0	24	1	59	3
Maldonado, Johnson City	2	4	.333	4.38	17	4	1	6	0	2	49.1	61	40	24	5	3	17	0	34	3
Martinez, Kingsport	0	0	.000	8.24	9	0	0	6	0	0	19.2	24	22	18	0	1	19	0	17	9
Mason, Bluefield	1	1	.500	4.60	11	2	1	3	0	1	29.1	36	20	15	3	0	6	0	14	1
Mehalko, Pulaski°	2	0	1.000	1.50	4	3	1	0	1	0	24	17	5	4	0	0	8	0	12	0
Mejia, Johnson City	1	1	.500	7.07	20	1	0	10	0	1	35.2	50	33	28	3	1	12	0	21	0
Milligen, Johnson City°	3	1	.750	3.67	9	7	0	1	0	0	41.2	53	24	17	4	0	18	1	18	0
Miquel, Bristol°	0	0	.000	4.15	2	2	0	0	0	0	8.2	6	4	4	1	1	5	0	9	0
Monteleone, Bristol	4	6	.400	3.89	12	12	0	0	0	0	71.2	66	41	31	8	1	23	0	52	4
A. Moody, Kingsport	2	1	.667	1.04	8	2	2	4	0	2	26	12	5	3	0	2	13	0	22	1
K. Moody, Pulaski°	6	4	.600	3.73	13	13	3	0	0	0	82	83	38	34	4	1	29	1	38	4
Moon, Johnson City	0	3	.000	8.10	7	2	0	1	0	0	20	32	19	18	2	0	18	0	10	2
Mulcahy, Bluefield°	5	0	1.000	3.49	22	2	1	12	0	6	49	43	21	19	2	1	23	0	52	3
Myers, Kingsport°	6	3	.667	4.12	13	13	1	0	0	0	74.1	68	49	34	1	4	69	0	86	12
Niemiec, Paintsville	2	0	1.000	3.71	10	2	0	5	0	1	26.2	28	14	11	0	3	15	0	23	12
Nordbrook, Pikeville	0	0	.000	4.50	1	0	0	0	0	0	2	3	1	1	0	0	1	0	1	0
Ortega, Pikeville°	7	1	.875	1.55	26	0	0	24	0	10	58	43	10	10	2	0	12	2	39	2
Page, 6 Eliza.-1 Pulaski	2	2	.500	6.48	7	4	0	1	0	0	25	30	21	18	4	0	10	0	7	2
Parham, Elizabethton°	6	2	.750	3.44	12	12	1	0	0	0	68	63	39	26	3	4	38	1	57	6
Pena, Pikeville°	0	2	.000	4.64	7	1	0	2	0	0	21.1	23	15	11	3	0	16	0	23	1
Pimentel, Kingsport	2	0	1.000	6.14	12	0	0	7	0	0	22	28	17	15	3	0	15	0	13	5

Pitcher—Club	W.	L.	Pct.	ERA.	G.	GS.	CG.	GF.	ShO.	Sv.	IP.	H.	R.	ER.	HR.	HB.	BB.	Int. BB.	SO.	WP.
Plunk, Paintsville	6	3	.667	4.64	12	8	4	2	0	0	64	63	35	33	2	3	30	0	59	9
Raubolt, Bristol	1	1	.500	6.26	12	5	1	4	0	1	27.1	27	21	19	1	1	27	0	28	1
Ream, Pikeville	2	4	.333	5.14	14	7	0	2	0	0	42	43	29	24	7	0	29	2	35	8
Rice, Pikeville	1	3	.250	5.65	14	5	0	8	0	0	43	44	35	27	4	3	27	1	29	6
Rijo, Paintsville	8	4	.667	2.50	13	12	6	1	3	0	79.1	76	33	22	6	0	22	0	66	6
Rivera, Pulaski	4	3	.571	3.89	23	0	0	19	0	5	41.2	44	26	18	2	4	17	3	41	6
Sanchez, Johnson City	2	4	.333	5.86	13	7	1	2	0	0	50.2	58	34	33	3	3	23	0	29	3
Sanders, Elizabethton	0	0	.000	10.38	4	0	0	1	0	0	4.1	12	8	5	1	1	3	0	1	0
Sawyer, Elizabethton	0	1	.000	6.86	9	2	0	5	0	0	19.2	24	19	15	3	2	10	0	13	1
Scarpetta, Pikeville°	5	3	.625	2.83	12	9	4	1	1	0	70	46	30	22	2	3	27	0	69	2
Sczesnak, Bluefield°	1	0	1.000	2.08	9	0	0	7	0	3	13	11	5	3	0	0	10	0	14	0
Shamblin, Elizabethton	2	1	.667	6.75	6	0	0	0	0	0	14.2	20	13	11	1	2	13	0	10	4
Smith, Elizabethton	1	7	.125	2.45	23	0	0	22	0	7	47.2	44	18	13	2	2	20	5	41	3
Sperto, Pulaski	1	4	.200	5.94	17	0	0	9	0	2	33.1	41	29	22	4	2	24	0	27	8
Suggs, Johnson City	1	0	1.000	2.45	7	1	0	2	0	0	18.1	5	6	5	0	2	20	0	17	1
Sullivan, Pikeville	0	1	.000	0.00	1	1	1	0	0	0	6.1	4	2	0	0	0	2	0	3	2
Tirado, Kingsport	0	5	.000	7.52	13	2	0	5	0	2	32.1	51	39	27	7	2	13	0	28	2
Torres, Pulaski	3	2	.600	9.00	9	5	1	2	0	0	25	25	27	25	3	0	20	0	18	2
Turnbull, Johnson City	9	4	.692	2.05	13	13	5	0	2	0	92.1	74	26	21	2	1	30	1	86	1
Unger, Paintsville°	5	2	.714	1.37	22	0	0	12	0	1	46	42	13	7	1	0	10	1	45	0
Van Gennep, Pulaski	0	0	.000	11.88	3	0	0	2	0	0	8.1	15	11	11	2	0	4	0	4	0
Watson, Pikeville	0	2	.000	5.06	2	2	1	0	0	0	10.2	12	7	6	2	1	6	0	7	2
Whitmore, Bristol	1	2	.333	5.60	11	3	0	5	0	0	27.1	34	23	17	0	4	15	0	12	4
B. Williams, Pikeville	3	5	.375	4.20	11	11	2	0	1	0	60	48	43	28	1	8	63	0	61	7
S. Williams, Pikeville	0	0	.000	7.32	8	1	0	2	0	0	19.2	18	25	16	3	1	23	1	15	3
Wilson, Bluefield°	4	1	.800	1.95	12	1	1	3	0	0	37	24	12	8	3	1	18	0	45	4
Winters, Pulaski	0	1	.000	11.03	10	1	0	7	0	0	23.2	32	30	29	2	1	24	0	9	3
Youmans, Kingsport	2	4	.333	6.18	10	9	0	1	0	0	39.1	35	39	27	3	2	39	0	31	11

BALKS—Concepcion, Myers, Rijo, Unger, 3 each; Crim, Crumley, Finnegan, Lackie, Leiter, Lynn, Mason, Parham, Pimentel, Raubolt, Turnbull, Youmans, 2 each; Barlow, Bautista, Blunt, Bosio, Brown, Candalaria, Cook, Corsi, Diez, Downs, Easley, Everett, Frey, George, Gooden, Gyarmati, Habyan, Kindred, Koch, Legumina, Maack, Monteleone, Pena, Plunk, Whitmore, B. Williams, Winters, 1 each.

COMBINATION SHUTOUTS—Legumina-Gordon, Cooper-Gordon, Bristol; Turnbull-Ortega, Milligan-Ortega, Blunt-Sanchez, Johnson City; Adams-Moody, Kingsport; Easley-Compagno, Lewis-Unger-Rijo, Paintsville.

NO-HIT GAME—None.

Gulf Coast League

SUMMER CLASS A CLASSIFICATION

CHAMPIONSHIP WINNERS IN PREVIOUS YEARS

1964—Sarasota Braves	.610	1971—Kansas City	.755
1965—Bradenton Astros	.632	1972—Chicago N.L. a	.651
1966—New York A.L.	.667	Kansas City a	.651
1967—Kansas City	.614	1973—Texas	.732
1968—Oakland	.650	1974—Chicago N.L.	.702
1969—Montreal	.585	1975—Texas	.774
1970—Chicago A.L.	.600		
1976—Texas	.704		
1977—Chicago-AL	.731		
1978—Texas	.600		
1979—Houston	.635		
1980—Kansas City-Blue	.635		
1981—Kansas City-Gold	.688		

(Note—Known as Sarasota Rookie League in 1964 and Florida Rookie League in 1965.) aDeclared co-champions; no playoff.

STANDING OF CLUBS AT CLOSE OF SEASON, AUGUST 31

Club	N.Y. AL	Chi. AL	Tex.	Atl.	Tor.	Chi. NL	S.D.	K.C.	Pitt.	Hou.	W.	L.	T.	Pct.	G.B.
New York-AL (Yankees)	....	3	4	5	4	4	6	5	6	5	42	21	0	.667	....
Chicago-AL (White Sox)	4	....	6	5	2	4	5	4	6	6	40	23	0	.635	2
Texas (Rangers)	2	1	....	5	4	4	5	4	5	5	36	27	0	.571	6
Atlanta (Braves)	3	2	3	....	4	4	2	5	5	4	32	31	0	.508	10
Toronto (Blue Jays)	3	4	3	2	....	3	3	4	4	4	30	33	0	.476	12
Chicago-NL (Cubs)	2	3	3	3	4	....	3	4	3	5	30	33	0	.476	12
San Diego (Padres)	2	3	2	4	4	4	....	3	2	5	29	34	0	.460	13
Kansas City (Royals)	2	3	2	2	4	4	4	....	3	4	28	35	0	.444	14
Pittsburgh (Pirates)	1	2	2	2	4	5	5	3	....	3	27	35	0	.435	14½
Houston (Astros)	2	2	2	3	3	1	1	3	3	....	20	42	0	.323	21½

Games played at Bradenton and Sarasota, Fla.

Major league affiliations in parentheses.

Regular-season attendance—4,428.

Managers: Atlanta, Pedro Gonzalez; Chicago-AL, John Boles; Chicago-NL, Jim Fairey; Houston, Jose Tartabull; Kansas City, Joe Jones; New York-AL, Carlos Tosca; Pittsburgh, Woody Huyke; San Diego, Manny Crespo; Texas, Tom Grieve; Toronto, Hector Torres.

All-Star Team: 1B—McGriff, New York-AL; 2B—Keeton, Chicago-AL; 3B—Dunston, Chicago-NL; SS—Rivera, Pittsburgh; OF—Boderick, Chicago-NL; Hodge, Houston; McLaughlin, Chicago-AL; C—Karcovice, Chicago-AL; P—DeVincenso, Chicago-AL; Rel. P—Coleman, San Diego; Manager—Boles, Chicago-AL.

(Compiled by Howe News Bureau, Boston, Mass.)

CLUB BATTING

Club	Pct.	G.	AB.	R.	OR.	H.	TB.	2B.	3B.	HR.	RBI.	GW.	SH.	SF.	HP.	BB.	Int. BB.	SO.	SB.	CS.	LOB.
Chicago-AL	.259	63	2060	327	261	533	712	85	14	22	265	32	26	30	17	280	5	440	115	51	492
New York-AL	.258	63	2094	350	249	541	731	85	15	25	303	33	12	22	27	305	4	382	100	37	516
Pittsburgh	.253	62	2095	243	281	529	694	67	22	18	207	18	2	20	19	147	3	359	76	40	432
Chicago-NL	.252	63	1957	262	259	494	606	59	16	7	200	20	12	20	19	171	3	358	198	84	343
Toronto	.245	63	2062	271	268	506	643	60	16	15	216	25	12	19	24	189	1	364	57	28	429
Kansas City	.244	63	2124	280	295	519	670	55	27	14	237	22	22	26	15	257	10	386	105	49	485
Houston	.243	62	2048	256	361	497	645	69	20	13	221	16	23	22	23	211	6	392	62	33	451
Texas	.242	63	2031	248	225	491	630	77	10	14	209	28	21	22	11	227	6	336	90	38	462
San Diego	.242	63	1977	237	285	478	592	61	13	9	178	23	20	12	19	223	4	381	123	54	423
Atlanta	.237	63	1990	247	237	472	624	56	18	20	213	24	23	19	23	218	7	381	73	37	441

INDIVIDUAL BATTING

(Leading Qualifiers for Batting Championship—170 or More Plate Appearances)

°Bats lefthanded.　　†Switch-hitter.

Player and Club	Pct.	G.	AB.	R.	H.	TB.	2B.	3B.	HR.	RBI.	GW.	SH.	SF.	HP.	BB.	Int. BB.	SO.	SB.	CS.
McLaughlin, David, Chicago-AL°	.350	63	237	48	83	97	9	1	1	25	5	2	4	3	35	2	29	32	14
Griffin, David, Atlanta	.327	61	208	33	68	103	11	3	6	39	5	0	5	5	30	1	15	3	2
Keeton, Garry, Chicago-AL	.323	54	192	37	62	78	8	1	2	26	3	5	2	3	28	0	24	8	6
Dunston, Shawon, Chicago-NL	.321	53	190	27	61	78	11	0	2	28	4	1	4	1	11	1	22	32	10
Boderick, Willie, Chicago-NL	.313	55	198	43	62	85	8	3	3	20	3	2	1	3	15	0	36	41	12
Allen, Edward, Kansas City	.307	37	150	32	46	52	0	3	0	13	1	0	0	3	19	0	38	27	9
Then, Hediberto, Pittsburgh	.306	43	144	23	44	68	7	1	5	23	0	0	2	6	21	1	24	11	7
Daugherty, Bill, San Diego	.301	45	156	19	47	72	13	0	4	35	4	0	3	3	23	2	32	8	2
Fernandez, Jose, Toronto†	.300	62	243	46	73	81	8	0	0	18	5	4	3	4	23	0	20	19	10
Aruca, Daniel, Houston°	.297	43	158	22	47	57	3	2	1	17	1	2	1	1	13	0	22	11	7

Departmental Leaders: G—McLaughlin, Monson, Nunez, 63; AB—Fernandez, Shuffield, 243; R—McLaughlin, 48; H—McLaughlin, 83; TB—Bolivar, Griffin, 103; 2B—Daugherty, 13; 3B—T. Castillo, P. Garcia, Shuffield, 5; HR—McGriff, 9; RBI—Nelson, McGriff, 41; GWRBI—Bolivar, McGriff, 6; SH—J. Walsh, 6; SF—Sandry, 6; HP—Then, 6; BB—McGriff, 48; SO—Karkovice, 73; SB—Boderick, 41; CS—McLaughlin, 14.

(All Players—Listed Alphabetically)

Player and Club	Pct.	G.	AB.	R.	H.	TB.	2B.	3B.	HR.	RBI.	GW.	SH.	SF.	HP.	BB.	Int. BB.	SO.	SB.	CS.
Aaron, Lawrence, Atlanta°	.320	36	103	16	33	40	4	0	1	10	1	0	1	0	18	1	21	5	2
Achique, Ramon, Toronto°	.130	35	100	6	13	22	3	0	2	8	0	0	1	0	5	0	41	0	0
Alcantara, Agapito, Texas	.071	6	14	1	1	1	0	0	0	0	0	0	0	0	1	0	6	0	0
Allen, Edward, Kansas City	.307	37	150	32	46	52	0	3	0	13	1	0	0	3	19	0	38	27	9
Allison, James, Texas†	.275	25	69	12	19	24	2	0	1	7	2	0	0	2	8	0	16	8	2
Ambrosino, Joseph, Texas°	.226	29	93	12	21	27	1	1	1	13	1	3	3	0	6	0	12	1	1

Player and Club	Pct.	G.	AB.	R.	H.	TB.	2B.	3B.	HR.	RBI.	GW.	SH.	SF.	HP.	BB.	Int. BB.	SO.	SB.	CS.
Antonetty, Elliott, Houston	.222	12	45	5	10	13	3	0	0	2	1	0	0	0	3	0	8	0	1
Aquino, F. Augusto, Texas*	.241	10	29	2	7	7	0	0	0	0	0	0	0	0	3	0	1	3	0
Aruca, Daniel, Houston*	.297	43	158	22	47	57	3	2	1	17	1	2	1	1	13	0	22	11	7
Atwood, Kevin, Chicago-NL*	.118	6	17	1	2	2	0	0	0	2	0	0	0	0	2	0	2	1	1
Aubin, Gerard, Pittsburgh	.200	8	30	4	6	16	1	0	3	10	1	0	1	0	4	0	8	1	2
Austin, Claude, Pittsburgh	.154	6	13	1	2	2	0	0	0	0	0	0	0	0	1	0	6	0	0
Bachmeier, Ronald, Chicago-NL†	.227	30	97	15	22	23	1	0	0	3	0	0	0	0	6	0	26	14	2
Baker, Kerry, Pittsburgh†	.147	24	68	7	10	10	0	0	0	4	0	0	2	0	8	0	14	4	3
Barringer, Scott, Pittsburgh*	.219	9	32	4	7	7	0	0	0	2	0	0	0	0	2	0	3	1	1
Battle, Kevin, Pittsburgh	.213	31	94	6	20	24	2	1	0	4	1	1	0	2	3	0	19	1	1
Ben, Elijah, Texas	.225	40	111	25	25	39	5	0	3	11	1	1	1	1	15	1	24	17	4
Boderick, Willie, Chicago-NL	.313	55	198	43	62	85	8	3	3	20	3	2	1	3	15	0	36	41	12
Bolivar, Esteban, Toronto	.281	62	235	31	66	103	8	4	7	37	6	0	1	3	20	1	33	11	2
Bonilla, Roberto, Pittsburgh†	.228	47	167	20	38	56	3	0	5	26	2	0	2	0	11	1	20	2	3
Borowski, Richard, New York-AL	.143	7	14	1	2	3	1	0	0	0	0	0	0	0	1	0	4	0	0
Botkin, Michael, Houston*	.287	35	122	18	35	38	3	0	0	11	0	4	1	0	13	1	12	3	0
Brennan, Edward, Texas	.314	41	121	13	38	48	7	0	1	20	4	0	2	2	13	0	12	1	3
Brim, Cecil, Texas	.029	16	35	2	1	1	0	0	0	0	0	0	0	0	4	0	17	1	1
Brittman, James, Kansas City*	.194	42	139	23	27	45	4	4	2	18	3	0	1	1	20	1	15	5	3
Brower, Robert, Texas	.287	36	122	25	35	46	7	2	0	7	2	0	0	3	14	0	24	19	3
Brown, Kenneth, Pittsburgh	.215	28	79	10	17	22	1	2	0	6	0	0	2	2	3	0	25	4	4
Brunenkant, Stephen, Texas	.325	37	126	18	41	49	5	0	1	18	2	0	1	1	11	0	15	2	0
Callahan, Daniel, San Diego	.500	16	2	0	1	2	1	0	0	0	0	0	0	0	0	0	1	0	0
Cannon, Thomas, San Diego	.197	49	152	16	30	31	1	0	0	8	1	1	0	2	25	0	49	6	3
Capellan, Rafael, Chicago-AL	.125	26	40	5	5	7	2	0	0	4	0	1	1	0	0	0	6	0	1
Carden, Allen, Atlanta*	.189	45	132	17	25	32	4	0	1	10	2	1	0	3	17	2	17	3	1
Cardieri, Ronald, Atlanta*	.222	14	36	5	8	9	1	0	0	2	0	0	0	0	4	1	4	1	0
Carmona, William, Toronto	.154	26	65	4	10	12	2	0	0	9	2	2	0	0	3	0	18	1	0
Carter, Richard, New York-AL	.274	38	135	25	37	47	8	1	0	20	2	2	0	3	18	0	13	8	4
Castillo, Carlos, San Diego	.227	43	141	12	32	40	5	0	1	8	0	0	1	3	11	0	28	2	4
Castillo, Thomas, Toronto	.291	60	206	26	60	79	6	5	1	30	1	2	4	3	29	0	28	3	2
Christenson, Kim, Chicago-AL	.267	60	217	42	58	84	11	3	3	28	3	2	4	1	25	1	30	8	3
Christy, Mark, San Diego	.000	9	2	0	0	0	0	0	0	0	0	0	0	0	2	0	2	0	0
Coleman, Ricky, San Diego	.272	37	136	26	37	51	5	3	1	19	2	2	0	0	15	0	14	22	3
Coleman, Randy, San Diego	.000	17	1	0	0	0	0	0	0	0	0	0	1	0	0	0	0	0	0
Collins, Jeff, San Diego	.000	19	3	0	0	0	0	0	0	0	0	0	0	0	0	0	1	0	0
Coss, David, Pittsburgh	.299	34	117	20	35	48	7	3	0	12	1	0	0	1	18	0	23	9	3
Cox, Dan, New York-AL	.347	23	49	10	17	18	1	0	0	5	1	0	0	1	8	0	5	3	0
Cunningham, Charles, Pittsburgh	.250	13	32	2	8	10	0	1	0	4	0	0	2	0	0	0	10	1	0
Cunningham, Herman, New York-AL	.234	41	146	28	34	44	5	1	1	23	4	0	2	3	23	1	36	3	1
Curry, Clinton, Texas	.222	35	108	10	24	32	3	1	1	15	2	1	3	0	7	0	21	3	1
Daniels, Samuel, San Diego	.000	13	4	0	0	0	0	0	0	0	0	0	0	0	1	0	2	1	0
Daugherty, Bill, San Diego	.301	45	156	19	47	72	13	0	4	35	4	0	3	3	23	2	32	8	2
Davila, Victor, Kansas City†	.209	29	91	7	19	20	1	0	0	8	0	0	1	0	4	0	10	0	0
Davis, Robert, Kansas City	.224	36	116	10	26	29	3	0	0	14	2	2	4	2	14	1	16	2	0
DelRosario, Manuel, San Diego†	.227	58	194	30	44	52	6	1	0	19	2	2	1	0	33	0	33	19	12
DelRosario, Sergio, San Diego	.000	9	2	0	0	0	0	0	0	0	0	0	0	0	0	0	1	0	0
DeLaRosa, Emilio, Texas	.130	17	46	2	6	6	0	0	0	1	0	3	0	1	0	0	9	1	2
Denis, Orlando, Houston	.283	51	184	18	52	65	11	1	0	20	0	1	1	3	14	0	20	1	2
DesJarden, Matthew, Kansas City†	.254	37	114	12	29	36	5	1	0	14	1	0	1	1	21	1	27	9	5
Diaz, Angel, Toronto	.201	45	149	16	30	41	3	1	2	20	1	0	1	4	10	0	40	0	2
Diaz, Maximiano, Chicago-AL	.235	17	34	4	8	10	0	1	0	6	1	2	2	0	9	0	7	0	0
Dollar, Rodney, Houston	.208	18	53	5	11	16	5	0	0	5	0	0	0	0	3	0	10	0	1
Donnelly, James, Houston*	.209	33	91	18	19	28	3	0	2	9	0	3	1	2	16	1	12	1	0
Dophied, Tracy, Houston*	.313	5	16	4	5	7	0	1	0	5	0	0	0	0	3	0	2	0	0
Duncan, Lindon, Texas	.100	8	20	1	2	3	1	0	0	0	0	0	0	0	5	2	5	0	0
Dunston, Shawon, Chicago-NL	.321	53	190	27	61	78	11	0	2	28	4	1	4	1	11	1	22	32	10
Edwards, Tracy, Atlanta†	.257	27	70	13	18	29	2	0	3	18	3	1	2	1	14	0	5	1	0
Elwess, Howard, Chicago-NL	.268	31	82	13	22	25	1	1	0	7	0	1	1	3	17	0	23	14	7
Espinal, Nelson, Houston	.190	13	42	8	8	10	2	0	0	6	1	0	0	1	7	0	8	3	1
Esser, Michael, Texas	.212	32	66	7	14	17	1	1	0	7	0	0	0	0	7	0	9	7	4
Estrada, Craig, San Diego	.257	62	218	18	56	71	9	3	0	15	1	1	2	2	11	0	23	11	3
Fasola, John, Pittsburgh	.250	2	4	0	1	1	0	0	0	1	0	0	1	0	0	0	1	0	0
Fernandez, Jose, Toronto†	.300	62	243	46	73	81	8	0	0	18	5	4	3	4	23	0	20	19	10
Ferrer, Jose, Pittsburgh	.250	26	80	8	20	25	2	0	1	6	0	0	1	2	4	0	13	1	0
Foit, James, Texas	.176	43	131	14	23	25	2	0	0	8	2	1	1	1	9	0	24	7	1
Freidhof, William, Kansas City	.279	49	179	19	50	71	5	2	4	28	5	0	3	0	24	1	26	5	2
Frierson, Jim, San Diego	.281	43	139	21	39	46	3	2	0	10	1	1	0	0	25	0	25	10	6
Garcia, Anthony, Chicago-NL	.234	43	145	16	34	42	8	0	0	8	0	1	0	2	9	0	14	8	5
Garcia, Paulino, Houston	.228	58	219	29	50	86	8	5	6	28	5	2	2	1	15	0	47	7	3
Gautier, Domingo, Atlanta	.186	22	43	3	8	9	1	0	0	2	0	0	0	0	4	0	10	4	1
Gergen, Robert, Texas	.229	23	70	4	16	18	2	0	0	3	0	0	0	3	5	0	5	1	2
Giordano, Donald, New York-AL	.169	22	65	12	11	12	1	0	0	3	1	0	0	0	15	1	12	4	0
Gonzalez, Fredi, New York-AL	.240	40	129	17	31	41	4	0	2	16	2	2	0	1	16	0	32	0	2
Goodman, Adolph, Chicago-NL	.218	26	87	9	19	24	5	0	0	6	1	2	0	0	3	0	14	2	2
Griffin, David, Atlanta	.327	61	208	31	68	103	11	3	6	39	5	0	5	5	30	1	15	3	2
Grullon, Pedro, Pittsburgh	.000	11	26	0	0	0	0	0	0	0	0	0	0	0	0	0	9	1	0
Guance, Johnny, Toronto†	.000	8	6	2	0	0	0	0	0	0	0	0	0	0	1	0	4	0	0
Harkins, James, San Diego	.333	13	6	0	2	2	0	0	0	0	0	0	0	0	0	0	1	0	0
Hausladen, Robert, Texas*	.328	40	116	10	38	48	10	0	0	20	3	1	1	3	18	0	19	3	1
Healy, Mark, Pittsburgh*	.163	25	80	7	13	15	0	1	0	6	0	0	0	0	12	0	11	1	0
Henderson, Gary, Toronto	.182	12	11	1	2	2	0	0	0	1	0	0	0	0	1	0	6	0	0
Hennessey, Brendan, Texas	.152	25	79	8	12	13	1	0	0	8	0	1	1	0	6	0	16	0	1
Hermsen, Mark, Pittsburgh*	.333	1	3	0	1	1	0	0	0	0	0	0	0	0	0	0	0	0	0
Hernandez, Gustavo, Chicago-AL	.125	20	40	3	5	5	0	0	0	2	1	0	0	1	4	0	17	2	1
Hodge, Simon, Houston	.252	59	234	24	59	75	6	2	2	27	2	0	2	1	7	0	47	7	4
Holecek, Joseph, Chicago-NL	.228	37	123	14	28	36	5	0	1	14	2	0	1	2	13	0	28	2	4
Howard, Randy, New York-AL	.255	46	145	25	37	45	4	2	0	20	1	3	3	1	17	0	20	4	0
Hunsuker, Mikel, Chicago-AL	.169	25	59	5	10	11	1	0	0	4	0	0	0	0	3	0	15	1	0
Infante, Alexis, Toronto	.292	37	137	17	40	51	7	2	0	15	3	0	3	0	9	0	15	6	2
Isaac, Johnny, Houston	.286	39	147	24	42	52	3	2	1	24	1	1	2	3	10	0	42	8	1
Jabalera, Guadalupe, Houston†	.175	34	97	10	17	18	1	0	0	7	0	0	0	5	9	0	22	4	2

Player and Club	Pct.	G.	AB.	R.	H.	TB.	2B.	3B.	HR.	RBI.	GW.	SH.	SF.	HP.	BB.	Int. BB.	SO.	SB.	CS.
Jobes, Craig, New York-AL	.000	2	0	0	0	0	0	0	0	1	0	0	1	0	1	0	0	0	0
Johnson, Hardis, Chicago-NL†	.059	7	17	0	1	3	0	1	0	0	0	0	0	0	2	0	5	0	1
Johnson, Timothy, Chicago-AL°	.197	39	127	8	25	38	4	0	3	18	3	1	0	0	4	0	36	0	0
Jones, Gary, Chicago-NL°	.349	29	106	29	37	42	3	1	0	12	1	1	0	0	17	0	16	18	5
Jones, Kevin, Chicago-AL°	.254	30	63	10	16	24	3	1	1	14	3	0	0	0	9	0	23	3	2
Karkovice, Ronald, Chicago-AL	.262	60	214	34	56	83	6	0	7	32	1	1	2	1	29	2	73	5	3
Keeton, Garry, Chicago-AL	.323	54	192	37	62	78	8	1	2	26	3	5	2	3	28	0	24	8	6
Kelly, Roberto, New York-AL	.198	31	86	13	17	23	1	1	1	18	1	0	3	0	10	0	18	3	3
Khalifa, Sammy, Pittsburgh	.080	6	25	1	2	2	0	0	0	0	0	0	0	0	3	0	4	1	0
King, Michael, New York-AL	.280	46	175	24	49	72	12	1	3	35	5	1	1	3	15	0	27	4	2
Koch, Bryan, Chicago-AL°	.300	17	10	0	3	3	0	0	0	0	0	0	0	0	0	0	3	1	0
Kohler, Robert, Texas°	.200	5	15	1	3	3	0	0	0	0	0	0	0	0	1	0	0	0	0
Lane, Ira, Houston	.197	26	66	10	13	17	0	2	0	5	1	0	0	0	14	0	24	1	0
Lautaret, Neil, Houston†	.185	18	54	8	10	10	0	0	0	5	1	0	0	1	12	0	19	0	1
Locke, Walton, Atlanta	.182	9	22	3	4	6	2	0	0	1	0	0	0	0	1	0	6	0	1
Lopez, Saul, Pittsburgh	.364	3	11	1	4	4	0	0	0	0	0	0	0	0	0	0	0	0	0
Lora, Cesar, Atlanta	.256	46	164	26	42	69	6	3	5	19	0	2	0	2	17	1	43	3	2
Lowe, Andre, Atlanta	.263	57	186	29	49	56	3	2	0	14	2	4	1	2	22	0	37	15	6
Mace, Jeffrey, Texas	.230	39	135	22	31	49	7	1	3	14	3	1	0	1	9	0	18	3	2
MacKay, Joey, New York-AL	.219	42	146	24	32	50	5	2	3	16	2	0	1	0	21	0	26	8	2
Marbrey, Ronald, New York-AL	.250	6	12	1	3	5	0	1	0	1	0	0	0	0	1	0	1	0	1
Marrero, Samuel, Chicago-NL	.108	14	37	6	4	4	0	0	0	4	0	0	0	1	0	0	9	3	1
Martinez, Luis, Pittsburgh	.325	31	114	12	37	47	8	1	0	11	1	0	0	0	4	0	12	1	2
Martinez, Modesto, Pittsburgh	.353	37	119	13	42	45	3	0	0	12	3	0	1	2	4	0	7	2	5
Martino, Martin, Kansas City°	.306	10	36	6	11	12	1	0	0	7	1	0	0	0	4	1	4	2	1
Massiah, Omar, Pittsburgh	.250	42	168	19	42	56	8	3	0	14	1	1	0	2	7	1	31	4	1
Mayse, Gregory, Atlanta	.200	14	30	0	6	7	1	0	0	2	0	0	0	0	3	0	4	2	1
McClain, Michael, San Diego	.000	13	5	0	0	0	0	0	0	0	0	0	0	0	0	0	4	0	0
McGee, Lawrence, Chicago-AL	.253	61	194	31	49	67	10	1	2	27	4	3	1	3	42	0	57	18	4
McGriff, Frederick, New York-AL°	.272	62	217	38	59	99	11	1	9	41	6	1	1	5	48	2	63	6	6
McLaughlin, David, Chicago-AL°	.350	63	237	48	83	97	9	1	1	25	5	2	4	3	35	2	29	32	14
McReddie, Warren, Texas	.273	28	66	4	18	24	4	1	0	6	1	2	1	0	12	2	6	1	0
Mena, Cesar, Pittsburgh	.250	1	4	0	1	1	0	0	0	0	0	0	0	0	0	0	1	0	0
Mercedes, Luis, Atlanta	.258	33	93	8	24	25	1	0	0	12	0	0	1	1	9	0	23	0	1
Meyer, Urban, Atlanta	.170	20	53	6	9	13	0	2	0	5	2	1	0	1	6	0	9	1	2
Miller, John, Houston	.298	37	124	13	37	45	6	1	0	13	1	3	2	1	8	0	17	1	3
Mims, James, Pittsburgh	.533	6	15	2	8	8	0	0	0	1	0	0	0	0	0	0	0	0	0
Miranda, Vladimir, Houston	.091	16	33	1	3	3	0	0	0	1	0	0	0	0	2	0	10	1	1
Mohl, Thomas, Pittsburgh	.280	15	50	1	14	20	2	2	0	7	0	0	0	1	4	0	10	1	1
Moncada, Rafael, Pittsburgh	.181	37	127	12	23	29	4	1	0	6	0	0	1	0	19	0	0	0	0
Monson, Eric, Kansas City	.289	63	235	31	68	87	5	4	2	34	4	0	4	0	38	1	43	13	6
Moreno, Jaime, San Diego	.290	16	62	9	18	23	5	0	0	8	1	0	0	1	4	0	6	2	1
Morin, Allen, Houston	.226	44	133	13	30	45	8	2	1	16	1	2	4	3	21	0	24	2	0
Morris, David, Atlanta	.207	62	213	24	44	61	10	2	1	20	1	5	2	3	18	0	38	12	4
Nelson, Darnell, New York-AL	.257	62	230	46	59	81	10	3	2	41	3	0	5	3	39	0	30	12	2
Nieves, Marcos, San Diego	.245	19	53	5	13	16	0	0	1	13	3	1	1	0	3	0	15	0	0
Nodell, Raymond, New York-AL†	.234	50	141	17	33	39	3	0	1	8	3	3	1	2	17	0	31	10	1
Nunez, Daniel, San Diego°	.255	63	235	29	60	67	3	2	0	12	1	3	1	2	24	0	43	25	12
Otstot, Scott, Atlanta	.129	28	70	3	9	9	0	0	0	7	0	5	0	0	5	0	12	0	0
Oxner, Stanley, Kansas City	.227	9	22	5	5	8	0	0	1	3	0	0	1	0	3	0	3	2	1
Palencia, Edwin, Toronto	.000	14	2	0	0	0	0	0	0	0	0	0	0	0	0	0	0	0	0
Palmer, Roscoe, Kansas City	.286	5	7	1	2	2	0	0	0	2	0	2	0	0	2	0	0	0	0
Palmore, Stanley, Kansas City	.237	14	59	7	14	19	1	2	0	3	0	0	0	0	3	0	14	4	0
Peake, Allen, Kansas City°	.240	25	75	7	18	25	2	1	1	10	1	2	1	0	15	0	18	0	1
Pena, Jorge, San Diego	.254	35	118	18	30	33	1	1	0	9	0	2	1	1	18	0	15	5	5
Peraza, Oswaldo, Toronto	.218	51	156	20	34	42	2	0	2	13	1	0	0	3	17	0	25	1	1
Perry, Glynn, New York-AL	.156	16	32	4	5	5	0	0	0	5	1	0	1	0	4	0	2	3	0
Perry, Scott, Texas	.000	1	2	0	0	0	0	0	0	0	0	0	0	0	0	0	0	0	0
Pettis, Stacey, Pittsburgh°	.265	11	34	6	9	11	0	1	0	3	1	0	0	1	3	0	8	7	1
Pino, Rolando, Chicago-AL	.217	53	175	33	38	57	12	2	1	20	2	1	5	1	36	0	38	16	6
Pirrucello, Mark, Kansas City°	.342	24	79	10	27	44	7	2	2	12	0	0	2	1	11	0	11	0	0
Piskol, Peter, New York-AL	.307	34	137	20	42	52	7	0	1	19	1	1	1	1	16	0	21	10	1
Portale, Joseph, New York-AL	.286	5	7	1	2	5	0	0	1	0	0	0	0	0	0	0	4	0	0
Porterfield, William, Texas°	.171	19	41	4	7	8	1	0	0	2	0	0	0	6	0	0	15	1	3
Ramos, Luis, Pittsburgh	.296	50	186	31	55	74	10	3	1	18	3	0	2	0	13	0	30	15	3
Reyes, Manuel, Houston	.182	13	22	0	4	4	0	0	0	3	0	0	1	0	4	0	8	2	0
Reynoso, Luis, New York-AL°	.176	11	17	3	3	3	0	0	0	0	0	0	0	0	1	0	6	0	0
Rivas, Pedro, San Diego	.174	60	207	17	36	47	6	1	1	14	5	1	1	3	11	2	55	2	2
Rivera, Jose, Pittsburgh	.292	51	185	24	54	68	7	2	1	23	4	0	3	0	13	0	21	4	3
Rivera, Jose, Chicago-NL°	.261	37	119	16	31	37	2	2	0	7	0	1	0	2	0	0	8	6	5
Roadcap, Steve, Chicago-NL†	.232	36	95	10	22	26	4	0	0	7	2	1	3	0	25	1	28	6	8
Roberts, Leon, Pittsburgh†	.304	6	23	4	7	8	1	0	0	1	0	0	0	0	2	0	4	4	0
Roberts, Jay, Atlanta	.186	58	183	14	34	49	6	3	1	24	5	1	3	1	19	0	60	6	5
Rodriguez, Radhames, Toronto†	.239	40	109	15	26	29	3	0	0	12	2	0	2	0	8	0	16	5	3
Roman, Cesar, Toronto	.272	49	147	18	40	49	9	0	0	16	2	3	1	2	17	0	20	0	1
Rossi, Domingo, Toronto†	.232	47	125	19	29	36	2	1	0	10	0	0	1	1	6	0	18	2	0
Russell, Anthony, New York-AL	.327	29	110	19	36	45	7	1	0	10	1	0	2	2	14	0	15	7	2
Sandry, William, Chicago-AL	.271	59	221	33	60	81	12	3	1	36	2	1	6	2	21	0	22	4	1
Sciacca, Christopher, Chicago-NL†	.204	51	181	11	37	46	3	3	0	21	0	1	3	2	7	0	44	10	5
Sherman, James, Houston	.279	19	68	9	19	27	4	2	0	6	0	0	3	1	11	2	8	3	1
Shuffield, Jack, Kansas City°	.255	61	243	46	62	78	3	5	1	23	1	1	1	1	31	2	30	13	8
Silva, James, New York-AL	.244	39	131	24	32	44	4	1	2	15	1	2	1	2	24	0	24	19	10
Simmons, James, Atlanta°	.244	33	90	19	22	22	0	0	0	3	0	1	0	1	11	1	13	5	3
Simmons, John, Atlanta	.167	7	18	1	3	3	0	0	0	0	0	0	0	0	3	0	4	1	0
Slate, Gregory, Texas	.343	15	35	2	12	12	0	0	0	3	0	0	0	0	5	0	2	0	0
Smith, James, Pittsburgh	.100	10	20	3	2	5	0	0	1	4	0	0	0	0	2	0	7	0	0
Smith, Randy, Kansas City	.167	4	6	1	1	1	0	0	0	0	0	0	0	0	1	0	2	0	0
Sorce, Samuel, Texas	.301	27	83	6	25	36	6	1	1	15	2	1	3	1	6	1	10	2	1
Sorel, Michael, Kansas City	.179	56	207	21	37	40	3	0	0	19	1	4	4	7	0	19	10	4
Speeney, Michael, New York-AL	.167	4	12	1	2	2	0	0	0	0	0	0	0	0	2	0	0	0	0
Stanley, Kevin, Kansas City°	.254	38	130	17	33	45	7	1	1	15	0	2	0	1	18	1	44	2	6
Stock, Kevin, Texas	.289	40	128	20	37	49	5	2	1	16	2	1	0	1	19	0	21	6	4

Player and Club	Pct.	G.	AB.	R.	H.	TB.	2B.	3B.	HR.	RBI.	GW.	SH.	SF.	HP.	BB.	Int. BB.	SO.	SB.	CS.
Stovall, Daryl, Chicago-AL	.105	17	38	1	4	4	0	0	0	1	0	0	0	0	8	0	13	0	0
Sturdivant, Darren, Kansas City	.167	24	60	5	10	14	4	0	0	5	0	3	3	1	10	0	17	1	0
Sutton, Mark, Texas	.200	39	95	12	19	24	2	0	1	9	1	4	1	0	12	0	18	1	0
Swinney, Steve, New York-AL°	.345	13	29	5	10	10	0	0	0	2	0	0	0	0	3	0	8	3	1
Swiski, Mark, Texas°	.213	29	75	11	16	21	5	0	0	8	0	1	3	0	21	0	11	2	2
Then, Hediberto, Pittsburgh	.306	43	144	23	44	68	7	1	5	23	0	0	2	6	21	1	24	11	7
Thomas, Andres, Atlanta	.259	44	143	18	37	44	2	1	1	14	0	1	2	0	7	0	20	8	3
Thomas, James, Houston†	.156	14	45	12	7	9	2	0	0	5	0	2	2	0	15	2	5	5	2
Thompson, Randolph, Pittsburgh	.156	18	45	2	7	11	1	0	1	2	0	0	0	0	4	0	19	0	0
Todman, Jens, Chicago-NL°	.235	33	98	11	23	26	1	1	0	14	2	1	2	1	10	1	19	2	4
Torres, Joaquin, Toronto	.261	62	207	32	54	63	5	2	0	16	2	1	1	3	32	0	40	9	5
Tribble, Lawrence, Chicago-NL	.278	46	151	17	42	48	4	1	0	18	1	0	2	1	6	0	18	18	6
Uresti, Guadalupe, Atlanta	.250	6	16	1	4	7	1	1	0	2	0	0	1	1	0	0	7	0	0
Velazquez, Juan, Chicago-NL	.250	33	96	12	24	33	2	2	1	14	2	0	1	0	18	0	13	11	3
Vizcaino, Tomas, Toronto†	.177	48	164	18	29	33	2	1	0	11	0	0	1	0	8	0	40	0	0
Wagner, Jeffrey, Atlanta	.214	37	117	10	25	31	1	1	1	9	1	1	0	2	10	0	33	3	3
Walsh, John, Chicago-AL	.211	48	95	14	20	25	5	0	0	11	2	6	1	1	16	0	20	9	5
Whalen, Larry, Chicago-NL†	.162	28	74	9	12	13	1	0	0	9	1	0	0	3	7	0	25	4	2
White, Marvin, New York-AL	.303	24	66	9	20	24	4	0	0	10	1	0	0	2	7	0	11	3	0
Whitehurst, Willis, Kansas City	.193	50	176	20	34	42	4	2	0	11	2	5	0	0	14	1	47	10	3
Williams, Kenneth, Chicago-AL	.298	31	104	19	31	38	2	1	1	11	2	1	2	1	10	0	27	9	4
Williams, Millard, New York-AL°	.200	5	5	0	1	1	0	0	0	1	0	0	0	0	1	0	2	0	0
Wilson, Lawrence, Chicago-NL	.244	17	41	3	10	12	0	1	0	5	1	0	1	0	1	0	8	6	1
Young, Stephen, Chicago-NL	.333	10	3	0	1	1	0	0	0	1	0	0	0	0	0	0	0	0	0

The following pitchers, listed alphabetically by club, with games in parentheses, had no plate appearances, primarily through use of designated hitters:

ATLANTA—Bormann, Michael (9); Britt, Wesley (15); Lineres, Felix (9); Maddock, Jim (11); Mehalko, Andrew (5); Melliand, James (4); Mortillaro, John (7); Napoleon, Esteban (11); Perez, Otilio (15); Rogers, Randy (14); Rosario, Maximo (10); Seitz, John (2); Sierra, Julio (10); Van Gennep, John (8); Ward, Duane (8).

CHICAGO-AL—Blanco, Domingo (7); Butler, Gregory (12); Concepcion, Jose (16); Correa, Edwin (10); Devincenzo, Richard (12); Gonzales, Gary (10); Howard, Fred (2); McKeon, Joel (4); Plasensia, Omar (4); Ruckebeil, Mark (10); Stacey, Shawn (10); Storer, Kevin (14); Taylor, Robert (14); Trujillo, Michael (1).

CHICAGO-NL—Adams, Andrew (15); Baker, Mark (10); Blevins, Bradley (3); Brown, Kelly (8); DeLeon, Socrates (13); German, Rene (12); Gordon, Rocetto (8); Moore, Edmund (3); Moore, Richard (21); Schwarz, Jeffrey (11); Trotter, Gregory (12); Volkman, John (11).

HOUSTON—Alburquerque, Claude (16); Ambrose, James (5); Blas, William (3); Corniel, Rafael (24); Espinoza, Ernesto (15); Heredia, Geysi (8); Lucas, Arbrey (7); Moore, Sam (13); Ortiz, Antonio (13); Polemir, Miguel (4); Severino, Leandro (12); Strasser, Richard (10); Traylor, Steven (9); Troncoso, Martin (13).

KANSAS CITY—Aube, Brian (3); Cusey, Michael (12); Czosek, David (21); Debord, Robert (16); Drizmala, Thomas (7); Leonard, Dennis (1); Morales, Edwin (13); Potestio, Douglas (13); Prado, Felipe (8); Sanchez, Israel (12); Serritella, John (11); Sielicki, Richard (12); Sparling, Donald (3); Steinberg, Scott (10); Walsh, James (12).

PITTSBURGH—Boren, Douglas (5); Catlett, Justin (8); Colina, Edgar (10); Cooke, John (4); Delarosa, David (3); Dryden, Jeffrey (8); Estrella, Orlando (9); Gonzales, Jose (3); Grudzinski, Gary (10); Holman, Shawn (7); Leon, Felix (7); Marte, Juan (1); Marty, Charles (1); Moronto, Orlando (7); Mott, Richard (7); Navarro, Francisco (5); Pol, Frank (9); Sanchez, Leopoldo (11); Simmons, Scott (7); Stanton, Bernard (9); Stinnett, James (8); Stone, Shawn (12).

NEW YORK-AL—Baldwin, John (5); Banes, David (6); Beahan, Scot (12); Bersano, Mark (9); Brock, Joe (2); Bryant, John (5); Compagno, Steven (3); Cruz, Pablo (1); Fletcher, Joseph (12); Herrera, Henry (14); Humphrey, Daryl (13); Inman, Ronald (3); Lewis, Larry (6); Marks, Jeffrey (3); Milton, Prescott (11); Nichols, Earl (2); Stidham, Clayton (9); Troester, Scott (13); Ubiera, Tomas (12).

SAN DIEGO—Patterson, Robert (8); Poston, Mark (2); Rodriguez, Efrain (10); Vazquez, Francisco (3).

TEXAS—Bass, Barry (6); Buckley, John (12); Clark, Robert (13); Dersin, Eric (6); Gordon, Kenneth (13); Guzman, Jose (12); Hendrick, Francisco (6); Hopkins, David (12); Johnson, Terrance (10); Joslin, Christopher (10); Kramer, Randall (2); Maki, Timothy (6); Mayfield, Montye (9); McLin, Larry (2); Rogers, Kenneth (2); Shulte, Todd (11); Ubri, Ramon (1); Waldron, Jose (6); Winbush, Michael (6); Zwolensky, Mitchell (9).

TORONTO—Alexander, Arsenio (13); Aquino, Luis (13); Castro, Eddy (9); Duncan, Ricky (10); Echarry, Ventura (14); Espinosa, Julio (15); Liendo, Dimas (14); Malave, Benito (9); Martinez, Juan (3); Mesa, Jose (13); Montana, Rick (10).

GRAND SLAM HOME RUNS—Daugherty, Kelly, McGriff, Nieves, Peskol, Pirruccello, Roberts, Sandry, 1 each.

AWARDED FIRST BASE ON CATCHER'S INTERFERENCE—Cox 2 (Diaz, Rivas); Daugherty (Denis); Roadcap (Diaz); Sorrell (Slate).

CLUB FIELDING

Club	Pct.	G.	PO.	A.	E.	DP.	PB.	Club	Pct.	G.	PO.	A.	E.	DP.	PB.
Texas	.958	63	1623	750	104	38	6	New York-AL	.943	63	1624	687	139	37	16
Toronto	.957	63	1598	670	103	34	16	Chicago-NL	.942	63	1581	661	137	46	18
Atlanta	.952	63	1583	694	114	50	10	Pittsburgh	.941	62	1602	662	143	54	9
Kansas City	.952	63	1676	785	123	52	26	San Diego	.936	63	1579	634	151	49	22
Chicago-AL	.946	63	1616	700	133	51	17	Houston	.926	62	1585	705	183	52	16

Triple Plays—Chicago-NL, Houston.

INDIVIDUAL FIELDING

FIRST BASEMEN

°Throws lefthanded.

Player and Club	Pct.	G.	PO.	A.	E.	DP.	Player and Club	Pct.	G.	PO.	A.	E.	DP.
Aaron, Atlanta	1.000	7	21	2	0	1	Goodman, Chicago-NL	1.000	1	5	1	0	0
Antonetty, Houston	.962	12	120	7	5	5	Griffin, Atlanta	.979	61	522	41	12	46
Aruca, Houston	.978	24	199	25	5	14	Holecek, Chicago-NL	.981	19	154	4	3	12
Atwood, Chicago-NL	1.000	4	23	1	0	2	Johnson, Chicago-AL°	.962	29	244	10	10	24
Battle, Pittsburgh	.982	12	102	8	2	11	McGriff, New York-AL°	.986	62	514	56	8	31
Bonilla, Pittsburgh	.962	43	318	36	14	30	McReddie, Texas°	.991	28	200	15	2	12
Brennan, Texas	.991	36	298	23	3	13	Moreno, San Diego	1.000	1	5	0	0	0
Brittman, Kansas City°	.988	16	145	13	2	6	Morin, Houston	.968	28	200	11	7	19
Carmona, Toronto	.966	5	27	1	1	1	Nieves, San Diego	.981	5	48	4	1	2
Cox, New York-AL	1.000	1	6	0	0	0	Peake, Kansas City°	1.000	24	219	8	0	19
Daugherty, San Diego	.951	17	130	7	7	14	Peraza, Toronto	1.000	1	4	0	0	0
Denis, Houston	1.000	1	2	0	0	1	Perry, New York-AL	.800	2	4	0	1	0
Diaz, Toronto	.935	3	29	0	2	3	Porterfield, Texas°	1.000	17	122	12	0	7
Dollar, Toronto	1.000	2	14	0	0	2	Rivas, San Diego	.979	40	315	15	7	23
Estrada, San Diego	1.000	3	18	3	0	0	Rodriguez, Toronto	1.000	1	4	0	0	0
FERNANDEZ, Toronto°	.991	58	541	20	5	28	Sandry, Chicago-AL	.981	35	290	24	6	20
Freidhof, Kansas City	.979	27	272	9	6	22	Stovall, Chicago-AL	.944	4	17	0	1	1
Frierson, San Diego	1.000	1	11	1	0	1	Thompson, Pittsburgh	.981	16	100	4	2	3
Garcia, Chicago-NL	.987	41	368	20	5	27							

SECOND BASEMEN

Player and Club	Pct.	G.	PO.	A.	E.	DP.	Player and Club	Pct.	G.	PO.	A.	E.	DP.
Ambrosino, Texas	.926	28	44	69	9	10	M. Martinez, Pittsburgh	.953	36	97	85	9	18
Austin, Pittsburgh	1.000	1	0	1	0	0	Nelson, New York-AL	.945	62	128	149	16	22
Bachmeier, Chicago-NL	.952	29	57	62	6	9	Pena, San Diego	.957	33	60	72	6	13
Capellan, Chicago-AL	.778	3	3	4	2	0	Perry, Texas	1.000	1	0	1	0	0
Davila, Kansas City	.973	10	23	13	1	4	Roberts, Pittsburgh	1.000	6	14	15	0	2
Espinal, Houston	.935	13	21	37	4	4	Roman, Toronto	.923	47	84	97	15	15
Estrada, San Diego	.925	33	56	79	11	14	Rossi, Toronto	1.000	3	2	1	0	0
Foit, Texas	1.000	5	13	11	0	3	Sorel, Kansas City	.938	56	139	179	21	37
Garcia, Houston	1.000	1	0	1	0	0	Stock, Texas	.949	14	23	14	2	1
Gautier, Atlanta	.928	18	37	27	5	10	Sutton, Texas	.910	29	39	62	10	11
Healy, Pittsburgh	.917	24	50	50	9	9	Thomas, Houston	.963	14	36	42	3	14
Jabalera, Houston	.933	27	68	58	9	16	Tribble, Chicago-NL	.911	8	16	25	4	5
Jones, Chicago-NL	.940	27	65	60	8	13	Vizcaino, Toronto	.962	23	28	48	3	4
Keeton, Chicago-AL	.954	51	140	110	12	23	Walsh, Chicago-AL	.953	19	28	33	3	7
Lautaret, Houston	.877	11	28	22	7	6	White, New York-AL	1.000	1	0	1	0	0
LOWE, Atlanta	.976	56	120	125	6	26	Wilson, Chicago-NL	1.000	3	1	4	0	0
L. Martinez, Pittsburgh	.857	3	4	2	1	0							

Triple Play—Wilson.

THIRD BASEMEN

Player and Club	Pct.	G.	PO.	A.	E.	DP.	Player and Club	Pct.	G.	PO.	A.	E.	DP.
Ambrosino, Texas	1.000	1	2	1	0	0	Lopez, Pittsburgh	.800	2	2	2	1	0
Battle, Pittsburgh	.923	17	16	32	4	1	L. Martinez, Pittsburgh	1.000	1	1	1	0	0
Borowski, New York-AL	.636	6	3	4	4	0	Mercedes, Atlanta	.829	31	22	41	13	3
Cannon, San Diego	.880	44	41	98	19	10	Miller, Houston	.832	37	43	56	20	1
Carden, Atlanta	.894	41	35	75	13	3	Monson, Kansas City	.892	63	58	140	24	10
Carmona, Toronto	.769	7	6	4	3	0	Nadal, Houston	.855	23	16	37	9	3
CHRISTENSON, Chicago-AL	.951	59	43	131	9	7	Piskol, New York-AL	.889	7	8	8	2	1
Cunningham, Pittsburgh	.742	9	4	19	8	0	Rivas, San Diego	.500	1	0	1	1	0
Curry, Texas	.667	6	4	4	4	0	Rodriquez, Toronto	.919	32	30	49	7	4
Dunston, Chicago-NL	.891	23	11	46	7	2	Rossi, Toronto	.912	35	35	68	10	2
Estrada, San Diego	.803	20	15	38	13	4	Sciacca, Chicago-NL	.908	19	14	45	6	3
A. Garcia, Chicago-NL	.800	1	1	3	1	0	Stock, Texas	.867	29	13	59	11	1
P. Garcia, Houston	.846	4	3	8	2	1	Swiski, Texas	.794	26	13	37	13	4
Hennessey, Texas	.839	14	3	23	5	1	Then, Pittsburgh	.872	40	32	70	15	5
Howard, New York-AL	.871	36	26	62	13	4	Tribble, Chicago-NL	.843	24	18	57	14	4
Hunsuker, Chicago-AL	.842	12	6	10	3	0	Walsh, Chicago-AL	.875	2	3	4	1	1
Lautaret, Houston	.643	5	1	8	5	0	White, New York-AL	.796	22	17	22	10	1

Triple Plays—Miller, Tribble.

SHORTSTOPS

Player and Club	Pct.	G.	PO.	A.	E.	DP.	Player and Club	Pct.	G.	PO.	A.	E.	DP.
Capellan, Chicago-AL	.900	18	10	26	4	1	Mayse, Atlanta	.842	11	13	19	6	6
Davila, Kansas City	.888	19	20	51	9	8	Meyer, Atlanta	.927	16	24	27	4	5
Del Rosario, San Diego	.834	58	65	131	39	19	Miranda, Houston	.800	9	10	26	9	3
Dunston, Chicago-NL	.887	29	50	83	17	12	Nadal, Houston	.765	8	6	7	4	1
Estrada, San Diego	.900	7	7	11	2	0	Pino, Chicago-AL	.856	53	75	163	40	26
Foit, Texas	.946	38	41	118	9	14	Piskol, New York-AL	.924	26	34	75	9	8
Garcia, Houston	.855	48	51	162	36	23	Rivera, Pittsburgh	.916	46	62	124	17	21
Gergen, Texas	.930	23	28	79	8	7	Rodriquez, Toronto	.844	7	5	22	5	2
Healy, Pittsburgh	.625	2	2	3	3	0	Sciacca, Chicago-NL	.874	31	49	83	19	17
Howard, New York-AL	.971	10	14	19	1	2	Speeney, New York-AL	.741	4	8	12	7	3
Infante, Toronto	.970	36	47	117	5	12	Sutton, Texas	.977	11	10	33	1	0
Jabalera, Houston	1.000	1	3	2	0	0	Thomas, Atlanta	.908	44	61	136	20	19
Keeton, Chicago-AL	.917	5	9	13	2	4	Vizcaino, Toronto	.897	27	36	68	12	8
Kelly, New York-AL	.868	28	46	79	19	7	WHITEHURST, Kansas City	.922	50	70	155	19	17
Khalifa, Pittsburgh	.905	6	12	26	4	5	Wilson, Chicago-NL	.923	7	7	17	2	3
L. Martinez, Pittsburgh	.854	11	11	30	7	5							

Triple Play—Sciacca.

OUTFIELDERS

Player and Club	Pct.	G.	PO.	A.	E.	DP.	Player and Club	Pct.	G.	PO.	A.	E.	DP.
Aaron, Atlanta	.906	22	28	1	3	0	DeLaRosa, Texas	.850	12	15	2	3	0
Alcantara, Texas	1.000	6	4	0	0	0	DesJarden, Kansas City°	.929	31	49	3	4	0
Allen, Kansas City	.911	35	69	3	7	1	Dophied, Houston	.909	3	9	1	1	0
Allison, Texas	1.000	21	32	1	0	0	Elwess, Chicago-NL	.982	29	49	5	1	0
Aquino, Texas°	1.000	7	10	1	0	0	Esser, Texas	.951	25	39	0	2	0
Aruca, Houston	.978	19	36	8	1	4	Fernandez, Toronto°	1.000	5	5	0	0	0
Aubin, Pittsburgh	1.000	8	8	0	0	1	Garcia, Houston	.800	4	4	0	1	0
Austin, Pittsburgh	1.000	4	9	1	0	1	Goodman, Chicago-NL	.962	24	48	3	2	1
Barringer, Pittsburgh	.750	2	3	0	1	0	Grullon, Pittsburgh	.909	8	8	2	1	0
Ben, Texas	.943	30	29	4	2	1	Guance, Toronto	.667	1	2	0	1	0
Boderick, Chicago-NL	.966	55	109	3	4	0	Hennessey, Texas	.857	5	5	1	1	0
Bolivar, Toronto	.967	62	139	6	5	0	Hermsen, Pittsburgh	1.000	1	1	0	0	0
Botkin, Houston	.963	33	69	10	3	2	Hernandez, Chicago-AL	.789	17	14	1	4	0
Brim, Texas	.667	11	4	0	2	0	Hodge, Houston	.922	58	87	8	8	2
Brower, Texas	1.000	32	53	3	0	0	Isaac, Houston	.968	39	85	5	3	0
Brown, Pittsburgh	.895	21	32	2	4	1	Johnson, Chicago-NL	.833	7	9	1	2	0
Carter, New York-AL	.958	34	66	2	3	0	Jones, Chicago-AL°	.919	22	33	1	3	0
C. Castillo, San Diego	.927	30	34	4	3	0	Kelly, New York-AL	1.000	1	1	0	0	0
T. Castillo, Toronto	.953	59	93	8	5	0	Kohler, Texas°	1.000	5	7	0	0	0
Coleman, San Diego	1.000	33	57	5	0	2	Lane, Houston	.909	18	19	1	2	0
Coss, Pittsburgh	.957	28	64	3	3	1	Lora, Atlanta	.948	47	104	5	6	2
Cox, New York-AL	1.000	22	25	4	0	1	Mace, Texas	.983	37	54	4	1	1
Cunningham, New York-AL	.909	40	46	4	5	0	MacKay, New York-AL	.951	42	68	10	4	1
Curry, Texas	1.000	20	16	2	0	0	Marrero, Chicago-NL	1.000	14	20	0	0	0
Daugherty, San Diego	.980	25	45	4	1	3	J. Martinez, Toronto	1.000	1	1	0	0	0

OUTFIELDERS—Continued

Player and Club	Pct.	G.	PO.	A.	E.	DP.
Martino, Kansas City	1.000	10	13	0	0	0
Massiah, Pittsburgh	.952	40	76	3	4	2
McGee, Chicago-AL	.966	56	82	3	3	1
McLaughlin, Chicago-AL	.971	61	93	6	3	2
Miranda, Houston	.000	1	0	0	1	0
Moncada, Pittsburgh	.960	37	68	4	3	2
MORRIS, Atlanta	.978	60	127	6	3	2
Nodell, San Diego	.941	46	74	6	5	0
Nunez, San Diego°	.975	60	109	9	3	1
Palmer, Kansas City	1.000	5	2	0	0	0
Palmore, Kansas City	.939	13	26	5	2	3
Perry, New York-AL	1.000	6	9	2	0	1
Pettis, Pittsburgh	.889	9	16	0	2	0
Ramos, Pittsburgh	.961	46	88	11	4	1
Reynoso, New York-AL	1.000	2	1	0	0	0
Rivera, Chicago-NL°	.969	34	60	3	2	1
Roberts, Atlanta	1.000	8	13	0	0	0
Rossi, Toronto	.667	1	2	0	1	0
Russell, New York-AL	.944	26	41	2	3	0
Sherman, Houston	.974	19	36	1	1	0
Shuffield, Kansas City°	.975	61	104	11	3	1
Silva, New York-AL	.986	35	68	5	1	0
Ja. Simmons, Atlanta	.975	32	36	3	1	1
Jo. Simmons, Atlanta	1.000	3	4	0	0	0
Smith, Kansas City	.800	3	4	0	1	0
Sorce, Texas	1.000	12	13	0	0	0
Stanley, Kansas City°	.934	38	54	3	4	1
Stovall, Chicago-AL	1.000	6	4	0	0	0
Todman, Chicago-NL°	.906	15	27	2	3	1
Torres, Toronto	.964	62	103	4	4	0
Wagner, Atlanta	.960	36	41	7	2	1
Walsh, Chicago-AL	.900	19	17	1	2	1
Whalen, Chicago-NL	.957	26	40	4	2	2
Williams, Chicago-AL	1.000	29	61	2	0	1
Wilson, Chicago-NL	1.000	1	1	0	0	0

Triple Plays—Botkin, Goodman.

CATCHERS

Player and Club	Pct.	G.	PO.	A.	E.	DP.	PB.
Achique, Toronto	1.000	2	2	0	0	0	0
Baker, Pittsburgh	.972	24	122	15	4	5	3
Brunenkant, Texas	.977	30	181	28	5	1	3
Cardieri, Atlanta	1.000	6	25	7	0	0	0
Davis, Kansas City	.980	29	156	37	4	3	13
Denis, Houston	.966	28	177	21	7	3	4
A. Diaz, Toronto	.979	25	126	14	3	0	9
M. Diaz, Chicago-AL	.949	15	68	7	4	2	4
Dollar, Houston	1.000	5	21	3	0	1	0
Donnelly, Houston	.958	25	137	22	7	0	7
Edwards, Atlanta	.959	24	94	23	5	2	3
Fasola, Pittsburgh	1.000	2	4	3	0	0	0
Ferrer, Pittsburgh	.972	23	116	21	4	0	5
Frierson, San Diego	.946	32	240	24	15	3	14
Giordano, New York-AL	.975	20	101	14	3	1	3
Gonzalez, New York-AL	.977	40	261	37	7	2	9
Hausladen, Texas	.972	27	162	13	5	0	1
Holecek, Chicago-NL	.778	6	7	0	2	0	0
Karkovice, Chicago-AL	.970	53	331	51	12	5	11
Keeton, Chicago-AL	1.000	1	1	4	0	1	0
King, New York-AL	.969	8	56	7	2	0	4
Koch, Chicago-AL	1.000	14	18	5	0	0	2
Locke, Atlanta	.945	9	49	3	3	0	0
Meyer, Atlanta	.833	1	4	1	1	0	0
Mims, Pittsburgh	1.000	6	30	2	0	1	0
Mohl, Pittsburgh	.971	9	64	3	2	1	0
Moreno, San Diego	.963	13	96	8	4	0	1
Nieves, San Diego	.933	4	12	2	1	0	1
Otstot, Atlanta	.987	28	124	32	2	0	6
Oxner, Kansas City	1.000	9	51	9	0	0	1
PERAZA, Toronto	.989	43	229	42	3	1	7
Pirruccello, Kansas City	.952	13	65	15	4	2	1
Portale, New York-AL	1.000	2	14	0	0	0	0
Reyes, Houston	.957	13	40	5	2	0	5
Rivas, San Diego	.970	17	116	12	4	0	6
Roadcap, Chicago-NL	.982	35	194	24	4	2	10
Jo. Simmons, Atlanta	1.000	4	12	3	0	0	0
Slate, Texas	.984	11	57	4	1	1	1
Smith, Pittsburgh	.953	10	35	6	2	0	1
Sorce, Texas	1.000	10	58	6	0	2	1
Sturdivant, Kansas City	.969	23	112	14	4	1	11
Tribble, Chicago-NL	1.000	3	10	3	0	0	0
Uresti, Atlanta	1.000	6	37	6	0	0	1
Velazquez, Chicago-NL	.934	31	147	22	12	0	8

Triple Plays—Dennis, Holecek.

PITCHERS

Player and Club	Pct.	G.	PO.	A.	E.	DP.
Adams, Chicago-NL	.875	15	4	3	1	0
Albuquerque, Houston	1.000	16	3	11	0	1
Alexander, Toronto	.889	13	2	6	1	0
Ambrose, Houston	1.000	5	0	3	0	0
Aquino, Toronto	1.000	13	3	12	0	0
Baker, Chicago-NL	1.000	10	3	10	0	0
Baldwin, New York-AL°	.750	5	2	1	1	0
Banes, New York-AL	.929	6	4	9	1	0
Bass, Texas	1.000	6	1	7	0	0
Beahan, New York-AL	.960	12	6	18	1	0
Bersano, New York-AL	.750	9	1	5	2	0
Blanco, Chicago-AL	1.000	7	1	0	0	0
Blas, Houston	1.000	3	0	3	0	0
Blevins, Chicago-NL	1.000	3	0	3	0	0
Boren, Pittsburgh	.667	5	1	1	1	0
Bormann, Atlanta	.824	9	3	11	3	2
Britt, Atlanta	1.000	15	1	5	0	0
Brown, Chicago-NL	.500	8	0	1	1	0
Bryant, New York-AL	1.000	5	1	2	0	0
Buckley, Texas	.900	12	3	6	1	0
Butler, Chicago-AL	1.000	12	10	12	0	1
Callahan, San Diego	.875	16	4	10	2	1
Castro, Toronto	.500	5	0	1	1	0
Catlett, Pittsburgh	.857	8	2	10	2	0
Christy, San Diego	.875	9	2	5	1	0
Clark, Texas°	.962	13	1	24	1	0
Coleman, San Diego	1.000	17	2	7	0	1
Colina, Pittsburgh	1.000	10	1	4	0	0
Collins, San Diego	1.000	19	5	4	0	0
Compagno, New York-AL°	1.000	3	0	2	0	0
Concepcion, Chicago-AL	1.000	16	1	4	0	0
Cooke, Pittsburgh	1.000	4	3	4	0	0
Corniel, Houston	.800	24	2	6	2	1
Correa, Chicago-AL	.923	10	5	7	1	1
Cusey, Kansas City	.923	12	2	10	1	0
Czosek, Kansas City	.947	21	2	16	1	2
Daniels, San Diego	.917	13	2	9	1	2
DeLeon, Chicago-NL	.750	13	2	1	1	0
Debord, Kansas City	1.000	16	4	3	0	0
DelRosario, San Diego	.857	9	3	3	1	0
DEVINCENZO, Chicago-AL°	1.000	12	5	21	0	1
Drizmala, Kansas City°	.833	7	1	4	1	0
Dryden, Pittsburgh	1.000	8	0	3	0	1
Duncan, Toronto	.895	10	1	16	2	1
Echarry, Toronto	.900	14	1	8	1	0
E. Espinoza, Houston	.818	16	12	24	8	1
J. Espinoza, Toronto	.955	15	4	17	1	1
Estrella, Pittsburgh	.833	9	3	2	1	0
Fletcher, New York-AL	.824	12	3	11	3	0
German, Chicago-NL	.957	12	2	20	1	2
G. Gonzales, Chicago-AL	.600	10	1	2	2	1
J. Gonzales, Pittsburgh	1.000	3	0	2	0	0
K. Gordon, Texas	.875	13	0	7	1	0
R. Gordon, Chicago-NL	.667	8	0	2	1	1
Grudzinski, Pittsburgh	1.000	10	5	4	0	0
Guzman, Texas	1.000	12	2	14	0	0
Harkins, San Diego	.952	13	2	18	1	0
Henderson, Toronto	1.000	8	1	1	0	0
Hendrick, Texas	1.000	6	0	1	0	0
Heredia, Houston	.857	8	1	5	1	0
Herrera, New York-AL	.778	14	3	4	2	1
Holman, Pittsburgh	1.000	7	3	7	0	0
Hopkins, Texas	1.000	12	9	12	0	3
Howard, Chicago-AL	1.000	2	0	1	0	0
Humphrey, New York-AL	.974	13	14	23	1	1
Inman, New York-AL°	.857	3	0	6	1	0
Johnson, Texas°	1.000	10	4	14	0	0
Joslin, Texas°	.857	10	3	3	1	0
Leon, Pittsburgh°	1.000	7	1	2	0	0
Leonard, Kansas City	1.000	1	0	1	0	0
Lewis, New York-AL	.857	6	2	10	2	0
Liendo, Toronto	.778	14	4	10	4	0
Lineres, Atlanta	1.000	9	3	5	0	0
Lucas, Houston	.889	7	3	5	1	1
Maddock, Atlanta°	.941	11	4	12	1	1
Maki, Texas	1.000	6	1	4	0	0
Malave, Toronto	.571	9	0	4	3	1
Marks, New York-AL°	1.000	3	0	1	0	0
Marty, Pittsburgh	1.000	1	1	4	0	0
Mayfield, Texas	.800	9	2	2	1	1
McClain, San Diego	.926	13	2	23	2	1
McKeon, Chicago-AL°	1.000	4	0	5	0	0
McLin, Texas°	1.000	12	3	8	0	1
Mehalko, Chicago-AL°	1.000	1	0	1	0	0
Melliand, Atlanta	1.000	4	1	7	0	0
Mesa, Houston	1.000	13	15	10	1	0
Milton, New York-AL	.917	11	5	6	1	0
Montana, Toronto°	1.000	10	1	3	0	0

PITCHERS—Continued

Player and Club	Pct.	G.	PO.	A.	E.	DP.	Player and Club	Pct.	G.	PO.	A.	E.	DP.
E. Moore, Chicago-NL	1.000	3	1	3	0	0	Shulte, Texas°	1.000	11	0	3	0	0
R. Moore, Chicago-NL	1.000	21	2	4	0	0	Sielicki, Kansas City	1.000	12	1	15	0	4
S. Moore, Houston	.947	13	4	14	1	0	Sierra, Atlanta	.889	10	1	7	1	2
Morales, Kansas City	1.000	13	1	8	0	0	Simmons, Pittsburgh°	.833	7	1	4	1	1
Moronta, Pittsburgh	1.000	7	0	4	0	0	Sorce, Texas	1.000	1	0	1	0	0
Mortillaro, Atlanta°	.900	7	3	6	1	0	Sparling, Kansas City	1.000	3	1	2	0	0
Mott, Pittsburgh	.667	7	1	1	1	0	Stacey, Chicago-AL	.833	10	0	5	1	0
Napoleon, Atlanta	1.000	11	3	7	0	0	Stanton, Pittsburgh	.667	9	0	2	1	0
Navarro, Pittsburgh	1.000	5	4	1	0	1	Steinberg, Kansas City	1.000	10	1	5	0	1
Ortiz, Houston	1.000	13	1	2	0	0	Stidham, New York-AL	.857	9	2	4	1	0
Palencia, Toronto	1.000	13	0	8	0	0	Stone, Pittsburgh	.846	12	4	7	2	1
Patterson, San Diego	.875	8	0	7	1	0	Storer, Chicago-AL	.833	14	1	9	2	0
Perez, Atlanta	1.000	15	2	6	0	0	Strasser, Houston	.870	10	6	14	3	1
Pol, Pittsburgh	.833	9	1	9	2	0	Taylor, Chicago-AL	.885	14	2	21	3	1
Polemir, Houston	1.000	4	1	3	0	0	Traylor, Houston°	.556	9	1	4	4	1
Poston, San Diego	1.000	2	0	2	0	0	Troester, New York-AL	.917	13	5	6	1	1
Potestio, Kansas City	.947	13	5	13	1	0	Troncoso, Houston	.955	13	8	13	1	0
Prado, Kansas City	1.000	8	1	1	0	0	Trotter, Chicago-NL	.900	12	2	16	2	3
Rodriguez, San Diego	1.000	10	3	12	0	0	Trujillo, Chicago-AL	1.000	1	0	2	0	0
K. Rogers, Texas°	1.000	2	0	1	0	0	Ubiera, New York-AL	.667	12	3	5	4	0
R. Rogers, Atlanta°	1.000	14	1	7	0	0	Van Gennep, Atlanta	.900	8	5	4	1	1
Rosario, Atlanta°	.857	10	1	11	2	1	Volkman, Chicago-NL	.857	11	0	6	1	0
Ruckebeil, Chicago-AL	1.000	10	0	2	0	0	Waldron, Texas	1.000	6	1	4	0	0
I. Sanchez, Kansas City°	.870	12	3	17	3	1	Walsh, Kansas City	1.000	12	1	6	0	0
L. Sanchez, Pittsburgh°	.778	11	0	7	2	0	Ward, Atlanta	1.000	8	2	10	0	1
Schwarz, Chicago-NL	.625	11	3	2	3	0	Winbush, Texas	1.000	6	0	7	0	1
Seitz, Atlanta	1.000	2	0	1	0	0	Young, Chicago-NL°	1.000	10	2	9	0	0
Serritella, Kansas City	.947	11	2	16	1	0	Zwolensky, Texas	1.000	9	1	2	0	0
Severino, Houston	1.000	12	2	4	0	0							

The following players do not have any recorded accepted chances at the positions indicated; therefore, are not listed in the fielding averages for those particular positions: Atwood, of; Aube, of, p; Ben, 1b; Brock, p; Carmona, of; Cunningham, p; DeLaRosa, p; Dersin, p; M. Diaz, p; Dollar, of; Guance, 2b; Infante, 2b; Kramer, p; Marte, p; Martinez, p; Morin, of; Nichols, p; Peraza, p; Perry, p; Plasensia, p; Rivera, 3b; Roman, c; Rossi, p; Stinnett, p; Swinney, of; Ubri, p; Vazquez, p.

CLUB PITCHING

Club	ERA.	G.	CG.	ShO.	Sv.	IP.	H.	R.	ER.	HR.	HB.	BB.	Int. BB.	SO.	WP.	Bk.
Texas	2.53	63	5	6	11	541.0	478	225	152	10	17	199	4	449	30	10
New York-AL	2.66	63	16	3	7	541.1	472	249	160	18	18	261	4	407	40	6
Chicago-NL	2.95	63	15	7	8	527.0	474	259	173	21	20	178	1	331	33	11
Atlanta	3.22	63	11	5	12	527.2	508	237	189	13	14	207	9	338	36	13
Chicago-AL	3.34	63	24	5	6	538.2	501	261	200	20	26	240	9	405	34	9
Pittsburgh	3.35	62	7	4	7	534.0	511	281	199	16	17	246	3	345	29	9
Toronto	3.40	63	17	7	2	532.2	466	268	201	14	18	210	1	340	40	20
San Diego	3.44	63	17	3	7	526.1	516	285	201	15	28	232	3	442	30	7
Kansas City	3.46	63	3	4	9	558.2	577	295	215	16	18	237	7	363	48	13
Houston	4.14	62	11	2	2	528.1	557	361	243	14	31	218	8	359	28	13

PITCHERS' RECORDS
(Leading Qualifiers for Earned-Run Average Leadership—50 or More Innings)

°Throws lefthanded.

Pitcher—Club	W.	L.	Pct.	ERA.	G.	GS.	CG.	GF.	ShO.	Sv.	IP.	H.	R.	ER.	HR.	HB.	BB.	Int. BB.	SO.	WP.
Hopkins, Texas	3	1	.750	1.67	12	6	0	2	0	0	54	45	13	10	1	2	21	0	37	2
Young, Chicago-NL°	5	2	.714	1.73	10	9	2	0	0	0	67.2	43	19	13	5	2	13	0	50	4
DeVincenzo, Chicago-AL°	9	1	.900	1.98	12	11	8	0	1	0	86.1	59	21	19	3	0	27	2	94	1
Duncan, Toronto	5	1	.833	2.04	10	9	1	0	1	0	61.2	50	19	14	1	1	23	0	36	2
Troncoso, Houston	5	4	.556	2.04	13	6	1	6	0	0	61.2	59	23	14	2	2	22	2	23	1
Clark, Texas°	6	3	.667	2.05	13	8	1	2	0	0	61.1	56	24	14	0	0	15	1	54	4
Guzman, Texas	5	4	.556	2.18	12	9	1	2	0	0	66	51	21	16	3	1	13	0	42	2
Potestio, Kansas City	3	3	.500	2.22	13	2	0	7	0	0	56.2	56	24	14	2	2	16	0	41	4
Van Gennep, Atlanta	2	2	.500	2.26	8	8	2	0	1	0	51.2	40	22	13	2	1	12	0	24	1
Beahan, New York-AL	7	1	.875	2.32	12	12	4	0	1	0	77.2	50	25	20	2	5	55	0	73	3

Departmental Leaders: G—Corniel, 24; GS—E. Espinosa, Harkins, S. Moore, 13; CG—DeVincenzo, Taylor, 8; GF—Corniel, R. Moore, 20; ShO—Mesa, 3; W—DeVincenzo, Humphrey, 9; L—E. Espinosa, Harkins, 9; Pct.—DeVincenzo, .900; Sv—Perez, 6; IP—Taylor, 95.1; H—Taylor, 100; R—E. Espinosa, 63; ER—E. Espinosa, 42; HR—Butler, Fletcher, Young, 5; HB—Butler, 7; BB—Beahan, 55; IBB—Corniel, Storer, Walsh, 3; SO—DeVincenzo, 94; WP—Montana, 15.

(All Pitchers—Listed Alphabetically)

Pitcher—Club	W.	L.	Pct.	ERA.	G.	GS.	CG.	GF.	ShO.	Sv.	IP.	H.	R.	ER.	HR.	HB.	BB.	Int. BB.	SO.	WP.
Adams, Chicago-NL	5	2	.714	2.06	15	4	1	7	0	3	48	50	26	11	1	0	22	0	30	5
Albuquerque, Houston	0	2	.000	5.63	16	0	0	6	0	0	32	41	33	20	0	3	16	0	21	2
Alexander, Toronto	2	2	.500	4.45	13	3	0	4	0	0	30.1	20	18	15	1	2	21	0	20	3
Ambrose, Houston	0	2	.000	3.38	5	2	0	3	0	0	18.2	15	10	7	0	0	2	0	11	1
Aquino, Toronto	4	7	.364	3.31	13	11	4	2	0	0	73.1	60	33	27	2	2	17	0	52	4
Aube, Kansas City	0	1	.000	47.25	2	0	0	0	0	0	1.1	5	7	7	0	0	2	0	1	1
Baker, Chicago-NL	4	4	.500	2.91	10	8	3	1	1	1	58.2	47	26	19	2	2	16	0	37	3
Baldwin, New York-AL°	1	1	.500	1.00	5	0	0	4	0	1	9	7	4	1	0	0	3	0	10	0
Banes, New York-AL	1	2	.333	1.64	6	6	0	0	0	0	33	30	13	6	1	1	19	0	27	6
Bass, Texas	3	0	1.000	2.18	6	6	1	0	1	0	33	23	9	8	1	0	9	0	28	1
Beahan, New York-AL	7	1	.875	2.32	12	12	4	0	1	0	77.2	50	25	20	2	5	55	0	73	3
Bersano, New York-AL	3	0	1.000	3.12	9	0	0	7	0	1	17.1	19	8	6	0	0	5	1	13	1
Blanco, Chicago-AL	0	0	.000	7.36	7	0	0	4	0	0	7.1	8	7	6	2	1	5	0	2	0
Blas, Houston	0	0	.000	1.13	3	0	0	1	0	1	8	6	4	1	0	0	2	0	6	1
Blevins, Chicago-NL	1	1	.500	2.45	3	3	1	0	0	0	18.1	23	8	5	0	1	6	0	7	0
Boren, Pittsburgh	0	3	.000	4.91	5	0	0	3	0	0	11	20	12	6	0	0	5	0	6	0
Bormann, Atlanta	4	2	.667	2.36	9	8	2	1	1	0	53.1	54	20	14	2	0	10	0	28	2
Britt, Atlanta	1	3	.250	3.55	15	0	0	13	0	4	25.1	27	17	10	1	1	10	2	22	3

Pitcher—Club	W.	L.	Pct.	ERA.	G.	GS.	CG.	GF.	ShO.	Sv.	IP.	H.	R.	ER.	HR.	HB.	BB.	Int. BB.	SO.	WP.
Brock, New York-AL	0	0	.000	5.40	2	0	0	0	0	0	1.2	5	3	1	0	1	2	0	1	0
Brown, Chicago-NL	0	2	.000	10.00	8	0	0	5	0	1	9	19	16	10	0	3	8	1	7	3
Bryant, New York-AL	1	0	1.000	3.65	5	2	0	1	0	1	12.1	8	6	5	0	0	14	0	7	0
Buckley, Texas	1	1	.500	2.63	12	4	0	4	0	2	41	43	23	12	0	0	15	0	35	3
Butler, Chicago-AL	6	3	.667	3.68	12	12	3	0	1	0	80.2	82	44	33	5	7	38	0	42	7
Callahan, San Diego	2	3	.400	3.31	16	3	1	4	0	2	54.1	51	30	20	0	2	23	0	39	4
Castro, Toronto	0	2	.000	4.50	5	0	0	5	0	0	6	5	4	3	1	0	4	0	5	2
Catlett, Pittsburgh	2	3	.400	2.63	8	8	2	0	1	0	41	40	21	12	2	0	15	0	23	0
Christy, San Diego	1	2	.333	3.05	9	4	1	1	1	0	38.1	33	19	13	1	5	19	0	30	0
Clark, Texas°	6	3	.667	2.05	13	8	1	2	0	0	61.1	56	24	14	0	0	15	1	54	4
Coleman, San Diego	4	1	.800	2.45	17	0	0	15	0	3	33	23	11	9	2	1	11	1	46	1
Colina, Pittsburgh	0	2	.000	6.75	10	0	0	7	0	1	14.2	22	11	11	1	0	6	1	6	0
Collins, San Diego	4	1	.800	3.65	19	0	0	19	0	2	24.2	25	12	10	2	3	13	1	22	3
Compagno, New York-AL°	0	0	.000	1.23	3	0	0	2	0	0	7.1	6	3	1	0	0	3	0	8	1
Concepcion, Chicago-AL	1	3	.250	4.28	16	0	0	5	0	2	40	47	23	19	0	0	34	1	31	8
Cooke, Pittsburgh	2	1	.667	3.65	4	0	0	3	0	1	12.1	11	6	5	0	0	3	0	9	2
Corniel, Houston	2	6	.250	3.93	24	0	0	20	0	1	36.2	44	33	16	1	2	14	3	29	2
Correa, Chicago-AL	5	2	.714	2.75	10	8	1	1	0	0	59	40	23	18	0	4	27	0	53	3
Cunningham, Pittsburgh	0	0	.000	0.00	3	0	0	2	0	0	3.2	2	1	0	0	2	3	0	1	0
Cusey, Kansas City	3	3	.500	4.26	12	12	0	0	0	0	57	65	34	27	2	4	21	0	20	5
Czosek, Kansas City	1	4	.200	3.30	21	0	0	19	0	1	30	31	12	11	0	0	14	2	17	1
Daniels, San Diego	5	4	.556	3.33	13	12	2	0	0	0	73	59	39	27	2	1	46	0	73	5
DeLeon, Chicago-NL	0	2	.000	5.16	13	0	0	6	0	0	29.2	42	24	17	3	1	6	0	9	1
Debord, Kansas City	4	2	.667	1.89	16	0	0	12	0	2	38	34	13	8	1	0	8	1	29	0
DelRosario, San Diego	0	1	.000	7.56	9	1	0	5	0	0	16.2	20	16	14	3	2	12	0	4	0
DeLaRosa, Pittsburgh	0	0	.000	13.50	3	0	0	2	0	0	4	6	6	6	0	0	3	0	1	0
Dersin, Texas	1	1	.500	9.39	6	0	0	2	0	0	7.2	11	9	8	0	2	4	0	5	1
DeVincenzo, Chicago-AL°	9	1	.900	1.98	12	11	8	0	1	0	86.1	59	21	19	3	0	27	2	94	1
Diaz, Chicago-AL	0	0	.000	4.50	1	0	0	1	0	0	2	2	1	1	0	0	2	0	1	1
Drizmala, Kansas City°	4	0	1.000	1.07	7	3	1	1	0	1	33.2	16	6	4	0	0	13	0	43	3
Dryden, Pittsburgh	1	2	.333	2.96	8	4	0	3	0	1	27.1	25	10	9	1	3	14	0	15	5
Duncan, Toronto	5	1	.833	2.04	10	9	1	0	1	0	61.2	50	19	14	1	1	23	0	36	2
Echarry, Toronto	0	2	.000	3.77	14	1	0	8	0	0	31	37	22	13	2	1	13	0	16	2
E. Espinoza, Houston	3	9	.250	4.83	15	13	3	0	1	0	78.1	84	63	42	0	4	35	0	50	4
J. Espinoza, Toronto	6	8	.429	3.07	15	12	5	3	2	1	88	75	37	30	3	1	21	1	65	2
Estrella, Pittsburgh	2	1	.667	3.62	9	3	0	4	0	0	32.1	28	14	13	2	1	18	0	22	2
Fernandez, Toronto	0	0	.000	0.00	1	0	0	1	0	0	2.1	1	0	0	0	0	0	0	3	0
Fletcher, New York-AL	6	5	.545	3.03	12	12	3	0	0	0	74.1	56	35	25	5	1	40	1	61	7
German, Chicago-NL	5	4	.556	2.70	12	11	3	0	1	0	76.2	62	32	23	1	2	12	0	41	2
G. Gonzales, Chicago-AL	2	3	.400	4.98	10	6	1	3	0	0	34.1	39	27	19	1	2	20	0	24	5
J. Gonzales, Pittsburgh	0	0	.000	4.00	3	0	0	0	0	0	9	13	7	4	0	2	2	0	5	0
K. Gordon, Texas	2	1	.667	4.58	13	0	0	8	0	0	19.2	20	13	10	2	0	13	0	9	2
R. Gordon, Chicago-NL	1	1	.500	3.12	8	2	0	2	0	0	17.1	15	11	6	1	0	6	0	16	3
Grudzinski, Pittsburgh	4	1	.800	3.51	10	9	0	0	0	0	51.1	49	29	20	1	2	28	0	45	7
Guzman, Texas	5	4	.556	2.18	12	9	1	2	0	0	66	51	21	16	3	1	13	0	42	2
Harkins, San Diego	3	9	.250	3.00	13	13	5	0	0	0	90	91	48	30	0	6	33	0	55	1
Henderson, Toronto	0	0	.000	5.25	8	0	0	4	0	0	12	15	12	7	0	0	4	0	1	2
Hendrick, Texas	0	0	.000	1.29	6	1	0	2	0	0	14	17	4	2	0	0	5	0	8	0
Heredia, Houston	0	5	.000	7.39	8	6	1	0	0	0	31.2	47	32	26	2	3	12	0	18	4
Herrera, New York-AL	4	0	1.000	4.44	14	0	0	10	0	1	24.1	26	14	12	3	1	12	1	20	1
Holman, Pittsburgh	5	1	.833	2.68	7	7	2	0	0	0	47	35	20	14	2	1	11	0	33	1
Hopkins, Texas	3	1	.750	1.67	12	6	0	2	0	0	54	45	13	10	1	2	21	0	37	2
Howard, Chicago-AL	2	0	1.000	3.75	2	2	0	0	0	0	12	12	5	5	0	0	2	0	8	2
Humphrey, New York-AL	9	4	.692	2.55	13	12	5	1	1	0	88.1	82	33	25	2	3	19	1	51	4
Inman, New York-AL°	1	0	1.000	0.47	3	2	1	1	0	1	19.1	16	5	1	0	0	2	0	14	1
Johnson, Texas°	4	4	.500	2.65	10	8	2	2	1	1	51	46	17	15	1	2	20	0	56	1
Joslin, Texas°	3	1	.750	0.76	10	4	0	5	0	2	35.2	19	7	3	0	0	18	1	45	0
Kramer, Texas°	0	0	.000	0.00	2	0	0	0	0	0	2.2	2	0	0	0	0	0	0	0	0
Leon, Pittsburgh°	0	4	.000	4.05	7	2	0	2	0	0	20	23	12	9	0	0	12	0	7	1
Leonard, Kansas City	0	1	.000	5.40	1	1	0	0	0	0	5	5	3	3	0	0	1	0	2	0
Lewis, New York-AL	5	1	.833	2.23	6	6	2	0	1	0	40.1	26	14	10	1	0	17	0	27	1
Liendo, Toronto	0	2	.000	4.11	14	3	0	5	0	0	30.2	34	21	14	0	2	14	0	14	1
Lineres, Atlanta	2	1	.667	3.41	9	1	0	5	0	1	29	21	11	11	1	1	12	0	19	3
Lucas, Houston	2	1	.667	3.18	7	4	1	2	0	0	34	30	12	12	2	3	7	0	34	1
Maddock, Atlanta°	4	6	.400	3.71	11	11	3	0	0	0	60.2	63	30	25	0	2	21	0	48	3
Maki, Texas	0	1	.000	2.65	6	4	0	0	0	0	17	14	6	5	0	0	6	0	11	0
Malave, Toronto	5	0	1.000	1.17	9	3	1	4	1	0	38.1	31	8	5	0	0	18	0	40	2
Marks, New York-AL°	0	0	.000	0.00	3	0	0	1	0	0	4	3	0	0	0	0	5	0	2	0
Marte, Pittsburgh	0	0	.000	0.00	1	0	0	0	0	0	1	0	0	0	0	1	2	0	0	0
Martinez, Toronto	0	0	.000	5.40	2	0	0	1	0	0	3.1	3	2	2	0	0	2	0	2	0
Marty, Pittsburgh	0	0	.000	0.00	1	0	0	0	0	0	5	2	0	0	0	0	3	0	3	0
Mayfield, Texas	0	1	.000	5.31	9	3	0	3	0	0	20.1	24	12	12	0	1	7	0	9	1
McClain, San Diego	3	5	.375	3.16	13	12	5	0	0	0	85.1	76	47	30	1	5	41	0	76	9
McKeon, Chicago-AL°	3	1	.750	1.86	4	4	3	0	2	0	29	22	7	6	0	0	2	0	43	0
McLin, Texas°	3	3	.500	3.24	12	7	0	1	0	0	50	38	29	18	2	3	27	0	41	7
Mehalko, Atlanta°	2	1	.667	2.63	5	1	0	1	0	0	13.2	14	5	4	0	0	5	1	7	1
Melliand, Atlanta	1	1	.500	3.57	4	3	0	1	0	0	17.2	25	8	7	0	0	5	0	14	0
Mesa, Houston	6	4	.600	2.70	13	12	6	1	3	1	83.1	58	34	25	1	6	20	0	40	2
Milton, New York-AL	2	2	.500	2.23	11	3	0	6	0	1	36.1	41	20	9	0	4	11	0	31	3
Montana, Toronto°	0	1	.000	13.85	10	1	0	1	0	0	13	17	24	20	1	2	26	0	9	15
E. Moore, Chicago-NL	1	1	.500	3.95	3	3	0	0	0	0	13.2	18	10	6	1	0	1	0	8	0
R. Moore, Chicago-NL	2	6	.250	2.06	21	0	0	20	0	2	35	33	13	8	0	2	4	0	32	1
S. Moore, Houston	2	6	.250	4.20	13	13	2	0	0	0	70.2	77	44	33	4	5	34	1	57	4
Morales, Kansas City	2	3	.400	4.53	13	8	0	3	0	1	49.2	50	28	25	4	1	35	0	36	4
Moronta, Pittsburgh	0	1	.000	7.20	7	0	0	4	0	0	10	13	14	8	2	0	6	1	6	0
Mortillaro, Atlanta°	2	4	.333	1.39	7	5	0	1	0	0	32.1	27	7	5	0	0	17	0	29	1
Mott, Pittsburgh	2	0	.000	5.40	7	0	0	3	0	0	21.2	21	14	13	2	0	12	0	13	1
Napoleon, Atlanta	3	0	1.000	3.29	11	1	0	5	0	0	27.1	27	10	10	2	1	18	1	10	3
Navarro, Pittsburgh	2	0	1.000	0.64	5	0	0	4	0	1	14	6	1	1	0	1	5	0	5	1
Nichols, New York-AL	0	0	.000	16.20	2	0	0	0	0	0	1.2	5	3	3	0	0	2	0	0	0
Ortiz, Houston	1	0	1.000	6.52	13	0	0	5	0	0	29	42	32	21	1	0	8	1	11	0
Palencia, Toronto	2	3	.400	3.83	13	8	0	4	0	0	51.2	54	30	22	2	1	21	0	28	2

Pitcher—Club	W.	L.	Pct.	ERA.	G.	GS.	CG.	GF.	ShO.	Sv.	IP.	H.	R.	ER.	HR.	HB.	BB.	Int. BB.	SO.	WP.
Patterson, San Diego	4	3	.571	2.94	8	6	3	1	0	0	52	60	18	17	1	0	7	1	65	3
Peraza, Toronto	0	1	.000	1.69	2	0	0	2	0	0	5.1	3	1	1	0	0	2	0	7	0
Perez, Atlanta	1	2	.333	3.24	15	1	1	9	0	6	41.2	42	21	15	1	1	11	1	23	4
Perry, New York-AL	0	0	.000	18.00	1	0	0	1	0	0	1	2	2	2	1	0	0	0	1	0
Plasensia, Chicago-AL	0	0	.000	6.43	4	0	0	2	0	0	7	10	6	5	1	0	5	0	4	1
Pol, Pittsburgh	1	6	.143	3.72	9	9	0	0	0	0	48.1	53	38	20	2	2	26	0	24	2
Polemir, Houston	0	2	.000	3.71	4	4	0	0	0	0	17	14	9	7	0	1	10	0	16	2
Poston, San Diego	0	0	.000	3.00	2	2	0	0	0	0	12	14	5	4	0	0	2	0	13	0
Potestio, Kansas City	3	3	.500	2.22	13	2	0	7	0	0	56.2	56	24	14	2	2	16	0	41	4
Prado, Kansas City	0	1	.000	7.24	8	0	0	4	0	1	13.2	17	13	11	0	3	9	0	6	5
Rodriguez, San Diego	3	5	.375	4.78	10	10	0	0	0	0	43.1	58	35	23	3	3	21	0	18	3
K. Rogers, Texas°	0	0	.000	0.00	2	0	0	0	0	0	3	0	0	0	0	0	0	0	4	0
R. Rogers, Atlanta°	3	0	1.000	1.17	14	1	0	11	0	1	30.2	25	4	4	0	1	10	1	28	2
Rosario, Atlanta°	4	4	.500	4.78	10	10	1	0	0	0	52.2	53	32	28	3	2	28	1	31	8
Rossi, Toronto	0	0	.000	11.57	1	0	0	1	0	0	2.1	3	3	3	0	0	4	0	2	1
Ruckebeil, Chicago-AL	2	2	.500	4.88	10	1	0	5	0	1	24	27	16	13	2	1	11	1	17	1
I. Sanchez, Kansas City°	3	5	.375	4.57	12	11	0	0	0	0	61	63	41	31	3	4	36	0	49	10
L. Sanchez, Pittsburgh°	2	0	1.000	1.63	11	1	0	6	0	2	27.2	26	10	5	0	1	9	0	22	1
Schwarz, Chicago-NL	2	5	.286	6.07	11	9	0	1	0	0	43	47	39	29	3	2	37	0	24	8
Seitz, Atlanta	2	0	1.000	0.00	2	0	0	2	0	0	7	4	0	0	0	1	1	0	7	1
Serritella, Kansas City	3	6	.333	3.94	11	11	1	0	0	0	64	57	39	28	1	1	29	0	38	4
Severino, Houston	0	1	.000	3.86	12	0	0	8	0	0	21	18	12	9	0	3	9	0	11	2
Shulte, Texas°	1	2	.333	1.80	11	0	0	10	0	3	20	19	7	4	0	0	8	0	26	1
Sielicki, Kansas City	2	3	.400	2.79	12	11	0	1	0	0	67.2	85	34	21	1	3	27	0	31	7
Sierra, Atlanta	1	2	.333	4.62	10	5	1	3	0	0	39	41	25	20	1	1	23	0	17	2
Simmons, Pittsburgh°	1	5	.167	4.15	7	6	1	1	1	1	34.2	38	20	16	0	0	16	0	21	0
Sorce, Texas	1	0	1.000	3.00	1	0	0	1	0	0	3	3	1	1	0	0	2	0	2	0
Sparling, Kansas City	1	1	.500	5.40	3	3	1	0	0	0	15	20	11	9	1	0	4	0	14	1
Stacey, Chicago-AL	1	0	1.000	3.58	10	5	0	4	0	0	27.2	23	17	11	0	6	32	0	23	2
Stanton, Pittsburgh	0	0	.000	0.75	9	0	0	5	0	0	12	5	1	1	0	0	11	0	14	1
Steinberg, Kansas City	0	1	.000	1.57	10	1	0	8	0	2	28.2	31	12	5	0	0	8	1	16	0
Stidham, New York-AL	2	2	.500	4.39	9	4	1	3	0	0	26.2	25	20	13	1	2	19	0	17	2
Stinnett, Pittsburgh	0	1	.000	3.24	8	0	0	6	0	0	8.1	7	4	3	0	0	7	1	5	0
Stone, Pittsburgh	5	2	.714	2.67	12	12	0	0	1	0	77.2	66	30	23	1	1	32	0	59	5
Storer, Chicago-AL	3	2	.600	3.71	14	1	0	12	0	2	26.2	29	14	11	2	1	16	3	18	0
Strasser, Houston	4	3	.571	2.44	10	10	3	0	0	0	66.1	56	28	18	1	3	24	1	54	1
Taylor, Chicago-AL	6	6	.500	3.12	14	12	8	2	0	1	95.1	100	48	33	4	4	15	2	39	2
Traylor, Houston	1	1	.500	6.56	9	4	0	0	0	0	23.1	24	26	17	1	2	23	0	18	3
Troester, New York-AL	0	0	.000	2.59	13	2	0	5	0	1	31.1	28	19	9	0	0	24	0	24	4
Troncoso, Houston	5	4	.556	2.04	13	6	1	6	0	0	61.2	59	23	14	2	2	22	2	23	1
Trotter, Chicago-NL	3	6	.333	2.35	12	12	4	0	2	0	80.1	57	27	21	3	2	27	0	56	3
Trujillo, Chicago-AL	0	0	.000	1.23	1	1	0	0	0	0	7.1	1	2	1	0	0	4	0	6	1
Ubiera, New York-AL	0	3	.000	2.80	12	2	0	5	0	0	35.1	37	22	11	2	0	9	0	20	6
Ubri, Texas°	0	0	.000	0.00	1	0	0	1	0	0	0	0	0	0	0	0	0	0	0	0
Van Gennep, Atlanta	2	2	.500	2.26	8	8	2	0	1	0	51.2	40	22	13	2	1	12	0	24	1
Vazquez, San Diego	0	0	.000	9.82	3	0	0	1	0	0	3.2	6	5	4	0	0	4	0	1	1
Volkman, Chicago-NL	1	2	.333	1.52	11	2	1	6	1	1	29.2	18	8	5	1	3	10	0	14	0
Waldron, Texas	0	1	.000	1.13	6	0	0	3	0	0	8	11	6	1	0	3	2	2	5	1
Walsh, Kansas City	2	1	.667	2.65	12	0	0	5	0	1	37.1	42	18	11	0	1	14	3	20	3
Ward, Atlanta	2	3	.400	4.53	8	8	1	0	0	0	45.2	45	25	23	0	3	24	1	31	2
Winbush, Texas	0	2	.000	6.08	6	3	0	1	0	0	13.1	16	15	9	0	1	11	0	6	3
Young Chicago-NL°	5	2	.714	1.73	10	9	2	0	0	0	67.2	43	19	13	5	2	13	0	50	4
Zwolensky, Texas	3	1	.750	1.77	9	0	0	8	0	3	20.1	20	9	4	0	2	3	0	26	1

BALKS—E. Espinosa, 6; Aquino, 5; Mesa, Rosario, Schwarz, Sielicki, 4 each; Alexander, Cusey, McClain, S. Moore, I. Sanchez, Sierra, 3 each; Castro, Correa, DeLeon, DeLaRosa, Guzman, Leon, Palencia, Patterson, Perez, Traylor, Young, 2 each; Baker, Banes, Bass, Bormann, Buckley, Callahan, Colina, Concepcion, DeVincenzo, Duncan, J. Espinosa, Estrella, German, G. Gonzales, K. Gordon, Harkins, Henderson, Herrera, Holman, Humphrey, Johnson, Maki, Mayfield, McLin, Montana, Morales, Mortillaro, Napoleon, Ortiz, Pol, Potestio, Ruckebeil, Severino, Stacey, Stidham, Stone, Storer, Taylor, Troester, Ubiera, Van Gennep, Volkman, Waldron, J. Walsh, 1 each.

COMBINATION SHUTOUTS—Ward-Perez, Mortillaro-Perez, Mortillaro-Perez-Mehalko-Rogers, Atlanta; Correa-Ruckebeil, Chicago-AL; Trotter-Moore, German-DeLeon, Chicago-NL; Espinosa-Troncoso, Houston; Serritella-Steinberg, Cusey-Prado, Morales-Steinberg, Drizmala-DeBord, Kansas City; Catlett-Navarro, Pittsburgh; McClain-DelRosario-Coleman, Callahan-Coleman, San Diego; Johnson-Clark, Buckley-Hopkins, McLin-Guzman, Guzman-Maki, Texas.

NO-HIT GAME—DeVincenzo, Chicago-AL, defeated Atlanta, 1-0, August 17 (five innings).

Pioneer League

SUMMER CLASS A CLASSIFICATION

CHAMPIONSHIP WINNERS IN PREVIOUS YEARS

1939—Twin Falls°	.581	1953—Ogden	.679
1940—Salt Lake City	.608	Salt Lake C. (4th)°	.527
Ogden (4th)°	.492	1954—Salt Lake City	.595
1941—Boise	.623	Great Falls (4th)°	.530
Ogden (2nd)°	.598	1955—Boise	.588
1942—Pocatello†	.690	Magic Valley (4th)°	.489
Boise	.683	1956—Boise	.561
1943-44-45—Did not operate.		1957—Salt Lake City	.650
1946—Twin Falls‡	.585	Billings†	.582
Salt Lake City†	.585	1958—Great Falls	.582
1947—Salt Lake City	.618	Boise†	.615
Twin Falls†	.600	1959—Boise	.633
1948—Pocatello	.611	Billings (2nd)°	.523
Twin Falls (2nd)°	.595	1960—Boise†	.686
1949—Twin Falls	.624	Idaho Falls	.650
Pocatello (3rd)°	.595	1961—Boise	.638
1950—Pocatello	.635	Great Falls°	.571
Billings (3rd)°	.571	1962—Boise§	.565
1951—Salt Lake City	.618	Billings†	.706
Great Falls (3rd)°	.559	1963—Idaho Falls	.702
1952—Pocatello	.595	Magic Valley†	.643
Idaho Falls (2nd)°	.573	1964—Treasure Valley	.615

1965—Treasure Valley	.530
1966—Ogden	.591
1967—Ogden	.621
1968—Ogden	.609
1969—Ogden	.620
1970—Idaho Falls	.629
1971—Great Falls	.643
1972—Billings	.694
1973—Billings	.629
1974—Idaho Falls	.569
1975—Great Falls	.577
1976—Great Falls	.577
1977—Lethbridge	.629
1978—Billings x	.735
1979—Helena	.623
Lethbridge y	.559
1980—Lethbridge y	.743
Billings	.629
1981—Calgary	.657
Butte y	.557

°Won four-club playoff. †Won split-season playoff. ‡Ended first half in tie with Salt Lake City and won one-game playoff. §Ended first half in tie with Billings and Great Falls and won playoff. xBillings (first place) defeated Idaho Falls (second place) in First Place-Second Place playoff. yLeague divided in Northern and Southern divisions; won two-club playoff.

STANDING OF CLUBS AT CLOSE OF SEASON, AUGUST 31
NORTHERN DIVISION

Club	M.H.	G.F.	Cal.	Leth.	I.F.	But.	Bil.	Hel.	W.	L.	T.	Pct.	G.B.
Medicine Hat (Blue Jays)	....	8	7	8	4	5	6	6	44	26	0	.629	......
Great Falls (Giants)	2	....	7	9	6	7	6	6	43	27	0	.614	1
Calgary (Expos)	3	3	....	4	3	2	4	6	25	45	0	.357	19
Lethbridge (Dodgers)	2	1	6	....	3	2	6	5	25	45	0	.357	19

SOUTHERN DIVISION

Club									W.	L.	T.	Pct.	G.B.
Idaho Falls (A's)	6	4	7	7	....	6	6	6	42	28	0	.600	......
Butte (Royals)	5	3	8	8	4	....	5	8	41	29	0	.586	1
Billings (Reds)	4	4	6	4	4	5	....	4	31	39	0	.443	11
Helena (Phillies)	4	4	4	5	4	2	6	....	29	41	0	.414	13

Major league affiliations in parentheses.

Playoff—Medicine Hat defeated Idaho Falls, three games to one, to win league championship.

Regular-Season Attendance—Billings, 63,931; Butte, 33,883; Calgary, 25,576; Great Falls, 67,044; Helena, 14,910; Idaho Falls, 22,497; Lethbridge, 21,645; Medicine Hat, 51,236; Total, 300,722. Playoffs, 4,075.

Managers: Billings, Marc Bombard; Butte, Thomas Jones; Calgary, Robert Reece; Great Falls, Ernest Rodriguez; Helena, Ronald Smith; Idaho Falls, Keith Lieppman; Lethbridge, Gary LaRocque; Medicine Hat, Duane Larson.

All-Star Team: 1B—Citari, Butte; 2B—Moreno, Calgary; 3B—Baham, Idaho Falls; SS—Clayton, Idaho Falls; OF—Daniels, Billings; Beauchamp, Medicine Hat; Cimo, Great Falls; C—Ramler, Calgary; P—Larkin, Great Falls; McCullers, Helena; Gorden, Medicine Hat; Manager—Jones, Butte.

(Compiled by William J. Weiss, League Statistician, San Mateo, Calif.)

CLUB BATTING

Club	Pct.	G.	AB.	R.	OR.	H.	TB.	2B.	3B.	HR.	RBI.	GW.	SH.	SF.	HP.	BB.	Int. BB.	SO.	SB.	CS.	LOB.
Idaho Falls	.316	70	2438	461	404	770	1052	132	24	34	388	38	43	20	16	313	31	385	86	38	573
Butte	.302	70	2483	539	378	751	1164	128	36	71	455	37	27	17	27	382	25	495	87	46	593
Medicine Hat	.287	70	2451	438	366	703	1029	113	18	59	387	36	31	24	23	305	23	505	66	29	559
Helena	.281	70	2364	351	403	664	874	95	8	33	296	26	21	16	14	251	24	513	105	52	499
Calgary	.276	70	2362	382	504	652	931	117	15	44	332	22	13	23	7	283	18	410	55	38	523
Great Falls	.266	70	2369	381	314	629	844	83	24	28	311	31	53	29	16	323	37	485	89	48	544
Lethbridge	.262	70	2390	328	449	627	784	86	13	15	296	24	35	15	22	282	19	464	62	32	590
Billings	.256	70	2325	296	358	596	790	102	10	24	249	30	34	15	20	289	29	480	98	32	575

INDIVIDUAL BATTING
(Leading Qualifiers for Batting Championship—189 or More Plate Appearances)

°Bats lefthanded.   †Switch-hitter.

Player and Club	Pct.	G.	AB.	R.	H.	TB.	2B.	3B.	HR.	RBI.	GW.	SH.	SF.	HP.	BB.	Int. BB.	SO.	SB.	CS.
Neuzil, Jeffrey, Butte	.379	68	253	69	96	125	6	7	3	41	2	7	0	1	36	0	28	11	8
Robles, Gregory, Idaho Falls°	.371	69	256	46	95	140	20	2	7	52	6	0	3	1	26	10	23	4	1
Daniels, Kalvoski, Billings°	.367	67	240	43	88	124	19	4	3	38	9	0	0	2	32	12	26	27	4
Johnston, Christopher, Med. Hat	.358	67	274	54	98	162	15	2	15	77	9	0	3	3	25	3	55	3	0
Baham, Leon, Idaho Falls†	.353	68	289	52	102	121	15	2	0	37	3	2	2	2	22	4	27	10	8
Clayton, Kenneth, Idaho Falls	.351	55	211	30	74	94	14	0	2	40	4	0	4	1	7	2	29	2	2
Walters, Kevin, Helena†	.344	57	186	25	64	83	10	0	3	35	4	0	7	1	35	7	12	6	1
Baier, Martin, Great Falls°	.342	61	199	27	68	91	8	0	5	39	4	2	3	2	26	13	21	4	2
Moreno, Armando, Calgary	.338	66	213	52	72	107	18	1	5	42	3	1	3	1	56	2	37	5	6
Chadwick, George, Calgary	.333	57	222	43	74	106	15	1	5	23	2	0	1	0	14	0	19	8	7

Departmental Leaders: G—Bates, Blackwell, Citari, 70; AB—Baham, 289; R—Citari, 75; H—Baham, 102; TB—Fielder, 176; 2B—Fielder, 28; 3B—Neuzil, 7; HR—Fielder, 20; RBI—Johnston, 77; GWRBI—Daniels, Johnston, 9; SH—Cimo, 11; SF—Walters, 7; HP—Fielder, 8; BB—Citari, 66; IBB—Baier, 13; SO—Jackson, 76; SB—Daniels, W. Davis, 27; CS—Leiva, 15.

(All Players—Listed Alphabetically)

Player and Club	Pct.	G.	AB.	R.	H.	TB.	2B.	3B.	HR.	RBI.	GW.	SH.	SF.	HP.	BB.	Int. BB.	SO.	SB.	CS.
Albino, William, Billings	.278	6	18	5	5	6	1	0	0	3	1	0	1	0	8	0	4	4	0
Anderson, David, Calgary°	.277	49	155	23	43	58	7	1	2	26	3	1	2	0	17	3	17	3	2
Baham, Leon, Idaho Falls†	.353	68	289	52	102	121	15	2	0	37	3	2	2	2	22	4	27	10	8
Baier, Martin, Great Falls°	.342	61	199	27	68	91	8	0	5	39	4	2	3	2	26	13	21	4	2
Bates, Kevin, Great Falls°	.311	70	251	45	78	107	11	6	2	45	3	5	4	1	45	6	46	15	8
Beauchamp, Kash, Medicine Hat	.318	68	286	57	91	118	8	5	3	40	6	3	1	0	22	2	37	12	8
Bippert, Douglas, Calgary	.265	40	117	13	31	43	3	0	3	16	0	1	2	0	9	0	21	3	0
Blackwell, Orlando, Great Falls†	.288	70	271	61	78	97	6	5	1	27	3	3	1	4	41	2	24	22	8
Borders, Patrick, Medicine Hat	.304	61	217	30	66	97	12	2	5	33	3	1	1	2	24	1	52	1	2
Browning, Thomas, Billings	.231	15	26	3	6	6	0	0	0	3	0	5	0	0	5	0	11	0	0
Cabell, William, Great Falls†	.172	35	29	8	5	8	1	1	0	0	0	1	0	0	5	0	11	3	4
Cain, Jerald, Lethbridge	.111	18	45	8	5	7	0	1	0	3	0	0	0	0	5	0	14	1	1
Calloway, Vaughn, Helena	.313	12	16	3	5	7	0	1	0	2	0	0	0	0	3	0	8	0	1
Campbell, Gregory, Great Falls	.000	2	7	1	0	0	0	0	0	2	0	0	1	0	1	0	3	0	0
Campbell, Steven, Idaho Falls	.346	49	156	36	54	81	9	3	4	32	2	6	2	0	17	1	18	6	3
Canseco, Jose, Idaho Falls	.263	28	57	13	15	24	3	0	2	7	0	0	0	0	9	0	13	3	0
Castro, Efren, Lethbridge	.182	32	110	12	20	39	2	1	5	17	2	0	0	0	9	0	28	0	0
Chadwick, George, Calgary	.333	57	222	43	74	106	15	1	5	23	2	0	1	0	14	0	19	8	7
Chapman, Ronald, Medicine Hat†	.275	63	247	57	68	96	10	3	4	35	3	2	2	3	50	5	50	26	7
Charles, Troy, Great Falls†	.318	39	132	29	42	54	5	2	1	9	0	3	2	0	17	0	42	6	0
Cimo, Matthew, Great Falls	.250	66	248	41	62	99	13	3	6	39	8	11	6	0	27	2	44	14	5
Citari, Joseph, Butte	.327	70	254	75	83	161	16	4	18	64	5	0	3	1	66	6	50	6	3
Clark, Gregory, Lethbridge°	.312	57	202	37	63	71	8	0	0	14	2	4	0	1	31	1	29	15	4
Clayton, Kenneth, Idaho Falls	.351	55	211	30	74	94	14	0	2	40	4	0	4	1	7	2	29	2	2
Culbertson, Curtis, Billings	.191	40	115	12	22	29	2	1	1	11	1	3	1	1	11	2	27	1	3
Daniels, Kalvoski, Billings°	.367	67	240	43	88	124	19	4	3	38	9	0	2	2	32	12	26	27	4
Davis, James, Billings	.230	48	135	13	31	35	1	0	1	9	1	0	0	2	22	1	27	5	2
Davis, William, Idaho Falls†	.268	69	254	64	68	82	7	2	1	21	2	9	0	2	48	3	45	27	6
DeSa, Gary, Billings	.167	8	24	1	4	4	0	0	0	2	0	0	0	0	0	0	6	0	0
Devone, Gregory, Helena	.267	25	45	8	12	15	1	1	0	3	0	0	0	0	8	1	14	4	1
Dickson, Richard, Great Falls†	.217	14	23	2	5	9	1	0	1	5	0	0	0	0	1	0	10	0	0
Duncan, Mariano, Lethbridge†	.236	30	55	9	13	21	3	1	1	8	1	0	1	1	8	0	21	1	2
Duvnjak, David, Calgary	.200	19	35	6	7	13	3	0	1	4	0	0	0	0	7	0	13	0	0
Dye, Mark, Idaho Falls	.214	12	14	5	3	6	0	0	1	2	0	0	0	0	2	0	3	1	0
Ellis, Thomas, Calgary†	.241	16	58	8	14	18	2	1	0	2	0	0	0	0	8	1	12	2	2
Empting, Michael, Great Falls	.276	61	196	33	54	74	8	0	4	21	2	7	3	1	23	1	29	4	2
Escribano, Eduardo, Idaho Falls	.000	10	1	0	0	0	0	0	0	0	0	0	0	0	0	0	1	0	0
Espinal, Feliz, Great Falls	.105	24	38	5	4	5	1	0	0	0	0	0	0	0	6	0	19	1	1
Evans, Anthony, Billings	.214	4	14	2	3	4	1	0	0	0	0	0	0	0	3	1	2	0	1
Farlow, Paul, Billings	.215	37	65	9	14	17	3	0	0	3	0	0	0	0	7	0	18	1	0
Faucette, Charles, Medicine Hat	.130	25	69	10	9	18	3	0	2	6	1	0	1	0	15	0	24	0	1
Fielder, Cecil, Butte	.322	69	273	73	88	176	28	0	20	68	4	0	1	8	37	7	62	3	0
Fischer, Todd, Idaho Falls	.000	36	0	0	0	0	0	0	0	0	0	1	0	0	0	0	0	0	0
Flores, Richard, Lethbridge†	.204	64	181	15	37	40	3	0	0	10	0	6	0	0	22	0	49	2	1
Fortaleza, Raymond, Calgary	.206	59	204	24	42	75	9	0	8	31	2	0	1	2	10	0	51	1	4
Fulgencio, Elvin, Billings	.218	27	55	4	12	13	1	0	0	5	0	1	1	0	4	1	13	0	1
Gatewood, Henry, Lethbridge	.236	15	55	3	13	14	1	0	0	6	0	1	0	0	4	0	7	0	0
Gerard, Mark, Medicine Hat°	.299	56	174	36	52	83	9	2	6	35	3	0	2	3	24	7	24	0	0
Gill, Shawn, Idaho Falls	.304	41	125	19	38	51	6	2	1	20	2	3	1	1	11	0	14	1	0
Gomez, Valentin, Lethbridge	.167	3	6	0	1	1	0	0	0	0	0	0	0	0	0	0	1	0	0
Gomez, Jose, Great Falls	.000	2	2	0	0	0	0	0	0	0	0	0	0	0	0	0	2	0	0
Gonzalez, Jose, Lethbridge	.301	55	209	35	63	91	14	1	4	47	2	3	2	1	15	1	45	11	6
Greene, Ricky, Great Falls	.231	45	117	16	27	32	3	1	0	8	0	1	0	0	16	1	34	0	2
Gregory, John, Lethbridge°	.298	67	248	25	74	91	12	1	1	44	4	2	4	0	30	10	30	0	1
Griffin, Gregory, Medicine Hat	.324	68	275	60	89	137	15	0	11	45	2	3	1	1	31	0	67	13	7
Groninger, Gehret, Billings	.246	27	57	8	14	16	2	0	0	5	0	3	0	0	15	0	11	4	0
Hall, Matthew, Butte	.315	47	162	36	51	81	11	2	5	26	3	2	0	3	18	0	21	2	3
Haney, Anthony, Calgary	.247	30	89	12	22	30	2	0	2	11	1	0	1	0	14	0	20	0	0
Hawley, Gary, Billings°	.167	13	18	1	3	8	2	0	1	3	0	3	0	0	2	0	1	0	0
Hempfield, Vaughn, Butte	.221	43	77	16	17	22	1	2	0	10	0	2	1	0	9	0	20	5	1
Henderson, Ramon, Helena	.235	18	34	2	8	9	1	0	0	0	0	0	0	0	3	0	8	0	1
Hill, Timothy, Lethbridge°	.291	43	148	15	43	57	7	2	1	23	3	1	0	1	15	2	33	4	1
Hoskins, Joseph, Calgary°	.329	39	140	19	46	54	3	1	1	28	1	2	0	0	9	0	15	7	2
Jackson, Kenneth, Helena	.252	62	218	38	55	81	11	0	5	28	1	0	1	2	32	3	76	13	3
Johnson, Todd, Helena	.273	38	143	22	39	58	4	0	5	23	3	0	2	0	7	2	40	1	2
Johnston, Christopher, Medicine Hat	.358	67	274	54	98	162	15	2	15	77	9	0	3	3	25	3	55	3	0
Jones, Scott, Billings	.111	8	9	0	1	1	0	0	0	0	0	2	0	0	3	0	6	0	1
Keeney, Steven, Great Falls°	.500	2	6	1	3	3	0	0	0	2	0	0	1	0	1	0	0	2	0
Keller, David, Billings	.298	61	208	36	62	96	13	0	7	40	2	0	3	4	30	1	55	7	1
Kennard, David, Helena	.241	57	191	30	46	55	4	1	1	27	2	4	2	2	23	4	24	10	4
Kimball, David, Medicine Hat	.182	21	55	7	10	15	2	0	1	6	1	1	1	3	4	0	14	0	0
Kochanski, Mark, Idaho Falls	.000	10	1	0	0	0	0	0	0	0	0	0	0	0	0	0	0	0	0
Konderla, Michael, Billings	.048	19	21	0	1	2	1	0	0	0	0	0	0	0	0	0	14	0	0
Korinek, Kurt, Butte	.242	22	66	9	16	22	4	1	0	8	0	0	0	4	8	0	17	1	0
Krupa, Thomas, Calgary°	.255	13	47	10	12	18	1	1	1	10	2	0	1	0	6	1	16	0	0
Kuziomko, Timothy, Medicine Hat	.176	29	51	6	9	10	1	0	0	5	0	3	0	2	5	0	16	0	0
Lavery, Michael, Medicine Hat	.263	38	95	18	25	40	6	0	3	15	2	2	3	0	17	1	24	0	1
Leiva, Jose, Helena	.316	59	225	33	71	76	5	0	0	29	5	4	1	0	28	0	26	24	15
Loard, Billy, Great Falls	.175	21	40	5	7	11	1	0	1	5	1	1	0	0	11	1	16	0	0
Loscalzo, Robert, Idaho Falls°	.363	56	146	29	53	81	7	6	3	20	3	4	1	0	21	3	26	3	3
Lukes, Louis, Helena	.203	27	59	3	12	15	0	0	1	10	0	0	0	0	5	0	34	0	1
Malone, Edward, Idaho Falls°	.195	40	87	18	17	22	5	0	0	9	1	2	2	0	15	0	23	5	3
Mangione, Mark, Lethbridge†	.150	37	107	8	16	18	2	0	0	6	1	2	1	0	8	0	27	0	1
Marin, Julio, Lethbridge	.263	43	133	19	35	41	4	1	0	18	3	1	1	1	21	1	27	1	2
Marr, Alan, Great Falls	.300	66	207	32	62	78	4	3	2	36	6	3	5	1	31	0	35	7	4
Martinez, Frank, Helena	.298	43	124	18	37	51	8	0	2	18	1	1	0	1	11	1	21	0	1
Mason, John, Medicine Hat†	.237	48	118	18	28	30	2	0	0	7	1	5	2	0	16	0	35	4	2
McGilvray, James, Great Falls	.333	3	6	2	2	5	0	0	1	2	1	0	0	0	0	0	0	0	0

Player and Club	Pct.	G.	AB.	R.	H.	TB.	2B.	3B.	HR.	RBI.	GW.	SH.	SF.	HP.	BB.	Int. BB.	SO.	SB.	CS.
McGraw, Gary, Idaho Falls	.133	6	15	5	2	6	1	0	1	2	1	1	0	0	5	0	3	1	0
Merenda, Robert, Great Falls*	.176	4	17	0	3	3	0	0	0	1	0	0	0	0	2	0	2	1	1
Michel, John, Idaho Falls*	.305	46	141	18	43	58	7	1	2	28	2	2	0	1	11	3	16	2	4
Mohr, Tom, Butte*	.250	14	20	3	5	6	1	0	0	6	0	0	0	1	7	0	7	0	0
Moore, Michael, Lethbridge	.240	18	50	2	12	12	0	0	0	6	0	0	1	0	5	1	4	0	0
Moreno, Armando, Calgary	.338	66	213	52	72	107	18	1	5	42	3	1	3	1	56	2	37	5	6
Morton, Mark, Great Falls*	.223	45	103	15	23	31	3	1	1	16	1	2	0	1	17	6	31	0	0
Moseley, Lester, Great Falls*	.186	38	102	13	19	21	2	0	0	7	0	2	0	0	12	1	30	2	2
Mota, Luis, Helena*	.272	53	191	32	52	76	11	2	3	24	2	0	1	2	11	0	45	11	4
Munson, Jay, Billings	1.000	1	1	0	1	1	0	0	0	0	0	0	0	0	0	1	0	0	0
Naber, Robert, Great Falls	.253	59	194	18	49	65	9	2	1	32	1	3	3	5	16	4	37	0	1
Nattiel, Michael, Billings	.150	23	40	2	6	9	3	0	0	3	0	1	0	0	2	0	13	1	1
Neuzil, Jeffrey, Butte	.379	68	253	69	96	125	6	7	3	41	2	7	0	1	36	0	28	11	8
Newsom, Gary, Lethbridge	.272	67	276	48	75	89	10	2	0	21	0	3	2	2	30	0	29	9	8
Nichols, Howard, Helena	.281	44	128	18	36	46	4	0	2	13	2	0	1	0	13	1	30	2	2
Odgers, Daniel, Helena	.325	65	252	35	82	103	16	1	1	30	3	4	1	2	9	0	19	10	5
Oquendo, Jorge, Idaho Falls*	.348	41	69	14	24	34	7	0	1	10	1	1	0	0	17	1	18	0	0
Oropeza, Clemente, Idaho Falls	.290	46	131	27	38	48	5	1	1	14	0	1	0	0	16	1	22	4	1
Ortega, Raymond, Helena	.266	42	128	24	34	63	8	0	7	24	1	3	0	1	17	1	38	1	1
Ortiz, Rafael, Billings	.000	19	3	0	0	0	0	0	0	0	0	0	0	0	0	0	2	0	0
Oxner, Stanley, Butte	.333	17	48	6	16	18	2	0	0	8	0	0	0	1	4	0	5	3	1
Paredes, Johnny, Helena	.305	34	105	17	32	41	4	1	1	7	0	0	0	0	13	1	10	6	1
Patterson, Kenneth, Butte†	.258	49	155	26	40	47	5	1	0	20	3	0	3	7	21	0	20	10	7
Phillips, William, Butte	.317	64	268	60	85	106	10	4	1	26	3	1	1	1	31	1	27	21	10
Posillico, James, Billings	.207	43	111	9	23	31	4	2	0	7	4	0	0	0	11	1	29	4	3
Proctor, Brice, Great Falls	.000	3	5	0	0	0	0	0	0	0	0	0	0	0	0	0	3	0	0
Pryor, Depew, Billings	.282	58	174	20	49	68	10	0	3	22	0	0	2	3	27	1	38	2	1
Radloff, Scott, Billings*	.000	4	4	0	0	0	0	0	0	0	0	0	0	0	0	0	3	0	0
Rainey, Scott, Great Falls	.250	17	36	4	9	10	1	0	0	1	0	3	0	1	5	0	4	2	0
Ramler, Steven, Calgary	.303	68	221	42	67	109	18	0	8	35	0	3	4	3	40	1	33	3	1
Reynolds, Timothy, Billings†	.222	13	27	1	6	10	1	0	1	1	1	2	0	1	0	0	8	0	0
Rhodes, Darrell, Medicine Hat	.222	45	99	11	22	28	4	1	0	8	0	3	1	0	13	0	18	6	0
Richards, Nicky, Butte	.323	29	65	15	21	47	3	1	7	27	2	1	0	0	14	0	14	1	1
Robles, Gregory, Idaho Falls*	.371	69	256	46	95	140	20	2	7	52	6	0	3	1	26	10	23	4	1
Robles, Jesus, Lethbridge	.100	12	30	1	3	3	0	0	0	3	0	1	0	2	0	18	1	0
Rojas, Octavio, Idaho Falls*	.217	16	23	5	5	5	0	0	0	4	1	2	1	0	4	0	9	0	0
Romano, Michael, Billings	.000	1	1	0	0	0	0	0	0	0	0	0	0	0	0	0	0	0	0
Ross, Keith, Helena*	.254	50	177	29	45	57	4	1	2	15	2	1	0	2	14	3	66	12	6
Rover, Vincent, Billings*	.277	61	202	24	56	69	9	2	0	19	5	1	1	4	25	7	29	10	4
Sambo, Ramon, Helena†	.333	19	33	7	11	12	1	0	0	1	0	2	0	0	5	0	9	5	1
Sanchez, Angel, Calgary	.194	46	134	21	26	36	4	3	0	12	1	2	0	0	22	0	22	6	0
Santiago, Eric, Calgary	.216	18	37	4	8	13	1	2	0	4	1	0	0	0	4	0	10	2	0
Scott, Timothy, Billings	.091	27	11	0	1	1	0	0	0	0	0	1	0	0	0	0	2	0	0
Shaddy, Christopher, Medicine Hat	.266	64	218	25	58	79	16	1	1	28	0	8	2	5	18	1	47	1	1
Shoemaker, Steven, Calgary*	.244	39	127	17	31	39	5	0	1	17	1	0	2	0	20	5	22	2	4
Skelton, Warren, Butte	.189	31	74	4	14	16	2	0	0	4	0	1	0	0	7	0	15	0	0
Smith, Christopher, Butte	.000	2	2	1	0	0	0	0	0	0	0	0	0	0	0	0	0	0	0
Smith, Henry, Helena	.214	16	42	2	9	9	0	0	0	1	0	0	0	1	0	5	18	0	0
Smith, Kelvin, Great Falls	.207	54	140	23	29	41	6	0	2	14	1	4	0	0	20	0	42	6	8
Snider, Van, Butte*	.300	67	237	46	71	121	13	5	9	53	6	2	1	1	28	7	63	5	4
Spagnola, Glenn, Billings*	.000	13	27	1	0	0	0	0	0	0	1	0	2	0	0	2	0	19	0	0
Spisok, Jeffery, Billings	.261	48	161	33	42	60	6	0	4	18	2	0	2	0	24	2	43	15	3
Steinmetz, Kevin, Billings	.259	64	251	22	65	78	10	0	1	21	1	6	3	1	10	0	14	8	3
Stenhouse, David, Medicine Hat	.305	51	187	30	57	89	4	2	8	34	3	0	1	0	28	2	30	0	0
Strickland, Terry, Calgary	.301	68	259	54	78	110	15	1	5	38	3	0	4	0	18	3	39	5	2
Swindle, Allen, Billings*	.000	22	4	0	0	0	0	0	0	0	0	0	1	0	0	1	0	2	0	0
Szekely, Joseph, Calgary*	.280	53	164	35	46	72	12	1	4	30	2	4	4	2	33	3	43	4	3
Tejada, Wilfredo, Helena	.193	26	57	4	11	14	3	0	0	4	0	2	1	0	8	0	15	0	1
Tennell, James, Butte	.347	50	147	31	51	68	8	3	1	33	4	4	1	0	25	1	20	2	2
Thomas, Richard, Idaho Falls	.284	62	197	34	56	81	15	2	2	43	3	5	5	2	39	2	39	5	2
Thompson, Craig, Lethbridge	.667	1	3	1	2	3	1	0	0	0	0	0	0	0	1	0	0	0	0
Toler, Gregory, Billings	.212	25	66	3	14	17	0	0	1	7	0	2	0	0	6	0	16	0	0
Trujillo, Louie, Billings	.412	29	17	4	7	10	3	0	0	4	0	1	0	0	1	0	2	0	0
Vest, James, Helena	.300	3	10	1	3	3	0	0	0	0	0	0	0	0	1	0	1	0	1
Wallace, Thomas, Butte	.235	42	115	15	27	43	3	5	1	17	2	2	1	1	23	0	46	10	3
Walters, Kevin, Helena†	.344	57	186	25	64	83	10	0	3	35	4	0	7	1	35	7	12	6	1
Washington, Keith, Helena	.233	18	43	3	10	12	0	0	1	3	0	2	0	0	2	0	20	0	1
Weinberger, Gary, Calgary*	.327	20	52	7	17	22	2	0	1	11	2	1	1	0	6	1	7	1	2
Wesley, Joseph, Lethbridge*	.174	17	23	5	4	4	0	0	0	2	0	0	0	0	6	0	8	0	0
West, Richard, Butte	.233	44	103	19	24	33	3	0	2	14	1	1	1	0	19	0	37	3	0
Wilder, David, Idaho Falls	.353	44	136	30	48	65	5	3	2	24	5	2	1	4	30	1	21	12	3
Wilks, Darryl, Billings	.273	64	220	40	60	75	10	1	1	23	3	0	1	0	36	0	39	9	4
Williams, Edward, Lethbridge	.313	63	224	41	70	82	10	1	0	32	1	3	2	9	32	0	36	7	3
Williams, Reginald, Lethbridge	.300	67	253	40	76	97	8	2	3	33	5	6	1	1	29	3	49	10	2
Wortmann, Russell, Idaho Falls	.271	42	129	16	35	53	6	0	4	22	1	3	0	0	12	0	34	0	2
Yari, John-David, Medicine Hat*	.244	37	86	19	21	27	6	0	0	13	2	0	3	1	13	1	12	0	0
Zawadzki, Corey, Calgary*	.249	54	209	24	52	68	9	2	1	19	0	2	0	1	21	1	36	7	5
Zerlang, Shane, Lethbridge*	.063	17	32	4	2	3	1	0	0	3	0	2	0	0	9	0	10	0	0

The following pitchers had no plate appearances, primarily through use of designated hitters, listed alphabetically by club, games in parentheses:

BUTTE—Chelini, Daniel (4); Dannewitz, Michael (19); Davis, John (14); Martinez, Arthur (17); McNamara, Edward (15); Moseley, Gregory (20); Sparling, Don (8); Stefani, Joseph (19), Steinberg, Scott (6); Vanderpohl, Arthur (16); Walberg, Mark (14); Ware, Duane (15); Wilder, William (20).

CALGARY—Bisnar, Andrew (16); Bridges, Troy (7); Drouillard, Victor (11); Glidewell, John (13); Marentette, Marcus (6); McKay, Troy (13); Mielke, Shawn (13); Morse, Robert (14); Nesmith, Steven (27); Pfeffer, Richard (14); Richards, Gregory (14); Schnatz, Rodney (20); Wuelling, Ronald (3); Zucco, Curtis (13).

GREAT FALLS—Bargerhuff, Brian (23); Blobaum, Jeffrey (15); Bockus, Randy (18); Burgermeister, Michael (1); Gendron, Robert (6); Hughes, John (6); Hummel, Dean (16); Larkin, Patrick (27); Larsen, Peter (4); Marks, Terrance (3); Mattson, Kurt (19); McKenna, Kevin (2); Morse, Randy (12); Norman, Scott (14); Taft, Dennie (13); Weir, James (14).

HELENA—Beal, Bron (18); Caraballo, Ramon (17); Coker, Kevin (15); Cole, Rodgers (13); Dickerson, Terry (10); Dombek, Damon (13); Hill, John (26); McCullers, Lance (13); Morton, Russell (4); Powell, John (16); Stout, Gregory (26); Weatherford, Brant (16).

IDAHO FALLS—Baehr, David (5); Bailey, James (3); Border, Mark (16); Brown, Eric (16); Conquest, Thomas (16); Farrow, Douglas (9); Gilbert, Angelo (8); Kendrick, Peter (5); Lambert, Timothy (13); Leiper, David (14); Mine, Gregory (11); Stevenson, Tenoa (6); Travers, Steven (7); Weatherman, David (9).

LETHBRIDGE—Burns, Ronald (15); Carne, Gregory (10); Cunningham, Michael (19); Encarnacion, Odalis (6); Galvez, Balvino (10); Gentle, Michael (14); Heuer, Mark (13); Kolb, Michael (27); Meeks, Timothy (14); Pinckard, Michael (12); Rodriguez, Miguel (3); Scudder, William (28); Sylvia, John (23); Veliz, Francisco (13).

MEDICINE HAT—Davis, Steven (13); Gilliam, Keith (14); Gorden, Daniel (22); Johnson, Ron (15); Kahle, Roger (13); Key, James (5); Mader, Perry (11); Patterson, Richard (12); Phillips, Timothy (13); Rightmire, Russell (7); Ruetter, Derrick (18); Walsh, David (13); Wells, David (12).

GRAND SLAM HOME RUNS—Ortega 2; S. Campbell, Chapman, Fielder, Fortaleza, Richards, 1 each.

AWARDED FIRST BASE ON CATCHER'S INTERFERENCE—Cimo 2 (Gill 2); Duvnjak (Tejada); Marin (Szekely); Marr (Gill); Nattiel (Marin); G. Robles (Lavery).

CLUB FIELDING

Club	Pct.	G.	PO.	A.	E.	DP.	PB.	Club	Pct.	G.	PO.	A.	E.	DP.	PB.
Great Falls	.9503	70	1896	781	140	66	22	Lethbridge	.945	70	1795	806	152	77	19
Idaho Falls	.9498	70	1810	820	139	63	13	Billings	.943	70	1803	704	152	52	22
Butte	.947	70	1824	850	150	58	12	Calgary	.941	70	1756	742	157	65	19
Medicine Hat	.945	70	1863	802	155	72	18	Helena	.938	70	1799	775	171	67	21

INDIVIDUAL FIELDING

°Throws lefthanded

FIRST BASEMEN

Player and Club	Pct.	G.	PO.	A.	E.	DP.	Player and Club	Pct.	G.	PO.	A.	E.	DP.
Anderson, Calgary	.959	27	219	15	10	17	Krupa, Calgary	.984	8	55	5	1	8
Baier, Great Falls°	.969	33	262	19	9	24	Marin, Lethbridge	.935	4	27	2	2	4
Campbell, Great Falls	.947	2	17	1	1	3	Martinez, Helena°	.963	10	74	5	3	7
Charles, Great Falls	.996	29	246	21	1	23	Michel, Idaho Falls	.984	8	54	6	1	5
Citari, Butte	.974	46	420	38	12	32	Morton, Great Falls	1.000	6	26	1	0	3
Clayton, Idaho Falls	1.000	9	73	7	0	5	Mota, Helena	.979	37	311	17	7	27
Ellis, Calgary	.949	7	71	3	4	6	Nichols, Helena	.929	4	26	0	2	2
Fielder, Butte	.985	25	247	18	4	22	Ortega, Helena	.987	27	223	10	3	20
Fortaleza, Calgary	.963	26	199	12	8	19	Radloff, Billings°	1.000	4	4	0	0	1
Gerard, Medicine Hat	.976	11	78	2	2	8	Richards, Butte	1.000	8	15	1	0	0
Greene, Great Falls	.977	16	79	7	2	8	ROBLES, Idaho Falls°	.991	62	511	36	5	43
Gregory, Lethbridge°	.988	67	617	44	8	62	Steinmetz, Billings	.988	11	74	7	1	5
Groninger, Billings	.889	1	8	0	1	1	Toler, Billings	1.000	1	7	0	0	0
Johnston, Medicine Hat	.973	62	583	37	17	58	Weinberger, Calgary°	.965	9	52	3	2	5
Keller, Billings°	.974	60	454	31	13	36							

SECOND BASEMEN

Player and Club	Pct.	G.	PO.	A.	E.	DP.	Player and Club	Pct.	G.	PO.	A.	E.	DP.
Bates, Great Falls	.950	67	127	179	16	40	Malone, Idaho Falls	1.000	1	1	2	0	0
Bippert, Calgary	1.000	1	2	4	0	3	Marr, Great Falls	1.000	2	1	1	0	1
Cabell, Great Falls	.897	11	13	13	3	4	Moreno, Calgary	.929	65	138	163	23	39
Chapman, Medicine Hat	.945	63	152	192	20	49	NEWSOM, Lethbridge	.970	67	173	210	12	55
Culbertson, Billings	.900	34	52	65	13	11	Paredes, Helena	.937	9	21	38	4	8
Davis, Idaho Falls	.937	68	135	179	21	44	Phillips, Butte	.955	64	141	202	16	31
DeSa, Billings	.879	7	14	15	4	3	Rhodes, Medicine Hat	.922	13	23	24	4	3
Duncan, Lethbridge	1.000	2	1	2	0	1	Sambo, Helena	.878	13	17	26	6	2
Dye, Idaho Falls	.800	3	2	2	1	0	Shaddy, Medicine Hat	1.000	1	2	0	0	0
Haney, Calgary	.867	13	23	16	6	2	Spisok, Billings	.929	42	98	85	14	15
Hempfield, Butte	.943	22	34	32	4	5	Thomas, Idaho Falls	1.000	3	3	3	0	1
Kennard, Helena	.963	57	114	171	11	40	E. Williams, Lethbridge	1.000	5	5	6	0	0

THIRD BASEMEN

Player and Club	Pct.	G.	PO.	A.	E.	DP.	Player and Club	Pct.	G.	PO.	A.	E.	DP.
Anderson, Calgary	.633	10	10	9	11	0	Paredes, Helena	.900	10	6	21	3	1
Blackwell, Great Falls	.882	9	5	10	2	0	Rhodes, Medicine Hat	.846	19	10	12	4	2
Borders, Medicine Hat	.826	49	23	96	25	9	Robles, Lethbridge	.556	5	1	4	4	0
Canseco, Idaho Falls	.857	14	1	17	3	2	Sanchez, Calgary	.860	44	34	77	18	3
Clayton, Idaho Falls	.846	29	19	47	12	7	Skelton, Butte	.880	31	14	30	6	1
Culbertson, Billings	.933	6	5	9	1	1	Smith, Helena	.783	12	6	12	5	2
Davis, Billings	1.000	1	0	1	0	0	Spisok, Billings	.889	4	2	6	1	1
Dye, Idaho Falls	1.000	5	5	6	0	1	Steinmetz, Billings	.840	54	35	70	20	2
Greene, Great Falls	.857	3	3	3	1	1	Strickland, Calgary	.895	21	17	34	6	4
Haney, Calgary	1.000	2	2	4	0	0	Tennell, Butte	.930	27	17	49	5	3
Kuziomko, Medicine Hat	.839	28	12	35	9	2	Thomas, Idaho Falls	1.000	1	0	1	0	0
Mangione, Lethbridge	.898	36	30	58	10	9	Toler, Billings	.897	16	12	23	4	0
Marr, Great Falls	.874	61	52	101	22	7	Washington, Calgary	.500	4	1	4	5	1
Morton, Great Falls	.700	14	8	6	6	0	Wesley, Lethbridge	.750	12	4	11	5	1
ODGERS, Helena	.890	52	52	86	17	11	West, Butte	.806	36	11	47	14	5
Oropeza, Idaho Falls	.933	42	29	69	7	4	E. Williams, Lethbridge	.821	38	26	61	19	5

SHORTSTOPS

Player and Club	Pct.	G.	PO.	A.	E.	DP.	Player and Club	Pct.	G.	PO.	A.	E.	DP.
Baham, Idaho Falls	.922	68	111	233	29	36	Marr, Great Falls	1.000	1	0	1	0	0
Bates, Great Falls	.667	1	1	1	1	0	Neuzil, Butte	.925	67	92	218	25	32
Blackwell, Great Falls	.931	61	118	177	22	37	Paredes, Helena	1.000	2	1	4	0	0
Davis, Billings	.881	18	17	35	7	7	Proctor, Great Falls	.333	1	0	1	2	0
Duncan, Lethbridge	.786	26	22	33	15	12	Rhodes, Medicine Hat	.900	14	11	25	4	10
Espinal, Great Falls	.840	15	13	29	8	7	Rover, Billings	.897	55	82	136	25	26
Evans, Billings	.750	4	4	11	5	3	Shaddy, Medicine Hat	.913	63	63	189	24	36
Flores, Lethbridge	.896	64	81	187	31	40	STRICKLAND, Calgary	.948	47	69	148	12	30
Haney, Calgary	.903	18	28	37	7	8	Thomas, Idaho Falls	.857	8	4	8	2	1
Hempfield, Butte	.773	12	8	9	5	3	Washington, Calgary	.889	15	13	27	5	7
Henderson, Helena	.857	13	10	20	5	8	West, Butte	.813	8	1	12	3	1
Jackson, Helena	.869	62	95	191	43	30							

OUTFIELDERS

Player and Club	Pct.	G.	PO.	A.	E.	DP.
Albino, Billings	1.000	6	5	0	0	0
Baier, Great Falls*	.500	2	0	1	1	0
Beauchamp, Medicine Hat	.960	68	115	4	5	0
Bippert, Calgary	.962	34	48	2	2	0
Cain, Lethbridge	1.000	15	10	0	0	0
Campbell, Idaho Falls	.954	45	56	6	3	2
Canseco, Idaho Falls	1.000	5	5	0	0	0
Chadwick, Calgary	.957	56	82	8	4	0
Charles, Great Falls	.750	3	3	0	1	0
Cimo, Great Falls	.964	66	123	10	5	1
Clark, Lethbridge	.957	49	64	3	3	0
Daniels, Billings	.956	66	104	4	5	0
Davis, Billings	.917	29	30	3	3	0
Devone, Helena	.909	21	10	0	1	0
Dickson, Great Falls	1.000	7	4	0	0	0
Ellis, Calgary	1.000	9	21	1	0	0
Farlow, Billings	.920	25	20	3	2	0
Faucette, Medicine Hat	.870	24	20	0	3	0
Fortaleza, Calgary	.938	9	12	3	1	1
Fulgencio, Billings	.900	18	17	1	2	0
Gerard, Medicine Hat*	1.000	2	1	0	0	0
Gomez, Lethbridge	1.000	2	2	0	0	0
Gonzalez, Lethbridge	.992	55	112	7	1	0
Greene, Great Falls	.909	20	18	2	2	0
Griffin, Medicine Hat	.960	68	138	6	6	2
Hall, Butte*	.917	44	60	6	6	0
Hempfield, Butte	1.000	3	3	0	0	0
Hill, Lethbridge	.895	30	31	3	4	0
Johnson, Helena	.953	38	57	4	3	1
Keeney, Great Falls	1.000	2	2	0	0	0
Korinek, Butte	.963	22	23	3	1	1
Leiva, Helena	.939	59	102	5	7	2
Loard, Great Falls	1.000	1	1	0	0	0
Loscalzo, Idaho Falls*	.951	48	53	5	3	1
Lukes, Helena	.963	25	25	1	1	0
Malone, Idaho Falls	.860	36	45	4	8	0
Mason, Medicine Hat	.943	45	48	2	3	0
McGraw, Idaho Falls	1.000	4	5	0	0	0
Merenda, Great Falls*	.857	4	5	1	1	0
Morton, Great Falls	.750	7	3	0	1	0
Moseley, Great Falls	.902	30	36	1	4	1
Mota, Helena*	1.000	12	20	0	0	0
Naber, Great Falls	.949	59	71	4	4	0
Nattiel, Billings	.875	11	7	0	1	0
Nichols, Helena	.774	35	37	4	12	2
Oquendo, Idaho Falls*	1.000	17	14	1	0	0
Patterson, Butte	.951	49	74	3	4	0
Phillips, Butte	1.000	2	3	1	0	1
Posillico, Billings	.927	34	34	4	3	1
Ramler, Calgary	.944	12	17	0	1	0
Rojas, Idaho Falls*	.667	14	2	0	1	0
Ross, Helena	.881	49	58	1	8	0
Santiago, Calgary	1.000	17	15	0	0	0
Shoemaker, Calgary	.935	37	66	6	5	0
Smith, Great Falls	.990	53	90	6	1	1
Snider, Butte	.926	66	99	14	9	2
Tennell, Butte	1.000	14	19	1	0	0
Thomas, Idaho Falls	.979	55	83	9	2	1
Vest, Helena	.800	3	4	0	1	0
Wallace, Butte	.927	39	35	3	3	0
Weinberger, Calgary*	1.000	7	9	2	0	0
Wilder, Idaho Falls	.925	44	70	4	6	0
Wilks, Billings*	.972	61	130	8	4	2
E. Williams, Lethbridge	1.000	5	6	1	0	1
R. Williams, Lethbridge	.956	65	141	12	7	2
Yari, Medicine Hat	.885	32	23	0	3	0
ZAWADZKI, Calgary*	1.000	50	99	9	0	1
Zerlang, Lethbridge*	1.000	9	7	0	0	0

CATCHERS

Player and Club	Pct.	G.	PO.	A.	E.	DP.	PB.
Calloway, Helena	1.000	9	18	1	0	0	0
Castro, Lethbridge	.973	19	100	10	3	2	6
Duvnjak, Calgary	.943	12	31	2	2	0	2
Empting, Great Falls	.990	61	436	45	5	1	16
Fortaleza, Calgary	.976	17	108	16	3	2	7
Gatewood, Lethbridge	.940	15	73	6	5	0	4
Gill, Idaho Falls	.987	41	267	33	4	0	9
Groninger, Billings	.992	20	115	8	1	4	4
Kimball, Medicine Hat	.971	21	118	16	4	0	4
Lavery, Medicine Hat	.983	17	105	10	2	0	5
Loard, Great Falls	1.000	8	23	2	0	0	3
Marin, Lethbridge	.976	28	139	23	4	3	9
McGilvray, Great Falls	.889	2	6	2	1	0	1
Moore, Lethbridge	.991	18	92	13	1	0	0
Ortega, Helena	1.000	11	57	5	0	1	2
Oxner, Butte	.938	14	66	10	5	0	1
PRYOR, Billings	.991	58	411	54	4	0	14
Rainey, Great Falls	.984	11	62	1	1	0	2
Ramler, Calgary	.984	52	276	37	5	3	10
Richards, Butte	.977	15	110	19	3	1	1
Romano, Billings	1.000	1	4	0	0	0	1
Smith, Butte	1.000	1	2	0	0	0	1
Stenhouse, Medicine Hat	.983	42	307	43	6	4	9
Szekely, Butte	.980	49	298	39	7	4	10
Tejada, Helena	.955	24	152	17	8	0	8
Toler, Billings	1.000	3	21	2	0	1	3
Walters, Helena	.979	43	284	38	7	5	11
Wortmann, Idaho Falls	.960	40	228	33	11	3	4

PITCHERS

Player and Club	Pct.	G.	PO.	A.	E.	DP.
Baehr, Idaho Falls	.333	5	0	1	2	0
Bailey, Idaho Falls	.500	3	0	1	1	0
Bargerhuff, Great Falls	.733	23	2	9	4	0
Beal, Helena	.875	18	0	7	1	0
Bippert, Calgary	1.000	3	0	1	0	0
Bisnar, Calgary	.800	16	1	7	2	0
Blobaum, Great Falls	.865	15	8	24	5	1
Bockus, Great Falls	.875	18	5	9	2	2
Border, Idaho Falls	1.000	16	2	4	0	1
Bridges, Lethbridge	1.000	7	0	3	0	0
Brown, Idaho Falls*	.750	16	1	5	2	0
Browning, Billings*	.875	14	5	23	4	1
Burgermeister, Great Falls	1.000	1	0	2	0	0
Burns, Lethbridge	.880	15	4	18	3	0
Caraballo, Helena	.800	17	0	8	2	0
Carne, Lethbridge*	1.000	10	0	2	0	0
Chelini, Butte	1.000	4	1	0	0	0
Coker, Helena	.750	15	1	5	2	0
Cole, Helena	.893	13	5	20	3	2
Conquest, Idaho Falls	.935	16	10	19	2	0
Cunningham, Lethbridge	.900	19	3	6	1	1
Dannewitz, Butte	.750	19	0	3	1	0
Davis, Butte	.813	14	4	9	3	0
Davis, Medicine Hat*	1.000	13	2	2	0	0
Dickerson, Helena*	1.000	10	0	1	0	0
Domhek, Helena*	1.000	13	1	8	0	0
Drouillard, Calgary	.857	11	3	3	1	0
Encarnacion, Lethbridge	1.000	6	1	1	0	0
Escribano, Idaho Falls	.900	9	1	8	1	0
Farrow, Idaho Falls	.750	9	1	5	2	0
Fischer, Idaho Falls	1.000	36	3	8	0	0
Galvez, Lethbridge	1.000	10	2	4	0	0
Gendron, Great Falls	1.000	6	0	4	0	0
Gentle, Lethbridge*	.882	14	4	11	2	0
Gilliam, Medicine Hat*	.970	14	7	25	1	1
Glidewell, Calgary	.818	13	4	5	2	0
Gorden, Medicine Hat	.889	22	2	6	1	0
Hawley, Lethbridge	1.000	13	1	9	0	1
Heuer, Lethbridge	.714	13	2	8	4	0
Hill, Helena	.846	26	2	9	2	0
Hughes, Great Falls*	.667	6	0	2	1	0
Hummel, Great Falls*	.923	15	4	20	2	3
Johnson, Medicine Hat	.765	15	4	9	4	0
Jones, Billings*	1.000	8	3	10	0	1
Kehle, Medicine Hat*	.600	13	1	2	2	0
Kendrick, Idaho Falls*	.818	5	0	9	2	0
Key, Medicine Hat*	.818	5	2	7	2	0
Kochanski, Idaho Falls	1.000	10	6	1	0	0
Kolb, Lethbridge	.889	27	3	13	2	1
Konderla, Billings	.778	19	3	11	4	3
Lambert, Idaho Falls	.778	13	5	9	4	3
LARKIN, Great Falls*	1.000	27	2	23	0	2
Larsen, Great Falls	1.000	4	1	0	0	0
Leiper, Idaho Falls*	.920	14	2	21	2	0
Mader, Medicine Hat	1.000	11	1	6	0	1
Martinez, Idaho Falls	1.000	17	0	4	0	0
Mattson, Great Falls	1.000	19	3	13	0	1
McCullers, Helena	1.000	13	5	18	2	0
McKay, Calgary	.897	13	10	16	3	1
McNamara, Butte	.800	15	5	15	5	0
Meeks, Lethbridge	.950	14	5	14	1	0
Mielke, Calgary	1.000	13	4	14	0	0
Mine, Helena	.500	10	0	1	1	0
Morse, Great Falls*	1.000	12	2	9	0	0
Morse, Calgary	1.000	14	1	4	0	2
Morton, Helena	1.000	4	2	3	0	1
Moseley, Butte	1.000	20	1	10	0	1
Nesmith, Calgary	.857	27	2	4	1	0

PITCHERS—Continued

Player and Club	Pct.	G.	PO.	A.	E.	DP.	Player and Club	Pct.	G.	PO.	A.	E.	DP.
Norman, Great Falls	1.000	14	3	12	0	1	Steinberg, Butte	1.000	6	0	1	0	0
Oropeza, Idaho Falls	1.000	1	0	1	0	0	Stevenson, Idaho Falls°	1.000	5	0	3	0	0
Ortiz, Billings	1.000	19	1	3	0	0	Stout, Helena	.900	26	3	6	1	1
Patterson, Medicine Hat	1.000	12	0	1	0	1	Swindle, Billings°	.786	22	2	9	3	1
Pfeffer, Calgary°	1.000	14	1	5	0	1	Sylvia, Lethbridge	.923	23	3	9	1	0
Phillips, Medicine Hat	.900	13	6	21	3	0	Taft, Great Falls°	.882	13	9	6	2	2
Pinckard, Lethbridge	.929	12	3	10	1	1	Travers, Idaho Falls	.833	7	1	4	1	0
Powell, Helena	1.000	16	0	6	0	0	Trujillo, Billings	.897	29	6	20	3	3
Reynolds, Billings	.929	13	10	16	2	3	Vanderpohl, Butte°	1.000	16	0	10	0	0
Richards, Calgary	.903	14	9	19	3	1	Veliz, Lethbridge°	1.000	13	0	2	0	0
Rightmire, Medicine Hat	.667	7	0	2	1	0	Walberg, Butte	.941	14	3	13	1	2
Rodriguez, Lethbridge	1.000	3	0	1	0	1	Walsh, Medicine Hat°	1.000	13	3	4	0	0
Ruetter, Medicine Hat°	1.000	18	2	9	0	1	Ware, Butte	.885	14	11	12	3	0
Schnatz, Calgary	.909	20	2	8	1	1	Weatherford, Helena	.875	16	0	7	1	1
Scott, Billings	.909	27	1	9	1	0	Weatherman, Idaho Falls	1.000	9	2	9	0	1
Scudder, Lethbridge	.800	28	1	11	3	2	Weir, Great Falls	.833	13	3	2	1	0
Spagnola, Billings	.947	13	5	13	1	0	Wells, Medicine Hat°	1.000	12	1	15	0	2
Sparling, Butte	.818	8	2	7	2	0	Wilder, Butte	.917	20	3	8	1	1
Stefani, Butte	.714	19	2	3	2	0	Zucco, Calgary°	.800	13	2	6	2	1

The following players do not have any recorded accepted chances at the positions indicated; therefore, are not listed in the fielding averages for those particular positions: Cabell, of; Escribano, of; Gilbert, p; Gomez, of; Marentette, p; Marks, p; Martinez, of; McKenna, p; Michel, 3b, of; Mohr, of; Munson, of; Paredes, of; Sambo, of; Thompson, of; West, 2b; Wortmann, 3b, of; Wuelling, p.

CLUB PITCHING

Club	ERA.	G.	CG.	ShO.	Sv.	IP.	H.	R.	ER.	HR.	HB.	BB.	Int. BB.	SO.	WP.	Bk.
Great Falls	3.26	70	8	3	20	632	627	314	229	32	17	284	20	516	34	6
Medicine Hat	3.71	70	12	4	13	621	627	366	256	44	13	310	16	513	51	6
Billings	3.95	70	7	5	11	601	669	358	264	14	22	261	29	538	41	3
Butte	4.46	70	6	2	9	608	673	378	301	38	13	268	29	445	43	6
Helena	4.55	70	7	3	13	599.2	602	403	303	35	24	369	19	481	52	6
Idaho Falls	4.88	70	10	2	10	603.1	721	404	327	37	17	288	34	473	38	6
Lethbridge	4.99	70	7	3	6	598.1	738	449	332	50	17	309	29	385	51	7
Calgary	5.81	70	11	0	6	585.1	735	504	378	58	22	339	30	386	33	5

PITCHERS' RECORDS

(Leading Qualifiers for Earned-Run Average Leadership — 56 or More Innings)

°Throws lefthanded.

Pitcher—Club	W.	L.	Pct.	ERA.	G.	GS.	CG.	GF.	ShO.	Sv.	IP.	H.	R.	ER.	HR.	HB.	BB.	Int. BB.	SO.	WP.
Fischer, Idaho Falls	8	2	.800	1.12	36	0	0	34	0	8	56.1	39	11	7	3	1	23	7	63	5
Trujillo, Billings	7	3	.700	1.91	29	2	1	15	0	1	70.2	59	27	15	0	3	39	6	71	4
Ruetter, Medicine Hat°	6	1	.857	2.02	18	4	2	6	0	1	62.1	48	17	14	2	1	19	1	43	3
Morse, Great Falls°	7	0	1.000	2.49	12	11	1	0	0	0	72.1	62	24	20	5	0	25	2	61	1
Reynolds, Billings	5	4	.556	3.03	13	13	1	0	1	0	86	83	37	29	2	4	19	3	63	4
Coker, Helena	3	4	.429	3.15	15	11	0	0	0	0	68.2	58	36	24	5	2	48	2	57	2
Cole, Helena	7	3	.700	3.22	13	12	5	0	1	0	86.2	76	43	31	4	0	27	1	69	6
Meeks, Lethbridge	7	4	.636	3.24	14	14	5	0	1	0	100	110	49	36	7	1	22	0	62	7
Blobaum, Great Falls	5	5	.500	3.36	15	15	5	0	2	0	96.1	105	43	36	3	9	31	1	66	3
Bargerhuff, Great Falls	4	1	.800	3.38	23	2	0	8	0	2	56	66	28	21	1	0	16	2	28	1

Departmental Leaders: G—Fischer, 36; GS—Blobaum, Burns, Hummel, 15; CG—Richards, 6; GF—Fischer, 34; ShO—Blobaum, 2; W—Gilliam, 10; L—Browning, McKay, 8; Pct.—Morse, 1.000; Sv—Larkin, 11; IP—Meeks, 100; H—Conquest, 119; R—Zucco, 63; ER—Davis, 55; HR—Richards, 12; HB—Blobaum, 9; BB—Dombek, 61; IBB—Moseley, Schnatz, 9; SO—Browning, 87; WP—Davis, 12.

(All Pitchers—Listed Alphabetically)

Pitcher—Club	W.	L.	Pct.	ERA.	G.	GS.	CG.	GF.	ShO.	Sv.	IP.	H.	R.	ER.	HR.	HB.	BB.	Int. BB.	SO.	WP.
Baehr, Idaho Falls	0	0	.000	13.50	5	0	0	0	0	0	3.1	5	6	5	0	0	7	0	4	0
Bailey, Idaho Falls	0	0	.000	6.43	3	0	0	0	0	0	7	7	5	5	0	1	8	0	6	1
Bargerhuff, Great Falls	4	1	.800	3.38	23	2	0	8	0	2	56	66	28	21	1	0	16	2	28	1
Beal, Helena	2	6	.250	4.93	18	9	0	3	0	1	65.2	75	49	36	5	2	44	3	51	9
Bippert, Calgary	0	0	.000	12.00	3	0	0	3	0	0	3	8	7	4	0	0	4	0	3	0
Bisnar, Calgary	1	5	.167	7.36	16	5	1	3	0	1	47.2	70	53	39	8	3	33	4	35	1
Blobaum, Great Falls	5	5	.500	3.36	15	15	5	0	2	0	96.1	105	43	36	3	9	31	1	66	3
Bockus, Great Falls	2	0	1.000	4.58	18	0	0	3	0	0	53	60	38	27	4	0	22	1	42	5
Border, Idaho Falls	2	1	.667	5.63	16	3	0	4	0	2	32	43	27	20	4	0	11	2	20	1
Bridges, Calgary	0	2	.000	9.00	7	1	0	1	0	0	18	25	25	18	1	1	12	1	4	1
Brown, Idaho Falls°	0	0	.000	6.91	16	0	0	2	0	0	28.2	30	27	22	3	1	29	3	20	2
Browning, Billings°	4	8	.333	3.89	14	14	3	0	0	0	88	96	53	38	2	3	41	2	87	3
Burgermeister, Great Falls	0	0	.000	7.71	1	0	0	0	0	0	2.1	4	2	2	1	0	0	0	1	0
Burns, Lethbridge	6	6	.500	5.13	15	15	2	0	0	0	80.2	104	61	46	8	1	24	2	35	7
Caraballo, Helena	0	1	.000	3.45	17	0	0	8	0	0	31.1	29	22	12	3	2	14	2	21	3
Carne, Lethbridge°	0	3	.000	14.29	10	4	0	0	0	0	17	36	33	27	2	1	18	1	14	2
Chelini, Butte	0	0	.000	3.00	4	0	0	4	0	0	6	8	3	2	0	0	4	0	3	1
Coker, Helena	3	4	.429	3.15	15	11	0	0	0	0	68.2	58	36	24	5	2	48	2	57	2
Cole, Helena	7	3	.700	3.22	13	12	5	0	1	0	86.2	76	43	31	4	0	27	1	69	6
Conquest, Idaho Falls	5	7	.417	4.00	16	13	2	1	0	0	90	119	55	40	1	2	16	4	52	6
Cunningham, Lethbridge	1	3	.250	4.26	19	4	0	3	0	1	50.2	60	28	24	3	0	30	3	25	3
Dannewitz, Butte	0	2	.000	5.11	19	0	0	10	0	2	37	35	27	21	3	0	15	1	35	2
J. Davis, Butte	7	1	.875	6.14	14	14	2	0	0	0	80.2	100	62	55	4	2	37	2	38	12
S. Davis, Medicine Hat°	5	1	.833	3.44	13	3	0	8	0	1	36.2	38	15	14	4	0	17	0	46	1
Dickerson, Helena°	0	0	.000	6.75	10	0	0	2	0	0	14.2	22	13	11	1	2	9	0	12	2
Dombek, Helena°	1	5	.167	7.13	13	13	0	0	0	0	48	55	47	38	1	5	61	0	49	9
Drouillard, Calgary	0	0	.000	4.88	11	0	0	1	0	0	24	28	24	13	3	1	21	2	7	3
Encarnacion, Lethbridge	0	0	.000	6.75	6	0	0	4	0	0	9.1	9	7	7	2	1	7	1	8	2
Escribano, Idaho Falls	5	1	.833	3.49	9	9	2	0	0	0	59.1	68	30	23	4	2	29	5	55	4
Farrow, Idaho Falls	0	1	.000	7.20	9	5	0	1	0	0	25	29	22	20	1	6	17	0	16	2

Pitcher—Club	W.	L.	Pct.	ERA	G.	GS.	CG.	GF.	ShO.	Sv.	IP.	H.	R.	ER.	HR.	HB.	BB.	Int. BB.	SO.	WP.
Fischer, Idaho Falls	8	2	.800	1.12	36	0	0	34	0	8	56.1	39	11	7	3	1	23	7	63	5
Galvez, Lethbridge	0	0	.000	5.75	10	0	0	5	0	0	20.1	33	21	13	3	1	17	2	11	2
Gendron, Great Falls	0	0	.000	1.13	6	0	0	2	0	0	8	8	2	1	0	0	3	3	8	0
Gentle, Lethbridge*	2	6	.250	7.41	14	14	0	0	0	0	58.1	70	56	48	7	3	37	2	42	4
Gilbert, Idaho Falls*	1	0	1.000	5.84	8	1	0	1	0	0	12.1	12	9	8	1	0	13	2	10	2
Gilliam, Medicine Hat*	10	2	.833	3.50	14	14	5	0	0	0	97.2	101	59	38	10	1	40	1	75	3
Glidewell, Calgary	3	6	.333	6.34	13	13	0	0	0	0	65.1	81	56	46	10	4	48	1	42	4
Gorden, Medicine Hat	6	1	.857	2.10	22	0	0	18	0	8	51.1	34	20	12	1	2	26	3	55	5
Hawley, Billings	2	6	.250	6.92	13	13	0	0	0	0	53.1	75	49	41	2	3	18	2	41	6
Heuer, Lethbridge	1	5	.167	8.13	13	6	0	1	0	0	31	56	41	28	5	2	21	0	14	2
Hill, Helena	4	5	.444	4.91	26	0	0	20	0	7	47.2	45	34	26	3	4	28	7	48	3
Hughes, Great Falls	1	0	1.000	2.89	6	0	0	3	0	0	9.1	10	3	3	0	0	7	0	12	1
Hummel, Great Falls*	3	5	.375	3.62	15	15	0	0	0	0	69.2	67	43	28	3	1	32	0	55	2
Johnson, Medicine Hat	6	7	.462	4.48	15	14	2	1	0	0	74.1	78	54	37	5	2	52	2	59	9
Jones, Billings*	3	3	.500	7.41	8	7	0	0	0	0	34	46	34	28	0	0	27	0	33	6
Kahle, Medicine Hat*	1	2	.333	3.27	13	4	0	2	0	0	41.1	47	24	15	4	3	20	1	34	7
Kendrick, Idaho Falls*	0	2	.000	6.30	5	4	0	0	0	0	20	36	19	14	1	1	12	0	15	5
Key, Medicine Hat*	2	1	.667	2.30	5	5	1	0	0	0	31.1	27	12	8	0	0	10	0	25	1
Kochanski, Idaho Falls	1	2	.333	11.87	10	4	0	2	0	0	30.1	53	47	40	2	1	22	2	19	4
Kolb, Lethbridge	5	1	.833	3.76	27	0	0	7	0	0	55	57	30	23	1	2	36	1	41	5
Konderla, Billings	3	6	.333	3.41	19	8	1	3	1	1	74	85	39	28	1	3	28	2	57	3
Lambert, Idaho Falls	6	4	.600	3.97	13	13	2	0	0	0	79.1	87	38	35	6	1	32	2	61	0
Larkin, Great Falls*	7	4	.636	2.14	27	0	0	23	0	11	46.1	37	14	11	3	1	21	2	58	0
Larsen, Great Falls	0	0	.000	7.94	4	0	0	4	0	0	5.2	9	5	5	0	1	4	0	2	0
Leiper, Idaho Falls*	9	3	.750	4.11	14	13	4	0	1	0	85.1	94	49	39	5	1	27	0	77	1
Mader, Medicine Hat	0	0	.000	3.96	11	1	0	3	0	0	25	22	15	11	2	0	16	1	22	2
Marentette, Calgary	0	0	.000	11.57	6	0	0	5	0	0	7	6	9	9	2	0	13	0	6	3
Marks, Great Falls	0	0	.000	11.25	3	0	0	0	0	0	4	8	7	5	1	0	6	0	4	1
Martinez, Butte	3	4	.429	4.15	17	0	0	17	0	0	21.2	18	10	10	0	1	9	2	35	1
Mattson, Great Falls	2	3	.400	0.74	19	0	0	12	0	5	36.2	26	7	3	1	0	17	5	36	5
McCullers, Helena	6	4	.600	3.72	13	13	2	0	1	0	87	89	44	36	5	2	33	2	62	5
McKay, Calgary	3	8	.273	5.63	13	13	2	0	0	0	72	72	61	45	4	4	54	4	44	6
McKenna, Great Falls	0	0	.000	5.40	2	0	0	0	0	0	5	7	3	3	0	0	2	0	4	0
McNamara, Butte	4	6	.400	4.73	15	13	0	0	0	0	80	96	59	42	5	4	30	5	39	3
Meeks, Lethbridge	7	4	.636	3.24	14	14	5	0	1	0	100	110	49	36	7	1	22	0	62	7
Mielke, Calgary	3	4	.429	4.70	13	11	2	2	0	0	69	82	48	36	5	3	31	0	68	0
Mine, Idaho Falls	2	2	.500	3.12	11	1	0	7	0	0	26	30	12	9	2	0	10	2	15	1
Ra. Morse, Great Falls*	7	0	1.000	2.49	12	11	1	0	0	0	72.1	62	24	20	5	0	25	2	61	1
Ro. Morse, Calgary	1	2	.333	6.04	14	0	0	4	0	0	22.1	30	20	15	0	2	16	1	14	2
Morton, Helena	1	3	.250	5.59	4	4	0	0	0	0	19.1	25	16	12	0	0	13	0	12	2
Moseley, Butte	3	0	1.000	2.98	20	1	0	8	0	2	48.1	54	28	16	3	0	31	9	36	4
Nesmith, Calgary	3	5	.375	3.41	27	0	0	22	0	5	34.1	46	25	13	2	0	14	4	18	0
Norman, Great Falls	6	4	.600	3.91	14	14	1	0	0	0	76	77	51	33	7	5	49	2	54	7
Oropeza, Idaho Falls	0	0	.000	9.00	1	0	0	1	0	0	1	2	1	1	0	0	0	1	0	0
Ortiz, Billings	0	0	.000	7.22	19	0	0	11	0	0	28.2	49	35	23	1	1	15	1	25	5
Patterson, Medicine Hat	0	0	.000	5.00	12	0	0	9	0	0	18	23	14	10	1	0	13	0	13	3
Pfeffer, Calgary*	0	0	.000	9.90	14	0	0	6	0	0	20	26	22	22	4	0	9	0	17	5
Phillips, Medicine Hat	3	5	.375	4.37	13	13	1	0	0	0	80.1	92	57	39	4	2	42	4	54	8
Pinckard, Lethbridge	0	7	.000	5.12	12	12	0	0	0	0	51	79	41	29	5	0	16	2	33	2
Powell, Helena	1	3	.250	4.25	16	2	0	4	0	1	36	26	27	17	0	2	35	1	31	3
Reynolds, Billings	5	4	.556	3.03	13	13	1	0	1	0	86	83	37	29	2	4	19	3	63	4
Richards, Billings	7	6	.538	3.44	14	14	6	0	0	0	99.1	118	49	38	12	1	23	3	57	3
Rightmire, Medicine Hat	0	1	.000	4.38	7	0	0	4	0	1	12.1	11	7	6	2	0	5	1	12	0
Rodriguez, Lethbridge	0	0	.000	2.25	3	0	0	3	0	0	4	3	1	1	0	0	2	0	2	3
Ruetter, Medicine Hat*	6	1	.857	2.02	18	4	2	6	0	1	62.1	48	17	14	2	1	19	1	43	3
Schnatz, Calgary	1	1	.500	8.04	20	0	0	12	0	0	28	44	30	25	0	3	31	9	17	2
Scott, Billings	4	2	.667	1.13	27	0	0	23	0	9	48	35	11	6	1	0	22	6	62	0
Scudder, Lethbridge	1	6	.143	2.70	28	0	0	25	0	5	46.2	47	27	14	1	3	29	8	55	3
Spagnola, Billings	3	6	.333	4.54	13	13	1	0	0	0	79.1	102	48	40	4	5	25	0	60	3
Sparling, Butte	5	1	.833	4.66	8	8	0	0	0	0	46.1	50	29	24	5	1	17	0	37	4
Stefani, Butte	0	2	.000	5.88	19	1	0	4	0	2	33.2	42	28	22	3	2	28	2	32	2
Steinberg, Butte	0	2	.000	8.03	6	0	0	1	0	0	12.1	20	13	11	1	2	7	1	8	2
Stevenson, Idaho Falls*	1	0	1.000	14.73	5	0	0	4	0	0	3.2	7	6	6	0	0	2	0	3	0
Stout, Helena	1	3	.250	4.53	26	0	0	19	0	4	47.2	46	29	24	3	1	24	1	37	4
Swindle, Billings*	0	1	.000	3.69	22	0	0	11	0	0	39	39	25	16	1	0	27	7	39	7
Sylvia, Lethbridge	2	4	.333	4.17	23	0	0	9	0	0	45.1	49	31	21	2	2	32	7	22	5
Taft, Great Falls*	5	4	.556	3.41	13	13	1	0	0	0	66	58	36	25	3	0	37	1	72	8
Travers, Idaho Falls	1	0	1.000	6.92	7	0	0	1	0	0	13	16	11	10	2	0	11	1	9	1
Trujillo, Billings	7	3	.700	1.91	29	2	1	15	0	1	70.2	59	27	15	0	3	39	6	71	4
Vanderpohl, Butte*	3	2	.600	2.89	16	3	0	6	0	1	37.1	29	15	12	0	0	29	1	36	4
Veliz, Lethbridge*	0	0	.000	4.66	13	0	0	8	0	0	29	25	21	15	4	0	18	0	21	4
Walberg, Butte	8	3	.727	4.89	14	12	1	0	0	0	73.2	84	49	40	7	1	24	1	54	1
Walsh, Medicine Hat*	1	2	.333	5.54	13	0	0	7	0	2	26	35	30	16	4	2	18	1	22	4
Ware, Butte	5	4	.556	3.76	14	14	3	0	0	0	88.2	99	44	37	7	0	20	0	64	4
Weatherford, Helena	3	4	.429	6.89	16	6	0	0	0	0	47	56	43	36	5	2	33	0	32	4
Weatherman, Idaho Falls	1	3	2.50	6.75	9	4	0	2	0	0	30.2	44	29	23	1	0	19	4	27	3
Weir, Great Falls	1	1	.500	2.13	13	0	0	7	0	2	25.1	23	8	6	0	0	12	1	13	0
Wells, Medicine Hat*	4	3	.571	5.18	12	12	1	0	1	0	64.1	71	42	37	5	0	32	1	53	5
Wilder, Butte	3	2	.600	1.91	20	4	0	13	0	2	42.1	38	11	9	0	0	17	5	28	3
Wuelling, Calgary*	0	0	.000	27.00	3	0	0	0	0	0	3	9	12	9	1	0	5	0	1	0
Zucco, Calgary*	3	6	.333	5.72	13	13	0	0	0	0	72.1	90	63	46	6	0	25	1	53	2

BALKS—Meeks, Taft, 3 each; Brown, Gilliam, Glidewell, McCullers, Walsh, Ware, Zucco, 2 each; Blobaum, Bockus, Border, Caraballo, Carne, Coker, Conquest, Cunningham, J. Davis, Dombek, Galvez, Gilbert, Heuer, Johnson, Jones, Kochanski, Konderla, Larkin, McNamara, Mielke, Moseley, Norman, Powell, Ruetter, Spagnola, Sparling, 1 each.

COMBINATION SHUTOUTS—Hawley-Trujillo-Swindle, Jones-Konderla, Reynolds-Scott, Billings; Vanderpohl-Moseley-Chelini, Walberg-Moseley-Stefani, Butte; Norman-Mattson, Great Falls; Coker-Hill, Helena; Leiper-Minc, Idaho Falls; Gentle-Sylvia, Meeks-Scudder, Lethbridge; Mader-Ruetter-Patterson, Ruetter-Davis, Wells-Gorden, Medicine Hat.

NO-HIT GAME—None.

AL OLIVER
● EXPOS ●
BATTING CHAMPION (.331)
TOTAL BASES (317)
HITS (204)
RBIs (109—tie)

DAVE KINGMAN
● METS ●
HOME RUNS (37)

DALE MURPHY
● BRAVES ●
RBIs (109—tie)

1982 N.L. LEADERS

STEVE CARLTON
● PHILLIES ●
WINS (23)
INNINGS (295.2)
STRIKEOUTS (286)
COMPLETE GAMES (19)
SHUTOUTS (6)

BRUCE SUTTER
● CARDINALS ●
SAVES (36)

STEVE ROGERS
● EXPOS ●
ERA (2.40)

ROBIN YOUNT
● BREWERS ●
HITS (210)
TOTAL BASES (367)
SLUGGING PCT. (.578)
DOUBLES (46—tie)

WILLIE WILSON
● ROYALS ●
BATTING CHAMPION (.332)
TRIPLES (15)

HAL McRAE
● ROYALS ●
RBIs (133)
DOUBLES (46—tie)

1982 A.L. LEADERS

LaMARR HOYT
● WHITE SOX ●
WINS (19)

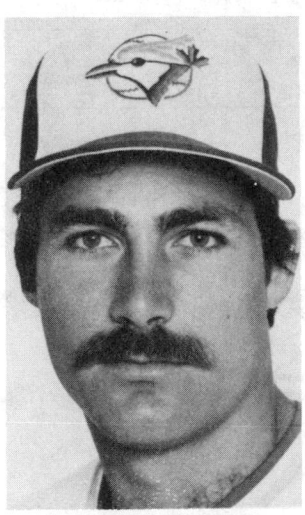

DAVE STIEB
● BLUE JAYS ●
COMPLETE GAMES (19)
SHUTOUTS (5)
INNINGS (288.1)

RICK SUTCLIFFE
● INDIANS ●
ERA (2.96)

1983 N.L. EASTERN DIVISION SLATE...

1983	EAST					
	AT CHICAGO	**AT MONTREAL**	**AT NEW YORK**	**AT PHILADELPHIA**	**AT PITTSBURGH**	**AT ST. LOUIS**
CHICAGO........		April 12, 14 June 24*, 25*, **26**, 27 Sept. 5, 6*, 7*	June 13*, 14*, 15* Aug. 12*, 13*, **14** Sept. 16*, 17, **18**	April 18*, 19*, 20* July 29*, 30*, **31** Aug. 1* Sept. 19*, 20	April 15*, 16, **17** June 20*, 21*, 22*, 23* Sept. 14*, 15*	June 17*, 18*, **19** Aug. 2*, 3*, 4* Sept. 30* Oct. 1, **2**
MONTREAL	April 5, 7 July 1, 2, **3**, 4-4 Sept. 12, 13		June 10*, 11*, **12** Aug. 2*, 3*, 4 Sept. 30* Oct. 1, **2**	May 26*, 27*, 28*, **29** June 28*, 29*, 30 Sept. 14*, 15*	June 13*, 14*, 15* Aug. 5*, 6, **7** Sept. 16*, 17*, **18**	May 12*, 13*, 14, **15** Aug. 15*, 16* Sept. 26*, 27*, 28*
NEW YORK	June 7, 8, 9 Aug. 5, 6, **7** Sept. 23, 24, **25**	June 17*, 18*, **19** Aug. 8*, 9*, 10* Sept. 9*, 10*, **11**		April 12, 13* July 1*, 2 (Tn), **3**, 4* Sept. 12*, 13*	May 12*, 13*, 14*, **15** Aug. 15*, 16 Sept. 27*, 28*, 29*	April 14*, 15*, 16*, **17** June 28*, 29*, 30* Sept. 21*, 22*
PHILADELPHIA	May 12, 13, 14, **15** Aug. 15, 16 Sept. 26, 27, 28	May 6*, 7, **8** June 20*, 21*, 22*, 23* Sept. 21*, 22*	April 5, 7 June 24*, 25, **26-26** Sept. 5*, 6*, 7*		June 17*, 18*, **19** Aug. 2*, 3*, 4* Sept. 9*, 10*, **11**	June 13*, 14*, 15* Aug. 5*, 6*, **7** Sept. 23*, 24, **25**
PITTSBURGH..	June 2, 3, 4, **5** June 28, 29, 30 Sept. 21, 22	June 7*, 8*, 9* Aug. 12*, 13, **14** Sept. 23*, 24, **25**	April 19*, 20* July 28*, 29*, 30, **31-31** Sept. 19*, 20	June 10*, 11*, **12** Aug. 8*, 9*, 10* Sept. 30* Oct. 1*, **2**		April 5, 6* June 24*, 25, **26**, 27* Sept. 5*, 6*, 7*
ST. LOUIS	June 10, 11, **12** Aug. 9, 10, 11 Sept. 9, 10, **11**	April 19, 20, 21 July 28*, 29*, 30*, **31** Sept. 19*, 20*	April 8*, 9, **10-10** June 21*, 22*, 23 Sept. 14*, 15*	June 7*, 8*, 9* Aug. 12*, 13*, **14** Sept. 16*, 17*, **18**	April 12, 13 July 1*, 2*, **3**, 4-4 Sept. 12*, 13*	
ATLANTA.......	May 17, 18 Aug. 18, 19, 20, **21**	May 3*, 4* July 8*, 9*, **10**, 11*	April 29*, 30 May **1** July 25*, 26*, 27	April 15*, 16*, **17** July 12*, 13*, 14*	May 30, 31* June 1* Aug. 26*, 27*, **28**	May 20*, 21*, **22** Aug. 23*, 24*, 25*
CINCINNATI ...	May 20, 21, **22** Aug. 22, 23, 24	April 29, 30 May **1-1** July 19*, 20*	May 6*, 7*, **8** July 12*, 13*, 14*	May 2*, 3*, 4* July 15*, 16*, **17**	May 17*, 18* Aug. 18*, 19*, 20*, **21**	May 30*, 31* June 1* Sept. 2*, 3*, **4**
HOUSTON.......	May 30, 31 June 1 Sept. 2, 3, **4**	April 26, 27 July 21*, 22*, 23*, **24**	May 2*, 3*, 4* July 8*, 9*, **10**	April 29*, 30 May **1** July 18*, 19*, 20*	May 20*, 21*, **22** Aug. 23*, 24*, 25*	May 17*, 18 Aug. 18*, 19*, 20*, **21**
LOS ANGELES	April 29, 30 May **1** July 25, 26, 27	May 17*, 18* Sept. 1*, 2*, 3*, **4**	May 20*, 21*, **22** Aug. 29*, 30*, 31*	May 23*, 24*, 25* Aug. 26*, 27*, **28**	April 22*, 23, **24** July 19*, 20*, 21*	April 25*, 26*, 27 July 22*, 23*, **24**
SAN DIEGO.....	April 26, 27, 28 July 22, 23, **24**	May 23*, 24*, 25* Aug. 26*, 27*, **28**	May 17*, 18*, 19* Sept. 2*, 3*, **4**	May 20*, 21, **22** Aug. 29*, 30*, 31*	April 29*, 30* May **1** July 25*, 26*, 27*	April 22*, 23*, **24** July 19*, 20*, 21*
SAN FRAN.	April 22, 23, **24** July 19, 20, 21	May 20*, 21, **22** Aug. 29*, 30*, 31*	May 23*, 24*, 25 Aug. 26*, 27*, **28**	May 16*, 17*, 18* Sept. 2*, 3*, **4**	April 26*, 27 July 22*, 23, **24-24**	April 29*, 30* May **1** July 25*, 26*, 27
1983	80 HOME DATES 0 NIGHTS	80 HOME DATES 52 NIGHTS	78 HOME DATES 52 NIGHTS	80 HOME DATES 63 NIGHTS	79 HOME DATES 56 NIGHTS	81 HOME DATES 59 NIGHTS

* NIGHT GAME
NIGHT GAME: Any game starting after 5:00 p.m.
HEAVY BLACK FIGURES DENOTE SUNDAY

AND COMPLETE WESTERN SCHEDULES

1983	AT ATLANTA	AT CINCINNATI	AT HOUSTON	AT LOS ANGELES	AT SAN DIEGO	AT SAN FRANCISCO
WEST						
CHICAGO........	May 26*, 27*, 28, **29** Aug. 29*, 30*	April 8*, 9, **10**, 11 Aug. 31* Sept. 1*	May 23*, 24*, 25* Aug. 26*, 27*, **28***	May 9*, 10* July 14*, 15*, 16*, **17**	May 6*, 7*, **8** July 11*, 12*, 13*	May 3*, 4 July 8*, 9, **10-10**
MONTREAL	May 9*, 10*, 11* July 15*, 16*, **17**	April 22*, 23*, **24** July 25*, 26*, 27*	April 15*, 16, **17** July 12*, 13*, 14*	April 8, 9, **10** Aug. 22*, 23*, 24	May 30*, 31* June 1* Aug. 19*, **21-21**	June 2*, 3*, 4, **5** Aug. 17*, 18*
NEW YORK	April 22*, 23*, **24** July 18*, 19*, 20*	April 26*, 27 July 21*, 22*, 23*, **24**	May 9*, 10*, 11* July 15*, 16*, **17***	June 2*, 3*, 4*, **5** Aug. 17*, 18*	May 27*, 28*, **29** Aug. 22*, 23*, 24*	May 30, 31* June 1* Aug. 19*, 20, **21**
PHILADELPHIA	April 26*, 27* July 21*, 22*, 23*, **24**	May 10*, 11* July 8*, 9*, **10**, 11*	April 22*, 23*, **24** July 26*, 27*, 28*	May 30*, 31* June 1* Aug. 19*, 20*, **21**	June 2, 3*, 4*, **5** Aug. 17*, 18	April 8*, 9, **10** Aug. 22*, 23*, 24
PITTSBURGH..	May 23*, 24*, 25* Sept. 2*, 3, **4**	May 26*, 27*, 28, **29** Aug. 29*, 30*	April 7*, 8*, 9*, **10** Aug. 31* Sept. 1	May 2*, 3*, 4* July 8*, 9*, **10**	May 9*, 10* July 14, 15*, 16*, **17**	May 6*, 7, **8** July 11*, 12*, 13
ST. LOUIS	June 2*, 3*, 4, **5** Aug. 31* Sept. 1*	May 23*, 24*, 25 Aug. 26*, 27, **28**	May 26*, 27*, 28*, **29** Aug. 29*, 30*	May 6*, 7*, **8** July 11*, 12*, 13*	May 3*, 4*, 5 July 8*, 9*, **10**	May 9*, 10* July 14*, 15*, 16, **17**
ATLANTA.......		April 4, 6* June 24 (Tn), 25* **26**, 27* Sept. 13*, 14*	May 12*, 13*, 14*, **15** June 20*, 21*, 22* Sept. 28*, 29*	June 14*, 15*, 16* Aug. 5*, 6*, **7** Sept. 9*, 10*, **11**	April 18*, 19*, 20* July 29*, 30*, **31** Sept. 30* Oct. 1*, **2**	June 17*, 18, **19** Aug. 1*, 2*, 3, 4* Sept. 7*, 8*
CINCINNATI ...	April 12*, 13* July 1*, 2*, **3**, 4* Sept. 20*, 21*, 22*		April 19*, 20*, 21* July 29*, 30*, **31*** Sept. 30* Oct. 1, **2***	June 17*, 18, **19** Aug. 1*, 2*, 3*, 4* Sept. 7*, 8*	June 14*, 15*, 16 Aug. 5*, 6 (Tn), **7** Sept. 9*, **11**	April 15*, 16, **17-17** June 20*, 21*, 22 Sept. 5, 6*
HOUSTON.......	May 5*, 6*, 7, **8** June 28*, 29*, 30* Sept. 5, 6*	June 3*, 4*, **5** Aug. 15*, 16*, 17* Sept. 16*, 17*, **18**		April 11*, 12*, 13* June 24*, 25*, **26** Sept. 19*, 20*, 21*	June 17*, 18*, **19** Aug. 1*, 2*, 3*, 4 Sept. 7*, 8	June 14*, 15, 16* Aug. 5*, 6, **7** Sept. 9*, 10, **11**
LOS ANGELES	June 7*, 8*, 9* Aug. 12*, 13*, **14** Sept. 23*, 24, **25**	June 10*, 11*, **12**, 13 Aug. 9*, 10*, 11* Sept. 26*, 27	April 5*, 6* July 1*, 2*, 3*, 4* Sept. 13*, 14*, 15*		May 12, 13*, 14, **15** June 28*, 29*, 30 Sept. 28*, 29*	April 18*, 19*, 20* July 29*, 30, **31** Sept. 16*, 17, **18**
SAN DIEGO.....	April 8*, 9, **10**, 11 Aug. 15*, 16 Sept. 16*, 17, **18**	June 7*, 8*, 9* Aug. 12*, 13*, **14** Sept. 23*, 24, **25**	June 10*, 11*, **12***, 13* Aug. 9*, 10*, 11* Sept. 26*, 27*	April 15*, 16*, **17** June 20*, 21*, 22*, 23 Sept. 5*, 6*		April 5, 6* June 24*, 25, **26-26** Sept. 19*, 20*, 21
SAN FRAN......	June 10 (Tn), 11*, **12** Aug. 9*, 10*, 11* Sept. 26*, 27*	May 12*, 13*, 14*, **15** June 28*, 29*, 30 Sept. 28*, 29	June 7*, 8*, 9* Aug. 12*, 13, **14*** Sept. 23*, 24*, **25***	May 26*, 27*, 28, **29** Aug. 15*, 16* Sept. 30* Oct. 1, **2**	April 12*, 13*, 14 July 1*, 2*, **3**, 4* Sept. 13*, 14*	
1983	80 HOME DATES 58 NIGHTS	80 HOME DATES 56 NIGHTS	81 HOME DATES 72 NIGHTS	81 HOME DATES 61 NIGHTS	79 HOME DATES 56 NIGHTS	78 HOME DATES 42 NIGHTS

JULY 6 — ALL STAR GAME AT CHICAGO (COMISKEY PARK)
AUGUST 1 — HALL OF FAME GAME AT COOPERSTOWN, N.Y. (St. Louis Cardinals vs. Baltimore Orioles)

1983 A.L. EASTERN DIVISION SLATE...

1983	EAST						
	AT MILWAUKEE	**AT DETROIT**	**AT CLEVELAND**	**AT TORONTO**	**AT BALTIMORE**	**AT NEW YORK**	**AT BOSTON**
MILWAUKEE...		June 20*, 21*, 22* Sept. 30* Oct. 1, **2**	July 1*, 2*, **3**, 4 Sept. 20*, 21*, 22*	April 12, 13, 14 Aug. 11*, 12*, 13, **14**	June 7*, 8*, 9* Sept. 16*, 17*, **18**, 19*	June 17*, 18*, **19** Sept. 12*, 13*, 14*	April 18, 20* July 29*, 30, **31** Aug. 1
DETROIT.........	June 27*, 28*, 29*, 30 Sept. 9*, 10*, **11**		June 17*, 18, **19-19** Sept. 5*, 7*	May 23, 24*, 25* Sept. 2 (Tn), 3, **4**	June 24*, 25*, **26** Sept. 27*, 28*, 29*	April 12, 13*, 14* Aug. 5*, 6*, **7**	June 6*, 7*, 8*, 9* Sept. 16*, 17, **18**
CLEVELAND ...	June 24*, 25*, **26** Sept. 27*, 28*, 29*	June 10*, 11, **12-12** Sept. 12*, 13*, 14*		April 19, 20 July 29*, 30, **31** Aug. 1	April 15, 16, **17**, 18* Aug. 8*, 9*, 10*	June 7*, 8* Sept. 23*, 24, **25**, 26*	June 20*, 21*, 22*, 23* Sept. 30* Oct. 1, **2**
TORONTO	May 16*, 17*, 18 Aug. 5*, 6, **7**	May 30* June 1*, 2 Aug. 26*, 27, **28**	May 12*, 13*, 14, **15** Aug. 15*, 16*, 17*		June 3*, 4*, **5**, 6* Aug. 23*, 24*, 25*	April 15*, 16, **17**, 18* Aug. 8*, 9*, 10	April 5, 7 Aug. 19*, 20, **21**, 22*
BALTIMORE....	June 13*, 14*, 15 Sept. 23*, 24*, **25**	July 1*, 2, **3**, 4 Sept. 20*, 21*, 22*	April 9, **10** Aug. 2 (Tn), 3*, 4*	May 19*, 20*, 21, **22** Aug. 31* Sept. 1		June 27*, 28*, 29*, 30* Sept. 9*, 10*, **11**	June 10*, 11, **12** Sept. 12*, 13*, 14*, 15*
NEW YORK	June 10*, 11*, **12** Sept. 5, 6*, 7*, 8*	May 16*, 17*, 18* Aug. 11*, 12*, 13*, **14**	June 13*, 14*, 15*, 16* Sept. 16*, 17*, **18**	April 9, **10** Aug. 2 (Tn), 3*, 4*	June 20*, 21*, 22* Sept. 30* Oct. 1*, **2**		June 24*, 25, **26** Sept. 19*, 20*, 21*
BOSTON.........	May 12*, 13*, 14*, **15** Aug. 15*, 16*, 17*	June 14*, 15*, 16* Sept. 23*, 24, **25**	June 27*, 28*, 29* Sept. 9*, 10, **11**	May 26*, 27*, 28, **29-29** Aug. 29, 30*	June 17*, 18*, **19** Sept. 5, 6*, 7*	July 1*, 2*, **3**, 4 Sept. 27*, 28*, 29*	
SEATTLE........	May 27*, 28*, **29**, 30 Aug. 22*, 23*	April 22*, 23, **24** July 26*, 27*, 28*	May 31* June 1*, 2* Aug. 19*, 20*, **21**	July 1, 2, **3**, 4* Sept. 20*, 21*	May 9*, 10*, 11* July 8*, 9*, **10**	June 3*, 4, **5**, 6* Aug. 24*, 25	May 6*, 7, **8** July 11*, 12*, 13*
OAKLAND	May 31* June 1*, 2 Aug. 19*, 20*, **21**	May 10*, 11*, 12 July 8*, 9*, **10**	June 3*, 4*, **5**, 6* Aug. 24*, 25	June 14*, 15*, 16* Sept. 9*, 10, **11**	May 6*, 7, **8** July 11*, 12*, 13*	May 27*, 28*, **29**, 30 Aug. 22*, 23*	May 3*, 4* July 14*, 15*, 16, **17**
CALIFORNIA ...	June 3*, 4, **5**, 6* Aug. 24*, 25	May 6*, 7, **8** July 11*, 12*, 13*	May 27*, 28*, **29**, 30 Aug. 22*, 23*	June 17*, 18, **19** Sept. 5*, 6*, 7*	May 3*, 4* July 14*, 15*, 16*, **17**	May 31* June 1*, 2* Aug. 19*, 20*, **21**	May 9*, 10*, 11* July 8*, 9, **10**
TEXAS	May 6*, 7, **8** July 18*, 19*, 20	May 19*, 20*, 21, **22** Aug. 31* Sept. 1*	April 12, 13, 14 Aug. 5*, 6*, **7**	May 2*, 3*, 4* July 8*, 9, **10**	April 19*, 20*, 21 July 29*, 30*, **31**	May 10*, 11* July 14*, 15*, 16, **17**	April 15*, 16, **17** Aug. 8*, 9*, 10*
KANSAS CITY	April 15, 16, **17** Aug. 2*, 3*, 4	April 19*, 20* July 29*, 30, **31-31**	May 10*, 11* July 14*, 15*, 16*, **17**	May 6*, 7, **8** July 18*, 19*, 20*	April 4, 6*, 7* Aug. 19*, 20, **21**	April 26*, 27* July 21*, 22*, 23*, **24**	May 17*, 18* Aug. 11*, 12*, 13, **14**
MINNESOTA ...	May 10*, 11 July 14*, 15*, 16*, **17**	May 27 (Tn), 28, **29** Aug. 29*, 30*	April 26, 27 July 21*, 22*, 23*, **24**	June 20*, 21*, 22 Sept. 30* Oct. 1, **2**	May 23*, 24*, 25* Aug. 26*, 27*, **28**	April 22*, 23, **24** July 18*, 19*, 20	May 19*, 20*, 21, **22** Aug. 31* Sept. 1*
CHICAGO.........	April 26*, 27* July 21*, 22*, 23*, **24**	April 8, 9, **10** Aug. 8*, 9*, 10*	April 22, 23, **24** July 18*, 19*, 20*	April 29*, 30 May **1** July 25*, 26*, 27*	May 16*, 17*, 18* Aug. 5*, 6*, **7**	May 13*, 14, **15** Aug. 15*, 16*, 17*	May 30*, 31* June 1* Sept. 2*, 3, **4**
1983	81 HOME DATES 53 NIGHTS	78 HOME DATES 51 NIGHTS	79 HOME DATES 54 NIGHTS	78 HOME DATES 43 NIGHTS	81 HOME DATES 62 NIGHTS	81 HOME DATES 56 NIGHTS	81 HOME DATES 51 NIGHTS

* NIGHT GAME
NIGHT GAME: Any game starting after 6:00 p.m.
HEAVY BLACK FIGURES DENOTE SUNDAY

AND COMPLETE WESTERN SCHEDULES

1983	WEST						
	AT SEATTLE	AT OAKLAND	AT CALIFORNIA	AT TEXAS	AT KANSAS CITY	AT MINNESOTA	AT CHICAGO
MILWAUKEE...	May 20*, 21*, 22 Aug. 29*, 30*, 31*	May 23*, 24*, 25 Aug. 26*, 27, 28	April 5*, 6*, 7* Sept. 2*, 3*, 4	April 22*, 23*, 24 July 11*, 12*, 13*	April 8*, 9, 10 Aug. 8*, 9*, 10*	April 29*, 30 May 1 July 25*, 26*, 27*	May 2*, 3*, 4* July 8*, 9, 10
DETROIT.........	May 3*, 4* July 14*, 15*, 16*, 17	April 29*, 30 May 1 July 18*, 19*, 20	April 27*, 28* July 21*, 22*, 23*, 24	June 3*, 4*, 5* Aug. 22*, 23*, 24*	May 13*, 14*, 15 Aug. 15*, 16*, 17*	April 5*, 6*, 7 Aug. 19*, 20*, 21	April 15*, 16, 17 Aug. 2*, 3*, 4*
CLEVELAND ...	May 23*, 24*, 25* Aug. 26*, 27*, 28	April 4*, 6, 7* Sept. 2*, 3, 4	May 20*, 21*, 22 Aug. 29*, 30*, 31*	May 16*, 17*, 18* Aug. 12*, 13*, 14*	April 29*, 30* May 1 July 25*, 26*, 27*	May 3*, 4*, 5 July 8*, 9*, 10	May 6*, 7, 8 July 11*, 12*, 13*
TORONTO	June 23*, 24*, 25*, 26 Sept. 13*, 14*	June 7*, 8, 9* Sept. 23*, 24, 25	June 10*, 11*, 12 Sept. 26*, 27*, 28*	April 26*, 27* July 21*, 22*, 23*, 24*	April 22*, 23*, 24 July 11*, 12*, 13*	June 28*, 29*, 30 Sept. 15*, 16*, 17	May 9*, 11* July 14*, 15*, 16, 17
BALTIMORE....	April 29*, 30* May 1 July 18*, 19*, 20	April 26*, 27* July 21*, 22*, 23, 24	April 22*, 23*, 24 July 25, 26*, 27*	May 13*, 14*, 15 Aug. 15*, 16*, 17*	May 26*, 27*, 28*, 29 Aug. 29*, 30*	May 30, 31* June 1* Sept. 2*, 3, 4	April 12, 14 Aug. 11*, 12*, 13*, 14
NEW YORK	April 5*, 6*, 7* Sept. 2*, 3*, 4	May 20*, 21, 22 Aug. 30*, 31* Sept. 1*	May 23*, 24*, 25* Aug. 26*, 27*, 28	April 29*, 30* May 1 July 25*, 26*, 27*	May 2*, 3*, 4* July 8*, 9*, 10	May 6*, 7*, 8 July 11*, 12*, 13*	April 19*, 20* July 29*, 30*, 31 Aug. 1*
BOSTON.........	April 26*, 27* July 21*, 22*, 23*, 24	April 22*, 23, 24 July 25*, 26*, 27*	April 29*, 30* May 1 July 18*, 19*, 20*	April 8*, 9*, 10 Aug. 2*, 3*, 4*	April 11*, 12*, 13* Aug. 5*, 6*, 7	June 3*, 4, 5 Aug. 23*, 24*, 25	May 23*, 24*, 25* Aug. 26*, 27, 28
SEATTLE........		May 13*, 14, 15 Aug. 8*, 9*, 10	April 11*, 12*, 13* Aug. 12*, 13*, 14	June 13*, 14*, 15* Sept. 22*, 23*, 24*, 25	June 17*, 18*, 19 Sept. 5*, 6*, 7*	April 18*, 19*, 20*, 21 July 29*, 30*, 31	June 20*, 21*, 22* Sept. 15*, 16*, 17*, 18
OAKLAND	April 14*, 15*, 16*, 17 Aug. 1*, 2*, 3*		April 18*, 19*, 20*, 21 July 29*, 30*, 31	June 24 (Tn), 25*, 26* Sept. 20*, 21*	June 20*, 21*, 22* Sept. 16*, 17*, 18	May 16*, 17*, 18* Aug. 4*, 5*, 6*, 7	June 17*, 18, 19 Sept. 5, 6*, 7*
CALIFORNIA...	May 17*, 18*, 19* Aug. 4*, 5*, 6*, 7	April 8*, 9, 10 Aug. 15*, 16*, 17*		June 20*, 21*, 22* Sept. 30* Oct. 1*, 2	June 23*, 24*, 25*, 26 Sept. 19*, 20*, 21*	April 14*, 15*, 16, 17 Aug. 1, 2*, 3*	June 13*, 14*, 15* Sept. 9*, 10*, 11
TEXAS	June 7*, 8*, 9* Sept. 9*, 10*, 11	July 1*, 2*, 3, 4* Sept. 13*, 14*, 15	June 27*, 28*, 29*, 30* Sept. 16*, 17*, 18		May 23*, 24*, 25* Aug. 25*, 26*, 27*, 28	June 10*, 11*, 12 Sept. 27*, 28*, 29	May 26*, 27*, 28*, 29 Aug. 29*, 30*
KANSAS CITY	June 10*, 11*, 12 Sept. 26*, 27*, 28*, 29*	June 27*, 28*, 29*, 30 Sept. 30* Oct. 1, 2	July 1*, 2*, 3, 4 Sept. 13*, 14*	May 30*, 31* June 1* Sept. 2*, 3*, 4		June 13*, 14*, 15* Sept. 9*, 10, 11	June 2*, 3*, 4, 5-5 Aug. 31* Sept. 1*
MINNESOTA...	April 8*, 9*, 10 Aug. 15*, 16*, 17*	April 12*, 13* Aug. 11*, 12*, 13, 14	May 13*, 14*, 15 Aug. 8*, 9*, 10*	June 16*, 17*, 18*, 19* Sept. 5*, 6*, 7*	June 7*, 8*, 9* Sept. 22*, 23*, 24*, 25		June 23, 24*, 25*, 26 Sept. 19*, 20*, 21*
CHICAGO........	June 27*, 28*, 29 Sept. 30* Oct. 1*, 2	June 10*, 11, 12-12 Sept. 27*, 28, 29*	June 7*, 8*, 9* Sept. 22*, 23*, 24, 25	April 4*, 5*, 6* Aug. 19 (Tn), 20*, 21*	May 20*, 21, 22 Aug. 22*, 23*, 24*	July 1*, 2*, 3, 4 Sept. 13*, 14*	
1983	81 HOME DATES 67 NIGHTS	80 HOME DATES 47 NIGHTS	81 HOME DATES 65 NIGHTS	79 HOME DATES 75 NIGHTS	81 HOME DATES 66 NIGHTS	81 HOME DATES 54 NIGHTS	80 HOME DATES 56 NIGHTS

JULY 6 — ALL STAR GAME AT CHICAGO (COMISKEY PARK)

AUGUST 1 — HALL OF FAME GAME AT COOPERSTOWN, N.Y. (St. Louis Cardinals vs. Baltimore Orioles)

Index to Contents

AMERICAN LEAGUE

NATIONAL LEAGUE

1982 Game Scores

1982 Game Scores

NATIONAL ASSOCIATION (MINOR LEAGUE) AVERAGES

Index to Minor League Clubs, Cities

NOTES

NOTES

NOTES